| True to the work of Yah Veh Elohim - Adonay - Eternal I AM - Creator - Judge. | True to the mission of Yah Shua Messiah - Adonay - Eternal I AM - Creator - Saviour. |

EDC HEBREW ENGLISH BIBLE

a literal translation and transliteration of Scripture

SERIES 3

Everday Church, Inc.

| True to the ministry of the Holy Spirit - Indwelling Paraclete - Endower of Spirituals - Birther of Eternal Life. | True to the enduements of the Holy Spirit - Ministries of Service - Energies of Dynamis - Attributes of Charismata. |

Ruach ha-kodesh

First Edition,
The AUTHORIZED KING JAMES VERSION of 1611 in exeGeses,
© 1992 by Herb Jahn, Exegete.

The Second Edition,
exeGeses ready research BIBLE,
© 1993 by Herb Jahn, Exegete.

The Third Edition,
exeGeses companion BIBLE,
© 1994 by Herb Jahn, Exegete.

This Fourth Edition,
exeGeses BIBLE,
© 1994 by Herb Jahn, Exegete.

Copyright © 2022 Everday Church, Inc.

All rights reserved. No part of this book may be reproduced, stored, or transmitted by any means—whether auditory, graphic, mechanical, or electronic—without written permission of both publisher and author, except in the case of brief excerpts used in critical articles and reviews. Unauthorized reproduction of any part of this work is illegal and is punishable by law.

ISBN: 978-1-63950-141-0 (sc)
ISBN: 978-1-63950-142-7 (e)

Because of the dynamic nature of the Internet, any web addresses or links contained in this book may have changed since publication and may no longer be valid. The views expressed in this work are solely those of the author and do not necessarily reflect the views of the publisher, and the publisher hereby disclaims any responsibility for them.

Writers Apex

Gateway Towards Success
8063 MADISON AVE #1252
Indianapolis, IN 46227
+13176596889
www.writersapex.com

LEXICON:

You will particularly appreciate the LEXICON beginning on page 1866. All the *exeGeses* are verifiable by the expository critiques in the LEXICON, and by Strong's Exhaustive Concordance.

The LEXICON thoroughly explains the importance of the word word – and why it is used in both verbal and nounal forms. The SUMMARIES give you a thorough digest of certain subjects and roots of words.

Now you can easily satisfy your desire for deeper research – for every word in the LEXICON is number coded to Strong's Exhaustive Concordance. This is especially helpful because more and more of the old reliable research materials are being republished, also number coded to Strong's Exhaustive Concordance.

My petition is that Adonay Yah Shua Messiah be pleased to place His seal on the work of my life by spiritually enriching the work of your life.

In the name of Adonay Yah Shua Messiah,
Herb Jahn, Exegete

I invite all exegetes to critique this *EDC Hebrew / English Bible* in the hope that future editions may be less imperfect.

Everyday Church give all credits to Herb Jahn, as we go forward with this future edition. Others in the future may be less imperfect. Also, "However" Isaiah 55:11 "So shall my word be that goeth forth out of my mouth: it shall not return unto me void, but it shall accomplish that wich I please, and it shall prosper in the thing where to I ser it."

Acknowledgement

*Thank you, Dawn,
for your
encouragement, endurance,
and
editorial excellence.*

TABLE OF CONTENTS

VOLUME FIVE:
EVANGELISMS

JOHN *YOCHANAN*	2
MATTHEW *MATIT'YAH - HA'LEVI*	70
MARK *MAKABI*	160
LUKE *UR*	216
ACTS	308

VOLUME SIX:
EPISTLES

ROMANS	400
1 CORINTHIANS	437
2 CORINTHIANS	472
GALATIANS	495
EPHESIANS	507
PHILIPPIANS	519
COLOSSIANS	528
1 THESSALONIANS	536
2 THESSALONIANS	544
1 TIMOTHY	548
2 TIMOTHY	558
TITUS	565
PHILEMON	569
HEBREWS	571
JAMES *YA'AKOV*	598
1 PETER *PETROS*	607
2 PETER *PETROS*	617
JUDE *Y'HUDAH*	623
1 JOHN *YOCHANAN*	626
2 JOHN *YOCHANAN*	635
3 JOHN *YOCHANAN*	637
REVELATION *HAGILU NATAN ELOHIM*	639

VOLUME SEVEN

LEXICON	684

VOLUME FIVE
EVANGELISMS

JOHN/YOCHANAN 1

GENESIS OF THE EVANGELISMS: GENEALOGY OF THE WORD

1 In the beginning was* the Word,
and the Word was* with *God* **Elohim**,
and *the Word was God* **Elohim was* the Word**.

2 The same was in the
beginning with *God* **Elohim**.

*was: in the sense of eternal being

THE WORD IS THE CREATOR

3 All *things were made by* **became through** him;
and *without* **apart from** him
was not any thing made **naught became**
that *was made* **became**.

4 In him was life;
and the life was the light of *men* **humanity**.

5 And the light *shineth* **manifesteth** in darkness;
and the darkness *comprehended* **overtook** it not.

THE WITNESS OF BAPTIZER YAHN

6 There *was* **became** a *man* **human**
sent **apostolized** from *God* **Elohim**,
whose name was *John* **Yahn**.

7 The same came *for a* **to** witness,
to *bear* witness *of* **concerning** the Light,
that all *men* through him might *believe* **trust**.

8 He was not that Light,
but *was sent* to *bear* witness *of* **concerning** that Light.

9 *That was* the true Light,
which lighteth every *man* **human**
that cometh into the *world* **cosmos**.

10 He was in the *world* **cosmos**,
and the *world was made by* **cosmos became through** him,
and the *world* **cosmos** knew him not.

11 He came unto his own,
and his own *received* **took** him not.

THE ELOHIM BIRTH

12 But as many as *received* **took** him,
to them gave he *power* **authority**
to become the *sons* **children** of *God* **Elohim**,
even to them that *believe on* **trust in** his name:

13 Which were *born* **birthed**,
not of blood, nor of the will of the flesh,
nor of the will of man,
but of *God* **Elohim**.

THE WORD BECAME FLESH

14 And the Word *was made* **became** flesh,
and *dwelt* **tabernacled** among us,
(and we *beheld* **saw** his glory,
the glory as of the only *begotten* **birthed** of the Father,)
full of *grace* **charism** and truth.

15 *John bare witness of* **Yahn witnessed concerning** him,
and cried, *saying* **wording**,
This was he of whom I *spake* **said**,
He that cometh after me
is preferred before **became ahead of** me:
for he was *before me* **first**.

16 And of his fulness have all we *received* **taken**,
and *grace* **charism** for *grace* **charism**.

17 For the *law* **torah** was given
by Moses **through Mosheh**,
but *grace* **charism** and truth
came by Jesus Christ **became
through Yah Shua Messiah**.

18 No *man* **one** hath seen *God* **Elohim**
at any time — **not ever**,
the only *begotten* **birthed** Son,
which is in the bosom of the Father,
he hath declared him.

BAPTIZER YAHN INTERROGATED

19 And this is the *record* **witness** of *John* **Yahn**,
when the *Jews* **Yah Hudiym**
sent **apostolized** priests and *Levites* **Leviym**
from *Jerusalem* **Yeru Shalem** to ask him, Who art thou?

20 And he *confessed* **professed**, and denied not;
but *confessed* **professed**, I am not the *Christ* **Messiah**.

21 And they asked him, *So* What *then*?
rt thou *Elias* **Eli Yah**?
And he *saith* **wordeth**, I am not.
Art thou that prophet?

GENESIS OF THE EVANGELISMS: GENEALOGY OF THE WORD

1 In the beginning was* the Word
and the Word was* with Elohim
and Elohim was* the Word:

2 he was*, in beginning, with Elohim.

*was: in the sense of eternal being

THE WORD IS THE CREATOR

3 All became through him;
and apart from him

JOHN/YOCHANAN 1

4 naught became that became:
   in him life was;
   and the life was the light of humanity:
5 the light manifested in darkness;
   and the darkness overtook it not.

THE WITNESS OF BAPTIZER YAHN

6 And so be it,
   a human apostolized from Elohim;
   his name, Yahn:
7 he comes to witness
   — to witness concerning the Light
   so that, through him, all trust:
8 he is not that Light
   — but witnesses concerning that Light
9 — the true light
   who lights every human coming into the cosmos.
10 He was in the cosmos
   and through him the cosmos became;
   and the cosmos knows him not:
11 he comes to his own,
   and his own take him not.

THE ELOHIM BIRTH

12 But as many as take him
   he gives authority to become the children of Elohim
   — to them who trust in his name:
13 who, neither of blood,
   nor of the will of the flesh,
   nor of the will of man,
   but of Elohim, are birthed.

THE WORD BECOMES FLESH

14 And the Word became flesh
   and tabernacles in us;
   and we see his glory
   — the glory as of the only birthed of the Father
   full of charism and truth.
15 Yahn witnesses concerning him, and cries,
   wording, This is he of whom I say,
   He coming after me, became ahead of me;
   for he was first:
16 and we all take of his fulness
   — and charism for charism.
17 For the torah was given through Mosheh;
   charism and truth became through Yah Shua Messiah.
18 No one has seen Elohim — not ever,
   the only birthed Son
   being in the bosom of the Father,
   he declares.

BAPTIZER YAHN INTERROGATED

19 And this is the witness of Yahn
   when the Yah Hudiym apostolize priests and Leviym
   from Yeru Shalem to ask him, Who are you?
20 And he professes, and denies not;
   but professes, I am not the Messiah.
21 And they ask him, So what? Are you Eli Yah?
   And he words, I am not.
   Are you that prophet?
   And he answered, No.
22 *Then* **So** said they unto him, Who art thou?
   that we may give an answer to them that sent us.
   What *sayest* **wordest** thou *of* **concerning** thyself?
23 He said,
   I *am* the voice of one crying in the wilderness,
   Make straight **Straighten** the way of *the Lord* **Yah Veh**,
   exactly as said the prophet *Esaias* **Yesha Yah**.
   Yesha Yah 40:3
24 And they which were *sent* **apostolized**
   were of the Pharisees.
25 And they asked him, and said unto him,
   So Why baptizest thou *then*,
   if thou be not *that Christ* **the Messiah**,
   nor *Elias* **Eli Yah**, neither that prophet?
26 *John* **Yahn** answered them, *saying* **wording**,
   I baptize in water:
   but there standeth one among you, whom ye know not;
27 He it is, who coming after me
   is preferred before **became ahead of** me,
   whose shoe's *latchet* **thongs** I am not worthy to unloose.
28 These *things were done* **became**
   in *Bethabara* **Beth Abara** beyond *Jordan* **Yarden**,
   where *John* **Yahn** was baptizing.

THE WORD IS THE LAMB OF ELOHIM

29 The next day
   John **Yahn** seeth *Jesus* **Yah Shua** coming unto him,
   and *saith* **wordeth**, Behold the Lamb of *God* **Elohim**,
   which taketh away the sin of the *world* **cosmos**.
30 This is he *of* **concerning** whom I said,
   After me cometh a man
   which *is preferred before* **became ahead of** me:
   for he was *before me* **first**.
31 And I knew him not:
   but that he should be *made* manifest to *Israel* **Yisra El**,
   therefore **so** am I come baptizing *with* **in** water.

THE WORD IS THE SON OF ELOHIM

32 And *John bare record* **Yahn witnessed**,

JOHN/YOCHANAN 1

saying **wording**,
I saw the Spirit descending from heaven *like* **as** a dove,
and it abode upon him.

33   And I knew him not:
but he that sent me to baptize *with* **in** water,
the same said unto me,
Upon whom **ever** thou shalt see the Spirit descending,
and *remaining* **abiding** on him,
the same is he
which baptizeth *with* **in** the *Holy Spirit* **Ruach ha-kodesh**.

34   And I saw, and *bare record* **witnessed**
that this is the Son of *God* **Elohim**.

YAH SHUA BEGINS HIS MINISTRY

35   Again the next day after *John* **Yahn** stood,
and two of his disciples;

36   And looking *upon Jesus* **at Yah Shua** as he walked,
he *saith* **wordeth**, Behold the Lamb of *God* **Elohim**!

37   And the two disciples heard him speak,
and they followed *Jesus* **Yah Shua**.

38   Then *Jesus* **Yah Shua** turned,
and saw them following,
and *saith* **wordeth** unto them, What seek ye?
They said unto him, Rabbi,
(which is to *say* **word**,
being *interpreted Master* **translated Doctor**,)
where *dwellest* **abidest** thou?

39   He *saith* **wordeth** unto them, Come and see.
They came and saw where he *dwelt* **abode**,
and abode with him that day:
for it was about the tenth hour.

THE WORD IS THE MESSIAH

40   One of the two which heard *John* **Yahn** speak,
and followed him, was *Andrew* **Andreas**,
Simon Peter's **Shimon Petros'** brother.

41   He first findeth his own brother *Simon* **Shimon**,
And he answers, No.

22   So they say to him, Who are you?
— to give an answer to them who send us.
What word you concerning yourself?

23   He says,
I — the voice of one crying in the wilderness,
Straighten the way of Yah Veh,
exactly as Yesha Yah the prophet says.
Yesha Yah 40:3

24   And those apostolized are of the Pharisees:

25   and they ask him, and say to him,
So why baptize you,
if you are neither the Messiah
nor Eli Yah nor the prophet?

26   Yahn answers them, wording,
I baptize in water:
but one stands among you whom ye know not;

27   he coming after me, became ahead of me;
of whom I am not worthy
to unloose the thongs of his shoes.

28   — these become in Beth Abara beyond Yarden,
where Yahn baptizes.

THE WORD IS THE LAMB OF ELOHIM

29   On the morrow
Yahn sees Yah Shua coming to him,
and words, Behold the Lamb of Elohim,
who takes away the sin of the cosmos!

30   This is he concerning whom I say,
After me comes a man, who became ahead of me;
because he was first:

31   and I knew him not
other than to manifest him to Yisra El,
so I come baptizing in water.

THE WORD IS THE SON OF ELOHIM

32   And Yahn witnesses, wording,
I saw the Spirit descending as a dove from the heavens;
and abiding upon him:

33   and I knew him not:
but he who sent me to baptize in water, said to me,
Upon whomever you see the Spirit descending,
and abiding on him,
is he who baptizes in the Holy Spirit.

34   — and I saw and witness,
that this is the Son of Elohim.

YAH SHUA BEGINS HIS MINISTRY

35   Again on the morrow
Yahn stands with two of his disciples;

36   and looking at Yah Shua walking;
he words, Behold the Lamb of Elohim!

37   And the two disciples hear him speak,
and they follow Yah Shua.

38   Then Yah Shua turns and sees them following
and words to them, What seek you?
They say to him, Rabbi!
— which words — translated, Doctor!
Where abide you?

39   He words to them, Come and see.
They go and see where he abides;
and abide with him that day
— for it is about the tenth hour.

THE WORD IS THE MESSIAH

40 Andreas the brother of Shimon Petros
— one of the two
who heard from Yahn and follows him
41 first finds his own brother Shimon,
and *saith* **wordeth** unto him, We have found the Messias,
which is, being *interpreted* **translated**,
the *Christ* **Messiah**.
42 And he brought him to *Jesus* **Yah Shua**.
And when *Jesus beheld* **Yah Shua looked at** him, he said,
Thou art *Simon* **Shimon** the son of *Jona* **Yonah**:
thou shalt be called *Cephas* **Kepha**,
which is by *interpretation* **translation**, *a Stone* **Petros**.
43 The day following
Jesus would **Yah Shua willed to** go
forth into *Galilee* **Galiyl**,
and findeth *Philip* **Philippos**,
and *saith* **wordeth** unto him, Follow me.
44 Now *Philip* **Philippos** was
of *Bethsaida* **Beth Sayad**,
the city of *Andrew* **Andreas** and *Peter* **Petros**.
45 *Philip* **Philippos** findeth *Nathanael* **Nathan El**,
and *saith* **wordeth** unto him, We have found him,
of whom *Moses* **Mosheh** in the *law* **torah**,
and the prophets, *did write* **scribed**,
Jesus **Yah Shua** of Nazareth, the son of *Joseph* **Yoseph**.
46 And *Nathanael said* **Nathan
El wordeth** unto him,
Can there *be* any good *thing come out of* **from** Nazareth?
Philip saith **Philippos wordeth** unto him, Come and see.
47 *Jesus* **Yah Shua** saw *Nathanael* **Nathan El**
coming to him,
and *saith of* **wordeth concerning** him,
Behold *truly* an *Israelite indeed* **Yisra Eliy**,
in whom is no *guile* **deception**!
48 *Nathanael saith* **Nathan El wordeth** unto him,
Whence knowest thou me?
Jesus **Yah Shua** answered and *said* **spake** unto him,
Before that Philip called **Ere Philippos
voiced out to** thee,
when thou wast under the fig tree, I saw thee.
49 *Nathanael* **Nathan El** answered
and *saith* **wordeth** unto him,
Rabbi, thou art the Son of *God* **Elohim**;
thou art the *King* **Sovereign** of *Israel* **Yisra El**.
50 *Jesus* **Yah Shua** answered
and *said* **spake** unto him,
Because I said unto thee, I saw thee under
the fig tree, *believest* **trustest** thou?
thou shalt see greater *things* than these.

51 And he *saith* **wordeth** unto him,
Verily, verily *I say* **Amen! Amen! I word** unto you,
Hereafter **From now on** ye shall see heaven open,
and the angels of *God* **Elohim**
ascending and descending
upon the Son of *man* **humanity**.

THE FIRST SIGN BY YAH SHUA

2 And the third day there *was* **became** a marriage
in *Cana* **Qanah** of *Galilee* **Galiyl**
and the mother of *Jesus* **Yah Shua** was there:
2 And both *Jesus* **Yah Shua**
was called, and his disciples,
to the marriage.
3 And when they *wanted* **lacked** wine,
the mother of *Jesus saith* **Yah Shua wordeth** unto him,
They have no wine.
4 *Jesus saith* **Yah Shua wordeth** unto her,
Woman, what have I to do with thee?
What *is that* to me and to you, woman?
mine hour is not yet come.
5 His mother *saith* **wordeth**
unto the *servants* **ministers**,
Whatsoever he *saith* **wordeth** unto you, do it.
6 And there were set there six waterpots of stone,
after the manner of the purifying
of the *Jews* **Yah Hudiym**,
containing two or three *firkins apiece* **measures each**.
7 *Jesus saith* **Yah Shua wordeth** unto them,
Fill the waterpots with water.
And they filled them *up* to the brim.
8 And he *saith* **wordeth** unto
them, *Draw out* **Bail** now,
and bear unto the *governor* **arch** of
the feast **entertainment**.
and words to him, We found the Messias!
— which translates, the Messiah.
42 And he brings him to Yah Shua:
and Yah Shua looks at him, and says,
You are Shimon the son of Yonah:
you are called Kepha!
— which translates, Petros.
43 On the morrow he wills to go to Galiyl
and finds Philippos;
and words to him, Follow me.
44 And Philippos is from Beth Sayad
the city of Andreas and Petros:
45 Philippos finds Nathan El, and words to him,
We found him
who was scribed by Mosheh in the torah

and in the prophets
— Yah Shua of Nazareth, the son of Yoseph.
46 And Nathan El words to him,
Can there be any good from Nazareth?
Philippos words to him, Come and see.
47 Yah Shua sees Nathan El coming to him,
and words concerning him,
Behold, truly an Yisra Eliy, in whom is no deception!
48 Nathan El words to him, Whence know you me?
Yah Shua answers him, speaking,
Ere Philippos voiced to you,
being under the fig tree, I saw you.
49 Nathan El answers him, wording,
Rabbi, you are the Son of Elohim! You
are the Sovereign of Yisra El!
50 Yah Shua answers him, speaking,
Because I say to you, I saw you under the fig tree,
trust you?
Greater than these you see.
51 And he words to him,
Amen! Amen! I word to you,
From now on you see the heavens opened,
and the angels of Elohim
ascending and descending on the Son of humanity.

THE FIRST SIGN BY YAH SHUA

2 And the third day
there is a marriage in Qanah, Galiyl;
and the mother of Yah Shua is there:
2 and they also call Yah Shua and his disciples
to the marriage.
3 And lacking wine,
the mother of Yah Shua words to him,
They have no wine.
4 Yah Shua words to her,
What *is that* to me and to you, woman?
My hour has not yet come.
5 His mother words to the ministers,
Whatever he words to you, do.
6 And there are six waterpots of stone
set according to the purifying of the Yah Hudiym
— each containing two or three measures.
7 Yah Shua words to them,
Fill the waterpots with water.
— and they fill them to the brim.
8 And he words to them, Bail now,
and bear to the arch of entertainment.
And they bare it.

9 When the *ruler* **arch** of *the feast* **entertainment**
had tasted the water that *was made* **became** wine,
and knew not whence it was:
(but the *servants* **ministers**
which *drew* **bailed** the water knew;)
the *governor* **arch** of *the feast* **entertainment**
called **voiced out to** the bridegroom,
10 And *saith* **wordeth** unto him,
Every *man* **human** at the beginning
doth set forth good wine;
and when *men* **ever they** have *well drunk* **intoxicated**,
then that which is worse **so the lesser**:
but thou hast *kept* **guarded** the good wine until now.
11 This beginning of *miracles* **signs**
did *Jesus* **Yah Shua** in *Cana* **Qanah** of *Galilee* **Galiyl**,
and manifested forth his glory;
and his disciples *believed on* **trusted in** him.

YAH SHUA CLEARS THE PRIESTAL PRECINCT

12 After this he *went down* **descended**
to *Capernaum* **Kaphar Nachum**,
he, and his mother, and his brethren, and his disciples:
and they *continued* **abode** there not many days.
13 And the *Jews' passover* **Yah Hudiym's pasach**
was *at hand* **near**,
and *Jesus* **Yah Shua**
went up **ascended** to *Jerusalem* **Yeru Shalem**.
14 And found in the *temple* **priestal precinct**
those that sold oxen and sheep and doves, and
the *changers of money* **coindealers** sitting:
15 And when he had made a *scourge* **whip**
of *small cords* **ropes**,
he *drove* **cast** them all out of the
temple **priestal precinct**,
and the sheep, and the oxen;
and poured out the *changers' money* **coindealer's coins**,
and *overthrew* **overturned** the tables;
16 And said unto them that sold doves,
Take these *things* hence;
make not my Father's house an house of merchandise.
17 And his disciples remembered
that it was *written* **scribed**,
The zeal of thine house hath *eaten* **consumed** me *up*.
Psalm 69:9

YAH SHUA PROPHESIES
HIS DEATH AND RESURRECTION

18 *Then* **So** answered the *Jews* **Yah Hudiym**
and said unto him,

	What sign shewest thou unto us,
	seeing that thou doest these *things*?
19	*Jesus* **Yah Shua** answered and said unto them,
	Destroy **Release** this *temple* **nave**,
	and in three days I *will* **shall** raise it *up*.
20	*Then* **So** said the *Jews* **Yah Hudiym**,
	Forty and six years was this *temple* **nave** in building,
	and *wilt* **shalt** thou *rear* **raise** it *up* in three days?
21	But he *spake* **worded**
	of **concerning** the *temple* **nave** of his body.
22	**So** When *therefore* he was risen from the dead,
	his disciples remembered
	that he had *said* **worded** this unto them;
	and they *believed* **trusted** the scripture,
	and the word which *Jesus* **Yah Shua** had said.

The Pasach Celebration

23	Now when he was in *Jerusalem* **Yeru Shalem**
	at the *passover* **pasach**, in the *feast day* **celebration**,
	many *believed* **trusted** in his name,
	when they saw the *miracles* **signs** which he did.
24	But *Jesus* **Yah Shua**
	did not commit **entrusted not** himself unto them,
	because he knew all *men*,
25	And needed not that any **one**
	should *testify of man* **witness concerning humanity**:
	for he knew what was in *man* **humanity**.

The Spirit Birth

3	There was a *man* **human** of the Pharisees,
	named Nicodemus,
	a ruler **an arch** of the *Jews* **Yah Hudiym**:
2	The same came to *Jesus* **Yah Shua** by night,
	and said unto him,
	— and they bear.
9	And the arch of entertainment
	tastes the water become wine,
	and knows not whence it is
	— but the ministers bailing the water know.
	And the arch of entertainment
	voices out to the bridegroom
10	and words to him,
	Every human, at the beginning, sets good wine;
	and whenever they intoxicate, then the lesser:
	you guarded the good wine until now.
11	Yah Shua does this beginning of signs
	in Qanah of Galiyl;

	and manifests his glory:
	and his disciples trust in him.

Yah Shua Clears The Priestal Precinct

12	After this he descends to Kaphar Nachum
	— he and his mother and his brothers and his disciples:
	and they abide there not many days.
13	And the pasach of the Yah Hudiym is near
	and Yah Shua ascends to Yeru Shalem;
14	and in the priestal precinct
	finds them who sell oxen and sheep and doves
	— and the coindealers sitting:
15	and he makes a whip of ropes
	and casts them all from the priestal precinct
	with the sheep and the oxen;
	and pours out the coins of the coindealers
	and overturns the tables;
16	and says to them who sell doves,
	Take these hence;
	make not the house of my Father
	a house of merchandise.
17	— and his disciples remember it is scribed,
	The zeal of your house consumes me. Psalm 69:9

Yah Shua Prophesies His Death And Resurrection

18	So the Yah Hudiym answer him, saying,
	What sign show you us, that you do these?
19	Yah Shua answers them, saying,
	Release this nave, and in three days I raise it.
20	So the Yah Hudiym say,
	Forty—six years to build this nave,
	and you, raise it in three days?
21	But he words concerning the nave of his body:
22	so when he rises from the dead,
	his disciples remember that he worded this to them;
	and they trust the scripture
	and the word Yah Shua said.

The Pasach Celebration

23	And as he is in Yeru Shalem,
	in the pasach, in the celebration,
	many trust in his name,
	seeing the signs he does:
24	and Yah Shua entrusts not himself to them
	because he knows all;
25	and needs no one to witness
	concerning humanity:
	for he knows what is in humanity.

JOHN/YOCHANAN 3

The Spirit Birth

3 And there is a human of the Pharisees;
his name, Nicodemus — an arch of the Yah Hudiym: 2
who comes to Yah Shua by night, and says to him,
Rabbi, we know that thou art a *teacher* **doctor**
come from *God* **Elohim**:
for no *man* **one** can do these *miracles*
signs that thou doest,
except *God* **unless Elohim** be with him.
3 *Jesus* **Yah Shua** answered and said unto him,
Verily, verily, I say **Amen! Amen! I word** unto thee,
Except a man **Unless one** be *born* **birthed** *again* **above**,
he cannot see the *kingdom*
sovereigndom of *God* **Elohim**.
4 Nicodemus *saith* **wordeth** unto him,
How can a *man* **human** be *born* **birthed** when he is old?
can he enter the second time into his mother's womb,
and be *born* **birthed**?
5 *Jesus* **Yah Shua** answered,
Verily, verily I say **Amen! Amen! I word** unto thee,
Except a man be **Unless one is birthed**
of water and of the Spirit
he cannot enter
into the *kingdom* **sovereigndom** of *God* **Elohim**.
6 That which is *born* **birthed** of the flesh is flesh;
and that which is *born* **birthed** of the Spirit is spirit.
7 Marvel not that I said unto thee,
Ye must be *born* **birthed** *again* **from above**.
8 The *wind bloweth* **Spirit puffeth**
where *it listeth* **he willeth**,
and thou hearest the *sound thereof* **voice of him**,
but *canst not tell* **knowest not**
whence it cometh, and whither it goeth:
so **thus** is every one that is *born* **birthed** of the Spirit.
9 Nicodemus answered and said unto him,
How can these *things* be?
10 *Jesus* **Yah Shua** answered and said unto him,
Art thou a *master* **doctor** of *Israel* **Yisra El**,
and knowest not these *things*?
11 *Verily, verily I say* **Amen!
Amen! I word** unto thee,
We speak that we do know,
and *testify* **witness** that we have seen;
and ye *receive* **take** not our witness.
12 If I have *told* **said to** you *of the* earthly *things*,
and ye *believe* **trust** not,
how shall ye *believe* **trust**,
if **whenever** I *tell* **say to** you of *the* heavenly *things*?
13 And no *man* **one** hath ascended up to heaven,
but **except** he that *came down* **descended** from heaven,
even the Son of *man* **humanity** which is in heaven.

Eternal Life

14 And **exactly** as *Moses* **Mosheh**
lifted up **exalted** the serpent in the wilderness,
even *so* **thus**
must the Son of *man* **humanity** be *lifted up* **exalted**:
15 That whosoever *believeth* **trusteth** in him
should not *perish* **destruct**, but have
eternal life. Yahn 12:30—34
16 For *God* so **Elohim** loved
the *world,* **cosmos thus:**
that he gave his only *begotten* **birthed** Son,
that whosoever *believeth* **trusteth** in him
should not *perish* **destruct**
but have *everlasting* **eternal** life.
17 For *God* **Elohim**
sent **apostolized** not his Son into the *world* **cosmos**
to *condemn* **judge** the *world* **cosmos**;
but that the *world* **cosmos** through him might be saved.
18 He that *believeth on* **trusteth in** him
is not *condemned* **judged**:
but he that *believeth* **trusteth** not
is *condemned* **judged** already,
because he hath not *believed* **trusted** in the name
of the only *begotten* **birthed** Son of *God* **Elohim**.
19 And this is the *condemnation* **judgment**,
that light is come into the *world* **cosmos**,
and men loved darkness rather than light,
because their *deeds* **works** were evil.
20 For every one that doeth evil hateth the light,
neither cometh to the light,
lest his *deeds* **works** should be reproved.
21 But he that doeth truth cometh to the light,
that his *deeds* **works** may be *made* manifest,
that they are *wrought* **worked** in *God* **Elohim**.

The Final Witness Of Baptizer Yahn

22 After these *things*
Rabbi, we know you are a doctor come from Elohim:
for no one can do these signs you do
unless Elohim be with him.
3 Yah Shua answers him, saying,
Amen! Amen! I word to you,
Unless one is birthed from above,

he cannot see the sovereigndom of Elohim.
4 Nicodemus words to him,
How can a human be birthed when he is old?
Can he enter the womb of his mother
a second time and be birthed?
5 Yah Shua answers,
Amen! Amen! I word to you,
Unless one is birthed of water and of the Spirit
he cannot enter the sovereigndom of Elohim:
6 that birthed of the flesh is flesh;
and that birthed of the Spirit is spirit:
7 marvel not that I say to you,
you need to be birthed from above.
8 The Spirit puffs where he wills
and you hear his voice;
but know not whence it comes and where it goes:
thus is everyone birthed of the Spirit.
9 Nicodemus answers him, saying,
How can these be?
10 Yah Shua answers him, saying,
You, a doctor of Yisra El, and know these not?
11 Amen! Amen! I word to you,
We speak what we know,
and witness what we see;
and you take not our witness:
12 if I say to you of the earthly, and you trust not,
how trust you, whenever I say to you of the heavenlies?
13 And no one ascends to the heavens,
except whoever descends from the heavens
— even the Son of humanity who is in the heavens.

Eternal Life

14 And exactly as Mosheh
exalted the serpent in the wilderness,
even thus must the Son of humanity be exalted:
15 so that whoever trusts in him
destructs not, but has eternal life.
Yahn 12:30—34
16 For Elohim loved the cosmos thus:
that he gave his only birthed Son;
that whoever trusts in him destructs not
but has eternal life.
17 For Elohim
apostolized not his Son into the cosmos
to judge the cosmos;
but that the cosmos be saved through him.
18 Whoever trusts in him is not judged;
but whoever trusts not is already judged:
because he trusts not
in the name of the only birthed Son of Elohim.
19 And this is the judgment:
light comes into the cosmos,
and men love darkness rather than light
because their works are evil.
20 For everyone doing evil hates the light;
and comes not to the light lest his works be reproved:
21 but whoever does truth comes to the light,
to manifest that his works are worked in Elohim.

The Final Witness Of Baptizer Yahn

22 After these,
came *Jesus* **Yah Shua** and his disciples
into the land of *Judaea* **Yah Hudah**;
and there he tarried with them, and baptized.
23 And *John* **Yahn** also was baptizing
in *Aenon* **Ainon** near to *Salim* **Shalem**,
because there was much water there:
and they came, and were baptized.
24 For *John* **Yahn**
was not yet cast into *prison* **the guardhouse**.
25 *Then* **So** there *arose* **became** a question
between some of *John's* **Yahn's** disciples and
the *Jews* **Yah Hudiym** about purifying.
26 And they came unto *John*
Yahn, and said unto him,
Rabbi, he that was with thee beyond *Jordan* **Yarden**,
to whom thou *barest witness* **witnessest**,
behold, the same baptizeth, and all *men* come to him.
27 *John* **Yahn** answered and said,
A *man* **Humanity** can *receive nothing* **take naught**,
except **unless** it be given him from heaven.
28 Ye yourselves *bear me witness*
witnessed, that I said,
I am not the *Christ* **Messiah**,
but that I am *sent before* **apostolized ahead of** him.
29 He that hath the bride is the bridegroom:
but the friend of the bridegroom,
which standeth and heareth him,
rejoiceth greatly **cheereth cheer**
because of the bridegroom's voice:
so this my joy *therefore* is fulfilled/**shalamed**.
30 He must *increase* **grow**,
but I must *decrease* **lessen**.
31 He that cometh from above is above all:
he that is of the earth is *earthly* **of the earth**,
and speaketh of the earth:
he that cometh from heaven is above all.

JOHN/YOCHANAN 4

32 And what he hath seen and heard,
that he *testifieth* **witnesseth**;
and no *man receiveth* **one taketh** his *testimony* **witness**.
33 He that hath *received* **taken**
his *testimony* **witness**
hath set to his seal that *God* **Elohim** is true.
34 For he whom *God* **Elohim** hath *sent* **apostolized**
speaketh the *words* **rhema** of *God* **Elohim**:
for *God* **Elohim** giveth not the Spirit
by measure unto him.
35 The Father loveth the Son,
and hath given all *things* into his hand.
36 He that *believeth on* **trusteth in** the Son
hath *everlasting* **eternal** life:
and he that *believeth not* **distrusteth** the Son
shall not see life;
but the wrath of *God* **Elohim** abideth on him.

Yah Shua Goes To Galiyl

4 **So** When *therefore the Lord* **Adonay** knew
how the Pharisees had heard
that *Jesus* **Yah Shua** made and baptized
many more disciples than *John* **Yahn**,
2 (Though *Jesus* **Yah Shua** himself baptized not,
but his disciples),
3 He left *Judaea* **Yah Hudah**,
and departed again into *Galilee* **Galiyl**

Yah Shua And The Shomeroniy

4 And he must *needs go* **pass**
through *Samaria* **Shomeron**.
5 *Then* **So** cometh he to a
city of *Samaria* **Shomeron**,
which is *called* **worded** Sychar,
near to the *parcel of ground* **field**
that *Jacob* **Yaaqov** gave to his son *Joseph* **Yoseph**.
6 Now *Jacob's well* **Yaaqov's fountain** was there.
Jesus therefore **So Yah Shua**,
being wearied with **belabored from** his journey,
sat thus on the well:
and it was about the sixth hour.
7 There cometh a woman of *Samaria* **Shomeron**
to *draw* **bail** water:
Jesus saith **Yah Shua wordeth** unto
her, Give me to drink.
8 (For his disciples were gone away unto the city
to *buy meat* **market for nourishment**).
9 *Then saith* **So** the woman of
Samaria — **a Shomeroniy**
wordeth unto him,

How is it that thou, being a *Jew* **Yah Hudiy**,
askest drink of me,
which am a woman *of Samaria* — **a Shomeroniy**?
for the *Jews have no dealings* **Yah Hudiym associate not**
Yah Shua and his disciples
go to the land of Yah Hudah;
and he tarries with them, and baptizes:
23 and Yahn also baptizes in Ainon near Shalem
because there is much water there:
and they come, and are baptized:
24 for Yahn is not yet cast into the guardhouse.
25 So there is a question
between some of the disciples of Yahn
and the Yah Hudiym about purifying:
26 and they go to Yahn, and say to him,
Rabbi, he who is with you beyond Yarden,
to whom you witness,
behold, he baptizes, and all go to him.
27 Yahn answers, saying,
Humanity can take naught
unless it is given him from the heavens.
28 You yourselves witnessed that I said,
I am not the Messiah;
but that I am apostolized ahead of him.
29 He who has the bride is the bridegroom:
but the friend of the bridegroom
who stands and hears him,
cheers with cheer
because of the voice of the bridegroom:
so this my joy is fulfilled/shalamed.
30 He must grow; and me to lessen:
31 He who comes from above is over all:
He who is of the earth is of the earth,
and speaks of the earth:
whoever comes from the heavens is over all.
32 And what he see and hears, he witnesses;
and no one takes his witness:
33 whoever takes his witness
sets his seal that Elohim is true:
34 for he whom Elohim apostolizes
speaks the rhema of Elohim:
for Elohim gives him not the Spirit by measure.
35 The Father loves the Son
and gives all into his hand.
36 He who trusts in the Son has eternal life:
and he who distrusts the Son sees not life;
but the wrath of Elohim abides on him.

Yah Shua Goes To Galiyl

4 So when Adonay knows

	that the Pharisees hear that Yah Shua
	makes and baptizes many more disciples than Yahn,
2	— though Yah Shua himself baptizes no one
	except his disciples,
3	he leaves Yah Hudah and
	departs again to Galiyl.

YAH SHUA AND THE SHOMERONIY

4	And he must pass through Shomeron:
5	so he goes to a city of Shomeron *worded* Sychar
	near the field Yaaqov gave his son Yoseph;
6	and the fountain of Yaaqov is there:
	so Yah Shua, belabored from his journey,
	sits thus on the well at about the sixth hour:
7	and a woman of Shomeron comes to bail water.
	Yah Shua words to her, Give me a drink.
8	— for his disciples had gone to the city
	to market for nourishment.
9	So the woman — a Shomeroniy words to him,
	How is it you, being a Yah Hudiy,
	ask drink of me, being a woman — a Shomeroniy?
	— for the Yah Hudiym associate not
	with the *Samaritans* **Shomeroniym**
10	*Jesus* **Yah Shua** answered and said unto her,
	If thou knewest the *gift* **gratuity** of *God* **Elohim**,
	and who it is that *saith* **wordeth** to thee,
	Give me to drink;
	thou *wouldest* **shouldest ever** have asked of him,
	and he *would* **should ever** have given thee living water.
11	The woman *saith* **wordeth** unto him,
	Sir **Adoni**, thou hast *nothing* **naught** to *draw* **bail** *with*,
	and the well is deep:
	so from whence *then* hast thou that living water?
12	Art thou greater than our father *Jacob* **Yaaqov**,
	which gave us the well, and drank thereof himself,
	and his *children* **sons**, and his *cattle* **stock**?
13	*Jesus* **Yah Shua** answered and said unto her,
	Whosoever drinketh of this water shall thirst again:
14	But whosoever drinketh of the water
	that I shall give him
	shall never **ever** thirst **unto the eons**;
	but the water that I shall give him
	shall be in him a *well* **fountain** of water
	springing up into *everlasting* **eternal** life.
15	The woman *saith* **wordeth** unto him,
	Sir **Adoni**, give me this water, that I thirst not,
	neither come hither to *draw* **bail**.
16	*Jesus saith* **Yah Shua wordeth** unto her,
	Go, *call* **voice out** to thy *husband* **man**, and come hither.
17	The woman answered and said,
	I have no *husband* **man**.
	Jesus said **Yah Shua worded** unto her,
	Thou hast well *said* **spoken**, I have no *husband* **man**:
18	For thou hast had five *husbands* **men**;
	and he whom thou now hast is not thy *husband* **man**:
	in that *saidst* **spakest** thou truly.
19	The woman *saith* **wordeth** unto him,
	Sir **Adoni**, I perceive that thou art a prophet.
20	Our fathers worshipped in this mountain;
	and ye *say* **word**, that in *Jerusalem* **Yeru Shalem**
	is the place where men *ought* **need** to worship.
21	*Jesus saith* **Yah Shua wordeth** unto her,
	Woman, *believe* **trust** me, the hour cometh,
	when ye shall neither in this mountain,
	nor yet at Jerusalem Yeru Shalem, worship the Father.
22	Ye worship ye know not what:
	we know what we worship:
	for salvation is of the *Jews* **Yah Hudiym**.
23	But the hour cometh, and now is,
	when the true worshippers
	shall worship the Father in spirit and in truth:
	for the Father seeketh such to worship him.
24	*God* **Elohim** is a Spirit:
	and they that worship him
	must worship him in spirit and in truth.
25	The woman *saith* **wordeth** unto him,
	I know that Messias cometh,
	which is *called Christ* **worded Messiah**:
	when **ever** he is come,
	he *will tell us* **shall evangelize** all *things* **us**.
26	*Jesus saith* **Yah Shua wordeth** unto her,
	I that speak **I AM speaketh** unto thee *am he*.
27	And upon this came his disciples,
	and marvelled that he *talked* **spake** with the woman:
	yet **indeed** no *man* **one** said, What seekest thou?
	or, Why *talkest* **speakest** thou with her?
28	**So** woman *then left* **forsook** her waterpot,
	and went her way into the city,
	and *saith* **wordeth** to the men,
29	Come, see a *man* **human**,
	which told me *all things that* — **as much as** ever I did:
	is not this the *Christ* **Messiah**?
30	*Then* **So** they went out of
	the city, and came unto him.
	with the Shomeroniym.
10	Yah Shua answers her, saying,
	If you knew the gratuity of Elohim,
	and who words to you, Give me a drink;
	you had ever asked of him,
	and he had ever given you living water.

JOHN/YOCHANAN 4

11 The woman words to him,
Adoni, you have naught to bail and the well is deep:
so where have you that living water?
12 Are you greater than our father Yaaqov,
who gave us the well,
from which he and his sons, and his stock drank?
13 Yah Shua answers her, saying,
Whoever drinks of this water thirsts again:
14 but whoever drinks of the water I give
never ever thirsts to the eons;
but the water I give
becomes a fountain of water in him
springing up to eternal life.
15 The woman words to him,
Adoni, give me this water
that I neither thirst nor come here to bail.
16 Yah Shua words to her,
Go, voice out to your man, and come here.
17 The woman answers, saying,
I have no man.
Yah Shua words to her, Well spoken, I have no man:
18 for you had five men;
and he whom you now have is not your man
— in that you speak truly.
19 The woman words to him,
Adoni, I perceive you are a prophet:
20 our fathers worshipped in this mountain;
and you word, that in Yeru Shalem
is the place men need to worship.
21 Yah Shua words to her,
Woman, trust me, the hour comes,
when you neither in this mountain
nor in Yeru Shalem worship the Father:
22 you worship what you know not;
we worship what we know:
for salvation is of the Yah Hudiym.
23 But an hour comes, and now is,
when the true worshippers
worship the Father in spirit and in truth:
for the Father seeks such to worship him.
24 Elohim is a Spirit:
and they who worship him
must worship him in spirit and in truth.
25 The woman words to him,
I know that Messias comes
— who is worded Messiah:
whenever he comes, he evangelizes us of all.
26 Yah Shua words to her, I AM speaks to you.
27 And upon this his disciples come,
and marvel that he speaks with the woman:
yet indeed no one says, What seek you?
or, Why speak to her?
28 So the woman forsakes her waterpot
and goes to the city and words to the men,
29 Come, see a human,
who told me as much as I ever did!
Is not this the Messiah?
30 — so they go from the city and come to him.

THE FOOD OF YAH SHUA

31 In *the mean while* **between**
his disciples *prayed* **asked** him,
saying **wording**, *Master* **Rabbi**, eat.
32 But he said unto them,
I have *meat* **food** to eat that ye know not of.
33 *Therefore said* **So worded**
the disciples one to another,
Hath any *man* **one** brought him *ought* to eat?
34 *Jesus saith* **Yah Shua wordeth** unto them,
My *meat* **food** is to do the will of him that sent me,
and to *finish* **complete/shalam** his work.
35 *Say* **Word** not ye, There are yet four months,
and *then* cometh harvest?
behold, I *say* **word** unto you,
Lift up your eyes, and *look on* **see** the *fields* **regions**;
for they are white already to harvest.
36 And he that *reapeth* **harvesteth**
receiveth wages **taketh reward**,
and gathereth fruit unto life eternal:
that both he that *soweth* **sporeth**
and he that *reapeth* **harvesteth**
may *rejoice* **cheer** together.
37 *And* **For** herein is that *saying* **word** true,
One *soweth* **sporeth**, and another *reapeth* **harvesteth**.
38 I *sent* **apostolized** you
to *reap* **harvest** that whereon ye bestowed no labour:
other men **others** laboured,
and ye are entered into their labours.
39 And many of the *Samaritans*
Shomeroniym of that city
believed on **trusted in** him
for the *saying* **word** of the woman,
which *testified* **witnessed**,
He *told me all that* **said to me** — *as much as* ever I did.

YAH SHUA AND THE SHOMERONIYM

40 So when the *Samaritans* **Shomeroniym**
were come unto him,
they *besought* **asked** him
that he *would tarry* **should abide** with them:

	and he abode there two days.		wording, Rabbi, eat.
41	And many more *believed* **trusted**	32	And he says to them,
	because of his own word;		I have food to eat that you know not.
42	And *said* **worded** unto the woman,	33	So the disciples word to one another,
	Now we *believe* **trust**, not because of thy *saying* **speech**:		Has anyone brought him to eat?
	for we have heard him ourselves,	34	Yah Shua words to them,
	and know that this is *indeed* **truly** the *Christ* **Messiah**,		My food is to do the will of him who sent me
	the Saviour of the *world* **cosmos**.		and to complete/shalam his work.
43	Now after two days he departed thence,	35	Word not, Yet four months, and harvest comes!
	and went into *Galilee* **Galiyl**.		Behold, I word to you,
44	For *Jesus* **Yah Shua** himself *testified* **witnessed**,		Lift your eyes, and see the regions;
	that a prophet hath no honour		for they are already white to harvest:
	in his own *country* **fatherland**.	36	and whoever harvests, takes reward;
45	*Then* **So** when he was come into *Galilee* **Galiyl**,		and gathers fruit to life eternal:
	the *Galilaeans* **Galiliy** received him,		so that both the sporer and the harvester
	having seen all *the things* that he did		cheer together.
	at *Jerusalem* **Yeru Shalem** at the *feast* **celebration**:	37	For herein is that word true,
	for they also went unto the *feast* **celebration**.		One spores, and another harvests.
		38	I apostolize you
	THE SECOND SIGN OF YAH SHUA		to harvest whereon you bestow no labour:
46	So *Jesus* **Yah Shua** came again		others labor, and you enter into their labors.
	into *Cana* **Qanah** of *Galilee* **Galiyl**,	39	And many of the Shomeroniym of that city
	where he made the water wine.		trust in him
	And there was a *certain nobleman* **sovereign**,		because of the word of the woman who witnessed,
	whose son was *sick* **frail** at *Capernaum*		He said to me as much as I ever did.
	Kaphar Nachum.		YAH SHUA AND THE SHOMERONIYM
47	When he heard that *Jesus* **Yah Shua**	40	And the Shomeroniym go to him,
	was come out of *Judaea* **Yah Hudah** into *Galilee* **Galiyl**,		and ask him to abide with them;
	he went unto him,		and he abides there two days:
	and *besought* **asked** him	41	and many more trust because of his own word.
	that he *would come down* **should**	42	And they word to the woman,
	descend, and heal his son:		Now we trust, not because of your speech:
	for he was *at the point of death* **about to die**.		for we hear him ourselves,
48	*Then* **So** said *Jesus* **Yah Shua** unto him,		and know that this is truly the Saviour of the cosmos
	Except **Unless** ye see signs and *wonders*		— the Messiah.
	omens, ye *will* **shall** not *believe* **trust**.	43	And after two days he departs from there,
49	The *nobleman saith*		and goes to Galiyl;
	sovereign wordeth unto him,	44	for Yah Shua himself witnessed
	Sir **Adoni**, *come down* **descend** ere my child die.		that a prophet has no honor in his own fatherland:
50	*Jesus saith* **Yah Shua wordeth** unto him,	45	so he goes to Galiyl, and
	Go thy way; thy son liveth.		the Galiliym receive him,
	And the *man believed* **human trusted** the word		seeing all he did at Yeru Shalem at the celebration;
	that *Jesus* **Yah Shua** had *spoken* **said** unto him,		for they also went to the celebration.
	and he went his way.		
51	And as he was *now going*		THE SECOND SIGN OF YAH SHUA
	down **already descending**,	46	So Yah Shua comes again into Qanah, Galiyl
	his servants met him,		where he made the water wine:
			and a sovereign whose son is frail at Kaphar Nachum
	The Food Of Yah Shua	47	hears that Yah Shua
31	In between, his disciples ask him,		

comes from Yah Hudah to Galiyl;
and he goes to him,
and asks him to descend and heal his son
for he is about to die.
48 So Yah Shua says to him,
Unless you see signs and omens, you trust not.
49 The sovereign words to him,
Adoni, descend ere my child die.
50 Yah Shua words to him,
Go your way; your son lives!
And the human trusts the word Yah Shua says to him
and he goes his way:
51 and as he descends, his servants meet him,
and *told* **evangelized** him *saying* **wording**,
Thy *son* **lad** liveth.
52 *Then* **So** enquired he of them
the hour *when* **in which** he began to amend.
And they said unto him,
Yesterday at the seventh hour the fever left him.
53 So the father knew that it was at the same hour,
in the which *Jesus* **Yah Shua** said unto him,
Thy son liveth:
and himself *believed* **trusted**, and his whole house.
54 This is again
the second *miracle* **sign** that *Jesus* **Yah Shua** did,
when he was come out of *Judaea* **Yah Hudah**
into *Galilee* **Galiyl**.

Yah Shua Heals On The Shabbath

5 After this
there was a *feast* **celebration** of the *Jews* **Yah Hudiym**;
and *Jesus* **Yah Shua**
went up **ascended** to *Jerusalem* **Yeru Shalem**.
2 Now there is at *Jerusalem* **Yeru Shalem**
by the sheep *market* **gate** a pool,
which is called in *the Hebrew tongue* **Hebraic**
Bethesda **Beth Hesed**,
having five *porches* **porticos**.
3 In these lay a *great* **vast**
multitude of *impotent folk* **frail**,
of blind, *halt* **lame**, withered,
waiting for the moving of the water.
4 For an angel *went down*
descended at a certain season
into the pool, and *troubled* **agitated** the
water: *so***whosoever** *then* **first**
after the *troubling* **agitating** of the water
stepped in **entered**
was made **became** whole of whatsoever disease he had.
5 And a *certain man* **human** was there,
which had *an infirmity* **a fraility** thirty and eight years.
6 When *Jesus* **Yah Shua** saw him lie,
and knew that he had been
now a long **already a vast** time in that case,
he *saith* **wordeth** unto him,
Wilt **Willest** thou *be made* **become** whole?
7 The *impotent man* **frail** answered him,
Sir **Adoni**, I have no *man* **human**,
when **whenever** the water is troubled,
to put me into the pool:
but while I am coming,
another *steppeth down before* **descendeth in front of** me.
8 *Jesus saith* **Yah Shua wordeth** unto him,
Rise, take up thy *bed* **pad**, and walk.
9 And *immediately* **straightway**
the *man was made* **human became** whole,
and took up his *bed* **pad**, and walked:
and *on* **in** the same day was the *sabbath* **shabbath**.
10 *So* The *Jews* **Yah Hudiym** therefore
said **worded** unto him that was cured,
It is the *sabbath day* **shabbath**:
it is not *lawful* **allowed** for thee to carry thy *bed* **pad**.
11 He answered them, He that made me whole,
the same said unto me, Take up thy *bed* **pad**, and walk.
12 *Then* **So** asked they him,
What *man* **human** is that which said unto thee,
Take up thy *bed* **pad**, and walk?
13 And he that was healed
wist **knew** not who it was:
for *Jesus* **Yah Shua** had conveyed himself
away, a multitude being in that place.
14 Afterward *Jesus* **Yah Shua**
findeth him in the *temple* **priestal precinct**,
and said unto him,
Behold, thou art *made* **become** whole:
sin no more,
lest *a* **somewhat** worse *thing come* **become** unto thee.
15 The *man* **human** departed,
and *told* **evangelized** the *Jews* **Yah Hudiym**
that it was *Jesus* **Yah Shua**, which had made him whole.
16 And *therefore* **because of this**
did the *Jews* **Yah Hudiym** persecute *Jesus* **Yah Shua**,
and sought to *slay* **slaughter** him,
because he had done these *things*
on **in** the *sabbath day* **shabbath**.
17 But *Jesus* **Yah Shua** answered them,
and evangelize him, wording, Your lad lives.
52 So he enquires of them
the hour he began to amend:
and they say to him,

EDC Hebrew / English Bible   JOHN/YOCHANAN 4, 5

      Yesterday at the seventh hour the fever left him.
53   So the father knows it is at the same hour
      Yah Shua said to him, Your son lives! —
      and he and his whole house trust.
54   This again is the second sign Yah Shua does,
      coming from Yah Hudah to Galiyl.

YAH SHUA HEALS ON THE SHABBATH

5   After these,
      there is a celebration of the Yah Hudiym;
      and Yah Shua ascends to Yeru Shalem:
2   and in Yeru Shalem by the sheep gate
      there is a pool, called in Hebraic, Beth Hesed;
      with five porticos:
3   and in these lie a vast multitude of the frail
      — blind, lame, withered;
      awaiting the moving of the water:
4   for at a certain season
      an angel descends into the pool
      and agitates the water;
      so whoever enters first
      after the agitating of the water
      becomes whole of whatever disease he has.
5   And there is a human
      who has a fraility thirty—eight years:
6   when Yah Shua sees him lie,
      and knowing he already is there a vast time, he
      words to him, Will you to become whole?
7   The frail answers him, Adoni, I have no human,
      whenever the water troubles,
      to put me into the pool:
      but as I go, another descends in front of me.
8   Yah Shua words to him,
      Rise, take your pad, and walk.
9   And straightway the human becomes whole,
      and takes his pad, and walks.
      — and that day is shabbath.
10   So the Yah Hudiym word to him who is cured,
      It is shabbath:
      you are not allowed to carry your pad.
11   He answers them, He who made me whole,
      said to me, Take your pad and walk.
12   So they ask him,
      What human said to you, Take your pad, and walk?
13   And he who is healed knows not who:
      for Yah Shua conveyed himself away
      — there being a multitude in that place.
14   After these
      Yah Shua finds him in the priestal precinct,
      and says to him,

      Behold, you have become whole:
      sin no more — lest somewhat worse becomes you.
15   The human departs,
      and evangelizes the Yah Hudiym
      that Yah Shua made him whole:
16   and because of this
      the Yah Hudiym persecute Yah Shua,
      and seek to slaughter him;
      because he does these in shabbath.
17   And Yah Shua answers them,
      My Father worketh hitherto, and I work.
18   *Therefore* **And because of this**
      the *Jews* **Yah Hudiym** sought the
      more to *kill* **slaughter** him,
      because he not only
      had *broken* **released** the *sabbath* **shabbath**,
      but *said* **worded** also that *God* **Elohim** was his Father,
      making himself equal with *God* **Elohim**.
      read: Philippians 2:5—8
19   *Then* **So** answered *Jesus* **Yah Shua** and said unto them,
      Verily, verily ! say **Amen! Amen! I word** unto you,
      The Son can do *nothing* **naught** of himself,
      but what he seeth the Father do:
      for what *things* soever he doeth,
      these also doeth the Son likewise.
20   For the Father *loveth* **befriendeth** the Son,
      and sheweth him all *things* that himself doeth:
      and he *will* **shall** shew him greater works than these,
      that ye may marvel.
21   For **exactly** as the Father raiseth *up* the dead,
      and *quickeneth* **enliveneth** them;
      even *so* **thus** the Son *quickeneth* **enliveneth**
      whom he *will* **willeth**.
22   For the Father judgeth no *man* **one**,
      but hath *committed* **given** all judgment unto the Son:
23   That all men should honour the Son,
      even **exactly** as they honour the Father.
      He that honoureth not the Son
      honoureth not the Father which hath sent him.
24   *Verily, verily ! say* **Amen! Amen! I word** unto you,
      He that heareth my word,
      and *believeth on* **trusteth** him that sent me,
      hath *everlasting* **eternal** life,
      and shall not come into *condemnation* **judgment**;
      but is *passed* **departed** from death unto life.
25   *Verily, verily, ! say* **Amen! Amen! I word** unto you,
      The hour is coming, and now is,

JOHN/YOCHANAN 5

when the dead
shall hear the voice of the Son of *God* **Elohim**:
and they that hear shall live.
26 For as the Father hath life in himself;
so **thus** hath he given to the Son to have life in himself;
27 And hath given him authority
to *execute* **do** judgment also,
because he is the Son of *man* **humanity**.

THE TWO RESURRECTIONS

28 Marvel not at this:
for the hour is coming, in the which
all that are in the *graves* **tombs** shall hear his voice,
29 And shall *come forth* **proceed**;
they that have done good,
unto the resurrection of life;
and they that have done evil,
unto the resurrection of *damnation* **judgment**.
30 I can of mine own self do *nothing* **naught**:
exactly as I hear, I judge: and my judgment is
just; because I seek not mine own will,
but the will of the Father which hath sent me.
31 *If* **Whenever** I *bear* witness
of **concerning** myself,
my witness is not true.
32 There is another
that *beareth witness of* **witnesseth concerning** me;
and I know that the witness
which he witnesseth *of* **concerning** me is true.
33 Ye *sent* **apostolized** unto *John* **Yahn**,
and he *bare witness* **witnessed** unto the truth.
34 But I *receive* **take** not *testimony* **witness**
from *man* **humanity**:
but these *things I say* **I word**, that ye might be saved.
35 He was a burning and a
shining light **manifest candle**:
and ye *were willing* **willed** for *a season* **an hour**
to *rejoice* **jump for joy** in his light.
36 But I have greater witness
than that of *John* **Yahn**:
for the works
which the Father hath given me to
finish **complete/shalam**,
the same works that I do, *bear* witness *of* **concerning** me,
that the Father hath *sent* **apostolized** me.
37 And the Father himself, which hath sent me,
hath *borne witness of* **witnessed concerning** me.
Ye have neither heard his voice *at any time* — **not ever**,
My Father works until now; and I work.
18 And because of this
the Yah Hudiym seek the more to slaughter him;
because he not only releases the shabbath,
but also words that Elohim is his Father
— making himself equal with Elohim.
read: Philippians 2:5—8
19 So Yah Shua answers them, saying,
Amen! Amen! I word to you,
the Son can do naught of himself,
except what he sees the Father do:
for whatever he does,
these also the Son likewise does:
20 for the Father befriends the Son,
and shows him all he himself does:
and shows him greater works than these
so that you marvel.
21 For exactly as the Father raises the dead
and enlivens them;
even thus the Son enlivens whom he wills.
22 For the Father judges no one,
but gives all judgment to the Son:
23 so that all men honor the Son,
exactly as they honor the Father:
he who honors not the Son
honors not the Father who sent him.
24 Amen! Amen! I word to you,
Whoever hears my word and trusts him who sent me
has eternal life and goes not into judgment;
but departs from death to life.
25 Amen! Amen! I word to you,
an hour comes — and now is
when the dead hear the voice of the Son of Elohim:
and whoever hears, lives.
26 For as the Father has life in himself;
thus he gives the Son to have life in himself;
27 and also gives him authority to do judgment
because he is the Son of humanity.

THE TWO RESURRECTIONS

28 Marvel not at this:
an hour comes,
wherein all who are in the tombs hear his voice,
29 and whoever does good,
proceeds to the resurrection of life;
and whoever does evil,
to the resurrection of judgment.
30 I, of my own self, can do naught:
exactly as I hear, I judge; and my judgment is just:
because I seek not my own will
but the will of the Father who sent me.
31 Whenever I witness concerning myself,

JOHN/YOCHANAN 5, 6

	my witness is not true:
32	another witnesses concerning me; and I know the witness he witnesses concerning me is true.
33	You apostolize to Yahn; and he witnesses to the truth:
34	but I take no witness from humanity; but I word these, that you be saved:
35	he was a burning and a manifest candle: and for an hour you willed to jump for joy in his light:
36	but I have greater witness than Yahn: for the works the Father gave me to complete/shalam — these works I do, they witness concerning me, that the Father apostolized me.
37	And the Father himself, who sent me, witnesses concerning me. You neither heard his voice — not ever, nor seen his *shape* **semblance**.
38	And ye have not his word abiding in you: for whom he hath *sent* **apostolized**, him ye *believe* **trust** not.
39	Search the scriptures; for in them ye think ye have eternal life: and they are they which *testify of* **witness concerning** me.
40	And ye will *to* not come to me, that ye might have life.
41	I *receive* **take** not *honour* **glory** from *men* **humanity**.
42	But I know you, that ye have not the love of *God* **Elohim** in you.
43	I am come in my Father's name, and ye *receive* **take** me not: *if* **whenever** another shall come in his own name, him ye *will receive* **shall take**.
44	How can ye *believe* **trust**, which *receive honour* **take glory** one of another, and seek not the *honour* **glory** that cometh from *God* **Elohim** only?
45	Do not think that I *will* **shall** accuse you to the Father: there is one that accuseth you, even *Moses* **Mosheh**, in whom ye *trust* **hope**. 46 For had ye *believed Moses* **trusted Mosheh**, ye *would* **should** have *believed* **trusted** me; for he *wrote of* **scribed concerning** me.
47	But if ye *believe* **trust** not his *writings* **scribings**, how shall ye *believe* **trust** my *words* **rhema**?

YAH SHUA FEEDS FIVE THOUSAND

6	After these *things* *Jesus* **Yah Shua** went over the sea of *Galilee* **Galiyl**, *which is the sea* of Tiberias.
2	And a *great* **vast** multitude followed him, because they saw his *miracles* **signs** which he did on them that were *diseased* **frail**.
3	And *Jesus* **Yah Shua** went up into a mountain, and there he sat with his disciples.
4	And the *passover* **pasach**, a *feast* **celebration** of the *Jews* **Yah Hudiym**, was nigh.
5	*When Jesus then* **Yah Shua** lifted *up* his eyes, and saw a *great company* **vast multitude** come unto him, he *saith* **wordeth** unto *Philip* **Philippos**, Whence shall we *buy* **market** bread, that these may eat?
6	And this he s*aid* **worded** to *prove* **test** him: for he himself knew what he *would* **should** do.
7	*Philip* **Philippos** answered him, Two hundred *pennyworth* **denarion** of bread is not sufficient for them, that *every one* **each** of them may take a little.
8	One of his disciples, *Andrew* **Andreas**, *Simon Peter's* **Shimon Petros'** brother *saith* **wordeth** unto him,
9	There is a *lad* **child** here, which hath five barley *loaves* **breads**, and two small *fishes* **broilings**: but what are they *among* **unto** so many?
10	And *Jesus* **Yah Shua** said, Make the *men sit down* **humans repose**. Now there was much *grass* **herbage** in the place. So the men *sat down* **reposed** in number about five thousand.
11	And *Jesus* **Yah Shua** took the *loaves* **breads**; and when he had *given thanks* **eucharistized**, he distributed to the disciples, and the disciples to them that *were set down* **reposed**; and likewise of the *fishes* **broilings** as much as they *would* **willed**.
12	When they were filled, he *said* **worded** unto his disciples, Gather *up* **together** the fragments that *remain* **superabound**, that *nothing be lost* **naught destruct**.
13	*Therefore* **So** they gathered them together, and filled twelve baskets with the fragments of the five barley *loaves* **breads**, which *remained* **superabounded** over and above unto them that had eaten.

JOHN/YOCHANAN 6

14   *Then* **So** those men,
      when they had seen the *miracle* **sign**
        that *Jesus* **Yah Shua** did, *said* **worded**,
       This is *of a truth* **truly** that prophet
    that should come into the *world* **cosmos**.
              nor saw his semblance:
38   nor have you his word abiding in you:
         for whom he apostolized, you trust not.
39   Search the scriptures;
     for in them you think you have eternal life:
   and these are those that witness concerning me.
40   And you will to not come to me, to have life.
41   I take no glory from humanity.
42   But I know you,
      that you have not the love of Elohim in you.
43   I come in the name of my Father,
              and you take me not:
    whenever another comes in his own name,
                him you take.
44   How can you trust
     — you who take glory of one another,
 and seek not the glory that comes from Elohim only?
45   Think not that I accuse you to the Father:
            there is one who accuses you,
       even Mosheh, in whom you hope:
46   for had you trusted Mosheh,
              you had trusted me;
          for he scribed concerning me:
47   but if you trust not his scribings,
            how trust you my rhema?

YAH SHUA FEEDS FIVE THOUSAND

6   After these
Yah Shua comes across the sea of Galiyl of Tiberias:
2   and a vast multitude follows him,
  because they see the signs he does on the frail:
3   and Yah Shua ascends the mountain;
           and sits there with his disciples:
4   and the pasach, a celebration
              of the Yah Hudiym,
                   is near.
5   Yah Shua, lifting his eyes,
      sees a vast multitude come to him;
           and words to Philippos,
   Where market we bread for these to eat?
6   — he words this to test him:
         for he himself knows what to do.
7   Philippos answers him,
        Two hundred denarion of bread
is not sufficient for each of them to take a little.
8   One of his disciples,
Andreas, the brother of Shimon Petros, words to him,
9   Here is a child
who has five barley breads and two small broilings:
          but what are they to so many?
10   And Yah Shua says, Have the humans repose.
     — and there is much herbage in the place:
the men repose — about five thousand in number.
11   And Yah Shua takes the
          breads and eucharistizes;
       and distributes to the disciples;
      and the disciples to those reposimg:
and likewise the broilings — as much as they will.
12   And when they are filled,
              he words to his disciples,
Gather together the fragments that superabound
        so that naught destructs.
13   So they gather them together;
             and fill twelve baskets
     with the fragments of the five barley breads
which superabounded over and above them who ate.
14   So those men,
   when they see the sign Yah Shua did, word,
This truly is that prophet to come into the cosmos.
15   *When Jesus therefore perceived*
             So Yah Shua knowing
      that they *would* **should** come and
          take **seize** him *by force*,
        to make him *a king* **sovereign**,
he departed again into a mountain himself alone.
16   And *when even was now come* **being evening**,
  his disciples *went down* **descended** unto the sea,
17   And *entered* **embarked** into a *ship* **sailer**,
            and went over the sea
    toward Capernaum **unto Kaphar Nachum**.
    And it *was now* **had already become** dark,
   and *Jesus* **Yah Shua** was not come to them.
18   And the sea *arose* **was roused**
by *reason* **the puffing** of a *great* **mega** wind *that blew*.

YAH SHUA WALKS ON THE SEA

19   So when they *had rowed* **were driven**
  about five and twenty or thirty *furlongs* **stadia**,
   they see *Jesus* **Yah Shua** walking on the sea,
   and *drawing* **being** nigh unto the *ship* **sailer**:
       and they were *afraid* **awestricken**.
20   But he *saith* **wordeth** unto them,
        It is *I* **I AM**; be not *afraid* **awed**.
21   *Then* **So** they *willingly*
        received **willed to take** him

into the *ship* **sailer**:
and *immediately* **straightway** the s*hip* **sailer**
was **became** at the land *whither* **into which** they went.

22 The day following, when the *people* **multitude**
which stood on the other side of the sea
saw that there was none other *boat* **skiff** there,
save **except** that one
whereinto his disciples *were entered* **embarked**,
and that *Jesus* **Yah Shua**
went not with his disciples into the *boat* **skiff**,
but that his disciples were gone away alone;

23 (Howbeit there came other
boats **skiffs** from Tiberias
nigh unto the place where they did eat bread,
after that *the Lord* **Adonay** had *given*
thanks **eucharistized**:)

24 **So** When the *people therefore* **multitude** saw
that *Jesus* **Yah Shua** was not there, neither his disciples,
they also *took shipping* **embarked into sailers**,
and came to *Capernaum* **Kaphar Nachum**,
seeking for *Jesus* **Yah Shua**.

25 And when they had found him
on the other side of the sea,
they said unto him, Rabbi,
when *camest* **becamest** thou hither?

26 *Jesus* **Yah Shua** answered them and said,
Verily, verily, I say **Amen! Amen! I word** unto you,
Ye seek me, not because ye saw the *miracles* **signs**,
but because ye did eat of the *loaves* **breads**,
and were *filled* **fed**.

27 *Labour* **Work** not for the *meat* **food**
which *perisheth* **destructeth**,
but for that *meat* **food**
which *endureth* **abideth** unto *everlasting* **eternal** life,
which the Son of *man* **humanity** shall give unto you:
for him hath *God* **Elohim** the Father sealed.

28 *Then* **So** said they unto him, What shall we do,
that we might work the works of *God* **Elohim**?

29 *Jesus* **Yah Shua** answered and said unto them,
This is the work of *God* **Elohim**,
that ye *believe on* **trust in** him
whom he hath *sent* **apostolized**.

30 **So** They said *therefore* unto him,
So What sign *shewest* **doest** thou *then*,
so that we may see, and *believe* **trust** thee?
what *dost* **workest** thou *work*?

31 Our fathers did eat manna
in the *desert* **wilderness**;
exactly as it is *written* **scribed**,
He gave them bread from heaven to eat.

Nechem Yah 9:5

32 *Then* **So Yah Shua** said unto them,
Verily, verily I say **Amen! Amen! I word** unto you,
Moses **Mosheh** gave you not that bread from heaven;
but my Father giveth you the true bread from heaven.

33 For the bread of *God* **Elohim**
is he which *cometh down* **descendeth** from heaven,
and giveth life unto the *world* **cosmos**.

34 *Then* **So** said they unto him, *Lord* **Adonay**,
evermore give us this bread.

15 So Yah Shua,
knowing that they come to seize him
to make him sovereign,
departs again into a mountain alone by himself:

16 and being evening,
his disciples descend to the sea

17 and embark in a sailer,
and go across the sea to Kaphar Nachum:
and being already dark,
Yah Shua had not come to them;

18 and the sea rouses by the
puffing of a mega wind.

Yah Shua Walks On The Sea

19 So driving onward
about twenty—five or thirty stadia;
and they see Yah Shua walking on the sea
and being near the sailer: and they are awestricken.

20 And he words to them,
I AM! Awe not!

21 So they will to take him into the sailer:
and straightway the sailer
is at the land they are going.

22 On the morrow,
the multitude stands across the sea
and sees no other skiff there
except that one wherein his disciples embarked;
and that Yah Shua
had not gone with his disciples in the skiff,
but that his disciples departed alone;

23 — however other skiffs come from Tiberias
near the place where they ate the breads
after Adonay eucharistized.

24 So when the multitude sees
that neither Yah Shua nor his disciples are there,
they also embark into sailers
and go to Kaphar Nachum seeking Yah Shua:

25 and they find him across the sea,
and they say to him, Rabbi, when became you here?

26 Yah Shua answers them, saying,

JOHN/YOCHANAN 6

      Amen! Amen! I word to you,
You seek me, not because you see the signs, but
because you ate the breads and are fed.
27 Work not for the food that destructs;
but for the food that abides to eternal life
which the Son of humanity gives you:
for Elohim the Father sealed him.
28 So they say to him,
What do we to work the works of Elohim?
29 Yah Shua answers them, saying,
This is the work of Elohim:
to trust in him whom he apostolized.
30 So they say to him,
So what sign do you, that we see and trust you?
What work you?
31 Our fathers ate manna in the wilderness;
exactly as scribed,
He gave them bread from the heavens
to eat. Nechem Yah 9:5
32 So Yah Shua says to them,
Amen! Amen! I word to you,
Mosheh gave you not that bread from the heavens;
but my Father gives you the true bread from the heavens:
33 for the bread of Elohim
is he who descends from the heavens
and gives life to the cosmos.
34 So they say to him, Adonay,
Give us evermore this bread.

YAH SHUA, THE LIVING BREAD

35 And *Jesus* **Yah Shua** said unto them,
I am **I AM** the bread of life:
he that cometh to me shall never hunger;
and he that *believeth on* **trusteth in** me
shall never — **not ever** thirst.
36 But I said unto you,
That ye also have seen me, and *believe* **trust** not.
37 All that the Father giveth me shall come to me;
and him that cometh to me
I *will in no wise cast out* **shall never eject**.
38 For I *came down* **descended** from heaven,
not to do mine own will, but the
will of him that sent me.
39 And this is the Father's will which hath sent me,
that of all which he hath given me
I should lose *nothing* **naught thereof**,
but should raise it *up* again at the *last* **final** day.
40 And this is the will of him that sent me,
that every one which seeth the Son, and
believeth on **trusteth in** him,
may have *everlasting* **eternal** life:
and I *will* **shall** raise him *up* at the *last* **final** day.
41 *The Jews then* **So the Yah Hudiym** murmured
at **concerning** him,
because he said,
I am **I AM** the bread
which *came down* **descended** from heaven.
42 And they *said* **worded**,
Is not this *Jesus* **Yah Shua**, the son of *Joseph* **Yoseph**,
whose father and mother we know?
So how is it *then* that he *saith* **wordeth**,
I *came down* **descended** from heaven?
43 *Jesus therefore* **So Yah Shua**
answered and said unto them,
Murmur not *among yourselves* **with one another**.
44 No *man* **one** can come to me,
except **unless** the Father which hath sent me draw him:
and I *will* **shall** raise him *up* at the *last* **final** day.
45 It is *written* **scribed** in the prophets,
And they shall be all *taught* **doctrinated** of *God* **Elohim**.
So Every *man therefore* **one** that hath heard,
and hath learned of the Father, cometh
unto me. Yesha Yah 54:13
46 Not that any *man* **one** hath seen the Father,
save **except** he which is of *God* **Elohim**,
he hath seen the Father.
47 *Verily, verily I say* **Amen!**
Amen! I word unto you,
He that *believeth on* **trusteth in** me
hath *everlasting* **eternal** life.
48 *I am* **I AM** that bread of life.
49 Your fathers did eat manna in the wilderness,
and are dead.
50 This is the bread
which *cometh down* **descendeth** from heaven,
that *a man* **anyone** may eat thereof, and not die.
51 *I am* **I AM** the living bread
which *came down* **descended** from heaven:
if any man **Whenever anyone** eat of this bread,
he shall live *for ever* **unto the eons**:
and the bread that I *will* **shall** give is my flesh,
which I *will* **shall** give for the life of the *world* **cosmos**.
52 *The Jews therefore* **So the Yah Hudiym**
strove among *themselves* **one another**, *saying* **wording**,
How can this man give us his flesh to eat?
53 *Then Jesus* **So Yah Shua** said unto them,
Verily, verily I say **Amen! Amen! I word** unto you,
Except **Unless** ye eat the flesh of
the Son of *man* **humanity**,
and drink his blood, ye have no life in you.

54	Whoso eateth my flesh, and drinketh my blood,
	hath eternal life;
	and I *will* **shall** raise him *up* at the *last* **final** day.
55	For my flesh is *meat indeed* **truly food**,
	and my blood is **truly** drink *indeed*.
56	He that eateth my flesh, and drinketh my blood,
	dwelleth **abideth** in me, and I in him.
57	**Exactly** As the living Father
	hath *sent* **apostolized** me,
	and I live *by* **through** the Father:
	thus he that eateth me, even he shall live *by* **through** me.
58	This is that bread

YAH SHUA, THE LIVING BREAD

35	And Yah Shua says to them,
	I AM the bread of life:
	whoever comes to me never famishes;
	and whoever trusts in me never thirsts — not ever.
36	But I say to you,
	that you also see me, and trust not:
37	all whom the Father gives me, come to me;
	and whoever comes to me, I never eject.
38	For I descended from the heavens
	— not to do my own will
	but the will of him who sent me.
39	And this is the will of the Father who sent me,
	of all whom he gave me, I lose none;
	but raise him again at the final day:
40	and this is the will of him who sent me,
	that everyone who sees the Son and trusts in him
	has eternal life:
	and I raise him at the final day.
41	So the Yah Hudiym murmur concerning him,
	because he said,
	I AM the bread that descended from the heavens.
42	And they word,
	Is not this Yah Shua the son of Yoseph,
	whose father and mother we know?
	So how words he, I descended from the heavens?
43	So Yah Shua answers them, saying,
	Murmur not with one another.
44	No one can come to me
	unless the Father who sent me draws him:
	and I raise him at the final day.
45	It is scribed in the prophets,
	And they all are doctrinated of Elohim.
	So everyone who hears,
	and learns of the Father, comes to me.
	Yesha Yah 54:13
46	Not that anyone has seen the Father,
	except he who is of Elohim; he has seen the Father.
47	Amen! Amen! I word to you,
	Whoever trusts in me has eternal life.
48	I AM that bread of life.
49	Your fathers ate manna in
	the wilderness, and died.
50	This is the bread that
	descended from the heavens,
	for anyone to eat thereof, and not die.
51	I AM the living bread
	descended from the heavens:
	whenever anyone eats of this bread,
	he lives to the eons:
	and the bread I give is my flesh,
	which I give for the life of the cosmos.
52	So the Yah Hudiym
	strive among one another, wording,
	How can this one give us his flesh to eat?
53	So Yah Shua says to them,
	Amen! Amen! I word to you,
	Unless you eat the flesh of the Son of humanity,
	and drink his blood, you have no life in you.
54	Whoever eats my flesh and drinks my blood
	has eternal life;
	and I raise him at the final day.
55	For my flesh is truly food,
	and my blood is truly drink.
56	Whoever eats my flesh and drinks my blood
	abides in me; and I in him.
57	Exactly as the living Father apostolized me
	— and I live through the Father;
	thus whoever eats me, even he lives through me.
58	This is that bread
	which *came down* **descended** from heaven:
	not **exactly** as your fathers did eat manna, and are dead:
	he that eateth of this bread
	shall live *for ever* **unto the eons**.
59	These *things* said he in the synagogue,
	as he *taught* **doctrinated** in
	Capernaum **Kaphar Nachum**.
60	**So** Many *therefore* of his disciples,
	when they had heard this, said,
	This is an hard *saying* **word**; who can hear it?
61	When *Jesus* **Yah Shua** knew in himself
	that his disciples murmured *at* **concerning** it,
	he said unto them, Doth this *offend* **scandalize** you?
62	*What and if —* **so whenever**
	ye shall see the Son of *man* **humanity**
	ascend *up* where he was before?
63	It is the spirit that *quickeneth* **enliveneth**;

JOHN/YOCHANAN 6, 7

the flesh *profiteth nothing* **benefiteth naught**:
the *words* **rhema** that I speak unto you,
they are spirit, and they are life.

64 But there are some of you that *believe* **trust** not.
For *Jesus* **Yah Shua** knew from the beginning
who they were that *believed* **trusted** not,
and who should betray him.

65 And he *said* **worded**,
Therefore **So** said I unto you,
that no *man* **one** can come unto me,
except **unless** it were given unto him of my Father.

66 From that time many of his disciples went back,
and walked no more with him.

THE WITNESS OF PETROS

67 *Then* **So** said *Jesus* **Yah Shua** unto the twelve,
will ye also go away?

68 *Then Simon Peter* **So Shimon Petros** answered him,
Lord **Adonay**, to whom shall we go?
thou hast the *words* **rhema** of eternal life.

69 And we *believe* **trust** and *are sure* **know**
that thou art *that Christ* **the Messiah**,
the Son of the living *God* **Elohim**.

70 *Jesus* **Yah Shua** answered them,
Have not I chosen you twelve,
and one of you is *a devil* **Diabolos**?

71 He *spake* **worded** of *Judas Iscariot* **Yah Hudah the urbanite**
the son of *Simon* **Shimon**:
for he it was that should betray him,
being one of the twelve.

7 After these *things*
Jesus **Yah Shua** walked in *Galilee* **Galiyl**:
for he *would* **willed to** not walk in *Jewry* **Yah Hudah**,
because the *Jews* **Yah Hudiym**
sought to *kill* **slaughter** him.

THE TABERNACLE STAKING CELEBRATION – SUKKOTH/BRUSH ARBORS

2 Now the *Jews' feast* **Yah Hudiy's celebration**
of *tabernacles* **tabernacle staking** was *at hand* **nigh**.

3 **So** His brethren *therefore* said unto him,
Depart hence, and go into *Judaea* **Yah Hudah**,
that thy disciples also may see the works that thou doest.

4 For there is no *man* **one**
that doeth *any thing* **aught** in secret,
and he himself seeketh to be known *openly* **boldly**.
If thou do these *things*,
shew **manifest** thyself to the *world* **cosmos**.

5 For neither did his brethren *believe* **trust** in him.

6 *Then Jesus said* **So Yah Shua worded** unto them,
My *time* **season** is not yet *come* **here**:
but your *time* **season** is alway *ready* **prepared**.

7 The *world* **cosmos** cannot hate you;
but me it hateth,
because I *testify of* **witness concerning** it,
that the works thereof are evil.

8 *Go* **Ascend** ye *up* unto this *feast* **celebration**:
I *go* **ascend** not *up* yet unto this *feast* **celebration**:
for my *time* **season** is not yet *full come* **fulfilled/shalamed**.

9 When he had said these words unto them,
he abode still in *Galilee* **Galiyl**.

10 But when his brethren were *gone up* **ascended**,
then *went* **ascended** he also *up*
unto the *feast* **celebration**,
not *openly* **manifestly**, but as it were in secret.

descended from the heavens:
not exactly as your fathers ate manna, and died:
whoever eats of this bread lives to the eons.

59 — he says these in the synagogue,
as he doctrinates in Kaphar Nachum.

60 So many of his disciples,
when they hear this, say,
This is a hard word; who can hear it?

61 Yah Shua knows in himself
that his disciples murmur concerning it,
and he says to them, Does this scandalize you?

62 — so whenever you see the Son of humanity
ascend where he was previously?

63 The spirit enlivens; the flesh benefits naught:
the rhema I speak to you are spirit and life:

64 but there are some of you who trust not.
— for Yah Shua knew from the beginning
who they are who trust not,
and who betrays him.

65 And he words, So say I to you,
no one can come to me,
unless it is given of my Father.

66 — from that time many of his disciples go back,
and walk no more with him.

THE WITNESS OF PETROS

67 So Yah Shua says to the twelve,
Will you also to go away?

68 So Shimon Petros answers him,
Adonay, to whom go we?
You have the rhema of eternal life:

69 and we trust and know that you are the Messiah,

the Son of the living Elohim.
70 Yah Shua answers them,
Have I not chosen you twelve — and
one of you is Diabolos?
71 He words of Yah Hudah
the urbanite — of Shimon:
for he is about to betray him, being one of the twelve.

7 After these Yah Shua walks in Galiyl:
for he wills to not walk in Yah Hudah,
because the Yah Hudiym seek to slaughter him.

THE TABERNACLE STAKING CELEBRATION —
SUKKOTH/BRUSH ARBORS

2 And the celebration of the Yah Hudiym
of tabernacle staking is near.
3 So his brothers say to him,
Depart hence, and go to Yah Hudah,
so that your disciples also see the works you do.
4 For no one does aught in secret,
and seeks for himself to be known boldly.
if you do these,
manifest yourself to the cosmos.
5 — for not even his brothers trust in him.
6 So Yah Shua words to them,
My season is not yet here:
but your season is always prepared.
7 The cosmos cannot hate you;
but it hates me — because I witness concerning it
that its works are evil.
8 You ascend to this celebration:
I ascend not yet to this celebration
for my season is not yet fulfilled/shalamed.
9 He says these words to them
and still abides in Galiyl:
10 and his brothers ascend,
then he also ascends to the celebration
— not manifestly, but as in secret.
11 Then **So** the *Jews* **Yah Hudiym**
sought him at the *feast* **celebration**,
and *said* **worded**, Where is he?
12 And there was much murmuring
among the *people* **multitude** concerning him:
for **indeed** some *said* **worded**, He is a good man:
others *said* **spake**, Nay;
but he *deceiveth* **seduceth** the *people* **multitude**.
13 **Howbeit Yet indeed**
no *man* **one** spake *openly* **of boldly about** him
for *fear* **awe** of the *Jews* **Yah Hudiym**.
14 *Now about* **Already** the
midst of the *feast* **celebration**

Jesus went up **Yah Shua ascended**
into the *temple* **priestal precinct**,
and *taught* **doctrinated**.
15 And the *Jews* **Yah Hudiym**
marvelled, *saying* **wording**,
How knoweth this *man letters* **one scribings**,
having never learned?
16 *Jesus* **Yah Shua** answered them, and said,
My doctrine is not mine, but his that sent me.
17 *If* **Whenever** any *man will*
one willeth to do his will,
he shall know *of* **concerning** the doctrine,
whether it be of *God* **Elohim**, or
whether I speak of myself.
18 He that speaketh of himself
seeketh his own glory:
but he that seeketh his glory that sent him,
the same is true,
and no *unrighteousness* **unjustness** is in him.
19 Did not *Moses* **Mosheh** give you the *law* **torah**,
and yet none of you *keepeth* **doeth** the *law* **torah**?
Why *go* **seek** ye *about* to *kill* **slaughter** me?
20 The *people* **multitude** answered and said,
Thou hast a *devil* **demon**:
who *goeth about* **seeketh** to *kill* **slaughter** thee?
21 *Jesus* **Yah Shua** answered and said unto them,
I have done one work, and ye all marvel.
22 *Moses therefore* **So Mosheh**
gave unto you circumcision;
(not because it is of *Moses* **Mosheh**, but of the fathers;)
and ye on the *sabbath day* **shabbath**
circumcise a *man* **human**.
23 If a *man* **human** on the *sabbath day* **shabbath**
receive **taketh** circumcision,
that the *law* **torah** of *Moses* **Mosheh**
should not be *broken* **released**;
are ye *angry* **choleric** at me,
because I have made a *man every whit* **human whole**
on the *sabbath day* **shabbath**?
24 Judge not according to *the appearance* **visage**,
but judge *righteous* **just** judgment.
25 *Then said* **So worded**
some of *them of Jerusalem* **the Yeru Shalemiym**,
Is not this he, whom they seek to *kill* **slaughter**?
26 But, *lo* **behold**, he speaketh boldly,
and they *say nothing* **word naught** unto him.
Do the *rulers* **archs** know *indeed* **truly**
that this is **truly** the *very Christ* **Messiah**?
27 *Howbeit* **Yet** we know this
man **one** whence he is:

but when *Christ* **ever the Messiah** cometh,
no *man* **one** knoweth whence he is.

YAH SHUA DOCTRINATES
IN THE PRIESTAL PRECINCT

28 *Then* **So** cried *Jesus* **Yah Shua**
in the *temple* **priestal precinct** as he *taught* **doctrinated**,
saying **wording**, Ye both know me,
and ye know whence *I am* **I AM**:
and I am not come of myself,
but he that *sent* **apostolized** me is true,
whom ye know not.

29 But I know him: for *I am*
from him **of him, I AM**,
and he hath sent me.

30 *Then* **So** they sought to *take* **seize** him:
but no *man* **one** laid hands on him,
because his hour was not yet come.

31 And many of the *people* **multitude**
believed on **trusted in** him, and *said* **worded**,
When *Christ* **ever the Messiah** cometh,
will **shall** he do *many* more *miracles* **signs** than these
which this *man* **one** hath done?

32 The Pharisees heard that the *people* **multitude**
murmured *such things* **these** concerning him;
and the Pharisees and the *chief* **arch** priests
sent officers **apostolized attendants** to *take* **seize** him.

11 So the Yah Hudiym seek him at the celebration
and word, Where is he?

12 And there is much murmuring
among the multitude concerning him:
for indeed some word, He is a good man.
Others speak, No; but he seduces the multitude.

13 Yet indeed no one speaks boldly about him
for awe of the Yah Hudiym.

14 Already midst the celebration
Yah Shua ascends into the priestal precinct
and doctrinates:

15 and the Yah Hudiym marvel, wording,
How knows this one scribings, not having learned?

16 Yah Shua answers them, saying,
My doctrine is not mine; but his who sent me:

17 whenever anyone wills to do his will,
he knows concerning the doctrine
— whether it be of Elohim,
or whether I speak of myself.

18 Whoever speaks of himself seeks his own glory:
but whoever seeks the glory of him who sent him,
that same *one* is true:
and there is no unjustness in him.

19 Gave not Mosheh you the torah?
And yet none of you does the torah!
Why seek you to slaughter me?

20 The multitude answers,
saying, You have a demon!
Who seeks to slaughter you?

21 Yah Shua answers them, saying,
I do one work and you all marvel:

22 so Mosheh gave you circumcision
— not because it is of Mosheh, but of the fathers:
and you in shabbath circumcise a human:

23 if a human, on shabbath, takes circumcision,
that the torah of Mosheh not be released;
are you choleric at me
because I make a human whole on shabbath?

24 Judge not according to visage,
but judge just judgment.

25 So some of the Yeru Shalemiym word,
Is not this he, whom they seek to slaughter?

26 But, behold, he speaks boldly
and they word naught to him.
Know the archs truly that this is truly the Messiah?

27 Yet this one, we know whence he is:
but whenever the Messiah comes
no one knows whence he is.

YAH SHUA DOCTRINATES
IN THE PRIESTAL PRECINCT

28 So in the priestal precinct
Yah Shua cries as he doctrinates,
wording, You both know me,
and you know whence I AM:
and I come not from myself,
but he who apostolized me is true
— whom you know not.

29 But I know him: for of him, I AM,
and he sent me.

30 So they seek to seize him:
but no one lays hands on him
because his hour is not yet come.

31 And many of the multitude trust in him
and word, Whenever the Messiah comes,
does he many more signs than these
which this one does?

32 The Pharisees hear that the multitude
murmur these concerning him;
and the Pharisees and the archpriests
apostolize attendants to seize him.

33 *Then* said *Jesus* **Yah Shua** unto them,
Yet a little *while* **time** am I with you,

	and *then* I go unto him that sent me.	47	*Then* **So** answered them the Pharisees, Are ye also *deceived* **seduced**?
34	Ye shall seek me, and shall not find me: and where I am, thither ye cannot come.	48	Have any of the *rulers* **archs** or of the Pharisees *believed on* **trusted in** him?
35	*Then* **So** said the *Jews* **Yah Hudiym** among themselves, Whither *will* **shall** he go, that we shall not find him? *will* **shall** he go unto the *dispersed* **Diaspora** among the *Gentiles* **Hellenes**, and *teach* **doctrinate** the *Gentiles* **Hellenes**?	49	But this *people* **multitude** who knoweth not the *law* **torah** are cursed.
		50	Nicodemus *saith* **wordeth** unto them, (he that came to *Jesus* **Yah Shua** by night, being one of them,)
36	What *manner of saying* **word** is this that he said, Ye shall seek me, and shall not find me: and where I am, thither ye cannot come?	51	Doth our *law* **torah** judge any *man* **human**, *before* **unless** it *first* hear him, and know what he doeth?
		52	They answered and said unto him, Art thou also of *Galilee* **Galiyl**? Search, and *look* **see**: for out of *Galilee* **Galiyl** ariseth no prophet.

The Invitation Of Yah Shua To Take The Holy Spirit

37	In the *last* **final** day, that *great* **mega** day of the *feast* **celebration**, *Jesus* **Yah Shua** stood and cried, *saying* **wording**, *If* **Whenever** any *man* **one** thirst, let him come unto me, and drink.	53	And *every man* **each** went unto his own house.
38	He that *believeth on* **trusteth in** me, **exactly** as the scripture hath said, out of his belly shall flow *rivers* **streams** of living water.	8	*Jesus* **But Yah Shua** went unto the mount of Olives.

The Adulteress

39	(But this *spake* **said** he *of* **concerning** the Spirit, which they that *believe on* **trust in** him should *receive* **take**: for the *Holy Spirit* **Ruach ha-kodesh** was not yet *given*; because that *Jesus* **Yah Shua** was not yet glorified.)	2	And *early in the morning* **at dawn** he came again into the *temple* **priestal precinct**, and all the people came unto him; and he sat down, and *taught* **doctrinated** them.
40	**So** Many of the *people* **multitude** *therefore*, when they heard this *saying* **word**, *said* **worded**, *Of a truth* **Truly** this is the Prophet.	3	And the scribes and Pharisees brought unto him a woman *taken* **overtaken** in adultery; and when they had set her in the midst,
41	Others *said* **worded**, This is the *Christ* **Messiah**. But some *said* **worded**, shall *Christ* **the Messiah** come out of *Galilee* **Galiyl**?	4	They *say* **word** unto him, *Master* **Doctor**, this woman was *taken* **overtaken** in adultery, in the very act.
		33	Yah Shua says to them, Yet a little time I am with you, and I go to him who sent me.
42	Hath not *indeed* the scripture said, That *Christ* **the Messiah** cometh of the *seed* **sperma** of David, and out of the *town* **village** of *Bethlehem* **Beth Lechem**, where David was? Michah 5:2	34	You seek me, and find me not: and where I am, you cannot come.
		35	So the Yah Hudiym say among themselves, Where goes he, that we find him not? Goes he to the diaspora among the Hellenes and doctrinates the Hellenes?
43	So there *was* **became** a *division* **schism** among the *people* **multitude** because of him.	36	What word is this he says, You seek me, and find me not: and, Where I am, you cannot come?
44	And some of them *would have taken* **willed to seize** him; but no *man* **one** laid hands on him.		

The Invitation Of Yah Shua To Take The Holy Spirit

45	*Then* **So** came the *officers* **attendants** to the *chief* **arch** priests and Pharisees; and they said unto them, Why have ye not brought him?	37	In the final day — that mega day of the celebration Yah Shua stands and cries, wording, whenever anyone thirsts, come to me and drink:
46	The *officers* **attendants** answered, Never **ever** *man* spake *a human* like this *man* **human**.	38	whoever trusts in me,

JOHN/YOCHANAN 8

exactly as the scripture says,
from his belly flows streams of living water.
39 And he says this concerning the Spirit
whom those trusting in him are about to take:
for the Holy Spirit is not yet
because Yah Shua is not yet glorified.
40 So many of the multitude,
when they hear this word,
word, Truly this is the Prophet.
41 Others word, This is the Messiah.
But some word, Comes the Messiah from Galiyl?
42 Indeed, says not the scripture,
The Messiah comes from the sperma of David
and from the village of Beth Lechem
where David was?
Michah 5:2
43 So there becomes a schism
among the multitude because of him:
44 and some of them will to seize him;
but no one lays hands on him.
45 So the attendants
go to the archpriests and Pharisees;
and say to them, Why bring you him not?
46 The attendants answer,
Never ever spoke a human as this human.
47 So the Pharisees answer them,
Are you also seduced?
48 Trust any of the archs or
of the Pharisees in him?
49 But this multitude who know not the torah
are cursed.
50 Nicodemus words to them
— who came to Yah Shua by night
— being one of them,
51 Judges our torah any human
unless it first hears him and knows what he does?
52 They answer him, saying,
Are you also of Galiyl?
Search and see! For no prophet rises from Galiyl.
53 And each goes to his own house
8 and Yah Shua goes to the mount of Olives.

THE ADULTERESS

2 And at dawn he goes again
to the priestal precinct
and all the people come to him;
and he sits and doctrinates them:
3 and the scribes and Pharisees
bring him a woman overtaken in adultery;
and they set her among them.

4 They word to him, Doctor,
this woman was overtaken in the
very act — adulterizing:
5 Now *Moses* **Mosheh** in the *law* **torah**
commanded **misvahed** us, that such should be stoned:
but what *sayest* **wordest** thou?
6 This they *said* **worded**, *tempting* **testing** him,
that they might have to accuse him.
But *Jesus* **Yah Shua** stooped *down*,
and with his finger *wrote on* **scribed in** the ground,
as though he heard them not.
7 So when they *continued* **abode** asking him,
he *lifted up* **unbent** himself, and said unto them,
He that is *without sin* **sinless** among you,
let him first cast a stone at her.
8 And again he stooped *down*,
and *wrote on* **scribed in** the ground.
9 And they which heard it,
being *convicted* **reproved** by their own conscience,
went out one by one,
beginning *at* **from** the *eldest* **elders**,
even unto the *last* **final**:
and *Jesus* **Yah Shua** was left alone,
and the woman standing in the midst.
10 When *Jesus* **Yah Shua** had
lifted up **unbent** himself,
and saw *none but* **no one except** the woman,
he said unto her, Woman,
where are those thine accusers?
hath no *man* **one** condemned thee?
11 She said, no *man* **one**, *Lord* **Adonay**.
And *Jesus* **Yah Shua** said unto her,
Neither do I condemn thee: go, and sin no more.
12 *Then* **So** spake *Jesus* **Yah Shua** again unto them,
saying **wording**,
I am **I AM** the light of the *world* **cosmos**:
he that followeth me shall not walk in darkness,
but shall have the light of life.
13 **So** The Pharisees *therefore* said unto him,
Thou *bearest record of* **witnessest concerning** thyself;
thy *record* **witness** is not true.
14 *Jesus* **Yah Shua** answered and said unto them,
Though I *bear record of* **witness concerning** myself,
yet my *record* **witness** is true:
for I know whence I came, and whither I go;
but ye *cannot tell* **know not** whence I come,
and whither I go.
15 Ye judge after the flesh; I judge no *man* **one**.
16 And yet *if* **whenever** I
judge, my judgment is true:

	for I am not alone, but I and the Father that sent me.	11	She says, No one, Adonay.
17	It is also *written* **scribed** in your *law* **torah**,		Yah Shua says to her,
	that the testimony witness of two men humans is true.		Neither condemn I you: go, and sin no more.
18	*I am one that bear witness of*	12	So again Yah Shua speaks to them,
	I AM witness concerning myself,		wording, I AM the light of the cosmos:
	and the Father that sent me		whoever follows me, walks not in darkness,
	beareth witness of **witnesseth concerning** me.		but has the light of life.
19	*Then said* **So worded** they	13	So the Pharisees say to him,
	unto him, Where is thy Father?		You witness concerning yourself;
	Jesus **Yah Shua** answered,		your witness is not true.
	Ye neither know me, nor my Father:	14	Yah Shua answers them, saying,
	if ye had known me,		Though I witness concerning myself,
	ye should have known my Father also.		yet my witness is true:
20	These *words* **rhema**		for I know whence I came, and where I go;
	spake *Jesus* **Yah Shua** in the treasury,		but you know not whence I came, and where I go.
	as he *taught* **doctrinated** in the *temple* **priestal precinct**	15	You judge after the flesh; I judge no one:
	and no *man laid hands on* **one seized** him;	16	and yet whenever I judge,
	for his hour was not yet come.		my judgment is true:
21	*Then* **So** said *Jesus* **Yah Shua** again unto them,		for I am not alone, but I and the Father who sent me.
	I go my way,	17	And also it is scribed in your torah,
	and ye shall seek me, and shall die in your sins:		The witness of two humans is true.
	whither I go, ye cannot come.	18	I AM witness concerning myself;
22	*Then said* **So worded** the *Jews* **Yah Hudiym**,		and the Father who sent me witnesses concerning me.
	will **shall** he *kill* **slaughter** himself?	19	So they word to him, Where is your Father?
	because he *saith* **wordeth**, Whither I go, ye cannot come.		Yah Shua answers,
23	And he said unto them,		You know neither me nor my Father:
	Ye are from beneath; I am from above:		had you known me,
5	and in the torah		you had known my Father also.
	Mosheh misvahs us to stone such:	20	Yah Shua speaks these rhema in the treasury
	but what word you?		as he doctrinates in the priestal precinct;
6	They word this to test him — to accuse him:		and no one seizes him
	and Yah Shua stoops		for his hour is not yet come.
	and with his finger scribes in the ground	21	So Yah Shua says to them again,
	as though he hears them not.		I go my way;
7	And they abide asking him,		and you seek me; and die in your sins:
	and he unbends himself and says to them,		where I go, you cannot come.
	The sinless among you,	22	So the Yah Hudiym word,
	cast the first stone at her.		Slaughters he himself?
8	Again he stoops and scribes in the ground;		Because he words, Where I go, you cannot come.
9	but they who hear:	23	And he says to them,
	— reproved by their own conscience		You are from below; I am from above:
	they go out one by one		ye are of this *world* **cosmos**;
	beginning from the elders even to the final;		I am not of this *world* **cosmos**.
	and Yah Shua is left alone	24	*So* I said *therefore* unto you,
	with the woman standing in the midst.		that ye shall die in your sins:
10	And Yah Shua unbends himself		for *if* **whenever** ye *believe* **trust** not that *I*
	and sees no one except the woman:		*am he* **I AM**, ye shall die in your sins.
	and he says to her,	25	*Then said* **So worded** they
	Woman, where are your accusers?		unto him, Who art thou?
	Is no one condemning you?		And *Jesus* **Yah Shua** saith unto them,

JOHN/YOCHANAN 8

Even the same
that I *said* **spake** unto you from the beginning.

26 I have *many things* **much**
to *say* **speak** and to judge
of **concerning** you:
but he that sent me is true;
and I *speak* **word** to the *world* **cosmos**
those *things* which I have heard of him.

27 They *understood* **knew** not
that he *spake* **worded** to them of the Father.

TRUTH LIBERATES

28 Then said *Jesus* **Yah Shua** unto them,
When **ever** ye have
lifted up **exalted** the Son of *man* **humanity**,
then shall ye know that *I am he* **I AM**,
and that I do *nothing* **naught** of myself;
but **exactly** as my Father hath *taught* **doctrinated** me,
I speak these *things*.

29 And he that sent me is with me:
the Father hath not *left* **forsaken** me alone;
for I do always those *things* that please him.

30 As he spake these words,
many *believed on* **trusted in** him.

31 Then said *Jesus* **So worded Yah Shua**
to those *Jews* **Yah Hudiym** which
believed on **trusted in** him,
If **Whenever** ye *continue* **abide** in my word,
then are ye *truly* my disciples *indeed*;

32 And ye shall know the truth,
and the truth shall *make* **liberate** you *free*.

33 They answered him, We be
Abraham's *seed* **sperma**,
and were never — **not ever**
in bondage **servient** to any *man* **one**:
how *sayest* **wordest** thou, Ye shall
be *made free* **liberated**?

34 *Jesus* **Yah Shua** answered them,
Verily, verily I say **Amen! Amen! I word** unto you,
Whosoever *committeth* **doeth** sin is the servant of sin.

35 And the servant abideth not in the house
for ever **unto the eons**:
but the Son abideth *for ever* **unto the eons**.

36 *If* **So whenever** the Son *therefore*
shall *make* **liberate** you *free*,
ye shall be *free* **liberated** indeed.

37 I know that ye are Abraham's *seed* **sperma**;
but ye seek to *kill* **slaughter** me, because
my word hath no place in you.

38 I speak that which I have seen with my Father:
and ye do that which ye have seen with your father.

39 They answered and said unto him,
Abraham is our father.
Jesus saith **Yah Shua wordeth** unto them,
If ye were Abraham's children,
ye *would* **should** do the works of Abraham.

40 But now ye seek to *kill* **slaughter** me,
a *man* **human** that hath *told you* **spoken** the truth,
which I have heard of *God* **Elohim**:
this did not Abraham.

41 Ye do the *deeds* **works** of your father.
Then **So** said they to him,
We be not *born* **birthed** of *fornication* **whoredom**;
we have one Father, even *God* **Elohim**.

42 *Jesus* **Yah Shua** said unto them,
If *God* **Elohim** were your Father,
ye *would* **should** love me:
for I proceeded *forth* and came from *God* **Elohim**;
neither came I of myself, but he *sent* **apostolized** me.

43 Why do ye not *understand* **know** my speech?
even because ye cannot hear my word.

44 Ye are of your father *the devil* **Diabolos**,
and the *lusts* **pantings** of your father ye will **to** do.
He was a murderer from the beginning,
and *abode* **stood** not in the truth,
because there is no truth in him.
When **ever** he speaketh a lie, he speaketh of his own:
for he is a liar, and the father of it.

you are of this cosmos; I am not of this cosmos:

24 so I say to you, that you die in your sins;
for whenever you trust not that I AM,
you die in your sins.

25 So they word to him, Who are you?
And Yah Shua says to them,
Even what I spoke to you from the beginning:

26 I have much to speak and
to judge concerning you:
but he who sent me is true;
and I word to the cosmos what I hear from him.

27 — they know not
that he words to them of the Father.

TRUTH LIBERATES

28 Then Yah Shua says to them,
Whenever you exalt the Son of humanity,
then you know that I AM
and that I do naught of myself:
exactly as my Father doctrinates me, these I speak:
29 and he who sent me is with me: the Father forsakes
me not alone; for I always do what pleases him.

30 — as he speaks these words, many trust in him.
31 So Yah Shua words
to the Yah Hudiym who trust in him,
Whenever you abide in my word
you are truly my disciples;
32 and you know the truth
and the truth liberates you.
33 They answer him, We are sperma of Abraham;
and never — not ever servient to anyone!
How word you, Become liberated?
34 Yah Shua answers them,
Amen! Amen! I word to you,
Whoever does sins is the servant of sin:
35 and the servant abides not
in the house to the eons:
but the Son abides to the eons:
36 so whenever the Son liberates you,
you become liberated indeed.
37 I know you are sperma of Abraham;
but you seek to slaughter me
because my word has no place in you:
38 I speak what I see with my Father:
and you do what you see with your father.
39 They answer him, saying,
Abraham is our father.
Yah Shua words to them,
If you were children of Abraham,
you had done the works of Abraham:
40 and now you seek to slaughter me,
a human who speaks the truth I heard from Elohim:
this Abraham did not:
41 you do the works of your father.
So they say to him,
We are not birthed of whoredom;
we have one Father — even Elohim.
42 Yah Shua says to them,
If Elohim were your Father, you had loved me:
for I proceeded and came from Elohim;
I came not from myself, but he apostolized me.
43 Why know you not my speech?
Even because you cannot hear my word.
44 You are of your father Diabolos
and the pantings of your father you will to do:
he is a murderer from the beginning;
and stands not in the truth
because there is no truth in him.
Whenever he speaks a lie, he speaks of his own:
for he is a liar, and the father thereof.
45 And because I *tell* **word** you the truth,
ye *believe* **trust** me not.
46 Which of you *convinceth*
reproveth me *of* **for** sin?
And if I *say* **word** the truth,
why do ye not *believe* **trust** me?
47 He that is of *God* **Elohim**
heareth *God's words* **the rhema of Elohim**:
so ye *therefore* hear them not,
because ye are not of *God* **Elohim**.
48 *Then* **So** answered the *Jews* **Yah Hudiym**,
and said unto him,
Say **Word** we not well
that thou art a *Samaritan* **Shomeroniy**,
and hast a *devil* **demon**?
49 *Jesus* **Yah Shua** answered,
I have not a *devil* **demon**;
but I honour my Father, and ye *do* dishonour me.
50 And I seek not mine own glory:
there is one that seeketh and judgeth.
51 *Verily, verily, I say* **Amen!
Amen! I word** unto you,
If **Whenever** any *man* keep **one guard** my *saying* **word**,
he shall never see death **unto the eons**.
52 *Then* **So** said the *Jews* **Yah Hudiym** unto him,
Now we know that thou hast a *devil* **demon**.
Abraham is dead, and the prophets;
and thou *sayest* **wordest**,
If **Whenever** *a man* keep **any one guard** my *saying* **word**,
he shall never taste of death **unto the eons**.
53 Art thou greater than our father Abraham,
which is dead? and the prophets are
dead: whom makest thou thyself?
54 *Jesus* **Yah Shua** answered,
If **Whenever** I *honour* **glorify** myself,
my *honour* **glory** is *nothing* **naught**:
it is my Father that *honoureth* **glorifieth** me;
of whom ye *say* **word**, that he is your *God* **Elohim**:
55 Yet ye have not known him; but I know him:
and *if* **whenever** I should say, I know him not,
I shall be a liar like unto you:
but I know him, and *keep* **guard** his *saying* **word**.
56 Your father Abraham
rejoiced **jumped for joy** to see my day: and
he saw it, and *was glad* **cheered**.

Yah Shua, The Eternal I Am

57 *Then* **So** said the *Jews* **Yah Hudiym** unto him,
Thou art not yet fifty years *old*,
and hast thou seen Abraham?
58 *Jesus* **Yah Shua** said unto them,
Verily, verily I say **Amen! Amen! I word** unto you,

JOHN/YOCHANAN 9

Before **Ere** Abraham *was* **became**, *I am* **I AM**.
59   *Then* **So** took they *up* stones to cast at him:
but *Jesus hid* **Yah Shua secreted** himself,
and went out of the *temple* **priestal precinct**,
going **passing** through the midst of them,
and *so* **thus** passed by.

YAH SHUA HEALS ONE BIRTHED BLIND

9   And as *Jesus passed* **passing** by,
he saw a *man* **human** which was blind from his birth.
2   And his disciples asked him, *saying* **wording**,
Master **Rabbi**, who did sin,
this man, or his parents, that he was *born* **birthed** blind?
3   *Jesus* **Yah Shua** answered,
Neither hath this man sinned, nor his parents:
but that the works of *God* **Elohim**
should be *made* manifest in him.
4   I must work the works of him that sent me,
while it is day:
the night cometh, when no *man* **one** can work.
5   *As long as* **Whenever** I am in the *world* **cosmos**,
I am **I AM** the light of the *world* **cosmos**.
6   When he had thus *spoken* **said**,
he spat on the ground, and made clay of the spittle,
and he *anointed* **supplied** the eyes of the blind *man*
with the clay,
7   And said unto him, Go,
wash in the pool of *Siloam* **Shiloach**,
(which *is by interpretation* **translates**, *Sent* **Apostolized**.)
So He went his way *therefore*,
and washed, and came seeing.
45   And because I word you the truth
you trust me not.
46   Which of you reproves me for sin?
And if I word the truth, why trust you me not?
47   Whoever is of Elohim,
hears the rhema of Elohim:
so you hear them not
because you are not of Elohim.
48   So the Yah Hudiym answer him, saying,
Word we not well,
that you are a Shomeroniy, and have a demon?
49   Yah Shua answers, I have no demon;
but I honor my Father, and you dishonor me:
50   and I seek not my own glory:
there is one who seeks and judges.
51   Amen! Amen! I word to you,
Whenever anyone guards my word,
he never sees death to the eons.
52   So the Yah Hudiym say to him,

Now we know you have a demon:
Abraham is dead — and the prophets;
and you word,
Whenever anyone guards my word,
he never tastes death to the eons.
53   Are you greater than our
father Abraham who died?
And the prophets who died?
Whom make you yourself?
54   Yah Shua answers,
Whenever I glorify myself, my glory is naught:
my Father glorifies me
— of whom you word that he is your Elohim:
55   yet you know him not; but I know him:
and whenever I say, I know him not,
I become a liar like you:
but I know him, and guard his word.
56   Your father Abraham
jumped for joy to see my day:
and he saw, and cheered.

YAH SHUA, THE ETERNAL I AM

57   So the Yah Hudiym say to him,
You are not yet fifty years
— and have you seen Abraham?
58   Yah Shua says to them,
Amen! Amen! I word to you,
Ere Abraham became, I AM.
59   So they take stones to cast at him:
but Yah Shua secretes himself,
and goes from the priestal precinct,
passing through their midst, and thus passes by.

YAH SHUA HEALS ONE BIRTHED BLIND

9   And passing by,
he sees a human who is blind from birth:
2   and his disciples ask him, wording,
Rabbi, who sinned, this man or his parents,
that he is birthed blind?
3   Yah Shua answers,
Neither this man sinned, nor his parents:
but to manifest the works of Elohim in him.
4   I must work the works of him who sent me
while it is day:
the night comes when no one can work.
5   Whenever I am in the cosmos,
I am the light of the cosmos.
6   Saying these,
he spits on the ground and makes clay from the spit;
and he supplies the eyes of the blind with the clay;

JOHN/YOCHANAN 9

7 and says to him, Go, wash
in the pool of Shiloach,
— which translates, Apostolized.
So he goes his way and washes and comes seeing:
8 **So** The neighbours *therefore*,
and they which before had seen him that he was blind,
said **worded**, Is not this he that sat and begged?
9 Some *said* **worded**, This is he: others *said*, He
is like him: but he *said* **worded**, I am *he*.
10 *Therefore said* **So worded** they unto him,
How were thine eyes opened?
11 He answered and said,
A *man* **human** that is *called Jesus* **worded Yah Shua**
made clay,
and *anointed* **supplied** mine eyes, and said unto me,
Go to the pool of *Siloam* **Shiloach**, and wash:
and I went and washed, and I *received sight* **saw**.
12 *Then* **So** said they unto him, Where is he?
He *said* **worded**, I know not.
13 They brought to the Pharisees
him that *aforetime* **once** was blind.
14 And it was the *sabbath day* **shabbath**
when *Jesus* **Yah Shua** made the clay,
and opened his eyes.
15 *Then* **So** again the Pharisees also asked him
how he *had received his sight* **saw**.
He said unto them, He put clay upon mine eyes,
and I washed, and *do* see.
16 *Therefore said* **So worded** some of the Pharisees,
This *man* **human** is not of *God* **Elohim**,
because he *keepeth* **guardeth** not
the sabbath day shabbath.
Others *said* **worded**,
How can a *man* **human** that is a sinner
do such *miracles* **signs**?
And there was a *division* **schism** among them.
17 They *say* **word** unto the blind man again,
What *sayest* **wordest** thou *of* **concerning** him,
that he hath opened thine eyes?
He said, He is a prophet.
18 But the *Jews* **Yah Hudiym** did not *believe* **trust**
concerning him,
that he had been blind, and *received his sight* **saw**,
until they *called* **voiced out**
to the parents of him that *had received his sight* **saw**.
19 And they asked them, *saying* **wording**,
Is this your son, who ye *say* **speak**
was *born* **birthed** blind?
So how *then* doth he now see?
20 His parents answered them and said,

We know that this is our son, and that
he was *born* **birthed** blind:
21 But by what means he now seeth, we know not;
or who hath opened his eyes, we know not:
he is *of age* **mature**; ask him:
he shall speak *for* **concerning** himself.
22 These words *spake* **said** his parents,
because they *feared* **awed** the *Jews* **Yah Hudiym**:
for the Jews Yah Hudiym had agreed covenanted already,
that *if* **whenever** any *man* **one**
did confess **professed** that he was *Christ* **Messiah**,
he should be *put out of the synagogue* **ex—synagogued**.
23 *Therefore* **So** said his parents,
He is *of age* **mature**; ask him.
24 *Then again* **Of a second time**
called voiced they out to the man human that was blind,
and said unto him, Give God Elohim the praise glory:
we know that this *man* **human** is a sinner.
25 He answered and said,
Whether he be a sinner or no, I know not:
8 So the neighbors
and whoever had previously seen that he was blind,
word, Is not this he who sat and begged?
9 Some word, This is he!
Others, He is like him!
But he words, I am!
10 So they word to him,
How were your eyes opened?
11 He answers, saying,
A human, worded Yah Shua, made clay,
and supplied my eyes, and said to me,
Go to the pool of Shiloach, and wash:
and I went and washed and I see.
12 So they say to him, Where is he?
He words, I know not.
13 They bring him who once *was* blind
to the Pharisees:
14 and it is shabbath
when Yah Shua makes the clay,
and opens his eyes.
15 So again the Pharisees also ask him
how he sees.
He says to them, He put clay on my eyes
and I washed and see.
16 So some of the Pharisees word,
This human is not of Elohim,
because he guards not the shabbath.
Others word,
How can a human — a sinner do such signs?
— and there is a schism among them.

31

17	They word to the blind man again, What word you concerning him who opened your eyes? He says, He is a prophet.
18	But the Yah Hudiym trust not concerning him that he was blind, and sees; until they voice out to the parents of him who sees:
19	and they ask them, wording, Is this your son, of whom you speak, who was birthed blind? so how sees he now?
20	His parents answer them, saying, We know this is our son; and that he was birthed blind:
21	but how he now sees, we know not; or who opened his eyes, we know not; he is mature; ask him: he speaks concerning himself.
22	— his parents say these words because they awe the Yah Hudiym: for the Yah Hudiym had already covenanted that whenever anyone professes Messiah, to ex—synagogue him.
23	So his parents say, He is mature; ask him.
24	They voice out a second time to the human who is blind, and say to him, Give Elohim the glory: we know this human is a sinner.
25	He answers, saying, Whether he is a sinner or not, I know not: one *thing* I know, that, whereas I was blind, now I see.
26	*Then* **And** said they to him again, What did he to thee? how opened he thine eyes?
27	He answered them, I have *told* **said to** you already, and ye did not hear: wherefore *would* **will** ye *to* hear it again? will ye also *to* be his disciples?
28	*Then* **So** they *reviled* **abused** him, and said, Thou art his disciple; but we are *Moses'* **Mosheh's** disciples.
29	We know that *God* **Elohim** spake unto *Moses* **Mosheh**: as for this *fellow*, we know not from whence he is.
30	The *man* **human** answered and said unto them, *Why* **Indeed** herein is a *marvellous thing* **marvel**, that ye know not from whence he is, and yet he hath opened mine eyes.
31	Now we know that *God* **Elohim** heareth not sinners: but *if* **whenever** any *man* be *a worshipper of God* **Elohim—revering**, and doeth his will, him he heareth.
32	*Since the world began* **From the first eon** was it not heard that any *man* **one** opened the eyes of one that was *born* **birthed** blind.
33	*If this man* **Unless this one** were *not* of *God* **Elohim**, he could do *nothing* **naught**.
34	They answered and said unto him, Thou wast altogether *born* **birthed** in sins, and dost thou *teach* **doctrinate** us? And they *cast him out* **ejected him**.

Yah Shua, The Son Of Elohim

35	*Jesus* **Yah Shua** heard that they had *cast* **ejected** him *out*; and when he had found him, he said unto him, Dost thou *believe on* **trust in** the Son of *God* **Elohim**?
36	He answered and said, Who is he, *Lord* **Adoni**, that I might *believe on* **trust in** him?
37	And *Jesus* **Yah Shua** said unto him, Thou hast both seen him, and it *is* **be** he that *talketh* **speaketh** with thee.
38	And he said, *Lord* **Adonay**, I *believe* **trust**. And he worshipped him.
39	And *Jesus* **Yah Shua** said, *For* **In** judgment I am come into this *world* **cosmos**, that they which see not might see; and that they which see might be *made* blind.
40	And some of the Pharisees which were with him heard these words, and said unto him, Are we blind also?
41	*Jesus* **Yah Shua** said unto them, If ye were blind, ye should have no sin: but now ye *say* **word**, We see; *therefore* **so** your sin *remaineth* **abideth**.

Yah Shua, The Good Shepherd

10	*Verily, verily, I say* **Amen!** **Amen! I word** unto you, He that entereth not *by* **through** the *door* **portal** into the sheepfold, but *climbeth up* **ascendeth** some other way, the same is a thief and a robber.
2	But he that entereth in *by* **through** the *door* **portal**

	is the shepherd of the sheep.
3	To him the *porter* **portalguard** openeth;
	and the sheep hear his voice:
	and he calleth his own sheep by name,
	and leadeth them out.
4	And when **ever** he putteth forth his own sheep,
	he goeth *before* **ahead of** them,
	and the sheep follow him: for they know his voice.
5	And *a stranger will* **another**
	shall they not follow,
	but *will* **shall** flee from him:
	for they know not the voice of *strangers* **another**.
6	This parable spake *Jesus* **Yah Shua** unto them:
	one I know, whereas I was blind, I now see.
26	And they say to him again, What did he to you?
	How opened he your eyes?
27	He answers them, I already said to you,
	and you heard not:
	Why will you to hear it again?
	Will you also to become his disciples?
28	So they abuse him and say,
	You are his disciple;
	but we are disciples of Mosheh:
29	we know Elohim spoke to Mosheh:
	as for this, we know not whence he is.
30	The human answers them, saying,
	Indeed herein is a marvel,
	that you know not whence he is,
	and yet he opened my eyes:
31	now we know that Elohim hears not sinners:
	but whenever any is reverent of Elohim
	and does his will,
	him he hears.
32	From the first eon it was not heard
	that anyone opens the eyes of one birthed blind.
33	Unless this one were of
	Elohim, he can do naught.
34	They answer him, saying,
	You are altogether birthed in sins!
	And you doctrinate us?
	— and they eject him.

Yah Shua, The Son Of Elohim

35	Yah Shua hears they ejected him;
	and when he finds him, he says to him,
	Trust you in the Son of Elohim?
36	He answers, saying, Who is he, Adoni,
	so that I trust in him?
37	And Yah Shua says to him,
	You have both seen him,
	and he who speaks with you is he.
38	And he says, Adonay, I trust.
	— and he worships him.
39	And Yah Shua says,
	I come to this cosmos in judgment,
	that whoever sees not, sees;
	and whoever sees, becomes blind.
40	And some of the Pharisees with him
	hear these words, and say to him,
	Are we also blind?
41	Yah Shua says to them,
	If you had been blind, you had no sin:
	but now you word, We see!
	so your sin abides.

Yah Shua, The Good Shepherd

10	Amen! Amen! I word to you,
	Whoever enters not the sheepfold through the portal,
	but ascends some other way,
	is a thief and a robber;
2	and whoever enters through the portal
	is the shepherd of the sheep:
3	the portalguard opens to him
	and the sheep hear his voice:
	and he calls his own sheep by name
	and leads them out:
4	and whenever he puts forth his own sheep
	he goes ahead of them;
	and the sheep follow him; for they know his voice:
5	and they follow not another; but flee from him:
	for they know not the voice of another.
6	— Yah Shua speaks this parable to them:
	but they *understood* **knew** not
	what *things they were which* he *spake* **told** unto them.

Yah Shua, The Portal

7	*Then* **So** said *Jesus* **Yah Shua** unto them again,
	Verily, verily, I say **Amen! Amen! I word**, unto you,
	I am **I AM** the *door* **portal** of the sheep.
8	All *that —* **As many as** ever came before me
	are thieves and robbers:
	but the sheep did not hear them.
9	*I am* **I AM** the *door* **portal**:
	by **through** me *if* **whenever** any *man* **one** enter in,
	he shall be saved,
	and shall go in and out, and find pasture.
10	The thief cometh not, *but*
	for **except** to *steal* **thieve**,
	and to *kill* **sacrifice**, and to destroy:
	I am come that they might have life,

and that they might have it
more abundantly **superabundantly**.

THE GOOD SHEPHERD PLACES HIS SOUL

11 *I am* **I AM** the good shepherd:
the good shepherd *giveth* **placeth**
his *life* **soul** for the sheep.
12 But he that is an hireling,
and not **being** the shepherd,
whose own the sheep are not, seeth the wolf coming,
and *leaveth* **forsaketh** the sheep, and fleeth:
and the wolf *catcheth* **seizeth** them,
and scattereth the sheep.
13 The hireling fleeth, because he is an hireling,
and *careth* **concerneth** not for the sheep.
14 *I am* **I AM** the good shepherd,
and know my sheep,
and am known of mine.
15 **Exactly** As the Father knoweth me,
even so know I the Father:
and I *lay down* **place** my *life* **soul** for the sheep.

OTHER SHEEP, ANOTHER COURTYARD:
ONE SHEPHERDDOM, ONE SHEPHERD

16 And other sheep I have,
which are not of this *fold* **courtyard**:
them also I must bring, and they shall hear my voice;
and there shall be one *fold* **shepherddom**,
and one shepherd.
17 *Therefore* **So** doth my Father love me,
because I *lay down* **place** my *life* **soul**,
that I might take it again.
18 No *man* **one** taketh it from me,
but I *lay* **place** it *down* of myself.
I have *power* **authority** to *lay it down* **place**,
and I have *power* **authority** to take it again.
This *commandment* **misvah**
have I *received* **taken** of my Father.
19 **So** There *was* **became** a *division* **schism**
therefore again
among the *Jews* **Yah Hudiym** for these *sayings* **words**.
20 And many of them *said* **worded**,
He hath a *devil* **demon**, and *is mad* **raveth**;
why hear ye him?
21 Others *said* **worded**,
These are not the *words* **rhema**
of *him that hath a devil* **one demonized**.
Can a *devil* **demon** open the eyes of the blind?

YAH SHUA, THE MESSIAH

22 And it *was* **became** at *Jerusalem* **Yeru Shalem**
the *feast of the dedication* **hanukkah**,
and it was *winter* **the downpour**.
23 And *Jesus* **Yah Shua**
walked in the *temple* **priestal precinct**
in *Solomon's porch* **Shelomoh's portico**.
24 *Then came* **So** the *Jews* **Yah Hudiym**
round about **surrounded him**, and
said **worded** unto him,
How long **Until when**
dost thou *make us to doubt* **lift our soul in suspense**?
If thou be the *Christ* **Messiah**, *tell*
say to us *plainly* **boldly**.

YAH SHUA AND FATHER ARE ONE

25 *Jesus* **Yah Shua** answered them,
I *told* **said to** you, and ye *believed* **trusted** not:
the works that I do in my Father's name,
they *bear* witness *of* **concerning** me.
26 But ye *believe* **trust** not,
because ye are not of my sheep,
but they know not what he tells them.

YAH SHUA, THE PORTAL

7 So Yah Shua says to them again, Amen!
Amen! I word, to you, I AM the portal of the sheep.
8 All — as many as ever came preceding me
are thieves and robbers:
but the sheep hear them not.
9 I AM the portal:
whenever anyone enters through me, he is saved;
and goes in and out, and finds pasture:
10 the thief comes not, except to thieve
and to sacrifice and to destroy:
I come that they have life,
and that they have it superabundantly.

THE GOOD SHEPHERD PLACES HIS SOUL

11 I AM the good shepherd;
the good shepherd places his soul for the sheep:
12 and a hireling, not being a shepherd,
whose own the sheep are not, sees the wolf coming;
and forsakes the sheep, and flees:
and the wolf seizes them, and scatters the sheep.
13 The hireling flees, because he is a hireling,
and not concerned for the sheep.
14 I AM the good shepherd and know my sheep;
and mine know me.

15 Exactly as the Father knows me,
even thus I know the Father:
and I place my soul for the sheep.

OTHER SHEEP, ANOTHER COURTYARD: ONE SHEPHERDDOM, ONE SHEPHERD

16 And I have other sheep, not of this courtyard:
I must also bring them;
and they hear my voice;
and there becomes one shepherddom
and one shepherd.
17 So my Father loves me,
because I place my soul — to take it again:
18 no one takes it from me; but I place it of myself:
I have authority to place,
and I have authority to take again:
I took this misvah from my Father.
19 — so again, there becomes a schism
among the Yah Hudiym for these words.
20 And many of them word,
He has a demon, and raves! Why hear him?
21 Others word,
These are not the rhema of one demonized:
Can a demon open the eyes of the blind?

YAH SHUA, THE MESSIAH

22 And the hanukkah becomes at Yeru Shalem;
and it is the downpour:
23 and Yah Shua walks in the priestal precinct
in the portico of Shelomoh.
24 So the Yah Hudiym surround him,
and word to him,
Until when lift you our soul in suspense?
If you are the Messiah, say to us boldly.

YAH SHUA AND FATHER ARE ONE

25 Yah Shua answers them,
I say to you, and you trust not:
the works I do in the name of my Father
witness concerning me:
26 but you trust not,
because you are not of my sheep,
exactly as I said unto you.
27 My sheep hear my voice, and I know them,
and they follow me:
28 And I give unto them eternal life;
and they shall never *perish* **destruct unto the eons**,
neither shall any *man* **one**
pluck **seize** them out of my hand.
29 My Father, which gave them
me, is greater than all;
and no *man* **one**
is able to *pluck* **seize** them out of my Father's hand.
30 I and *my* **the** Father are one.

YAH SHUA ACCUSED OF BLASPHEMY

31 *Then* **So** the *Jews* took up **Yah
Hudiym bore** stones again
to stone him.
32 *Jesus* **Yah Shua** answered them,
Many good works have I shewed you from my Father;
for which of those works do ye stone me?
33 The *Jews* **Yah Hudiym**
answered him, *saying* **wording**,
For a good work we stone thee not; but for blasphemy;
and because that thou, being *a man* **human**,
makest thyself *God* **Elohim**.
Philippians 2:5—8
34 *Jesus* **Yah Shua** answered them,
Is it not *written* **scribed** in your *law* **torah**,
I said, Ye are *gods* **elohim**?
Psalm 82:6
35 If he called them *gods* **elohim**,
unto whom the word of *God came* **Elohim became**,
and the scripture cannot be *broken* **released**;
36 *Say* **Word** ye of him,
whom the Father hath *sanctified* **hallowed**,
and *sent* **apostolized** into the *world* **cosmos**,
Thou blasphemest;
because I said, *I am* **I AM** the Son of *God* **Elohim**?
37 If I do not the works of my Father,
believe **trust** me not.
38 But if I do, though ye *believe* **trust** not me,
believe **trust** the works:
that ye may know, and *believe* **trust**,
that the Father is in me, and I in him.
39 *Therefore* **So** they sought
again to *take* **seize** him:
but he escaped out of their hand,
40 And went away again
beyond Jordan **over Yarden**
into the place where *John* **Yahn** at first baptized;
and there he abode.
41 And many resorted unto him, and *said* **worded**,
Indeed, *John* **Yahn** did no *miracle* **sign**:
but all *things that John spake of*
Yahn said about this man
were true.
42 And many *believed on* **trusted in** him there.

JOHN/YOCHANAN 11 — EDC Hebrew / English Bible

El Azar Dies

11 Now *a certain man* **someone** was *sick* **frail**,
named Lazarus — **El Azar**, of *Bethany* **Beth Ania**,
the town of *Mary* **Miryam** and her sister Martha.

2 (It was that *Mary* **Miryam**
which anointed *the Lord* **Adonay** with *ointment* **myrrh**,
and *wiped* **squeezedried** his feet with her hair,
whose brother *Lazarus* **El Azar** was *sick* **frail**.)

3 *Therefore* **So** his sisters *sent*
apostolized unto him,
saying **wording**, *Lord* **Adonay**, behold,
he whom thou *lovest* **befriendest** is *sick* **frail**.

4 When *Jesus* **Yah Shua** heard that, he said,
This *sickness* **frailty** is not unto death,
but for the glory of *God* **Elohim**,
that the Son of *God* **Elohim** might be glorified thereby.

5 Now *Jesus* **Yah Shua** loved Martha,
and her sister, and *Lazarus* **El Azar**.

6 **So** When he had heard
therefore that he was *sick* **frail**,
he abode two days still in the same place where he was.

7 Then after that *saith* **wordeth** he to his disciples,
Let us go into *Judaea* **Yah Hudah** again.

8 His disciples *say* **word** unto him, *Master* **Rabbi**,
the *Jews of late* **Yah Hudiym now** sought to stone thee;
and goest thou thither again?

exactly as I say to you.

27 My sheep hear my voice and I know them;
and they follow me:

28 and I give them eternal life;
and they neither destruct to the eons,
nor anyone seize them from my hand.

29 My Father who gave them
to me, is greater than all;
and no one can seize them from the hand of my Father.

30 I and the Father are one.

Yah Shua Accused Of Blasphemy

31 So again the Yah Hudiym
bear stones to stone him.

32 Yah Shua answers them,
I show you many good works from my Father;
for which of those works stone you me?

33 The Yah Hudiym answer him, wording,
For a good work we stone you not;
but for blasphemy;
and because you, being human,
make yourself Elohim.

Philippians 2:5—8

34 Yah Shua answers them,
Is it not scribed in your torah,
I say, You are elohim?

Psalm 82:6

35 If he called them elohim,
to whom the word of Elohim became
— and the scripture cannot be released

36 word you of him whom the Father hallowed
and apostolized into the cosmos,
You blaspheme!
— because I say, I AM the Son of Elohim?

37 If I do not the works of my Father,
trust me not:

38 but if I do, though you trust me not,
trust the works:
so that you know and trust
that the Father is in me, and I in him.

39 So again they seek to seize him;
but he escapes from their hand

40 and goes again across Yarden
to the place Yahn first baptized;
and there he abides.

41 And many resort to him, and word,
Indeed, Yahn did no sign:
but all Yahn says about this man is true.

42 — and many trust in him there.

El Azar Dies

11 And someone frail, El Azar of Beth Ania
of the town of Miryam and her sister Martha:

2 — that Miryam who
anointed Adonay with myrrh
and squeezedried his feet with her hair
whose brother El Azar is frail.

3 So his sisters apostolize to him,
wording, Adonay, behold,
he whom you befriend is frail.

4 When Yah Shua hears, he says,
This frailty is not to death; but for the glory of Elohim
and thereby glorifies the Son of Elohim.

5 And Yah Shua loves Martha
and her sister and El Azar:

6 and he hears he is frail:
so he still abides two days in the same place he is:

7 then after that he words to his disciples,
We go to Yah Hudah again.

8 His disciples word to him, Rabbi,
the Yah Hudiym now seek to stone you!
And go you there again?

9 *Jesus* **Yah Shua** answered,

Are there **indeed** not twelve hours in the day?
If **Whenever** any *man* **one** walk in
the day, he stumbleth not,
because he seeth the light of this *world* **cosmos**.

10 But *if* **whenever** a man walk
in the night, he stumbleth,
because there is no light in him.

11 These *things* said he:
and after that he *saith* **wordeth** unto them,
Our friend *Lazarus* **El Azar** sleepeth;
but I go, that I may awake him out of sleep.

12 *Then* **So** said his disciples,
Lord **Adonay**, if he sleep, he shall *do well* **be saved**.

13 Howbeit *Jesus* **Yah Shua**
spake of **said concerning** his death:
but they thought that he had *spoken* **worded**
of taking of rest **about sleeping** in *sleep* **slumber**.

14 Then said *Jesus* **Yah Shua**
unto them *plainly* **boldly**,
Lazarus **El Azar** is dead.

15 And I am glad for your
sakes that I was not there,
to the intent **that** ye may *believe* **trust**;
nevertheless **yet** let us go unto him.

16 *Then* **So** said *Thomas* **Taom**,
which is *called Didymus* **worded Twin**,
unto his *fellowdisciples* **co—disciples**,
Let us also go, that we may die with him.

17 *Then* **So** when *Jesus* **Yah Shua** came,
he found
that he had lain in the *grave* **tomb** four days already.

18 Now *Bethany* **Beth Ania**
was nigh unto *Jerusalem* **Yeru Shalem**,
about fifteen *furlongs* **stadia** off:

19 And many of the *Jews* **Yah Hudiym**
came to *them around* Martha and *Mary* **Miryam**,
to *comfort* **console** them concerning their brother.

20 *Then* **So** Martha,
as soon as she heard that *Jesus* **Yah Shua** was coming,
went and met him:
but *Mary* **Miryam** sat still in the house.

21 *Then* **So** said Martha unto
Jesus **Yah Shua**, *Lord* **Adonay**,
if thou hadst been here, my brother had not died.

22 But I know, that even now,
whatsoever — **as much as ever**
thou *wilt* **shalt** ask of *God* **Elohim**,
God will **Elohim shall** give it thee.

23 *Jesus saith* **Yah Shua wordeth** unto her,
Thy brother shall rise *again*.

24 Martha *saith* **wordeth** unto him,
I know that he shall rise *again*
in the resurrection at the *last* **final** day.

Yah Shua, The Resurrection And The Life

25 *Jesus* **Yah Shua** said unto her,
I am **I AM** the resurrection, and the life:
he that *believeth* **trusteth** in me,
though he were dead, yet shall he live:

26 And whosoever liveth and
believeth **trusteth** in me
shall never die **unto the eons**.
Believest **Trustest** thou this?

27 She *saith* **wordeth** unto him, Yea, *Lord* **Adonay**:
I *believe* **trust** that thou art the *Christ* **Messiah**,
the Son of *God* **Elohim**,
which should come into the *world* **cosmos**.

28 And when she had so said, she went her way,
and *called Mary* **voiced out to**
Miryam her sister secretly,
saying, The *Master* **Doctor** is *come* **here**
and *calleth for* **voiceth out to** thee.

29 As soon as she heard that,
she arose quickly, and came unto him.

30 Now *Jesus* **Yah Shua** was
not yet come into the town,
but was in that place where Martha met him.

31 So The *Jews* **Yah Hudiym** *then* which were
with her in the house, and *comforted* **consoled**
her, when they saw *Mary* **Miryam**,
that she rose *up hastily* **quickly** and went *out*,
followed her, *saying* **wording**,
She goeth unto the *grave* **tomb** to weep there.

32 *Then* **So** when *Mary* **Miryam** was come
where *Jesus* **Yah Shua** was, and saw him,

9 Yah Shua answers,
Are there not indeed twelve hours in the day?
Whenever anyone walks in the day, he stumbles not,
because he sees the light of this cosmos:

10 but whenever a man walks in the night,
he stumbles,
because there is no light in him.

11 He says these:
and after this he words to them,
Our friend El Azar sleeps;
but I go to waken him from sleep.

12 So his disciples say,
Adonay, if he sleeps, he is saved.

13 — howbeit Yah Shua says concerning his death:
but they thought he words about sleeping in slumber.

14 Then Yah Shua says to them boldly, El Azar died:
15 and for your sakes I am glad I was not there
— so that you trust; still we go to him.
16 So Taom, who is worded Twin,
says to his co—disciples,
We also go, to die with him.
17 So when Yah Shua comes,
he finds he already laid in the tomb four days.
18 Now Beth Ania is near Yeru Shalem
— of about fifteen stadia:
19 and many of the Yah Hudiym
go to them around Martha and Miryam, to
console them concerning their brother.
20 So Martha,
as soon as she hears Yah Shua is coming,
goes to meet him:
but Miryam still sits in the house.
21 So Martha says to Yah Shua, Adonay,
if you had been here, my brother had not died:
22 but I know, even now,
— as much as ever you ask of Elohim,
Elohim gives you.
23 Yah Shua words to her, Your brother rises.
24 Martha words to him,
I know he rises in the resurrection at the final day.

YAH SHUA, THE RESURRECTION AND THE LIFE

25 Yah Shua says to her,
I AM the resurrection and the life:
whoever trusts in me,
though he dies, he still lives:
26 and whoever lives and trusts in me
never dies to the eons.
Trust you this?
27 She words to him, Yes, Adonay:
I trust that you are the Messiah
— the Son of Elohim who comes to the cosmos.
28 And saying these, she goes her way,
and voices out to Miryam her sister secretly,
saying, The Doctor is here and voices out to you.
29 As soon as she hears that
she rises quickly and comes to him:
30 and Yah Shua has not yet come to the town,
but is in the place Martha met him.
31 So the Yah Hudiym with her in the house
who are consolling her,
when they see Miryam rise quickly and go,
they follow her, wording,
She goes to the tomb to weep there.
32 So Miryam goes where
Yah Shua is, and sees him,
she fell *down at* **to** his feet, *saying* **wording** unto him,
Lord **Adonay**, if thou hadst been here,
my brother had not died.
33 **So** When *Jesus therefore*
Yah Shua saw her weeping,
and the *Jews* **Yah Hudiym** also weeping
which came with her,
he *groaned* **sighed** in the spirit, and was troubled.
34 And said, Where have ye *laid* **placed** him?
They said worded unto him, Lord Adonay, come and see.
35 *Jesus* **Yah Shua** wept.
36 *Then said* **So worded** the *Jews* **Yah Hudiym**,
Behold how he *loved* **befriended** him!
37 And some of them said,
Could not this man, which opened the eyes of the blind,
have caused that even this man should not have died?
38 *Jesus therefore* **So** again **Yah Shua**
groaning **sighing** in himself cometh to the *grave* **tomb**.
It was a *cave* **grotto**, and a stone lay upon it.
39 *Jesus said* **Yah Shua worded**,
Take ye away the stone.
Martha, the sister of him that was dead,
saith **wordeth** unto him,
Lord **Adonay**, *by this time* **already** he stinketh:
for he hath been dead four days.
40 *Jesus saith* **Yah Shua wordeth** unto her,
Said I not unto thee, that,
if **whenever** thou *wouldest believe* **shouldest trust**,
thou shouldest see the glory of *God* **Elohim**?
41 *Then* **So** they took away the stone
from the place where the dead was laid.
And *Jesus* **Yah Shua** lifted *up* his eyes, and said,
Father, I thank eucharistize thee
that thou hast heard me.
42 And I knew that thou hearest me always:
but because of the *people* **multitude** which stand by
I said it, that they may *believe* **trust**
that thou hast *sent* **apostolized** me.
43 And when he thus had *spoken* **said**,
he cried with a *loud* **mega** voice,
Lazarus **El Azar**, come forth.
44 And he that was dead came forth,
bound hand and foot with *graveclothes* **swathes**:
and his face was bound about with a napkin sudarium.
Jesus saith **Yah Shua wordeth** unto them,
Loose **Release** him, and let him go.
45 *Then* **So** many of the *Jews* **Yah Hudiym**

which came to *Mary* **Miryam**,
and had seen the thing *that* which *Jesus* **Yah Shua** did,
believed on **trusted in** him.

46 But some of them went
their ways to the Pharisees,
and *told* **said to** them
what *things Jesus* **Yah Shua** had done.

47 *Then* **So** gathered the *chief*
arch priests and the Pharisees
a *council* **sanhedrim**,
and *said* **worded**, What do we?
for this *man* **human** doeth many *miracles* **signs**.

48 *If* **Whenever** we *let* **allow** him thus *alone*,
all *men will believe on* everyone shall trust in him:
and the Romans shall come
and take away both our place and *nation* **goyim**.

49 And one of them, *named* Caiaphas,
being the *high* **arch** priest that same year,
said unto them, Ye know *nothing at all* **not aught**,

50 Nor *consider* **reason**
that it is *expedient* **benefical** for us,
that one *man* **human** should die for the people,
and that the whole nation perish goyim destruct not.

51 And this *spake* **said** he not of himself:
but being *high* **arch** priest that year,
he prophesied
that Jesus Yah Shua should die for that nation goyim;

52 And not for that *nation* **goyim** only,
but that also he should gather together in one
the children of *God* **Elohim** that were scattered abroad.

she falls to his feet, wording to him,
Adonay, if you had been here,
my brother had not died.

33 So when Yah Shua sees her weeping,
and the Yah Hudiym coming with her
also weeping,
he sighs in spirit, and is troubled:

34 and says, Where have you placed him?
They word to him, Adonay, come and see.

35 Yah Shua weeps.

36 So the Yah Hudiym word,
Behold how he befriends him!

37 And some of them say,
Could not this man, who opens the eyes of the blind,
even cause this one not to die?

38 So again, Yah Shua sighing in himself,
goes to the tomb — a grotto;
and a stone lies thereon.

39 Yah Shua words, Take away the stone.

Martha, the sister of him who died, words to him,
Adonay, he already stinks — for it is four days.

40 Yah Shua words to her,
Said I not to you,
Whenever you trust, you see the glory of Elohim?

41 So they take away the stone
from the place the dead lies:
and Yah Shua lifts his eyes, and says,
Father, I eucharistize you that you hear me:

42 and I know that you hear me always:
but I say it because of the multitude standing by
— that they trust that you apostolized me.

43 And saying thus, he cries with a mega voice,
El Azar, come forth!

44 And he who was dead comes forth,
bound hand and foot with swathes:
and his face bound with a sudarium.
Yah Shua words to them,
Release him, and let him go.

45 So many of the Yah Hudiym
who come to Miryam
seeing what Yah Shua did, trust in him:

46 but some of them go their ways to the Pharisees,
and say to them what Yah Shua did.

47 So the archpriests and the Pharisees
gather a sanhedrim, and word,
What do we? For this human does many signs.

48 Whenever we thus allow him,
everyone trusts in him:
and the Romans come and take
both our place and goyim.

49 And one of them, Caiaphas,
being the archpriest that same year,
says to them, You neither know aught;

50 nor reason that it is benefical for us
that one human die for the people; and
that the whole goyim not destruct.

51 And he says this not of himself:
but being archpriest that year
he prophesies that Yah Shua dies for that goyim;

52 and not only for that goyim,
but that he also gathers together in one
the children of Elohim who are scattered abroad.

53 *Then* **So** from that day *forth*
they took counsel together
for to *put him to death* **slaughter** him.

54 *Jesus* **So Yah Shua** *therefore*
walked no more *openly* **boldly** among
the *Jews* **Yah Hudiym**;
but went thence

JOHN/YOCHANAN 11

unto a *country* **region** near to the wilderness,
into a city *called Ephraim* **worded Ephrayim**,
and there *continued* **tarried** with his disciples.

55 And the *Jews' passover* **Yah Hudiy's pasach**
was nigh *at* hand:
and many *went out of the country up*
ascended from the region
to *Jerusalem* **Yeru Shalem**
before **preceding** the *passover* **pasach**,
to *purify* **hallow** themselves.

56 *Then* **So** sought they for *Jesus* **Yah Shua**,
and *spake among themselves* **worded with each other**,
as they stood in the *temple* **priestal precinct**,
What think ye,
that he *will* **shall** not come to the *feast* **celebration**?

57 Now both the *chief* **arch**
priests and the Pharisees
had given a *commandment* **misvah**,
that, *if* **whenever** any *man* **one** knew where he were,
he should *shew* **disclose** it, that
they might *take* **seize** him.

MIRYAM ANOINTS YAH SHUA

12 *Then Jesus* **So Yah Shua**
six days before the *passover* **pasach**
came to *Bethany* **Beth Ania**, where *Lazarus* **El Azar** was,
which had been dead, whom he raised from the dead.

2 There they made him a supper;
and Martha *served* **ministered**:
but *Lazarus* **El Azar** was one of them
that *sat at the table* **reposed** with him.

3 *Then* **So** took *Mary* **Miryam**
a *pound* **litra** of *ointment* **myrrh** of *spikenard* **nard**,
very costly **trustworthy and vastly precious**,
and anointed the feet of *Jesus* **Yah Shua**,
and *wiped* **squeezedried** his feet with her hair:
and the house was filled
with the *odour* **fragrance** of the *ointment* **myrrh**.

4 *Then saith* **So wordeth** one of his disciples,
Judas Iscariot **Yah Hudah the urbanite**, *Simon's*
Shimon's son, which should betray him,

5 Why was not this *ointment* **myrrh** sold
for three hundred *pence* **denarion**,
and given to the poor?

6 This he said,
not that he *cared* **was concerned** for the poor;
but because he was a thief, and had the bag,
and bare what was put therein.

7 *Then* **So** said *Jesus* **Yah
Shua**, *Let* **Allow** her *alone*:

against **to** the day of my *burying* **embalming**
hath she *kept* **guarded** this.

8 For the poor always ye have with you;
but me ye have not always.

9 **So** Much *people* **multitude**
of the *Jews* **Yah Hudiym**
therefore knew that he was there:
and they came not for *Jesus'* **Yah Shua's** sake only,
but that they might see *Lazarus* **El Azar** also,
whom he had raised from the dead.

10 But the *chief* **arch** priests *consulted* **counseled**
that they might
put *Lazarus* **slaughter El Azar** also *to death*;

11 Because that *by reason* **because** of him
many of the *Jews* **Yah Hudiym** went *away*, and
believed on Jesus **trusted in Yah Shua**.

THE TRIUMPHAL ENTRY OF YAH SHUA

12 On the next day much *people* **multitude**
that were come to the *feast* **celebration**,
when they heard that *Jesus* **Yah Shua**
was coming to *Jerusalem* **Yeru Shalem**

13 Took branches of *palm trees* **phoinix**,
and went forth to meet him,
and cried, *Hosanna:* **Hoshia Na!**
Blessed is **Eulogized**
— the *King* **Sovereign** of *Israel* **Yisra El**
that cometh in the name of *the Lord* **Yah Veh**.

14 And *Jesus* **Yah Shua**,
when he had found a *young ass* **burrito**, sat thereon;
exactly as *it is written* **scribed**,

53 So from that day
they counsel together to slaughter him:

54 So Yah Shua walks boldly no more
among the Yah Hudiym;
but goes to a region near the wilderness
— to a city worded Ephrayim;
and tarries there with his disciples.

55 And the pasach of the Yah Hudiy is near:
and many ascend from the region to Yeru Shalem
to hallow themselves preceding the pasach.

56 So they seek for Yah Shua;
and word with each other
as they stand in the priestal precinct,
What think you,
that he comes not to the celebration?

57 Both the archpriests and the Pharisees
give a misvah,
that whenever anyone knows where he is,
that he discloses it, so as to seize him.

Miryam Anoints Yah Shua

12 So six days prior to the pasach
Yah Shua goes to Beth Ania where El Azar is
— who died — whom he raised from the dead.
2 They make him a supper there;
and Martha ministers:
and El Azar is one of them reposing with him.
3 So Miryam takes a litra of myrrh of nard
— trustworthy and vastly precious
and anoints the feet of Yah Shua
and *squeezed*ries his feet with her hair:
and the house fills with the fragrance of the myrrh.
4 So one of his disciples *words*
— Yah Hudah the urbanite of Shimon
who is to betray him,
5 Why was not this myrrh sold
for three hundred denarion
and given to the poor?
6 — he says this,
not that he is concerned for the poor;
but because he is a thief and has the bag
and bears what is put therein.
7 So Yah Shua says, Allow her:
she guards this to the day of my embalming:
8 for you have the poor with you always;
but me you have not always.
9 So a vast multitude of the Yah Hudiym
knows he is there:
and they come, not only for sake of Yah Shua
but also to see El Azar whom he raised from the dead:
10 and the archpriests counsel
to also slaughter El Azar;
11 because, because of him,
many of the Yah Hudiym go and trust in Yah Shua.

The Triumphal Entry Of Yah Shua

12 On the morrow,
a vast multitude who come to the celebration,
when they hear that Yah Shua comes to Yeru Shalem,
13 they take branches of phoinix and go meet him,
and cry, Hoshia Na!
Eulogized — he who comes in the name of Yah Veh
— the Sovereign of Yisra El.
14 And Yah Shua finds a burrito and sits thereon;
exactly as scribed,
15 *Fear* **Awe** not, daughter of *Sion* **Siyon**:
behold, thy *King* **Sovereign** cometh,
sitting on *an ass's* **a burro's** colt.
Psalm 118:25, 26; Zechar Yah 9:9

16 These *things understood* **knew** not his disciples
at the first:
but when *Jesus* **Yah Shua** was glorified,
then remembered they
that these *things* were *written* **scribed** of him,
and that they had done these *things* unto him.
17 **So** The *people* **multitude**
therefore that was with him
when he *called Lazarus* **voiced out to El Azar**
out of his *grave* **tomb**, and raised him from the dead,
bare record **witnessed**.
18 For this cause the *people*
multitude also met him,
for that they heard that he had done this *miracle* **sign**.
19 **So** The Pharisees *therefore*
said among themselves,
Perceive **See** ye how ye *prevail nothing* **benefit naught**?
behold, the *world* **cosmos** is gone after him.

Hellenes Will To See Yah Shua

20 And there were *certain Greeks* **some Hellenes**
among **of** them that *came up* **ascended** to worship
at the *feast* **celebration**:
21 *The same* **So these** came
therefore to *Philip* **Philippos**,
which was of *Bethsaida* **Beth Sayad**, *Galilee* **Galiyl**,
and *desired* **asked** him, *saying* **wording**,
Sir Lord **Adoni**, we *would* **will to** see *Jesus* **Yah Shua**.
22 *Philip* **Philippos** cometh
and *telleth Andrew* **wordeth to Andreas**:
and again *Andrew* **Andreas** and *Philip* **Philippos**
tell Jesus **word to Yah Shua**.

Yah Shua Prophesies
His Death And Glorification

23 And *Jesus* **Yah Shua** answered
them, *saying* **wording**,
The hour is come,
that the Son of *man* **humanity** should be glorified.
24 *Verily, verily, I say* **Amen!
Amen! I word** unto you,
Except **Unless** a *corn* **kernal** of *wheat* **grain**
fall into the ground and die, it abideth alone:
but *if* **whenever** it die, it bringeth forth much fruit.
25 He that *loveth* **befriendeth**
his *life* **soul** shall lose it;
and he that hateth his *life* **soul** in this *world*
cosmos shall *keep* **guard** it unto life eternal.
26 *If* **Whenever** any *man serve* **one minister to** me,
let him follow me;

JOHN/YOCHANAN 12

and where I am, there shall also my *servant* **minister** be:
if **whenever** any *man* serve *one* **minister** *to* me,
him *will* **shall** my Father honour.

27 Now is my soul troubled; and what shall I say?
Father, save me from this hour:
but for this cause came I unto this hour.

28 Father, glorify thy name.
Then **So** came there a voice from heaven, saying,
I have both glorified *it*, and *will* **shall** glorify *it* again.

29 **So**The *people* **multitude** *therefore*,
that stood by, and heard it,
said **worded** that *it thundered* **thunder became**:
others *said* **worded**, An angel spake to him.

THE ARCH OF THE COSMOS EJECTED: YAH SHUA EXALTED

30 *Jesus* **Yah Shua** answered and said,
This voice *came* **became** not because of me,
but for your sakes.

31 Now is the judgment of this *world* **cosmos**:
now shall the *prince* **arch** of this *world* **cosmos**
be *cast out* **ejected**.

32 And I, *if* **whenever** I be *lifted up* **exalted** from the earth,
will **shall** draw all men unto me.

33 This he *said* **worded**,
signifying what death he should die.
Loukas 10:18, Revelation 12:7—12

34 The *people* **multitude** answered him,
We have heard out of the *law* **torah**
that *Christ* **the Messiah** abideth *forever* **unto the eons**:
and how *sayest* **wordest** thou,
The Son of *man* **humanity** must be *lifted up* **exalted**?
who is this Son of *man* **humanity**?

35 *Then Jesus* **So Yah Shua** said unto them,
Yet a little *while* **time** is the light with you.

15 Awe not, daughter of Siyon!
Behold, your Sovereign comes,
sitting on a colt of a burro.
Psalm 118:25, 26; Zechar Yah 9:9

16 At first, His disciples knew these not:
but when Yah Shua was glorified
then they remember these that are scribed of him;
and that they had done these to him.

17 So the multitude with him
witness that he voiced El Azar from his tomb
and raised him from the dead,

18 for this cause the multitude also meet him,
for they hear he had done this sign.

19 So the Pharisees say among themselves,
See how you benefit naught?
Behold, the cosmos goes after him!

HELLENES WILL TO SEE YAH SHUA

20 And some Hellenes
ascend to worship at the celebration:

21 so they come to Philippos
who is of Beth Sayad, Galiyl,
and ask him, wording,
Adoni, we will to see Yah Shua.

22 Philippos goes and words to Andreas:
and again Andreas and Philippos word to Yah Shua.

YAH SHUA PROPHESIES HIS DEATH AND GLORIFICATION

23 And Yah Shua answers them, wording,
The hour is come to glorify the Son of humanity.

24 Amen! Amen! I word to you,
Unless a kernal of grain
falls to the ground and dies, it abides alone:
but whenever it dies, it brings forth much fruit.

25 Whoever befriends his soul,
loses it;
and whoever hates his soul in this cosmos,
guards it to life eternal:

26 whenever anyone ministers to me, follow me;
and where I am, there also is my minister:
whenever anyone ministers to me,
him my Father honors.

27 Now my soul troubles; And what say I?
Father, save me from this hour?
But for this cause, I come to this hour.

28 Father, glorify your name.
So a voice comes from the heavens, saying,
I both glorified, and glorify again.

29 So the multitude who stand by and hear,
word that thunder became:
others word, An angel speaks to him.

THE ARCH OF THE COSMOS EJECTED: YAH SHUA EXALTED

30 Yah Shua answers, saying,
This voice became not for my sake;
but for your sake.

31 Now is the judgment of this cosmos;
now is the arch of this cosmos ejected:

32 and I, whenever I am exalted from the earth,
draw all men to me.

33 — he words this, signifying what death he dies.
Loukas 10:18, Revelation 12:7—12

JOHN/YOCHANAN 12

34 The multitude answers him,
We hear from the torah
that the Messiah abides to the eons:
and how word you,
The Son of humanity must be exalted?
Who is this Son of humanity?

35 So Yah Shua says to them,
Yet a little time the light is with you:
Walk while ye have the light,
lest darkness *come upon* **overtake** you:
for he that walketh in darkness
knoweth not whither he goeth.

36 While ye have light, *believe* **trust** in the light,
that ye may be the *children* **sons** of light.
These *things* spake *Jesus* **Yah Shua**, and departed,
and *did hide* **secreted** himself from them.

37 But though he had done so many *miracles* **signs**
before **in front of** them,
yet they *believed* **trusted** not *on* **in** him:

38 That the *saying* **word** of
Esaias **Yesha Yah** the prophet
might be fulfilled/**shalamed** which he *spake* **said**,
Lord, who hath *believed* **trusted** our report?
and to whom hath the arm of *the Lord* **Yah Veh**
been *revealed* **unveiled**?
Yesha Yah 53:1

39 *Therefore* **So** they could not *believe* **trust**,
because that *Esaias* **Yesha Yah** said again,

40 He hath blinded their eyes,
and *hardened* **petrified** their heart;
that they should not see with their eyes,
nor *understand* **comprehend** with their heart,
and *be converted* **return**, and I should heal them.

41 These *things* said *Esaias* **Yesha Yah**,
when he saw his glory, and spake *of*
concerning him. Yesha Yah 6:1

42 *Nevertheless* **Yet indeed**,
among the chief rulers **even of the archs** also
many *believed on* **trusted in** him;
but because of the Pharisees they
did not *confess* **profess** him,
lest they should be
put out of the synagogue **ex—synagogued**:

43 For they loved the *praise*
glory of *men* **humanity**
more than the *praise* **glory** of *God* **Elohim**.

44 *Jesus* **Yah Shua** cried and said,
He that *believeth on* **trusteth in** me,
believeth not on **trusteth not in** me,
but *on* **in** him that sent me.

45 And he that seeth me seeth him that sent me.

46 I am come a light into the *world* **cosmos**,
that whosoever *believeth on* **trusteth in**
me should not abide in darkness.

47 And *if* **whenever** any *man*
one hear my *words* **rhema**,
and *believe* **trust** not,
I judge him not:
for I came not to judge the *world* **cosmos**,
but to save the *world* **cosmos**.

48 He that *rejecteth* **setteth** me **aside**,
and *receiveth* **taketh** not my *words* **rhema**,
hath one that judgeth him:
the word that I have spoken,
the same shall judge him in the *last* **final** day.

49 For I have not spoken of myself;
but the Father which sent me,
he gave me a *commandment* **misvah**,
what I should say, and what I should speak.

50 And I know that his *commandment* **misvah**
is life *everlasting* **eternal**:
So whatsoever I speak *therefore*,
even **exactly** as the Father said unto me, *so* **thus** I speak.

THE FINAL NIGHT OF
YAH SHUA: THE FINAL SUPPER

13 Now *before* **preceding**
the *feast* **celebration** of the *passover* **pasach**,
when *Jesus* **Yah Shua** knew that his hour was come
that he should depart out of this *world* **cosmos**
unto the Father,
having loved his own which were in the *world* **cosmos**,
he loved them unto the *end* **completion/shalom**.

YAH SHUA PURIFIES
THE FEET OF THE DISCIPLES

2 And supper *being ended* **having become**,
the *devil* **Diabolos** having *now* **already** put into the heart
of *Judas Iscariot* **Yah Hudah the urbanite**,
Simon's **Shimon's** son, to betray him;

3 *Jesus* **Yah Shua**, knowing that the Father
had given all *things* into his hands,
and that he was come from *God* **Elohim**,
and went to *God* **Elohim**;
Walk while you have the light
lest darkness overtake you:
for whoever walks in darkness
knows not where he goes.

36 While you have light, trust in the light
that you become sons of light.

JOHN/YOCHANAN 12, 13

Yah Shua speaks these and departs
and secrets himself from them.
37 But though he does so
many signs in front of them
yet they trust not in him:
38 to fulfill/shalam the word
of Yesha Yah the prophet
wherein he says,
Who trusts our report?
And to whom is the arm of Yah Veh unveiled?
Yesha Yah 53:1
39 So they cannot trust,
because Yesha Yah says again,
40 He blinds their eyes,
and petrifies their heart;
that they neither see with their eyes
nor comprehend with their heart
and return, and I heal them.
41 Yesha Yah said these when he saw his glory,
and spoke concerning him.
Yesha Yah 6:1
42 Yet indeed,
even many of the archs also trust in him;
but because of the Pharisees, they profess him not,
lest they become ex—synagogued:
43 for they love the glory of humanity
more than the glory of Elohim.
44 Yah Shua cries and says,
Whoever trusts in me,
trusts not in me,
but in him who sent me:
45 and whoever sees me,
sees him who sent me.
46 I come — a light to the cosmos;
that whoever trusts in me
abides not in darkness:
47 and whenever anyone hears my rhema
and trusts not
I judge him not:
for I come not to judge the cosmos
but to save the cosmos.
48 Whoever sets me aside and takes not my rhema
has one who judges him:
the word I speak judges him in the final day.
49 For I speak not of myself;
but the Father who sent me gave me a misvah
— what to say, and what to speak:
50 and I know his misvah is life eternal:
so whatever I speak
exactly as the Father said to me, thus I speak.

THE FINAL NIGHT OF YAH SHUA:
THE FINAL SUPPER

13 Preceding the celebration of the pasach,
Yah Shua, knowing his hour
to depart from this cosmos to the Father is come,
loving his own who are in the cosmos,
he loves them to the completion/shalom.

YAH SHUA PURIFIES
THE FEET OF THE DISCIPLES

2 And being supper;
Diabolos having already put into the heart
of Yah Hudah the urbanite the son of Shimon
to betray him;
3 Yah Shua,
knowing that the Father gave all into his hands
and that he comes from Elohim
and goes to Elohim,
4 He riseth from supper,
and *laid aside* **placed** his *garments* **clothing**;
and took a *towel* **linen**, and girded himself.
5 *After that Then* **So** he
poureth water into a bason,
and began to wash the disciples' feet,
and to *wipe* **squeezedry** them
with the *towel* **linen** wherewith he was girded.
6 *Then* **So** cometh he to
Simon Peter **Shimon Petros**:
and *Peter saith* **Petros wordeth** unto him,
Lord **Adonay**, dost thou wash my feet?
7 *Jesus* **Yah Shua** answered and said unto him,
What I do thou knowest not now;
but thou shalt know *hereafter* **after this**.
8 *Peter saith* **Petros wordeth** unto him,
Thou shalt never wash my feet **unto the eons**.
Jesus **Yah Shua** answered him,
If **Unless** I wash thee *not*, thou hast no part with me.
9 *Simon Peter saith* **Shimon
Petros wordeth** unto him,
Lord **Adonay**, not my feet only,
but also my hands and my head.
10 *Jesus saith* **Yah Shua wordeth** to him,
He that is *washed* **bathed**
needeth not *save* **except** to wash his feet,
but is *clean* **pure** every whit:
and ye are *clean* **pure**, but **indeed** not all.
11 For he knew who should betray him;
Therefore **So** said he, Ye are not all *clean* **pure**.

Foot Purifying Example

12 So after he had washed their feet,
and had taken his *garments* **clothing**,
and *was set down* **reposed** again,
he said unto them, Know ye what I have done to you?

13 Ye *call* **voice out** to me
Master **Doctor** and *Lord* **Adonay**: and
ye *say* **word** well; for *so* I am.

14 **So** If I *then*, your *Lord*
Adonay and *Master* **Doctor**,
have washed your feet;
ye also *ought* **are indebted** to wash one another's feet.

15 For I have given you an example,
that ye should do **exactly** as I have done to you.

16 *Verily, verily, I say* **Amen!**
Amen! I word unto you,
The servant is not greater than his lord;
neither he that is *sent* **apostolized**
greater than he that sent him.

17 If ye know these *things*,
happy **blessed** are ye *if* **whenever** ye do them.

18 I *speak* **word** not *of* **concerning** you all:
I know whom I have chosen:
but that the scripture may be fulfilled/**shalamed**,
He that eateth bread with me
hath lifted *up* his heel against me.
Psalm 41:9

19 Now I *tell* **word to** you
before **ere** it *come* **becometh**,
that, when *ever* it *is come to pass* **becometh**,
ye may *believe* **trust** that *I am he* **I AM**.

20 *Verily, verily, I say* **Amen!**
Amen! I word unto you,
He that *receiveth* **taketh** whomsoever I send
receiveth **taketh** me;
and he that *receiveth* **taketh** me
receiveth **taketh** him that sent me.

21 When *Jesus* **Yah Shua** had thus said,
he was troubled in spirit, and *testified* **witnessed**,
and said,
Verily, verily, I say **Amen! Amen! I word** unto you,
that one of you shall betray me.

22 *Then* **So** the disciples looked one on another,
doubting of **perplexed about** whom he *spake* **worded**.

23 Now there was *leaning* **reposing**
on *Jesus'* **in Yah Shua's** bosom
one of his disciples, whom *Jesus* **Yah Shua** loved.

24 *Simon Peter therefore* **So**
Shimon Petros beckoned to him,
that he should ask who it should be
of **concerning** whom he *spake* **worded**.

25 He *then lying* **so falling** on
Jesus' breast **Yah Shua's chest**
saith **wordeth** unto him, *Lord* **Adonay**, who is it?

4 he rises from supper and places his clothing;
and takes a linen and girds himself:

5 so he pours water into a bason
and begins to wash the feet of the disciples;
and to squeezedry them
with the linen he is girt.

6 So he comes to Shimon Petros:
and Petros words to him,
Adonay, you — wash my feet?

7 Yah Shua answers him, saying,
What I do you know not now;
but after this you know.

8 Petros words to him,
You wash not my feet to the eons.
Yah Shua answers him,
Unless I wash you, you have no part with me.

9 Shimon Petros words to him,
Adonay, not only my feet
but also my hands and my head.

10 Yah Shua words to him,
Whoever bathes, need not wash, except his feet,
but is wholly pure:
and you are pure — but indeed not all.

11 — for he knows who is to betray him;
so he says, You are not all pure.

Foot Purifying Example

12 After he washes their feet,
and takes his clothing and reposes again,
he says to them, Know you what I did to you?

13 You voice out to me, Doctor and Adonay:
and you word well; for I am.

14 So if I, your Adonay and Doctor, wash your feet;
you also are indebted to wash the feet of one another:

15 for I give you an example
to do exactly as I do to you.

16 Amen! Amen! I word to you,
Neither is the servant greater than his adoni;
nor the apostolized greater than he who sent him.

17 If you know these,
blessed — whenever you do them.

18 I word not concerning you all:
I know whom I chose:
except to fulfill/shalam the scripture,
He who eats bread with me
lifts his heel against me.

JOHN/YOCHANAN 13

Psalm 41:9

19 Now I word to you ere it becomes,
so, whenever it becomes, you trust that I AM.
20 Amen! Amen! I word to you,
Whoever takes whomever I send, takes me;
and whoever takes me, takes him who sent me.
21 Saying thus, Yah Shua is troubled in spirit,
and witnesses, and says,
Amen! Amen! I word to you,
that one of you betrays me.
22 So the disciples look at one another,
perplexed about whom he words:
23 and reposing in the bosom of Yah Shua
is one of his disciples whom Yah Shua loves:
24 so Shimon Petros beckons him
to ask who it is concerning whom he words.
25 Then, falling on the chest of Yah Shua,
he words to him, Adonay, who is it?
26 *Jesus* **Yah Shua** answered, He it is,
to whom I shall give a *sop* **morsel**,
when I have *dipped* **baptized** it.
And when he had *dipped* **baptized** the *sop* **morsel**,
he gave it to *Judas Iscariot* **Yah Hudah the urbanite**
the son of *Simon* **Shimon**.

SATAN ENTERS YAH HUDAH

27 And after the *sop* **morsel**
then Satan entered into him.
Then said Jesus **So worded Yah Shua** unto
him, That thou doest, do quickly.
28 Now no *man at the table* **one reposing**
knew for what *intent* he *spake* **said** this unto him.
29 For some *of them* thought,
because *Judas* **Yah Hudah** had the bag,
that *Jesus* **Yah Shua** had *said* **worded** unto him,
Buy **Market** for those *things* that we have need of
against **unto** the *feast* **celebration**;
or, that he should give *something* **somewhat** to the poor.
30 So He *then* having *received* **taken** the *sop* **morsel**
went *immediately* **straightway** out: and it was night.
31 *Therefore* **So**, when he was gone out,
Jesus said **Yah Shua worded**,
Now is the Son of *man* **humanity** glorified,
and *God* **Elohim** is glorified in him.
32 If *God* **Elohim** be glorified in him,
God **Elohim** shall also glorify him in himself,
and shall straightway glorify him.
33 Little children, yet a little while I am with you.
Ye shall seek me:
and **exactly** as I said unto the *Jews* **Yah Hudiym**,

Whither I go, ye cannot come;
so now I say **I also word** to you.

A NEW MISVAH

34 A new *commandment* **misvah** I give unto you,
That ye love one another;
exactly as I have loved you, that ye also love one another.
35 By this shall *all men* **everyone** know
that ye are my disciples,
if **whenever** ye have love *one to* **in one** another.
36 *Simon Peter said* **Shimon
Petros worded** unto him,
Lord **Adonay**, whither goest thou?
Jesus **Yah Shua** answered him,
Whither I go, thou canst not follow me now;
but thou shalt follow me afterwards.
37 *Peter said* **Petros worded** unto him,
Lord **Adonay**, why cannot I follow thee now?
I *will lay down* **shall place** my *life* **soul** for thy sake.
38 *Jesus* **Yah Shua** answered him,
Wilt **Shalt** thou *lay down* **place** thy *life* **soul** for my sake?
Verily, verily, I say **Amen! Amen! I word** unto thee,
The *cock* **rooster** shall not *crow* **voice**,
till thou hast **utterly** denied me thrice.

YAH SHUA PROMISES HIS PAROUSIA

14 Let not your heart be troubled:
ye *believe* **trust** in *God* **Elohim**, *believe* **trust** also in me.
2 In my Father's house are
many *mansions* **abodes**:
if *it were* not *so*, *I would* **should** have *told* **said to** you.
I *go* **depart** to prepare a place for you.
3 And *if* **whenever** I *go* **depart**
and prepare a place for you,
I *will* **shall** come again,
and *receive* **take** you unto myself;
that where I am, there ye may be also.
4 And whither I go ye know, and the way ye know.
5 *Thomas saith* **Taom wordeth**
unto him, Lord **Adoni**,
we know not whither thou goest;
and how can we know the way?
6 *Jesus saith* **Yah Shua wordeth** unto him,
I am **I AM** the way, the truth, and the life:
no *man* **one** cometh unto the Father, *but* **except** by me.
7 If ye had known me,
ye should have known my Father also:
and from henceforth ye know him, and have seen him.
8 *Philip saith* **Philippos wordeth** unto him,
26 Yah Shua answers, It is he,

to whom I give a morsel when I baptize it.
— and he baptizes the morsel
and gives it to Yah Hudah the urbanite of Shimon.

Satan Enters Yah Hudah

27 And after the morsel, then Satan enters him:
and Yah Shua words to him,
What you do, do quickly.
28 And no one reposing
knows why he says this to him.
29 For some think,
because Yah Hudah had the bag,
that Yah Shua words to him,
Market what we need for the the celebration;
or to give somewhat to the poor.
30 So he takes the morsel
and straightway goes: and it is night.
31 So when he goes, Yah Shua words,
Now the Son of humanity is glorifiedl
and Elohim is glorified in him:
32 if Elohim is glorified in him,
Elohim also glorifies him in himself,
and straightway glorifies him.
33 Little children, yet a little I am with you.
You seek me:
and exactly as I say to the Yah Hudiym,
Where I go, you cannot come;
— I also word to you.

A New Misvah

34 A new misvah I give you — to love one another;
exactly as I love you, you also love one another:
35 by this everyone knows you are my disciples
— whenever you have love in one another.
36 Shimon Petros words to him,
Adonay, where go you?
Yah Shua answers him,
Where I go, you cannot follow me now
— but follow me afterwards.
37 Petros words to him,
Adonay, why cannot I follow you now?
I place my soul for your sake.
38 Yah Shua answers him,
You, place your soul for my sake?
Amen! Amen! I word to you,
The rooster voices not,
until you utterly deny me thrice.

Yah Shua Promises His Parousia

14 Trouble not your heart:
you trust in Elohim; trust also in me.
2 In the house of my Father are many abodes:
and if it not, I had said to you.
I depart to prepare a place for you:
3 and whenever I depart and
prepare a place for you
I come again and take you to myself;
that where I am, you also are.
4 And where I go you know,
and the way you know.
5 Taom words to him, Adoni,
we know not where you go;
and how can we know the way?
6 Yah Shua words to him,
I AM the way, the truth, and the life:
no one comes to the Father, except by me.
7 If you had known me,
you had also known my Father:
and from henceforth you know him and see him.
8 Philippos words to him,
Lord **Adoni**, shew us the Father,
and it *sufficeth* **satisfieth** us.
9 *Jesus saith* **Yah Shua wordeth** unto him,
Have I been so long time with you,
and yet hast thou not known me, *Philip* **Philippos**?
he that hath seen me hath seen the Father;
and how *sayest* **wordest** thou *then*, Shew us the Father?
10 *Believest* **trustest** thou not
that I am in the Father,
and the Father in me?
the *words* **rhema** that I speak unto you
I speak not of myself:
but the Father that *dwelleth* **abideth** in me,
he doeth the works.
11 *Believe* **Trust** me that I *am* in the Father,
and the Father in me:
or else **but if not**
believe **trust** me for the very works' sake.
12 *Verily, verily, I say* **Amen!
Amen! I word** unto you,
He that *believeth on* **trusteth in** me,
the works that I do shall he do also;
and greater works than these shall he do;
because I go unto my Father.
13 And whatsoever ye shall ask in my name,
that *will* **shall** I do,
that the Father may be glorified in the Son.
14 *If* **Whenever** — **whatever**
ye shall ask *any thing* in my name, I *will* **shall** do it.
15 *If* **Whenever** ye love me,

JOHN/YOCHANAN 14

keep **guard** my *commandments* **misvoth**.

YAH SHUA PROMISES THE PARACLETE

16 And I *will pray* **shall ask** the Father,
and he shall give you another *Comforter* **Paraclete**,
that he may abide with you *for ever* **unto the eons**;

17 Even the Spirit of truth;
whom the *world* **cosmos** cannot *receive* **take**,
because it seeth him not, neither knoweth him:
but ye know him;
for he *dwelleth* **abideth** with you, and shall be in you.

18 I *will* **shall** not *leave* **forsake**
you *comfortless* **orphaned**:
I *will* **shall** come to you.

19 Yet a little *while*,
and the *world* **cosmos** seeth me no more;
but ye see me: because I live, ye shall live also.

20 At that day ye shall know
that I *am* in my Father,
and ye in me, and I in you.

21 He that hath my *commandments* **misvoth**,
and *keepeth* **guardeth** them, he it is that loveth me:
and he that loveth me shall be loved of my Father,
and I *will* **shall** love him,
and *will* **shall** manifest myself to him.

22 *Judas saith* **Yah Hudah wordeth** unto him,
not *Iscariot* **the urbanite**,
Lord **Adonay**, how *is* **be** it
that thou *wilt* **art about to** manifest thyself unto us,
and *indeed* not unto the *world* **cosmos**?

23 *Jesus* **Yah Shua** answered and said unto him,
If a man **Whenever anyone** love me,
he *will keep* **shall guard** my words:
and my Father *will* **shall** love him,
and we *will* **shall** come unto him,
and make our abode with him.

24 He that loveth me not
keepeth **guardeth** not my *sayings* **words**:
and the word which ye hear is not mine,
but the Father's which sent me.

25 These *things* have I spoken unto you,
being yet present **abiding** with you.

26 But the *Comforter* **Paraclete**, which
is the *Holy Spirit* **Ruach ha-kodesh**,
whom the Father *will* **shall** send in my name,
he shall *teach* **doctrinate** you all *things*,
and *bring all things to your remembrance* **remind you**,
whatsoever I have said unto you.

YAH SHUA BESTOWS HIS UNITY

27 *Peace* **Shalom** I *leave* **release** with you,
my *peace* **shalom** I give unto you:
not *exactly* as the *world* **cosmos** giveth, give I unto you.
Let not your heart be troubled,
neither let it *be afraid* **coward**.
Adoni, show us the Father, and it satisfies us.

9 Yah Shua words to him,
Am I so long a time with you,
and yet you know me not, Philippos?
Whoever has seen me has seen the Father!
And how word you, Show us the Father?

10 Trust you not that I am in the Father,
and the Father in me?
The rhema I speak to you, I speak not from myself:
but the Father who abides in me
— he does the works.

11 Trust me:
I in the Father, and the Father in me:
but if not, trust me for sake of the very works.

12 Amen! Amen! I word to you,
Whoever trusts in me,
also does the works I do;
and greater works than these, he does;
because I go to my Father.

13 And whatever you ask in my name, this I do,
to glorify the Father in the Son.

14 Whenever — whatever
you ask in my name, I do.

15 Whenever you love me, guard my misvoth.

YAH SHUA PROMISES THE PARACLETE

16 I ask the Father;
and he gives you another Paraclete
to abide with you to the eons;

17 even the Spirit of truth;
whom the cosmos cannot take
because it neither sees him, nor knows him:
but you know him;
for he abides with you, being in you.

18 I forsake you not orphaned; I come to you:

19 yet a little, and the cosmos sees me no more;
but you see me: because I live, you live also.

20 At that day you know
— I in my Father, and you in me, and I in you.

21 Whoever has my misvoth and guards them
loves me:
and whoever loves me is loved by my Father;
and I love him and manifest myself to him.

22 Yah Hudah words to him — not the urbanite,
Adonay, how is it
that you are about to manifest yourself to us,
and not indeed to the cosmos?
23 Yah Shua answers him, saying,
whenever anyone loves me, he guards my words;
and my Father loves him:
and we come to him and make our abode with him.
24 Whoever loves me not, guards not my words:
and the word you hear is not mine
but of the Father who sent me.
25 I speak these to you, abiding with you.
26 And the Paraclete — the Holy Spirit
whom the Father sends in my name,
he doctrinates you all;
and reminds you of whatever I said to you.

Yah Shua Bestows His Unity

27 I release shalom with you;
my shalom I give to you:
not exactly as the cosmos gives, give I you:
neither trouble your heart; nor cower.
28 Ye have heard how I said unto you,
I go away, and come again unto you.
If ye loved me, ye *would rejoice* **should cheer**,
because I said, I go unto the Father:
for my Father is greater than I.
29 And now I have *told* **said to** you
before **ere** it *come to pass* **become**,
that, when *ever* it *is come to pass* **becometh**,
ye might *believe* **trust**.
30 Hereafter I *will* **shall** not
talk **speak** much with you:
for the *prince* **arch** of this *world* **cosmos** cometh,
and hath *nothing* **naught** in me.
31 But that the *world* **cosmos** may know
that I love the Father;
and **exactly** as the Father
gave **misvahed** me *commandment*,
even *so* **thus** I do.
Arise, let us go hence.

Abiding In The Vine

15 *I am* **I AM** the true vine,
and my Father is the *husbandman* **cultivator**.
2 Every branch in me that beareth not fruit
he taketh away:
and every branch that beareth fruit,
he *purgeth* **purifieth** it,
that it may *bring forth* **bear** *much* **more** fruit.

Now **Already** ye are *clean* **pure** through the word
which I have spoken unto you.
4 **Exactly** as the branch cannot bear fruit of itself,
except **unless** it abide in the vine;
no more **thus neither** can ye,
except **unless** ye abide in me.
5 *I am* **I AM** the vine, ye are the branches:
He that abideth in me, and I in him,
the same *bringeth forth* **beareth** much fruit:
for *without* **apart from** me ye can do *nothing* **naught**.
6 *If a man* **Unless anyone** abide *not* in me,
he is cast *forth* as a branch, and is withered;
and men gather them,
and cast them into the fire, and they are burned.
7 *If* **Whenever** ye abide in me,
and my *words* **rhema** abide in you,
ye shall ask what ye will, and it shall be *done* unto you.
8 Herein is my Father glorified,
that ye bear much fruit;
so shall ye be my disciples.
9 **Exactly** As the Father hath loved me,
so have I loved you:
continue **abide** ye in my love.
10 *If* **Whenever** ye *keep* **guard**
my *commandments* **misvoth**,
ye shall abide in my love;
even **exactly** as I have *kept* **guarded**
my Father's *commandments* **misvoth**,
and abide in his love.
11 These *things* have I spoken unto you,
that my *joy* **cheer** might *remain* **abide** in you,
and that your *joy* **cheer** might be full.
12 This is my *commandment* **misvah**,
That ye love one another, **exactly** as I have loved you.
13 Greater love hath no *man* **one** than this,
that *a man lay down* **one place** his
life **soul** for his friends.
14 Ye are my friends, *if* **whenever** ye do
whatsoever **as much as ever** I *command* **misvah** you.

THE NEW RELATIONSHIP

15 Henceforth I *call* **word** you not servants;
for the servant knoweth not what his lord doeth:
but I have *called* **said** you friends;
for all *things* that I have heard of my Father
I have made known unto you.
16 Ye have not chosen me, but I have chosen you,
and *ordained* **set** you,
that ye should go and *bring forth* **bear** fruit,
and that your fruit should *remain* **abide**:
that whatsoever ye shall ask of the Father in my name,

	he may give it you.
17	These *things* I *command* **misvah** you,
	that ye love one another.
18	If the *world* **cosmos** hate you,
	ye know that it hated me *before it hated you* **first**.
19	If ye were of the *world* **cosmos**,
28	You heard me say to you,
	I go away, and come again to you.
	If you love me, cheer!
	— because I say, I go to the Father:
	for my Father is greater than I.
29	And now I say to you, ere it becomes,
	that, whenever it becomes, you trust.
30	Hereafter I speak not much with you:
	for the arch of this cosmos comes,
	and has naught in me.
31	But so that the cosmos
	knows that I love the Father,
	and exactly as the Father misvahed me,
	even thus I do.
	Rise, we go hence.

ABIDING IN THE VINE

15	I AM the true vine,
	and my Father the cultivator.
2	Every branch in me that bears not fruit
	he takes away:
	and every branch that bears fruit,
	he purifies to bear much more fruit.
	Already you are pure
	through the word I spoke to you.
4	Exactly as the branch cannot bear fruit of itself
	unless it abide in the vine;
	thus neither can you
	unless you abide in me.
5	I AM the vine, you are the branches:
	whoever abides in me, and I in him,
	the same bears much fruit:
	for apart from me you can do naught.
6	Unless anyone abides in me,
	he is cast as a branch and withers;
	and men gather them
	and cast them into the fire and burn them.
7	Whenever you abide in me,
	and my rhema abides in you
	ask what you will, and thus it becomes to you.
8	Herein is my Father glorified
	— that you bear much fruit;
	thus you become my disciples.
9	Exactly as the Father loves me, thus I love you:
	you, abide in my love.
10	Whenever you guard my misvoth,
	you abide in my love;
	even exactly as I guard the misvoth of my Father,
	and abide in his love.
11	I speak these to you,
	so that my cheer abides in you,
	and to fill your cheer.
12	This is my misvah,
	to love one another, exactly as I love you.
13	Greater love has no one than this,
	than to place his soul for his friends:
14	you are my friends,
	whenever you do as much as ever I misvah you.

THE NEW RELATIONSHIP

15	Henceforth I word you not, servants;
	for the servant knows not what his adoni does:
	but I say of you, friends;
	for all I heard of my Father I made known to you.
16	You chose me not, but I chose you,
	and set you to go and bear fruit,
	and that your fruit abide:
	that whatever you ask of the Father in my name,
	he gives you.
17	These I misvah you:
	to love one another.
18	If the cosmos hates you,
	you know it hated me first.
19	If you are of the cosmos,
	the *world* **cosmos**
	would love **should ever befriend** his own:
	but because ye are not of the *world* **cosmos**,
	but I have chosen you out of the *world* **cosmos**,
	Therefore **So** the *world* **cosmos** hateth you.
20	Remember the word that I said unto you,
	The servant is not greater than his *lord*
	adoni. If they have persecuted me,
	they *will* **shall** also persecute you;
	if they have *kept* **guarded** my *saying* **word**,
	they *will keep* **shall guard** yours also.
21	But all these *things*
	will **shall** they do unto you for my name's sake,
	because they know not him that sent me.
22	If I had not come and spoken unto them,
	they had not had sin:
	but now they have no *cloak* **pretext** for their sin.
23	He that hateth me hateth my Father also.
24	If I had not done among them
	the works which none other man did,

they had not had sin:
but now have they both seen and hated
both me and my Father.
25 But this *cometh to pass* **becometh**,
that the word might be fulfilled/shalamed
that is *written* **scribed** in their *law* **torah**,
They hated me *without a cause*
gratuitously. Psalms 35:19, 69:4
26 But when **ever** the *Comforter* **Paraclete** is come,
whom I *will* **shall** send unto you from the Father,
even the Spirit of truth,
which proceedeth from the Father,
he shall *testify of* **witness concerning** me:
27 And ye also shall *bear* witness,
because ye have been with me from the beginning.

Ex—Synogoguing And Martyrdom

16 These *things* have I spoken unto you,
that ye should not be *offended* **scandalized**.
2 They shall *put* **ex—synogogue**
you *out of the synagogues*:
yea, **yet** the *time* **hour** cometh,
that whosoever *killeth* **slaughtereth** you *will* **shall** think
that he *doeth God service* **offereth Elohim liturgy**.
3 And these *things will* **shall** they do unto you,
because they have not known the Father, nor me.
4 But these *things* have I *told* **spoken unto** you,
that when **ever** the *time* **hour** shall *come* **become**,
ye may remember that I told you of them.
And these *things* I said not unto you
at **from** the beginning,
because I was with you.
5 But now I go my way to him that sent me;
and none of you asketh me, Whither goest thou?
6 But because I have *said*
spoken these *things* unto you,
sorrow hath filled your heart **full**.

The Ministry Of The Paraclete

7 *Nevertheless I tell* **Yet I word** you the truth;
It is *expedient* **beneficial** for you that I go away:
for *if* **whenever** I go not away,
the *Comforter will* **Paraclete shall** not come unto you;
but *if* **whenever** I depart, I *will* **shall** send him unto you.
8 And when he is come,
he *will* **shall** reprove the *world* **cosmos**
of **concerning** sin,
and *of righteousness* **concerning justness**,
and *of* **concerning** judgment:
9 *Of sin* **Concerning sin indeed**,
because they *believe* **trust** not *on* **in** me;
10 *Of righteousness* **Concerning justness**,
because I go to my Father, and ye see me no more;
11 *Of* **Concerning** judgment,
because the *prince* **arch** of this *world* **cosmos** is judged.
12 I have yet *many things*
much to *say* **word** unto you,
but ye cannot bear them now.
13 Howbeit when **ever** he, the
Spirit of truth, is come,
he *will* **shall** guide you into all truth:
for he shall not speak of himself;
but whatsoever he shall hear, that shall he speak:
and he *will shew* **shall evangelize** you
things **those** to come.
the cosmos ever befriends his own:
but because you are not of the cosmos,
but I chose you from the cosmos,
because of this the cosmos hates you.
20 Remember the word I said to you,
The servant is not greater than his adoni.
If they persecute me, they also persecute you;
if they guard my word, they guard yours also.
21 But they do all these to you for sake of my name,
because they know not him who sent me.
22 If I had not come and spoken to them,
they had not had sin:
but now they have no pretext for their sin.
23 Whoever hates me hates my Father also.
24 If I had not done among them
the works which no other man did,
they had not had sin:
but now have they both seen and hated
both me and my Father.
25 But this becomes,
to fulfill/shalam the word scribed in their torah,
They hated me gratuitously.
Psalms 35:19, 69:4
26 And whenever the Paraclete comes
— whom I send you from the Father
— even the Spirit of truth
who proceeds from the Father,
he witnesses concerning me:
27 and you also witness,
because you were with me from the beginning.

Ex—Synogoguing And Martyrdom

16 I have spoken these to you,
that you not be scandalized.
2 They ex—synogogue you:

JOHN/YOCHANAN 16

yet the hour comes that whoever slaughters you
thinks he offers Elohim liturgy:
3 and they do these to you
because they know neither the Father, nor me:
4 but I have spoken these to you,
that whenever the hour becomes,
to remember that I told you of them.
And I said these not to you from the beginning
because I was with you.
5 But now I go my way to him who sent me;
and none of you asks me, Where go you?
6 But because I have spoken these to you,
sorrow fills your heart full.

THE MINISTRY OF THE PARACLETE

7 Yet I word you the truth;
It is beneficial for you that I go away:
for whenever I go not away,
the Paraclete comes not to you:
but whenever I depart, I send him to you:
8 and when he comes, he reproves the cosmos
concerning sin,
and concerning justness,
and concerning judgment.
9 Concerning sin indeed,
because they trust not in me;
10 concerning justness,
because I go to my Father, and you see me no more;
11 concerning judgment,
because the arch of this cosmos is judged.
12 I still have much to word to you,
but you cannot bear them now.
13 However, whenever the Spirit of truth comes,
he guides you into all truth:
for he speaks not of himself;
but whatever he hears, he speaks
and he evangelizes you of those to come.
14 He shall glorify me:
for he shall *receive* **take** of mine,
and shall *shew* **evangelize** it unto you.

YAH SHUA PROPHESIES HIS DEATH, RESURRECTION, AND PAROUSIA

15 All *things that* — **as much as** the Father hath are mine:
Therefore **So** said I, that he shall take of mine,
and shall *shew* **evangelize** it unto you.
16 A little *while*, and ye shall not see me:
and again, a little *while*, and ye shall see
me, because I go to the Father.

17 *Then* **So** said some of his disciples
among themselves **to one another**,
What is this that he *saith* **wordeth** unto us,
A little *while*, and ye shall not see me:
and again, a little *while*, and ye shall see me:
and, Because I go to the Father?
18 **So** They *said* **worded** *therefore*,
What is this that he *saith* **wordeth**, A little *while*?
we *cannot tell* **know not** what he *saith* **wordeth**.
19 Now *Jesus* **Yah Shua** knew
that they *were desirous* **willed** to ask him,
and said unto them,
Do ye enquire among yourselves
Seek ye with one another
of **concerning** that I said,
A little *while*, and ye shall not see me:
and again, a little *while*, and ye shall see me?
20 *Verily, verily, I say* **Amen!**
Amen! I word unto you,
That ye shall weep and lament,
but the *world* **cosmos** shall *rejoice* **cheer**:
and ye shall be sorrowful,
but your sorrow shall *be turned into joy* **become cheer**.
21 A woman when **ever** she *is in travail* **births**
hath sorrow,
because her hour is come:
but *as soon as* **whenever**
she *is delivered of* **beareth** the child,
she remembereth no more the anguish,
for *joy* **cheer**
that a *man* **human** is *born* **birthed**
into the *world* **cosmos**.
22 And **so indeed** ye now *therefore* have sorrow:
but I *will* **shall** see you again,
and your heart shall *rejoice* **cheer**,
and your *joy* **cheer** no *man* **one** taketh from you.
23 And in that day ye shall ask me *nothing* **naught**.
Verily, verily, I say **Amen! Amen! I word**
unto you, *Whatsoever* **As much as ever**
ye shall ask the Father in my name,
he *will* **shall** give it you.
24 Hitherto have ye asked
nothing **naught** in my name:
ask, and ye shall *receive* **take**
that your *joy* **cheer** may be *full* **fulfilled/shalamed**.
25 These *things* have I spoken unto you in proverbs:
but the *time* **hour** cometh,
when I shall no more speak unto you in proverbs,
but I shall *shew* **evangelize** you *plainly* **boldly**
of **concerning** the Father.

26	At that day ye shall ask in my name:		but whenever she bears the child,
	and I *say* **word** not unto you,		she remembers no more the anguish,
	that I *will pray* **shall ask** the Father for you:		for cheer that a human is birthed into the cosmos.
27	For the Father himself *loveth* **befriendeth** you,	22	And so indeed, you now have sorrow:
	because ye have *loved* **befriended** me,		but I see you again, and your heart cheers,
	and have *believed* **trusted**		and no one takes your cheer from you:
	that I came out from *God* **Elohim**.	23	and in that day you ask me naught.
28	I came forth from the Father,		Amen! Amen! I word to you,

26   At that day ye shall ask in my name:
and I *say* **word** not unto you,
that I *will pray* **shall ask** the Father for you:

27   For the Father himself *loveth* **befriendeth** you,
because ye have *loved* **befriended** me,
and have *believed* **trusted**
that I came out from *God* **Elohim**.

28   I came forth from the Father,
and am come into the *world* **cosmos**:
again, I leave the *world* **cosmos**, and go to the Father.

29   His disciples *said* **worded** unto him,
Lo **Behold**, now speakest thou *plainly* **boldly**,
and *speakest* **wordest** no proverb.

30   Now *are we sure* **know**
that thou knowest all *things*,
and needest not that any *man* should ask thee:
by **in** this we *believe* **trust**
that thou camest forth from *God* **Elohim**.

31   *Jesus* **Yah Shua** answered them,
Do ye now *believe* **trust**?

32   Behold, the hour cometh, yea, is now come,

14   He glorifies me:
for he takes of mine and evangelizes to you.

Yah Shua Prophesies His Death, Resurrection, And Parousia

15   All — as much as the Father has is mine.
So I say,
He takes of mine, and evangelizes you.

16   A little, and you see me not;
and again, A little, and you see me;
because I go to the Father.

17   So some of his disciples say to one another,
What is this that he words to us,
A little, and you see me not:
and again, A little, and you see me;
and, Because I go to the Father?

18   So they word,
What is this that he words, A little?
We know not what he words.

19   Yah Shua knows that they will to ask him,
and says to them,
Seek you with one another concerning what I say,
A little, and you see me not:
and again, A little, and you see me?

20   Amen! Amen! I word to you,
You weep and lament, but the cosmos cheers:
and you sorrow, but your sorrow becomes cheer.

21   A woman, whenever she births, sorrows,
because her hour is come:
but whenever she bears the child,
she remembers no more the anguish,
for cheer that a human is birthed into the cosmos.

22   And so indeed, you now have sorrow:
but I see you again, and your heart cheers,
and no one takes your cheer from you:

23   and in that day you ask me naught.
Amen! Amen! I word to you,
As much as ever you ask the Father in my name,
he gives you.

24   Until now, you asked naught in my name:
ask and take to fulfill/shalam your cheer.

25   I speak these to you in proverbs:
but the hour comes,
when I no more speak to you in proverbs,
but I evangelize you boldly concerning the Father.

26   At that day you ask in my name:
and I word not to you,
that I ask the Father for you:

27   for the Father himself befriends you,
because you befriend me,
and trust that I came from Elohim.

28   I came from the Father
and came into the cosmos:
again, I leave the cosmos, and go to the Father.

29   His disciples word to him,
Behold, now you speak boldly and word no proverb:

30   now we know that you know all,
and need no one to ask you:
in this we trust — that you came from Elohim.

31   Yah Shua answers them, Trust you now?

32   Behold, the hour comes, yes, now comes,
that ye shall be scattered, *every man* **each** to his own,
and shall *leave* **forsake** me alone:
and yet I am not alone, because the Father is with me.

33   These *things* I have spoken unto you
that in me ye might have *peace* **shalom**.
In the *world* **cosmos** ye shall have tribulation:
but *be of good cheer;* **Courage**!
I have *overcome* **triumphed over** the *world* **cosmos**.

The Prayer Of Yah Shua To The Father

17   These words spake *Jesus* **Yah Shua**,
and lifted *up* his eyes to heaven, and said,
Father, the hour is come; glorify thy Son,
that thy Son also may glorify thee:

2   **Exactly** As thou hast given him *power* **authority**
over all flesh,
that he should give eternal life
to as many as thou hast given him.

JOHN/YOCHANAN 17

3 And this is life eternal,
that they might know thee the only true *God* **Elohim**,
and *Jesus Christ* **Yah Shua Messiah**,
whom thou hast *sent* **apostolized**.
4 I have glorified thee on the earth:
I have *finished* **completed/shalamed** the work
which thou gavest me to do.
5 And now, O Father, glorify
thou me with thine own self
with the glory which I had with thee
before **ere** the *world* **cosmos** was.
6 I have manifested thy name
unto *the men* **humanity**
which thou gavest me out of the *world* **cosmos**:
thine they were, and thou gavest them me;
and they have *kept* **guarded** thy word.
7 Now they have known that all *things*
whatsoever — **as much as ever** thou hast given me
are of thee.
8 For I have given unto them
the *words* **rhema** which thou gavest me;
and they have *received* **taken** them,
and have known *surely* **truly** that I came out from thee,
and they have *believed* **trusted**
that thou didst *send* **apostolize** me.
9 I *pray* **ask** for them: I *pray*
ask not for the *world* **cosmos**,
but for them which thou hast given
me; for they are thine.
10 And all mine are thine, and thine are mine;
and I am glorified in them.
11 And now I am no more in the *world* **cosmos**,
but these are in the *world* **cosmos**,
and I come to thee. Holy Father,
keep through **guard in** thine own name
those whom thou hast given me,
that they may be one, **exactly** as we *are*.
12 While I was with them in the *world* **cosmos**,
I *kept* **guarded** them in thy name:
those that thou gavest me I have *kept* **guarded**,
and none of them is lost,
but **except** the son of *perdition* **destruction**;
that the scripture might be fulfilled/**shalamed**.
13 And now come I to thee;
and these *things* I speak in the *world* **cosmos**,
that they might have my *joy* **cheer**
fulfilled/**shalamed** in themselves.
14 I have given them thy word;
and the *world* **cosmos** hath hated them,
because they are not of the *world* **cosmos**,
even **exactly** as I am not of the *world* **cosmos**.
15 I *pray* **ask** not
that thou shouldest take them out of the *world* **cosmos**,
but that thou shouldest *keep* **guard** them from the evil.
16 They are not of the *world* **cosmos**,
even **exactly** as I am not of the *world* **cosmos**.
17 *Sanctify* **Hallow** them *through* **in** thy truth:
thy word is truth.
18 **Exactly** As thou hast *sent* **apostolized** me
into the *world* **cosmos**,
even so have I also sent them into the *world* **cosmos**.
19 And for their sakes I *sanctify* **hallow** myself,
that they also might be *sanctified* **hallowed**
through **in** the truth.

The Prayer Of Yah Shua For Future Trusters

20 Neither *pray* **ask** I for these *alone* **only**,
that you scatter — each to his own,
and forsake me alone:
and yet I am not alone, because the Father is with me. 33
I speak these to you that you have shalom in me.
In the cosmos you have tribulation:
but, Courage! I triumph over the cosmos.

The Prayer Of Yah Shua To The Father

17 Yah Shua speaks these words
and lifts his eyes to the heavens, and says,
Father, the hour is come; glorify your Son,
so that your Son also glorifies you:
2 exactly as you gave him authority over all flesh
to give eternal life to as many as you give him.
3 And this is life eternal:
that they know you the only true Elohim,
and Yah Shua Messiah whom you apostolized.
4 I glorified you on the earth:
I completed/shalamed the work you gave me to do.
5 And now, O Father,
glorify me with your own self
with the glory I had with you ere the cosmos was.
6 I manifested your name to humanity
whom you gave me from the cosmos:
yours they are, and you gave them me;
and they guarded your word.
7 Now they know that all
— as much as ever you gave me are of you:
8 for I gave them the rhema you gave me;
and they took them;
and know truly that I come from you;
and they trust that you apostolized me.

9	I ask for them: I ask not for the cosmos,
	but for those you gave me;
	for they are yours:
10	and all mine are yours, and yours are mine;
	and I am glorified in them.
11	And now I am no more in the cosmos;
	but these are in the cosmos:
	and I come to you. Holy Father,
	guard in your own name
	those whom you gave me,
	that they be one, exactly as we.
12	When I was with them in the cosmos
	I guarded them in your name:
	those you gave me, I guarded;
	and none of them is lost
	except the son of destruction
	— to fulfill/shalam the scripture.
13	And now I come to you;
	and I speak these in the cosmos,
	to fulfill/shalam my cheer in them.
14	I gave them your word;
	and the cosmos hates them
	because they are not of the cosmos
	— even exactly as I am not of the cosmos.
15	I ask you not to take them from the cosmos,
	but to guard them from the evil.
16	They are not of the cosmos
	even exactly as I am not of the cosmos.
17	Hallow them in your truth:
	your word is truth.
18	Exactly as you apostolized me into the cosmos,
	even so I also sent them into the cosmos.
19	And for their sakes I hallow myself,
	that they also be hallowed in the truth.

The Prayer Of Yah Shua For Future Trusters

20	And I ask not for these only,
	but for them also
	which shall *believe on* **trust in** me through their word;
21	That they all may be one;
	exactly as thou, Father, *art* in me, and I in thee,
	that they also may be one in us:
	that the *world* **cosmos** may *believe* **trust**
	that thou hast *sent* **apostolized** me.
22	And the glory which thou gavest me
	I have given them;
	that they may be one, even **exactly** as we are one:
23	I in them, and thou in me,
	that they may be *made perfect* **completed/shalamed** in one;
	and that the *world* **cosmos** may know
	that thou hast *sent* **apostolized** me,
	and hast loved them, as thou hast loved me.
24	Father, I will that they also,
	whom thou hast given me,
	be with me where I am;
	that they may *behold* **see** my glory,
	which thou hast given me:
	for thou lovedst me
	before **ere** the foundation of the *world* **cosmos**.
25	O *righteous* **just** Father,
	the *world* **cosmos** hath not known thee:
	but I have known thee,
	and these have known
	that thou hast *sent* **apostolized** me.
26	And I have declared unto them thy name,
	and *will* **shall** declare it:
	that the love wherewith thou hast loved me
	may be in them,
	and I in them.

Yah Shua In The Garden

18	When *Jesus* **Yah Shua** had
	spoken **said** these words,
	he went forth with his disciples
	over the brook *Cedron* **Qidron**, where was a garden,
	into the which he entered, and his disciples.
2	And *Judas* **Yah Hudah**
	also, which betrayed him,
	knew the place:
	for *Jesus ofttimes* **Yah Shua often**
	resorted **gathered** thither with his disciples.

Yah Hudah Betrays Yah Shua

3	*Judas then* **So Yah Hudah**,
	having *received* **taken**
	a *band of men* **squad** and *officers* **attendants**
	from the *chief* **arch** priests and Pharisees,
	cometh thither
	with lanterns and *torches* **lamps** and weapons.
4	*Jesus therefore* **So Yah Shua**,
	knowing all *things* that should come upon him,
	went *forth*, and said unto them, Whom seek ye?
5	They answered him,
	Jesus of Nazareth **Yah Shua the Nazarene**.
	Jesus saith **Yah Shua wordeth** unto them, *I am he* **I AM**.
	And *Judas* **Yah Hudah** also, which betrayed him,
	stood with them.

JOHN/YOCHANAN 18

6 So As soon then as he had
said unto them, *I am he* **I AM**,
they went backward, and fell to unto the ground.
7 *Then* **So** asked he them again, Whom seek ye?
And they said, *Jesus of Nazareth*
Yah Shua the Nazarene.
8 *Jesus* **Yah Shua** answered,
I have *told* **said** to you that *I am he* **I AM**:
so if **therefore** ye seek me, *let* **release**
these *to* go their way:
9 That the *saying* might **word**
be fulfilled/**shalamed**,
which he *spake* **said**,
Of them which thou gavest me have I lost none.
10 *Then Simon Peter* **So Shimon
Petros** having a sword
drew it, and smote the *high* **arch** priest's servant,
and *cut off* **amputated** his right ear **lobe**.
The servant's name was *Malchus* **Melech**.
11 *Then* **So** said *Jesus* **Yah Shua** unto *Peter* **Petros**,
Put *up* thy sword into the sheath:
the cup which my Father hath given me,
shall I not drink it?

YAH SHUA ARRESTED

12 *Then* **So** the *band* **squad**
and the *captain* **chiliarch**
and *officers* **attendants** of the *Jews* **Yah Hudiym**
took *Jesus* **Yah Shua**, and bound him,
13 And led him away to *Annas* **Hanan Yah** first;
for he was father in law to Caiaphas,
but also for them who trust in me through their word;
21 that they all be one;
exactly as you, Father in me; and I in you;
that they also be one in us:
that the cosmos trust that you apostolized me.
22 And the glory you gave me, I gave them;
that they be one, even exactly as we are one:
23 I in them, and you in me,
that they be completed/shalamed in one;
and that the cosmos know that you apostolized me,
and loved them as you loved me.
24 Father, I will that whomever you gave me
also be with me where I am;
to see my glory that you gave me:
for you loved me ere the foundation of the cosmos.
25 O just Father,
the cosmos knows you not; but I know you:
and these know that you apostolized me:
26 and I declared your name to them;

and declare
that the love with which you love me be in them;
and I in them.

YAH SHUA IN THE GARDEN

18 Having said these words,
Yah Shua goes with his disciples
across the brook Qidron to a garden,
which he and his disciples enter:
2 and Yah Hudah also, who betrays him,
knows the place:
for Yah Shua often gathered there with his disciples.

YAH HUDAH BETRAYS YAH SHUA

3 So Yah Hudah takes a squad
and attendants of the archpriests and Pharisees,
and goes there
with lanterns and lamps and weapons.
4 So Yah Shua, knowing all
that is to come upon him,
goes and says to them, Whom seek you?
5 They answer him, Yah Shua the Nazarene.
Yah Shua words to them, I AM.
And Yah Hudah, who betrays him,
also stands with them:
6 so when he says to them, I AM,
they go backward, and fall to to the ground.
7 So he asks them again, Whom seek you?
And they say, Yah Shua the Nazarene.
8 Yah Shua answers, I say to you, I AM:
so if you seek me, release these to go their way.
9 — to fulfill/shalam the word he had said,
Of them you gave me, I lost none.
10 So Shimon Petros, holding a sword,
draws it, and smites the servant of the archpriest,
and amputates his right ear lobe.
— the name of the servant, Melech.
11 So Yah Shua says to Petros,
Put your sword into the sheath:
the cup my Father gives me, am I not to drink?

YAH SHUA ARRESTED

12 So the squad and the chiliarch
and attendants of the Yah Hudiym
take Yah Shua, and bind him;
13 and lead him away to Hanan Yah first;
for he is father in law to Caiaphas,
which was the *high* **arch** priest that same year.
14 Now Caiaphas was he,
which *gave counsel to* **counseled** the *Jews* **Yah Hudiym**,

that it was *expedient* **beneficial**
that one *man* **human** should *die* **be destroyed**
for the people.

THE FIRST DENIAL OF PETROS

15 And *Simon Peter* **Shimon Petros** followed *Jesus* **Yah Shua**,
and so did another disciple:
that disciple
was *known unto* **acquainted with** the *high* **arch** priest,
and went in with *Jesus* **Yah Shua**
into the palace of the *high* **arch** priest.
16 But *Peter* **Petros** stood at
the *door* **portal** without.
Then **So** went out that other disciple,
which was *known* **acquainted**
unto **with** the *high* **arch** priest,
and *spake* **said** unto her that kept
the *door* — **the portalguard**,
and brought in *Peter* **Petros**.
17 *Then saith* **So wordeth** the *damsel* **lass**
that kept the door — **the portalguard** unto *Peter* **Petros**,
Art not thou also one of this *man's* **human's** disciples?
He *saith* **wordeth**, *I am not* **Not I**.
18 And the servants and *officers*
attendants stood there,
who had made a fire of coals; for it was cold:
and they warmed themselves:
and *Peter* **Petros** stood with them, and warmed himself.

THE WITNESS OF YAH SHUA

19 *So* The *high* **arch** priest
then asked *Jesus* **Yah Shua**
of **concerning** his disciples, and *of*
concerning his doctrine.
20 *Jesus* **Yah Shua** answered him,
I spake *openly* **boldly** to the *world* **cosmos**;
I ever taught in the synagogue,
and in the *temple* **priestal precinct**,
whither the *Jews* **Yah Hudiym**
always *resort* **come together on all sides**;
and in secret have I *said nothing* **spoken naught**.
21 Why askest thou me? ask them which heard me,
what I have *said* **spoken** unto them:
behold, they know what I said.
22 And when he had thus *spoken* **said**,
one of the *officers which stood by* **attendants present**
struck Jesus with the palm of his hand
gave Yah Shua a slap, saying,
Answerest thou the *high* **arch** priest *so* **thus**?

23 *Jesus* **Yah Shua** answered him,
If I have spoken *evil* **evily**,
bear witness *of* **concerning** the evil:
but if well, why *smitest* **floggest** thou me?
24 Now *Annas* **Hanan Yah**
had *sent* **apostolized** him
bound unto Caiaphas the *high* **arch** priest.

THE SECOND DENIAL OF PETROS

25 And *Simon Peter* **Shimon Petros**
stood and warmed himself.
So They said *therefore* unto him,
Art not thou also one of his disciples?
He denied it, and said, *I am not* **Not I**.

THE THIRD DENIAL OF PETROS

26 One of the servants of the *high* **arch** priest,
being his *kinsman* **kin**
whose ear *Peter cut off* **Petros amputated**,
saith **wordeth**, Did not I see thee
in the garden with him?
27 *Peter* **So Petros** *then* denied again:
and *immediately* **straightway** the
cock *crew* **rooster voiced**.

THE TRIAL OF YAH SHUA

28 *Then* **So** led they *Jesus* **Yah Shua** from Caiaphas
unto the *hall of judgment* **praetorium**:
and it was early **morning**;
and they themselves
went not into the *judgment hall* **praetorium**,
lest they should be defiled;
but that they might eat the *passover* **pasach**.
29 *Pilate then* **So Pilatos** went
out unto them, and said,
What accusation bring ye against this *man* **human**?
30 They answered and said unto him,
If **Unless** he were *not a malefactor* **an evildoer**,
we *would* **should** not have delivered him *up* unto thee.
who is the archpriest that same year
14 — the Caiaphas who counseled the Yah Hudiym
that it is beneficial
to destroy one human for the people.

THE FIRST DENIAL OF PETROS

15 And Shimon Petros and that other disciple
follow Yah Shua:
and that disciple is acquainted with the archpriest;
and goes with Yah Shua
into the palace of the archpriest.

JOHN/YOCHANAN 18

16 But Petros stands outside at the portal:
so that other disciple,
who is acquainted with the archpriest,
goes out and says to the portal guard
to bring in Petros.
17 So the lass — the portal guard words to Petros,
Are not you also one of the disciples of this human?
He words, Not I.
18 And the servants and attendants
make a fire of coals and stand there; for it is cold:
and they warm themselves:
and Petros stands with them, and warms himself.

The Witness Of Yah Shua

19 So the archpriest asks Yah Shua
concerning his disciples and concerning his doctrine.
20 Yah Shua answers him,
I spoke boldly to the cosmos;
I ever taught in the synagogue
and in the priestal precinct
where the Yah Hudiym always come together;
and I spoke naught in secret.
21 Why ask me?
Ask them who heard me speak to them:
behold, they know what I said.
22 And when he says thus,
one of the attendants present gives Yah Shua a slap,
saying, Answer you the archpriest thus?
23 Yah Shua answers him,
If I have spoken evilly, witness concerning the evil:
but if well, why flog me?
24 — so Hanan Yah apostolizes to bind him
to Caiaphas the archpriest.

The Second Denial Of Petros

25 And Shimon Petros stands and warms himself.
So they say to him,
Are not you also one of his disciples?
He denies and says, Not I.

The Third Denial Of Petros

26 One of the servants of the archpriest,
being kin of him whose ear Petros amputated,
words, Saw I not you in the garden with him?
27 So Petros denies again:
— and straightway the rooster voices.

The Trial Of Yah Shua

28 So they lead Yah Shua
from Caiaphas to the praetorium:
and it is early morning;
and they themselves enter not the praetorium,
lest they defile themselves to eat the pasach.
29 So Pilatos goes to them, and says,
What accusation bring you against this human?
30 They answer him, saying,
Unless he were an evildoer,
we had not delivered him to you.
31 *Then* So said *Pilate* **Pilatos**
unto them, Take ye him,
and judge him according to your *law* **torah**.
The Jews therefore **So the Yah Hudiym** said unto him,
It is not *lawful* **allowed** for us
to *put any man to death* **slaughter anyone**:
32 That the *saying* **word** of *Jesus* **Yah Shua**
might be fulfilled/shalamed, which he *spake* **said**,
signifying what death he *should* **is about to** die.
33 *Then Pilate* **So Pilatos**
entered into the *judgment hall* **praetorium** again,
and *called Jesus* **voiced out to Yah Shua**,
and said unto him,
Art thou the *King* **Sovereign** of the *Jews* **Yah Hudiym**?
34 *Jesus* **Yah Shua** answered him,
Sayest **Wordest** thou this *thing* of thyself,
or did others *tell* **say** it *to* thee *of* **concerning** me?
35 *Pilate* **Pilatos** answered, Am I a *Jew* **Yah Hudiy**?
Thine own *nation* **goyim** and the *chief* **arch** priests
have delivered thee unto me: what hast thou done?
36 *Jesus* **Yah Shua** answered,
My *kingdom* **sovereigndom** is not of this *world* **cosmos**:
if my *kingdom* **sovereigndom** were of this *world* **cosmos**,
then would **had** my *servants fight* **attendants agonized**,
that I should not be delivered to the *Jews* **Yah Hudiym**:
but now is my *kingdom* **sovereigndom** not from hence.
37 *Pilate therefore* **So Pilatos** said unto him,
So Art thou a *king then* **sovereign**?
Jesus **Yah Shua** answered,
Thou *sayest* **wordest** that I am a *king* **sovereign**.
To this end was I *born* **birthed**,
and *for* **to** this cause came I into the *world* **cosmos**,
that I should *bear* witness unto the truth.
Every one that is of the truth heareth my voice.
38 *Pilate saith* **Pilatos wordeth**
unto him, What is truth?
And when he had said this,

he went out again unto the *Jews* **Yah Hudiym**,
and *saith* **wordeth** unto them,
I find in him no *fault* **cause** at all.
39 But ye have a custom,
that I should release unto you one at the *passover* **pasach**:
will **so shall** ye *therefore* that I release unto you
the *King* **Sovereign** of the *Jews* **Yah Hudiym**?

Yah Hudiym Demand Yah Shua

40 *Then* **So** cried they all again, *saying* **wording**,
Not this man, but *Barabbas* **Bar Abbas**.
Now Barabbas **Bar Abbas** was a robber.

Yah Shua Wreathed

19 *Then Pilate therefore* **So then,**
Pilatos took *Jesus* **Yah Shua**,
and scourged him.
2 And the *soldiers* **warriors**
platted **braided** a *crown* **wreath** of thorns,
and put it on his head,
and they *put on* **arrayed** him *a* **in** purple *robe* **clothing**,
3 And *said* **worded**, *Hail* **Cheers**,
King **Sovereign** of the *Jews* **Yah Hudiym**!
and they *smote him with their hands* **gave him a slap**.
4 *Pilate therefore* **So Pilatos** went *forth* again,
and *saith* **wordeth** unto them, Behold,
I bring him forth to you,
that ye may know that I find no *fault* **cause** in him.
5 *Then* **So** came *Jesus forth* **Yah Shua**,
wearing **bearing** the *crown* **wreath** of thorns,
and the purple *robe* **clothing**.
And *Pilate saith* **Pilatos wordeth** unto them,
Behold the *man* **human**!
6 **So** When the *chief* **arch** priests *therefore*
and *officers* **attendants** saw him,
they cried out, *saying* **wording**,
Crucify him, crucify him. **Stake! Stake!**
Pilate saith **Pilatos wordeth** unto them,
Take ye him, and *crucify him* **stake**:
for I find no *fault* **cause** in him.
7 The *Jews* **Yah Hudiym** answered him,
31 So Pilatos says to them, You take him
and judge him according to your torah.
So the Yah Hudiym say to him,
We are not allowed to slaughter anyone:
32 — to fulfill/shalam the word of Yah Shua
that he said
signifying by which death he is about to die.

33 So Pilatos enters the praetorium again,
and voices out to Yah Shua, and says to him,
Are you the Sovereign of the Yah Hudiym?
34 Yah Shua answers him,
Word you this of yourself?
Or say others to you concerning me?
35 Pilatos answers, Am I a Yah Hudiy?
Your own goyim and the archpriests
delivered you to me.
What did you?
36 Yah Shua answers,
My sovereigndom is not of this cosmos:
if my sovereigndom were of this cosmos,
my attendants had ever agonized
that I not be delivered to the Yah Hudiym:
but now my sovereigndom is not from here.
37 So Pilatos says to him,
So, are you a sovereign?
Yah Shua answers,
You word that I am a sovereign.
To this end I was birthed,
and to this cause I came into the cosmos
— to witness to the truth.
Everyone who is of the truth hears my voice.
38 Pilatos words to him, What is truth?
And when he says this
he again goes to the Yah Hudiym and words to them,
I find in him no cause at all:
39 but you have a custom,
that I release one to you at the pasach:
so is it your will that I release to you
the Sovereign of the Yah Hudiym?

Yah Hudiym Demand Yah Shua

40 So again they all cry, wording,
Not this man, but Bar Abbas.
— Bar Abbas is a robber.

Yah Shua Wreathed

19 So then,
Pilatos takes Yah Shua and scourges him:
2 and the warriors braid a wreath of thorns
and put it on his head;
and they array him in purple clothing;
3 and word, Cheers!
Sovereign of the Yah Hudiym!
— and they give him a slap.
4 Pilatos goes again and words to them,
Behold, I bring him to you,

JOHN/YOCHANAN 19

so that you know I find no cause in him.
5 So Yah Shua comes
bearing the wreath of thorns and the purple clothing:
and Pilatos words to them, Behold the human!
6 So when the archpriests and attendants see him
they cry out, wording, Stake! Stake!
Pilatos words to them, You take him, and stake:
for I find no cause in him.
7 The Yah Hudiym answer him,

We have a *law* **torah**,
and by our *law* **torah** he *ought* **is indebted** to die,
because he made himself the Son of *God* **Elohim**.
8 **So** When *Pilate* **Pilatos**
therefore heard that *saying* **word**,
he was the more *afraid* **awestricken**;
9 And went again into the
judgment hall **praetorium**,
and *saith* **wordeth** unto *Jesus* **Yah Shua**,
Whence art thou?
But *Jesus* **Yah Shua** gave him no answer.
10 *then saith Pilate* **So Pilatos wordeth** unto him,
Speakest thou not unto me?
knowest thou not
that I have *power* **authority** to *crucify* **stake** thee,
and have *power* **authority** to release thee?
11 *Jesus* **Yah Shua** answered,
Thou couldest have no *power* **authority** at all against me,
except it were given thee from above:
Therefore **So** he that delivered me unto thee
hath the greater sin.
12 And from thenceforth
Pilate **Pilatos** sought to release him:
but the *Jews* **Yah Hudiym** cried out, *saying* **wording**,
If **Whenever** thou *let this man go* **release this one**,
thou art not *Caesar's* **the kaisar's** friend:
whosoever maketh himself a *king* **sovereign**
speaketh against Caesar **contradicteth the kaisar**.
13 **So** When *Pilate* **Pilatos**
therefore heard that *saying*,
he brought *Jesus* **Yah Shua** forth,
and sat down in the *judgment seat* **bamah**
in a place that is *called* **worded** the Pavement,
but in *the Hebrew* **Hebraic**, Gabbatha.
14 And it was the preparation
of the *passover* **pasach**,
and about the sixth hour:
and he *saith* **wordeth** unto the *Jews* **Yah Hudiym**,
Behold your *king* **sovereign**!
15 But they cried out,
Away *with him*, away *with him*, *crucify* **stake** him.
Pilate saith **Pilatos wordeth** unto them,
Shall I *crucify* your King **Stake your Sovereign**?
The *chief* **arch** priests answered,
We have no *king but Caesar* **sovereign except the kaisar**.

YAH SHUA STAKED

16 **So** Then delivered he him *therefore* unto them
to be *crucified* **staked**.
And they took *Jesus* **Yah Shua**, and led him away.
17 And he bearing his *cross*
stake went forth into a place
called **worded** the place of a *skull* **cranium**,
which is *called* **worded** in *the Hebrew* **Hebraic**,
Golgotha **Golgoleth**:
18 Where they *crucified* **staked** him,
and two other with him, on either side one,
and *Jesus* **Yah Shua** in the midst.
19 And *Pilate wrote* **Pilatos scribed** a title,
and put it on the *cross* **stake**.
And the *writing* **scribing** was

JESUS OF NAZARETH YAH SHUA THE
NAZARENE THE KING SOVEREIGN
OF THE JEWS YAH HUDIYM.

20 **So** This title *then* read many
of the *Jews* **Yah Hudiym**:
for the place where *Jesus* **Yah Shua** was *crucified* **staked**
was nigh to the city:
and it was *written* **scribed** in *Hebrew* **Hebraic**,
and *Greek* **Hellenic**, and *Latin* **Romaic**.
21 *Then said* **So worded**
the *chief* **arch** priests of the *Jews* **Yah Hudiym**
to *Pilate* **Pilatos**, *Write* **Scribe** not,
The *King* **Sovereign** of the *Jews* **Yah Hudiym**;
but that he said,
I am *King* **Sovereign** of the *Jews* **Yah Hudiym**.
22 *Pilate* **Pilatos** answered,
What I have *written* **scribed** I have *written* **scribed**.

WARRIORS GAMBLE OVER THE GARMENTS OF YAH SHUA

23 *Then* **So** the *soldiers* **warriors**,
when they had *crucified Jesus* **staked Yah Shua**,
took his *garments* **clothing**, and made four parts,
to *every soldier* **each warrior** a part;
and also his *coat* **tunic**:
now the *coat* **tunic** was *without seam* **seamless**,

24   woven from the top.
So They said *therefore* among
themselves **each other**,
We have a torah,
and by our torah he is indebted to die
because he makes himself the Son of Elohim.
8   So when Pilatos hears that word
he is the more awestricken;
9   and goes again into the praetorium,
and words to Yah Shua, Whence are you?
— but Yah Shua gives him no answer.
10   So then Pilatos words to
him, Speak you not to me?
Know you not that I have authority to stake you,
and I have authority to release you?
11   Yah Shua answers,
You have no authority at all against me,
unless given you from above:
so whoever delivered me to you
has the greater sin.
12   And from then on Pilatos seeks to release him:
but the Yah Hudiym cry out, wording,
Whenever you release this one,
you are no friend of the kaisar:
whoever makes himself a sovereign
contradicts the kaisar.
13   So when Pilatos hears that,
he brings Yah Shua forth, and sits in the bamah
— in a place worded, the Pavement;
and in Hebraic, Gabbatha.
14   And it is the preparation of the pasach,
and about the sixth hour:
and he words to the Yah Hudiym,
Behold your sovereign!
15   And they cry out, Away! Away! Stake him!
Pilatos words to them, Stake your Sovereign?
The archpriests answer,
We have no sovereign except the kaisar.

Yah Shua Staked

16   So then he delivers him to them to stake:
and they take Yah Shua, and lead him away:
17   and bearing his stake he goes to a place
worded, the Place of a Cranium,
which in Hebraic, is worded, Golgoleth:
18   where they stake him —
and two others with him
— one on either side and Yah Shua in the midst.

19   And Pilatos scribes a title,
and puts it on the stake:
and the scribing is:

Yah Shua The Nazarene The Sovereign Of The Yah Hudiym.

20   So many of the Yah Hudiym read this title:
for the place they stake Yah Shua is near the city:
and it is scribed in Hebraic and Hellenic and Romaic.
21   So the archpriests of the Yah Hudiym
word to Pilatos, Scribe not,
The Sovereign of the Yah Hudiym;
but, He says I am Sovereign of the Yah Hudiym.
22   Pilatos answers, What I scribed I scribed.

Warriors Gamble Over The Garments Of Yah Shua

23   So when the warriors stake Yah Shua,
they take his clothing, and make four parts
— a part to each warrior; and also his tunic:
and the tunic is seamless, woven from the top.
24   So they say among each other,

Let us not *rend* **split** it, but cast lots for it,
whose it shall be:
that the scripture might be fulfilled/**shalamed**,
which *saith* **wordeth**,
They *parted* **divided** my *raiment* **garment** among them,
and for my *vesture* **garments** they *did* cast lots.
So These *things* **indeed** *therefore* the
soldiers **warriors** did. Psalm 22:18

Yah Shua Presents His Mother To Yahn

25   Now there stood by the *cross*
stake of *Jesus* **Yah Shua**
his mother, and his mother's sister,
Mary the wife of Cleophas **Miryam of Clopas**,
and *Mary* **Miryam the** Magdalene.
26   **So** When *Jesus* **Yah Shua**
therefore saw his mother,
and the disciple *standing by* **present**, whom he loved,
he *saith* **wordeth** unto his mother,
Woman, behold thy son!
27   Then *saith* **wordeth** he to the disciple,
Behold thy mother!
And from that hour
that disciple took her unto his own *home*.

JOHN/YOCHANAN 19

YAH SHUA THIRSTS

28 After this, *Jesus* **Yah Shua**
knowing that all *things*
were *now accomplished* **already completed/shalamed**,
that the scripture might be *fulfilled*
completed/shalamed,
saith **wordeth**, I thirst.

29 Now there was set a vessel full of vinegar:
and they filled a spunge with vinegar,
and put it upon hyssop, and *put* **offered** it to his mouth.

30 So When *Jesus* **Yah Shua** therefore
had *received* **taken** the vinegar,
he said, It is *finished* **completed/shalamed***:
and he *bowed* **reclined** his head,
and *gave up the ghost* **surrendered his spirit**.

*see SUMMARY, SHALAM

PROPHESIES FULFILLED

31 So The *Jews* **Yah Hudiym** therefore,
because it was the preparation,
that the bodies should not *remain* **abide**
upon the *cross* **stake** on the *sabbath day* **shabbath**,
(for that *sabbath day* **shabbath** was *an high* **a mega** day,)
besought Pilate **asked Pilatos** that
their legs might be broken,
and that they might be taken away.

32 *Then* **So** came the *soldiers* **warriors**,
and **indeed** brake the legs of the first,
and of the other which was *crucified* **staked** with him.

33 But when they came to *Jesus* **Yah Shua**,
and saw that he was dead already,
they brake not his legs:

34 But one of the *soldiers* **warriors** with a spear
pierced his side,
and *forthwith* **straightway** came
there out blood and water.

35 And he that saw it *bare record* **witnessed**,
and his *record* **witness** is true:
and he knoweth that he *saith* **wordeth** true,
that ye might *believe* **trust**.

36 For these *things were done* **became**,
that the scripture should be fulfilled/**shalamed**,
A **No** bone of him shall *not be broken* **be shattered**.

37 And again another scripture *saith* **wordeth**,
They shall *look on* **see unto** him whom they pierced.
Psalm 34:20, Zechar Yah 12:10

THE BODY OF YAH SHUA TAKEN

38 And after this *Joseph* **Yoseph**
of *Arimathaea* **Ramah**,
being a disciple of *Jesus* **Yah Shua**,
but secretly for *fear* **awe** of the *Jews* **Yah Hudiym**,
besought Pilate **asked Pilatos**
that he might take *away* the body of *Jesus* **Yah Shua**:
and *Pilate gave* **Pilatos permitted** him *leave*.
So He came *therefore*, and took the
body of *Jesus* **Yah Shua**.

39 And there came also Nicodemus,
which at the first came to *Jesus* **Yah Shua** by night,
and brought a mixture of myrrh and aloes,
about an hundred *pound weight* **litra**.

40 *Then* **So** took they the body of *Jesus* **Yah Shua**,
and *wound* **bound** it in linen clothes
with the *spices* **aromatics**,
exactly as the *manner* **custom** of the *Jews* **Yah Hudiym**
is to *bury* **embalm**.

Split it not, but cast lots for it, whose it becomes:
— to fulfill/shalam the scripture, wording,
They divided my garment among them;
and for my garments they cast lots.
— so these indeed the warriors did.
Psalm 22:18

YAH SHUA PRESENTS HIS MOTHER TO YAHN

25 And standing by the stake of Yah Shua
are his mother,
and the sister of his mother, Miryam of Clopas,
and Miryam the Magdalene.

26 So Yah Shua seeing his mother present
— and the disciple whom he loves,
he words to his mother, Woman, behold your son!

27 then he words to the disciple,
Behold your mother!
And from that hour
that disciple takes her to his own.

YAH SHUA THIRSTS

28 After this,
Yah Shua, knowing that all are completed/shalamed
— to complete/shalam the scripture, words, I thirst.

29 So they set a vessel full of vinegar:
and fill a sponge with vinegar and put it on hyssop
and offer it to his mouth.

30 So when Yah Shua takes the vinegar,
he says, Completed/Shalamed*:
and he reclines his head and surrenders his spirit.

*see SUMMARY, SHALAM
PROPHESIES FULFILLED

31	So the Yah Hudiym, because it is the preparation, that the bodies not abide on the stake on the shabbath — for that shabbath is a mega day ask Pilatos to break their legs and take them away.		

31 So the Yah Hudiym, because
it is the preparation,
that the bodies not abide on the stake on the
shabbath — for that shabbath is a mega day
ask Pilatos to break their legs and take them away.
32 So the warriors come,
and indeed break the legs of the first
and of the other staked with him:
33 but when they come to Yah Shua
and see that he is already dead,
they break not his legs:
34 but one of the warriors
pierces his side with a spear,
and straightway blood and water come forth.
35 And he who sees, witnesses;
and his witness is true:
and he knows that he words true, so that you trust.
36 For these became to fulfill/shalam the scripture,
No bone of him shatters.
37 And again another scripture words,
They see him whom they pierce.
Psalm 34:20, Zechar Yah 12:10

The Body Of Yah Shua Taken

38 And after this,
Yoseph of Ramah, being a disciple of Yah Shua,
but for awe of the Yah Hudiym,
secretly asks of Pilatos
to take the body of Yah Shua:
and Pilatos allows him.
So he comes, and takes the body of Yah Shua:
39 and Nicodemus also comes
— who at the first came to Yah Shua by night
and brings a mixture of myrrh and aloes
— about a hundred litra.
40 So they take the body of Yah Shua
and bind it in linen cloths with the aromatics,
exactly as the custom of the Yah Hudiym to embalm.

Yah Shua Entombed

41 Now in the place where he was *crucified* **staked**
there was a garden;
and in the garden a new *sepulchre* **tomb**,
wherein *was never man yet laid* **no
one had ever been placed**.
42 **So** There *laid* **placed** they
Jesus **Yah Shua** *therefore*
because of the *Jews'* **Yah Hudiy** preparation day;
for the *sepulchre* **tomb** was nigh at hand.

Yah Shua Disentombed

20 On The first *day* of the *week* **shabbaths**
cometh *Mary* **Miryam the** Magdalene
in the early **morning**, when it was yet dark,
unto the *sepulchre* **tomb**,
and seeth the stone taken away from the *sepulchre* **tomb**.
2 *Then* **So** she runneth,
and cometh to *Simon Peter* **Shimon Petros**,
and to the other disciple,
whom *Jesus loved* **Yah Shua befriended**,
and *saith* **wordeth** unto them,
They have taken away *the Lord* **Adonay**
out of the *sepulchre* **tomb**,
and we know not where they have *laid* **placed** him.
3 *Peter therefore* **So Petros** went *forth*,
and that other disciple,
and came to the *sepulchre* **tomb**.
4 *So* **And** they ran both together:
and the other disciple did outrun *Peter* **Petros**,
and came first to the *sepulchre* **tomb**.
5 And he stooping *down*, and looking in,
saw the linen clothes lying; yet **indeed** went he not in.
6 *Then* **So** cometh *Simon Peter*
Shimon Petros following him,
and went into the *sepulchre* **tomb**,
and seeth the linen clothes lie,
7 And the *napkin* **sudarium**,
that was about his head,
not lying with the linen clothes,
but wrapped together in a place *by itself* **apart**.
8 **So** Then went in also that other disciple,
which came first to the *sepulchre* **tomb**,
and he saw, and *believed* **trusted**.
9 For as yet they knew not the scripture,
that he must rise *again* from the dead.
10 *Then* **So** the disciples went away again
unto their own *home*.

The Resurrected Yah Shua Appears To Miryam

11 But *Mary* **Miryam** stood without
at the *sepulchre* **tomb** weeping:
and as she wept,
she stooped *down, and looked* into the *sepulchre* **tomb**,
12 And seeth two angels in white sitting,
the one at the head, and the other at the feet,
where the body of *Jesus* **Yah Shua** had lain.
13 And they *say* **word** unto her,
Woman, why weepest thou?

JOHN/YOCHANAN 20

She *saith* **wordeth** unto them,
Because they have taken away my *Lord* **Adonay**,
and I know not where they have *laid* **placed** him.

14 And when she had thus said,
she turned herself *back*,
and saw *Jesus* **Yah Shua** standing,
and knew not that it was *Jesus* **Yah Shua**.

15 *Jesus saith* **Yah Shua wordeth** unto her,
Woman, why weepest thou? whom seekest thou?
She, *supposing* **thinking** him to be the gardener,
saith **wordeth** unto him,
Sir Lord **Adoni**, if thou have borne him hence,
tell me where thou hast *laid* **placed** him,
and I *will* **shall** take him away.

16 *Jesus saith* **Yah Shua wordeth**
unto her, *Mary* **Miryam**.
She turned herself, and *saith* **wordeth** unto him,
Rabboni; which is to *say* **word**, *Master* **Doctor**.

17 *Jesus saith* **Yah Shua wordeth**
unto her, Touch me not;
for I am not yet ascended to my Father:
but go to my brethren, and say unto them,
I ascend unto my Father, and your Father;
and to my *God* **Elohim**, and your *God* **Elohim**.

18 *Mary* **Miryam the** Magdalene came
and *told* **evangelized** the disciples
that she had seen *the Lord* **Adonay**,
and that he had *spoken* **said** these *things* unto her.

Yah Shua Entombed

41 And there is a garden in the place he was staked;
and in the garden
a new tomb wherein no one had ever been placed:

42 so they place Yah Shua there
because of the Yah Hudiy preparation day;
for the tomb is near at hand.

Yah Shua Disentombed

20 On the first of the shabbaths
in the early morning while it is still dark
Miryam the Magdalene goes to the tomb,
and sees the stone taken from the tomb.

2 So she runs and goes to Shimon Petros
and to the other disciple whom Yah Shua befriended
and words to them,
They took Adonay from the tomb,
and we know not where they placed him.

3 So Petros and that other disciple go
and come to the tomb

4 — and they both run together:
and the other disciple outruns Petros,
and comes to the tomb first:

5 and he stoops and looks
and sees the linen clothes lying;
yet indeed he goes not in.

6 So Shimon Petros comes following him
and enters the tomb;
and sees the linen clothes lying:

7 and the sudarium which was around his head
not lying with the linen clothes
but wrapped together in a place apart.

8 So then that other disciple also goes in
who had come to the tomb first:
and he sees and trusts.

9 — for as yet they know not the scripture
that he must rise from the dead.

10 — so the disciples go again to their own.

The Resurrected Yah Shua Appears To Miryam

11 And Miryam stands outside the tomb weeping:
and as she weeps, she stoops into the tomb,

12 and sees two angels in white sitting;
the one at the head and the other at the feet,
where the body of Yah Shua had lain.

13 And they word to her, Woman, why weep you?
She words to them,
Because they took my Adonay
and I know not where they placed him.

14 And when she says thus,
she turns and sees Yah Shua standing;
and knows not it is Yah Shua.

15 Yah Shua words to her,
Woman, why weep you? Whom seek you?
She, thinking him to be the gardener, words to him,
Adoni, if you bore him hence,
tell me where you placed him, and I take him away.

16 Yah Shua words to her, Miryam.
She turns herself, and words to him, Rabboni!
— which is to word, Doctor.

17 Yah Shua words to her, Touch me not;
for I have not yet ascended to my Father:
but go to my brothers, and say to them,
I ascend to my Father, and your Father;
and to my Elohim, and your Elohim.

18 Miryam the Magdalene comes
and evangelizes the disciples that she saw Adonay
and that he said these to her.

THE RESURRECTED YAH SHUA APPEARS TO TEN DISCIPLES

19 *Then* **So** the same day at evening,
being the first *day* of the *week* **shabbaths**,
when the *doors* **portals** were shut
where the disciples were assembled
for *fear* **awe** of the *Jews* **Yah Hudiym**,
came *Jesus* **Yah Shua** and stood in the midst,
and *saith* **wordeth** unto them,
Peace **Shalom** be unto you.

20 And when he had so said,
he shewed unto them his hands and his side.
Then were **So** the disciples *glad* **cheered**,
when they saw *the Lord* **Adonay**.

21 *Then* **So** said *Jesus* **Yah Shua** to them again,
Peace **Shalom** be unto you:
exactly as my Father hath *sent* **apostolized** me,
even so send I you.

THE RESURRECTED YAH SHUA BESTOWS THE HOLY SPIRIT

22 And when he had said this,
he *breathed on* **puffed into** them,
and *saith* **wordeth** unto them,
Receive **Take** ye the *Holy Spirit* **Ruach ha-kodesh**:

23 Whosesoever sins ye *remit* **release**,
they are *remitted* **released** unto them;
and whosesoever sins ye *retain* **hold**,
they are *retained* **held**.

TAOM APPEARS

24 But *Thomas* **Taom**,
one of the twelve, *called Didymus* **worded Twin**,
was not with them when *Jesus* **Yah Shua** came.

25 **So** The other disciples *therefore*
said **worded** unto him,
We have seen *the Lord* **Adonay**.
But he said unto them,
Except **Unless** I shall see in his hands
the *print* **imprint** of the nails,
and put my finger into the *print* **imprint** of the nails,
and thrust my hand into his side,
I *will* **shall** not *believe* **trust**.

THE RESURRECTED YAH SHUA APPEARS TO ELEVEN DISCIPLES

26 And after eight days again
his disciples were within,
and *Thomas* **Taom** with them:
then came *Jesus* **Yah Shua**, the *doors* **portals** being shut,
and stood in the midst, and said,
Peace **Shalom** be unto you.

27 Then *saith* **So wordeth** he to *Thomas* **Taom**,
Reach **Bear** hither thy finger,
and *behold* **see** my hands;
and *reach* **bear** hither thy hand,
and thrust it into my side:
and be not *faithless* **trustless**, but *believing* **trusting**.

THE WITNESS OF TAOM TO THE DEITY OF YAH SHUA

28 And *Thomas* **Taom**
answered and said unto him,
My *Lord* **Adonay** and my *God* **Elohim**.

29 *Jesus saith* **Yah Shua wordeth** unto him,
Thomas **Taom**,
because thou hast seen me, thou hast *believed* **trusted**:
blessed are they that have not seen,
and yet have *believed* **trusted**.

30 And many other signs *truly*
indeed did *Jesus* **Yah Shua**
in the *presence* **sight** of his disciples,
which are not *written* **scribed** in this *book* **scroll**:

31 But these are *written* **scribed**,
that ye might *believe* **trust**
that *Jesus* **Yah Shua** is the *Christ* **Messiah**,
the Son of *God* **Elohim**;
and that *believing* **trusting**
ye might have life *through* **in** his name.

THE RESURRECTED YAH MANIFESTS HIMSELF AGAIN

21 After these *things*
Jesus shewed **Yah Shua manifested** himself again
to the disciples at the sea of Tiberias;
and *on this wise shewed* **thus manifested** he himself.

2 There were together *Simon*
Peter **Shimon Petros**,
and *Thomas called Didymus* **Taom worded Twin**,
and *Nathanael* **Nathan El** of *Cana*
Qanah in *Galilee* **Galiyl**,
and the sons of Zebedee, and two other of his disciples.

THE RESURRECTED YAH SHUA APPEARS TO TEN DISCIPLES

19 So the same day at evening,
being the first of the shabbaths,
the portals where the disciples assemble

being shut for awe of the Yah Hudiym,
Yah Shua comes and stands in their midst,
and words to them, Shalom to you.
20 And when he thus says,
he shows them his hands and his side;
so the disciples cheer when they see Adonay.
21 So again Yah Shua says to them, Shalom to you:
exactly as my Father apostolized me,
even thus I send you.

THE RESURRECTED YAH SHUA BESTOWS THE HOLY SPIRIT

22 And when he says this,
he puffs into them and words to them,
You, take the Holy Spirit:
23 whosoever sins you release, are released to them;
and whose ever sins you hold, are held.

TAOM APPEARS

24 And Taom, one of the twelve, worded Twin,
was not with them when Yah Shua came:
25 so the other disciples word to him,
We saw Adonay.
And he says to them,
Unless I see in his hands the imprint of the nails,
and put my finger into the imprint of the nails,
and thrust my hand into his side,
I trust not.

THE RESURRECTED YAH SHUA APPEARS TO ELEVEN DISCIPLES

26 And again after eight days
his disciples are inside
and Taom with them:
Yah Shua comes, the portals being shut,
and stands among them, and says,
Shalom to you.
27 Then he words to Taom,
Bear here your finger and see my hands;
and bear here your hand and thrust into my side:
and be not trustless, but trusting.

THE WITNESS OF TAOM TO THE DEITY OF YAH SHUA

28 And Taom answers him, saying,
My Adonay and my Elohim.
29 Yah Shua words to him,
Taom, because you see me, you trust:
blessed — whoever see not and still trust.
30 And indeed Yah Shua did many other signs
in the sight of his disciples,
which are not scribed in this scroll:
31 but these are scribed so that you trust
that Yah Shua is the Messiah the Son of Elohim;
and that trusting you have life in his name.

THE RESURRECTED YAH SHUA MANIFESTS HIMSELF AGAIN

21 After these
Yah Shua manifests himself again
to the disciples at the sea of Tiberias;
and he manifests himself thus:
2 Shimon Petros and Taom — worded Twin
and Nathan El of Qanah, Galiyl
and the sons of Zebedee
and two of his other disciples are together.
3 *Simon Peter saith* **Shimon Petros wordeth** unto them,
I go a fishing.
They *say* **word** unto him, We also *go* **come** with thee.
They went forth, and *entered* **ascended**
into a *ship immediately* **sailer straightway**;
and that night they caught *nothing* **naught**.
3 Shimon Petros words to them,
I go a fishing.
They word to him, We also go with you.
— and straightway they go and ascend into a sailer;
and that night they catch naught.

CASTING THE NET

4 Already being early morning,
Yah Shua stands on the shore:
but the disciples know not it is Yah Shua:
5 so Yah Shua words to them,
Children, have you any eats?
They answer him, No.
6 And he says to them,
Cast the net on the right part of the sailer, and find.
So they cast;
and now they are not able to draw
because of the multitude of fishes.
7 So that disciple whom Yah Shua loves
words to Petros, It is Adonay.
Now when Shimon Petros hears it is Adonay,
he girds his outer fishing enduement to him
— for he is naked
and casts himself into the sea:
8 and the other disciples come in a skiff
— for they are not far from land
but as it were two hundred cubits
dragging the net with fishes:

9	so as soon as they come to land, they see a fire of coals and broilings laid thereon and bread.	7	*Therefore* **So** that disciple whom *Jesus* **Yah Shua** loved *saith* **wordeth** unto *Peter* **Petros**, It is *the Lord* **Adonay**. Now when *Simon Peter* **Shimon Petros** heard that it was *the Lord* **Adonay**, he girt his fisher's *coat* **outer enduement** unto him, (for he was naked,) and did cast himself into the sea.
10	Yah Shua words to them, Bring of the broilings you now caught.		
11	Shimon Petros ascends and draws the net full of mega fishes — a hundred and fifty—three to land: and though there are so many, yet the net splits not.	8	And the other disciples came in a *little ship* **skiff**; (for they were not far from land, but as it were two hundred cubits,) dragging the net with fishes.
12	Yah Shua words to them, Come and dine. And none of the disciples dare ask him, Who are you? — knowing it is Adonay.	9	**So** As soon *then* as they were come to land, they saw a fire of coals there, and *fish* **broilings** laid thereon, and bread.
13	So Yah Shua comes and takes bread and gives them; and likewise the broilings:	10	*Jesus saith* **Yah Shua wordeth** unto them, Bring of the *fish* **broilings** which ye have now caught.
14	this is already the third time Yah Shua shows himself to his disciples after he rose from the dead.	11	*Simon Peter went up* **Shimon Petros ascended**, and drew the net to land full of *great* **mega** fishes, an hundred and fifty and three: and for all there were so many, yet was not the net *broken* **split**.

Love Vs Befriend

15	So they dine, and Yah Shua words to Shimon Petros, Shimon son of Yonah, love you me much more than these? He words to him, Yes, Adonay; you know I befriend you. He words to him, Feed my lambs.	12	*Jesus saith* **Yah Shua wordeth** unto them, Come and dine. And none of the disciples durst ask him, Who art thou? knowing that it was *the Lord* **Adonay**.
16	He words to him again the second time, Shimon, son of Yonah love you me? He words to him, Yes, Adonay; you know I befriend you. He words to him, Shepherd my sheep.	13	*Jesus then* **So Yah Shua** cometh, and taketh bread, and giveth them, and *fish* **broilings** likewise.
17	He words to him the third time,	14	This is *now* **already** the third time that *Jesus* **Yah Shua** shewed himself to his disciples, after that he was risen from the dead.

Casting The Net

4	*But when the* **Yet early** morning *was now come* **having already become**, *Jesus* **Yah Shua** stood on the shore: but the disciples knew not that it was *Jesus* **Yah Shua**.		

Love vs Befriend

5	*Then Jesus saith* **So Yah Shua wordeth** unto them, Children, have ye any *meat* **eats**? They answered him, No.	15	So when they had dined, *Jesus* **Yah Shua** *saith* **wordeth** to *Simon Peter* **Shimon Petros**, *Simon* **Shimon**, son of *Jonas* **Yonah**, lovest thou me **much** more than these? He *saith* **wordeth** unto him, Yea, *Lord* **Adonay**; thou knowest that I *love* **befriend** thee. He *saith* **wordeth** unto him, Feed my lambs.
6	And he said unto them, Cast the net on the right *side* **part** of the *ship* **sailer**, and *ye* shall find. **So** They cast *therefore*, and now they were not able to draw it for the multitude of fishes.	16	He *saith* **wordeth** to him again the second time, *Simon* **Shimon**, son of *Jonas* **Yonah**, lovest thou me? He *saith* **wordeth** unto him, Yea, *Lord* **Adonay**; thou knowest that I *love* **befriend** thee. He *saith* **wordeth** unto him, *Feed* **Shepherd** my sheep.
		17	He *saith* **wordeth** unto him the third time, *Simon* **Shimon**, son of *Jonas* **Yonah**,

JOHN/YOCHANAN 21

lovest **befriendest** thou me?
Peter **Petros** was *grieved* **sorrowed**
because he said unto him the third time,
Lovest **Befriendest** thou me?
And he said unto him, *Lord* **Adonay**,
thou knowest all *things*;
thou knowest that I *love* **befriend** thee.
Jesus saith **Yah Shua wordeth** unto him, Feed my sheep.

YAH SHUA PROPHESIES
THE MARTYRDOM OF PETROS

18 *Verily, verily, I say* **Amen!**
Amen! I word unto thee,
When thou wast young, thou girdedst thyself,
and walkedst whither thou *wouldest* **willest**:
but when **ever** thou shalt *be old* **senesce**, thou
shalt *stretch forth* **spread** thy hands,
and another shall gird thee,
and *carry* **bear** thee whither thou *wouldest* **willest** not.
19 This *spake* **said** he,
signifying by what death he should glorify *God* **Elohim**.
And when he had *spoken* **said** this,
he *saith* **wordeth** unto him, Follow me.
20 Then *Peter* **Petros**, turning *about* **around**,
seeth the disciple whom *Jesus* **Yah Shua** loved following;
which also leaned **who had reposed**
on his *breast* **chest** at supper, and said,
Lord **Adonay**, which is he that
betrayeth thee? Yahn 13:21—25
21 *Peter* **Petros** seeing him
saith **wordeth** to *Jesus* **Yah Shua**,
Lord **Adonay**, and what *shall this man do* **about this one**?
22 *Jesus saith* **Yah Shua wordeth** unto him,
If **Whenever** I will that he *tarry* **abide** till I come,
what is that to thee?
follow thou me.
23 *Then* **So** went this *saying abroad* **word**
among **unto** the brethren,
that that disciple should not die:
yet *Jesus* **Yah Shua** said not unto him,
He shall not die;
but, *If* **whenever** I will that he *tarry* **abide** till I come,
what is that to thee?

CONCLUSION

24 This is the disciple
which *testifieth of* **witnesseth about** these *things*,
and wrote these *things*:
and we know that his *testimony* **witness** is true.
25 And there are also many *other things* **others**
which *Jesus* — **as much as Yah Shua** did,
the which,
if **whenever** they should be *written* **scribed** every one,
I suppose that even the *world* **cosmos** itself
could not contain the *books* **scrolls**
that should be *written* **scribed**.
Amen.
Shimon, son of Yonah, befriend you me?
Petros sorrows
because he said to him the third time,
Befriend you me?
And he says to him, Adonay, you know all:
you know I befriend you.
Yah Shua words to him, Feed my sheep.

YAH SHUA PROPHESIES
THE MARTYRDOM OF PETROS

18 Amen! Amen! I word to you,
When you were young, you girded yourself
and walked where you willed:
but whenever you senesce
you spread your hands;
and another girds you,
and bears you where you will not.
19 He says this
to signify by what death he is to glorify Elohim:
and when he says this, he words to him, Follow me.
20 Petros, turning around
sees the disciple Yah Shua loves following
— who had reposed on his chest at supper
and said, Adonay, who is he that betrays you?
Yahn 13:21—25
21 Seeing him, Petros words to Yah Shua,
Adonay, and what about this one?
22 Yah Shua words to him,
Whenever I will him to abide until I come,
what is that to you?
You, follow me.

23 So this word goes to the brothers,
that that disciple dies not:
yet Yah Shua said not to him, He dies not;
but, whenever I will him to abide until I come,
what is that to you?

Conclusion

24 This is the disciple
who witnesses concerning these and writes these:
and we know his witness is true.
25 And there are also many others
— as much as Yah Shua did
which, whenever they be scribed one by one,
I suppose that not even the cosmos itself
has space for the scrolls scribed.
Amen.

MATTHEW/MATIT'YAH - HA'LEVI 1

THE GENESIS OF YAH SHUA

1 The *book* **scroll** of the *generation* **genesis** of *Jesus Christ* **Yah Shua Messiah**, the son of David, the son of Abraham.

FOURTEEN GENERATIONS: ABRAHAM TO DAVID

2 Abraham *begat* **birthed** *Isaac* **Yischaq**; and *Isaac* **Yischaq** *begat* **birthed** *Jacob* **Yaaqov**; and *Jacob* **Yaaqov** *begat* **birthed** *Judas* **Yah Hudah** and his brethren;

3 And *Judas* **Yah Hudah** *begat* **birthed** *Phares* **Peres** and *Zara* **Zerach** of *Thamar* **Tamar**; and *Phares* **Peres** *begat* **birthed** *Esrom* **Hesron**; and *Esrom* **Hesron** *begat* **birthed** *Aram* **Ram**;

4 And *Aram* **Ram** *begat* **birthed** *Aminadab* **Ammi Nadab**; and *Aminadab* **Ammi Nadab** *begat* **birthed** *Naasson* **Nachshon**; and *Naasson* **Nachshon** *begat* **birthed** *Salmon*;

5 And *Salmon* *begat* **birthed** *Booz* **Boaz** of Rachab; and *Booz* **Boaz** *begat* **birthed** *Obed* of Ruth; and *Obed* *begat* **birthed** *Jesse* **Yishay**;

6 And *Jesse* **Yishay** *begat* **birthed** David the *king* **sovereign**;

FOURTEEN GENERATIONS: TO THE BABEL EXILE

and David the *king* **sovereign** *begat* **birthed** *Solomon* **Shelomoh** *of her that had been the wife of Urias* **of Uri Yah's**;

7 And *Solomon* **Shelomoh** *begat* **birthed** *Roboam* **Rechab Am**; and *Roboam* **Rechab Am** *begat* **birthed** *Abia* **Abi Yah**; and *Abia* **Abi Yah** *begat* **birthed** Asa;

8 And Asa *begat* **birthed** *Josaphat* **Yah Shaphat**; and *Josaphat* **Yah Shaphat** *begat* **birthed** *Joram* **Yoram**; and *Joram* **Yoram** *begat* **birthed** *Ozias* **Uzzi Yah**;

9 And *Ozias* **Uzzi Yah** *begat* **birthed** *Joatham* **Yah Tham**; and *Joatham* **Yah Tham** *begat* **birthed** Achaz; and Achaz *begat* **birthed** *Ezekias* **Yechizq Yah**;

10 And *Ezekias* **Yechizq Yah** *begat* **birthed** *Manasses* **Menash sheh**; and *Manasses* **Menash Sheh** *begat* **birthed** Amon; and Amon *begat* **birthed** *Josias* **Yoshi Yah**;

11 And *Josias* **Yoshi Yah** *begat* **birthed** *Jechonias* **Yechon Yah** and his brethren, about the time they were *carried away* **exiled** to *Babylon* **Babel**:

FOURTEEN GENERATIONS: TO THE MESSIAH

12 And after they were *brought* **exiled** to *Babylon* **Babel**, *Jechonias* **Yechon Yah** *begat* **birthed** *Salathiel* **Shealti El**; and *Salathiel* **Shealti El** *begat* **birthed** *Zorobabel* **Zerub Babel**;

13 And *Zorobabel* **Zerub Babel** *begat* **birthed** *Abiud* **Abi Hud**; and *Abiud* **Abi Hud** *begat* **birthed** *Eliakim* **El Yaqim**; and *Eliakim* **El Yaqim** *begat* **birthed** *Azor* **Azzur**;

14 And *Azor* **Azzur** *begat* **birthed** *Sadoc* **Sadoq**; and *Sadoc* **Sadoq** *begat* **birthed** *Achim* **Yah Qim**; and *Achim* **Yah Qim** *begat* **birthed** *Eliud* **Eli Ud**;

15 And *Eliud* **Eli Ud** *begat* **birthed** *Eleazar* **El Azar**; and *Eleazar* **El Azar** *begat* **birthed** *Matthan* **Mattan**; and *Matthan* **Mattan** *begat* **birthed** *Jacob* **Yaaqov**;

16 And *Jacob* **Yaaqov** *begat* **birthed** *Joseph* **Yoseph** the *husband* **man** of *Mary* **Miryam**, of whom was *born* **birthed** *Jesus* **Yah Shua**, who is *called Christ* **worded Messiah**.

FORTY-TWO GENERATIONS: SUMMARY

17 So all the generations from Abraham to David are fourteen generations; and from David until the *carrying away* **exile** into *Babylon* **Babel** are fourteen generations; and from the *carrying away* **exile** into *Babylon* **Babel** unto *Christ* **the Messiah** are fourteen generations.

YAH SHUA MESSIAH BIRTHED BY THE HOLY SPIRIT

18 Now the birth of *Jesus Christ* **Yah Shua Messiah** was *on this wise* **thus**: When *as* **indeed** his mother *Mary* **Miryam** was espoused to *Joseph* **Yoseph**, before they came together, she was found *with child* **having in womb** of the *Holy Spirit* **Ruach ha-kodesh**.

19 *Then Joseph* **So Yoseph** her *husband* **man**, being *a* just *man*, and *not willing to* **having willed to not** *make her a publick example* **expose her**,

The Genesis Of Yah Shua

1 The scroll of the genesis of Yah Shua Messiah, the son of David, the son of Abraham.

Fourteen Generations: Abraham To David

2 Abraham births Yischaq,
and Yischaq births Yaaqov,
and Yaaqov births Yah Hudah and his brothers,
3 and Yah Hudah births
Peres and Zerach of Tamar,
and Peres births Hesron,
and Hesron births Ram,
4 and Ram births Ammi Nadab,
and Ammi Nadab births Nachshon,
and Nachshon births Salmon,
5 and Salmon births Boaz of Rachab,
and Boaz births Obed of Ruth,
and Obed births Yishay,
6 and Yishay births David the sovereign,

FOURTEEN GENERATIONS: TO THE BABEL EXILE and David the sovereign births Shelomoh of the *woman of* Uri Yah,
7 and Shelomoh births Rechab Am,
and Rechab Am births Abi Yah,
and Abi Yah births Asa,
8 and Asa births Yah Shaphat, and Yah Shaphat births Yoram, and Yoram births Uzzi Yah,
9 and Uzzi Yah births Yah Tham, and Yah Tham births Achaz, and Achaz births Yechizq Yah,
10 and Yechizq Yah births Menash Sheh,
and Menash Sheh births Amon,
and Amon births Yoshi Yah,
11 and Yoshi Yah births Yechon Yah and his brothers
about the time they are exiled to Babel,

Fourteen Generations: To The Messiah

12 and after the exile to Babel
Yechon Yah births Shealti El,
and Shealti El births Zerub Babel,
13 and Zerub Babel births Abi Hud, and Abi Hud births El Yaqim, and El Yaqim births Azzur,
14 and Azzur births Sadoq, and Sadoq births Yah Qim, and Yah Qim births Eli Ud,
15 and Eli Ud births El Azar, and El Azar births Mattan, and Mattan births Yaaqov,
16 and Yaaqov births Yoseph the man of Miryam of whom is birthed Yah Shua, who is worded Messiah.

Forty–Two Generations: Summary

17 So all the generations from Abraham to David
are fourteen generations;
and from David until the exile into Babel
are fourteen generations;
and from the exile into Babel to the Messiah
are fourteen generations.

Yah Shua Messiah Birthed By The Holy Spirit

18 Now the birth of Yah Shua Messiah is thus:
When indeed his mother Miryam espouses to Yoseph
— ere they come together,
she finds having in womb of the Holy Spirit.
19 So Yoseph her man, being just,
wills to not expose her,
was minded **had willed** to *put* **release** her *away privily* **secretly**.
20 But while he *thought* **pondered** on these *things*,
behold, the angel of *the Lord* **Yah Veh**
appeared **manifested** unto him in a dream,
saying **wording**, *Joseph* **Yoseph**, thou son of David,
fear **awe** not to take unto thee
Mary **Miryam** thy *wife* **woman**:
for that which is *conceived* **birthed** in her
is of the *Holy Spirit* **Ruach ha-kodesh**.
21 And she shall *bring forth* **birth** a son,
and thou shalt call his name *Jesus* **Yah Shua**:
for he shall save his people from their sins.

Yah Shua Messiah Virgin Birthed

22 Now all this *was done* **became**,
that it might be fulfilled/shalamed
which was *spoken of the Lord* **rhetorized by Yah Veh**
by **through** the prophet, *saying* **wording**,
23 Behold, a virgin shall *be with child* **have in womb**,
and shall *bring forth* **birth** a son,
and they shall call his name *Emmanuel* **Immanu El**,
which *being interpreted is* **translates**,
God **Elohim** with us.
Yesha Yah 7:14
24 *Then Joseph being raised* **And Yoseph, rousing** from sleep
did as the angel of *the Lord* **Yah Veh**
had *bidden* **ordered** him,
and took unto him his *wife* **woman**:
25 And knew her not
till she had *brought forth* **birthed** her
firstborn **firstbirthed** son:
and he called his name *Jesus* **Yah Shua**.

MATTHEW/MATIT'YAH - HA'LEVI 2

The Visit Of The Magi

2 Now when *Jesus* **Yah Shua** was *born* **birthed**
in *Bethlehem* **Beth Lechem** of *Judaea* **Yah Hudah**
in the days of Herod the *king* **sovereign**,
behold, there came *wise men* **magi**
from the *east* **rising** to *Jerusalem* **Yeru Shalem**,

2 *Saying* **Wording**,
Where is he
that is *born* **birthed** *king* **sovereign**
of the *Jews* **Yah Hudiym**?
for we have seen his star in the *east* **rising**,
and are come to worship him.

3 When Herod the *king* **sovereign**
had heard these *things*,
he was troubled and all *Jerusalem*
Yeru Shalem with him.

4 And when he had gathered
all the *chief* **arch** priests
and scribes of the people together,
he *demanded* **inquired** of them
where *Christ* **the Messiah** should be *born* **birthed**.

5 And they said unto him,
In *Bethlehem* **Beth Lechem** of *Judaea* **Yah Hudah**:
for thus it is *written by* **scribed through** the prophet,

6 And thou *Bethlehem* **Beth Lechem**,
in the land of *Juda* **Yah Hudah**,
art not the least
among the *princes* **governors** of *Juda* **Yah Hudah**:
for out of thee shall come a Governor,
that shall *rule* **shepherd** my people *Israel* **Yisra El**.
Michah 5:2

7 Then Herod,
when he had *privily* **secretly** called the *wise men* **magi**,
enquired of them *diligently* **precisely**
what time the star *appeared* **manifested**.

8 And he sent them to *Bethlehem*
Beth Lechem, and said,
Go and *search diligently* **investigate precisely**
for the young child;
and when ye have found him,
bring me word again **evangelize me**,
that I may come and worship him also.

9 When they had heard the
king **sovereign**, they departed;
and, *lo* **behold**, the star,
which they saw in the *east* **rising**, went before them,
till it came and stood over where the young child was.

10 When they saw the star, they *rejoiced* **cheered**
with exceeding great joy **an extremely mega cheer**.

11 And when they were come into the house,
they saw the young child with *Mary* **Miryam** his mother,
and fell *down*, and worshipped him:
and when they had opened their treasures,
they *presented* **offered** unto him *gifts* **oblations**;

but wills to release her secretly.

20 And pondering these, behold,
the angel of Yah Veh manifests to him in a dream,
wording, Yoseph, you son of David,
awe not to take Miryam your woman to yourself:
for that birthing in her is of the Holy Spirit.

21 And she is to birth a son;
and you, call his name Yah Shua:
for he saves his people from their sins.

Yah Shua Messiah Virgin Birthed

22 Now all this became,
to fulfill/shalam that rhetorized by Yah Veh
through the prophet, wording,

23 Behold, a virgin has in womb and births a son;
and they call his name Immanu El,
which translates, Elohim with us.
Yesha Yah 7:14

24 And Yoseph, rousing from sleep
does as the angel of Yah Veh orders him,
and takes his woman to him:

25 and knows her not
until she births her firstbirthed son:
and he calls his name Yah Shua.

The Visit Of The Magi

2 And Yah Shua is birthed
in Beth Lechem, Yah Hudah
in the days of Herod the sovereign.
Behold, magi come from the rising to Yeru Shalem,

2 wording, Where is he
who is birthed sovereign of the Yah Hudiym?
For we saw his star in the rising
and come to worship him.

3 When Herod the sovereign hears these,
he is troubled — and all Yeru Shalem with him:

4 and he gathers all the archpriests
and scribes of the people together;
and inquires of them where the Messiah is birthed.

5 And they say to him,
In Beth Lechem, Yah Hudah:
for thus it is scribed through the prophet,

6 And you Beth Lechem, in
the land of Yah Hudah,
are not the least among the governors of Yah Hudah:

for from you comes a Governor,
to shepherd my people Yisra El.
Michah 5:2
7   Then Herod secretly calls the magi
and enquires of them
precisely the time the star manifested.
8   And he sends them to Beth Lechem, and says,
Go and investigate precisely for the young child;
and when you find him, evangelize me;
and I also come and worship him.
9   And they hear the sovereign, and depart;
and behold,
the star they see in the rising, precedes them,
until it goes and stands over the young child:
10   and they see the star
and cheer an extremely mega cheer.
11   And they enter the house,
and see the young child with Miryam his mother,
and fall and worship him:
and they open their treasures and offer him oblations
gold, and frankincense, and myrrh.
12   And being *warned of God* **oracled** in a dream
that they should not return to Herod,
they departed into their own *country* **region**
through another way.

Yoseph, Miryam, And Yah Shua Flee To Misrayim

13   And when they were departed, behold,
the angel of *the Lord appeareth* **Yah Veh manifesteth**
to *Joseph* **Yoseph** in a dream, *saying* **wording**,
Arise, and take the young child and his mother,
and flee into *Egypt* **Misrayim**,
and be thou there until I *bring* **say to** thee *word*:
for Herod *will* **shall** seek the young child to destroy him.
14   When he arose,
he took the young child and his mother by night,
and departed into *Egypt* **Misrayim**:
15   And was there until the death of Herod:
that it might be fulfilled/shalamed
which was *spoken* **rhetorized**
of *the Lord by* **Yah Veh through** the prophet,
saying **wording**,
Out of *Egypt* **Misrayim** have I called my son.
Hoshea 11:1
16   Then Herod,
when he saw that he was mocked of the *wise men* **magi**,
was *exceeding wroth* **extremely furious**,
and *sent forth* **apostolized**,
and *slew* **took out** all the *children* **lads**

that were in *Bethlehem* **Beth Lechem**,
and in all the *coasts* **boundaries** *thereof*,
from two years *old* and under,
according to the time
which he had *diligently* **precisely** enquired
of the *wise men* **magi**.
17   Then was fulfilled/shalamed that which was
spoken **rhetorized** by *Jeremy* **Yirme Yah** the prophet,
saying **wording**,
18   In *Rama* **Ramah** was there a voice heard,
lamentation, and weeping,
and *great mourning* **much grieving**,
Rachel weeping for her children,
and *would* **willed to** not be comforted,
because they are not. Yirme Yah 31:5

Yoseph, Miryam, And Yah Shua Go To Nazareth

19   But when Herod was dead,
behold, an angel of *the Lord* **Yah Veh**
appeareth **manifesteth** in a dream
to *Joseph* **Yoseph** in *Egypt* **Misrayim**,
20   *Saying* **Wording**, Arise,
and take the young child and his mother,
and go into the land of *Israel* **Yisra El**:
for they *are dead* **have died**
which sought the young child's *life* **soul**.
21   And he arose, and took the
young child and his mother,
and came into the land of *Israel* **Yisra El**.
22   But when he heard
that Archelaus did reign in *Judaea* **Yah Hudah**
in the room of **for** his father Herod,
he was *afraid* **awestricken** to go thither:
notwithstanding, being *warned of*
God **oracled** in a dream,
he *turned aside* **departed** into the parts of *Galilee* **Galiyl**:
23   And he came and *dwelt* **settled**
in a city *called* **worded** Nazareth:
that it might be fulfilled/shalamed
which was *spoken by* **rhetorized through** the prophets,
He shall be called a Nazarene.
cp Yesha Yah 11:1

Yahn The Baptizer Preaches Repentance

3   In those days came *John*
Yahn the *Baptist* **Baptizer**,
preaching in the wilderness of *Judaea* **Yah Hudah**,
2   And *saying* **wording**, Repent *ye*:

for the *kingdom* **sovereigndom** of *heaven* **the heavens**
is at hand **approacheth**.
3 For this is he that was *spoken* **rhetorized**
of **by** the prophet *Esaias* **Yesha Yah**, *saying* **wording**,
The voice of one crying in the wilderness,
Prepare ye the way of *the Lord* **Yah Veh**,
make his paths straight.
— gold and frankincense and myrrh.
12 And in a dream
being oracled to not return to Herod
they depart to their own region
through another way.

Yoseph, Miryam, And Yah Shua Flee To Misrayim

13 And they depart, and behold,
the angel of Yah Veh manifests to Yoseph in a dream,
wording, Rise;
take the young child and his mother
and flee to Misrayim,
and be there until I say to you:
for Herod seeks to destroy the young child.
14 And he rises,
and takes the young child and his mother by night,
and departs to Misrayim;
15 and is there until the death of Herod:
to fulfill/shalam
that rhetorized by Yah Veh through the prophet,
wording, From Misrayim I call my son.
Hoshea 11:1
16 Then Herod, seeing he is mocked by the magi,
is extremely furious;
and apostolizes and takes out all the lads
in Beth Lechem and in all the boundaries
from two years and under
— according to the time
he precisely enquired of the magi.
17 — Then he fulfills/shalams
what Yirme Yah the prophet rhetorized, wording,
18 In Ramah a voice is heard:
lamentation and weeping and much grieving;
Rachel weeping for her children;
and wills to not be comforted because
they are not. Yirme Yah 31:5

Yoseph, Miryam, And Yah Shua Go To Nazareth

19 And Herod dies; and behold,
an angel of Yah Veh manifests in a dream
to Yoseph in Misrayim,
20 wording, Rise,
Take the young child and his mother
and go to the land of Yisra El:
for whoever sought the soul of the
young child have died.
21 And he rises,
and takes the young child and his mother
and goes to the land of Yisra El:
22 and he hears that Archelaus
reigns in Yah Hudah
in the stead of his father Herod;
and he is awestricken to go there: but being oracled
in a dream, he departs to the parts of Galiyl:
23 and he goes and settles in
a city worded Nazareth:
to fulfill/shalam that rhetorized through the prophets,
He is called a Nazarene.
cp Yesha Yah 11:1

Yahn The Baptizer Preaches Repentance

3 In those days, Yahn the Baptizer
comes preaching in the wilderness of Yah Hudah,
2 and wording, Repent!
For the sovereigndom of the the heavens approaches.
3 — for this is he
who is rhetorized by the prophet Yesha Yah,
wording, The voice of one crying in the wilderness,
Prepare the way of Yah Veh
make his paths straight.
Yesha Yah 40:3
4 And the same *John* **Yahn**
had his *raiment* **enduement** of camel's hair,
and a leathern girdle about his loins;
and his *meat* **nourishment** was locusts and wild honey.
5 Then *went out* **proceeded** to him
Jerusalem **Yeru Shalem**, and all *Judaea* **Yah Hudah**,
and all the region round about *Jordan* **Yarden**,
6 And were baptized of him in *Jordan* **Yarden**,
confessing their sins.

Yahn The Baptizer Derides The Pharisees And Sadoqiym

7 But when he saw
many of the Pharisees and *Sadducees* **Sadoqiym**
come to his baptism,
he said unto them, O *generation* **progeny** of vipers,
who hath *warned* **exemplified** you
to flee from the wrath *to come* **about to be**?
8 *Bring forth* **So produce** therefore

MATTHEW/MATIT'YAH - HA'LEVI 3, 4

fruits *meet* **worthy** for repentance:

9 And think not to *say* **word** within yourselves,
We have Abraham to our father:
for I *say* **word** unto you,
that *God* **Elohim** is able of these stones
to raise *up* children unto Abraham.

10 And *now* **already** also
the axe is laid unto the root of the trees:
therefore **so** every tree
which *bringeth* **produceth** not *forth* good fruit
is *hewn down* **exscinded**, and cast into the fire.

11 I indeed baptize you *with*
in water unto repentance:
but he that cometh after me is mightier than I,
whose shoes I am not *worthy* **adequate** to bear:
he shall baptize you
with **in** the *Holy Spirit* **Ruach ha-kodesh**, and *with* fire:

12 Whose *winnowing* fan is in his hand,
and he *will* **shall** throughly purge his **threshing** floor,
and gather **together** his *wheat* **grain**
into the *garner* **granary**;
but he *will* **shall** burn *up* the chaff
with unquenchable fire.

Yahn The Baptizer Baptizes Yah Shua

13 Then cometh *Jesus* **Yah Shua**
from *Galilee* **Galiyl** to *Jordan* **Yarden** unto *John* **Yahn**,
to be baptized of him.

14 But *John* **Yahn** forbad him, *saying* **wording**,
I have need to be baptized of thee,
and comest thou to me?

15 And *Jesus* **Yah Shua** answering said unto him,
Suffer **Allow** it to be so now:
for thus it *becometh* **befitteth** us
to fulfill/**shalam** all *righteousness* **justness**.
Then he *suffered* **allowed** him.

16 And *Jesus* **Yah Shua**, when he was baptized,
went up **ascended** straightway out of the water:
and, *lo* **behold**, the heavens were opened unto him,
and he saw the Spirit of *God* **Elohim**
descending *like* **as** a dove,
and lighting upon him:

17 And *lo* **behold,** a voice from *heaven* **the heavens**,
saying **wording**, This is my beloved Son,
in **of** whom I *am well pleased* **well—approve**.

Yah Shua Tested By Diabolos

4 Then was *Jesus led up* **Yah Shua brought** of the spirit
into the wilderness
to be *tempted* **tested** of *the devil* **Diabolos**.

2 And when he had fasted
forty days and forty nights,
he was afterward an hungred.

3 And when the *tempter*
tester came to him, he said,
If thou be the Son of *God* **Elohim**,
command **say** that these stones *be made* **become** bread.

4 But he answered and said, It is *written* **scribed**,
man **Humanity** shall not live by bread alone,
but by every *word* **rhema**
that proceedeth *out of* **through** the mouth
of *God* **Yah Veh**. Deuteronomy 8:3

5 Then *the devil* **Diabolos**
taketh him *up* into the holy city,
and setteth him
on a *pinnacle* **wing** of the *temple* **priestal precinct**,

6 And *saith* **wordeth** unto him,

4 And this Yahn has his enduement of camel hair
and a leather girdle around his loins;
and his nourishment is locusts and wild honey:

5 Then Yeru Shalem and all Yah Hudah
and all the region all around Yarden proceed to him;

6 and confessing their sins,
he baptizes them in Yarden.

Yahn The Baptizer Derides The Pharisees And Sadoqiym

7 But he sees many of the Pharisees and Sadoqiym
come to his baptism:
and he says to them, O progeny of vipers,
who exemplifies you to flee from the wrath about to be?

8 So produce fruits worthy of repentance:

9 and think not to word within yourselves,
We have Abraham to our father:
for I word to you,
that Elohim is able to raise children to Abraham
from these stones:

10 and also
the axe is already laid to the root of the trees:
so every tree not producing good fruit
is exscinded and cast into the fire.

11 I indeed baptize you in water to repentance:
but he coming after me is mightier than I,
whose shoes I am not adequate to bear: he
baptizes you in the Holy Spirit and fire:

12 whose winnowing fan is in his hand;
and he throughly purges his threshing floor,
and gathers his grain into the granary;
but he burns the chaff with unquenchable fire.

MATTHEW/MATIT'YAH - HA'LEVI 4

YAHN THE BAPTIZER BAPTIZES YAH SHUA

13 Then Yah Shua comes from Galiyl to Yarden
— to Yahn — to be baptized by him.
14 But Yahn forbids him, wording,
I need to be baptized by you
— and you come to me?
15 And Yah Shua answers him, saying,
Allow it for now:
for thus it befits us to fulfill/shalam all justness.
Then he allows him
16 and baptizes Yah Shua:
and he ascends straightway from the water:
and behold, the the heavens open to him,
and he sees the Spirit of Elohim descending,
as a dove, and lighting upon him:
17 and behold, a voice from the the heavenss,
wording, This is my beloved Son,
of whom I well—approve.

YAH SHUA TESTED BY DIABOLOS

4 Then the spirit brings Yah
Shua to the wilderness
to be tested by Diabolos:
2 and he fasts forty days and forty nights
and afterward famishes.
3 And the tester comes to him, and says,
If you are the Son of Elohim,
say that these stones become bread.
4 But he answers, saying, It is scribed,
Humanity lives, not by bread alone,
but by every rhema
proceeding through the mouth of
Yah Veh. Deuteronomy 8:3
5 Then Diabolos takes him to the holy city
and sets him on a wing of the priestal precinct;
6 and words to him,
If thou be the Son of *God* **Elohim**, cast thyself down:
for it is *written* **scribed**,
He shall *give* **misvah** his angels *charge* concerning thee:
and in their hands they shall bear thee *up*,
lest *at any time* **ever** thou dash thy foot
against a stone. Psalm 91:11, 12
7 *Jesus* **Yah Shua** said unto him,
It is *written* **scribed** again,
Thou shalt not *tempt* **test** *the Lord* **Yah Veh**
thy *God* **Elohim**. Deuteronomy 6:16
8 Again, *the devil* **Diabolos** taketh him *up*
into an *exceeding* **extremely** high mountain,
and sheweth him

all the *kingdoms* **sovereigndoms** of the *world* **cosmos**,
and the glory of them;
9 And *saith* **wordeth** unto him,
All these *things will* **shall** I give thee,
if **whenever** thou *wilt* **shalt** fall *down* and worship me.
10 Then *saith Jesus* **wordeth Yah Shua** unto him,
Get thee hence **Go**, Satan: for it is *written* **scribed**,
Thou shalt worship *the Lord* **Yah Veh** thy *God* **Elohim**,
and him only shalt thou *serve* **liturgize**.
Deuteronomy 6:13, 10:20
11 Then *the devil leaveth* **Diabolos forsaketh** him,
and, behold, angels came and ministered unto him.
12 Now when *Jesus* **Yah Shua** had heard
that *John* **Yahn** was *cast into prison* **betrayed**,
he departed into *Galilee* **Galiyl**;
13 And leaving Nazareth, he came
and *dwelt* **settled** in *Capernaum* **Kaphar Nachum**,
which is *upon* **at** the *sea coast* **seaside**,
in the *borders* **boundaries**
of *Zabulon* **Zebulun** and *Nephthalim* **Naphtali**:
14 That it might be fulfilled/shalamed
which was *spoken* **rhetorized**
by Essias **through Yesha Yah** the
prophet, *saying* **wording**,
15 The land of *Zabulon* **Zebulun**,
and the land of *Nephthalim* **Naphtali**,
by the way of the sea, beyond *Jordan* **Yarden**,
Galilee **Galiyl** of the *Gentiles* **goyim**;
16 The people which sat in darkness
saw *great* **a mega** light;
and to them which sat in the region and shadow of death
light is *sprung up* **risen**.
Yesha Yah 9:1, 2

YAH SHUA PREACHES, REPENT!

17 From that time *Jesus* **Yah Shua** began to preach,
and to *say* **word**, Repent:
for the *kingdom* **sovereigndom** of *heaven* **the heavens**
is at hand **approacheth**.

YAH SHUA CALLS PETROS AND ANDREAS

18 And *Jesus* **Yah Shua**, walking
by the sea of *Galilee* **Galiyl**,
saw two brethren,
Simon called Peter **Shimon worded Petros**,
and *Andrew* **Andreas** his brother,
casting a net into the sea: for they were fishers.
19 And he *saith* **wordeth** unto them,
Follow **Come after** me,
and I *will* **shall** make you fishers of *men* **humanity**.

20 And they straightway *left* **forsook** their nets,
and followed him.

YAH SHUA CALLS YAAQOVOS AND YAHN

21 And *going on* **advancing** from thence,
he saw other two brethren,
James **Yaaqovos** *the son* of *Zebedee* **Zabdi**,
and *John* **Yahn** his brother,
in a *ship* **sailer** with *Zebedee* **Zabdi** their father,
mending **preparing** their nets; and he called them.
22 And they *immediately* **straightway**
left **forsook** the *ship* **sailer** and their father,
and followed him.
23 And *Jesus* **Yah Shua** went
about all *Galilee* **Galiyl**,
teaching **doctrinating** in their synagogues,
and preaching
the *gospel* **evangelism** of the *kingdom* **sovereigndom**,
and *healing all manner of sickness* **curing every disease**
and *all manner of disease* **every debility**
among the people.
If you are the Son of Elohim, cast yourself down:
for it is scribed,
He misvahs his angels concerning you:
and in their hands they bear you;
lest ever you dash your foot against a stone.
Psalm 91:11, 12
7 Yah Shua says to him, It is scribed again,
Test not Yah Veh your Elohim.
Deuteronomy 6:16
8 Again,
Diabolos takes him to an extremely high mountain
and shows him all the sovereigndoms of the cosmos
and their glory;
9 and words to him,
All these I give you,
whenever you fall and worship me.
10 Then Yah Shua words to him,
Go, Satan: for it is scribed,
Worship Yah Veh your Elohim,
and liturgize him only.
Deuteronomy 6:13, 10:20
11 Then Diabolos forsakes him:
and behold, angels come and minister to him.
12 And Yah Shua hears that Yahn is betrayed;
and he departs to Galiyl;
13 and leaving Nazareth
he goes and settles in Kaphar Nachum
at the seaside
in the boundaries of Zebulun and Naphtali:
14 to fulfill/shalam that rhetorized
through Yesha Yah the prophet, wording,
15 The land of Zebulun and the land of Naphtali
by the way of the sea, beyond Yarden,
Galiyl of the goyim:
16 the people sitting in darkness
see a mega light;
and to them sitting in the region and shadow of death
light rises.
Yesha Yah 9:1, 2

YAH SHUA PREACHES, REPENT!

17 From that time Yah Shua
begins to preach and to word,
Repent!
For the sovereigndom of the the heavens approaches.

YAH SHUA CALLS PETROS AND ANDREAS

18 And walking by the sea of Galiyl,
Yah Shua sees two brothers,
Shimon worded Petros and Andreas his brother
casting a net into the sea: for they are fishers:
19 and he words to them, Come after me;
and I make you fishers of humanity.
20 — and straightway
they forsake their nets and follow him.

YAH SHUA CALLS YAAQOVOS AND YAHN

21 And advancing from there
he sees two other brothers
— Yaaqovos of Zabdi and his brother Yahn
preparing their nets in a sailer with Zabdi their father:
and he calls them.
22 — and straightway
they forsake the sailer and their father
and follow him.
23 And Yah Shua goes all around Galiyl
— doctrinating in their synagogues,
and preaching the evangelism of the sovereigndom
and curing every disease and every debility
among the people:
24 And his fame went *throughout* **into** all Syria:
and they *brought* **offered** unto him
all *sick people* **that were ill**
that were *taken* **held** with divers diseases and torments,
and those which were *possessed with devils* **demonized**,
and those which were lunatick,
and those that *had the palsy* **were paralytic**;
and he *healed* **cured** them.
25 And there followed him

great **vast** multitudes of people from *Galilee* **Galiyl**,
and from Decapolis, and from *Jerusalem* **Yeru Shalem**,
and from *Judaea* **Yah Hudah**,
and from beyond *Jordan* **Yarden**.

The Mountain Message Of Yah Shua: The Beatitudes

5 And seeing the multitudes,
he *went up* **ascended** into a mountain:
and when he was set, his disciples came unto him:

2 And he opened his mouth,
and *taught* **doctrined** them, *saying* **wording**,

3 Blessed are the poor in spirit:
for theirs is the *kingdom* **sovereigndom**
of *heaven* **the heavens**.

4 Blessed are they that mourn:
for they shall be comforted.

5 Blessed are the meek:
for they shall inherit the earth.

6 Blessed are they
which do hunger and thirst after *righteousness* **justness**:
for they shall be filled.

7 Blessed are the merciful:
for they shall obtain mercy.

8 Blessed are the pure in heart:
for they shall see *God* **Elohim**.

9 Blessed are *the peacemakers* **they who shalam**:
for they shall be called the *children* **sons** of *God* **Elohim**.

10 Blessed are they
which are persecuted for *righteousness'* **justness'** sake:
for theirs
is the *kingdom* **sovereigndom** of *heaven* **the heavens**.

11 Blessed are ye,
When **ever** men shall *revile* **reproach** you,
and persecute you,
and shall say *all manner of* **every** evil **rhema**
against you falsely, for my sake.

12 *Rejoice* **Cheer**, and *be
exceeding glad* **jump for joy**:
for *great* **vast** is your reward in *heaven* **the heavens**:
for *so* **thus** persecuted they the prophets
which were before you.

The Position Of The Truster

13 Ye are the salt of the earth:
but *if* **whenever**
the salt have *lost his savour* **become insipid**,
wherewith **wherein** shall it be salted?
it is thenceforth *good* **not able** for *nothing* **naught**,
but to be cast out,

and to be *trodden under foot*
trampled of *men* **humanity**.

14 Ye are the light of the *world* **cosmos**.
A city that is set on *an hill* **a mountain**
cannot be *hid* **secreted**.

15 Neither do men *light* **burn** a candle,
and put it under a *bushel* **measure**,
but **rather** on a *candlestick* **menorah**;
and it *giveth light* **radiateth** unto
all that are in the house.

16 Let your light *so shine* **thus radiate**
before men **in front of humanity**,
that they may see your good works,
and glorify your Father which is in *heaven* **the heavens**.

Yah Shua Fulfills The Torah

17 *Think* **Presume** not that I am come
to *destroy* **disintegrate** the *law* **torah**, or the prophets:
I am not come to *destroy* **disintegrate**,
but **rather** to fulfill/**shalam**.

18 For *verily I say* **Amen! I word** unto you,
Till heaven and earth pass,
one *jot* **iota** or one tittle
shall *in no wise* **never no way** pass from the *law* **torah**,
till all *be fulfilled*/**shalamed becometh**.

19 **So** Whosoever *therefore* shall *break* **release**
one of these least *commandments* **misvoth**,

24 and his fame goes to all Syria:
and they offer him all who are ill
— who are held with divers diseases and torments
— demonized, lunatic, paralytic;
and he cures them.

25 And vast multitudes of people from Galiyl,
and from Decapolis, and from Yeru Shalem,
and from Yah Hudah, and from beyond Yarden
follow him.

The Mountain Message Of Yah Shua: The Beatitudes

5 And seeing the multitudes,
he ascends a mountain and sits:
his disciples come to him:

2 and he opens his mouth and doctrines them,
wording,

3 Blessed — the poor in spirit:
for theirs is the sovereigndom of the the heavens.

4 Blessed — they who mourn:
for they are comforted.

5 Blessed — the meek:
for they inherit the earth.

6	Blessed — they who famish
	and thirst after justness:
	for they are filled.
7	Blessed — the merciful:
	for they obtain mercy.
8	Blessed — the pure in heart:
	for they see Elohim.
9	Blessed — they who shalam:
	for they are called the sons of Elohim.
10	Blessed — those persecuted for sake of justness:
	for theirs is the sovereigndom of the the heavens.
11	Blessed — you,
	whenever men reproach you and persecute you,
	and say every evil rhema against you falsely
	for my sake.
12	Cheer, and jump for joy!
	For vast is your reward in the the heavens:
	for thus they persecuted the prophets preceding you.

The Position Of The Truster

13	You are the salt of the earth:
	but whenever the salt becomes insipid,
	with what salt we?
	It is able for naught but to cast out,
	and for humanity to trample.
14	You are the light of the cosmos.
	Neither can a city set on a mountain be secreted;
15	nor men burn a candle and
	put it under a measure;
	but rather on a menorah;
	and it radiates to all in the house.
16	Thus radiate your light in front of humanity;
	so they see your good works
	and glorify your Father in the heavens.

Yah Shua Fulfills The Torah

17	Presume not
	that I come to disintegrate the torah or the prophets:
	I come not to disintegrate; rather to fulfill/shalam.
18	For Amen! I word to you,
	Until the heavens and earth pass,
	not one iota or one tittle
	never no way passes from the torah
	until all becomes.
19	So whoever releases one of these least misvoth,
	and shall *teach men so* **doctrinate humanity thus**,
	he shall be called the least
	in the *kingdom* **sovereigndom** of *heaven* **the heavens**:
	but whosoever shall do and *teach* **doctrinate** them,
	the same shall be called *great* **mega**
	in the *kingdom* **sovereigndom** of *heaven* **the heavens**.
20	For I *say* **word** unto you,
	That *except* **unless ever** your *righteousness* **justness**
	shall *exceed the righteousness* **superabound much more**
	of **than** the scribes and Pharisees,
	ye shall *in no case* **no way** enter
	into the *kingdom* **sovereigndom** of *heaven* **the heavens**.

The Value System Of Yah Shua: Murder, Rage, Slander

21	Ye have heard that it was *said* **rhetorized**
	of them of old time **to the ancients**,
	Thou shalt not *kill* **murder**;
	and whosoever shall *kill* **murder**
	shall be *in danger of* **subject to** the judgment:
22	But I *say* **word** unto you,
	That *whosoever* **everyone**
	who is *angry* **wroth** with his brother
	without a cause **in vain**
	shall be *in danger of* **subject to** the judgment:
	and whosoever shall say to his brother, *Raca* **Req**,
	shall be *in danger of* **subject to** the *council* **sanhedrim**:
	but whosoever shall say, Thou fool,
	shall be *in danger of* **subject to**
	hell **Gay Hinnom/the Valley of Burning** fire.

Forgiving

23	*Therefore if* **So whenever** thou
	bring **offer** thy *gift* **oblation**
	to **at** the *sacrifice* **altar**,
	and there rememberest
	that thy brother hath *ought* **somewhat** against thee;
24	*Leave* **Release** there thy *gift* **oblation**
	before **in front of** the *sacrifice* **altar**,
	and go thy way;
	first be reconciled to thy brother,
	and then come and offer thy *gift* **oblation**.

Settling Out Of Court

25	Agree with thine adversary quickly,
	whiles thou art in the way with him;
	lest *at any time* **ever**
	the adversary deliver thee to the judge,
	and the judge deliver thee to the *officer* **attendant**,
	and thou be cast into *prison* **a guardhouse**.
26	*Verily I say* **Amen! I word** unto thee,
	Thou shalt *by no means* **never no way** come out thence,
	till thou hast *paid* **given back**
	the *uttermost farthing* **final quarter**.

MATTHEW/MATIT'YAH - HA'LEVI 5

ADULTERIZING

27 Ye have heard that it was *said* **rhetorized** *by them of old time* **to the ancients**, *Thou shalt not commit adultery* **adulterize not**: Exodus 20:14, Deuteronomy 5:18
28 But I *say* **word** unto you, That whosoever *looketh on* **all who observe** a woman to *lust* **pant** after her hath *committed adultery* **adulterized** with her already in his heart.

AVOIDING GAY HINNOM/ THE VALLEY OF BURNING

29 And if thy right eye *offend* **scandalize** thee, pluck it *out*, and cast it from thee: for it is *profitable* **beneficial** for thee that one of thy members should *perish* **destruct**, and not that thy whole body should be cast into *hell* **Gay Hinnom/the valley of burning**.
30 And if thy right hand *offend* **scandalize** thee, *cut* **exscind** it *off*, and cast it from thee: for it is *profitable* **beneficial** for thee that one of thy members should *perish* **destruct**, and not that thy whole body should be cast into *hell* **Gay Hinnom/the Valley of Burning**.

DIVORCE

31 It hath been *said* **rhetorized**, Whosoever shall *put away* **release** his *wife* **woman**, let him give her a *writing* **scroll** of *divorcement* **apostasy**: Deuteronomy 24:1
32 But I *say* **word** unto you, and doctrinates humanity thus, is called the least in the sovereigndom of the heavens: but whoever does and doctrinates them, is called mega in the sovereigndom of the heavens.
20 For I word to you, That unless ever your justness superabounds much more than the scribes and Pharisees, you no way enter the sovereigndom of the heavens.

THE VALUE SYSTEM OF YAH SHUA: MURDER, RAGE, SLANDER

21 You heard it rhetorized to the ancients, Murder not; and whoever murders becomes subject to the judgment.
22 But I word to you, That everyone wroth with his brother in vain becomes subject to the judgment: and whoever says to his brother, Req! becomes subject to the sanhedrim: but whoever says, Fool! becomes subject to the fire of Gay Hinnom/the Valley of Burning.

FORGIVING

23 So whenever you offer your oblation at the sacrifice altar, and there remember that your brother has somewhat against you;
24 release your oblation in front of the sacrifice altar, and go your way; first reconcile to your brother, and then come and offer your oblation.

SETTLING OUT OF COURT

25 Agree with your adversary quickly while you are with him in the way: lest ever the adversary deliver you to the judge; and the judge deliver you to the attendant; and cast you into a guardhouse.
26 Amen! I word to you, You never no way come from there, until you give back the final quarter.

ADULTERIZING

27 You heard it rhetorized to the ancients, Adulterize not: Exodus 20:14, Deuteronomy 5:18
28 But I word to you, That whoever observes a woman — to pant after her already adulterizes with her in his heart.

AVOIDING GAY HINNOM/ THE VALLEY OF BURNING

29 And if your right eye scandalizes you pluck it out and cast it from you: for it is beneficial for you that one of your members destruct, and not your whole body cast into Gay Hinnom/the Valley of Burning.
30 And if your right hand scandalizes you, exscind it and cast it from you: for it is beneficial for you that one of your members destruct,

and not your whole body
cast into Gay Hinnom/the Valley of Burning.

DIVORCE

31 It was rhetorized,
Whoever releases his woman,
give her a scroll of apostasy.
Deuteronomy 24:1

32 But I word to you,
That whosoever shall *put away* **release** his *wife* **woman**,
saving **except**
for the *cause* **word** of *fornication* **whoredom**,
causeth her to *commit adultery* **adulterize**:
and whosoever shall marry her that is *divorced* **released**,
committeth adultery **adulterizeth**.

OATHING

33 Again, ye have heard that it
hath been *said* **rhetorized**
by them of old time **to the ancients**,
Thou shalt not *forswear thyself* **oath**,
but shalt *perform* **give back** unto *the Lord* **Yah Veh**
thine oaths:
Leviticus 19:12, Numbers 30:2, Deuteronomy 23:21

34 But I *say* **word** unto you, *Swear* **Oath** not at all;
neither *by heaven* **in the heavens**;
for it is *God's* **Elohim's** throne:

35 Nor *by* **in** the earth; for it is his footstool:
neither *by Jerusalem* **in Yeru Shalem**;
for it is the city of the *great king* **mega sovereign**.

36 Neither shalt thou *swear by* **oath in** thy head,
because thou canst not make one hair white or black.

37 But let your *communication* **word** be,
Yea, yea; Nay, nay:
for whatsoever is more **superabundant** than these
cometh **is** of evil.

RETALIATION

38 Ye have heard that it hath been *said* **rhetorized**,
An eye for an eye, and a tooth for a tooth:
Exodus 21:22—27, Leviticus 24:19, 20,
Deuteronomy 19:21

39 But I *say* **word** unto you, That ye resist not evil:
but whosoever shall *smite* **slap** thee on thy right cheek,
turn to him the other also.

40 And *if any man* **to whoever**
will sue thee at the law **willeth to have thee judged**,
and take away thy *coat* **tunic**,
let him have **release** thy *cloak* **garment** also.

41 And whosoever shall compel thee to go a mile,
go with him twain.

42 Give to him that asketh thee,
and from him that *would* **willeth to** borrow of thee
turn not thou away.

LOVING YOUR ENEMY

43 Ye have heard that it hath been *said* **rhetorized**,
Thou shalt love thy neighbour, and hate thine enemy.
Leviticus 19:18, Psalm 139:21, 22

44 But I *say* **word** unto you, Love your enemies,
bless **eulogize** them that curse you,
do good to them that hate you,
and pray for them which *despitefully use* **threaten** you,
and persecute you;

45 That ye may be the *children* **sons** of your Father
which is in *heaven* **the heavens**:
for he maketh his sun to rise on
the evil and on the good,
and *sendeth rain* **raineth** on the just and on the unjust.

46 For *if* **whenever** ye love them which love you,
what reward have ye?
do not **indeed**
even the *publicans* **customs agents** the same?

47 And *if* **whenever** ye salute your brethren only,
what do ye *more than others* **so superabundantly**?
do not **indeed**
even the *publicans* **so customs agents thus**?

48 *So* Be ye *therefore perfect* **complete/at shalom**,
even **exactly**
as your Father which is in *heaven* **the heavens**
is *perfect* **complete/at shalom**.

DOING MERCIES

6 *Take* heed that ye do not your *alms* **mercies**
before men **in front of humanity**,
to be *seen* **observed** of them:
otherwise **and if not** ye have no reward of your Father
which is in *heaven* **the heavens**.

2 *Therefore* **So** when **ever** thou
doest *thine alms* **thy mercies**,
do not sound a trumpet before **trump not ahead of** thee,
exactly as the hypocrites do
in the synagogues and in the streets,
that they may have glory of *men* **humanity**.
Verily I say **Amen! I word** unto you,
They have their reward.
Whoever releases his woman,
except for the word of whoredom,
causes her to adulterize:
and whoever marries her who is released,

adulterizes.

OATHING

33 Again, you heard it rhetorized to the ancients,
Oath not;
but give back your oaths to Yah Veh.
Leviticus 19:12, Numbers 30:2, Deuteronomy 23:21
34 But I word to you, Oath not at all;
neither in the the heavens;
for it is the throne of Elohim:
35 nor in the earth;
for it is the stool of his feet:
nor in Yeru Shalem;
for it is the city of the mega sovereign:
36 nor oath in your head,
because you cannot make one hair white or black:
37 but thus be your word, Yes, yes; No, no:
for whatever is more superabundant than these
is of evil.

RETALIATION

38 You heard it rhetorized,
An eye for an eye, and a tooth for a tooth:
Exodus 21:22—27, Leviticus 24:19,
20, Deuteronomy 19:21
39 But I word to you, Resist not evil:
but whoever slaps you on your right cheek,
also turn the other to him:
40 and to whoever wills to have you judged
to take away your tunic, release your garment also:
41 and whoever compels you to go a mile,
go with him two.
42 To him who asks, give;,
and from him who wills to borrow of you,
turn not away.

LOVING YOUR ENEMY

43 You heard it rhetorized,
Love your neighbor, and hate your enemy.
Leviticus 19:18, Psalm 139:21, 22
44 But I word to you, Love your enemies;
eulogize them who curse you;
do good to them who hate you;
and pray for them
who threaten you and persecute you;
45 so that you become
the sons of your Father in the the heavens:
for his sun rises on the evil and on the good;
and rains on the just and on the unjust.
46 For whenever you love them who love you,
what reward have you?
Do not indeed even the customs agents the same?
47 And whenever you salute your brothers only,
what do you so superabundantly?
Do not indeed even the customs agents thus?
48 So be complete/at shalom,
exactly as your Father is in the the heavens
is complete/at shalom.

DOING MERCIES

6 Heed to not do your mercies
in front of humanity
to be observed of them:
and if not,
you have no reward of your Father in the the heavens:
2 so whenever you do your mercies,
trump not ahead of you
exactly as the hypocrites
in the synagogues and in the streets,
to be glorified by humanity.
Amen! I word to you, they have their reward.
3 But when thou doest *alms* **mercies**,
let not thy left *hand* know what thy right *hand* doeth:
4 That *thine alms* **thy mercies** may be in secret:
and thy Father which *seeth* **observeth** in secret
himself shall *reward* **give** thee *openly* **manifestly**.

PRAYER

5 And when **ever** thou prayest,
thou shalt not be **exactly** as the hypocrites *are*:
for they *love* **befriend** to pray standing in the synagogues
and in the corners of the *streets* **broadways**,
that they may be *seen of men* **manifest to humanity**.
Verily ! say **Amen! I word** unto you,
They have their reward.
6 But thou, when **ever** thou prayest,
enter into thy *closet* **pantry**,
and when thou hast shut thy *door* **portal**,
pray to thy Father which is in secret;
and thy Father which *seeth* **observeth** in secret
shall *reward* **give** thee *openly* **manifestly**.
7 But when ye pray, use not vain repetitions,
exactly as the *heathen* **goyim** *do*:
for they think that they shall be heard
for their *much speaking* **polylogy**.
8 **So** Be not ye *therefore* like unto them:
for your Father knoweth what *things* ye have need of,
before **ere** ye ask him.
3 But when you do mercies,
let not your left know what your right does:

4	so your mercies are in secret: and your Father who observes in secret himself gives you manifestly.

PRAYER

5   And whenever you pray,
be not exactly as the hypocrites:
for they befriend to pray standing in the synagogues
and in the corners of the broadways
to manifest to humanity.
Amen! I word to you, they have their reward.

6   But you, whenever you pray,
enter your pantry and shut your portal;
pray to your Father in secret;
and your Father who observes in secret
gives you manifestly:

7   but in praying
use not vain repetitions exactly as the goyim: for
they think they are heard for their polylogy:

8   So you, liken not to them:
for your Father knows what you need
ere you ask him.

A PRAYER EXAMPLE

9   *After this manner therefore* **So** pray ye **thus**:
Our Father *which art* in *heaven* **the heavens**,
Hallowed be thy name.

10   Thy *kingdom* **sovereigndom** come.
Thy will *be done* **become** in earth, as it is in heaven.

11   Give us this day our *daily* bread **of subsistance**.

12   And forgive us our debts,
as we forgive our debtors.

13   And *lead* **bring** us not into *temptation* **testing**,
but *deliver* **rescue** us from evil:
For thine is the *kingdom* **sovereigndom**,
and the *power* **dynamis**, and the
glory, *for ever* **unto the eons**.
Amen.

FORGIVING

14   For *if* **whenever** ye forgive
men **humanity** their *trespasses* **backslidings**,
your heavenly Father *will* **shall** also forgive you:

15   But *if* **whenever** ye forgive not *men* **humanity**
their *trespasses* **backslidings**,
neither *will* **shall** your Father
forgive your *trespasses* **backslidings**.

FASTING

16   Moreover when *ever* ye fast,
be not, **exactly** as the hypocrites,
of a sad countenance — **sullen**:
for they *disfigure* **camouflage** their faces,
that they may *appear* **manifest** unto
men **humanity** to fast.
Verily ! say **Amen! I word** unto you,
They have their reward.

17   But thou, when thou fastest,
anoint thine head, and wash thy face;

18   That thou *appear* **manifest**
not unto *men* **humanity** to fast,
but unto thy Father which is in secret:
and thy Father, which *seeth* **observeth** in secret,
shall reward thee *openly* **manifestly**.

TREASURING TREASURES

19   *Lay* **Treasure** not *up* for yourselves
treasures upon earth,
where moth and rust *doth corrupt* **dissolve**,
and where thieves break through and steal:

20   But *lay up* **treasure** for
yourselves treasures in heaven,
where neither moth nor rust *doth corrupt* **dissolveth**,
and where thieves do not break through nor steal:

21   For where your treasure is,
there *will* **shall** your heart be also.

THE EYE

22   The *light* **candle** of the body is the eye:
if therefore **so whenever** thine eye be *single* **clear**,
thy whole body shall be *full of light* **brightly lighted**.

23   But *if* **whenever** thine eye be evil,

A PRAYER EXAMPLE

9   So pray thus:
Our Father in the heavens hallowed be your name:

10   your sovereigndom come;
your will become in earth as in the heavens:

11   give us this day our bread of subsistance:

12   and forgive us our debts
as we also forgive our debtors:

13   and bring us not into testing
but rescue us from evil:
for yours is the sovereigndom
and the dynamis and the glory to the eons.
Amen.

FORGIVING

14   For whenever
you forgive humanity their backslidings,

15   your heavenly Father also forgives you:
but whenever you forgive not
humanity their backslidings,
your Father forgives not your backslidings.

Fasting

16   Moreover whenever you fast,
be not exactly as the hypocrites — sullen:
for they camouflage their faces,
to manifest to humanity they fast.
Amen! I word to you,
They have their reward.
17   But you, when you fast,
anoint your head and wash your face;
18   that you not to manifest
to humanity that you fast,
but to your Father in secret:
and your Father who observes in secret
rewards you manifestly.

Treasuring Treasures

19   Treasure not for yourselves treasures on earth;
where moth and rust dissolve
and where thieves break through and steal:
20   but treasure for yourselves
treasures in the heavens;
where neither moth nor rust dissolve
and where thieves neither break through nor steal:
21   for where your treasure is,
there your heart is also.

The Eye

22   The candle of the body is the eye:
so whenever your eye is clear,
your whole body becomes brightly lit:
23   but whenever your eye is evil
thy whole body shall be *full of darkness* **dark**.
So **If** *therefore* the light that is in thee be darkness,
how *great* **vast** is that darkness!

Serving Two Adonim

24   No *man* **one** can serve two *masters* **adonim**:
for either he *will* **shall** hate the one,
and love the other;
or else he *will hold to* **shall uphold** the one,
and *despise* **disesteem** the other.
Ye cannot serve *God* **Elohim** and mammon.
25   *Therefore* **So** I *say* **word** unto you,
Take no thought **Be not anxious** for your *life* **soul**,
what ye shall eat, or what ye shall drink;
nor yet for your body, what ye shall *put on* **endue**.
Is not *indeed*
the *life* **soul** *much* more than *meat* **nourishment**,
and the body than *raiment* **enduement**?
26   *Behold* **Look at** the *fowls*
flyers of the *air* **heaven**:
for they *sow* **spore** not, neither do they *reap* **harvest**,
nor gather *together* into *barns* **granaries**;
yet your heavenly Father *feedeth* **nourisheth** them.
Are ye not *much better* **more surpassing** than they?
27   Which of you by *taking thought* **anxiety**
can add one cubit unto his *stature* **maturity**?
28   And why *take ye thought* **be ye anxious**
for *raiment* **enduement**?
Consider the lilies of the field, how they grow;
they *toil* **labour** not, neither do they spin:
29   And yet I *say* **word** unto you,
That even *Solomon* **Shelomoh** in all his glory
was not arrayed *like* **as** one of these.
30   *Wherefore*, **but** if *God* so **Elohim**
thus clothe the *grass* **herbage** of the field,
which to day is, and to morrow is cast into the oven,
shall he not much more *clothe* you,
O ye of little *faith* **trust**?
31   *Therefore take no thought* **So be not anxious**,
saying **wording**,
What shall we eat? or, What shall we drink?
or, Wherewithal shall we be *clothed* **arrayed**?
32   (For after all these *things* do
the *Gentiles* **goyim** seek:)
for your heavenly Father knoweth
that ye have need of all these *things*.

The Provision Of Yah Shua

33   But seek ye first
the *kingdom* **sovereigndom** of *God* **Elohim**,
and his *righteousness* **justness**;
and all these *things* shall be added unto you.
34   *Take therefore no thought* **So be not anxious**
for the morrow:
for the morrow
shall *take thought for the things* **be anxious** of itself.
Sufficient unto the day is the *evil* **malice** thereof.

Judging

7   Judge not, that ye be not judged.
2   For *with* **in** what judgment
ye judge, ye shall be judged:
and *with* **in** what measure ye *mete* **measure**,
it shall be *measured* **remeasured** to you *again*.

Twigs And Beams

3 And why *beholdest* **lookest**
thou **at** the *mote* **twig**
that is in thy brother's eye,
but *considerest* **perceivest** not the beam
that is in thine own eye?
4 Or how *wilt* **shalt** thou say to thy brother,
Let **Allow** me
pull out **to eject** the *mote* **twig** out of thine eye;
and, behold, a beam is in thine own eye?
5 Thou hypocrite,
first *cast out* **eject** the beam out of thine own eye;
and then shalt thou see clearly
to *cast out* **eject** the *mote* **twig** out of thy brother's eye.

Giving, Asking, Seeking, And Knocking

6 Give not that which is holy
unto the *dogs* **hounds**,
neither cast ye your pearls *before* **in front of** swine,
lest **ever** they trample them *under* **at** their feet,
and turn again and *rend* **tear** you.
7 Ask, and it shall be given you;
seek, and ye shall find;
knock, and it shall be opened unto you:
your whole body becomes dark:
so whenever the light in you becomes darkness
— how vast that darkness!

Serving Two Adonim

24 No one can serve two adonim:
for either he hates the one and loves the other;
or else he upholds the one and disesteems the other:
you cannot serve Elohim and mammon.
25 So I word to you, neither
be anxious for your soul
— what you eat or what you drink;
nor yet for your body
— what you endue.
Is not indeed the soul much more than nourishment?
And the body than enduement?
26 Look at the flyers of the heavens:
for they neither spore nor harvest
nor gather together into granaries;
yet your Father of the heavenlies nourishes them.
Surpass you not them?
27 Who of you, by anxiety,
is able to add one cubit to his maturity?
28 And why be anxious about enduement?
Consider the lilies of the field, how they
grow; they neither labor nor spin:
29 and yet I word to you,
that even Shelomoh in all his glory
arrayed not as one of these.
30 But if Elohim thus clothes
the herbage of the field
— which today is, and tomorrow cast into the oven
— how not much more You, O you of little trust?
31 So be not anxious, wording,
What eat we? or, What drink we?
or, With what array we?
32 For the goyim seek after all these:
for your Father of the heavenlies
knows you need all these.

The Provision Of Yah Shua

33 But first
seek the sovereigndom of Elohim and his justness;
and all these add to you.
34 So be not anxious for the morrow:
for the morrow has its own anxieties.
Each day has sufficient malice.

Judging

7 Judge not, so you are not judged.
2 For in what judgment you judge,
you are judged:
and in what measure you measure,
is remeasured to you.

Twigs And Beams

3 And why look at the twig
in the eye of your brother,
but perceive not the beam in your own eye?
4 Or, how say you to your brother,
Allow me to eject the twig from your eye;
and behold, a beam in your own eye?
5 You hypocrite!
First eject the beam from your own eye;
and then you see clearly
to eject the twig from the eye of your brother.

Giving, Asking, Seeking, And Knocking

6 Neither give the holy to the hounds
nor cast you your pearls in front of swine;
lest ever they trample them at their feet
and turn and rip you *apart*.
7 Ask, and you are given;
seek, and you find;

knock, and it opens to you:
8 For every one that asketh *receiveth* **taketh**;
and he that seeketh findeth;
and to him that knocketh it shall be opened.
9 Or what *man* **human** is there of you,
whom *if* **whenever** his son ask bread,
will **shall** he give him a stone?
10 Or *if* **whenever** he ask a fish,
will **shall** he give him a serpent?
11 *So* **If** ye *then*, being evil,
know how to give good gifts unto your children,
how much more
shall your Father which is in *heaven* **the heavens**
give good *things* to them that ask him?

THE GOLDEN RULE

12 *Therefore* **So** all
things whatsoever ye would — **as much as ever ye** will
that *men* **humanity** should do to you,
do ye even so thus to them:
for this is the *law* **torah** and the prophets.

GATES

13 Enter ye in *at* **through** the *strait* **narrow** gate:
for wide is the gate, and broad is the
way, that leadeth to destruction,
and many there be which *go in thereat* **enter therein**:
14 Because *strait* **narrow** is the gate,
and *narrow* **tribulated** is the way,
which leadeth unto life,
and few there be that find it.

PSEUDO PROPHETS

15 *Beware* **But take heed** of *false* **pseudo** prophets,
which come to you in sheep's *clothing* **enduement**,
but inwardly they are *ravening* **rapacious** wolves.
16 Ye shall know them by their fruits.
Do men gather **they** grapes of thorns,
or figs of *thistles* **briers**?
17 Even *so* **thus** every good tree
bringeth forth **produceth** good fruit;
but a *corrupt* **putrefied** tree
bringeth forth **produceth** evil fruit.
18 A good tree cannot *bring
forth* **produce** evil fruit,
neither can a *corrupt* **putrefied** tree
bring forth **produce** good fruit.
19 Every tree that *bringeth*
produceth not *forth* good fruit
is *hewn down* **exscinded**, and cast into the fire.
20 *Wherefore* **So then** by their
fruits ye shall know them.

PSEUDO PROFESSORS

21 Not every one that *saith* **wordeth** unto me,
Lord **Adonay**, Lord **Adonay**,
shall enter into
the *kingdom* **sovereigndom** of *heaven* **the heavens**;
but he that doeth the will of my Father
which is in *heaven* **the heavens**.
22 Many *will* **shall** say to me in that day,
Lord **Adonay**, Lord **Adonay**,
have we not prophesied in thy name?
and in thy name *have cast out devils* **ejected demons**?
and in thy name done many *wonderful works* **dynamis**?
23 And then *will* **shall** I profess unto them,
I never **ever** knew you:
depart from me, ye that *work iniquity* **violate the torah**.

BUILDING

24 *Therefore whosoever* **So everyone
who** heareth these *sayings* **words** of mine,
and doeth them,
I *will* **shall** liken him unto a *wise* **thoughtful** man,
which built his house upon a rock:
25 And the rain descended, and
the *floods* **streams** came,
and the winds *blew* **puffed**, and beat upon that house;
and it fell not: for it was founded upon a rock.
26 And every one that heareth
these sayings of mine,
and doeth them not,
shall be likened unto a foolish man,
which built his house upon the sand:
27 And the rain descended, and
the *floods* **streams** came,
and the winds *blew* **puffed**,
and *beat* **dashed** upon that house;
and it fell: and *great* **mega** was the *fall* **downfall** of it.
28 And *so be* it *came to pass*,
when *Jesus* **Yah Shua**
had *ended* **completed/shalamed** these *sayings* **words**,
8 for everyone who asks, takes;
and whoever seeks, finds;
and whoever knocks, it opens.
9 Or what human of you,
whenever his son asks bread,
gives him a stone?
10 Or whenever he asks a fish,
gives him a serpent?

11 So if you, being evil,
know how to give good gifts to your children,
how much more your Father in the heavens
gives good to them who ask him?

THE GOLDEN RULE

12 So all — as much as ever you will
that humanity does to you,
you do even thus to them:
for this is the torah and the prophets.

GATES

13 Enter through the narrow gate:
for wide the gate and broad the way
leading to destruction;
and many who enter therein:
14 because narrow the gate and tribulated the way,
leading to life;
and few are they who find it.

PSEUDO PROPHETS

15 But take heed of pseudo prophets
who come to you in the enduement of sheep;
but inwardly are rapacious wolves:
16 you know them by their fruits.
Gather they grapes of thorns?
Or figs of briers?
17 Even thus every good tree produces good fruit;
but a putrefied tree produces evil fruit.
18 A good tree cannot produce evil fruit;
and a putrefied tree cannot produce good fruit:
19 every tree not producing good fruit is exscinded
and cast in the fire.
20 So then you know them by their fruits.

PSEUDO PROFESSORS

21 Not everyone who words
to me, Adonay! Adonay!
enters the sovereigndom of the heavens;
but whoever does the will
of my Father in the heavens.
22 Many say to me in that day, Adonay! Adonay!
Prophesied we not in your name?
And ejected demons in your name?
And done many dynamis in your name?
23 And then I profess to them,
I never ever knew you:
depart from me, you who violate the torah.

BUILDING

24 So everyone
— whoever hears my words and does them,
I liken to a thoughtful man,
who builds his house on a rock:
25 and the rain descends and the streams come
and the winds puff and beat on that house;
and it falls not: for it is founded on a rock.
26 And whoever hears these sayings of mine
and does them not,
is likened to a foolish man
who builds his house on sand:
27 and the rains descend and the streams come
and the winds puff and dash on that house;
and it falls: and mega is the downfall.
28 And so be it,
when Yah Shua completes/shalams these words
the *people* **multitude** were astonished at his doctrine:
29 For he *taught* **doctrinated**
them as *one* having authority,
and not as the scribes.

YAH SHUA CLEANSES A LEPER

8 When he
was come down **descended** from the mountain,
great **vast** multitudes followed him.
2 And, behold, there came a
leper and worshipped him,
saying **wording**, Lord **Adonay**, *if whenever* thou
wilt, thou canst *make* **purify** me *clean*.
3 And *Jesus put forth* **Yah Shua spread** his hand
and touched him, *saying* **wording**,
I will; be thou *clean* **pure**.
And *immediately* **straightway**
his leprosy was *cleansed* **purified**.
4 And *Jesus saith* **Yah Shua wordeth** unto him,
See thou *tell* **say to** no *man* **one**;
but go thy way, shew thyself to the priest,
and offer the *gift* **oblation**
that *Moses commanded* **Mosheh ordered**,
for a *testimony* **witness** unto them.

YAH SHUA HEALS A PARALYTIC

5 And when *Jesus* **Yah Shua**
was entered into *Capernaum* **Kaphar Nachum**,
there came unto him a centurion, beseeching him,
6 And *saying* **wording**, Lord **Adonay**,
my *servant* **lad** lieth at home *sick of the palsy* **paralyzed**,
grievously tormented **excessively tortured**.

MATTHEW/MATIT'YAH - HA'LEVI 8

7 And *Jesus saith* **Yah Shua wordeth** unto him,
I *will* **shall** come and *heal* **will shall cure** him.

8 The centurion answered and said, *Lord* **Adonay**,
I am not *worthy* **adequate**
that thou shouldest *come* **enter** under my *roof* **thatch**:
but *speak* **say** the word only,
and my *servant* **lad** shall be healed.

9 For I am a *man* **human** under authority,
having *soldiers* **warriors** under me:
and I *say* **word** to this man, Go, and he goeth;
and to another, Come, and he cometh;
and to my servant, Do this, and he doeth *it*.

10 When *Jesus* **Yah Shua** heard it, he marvelled,
and said to them that followed,
Verily I say **Amen! I word** unto you,
I have not found so *great faith* **much trust**,
no, not *even* in *Israel* **Yisra El**.

11 And I *say* **word** unto you,
That many shall come
from the *east* **rising** and *west* **the lowering**,
and shall *sit down* **recline** with Abraham,
and *Isaac* **Yischaq**, and *Jacob* **Yaaqov**,
in the *kingdom* **sovereigndom** of *heaven* **the heavens**.

12 But the *children* **sons** of the
kingdom **sovereigndom**
shall be *cast out* **ejected** into outer darkness:
there shall be weeping and gnashing of teeth.

13 And *Jesus* **Yah Shua** said unto the centurion,
Go thy way;
and as thou hast *believed* **trusted**,
so be it *done* unto thee.
And his *servant* **lad** was healed in the selfsame hour.

YAH SHUA ALLEVIATES A FEVER

14 And when *Jesus* **Yah Shua**
was come into *Peter's* **Petros'** house,
he saw his *wife's mother* **mother in law** laid,
and *sick of a fever* **fevered**.

15 And he touched her hand,
and the fever *left* **forsook** her:
and she arose, and ministered unto them.

YAH SHUA EJECTS DEMONIZED SPIRITS

16 *When the even was come* **Being evening**,
they *brought* **offered** unto him
many that were *possessed with devils* **demonized**:
and he *cast out* **ejected** the spirits with his word,
and *healed* **cured** all that were *sick* **ill**:

17 That it might be fulfilled/**shalamed**
which was *spoken* **rhetorized**
by *Esaias* **through Yesha Yah** the
prophet, *saying* **wording**,
Himself took our *infirmities* **frailties**,
and bare our *sicknesses* **diseases**.
the multitude is astonished at his doctrine: 29
for he doctrinates them as having authority
and not as the scribes.

YAH SHUA CLEANSES A LEPER

8 And he descends from the mountain
and vast multitudes follow him:

2 and behold, a leper comes and worships him;
wording, Adonay,
whenever you will, you can purify me.

3 And Yah Shua spreads his
hand and touches him,
wording, I will! Purify!
— and straightway his leprosy purifies.

4 And Yah Shua words to him,
See that you say to no one;
but go your way, show yourself to the priest,
and offer the oblation Mosheh ordered
for a witness to them.

YAH SHUA HEALS A PARALYTIC

5 And Yah Shua enters Kaphar Nachum,
and a centurion comes to him, beseeching him,

6 and wording, Adonay,
my lad lies at home paralyzed — excessively tortured.

7 And Yah Shua words to him,
I come and cure him.

8 The centurion answers, saying, Adonay,
I am not adequate that you enter under my thatch:
but only say the word, and my lad heals:

9 for I also am a human under authority,
having warriors under me:
and I word to this man, Go! — and he goes;
and to another, Come! — and he comes;
and to my servant, Do this! — and he does.

10 And Yah Shua hears, and marvels;
and says to them who follow,
Amen! I word to you,
I find not this much trust
— no, not even in Yisra El:

11 and I word to you,
that many come from the rising and the lowering
and recline with Abraham and Yischaq and Yaaqov
in the sovereigndom of the heavens:

12 but the sons of the sovereigndom

are ejected into outer darkness: with
weeping and gnashing of teeth.

13 And Yah Shua says to the centurion,
Go your way; and as you trust, so be it to you.
— and his servant lad is healed in that hour.

Yah Shua Alleviates A Fever

14 And Yah Shua goes to the house of Petros;
and he sees his mother in law lying fevered:
15 he touches her hand and the fever forsakes her;
and she rises and ministers to them.

Yah Shua Ejects Demonized Spirits

16 And being evening,
they offer him many demonized;
and he ejects the spirits with his word
and cures all the ill:
17 to fulfill/shalam
what Yesha Yah the prophet rhetorized,
wording,
Himself took our frailities and bore
our diseases. Yesha Yah 53:4

Following Yah Shua

18 Now when *Jesus* **Yah Shua**
saw *great* **vast** multitudes about him,
he *gave commandment* **summoned**
to depart unto the other side.
19 And a certain scribe came, and said unto him,
Master **Doctor**,
I *will* **shall** follow thee whithersoever thou goest.
20 And *Jesus saith* **Yah Shua wordeth** unto him,
The foxes have *holes* **burrrows**,
and the *birds* **flyers** of the *air* **heaven** have nests;
but the Son of *man* **humanity**
hath not where to *lay* **recline** his head.
21 And another of his disciples said unto him,
Lord **Adonay**, *suffer* **allow** me first
to go and *bury* **entomb** my father.
22 But *Jesus* **Yah Shua** said unto him, Follow me;
and *let* **allow** the dead *bury* **to entomb** their dead.

Yah Shua Rebukes The Winds And The Sea

23 And when he *was entered*
embarked into a *ship* **sailer**,
his disciples followed him.
24 And, behold,
there *arose* **became** a *great tempest*
mega quake in the sea,
insomuch that
the *ship* **sailer** was *covered with* **veiled by** the waves:
but he was asleep.
25 And his disciples came to
him, and *awoke* **roused** him,
saying **wording**, Lord **Adonay**, save us:
we *perish* **destruct**.
26 And he *saith* **wordeth** unto them,
Why are ye *fearful* **cowardly**, O ye of little *faith* **trust**?
Then he arose, and rebuked the winds and the sea;
and there *was* **became** a *great* **mega** calm.
27 But the *men* **humans**
marvelled, *saying* **wording**,
What manner of man is this,
that even the winds and the sea obey him!

Yah Shua Ejects Demons

28 And when he was come to the other side
into the *country* **region** of the *Gergesenes* **Girgashiym**,
there met him two *possessed with devils* **demonized**,
coming out of the tombs,
exceeding fierce **extremely furious**,
so that no *man* **one** might **be able**
to pass *by* **through** that way.
29 And, behold, they cried out, *saying* **wording**,
What have we to do with thee, *Jesus* **Yah Shua**,
thou Son of *God* **Elohim**?
art thou come hither
to *torment* **torture** us *before* **ere** the *time* **season**?
30 And there was *a good way* **afar** off from them
an herd **a drove** of many swine feeding.
31 So the *devils* **demons** besought
him, *saying* **wording**,
If thou *cast* **eject** us *out*,
suffer **allow** us to go away into the *herd* **drove** of swine.
32 And he said unto them, Go.
And when they were come out,
they went into the *herd* **drove** of swine:
and, behold, the whole *herd* **drove** of swine
ran violently down a *steep place* **cliff** into the sea,
and *perished* **died** in the waters.
33 And they that *kept* **fed** them fled,
and went their ways into the city,
and *told every thing* **evangelized all**,
and what was befallen
to the *possessed of the devils* **demonized**.
34 And, behold,
the whole city came out to meet *Jesus* **Yah Shua**:
and when they saw him,
they besought him that he *would* **should** depart
out of their *coasts* **boundaries**.

MATTHEW/MATIT'YAH - HA'LEVI 8, 9

9 And he *entered* **embarked** into a *ship* **sailer**,
and passed over, and came into his own city.

YAH SHUA HEALS A PARALYTIC

2 And, behold, they *brought* **offered** to him
a *man sick of the palsy* **paralytic**, lying on a bed:
and *Jesus* **Yah Shua** seeing their *faith* **trust**
said unto the *sick of the palsy* **paralytic**;
Son, be of good cheer **Courage, child**;
thy sins be forgiven thee.

FOLLOWING YAH SHUA

18 And Yah Shua sees vast multitudes around him;
and he summons to depart across:
19 and some scribe comes and says to him,
Doctor, I follow you wherever you go.
20 And Yah Shua words to him,
The foxes have burrrows,
and the flyers of the heavens nests;
but the Son of humanity
has nowhere to recline his head.
21 And another of his disciples says to him,
Adonay, first allow me to go and entomb my father.
22 And Yah Shua says to him, Follow me;
and allow the dead to entomb their dead.

YAH SHUA REBUKES THE WINDS AND THE SEA

23 And he embarks into a sailer
and his disciples follow him:
24 and behold, a mega quake becomes in the sea,
so that the sailer is veiled by the waves:
but he sleeps.
25 And his disciples come to him and rouse him,
wording, Adonay, save us! We destruct!
26 And he words to them,
Why are you cowardly, O you of little trust?
— then he rises, and rebukes the winds and the sea
and there becomes a mega calm.
27 And the humans marvel, wording,
What manner is this,
that even the winds and the sea obey him?

YAH SHUA EJECTS DEMONS

28 And he goes across
to the region of the Girgashiym;
and two demonized meet him
coming from the tombs — extremely furious
so that no one is able to pass through that way:
29 and behold, they cry out wording,
What have we to do with you Yah Shua
— you Son of Elohim?
Come you here to torture us ere the season?
30 And afar from them
a drove of many swine is feeding:
31 and the demons beseech him, wording,
If you eject us, allow us to go into the drove of swine.
32 And he says to them, Go.
— and they come out and go into the drove of swine:
and behold, the whole drove of swine
runs violently down a cliff into the sea
and dies in the waters:
33 and they who feed them flee
and go their ways to the city and evangelize all;
and what befell to the demonized:
34 and behold,
the whole city comes to meet Yah Shua:
and they see him, and beseech him
to depart from their boundaries:

9 — and he embarks in a sailer,
and passes over, and goes to his own city.

YAH SHUA HEALS A PARALYTIC

2 And behold,
they offer him a paralytic lying on a bed:
and seeing their trust
Yah Shua says to the paralytic;
Courage, child; your sins are forgiven.

SCRIBES ACCUSE YAH SHUA OF BLASPHEMY

3 And, behold,
certain **some** of the scribes said within themselves,
This *man* blasphemeth.
4 And *Jesus* **Yah Shua**,
knowing their *thoughts* **deliberations** said,
Wherefore *think* **ponder** ye evil in your hearts?
5 For whether is easier, to say,
Thy sins be forgiven thee;
or to say, Arise, and walk?
6 But that ye may know that
the Son of *man* **humanity**
hath *power* **authority** on earth to forgive sins,
(then *saith* **wordeth** he to the *sick of the palsy* **paralytic**,)
Arise, take *up* thy bed, and go unto thine house.
7 And he arose, and departed to his house.
8 But when the multitudes saw it,
they marvelled, and glorified *God* **Elohim**,
which had given such *power* **authority**
unto *men* **humanity**.

Matthaios Follows Yah Shua

9 And as *Jesus* **Yah Shua**
passed *forth* from thence,
he saw a *man* **human**
named Matthew **worded Matthaios**,
sitting at the *receipt of* custom:
and he *saith* **wordeth** unto him, Follow me.
And he arose, and followed him.

Pharisees Question The Disciples

10 And **so be** it *came to pass*,
as *Jesus sat at meat* **Yah Shua reposed** in the house,
behold, many *publicans* **customs agents** and sinners
came and *sat down* **reposed** with him and his disciples.
11 And when the Pharisees saw it,
they said unto his disciples,
Why eateth your *Master* **Doctor**
with *publicans* **customs agents** and sinners?
12 But when *Jesus* **Yah Shua** heard that,
he said unto them,
They that be *whole* **able** need not a *physician* **healer**,
but they that are *sick* **ill**.
13 But go ye and learn what that *meaneth* **is**,
I will *have* mercy, and not sacrifice:
for I am not come to call the *righteous* **just**,
but sinners to repentance.
14 Then came to him the disciples of *John* **Yahn**,
saying **wording**,
Why do we and the Pharisees fast *oft* **much**,
but thy disciples fast not?
15 And *Jesus* **Yah Shua** said unto them,
Can the *children* **sons** of the bridechamber mourn,
as long as the bridegroom is with them?
but the days *will* **shall** come,
When **ever** the bridegroom shall be taken from them,
and then shall they fast.

The Parable Of Garments

16 No *man* **one** putteth a *piece*
patch of *new* **unfulled** cloth
unto an old garment,
for that *which is put in to fill it up* **fulness**
taketh from the garment,
and the *rent is made* **split becometh** worse.

The Parable Of Skins

17 Neither do men put new
wine into old *bottles* **skins**:
else **and if not** the *bottles break* **skins burst**,
and the wine *runneth out* **poureth**,
and the *bottles perish* **skins destruct**:
but they put new wine into new *bottles* **skins**,
and both are preserved.

The Dead Daughter Of An Arch

18 While he spake these *things* unto them, behold,
there came *a certain ruler* **an arch**, and worshipped him,
saying **wording**, My daughter is even now dead:
but come and *lay* **put** thy hand upon her,
and she shall live.
19 And *Jesus* **Yah Shua** arose, and followed him,
and so did his disciples.

Yah Shua Heals A Hemorrhage

20 And, behold, a woman,
which *was diseased with an issue of blood* **hemorrhaged**
twelve years, came behind him,
and touched the *hem* **edge** of his garment:

Scribes Accuse Yah Shua Of Blasphemy

3 And behold,
some of the scribes say within themselves,
This *one* blasphemes.
4 And Yah Shua, knowing
their deliberations, says,
Why ponder evil in your hearts?
5 For which is easier to say, Your sins are forgiven?
or to say, Rise, and walk?
6 But so you know that the Son of humanity
has authority on earth to forgive sins,
— then he words to the paralytic,
Rise, take your bed, and go to your house.
7 — and he rises and departs to his house.
8 And the multitudes see and
marvel and glorify Elohim,
who gives such authority to humanity.

Matthaios Follows Yah Shua

9 And Yah Shua passes from there
and sees a human worded Matthaios
sitting at the custom:
and he words to him, Follow me.
— and he rises, and follows him.

Pharisees Question The Disciples

10 And so be it, as Yah Shua reposes in the house,
and behold, many customs agents and sinners
come and repose with him and his disciples.

11 And when the Pharisees see,
they say to his disciples,
Your Doctor,
why eats he with customs agents and sinners?
12 And Yah Shua hears, and says to them,
The able need no healer,
but they who are ill:
13 but you go and learn what this is,
I will mercy and not sacrifice:
for I come not to call the just;
but sinners to repentance.
14 Then the disciples of Yahn
come to him, wording,
Why do we and the Pharisees fast much,
but your disciples fast not?
15 And Yah Shua says to them,
Can the sons of the bridechamber mourn,
as long as the bridegroom is with them?
But days come,
whenever the bridegroom is taken from them,
then they fast.

The Parable Of Garments

16 No one puts a patch of unfulled cloth
to an old garment;
for that fulness takes from the garment
and the split becomes worse.

The Parable Of Skins

17 Men put not new wine into old skins:
and if not, the skins burst and the wine pours
and the skins destruct:
but they put new wine into new skins,
and preserve both.

The Dead Daughter Of An Arch

18 While he speaks these to them, behold,
an arch comes and worships him,
wording, My daughter has even died:
but come and put your hand on her, and she lives.
19 — and Yah Shua rises, and follows him
— and also his disciples.

Yah Shua Heals A Hemorrhage

20 And behold,
a woman hemorrhaging twelve years
comes behind him,
and touches the edge of his garment:
21 For she *said* **worded** within herself,
if **whenever** I may *but* **only** touch his garment,
I shall be *whole* **saved**.
22 But *Jesus* **Yah Shua** turned *him about*,
and when he saw her, he said,
Daughter, *be of good comfort* **courage**;
thy *faith* **trust** hath *made* **saved** thee *whole*.
And the woman was *made whole* **saved** from that hour.

Yah Shua Resurrects The Daughter Of The Arch

23 And when *Jesus* **Yah Shua**
came into the *ruler's* **arch's** house,
and saw the *minstrels* **flutists**
and the *people making a noise* **multitude tumulting**,
24 He *said* **worded** unto them, *Give place* **Depart**:
for the *maid* **maiden** is not dead, but sleepeth.
And they *laughed* **ridiculed** him *to scorn*.
25 But when the *people* **multitude**
were put forth **was ejected**,
he *went in* **entered**,
and *took* **overpowered** her by the hand,
and the *maid* **maiden** arose.
26 And the fame thereof went
abroad into all that land.

Yah Shua Opens Blind Eyes

27 And when *Jesus departed*
Yah Shua passed thence,
two blind men followed him,
crying, and *saying* **wording**,
Thou son of David, *have* mercy *on* us.
28 And when he was come into the house,
the blind men came to him:
and *Jesus saith* **Yah Shua wordeth** unto them,
Believe **Trust** ye that I am able to do this?
They *said* **worded** unto him, Yea, *Lord* **Adonay**.
29 Then touched he their eyes, *saying* **wording**,
According to your *faith* **trust** be it unto you.
30 And their eyes were opened;
and *Jesus* **Yah Shua**
straitly charged **sternly enjoined** them, *saying* **wording**,
See that no *man* **one** know it.
31 But they, when they were departed,
spread abroad his fame **reported about him**
in all that *country* **land**.

Yah Shua Ejects A Demon

32 As they went out, behold,
they *brought* **offered** to him a *dumb man* **mute human**
possessed with a devil **demonized**.
33 And when the *devil* **demon** was *cast out* **ejected**,

the *dumb* **mute** spake:
and the multitudes marvelled, *saying* **wording**,
It was never *so seen* **ever thus**
manifested in *Israel* **Yisra El**.
34 But the Pharisees *said* **worded**,
He *casteth out devils* **ejecteth demons**
through **in** the *prince* **arch** of *the devils* **demons**.

Yah Shua Has A Sympathetic Spleen

35 And *Jesus* **Yah Shua**
went about all the cities and villages,
teaching **doctrinating** in their synagogues,
and preaching
the *gospel* **evangelism** of the *kingdom* **sovereigndom**,
and *healing* **curing** every *sickness* **disease**
and every *disease* **debility** among the people.
36 But when he saw the multitudes,
he *was moved with compassion* **had
a sympathetic spleen**
on **for** them, because they fainted,
and were *scattered abroad* **tossed about**,
as sheep having no shepherd.
37 *Then saith* **So wordeth** he unto his disciples,
The harvest *truly* **indeed** is *plenteous* **vast**,
but the *labourers* **workers** are few;
38 *Pray* **So petition** ye *therefore*
the *Lord* **Adonay** of the harvest,
that he *will send* **shall cast** forth *labourers* **workers**
into his harvest.

Yah Shua Authorizes
His Twelve Disciples

10 And when he had called unto him
his twelve disciples,
he gave them *power* **authority** against
unclean **impure** spirits,
so as to *cast* **eject** them *out*,
and to *heal all manner of sickness* **cure every disease**
and *all manner of disease* **every debility**.
21 — for she words within herself,
whenever I only touch his garment, I am saved.
22 And Yah Shua turns and sees her, and says,
Daughter, courage! Your trust saves you.
— and the woman is saved from that hour.

Yah Shua Resurrects
The Daughter Of The Arch

23 And Yah Shua comes to the house of the arch
and sees the flutists and the multitude tumulting;

24 and he words to them, Depart:
for the maiden is not dead, but sleeps.
— and they ridicule him.
25 But they eject the multitude;
and he enters and overpowers her by the hand;
and the maiden rises.
26 — and the fame thereof goes to all that land.

Yah Shua Opens Blind Eyes

27 And Yah Shua passes there;
and two blind men follow him, crying, and wording,
You, son of David, mercy us.
28 And he goes to the house,
and the blind men come to him:
and Yah Shua words to them,
Trust you that I am able to do this?
They word to him, Yes, Adonay.
29 Then he touches their eyes, wording,
According to your trust, so be it to you.
30 And their eyes open;
and Yah Shua sternly enjoins them,
wording, See that no one knows.
31 — but they depart
and report about him in all that land.

Yah Shua Ejects A Demon

32 As they go, behold,
they offer him a mute human — demonized:
33 and he ejects the demon and the mute speaks:
and the multitudes marvel, wording,
It was never ever thus manifested in Yisra El.
34 But the Pharisees word,
He ejects demons in the arch of demons.

Yah Shua Has A Sympathetic Spleen

35 And Yah Shua goes around
all the cities and villages
— doctrinating in their synagogues
and preaching the evangelism of the sovereigndom;
and curing every disease
and every debility among the people:
36 and he sees the multitudes
and has a sympathetic spleen for them
— because they faint
— tossed about as sheep having no shepherd.
37 Then he words to his disciples,
The harvest indeed is vast, but the workers few;
38 so petition Adonay of the harvest
to cast workers into his harvest.

MATTHEW/MATIT'YAH - HA'LEVI 10

YAH SHUA AUTHORIZES HIS TWELVE DISCIPLES

10 And he calls his twelve disciples to him
and gives them authority against impure spirits
so as to eject them;
and to cure every disease and every debility.

THE NAMES OF THE TWELVE APOSTLES

2 Now the names of the twelve apostles are these;
The first, *Simon* **Shimon**,
who is *called Peter* **worded Petros**,
and *Andrew* **Andreas** his brother;
James **Yaaqovos** the son of *Zebedee* **Zabdi**,
and *John* **Yahn** his brother;
3 *Philip* **Philippos**, and *Bartholomew* **Bar Talmay**;
Thomas **Taom**,
and *Matthew* **Matthaios** the *publican* **customs agent**;
James **Yaaqovos** the son of *Alphaeus* **Heleph**,
and Lebbaeus, *whose surname was* **called** Thaddaeus;
4 *Simon* **Shimon** the *Canaanite* **Kenaaniy**,
and *Judas Iscariot* **Yah Hudah the urbanite**,
who also betrayed him.

YAH SHUA APOSTOLIZES HIS APOSTLES

5 These twelve *Jesus sent forth*
Yah Shua apostolized,
and *commanded* **evangelized** them, *saying* **wording**,
Go not into the way of the *Gentiles* **goyim**,
and into any city of the *Samaritans* **Shomeroniym**
enter ye not:
6 But go rather
to the lost sheep of the house of *Israel* **Yisra El**.
7 And as ye go, preach, *saying* **wording**,
The *kingdom* **sovereigndom** of *heaven* **the heavens**
is at hand **approacheth**.
8 *Heal* **Cure** the *sick* **frail**,
cleanse **purify** the lepers,
raise the dead, *cast out devils* **eject demons**:
freely **gratuitously** ye have *received* **taken**,
freely **gratuitously** give.

THE POSSESSIONS OF AN APOSTLE

9 *Provide* **Acquire** neither gold, nor silver,
nor *brass* **copper** in your *purses* **girdles**,
10 Nor *scrip for your journey* **wallet in the way**,
neither two *coats* **tunics**, neither shoes, nor
yet *staves* **rods**: for the *workman* **worker**
is worthy of his *meat* **nourishment**.

THE HOME OF AN APOSTLE

11 And into whatsoever city or
town **village** ye shall enter,
enquire **interrogate** who in it is worthy;
and there abide till ye go thence.
12 And when ye *come* **enter** into an house, salute it.
13 And *if* **whenever indeed** the house be worthy,
let your *peace* **shalom** come upon it:
but *if* **whenever** it be not worthy,
let your *peace return* **shalom turn again** to you.
14 And whosoever — **whenever**
they shall not receive you,
nor hear your words,
when ye depart out of that house or city,
shake off the dust of your feet.
15 *Verily I say* **Amen! I word** unto you,
It shall be more tolerable
for the land of *Sodom* **Sedom** and *Gomorrha* **Amorah**
in the day of judgment, than for that city.
16 Behold, I *send* **apostolize** you *forth*
as sheep in the midst of wolves:
So be ye *therefore wise* **thoughtful** as serpents,
and *harmless* **unadulterated** as doves.

YAH SHUA PROPHESIES BETRAYAL

17 But *beware of men* **heed humanity**:
for they *will deliver* **shall betray** you
up to the *councils* **sanhedrim**,
and they *will* **shall** scourge you in their synagogues;
18 And *ye* shall be brought
before governors and *kings* **sovereigns** for my sake,
for **in** a *testimony* **witness** against them
and the *Gentiles* **goyim**.
19 But when **ever** they *deliver* **betray** you *up*,
take no thought **be not anxious**
how or what ye shall speak:
for it shall be given you in that same hour
what ye shall speak.
20 For it is not ye that speak,
but the Spirit of your Father which speaketh in you.

YAH SHUA PROPHESIES FAMILY TRAITORS

21 And the brother shall *deliver*
up **betray** the brother
to death,

THE NAMES OF THE TWELVE APOSTLES

2 And these are the names of the twelve apostles:
The first, Shimon, worded Petros;

and his brother Andreas;
Yaaqovos of Zabdi and his brother Yahn;
3   Philippos and Bar Talmay;
Taom and Matthaios the customs agent;
Yaaqovos of Heleph and Lebbaeus called Thaddaeus;
4   Shimon the Kenaaniy and
Yah Hudah the urbanite
— who also betrays him.

Yah Shua Apostolizes His Apostles

5   Yah Shua apostolizes these twelve
and evangelizes them,
wording, Neither go the way of the goyim;
nor enter any city of the Shomeroniym:
6   but go rather
to the lost sheep of the house of Yisra El:
7   and preach as you go, wording,
The sovereigndom of the heavens approaches.
8   Cure the frail; purify the lepers;
raise the dead; eject demons:
gratuitously you have taken; gratuitously give.

The Possessions Of An Apostle

9   Acquire neither gold nor silver
nor copper in your girdles
10   nor wallet in the way
nor two tunics nor shoes nor rod:
for the worker is worthy of his nourishment.

The Home Of An Apostle

11   And into whatever city or village you enter,
interrogate who therein is worthy;
and abide there until you go:
12   and when you enter a house, salute:
13   and indeed whenever the house is worthy,
your shalom comes upon it:
but whenever it is not worthy your
shalom returns to you:
14   and whoever — whenever
they neither receive you
nor hear your words
when you depart from that house or city
shake the dust off your feet.
15   Amen! I word to you,
that in the day of judgment
it becomes more tolerable
for the land of Sedom and Amorah
than for that city.
16   Behold, I apostolize you as sheep among wolves:
so be thoughtful as serpents,
and unadulterated as doves.

Yah Shua Prophesies Betrayal

17   But heed humanity:
for they betray you to the sanhedrim;
and they scourge you in their synagogues;
18   and bring you in front of
governors and sovereigns
for my sake,
in a witness against them and the goyim.
19   And whenever they betray you
be not anxious how or what to speak:
for in that same hour you are given what to speak:
20   for it is not you who speaks,
but the Spirit of your Father who speaks in you.

Yah Shua Prophesies Family Traitors

21   And the brother betrays the brother to death;
and the father the child:
and the children shall *rise up against*
attack their parents,
and cause them to be *put to death* **deathified**.
22   And ye shall be hated of all
men for my name's sake:
but he that *endureth* **abideth** to the
end **completion/shalom**
shall be saved.
23   But when **ever** they persecute you in this city,
flee ye into another:
for *verily I say* **Amen! I word** unto you,
Ye shall *not* **never no way**
have *gone over* **completed/shalamed**
the cities of *Israel* **Yisra El**
till **ever** the Son of *man* **humanity** be come.

Service Ranks

24   The disciple is not above his *master* **doctor**,
nor the servant above his *Lord* **Adoni**.
25   It is enough for the disciple
that he be as his *master* **doctor**,
and the servant as his *Lord* **Adoni**.
If they have called the *master of the house* **housedespotes**
Beelzebub **Baal Zebub**,
how much more shall they *call* them of his household?
26   *Fear* **So awe** them not *therefore*:
for *there is nothing covered* **naught that shall be veiled**,
that shall not be *revealed* **unveiled**;
and *hid* **secret**, that shall not be known.
27   What I *tell* **word to** you in darkness,
that *speak* **say** ye in light:
and what ye hear in the ear,

MATTHEW/MATIT'YAH - HA'LEVI 10 — EDC Hebrew / English Bible

28   that preach ye upon the housetops.
28   And *fear* **awe** not them which
kill **slaughter** the body,
but are not able to *kill* **slaughter** the soul:
but rather *fear* **awe** him
which is able to destroy both soul and body in
hell Gay Hinnom/the valley of burning.
29   Are not **indeed** two sparrows
sold for *a farthing* **an assarion**?
and **not** one of them shall *not* fall on the ground
without your Father.
30   But the very hairs of your
head are all numbered.
31   *Fear* **So awe** ye not *therefore*,
ye *are of more value than* **surpass** many sparrows.

HOMOLOGIZING

32   **So all —** Whosoever *therefore*
shall *confess* **profess** me
before men **in front of humanity**,
him *will* **shall** I *confess* **profess** also
before **in front of** my Father
which is in *heaven* **the heavens**.
33   But whosoever shall deny me
before men **in front of humanity**,
him *will* **shall** I also deny *before* **in front of** my Father
which is in *heaven* **the heavens**.
34   *Think* **Presume** not
that I am come to *send peace* **put shalom** on earth:
I came not to *send peace* **put shalom**, but a sword.
35   For I am come to *set a man
at variance* **alienate a human**
against his father,
and the daughter against her mother,
and the *daughter in law* **bride** against her mother in law.
36   And a *man's* **human's** foes
shall be they of his own household.
37   He that *loveth* **befriendeth**
father or mother more than me
is not worthy of me:
and he that *loveth* **befriendeth** son
or daughter more than me
is not worthy of me.
38   And he that taketh not his *cross* **stake**,
and followeth after me,
is not worthy of me.

THE SOUL

39   He that findeth his *life* **soul** shall lose it:
and he that loseth his *life* **soul** for my sake shall find it.

40   He that receiveth you receiveth me,
and he that receiveth me
receiveth him that *sent* **apostolized** me.
41   He that receiveth a prophet
in the name of a prophet
shall *receive* **take** a prophet's reward;
and he that receiveth *a righteous man* **the just**
in the name of *a righteous man* **the just**
shall *receive a righteous man's* **take the just's** reward.
and the father the child:
and the children attack their parents;
and have them deathified:
22   and you are hated of all for sake of my name:
but whoever abides to the completion/shalom is saved.
23   And whenever they persecute you in this city
flee to another.
For Amen! I word to you,
You never no way complete/shalam the cities of Yisra El
until ever the Son of humanity comes.

SERVICE RANKS

24   Neither is the disciple above his doctor
nor the servant above his Adoni:
25   it is enough for the disciple to be as his doctor
and the servant as his adoni.
If they call the housedespotes Baal Zebub,
how much more they them of his household?
26   So awe them not:
for naught becomes veiled, that is not unveiled;
and secret, that is not known.
27   What I word to you in darkness,
say in the light:
and what you hear in the ear,
preach on the housetops.
28   And awe not them who slaughter the body,
but are not able to slaughter the soul:
but rather awe him
who is able to destroy both soul and body
in Gay Hinnom/the Valley of Burning.
29   Are not indeed two sparrows
sold for an assarion?
and not one of them falls on the ground
without your Father:
30   but the very hairs of your
head are all numbered.
31   So awe not: you surpass many sparrows.

HOMOLOGIZING

32   So all —
whoever professes me in front of humanity

I also profess
in front of my Father in the heavens:
33 but whoever denies me in front of humanity
I also deny in front of my Father in the heavens.
34 Presume not that I come to put shalom on earth:
I come not to put shalom — but a sword.
35 For I come to alienate a
human against his father
and the daughter against her mother
and the bride against her mother in law:
36 and the foes of a human
are they of his own household.
37 Whoever befriends father
or mother more than me
is not worthy of me:
and whoever befriends son or daughter more than me
is not worthy of me:
38 and whoever takes not his stake
and follows after me is not worthy of me.

THE SOUL

39 Whoever finds his soul loses it;
and whoever loses his soul for my sake finds it:
40 whoever receives you
receives me;
and whoever receives me
receives him who apostolized me;
41 whoever receives a prophet
in the name of a prophet
takes the reward of a prophet;
and whoever receives the just in the name of the just
takes the reward of the just:
42 And whosoever shall give to drink
unto one of these little ones
a cup of cold *water* only in the name of a disciple,
verily ! say **Amen! I word** unto you,
he shall *in no wise* **never no way** lose his reward.

YAHN THE BAPTIZER IN PRISON

11 And **so be** it *came to pass*,
when *Jesus* **Yah Shua** had *made an*
end **completed/shalamed**
of commanding **ordaining** his twelve disciples,
he departed thence
to *teach* **doctrinate** and to preach in their cities.
2 Now when *John* **Yahn** had heard in the prison
the works of *Christ* **the Messiah**,
he sent two of his disciples,
3 And said unto him, Art
thou he that should come,
or *do* **await** we *look for* another?
4 *Jesus* **Yah Shua** answered and said unto them,
Go and *shew John again* **evangelize Yahn** those
things which ye do hear and *see* **observe**:
5 The blind *receive their sight*
see, and the lame walk,
the lepers are *cleansed* **purified**, and the
deaf **mute** hear, the dead are raised *up*,
and the poor *have the gospel preached*
to them **are evangelized**.
6 And blessed *is he*,
— whosoever shall not be *offended* **scandalized** in me.

THE WITNESS OF YAH SHUA
CONCERNING YAHN THE BAPTIZER

7 And as they departed,
Jesus **Yah Shua** began to *say* **word** unto the multitudes
concerning *John* **Yahn**,
What went ye out into the wilderness to *see* **observe**?
A reed shaken *with* **by** the wind?
8 But what went ye out for to see?
A *man* **human**
clothed in *soft raiment* **effeminate garment**?
behold, they that *wear soft clothing* **bear the effeminate**
are in *kings'* **sovereign's** houses.
9 But what went ye out for to see? A prophet?
yea, I *say* **word** unto you,
and more **superabundantly** than a prophet.
10 For this is he,
of **concerning** whom it is *written* **scribed**,
Behold, I *send* **apostolize** my *messenger* **angel**
before **in front of** thy face,
which shall prepare thy way *before* **preceding**
thee. Yesha Yah 40:3, Malachi 3:1
11 *Verily !* say **Amen! I word** unto you,
Among them that are *born* **birthed** of women
there hath not risen
a greater than *John* **Yahn** the *Baptist* **Baptizer**:
notwithstanding **but** he that is least
in the *kingdom* **sovereigndom** of *heaven* **the heavens**
is greater than he.
12 And from the days of *John*
Yahn the *Baptist* **Baptizer**
until now
the *kingdom* **sovereigndom** of *heaven* **the heavens**
suffereth violence **is taken by force**,
and the *violent* **enforcers** take it *by force*.
13 For all the prophets and the *law* **torah**
prophesied until *John* **Yahn**.
14 And if ye will **to receive it**,

this is *Elias* **Eli Yah**, which was for to come.
15 He that hath ears to hear, let him hear.
16 But whereunto shall I liken this generation?
It is like unto children sitting in the markets,
and calling unto their *fellows* **comrades**,
17 And *saying* **wording**,
We have *piped* **fluted** unto you,
and ye have not danced;
we have *mourned* **lamented** unto you,
and ye have not *lamented* **chopped**.
18 For *John* **Yahn** came neither
eating nor drinking,
and they *say* **word**, He hath a *devil* **demon**.
19 The Son of *man* **humanity**
came eating and drinking,
and they *say* **word**,
Behold, a *man gluttonous* **human glutton**, and a winebibber,
a friend of *publicans* **customs agents** and sinners.
But wisdom is justified of her children.
42 and whoever gives drink
to one of these little ones
— only a cup of cold in the name of a disciple
Amen! I word to you,
he never no way loses his reward.

Yahn The Baptizer In Prison

11 And so be it, when Yah Shua completes/shalams
ordaining his twelve disciples,
he departs to doctrinate and to preach in their cities:
2 and in prison
Yahn hears of the works of the Messiah;
and he sends two of his disciples
3 who say to him,
Are you he who comes? Or await we another?
4 Yah Shua answers them, saying,
Go and evangelize Yahn
what you hear and observe:
5 the blind see and the lame walk;
the lepers purify and the mute hear;
the dead rise and the poor are evangelized:
6 and blessed — whoever
is not scandalized in me.

The Witness Of Yah Shua Concerning Yahn The Baptizer

7 And as they depart,
Yah Shua begins to word to the multitudes
concerning Yahn,
What went you out into the wilderness to observe?
A reed shaken by the wind?
8 But what went you out to see?
A human clothed in effeminate garment?
Behold, whoever bear the effeminate
are in houses of sovereigns.
9 But what went you out to see?
A prophet?
Yes, I word to you,
and superabundantly more than a prophet.
10 For this is he concerning whom it is scribed,
Behold, I apostolize my angel in front of your face
who prepares your way preceding you.
Yesha Yah 40:3, Malachi 3:1
11 Amen! I word to you,
Among them birthed of women
a greater than Yahn the Baptizer has not risen:
but whoever is least
in the sovereigndom of the heavens
is greater than he.
12 And from the days of Yahn
the Baptizer until now
the sovereigndom of the heavens is taken by force:
and the enforcers take it.
13 For all the prophets and the torah
prophesied until Yahn:
14 and if you will to receive it,
this is Eli Yah, who was to come.
15 Whoever has ears to hear, hear!
16 But to what liken I this generation?
It is likened to children sitting in the markets
and calling to their comrades
17 and wording,
We flute to you and you dance not;
we lament to you and you chop not.
18 For Yahn comes neither eating nor drinking
and they word, He has a demon:
19 the Son of humanity comes eating and drinking
and they word,
Behold, a human glutton and a winebibber,
a friend of customs agents and sinners.
But wisdom is justified of her children.

Yah Shua Reproaches The Cities

20 Then began he to *upbraid* **reproach** the cities
wherein most of his *mighty works* **dynamis**
were *done* **became**,
because they repented not:
21 Woe unto thee, Chorazin!
woe unto thee, *Bethsaida* **Beth Sayad**!
for if the *mighty works* **dynamis**,

which *were done* **became** in you,
had *been done* **become** in *Tyre* **Sor** and Sidon,
they *would* **should** have repented long ago
in *sackcloth* **saq** and ashes.

22 But *! say* **Moreover I word** unto you,
It shall be more tolerable for *Tyre* **Sor** and Sidon
at **in** the day of judgment, than for you.

23 And thou, *Capernaum* **Kaphar Nachum**,
which art exalted unto *the* **the** heaven,
shalt be brought down to *hell* **sheol/hades**:
for if the *mighty works* **dynamis**,
which *have been done* **became** in thee,
had *been done* **become** in *Sodom* **Sedom**,
it *would* **should** have *remained* **abode** until this day.

24 But *! say* **Moreover I word** unto you,
That it shall be more tolerable
for the land of *Sodom* **Sedom** in the day of judgment,
than for thee.

Yah Shua Homologizes The Father

25 At that *time* **season**,
Jesus **Yah Shua** answered and said,
I *thank* **confess** thee, O Father,
Lord **Adonay** of *the* **the** heaven and *the* **the** earth,
because thou hast *hid* **secreted** these *things* from
the wise and *prudent* **comprehending**, and
hast *revealed* **unveiled** them unto babes.

26 Even so **Yes**, Father:
for *so* **thus** it *seemeth good* **became well—approved**
in *thy sight* **front of thee**.

27 All *things* are delivered unto me of my Father:
and no *man* **one** knoweth the Son, *but* **except** the Father;
neither knoweth any *man* **one** the Father,
save **except** the Son,
and he to whomsoever the Son *will*
reveal **shall unveil** him.

The Invitation Of Yah Shua To Rest

28 Come unto me,
all ye that labour and are *heavy laden* **overburdened**,
and I *will give you* **shall** rest **you**.

29 Take my yoke upon you, and learn of me;
for I am meek and *lowly* **humble** in heart:
and *ye* shall find rest unto your souls.

30 For my yoke is *easy* **kind**,
and my burden is light.

Yah Shua, Adonay Of The Shabbath

12 At that *time* **season**
Jesus **Yah Shua** went on the *sabbath day* **shabbath**
through the *corn* **spores**;
and his disciples were an hungred,
and began to pluck the *ears of corn* **cobs** and to eat.

2 But when the Pharisees
saw it, they said unto him,
Behold,
thy disciples do that which is not *lawful* **allowed** to do
upon the sabbath day **in shabbath**.

3 But he said unto them,
Have ye not read what David did,
when he was an hungred, and they that were with him;

4 How he entered into the house of *God* **Elohim**,
and did eat the *shewbread* **prothesis bread**,
which was not *lawful* **allowed** for him to eat,
neither for them which were with him,
but **except** only for the priests?

5 Or have ye not read in the *law* **torah**,
how that on the *sabbath days* **shabbaths**
the priests in the *temple* **priestal precinct**
profane the *sabbath* **shabbath**,
and are *blameless* **unaccused**?

6 But I *say* **word** unto you,
That *in this place is one greater than the temple*
a greater than the priestal precinct is here.

7 But if ye had known what this *meaneth* **be**,
I will have mercy, and not sacrifice,

Yah Shua Reproaches The Cities

20 Then he begins to reproach the cities
wherein most of his dynamis became,
because they repent not.

21 Woe to you, Chorazin!
Woe to you, Beth Sayad!
for if the dynamis that became in you,
had become in Sor and Sidon,
they had repented long ago in saq and ashes.

22 Moreover I word to you,
It becomes more tolerable for Sor and Sidon
in the day of judgment, than for you.

23 And you, Kaphar Nachum
— exalted to the heavens to descend to sheol/hades:
for if the dynamis that became in you
had become in Sedom,
it had abode until this day.

24 Moreover I word to you,
that in the day of judgment
it becomes more tolerable for the land of Sedom,
than for you.

Yah Shua Homologizes The Father

25   At that season, Yah Shua answers, saying,
I confess you, O Father,
Adonay of the heavens and the earth,
because you secrete these
from the wise and comprehending
and unveil them to babes.
26   Yes, Father:
for thus it becomes well—approved in front of you.
27   All are delivered to me by my Father:
and neither knows anyone the Son,
except the Father;
nor knows anyone the Father, except the Son
— and he to whomever the Son wills to unveil him.

The Invitation Of Yah Shua To Rest

28   Come to me
all you belabored and overburdened
and I rest you:
29   take my yoke upon you and learn of me;
for I am meek and humble in heart:
and find rest to your souls:
30   for my yoke is kind and my burden light.

Yah Shua, Adonay Of The Shabbath

12   At that season, on the shabbath,
Yah Shua goes through the spores;
and his disciples famish
and begin to pluck the cobs and eat.
2   And the Pharisees see, and say to him,
Behold, your disciples do
what is not allowed to do in shabbath.
3   And he says to them,
Read you not what David did
when he famished — he and those with him;
4   how he entered the house of Elohim
and ate the prothesis bread
— which neither he is allowed to eat
nor them with him
— except only the priests?
5   Or read you not in the torah,
how that in the shabbaths
the priests in the priestal precinct
profane the shabbath and are unaccused?
6   But I word to you,
That a greater than the priestal precinct is here.
7   But if you had known what this is,
I will mercy, and not sacrifice,
ye *would* **should** not
have *condemned* **adjudged** the *guiltless* **unaccused**.
8   For the Son of *man* **humanity** is *Lord* **Adonay**
even of the *sabbath day* **shabbath**. Hoshea 6:6

Yah Shua Heals On The Shabbath

9   And when he was departed thence,
he went into their synagogue:
10   And, behold,
there was a *man* **human** which had his hand withered.
And they asked him, *saying* **wording**,
Is it *lawful* **allowed**
to *heal* **cure** on the *sabbath days* **shabbaths**?
that they might accuse him.
11   And he said unto them,
What *man* **human** shall there be *among* **of** you,
that shall have one sheep,
and *if* **whenever** it fall into a *pit* **cistern**
on the *sabbath day* **shabbaths**,
will **shall** he not *lay hold on* **indeed, overpower** it,
and lift it out?
12   *So* How much *then*
is *a man better than* **a human surpasseth** a sheep?
Wherefore **So** it is *lawful* **allowable** to do well
on the *sabbath days* **shabbaths**.
13   Then *saith* **wordeth** he to the *man* **human**,
Stretch forth **Spread** thine hand.
And he *stretched* **spreads** it *forth*;
and it was restored whole, like as the other.
14   *Then* **And** the Pharisees went out,
and *held a* **took** council against him,
how they might destroy him.

Yah Shua Cures The Multitudes

15   But when *Jesus* **Yah Shua** knew it,
he withdrew himself from thence:
and *great* **vast** multitudes followed him,
and he *healed* **cured** them all;
16   And *charged* **admonished** them
that they should not make him *known* **manifest**:
17   That it might be fulfilled/shalamed
which was *spoken* **rhetorized**
by Esaias **through Yesha Yah** the
prophet, *saying* **wording**,
18   Behold my *servant* **lad**, whom I have chosen;
my beloved,
in **of** whom my soul *is well pleased* **well—approveth**:
I *will* **shall** put my spirit upon him,
and he shall shew judgment to the *Gentiles* **goyim**.
19   He shall not strive, nor cry;
neither shall any *man* **one** hear his voice

	in the *streets* **broadways**.
20	A *bruised* **crushed** reed shall he not break,
	and smoking *flax* **linen** shall he not quench,
	till he send forth judgment unto *victory* **triumph**.
21	And in his name shall the
	Gentiles trust **goyim hope**.
	Yesha Yah 42:1—4
22	Then was *brought* **offered** unto him
	one *possessed with a devil* **demonized**,
	blind, and *dumb* **mute**:
	and he *healed* **cured** him,
	insomuch that
	the blind and *dumb* **mute** both spake and *saw* **observed**.
23	And all the *people* **multitude**
	were *amazed* **astounded**,
	and *said* **worded**, Is not this the son of David?

Pharisees Blaspheme The Holy Spirit

24	But when the Pharisees heard it, they said,
	This *fellow* doth not *cast out devils* **eject demons**,
	but by Beelzebub **except in Baal Zebub**
	the *prince* **arch** of the *devils* **demons**.
25	And *Jesus* **Yah Shua** knew
	their *thoughts* **deliberations**,
	and said unto them,
	Every *kingdom* **sovereigndom** divided against itself
	is brought to desolation **shall desolate**;
	and every city or house divided against itself
	shall not stand:
26	And if Satan *cast out* **eject** Satan,
	he *is divided* **divideth** against himself;
	so how shall *then* his *kingdom* **sovereigndom** stand?
27	And if I *by Beelzebub* **in Baal Zebub**
	cast out devils **eject demons**,
	you had not adjudged the unaccused.
8	For the Son of humanity is Adonay
	even of the shabbath.
	Hoshea 6:6

Yah Shua Heals On The Shabbath

9	And he departs from there
	and enters their synagogue:
10	and behold, a human whose hand is withered.
	And they ask him, wording,
	Is it allowed to cure in the shabbaths?
	— to accuse him.
11	And he says to them,
	What human of you, having one sheep,
	and whenever it falls into a cistern in the shabbaths
	overpowers he not indeed it and lifts it out?

12	So how much a human surpasses a sheep?
	So it is allowed to do well in the shabbaths.
13	Then he words to the human, Spread your hand.
	— and he spreads; and it restores whole, as the other.
14	And the Pharisees go,
	and take council against him on how to destroy him.

Yah Shua Cures The Multitudes

15	And Yah Shua knows
	and withdraws himself from there:
	and vast multitudes follow him and he cures them all:
16	and admonishes them to
	not make him manifest:
17	to fulfill/shalam that
	rhetorized through Yesha Yah the prophet, wording,
18	Behold my lad, whom I chose;
	my beloved of whom my soul well—approves:
	I put my spirit on him
	and he shows judgment to the goyim:
19	he neither strives, nor cries;
	nor anyone hear his voice in the broadways:
20	he neither breaks a crushed reed
	nor quenches a smoking linen
	until he sends judgment to triumph:
21	and in his name, the goyim hope.
	Yesha Yah 42:1—4
22	Then they offer him
	someone demonized, blind and mute;
	and he cures him
	so that the blind and mute both speaks and observes.
23	And all the multitude is astounded,
	and word, Is not this the son of David?

Pharisees Blaspheme The Holy Spirit

24	But the Pharisees hear, and say,
	This *one* ejects not demons,
	except in Baal Zebub the arch of demons.
25	And Yah Shua knows their deliberations,
	and says to them,
	Every sovereigndom divided against itself
	desolates;
	and every city or house divided against itself
	stands not:
26	and if Satan ejects Satan,
	he divides against himself:
	so how stands his sovereigndom?
27	And if I eject demons in Baal Zebub,
	by **in** whom do your *children cast* **sons eject** *them* **out**?
	Therefore **So** they shall be your judges.
28	But if I *cast out devils* **eject demons**

MATTHEW/MATIT'YAH - HA'LEVI 12

by **in** the Spirit of *God* **Elohim**,
then the *kingdom* **sovereigndom** of *God* **Elohim**
is come unto **has arrived upon** you.

29 how can *any* **one** enter
into a strong man's house,
and *spoil* **plunder** his *goods* **vessels**,
except **unless** he first bind the strong man?
and then he *will spoil* **shall plunder** his house.

30 He that is not with me is against me;
and he that gathereth not with me scattereth *abroad*.

THE UNFORGIVEN SIN

31 *Wherefore* **Because of this** I *say* **word** unto you,
All manner of **Every** sin and blasphemy
shall be forgiven unto *men* **humanity**:
but the blasphemy *against* **of** the
Holy Spirit **Ruach ha-kodesh**
shall not be forgiven unto *men* **humanity**.

32 And whosoever *speaketh* **sayeth** a word
against the Son of *man* **humanity**,
it shall be forgiven him:
but whosoever *speaketh* **sayeth** against
the *Holy Spirit* **Ruach ha-kodesh**,
it shall not be forgiven him,
neither in this *world* **eon**,
neither in the *world to come* **about to be**.

33 Either make the tree good, and his fruit good;
or else make the tree *corrupt* **putrefied**,
and his fruit *corrupt* **putrefied**:
for the tree is known by his fruit.

YAH SHUA DENOUNCES THE SCRIBES AND PHARISEES

34 O *generation* **progeny** of vipers,
how can ye, being evil, speak good *things*?
for out of the **super** abundance of the heart
the mouth speaketh.

35 A good *man* **human**
out of the good treasure of the heart
bringeth forth good things **ejecteth good**:
and an evil *man* **human** out of the evil treasure
bringeth forth evil things **ejecteth evil**.

36 But I *say* **word** unto you,
That every idle *word* **rhema**
that men **whatever humanity** shall speak,
they shall *give account* **render word**
thereof **concerning it**
in the day of judgment.

37 For by thy words thou shalt be justified,
and by thy words thou shalt be *condemned* **adjudged**.

YAH SHUA PROPHESIES HIS DEATH AND RESURRECTION

38 Then *certain* **some** of the
scribes and of the Pharisees
answered, *saying* **wording**, *Master* **Doctor**,
we *would* **will to** see a sign from thee.

39 But he answered and said unto them,
An evil and adulterous generation seeketh after a sign;
and there shall no sign be given to it,
but **except** the sign of the prophet *Jonas* **Yonah**:

40 For **exactly** as *Jonas* **Yonah**
was three days and three nights
in the *whale's* **monster's** belly;
so **thus** shall the Son of *man* **humanity**
be three days and three nights in the heart of the earth.

YAH SHUA PROPHESIES CONDEMNATION

41 *The men of Nineveh* **Men — Nineviy**
shall rise in judgment with this generation,
and shall condemn it:
because they repented
at **in** the preaching of *Jonas* **Yonah**; and, behold,
a greater **much more** than *Jonas* **Yonah** is here.

42 The *queen* **sovereigness** of the south
shall rise *up* in the judgment with this generation,
and shall condemn it:
for she came
from the *uttermost parts* **extremities** of the earth
to hear the wisdom of *Solomon* **Shelomoh**; and, behold,
a greater **much more** than *Solomon* **Shelomoh** is here.

IMPURE SPIRITS

43 When **ever** the *unclean* **impure** spirit
is gone out of a *man* **human**,
he *walketh* **passeth** through *dry* **waterless** places,
seeking rest, and findeth none.

in whom do your sons eject?
So they become your judges.

28 But if I eject demons in the Spirit of Elohim,
then the sovereigndom of Elohim arrives upon you.

29 How can any enter the house of a strong man,
and plunder his vessels,
unless he first bind the strong man?
— and then he plunders his house.

30 Whoever is not with me, is against me;
and whoever gathers not with me scatters.

THE UNFORGIVEN SIN

31 Because of this I word to you,

Every sin and blasphemy is forgiven humanity:
but the blasphemy of the Holy Spirit
is not forgiven humanity:
32 and whoever says a word
against the Son of humanity,
is forgiven:
but whoever says against the Holy Spirit,
is not forgiven
— neither in this eon nor in the about to be.
33 Either make the tree good and his fruit good;
or else make the tree putrefied and his fruit putrefied:
— for the tree is known by its fruit.

Yah Shua Denounces
The Scribes And Pharisees

34 O progeny of vipers,
how can you, being evil, speak good?
For the mouth speaks
from the super abundance of the heart:
35 a good human from the
good treasure of the heart
ejects good:
and an evil human from the evil treasure
ejects evil.
36 But I word to you,
That every idle rhema — whatever humanity speaks,
renders word concerning it in the day of judgment:
37 for by your words you are justified;
and by your words you are adjudged.

Yah Shua Prophesies
His Death And Resurrection

38 Then some of the scribes and Pharisees answer,
wording, Doctor, we will to see a sign from you.
39 But he answers them, saying,
An evil and adulterous generation seeks after a sign;
and no sign is given
except the sign of the prophet Yonah:
40 for exactly as Yonah
was three days and three nights in
the belly of the monster;
thus is the Son of humanity
three days and three nights in the heart of the earth.

Yah Shua Prophesies Condemnation

41 Men — Nineviy
rise in judgment with this generation
and condemn it:
because they repented in the preaching of Yonah;
and behold, much more than Yonah is here.

42 The sovereigness of the south
rises in the judgment with this generation,
and condemns it:
for she came from the extremities of the earth
to hear the wisdom of Shelomoh;
and behold, much more than Shelomoh is here.

Impure Spirits

43 Whenever the impure
spirit comes from a human
he passes through waterless places,
seeks rest, and finds none.
44 Then he *saith* **wordeth**,
I *will* **shall** return into my house
from whence I came *out*;
and when he is come,
he findeth it empty, swept, and *garnished* **adorned**.
45 Then goeth he,
and taketh with himself seven other spirits
more *wicked* **evil** than himself,
and they enter *in* and *dwell* **settle** there:
and the *last* **final** state of that *man* **human**
is **becometh** worse than the first.
Even *so* **thus**
shall it be also unto this *wicked* **evil** generation.

Relationship With Yah Shua

46 While he yet *talked* **spoke**
to the *people* **multitudes**,
behold, his mother and his brethren stood
without, *desiring* **seeking** to speak with him.
47 *Then* **And some** one said unto him, Behold,
thy mother and thy brethren stand without,
desiring **seeking** to speak with thee.
48 But he answered and said
unto him that told him,
Who is my mother? and who are my brethren?
49 And he *stretched forth* **spread** his hand
toward his disciples, and said, Behold
my mother and my brethren!
50 For whosoever shall do the will of my Father
which is in *heaven* **the heavens**,
the same is my brother, and sister, and mother.

The Parables Of The Sovereigndom

13 The same day went *Jesus*
Yah Shua out of the house,
and sat by the sea side.
2 And *great* **vast** multitudes
were gathered together unto him,

MATTHEW/MATIT'YAH - HA'LEVI 12, 13

so that he *went* **embarked** into a *ship* **sailer**, and sat;
and the whole multitude stood on the shore.

THE PARABLE OF THE SPORER

3 And he spake *many things* **much** unto them in parables,
saying **wording**,
Behold, a *sower* **sporer** went forth to *sow* **spore**;
4 And *when he sowed* **in his sporing**,
some *seeds* **indeed** fell by the way side,
and the *fowls* **flyers** came and devoured them *up*:
5 *Some* **Others** fell upon *stony places* **rocky**,
where they had not much *earth* **soil**:
and *forthwith* **straightway** they sprung *up*,
because they had no *deepness* **depth** of *earth* **soil**:
6 And when the sun *was up*
rose, they were scorched;
and because they had no root, they withered *away*.
7 And *some* **others** fell among thorns;
and the thorns *sprung up* **ascended**, and choked them:
8 But other fell into good *ground* **soil**,
and *brought forth* **gave** fruit,
some **indeed** an hundredfold,
some sixtyfold, some thirtyfold.
9 Who hath ears to hear, let him hear.

WHY PARABLES?

10 And the disciples came, and said unto him,
Why speakest thou unto them in parables?
11 He answered and said unto them,
Because it is given unto you to know the mysteries
of the *kingdom* **sovereigndom** of *heaven* **the heavens**,
but to them it is not given.
12 For whosoever hath, to him shall be given,
and he shall *have more abundance*
superabound: but whosoever hath not,
from him shall be taken away even that he hath.
13 *Therefore* **So** speak I to them in parables:
because **in observing**, they *seeing see* **observe**
not; and hearing they hear not,
neither do they *understand* **comprehend**.
14 And in them
is fulfilled/**shalamed** the prophecy of *Esaias* **Yesha Yah**,
which *saith* **wordeth**,
By hearing ye shall hear,
and shall *not understand* **never no way comprehend**;
and *seeing* **observing**, ye shall *see* **observe**,
and shall *not* **never no way** perceive:
15 For this people's heart is *waxed gross* **calloused**,
and their ears are dull of hearing,

44 Then he words, I return to
my house whence I come.
— and when he comes
he finds it empty, swept and adorned.
45 Then he goes and takes
seven other spirits with him
— more evil than himself;
and they enter and settle there:
and the final state of that human
becomes worse than the first.
Even so be it also to this evil generation.

RELATIONSHIP WITH YAH SHUA

46 And he still speaks to the multitudes;
and behold, his mother and his brothers stand outside
seeking to speak with him:
47 and someone says to him, Behold,
your mother and your brothers stand
outside, seeking to speak with you.
48 But he answers, saying to him who told him,
Who is my mother? And who are my brothers?
49 — and he spreads his hand toward his disciples
and says, Behold my mother and my brothers!
50 For whoever does the will
of my Father in the heavens,
the same is my brother and sister and mother.

THE PARABLES OF THE SOVEREIGNDOM

13 And in that day Yah Shua comes from the house
and sits by the sea side:
2 and vast multitudes gather together to him;
and so he embarks in a sailer, and sits;
and the whole multitude stands on the shore.

THE PARABLE OF THE SPORER

3 And he speaks much to them in parables,
wording, Behold, a sporer comes to spore:
4 and in his sporing,
some indeed falls by the way side;
and the flyers come and devour them.
5 Others fall on rocky, where
they have not much soil;
and straightway they spring up
because they have no depth of soil:
6 and the sun rises and they scorch;
and because they have no root, they wither.
7 And others fall among thorns;
and the thorns ascend and choke them.
8 And others fall on good soil and give fruit:
some indeed a hundredfold;
some sixtyfold; some thirtyfold.

9 Whoever has ears to hear, Hear.

Why Parables?

10 And the disciples come and say to him,
Why speak you to them in parables?
11 He answers them, saying,
Because you are given to know the mysteries
of the sovereigndom of the heavens;
but they are not given:
12 for whoever has, is given; and superabounds:
but whoever has not,
even what he has is taken away.
13 So I speak to them in parables:
because in observing, they observe not;
and hearing, they hear not;
and they comprehend not.
14 And in them is fulfilled/shalamed
the prophecy of Yesha Yah
— which words, By hearing you hear,
and no way comprehend;
— and by observing you observe,
and no way perceive:
15 for this people callous their heart
and dull their ears from hearing
and their eyes they have *closed* **shut**;
lest *at any time* **ever** they should see with their eyes
and hear with their ears,
and should *understand* **comprehend** with their heart,
and should *be converted* **turn around**,
and I should heal them.
Yesha Yah 6:9,10
16 But blessed *are* your eyes, for they *see* **observe**:
and your ears, for they hear.
17 For *verily I say* **Amen! I word** unto you,
That many prophets and *righteous men* **just**
have *desired* **panted**
to *see* **observe** those *things* which ye see,
and have not seen them;
and to hear those *things* which ye hear,
and have not heard them.
18 **So** Hear ye *therefore* the
parable of the *sower* **sporer**.

The Parable Explained

19 When any one
heareth the word of the *kingdom* **sovereigndom**,
and *understandeth* **comprehendeth** it not,
then cometh the *wicked* **evil** one,
and *catcheth away* **seizeth** that
which was *sown* **spored** in his heart.
This is he
which *received seed* **was** *sown* **spored** by the way side.
20 But he that *received the seed* **spored**
into the *stony places* **rocky**,
the same is he that heareth the word,
and *anon* **straightway** with *joy receiveth* **cheer taketh** it;
21 Yet hath he not root in himself,
but *dureth for a while* **is temporary**:
for when tribulation or persecution *ariseth* **become**
because of the word,
by and by **straightway** he is *offended* **scandalized**.
22 He also that *received seed*
among **spored in** the thorns
is he that heareth the word;
and the *care* **anxiety** of this *world* **eon**,
and the deceitfulness of riches,
choke **strangle** the word, and he becometh unfruitful.
23 But he that *received seed* **spored**
into the good *ground* **soil**
is he that heareth the word,
and *understandeth it* **comprehendeth**;
which *also* **now** beareth fruit,
and *bringeth forth* **produceth**,
some **indeed** an hundredfold, some sixty, some thirty.

The Parable Of The Darnel And Sperma

24 Another parable *put* **set** he forth unto them,
saying **wording**,
The *kingdom* **sovereigndom** of *heaven* **the heavens**
is likened unto a *man* **human**
which *sowed* **spored** good *seed* **sperma** in his field:
25 But while *men* **humanity** slept,
his enemy came
and *sowed tares* **spored darnel** among the *wheat* **grain**,
and went his way.
26 But when the *blade was*
sprung up **herbage sprouted**,
and *brought forth* **produced** fruit,
then *appeared* **manifested** the *tares* **darnel** also.
27 So the servants of the
householder **housedespotes**
came and said unto him, *Sir Lord* **Adoni**,
didst not **indeed** thou *sow* **spore**
good *seed* **sperma** in thy field?
from **So** whence *then* hath it *tares* **darnel**?
28 He said unto them,
An enemy — *a* **human** hath done this.
The servants said unto him,
So Wilt thou *then* that we go and gather them *up*?
29 But he said, Nay;

MATTHEW/MATIT'YAH - HA'LEVI 13

lest while **ever** ye gather *up* the *tares* **darnel**,
ye *root up* **uproot** also the *wheat* **grain**
with them **simultaneously**.
30 *Let* **Allow** both grow together until the harvest:
and in the *time* **season** of harvest
I *will* **shall** say to the *reapers* **harvesters**,
Gather ye together first the *tares* **darnel**,
and bind them in bundles to burn them:
but gather **together** the *wheat* **grain**
into my *barn* **granary**.
and shut their eyes
— lest ever they see with their eyes
and hear with their ears
and comprehend with their heart and
turn around; and I heal them.
Yesha Yah 6:9,10
16 But blessed — your eyes; for they observe:
and your ears; for they hear.
17 For Amen! I word to you,
That many prophets and just
panted to observe what you see;
and saw them not:
and to hear what you hear;
and heard them not:
18 so hear the parable of the sporer.

THE PARABLE EXPLAINED

19 When anyone hears the
word of the sovereigndom
and comprehends not,
the evil one comes
and seizes what is spored in his heart:
this is that spored by the way side.
20 And that spored on the rocky
is whoever hears the word:
and straightway takes it with cheer;
21 yet has he no root in himself but is temporary:
for when tribulation or persecution become
because of the word,
he is straightway scandalized.
22 And that spored in the thorns
is whoever hears the word:
and the anxiety of this eon
and the deceitfulness of riches
strangle the word;
and he becomes unfruitful.
23 And that spored in the good soil
is whoever hears the word and comprehends:
and now bears fruit and produces
— some indeed a hundredfold;
some sixty; some thirty.

THE PARABLE OF THE DARNEL AND SPERMA

24 He sets them another parable, wording,
The sovereigndom of the heavens
is likened to a human
who spores good sperma in his field:
25 and while humanity sleeps
his enemy comes and spores darnel among the grain
and goes his way:
26 and when the herbage
sprouts and produces fruit,
then the darnel also manifests:
27 and the servants of the housedespotes
come and say to him, Adoni,
spored you not indeed good sperma in your field?
So why has it darnel?
28 He says to them, An enemy — a human did this.
The servants say to him,
So will you that we go and gather them?
29 And he says, No;
lest in gathering the darnel
you also uproot the grain simultaneously:
30 allow both to grow together until the harvest:
and in the season of harvest I say to the harvesters,
First gather the darnel
and bind them in bundles to burn:
and gather the grain into my granary.

THE PARABLE OF THE MUSTARD KERNEL

31 Another parable *put* **set** he *forth* unto them,
saying **wording**,
The *kingdom* **sovereigndom** of *heaven* **the heavens**
is like to a *grain* **kernal** of mustard *seed*,
which a *man* **human** took, and *sowed* **spored** in his field:
32 Which indeed is the least of all *seeds* **spermas**:
but when **ever** it is grown,
it is the greatest among herbs, and becometh a tree,
so that the *birds* **flyers** of the *air* **heavens**
come and *lodge* **nest** in the branches thereof.

THE PARABLE OF FERMENTATION

33 Another parable spake he unto them;
The *kingdom* **sovereigndom** of *heaven* **the heavens**
is like unto *leaven* **fermentation**, which a woman took,
and hid in three *measures* **seahs** of *meal* **flour**,
till the whole was *leavened* **fermented**.

THE PURPOSE OF PARABLES

34 All these *things* spake *Jesus* **Yah Shua**
unto the multitude in parables;

and *without* **apart from** a parable
spake he not unto them:
35 That it might be *fulfilled*/**shalamed**
which was *spoken by* **rhetorized through** the prophet,
saying **wording**, I *will* **shall** open my mouth in parables;
I *will* **shall** utter *things* **those**
which have been *kept secret* **secreted**
from the foundation of the *world* **cosmos**.
Psalm 78:2

The Parable Of The Darnel And Sperma Explained

36 Then *Jesus sent* **Yah Shua released** the multitude *away*,
and went into the house:
and his disciples came unto him, *saying* **wording**,
Declare unto us the parable of the
tares **darnel** of the field.
37 He answered and said unto them,
He that *soweth* **sporeth** the good *seed* **sperma**
is the Son of *man* **humanity**;
38 The field is the *world* **cosmos**;
the good *seed* **sperma**
are the *children* **sons** of the *kingdom* **sovereigndom**;
but the *tares* **darnel**
are the *children* **sons** of the *wicked one* **evil**;
39 The enemy that *sowed* **spored**
them is *the devil* **Diabolos**;
the harvest is the *end* **completion/ shalom** of the *world* **eon**;
and the *reapers* **harvesters** are the angels.
40 *So exactly* **As therefore** the
tares **darnel** are gathered
and burned in the fire;
so **thus** shall it be
in the *end* **completion/shalom** of this *world* **eon**.
41 The Son of *man* **humanity**
shall *send forth* **apostolize** his angels,
and they shall gather out of his *kingdom* **sovereigndom**
all *things* **those** that *offend* **scandalize**,
and them which *do iniquity* **violate the torah**;
42 And shall cast them into a furnace of fire:
there shall be wailing and gnashing of teeth.
43 Then shall the *righteous* **just**
shine forth **resplend** as the sun
in the *kingdom* **sovereigndom** of their Father.
Who hath ears to hear, let him hear.
Apocalypse 14:14—20

The Parable Of The Secreted Treasure

44 Again,
the *kingdom* **sovereigndom** of *heaven* **the heavens**
is like unto treasure *hid* **secreted** in a field;
the which when a *man* **human** hath found,
he *hideth* **secreteth**,
and for *joy* **cheer** thereof
goeth and selleth all *that* — **as much as** he hath,
and *buyeth* **marketeth** that field.

The Parable Of The Precious Pearl

45 Again,
the *kingdom* **sovereigndom** of *heaven* **the heavens**
is like unto a *merchant man* **human merchant**,
seeking goodly pearls:
46 Who, when he had found one pearl
of great price **vastly precious**,
went and sold all *that* — **as much as** he had,
and *bought* **marketed** it.

The Parable Of The Mustard Kernel

31 He sets them another parable, wording,
The sovereigndom of the heavens
is likened to a kernal of mustard;
which a human takes and spores in his field:
32 which indeed is the least of all spermas:
but whenever it is grown
it is the greatest among herbs;
and becomes a tree:
so that the flyers of the heavens
come and nest in the branches thereof.

The Parable Of Fermentation

33 He speaks another parable to them:
The sovereigndom of the heavens
is likened to fermentation;
that a woman takes and hides in three seahs of flour
until the whole is fermented.

The Purpose Of Parables

34 Yah Shua speaks all these to the multitude
in parables;
and speaks not to them apart from a parable:
35 to fulfill/shalam
that rhetorized through the prophet,
wording, I open my mouth in parables:
I utter those which have been secreted
from the foundation of the cosmos.
Psalm 78:2

The Parable Of The Darnel And Sperma Explained

36 Then Yah Shua releases the multitude
and goes in the house:
and his disciples come to him, wording,
Declare to us the parable of the darnel of the field.
37 He answers them, saying,
He who spores the good sperma
is the Son of humanity:
38 the field is the cosmos;
the good sperma are the sons of the sovereigndom;
and the darnel are the sons of the evil;
39 the enemy who spores them is Diabolos;
the harvest is the completion/shalom of the eon;
and the harvesters are the angels:
40 so exactly as the darnel are gathered
and burned in the fire,
so be it in the completion/shalom of this eon.
41 The Son of humanity apostolizes his angels,
and from his sovereigndom
they gather all who scandalize
and who violate the torah;
42 and cast them into a furnace of fire:
and there becomes wailing and gnashing of teeth.
43 Then the just resplend as the sun
in the sovereigndom of their Father. Whoever
has ears to hear, hear. Apocalypse 14:14—20

The Parable Of The Secreted Treasure

44 Again, the sovereigndom of the heavens
is likened to treasure secreted in a field:
which, when a human finds, he secretes;
and for cheer thereof
goes and sells all — as much as he has,
and markets that field.

The Parable Of The Precious Pearl

45 Again, the sovereigndom of the heavens
is likened to a human merchant
seeking goodly pearls:
46 who, when he finds one pearl, vastly precious,
goes and sells all — as much as he has
and markets it.

The Parable Of The Net

47 Again,
the *kingdom* **sovereigndom** of *heaven* **the heavens**
is like unto a net, that was cast into the sea,
and gathered **together** of every *kind* **genos**:
48 Which, when it was full, they drew to shore,
and sat down, and gathered the good into vessels,
but cast the *bad* **putrefied** away.

The Completion/Shalom Of The Eon

49 So shall it be
at the *end* **completion/shalom** of the *world* **eon**:
the angels shall come forth,
and *sever* **set apart** the *wicked* **evil** from among the just,
50 And shall cast them into the furnace of fire:
there shall be wailing and gnashing of teeth.
51 *Jesus saith* **Yah Shua wordeth** unto them,
Have ye *understood* **comprehended** all these *things*?
They *say* **word** unto him, Yea, *Lord* **Adonay**.

The Parable Of The Housedespotes

52 *Then* **And** said he unto them,
Therefore **So** every scribe which is *instructed* **discipled**
unto the *kingdom* **sovereigndom** of *heaven* **the heavens**
is like unto a *man that is an householder*
human housedespotes,
which *bringeth forth* **ejecteth** out of his treasure
things new and old.

Yah Shua Rejected In His Fatherland

53 And it *came to pass* **became**,
that when *Jesus* **Yah Shua**
had *finished* **completed/shalamed** these parables,
he departed thence.
54 And when he was come
into his *own country* **fatherland**,
he *taught* **doctrinated** them in their synagogue,
insomuch that they were astonished, and *said* **worded**,
Whence hath this man this wisdom,
and these *mighty works* **dynamis**?
55 Is not this the carpenter's son?
is not his mother *called Mary* **indeed worded Miryam**?
and his brethren, *James* **Yaaqovos**, and *Joses* **Yoses**,
and *Simon* **Shimon**, and *Judas* **Yah Hudah**?
56 And his sisters, are they not **indeed** all with us?
So Whence *then* hath this man all these *things*?
57 And they were *offended* **scandalized** in him.
But *Jesus* **Yah Shua** said unto them,
A prophet is not *without honour* **dishonoured**,
save **except** in his own *country* **fatherland**,
and in his own house.
58 And he did not many *mighty*
works **dynamis** there
because of their *unbelief* **trustlessness**.

Yahn The Baptizer Beheaded

14 At that *time* **season**
Herod the tetrarch heard of the fame of *Jesus* **Yah Shua**,
2 And said unto his *servants* **lads**,
This is *John* **Yahn** the *Baptist* **Baptizer**;
he is risen from the dead;
and *therefore* **because of this**
mighty works **dynamis**
do shew forth themselves **energizeth** in him.
3 For Herod had *laid hold on*
John **overpowered Yahn**,
and bound him,
and put him in *prison* **a guardhouse** for Herodias' sake,
his brother *Philip's wife* **Philippos' woman**.
4 For *John said* **Yahn worded** unto him,
It is not *lawful* **allowed** for thee to have her.
5 And when he *would* **willed**
to have *put* **slaughtered** him *to death*,
he *feared* **awed** the multitude,
because they *counted* **regarded** him as a prophet.
6 But when Herod's birthday was *kept* **brought**,
the daughter of Herodias
danced *before them* **in their midst**,
and pleased Herod.
7 Whereupon he *promised* **professed** with an oath
to give her whatsoever she *would* **should** ask.
8 And she,
being *before instructed* **previously instigated**
of **by** her mother, said,
Give me here *John Baptist's* **Yahn the Baptizer's** head
in **on** *a charger* **platter**.

The Parable Of The Net

47 Again, the sovereigndom of the heavens
is likened to a net cast into the sea:
and gathers together of every genos:
48 which, when it fills full, they draw to shore;
and sit down, and gather the good in vessels,
but cast out the putrefied.

The Completion/Shalom Of The Eon

49 So be it at the completion/shalom of the eon:
the angels come
and set the evil apart from among the just
50 and cast them into the furnace of fire:
there becomes wailing and gnashing of teeth.
51 Yah Shua words to them,
Comprehend you all these?
They word to him, Yes, Adonay.

The Parable Of The Housedespotes

52 And he says to them,
So every scribe
discipled to the sovereigndom of the heavens
is likened to a human housedespotes
who ejects new and old from his treasure.

Yah Shua Rejected In His Fatherland

53 And so be it,
when Yah Shua completes/shalams these parables
he departs from there
54 and comes to his fatherland
and doctrinates in their synagogue,
so that they are astonished, and word,
Whence has this man this wisdom
and these dynamis?
55 Is not this the son of the carpenter?
Is not his mother indeed worded Miryam?
And his brothers, Yaaqovos and Yoses
and Shimon and Yah Hudah?
56 And his sisters, are they not indeed all with us?
So whence has this man all these?
57 — and they are scandalized in him.
And Yah Shua says to them,
A prophet is not dishonored
except in his own fatherland and in his own house.
58 — and he did not many dynamis there
because of their trustlessness.

Yahn The Baptizer Beheaded

14 At that season
Herod the tetrarch hears of the fame of Yah Shua,
2 and says to his lads,
This is Yahn the Baptizer; he is risen from the dead;
and because of this, dynamis energizes in him.
3 For Herod had overpowered Yahn,
and bound him,
and put him in a guardhouse for sake of Herodias
the woman of his brother Philippos:
4 for Yahn had worded to him,
You are not allowed to have her!
5 — and he wills to slaughter him
but he awes the multitude
because they regard him as a prophet.
6 But the birthday of Herod is brought on;
and the daughter of Herodias dances among them
and pleases Herod:
7 whereupon he professes with an oath
to give her whatever she asks.

MATTHEW/MATIT'YAH - HA'LEVI 14

8 And she,
being previously instigated by her mother,
Give me here, she says,
the head of *Yahn* the Baptizer on a platter.
9 And the *king was sorry* **sovereign sorrowed**:
nevertheless for the oath's sake,
and them which *sat* **reposed** with him *at meat*,
he *commanded* **summoned** it to be given her.
10 And he sent,
and beheaded *John* **Yahn** in the *prison* **guardhouse**.
11 And his head was brought
in **on** a *charger* **platter**,
and given to the *damsel* **maiden**:
and she brought it to her mother.
12 And his disciples came,
and took *up* the body, and *buried* **entombed** it,
and went and *told Jesus* **evangelized Yah Shua**.
13 When *Jesus* **Yah Shua** heard of it,
he departed thence *by ship* **in a sailer**
into a *desert* **desolate** place *apart* **privately**:
and when the *people* **multitude** had heard thereof,
they followed him on foot out of the cities.
14 And *Jesus* **Yah Shua** went forth,
and saw a great vast multitude,
and *was moved with compassion*
had a sympathetic spleen
toward them,
and he *healed* **cured** their *sick* **infirm**.

Yah Shua Feeds Five Thousand

15 And *when it was* **being** evening,
his disciples came to him, *saying* **wording**,
This is a *desert* **desolate** place,
and the *time* **hour** is *now* **already** past;
send **release** the multitude *away*,
that they may go into the villages,
and *buy* **market** themselves *victuals* **food**.
16 But *Jesus* **Yah Shua** said unto them,
They need not depart; give ye them to eat.
17 And they *say* **word** unto him,
We have *naught* here *but* **except only** five *loaves* **breads**,
and two fishes.
18 He said, Bring them hither to me.
19 And he *commanded* **summoned** the multitude
to *sit down* **recline** on the *grass* **herbage**,
and took the five *loaves* **breads**, and the two fishes,
and looking *up* to the *heaven* **heavens**,
he *blessed* **eulogized**, and brake,
and gave the *loaves* **breads** to his disciples,
and the disciples to the multitude.

20 And they did all eat, and were filled:
and they took *up*
of the fragments that *remained* **superabounded**
twelve baskets full.
21 And they that had eaten
were about five thousand men,
beside **apart from** women and children.
22 And straightway *Jesus* **Yah Shua**
constrained **compelled** his disciples to
get **embark** into a *ship* **sailer**,
and to go before him unto the other side, while
he *sent* **released** the multitudes *away*.

Yah Shua Walks On The Sea

23 And when he had *sent*
released the multitudes *away*,
he *went up* **ascended** into a mountain
apart **privately** to pray:
and *when the* **being** evening *was come*,
he was there alone.
24 But the *ship* **sailer**
was *now* **already** in the midst of the sea,
tossed with **tortured by** waves:
for the wind was contrary.
25 And in the fourth *watch* **guard** of the night
Jesus **Yah Shua** went unto them, walking on the sea.
26 And when the disciples saw
him walking on the sea,
they were troubled, *saying* **wording**,
It is a *spirit* **phantasm**;
and they cried out for *fear* **awe**.
27 But straightway *Jesus* **Yah
Shua** spake unto them,
saying **wording**, Be of good cheer; **Courage!**
it is I **I AM**; *be not afraid* **Awe not**.

Petros Walks On The Sea

28 And *Peter* **Petros** answered him and said,
Lord **Adonay**, if it be thou,
bid **summon** me come unto thee on the water.
9 And the sovereign sorrows:
nevertheless for sake of the oath
and them who repose with him,
he summons to give it to her:
10 and he sends and beheads
Yahn in the guardhouse:
11 and they bring his head on a platter
and give it to the maiden:
and she brings it to her mother.
12 And his disciples come

and take the body and entomb it;
and go and evangelize to Yah Shua.

13 When Yah Shua hears
he departs in a sailer privately to a desolate place:
and when the multitude hears thereof
they follow him on foot from the cities:

14 and Yah Shua goes and
sees a great vast multitude
and has a sympathetic spleen toward
them; and he cures their infirm.

YAH SHUA FEEDS FIVE THOUSAND

15 And being evening;
his disciples come to him, wording,
This is a desolate place and the hour is already past;
release the multitude to go to the villages
and market themselves food.

16 And Yah Shua says to them,
They need not depart; you give them to eat.

17 And they word to him,
We have naught here
except only five breads and two fishes.

18 He says, Bring them here to me.

19 — and he summons the multitude
to recline on the herbage;
and takes the five breads and the two fishes;
and looking to the heavens,
he eulogizes and breaks
and gives the breads to his disciples
— and the disciples to the multitude.

20 And they all eat, and fill up:
and they take twelve baskets full of the
fragments that superabound:

21 and there are about five thousand men who eat
apart from women and children.

22 And straightway
Yah Shua compels his disciples to embark into a sailer
and to precede him across
while he releases the multitudes.

YAH SHUA WALKS ON THE SEA

23 And he releases the multitudes
and ascends to a mountain privately to pray:
and being evening; and he is there alone:

24 and the sailer is already midst the sea
tortured by waves — for the wind is contrary:

25 and in the fourth guard of the night
Yah Shua goes to them, walking on the sea.

26 And the disciples see him walking on the sea
and they are troubled, wording,
It is a phantasm!
— and they cry out for awe.

27 But straightway Yah Shua speaks to them,
wording, Courage! I AM; Awe not!

PETROS WALKS ON THE SEA

28 And Petros answers him, saying,
Adonay, if it is you,
summon me to come to you on the water.

29 And he said, Come.
And when *Peter* **Petros**
was come down **descended** out of the *ship* **sailer**,
he walked on the water, to go to *Jesus* **Yah Shua**.

30 But when he saw **observed** the wind
boisterous **mighty**,
he *was afraid* **awed**;
and beginning to *sink* **submerge**, he cried,
saying **wording**, *Lord* **Adonay**, save me.

31 And *immediately* **straightway**
Jesus stretched forth **Yah Shua spread** his hand,
and *caught* **took hold of** him,
and *said* **worded** unto him, O thou of little *faith* **trust**,
wherefore **why** didst thou doubt?

32 And when they *were* **had**
come **embarked** into the *ship* **sailer**,
the wind *ceased* **relaxed**.

33 *Then* **And** they that were in the *ship* **sailer**
came and worshipped him, *saying* **wording**, Of a
truth **Truly** thou art the Son of *God* **Elohim**.

34 And when they were gone over,
they came into the land of *Gennesaret* **Kinneroth**.

35 And when the men of that place
had knowledge of him,
they *sent out* **apostolized**
into all that country round about,
and *brought* **offered** unto him all that were *diseased* **ill**;

36 And besought him
that they might only touch the *hem* **edge** of his garment:
and as many as touched
were *made perfectly whole* **saved**.

MISVAH VS TRADITION

15 Then came to *Jesus* **Yah
Shua** scribes and Pharisees,
which were of *Jerusalem* **Yeru Shalem**, *saying* **wording**,

2 Why do thy disciples
transgress the tradition of the elders?
for they wash not their hands when **ever** they eat bread.

3 But he answered and said unto them,
Why do ye also

MATTHEW/MATIT'YAH - HA'LEVI 15

transgress the *commandment* **misvah** of *God* **Elohim**
by **for** your tradition?
4 For *God commanded* **Elohim misvahed**,
saying **wording**, Honour thy father and mother:
and, He that *curseth* **vilifieth** father or mother,
let him die the death.
5 But ye *say* **word**,
Whosoever shall say to his father or his mother,
It is a gift **An oblation**,
by whatsoever
thou mightest be *profited* **benefited** by me;
6 And **in no way** honour not
his father or his mother,
he shall be free.
Thus have ye *made* **invalidated**
the *commandment* **misvah** of *God* **Elohim** *of none effect*
by **for** your tradition.
Exodus 20:12, 21:17
7 Ye hypocrites,
well did *Esaias* **Yesha Yah** prophesy *of* **concerning** you,
saying **wording**,
This people
draweth nigh unto **approacheth** me with their mouth,
and honoureth me with their lips;
but their heart is far from me.
9 But in vain they do *worship* **venerate** me,
teaching **doctrinating** for doctrines
the *commandments* **misvoth** of *men*
humanity. Yesha Yah 29:13
10 And he called the multitude,
and said unto them,
Hear, and *understand* **comprehend**:
11 Not that which *goeth* **entereth** into the mouth
defileth **profaneth** a *man* **human**;
but that which *cometh* **proceedeth** out of the mouth,
this *defileth* **profaneth** a *man* **human**.
12 Then came his disciples, and said unto him,
Knowest thou that the Pharisees
were *offended* **scandalized**,
after they heard this *saying* **word**?
13 But he answered and said,
Every plant, which my heavenly Father hath not planted,
shall be *rooted up* **uprooted**.
29 And he says, Come.
And Petros descends from the sailer;
and he walks on the water to go to Yah Shua:
30 but he observes the mighty wind, and he awes;
and beginning to submerge,
he cries, wording, Adonay, save me!
31 And straightway Yah Shua spreads his hand,
and takes hold of him, and words to him,
O you of little trust! Why doubt you?
32 And they embark into the sailer
and the wind relaxes:
33 and they in the sailer come and worship him,
wording, Truly you are the Son of Elohim.
34 And they go over
and come to the land of Kinneroth:
35 and the men of that place know about him
and they apostolize all around that country;
and offer him all who are ill;
36 and beseech him
to only touch the edge of his garment:
and as many as touch are saved.

Misvah vs Tradition

15 Then the scribes and Pharisees of Yeru Shalem
come to Yah Shua, wording,
2 Why transgress your disciples
the tradition of the elders?
For they wash not their hands
whenever they eat bread.
3 And he answers them, saying,
Why transgress you also the misvah of Elohim
for your tradition?
4 For Elohim misvahed, wording,
Honor your father and mother:
and, Whoever vilifies father or mother,
deathify him to death.
5 But you word,
Whoever says to his father or his mother,
An oblation — by whatever you benefit by me;
6 and in no way honors his father or his mother.
— thus you invalidate the misvah of Elohim
for your tradition.
Exodus 20:12, 21:17
7 You hypocrites,
Yesha Yah prophesied well concerning you, wording,
8 This people approaches me with their mouth
and honors me with their lips;
but their heart is far from me:
9 and in vain they venerate me,
doctrinating for doctrines the misvoth of humanity.
Yesha Yah 29:13
10 And he calls the multitude, and says to them,
Hear, and comprehend:
11 not what enters the mouth
profanes a human;
but what proceeds from the mouth
profanes a human.

12	Then his disciples come and say to him, Know you that the Pharisees are scandalized after they hear this word?
13	And he answers, saying, Every plant my Father of the heavenlies has not planted, uproots.
14	Let **Allow** them *alone*: they be blind *leaders* **guides** of the blind. And *if* **whenever** the blind *lead* **guide** the blind, both shall fall into the *ditch* **cistern**.
15	*Then* **So** answered *Peter* **Petros** and said unto him, Declare unto us this parable.

ENTERING THE MOUTH VS PROCEEDING FROM THE MOUTH

16	And *Jesus* **Yah Shua** said, Are ye also yet *without understanding* **noncomprehending**?
17	Do not ye yet *understand* **comprehend**, that *whatsoever* **all that** entereth *in* at the mouth *goeth* **passeth** into the belly, and is *cast out* **ejected** into the *draught* **privy**?
18	But those *things* which proceed out of the mouth come *forth* from the heart; and they *defile* **profane** the *man* **human**.

FROM THE HEART VS FROM THE MOUTH

19	For out of the heart proceed evil *thoughts* **reasonings**, murders, adulteries, *fornications* **whoredoms**, thefts, *false* **pseudo** witness, blasphemies:
20	These are *the things* **those** which *defile* **profane** a *man* **human**: but to eat with unwashen hands *defileth* **profaneth** not a *man* **human**.

YAH SHUA EJECTS A DEMON

21	*Then Jesus* **So Yah Shua** went thence, and departed into the *coasts* **parts** of *Tyre* **Sor** and Sidon.
22	And, behold, a woman *of Canaan* — **a Kenaaniy** came out of the same *coasts* **boundaries**, and cried unto him, *saying* **wording**, *Have mercy on* **Mercy** me, O *Lord* **Adonay**, thou son of David; my daughter *is grievously vexed with a devil* **evilly demonized**.
23	But he answered her not a word. And his disciples came and *besought* **asked** him, *saying* **wording**, *Send her away* **Release her**; for she crieth after us.
24	But he answered and said, I am not *sent* **apostolized** *but* **except only** unto the lost sheep of the house of *Israel* **Yisra El**.
25	*Then* came she and worshipped him, *saying* **wording**, *Lord* **Adonay**, help me.
26	But he answered and said, It is not *meet* **good** to take the children's bread, and to cast it to *dogs* **puppies**.
27	And she said, *Truth* **Yea**, *Lord* **Adonay**: yet **indeed** the *dogs* **puppies** eat of the crumbs which fall from their *masters'* **adoni's** table.
28	Then *Jesus* **Yah Shua** answered and said unto her, O woman, *great* **mega** is thy *faith* **trust**: be it unto thee even as thou *wilt* **willest**. And her daughter was made whole from that very hour.

YAH SHUA CURES THE MULTITUDES

29	And *Jesus* **Yah Shua** departed from thence, and came nigh unto the sea of *Galilee* **Galiyl**; and *went up* **ascended** into a mountain, and sat down there.
30	And *great* **vast** multitudes came unto him, having with them those that were lame, blind, *dumb* **mute**, maimed, and many others, and *cast* **tossed** them *down* at *Jesus'* **Yah Shua's** feet; and he *healed* **cured** them:
31	Insomuch that the multitude *wondered* **marvelled**, when they *saw* **observed** the *dumb* **mute** to speak, the maimed to be whole, the lame to walk, and the blind to *see* **observe**: and they glorified the *God* **Elohim** of *Israel* **Yisra El**.

YAH SHUA FEEDS FOUR THOUSAND

32	*Then Jesus* **So Yah Shua** called his disciples unto him, and said, I have *compassion* **a sympathetic spleen** on the multitude, because they *continue* **already abide** with me *now* three days, and have *nothing* **naught** to eat: and I will **to** not *send* **release** them *away* fasting, lest **ever** they faint in the way.
14	Allow them: they are blind guides of the blind:

and whenever the blind guide the blind
both fall into the cistern.
15 So Petros answers him, saying,
Declare this parable to us.

ENTERING THE MOUTH VS PROCEEDING FROM THE MOUTH

16 And Yah Shua says,
Are you also yet noncomprehending?
17 Comprehend you not yet
that all that enters the mouth
passes into the belly and ejects into the privy?
18 But whatever proceeds from the mouth
comes from the heart and profanes the human.

FROM THE HEART VS FROM THE MOUTH

19 For from the heart proceed evil reasonings,
murders, adulteries, whoredoms, thefts,
pseudo witnesses, blasphemies:
20 these are those that profane a human:
but to eat with unwashed hands
profanes not a human.

YAH SHUA EJECTS A DEMON

21 And Yah Shua goes there
and departs to the parts of Sor and Sidon:
22 and behold, a woman — a Kenaaniy
comes from the same boundaries,
and cries to him, wording,
Mercy me, O Adonay, you son of David;
my daughter is evilly demonized.
23 But he answers her not a word:
and his disciples come and ask him,
wording, Release her; for she cries after us.
24 But he answers, saying, I am not apostolized
except only to the lost sheep of the house of Yisra El.
25 She comes and worships him,
wording, Adonay, help me.
26 But he answers, saying,
It is not good to take the bread of children
and to cast it to puppies.
27 And she says, Yes, Adonay:
yet indeed the puppies eat of the crumbs
that fall from the table of their adoni.
28 Then Yah Shua answers her, saying,
O woman, how mega your trust:
so be it to you even as you will.
— and her daughter is whole from that very hour.

YAH SHUA CURES THE MULTITUDES

29 And Yah Shua departs from there and comes near
the sea of Galiyl; and ascends a mountain and sits:
30 and vast multitudes come to him;
having the lame, blind, mute, maimed
and many others with them,
and they toss them at the feet of Yah Shua;
and he cures them:
31 so that the multitude marvels
— observing mute speaking,
maimed whole, lame walking,
and the blind observing:
and they glorify the Elohim of Yisra El.

YAH SHUA FEEDS FOUR THOUSAND

32 And Yah Shua calls his
disciples to him, and says,
I have a sympathetic spleen on the multitude;
because they already abide with me three days
and have naught to eat:
and I will to not release them fasting
— lest ever they faint in the way.
33 And his disciples *say* **word** unto him,
Whence should we have so much bread
in the wilderness,
as to fill so *great* **vast** a multitude?
34 And *Jesus saith* **Yah Shua wordeth** unto them,
How many *loaves* **breads** have ye?
And they said, Seven, and a few *little fishes* **fishling**.
35 And he *commanded* **summoned** the multitude
to *sit down* **repose** on the *ground* **soil**.
36 And he took the seven
loaves **breads** and the fishes,
and *gave thanks* **eucharistized**,
and brake them, and gave to his disciples,
and the dsciples to the multitude.
37 And they did all eat, and were filled:
and they took *up* of the *broken meat* **fragments**
that *was left* **superabounded** seven baskets full.
38 And they that did eat were four thousand men,
beside **apart from** women and children.
39 And he *sent away* **released** the multitude,
and *took ship* **embarked into a sailer**,
and came into the *coasts* **boundaries** of Magdala.

Yah Shua Rebukes The Pharisees And The Sadoqiym

16 The Pharisees *also* with the *Sadducees* **Sadoqiym** came, and *tempting* **testing, desired** **asked** him that he *would* **should** shew them a sign from **the** heaven.
2 He answered and said unto them, When it is **Being** evening, ye *say* **word**, It will *be* fair weather: for the *sky* **heaven** is *red* **fiery**.
3 And in the early morning, It will be foul weather **Downpour** to day: for the *sky* **heaven** is *red* **fiery** and *lowring* **gloomy**. O ye hypocrites, ye can **indeed know** **to** discern the face of the *sky* **heaven**; but can ye not discern the signs of the *times* **seasons**?
4 *A wicked* **An evil** and adulterous generation seeketh *after* a sign; and there shall no sign be given unto it, *but* **except** the sign of the prophet *Jonas* **Yonah**. And he left them, and departed.

Yah Shua Interprets The Parable Of Fermentation

5 And when his disciples were come to the other side, they had forgotten to take bread.
6 *Then Jesus* **And Yah Shua** said unto them, *Take heed* **See** and *beware of* **heed** the *leaven* **fermentation** of the Pharisees and of the *Sadducees* **Sadoqiym**.
7 And they reasoned among themselves, *saying* **wording**, *It is* because we have taken no bread.
8 *Which when Jesus perceived* **And Yah Shua, knowing,** he said unto them, O ye of little *faith* **trust**, why reason ye among yourselves, because ye have *brought* **taken** no bread?
9 Do ye not yet *understand* **comprehend**, neither remember the five *loaves* **breads** of the five thousand, and how many baskets ye took *up*?
10 Neither the seven *loaves* **breads** of the four thousand, and how many baskets ye took *up*?
11 How is it that ye do not *understand* **comprehend** that I *spake* **said** it not to you concerning bread, that ye should *beware of* **heed** the *leaven* **fermentation** of the Pharisees and of the *Sadducees* **Sadoqiym**?
12 Then *understood* **comprehended** they how that he *bade* **said to** them not *beware of* **heed** the *leaven* **fermentation** of bread, but of the doctrine of the Pharisees and of the *Sadducees* **Sadoqiym**.

Opinions Concerning Yah Shua

13 When *Jesus* **Yah Shua** came into the *coasts* **parts** of *Caesarea Philippi* **Kaisaria Philippos**, he asked his disciples, *saying* **wording**, Whom do *men say* **humanity word** that I the Son of *man* **humanity** am?
33 And his disciples word to him, Whence we have so much bread in the wilderness to fill so vast a multitude?
34 And Yah Shua words to them, How many breads have you? And they say, Seven, and a few fishling.
35 And he summons the multitude to repose on the soil:
36 and he takes the seven breads and the fishes, and eucharistizes and breaks and gives to his disciples; and his disciples to the multitude.
37 and they all eat, and fill: and they take seven baskets full of the fragments that superabound:
38 and four thousand men eat apart from women and children.
39 And he releases the multitude and embarks in a sailer and goes to the boundaries of Magdala.

Yah Shua Rebukes The Pharisees And The Sadoqiym

16 And the Pharisees and Sadoqiym come testing; and ask him to show them a sign from the heavens.
2 He answers them, saying, And being evening, you word, Fair weather! — for the heavens are fiery:
3 and in the early morning, Downpour today! — for the heavens are fiery and gloomy. Hypocrites! You indeed know to discern the face of the heavens; but the signs of the seasons you cannot.
4 An evil and adulterous generation seeks a sign; and no sign is given except the sign of the prophet Yonah.

MATTHEW/MATIT'YAH - HA'LEVI 16

— and he leaves them, and departs.

YAH SHUA INTERPRETS THE PARABLE OF FERMENTATION

5 And his disciples go across; and they forget to take bread:

6 and Yah Shua says to them, See and heed the fermentation of the Pharisees and of the Sadoqiym.

7 And they reason among themselves, wording, Because we took no bread.

8 And Yah Shua, knowing, says to them, O you of little trust! Why reason you among yourselves, because you took no bread?

9 Comprehend you not yet? Neither remember the five breads of the five thousand — and how many baskets you took?

10 nor the seven breads of the four thousand — and how many baskets you took?

11 How is it that you comprehend not that I say not to you concerning bread — but to heed the fermentation of the Pharisees and of the Sadoqiym?

12 Then they comprehend that he says not to them to heed the fermentation of bread, but of the doctrine of the Pharisees and of the Sadoqiym.

OPINIONS CONCERNING YAH SHUA

13 And Yah Shua enters the parts of Kaisaria Philippos; and asks his disciples, wording, Whom words humanity me the Son of humanity to be?

14 And they said, Some **indeed**, *say that thou art John* **Yahn** the *Baptist* **Baptizer**: *some Elias* **others, Eli Yah**; and others, *Jeremias* **Yirme Yah**, or one of the prophets.

THE WITNESS OF PETROS CONCERNING YAH SHUA

15 He *saith* **wordeth** unto them, But whom *say* **word** ye that I am?

16 And *Simon Peter* **Shimon Petros** answered and said, Thou art the *Christ* **Messiah**, the Son of the living *God* **Elohim**.

17 And *Jesus* **Yah Shua** answered and said unto him, Blessed *art* thou, *Simon Barjona* **Shimon Bar Yonah**: for flesh and blood hath not *revealed* **unveiled** it unto thee, but my Father which is in *heaven* **the heavens**.

18 And I *say* **word** also unto thee, That thou art *Peter* **Petros/Rock**, and upon this rock/petra I *will* **shall** build my *church* **ecclesia**; and the gates of *hell* **sheol/hades** shall not *prevail against* **overpower** it.

19 And I *will* **shall** give unto thee the keys of the *kingdom* **sovereigndom** of *heaven* **the heavens**: and whatsoever thou shalt bind on earth shall be bound in *heaven* **the heavens**: and whatsoever thou shalt *loose* **release** on earth shall be *loosed* **released** in *heaven* **the heavens**.

20 Then charged he his disciples that they should *tell* **say to** no *man* **one** that he was *Jesus* **Yah Shua** the *Christ* **Messiah**.

YAH SHUA PROPHESIES HIS DEATH AND RESURRECTION

21 From *that time forth* **then** began *Jesus* **Yah Shua** to shew unto his disciples, how that he must go unto *Jerusalem* **Yeru Shalem**, and suffer *many things* **much** of the elders and *chief* **arch** priests and scribes, and be *killed* **slaughtered**, and be raised again the third day.

22 *Then Peter* **And Petros** took him, and began to rebuke him, *saying* **wording**, *Be it far from* **Kapur/Atone** unto thee, *Lord* **Adonay**: this shall *not* **never no way** be unto thee.

23 But he turned, and said unto *Peter* **Petros**, *Get* **Go** thee behind me, Satan: thou art *an offence* **a scandal** unto me: for thou *savourest* **mindest** not *the things* **those** that be of *God* **Elohim**, but those that be of *men* **humanity**.

24 Then said *Jesus* **Yah Shua** unto his disciples, If any *man will* **willeth to** come after me, let him *utterly* deny himself, and take *up* his *cross* **stake**, and follow me.

LOSE THE SOUL TO FIND THE SOUL

25 For whosoever *will* **willeth to** save his *life* **soul** shall lose it:

and whosoever *will* **shall** lose his *life* **soul** for my sake shall find it.

26 For what is a *man profited* **human benefited**,
if **whenever** he shall gain the whole *world* **cosmos**,
and lose his own soul?
or what shall a *man* **human** give
in exchange for his soul?

27 For the Son of *man* **humanity** shall come
in the glory of his Father with his angels;
and then he shall *reward every man* **give each**
according to his *works* **acts**.

28 *Verily I say* **Amen! I word** unto you,
There be some standing here,
which shall *not* **never no way** taste of death,
till they see the Son of *man* **humanity**
coming in his *kingdom* **sovereigndom**.

THE METAMORPHOSIS OF YAH SHUA

17 And after six days *Jesus* **Yah Shua** taketh *Peter* **Petros**,
James **Yaaqovos**, and *John* **Yahn** his brother,
and bringeth them *up* into an high mountain
apart **privately**,

2 And was *transfigured* **metamorphosed**
before **in front of** them:
and his face *did shine* **radiated** as the sun,

14 And they say,
Some indeed, Yahn the Baptizer:
others, Eli Yah:
and others, Yirme Yah:
or, One of the prophets.

THE WITNESS OF PETROS CONCERNING YAH SHUA

15 He words to them,
And You, whom word you me to be?

16 And Shimon Petros answers, saying,
You are the Messiah, the Son of the living Elohim.

17 And Yah Shua answers him, saying,
Blessed — you, Shimon Bar Yonah:
for flesh and blood unveiled not to you
but my Father in the heavens.

18 And I also word to you,
that you are Petros/Rock:
and on this rock/petra I build my ecclesia;
and the gates of sheol/hades overpower it not:

19 and I give you the keys
of the sovereigndom of the heavens: and
whatever you bind on earth becomes bound
in the heavens: and whatever you release on
earth becomes released in the heavens.

20 Then he charges his disciples
to say to no one that he is Yah Shua the Messiah.

YAH SHUA PROPHESIES HIS DEATH AND RESURRECTION

21 From then
Yah Shua begins to show his disciples
how he must go to Yeru Shalem;
and suffer much
from the elders and archpriests and scribes
— slaughtered and rise again the third day.

22 And Petros takes him and begins to rebuke him,
wording, Kapur/Atone to you, Adonay:
this never no way becomes you.

23 And he turns to Petros, saying,
Go you behind me, Satan!
You are a scandal to me:
for you mind not those of Elohim
but those of humanity.

24 Then Yah Shua says to his disciples,
If anyone wills to come after me,
he is to utterly deny himself,
and take his stake and follow me.

LOSE THE SOUL TO FIND THE SOUL

25 For whoever wills to save his soul, loses it:
and whoever loses his soul for my sake, finds it:

26 for what is a human benefited
whenever he gains the whole cosmos
and loses his own soul?
Or what gives a human in exchange for his soul?

27 For the Son of humanity comes
in the glory of his Father with his angels;
and then he gives each according to his acts.

28 Amen! I word to you,
Some standing here never no way taste death
until they see the Son of humanity
coming in his sovereigndom.

THE METAMORPHOSIS OF YAH SHUA

17 And after six days
Yah Shua takes Petros,
Yaaqovos, and Yahn his brother,
and privately brings them to a high mountain;

2 and is metamorphosed in front of them:
and his face radiates as the sun

and his *raiment was* **garment became** white as the light.

MATTHEW/MATIT'YAH - HA'LEVI 17

3 And, behold, there appeared unto them
Moses **Mosheh** and *Elias* **Eli Yah** talking with him.
4 *Then* **And** answered *Peter* **Petros**,
and said unto *Jesus* **Yah Shua**,
Lord **Adonay**, it is good for us to be here:
if thou *wilt* **willest**, let us make here three tabernacles;
one for thee,
and one for *Moses* **Mosheh**, and one for *Elias* **Eli Yah**.
5 While he yet spake, behold,
a *bright* **brightly lighted** cloud overshadowed them:
and behold a voice out of the cloud,
which *said* **wording**, This is my beloved Son,
in **of** whom I *am well pleased* **well—approve**;
hear ye him.
6 And when the disciples heard
it, they fell on their face,
and were *sore afraid* **extremely awestricken**.
7 And *Jesus* **Yah Shua** came and touched them,
and said, Arise, and be not *afraid* **awestricken**.
8 And when they had lifted *up* their eyes,
they saw no *man* **one**, save *Jesus* **except Yah Shua** only.
9 And as they *came down*
descended from the mountain,
Jesus charged **Yah Shua misvahed** them, *saying* **wording**,
Tell **Say** the vision to no *man* **one**,
until the Son of *man* **humanity** be
risen *again* from the dead.

Yahn The Baptizer Is The Eli Yah To Come

10 And his disciples asked him, *saying* **wording**,
So Why *then say* **word** the scribes
that *Elias* **Eli Yah** must first come?
11 And *Jesus* **Yah Shua** answered
and said unto them,
Elias truly **Eli Yah indeed** shall *first* come **first**,
and restore all *things*.
12 But I *say* **word** unto you,
That *Elias* **Eli Yah** is come already,
and they knew him not,
but have done *unto* **in** him
whatsoever **as much as** they *listed* **willed**.
Likewise **Thus** shall also
the Son of *man* **humanity** suffer of them.
13 Then the disciples *understood* **comprehended**
that he *spake* **said** unto them
of John **concerning Yahn** the *Baptist* **Baptizer**.

Yah Shua Rebukes A Demon

14 And when they were come to the multitude,
there came to him a *certain man* **human**,
kneeling *down* to him, and *saying* **wording**,
15 *Lord* **Adonay**, have mercy *on* my son:
for he is lunatick, and *sore vexed* **suffereth evilly**:
for *ofttimes* he falleth **often** into the fire,
and *oft* **often** into the water.
16 And I *brought* **offered** him to thy disciples,
and they could not cure him.
17 *Then Jesus* **So Yah Shua** answered and said,
O *faithless* **trustless**
and *perverse* **thoroughly perverted** generation,
how long **until when** shall I be with you?
how long **until when** shall I *suffer* **tolerate** you?
bring him hither to me.
18 And *Jesus* **Yah Shua** rebuked the *devil* **demon**;
and he departed out of him:
and the *child* **lad** was cured from that very hour.
19 Then **So** came the disciples to *Jesus* **Yah Shua**
apart **privately**, and said,
Why could not we *cast* **eject** him *out*?
20 And *Jesus* **Yah Shua** said unto them,
Because of your *unbelief* **trustlessness**:
for verily I say **Amen! I word** unto you,
if **whenever** ye have *faith* **trust**
as a *grain* **kernal** of mustard *seed*,
ye shall say unto this mountain,
Remove **Depart** hence to yonder place;
and it shall *remove* **depart**;
and *nothing* **naught** shall be impossible unto you.
21 Howbeit this *kind goeth*
genos proceedeth not *out*
but by **except in** prayer and fasting.
and his garment becomes white as the light:
3 and behold, Mosheh and
Eli Yah appear to them,
talking with him.
4 And Petros answers Yah Shua, saying,
Adonay, it is good for us to be here:
if you will, we make three tabernacles here;
one for you and one for Mosheh and one for Eli Yah.
5 While he still speaks, behold,
a brightly lighted cloud overshadows them:
and behold, a voice from the cloud, wording,
This is my beloved Son, of whom I well—approve:
Hear him!
6 — and the disciples hear
and they fall on their face
and are extremely awestricken.
7 And Yah Shua comes and touches them,
and says, Rise! and, Be not awestricken!
8 And they lift their eyes and see no one

9 And as they descend the mountain,
Yah Shua misvahs them, wording,
Say the vision to no one,
until the Son of humanity rises from the dead.

Yahn The Baptizer Is The Eli Yah To Come

10 And his disciples ask him, wording,
So why word the scribes that Eli Yah must first come?
11 And Yah Shua answers them, saying,
Eli Yah indeed comes first and restores all:
12 and I word to you,
that Eli Yah has already come:
and they know him not
but did in him as much as they willed:
Thus also the Son of humanity suffers of them.
13 Then the disciples comprehend
that he says to them concerning Yahn the Baptizer.

Yah Shua Rebukes A Demon

14 And they go to the multitude,
and a human comes to him
— kneeling to him, and wording,
15 Adonay, mercy my son:
for he is lunatick and suffers evilly:
for he falls often into the fire and often into the water:
16 and I offered him to your disciples,
and they cannot cure him.
17 So Yah Shua answers, saying,
O trustless and thoroughly perverted generation!
Until when am I with you? Until when tolerate I you?
Bring him here to me.
18 And Yah Shua rebukes the demon;
and he departs from him:
and the lad is cured from that very hour.
19 Then the disciples come to Yah Shua privately,
and say, Why could we not eject him?
20 And Yah Shua says to them,
Because of your trustlessness!
Amen! I word to you,
whenever you have trust as a kernal of mustard,
you say to this mountain,
Depart hence to yonder place!
— it departs:
— and naught is impossible to you
21 — and this genos proceeds not
except in prayer and fasting.

Yah Shua Prophesies His Death And Resurrection

22 And while they *abode* **remained** in *Galilee* **Galiyl**,
Jesus **Yah Shua** said unto them,
The Son of *man* **humanity**
shall be betrayed into the hands of *men* **humanity**:
23 And they shall *kill* **slaughter** him,
and the third day he shall *be raised again* **rise**.
And they were *exceeding sorry* **extremely sorrowed**.

The Double Drachma

24 And when they were come
to *Capernaum* **Kaphar Nachum**,
they that *received* **took**
tribute money **the double drachma**
came to *Peter* **Petros**, and said,
Doth not your *master* **doctor**
pay tribute **complete/shalam the double drachma**?
25 He *saith* **wordeth**, Yes.
And when he *was come* **had entered** into the house,
Jesus prevented **Yah Shua anticipated** him,
saying **wording**, What thinkest thou, *Simon* **Shimon**?
of whom do the *kings* **sovereigns** of the earth
take *custom* **completion/shalom** or tribute?
of their own *children* **sons**, or of *strangers* **others**?
26 *Peter saith* **Petros wordeth** unto him,
Of *strangers* **others**.
Jesus **Yah Shua** saith unto him,
Then **indeed** are the *children free* **sons liberated**.
27 *Notwithstanding* **But**,
lest we should *offend* **scandalize** them, go
thou to the sea, and cast an hook,
and take *up* the fish that first *cometh up* **ascendeth**;
and when thou hast opened his mouth,
thou shalt find a *piece of money* **stater**:
that take, and give unto them for me and thee.

The Greatest In The Sovereigndom Of The Heavens

18 At the same *time* **hour**
came the disciples unto *Jesus* **Yah Shua**, *saying* **wording**,
So Who is the greatest
in the *kingdom* **sovereigndom** of *heaven* **the heavens**?
2 And *Jesus* **Yah Shua** called
a little child unto him,
and set him in the midst of them,
3 And said, *verily I say* **Amen! I word** unto you,
Except **Unless** ye *be converted* **turn**,

and become as little children,
ye shall *not* **never no way** enter
into the *kingdom* **sovereigndom** of *heaven* **the heavens**.
4 **So** Whosoever *therefore*
shall humble himself as this little child,
the same is greatest
in the *kingdom* **sovereigndom** of *heaven* **the heavens**.
5 And whoso shall receive one
such little child in my name
receiveth me.
6 But whoso shall *offend* **scandalize**
one of these little ones which *believe* **trust** in me,
it were *better* **beneficial** for him
that a millstone **turned by a burro**
were *drowned* **submerged**
in the depth of the sea.
7 Woe unto the *world* **cosmos**
because of *offences* **scandals**!
for it *must needs* be **necessary** that
offences **scandals** come;
but **however** woe to that *man* **human**
by whom the *offence* **scandal** cometh!

Avoiding Scandalizings

8 *Wherefore* **And**
if thy hand or thy foot *offend* **scandalize** thee,
cut **exscind** them *off*, and cast them from thee:
it is *better* **well** for thee
to enter into life *halt* **lame** or maimed,
rather than having two hands or two feet
to be cast into *everlasting* **eternal** fire.
9 And if thine eye *offend* **scandalize** thee,
pluck it *out*, and cast it from thee:
it is *better* **well** for thee
to enter into life *with one eye* **one—eyed**,
rather than having two eyes to be cast
into *hell* **Gay Hinnom/the Valley of Burning** fire.

Yah Shua Prophesies
His Death And Resurrection

22 And they remain in Galiyl,
and Yah Shua says to them,
The Son of humanity
is about to be betrayed into the hands of humanity:
23 and they slaughter him;
and the third day he rises.
— and they are extremely sorrowed.

The Double Drachma

24 And they come to Kaphar Nachum:
and they who take the double drachma
come to Petros, and say,
Your doctor
— completes/shalams he not the double drachma?
25 He words, Yes.
And he enters the house;
and Yah Shua anticipates him,
wording, What think you, Shimon?
Of whom do the sovereigns of the earth
take completion/shalom or tribute?
— Of their own sons? Or of others?
26 Petros words to him, Of others.
Yah Shua says to him,
Then indeed the sons are liberated:
27 but lest we scandalize them,
go to the sea and cast a hook;
and take the first fish that ascends;
and when you open his mouth, you find a stater:
take that, and give to them for me and you.

The Greatest In The
Sovereigndom Of The Heavens

18 At the same hour
the disciples come to Yah Shua, wording,
Who then is the greatest
in the sovereigndom of the heavens?
2 And Yah Shua calls a little child to him,
and sets him midst them,
3 and says, Amen! I word to you,
Unless you turn and become as little children,
you never no way enter the sovereigndom of the heavens.
4 So whoever
humbles himself as this little child,
the same is greatest in the sovereigndom of the heavens:
5 and whoever
receives one such little child in my name,
receives me:
6 and whoever scandalizes
one of these little ones who trust in me,
it is beneficial for him
that a millstone turned by a burro
hang around his neck,
and that he submerge into the depth of the sea.
7 Woe to the cosmos because of scandals!
for of necessity, scandals come;
however woe to that human
by whom the scandal comes!

Avoiding Scandalizings

8 And if your hand or your foot scandalizes you,
exscind them and cast them from you:
it is well for you
to enter life lame or maimed,
rather than having two hands or two feet
and cast into eternal fire.

9 And if your eye scandalizes you,
pluck it and cast it from you:
it is well for you to enter life one—eyed
rather than having two eyes cast into the fire
of Gay Hinnom/the Valley of Burning.

10 *Take heed* **See** that ye *despise* **disesteem** not
one of these little ones;
for I *say* **word** unto you,
That in *heaven* **the heavens**
their angels *do always* **through all time**
behold **see** the face of my Father
which is in *heaven* **the heavens**.

11 For the Son of *man* **humanity**
is come to save that which was lost.

The Parable Of The Wandering Sheep

12 How think ye?
if man have **whenever any human**
become an hundred sheep,
and one of them *be gone astray* **wander**,
doth he not *leave* **forsake** the ninety and nine,
and goeth into the mountains,
and seeketh that which *is gone astray* **wandereth**?

13 And *if* **whenever** so be that he find it,
verily ! *say* **Amen! I word** unto you,
he *rejoiceth* **cheereth** more of that *sheep*,
than of the ninety and nine
which *went* **wandered** not *astray*.

14 Even *so* **thus** it is not the
will **in front** of your Father
which is in *heaven* **the heavens**,
that one of these little ones should *perish* **be lost**.

A Sinning Brother

15 *Moreover if* **And whenever** thy brother
shall *trespass against* **sin unto** thee,
go and *tell* **reprove** him *his fault*
between thee and him alone:
if **whenever** he shall hear thee, thou
hast gained thy brother.

16 But *if* **whenever** he *will* **shall** not hear thee,
then take with thee one or two more,
that in the mouth of two or three witnesses
every *word* **rhema** may be established.

17 And *if* **whenever** he shall
neglect **refuse** to hear them,
tell **say** it unto the *church* **ecclesia**:
but *if* **whenever** he *neglect* **refuse** to
hear the *church* **ecclesia**,
let him be unto thee *exactly* **as** *an*
heathen man **the goyim**
and a *publican* **customs agent**.

Binding And Releasing

18 *Verily !* *say* **Amen! I word** unto you,
Whatsoever ye shall bind on earth
shall be bound in **the** heaven:
and whatsoever ye shall *loose* **release** on earth
shall be *loosed* **released** in **the** heaven.

Symphonizing Trust

19 Again I *say* **word** unto you,
That *if* **whenever** two of you
shall *agree* **symphonize** on earth
as touching **concerning** any *thing* **matter**
that they shall ask,
it shall *be done* **become** for them of my Father
which is in *heaven* **the heavens**.

20 For where two or three
are gathered together in my name,
there am I in the midst of them.

The Parable On Forgiveness

21 Then came *Peter* **Petros** to him, and said,
Lord **Adonay**,
how oft shall my brother sin *against* **unto** me,
and I forgive him? till seven times?

22 *Jesus saith* **Yah Shua wordeth** unto him,
I *say* **word** not unto thee, Until seven times:
but, Until seventy times seven.

23 *Therefore* **So**
is the *kingdom* **sovereigndom** of *heaven* **the heavens**
likened unto a *certain king* **human sovereign**,
which *would* **willed**
to *take account* **reckon word** of his servants.

24 And when he had begun to reckon,
one was brought unto him,
which *owed him* **a debtor of**
ten thousand talents **a myriad talent weights**.

25 But *forasmuch* as he had not to *pay* **give**,
his *Lord commanded* **adoni summoned** him to be sold,
and his *wife* **woman**, and children,
and all *that —* **as much as** he had,

and *payment to be made* **given back**.
10 See that you not disesteem
one of these little ones;
for I word to you,
That in the heavens, through all time,
their angels see the face of my Father in the heavens.
11 For the Son of humanity comes to save the lost.

THE PARABLE OF THE WANDERING SHEEP

12 How think you?
Whenever any human becomes a hundred sheep
and one of them wanders,
forsakes he not the ninety—nine,
and goes to the mountains,
and seeks that which wanders?
13 And so be it, whenever he finds it,
Amen! I word to you,
he cheers more over it
than of the ninety—nine who wander not.
14 Even thus it is not the will
in front of your Father in the heavens,
that one of these little ones be lost.

A SINNING BROTHER

15 And whenever your brother sins to you,
go and reprove him between you and him alone:
whenever he hears you, you gain your brother:
16 but whenever he hears you not
take one or two more with you;
so that in the mouth of two or three witnesses
you establish every rhema:
17 and whenever he refuses to hear them,
say it to the ecclesia:
and whenever he refuses to hear the ecclesia,
he becomes to you
exactly as the goyim and a customs agent.

BINDING AND RELEASING

18 Amen! I word to you,
Whatever you bind on earth
becomes bound in the heavens:
whatever you release on earth
becomes released in the heavens.

SYMPHONIZING TRUST

19 Again I word to you,
That whenever two of you symphonize on earth
concerning any matter — whatever they ask
it becomes for them
from my Father in the heavens:
20 for where two or three
gather together in my name,
I am there midst them.

THE PARABLE ON FORGIVENESS

21 Then Petros comes to him, saying,
Adonay, how often sins my brother to me,
and I forgive him?
Until seven times?
22 Yah Shua words to him,
I word not to you, Until seven times:
but, Until seventy times seven.
23 So the sovereigndom of the heavens
is likened to a human sovereign,
who wills to reckon word of his servants:
24 and he begins to reckon;
they bring him a debtor of a myriad talent weights.
25 and having naught to give,
his adoni summons to sell him
and his woman and children,
and all — as much as he has
and to give back.
26 **So** The servant *therefore* fell *down*,
and worshipped him, *saying* **wording**, Lord **Adoni**,
have patience with me, and I *will pay* **shall give** thee all.
27 *Then* **And** the *lord* **adoni** of that servant
was moved with compassion **had a sympathetic spleen**,
and *loosed* **released** him, and forgave him the debt.
28 But the same servant went out,
and found one of his *fellowservants* **co—servants**,
which *owed him* **was indebted**
an hundred *pence* **denarion**:
and he *laid hands on* **overpowered** him,
and *took* **strangled** him *by the throat*, *saying* **wording**,
Pay **Give** me *that thou owest* **thy debt**.
29 And his *fellowservant* **co—servant**
fell *down at* **to** his feet,
and besought him, *saying* **wording**,
Have patience with me, and I *will pay* **shall give** thee all.
30 And he *would* **willed** not:
but went and cast him into *prison* **a guardhouse**,
till he should *pay* **give** the debt.
31 So when his *fellowservants* **co—servants** saw
what *was done* **had become**,
they were *very sorry* **extremely sorrowed**,
and came and told unto their *lord* **adoni**
all that *was done* **had become**.
32 Then his *lord* **adoni**, after
that he had called him,
said **worded** unto him, O thou *wicked* **evil** servant,

	I forgave thee all that debt,
	because thou *desiredst* **besoughtest** me:
33	Shouldest not thou also
	have *had compassion on* **mercied**
	thy *fellowservant* **co—servant**,
	even as I *had pity on* **mercied** thee?
34	And his *lord* **adoni** was wroth,
	and delivered him to the *tormentors* **torturers**,
	till he should *pay* **give**
	all that was *due* **indebted** unto him.
35	*So* **Thus** likewise
	shall my *heavenly* Father **in the heavenlies**
	do also unto you,
	if **unless** ye from your hearts
	forgive not *every one* **each** his brother
	their *trespasses* **backslidings**.

19 And *so be*it *came to pass*,
that when *Jesus* **Yah Shua**
had *finished* **completed/shalamed** these *sayings* **words**,
he departed from *Galilee* **Galiyl**,
and came into the *coasts* **boundaries**
of *Judaea* **Yah Hudah** beyond *Jordan* **Yarden**;

2 And *great* **vast** multitudes followed him;
and he *healed* **cured** them there.

Releasing A Woman

3 The Pharisees also came unto him,
tempting **testing** him, and *saying* **wording** unto him,
Is it *lawful* **allowed** for a *man* **human**
to *put away* **release** his *wife* **woman** for every cause?

4 And he answered and said unto them,
Have ye not read,
that he which *made* **created** *them* at the beginning
made **created** them male and female,

5 And said, For this cause
a *man* **human** shall leave father and mother,
and shall *cleave* **adhere** to his *wife* **woman**:
and they twain shall be one flesh?

6 *Wherefore* **So** they are no
more twain, but one flesh.
So What *therefore*
God **Elohim** hath *joined together* **co—yoked**,
let not *man put asunder* **humanity separate**.

7 They *say* **word** unto him,
So Why did *Moses* **Mosheh** then *command* **misvah**
to give a *writing* **scroll** of *divorcement* **apostasy**,
and to *put* **release** her *away*?

8 He *saith* **wordeth** unto them, *Moses* **Mosheh**,
because of *the hardness of* your *hearts*
hardheartedness, *suffered* **permitted** you

to *put away* **release** your *wives* **women**:
but from the beginning it *was* **became** not *so* **thus**.

9 And I *say* **word** unto you,
Whosoever shall *put away* **release** his *wife* **woman**,

26 So the servant falls and worships him,
wording, Adoni,
have patience with me and I give you all.

27 And the adoni of that servant
has a sympathetic spleen,
and releases him, and forgives his debt.

28 But the same servant goes
and finds one of his co—servants
who is indebted a hundred denarion:
and he overpowers him and strangles him,
wording, Give me your debt.

29 And his co—servant falls to his feet,
and beseeches him, wording,
Have patience with me and I give you all.

30 And he wills not:
but goes and casts him into a guardhouse
until he gives the debt.

31 So when his co—servants see what became,
they are extremely sorrowed,
and come and tell their adoni all that became.

32 Then his adoni, after he calls him, words to him,
O you evil servant,
I forgave you all that debt because you besought me:

33 Ought you not also mercy your co—servant
even as I mercied you?

34 — and his adoni is wroth
and delivers him to the torturers,
until he gives all he is indebted.

35 Thus likewise
my Father in the heavenlies does also to you
unless from your hearts
you each forgive your brother
his backslidings.

19 And so be it,
Yah Shua completes/shalams these words,
and departs from Galiyl
and goes to the boundaries of Yah Hudah
beyond Yarden;

2 and vast multitudes follow him;
and he cures them there.

Releasing A Woman

3 The Pharisees also come to him,
testing him and wording to him,
Is a human allowed to release his woman
for every cause?

4	And he answers them, saying, Read you not that he who created at the beginning created them male and female,		and the disciples rebuked them.
5	and said, For this cause a human leaves father and mother and adheres to his woman: and they two become one flesh?	14	But *Jesus* **Yah Shua** said, *Suffer* **Allow** little children, and forbid them not, to come unto me: for of such is the *kingdom* **sovereigndom** of *heaven* **the heavens**.
6	So they are no more two — yet one flesh. So what Elohim co—yokes, humanity is not to separate.	15	And he *laid* **put** his hands on them, and departed thence.

Eternal Life

7	They word to him, So why misvahed Mosheh to give a scroll of apostasy to release her?
8	He words to them, Because of your hard heartedness, Mosheh allowed you to release your women: but from the beginning it was not thus.
9	And I word to you, Whoever releases his woman except it be for *fornication* **whoredom**, and shall marry another, *committeth adultery* **adulterizeth**: and whoso **ever** marrieth her which is *put away* **released**, *doth commit adultery* **adulterizeth**.
10	His disciples *say* **word** unto him, If the case of the *man* **human** be *so* **thus** with his *wife* **woman**, it is not *good* **beneficial** to marry.
11	But he said unto them, All *men* cannot *receive* **accept** this *saying* **word**, *save* **rather** they to whom it is given.

16	And, behold, one came and said unto him, Good *Master* **Doctor**, what good *thing* shall I do, that I may have eternal life?
17	And he said unto him, Why *callest* **wordest** thou me good? there is none good *but* **except** one, *that is*, *God* **Elohim**: but if thou *wilt* **willest to** enter into life, keep **guard** the *commandments* **misvoth**.
18	He *saith* **wordeth** unto him, Which? *Jesus* **Yah Shua** said, Thou shalt *do no* **not** murder, Thou shalt not *commit adultery* **adulterize**, Thou shalt not steal, Thou shalt not *bear false* **pseudo** witness,
19	Honour thy father and thy mother: and, Thou shalt love thy neighbour as thyself.
20	The *young man said* **youth worded** unto him, All these *things* have I *kept* **guarded** from my youth *up*: what lack I yet?
21	*Jesus* **Yah Shua** said unto him, If thou *wilt* **willest to** be *perfect* **complete/at shalom**, go and sell that thou hast, and give to the poor, and thou shalt have treasure in the heaven: and come and follow me.
22	But when the *young man* **youth** heard that *saying* **word**, he went away sorrowful: for he had *great* **vast** possessions.

Eunuchs

12	For there are some eunuchs, *which were so born* **thus birthed** from their mother's womb: and there are some eunuchs, *which were made eunuchs* **eunuchized** of *men* **humanity**: and there be eunuchs, which have *made* **eunuchized** themselves *eunuchs* for the *kingdom* **sovereigndom** of *heaven's* **the heavens'** sake. He that is able to *receive* **accept** it, let him *receive* **accept** it.

The Rich And The Sovereigndom

23	*Then* **So** said *Jesus* **Yah Shua** unto his disciples, *Verily I say* **Amen! I word** unto you, That a rich man shall *hardly* **with difficulty** enter into the *kingdom* **sovereigndom** of *heaven* **the heavens**.
24	And again I *say* **word** unto you, It is easier for a *camel* **rope*** to *go* **pass** through the eye of a needle, than for a rich man to enter

Yah Shua Receives Little Children

13	Then were there *brought* **offered** unto him little children, that he should put his hands on them, and pray:

into the *kingdom* **sovereigndom** of
God **Elohim**. *rope: see Lamsa
25 When his disciples heard it,
they were *exceedingly amazed* **extremely astonished**,
saying **wording**, Who then can be saved?
— except for whoredom
and marries another, adulterizes:
and whoever marries her who is released, adulterizes.
10 His disciples word to him,
If the case of the human with the woman is thus,
it is not beneficial to marry.
11 But he says to them,
All cannot accept this word
— rather they to whom it is given.

Eunuchs

12 For there are eunuchs
thus birthed from the womb of their mother:
and there are eunuchs eunuchized by humanity:
and there are eunuchs eunuchized by themselves
for sake of the sovereigndom of the heavens.
Whoever is able to accept, accept.

Yah Shua Receives Little Children

13 Then they offer him little children
to put his hands on, and pray:
and the disciples rebuke them.
14 But Yah Shua says, Allow little children;
and forbid them not to come to me:
for of such is the sovereigndom of the heavens.
15 — and he puts his hands on them and departs.

Eternal Life

16 And behold, one comes to him, saying,
Good Doctor, what good do I to have eternal life?
17 And he says to him,
Why word you me, good?
None is good except one — Elohim:
but if you will to enter life, guard the misvoth.
18 He words to him, Which?
Yah Shua says,
Murder not:
Adulterize not:
Steal not:
Pseudo witness not:
19 Honor your father and your mother:
and, Love your neighbor as yourself.
20 The youth words to him,
I guarded all these from my youth:
What lack I still?

21 Yah Shua says to him,
If you will to be complete/at shalom,
go and sell what you have and give to the poor;
and have treasure in the heavens:
and come and follow me.
22 But the youth hears that word,
and goes away sorrowful:
for he has vast possessions.

The Rich And The Sovereigndom

23 So Yah Shua says to his disciples,
Amen! I word to you,
That a rich man difficultly enters
the sovereigndom of the heavens.
24 And again I word to you,
It is easier for a rope*
to pass through the eye of a needle,
than for a rich man to enter
the sovereigndom of Elohim.
*rope: see Lamsa
25 When his disciples hear,
they are extremely astonished,
wording, Who then can be saved?
26 But *Jesus beheld them* **Yah Shua looked**,
and said unto them,
With *men* **humanity** this is impossible;
but with *God* **Elohim** all *things* are possible.

The Cost Of Discipleship

27 Then answered *Peter* **Petros** and said unto him,
Behold, we have forsaken all, and followed
thee; what **then** shall we have *therefore*?
28 And *Jesus* **Yah Shua** said unto them,
Verily I say **Amen! I word** unto you,
That ye which have followed me,
in the *regeneration* **regenesis,**
when **ever** the Son of *man* **humanity**
shall sit in the throne of his glory,
ye also shall sit upon twelve thrones,
judging the twelve *tribes* **scions** of *Israel* **Yisra El**.
29 And every one that hath forsaken houses,
or brethren, or sisters, or father, or mother,
or *wife* **woman**, or children, or lands,
for my name's sake,
shall *receive* **take** an hundredfold,
and shall inherit *everlasting* **eternal** life.
30 But many that are first shall be *last* **final**;
and the *last* **final** shall be first.

The Parable Of The Vineyard Workers

20 For the *kingdom* **sovereigndom**
of *heaven* **the heavens**
is like unto a *man* **human**
that is an *householder* **housedespotes**,
which went out **simultaneously** early in the morning
to hire *labourers* **workers** into his vineyard.
2 And when he had *agreed* **symphonized**
with the *labourers* **workers** for a *penny* **denarion** a day,
he *sent* **apostolized** them into his vineyard.
3 And he went out about the third hour,
and saw others standing idle in the *marketplace* **market**,
4 And said unto them; Go
ye also into the vineyard,
and whatsoever is *right* **just** I *will* **shall**
give you. And they went their way.
5 Again he went out about
the sixth and ninth hour,
and did likewise.
6 And about the eleventh hour he went out,
and found others standing idle,
and *saith* **wordeth** unto them,
Why stand ye here all the day idle?
7 They *say* **word** unto him,
Because no *man* **one** hath hired us.
He *saith* **wordeth** unto them,
Go ye also into the vineyard;
and whatsoever is *right* **just**, that shall ye *receive* **take**.
8 So when even was come **being evening**,
the *lord* **adoni** of the vineyard
saith **wordeth** unto his *steward* **manager**,
Call the *labourers* **workers**, and give them their hire,
beginning from the *last* **final** unto the first.
9 And when they came
that were hired about the eleventh hour,
they *received every man* **each took** a *penny* **denarion**.
10 But when the first came,
they *supposed* **presumed**
that they should have *received* **taken much** more;
and they likewise
received every man **each took** a *penny* **denarion**.
11 And when they had *received* **taken** it,
they murmured
against the *goodman of the house* **housedespotes**,
12 *saying* **wording**,
These *last* **final** have *wrought* **produced** but one hour,
and thou hast made them equal unto us,
which have borne the burden and heat of the day.
13 But he answered one of them, and said,
Friend **Comrade**, I *do* **injure** thee *no wrong* **not**:
didst not thou *agree indeed* **symphonize** with me
for a *penny* **denarion**?
14 Take that thine is, and go thy way:
I *will* give unto this *last* **final**, even as unto thee.
15 Is it not *lawful* **allowed** for me
to do what I will with mine own?
26 But Yah Shua looks, and says,
With humanity this is impossible;
but with Elohim all are possible.

The Cost Of Discipleship

27 Then Petros answers him, saying,
Behold, we forsook all, and follow you;
what then, have we?
28 And Yah Shua say to them,
Amen! I word to you — to you who follow me:
In the regenesis,
when the Son of humanity
sits on the throne of his glory,
you also sit on twelve thrones
judging the twelve scions of Yisra El:
29 and everyone who forsakes houses
or brothers or sisters or father or mother
or woman or children or lands
for sake of my name;
takes a hundredfold and inherits eternal life:
30 but many who are first become final;
and the final first.

The Parable Of The Vineyard Workers

20 For the sovereigndom of the heavens
is likened to a human — a housedespotes
who goes simultaneously early in the morning
to hire workers into his vineyard:
2 and he symphonizes with the workers
for a denarion a day;
and apostolizes them to his vineyard.
3 And about the third hour
he goes and sees others standing idle in the market
4 and says to them, You also go to the vineyard,
and I give you whatever is just.
— and they go their way.
5 Again about the sixth and ninth hour
he goes and does likewise.
6 And about the eleventh hour
he goes and finds others standing idle,
and words to them,
Why stand you here idle all the day?
7 They word to him, Because no one hires us.

He words to them,
You also go into the vineyard;
and whatever is just, you take.

8 And being evening;
the adoni of the vineyard words to his manager,
Call the workers, and give them their hire,
beginning from the final to the first.

9 And those hired about the eleventh hour, come;
and they each take a denarion.

10 And the first come;
and they presume to take much more;
and they likewise each take a denarion.

11 And they take it,
and murmur against the housedespotes,

12 wording, These final produced but one hour:
and you make them equal to us
who bore the burden and heat of the day.

13 And he answers one of them, saying,
Comrade, I injure you not.
Symphonized you not with me
indeed for a denarion?

14 Take what is yours and go your way:
I give to this final, even as to you.

15 Am I not allowed to do
what I will with my own?
Is your eye evil because I am good?

16 *So* **Thus** the *last* **final** shall be first,
and the first *last* **final**:
for many be called, but few *chosen* **selected**.

Yah Shua Prophesies
His Death And Resurrection

17 And *Jesus* **Yah Shua**
going up **ascending** to *Jerusalem* **Yeru Shalem**
took the twelve disciples *apart* **privately** in the way,
and said unto them,

18 Behold, we *go up* **ascend**
to *Jerusalem* **Yeru Shalem**;
and the Son of *man* **humanity** shall be betrayed
unto the *chief* **arch** priests and unto the scribes,
and they shall condemn him to death,

19 And shall *deliver* **betray**
him to the *Gentiles* **goyim**
to mock, and to scourge, and to *crucify* him
stake: and the third day he shall rise *again*.

Priority Positions

20 Then came to him
the mother of *Zebedee's children* **Zabdi's sons**
with her sons, worshipping him,
and *desiring a certain thing* **asking somewhat** of him.

21 And he said unto her, What *wilt* **willest** thou?
She *saith* **wordeth** unto him,
Grant **Say** that these my two sons may sit,
the one *on* **at** thy right *hand*,
and the *other on* **one at** the left,
in thy *kingdom* **sovereigndom**.

22 But *Jesus* **Yah Shua** answered and said,
Ye know not what ye ask.
Are ye able to drink of the cup
that I shall drink of,
and *to be* baptized with the baptism
that I am baptized with?
They *say* **word** unto him, We are able.

23 And he *saith* **wordeth** unto them,
Ye shall drink indeed of my cup,
and be baptized
with the baptism that I am baptized with:
but to sit *on* **at** my right *hand*, and *on* **at** my left,
is not mine to give,
but it shall be given to them
for whom it is prepared of by my Father.

The Ten Indignant Disciples

24 And when the ten heard it,
they were *moved with indignation* **indignified**
against **concerning** the two brethren.

25 But *Jesus* **Yah Shua** called
them unto him, and said,
Ye know that the *princes* **archs** of the *Gentiles* **goyim**
exercise dominion over **rule over** them,
and they that are *great* **mega**
exercise authority upon **authorize over** them.

26 But it shall not be *so* **thus** among you:
but whosoever *will* **willeth** to *be great* **mega** among you,
let him be your minister;

27 And whosoever *will* **willeth**
to *be chief* **first** among you,
let him be your servant:

28 *Even* **Exactly** as the Son of *man* **humanity**
came not to be ministered unto, but to minister,
and to give his *life* **soul** a *ransom* **redemption** for many.

Yah Shua Heals Two Blind

29 And as they *departed*
proceeded from *Jericho* **Yericho**,
a *great* **vast** multitude followed him.

30 And, behold, two blind
men sitting by the way side,
when they heard that *Jesus* **Yah Shua** passed by,

cried out, *saying* **wording**, *Have mercy on* **Mercy** us,
O *Lord* **Adonay**, thou son of David.
31 And the multitude rebuked them,
because that they should *hold their peace* **hush**:
but they cried the more, *saying* **wording**,
Have mercy on **Mercy** us,
O *Lord* **Adonay**, thou son of David.
32 And *Jesus* **Yah Shua** stood still,
and *called* **voiced out to** them, and said,
What will ye that I shall do unto you?
33 They *say* **word** unto him,
Lord **Adonay**, that our eyes may be opened.
16 Thus the final become first,
and the first final:
for many be called but few selected.

YAH SHUA PROPHESIES
HIS DEATH AND RESURRECTION

17 And Yah Shua ascends to Yeru Shalem
and takes the twelve disciples privately in the way
and says to them,
18 Behold, we ascend to Yeru Shalem
for the betrayal of the Son of humanity
to the archpriests and to the scribes
to condemn him to death
19 — to betray him to the goyim
to mock and to scourge and to stake:
and the third day he rises.

PRIORITY POSITIONS

20 Then the mother of the sons of Zabdi
comes to him with her sons,
worshipping him and asking somewhat of him.
21 And he says to her, What will you?
She words to him,
Say that these my two sons sit,
the one at your right and the one at the left
in your sovereigndom.
22 But Yah Shua answers, saying,
You know not what you ask:
Are you able to drink of the cup I am about to drink?
And baptized with the baptism
I am about to be baptized?
They word to him, We are able.
23 And he words to them,
You indeed drink of my cup,
and baptize with the baptism I am about to be baptized:
but to sit at my right and at my left
is not mine to give:
but it is given to them

for whom it is prepared by my Father.

THE TEN INDIGNANT DISCIPLES

24 And the ten hear it,
and are indignified concerning the two brothers.
25 And Yah Shua calls them to him, and says,
You know that the archs of the goyim rule over them;
and they who are mega authorize over them.
26 But so be it not among you:
but whoever wills to be mega among you,
becomes your minister;
27 and whoever wills to be first among you,
becomes your servant.
28 Exactly as the Son of humanity
comes not to be ministered unto, but to minister:
and to give his soul a redemption for many.

YAH SHUA HEALS TWO BLIND

29 And as they proceed from Yericho
a vast multitude follows him:
30 and behold, two blind men
sitting by the way side,
hear that Yah Shua passes by,
and they cry out, wording,
Mercy us, O Adonay, you son of David.
31 — and the multitude rebukes them to hush.
But they cry out the more, wording,
Mercy us, O Adonay, you son of David.
32 And Yah Shua stands still
and voices out to them, saying,
What will you that I do to you?
33 They word to him,
Adonay, that our eyes be opened.
34 So *Jesus* **Yah Shua**
had *compassion* **a sympathetic spleen** on them,
and touched their eyes:
and *immediately* **straightway** their
eyes *received sight* **saw**,
and they followed him.

THE TRIUMPHAL ENTRY OF YAH SHUA

21 And when they
drew nigh **approached** unto *Jerusalem* **Yeru Shalem**,
and were come to *Bethphage* **Beth Pag**,
unto the mount of Olives,
then *sent Jesus* **Yah Shua apostolized** two disciples,
2 *Saying* **Wording** unto them,
Go into the village over against you,
and straightway ye shall find *an ass* **a burro** tied,
and a colt with her:

loose **release** them, and bring them unto me.

3 And *if* **whenever** any *man* **one** say ought unto you, ye shall say, *the Lord* **Adonay** hath need of them; and straightway he *will send* **shall apostolize** them.

4 All this *was done* **became**, that it might be fulfilled/shalamed which was *spoken by* **rhetorized through** the prophet, *saying* **wording**,

5 *Tell* **Say** ye the daughter of *Sion* **Siyon**, Behold, thy *king* **sovereign** cometh unto thee, meek, and *sitting* **mounted** upon *an ass* **a burro**, and a colt the *foal* **son** of *an ass* **a burro**. Zechar Yah 9:9

6 And the disciples went, and did **exactly** as *Jesus commanded* **Yah Shua ordered** them,

7 And brought the *ass* **burro**, and the colt, and put on them their *clothes* **garments**, and they set him thereon.

8 And a *very great* **vast** multitude spread their garments in the way; others cut down branches from the trees, and *strawed* **spread** them in the way.

9 And the multitudes that went before, and that followed, cried, *saying* **wording**, *Hosanna* **Hoshia Na** to the son of David: *Blessed* **Eulogized** is he that cometh in the name of *the Lord* **Yah Veh**; *Hosanna* **Hoshia Na** in the *highest* **highests**. Psalm 118:25, 26

10 And when he *was come* **entered** into *Jerusalem* **Yeru Shalem**, all the city *was moved* **quaked**, *saying* **wording**, Who is this?

11 And the multitude *said* **worded**, This is *Jesus* **Yah Shua** the prophet of Nazareth of *Galilee* **Galiyl**.

YAH SHUA CLEANSES THE PRIESTAL PRECINCT

12 And *Jesus went into* **Yah Shua entered** the *temple* **priestal precinct** of *God* **Elohim**, and *cast out* **ejected** all them that sold and *bought* **marketed** in the *temple* **priestal precinct**, and *overthrew* **upset** the tables of the *moneychangers* **coindealers**, and the *seats* **cathedras** of them that sold doves,

13 And *said* **worded** unto them, It is *written* **scribed**, My house shall be called the house of prayer; but ye have made it a *den* **grotto** of *thieves* **robbers**. Yesha Yah 56:7

YAH SHUA CURES THE BLIND AND THE LAME

14 And the blind and the lame came to him in the *temple* **priestal precinct**; and he *healed* **cured** them.

15 And when the *chief* **arch** priests and scribes saw the *wonderful things* **marvels** that he did, and the *children* **lads** crying in the *temple* **priestal precinct**, and *saying* **wording**, *Hosanna* **Hoshia Na** to the son of David; they *were sore displeased* **indignified**, Psalm 118:25, 26

16 And said unto him, Hearest thou what these *say* **word**? And *Jesus saith* **Yah Shua wordeth** unto them, Yea; have ye never ever read, out of the mouth of babes and *sucklings* **nipplers** thou hast *perfected praise* **prepared halal**? Psalm 8:2

34 So Yah Shua has a sympathetic spleen on them and touches their eyes: and straightway their eyes see and they follow him.

THE TRIUMPHAL ENTRY OF YAH SHUA

21 And they approach Yeru Shalem, and go to Beth Pag, to the mount of Olives. Then Yah Shua apostolizes two disciples,

2 wording to them, Go into the village opposite you; and straightway you find a burro tied with a colt: release them, and bring them to me:

3 and whenever anyone says aught to you, say, Adonay needs them. — and straightway he apostolizes them.

4 All this is to fulfill/shalam what the prophet rhetorized, wording,

5 Say you the daughter of Siyon, Behold, your sovereign comes to you — meek and mounted on a burro with a colt the son of a burro. Zechar Yah 9:9

6 And the disciples go and do exactly as Yah Shua orders them;

7 and bring the burro and the colt, and put their garments on them; and they set him on them.

8 And vast multitude

spreads their garments in the way;
others cut down branches from the trees
and spread them in the way:
9 and the multitudes preceding
and following cry out,
wording, Hoshia Na to the son of David:
Eulogized — he who comes in the name of Yah Veh;
Hoshia Na in the highests.
Psalm 118:25, 26
10 And he enters Yeru Shalem;
and all the city quakes,
wording, Who is this?
11 And the multitude words,
This is Yah Shua the prophet of Nazareth, Galiyl.

YAH SHUA CLEANSES THE PRIESTAL PRECINCT

12 And Yah Shua enters the
priestal precinct of Elohim
and ejects all who sell and market
in the priestal precinct;
and upsets the tables of the coindealers
and the cathedras of them who sell doves.
13 And words to them, It is scribed,
My house is called the house of prayer;
but you make it a grotto of robbers.
Yesha Yah 56:7

YAH SHUA CURES THE BLIND AND THE LAME

14 And the blind and the lame
come to him in the priestal precinct
and he cures them.
15 And the archpriests and scribes
see the marvels he does:
and the lads crying in the priestal precinct,
and wording, Hoshia Na to the son of David
— they indignify.
Psalm 118:25, 26
16 And they say to him,
Hear you what these are wording?
And Yah Shua words to them, Yes;
have you never ever read,
From the mouth of babes and nipplers
you prepare halal?
Psalm 8:2
17 And he left them,
and went out of the city into *Bethany* **Beth Ania**;
and he *lodged* **camped** there.

YAH SHUA CURSES THE FIG TREE

18 *Now* **But** in the **early** morning
as he returned into the city,
he hungered.
19 And when he saw a fig tree
in the way, he came to it,
and found *nothing* **naught** thereon,
but **except** leaves only,
and *said* **worded** unto it,
Let no fruit *grow on* **become from** thee
henceforward for ever **unto the eons**.
And *presently* **immediately** the fig tree withered away.
20 And when the disciples saw it,
they marvelled, *saying* **wording**,
How *soon is* **immediately** the fig tree withered *away*!
21 *Jesus* **Yah Shua** answered and said unto them,
Verily ! *say* **Amen! I word** unto you,
if **whenever** ye have *faith* **trust**, and doubt not,
ye shall not only do this *which is done* to the fig tree,
but also *if* **whenever** ye shall say unto this mountain,
Be thou removed, and be thou cast into the sea;
it shall be *done*.
22 And all *things*,
whatsoever — **as much as ever** ye shall ask in prayer,
believing **trusting**, ye shall *receive* **take**.

ARCH PRIESTS AND PRESBYTERS
OF THE PEOPLE QUESTION
THE AUTHORITY OF YAH SHUA

23 And when he was come
into the *temple* **priestal precinct**,
the *chief* **arch** priests and the elders of the people
came unto him as he was *teaching* **doctrinating**,
and *said* **worded**,
By **In** what authority doest thou these *things*?
and who gave thee this authority?
24 And *Jesus* **Yah Shua** answered
and said unto them,
I also *will* **shall** ask you one *thing* **word**,
which *if* **whenever** ye tell me,
I *in like wise will tell* **shall also say to** you
by **in** what authority I do these *things*.
25 The baptism of *John* **Yahn**, whence was it?
from **of the** heaven, or of *men* **humanity**?
And they reasoned with themselves, *saying* **speaking**,
if **whenever** we shall say, From **Of the** heaven;
he *will* **shall** say unto us,
So **Why** did ye not *then believe* **trust** him?
26 But *if* **whenever** we shall say, Of *men* **humanity**;
we *fear* **awe** the *people* **multitudes**;
for all *hold John* **regard Yahn** as a prophet.
27 And they answered *Jesus* **Yah Shua**, and said,
We *cannot tell* **know not**.

And he said unto them,
Neither *tell* **word** I you
by **in** what authority I do these *things*.

THE PARABLE OF THE TWO CHILDREN

28 But what think ye?
A *certain man* **human** had two *sons* **children**;
and he came to the first, and said,
Son **Child**, go work to day in my vineyard.
29 He answered and said, I will not:
but afterward he *repented* **regretted**, and went.
30 And he came to the second, and said likewise.
And he answered and said, I go, *sir* **adoni**: and went not.
31 Whether of them twain
did the will of his father?
They *say* **word** unto him, The first.
Jesus saith **Yah Shua speaketh** unto them,
Verily *! say* **Amen! I word** unto you,
That
the *publicans* **customs agents** and the *harlots* **whores**
go into the *kingdom* **sovereigndom** of *God* **Elohim**
before **preceding** you.
32 For *John* **Yahn** came unto you
in the way of *righteousness* **justness**,
and ye *believed* **trusted** him not:
but the *publicans* **customs agents** and the *harlots* **whores**
believed **trusted** him:
and ye, when ye had seen it,
repented **regretted** not afterward,
that ye might *believe* **trust** him.
17 And he leaves them
and goes from the city to Beth Ania
— and there he camps.

YAH SHUA CURSES THE FIG TREE

18 But in the early morning,
he returns to the city, famished.
19 And he sees a fig tree in the way
and comes to it,
and finds naught thereon except leaves only:
and he words to it,
No fruit becomes from you to the eons.
— and immediately the fig tree withers.
20 And the disciples see and marvel, wording,
How immediately the fig tree withers!
21 Yah Shua answers them, saying,
Amen! I word to you,
Whenever you have trust, and doubt not,
you not only do this to the fig tree,
but also, whenever you say to this mountain,

Remove! And be cast into the sea!
— so be it.
22 And all — as much as ever you ask in prayer,
trusting, you take.

ARCHPRIESTS AND PRESBYTERS OF THE PEOPLE QUESTION THE AUTHORITY OF YAH SHUA

23 And he comes to the priestal precinct:
and the archpriests and the elders of the people
come to him as he doctrinates, and they word,
In what authority do you these?
and, Who gives you this authority?
24 And Yah Shua answers them, saying,
I also ask you one word,
which, whenever you tell me,
I also say to you in what authority I do these.
25 The baptism of Yahn, whence is it
— Of the heavens? Or of humanity?
And they reason with themselves, speaking,
Whenever we say, Of the heavens;
he says to us, So why trust you not him?
26 But whenever we say, Of humanity;
we awe the multitudes;
for all regard Yahn as a prophet.
27 — and they answer Yah Shua, saying,
We know not.
And he says to them,
And I word not in what authority I do these.

THE PARABLE OF THE TWO CHILDREN

28 But what think you?
A human has two children:
and he comes to the first and says,
Child, go work today in my vineyard.
29 He answers, saying, I will not
— but afterward he regrets, and goes.
30 And he comes to the second, and says likewise.
And he answers, saying, I go, adoni: and goes not.
31 Which of the two does the will of his father?
They word to him, The first.
Yah Shua speaks to them,
Amen! I word to you,
That the customs agents and the whores
precede you into the sovereigndom of Elohim.
32 For Yahn came to you in the way of justness,
and you trusted him not:
but the customs agents and the whores trusted him:
and you, when you saw,
regretted not afterward to trust him.

MATTHEW/MATIT'YAH - HA'LEVI 21, 22

THE PARABLE OF THE VINEYARD

33 Hear another parable:
There was a *certain householder* **human housedespotes**,
which planted a vineyard, and hedged it round about,
and digged a *winepress* **trough** in it, and built a tower,
and *let* **leased** it out to *husbandmen* **cultivators**,
and went *into a far country* **abroad**:

34 And when the *time* **season** of the fruit
drew near **approached**,
he *sent* **apostolized** his servants
to the *husbandmen* **cultivators**,
that they might *receive* **take** the fruits of it.

35 And the *husbandmen*
cultivators took his servants
and *beat* **indeed flogged** one,
and *killed* **slaughtered** another, and stoned another.

36 Again, he *sent* **apostolized** other servants
much more than the first:
and they did unto them likewise.

37 But *last of all* **afterward**
he *sent* **apostolized** unto them his son, *saying* **wording**,
They *will reverence* **shall respect** my son.

38 But when the *husbandmen*
cultivators saw the son,
they said among themselves, This is the heir;
come, let us *kill* **slaughter** him,
and let us seize on his inheritance.

39 And they *caught* **took** him,
and *cast* **ejected** him out of the vineyard,
and *slew* **slaughtered** him.

40 *So* **When** the *lord* **adoni**
therefore of the vineyard cometh,
what *will* **shall** he do
unto those *husbandmen* **cultivators**?

41 They *say* **word** unto him,
He *will miserably* **shall evilly** destroy
those *wicked* **evil** men,
and *will let out* **shall lease** his vineyard
unto other *husbandmen* **cultivators**,
which shall *render* **give** him the fruits in their seasons.

42 *Jesus saith* **Yah Shua wordeth** unto them,
Did ye never **ever** read in the scriptures,
The stone which the builders *rejected* **disapproved**,
the same is become the head of the corner:
this is *the Lord's doing* **Yah Veh's becoming**,
and it is marvellous in our eyes?
Psalm 118:22, 23

43 *Therefore say* **So word** I unto you,
The *kingdom* **sovereigndom** of *God* **Elohim**
shall be taken from you,
and given to a *nation* **goyim**
bringing forth **producing** the fruits thereof.

44 And whosoever shall fall on this stone
shall be *broken* **crushed**:
but on whomsoever it shall fall,
it will grind him to powder **shall be pulverized**. Yesha Yah 8:14

45 And when the *chief* **arch** priests and Pharisees
had heard his parables,
they *perceived* **knew**
that he *spake of* **worded concerning** them.

46 But when they sought to lay hands on him,
they *feared* **awed** the multitude,
because they *took* **regarded** him *for* **as** a prophet.

THE PARABLE OF THE MARRIAGE FEAST

22 And *Jesus* **Yah Shua** answered
and *spake* **said** unto them again by parables,
and said **wording**,

2 The *kingdom* **sovereigndom**
of *heaven* **the heavens**
is like unto a *certain king* **human sovereign**,
which made a marriage for his son,

3 And *sent forth* **apostolized** his servants
to call them that were bidden to the *wedding* **marriage**:
and they *would* **willed to** not come.

4 Again, he *sent forth* **apostolized** other servants,
saying **wording**, Tell them which are bidden,
Behold, I have prepared my dinner:
my *oxen* **bulls** and my fatlings are *killed* **sacrificed**,
and all *things* are *ready* **prepared**:
come unto the marriage.

5 But they *made light of* **disregarded**
it, and went their ways,
one **indeed** to his *farm* **field**, another
to his merchandise:

THE PARABLE OF THE VINEYARD

33 Hear another parable:
A human housedespotes,
plants a vineyard and hedges it all around
and digs a trough in it and builds a tower
and leases it to cultivators and goes abroad:

34 and the season of the fruit approaches
and he apostolizes his servants to the cultivators
to take of the fruits:

35 and the cultivators take his servants;
and indeed flog one
and slaughter another and stone another.

36 Again, he apostolizes other servants

much more than the first:
and they do to them likewise.

37 And afterward he apostolizes his son to them,
wording, They respect my son.

38 But the cultivators see the son,
and they say among themselves, This is the heir!
Come! Slaughter him! Seize his inheritance!

39 And they take him
and eject him from the vineyard and slaughter him.

40 So when the adoni of the vineyard comes,
what does he to those cultivators?

41 They word to him,
He evilly destroys those evil men,
and leases his vineyard to other cultivators
who give him the fruits in their seasons.

42 Yah Shua words to them,
Read you never ever in the scriptures,
The stone the builders disapprove,
the same becomes the head of the corner:
this becomes of Yah Vah
and it is marvellous in our eyes?
Psalm 118:22, 23

43 So I word to you,
The sovereigndom of Elohim is taken from you and
given to a goyim producing the fruits thereof.

44 And whoever falls on this stone crushes:
but on whomever it falls, pulverizes. Yesha Yah 8:14

45 And the archpriests and Pharisees
hear his parables,
and they know he words concerning them:

46 and they seek to lay hands on him,
but they awe the multitude
because they regard him as a prophet.

THE PARABLE OF THE MARRIAGE FEAST

22 And again Yah Shua answers them by parables,
wording,

2 The sovereigndom of the heavens
is likened to a human sovereign
who makes a marriage for his son:

3 and he apostolizes his servants
to call those bidden to the marriage:
and they will to not come.

4 Again, he apostolizes other servants,
wording, Tell those bidden,
Behold, I prepared my dinner:
my bulls and my fatlings are sacrificed
and all are prepared:
come to the marriage.

5 And they disregard, and go their ways:
one indeed to his field; another to his merchandise;

6 And the *remnant took* **rest**
overpowered his servants,
and *entreated* **insulted** them *spitefully*,
and *slew* **slaughtered** them.

7 But when the *king* **sovereign** heard thereof,
he was wroth:
and he sent *forth* his *armies* **warriors**,
and destroyed those murderers, and burned *up* their city.

8 Then *saith* **wordeth** he to his servants,
The *wedding* **marriage** is *ready* **indeed prepared**,
but they which were bidden were not worthy.

9 **So** Go ye *therefore* into the highways,
and as many as **ever** ye shall find, bid to the marriage.

10 *So* **And** those servants went
out into the highways,
and gathered together all as many as they found,
both *bad* **evil** and good:
and the *wedding* **marriage** was *furnished* **filled**
with *guests* **those reposing**.

11 And when the *king came in* **sovereign entered**
to *see the guests* **observe those reposing**,
he saw there a *man* **human** which had not *on* **endued**
a *wedding garment* **marriage enduement**:

12 And he *saith* **wordeth** unto
him, *Friend* **Comrade**,
how *camest* **enterest** thou in hither
not having a *wedding garment* **marriage enduement**?
And he was *speechless* **muzzled**.

13 Then said the *king* **sovereign**
to the *servants* **ministers**,
Bind him hand and foot, and take him away,
and *cast* **eject** him into outer darkness,
there shall be weeping and gnashing of teeth.

14 For many are called, but few are *chosen* **selected**.

THE HERODIANS TEST YAH SHUA

15 Then went the Pharisees, and took counsel
how they might *entangle* **ensnare** him in *his talk* **word**.

16 And they *sent out* **apostolized** unto him
their disciples with the Herodians, *saying* **wording**,
Master **Doctor**, we know that thou art true,
and *teachest* **doctrinatest** the way
of *God* **Elohim** in truth,
neither *carest* **concernest** thou for any *man* **one**:
for thou *regardest* **lookest** not
on the *person* **face** of *men* **humanity**.

17 *Tell* **So say to** us *therefore*, What thinkest thou?
Is it *lawful* **allowed** to give tribute
unto *Caesar* **the Kaisar**,

MATTHEW/MATIT'YAH - HA'LEVI 22

or not?
18 But *Jesus* **Yah Shua**
perceived **knew** their *wickedness* **evil**, and said,
Why *tempt* **test** ye me, ye hypocrites?
19 Shew me the tribute *money* **coin**.
And they *brought* **offered** unto him a *penny* **denarion**.
20 And he *saith* **wordeth** unto them,
Whose is this *image* **icon** and *superscription* **epigraph**?
21 They *say* **word** unto him, *Caesar's* **The Kaisar's**.
Then *saith* **wordeth** he unto them,
Render therefore **So give**
unto Caesar the things which are Caesar's
the Kaisar's to the Kaisar;
and *unto God the things that are God's*
Elohim's to Elohim.
22 When they had heard these
words, they marvelled,
and *left* **forsook** him, and went their way.

THE SADOQIYM TEST YAH SHUA

23 The same day came to him
the *Sadducees* **Sadoqiym**,
which *say* **word** that there is no resurrection,
and asked him,
24 *Saying* **Wording**, *Master* **Doctor**,
Moses **Mosheh** said,
if **whenever** *a man* **one** die, having no children,
his brother shall marry his *wife* **woman**,
and raise *up seed* **sperma** unto his brother.
25 Now there were with us seven brethren:
and the first, when he had married *a wife, deceased* **died**,
and, having no *issue* **sperma**,
left **forsook** his *wife* **woman** unto his brother:
26 Likewise the second also,
and the third, unto the seventh.
27 And *last of all* **afterward** the woman died also.
Genesis 38:8—10
28 *Therefore* **So** in the resurrection
whose *wife* **woman** shall she be of the seven?
for they all had her.
6 and the rest overpower his servants
and insult them and slaughter them.
7 And the sovereign hears, and he is wroth:
and he sends his warriors
and destroys those murderers and burns their city.
8 Then he words to his servants,
The marriage is indeed prepared
and they who are bidden are not worthy:
9 so go into the highways,
and as many as ever you find, bid to the marriage.
10 And those servants go into the highways
and gather all — as many as they find
— both evil and good:
and the marriage fills up with those reposing.
11 And the sovereign enters
to observe those reposing:
and there he sees a human
not endued in a marriage enduement:
12 and he words to him, Comrade,
how entered you here, not having
a marriage enduement?
— and he is muzzled.
13 Then the sovereign says to the ministers,
Bind him hand and foot and take him away
and eject him into outer darkness;
there becomes weeping and gnashing of teeth:
14 for many are called, but few are selected.

THE HERODIANS TEST YAH SHUA

15 Then the Pharisees go and take counsel
on how to ensnare him in words:
16 and they apostolize
their disciples with the Herodians to him,
wording, Doctor, we know you are true,
and doctrinate the way of Elohim in truth;
and you concern not about anyone:
for you look not on the face of humanity:
17 so say to us, What think you?
Is it allowed to give tribute to the Kaisar — or not?
18 But Yah Shua, knowing their evil,
says, Why test you me, you hypocrites?
19 Show me the tribute coin.
— and they offer him a denarion.
20 And he words to them,
Whose is this icon and epigraph?
21 They word to him, Of the Kaisar.
Then he words to them,
So give that of the Kaisar to the Kaisar;
and that of Elohim to Elohim.
22 And they hear these and marvel
and forsake him and go their way.

THE SADOQIYM TEST YAH SHUA

23 The same day the Sadoqiym come to him
— who word that there is no resurrection,
and ask him,
24 wording, Doctor, Mosheh says,
Whenever anyone dies, having no children,
his brother marries his woman
and raises sperma to his brother:

25	and there are seven brothers with us: and the first, marries and dies; and having no *sperma*, forsakes his woman to his brother:	40	*On* **In** these two *commandments* **misvoth** hang all the *law* **torah** and the prophets. Deuteronomy 6:5, Leviticus 19:18
26	likewise the second also and the third, to the seventh:		YAH SHUA TESTS THE PHARISEES
27	and afterward the woman also dies. Genesis 38:8—10	41	While the Pharisees were gathered together, *Jesus* **Yah Shua** asked them,
28	So in the resurrection, of the seven, whose woman becomes she? — for they all had her.	42	*Saying* **Wording**, What think ye *of Christ* **concerning the Messiah**? whose son is he? They *say* **word** unto him, The son of David.
29	*Jesus* **Yah Shua** answered and said unto them, Ye *do err* **wander**, not knowing the scriptures, nor the *power* **dynamis** of *God* **Elohim**.	43	He *saith* **wordeth** unto them, *So* How then doth David in spirit call him *Lord* **Adonay**, *saying* **wording**,
30	For in the resurrection they neither marry, nor are *given in marriage* **married off**, but are as the angels of *God* **Elohim** in *the* heaven.	44	*The LORD said* **An oracle of Yah Veh** unto my *Lord* **Adonay**, Sit thou *on* **at** my right *hand*, till I *make* **place** thine enemies thy footstool?
31	But *as touching* **concerning** the resurrection of the dead, have ye not read that which was *spoken* **rhetorized** unto you by *God* **Elohim**, *saying* **wording**,	45	*So* If David *then* call him *Lord* **Adonay**, how is he his son? Psalm 110:1
32	*I am* **I AM** the *God* **Elohim** of Abraham, and the *God* **Elohim** of Isaac **Yischaq**, and the *God* **Elohim** of Jacob **Yaaqov**? *God* **Elohim** is not the *God* **Elohim** of the dead, but of the living.	46	And no *man* **one** was able to answer him a word, neither durst any *man* **one** from that day *forth* ask him any more questions.
33	And when the multitude heard this, they were astonished at his doctrine. Exodus 3:6		THE PSEUDO RELIGION OF THE PHARISEES
	THE PHARISEES TEST YAH SHUA	**23**	Then spake *Jesus* **Yah Shua** to the multitude, and to his disciples,
34	But when the Pharisees had heard that he had *put* **muzzled** the *Sadducees* **Sadoqiym** to silence, they were gathered together.	2	*Saying* **Wording**, The scribes and the Pharisees sit in *Moses' seat* **Mosheh's cathedra**:
35	*Then* **So** one of them, *which was a lawyer* **a torahist**, asked him a question, *tempting* **testing** him, and *saying* **wording**,	3	*So* All *therefore whatsoever* — **as much as ever** they *bid you observe* **say to you to guard**, that *observe* **guard** and do; but do not ye after their works: for they *say* **word**, and do not.
36	*Master* **Doctor**, which is the *great commandment* **mega misvah** in the *law* **torah**?	4	For they bind heavy burdens and *grievous to be borne* **oppressive**, and *put* **place** them on *men's* **humanity's** shoulders; but they themselves will *to* not *move* **wag** them with one of their fingers.
37	*Jesus* **Yah Shua** said unto him, Thou shalt love *the Lord* **Yah Veh** thy *God* **Elohim** *with* **in** all thy heart, and *with* **in** all thy soul, and *with* **in** all thy mind.	5	But all their works they do for to be *seen* **observed** of *men* **humanity**: they *make broad* **broaden** their phylacteries, and *enlarge* **magnify** the *borders* **edges** of their garments,
38	This is the first and *great commandment* **mega misvah**.	29	Yah Shua answers them, saying, You wander, neither knowing the scriptures nor the dynamis of Elohim:
39	And the second is like unto it, Thou shalt love thy neighbour as thyself.		

MATTHEW/MATIT'YAH - HA'LEVI 23

30 for in the resurrection
they neither marry nor are married off;
but are as the angels of Elohim in the heavens.
31 But concerning the resurrection of the dead:
Read you not what Elohim rhetorized, wording,
32 I AM the Elohim of Abraham
and the Elohim of Yischaq
and the Elohim of Yaaqov?
Elohim is not the Elohim of the dead; but of the living.
33 — and when the multitude hears this,
they are astonished at his doctrine.
Exodus 3:6

THE PHARISEES TEST YAH SHUA

34 But the Pharisees hear he
muzzled the Sadoqiym,
and they gather together to him:
35 and one of them, a torahist,
asks him a question; testing him, and wording,
36 Doctor, which is the mega misvah in the torah?
37 Yah Shua says to him,
Love Yah Veh your Elohim in all your heart
and in all your soul and in all your mind
38 — this is the first and mega misvah:
39 and the second is likened to it,
Love your neighbor as yourself:
40 — in these two misvoth
hang all the torah and the prophets.
Deuteronomy 6:5, Leviticus 19:18

YAH SHUA TESTS THE PHARISEES

41 And the Pharisees gather together;
and Yah Shua asks them,
42 wording,
What think you concerning the Messiah?
Whose son is he?
They word to him, Of David.
43 He words to them,
So how, in spirit, calls David him Adonay
wording,
44 An oracle of Yah Veh to my Adonay:
Sit at my right,
until I place your enemies a stool for your feet?
45 So if David calls him Adonay, how is he his son?
Psalm 110:1
46 And no one is able to answer him a word,
and from that day
no one dares ask him any more questions.

THE PSEUDO RELIGION OF THE PHARISEES

23 Then Yah Shua speaks to the multitude
and to his disciples,
2 wording,
The scribes and the Pharisees
sit in the cathedra of Mosheh:
3 so all — as much as ever
they say to you to guard,
guard and do;
but after their works, do not:
for they word, and do not:
4 for they bind heavy and oppressive burdens
and place them on the shoulders of humanity;
but they themselves
will to not wag them with one of their fingers:
5 but they do all their works
to be observed of humanity:
they broaden their phylacteries
and magnify the edges of their garments;
6 And *love* **befriend**
the *uppermost rooms* **preeminent resposings**
at *feasts* **suppers**,
and the *chief seats* **preeminent cathedras**
in the synagogues,
7 And *greetings* **salutations** in the markets,
and to be called of *men* **humanity**, Rabbi, Rabbi.

HONORARY TITLES RESERVED FOR DEITY

8 But be not ye called Rabbi:
for one is your Rabbi, even *Christ* **the Messiah**;
and all ye are brethren.
9 And call no man your father upon the earth:
for one is your Father, which is in *heaven* **the heavens**.
10 Neither be ye called *masters* **tutors**:
for one is your *Master* **tutor**, even *Christ* **the Messiah**.
11 But he that is greatest among you
shall be your *servant* **minister**.
12 And whosoever shall exalt himself
shall be *abased* **humbled**;
and he that shall humble himself shall be exalted.

YAH SHUA DENOUNCES THE PHARISEES

13 But woe unto you, scribes
and Pharisees, hypocrites!
for ye shut *up*
the *kingdom* **sovereigndom** of *heaven* **the heavens**
against men **in front of humanity**:
for ye neither *go in yourselves* **enter**,

14 Woe unto you, scribes and
Pharisees, hypocrites!
for ye devour widows' houses,
and for a *pretence* **pretext** make *long* **far out** prayer:
therefore **because of this** ye shall *receive* **take**
the *greater damnation* **superabundant judgment**.

15 Woe unto you, scribes and
Pharisees, hypocrites!
for ye *compass* **go about the** sea and *land* **the dry**
to make one proselyte,
and when *ever* he *is made* **becometh**,
ye make him *twofold more* **double**
the child of *hell* **Gay Hinnom/the Valley of Burning**
than yourselves.

16 Woe unto you, ye blind guides, which *say* **word**,
Whosoever shall *swear* **oath**
by **in** the *temple* **nave**,
it is *nothing* **naught**;
but whosoever shall *swear* **oath**
by **in** the gold of the *temple* **nave**,
he is a debtor!

17 Ye fools and blind: for whether is greater,
the gold,
or the *temple* **nave** that *sanctifieth* **halloweth** the gold?

18 And, Whosoever shall *swear* **oath**
by **in** the *sacrifice* **altar**,
it is *nothing* **naught**;
but whosoever *sweareth* **oatheth**
by **in** the *gift* **oblation** that is upon it,
he is *guilty* **a debtor**.

19 Ye fools and blind: for whether is greater,
the *gift* **oblation**,
or the *sacrifice* **altar**
that *sanctifieth* **halloweth** the *gift* **oblation**?

20 *So* **Whoso** *therefore* shall *swear* **oath**
by **in** the *sacrifice* **altar**,
sweareth by **oatheth in** it, and *by* **in** all *things* thereon.

21 And whoso shall *swear* **oath**
by **in** the *temple* **nave**,
sweareth by **oatheth in** it,
and *by* **in** him that *dwelleth* **settleth** therein.

22 And he that shall *swear* **oath**
by **in the** heaven,
sweareth by **oatheth in** the throne of *God* **Elohim**,
and *by* **in** him that sitteth thereon.

23 Woe unto you, scribes and
Pharisees, hypocrites!
for ye pay tithe of mint and anise and *cummin* **kammon**,
and have *omitted* **forsaken**
the weightier matters of the *law* **torah**,
the judgment, **and the** mercy, and *faith* **the trust**:
these *ought* **needed** ye to have done,
and not to *leave the other* **forsake those** undone.

24 Ye blind guides,
which strain at a gnat, and swallow a camel.

6 and befriend the preeminent
resposings at suppers
and the preeminent cathedras in the synagogues

7 and salutations in the markets;
and to be called by humanity, Rabbi, Rabbi.

HONORARY TITLES RESERVED FOR DEITY

8 And you, neither call yourselves Rabbi:
for one is your Rabbi — even the Messiah
and all you are brothers:

9 nor call any man on the earth your father;
for one is your Father — in the heavens:

10 nor be called tutors;
for one is your tutor, even the Messiah.

11 But whoever is greatest among you
becomes your minister:

12 and whoever exalts himself becomes humbled;
and whoever humbles himself, exalts.

YAH SHUA DENOUNCES THE PHARISEES

13 But woe to you, scribes
and Pharisees! Hypocrites!
For you shut the sovereigndom of the heavens
in front of humanity:
for neither you enter
nor allow those entering to enter.

14 Woe to you, scribes and Pharisees! Hypocrites!
For you devour houses of widows
and for a pretext make far out prayers:
because of this you take the superabundant judgment.

15 Woe to you, scribes and Pharisees! Hypocrites!
For you go all around the sea and the dry
to make one proselyte,
and whenever he becomes,
you make him a double child
of Gay Hinnom/the Valley of Burning
more than yourselves.

16 Woe to You, you blind guides, who word,
Whoever oaths in the nave,
it is naught;
but whoever oaths in the gold of the nave,
is a debtor.

17 You fools and blind:

	for which is greater,
	The gold?
	Or the nave that hallows the gold?
18	And, Whoever oaths in the sacrifice altar,
	it is naught;
	but whoever oaths in the oblation thereon,
	is a debtor.
19	You fools and blind:

19 You fools and blind:
for which is greater,
The oblation?
Or the sacrifice altar that hallows the oblation?
20 So whoever oaths in the sacrifice altar,
oaths in it, and in all thereon:
21 and whoever oaths in the nave,
oaths in it,
and in him who settles therein:
22 and whoever oaths in the heavens,
oaths in the throne of Elohim, and
in him who sits thereon.
23 Woe to you, scribes and Pharisees! Hypocrites!
For you pay tithes of mint and anise and kammon,
and forsake the weightier matters of the torah
— the judgment and the mercy and the trust:
these you need to do
and not forsake those undone.
24 You blind guides
who strain at a gnat and swallow a camel.
25 Woe unto you, scribes and
Pharisees, hypocrites!
for ye *make clean* **purify**
the *outside of the cup* **cup outwardly** and *of* the platter,
but *within* **inwardly**
they are full of *extortion* **plunder** and *excess* **unrestraint**.
26 Thou blind Pharisee,
cleanse **purify** first
that which is within the **inward** cup and platter,
that *the outside* **outwardly**
of them **they** may be *clean* **purified** also.
27 Woe unto you, scribes and
Pharisees, hypocrites!
for ye are like unto
whited sepulchres **whitewashed tombs**, which indeed
appear **manifest** beautiful *outward* **outwardly**,
but are *within* **inwardly** full of dead *men's* bones,
and of all *uncleanness* **impurity**.
28 Even *so* **thus indeed** ye also
outwardly *appear righteous* **manifest**
just unto *men* **humanity**,
but *within* **inwardly** ye are full of hypocrisy
and *iniquity* **torah violations**.

29 Woe unto you, scribes and
Pharisees, hypocrites!
because ye build the tombs of the prophets,
and *garnish* **adorn**
the *sepulchres* **tombs** of the *righteous* **just**,
30 And *say* **word**,
If we had been in the days of our fathers,
we *would* **should** not have been
partakers **communicants** with them
in the blood of the prophets.
31 *Wherefore ye be witnesses* **So**
ye witness unto yourselves,
that ye are the *children* **sons** of them
which *killed* **murdered** the prophets.
32 *Fill ye up then* **Fulfill/Shalam**
the measure of your fathers.
33 Ye serpents, ye *generation* **progeny** of vipers,
how can ye *escape* **flee** the *damnation* **judgment**
of *hell* **Gay Hinnom/the Valley of Burning**?
34 *Wherefore* **Because of this**, behold,
I *send* **apostolize** unto you prophets,
and wise men, and scribes:
and some of them
ye shall *kill* **slaughter** and *crucify* **stake**;
and some of them shall ye scourge in your synagogues,
and persecute them from city to city:
35 That upon you may come
all the *righteous* **just** blood
shed **poured** upon the earth,
from the blood of *righteous* **just** Abel
unto the blood of *Zacharias* **Zechar Yah**
son of *Barachias* **Berech Yah**,
whom ye *slew* **murdered**
between the *temple* **nave** and the **sacrifice** altar.
36 *Verily !* *say* **Amen! I word** unto you,
All these *things* shall come upon this generation.

YAH SHUA LAMENTS OVER YERU SHALEM

37 O *Jerusalem, Jerusalem*
Yeru Shalem, Yeru Shalem,
thou that *killest* **slaughterest** the prophets,
and stonest them which are *sent* **apostolized** unto thee,
how often *would* have **I willed**
gathered **to gather** thy children together,
even *as* **in the manner**
a hen gathereth her *chickens* **young** under her wings,
and ye *would* **willed** not!
38 Behold, your house is *left*
forsaken unto you desolate.
39 For I *say* **word** unto you,

Ye shall *not* **never no way** see me henceforth,
till ye shall say, *Blessed* **Eulogized** is he
that cometh in the name of *the Lord* **Yah Veh**.

Yah Shua Prophesies Disintegration Of The Priestal Precinct

24 And *Jesus* **Yah Shua** went *out*,
and departed from the *temple* **priestal precinct**:
and his disciples came to him for to shew him
the *buildings* **edifices** of the *temple* **priestal precinct**.

2 And *Jesus* **Yah Shua** said unto them,
See ye not all these *things*?
verily I say **Amen! I word** unto you,
There shall *not* **never no way** be *left* **allowed** here
one stone upon another,
that shall *not* **never no way** be
thrown down **disintegrated**.

25 Woe to you, scribes and Pharisees! Hypocrites!
For outwardly
you purify the cup and the platter;
but inwardly
they are full of plunder and unrestraint.

26 Blind Pharisee!
First purify the inward cup and platter,
so that it also becomes purified outwardly.

27 Woe to you, scribes and Pharisees! Hypocrites!
For you are likened to whitewashed tombs
which outwardly indeed manifest beauty
but inwardly are full of dead bones
and of all impurity.

28 Even thus indeed
outwardly you also manifest as just
unto humanity,
but inwardly you are full of hypocrisy
and torah violations.

29 Woe to you, scribes and Pharisees! Hypocrites!
For you build the tombs of the prophets
and adorn the tombs of the just;

30 and word,
If we had been in the days of our fathers,
we had not been communicants with them
in the blood of the prophets.

31 So you witness to yourselves
that you are the sons
of them who murdered the prophets:

32 and you — you fulfill/shalam
the measure of your fathers.

33 You serpents! You progeny of vipers!
How can you flee the judgment
of Gay Hinnom/the Valley of Burning?

34 Because of this, behold, I apostolize to you
prophets and wise men and scribes:
and of them, you slaughter and stake
and of them, you scourge in your synagogues
and persecute from city to city:

35 so that all the just blood poured on the earth
comes upon you
— from the blood of just Abel
— to the blood of Zechar Yah son of Berech Yah
whom you murdered
between the nave and the sacrifice altar.

36 Amen! I word to you,
All these come upon this generation.

Yah Shua Laments Over Yeru Shalem

37 O, Yeru Shalem! Yeru Shalem!
— you who slaughter the prophets
and stone them apostolized to you!
how often I willed to gather your children together
— even in the manner
a hen gathers her young under her wings
— and you willed not!

38 Behold, your house is forsaken to you, desolate.

39 For I word to you,
You never no way see me henceforth,
until you say,
Eulogized — he who comes in the name of Yah Veh.

Yah Shua Prophesies Disintegration Of The Priestal Precinct

24 And Yah Shua goes
and departs from the priestal precinct:
and his disciples come to him
to shew him the edifices of the priestal precinct.

2 And Yah Shua says to them,
See you not all these?
Amen! I word to you,
Never no way is stone upon stone allowed,
that never no way disintegrates.

The Mount Of Olives Speech Of Yah Shua

3 And as he sat upon the mount of Olives,
the disciples came unto him privately,
saying **wording**, Tell us,
when shall these *things* be?
and what shall be the sign of thy *coming* **parousia**,
and of the *end* **completion/shalom** of the *world* **eon**?

4 And *Jesus* **Yah Shua** answered
and said unto them,

MATTHEW/MATIT'YAH - HA'LEVI 24

Take heed that no man **Look, lest anyone** deceive you.
5   For many shall come in
my name, *saying* **wording**,
I am Christ **I AM the Messiah**;
and shall *deceive* **seduce** many.
6   And ye shall **be about**
to hear of wars and rumours of wars:
see that ye *be not troubled* **lament**:
for all these *things* must *come to pass* **become**,
but the *end* **completion/shalom** is not yet.
7   For *nation* **goyim** shall
rise against *nation* **goyim**,
and *kingdom* **sovereigndom** against
kingdom **sovereigndom**
and there shall be famines, and pestilences,
and *earthquakes* **quakes**, in divers places.
8   All these are the beginning of *sorrows* **travail**.
9   Then shall they *deliver* **betray** you *up*
to be afflicted **unto affliction**,
and shall *kill* **slaughter** you:
and ye shall be hated of all *nations* **goyim**
for my name's sake.
10   And then shall many be *offended* **scandalized**,
and shall betray one another, and shall hate one another.
11   And many *false* **pseudo** prophets shall rise,
and shall *deceive* **seduce** many.
12   And because
iniquity **torah violations** shall *abound* **multiply**,
the love of many shall *wax* **breathe** cold.
13   But he
that shall *endure* **abide** unto the
end **completion/shalom**,
the same shall be saved.
14   And this
gospel **evangelism** of the *kingdom* **sovereigndom**
shall be preached in all the world
for **in** a witness unto all *nations* **goyim**;
and then shall the *end* **completion/shalom** come.

THE GREAT TRIBULATION

15   **So** When **ever** ye *therefore*
shall see the abomination of desolation,
spoken of **rhetorized**
by Daniel **through Dani El** the prophet,
stand in the holy place,
(whoso readeth, let him *understand* **comprehend**:)
16   Then let them which be in *Judaea* **Yah Hudah**
flee into the mountains:
17   Let him which is on the housetop
not *come down* **descend**
to take *any thing* **somewhat** out of his house:
18   Neither let him which is in the field
return back to take his *clothes* **garments**.
19   And woe unto them that *are*
with child **have in womb**,
and to them that *give suck* **nipple** in those days!
20   But pray ye that your flight
be not in the *winter* **downpour**,
neither *on* **in** the *sabbath day* **shabbath**:
21   For then shall be *great* **mega** tribulation,
such as *was* **became** not
since **from** the beginning of the *world* **cosmos**
to *this time* **now**,
no, nor *ever* shall **no way** be.
22   And except those days should be shortened,
there should **not** no flesh *ever* be saved:
but **except** for the *elect's* **select's** sake
those days shall be shortened.
Dani El 9:27, 11:31, 12:11
23   Then *if* **whenever** any *man*
one shall say unto you,
lo **Behold**, *here is Christ* **here — the Messiah**, or there;
believe it **trust** not.
24   For there shall arise *false*
Christs **pseudo messiahs**,
and *false* **pseudo** prophets,
and shall *shew* **give** *great* **mega**
signs and *wonders* **omens**;

THE MOUNT OF OLIVES SPEECH OF YAH SHUA

3   And he sits on the mount of Olives
and the disciples come to him privately,
wording, Tell us,
When become these?
And what is the sign of your parousia?
And of the completion/shalom of the eon?
4   And Yah Shua answers them, saying,
Look, lest anyone deceive you:
5   for many come in my name,
wording, I AM the Messiah!
— and seduce many:
6   and you are about to hear
of wars and rumours of wars:
see that you not lament:
for all these must become;
but the completion/shalom is not yet.
7   For goyim rises against goyim,
and sovereigndom against sovereigndom
and so be it, famines and pestilences
and quakes in divers places

8   — all these are the beginning of travail.
9   Then they betray you to affliction,
and slaughter you:
and you become hated of all goyim
for sake of my name:
10   and then they scandalize many
and betray one another and hate one another:
11   and many pseudo prophets
rise, and seduce many:
12   and because torah violations multiply,
the love of many breathes cold:
13   but whoever abides to the
completion/shalom is saved.
14   And this evangelism of the sovereigndom
is preached in all the world in a witness to all goyim;
and then comes the completion/shalom.

THE GREAT TRIBULATION

15   So whenever you see the
abomination of desolation
rhetorized through Dani El the prophet
stand in the holy place
— whoever reads, comprehend
16   Then whoever is in Yah
Hudah, flee to the mountains:
17   whoever is on the housetop
descend not to take somewhat from his house:
18   Then whoever is in the field
return not to take his garments:
19   and woe to them who have in womb
and to them who nipple in those days!
20   And pray that your flight becomes
neither in downpour nor in shabbath:
21   for then becomes mega tribulation
such as became not from the beginning of the cosmos
to now,
no, nor no way becomes:
22   and except those days shorten,
no flesh is no way ever saved:
and except for sake of the select
those days are shortened.
Dani El 9:27, 11:31, 12:11
23   Then whenever anyone says to you,
Behold, here — the Messiah! or, There!
— trust them not.
24   For pseudo messiahs and pseudo prophets rise;
and they give mega signs and omens;
insomuch that, if it *were* possible,
they shall *deceive* **seduce** the very *elect* **select**.
25   Behold, I have *told you before* **foretold you**.

26   *Wherefore if* **So whenever**
they shall say unto you,
Behold, he is in the *desert* **wilderness**;
go not forth:
behold, he is in the *secret chambers* **pantry**;
believe it **trust** not.

THE PAROUSIA OF YAH SHUA

27   For **exactly**
as the lightning cometh out of the *east* **rising**,
and *shineth* **manifesteth** even unto the *west* **lowering**;
so **thus** shall also
the *coming* **parousia** of the Son of *man* **humanity** be.
28   For wheresoever the carcase is,
there *will* **shall** the eagles be gathered together.

POST-TRIBULATION OMENS

29   *Immediately* **Straightway**
after the tribulation of those days
shall the sun be darkened,
and the moon shall not give her *light* **brilliance**,
and the stars shall fall from *heaven* **the heavens**,
and the *powers* **dynamis** of the heavens shall be shaken:

THE PAROUSIA

30   And then shall *appear* **manifest**
the sign of the Son of *man* **humanity** in *the* **the** heaven:
and then
shall all the *tribes* **scions** of the earth *mourn* **chop**,
and they shall see the Son of *man* **humanity**
coming in the clouds of *the* **the** heaven
with *power* **dynamis** and *great* **vast** glory.
31   And he shall *send* **apostolize** his angels
with a *great sound* **mega voice** of a trumpet,
and they shall gather together
his *elect* **select** from the four winds,
from *one end* **the extremities** of *heaven* **the heavens**
to *the other* **their extremities**.

PRE-PAROUSIA SIGNS

32   Now learn a parable of the fig tree;
When **ever** his branch *is yet* **becometh already** tender,
and *putteth forth* **sprouteth** leaves,
ye know that *summer* **warmth** is nigh:
33   *So* **Thus** likewise ye,
when **ever** ye shall see all these *things*,
know that it is near, even at the *doors* **portals**.
34   *Verily I say* **Amen!** I word unto you,
This generation shall *not* **never no way** pass,
till all these *things* be fulfilled/shalamed.

35   **The** heaven and earth shall pass *away*,
but my words shall *not* **never no way** pass *away*.
36   But *of* **concerning** that day and hour
knoweth no *man* **one**,
no, not the angels of *heaven* **the heavens**,
but **except** my Father only.
37   But **exactly** as the days of *Noe were* **Noach**,
so **thus** shall also
the *coming* **parousia** of the Son of *man* **humanity** be.
38   For **exactly** as in the days *that were*
before **preceding** the *flood* **cataclysm**
they were eating and drinking,
marrying and *giving in marriage* **marrying off**,
until the day that *Noe* **Noach** entered into the ark,
39   And knew not until the *flood* **cataclysm** came,
and took them all *away*;
so **thus** shall also
the *coming* **parousia** of the Son of *man* **humanity** be.
40   Then shall two be in the field;
the one shall be taken,
and the *other left* **one be forsaken**.
41   Two *women* shall be grinding *at* **in** the mill;
the one shall be taken,
and the *other left* **one be forsaken**.
42   **So** Watch *therefore*:
for ye know not what hour
your *Lord doth come* **Adonay cometh**.
43   But know this,
that if the *goodman of the house* **housedespotes**
had known
in what *watch* **guard** the thief *would* **should** come,

so as, if possible, to seduce the very select.
25   Behold, I foretell you.
26   So whenever they say to you,
Behold, in the wilderness! — go not forth:
Behold, in the pantry! — trust not.

The Parousia Of Yah Shua

27   For exactly as the lightning
comes from the rising
and manifests even to the lowering
— thus also
becomes the parousia of the Son of humanity
28   for wherever the carcase,
the eagles gather together.

Post–Tribulation Omens

29   Straightway after the tribulation of those days
the sun darkens
and the moon gives not her brilliance
and the stars fall from the heavens
and the dynamis of the heavens shakes.

The Parousia

30   And then the sign of the Son of humanity
manifests in the heavens:
and then all the scions of the earth chop:
and they see the Son of humanity
coming in the clouds of the heavens
with dynamis and vast glory:
31   and he apostolizes his angels
with a mega voice of a trumpet:
and they gather together
his select from the four winds
— from the extremities of the heavens
to their extremities.

Pre–Parousia Signs

32   Now learn a parable of the fig tree;
Whenever his branch
becomes already tender and sprouts leaves
you know warmth is near:
33   thus likewise you,
whenever you see all these,
know it is near — even at the portals.
34   Amen! I word to you,
This generation never no way passes
until all these fulfill:
35   the heavens and earth pass
but my words never no way pass:
36   but concerning that day and hour
no one knows
— no, not the angels of the heavens,
except my Father only.
37   But exactly as the days of Noach,
thus also becomes the parousia
of the Son of humanity.
38   For exactly as in the days
preceding the cataclysm
— eating and drinking, marrying and marrying off,
until the day Noach entered the ark;
39   and knew not until the cataclysm came
and took them all;
thus also
becomes the parousia of the Son of humanity.
40   Then two, being in the field;
the one taken and the one forsaken:
41   two grinding in the mill;
the one taken, and the one forsaken.

42 So watch!
For you know not what hour your Adonay comes.
43 But know this,
that if the *housedespotes*
had known in what guard the thief comes,
he *would* **should** have watched,
and *would* **should** not have *suffered* **allowed** his house
to be broken *up* **through**.
44 *Therefore* **So** be ye also *ready* **prepared**:
for in such an hour as ye think not the
Son of *man* **humanity** cometh.
45 **So** Who then
is a *faithful* **trustworthy** and *wise* **thoughtful** servant,
whom his *lord* **adoni**
hath *made* **seated** ruler over his *household* **therapy**,
to give them *meat* **nourishment** in due season?
46 Blessed *is* that servant, whom his *lord* **adoni**,
when he cometh shall find *so* **thus** doing.
47 *Verily ! say* **Amen! I word** unto you,
That he shall *make* **seat** him *ruler*
over all his *goods* **holdings**.
48 But *and if* **whenever** that evil
servant shall say in his heart,
My *lord delayeth* **adoni taketh** his **time** coming;
49 And shall begin
to *smite* **strike** his *fellowservants* **co—servants**,
and to eat and drink with the *drunken* **intoxicated**;
50 the *lord* **adoni** of that servant shall come
in a day when he *looketh* **expecteth** not *for him*,
and in an hour that he *is not aware of* **knoweth not**,
51 And shall *cut* **dichotomize** him *asunder*,
and *appoint him* **place** his portion with the hypocrites:
there shall be weeping and gnashing of teeth.

The Parable Of The Ten Virgins

25 Then shall the *kingdom*
sovereigndom of *heaven* **the heavens**
be likened unto ten virgins, which took their lamps,
and went *forth* to meet the bridegroom.
2 And five of them were *wise* **thoughtful**,
and five were foolish.
3 They that were foolish took their lamps,
and took no **olive** oil with them:
4 But the *wise* **thoughtful**
took **olive** oil in their vessels with their lamps.
5 *While* **But** the bridegroom
tarried **took his time**,
they all slumbered and slept.
6 And at midnight there *was* **became** a cry *made*,
Behold, the bridegroom cometh; go ye out to meet him.

7 Then all those virgins arose,
and *trimmed* **adorned** their lamps.
8 And the foolish said unto the *wise* **thoughtful**,
Give us of your **olive** oil;
for our lamps are *gone out* **quenched**.
9 But the *wise* **thoughtful** answered,
saying **wording**, Not so;
lest **ever** there be not *enough* **sufficient** for us and you:
but go ye rather to them that sell,
and *buy* **market** for yourselves.
10 And while they went to *buy* **market**,
the bridegroom came;
and they that were *ready* **prepared**
went in **entered** with him to the marriage:
and the *door* **portal** was shut.
11 Afterward came also the
other **rest of the** virgins,
saying **wording**, *Lord* **Adoni**, *Lord* **Adoni**, open to us.
12 But he answered and said,
Verily ! say **Amen! I word** unto you,
I know you not.
13 **So** Watch *therefore*,
for ye know neither the day nor the hour
wherein the Son of *man* **humanity** cometh.

The Investment Test

14 For *the kingdom of heaven*
is **exactly** as a *man* **human**
travelling into a far country **going abroad**,
who called his own servants,
and delivered unto them his *goods* **holdings**.
15 And unto one **indeed**
he gave five *talents* **talent weights**,
to another two, and to another one;
to *every man* **each**
according to his several *ability* **dynamis**;
and straightway *took his journey* **went abroad**.
16 *Then* **And** he that had *received* **taken**
the five *talents* **talent weights**
went and *traded with* **worked in** the same,
he had watched,
and had not allowed his house to be broken through.
44 So you also, be prepared:
for in such a hour as you think not
the Son of humanity comes.
45 Who then is a trustworthy
and thoughtful servant,
whom his adoni seats ruler over his therapy
to give them nourishment in due season?
46 Blessed — that servant, whom,

MATTHEW/MATIT'YAH - HA'LEVI 25

when his adoni comes, finds him thus doing.
47 Amen! I word to you,
He seats him over all his holdings.
48 But whenever that evil servant says in his heart,
My adoni takes his time coming;
49 and begins to strike his co—servants
and to eat and drink with the intoxicated;
50 the adoni of that servant
comes in a day when he expects not
and in an hour he knows not;
51 and dichotomizes him
and places his portion with the hypocrites:
there is weeping and gnashing of teeth.

THE PARABLE OF THE TEN VIRGINS

25 Then the sovereigndom of the heavens
is likened to ten virgins who take their lamps
and go to meet the bridegroom:
2 and five are thoughtful, and five are foolish:
3 the foolish take their lamps,
and take no olive oil with them:
4 but the thoughtful
take olive oil in their vessels with their lamps:
5 but the bridegroom takes his time
and they all slumber and sleep:
6 and at midnight there becomes a cry,
Behold, the bridegroom comes! Go meet him!
7 Then all those virgins rise
and adorn their lamps:
8 and the foolish say to the thoughtful,
Give us of your olive oil, for our lamps are quenched.
9 And the thoughtful answer, wording, Not so;
lest ever there is not sufficient for us and you:
but go rather to them who sell
and market for yourselves.
10 And while they go to market,
the bridegroom comes;
and the prepared enter with him to the marriage:
and they shut the portal.
11 Afterward the rest of the virgins also come,
wording, Adoni, Adoni, open to us.
12 And he answers, saying,
Amen! I word to you, I know you not.
13 So watch:
for you know neither the day nor the hour
wherein the Son of humanity comes.

THE INVESTMENT TEST

14 For exactly as a human going abroad,
he calls his own servants,
and delivers his holdings to them:
15 and indeed he gives one five talent weights,
another two, and another one;
— each according to his several dynamis;
and straightway goes abroad.
16 And he who took the five talent weights
goes and works them,
and *made them* **produced**
other *five talents* **talent weights**.
17 And likewise he that had *received* two,
he also gained other two.
18 But he that had *received* **taken** one
went and digged in the *earth* **soil**,
and *hid* **secreted** his *lord's money* **adoni's silver**.
19 After a *long* **vast** time
the *lord* **adoni** of those servants cometh,
and reckoneth **words** with them.
20 And *so* he that had *received*
taken five *talents* **talent weights**
came and *brought* **offered** other
five *talents* **talent weights**,
saying **wording**, *Lord* **Adoni**,
thou deliveredst unto me five *talents* **talent weights**:
behold, I have gained beside them
five *talents more* **other talent weights**.
21 His *lord* **adoni** said unto him,
Well done, thou good and *faithful* **trustworthy** servant:
thou hast been *faithful* **trustworthy**
over a *few things* **little**,
I will make **shall seat** thee *ruler* over *many things* **much**:
enter thou into the *joy* **cheer** of thy *lord* **adoni**.
22 He also that had *received* **taken** two
talents **talent weights** came and said, *Lord* **Adoni**,
thou deliveredst unto me two *talents* **talent weights**:
behold, I have gained two other *talents* **talent weights**
beside them.
23 His *lord* **adoni** said unto him,
Well done, good and *faithful* **trustworthy** servant;
thou hast been *faithful* **trustworthy**
over *a few things* **little**,
I will make **shall seat** thee *ruler* over *many things* **much**:
enter thou into the *joy* **cheer** of thy *lord* **adoni**.
24 Then he which had *received* **taken**
the one *talent* **talent weight**
came and said, *Lord* **Adoni**,
I knew thee that thou art an hard *man* **human**,
reaping **harvesting** where thou hast not *sown* **spored**,
and gathering **together**
where thou hast not *strawed* **scattered**:
25 And I was *afraid* **awestricken**,

and went and *hid* **secreted** thy talent **weight**
in the *earth* **soil**:
lo **behold**, there thou hast that is thine.
26 His *lord* **adoni** answered and said unto him,
Thou *wicked* **evil** and slothful servant,
thou knewest that I *reap* **harvest**
where I *sowed* **spored** not,
and gather **together** where I have not *strawed* **scattered**:
27 **So** Thou *oughtest* **needest** *therefore*
to have put my *money* **silver** to the exchangers,
and *then* at my coming
I should have received mine own with *usury* **interest**.
28 **So** Take *therefore* the talent **weight** from him,
and give it unto him
which hath ten *talents* **talent weights**.
29 For unto every one that hath shall be given,
and he shall have **super** abundance:
but from him that hath not
shall be taken away even that which he hath.
30 And *cast* **eject** ye the
unprofitable **useless** servant
into outer darkness:
there shall be weeping and gnashing of teeth.

Yah Shua Tests The Goyim

31 When **ever** the Son of *man* **humanity**
shall come in his glory, and all the holy angels with him,
Then shall he sit upon the throne of his glory:
32 And *before* **in front of** him
shall be gathered all *nations* **goyim**:
and he shall *separate* **set apart** them one from another,
exactly as a shepherd
divideth **setteth apart** his sheep from the goats:
33 And he **indeed** shall set the
sheep *on* **at** his right *hand*,
but the goats *on* **at** the left.
34 Then shall the *king* **sovereign** say
unto them *on* **at** his right *hand*,
Come, ye *blessed* **eulogized** of my Father,
inherit the *kingdom* **sovereigndom** prepared for you
and produces another five talent weights:
17 and likewise he who *took*
two, also gains another two:
18 but he who took one, goes and digs in the soil
and secretes the silver of his adoni.
19 After a vast time the adoni of those servants
comes and reckons words with them.
20 And he who took five talent weights
comes and offers another five talent weights;
wording, Adoni,

you delivered five talent weights to me:
behold,
I gained another five talent weights beside them.
21 His adoni says to him,
Well done, you good and trustworthy servant:
you are trustworthy over a little;
I seat you over much:
enter the cheer of your adoni.
22 And he who took two talent weights
comes and says, Adoni,
you delivered two talent weights to me:
behold,
I gained another two talent weights beside them.
23 His adoni says to him,
Well done, good and trustworthy servant;
you are trustworthy over a little,
I seat you over much:
enter the cheer of your adoni.
24 He who took the one talent weight
comes and says, Adoni,
I know you, that you are a hard human,
harvesting where you spore not,
and gathering together where you scatter not:
25 and being awestricken,
I went and secreted your talent weight in the soil:
behold, you have your own.
26 His adoni answers him, saying,
You evil and slothful servant,
you know I harvest where I spore not,
and gather together where I scatter not:
27 so you needed to put my
silver to the exchangers,
and then at my coming
I had received my own with interest.
28 So take the talent weight from him,
and give to him who has ten talent weights.
29 For to everyone who has, is given;
and he has super abundance:
but from him who has not
is taken away even what he has.
30 And eject the useless
servant into outer darkness:
there becomes weeping and gnashing of teeth.

Yah Shua Tests The Goyim

31 Whenever the Son of humanity
comes in his glory — with all the holy angels,
then he sits on the throne of his glory:
32 and all goyim gather in front of him:
and he sets them apart one from another,

exactly as a shepherd
sets apart his sheep from the goats:
33 and indeed he sets the sheep at his right
and the goats at the left.
34 Then the sovereign says to them at his right,
Come, you eulogized of my Father,
inherit the sovereigndom prepared for you
from the foundation of the *world* **cosmos**:
35 For I was an hungred, and ye gave me *meat* **eats**:
I was thirsty, and ye gave me drink:
I was a stranger, and ye *took* **gathered** me in:
36 Naked, and ye *clothed* **arrayed** me:
I was *sick* **frail**, and ye visited me:
I was in *prison* **a guardhouse**, and ye came unto me.
37 Then shall the *righteous* **just** answer him,
saying **wording**, *Lord* **Adonay**,
when saw we thee an hungred, and *fed* **nourished** thee?
or thirsty, and gave thee drink?
38 When saw we thee a stranger,
and *took* **gathered** thee in?
or naked, and *clothed* **arrayed** thee?
39 Or when saw we thee *sick* **frail**,
or in *prison* **a guardhouse**,
and came unto thee?
40 And the *king* **sovereign** shall answer
and say unto them,
Verily ! *say* **Amen! I word** unto you,
Inasmuch as ye have done it
unto one of the least of these my brethren,
ye have done it unto me.
41 Then shall he say also unto
them *on* **at** the left *hand*,
Depart from me, ye cursed, into *everlasting* **eternal** fire,
prepared for *the devil* **Diabolos** and his angels:
42 For I was an hungred, and
ye gave me no *meat* **eats**:
I was thirsty, and ye gave me no drink:
43 I was a stranger, and ye *took* **gathered** me not in:
naked, and ye *clothed* **arrayed** me not:
sick **frail**, and in *prison* **a guardhouse**,
and ye visited me not.
44 Then shall they also answer
him, *saying* **wording**,
Lord **Adonay**,
when saw we thee an hungred, or athirst, or a stranger,
or naked, or *sick* **frail**, or in *prison* **a guardhouse**,
and did not minister unto thee?
45 Then shall he answer them, *saying* **wording**,
Verily ! *say* **Amen! I word** unto you,
Inasmuch as ye did it not to one of the least of these,
ye did it not to me.
46 And these shall go *away*
into *everlasting* **eternal** punishment: but
the *righteous* **just** into life eternal.

YAH SHUA PROPHESIES HIS STAKING

26 And **so be**it *came to pass*,
when *Jesus* **Yah Shua**
had *finished* **completed/shalamed**
all these *sayings* **words**,
he said unto his disciples,
2 Ye know that after two days
is the *feast of the passover* **pasach**,
and the Son of *man* **humanity**
is betrayed to be *crucified* **staked**.

THE PLOT TO SLAUGHTER YAH SHUA

3 Then assembled together the *chief* **arch** priests,
and the scribes, and the elders of the people,
unto the *palace* **courtyard** of the *high* **arch** priest,
who was *called* **worded** Caiaphas,
4 And *consulted* **counseled together**
that they might take Jesus **to overpower Yah Shua**
by *subtilty* **deception**,
and *kill* **slaughter** him.
5 But they *said* **worded**,
Not *on* **in** the *feast day* **celebration**,
lest there be *an uproar* **a tumult** among the people.

A WOMAN ANOINTS YAH SHUA

6 *Now when Jesus* **But Yah Shua**
was in *Bethany* **Beth Ania**,
in the house of *Simon* **Shimon** the leper,
7 There came unto him a
woman having an alabaster *box*
of very precious *ointment* **myrrh**,
and poured it on his head, as he *sat at meat* **reposed**.
8 But when his disciples saw it,
they *had indignation* **indignified**, *saying* **wording**,
To what purpose is this *waste* **destruction**?
9 For this *ointment* **myrrh**
might have been sold for much,
and given to the poor.
10 *When Jesus understood* it
But Yah Shua knowing,
he said unto them,
from the foundation of the cosmos:
35 for I famished, and you gave me eats; I thirsted, and
you gave me drink; a stranger, and you gathered me in;
36 naked, and you arrayed me;

	frail, and you visited me;
	in a guardhouse, and you came to me.
37	Then the just answer him, wording, Adonay,
	When saw we you famishing, and nourished you?
	Or thirsting, and gave you drink?
38	When saw we you a stranger,
	and gathered you in?
	Or naked, and arrayed you?
39	Or when saw we you frail?
	Or in a guardhouse, and came to you?
40	And the sovereign answers them, saying,
	Amen! I word to you,
	As you did
	to one of the least of these my brothers,
	you did to me.
41	Then he also says to them at the left,
	Depart from me, you cursed, into eternal fire,
	prepared for Diabolos and his angels:
42	for I famished, and you gave me no eats;
	I thirsted, and you gave me no drink;
43	a stranger, and you gathered me not in;
	naked, and you arrayed me not;
	frail, and in a guardhouse, and you visited me not.
44	Then they also answer him, wording,
	Adonay, when saw we you famishing or thirsting?
	Or a stranger or naked or frail or in a guardhouse
	and ministered not to you?
45	Then he answers them, wording,
	Amen! I word to you,
	As you did it not to one of the least of these,
	you did it not to me:
46	and these go to eternal punishment:
	but the just to life eternal.

Yah Shua Prophesies His Staking

26 And so be it,
when Yah Shua completes/shalams all these words,
he says to his disciples,

2 You know that after two days is the pasach,
and the Son of humanity is betrayed to staking.

The Plot To Slaughter Yah Shua

3 Then the archpriests and the scribes
and the elders of the people assemble together
in the courtyard of the archpriest worded Caiaphas:

4 and they counsel together
on how to overpower Yah Shua by deception
and slaughter him:

5 but they word, Not in the celebration
lest there be a tumult among the people.

A Woman Anoints Yah Shua

6 But Yah Shua is in Beth Ania
in the house of Shimon the leper,

7 and a woman comes to him
having an alabaster of very precious myrrh
and as he reposes, pours it on his head.

8 But his disciples see it, and are indignified,
wording, What is the purpose of this destruction?

9 For this myrrh could have been sold for much
and given to the poor.

10 But knowing, Yah Shua says to them,
Why *trouble* **belabour and embarrass** ye the woman?
for she hath *wrought* **worked** a good work *upon* **unto** me.

11 For ye have the poor always with you;
but me ye have not always.

12 For in that she hath
poured this *ointment* **myrrh** on my body, she
did it *for* **unto** my *burial* **embalming**.

13 *Verily ! say* **Amen! I word** unto you,
Wheresoever this *gospel* **evangelism** shall be preached
in the whole *world* **cosmos**,
there shall also this, that this woman hath done,
be *told for* **spoken unto** a memorial of her.

Yah Hudah Seeks A Bribe

14 Then one of the twelve,
called Judas Iscariot **worded Yah Hudah the urbanite**,
went unto the *chief* **arch** priests,

15 And said unto them,
What will ye **to** give me,
and I *will* **shall** deliver him unto you?
And they covenanted with him for thirty *pieces of* silver.

16 And from *that time* **then**
he sought opportunity to betray him.

The Final Pasach Of Yah Shua

17 Now the first day
of the *feast of unleavened bread* **matsah**
the disciples came to *Jesus* **Yah Shua**,
saying **wording** unto him,
Where *wilt* **willest** thou that we prepare for thee
to eat the *passover* **pasach**?

18 And he said, Go into the
city to *such a man* **so and so**,
and say unto him, The *Master saith* **Doctor
wordeth**, My *time* **season** is *at hand* **nigh**;
I *will keep* **shall do** the *passover* **pasach** at thy house
with my disciples.

19 And the disciples did

as *Jesus* **Yah Shua** had *appointed* **ordered** them;
and they *made ready* **prepared** the *passover* **pasach**.
20 Now when *the even was come* **being evening**,
he *sat down* **reposed** with the twelve.
21 And as they did eat, he said,
Verily ! say **Amen! I word** unto you,
that one of you shall betray me.
22 And they were *exceeding* **extremely** sorrowful,
and began *every one* **each** of them to *say* **word** unto him,
Lord **Adonay**, is it I?
23 And he answered and said,
He that *dippeth* **baptizeth** his hand with me in the dish,
the same shall betray me.
24 The Son of *man* **humanity indeed** goeth
exactly as it is *written of* **scribed concerning** him:
but woe unto that *man* **human**
by **through** whom the Son of *man* **humanity** is betrayed!
it had been good for that *man* **human**
if he had not been *born* **birthed**.
25 Then *Judas* **But Yah Hudah**,
which betrayed him,
answered and said, *Master* **Rabbi**, is it I?
He *said* **worded** unto him, Thou hast said.

The Final Eucharist Of Yah Shua

26 And as they were eating,
Jesus **Yah Shua** took bread,
and *blessed* it **eulogized** and brake it,
and gave it to the disciples, and said,
Take, eat; this is my body.
27 And he took the cup, and
gave thanks **eucharistized**,
and gave it to them, *saying* **wording**, Drink ye all of it;
28 For this is my blood of the
new *testament* **covenant**,
which is *shed* **poured** for many
for **unto** the *remission* **forgiveness** of sins.
29 But I *say* **word** unto you,
I *will* **shall** *not* **never no way** drink henceforth
of this *fruit* **produce** of the vine,
until that day when I drink it new with you
in my Father's *kingdom* **sovereigndom**.
30 And when they had *sung an hymn* **hymned**,
they went out into the mount of Olives.
Why belabor and embarrass the woman?
For she works a good work to me:
11 for you have the poor with you always;
but me you have not always:
12 for in pouring this myrrh on my body
she does it to my embalming.

13 Amen! I word to you,
Wherever this evangelism is preached
in the whole cosmos,
this also, what this woman did,
is spoken to her memorial.

Yah Hudah Seeks A Bribe

14 Then one of the twelve,
worded Yah Hudah the urbanite,
goes to the archpriests,
15 and says to them,
What will you to give me to deliver him to you?
— and they covenant with him for thirty silver
16 — and from then
he seeks opportunity to betray him.

The Final Pasach Of Yah Shua

17 But on the first of matsah
the disciples come to Yah Shua, wording to him,
Where will you have us prepare for you
to eat the pasach?
18 And he says, Go into the city to so and so
and say to him,
The Doctor words, My season is near;
I do the pasach at your house with my disciples.
19 And the disciples do as Yah Shua orders them
and they prepare the pasach:
20 and being evening,
he reposes with the twelve.
21 And as they eat, he says,
Amen! I word to you,
that one of you betrays me.
22 And they are extremely sorrowful,
and each of them begins to word to him,
Adonay, is it I?
23 And he answers, saying,
He who baptizes his hand in the dish with me,
the same betrays me.
24 The Son of humanity indeed goes
exactly as scribed concerning him:
but woe to that human
through whom the Son of humanity is betrayed!
it had been good for that human
if he had not been birthed.
25 But Yah Hudah, who betrays him,
answers, saying, Rabbi, is it I?
He words to him, You said.

The Final Eucharist Of Yah Shua

26 And as they eat, Yah Shua takes bread,

and eulogizes and breaks,
and gives it to the disciples, and says,
Take, eat; this is my body.

27 And he takes the cup, and eucharistizes,
and gives it to them, wording,
Drink thereof — all:

28 for this is my blood of the new covenant
poured for many to the forgiveness of sins.

29 But I word to you,
I never no way drink henceforth
of this produce of the vine,
until that day I drink it anew with you
in the sovereigndom of my Father.

30 — and they hymn, and go
to the mount of Olives.

31 Then *saith Jesus* **wordeth Yah Shua** unto them,
All ye shall be *offended because of* **scandalized in** me
this night:
for it is *written* **scribed**, I *will* **shall** smite the shepherd,
and the sheep of the *flock* **shepherddom**
shall be scattered *abroad*.

32 But after I am risen *again*,
I *will go before* **shall precede** you into
Galilee **Galiyl**. Zechar Yah 13:7

33 *Peter* **Petros** answered and said unto him,
Though all *men* shall be *offended* **scandalized**
because of **in** thee,
yet *will* **shall** I never *ever* be *offended* **scandalized**.

34 *Jesus* **Yah Shua** said unto him,
Verily ! say **Amen! I word** unto thee,
That this night, *before* **ere** the *cock crow* **rooster voiceth**,
thou shalt *utterly* deny me thrice.

35 *Peter said* **Petros worded** unto him,
Though *! should* **And if I must** die with thee,
yet *will* **shall** I not *ever* **utterly** deny thee.
Likewise also said all the disciples.

Yah Shua In Gath Shemen

36 Then cometh *Jesus* **Yah Shua** with them
unto a *place* **parcel**
called *Gethsemane* **worded Gath Shemen**,
and *saith* **wordeth** unto the disciples,
Sit ye here, while I go and pray yonder.

37 And he took with him *Peter* **Petros**
and the two sons of *Zebedee* **Zabdi**,
and began to be sorrowful and *very heavy* **to heave**.

38 Then *saith* **wordeth** he unto them,
My soul is exceeding sorrowful, even unto death:
tarry **abide** ye here, and watch with me.

39 And he *went a little farther* **proceeded**,
and fell on his face, and prayed, *saying* **wording**,
O my Father, if it be possible, let this cup pass from me:
nevertheless **however** not as I will,
but as thou *wilt* **willest**.

40 And he cometh unto the disciples,
and findeth them asleep,
and *saith* **wordeth** unto *Peter* **Petros**,
What **Thus**, could ye not watch with me one hour?

41 Watch and pray,
that ye enter not into *temptation* **testing**:
the spirit indeed is *willing* **eager**,
but the flesh *is weak* **frail**.

42 He went away again the
second time, and prayed,
saying **wording**, O my Father,
if this cup may *not* pass **not** away from me,
except **unless** I drink it,
thy *will* **shall** be *done*.

43 And he came and found them asleep again:
for their eyes were heavy.

44 And he left them, and went away again,
and prayed the third time, saying the same words.

45 Then cometh he to his disciples, and *saith* **wordeth**
unto them, Sleep on *now*, and *take your* rest:
behold, the hour *is at hand* **approacheth**,
and the Son of *man* **humanity**
is betrayed into the hands of sinners.

46 Rise, let us be going: behold,
he *is at hand* **approacheth** that
doth betray **betrayeth** me.

The Betrayal And Arrest Of Yah Shua

47 And while he yet spake, *lo* **behold**,
Judas **Yah Hudah**, one of the twelve, came,
and with him
a *great* **vast** multitude with swords and staves,
from the *chief* **arch** priests and elders of the people.

48 Now he that betrayed him gave them a sign,
saying **wording**, Whomsoever I shall kiss,
that same is he: *hold* **overpower** him *fast*.

49 And *forthwith* **straightway**
he came to *Jesus* **Yah Shua**,
and said, *Hail* **Cheers**, *master* **Rabbi**;
and **ardently** kissed him.

50 And *Jesus* **Yah Shua** said unto him,
Friend **Comrade**, wherefore art thou *come* **here**?

31 Then Yah Shua words to them,
All you scandalize in me this night:
for it is scribed, I smite the shepherd,
and the sheep of the shepherddom scatter:

32 but after I rise, I precede you into Galiyl.
Zechar Yah 13:7
33 Petros answers him, saying,
Though all scandalize in you,
yet I never ever scandalize.
34 Yah Shua says to him,
Amen! I word to you,
This night, ere the rooster voices,
you utterly deny me thrice.
35 Petros words to him,
And if I must die with you,
I never ever utterly deny you.
— likewise also say all the disciples.

YAH SHUA IN GATH SHEMEN

36 Then Yah Shua goes with them
to a parcel worded Gath Shemen;
and words to the disciples,
You sit here, while I go yonder and pray.
37 And he takes Petros
and the two sons of Zabdi with him,
and begins to sorrow and to heave:
38 then he words to them,
My soul sorrows exceedingly — even to death:
you abide here and watch with me.
39 And he proceeds and falls on his face
and prays, wording, O my Father,
if possible, pass this cup from me
— however, not as I will — but as you will.
40 And he comes to the disciples,
and finds them sleeping;
and words to Petros,
Thus, can you not watch with me one hour?
41 Watch and pray, that you not enter into testing:
the spirit indeed is eager; but the flesh, frail.
42 He goes again the second time, and prays,
wording, O my Father,
if this cup not pass from me unless I drink it,
your will become.
43 And he comes, and again finds them sleeping:
for their eyes are heavy:
44 and he leaves them and goes again
and prays the third time, saying the same words.
45 Then he comes to his
disciples and words to them,
Sleep on! and, Rest!
Behold, the hour approaches,
to betray the Son of humanity
into the hands of sinners.
46 Rise! We go!
Behold, he who betrays me approaches.

THE BETRAYAL AND ARREST OF YAH SHUA

47 And as he yet speaks, behold,
Yah Hudah, one of the twelve, comes,
and with him
a vast multitude with swords and staves
from the archpriests and elders of the people.
48 And he who betrays him gives them a sign,
wording, Whomever I kiss, that same is he.
Overpower him.
49 And straightway he comes to Yah Shua,
and says, Cheers, Rabbi!
— and ardently kisses him.
50 And Yah Shua says to him,
Comrade, why are you here?
Then came they, and laid hands on *Jesus* **Yah Shua**
and *took* **overpowered** him.
51 And, behold,
one of them which were with *Jesus* **Yah Shua**
stretched out **spread** his hand,
and *drew* **withdrew** his sword,
and *struck* **smote** a servant of the *high* **arch** priest's,
and *smote off* **removed** his ear **lobe**.
52 Then *said Jesus* **worded Yah Shua** unto him,
Put up again **Return** thy sword into his place:
for all they that take the sword
shall *perish with* **destruct in** the sword.
53 Thinkest thou
that I cannot now *pray to* **beseech** my Father,
and he shall presently give me
much more than twelve legions of angels?
54 *But* how *then* shall the
scriptures be fulfilled/**shalamed**,
that thus it must be?
55 In that same hour said *Jesus*
Yah Shua to the multitudes,
Are ye come out as against a *thief* **robber**
with swords and staves for to take me?
I sat daily with you
teaching **doctrinating** in the *temple* **priestal precinct**,
and ye *laid no hold on* **overpowered** me **not**.
56 But all this *was done* **became**,
that the scriptures of the prophets
might be fulfilled/**shalamed**.
Then all the disciples forsook him, and fled.

YAH SHUA FACES THE ARCH PRIEST

57 And they that had
laid hold on Jesus **overpowered Yah Shua**

led him away to Caiaphas the *high* **arch** priest,
where the scribes and the elders
were assembled **together**.

58 But *Peter* **Petros** followed him **from** afar *off*
unto the *high* **arch** priest's *palace* **courtyard**,
and *went in* **entered**,
and sat with the *servants* **attendants**,
to see the *end* **completion/shalom**.

59 Now the *chief* **arch** priests, and elders,
and all the *council* **sanhedrim**,
sought *false* **pseudo** witness against *Jesus* **Yah Shua**,
to *put* **deathify** him *to death*;

60 But found none:
yea, though many *false* **pseudo** witnesses came,
yet found they none.
At the last **Afterward** came two *false* **pseudo** witnesses,

61 And said, This *fellow* said,
I am able
to *destroy* **disintegrate** the *temple* **nave** of *God* **Elohim**,
and to build it *in* **through** three days.

62 And the *high* **arch** priest
arose, and said unto him,
Answerest thou *nothing* **naught**?
what is it which these witness against thee?

63 But *Jesus held his peace* **Yah Shua hushed**.
And the *high* **arch** priest answered and said unto him,
I *adjure* **exorcise** thee by the living *God* **Elohim**,
that thou *tell* **say to** us
whether thou be the *Christ* **Messiah**,
the Son of *God* **Elohim**.

64 *Jesus saith* **Yah Shua wordeth** unto him,
Thou hast said:
nevertheless **moreover** I *say* **word** unto you,
Hereafter **From now on** shall ye see
the Son of *man* **humanity**
sitting *on* **at** the right hand of *power* **the dynamis**,
and coming in the clouds of **the** heaven.

65 Then the *high* **arch** priest
rent **ripped** his clothes,
saying **wording**, He hath *spoken blasphemy* **blasphemed**;
what further need have we of witnesses?
behold, now ye have heard his blasphemy.

66 What think ye?
They answered and said, He is *guilty of* **subject to** death.

67 Then did they spit in his face,
and *buffeted* **punched** him;
and others *smote* **slapped** him
with the palms of their hands,

68 *Saying* **Wording**,
Prophesy unto us, thou *Christ* **Messiah**,

Who is he that smote thee?
They come and lay hands on Yah Shua
and overpower him:

51 and behold, one of them with Yah Shua
spreads his hand and draws his sword
and smites a servant of the archpriest
and removes his ear lobe.

52 Then Yah Shua words to him,
Return your sword to its place:
for all who take the sword destruct in the sword.

53 Think you
that I am not able now to beseech my Father,
and he presently gives me
much more than twelve legions of angels?

54 How then are the scriptures fulfilled/shalamed,
that it must be thus?

55 In that same hour
Yah Shua says to the multitudes,
Come you as upon a robber
to take me with swords and staves?
I sat daily with you
doctrinating in the priestal precinct,
and you overpowered me not.

56 — but all this becomes
to fulfill/shalam the scriptures of the prophets.
— then all the disciples forsake him, and flee.

YAH SHUA FACES THE ARCHPRIEST

57 And they who overpowers Yah Shua
lead him to Caiaphas the archpriest,
where the scribes and the elders assemble together:

58 and Petros follows him from afar
to the courtyard of the archpriest;
and enters and sits with the attendants
to see the completion/shalom.

59 And the archpriests and elders
and all the sanhedrim
seek pseudo witnesses against Yah Shua
to deathify him;

60 but find none
— yes, though many pseudo witnesses come,
yet they find none.
Afterward two pseudo witnesses come,

61 and say, This one says,
I am able to disintegrate the nave of Elohim
and to build it through three days.

62 And the archpriest rises, and says to him,
Answer you naught?
What witness these against you?

63 — but Yah Shua hushes.

And the archpriest answers him, saying,
I exorcise you by the living Elohim,
to say to us
whether you be the Messiah, the Son of Elohim.
64 Yah Shua words to him, You said!
Moreover I word to you,
From now on you see the Son of humanity
sitting at the right of the *dynamis*,
and coming in the clouds of the heavens.
65 Then the archpriest rips his clothes,
wording, He blasphemes!
What further need have we of witnesses?
Behold, now you heard his blasphemy!
66 What think you?
They answer, saying, He is subject to death.
67 — then they spit in his face and punch him.
And others slap him,
68 Wording, Prophesy to us, you Messiah,
Who smote you?

THE FIRST DENIAL OF PETROS

69 Now *Peter* **Petros** sat without
in the *palace* **courtyard**:
and a *damsel* **lass** came unto him, *saying* **wording**,
Thou also wast with *Jesus* **Yah Shua** of *Galilee* **Galiyl**.
70 But he denied *before them* **in front of all**,
saying **wording**, I know not what thou *sayest* **speakest**.

THE SECOND DENIAL OF PETROS

71 And when he was gone out into the *porch* **gate**,
another *maid* saw him,
and *said* **worded** unto them that were there,
This *fellow*
was also with *Jesus of Nazareth* **Yah Shua the Nazarene**.
72 And again he denied with an oath,
I *do not* know *not* the *man* **human**.

THE THIRD DENIAL OF PETROS

73 And after a while came
unto him they that stood by,
and said to *Peter* **Petros**,
Surely **Truly** thou also art one of them;
for thy speech *bewrayeth* **maketh** thee *evident*.
74 Then began he to curse and
to *swear* **anathematize**,
saying, I know not the *man* **human**.
And *immediately* **straightway**
the *cock crew* **rooster voiced**.
75 And *Peter* **Petros** remembered
the *word* **rhema** of *Jesus* **Yah Shua**, which said unto him,

Before **Ere** the *cock crow* **rooster voiceth**,
thou shalt **utterly** deny me thrice.
And he went out, and wept bitterly.

YAH SHUA FACES PILATOS

27 *When the* **And being early** morning *was come*,
all the *chief* **arch** priests and elders of the people
took counsel against *Jesus* **Yah Shua**
to *put* **deathify** him *to death*:
2 And when they had bound
him, they led him away,
and delivered him to Pontius *Pilate* **Pilatos** the governor.

THE REGRET OF YAH HUDAH

3 Then *Judas* **Yah Hudah**,
which had betrayed him,
when he saw that he was condemned,
repented himself **regretted**,
and brought again the thirty *pieces of* silver
to the *chief* **arch** priests and elders,
4 *Saying* **Wording**, I have sinned
in that I have betrayed *the innocent* **guiltless** blood.
And they said, What is that to us? see thou to that.
5 And he *cast down* **tossed** the *pieces of* silver
in the *temple* **nave**,
and departed, and went and *hanged* **strangled** himself.
6 And the *chief* **arch** priests took the silver *pieces*,
and said, It is not *lawful for* **allowed**
to put them into the *treasury* **qurban**,
because it is the price of blood.
7 And they took counsel,
and *bought with* **marketed of** them the potter's field,
to *bury* **entomb** strangers *in*.
8 *Wherefore* **So** that field was called,
The field of blood, unto this day.
9 Then was fulfilled/**shalamed**
that which was *spoken* **rhetorized**
by Jeremy **through Yirme Yah** the prophet,
saying **wording**, And they took the thirty *pieces of* silver,
the price of him that was *valued* **priced**,
whom they of the *children* **sons** of *Israel* **Yisra El**
did value **priced**;
10 And gave them *for* **unto** the potter's field,
exactly as *the Lord appointed* **Yah Veh ordered** me.
cp Zechar Yah 11:12,13
11 And *Jesus* **Yah Shua**
stood *before* **in front of** the governor:
and the governor asked him, *saying* **wording**,
Art thou the *king* **sovereign** of the *Jews* **Yah Hudiym**?
And *Jesus* **Yah Shua** said unto him,

	Thou *sayest* **wordest**.
12	And *when he was* **in his being** accused
	of the *chief* **arch** priests and elders,
	he answered *nothing* **naught**.
13	Then *said Pilate* **worded Pilatos** unto him,
	Hearest thou not
	how *many things* **much** they witness against thee?

THE FIRST DENIAL OF PETROS

69	And Petros sits outside in the courtyard:
	and a lass comes to him, wording,
	You also are with Yah Shua of Galiyl.
70	And he denies in front of all,
	wording, I know not what you speak.

THE SECOND DENIAL OF PETROS

71	And he goes to the gate, and another sees him:
	and words to them who are there,
	This *one* also was with Yah Shua the Nazarene.
72	And again he denies with an oath,
	I know not the human.

THE THIRD DENIAL OF PETROS

73	And after a little,
	those standing by come to Petros,
	and say, Truly you also are one of them;
	for your speech makes you evident.
74	Then he begins to curse and to anathematize,
	I know not the human.
	— and straightway the rooster voices.
75	And Petros remembers the rhema of Yah Shua,
	saying to him,
	Ere the rooster voices,
	you utterly deny me thrice.
	— and he goes and weeps bitterly.

YAH SHUA FACES PILATOS

27	And being early morning,
	all the archpriests and elders of the people
	take counsel against Yah Shua to deathify him:
2	and they bind him and lead him away
	and deliver him to Pontius Pilatos the governor.

THE REGRET OF YAH HUDAH

3	Then Yah Hudah, who betrayed him,
	seeing he is condemned, regrets,
	and brings again the thirty silvers
	to the archpriests and elders;
4	wording, I sinned in betraying guiltless blood.

	And they say, What is that to us? You see to that.
5	— and he tosses the silver in the nave
	and departs and goes and strangles himself.
6	And the archpriests takes the silver, and say,
	It is not allowed to put them into the qurban
	because it is the price of blood.
7	And they take counsel,
	and they market of them
	the field of the potter to entomb strangers:
8	so that field is called, The field of blood,
	to this day.
9	— then to fulfill/shalam
	what Yirme Yah the prophet rhetorized,
	wording, And they take the thirty silvers
	the price of him who is priced
	— whom they of the sons of Yisra El priced;
10	and give them to the field of the potter
	exactly as Yah Veh ordered me.
	cp Zechar Yah 11:12,13
11	And Yah Shua stands in front of the governor:
	and the governor asks him, wording,
	Are you the sovereign of the Yah Hudiym?
	And Yah Shua say to him, You worded.
12	— and in his being accused
	by the archpriests and elders,
	he answers naught.
13	Then Pilatos words to him,
	Hear you not how much they witness against you?
14	And he answered him
	to never a word **not even a rhema**;
	insomuch that the governor marvelled *greatly* **extremely**.
15	Now at that *feast* **celebration**
	the governor was *wont* **accustomed**
	to release unto the *people* **multitude** a prisoner,
	whom they *would* **willed**.
16	And they had then *a notable*
	an eminent prisoner,
	called Barabbas **worded Bar Abbas**.
17	*Therefore* **So** when they were gathered together,
	Pilate **Pilatos** said unto them,
	Whom *will* **shall** ye that I release unto you?
	Barabbas **Bar Abbas**,
	or *Jesus* **Yah Shua**
	which is *called Christ* **worded Messiah**?
18	For he knew
	that for envy they had delivered him.
19	When he was set down on
	the *judgment seat* **bamah**,
	his *wife* sent **woman apostolized** unto him,
	saying **wording**,

MATTHEW/MATIT'YAH - HA'LEVI 27

Have thou *nothing* **naught** to do with that just man:
for I have suffered *many things* **much** this day in a dream
because of him.

20 But the *chief* **arch** priests and elders
persuaded **convinced** the multitude
that they should ask *Barabbas* **Bar Abbas**,
and destroy *Jesus* **Yah Shua**.

21 The governor answered and said unto them,
Whether of the twain will ye that I release unto you?
They said, *Barabbas* **Bar Abbas**.

22 *Pilate saith* **Pilatos wordeth** unto them,
So What shall I do *then* with *Jesus* **Yah Shua**
which is *called Christ* **worded Messiah**?
They all *say* **word** unto him, Let him be *crucified* **Stake**.

23 And the governor said,
Why **Indeed**, what evil hath he done?
But they cried out *the more* **superabundantly**,
saying **wording**, Let him be *crucified* **Stake**.

24 When *Pilate* **Pilatos** saw
that he could *prevail nothing* **not benefit naught**,
but that rather a *tumult was made* **riot became**,
he took water,
and washed his hands *before* **in front of** the multitude,
saying **wording**,
I am *innocent* **guiltless** of the blood of this just person:
see ye to it.

25 *Then* **And** answered all the people, and said,
His blood *be* on us, and on our children.

Bar Abbas Released, Yah Shua Betrayed

26 Then released he *Barabbas*
Bar Abbas unto them:
and when he had *scourged Jesus* **whipped Yah
Shua**, he delivered him to be *crucified* **staked**.

27 Then the *soldiers* **warriors** of the governor
took *Jesus* **Yah Shua** into the *common hall* **praetorium**,
and gathered **together** unto him
the whole *band* **squad** of soldiers.

28 And they stripped him, and
put on him a scarlet robe.

29 And when they had
platted **braided** a *crown* **wreath** of thorns,
they put it upon his head, and a reed in his right *hand*:
and they *bowed the knee before* **kneeled in front of** him,
and mocked him, *saying* **wording**, *Hail* **Cheers**,
king **sovereign** of the *Jews* **Yah Hudiym**!

30 And they spit upon him, and took the reed,
and *smote* **struck** him on the head.

31 And after that they had mocked him,
they *took* **stripped** the robe *off* from him,
and *put* **endued** his own *raiment* **garment** on him,
and led him away to *crucify* **stake** him.

32 And as they came out,
they found a *man of Cyrene* **human — a Cyrenian**,
Simon **Shimon** by name:
him they compelled to bear his *cross* **stake**.

33 And when they were come unto a place
called Golgotha **worded Golgoleth**,
that is to *say* **word**, *a place of a skull* **cranium place**,

34 They gave him vinegar to
drink mingled with *gall* **choler**:
and when he had tasted thereof,
he *would* **willed to** not drink.

14 And he answers him not even a rhema;
so that the governor marvels extremely.

15 And at that celebration
the governor is accustomed
to release a prisoner to the multitude
— whom they will:

16 and then hey have an eminent prisoner,
worded Bar Abbas.

17 So they gather together,
and Pilatos says to them,
Whom will you that I release to you?
Bar Abbas? Or Yah Shua, worded Messiah?

18 — for he knows they deliver
him because of envy.

19 As he sits on the bamah,
his woman apostolizes him,
wording, Have naught to do with that just man:
for I suffered much this day in a dream
because of him.

20 But the archpriests and elders
convince the multitude to ask for Bar Abbas
and destroy Yah Shua.

21 The governor answers them, saying,
Which of the two will you that I release to you?
They say, Bar Abbas.

22 Pilatos words to them,
What then do I with Yah Shua who is worded Messiah?
They all word to him, Stake!

23 And the governor says,
Indeed, what evil has he done?
But they cry out superabundantly, wording, Stake!

24 And Pilatos sees he cannot benefit aught,
but rather, a riot becomes,
he takes water,
and washes his hands in front of the multitude,
wording,

I am guiltless of the blood of this just person:
you see to it.

25 And all the people answer, saying,
His blood — on us and on our children.

Bar Abbas Released, Yah Shua Betrayed

26 Then he releases Bar Abbas to them:
and he whips Yah Shua,
and delivers him to stake.

27 Then the warriors of the governor
take Yah Shua into the praetorium,
and gather the whole squad of soldiers to him:

28 and they strip him, and
put a scarlet robe on him:

29 and they braid a wreath of thorns,
and put it on his head; and a reed in his right:
and they kneel in front of him, and mock him,
wording, Cheers, sovereign of the Yah Hudiym!

30 And they spit on him
and take the reed and strike him on the head:

31 and after they mock him
they strip off the robe
and endue his own garment on him;
and lead him away to stake him.

32 And as they come out,
they find a human — a Cyrenian, Shimon by name:
and they compel him to bear his stake.

33 And they come to a place worded Golgoleth
— worded, Cranium Place;

34 they give him vinegar mingled with choler
to drink;
and he tastes thereof, and wills to not drink.

Yah Shua Is Staked

35 And they *crucified* **staked** him,
and *parted* **divided** his garments, casting lots:
that it might be fulfilled/shalamed
which was *spoken* **rhetorized** by the prophet,
They *parted* **divided** my garments among them,
and upon my *vesture did* **garment** they cast lots.
Psalm 22:18

36 And sitting down they
watched **guarded** him there;

37 And *set up over* **put above** his head
his accusation *written* **scribed**,
THIS IS *JESUS* **YAH SHUA**
THE *KING* **SOVEREIGN** OF THE
JEWS **YAH HUDIYM**.

38 Then were there two *thieves* **robbers**
crucified **staked** with him,
one *on* **at** the right *hand*, and *another on* **one at** the left.

39 And they that passed by
reviled **blasphemed** him,
wagging their heads,

40 And *saying* **wording**,
Thou that *destroyest* **disintegratest** the *temple* **nave**,
and buildest it in three days, save thyself.
If thou be the Son of *God* **Elohim**,
come down **descend** from the *cross* **stake**.

41 Likewise also the *chief*
arch priests mocking him,
with the scribes and elders, *said* **worded**,

42 He saved others; himself he cannot save.
If he be the *king* **sovereign** of *Israel* **Yisra El**,
let him now *come down* **descend** from the *cross* **stake**,
and we *will believe* **shall trust in** him.

43 He *trusted* **confided** in *God* **Elohim**;
let him *deliver* **rescue** him now,
if he *will have him* **willeth**:
for he said, I am the Son of *God* **Elohim**.

44 The thieves also,
which were *crucified* **staked** with him,
cast the same in his teeth **reproached him**.

45 Now from the sixth hour
there *was* **became** darkness over all the *land* **earth**
unto the ninth hour.

46 And about the ninth hour
Jesus **Yah Shua** cried with a *loud* **mega** voice,
saying **wording**,
Eli, Eli, lama sabachthani?
that is *to say*,
My *God* **Elohim**, my *God* **Elohim**,
why hast thou forsaken me?
Psalm 22:1

47 Some of them that stood there,
when they heard that, *said* **worded**,
This *man calleth for Elias* **voiceth to Eli Yah**.

48 And straightway one of
them ran, and took a spunge,
and filled it with vinegar, and put it on a reed,
and gave him to drink.

49 The rest *said* **worded**, *Let be* **Allow**,
let us see
whether *Elias will* **Eli Yah shall** come to save him.

50 *Jesus* **Yah Shua**,
when he had cried again with a *loud* **mega** voice,
yielded up the ghost **released his spirit**.

Material And Physical Reactions

51 And, behold,
the veil of the *temple* **nave** was *rent* **split** in twain
from *the top to the bottom* **above to downward**;
and the earth *did quake* **quaked**, and the rocks *rent* **split**;
52 And the *graves* **tombs** were opened;
and many bodies of the *saints* **holy** which slept arose,
53 And came out of the *graves* **tombs**
after his *resurrection* **rising**,
and *went* **entered** into the holy city,
and *appeared* **manifested** unto many.
54 Now when the centurion,
and they that were with him,
watching Jesus **guarding Yah Shua**,
saw the *earthquake* **quake**,
and those *things* that *were done* **became**,
they *feared greatly* **awed extremely**, *saying* **wording**,
Truly this was the Son of *God* **Elohim**.

Yah Shua Is Staked

35 And they stake him,
and divide his garments, casting lots:
to fulfill/shalam what the prophet rhetorized,
They divided my garments among them
and upon my garment they cast lots.
Psalm 22:18
36 And sitting down they guard him there:
37 and above his head put his accusation scribed,

This Is Yah Shua The Sovereign Of The Yah Hudiym.

38 Then they stake two robbers with him,
one at the right and one at the left.
39 And those passing by blaspheme him,
wagging their heads
40 and wording,
You who disintegrates the nave
and builds it in three days, save yourself!
If you are the Son of Elohim, descend from the stake!
41 Likewise also the archpriests
with the scribes and elders mock him, wording,
42 He saved others; himself he cannot save.
If he be the sovereign of Yisra El,
have him now descend from the stake;
and we trust in him.
43 He confides in Elohim;
have him rescue him now — if he wills:
for he says, I am the Son of Elohim.
44 — the thieves staked with
him also reproach him.
45 And from the sixth hour
darkness becomes over all the earth
to the ninth hour:
46 and about the ninth hour
Yah Shua cries with a mega voice, wording,
Eli, Eli, lama sabachthani?
that is,
My Elohim, my Elohim,
why forsake you me?
Psalm 22:1
47 Some of them standing there, hearing that,
word, This one voices to Eli Yah.
48 And straightway one of them runs
and takes a spunge and fills it with vinegar
and puts it on a reed and gives him to drink.
49 The rest word, Allow!
We see whether Eli Yah comes to save him.
50 And again Yah Shua cries with a mega voice
and releases his spirit.

Material And Physical Reactions

51 And behold,
the veil of the nave splits in two
from above to downward;
and the earth quakes and the rocks split
52 and the tombs open;
and many bodies of the sleeping holy rise;
53 and come from the tombs after his rising
and enter the holy city and manifest to many.
54 And the centurion
and those with him guarding Yah Shua
see the quake and all that becomes;
and they awe extremely, wording,
Truly this is the Son of Elohim.
55 And many women were there
beholding **observing from** afar *off*,
which followed *Jesus* **Yah Shua** from *Galilee* **Galiyl**,
ministering unto him:
56 Among which was *Mary*
Miryam the Magdalene,
and *Mary* **Miryam**
the mother of *James* **Yaaqovos** and *Joses* **Yoses**,
and the mother of *Zebedee's children* **Zabdi's sons**.

Yah Shua Entombed

57 *When the even was come* **And being evening**,
there came a rich *man* **human** of *Arimathaea* **Ramah**,
named *Joseph* **Yoseph**,

who also himself
was *Jesus' disciple* **discipled by Yah Shua**:
58 He went to *Pilate* **Pilatos**,
and *begged* **asked** the body of *Jesus* **Yah Shua**.
Then *Pilate* **Pilatos**
commanded **summoned** the body to be *delivered* **given**.
59 And when *Joseph* **Yoseph** had taken the body,
he *wrapped* **entwined** it in *a clean* **pure** linen *cloth*,
60 And laid it in his own new tomb,
which he had *hewn* **quarried** out in the rock:
and he rolled a *great* **mega** stone
to the *door* **portal** of the *sepulchre* **tomb**,
and departed.
61 And there was *Mary* **Miryam the** Magdalene,
and the other *Mary* **Miryam**,
sitting over against the *sepulchre* **tomb**.

THE TOMB SEALED AND GUARDED

62 *Now the next day* **And being evening**,
that followed **after** the day of the preparation,
the *chief* **arch** priests and Pharisees
came **gathered** together unto *Pilate* **Pilatos**,
63 *saying* **wording**, Sir **Adoni**,
we remember that that *deceiver* **seducer** said,
while he was yet alive,
After three days I *will* **shall** rise *again*.
64 *Command therefore* **So Summon**
that the *sepulchre* **tomb** be *made sure* **secured**
until the third day,
lest *ever* his disciples come by night, and steal him away,
and say unto the people, He is risen from the dead:
so the *last error* **final deception**
shall be worse than the first.
65 *Pilate* **Pilatos** said unto them,
Ye have a *watch* **custodian**:
go your way, *make* **secure** it *as sure as ye* **know**.
66 So they went,
and *made the sepulchre sure* **secured the tomb**,
sealing the stone, and setting a *watch* **custodian**.

YAH SHUA IS RESURRECTED

28 In the *end* **eve** of the *sabbath* **shabbaths**,
as it began to dawn
toward **unto** the first *day* of the *week* **shabbaths**,
came *Mary* **Miryam the** Magdalene
and the other *Mary* **Miryam**
to *see* **observe** the *sepulchre* **tomb**.
2 And, behold,
there *was a great earthquake* **became a mega quake**:
for the angel of *the Lord* **Yah Veh**
descended from **the** heaven,
and came and rolled back the stone
from the *door* **portal**,
and sat upon it.
3 His countenance was *like* **as** lightning,
and his *raiment* **enduement** white as snow:
4 And for *fear* **awe** of him
the *keepers did shake* **guards quaked**,
and became as dead *men*
5 And the angel answered
and said unto the women,
Fear not ye **Be ye not awestricken**:
for I know that ye seek *Jesus* **Yah Shua**,
which was *crucified* **staked**.
6 He is not here: for he is risen, **exactly** as he said.
Come, see the place where *the Lord* **Adonay** lay.
7 And go quickly,
and *tell* **say to** his disciples that he is risen from the dead;
and, behold, he *goeth before* **precedes**
you into *Galilee* **Galiyl**;
there shall ye see him:
lo **behold**, I have *told* **said to** you.
55 And many women
who had followed Yah Shua from Galiyl
who ministered to him
observe from afar
56 — among whom are Miryam the Magdalene,
and Miryam the mother of Yaaqovos and Yoses,
and the mother of the sons of Zabdi.

YAH SHUA ENTOMBED

57 And being evening,
a rich human of Ramah named Yoseph comes
— who himself was also discipled by Yah Shua:
58 he goes to Pilatos
and asks for the body of Yah Shua:
then Pilatos summons the body to be given.
59 And Yoseph takes the body
and entwines it in pure linen;
60 and lays it in his own new tomb
which he quarried in the rock:
and he rolls a mega stone to the portal of the tomb
and departs:
61 and Miryam the Magdalene
and the other Miryam
sit opposite the tomb.

THE TOMB SEALED AND GUARDED

62 And on the morrow after
the day of the preparation

MATTHEW/MATIT'YAH - HA'LEVI 28

the archpriests and Pharisees gather together to Pilatos,
63 wording, Adoni,
we remember that seducer say,
while he was still alive,
After three days I rise.
64 So summon to secure the
tomb until the third day
— lest ever his disciples come by night
and steal him away and say to the people,
He rose from the dead!
— and the final deception is worse than the first.
65 Pilatos say to them, You have a custodian:
go your way, secure it as you know.
66 So they go and secure the tomb;
sealing the stone and setting a custodian.

YAH SHUA RESURRECTED

28 In the eve of the shabbaths
as it begins to dawn to the first of the shabbaths,
Miryam the Magdalene and the other Miryam
go to observe the tomb.
2 And behold, there is a mega quake:
for the angel of Yah Veh descends from the heavens
and comes and rolls the stone from the portal
and sits on it:
3 his countenance is as lightning
and his enduement white as snow:
4 and the guards quake in awe of him
and become as dead.
5 And the angel answers the women, saying,
Awe not:
for I know you seek Yah Shua who was staked:
6 he is not here: for he rose exactly as he said:
come, see the place where Adonay lay:
7 and go quickly
and say to his disciples that he rose from the dead;
and behold, he precedes you into Galiyl;
and there you see him:
behold, I have said to you.
8 And they departed quickly
from the *sepulchre* **tomb**
with *fear* **awe** and *great joy* **mega cheer**;
and did run to *bring* **evangelize** his disciples *word*.
9 And as they went to *tell* **evangelize** his disciples,
behold, *Jesus* **Yah Shua** met them, *saying* **wording**,
All hail **Cheers**.
And they came and *held* **overpowered** him by the feet,
and worshipped him.
10 Then *said Jesus* **worded Yah Shua** unto them,
Be **Awe** not *afraid*:

go *tell* **evangelize** my brethren
that they go into *Galilee* **Galiyl**,
and there shall they see me.

WARRIORS BRIBED TO DENY THE RESURRECTION

11 Now when they were going, behold,
some of the *watch* **custodians** came into the city,
and *shewed* **evangelized** unto the *chief* **arch** priests
all *the things* **those** that *were done* **became**.
12 And when they were assembled with the elders,
and had taken counsel,
they gave *large money* **ample silver**
unto the *soldiers* **warriors**,
13 *saying* **wording**, Say ye,
His disciples came by night,
and stole him away while we slept.
14 And *if this come to the governor's ears*
whenever the governor hears,
we *will persuade* **shall convince** him,
and *secure you* **make you unanxious**.
15 So they took the *money* **silver**,
and did as they were *taught* **doctrinated**: and
this *saying* **word** is commonly reported among
the *Jews* **Yah Hudiym** until this day.
16 *Then* **And** the eleven disciples
went away into *Galilee* **Galiyl**,
into a mountain
where *Jesus* **Yah Shua** had *appointed* **ordained** them.
17 And when they saw him, they worshipped him:
but some doubted.

THE FINAL MISVAH OF YAH SHUA

18 And *Jesus* **Yah Shua** came and spake unto them,
saying **wording**,
All *power* **authority** is given unto me
in heaven and in earth.
19 **So** Go ye *therefore*, and *teach*
disciple all *nations* **goyim**,
baptizing them in the name* of the Father,
and of the Son,
and of the *Holy Spirit* **Ruach ha-kodesh**:
20 *Teaching* **Doctrinating** them to *observe* **guard**
all *things whatsoever* — **as much as ever**
I have *commanded* **misvahed** you:
and, *lo* **behold**, I am with you *alway* **all days**,
even unto the *end* **completion/shalom** of the *world* **eon**.
Amen.
*name: Exodus 3:3—15, Yesha Yah 42:8, Yahn 8:58

8	And they depart quickly from the tomb with awe and mega cheer; and run to evangelize his disciples.
9	And as they go to evangelize his disciples, behold, Yah Shua meets them, wording, Cheers! — and they come and overpower him by the feet and worship him.
10	Then Yah Shua words to them, Awe not: go evangelize my brothers to go to Galiyl and see me there.

Warriors Bribed To Deny The Resurrection

11	And as they go, behold, some of the custodians come to the city, and evangelize to the archpriests all that became.
12	And they assemble with the elders and take counsel; they give ample silver to the warriors,
13	wording, Say, His disciples came by night, and stole him away while we slept:
14	and whenever the governor hears, we convince him, and make you unanxious.
15	So they take the silver and do as they are doctrinated: and this word is commonly reported among the Yah Hudiym until this day.
16	And the eleven disciples go to Galiyl — to a mountain where Yah Shua ordained them
17	— and they see him and worship him — but some doubt.

The Final Misvah Of Yah Shua

18	And Yah Shua comes and speaks to them, wording, All authority is given me in the heavens and in earth.
19	So go and disciple all goyim, baptizing them in the name* of the Father, and of the Son, and of the Holy Spirit:
20	doctrinating them to guard all — as much as ever I misvahed you: and behold, I am with you all days — even to the completion/shalom of the eon. Amen.

*name: Exodus 3:3—15, Yesha Yah 42:8, Yahn 8:58

YAH SHUA MESSIAH, THE SON OF ELOHIM

1 The beginning of the *gospel* **evangelism**
of *Jesus Christ* **Yah Shua Messiah**,
the Son of *God* **Elohim**;

2 As it is *written* **scribed** in the prophets, Behold,
I *send* **apostolize** my *messenger* **angel**
before **preceding** thy face,
which shall prepare thy way *before* **in front of** thee.

3 The voice of one crying in the wilderness,
Prepare ye the way of *the Lord* **Yah Veh**,
make his paths straight.
Malachi 3:1, Yesha Yah 40:3

YAHN THE BAPTIZER

4 **And so be it,** *John* **Yahn** did
baptize in the wilderness,
and *preach* **preaching** the baptism of repentance
for the *remission* **forgiveness** of sins.

5 And there *went out* **proceeded** unto him
all the *land* **region** of *Judaea* **Yah Hudah**,
and *they of Jerusalem* **the Yeru Shalemiym**,
and were all baptized of him
in the *river* **stream** of *Jordan* **Yarden**,
confessing **homologizing** their sins.

6 And *John* **Yahn** was *clothed*
endued with camel's hair,
and with a girdle of *a skin* **leather** about his
loins; and he did eat locusts and wild honey;

7 And preached, *saying* **wording**,
There cometh one mightier than I after
me, the *latchet* **thongs** of whose shoes
I am not worthy to stoop down and *unloose* **release**.

8 I indeed have baptized you *with* **in** water:
but he shall baptize you *with* **in** the
Holy Spirit **Ruach ha-kodesh**.

YAHN BAPTIZES YAH SHUA

9 And **so be it** *came to pass* in those days,
that *Jesus* **Yah Shua** came from
Nazareth of *Galilee* **Galiyl**,
and was baptized of *John* **Yahn** in *Jordan* **Yarden**.

HOLY SPIRIT DESCENDS ON YAH SHUA

10 And straightway
coming up **ascending** out of the water,
he saw the heavens *opened* **split**,
and the Spirit *like* **as** a dove descending upon him:

11 And there *came* **became** a voice
from *heaven* **the heavens**,
saying, Thou art my beloved Son,
in whom I *am well pleased* **well—approve**.

SATAN TESTS YAH SHUA

12 And *immediately* **straightway**
the spirit *driveth* **casteth** him into the wilderness.

13 And he was there in the wilderness forty days,
tempted **tested** of Satan; and was with the wild beasts;
and the angels ministered unto him.

YAH SHUA PREACHES THE SOVEREIGNDOM OF ELOHIM

14 Now after that *John* **Yahn**
was *put in prison* **betrayed**,
Jesus **Yah Shua** came into *Galilee* **Galiyl**,
preaching the *gospel* **evangelism**
of the *kingdom* **sovereigndom** of *God* **Elohim**,

15 And *saying* **wording**, The *time*
season is fulfilled/shalamed,
and the *kingdom* **sovereigndom** of *God* **Elohim**
is at hand **approacheth**:
repent ye, and *believe* **trust in** the *gospel* **evangelism**.

16 Now as he walked by the sea of *Galilee* **Galiyl**,
he saw *Simon* **Shimon** and *Andrews* **Andreas** his brother
casting a net into the sea: for they were fishers.

17 And *Jesus* **Yah Shua** said
unto them, Come ye after me,
and I *will* **shall** make you
to become fishers of *men* **humanity**.

18 And straightway they forsook their nets,
and followed him.

19 And when he had
gone a little farther **advanced** thence,
he saw *James* **Yaaqovos** *the son* of *Zebedee* **Zabdi**,
and *John* **Yahn** his brother,
who also were in the *ship* **sailer**
mending **preparing** their nets.

20 And straightway he called them:
and they *left* **forsook** their father *Zebedee* **Zabdi**
in the *ship* **sailer**
with the *hired servants* **hirelings**, and went after him.

YAH SHUA DOCTRINATES IN THE SYNAGOGUE

21 And they *went into* **entered**
Capernaum **Kaphar Nachum**;
and straightway on the *sabbath day* **shabbaths**

Yah Shua Messiah, The Son Of Elohim

1 The beginning of the evangelism
of Yah Shua Messiah, the Son of Elohim

2 as scribed in the prophets,
Behold,
I apostolize my angel preceding your face
who prepares your way in front of you

3 — the voice of one crying in the wilderness,
Prepare the way of Yah Veh,
make his paths straight.
Malachi 3:1, Yesha Yah 40:3

Yahn The Baptizer

4 And so be it,
Yahn baptizes in the wilderness
and preaches the baptism of repentance
for the forgiveness of sins:

5 and all the region of Yah Hudah
and the Yeru Shalemiym proceed to him;
and he baptizes them all in the stream of Yarden,
homologizing their sins.

6 And Yahn endues with camel hair
and a leather girdle around his loins;
and he eats locusts and wild honey:

7 and preaches, wording,
One comes after me, mightier than I,
whose shoe thongs
I am not worthy to stoop down and release.

8 I indeed baptize you in water:
but he baptizes you in the Holy Spirit.

Yahn Baptizes Yah Shua

9 And so be it, in those days,
Yah Shua comes from Nazareth, Galiyl,
and Yahn baptizes him in Yarden.

Holy Spirit Descends On Yah Shua

10 And straightway, ascending from the water,
he sees the heavens split,
and the Spirit as a dove descending on him:

11 and a voice becomes from the heavens,
You are my beloved Son in whom I well—approve.

Satan Tests Yah Shua

12 And straightway
the Spirit casts him in the wilderness:

13 and there he is, in the wilderness forty days,
tested of Satan;
and is with the wild beasts;
and the angels minister to him.

Yah Shua Preaches The Sovereigndom Of Elohim

14 And after Yahn is betrayed,
Yah Shua goes to Galiyl
preaching the evangelism
of the sovereigndom of Elohim:

15 and wording, The season fulfills/shalams,
and the sovereigndom of Elohim approaches:
repent, and trust in the evangelism.

16 And as he walks by the sea of Galiyl
he sees Shimon and Andreas his brother
casting a net into the sea — for they are fishers:

17 and Yah Shua says to them, Come after me,
and I make you to become fishers of humanity.

18 — and straightway they forsake their nets
and follow him.

19 And as he advances there,
he see Yaaqovos of Zabdi and his brother Yahn
also in the sailer preparing their nets

20 and straightway he calls them:
and they forsake their father Zabdi in the sailer
with the hirelings — and goes after him.

Yah Shua Doctrinates In The Synagogue

21 And they enter Kaphar Nachum;
and straightway on the shabbaths
he entered into the synagogue, and *taught* **doctrinated**.

22 And they were astonished at his doctrine:
for he *taught* **doctrinated** them as
one that had authority,
and not as the scribes.

Yah Shua Rebukes An Impure Spirit

23 And there was in their synagogue
a *man* **human** with an *unclean* **impure** spirit;
and he *cried out* **screamed**,

24 *saying* **wording**, Let us alone **Aha!**;
what have we to do with thee,
thou *Jesus of Nazareth* **Yah Shua the Nazarene**?
art thou come to destroy us?
I know thee who thou art, the Holy One of *God* **Elohim**.

25 And *Jesus* **Yah Shua** rebuked
him, *saying* **wording**,
Hold thy peace **Muzzle**, and come out of him.

26 And when the *unclean* **impure** spirit
had *torn* **convulsed** him,
and cried with a *loud* **mega** voice, he came out of him.

27 And they were all *amazed* **astonished**,
insomuch that they *questioned*
disputed among themselves,

MARK/MAKABI 1

saying **wording**,
What *thing* is this? what new doctrine is this?
for with authority *commandeth* **ordereth** he
even the *unclean* **impure** spirits,
and they *do* obey him.

28   And immediately his fame spread abroad
throughout **into** all the region round
about *Galilee* **Galiyl**.

YAH SHUA CURES THE MOTHER
IN LAW OF SHIMON

29   And *forthwith* **straightway**,
when they were come out of the synagogue
they entered
into the house of *Simon* **Shimon** and *Andrew* **Andreas**,
with *James* **Yaaqovos** and *John* **Yahn**.

30   But *Simon's wife's mother*
Shimon's mother in law
lay *sick of a fever* **fevered**,
and *anon* **straightway** they *tell* **word to** him *of* **about** her.

31   And he came and *took*
overpowered her by the hand,
and lifted her *up*;
and *immediately* **straightway** the fever *left* **forsook** her,
and she ministered unto them.

YAH SHUA CASTS OUT DEMONS AND CURES

32   And *at even* **being evening**,
when the sun *did* set,
they brought unto him all that were *diseased* **ill**, and
them that were *possessed with devils* **demonized**.

33   And all the city was gathered
together at the *door* **portal**.

34   And he *healed* **cured** many
that were *sick* **ill** of divers diseases,
and cast out many *devils* **demons**;
and *suffered* **allowed** not the *devils* **demons** to speak,
because they knew him.

YAH SHUA PRAYS AND PREACHES

35   And in the **early** morning,
rising *up a great while before day* **extremely night**,
he went out, and departed into a *solitary* **desolate** place,
and there prayed.

36   And *Simon* **Shimon** and
they that were with him
followed after him.

37   And when they had found him,
they *said* **worded** unto him, All *men* seek for thee.

38   And he *said* **worded** unto them,
Let us go into the *next towns* **nearby villages**,

that I may preach there also: for
therefore **this** came I forth.

39   And he preached in their synagogues
throughout **in** all *Galilee* **Galiyl**,
and cast out *devils* **demons**.

YAH SHUA PURIFIES A LEPER

40   And there came a leper to him, beseeching him,
and kneeling down to him,
and *saying* **wording** unto him,
If **Whenever** thou *wilt* **willest**,
thou canst *make* **purify** me *clean*.

41   And *Jesus* **Yah Shua**,
moved with *compassion* **sympathetic spleen**,
put forth **spread** his hand, and touched him,
and *saith* **wordeth** unto him,
I will; be thou *clean* **purified**.

42   And as soon as he had *spoken* **said**,
immediately **straightway** the leprosy departed from him,
and he was *cleansed* **purified**.

he enters the synagogue and doctrinates:

22   and they are astonished at his doctrine:
for he doctrinates them as one having authority
and not as the scribes.

YAH SHUA REBUKES AN IMPURE SPIRIT

23   And in their synagogue
there is a human with an impure spirit;
and he screams,

24   wording, Aha!
What have we to do with you
— Yah Shua, Nazarene?
Come you to destroy us?
I know you, who you are — the Holy One of Elohim.

25   And Yah Shua rebukes him, wording,
Muzzle! and, Come from him!

26   — and as the impure spirit convulses him
he cries with a mega voice and comes from him.

27   And they are all astonished,
so that they dispute among themselves, wording,
What is this? What new doctrine is this?
For with authority he orders even the impure spirits
and they obey him.

28   — and immediately his fame spreads abroad
into all the region all around Galiyl.

YAH SHUA CURES THE MOTHER
IN LAW OF SHIMON

29   And straightway, as they
come from the synagogue,

	they enter the house of Shimon and Andreas with Yaaqovos and Yahn:
30	and the mother in law of Shimon lies fevered; and straightway they word to him about her:
31	and he comes and overpowers her by the hand and lifts her; and straightway the fever forsakes her and she ministers to them.

Yah Shua Casts Out Demons And Cures

32	And being evening, as the sun sets, they bring him all the ill and the demonized:
33	and all the city gathers together at the portal:
34	and he cures many who are ill of divers diseases and casts out many demons; and allows not the demons to speak because they know him.

Yah Shua Prays And Preaches

35	And very early morning, still extremely night, he rises and goes and departs to a desolate place; and there he prays:
36	and Shimon and those with him follow after him:
37	and they find him, and they word to him, All seek for you.
38	And he words to them, We go to the nearby villages, to preach there also: for this I have come.
39	— and he preaches in their synagogues in all Galiyl and cast out demons.

Yah Shua Purifies A Leper

40	And a leper comes to him, beseeching him, and kneeling down to him, words to him, Whenever you will, you can purify me.
41	And Yah Shua, with sympathetic spleen, spreads his hand and touches him, and words to him, I will! Purify!
42	— and as soon as he says, straightway the leprosy departs from him and he purifies.
43	And he *straitly charged* **sternly enjoined** him, and *forthwith sent* **straightway cast** him *away* **forth**;
44	And *saith* **wordeth** unto him, See thou say *nothing* **naught** to any *man* **one**: but go thy way, shew thyself to the priest, and offer for thy *cleansing* **purifying** those *things* which *Moses commanded* **Mosheh ordered**, *for* **in** a *testimony* **witness** unto them.
45	But he went out, and began to *publish* **preach** it much, and to *blaze abroad* **report** the *matter* **word**, insomuch that *Jesus* **Yah Shua** could no more *openly* **manifestly** enter into the city, but was without in *desert* **desolate** places: and they came to him from every quarter.

Yah Shua Cures A Paralytic

2	And again he entered into *Capernaum* **Kaphar Nachum** after *some* days; and it was *noised* **heard** that he was in the house.
2	And straightway many were gathered together, insomuch that there was no *more* room to *receive* **place** them, no, not *so much as* **even** about the *door* **portal**: and he *preached* **spoke** the word unto them.
3	And they come unto him, bringing *one sick of the palsy* **a paralytic**, which was borne of four.
4	And when they could not come nigh unto him for the *press* **multitude**, they uncovered the *roof* **thatch** where he was: and when they had broken it *up*, they *let down* **lowered** the *bed* **pad** wherein the *sick of the palsy* **a paralytic** lay.
5	When *Jesus* **Yah Shua** saw their *faith* **trust**, he *said* **worded** unto the *sick of the palsy* **a paralytic**, *Son*, **Child**, thy sins be forgiven thee.
6	But there were *certain* **some** of the scribes sitting there, and reasoning in their hearts,
7	Why doth this man thus speak blasphemies? who can forgive sins *but God only* **except one — Elohim**? Yesha Yah 43:25
8	And *immediately* **straightway** *when Jesus perceived* **Yah Shua knowing** in his spirit that they *so* **thus** reasoned within themselves, he said unto them, Why reason ye these *things* in your hearts?
9	Whether is it easier to say to the *sick of the palsy* **a paralytic**, Thy sins be forgiven thee; or to say, Arise, and take *up* thy *bed* **pad**, and walk?
10	But that ye may know that the Son of *man* **humanity**

hath *power* **authority** on earth to forgive sins,
(he *saith* **wordeth** to the *sick of the palsy* **a paralytic**,)
11 I *say* **word** unto thee, Arise,
and take *up* thy *bed* **pad**,
and go thy way into thine house.
12 And *immediately* **straightway** he arose,
took *up* the *bed* **pad**,
and went forth *before* **in front of** them all;
insomuch that they were all *amazed* **astounded**,
and glorified *God* **Elohim**, *saying* **wording**,
We never *ever* saw it *on this fashion* **thus**.

Levi Follows Yah Shua

13 And he went *forth* again by the sea side;
and all the multitude *resorted* **came** unto
him, and he *taught* **doctrinated** them.
14 And as he passed by,
he saw Levi *the son* of *Alphaeus* **Heleph**
sitting at the *receipt of custom* **customs**,
and *said* **worded** unto him, Follow me.
And he arose and followed him.

Yah Shua Reposes With Customs Agents And Sinners

15 And *so be* it *came to pass*, that,
as *Jesus sat at meat* **Yah Shua reposed** in his house,
many *publicans* **customs agents** and sinners
sat **reposed** also together
with *Jesus* **Yah Shua** and his disciples:
for there were many, and they followed him.
43 And he sternly enjoins him
and straightway casts him forth
44 and words to him,
See that you say naught to anyone:
but go your way, show yourself to the priest,
and for your purifying,
offer what Mosheh ordered in a witness to them.
45 But he goes, and begins to preach much,
and to report the word,
so that Yah Shua
can no more manifestly enter the city,
but is outside in desolate places:
and they come to him from every quarter.

Yah Shua Cures A Paralytic

2 And again, days after,
he enters Kaphar Nachum;
and they hear he is in the house:
2 and straightway many gather together
so that there is no more room to place them
— no, not even around the portal:
and he speaks the word to them.
3 And they come to him
and bring a paralytic who is borne by four:
4 and they cannot approach him
because of the multitude;
and they uncover the thatch where he is:
and they break it,
and lower the pad wherein the paralytic lies.
5 And Yah Shua sees their trust
and he words to the paralytic,
Child, your sins be forgiven you.
6 And some of the scribes sitting there
reason in their hearts,
7 Why does this man thus speak blasphemies?
Who can forgive sins except one —
Elohim? Yesha Yah 43:25
8 And straightway Yah Shua,
knowing in his spirit,
that they reason thus within themselves,
he says to them,
Why reason you these in your hearts?
9 Which is it easier to say to the paralytic,
Your sins be forgiven you?
or to say, Rise and take your pad and walk?
10 But so that you know that the Son of humanity
has authority on earth to forgive sins
— he words to the paralytic,
11 I word to you, Rise and take your pad
and go your way to your house.
12 — and straightway he rises, takes the pad,
and goes in front of them all;
so that they are all astounded, and glorify Elohim,
wording, We never ever saw it thus.

Levi Follows Yah Shua

13 And again he goes by the sea side;
and all the multitude comes to him
and he doctrinates them.
14 And as he passes by
he sees Levi of Heleph sitting at the customs
and words to him, Follow me.
— and he rises and follows him.

Yah Shua Reposes With Customs Agents And Sinners

15 And so be it,
as Yah Shua reposes in his house,
many customs agents and sinners
also repose together with Yah Shua and his disciples:

for they are many, and they follow him.

16 And when the scribes and Pharisees
saw him eat with *publicans* **customs agents** and sinners,
they *said* **worded** unto his disciples,
How is it that he eateth and drinketh
with *publicans* **customs agents** and sinners?

17 When *Jesus* **Yah Shua** heard it, he *saith*
wordeth unto them, They that are *whole* **able**
have no need of the *physician* **healer**,
but they that are *sick* **ill**:
I came not to call the *righteous* **just**,
but sinners to repentance.

FASTING

18 And the disciples of *John*
Yahn and of the Pharisees
used to fast:
and they come and *say* **word** unto him,
Why do the disciples of *John* **Yahn**
and of the Pharisees fast,
but thy disciples fast not?

19 And *Jesus* **Yah Shua** said unto them,
Can the *children* **sons** of the bridechamber fast,
while **during the time** the bridegroom is with them?
as long *time* as they have the bridegroom with them,
they cannot fast.

20 But the days *will* **shall** come,
when the bridegroom shall be taken away from them,
and then shall they fast in those days.

PATCHING

21 No *man* **one**
also seweth a piece of *new* **unfulled** cloth
on an old garment:
else **but if not** the *new piece that filled it up* **fullness**
taketh away from the old,
and the *rent is made* **split becometh** worse.

NEW WINE, NEW SKINS

22 And no *man* **one**
putteth new wine into old *bottles* **skins**:
else **but if not** the new wine doth burst the *bottles* **skins**,
and the wine is *spilled* **poured**,
and the *bottles will be marred* **skins shall destruct**:
but new wine must be put into new *bottles* **skins**.

YAH SHUA, ADONAY OF THE SHABBATH

23 And *so be* it *came to pass*,
that he *went* **passed** through the *corn fields* **spores**
on the *sabbath day* **shabbaths**;
and his disciples began, as they *went* **made their way**,
to pluck *the ears of corn*.

24 And the Pharisees *said*
worded unto him, Behold,
why do they on the *sabbath day* **shabbaths**
that which is not *lawful* **allowed**?

25 And he *said* **worded** unto them,
Have ye never *ever* read what David did,
when he had need, and *was an hungred* **famished**,
he, and they that were with him?

26 How he *went into* **entered**
the house of *God* **Elohim**
in the days of *Abiathar* **Abi Athar** the *high* **arch** priest,
and did eat the *shewbread* **prothesis bread**,
which is not *lawful* **allowed** to eat
but **except** for the priests,
and gave also to them which were with him?
Leviticus 24:5—9

27 And he *said* **worded** unto them,
The *sabbath* **shabbaths**
was made **became** for *man* **humanity**,
and not *man* **humanity** for the *sabbath* **shabbaths**:

28 *Therefore* **So then** the Son of *man* **humanity**
is *Lord* **Adonay** also of the *sabbath* **shabbath**.

YAH SHUA CURES ON THE SHABBATH

3 And he entered again into the synagogue;
and there was a *man* **human** there
which had a withered hand.

2 And they *watched* **observed** him,
whether he *would heal* **should cure** him
on the *sabbath day* **shabbaths**;
that they might accuse him.

3 And he *saith* **wordeth**
unto the *man* **human** which had the withered hand,
Stand *forth* **in our midst**.

4 And he *saith* **wordeth** unto them,

16 And the scribes and Pharisees
see him eat with customs agents and sinners,
and they word to his disciples,
How is it that he eats and drinks
with customs agents and sinners?

17 And Yah Shua hears, and he words to them,
The able need no healer, but they who are ill:
I come not to call the just, but sinners to repentance.

FASTING

18 And the disciples of Yahn
and of the Pharisees fast:
and they come and word to him,

Why fast the disciples of Yahn and of the Pharisees
and your disciples fast not?
19 And Yah Shua says to them,
Can the sons of the bridechamber fast
during the time the bridegroom is with them?
As long time as they have the bridegroom with them,
they cannot fast:
20 but days come,
when the bridegroom is taken from them,
and then in those days they fast.

PATCHING

21 No one sows a piece of unfulled cloth
on an old garment:
but if not, the fullness takes away from the old,
and the split becomes worse.

NEW WINE, NEW SKINS

22 And no one puts new wine into old skins:
but if not, the new wine bursts the skins;
and the wine pours and the skins destruct:
— but new wine must be put into new skins.

YAH SHUA, ADONAY OF THE SHABBATH

23 And so be it,
he passes through the spores on the shabbaths;
and as they make their way
his disciples begin to pluck.
24 And the Pharisees word to him, Behold,
why do they what is not allowed on the shabbaths?
25 And he words to them,
Have you never ever read what David did
when he had need, and famished?
— he, and those with him?
26 How he entered the house of Elohim
in the days of Abi Athar the archpriest,
and ate the prothesis bread,
which is not allowed to eat — except for the priests,
and also gave to them with him?
Leviticus 24:5—9
27 And he words to them,
The shabbaths became for humanity
and not humanity for the shabbaths:
28 So then the Son of humanity
is also Adonay of the shabbath.

YAH SHUA CURES ON THE SHABBATH

3 And again he enters the synagogue;
and there is a human with a withered hand;
2 and they observe,
whether he cures him on the shabbaths;
to accuse him.
3 And he words to the human
with the withered hand,
Stand midst us.
4 And he words to them,
Is it *lawful* **allowed** to do good on
the *sabbath days* **shabbaths**,
or to do evil?
to save *life* **soul**, or to *kill* **slaughter**?
But they *held their peace* **hushed**.
5 And when he had looked round about on them
with *anger* **wrath**,
being grieved for the *hardness*
petrifaction of their hearts,
he *saith* **wordeth** unto the *man* **human**,
Stretch forth **Spread** thine hand.
And he *stretched it out* **spread**:
and his hand was restored whole as the other.
6 And the Pharisees went *forth*,
and straightway
took **made** counsel with the Herodians against him,
how they might destroy him.
7 But *Jesus* **Yah Shua**
withdrew himself with his disciples to the sea:
and a *great* **vast** multitude from *Galilee* **Galiyl**
followed him,
and from *Judaea* **Yah Hudah**,
8 And from *Jerusalem* **Yeru Shalem**,
and from *Idumaea* **Edom**,
and from beyond *Jordan* **Yarden**;
and they about *Tyre* **Sor** and Sidon,
a *great* **vast** multitude,
when they had heard
what great things **as much as** he did,
came unto him.
9 And he *spake* **said** to his disciples,
that a *small ship* **skiff** should wait on him
because of the multitude,
lest they should *throng* **tribulate** him.
10 For he had *healed* **cured** many;
insomuch
that they *pressed* **fell** upon him for to touch him,
as many as had *plagues* **scourges**.
11 And *unclean* **impure** spirits,
when they *saw* **observed** him,
fell down before **prostrated in front of** him,
and cried, *saying* **wording**,
Thou art the Son of *God* **Elohim**.
12 And he *straitly charged* **admonished** them
that they should not make him *known* **manifest**.

Yah Shua Ordains The Twelve

13 And he *goeth up* **ascendeth** into a mountain,
and calleth unto him whom he *would* **willed**:
and they came unto him.

14 And he ordained twelve,
that they should be with him,
and that he might *send* **apostolize** them *forth* to preach,

15 And to have *power* **authority**
to *heal sicknesses* **cure diseases**,
and to cast out *devils* **demons**:

16 And *Simon* **to Shimon**
he *surnamed Peter* **added the name Petros**;

17 And *James the son of Zebedee* **Yaaqovos of Zabdi**,
and *John* **Yahn** the brother of *James* **Yaaqovos**;
and he *surnamed them* **added the names**
Boanerges **Ben Regaz**,
which is, The sons of thunder:

18 And *Andrew* **Andreas**, and *Philip* **Philippos**,
and *Bartholomew* **Bar Talmay**, and *Matthew* **Matthaios**,
and *Thomas* **Taom**,
and *James the son* **Yaaqovos** of *Alphaeus* **Heleph**,
and Thaddaeus,
and *Simon* **Shimon** the *Canaanite* **Kenaaniy**,

19 And *Judas Iscariot* **Yah Hudah the urbanite**,
which also betrayed him:
and they went into an house.

20 And the multitude cometh together again,
so that they could not so much as **even** eat bread.

21 And when his friends heard of it,
they went out to *lay hold on* **overpower** him:
for they *said* **worded**, He is *beside himself* **astounded**.

Yah Shua Accused Of Having Baal Zebub

22 And the scribes
which came down from *Jerusalem* **Yeru Shalem**
Is it allowed on the shabbaths
to do good? Or to do evil?
To save soul? Or to slaughter?
— but they hush.

5 And he looks all around them with wrath
being grieved for the petrifaction of their hearts;
he words to the human, Spread your hand!
— and he spreads
and his hand restores, whole as the other.

6 And the Pharisees go,
and straightway make counsel against him
with the Herodians
— how to destroy him.

7 But Yah Shua, with his disciples,
withdraws himself to the sea:
and a vast multitude follows him
— from Galiyl and from Yah Hudah

8 and from Yeru Shalem and from Edom
and from beyond Yarden:
and those around Sor and Sidon, a vast multitude,
having heard as much as he did, come to him.

9 And because of the multitude,
he says to his disciples, for a skiff to await him;
lest they tribulate him:

10 for he cures many;
so that they fall on him to touch him:
and as many as have scourges

11 and impure spirits,
when they observe him, prostrate in front of him,
and cry, wording, You are the Son of Elohim.

12 — and he admonishes them
to not make him manifest.

Yah Shua Ordains The Twelve

13 And he ascends a mountain
and calls whom he wills to himself;
and they come to him:

14 and he ordains twelve to be with him
— to apostolize them to preach

15 and to have authority to cure diseases
and to cast out demons.

16 And to Shimon he adds the name Petros:

17 and to Yaaqovos of Zabdi
and Yahn the brother of Yaaqovos
he adds the names Ben Regaz,
which is, Sons of thunder:

18 and Andreas and Philippos and Bar Talmay
and Matthaios and Taom and Yaaqovos of Heleph
and Thaddaeus and Shimon the Kenaaniy

19 and Yah Hudah the urbanite
who also betrays him;
— and they come to a house.

20 And the multitude comes together again
so that they cannot so much as even eat bread:

21 and his friends hear of it
and come to overpower him:
for they word, He is astounded.

Yah Shua Accused Of Having Baal Zebub

22 And the scribes from Yeru Shalem descend
said **spake**, He hath *Beelzebub* **Baal Zebub**,
and *by* **in** the *prince* **arch** of *the devils* **demons**
casteth he *out devils* **demons**.

23 And he called them unto him,

and *said* **worded** unto them in parables,
How can Satan cast out Satan?

24 And *if* **whenever** a *kingdom* **sovereigndom**
be divided against itself,
that *kingdom* **sovereigndom** cannot stand.

25 And *if* **whenever** a house
be divided against itself,
that house cannot stand.

26 And if Satan rise *up* against
himself, and be divided,
he cannot stand, but hath *an end* **a completion**.

27 No *man* **one** can enter
into *a strong man's* **the** house **of the mighty**,
and *spoil* **throughly plunder** his *goods* **vessels**,
except **unless** he *will* **shall** first bind
the *strong man* **mighty**;
and then he *will spoil* **shall throughly plunder** his house.

THE UNFORGIVEN SIN

28 *Verily I say* **Amen! I word** unto you,
All sins shall be forgiven unto the
sons of *men* **humanity**,
and blasphemies
wherewith soever **as much as ever** they shall blaspheme:

29 But he that shall blaspheme against
the *Holy Spirit* **Ruach ha-kodesh**
hath never forgiveness **unto the eons**,
but is *in danger of* **subject to** eternal
damnation **judgment**.

30 Because they *said* **worded**,
He hath an *unclean* **impure** spirit.

MOTHER AND BRETHREN SEEK YAH SHUA

31 There came then his brethren and his mother,
and, standing without,
sent **apostolized** unto him, *calling* **voicing to** him.

32 And the multitude sat about him,
and they said unto him, Behold,
thy mother and thy brethren without seek for thee.

33 And he answered them, *saying* **wording**,
Who is my mother, or my brethren?

34 And he looked round about
on them which sat about him,
and *said* **worded**, Behold my mother and my brethren!

35 For whosoever shall do the will of *God* **Elohim**,
the same **this** is my brother, and my sister, and mother.

4 And he began again
to *teach* **doctrinate** by the sea side:
and there was gathered **together** unto him
a *great* **vast** multitude,
so that he *entered* **embarked** into a *ship* **sailer**,
and sat in the sea;
and the whole multitude was by the sea on the land.

2 And he taught **doctrinated** them
many things by **much in** parables,
and *said* **worded** unto them in his doctrine,

THE PARABLE OF THE SPORER

3 Hearken; Behold,
there went out a *sower* **sporer** to *sow* **spore**:

4 And it *came to pass* **became**,
as he sowed **in his sporing**,
some **indeed** fell by the way side,
and the *fowls* **flyers** of the *air* **heaven**
came and devoured it *up*.

5 And *some* **others** fell on *stony ground* **rocky**,
where it had not much *earth* **soil**;
and *immediately* **straightway** it sprang *up*,
because it had no depth of *earth* **soil**:

6 But when the sun was *up* **risen**, it was scorched;
and because it had no root, it withered away.

7 And *some* **others** fell among thorns,
and the thorns *grew up* **ascended**,
and *choked* **strangled** it,
and it *yielded* **gave** no fruit.

8 And other fell on good *ground* **soil**,
and *did yield* **gave** fruit
that *sprang up* **ascended** and *increased* **grew**;
and brought forth, *some* **one** thirty,
and *some* **one** sixty, and *some* **one** an hundred.

9 And he *said* **worded** unto them,
He that hath ears to hear, let him hear.

THE PURPOSE OF PARABLES

10 And when he was alone,
they that were about him with the twelve
asked of him the parable.
and speak, He has Baal Zebub!
— and, In the arch of demons he casts demons.

23 And he calls them to him
and words to them in parables: How
can Satan cast out Satan?

24 — and, whenever a sovereigndom
divides against itself,
that sovereigndom cannot stand!

25 — and, Whenever a house divides against itself,
that house cannot stand!

26 — and, If Satan rises and
divides against himself,
he cannot stand — but has a completion.

27 No one can enter the house of the mighty;
and throughly plunder his vessels
unless he first binds the mighty;
and then he throughly plunders his house.

THE UNFORGIVEN SIN

28 Amen! I word to you,
All sins are forgiven the sons of humanity,
and blasphemies — as much as ever they blaspheme:
29 but whoever blasphemes against the Holy Spirit
never has forgiveness to the eons
but is subject to eternal judgment
30 — because they word, He has an impure spirit.

MOTHER AND BROTHERS SEEK YAH SHUA

31 So his brothers and his mother come;
and standing outside,
apostolize to him — voicing to him:
32 and the multitude sits
around him and says to him,
Behold,
your mother and your brothers outside seek for you.
33 And he answers them, wording,
Who is my mother? Or my brothers?
34 And he looks around on
those who sit around him,
and words, Behold my mother and my brothers!
35 For whoever does the will of Elohim
— this is my brother and my sister and mother.

4 And again he begins to
doctrinate by the sea side:
and a vast multitude gathers to him
so that he embarks into a sailer and sits in the sea;
and the whole multitude is by the sea on the land:
2 and he doctrinates them much in parables
and words to them in his doctrine.

THE PARABLE OF THE SPORER

3 Hearken; Behold, a sporer goes sporing:
4 and so be it, in his sporing,
some indeed falls by the way side;
and the flyers of the heavens come and devour.
5 And others fall on rocky
where it has not much soil;
and straightway it springs
because it has no depth of soil:
6 but the sun rises and scorches;
and because it has no root, withers away.
7 And others fall among thorns;
and the thorns ascend and strangle;
and it gives no fruit.
8 And others falls on good soil;
and gives fruit that ascends and grows;
and brings forth
— one thirty and one sixty and one a hundred.
9 And he words to them,
Whoever has ears to hear, hearken.

THE PURPOSE OF PARABLES

10 And when he is alone,
those around him with the twelve
ask him about the parable.
11 And he *said* **worded** unto them,
Unto you it is given to know the mystery
of the *kingdom* **sovereigndom** of *God* **Elohim**:
but unto them that are without,
all these *things are done* **become** in parables:
12 That *seeing* **observing** they may *see* **observe**,
and not perceive;
and hearing they may hear,
and not *understand* **comprehend**;
lest *at any time* **ever** they should *be converted* **turn**,
and their sins should be forgiven them.
Yesha Yah 6:9, 10

THE PARABLE OF THE SPORER INTERPRETED

13 And he *said* **worded** unto them,
Know ye not this parable?
and how then *will* **shall** ye know all parables?
14 The *sower soweth* **sporer sporeth** the word.
15 And these are they by the way side,
where the word is *sown* **spored**;
but when they have heard,
Satan cometh *immediately* **straightway**,
and taketh away the word
that was *sown* **spored** in their hearts.
16 And these are they likewise
which are *sown* **spored** on *stony ground* **rocky**;
who, when they have heard the word,
immediately **straightway**
receive **take** it with *gladness* **cheer**;
17 And have no root in themselves,
and so endure *but for a time* **temporarily**:
afterward **then**, when *affliction*
tribulation or persecution
ariseth **becometh** for the word's sake,
immediately **straightway** they are *offended* **scandalized**.
18 And these are they which are
sown **spored** among thorns;

such as hear the word,
19   And the *cares* **anxieties** of this *world* **eon**,
and the deceitfulness of riches,
and the *lusts of other things* **remaining pantings** entering *in*,
choke **strangle** the word, and it becometh unfruitful.
20   And these are they
which are *sown* **spored** on good *ground* **soil**;
such as hear the word, and receive it,
and *bring forth* **bear** fruit, *some* **one** thirtyfold,
some **one** sixty, and *some* **one** an hundred.

THE PARABLE OF THE CANDLE

21   And he *said* **worded** unto them,
Is a candle brought to be put under a *bushel* **measure**,
or under a bed?
and not *to be set* **put** on a *candlestick* **menorah**?
22   For there is *nothing hid* **naught secreted**,
which shall not **lest it shall** be manifested;
neither *was any thing* **hath ought**
kept secret **become secreted**,
but that it should *come abroad* **become manifested**.
23   If any *man* **one** have ears to hear, let him hear.
24   And he *said* **worded** unto them,
Take heed **Observe** what ye hear:
with **in** what measure ye *mete* **measure**,
it shall be measured to you:
and unto you that hear shall *more* be *given* **added**.
25   For he that hath, to him shall be given:
and he that hath not,
from him shall be taken even that which he hath.

SPORE SEASON AND HARVEST

26   And he *said* **worded**, *So* **Even thus**
is the *kingdom* **sovereigndom** of *God* **Elohim**,
as *if* **whenever** a *man* **human**
should cast *seed* **spores** into the *ground* **soil**;
27   And should sleep, and rise night and day,
and the *seed* **spores** should *spring* **sprout** and grow *up*,
he knoweth not how.
28   For the earth *bringeth forth* **beareth** fruit
of herself **automatically**;
first the *blade* **herbage**, then the *ear* **kernel**,
after that the full *corn* **grain** in the *ear* **kernel**.
29   But when the fruit is *brought forth* **delivered**,
immediately **straightway**
he *putteth in* **apostolizeth** the sickle,
because the harvest is *come* **here**.
11   And he words to them,
You are given to know the mystery
of the sovereigndom of Elohim:
but to them outside,
all these become in parables:
12   that observing, they observe and perceive not;
and hearing, they hear and comprehend not — lest ever
they turn, and their sins be forgiven. Yesha Yah 6:9, 10

THE PARABLE OF THE SPORER INTERPRETED

13   And he words to them,
Know you not this parable?
and, How then know you all parables?
14   The sporer spores the word:
15   And these are those by the way side
where the word is spored;
but when they hear, Satan comes straightway,
and takes away the word spored in their hearts.
16   And likewise, these are they spored on rocky:
who, when they hear the word,
straightway take it with cheer;
17   and have no root in themselves,
and so endure temporarily:
so when tribulation or persecution become
because of the word,
straightway they scandalize.
18   And these are they spored among thorns;
such as hear the word:
19   and the anxieties of this eon
and the deceitfulness of riches
and the remaining pantings enter
and strangle the word;
and it becomes unfruitful.
20   And these are they spored on good soil:
such as hear the word, and receive, and bear fruit; —
one thirtyfold and one sixty and one a hundred.

THE PARABLE OF THE CANDLE

21   And he words to them,
Comes the candle to be put under a measure?
Or under a bed?
And not put on a menorah?
22   For naught is secreted, lest
it become manifested;
and naught secreted, but to become manifested.
23   If anyone has ears to hear, hear!
24   And he words to them, Observe what you hear:
in what measure you measure, is measured to you:
and to you who hear is added:
25   for whoever has, is given:
and whoever has not, is taken even what he has.

Spore Season And Harvest

26 And he words,
Even thus is the sovereigndom of Elohim,
as whenever a human casts spores into the soil;
27 and sleeps, and rises night and day,
and the spores sprout and grow, he knows not how:
28 for the earth bears fruit automatically:
first the herbage, then the kernel, after
that the full grain in the kernel.
29 and whenever the fruit is delivered,
straightway he apostolizes the sickle
because the harvest is here.

The Parable Of The Mustard Kernel

30 And he *said* **worded**, Whereunto shall we liken
the *kingdom* **sovereigndom** of *God* **Elohim**?
or with what *comparison* **parable**
shall we *compare it* **cast along side**?
31 It is like a *grain* **kernel** of mustard *seed*,
which, when it is *sown* **spored** in the earth,
is less than all the *seeds* **sperma** that be in the earth:
32 But when it is *sown* **spored**,
it *groweth up* **ascendeth**,
and becometh greater than all herbs,
and *shooteth out great* **produceth more mega** branches;
so that the *fowls* **flyers** of the *air* **heaven**
may *lodge* **nest** under the shadow of it.

Yah Shua Explains The Parables

33 And with many such parables
spake he the word unto them,
exactly as they were able to hear it.
34 But *without* **apart from** a parable
spake he not unto them:
and when they were alone,
he *expounded* **explained** all *things* to his disciples.

Yah Shua Stills The Mega Whirlwind

35 And the same day,
when the *even was come* **being evening**,
he *saith* **wordeth** unto them,
Let us pass *over* **through** unto the other side.
36 And when they had *sent
away* **released** the multitude,
they took him even as he was in the *ship* **sailer**. And
there were also with him other *little ships* **skiffs**.
37 And there *arose* **became**
a *great storm of wind* **mega whirlwind**, and
the waves beat into the *ship* **sailer**,
so that it was *now* **already** full.
38 And he was in the *hinder part of the ship* **stern**,
asleep on a pillow:
and they *awake* **rouse** him, and *say* **word** unto him,
Master **Doctor**, *carest* **art** thou not **concerned**
that we *perish* **destruct**?
39 And he arose, and rebuked the wind,
and said unto the sea, *Peace* **Hush**, *be still* **muzzle**.
And the wind *ceased* **relaxed**,
and there *was a great* **became a mega** calm.
40 And he said unto them,
Why are ye *so fearful* **thus cowardly**? how
is it that ye have no *faith* **trust**?
41 And they *feared exceedingly* **awed a mega awe**,
and *said* **worded** one to another,
What manner of man **Who then** is this,
that even the wind and the sea obey him?

Yah Shua Ejects An Impure Spirit Of Demons

5 And they came over unto
the other side of the sea,
into the *country* **region** of the Gadarenes.
2 And when he was come out of the *ship* **sailer**,
immediately **straightway** there met him out of the
tombs a *man* **human** with an *unclean* **impure** spirit,
3 Who had his *dwelling*
settlement among the tombs;
and no *man* **one** could bind him,
no, not *even* with *chains* **fetters**:
4 Because that he had been often bound
with *fetters* **shackles** and *chains* **fetters**,
and the *chains* **fetters**
had been *plucked asunder* **drawn apart** by him,
and the *fetters broken in pieces* **shackles shattered**:
neither could any *man* **one** tame him.
5 And *always* **continually**, night and day,
he was in the mountains, and in the tombs,
crying, and cutting himself with stones.
6 But when he saw *Jesus* **Yah Shua** from afar *off*,
he ran and worshipped him,
7 And cried with a *loud* **mega** voice, and said,
What have I to do with thee, *Jesus* **Yah Shua**,
thou Son of *the most high God* **El Elyon**?
I *adjure* **oath** thee by *God* **Elohim**,
that thou *torment* **torture** me not.
8 For he *said* **worded** unto him,
Come out of the *man* **human**, thou
unclean **impure** spirit.
9 And he asked him, What is thy name?

The Parable Of The Mustard Kernel

30 And he words,
Whereto liken we the sovereigndom of Elohim?
Or with what parable cast we along side?
31 As a kernel of mustard,
which, when it is spored in the earth,
is less than all the sperma on the earth:
32 and when it spores
it ascends and becomes greater than all herbs;
and produces more mega branches;
so that the flyers of the heavens
can nest under its shadow.

Yah Shua Explains The Parables

33 And with many such parables
he speaks the word to them
exactly as they are able to hear:
34 but he speaks not to them apart from a parable:
and when they are alone
he explains all to his disciples.

Yah Shua Stills The Mega Whirlwind

35 And the same day, being evening,
he words to them,
We pass through across.
36 And they release the multitude
and they take him even as he is in the sailer:
and there are also other skiffs with him:
37 and a mega whirlwind becomes
and the waves beat into the sailer
so that it is already full:
38 and he is in the stern, asleep on a pillow:
and they rouse him, and word to him,
Doctor, concern you not that we destruct?
39 And he rises, and rebukes the wind,
and says to the sea, Hush! Muzzle!
— and the wind relaxes and there is a mega calm.
40 And he says to them,
Why are you thus cowardly?
How is it you have no trust?
41 And they awe a mega awe,
and word to one another,
Who then is this,
that even the wind and the sea obey him?

Yah Shua Ejects An Impure Spirit Of Demons

5 And they go across the sea
to the region of the Gadarenes;
2 and he comes from the sailer:
and straightway, from the tombs,
a human with an impure spirit meets him
3 who has his settlement among the tombs;
and no one can bind him
— no, not even with fetters:
4 because he was often bound
with shackles and fetters;
and he drew apart the fetters
and shattered the shackles;
and no one could tame him:
5 and continually, night and day,
he is in the mountains, and in the tombs,
crying, and cutting himself with stones.
6 And seeing Yah Shua from afar,
he runs and worships him;
7 and cries with a mega voice, and says,
What have I to do with you,
Yah Shua, you Son of El Elyon?
I oath you by Elohim, that you not torture me.
8 For he words to him,
Come from the human, you impure spirit.
9 And he asks him, What is your name?
And he answered, *saying* **wording**,
My name is Legion: for we are many.
10 And he besought him much
that he *would* **should** not *send* **apostolize** them *away*
out of the *country* **region**.
11 Now there was there nigh unto the mountains
a *great herd* **mega drove** of swine feeding.
12 And all the *devils* **demons** besought him,
saying **wording**,
Send us into the swine, that we may enter into them.
13 And *forthwith* **straightway**
Jesus gave **Yah Shua allowed** them *leave*.
And the *unclean* **impure** spirits went out,
and entered into the swine:
and the *herd* **drove** ran violently down a *steep place* **cliff**
into the sea,
(they were about two thousand;)
and were *choked* **strangled** in the sea.
14 And they that fed the swine fled,
and *told* **evangelized** it in the city,
and in the *country* **field**.
And they went *out* to see what it was
that *was done* **had become**.
15 And they come to *Jesus* **Yah Shua**,
and *see* **observe** him
that was *possessed with the devil* **demonized**,
and had the legion,

	sitting, and clothed, and *in his right mind* **sound minded**: and they were *afraid* **awestricken**.
16	And they that saw it *told* **declared** them how it *befell* **became** to him that was *possessed with the devil* **demonized**, and also concerning the swine.
17	And they began to *pray* **beseech** him to depart out of their *coasts* **boundries**.
18	And when he *was come* **embarked** into the *ship* **sailer**, he that had been *possessed with the devil* **demonized** *prayed* **besought** him that he might be with him.
19	Howbeit *Jesus suffered* **Yah Shua allowed** him not, but *saith* **wordeth** unto him, Go home to thy friends, and *tell* **evangelize** them *how great things the Lord* **as much as Adonay** hath done for thee, and hath *had compassion on* **mercied** thee.
20	And he departed, and began to *publish* **preach** in Decapolis *how great things Jesus* **as much as Yah Shua** had done for him: and all *men* did marvel.

The Daughterling Of Yair In Her Final Extremity

21	And when *Jesus* **Yah Shua** *was* passed *over* **through** again by *ship* **sailer** unto the other side, *much people* **vast multitudes** gathered unto him: and he was nigh unto the sea.
22	And, behold, there cometh one of the *rulers of the synagogue* **synagogue archs**, *Jairus* **Yair** by name; and when he saw him, he fell at his feet,
23	And besought him *greatly* **much**, *saying* **wording**, My *little daughter* **daughterling** *lieth at the point of death* **is in her final extremity**: I pray thee, come and *lay* **put** thy hands on her, that she may be *healed* **saved**; and she shall live.
24	And *Jesus* **Yah Shua** went with him; and *much people* **vast multitudes** followed him, and thronged him.

Yah Shua Heals A Flux

25	And a *certain* woman, which had *an issue* **a flux** of blood twelve years,
26	And had suffered *many things* **much** by many *physicians* **healers**, and had spent all that she had, and *was nothing bettered* **benefited naught**, but rather grew worse,
27	When she had heard *of Jesus* **about Yah Shua**, came in the *press* **multitude** behind, and touched his garment.
28	For she *said* **worded**,

And he answers, wording, My name is Legion: for we are many.

10	— and he beseeches him much to not apostolize them from the region.
11	And near the mountains a mega drove of swine is feeding:
12	and all the demons beseech him, wording, Send us into the swine, to enter them.
13	And straightway Yah Shua allows them: and the impure spirits go and enter the swine: and the drove runs violently down a cliff into the sea — about two thousand strangle in the sea.
14	And they who feed the swine flee, and evangelize it in the city and in the field: and they come to see what became:
15	and they come to Yah Shua, and observe the demonized who had the legion sitting and clothed and sound minded: and they are awestricken.
16	And they who saw declare how it became to the demoniac and also concerning the swine:
17	and they begin to beseech him to depart from their boundries.
18	And he embarks into the sailer: and the demoniac beseeches to be with him:
19	and Yah Shua allows him not, but words to him, Go home to your friends, and evangelize them as much as Adonay did for you, and mercied you.
20	— and he departs and begins to preach in Decapolis as much as Yah Shua did for him: and all marvel.

The Daughterling Of Yair In Her Final Extremity

21	And again by sailer, Yah Shua passes across: and vast multitudes gather to him: and he is near the sea.
22	And behold,

one of the synagogue *archs* comes — Yair by name;
and he sees him and falls at his feet
23 and beseeches him much, wording,
My *daughterling* is in her final extremity:
I pray you, come and put your hands on her,
to save her, and she lives.
24 — and Yah Shua goes with him;
and vast multitudes follow him and throng him.

Yah Shua Heals A Flux

25 And a woman, having a
flux of blood twelve years,
26 who suffered much by many healers
and spent all she had and benefited naught;
and rather grew worse:
27 she hears about Yah Shua;
and comes in the multitude behind
and touches his garment
28 — for she words,
If I may touch but his clothes, I shall be *whole* **saved**.
29 And straightway
the fountain of her blood was dried *up*;
and she *felt* **knew** in her body
that she was healed of that *plague* **scourge**.
30 And *Jesus immediately* **Yah Shua straightway**
knowing in himself
that *virtue* **dynamis** had gone out of him,
turned him about in the *press* **multitude**,
and *said* **worded**, Who touched my clothes?
31 And his disciples *said* **worded** unto him,
Thou *seest* **observest** the multitude thronging thee,
and *sayest* **wordest** thou, Who touched me?
32 And he looked round about
to see her that had done this *thing*.
33 But the woman *fearing* **awing** and trembling,
knowing what *was done* **became** in her,
came and *fell down before* **prostrated in front of** him,
and *told* **said to** him all the truth.
34 And he said unto her, Daughter,
thy *faith* **trust** hath *made* **saved** thee *whole*;
go in *peace* **shalom**, and be whole of thy *plague* **scourge**.

The Daughterling Of Yair Rises

35 While he yet spake,
there came
from the *ruler* **arch** of the *synagogue's house* **synagogue**
certain which said *wording*, Thy daughter is dead:
why *troublest* **harrassest** thou the *Master* **Doctor**
any further?
36 *As soon as Jesus* **Straightway when Yah Shua**
heard the word that was spoken,
he *saith* **wordeth** unto the *ruler* **arch** of the synagogue,
Be *Awe* not *afraid*, only believe **trust**.
37 And he *suffered* **allowed**
no *man* **one** to follow *with* him,
save Peter **except Petros**, and *James* **Yaaqovos**,
and *John* **Yahn** the brother of *James* **Yaaqovos**.
38 And he cometh to the house
of the *ruler* **arch** of the *synagogue* **synagogue**,
and *seeth* **observeth** the tumult,
and them that wept and *wailed greatly* **halooed much**.
39 And when he *was come in* **entered**,
he *saith* **wordeth** unto them,
Why make ye this *ado* **tumult**, and weep? the
damsel **child** is not dead, but sleepeth.

The Daughterling Of Yair Lives

40 And they *laughed* **ridiculed** him *to scorn*.
But when he had *put* **cast** them all out,
he taketh the father and the mother of the *damsel* **child**,
and them that were with him,
and entereth *in*
where the *damsel was lying* **child reposed**.
41 And he *took* **overpowered** the *damsel* **child**
by the hand,
and *said* **wordeth** unto her, *Talitha cumi* **Taleh quwm**;
which is, being *interpreted* **translated**,
Damsel **Maiden**, I *say* **word** unto thee, arise.
42 And straightway the *damsel* **maiden** arose,
and walked;
for she was of the age of twelve years.
And they were *astonished* **astounded**
with a *great astonishment* **mega ecstasis**.
43 And he charged them *straitly* **much**
that no *man* **one** should know it;
and *commanded* **said**
that something should be given her to eat.

Yah Shua Dishonoured In His Fatherland

6 And he went out from thence,
and came into his *own country* **fatherland**;
and his disciples follow him.
2 And when the *sabbath day* **shabbath**
was come **became**,
he began to *teach* **doctrinate** in the synagogue:
and many hearing him were astonished, *saying* **wording**,
From whence hath this man these *things*?
and what wisdom is this which is given unto him,
that even such *mighty works* **dynamis**

are *wrought* **become** by his hands?
3 Is not this the carpenter,
the son of *Mary* **Miryam**,
If I even touch his clothes, I am saved.
29 — and straightway the
fountain of her blood dries;
and she knows in her body that her scourge is healed.
30 And straightway, Yah Shua,
knowing in himself that dynamis goes from him,
turns around in the multitude,
and words, Who touched my clothes?
31 And his disciples word to him,
You observe the multitude thronging you;
and word you, Who touched me?
32 And he looks around to see her who did this:
33 and the woman, awing and trembling,
knowing what became in her,
comes and prostrates in front of him,
and says all the truth to him.
34 And he says to her, Daughter,
your trust saves you;
go in shalom, and be whole of your scourge.

The Daughterling Of Yair Rises

35 While he yet speaks,
they of the arch of the synagogue, come wording,
Your daughter is dead:
Why harrass the Doctor any further?
36 Straightway Yah Shua hears the word spoken,
and he words to the arch of the synagogue,
Awe not! Only trust!
37 — and he allows no one to follow with him
except Petros and Yaaqovos
and Yahn the brother of Yaaqovos:
38 and he comes to the house
of the arch of the synagogue;
and observes the tumult
and them who weep and haloo much.
39 And he enters and words to them,
Why make you this tumult, and weep?
The child is not dead, but sleeps.
40 — and they ridicule him.

The Daughterling Of Yair Lives

And he casts them all out
and takes the father and the mother of the child
and those with him,
and enters where the child reposes:
41 and he overpowers the child by the hand,
and words to her, Taleh quwm;
which is, being translated,
Maiden, I word to you, Rise.
42 — and straightway the maiden rises and walks
— for she is of the age of twelve years.
And they are astounded with a mega ecstasis.
43 And he charges them
much, that no one know it;
and says to give her somewhat to eat.

Yah Shua Dishonored In His Fatherland

6 And he goes from there,
and comes to his fatherland;
and his disciples follow him.
2 And so be it, shabbath;
and he begins to doctrinate in the synagogue.
And many hearing him are astonished,
wording, Whence has this one all these?
and, What wisdom is given him
that even such dynamis becomes by his hands?
3 Is not this the carpenter the son of Miryam
the brother of *James* **Yaaqovos**, and *Joses* **Yoses**,
and of *Juda* **Yah Hudah**, and *Simon* **Shimon**?
and are not his sisters here with us?
And they were *offended* **scandalized** at him.
4 But *Jesus said* **Yah Shua worded** unto them,
A prophet is not *without honour* **dishonoured**,
but **except** in his *own country* **fatherland**,
and among his own kin, and in his own house.
5 And he could there do no *mighty work* **dynamis**,
save **except** that
he *laid* **put** his hands upon a few sick folk,
and *healed* **cured** them.
6 And he marvelled
because of their *unbelief* **trustlessness**.
And he went round about the villages,
teaching **doctrinating**.

The Twelve Have Authority Over Impure Spirits

7 And he called unto him the twelve,
and began to *send* **apostolize** them *forth* by two and two;
and gave them *power* **authority** over
unclean **impure** spirits;
8 And *commanded* **evangelized** them
that they should take *nothing* **naught**
for their *journey* **way**,
save **except** a *staff* **rod** only;
no *scrip* **wallet**, no bread,
no *money* **copper** in their *purse* **girdle**:
9 But be *shod* **tied** with sandals;

MARK/MAKABI 6

and not *put on* **endue** two *coats* **tunics**.
10 And he *said* **worded** unto them,
In what place soever ye enter into an house,
there abide till ye depart from that place.
11 And *whosoever shall not*
as many as ever shall neither receive you,
nor hear you,
when ye depart thence, shake off
the dust under your feet
for a *testimony* **witness** against them.
Verily I say **Amen! I word** unto you,
It shall be more tolerable
for *Sodom* **Sedom** and *Gomorrha* **Amorah**
in the day of judgment,
than for that city.
12 And they went *out*,
and preached that men should repent.
13 And they cast out many *devils* **demons**,
and anointed with **olive** oil many that were sick,
and *healed* **cured** them.

Herod Fears Yahn The Baptizer

14 And *king* **sovereign** Herod heard of him;
(for his name *was* **became** spread *abroad* **manifestly**:)
and he *said* **worded**,
That *John* **Yahn** the *Baptist* **Baptizer**
was risen from the dead,
and *therefore* **because of this**
mighty works **dynamis**
do shew forth themselves **energizeth** in him.
15 Others *said* **worded**, That it is *Elias* **Eli Yah**.
And others *said* **worded**, That it is a prophet,
or as one of the prophets.
16 But when Herod heard thereof, he said,
It **He** is *John* **Yahn**, whom I beheaded:
he is risen from the dead.
17 For Herod himself had *sent forth* **apostolized**
and *laid hold upon John* **overpowered Yahn**,
and bound him in *prison* **the guardhouse**
for Herodias' sake,
his brother *Philip's wife* **Philippos' woman**:
for he had married her.
18 For *John* **Yahn** had *said* **worded** unto Herod,
It is not *lawful* **allowed** for thee
to have thy brother's *wife* **woman**.
19 *Therefore* **But**
Herodias *had a quarrel against* **begrudged** him,
and *would* **willed to** have *killed* **slaughtered** him;
but she could not:
20 For Herod *feared John* **awed Yahn**,

knowing that he was a just man and an holy,
and *observed* **guarded** him;
and when he heard him, he did *many things* **much**,
and heard him *gladly* **with pleasure**.

and brother of Yaaqovos and Yoses
and Yah Hudah and Shimon?
and, Are not his sisters here with us?
— and they are scandalized at him.
4 But Yah Shua words to them,
A prophet is not dishonored except in his fatherland
and among his own kin and in his own house.
5 — and he can do no dynamis there;
except he puts his hands upon a few sick folk
and cures them:
6 and he marvels because of their trustlessness.
— and he goes doctrinating around the villages.

The Twelve Have Authority Over Impure Spirits

7 And he calls the twelve to him
and begins to apostolize them two by two; and
gives them authority over impure spirits;
8 and evangelizes them to
take naught for their way
except only a rod
— no wallet, no bread, no copper in their girdle:
9 but tie on sandals; and not endue two tunics.
10 And he words to them,
Wherever you enter a house,
abide there until you depart:
11 and as many as ever
neither receive you nor hear you,
when you depart, shake off the dust under your feet
for a witness against them.
Amen! I word to you,
It is more tolerable in the day of judgment,
for Sedom and Amorah than for that city.
12 And they go and preach for men to repent:
13 and they cast out many demons
and anoint many sick with olive oil and cure them.

Herod Fears Yahn The Baptizer

14 And sovereign Herod hears of him;
— for his name is spread manifestly:
and he words,
Yahn the Baptizer rises from the dead
and because of this dynamis energizes in him.
15 Others word, He is Eli Yah.
And others word, He is a prophet.

Or, As one of the prophets.

16 And Herod hears thereof, and says,
He is Yahn, whom I beheaded:
he rose from the dead.
17 — for Herod himself had apostolized
and overpowered Yahn,
and bound him in the guardhouse
for sake of Herodias
the woman of his brother Philippos
— because he had married her.
18 — for Yahn had worded to Herod,
You are not allowed
to have the woman of your brother.
19 — but Herodias begrudged him
and willed to slaughter him;
but she could not:
20 for Herod awed Yahn,
knowing he was a just and holy man;
and guarded him;
and he heard him and did much;
and heard him with pleasure.

The Birthday Supper Of Herod

21 And when *a convenient* **an opportune** day
was come **became**,
that Herod on his birthday
made **prepared** a supper to his *lords* **magistrates**,
high captains **chiliarchs**,
and *chief estates* **preeminent** of *Galilee* **Galiyl**;
22 And when the daughter of the said Herodias
came in **entered**, and danced,
and pleased Herod and them that *sat* **reposed** with him,
the *king* **sovereign** said unto the *damsel* **maiden**,
Ask of me whatsoever thou *wilt* **willest**,
and I *will* **shall** give it thee.
23 And he *sware* **oathed** unto her,
Whatsoever thou shalt ask of me, I *will* **shall** give it thee,
unto the half of my *kingdom* **sovereigndom**.
24 And she went *forth*, and said unto her mother,
What shall I ask?
And she said,
The head of *John* **Yahn** the *Baptist* **Baptizer**.
25 And she *came in* **entered** straightway
with *haste* **diligence**
unto the *king* **sovereign** and asked, *saying* **wording**,
I will that thou give me
by and by in **immediately on** a *charger* **platter**
the head of *John* **Yahn** the *Baptist* **Baptizer**.
26 And the *king* **sovereign**
was exceeding sorry **became extremely sorrowful**;
yet for his oath's sake,
and for their sakes which *sat* **reposed** with him,
he *would* **willed to** not *reject her* **set her aside**.

Herod Has Yahn The Baptizer Beheaded

27 And *immediately* **straightway**
the *king* **sovereign**
sent an executioner **apostolized a speculator**,
and *commanded* **ordered** his head to be brought:
and he went
and beheaded him in the *prison* **guardhouse**,
28 And brought his head *in* **on** a *charger* **platter**,
and gave it to the *damsel* **maiden**:
and the *damsel* **maiden** gave it to her mother.
29 And when his disciples heard of it,
they came and took *up* his *corpse* **carcase**,
and *laid* **placed** it in a tomb.

Apostles Evangelize To Yah Shua

30 And the apostles
gathered themselves together unto *Jesus* **Yah Shua**,
and *told* **evangelized** him all *things*,
both *what* **as much as** they had done,
and *what* **as much as** they had *taught* **doctrinated**.
31 And he said unto them,
Come ye yourselves apart into a *desert* **desolate** place,
and rest a *while* **little**:
for there were many coming and going,
and they had no *leisure* **opportunity** so much as to eat.
32 And they departed into a *desert* **desolate** place
by *ship* **sailer** privately.
33 And the *people* **multitude**
saw them *departing* **going**,
and many knew him,
and *ran afoot* **crushed together** thither out of all cities,
and *outwent* **preceded** them,
and came together unto him.

Yah Shua Feeds Five Thousand

34 And *Jesus* **Yah Shua**, when he came out,
saw *much people* **vast multitudes**,
and *was moved with compassion*
had a sympathetic spleen
toward them,
because they were as sheep not having a shepherd:
and he began
to *teach* **doctrinate** them *many things* **much**.
35 And when the *day* **hour**
was now far **became already much** spent,
his disciples came unto him, and *said* **worded**,

This is a *desert* **desolate** place,
and *now* **already** the *time* **hour** is *far passed* **much**:
36 *Send* **Release** them *away*, that they may go
into the *country round about* **surrounding fields**,
and into the villages, and *buy* **market** themselves bread:
for they have *nothing* **naught** to eat.

THE BIRTHDAY SUPPER OF HEROD

21 And so be it, an opportune day:
and on his birthday
Herod prepares a supper to his magistrates,
chiliarchs and preeminent of Galiyl:
22 and the daughter of Herodias enters and dances;
and pleases Herod and those who repose with him.
And the sovereign says to the maiden,
Ask of me whatever you will, and I give you.
23 — and he oaths to her,
Whatever you ask of me,
I give You, to the half of my sovereigndom.
24 And she goes, and says to
her mother, What ask I?
And she says, The head of Yahn the Baptizer.
25 And straightway she enters with diligence
to the sovereign and asks, wording,
I will that you give me, immediately on a platter,
the head of Yahn the Baptizer.
26 And the sovereign becomes
extremely sorrowful;
yet for sake of his oath,
and for the sakes of them who repose with him,
he wills to not set her aside.

HEROD HAS YAHN THE BAPTIZER BEHEADED

27 And straightway
the sovereign apostolizes a speculator
and orders him to bring his head:
and he goes and beheads him in the guardhouse;
28 and brings his head on a platter
and gives it to the maiden:
and the maiden gives it to her mother:
29 and his disciples hear thereof
and come and take his carcase and place it in a tomb.

APOSTLES EVANGELIZE TO YAH SHUA

30 And the apostles gather together to Yah Shua
and evangelize all to him
— both as much as they do
and as much as they doctrinate.
31 And he says to them,
Come apart into a desolate place and rest a little.
— for many come and go
and they have no opportunity so much as to eat.
32 And they depart to a desolate place
by sailer privately;
33 and the multitude sees them go,
and many know him,
and crush together there from all cities,
and precede them and come together to him.

YAH SHUA FEEDS FIVE THOUSAND

34 And Yah Shua comes and sees vast multitudes;
and has a sympathetic spleen toward them
because they are as sheep not having a shepherd:
and he begins to doctrinate them much.
35 And already the hour being much
and his disciples come to him, and word,
This is a desolate place,
and already the hour is much:
36 release them to go
to the surrounding fields and to the villages
to market bread for themselves;
for they have naught to eat.
37 He answered and said unto
them, Give ye them to eat.
And they *say* **word** unto him,
shall we go and *buy* **market**
two hundred *pennyworth* **denarion** of bread,
and give them to eat?
38 He *saith* **wordeth** unto them,
How many *loaves* **breads** have ye? go and see.
And when they knew, they *say* **word**,
Five, and two fishes.
39 And he *commanded* **ordered** them
to make all *sit down* **recline**
by companies **symposium by symposium**
upon the green *grass* **herbage**.
40 And they *sat down in ranks* **reposed row by row**,
by hundreds, and by fifties.
41 And when he had taken
the five *loaves* **breads** and the two fishes,
he looked *up* to the heaven,
and *blessed* **eulogized**, and brake the *loaves* **breads**,
and gave them to his disciples to set *before* **by** them;
and the two fishes divided he among them all.
42 And they did all eat, and were *filled* **fed**.
43 And they took *up* twelve
baskets full of the fragments,
and of the fishes.
44 And they that did eat of the *loaves* **breads**
were about five thousand men.

YAH SHUA WALKS ON THE SEA

45 And straightway
he *constrained* **compelled** his disciples
to *get* **embark** into the *ship* **sailer**,
and to go to the other side
before **preceding** unto *Bethsaida* **Beth Sayad**,
while he *sent away* **released** the *people* **multitudes**.

46 And when he had *sent* **bid** them *away* **farewell**,
he departed into a mountain to pray.

47 And *when even was come* **being evening**,
the *ship* **sailer** was in the midst of the sea,
and he alone on the land.

48 And he saw them *toiling* **torturing** in rowing;
for the wind was contrary unto them:
and about the fourth *watch* **guard** of the night
he cometh unto them, walking upon the sea,
and *would* **willed to** have passed by them.

49 But when they saw him walking upon the sea,
they *supposed* **thought** it had been a *spirit*
it **phantasm**, and *cried out* **screamed**:

50 For they all saw him, and were troubled.
And *immediately* **straightway** he
talked **spoke** with them,
and *saith* **wordeth** unto them,
Be of good cheer: it is I; **Courage! I AM!**
be not afraid **Awe not**.

51 And he *went up* **ascended** unto them
into the *ship* **sailer**;
and the wind *ceased* **relaxed**:
and they were *sore amazed* **astounded** in themselves
beyond measure **very superabundantly**,
and *wondered* **marvelled**.

52 For they *considered* **comprehended** not
the miracle of the loaves **about the breads**:
for their heart was *hardened* **petrified**.

YAH SHUA SAVES AT KINNORETH

53 And when they had passed over,
they came into the land of *Gennesaret* **Kinneroth**,
and *drew to the shore* **moored**.

54 And when they were come out of the *ship* **sailer**,
straightway they knew him,

55 And ran through that
whole region round about,
and began to carry about in *beds* **pads**
those that were *sick* **ill**,
where they heard he was.

56 And whithersoever he entered,
into villages, or cities, or *country* **fields**,
they *laid* **placed** the *sick* **frail** in the *streets* **markets**,
and besought him that they might touch
if it were but the *border* **edge** of his garment:
and as many as touched him were
made whole **ever saved**.

37 He answers them, saying, You give them to eat.
And they word to him,
Go we and market two hundred denarion of bread
and give them to eat?

38 He words to them,
How many breads have you? Go and see!
And knowing, they word, Five; and two fishes.

39 And he orders them all to recline
symposium by symposium on the green herbage:

40 and they repose row by row
— by hundreds and by fifties.

41 And he takes the five breads and the two fishes,
looks to the heavens and eulogizes,
and breaks the breads
and gives them to his disciples to set by them;
and he divides the two fishes among them all:

42 and they all eat and are fed:

43 and they take twelve baskets full
of the fragments and of the fishes:

44 and they who eat of the breads
are about five thousand men.

YAH SHUA WALKS ON THE SEA

45 And straightway
he compels his disciples to embark into the sailer
and to precede across to Beth Sayad,
until he releases the multitudes:

46 and he bids them farewell
and departs to a mountain to pray:

47 and being evening,
and the sailer is midst the sea and
he is alone on the land:

48 and he sees them tortured in rowing;
for the wind is contrary to them:
and at about the fourth guard of the night,
he comes to them, walking upon the sea,
and wills to pass by them:

49 and they see him walking on the sea
and think it is a phantasm, and they scream:

50 for they all see him and are troubled.
And straightway he speaks with them,
and words to them,
Courage! I AM! Awe not!

51 — and he ascends to them into the sailer;
and the wind relaxes:

and they are very superabundantly
astounded in themselves and marvel:
52 for they comprehended not about the breads:
for their heart is petrified.

YAH SHUA SAVES AT KINNORETH

53 And they pass over
and come to the land of Kinneroth,
and moore there:
54 and as they come from the sailer
straightway they know him;
55 and run all around that whole region all around,
and begin to carry the ill around in pads
to wherever they hear he is:
56 and wherever he enters
— villages or cities or fields
they place the frail in the markets
and beseech him
if only to touch the edge of his garment:
and as many as touch him are ever saved.

YAH SHUA ADMONISHES THE PHARISEES

7 Then *came* **gathered** together
unto him the Pharisees,
and *certain* **some** of the scribes,
which came from *Jerusalem* **Yeru Shalem**.
2 And when they saw some
of his disciples eat bread
with *defiled* **profane**,
that is *to say*, with unwashen hands,
they found fault.
3 For the Pharisees, and all the *Jews* **Yah Hudiym**,
except **unless** they wash their hands *oft* **to the fist**,
eat not, *holding* **empowering** the tradition of the elders.
4 And when they come from the market,
except **unless** they *wash* **baptize**, they eat
not. And many other *things* there be,
which they have received to *hold* **empower**,
as the *washing* **baptism** of cups, and pots,
brasen vessels **copperware**, and of *tables* **beds**.
5 Then the Pharisees and scribes asked him,
Why walk not thy disciples
according to the tradition of the elders,
but eat bread with unwashen hands?
6 He answered and said unto them,
Well hath *Esaias* **Yesha Yah** prophesied
of **concerning** you hypocrites,
as it is *written* **scribed**,
This people honoureth me with their lips,
but their heart is far from me.
7 Howbeit in vain do they *worship* **venerate** me,
teaching **doctrinating** for doctrines
the *commandments* **misvoth** of *men*
humanity. Yesha Yah 29:13
8 For *laying aside* **forsaking**
the *commandment* **misvoth** of *God* **Elohim**,
ye *hold* **empower** the tradition of *men* **humanity**,
as the *washing* **baptism** of pots and cups:
and many other such like *things* ye do.
9 And he *said* **worded** unto them,
Full well ye *reject* **set aside**
the *commandment* **misvah** of *God* **Elohim**,
that ye may *keep* **guard** your own tradition.
10 For *Moses* **Mosheh** said,
Honour thy father and thy mother;
and, Whoso *curseth* **vilifieth** father or mother,
let him die the death:
Exodus 20:12, 21:17, Leviticus 20:9
11 But ye *say* **word**,
if **whenever** a *man* **human** shall say
to his father or mother,
It is *Corban* **Qurban**,
that is to say **which is**, *a gift* **Oblation**,
by whatsoever thou mightest be
profited **benefited** by *me*;
he shall be free.
12 And ye *suffer* **allow** him no more
to do ought for his father or his mother;
13 *Making* **Invalidating** the word of *God* **Elohim**
of none effect
through your tradition, which ye
have *delivered* **betrayed**:
and many such like *things* do ye.

ENTERING IN VS PROCEEDING OUT

14 And when he had called
all the *people* **multitude**
unto him, he *said* **worded** unto them,
Hearken unto me *every one* **all** of you,
and *understand* **comprehend**:
15 There is *nothing* **naught**
from without a *man* **human**,
that entering into him can *defile* **profane** him:
but *the things* **those** which *come* **proceed** out of him,
those are they that *defile* **profane** the *man* **human**.
16 If any *man* **one** have ears to hear, let him hear.
17 And when he was entered into the house
from the *people* **multitude**,
his disciples asked him concerning the parable.
18 And he *saith* **wordeth** unto them,

Are ye *so* **thus**
without understanding **uncomprehending** also?
Do ye not *perceive* **comprehend**,
that *whatsoever thing* **all that** from without
entereth *into* the *man* **human**,
it cannot *defile* **profane** him;

Yah Shua Admonishes The Pharisees

7 And the Pharisees and some of the scribes
come from Yeru Shalem
and gather together to him:
2 and they see some of his disciples eat bread
with profane, that is, unwashed hands,
and they find fault:
3 for the Pharisees and all
the Yah Hudiym eat not
unless they wash their hands to the fist;
thus empowering the tradition of the elders:
4 and coming from the market,
eat not unless they baptize:
and there be many others
which they receive to empower
— as the baptism of cups and pots
and copperware and beds.
5 Then the Pharisees and scribes ask him,
Why walk not your disciples
according to the tradition of the elders
— but eat bread with unwashed hands?
6 He answers them, saying,
Well prophesied Yesha Yah
concerning you hypocrites;
as scribed, This people honor me with their lips
but their heart is far from me;
7 and in vain they venerate me
doctrinating for doctrines the misvoth of humanity.
Yesha Yah 29:13
8 For, forsaking the misvoth of Elohim
you empower the tradition of humanity
— as the baptism of pots and cups and
you do many others like such.
9 And he words to them,
You full well set aside the misvah of Elohim
to guard your own tradition:
10 for Mosheh said,
Honor your father and your mother;
and, Whoever vilifies father or mother,
dies the death.
Exodus 20:12, 21:17, Leviticus 20:9
11 But you word,
Whenever a human says to his father or mother,
Qurban! which is, Oblation,
by whatever you benefit;
12 and you allow him no more
to do aught for his father or his mother;
13 invalidating the word of Elohim
through your tradition — which you
betray: and you do many like such.

Entering In vs Proceeding Out

14 And he calls all the multitude
and words to them,
Hearken to me, all of you, and comprehend:
15 naught entering a human from outside,
can profane him:
but those that proceed from him
— these are those that profane the human.
16 If anyone has ears to hear, Hear.
17 And he enters the house from the multitude;
and his disciples ask him concerning the parable:
18 and he words to them,
Are you also thus uncomprehending?
Comprehend you not
that all that enters the human from outside
cannot profane him;
19 Because it entereth not into his heart,
but into the belly,
and *goeth out* **proceedeth** into the *draught* **privy**,
purging **purifying** all *meats* **food**?
20 And he *said* **worded**,
That which *cometh* **departeth** out of the *man* **human**,
that *defileth* **profaneth** the *man* **human**.
21 For from within, out of the
heart of *men* **humanity**,
proceed evil thoughts, adulteries,
fornications **whoredoms**, murders,
22 Thefts, *covetousness* **avarices**,
wickedness **evils**, deceit, lasciviousness,
an evil eye **maliciousness**, blasphemy,
pride, *foolishness* **thoughtlessness**:
23 All these *evil things* **maliciousnesses**
come **proceed** from within,
and *defile* **profane** the *man* **human**.

Yah Shua Casts Out A Demon

24 And from thence he arose,
and went into the borders of *Tyre* **Sor** and Sidon,
and entered into an house,
and *would have* **willed that** no *man* **one** know it:
but he could not be hid.
25 For a *certain* woman,

whose *young daughter* **daughterling**
had an *unclean* **impure** spirit,
heard *of* **concerning** him,
and came and *fell* **prostrated** at his feet:
26 The woman was a *Greek* **Hellenist**,
a *Syrophenician* **Syrophoinissian** by *nation* **genos**;
and she *besought* **asked** him
that he *would* **should** cast forth the *devil* **demon**
out of her daughter.
27 But *Jesus* **Yah Shua** said unto her,
Let **Allow** the children first be *filled* **fed**:
for it is not *meet* **good** to take the children's bread,
and to cast it unto the *dogs* **puppies**.
28 And she answered and *said* **worded** unto him,
Yes, *Lord* **Adonay**:
yet **indeed** the *dogs* **puppies** under the table
eat of the children's crumbs.
29 And he said unto her, For
this *saying* **word** go thy way;
the *devil* **demon** is gone out of thy daughter.
30 And when she was come to her house,
she found the *devil* **demon** gone out, and
her daughter *laid* **put** upon the bed.
31 And again, departing from the *coasts* **boundries**
of *Tyre* **Sor** and Sidon,
he came unto the sea of *Galilee* **Galiyl**,
through the midst of the *coasts* **boundries** of Decapolis.

Yah Shua Heals A Tongue–Tied Mute

32 And they bring unto him
one that was *deaf* **mute**,
and *had an impediment in his*
speech **could hardly speak**;
and they beseech him to put his hand upon him.
33 And he took him *aside* from the multitude,
and put his fingers into his ears,
and he spit, and touched his tongue;
34 And looking *up* to the heaven, he sighed,
and *saith* **wordeth** unto him, Ephphatha,
that is, Be opened.
35 And straightway his ears were opened,
and the *string* **bond** of his tongue was *loosed* **released**,
and he spake *plain* **straightforwardly**.
36 And he charged them
that they should *tell no man* **say to no one**:
but *the more* **as much as** he charged them,
so much the more *a great deal* **superabundantly**
they *published it* **preached**;
37 And were
beyond measure **superabundantly** astonished,

saying **wording**, He hath done all *things* well:
he maketh both the *deaf* **mute** to hear,
and the *dumb* **speechless** to speak.

Yah Shua Feeds Four Thousand

8 In those days the multitude being very great,
and having *nothing* **naught** to eat,
Jesus **Yah Shua** called his disciples unto him,
and *saith* **wordeth** unto them,
19 because it enters not his heart
but the belly;
and proceeds into the privy purifying all food?
20 And he words,
That which departs from the human,
profanes the human.
21 For from within, from the heart of humanity,
proceed evil thoughts,
adulteries, whoredoms, murders,
22 thefts, avarices, evils, deceit, lasciviousness,
maliciousness, blasphemy, pride, thoughtlessness:
23 all these maliciousnesses proceed from within
and profane the human.

Yah Shua Casts Out A Demon

24 And from there he rises
and goes to the borders of Sor and Sidon,
and enters a house, and wills that no one know:
but they cannot hide him.
25 For a woman,
whose daughterling has an impure spirit
hears concerning him,
and comes and prostrates at his feet:
26 the woman is a Hellenist,
a Syrophoinissian by genos;
and she asks him to cast the demon
from her daughter.
27 But Yah Shua says to her,
First allow the children be fed:
for it is not good to take the bread of children,
and to cast it to the puppies.
28 And she answers him, wording,
Yes, Adonay:
yet indeed the puppies under the table
eat the crumbs of the children.
29 And he says to her, For this word go your way;
the demon is gone from your daughter.
30 — and she goes to her house
and finds the demon gone
and her daughter put upon the bed.
31 And again,

he departs from the boundries of Sor and Sidon,
and goes to the sea of Galiyl,
midst the boundries of Decapolis.

Yah Shua Heals A Tongue–Tied Mute

32 And they bring him a mute
who can hardly speak;
and they beseech him to put his hand on him:
33 and he takes him from the multitude
and puts his fingers into his ears and
he spits and touches his tongue;
34 and looks to the heavens and sighs,
and words to him, Ephphatha — which is, Open!
35 And straightway his ears open
and the bond of his tongue releases
and he speaks straightforwardly.
36 And he charges them to say to no one:
but as much as he charges them,
so much the more superabundantly they preach;
37 and are superabundantly astonished,
wording, He does all well:
he makes both the mute to hear
and the speechless to speak.

Yah Shua Feeds Four Thousand

8 In those days, the multitude being very great,
and having naught to eat,
Yah Shua calls his disciples and words to them,
2 I have *compassion* **a sympathetic spleen**
on the multitude,
because
they have *now been* **already abode** with me three days,
and have *nothing* **naught** to eat:
3 And *if* **whenever** I *send*
release them *away* fasting
to their own houses,
they *will* **shall** faint by the way:
for *divers* **some** of them came from far.
4 And his disciples answered him,
From whence can *a man satisfy* **anyone fill** these men
with bread here in the wilderness?
5 And he asked them, How
many *loaves* **breads** have ye?
And they said, Seven.
6 And he *commanded* **evangelized**
the *people* **multitude**
to *sit down* **repose** on the *ground* **soil**:
and he took the seven *loaves* **breads**,
and *gave thanks* **eucharistized** and brake,
and gave to his disciples to set *before* **by** them;
and they did set them
before **to** the *people* **multitude**.
7 And they had a few small fishes:
and he *blessed* **eulogized**,
and *commanded* **said** to set them also *before them*.
8 So they did eat, and were *filled* **fed**:
and they took *up* of the
broken meat that was left **superabundant fragments**,
seven baskets.
9 And they that had eaten
were about four thousand:
and he *sent* **released** them *away*.
10 And straightway
he *entered* **embarked** into a *ship* **sailer**
with his disciples,
and came into the parts of Dalmanutha.

The Pharisees Seek A Sign

11 And the Pharisees came *forth*,
and began to *question* **dispute** with him,
seeking of him a sign from **the** heaven,
tempting **testing** him.
12 And he sighed deeply in his
spirit, and *saith* **wordeth**,
Why doth this generation seek after a sign?
Verily I say **Amen! I word** unto you,
There shall no sign be given unto this generation.

Yah Shua Interprets
The Parable Of Fermentation

13 And he *left* **released** them,
and *entering* **embarking** into the *ship* **sailer** again
departed to the other side.
14 Now the disciples had forgotten to take bread,
neither had they in the *ship* **sailer** with
them *more than* **except** one *loaf* **bead**.
15 And he charged them, *saying*
wording, *Take heed* **See**,
beware **observe** of the *leaven* **fermentation**
of the Pharisees,
and of the *leaven* **fermentation** of Herod.
16 And they reasoned among
themselves **one another**,
saying **wording**, because we have no bread.
17 And when *Jesus* **Yah Shua** knew it,
he *saith* **wordeth** unto them,
Why reason ye, because ye have no bread?
perceive ye not yet,
neither *understand* **comprehend**?
have ye your heart yet *hardened* **petrified**?

MARK/MAKABI 8

18 Having eyes, *see* **observe** ye not?
and having ears, hear ye not? and do ye not remember?
19 When I brake the five *loaves* **breads**
among five thousand,
how many baskets full of fragments took ye *up*?
They *say* **word** unto him, Twelve.
20 And when the seven among four thousand,
how many baskets full of fragments took ye *up*?
And they said, Seven.
21 And he *said* **worded** unto them,
How is it that ye do not *understand* **comprehend**?
2 I have a sympathetic spleen on the multitude
because they already abide with me three days
and have naught to eat:
3 and whenever I release them
to their own houses fasting
they faint by the way:
for some of them come from afar.
4 And his disciples answer him,
Whence can anyone fill these men with bread
here in the wilderness?
5 And he asks them, How many breads have you?
And they say, Seven.
6 And he evangelizes the multitude
to repose on the soil:
and he takes the seven breads
and eucharistizes and breaks
and gives to his disciples to set by them;
and they set them to the multitude.
7 And they have a few small fishes:
and he eulogizes, and says to set them also:
8 so they eat, and are fed:
and they take seven baskets
of the superabundant fragments:
9 and they who eat are about four thousand:
and he releases them.
10 And straightway
he embarks in a sailer with his disciples,
and goes to the parts of Dalmanutha.

THE PHARISEES SEEK A SIGN

11 And the Pharisees come
and begin to dispute with him,
seeking a sign from the heavens — testing him.
12 And he sighs deeply in his spirit, and words,
Why seeks this generation after a sign?
Amen! I word to you,
no sign is given this generation.

YAH SHUA INTERPRETS THE PARABLE OF FERMENTATION

13 And he releases them,
and embarks in the sailer again
and departs across:
14 and the disciples forget to take bread,
and they have none in the sailer with them
except one bead.
15 And he charges them, wording, See!
observe the fermentation of the Pharisees
and the fermentation of Herod.
16 And they reason among one another,
wording, Because we have no bread.
17 And Yah Shua knows, and words to them,
Why reason you, because you have no bread?
Perceive you not yet? Comprehend you not?
Petrify you still your heart?
18 Having eyes, observe you not?
And having ears, hear you not?
And remember you not,
19 when I broke the five breads
among five thousand,
how many baskets full of fragments took you?
They word to him, Twelve.
20 And the seven among four thousand,
how many baskets full of fragments took you?
And they say, Seven.
21 And he words to them,
How is it that you comprehend not?

YAH SHUA HEALS A BLIND

22 And he cometh to *Bethsaida* **Beth Sayad**;
and they bring a blind *man* unto him,
and besought him to touch him.
23 And he took the blind *man* by the hand,
and led him out of the *town* **village**;
and when he had spit on his eyes,
and put his hands upon him,
he asked him if he *saw ought* **observed anyone**.
24 And he looked *up*, and *said* **worded**,
I *see men* **observe humans** as trees, walking.
25 *After that* **Then** he put his
hands again upon his eyes,
and made him look *up*: and he was restored,
and *saw every man* **looked at everyone** clearly.
26 And he *sent* **apostolized** him *away* to his house,
saying **wording**, Neither *go into* **enter** the *town* **village**,
nor *tell* **say** it to any in the *town* **village**.

THE WITNESS OF PETROS
CONCERNING YAH SHUA

27 And *Jesus* **Yah Shua** went *out*, and his disciples,
into the *towns* **villages**
of *Caesarea Philippi* **Kaisaria Philippos**:
and *by* **on** the way he asked his disciples,
saying **wording** unto them,
Whom do *men say that I am* **humanity speak me to be**?
28 And they answered, *John*
Yahn the *Baptist* **Baptizer**;
but *some* **others** say, *Elias* **Eli Yah**;
and others, One of the prophets.
29 And he *saith* **wordeth** unto them,
But whom *say ye that I am* **word ye me to be**?
And *Peter* **Petros** answereth and
saith **wordeth** unto him,
Thou art the *Christ* **Messiah**.
30 And he *charged* **admonished** them
that they should *tell* **word** no *man* **of one about** him.

YAH SHUA PROPHESIES
HIS DEATH AND RESURRECTION

31 And he began to *teach* **doctrinate** them,
that the Son of *man* **humanity** must
suffer *many things* **much**,
and be *rejected* **disapproved** of the elders,
and of the *chief priests*,**archpriests** and scribes,
and be *killed* **slaughtered**, and
after three days rise again.
32 And he spake that *saying openly* **word boldly**.
And *Peter* **Petros** took him, and began to rebuke him.
33 But when he had turned about
and *looked on* **saw** his disciples,
he rebuked *Peter* **Petros**, *saying* **wording**,
Get thee behind me, Satan:
for thou *savourest* **mindest** not
the things **those** that be of *God* **Elohim**,
but *the things* **those** that be of *men* **humanity**.

LOSING THE SOUL TO SAVE THE SOUL

34 And when he had called the *people* **multitude**
unto him with his disciples also, he said unto them,
Whosoever come after me, let him deny himself,
and take *up* his *cross* **stake**, and follow me.
35 For whosoever *will* **willeth to** save his *life* **soul**
shall lose it;
but whosoever shall lose his *life* **soul** for my sake
and the *gospel's* **evangelism's**,
the **this** same shall save it.
36 For what shall it *profit* **benefit** a *man* **human**,
if **whenever** he shall gain the whole *world* **cosmos**,
and lose his own soul?
37 Or what shall a *man* **human** give
in exchange for his soul?
38 Whosoever *therefore* **indeed**
shall *be ashamed* **shame** of me and of my words
in this adulterous and sinful generation;
of him also shall the Son of *man be
ashamed* **humanity shame**,
when he cometh
in the glory of his Father with the holy angels.

THE METAMORPHOSIS OF YAH SHUA

9 And he *said* **worded** unto them,
Verily I say **Amen! I word** unto you,
That there be some of them that stand here,
which shall not taste of death,

YAH SHUA HEALS A BLIND

22 And he goes to Beth Sayad;
and they bring him someone blind
and beseech him to touch him:
23 and he takes the blind by the hand
and leads him from the village;
and he spits on his eyes and puts his hands on him,
and he asks him if he observes anyone.
24 And he looks, and words,
I observe humans as trees, walking.
25 Then again he puts his hands on his eyes,
and has him look:
and he is restored, and looks at everyone clearly:
26 and he apostolizes him to his house,
wording, Neither enter the village,
nor say it to any in the village.

THE WITNESS OF PETROS
CONCERNING YAH SHUA

27 And Yah Shua and his disciples
go to the villages of Kaisaria, Philippos:
and on the way he asks his disciples,
wording to them,
Whom do humanity speak me to be?
28 And they answer, Yahn the Baptizer;
and others say, Eli Yah;
but others, One of the prophets.
29 And he words to them,
And You, whom word you me to be?
And Petros answers him, wording,
You are the Messiah!

30 — and he admonishes them
to word to no one about him.

YAH SHUA PROPHESIES HIS DEATH AND RESURRECTION

31 And he begins to doctrinate them
that the Son of humanity must suffer much;
and be disapproved of the elders
and of the archpriests and scribes;
and be slaughtered
and after three days rise:

32 and he speaks that word boldly.
— and Petros takes him and begins to rebuke him.

33 But he turns around and sees his disciples
and he rebukes Petros, wording,
Get behind me, Satan:
for you mind not those of Elohim,
but those of humanity.

LOSING THE SOUL TO SAVE THE SOUL

34 And he calls the multitude with his disciples
and says to them,
Whoever comes after me
denies himself and takes his stake and follows me.

35 For whoever wills to save his soul,
loses it;
but whoever loses his soul
because of me and the evangelism,
saves it.

36 For what is a human benefited
whenever he gains the whole cosmos
and loses his own soul?

37 Or what gives a human in exchange for his soul?

38 Whoever indeed
shames of me and of my words
in this adulterous and sinful generation;
of him also the Son of humanity shames
when he comes in the glory of his Father
with the holy angels.

THE METAMORPHOSIS OF YAH SHUA

9 And he words to them,
Amen! I word to you,
some of those standing here taste not of death
till they have seen
the *kingdom* **sovereigndom** of *God* **Elohim**
come *with power* **in dynamis**.

2 And after six days *Jesus*
Yah Shua taketh with him
Peter **Petros**, and *James* **Yaaqovos**, and *John* **Yahn**,
and *leadeth* **bringeth** them up into an high mountain
apart by themselves **alone**:
and he was *transfigured* **metamorphosed**
before **in front of** them.

3 And his raiment became *shining* **gleaming**,
exceeding **very** white as snow;
so as no fuller on earth can white them.

4 And there appeared unto them
Elias **Eli Yah** with *Moses* **Mosheh**:
and they were talking with *Jesus* **Yah Shua**.

5 And *Peter* **Petros** answered
and *said* **worded** to *Jesus* **Yah Shua**,
Master **Rabbi**, it is good for us to be here:
and let us make three tabernacles;
one for thee,
and one for *Moses* **Mosheh**, and one for *Elias* **Eli Yah**.

6 For he *wist* **knew** not what to *say* **speak**;
for they were *sore afraid* **utterly frightened**.

7 And *there was* **so be it**,
a cloud *that* overshadowed them:
and a voice *came* out of the cloud, *saying* **wording**,
This is my beloved Son: hear him.

8 And suddenly, when they
had looked round about,
they saw no *man* **one** any more,
save *Jesus* **but Yah Shua** only with themselves.

9 And as they came down from the mountain,
he charged them that they should
tell **declare to** no *man* **one**
what *things* they had seen,
till **except when** the Son of *man* **humanity**
were risen from the dead.

10 And they *kept* **empowered** that *saying* **word**
with themselves,
questioning one with another **disputing**
what the rising from the dead should mean.

11 And they asked him, *saying* **wording**,
Why *say* **word** the scribes
that *Elias* **Eli Yah** must first come?

12 And he answered and *told* **said to** them,
Elias verily **Eli Yah indeed** cometh first,
and restoreth all *things*;
and how it is *written* **scribed**
of the Son of *man* **humanity**,
that he must suffer *many things* **much**,
and be set at nought.

13 But I *say* **word** unto you,
That *Elias* **Eli Yah** is indeed come,
and they have done unto him
whatsoever **as much as** they *listed* **willed**,

EDC Hebrew / English Bible   MARK/MAKABI 9

       exactly as it is *written* **scribed** of him.
            Malachi 4:5, 6

Yah Shua Casts Out A Demon

14   And when he came to his disciples,
    he saw a *great* **vast** multitude about them,
   and the scribes *questioning* **disputing** with them.
15   And straightway all the *people* **multitude**,
      when they *beheld* **saw** him,
     were *greatly amazed* **utterly astonished**,
      and running to him saluted him.
16   And he asked the scribes,
     What *question* **dispute** ye with them?
17   And one of the multitude answered and said,
  Master **Doctor**, I have brought unto thee my
   son, which hath a *dumb* **speechless** spirit;
18   And wheresoever he *taketh* **overtaketh** him,
        he teareth him:
   and he foameth, and gnasheth with his teeth,
     and *pineth* **withereth** away:
    and I spake to thy disciples that
      they should cast him out;
        and they could not.
19   He answereth him, and *saith* **wordeth**,
     O *faithless* **trustless** generation,
  how long **until when** shall I be with you?
 how long **until when** shall I *suffer* **tolerate** you?
       bring him unto me.
        until they see
  the sovereigndom of Elohim come in dynamis.
2   And after six days, Yah Shua takes
    Petros and Yaaqovos and Yahn with him
   and brings them to a high mountain alone:
    and he is metamorphosed in front of them:
3   and his raiment becomes gleaming
       — very white as snow
  as no fuller on earth can whiten them:
4   and Eli Yah with Mosheh appears to them
      and they talk with Yah Shua.
5   And Petros answers Yah Shua, wording,
   Rabbi, it is good for us to be here;
     and we make three tabernacles:
 one for you and one for Mosheh and one for Eli Yah.
6   — for he knows not what to speak
      for they are utterly frightened.
7   And so be it, a cloud overshadows them:
   and a voice from the cloud, words,
    This is my beloved Son! Hear him!
8   — and suddenly, as they look around
      they see no one any more

      but Yah Shua only with them.
9   And as they descend the mountain
  he charges them to declare to no one what they saw,
except when the Son of humanity rises from the dead:
10   and they empower that word with themselves
  disputing what the rising from the dead means.
11   And they ask him, wording,
 Why word the scribes that Eli Yah must first come?
12   And he answers them, saying,
  Eli Yah indeed comes first and restores all;
 and how it is scribed of the Son of humanity
   to suffer much and be set at naught.
13   But I word to you,
    That Eli Yah indeed has come,
 and they did to him as much as they willed
    exactly as it is scribed of him.
       Malachi 4:5, 6

Yah Shua Casts Out A Demon

14   And he comes to his disciples
  and he sees a vast multitude around them;
   and the scribes disputing with them:
15   and straightway, when they see him,
   all the multitude is utterly astonished,
    and running to him salute him.
16   And he asks the scribes,
     What dispute you with them?
17   And one of the multitude answers, saying,
    Doctor, I bring my son to you
    who has a speechless spirit;
18   and wherever he overtakes him, he tears him:
   and he foams and gnashes with his teeth
       and withers away:
   and I spoke to your disciples to cast him out;
       and they cannot.
19   He answers him, wording,
     O trustless generation,
Until when am I with you? Until when tolerate I you?
       Bring him to me.
20   And they brought him unto him:
     and when he saw him,
 straightway the spirit *tare* **convulsed** him;
and he fell on the *ground* **soil**, and wallowed foaming.
21   And he asked his father,
   How *long is it ago* **much time**
   since this *came unto* **became** him?
And he said, Of a child **Since childhood**.
22   And *ofttimes* **often** it hath cast him into the fire,
    and into the waters, to destroy him:
    but if thou canst do *any thing* **aught**,

have *compassion* **a sympathetic spleen** on us, and help us.
23 *Jesus* **Yah Shua** said unto him,
If thou canst *believe* **trust**,
all *things* are possible to him that *believeth* **trusteth**.
24 And straightway the father
of the child cried out,
and *said* **worded** with tears, *Lord* **Adonay**, I *believe* **trust**;
help thou *mine unbelief* **my trustlessness**.
25 When *Jesus* **Yah Shua** saw
that the *people* **multitude** came running together,
he rebuked the *foul* **impure** spirit,
saying **wording** unto him,
Thou *dumb* **speechless** and deaf spirit,
I *charge* **order** thee,
come out of him, and enter no more into him.
26 And *the spirit* **having** cried,
and *rent* **having convulsed** him *sore* **much**,
and came out of him: and he *was* **became** as one dead;
insomuch that many *said* **worded**, He is dead.
27 But *Jesus* **Yah Shua**
took **overpowered** him by the hand,
and lifted him *up*; and he arose.
28 And when he was come into the house,
his disciples asked him privately, Why
could not we cast him out?
29 And he said unto them,
This *kind* **genos** can come forth by *nothing* **naught**,
but **except** by prayer and fasting.

Yah Shua Prophesies His Death And Resurrection

30 And they departed thence,
and passed through *Galilee* **Galiyl**;
and he *would* **willed**
not that any man **that no one** should know it.
31 For he *taught* **doctrinated** his disciples,
and *said* **worded** unto them,
The Son of *man* **humanity**
is *delivered* **betrayed** into the hands of men,
and they shall *kill* **slaughter** him;
and after that he is *killed* **slaughtered**,
he shall rise the third day.
32 But they *understood* **knew**
not that *saying* **rhema**,
and were *afraid* **awestricken** to ask him.

The First Are Final

33 And he came to *Capernaum* **Kaphar Nachum**:
and being in the house he asked them,
What was it that ye *disputed* **reasoned** among yourselves
by **on** the way?
34 But they *held their peace* **hushed**:
for *by* **on** the way they had *disputed* **reasoned**
among *themselves* **one another**,
who should be the greatest.
35 And he sat *down*, and
called **voiced to** the twelve,
and *saith* **wordeth** unto them,
If any *man desire* **one willeth** to be first,
the same shall be *last* **final** of all,
and *servant* **minister** of all.
36 And he took a child, and set
him in the midst of them:
and when he had taken him in his arms,
he said unto them,
37 Whosoever shall receive one of such children
in my name,
receiveth me:
and whosoever shall receive me,
receiveth not me, but him that *sent* **apostolized** me.
38 And *John* **Yahn** answered him, *saying* **wording**,
Master **Doctor**,
we saw one casting out *devils* **demons** in thy name,
and he followeth not us:
and we forbad him, because he followeth not us.
20 And they bring him to him:
and straightway, when he sees him,
the spirit convulses him;
and he falls on the soil and wallows foaming:
21 and he asks his father,
How much time since this became him?
And he says, Since childhood:
22 and often it has casts him into the fire
and into the waters to destroy him:
but if you can do aught,
have a sympathetic spleen on us and help us.
23 Yah Shua says to him, If you can trust!
All is possible to him who trusts.
24 And straightway the father of the child cries out
and words with tears, Adonay, I trust!
Help my trustlessness!
25 Yah Shua sees the multitude
come running together
and rebukes the impure spirit, wording to him,
You speechless and deaf spirit,
I order you, come from him and enter him no more.
26 And crying and convulsing him much
it comes from him:
and he becomes as one dead;

so that many word, He is dead!
27 But Yah Shua overpowers him by the hand
and lifts him and he rises.
28 And he comes into the house,
and his disciples ask him privately,
Why could not we cast him out?
29 And he says to them,
This genos can come forth in naught,
except by prayer and fasting.

Yah Shua Prophesies His Death And Resurrection

30 And they depart from there
and pass through Galiyl;
and he wills that no one know:
31 for he doctrinates his
disciples, and words to them,
The Son of humanity
is betrayed into the hands of men;
and they slaughter him;
and after he is slaughtered, the third day he rises.
32 — but they know not that rhema,
and are awestricken to ask him.

The First Are Final

33 And he goes to Kaphar Nachum:
and being in the house he asks them,
What reasoned you among yourselves on the way?
34 But they hush:
for on the way they reasoned among one another
who is the greatest.
35 And he sits,
and voices to the twelve, and words to them,
If anyone wills to be first,
the same becomes final of all, and minister of all.
36 And he takes a child and
sets him in their midst:
and he takes him in his arms, and he says to them,
37 Whoever receives one of such children
in my name,
receives me:
and whoever receives me,
receives not me, but him who apostolized me.
38 And Yahn answers him, wording, Doctor,
we saw one casting out demons in your name;
and he follows us not:
and we forbad him because he follows us not.
39 But *Jesus* **Yah Shua** said, Forbid him not:
for there is no *man* **one**
which shall do *a miracle* **dynamis** in my name,
that can *lightly speak evil of* **quickly vilify** me.
40 For he that is not against us is on our part.

Never Scandalize

41 For whosoever shall give
you a cup of water to drink
in my name,
because ye belong to *Christ* **Messiah**,
verily I say **Amen! I word** unto you,
he shall not lose his reward.
42 And whosoever shall *offend* **scandalize**
one of these little ones that *believe* **trust** in me,
it is *better* **good** for him
that a millstone were hanged *about* **around** his neck,
and he were cast into the sea.

Amputate When Necessary

43 And *if* **whenever** thy hand
offend **scandalize** thee,
cut it off **amputate**:
it is *better* **good** for thee to enter into life maimed,
than having two hands to go into
hell **Gay Hinnom/the valley of burning**,
into the fire *that never shall be quenched* **unquenchable**:
44 Where their *worm* **maggot** dieth not,
and the fire is not quenched.
45 And *if* **whenever** thy foot
offend **scandalize** thee,
cut it off **amputate**:
it is *better* **good** for thee to enter *halt* **lame** into life,
than having two feet to be cast into
hell **Gay Hinnom/the valley of burning**,
into the fire *that never shall be quenched* **unquenchable**:
46 Where their *worm* **maggot** dieth not,
and the fire is not quenched.
47 And *if* **whenever** thine eye
offend **scandalize** thee,
pluck **cast** it out:
it is *better* **good** for thee
to enter into the *kingdom* **sovereigndom** of *God* **Elohim**
with one eye **one—eyed**,
than having two eyes to be cast into
hell **Gay Hinnom/the valley of burning** fire:
48 Where their *worm* **maggot** dieth not,
and the fire is not quenched.
49 For every one shall be salted with fire,
and every sacrifice shall be salted with salt.
50 Salt is good:
but *if* **whenever** the salt *have lost his*
saltness **become saltless**,

wherewith *will* **shall** ye season it?
Have salt in yourselves,
and *have peace* **shalom** one with another.

MARRIAGE AND DIVORCE

10 And he arose from thence,
and cometh into the *coasts* **boundaries**
of *Judaea* **Yah Hudah**
by the farther side of Jordan **across Yarden**:
and the *people resort* **multitude go** unto him again;
and, as he was *wont* **accustomed**,
he *taught* **doctrinated** them again.
2 And the Pharisees came to him, and asked him,
Is it *lawful* **allowed**
for a man to *put away* **release** his *wife* **woman**?
tempting **testing** him.
3 And he answered and said unto them,
What did *Moses command* **Mosheh misvah** you?
4 And they said, *Moses suffered* **Mosheh allowed**
to *write* **scribe** a *bill* **scroll** of *divorcement*
apostasy, and to *put* **release** her *away*.
5 And *Jesus* **Yah Shua** answered
and said unto them,
For *the hardness of* your *heart* **hardheartedness**
he *wrote* **scribed** you this *precept* **misvah**.
6 But from the beginning of the creation
God **Elohim** made them male and female.
7 For this cause
shall a *man* **human** leave his father and mother,
and *cleave* **adhere** to his *wife* **woman**;
39 But Yah Shua says, Forbid him not:
for no one doing dynamis in my name,
can quickly vilify me:
40 for whoever is not against us is on our part.

NEVER SCANDALIZE

41 For whoever gives you a cup of water to drink
in my name,
because you belong to Messiah,
Amen! I word to you,
he loses not his reward:
42 and whoever scandalizes
one of these little ones who trust in me,
it is good for him
to hang a millstone around his neck,
and cast him in the sea.

AMPUTATE WHEN NECESSARY

43 And whenever your hand scandalizes you,
amputate:
it is good for you to enter life maimed,
rather than two hands
go in Gay Hinnom/the Valley of Burning
— into the fire unquenchable:
44 where their maggot dies not
and the fire quenches not.
45 And whenever your foot scandalizes you,
amputate:
it is good for you to enter life lame,
rather than two feet
cast in Gay Hinnom/the Valley of Burning
— in the fire unquenchable:
46 where their maggot dies not
and the fire quenches not.
47 And whenever your eye scandalizes you,
cast it out:
it is good for you
to enter the sovereigndom of Elohim one—eyed,
rather than two eyes
cast in Gay Hinnom/the Valley of Burning fire:
48 where their maggot dies not,
and the fire quenches not.
49 For everyone is to be salted with fire
and every sacrifice salted with salt:
50 salt is good:
but whenever the salt becomes saltless,
in what season you?
Have salt in yourselves,
and shalam one another.

MARRIAGE AND DIVORCE

10 And he rises from there,
and enters the boundaries of Yah Hudah
across Yarden:
and again the multitude comes to him;
and, as accustomed, he again doctrinates them.
2 And the Pharisees come to him, and ask him,
Is a man allowed to release his woman?
— testing him.
3 And he answers them, saying,
What misvahed Mosheh?
4 And they say,
Mosheh allowed to scribe a scroll of apostasy,
and to release her.
5 And Yah Shua answers them, saying,
Because of your hardheartedness
he scribed you this misvah:
6 but from the beginning of the creation
Elohim made them male and female.

| 7 | For this cause a human
leaves his father and mother
and adheres to his woman
| 8 | And they twain shall be *into* one flesh:
so then they are no more twain, but one flesh.
| 9 | *So* What *therefore*
God **Elohim** hath *joined together* **co—yoked**, let
not *man put asunder* **humanity separate**.
| 10 | And in the house his disciples asked him again
of **concerning** the same matter.
| 11 | And he *saith* **wordeth** unto them,
Whosoever shall *put away* **release** his *wife* **woman**
and marry another,
committeth adultery **adulterizeth** against her.
| 12 | And *if* **whenever** a woman
shall *put away* **release** her man,
and be married to another,
she *committeth adultery* **adulterizeth**.

YAH SHUA EULOGIZES YOUNG CHILDREN

| 13 | And they *brought* **offered**
young children to him,
that he should touch them:
and his disciples rebuked those
that *brought* **offered** them.
| 14 | But when *Jesus* **Yah Shua** saw it,
he *was much displeased* **indignified**, and said unto them,
Suffer **Allow** the little children to come unto me,
and forbid them not:
for of such is the *kingdom* **sovereigndom** of *God* **Elohim**.
| 15 | *Verily I say* **Amen! I word** unto you,
Whosoever shall not receive
the *kingdom* **sovereigndom** of *God*
Elohim as a little child,
he shall not enter therein.
| 16 | And he took them *up* in his arms,
put his hands upon them, and *blessed* **eulogized** them.

WEALTHY BUT LOST

| 17 | And when he *was gone forth*
departed into the way,
there came one running, and kneeled to him,
and asked him, Good *Master* **Doctor**,
what shall I do that I may inherit eternal life?
| 18 | And *Jesus* **Yah Shua** said unto him,
Why *callest* **wordest** thou me good?
there is none good *but* **except** one, *that is, God* **Elohim**.
| 19 | Thou knowest the *commandments* **misvoth**,
Do not commit adultery **adulterize not**,
Do not kill **murder not**,
Do not steal **not**,
Do not bear false **pseudo** witness **not**,
Defraud not,
Honour thy father and mother.
| 20 | And he answered and said
unto him, *Master* **Doctor**,
all these have I *observed* **guarded** from my youth.
| 21 | *Then Jesus* **And Yah Shua**
beholding **looking at** him loved him,
and said unto him, One *thing* thou lackest:
go thy way, sell *whatsoever* **as much as** thou hast,
and give to the poor,
and thou shalt have treasure in heaven:
and come, take *up* the *cross* **stake**, and follow me.
| 22 | And he was *sad* **gloomy** at that *saying* **word**,
and went away *grieved* **sorrowed**:
for he had *great* **vast** possessions.

YAH SHUA AND RICHES

| 23 | And *Jesus* **Yah Shua** looked round about,
and *saith* **wordeth** unto his disciples,
How *hardly* **difficultly** shall they that have riches
enter into the *kingdom* **sovereigndom** of *God* **Elohim**!
| 24 | And the disciples *were* astonished at his words.
But *Jesus* **Yah Shua** answereth again,
and *saith* **wordeth** unto them,
Children, how *hard* **difficult** is it
for them that *trust* **confide** in riches
to enter into the *kingdom* **sovereigndom** of *God* **Elohim**!
| 25 | It is easier for a *camel* **rope***
to *go* **pass** through the eye of a needle,
than for a rich man
to enter into the *kingdom* **sovereigndom** of *God* **Elohim**.

*see Lamsa

| 26 | And they *were* astonished *out*
of measure **superabundantly**,
| 8 | and the two become into one flesh:
that they are no more two, but one flesh.
| 9 | So what Elohim co—yokes,
humanity is not to separate.
| 10 | And in the house his disciples ask him again
concerning the same matter:
| 11 | and he words to them,
Whoever releases his woman
and marries another,
adulterizes against her:
| 12 | and whenever a woman releases her man
and marries another,
she adulterizes.

MARK/MAKABI 10

YAH SHUA EULOGIZES YOUNG CHILDREN

13 And they offer him young children to touch:
and his disciples rebuke those who offer them.
14 But Yah Shua sees, and he indignifies,
and says to them,
Allow the little children to come to me
and forbid them not:
for of such is the sovereigndom of Elohim.
15 Amen! I word to you,
Whoever receives not the sovereigndom of Elohim
as a little child,
enters not therein.
16 — and he takes them in his arms,
puts his hands on them and eulogizes them.

WEALTHY BUT LOST

17 And as he departs in the way,
someone comes running and kneels to him,
and asks him, Good Doctor,
what do I to inherit eternal life?
18 And Yah Shua says to him,
Why word you me good?
None is good except one, Elohim.
19 You know the misvoth,
Adulterize not!
Murder not!
Steal not!
Pseudo witness not!
Defraud not!
Honor your father and mother!
20 And he answers him, saying, Doctor,
I guarded all these from my youth.
21 And Yah Shua, looking at him, loves him,
and says to him, You lack One:
go your way, sell as much as you have,
and give to the poor,
and you have treasure in the heavens:
and come, follow me, take the stake.
22 And he is gloomy at that
word, and goes away sorrowed:
for he has vast possessions.

YAH SHUA AND RICHES

23 And Yah Shua looks around
and words to his disciples,
How difficultly they who have riches
enter the sovereigndom of Elohim!
24 — and the disciples astonish at his words.
And again Yah Shua answers them, wording,
Children, how difficult for them who confide in riches
to enter the sovereigndom of Elohim!
25 It is easier for a rope*
to pass through the eye of a needle,
than for a rich man
to enter the sovereigndom of Elohim.

*see Lamsa

26 And they superabundantly astonish
saying **wording** among themselves,
Who *then* can be saved?
27 And *Jesus* **Yah Shua** looking
upon them *saith* **wordeth**,
With *men* **humanity** it is impossible,
but not with *God* **Elohim**:
for with *God* **Elohim** all *things* are possible.
28 *Then Peter* **And Petros**
began to *say* **word** unto him,
Lo **Behold**,
we have *left* **forsaken** all, and have followed thee.
29 And *Jesus* **Yah Shua** answered and said,
Verily I say **Amen! I word** unto you,
There is no *man* **one** that hath *left* **forsaken** house,
or brethren, or sisters, or father, or mother,
or *wife* **woman**, or children, or *lands* **fields**,
for my sake, and the *gospel's* **evangelism's**,
30 But he shall *receive* **take** an hundredfold
now in this *time* **season**,
houses,
and brethren, and sisters, and mothers, and children,
and *lands* **fields**, with persecutions;
and in the *world* **eons** to come eternal life.
31 But many that are first shall be *last* **final**;
and the *last* **final** first.

YAH SHUA PROPHESIES
HIS DEATH AND RESURRECTION

32 And they were in the way
going up **ascending** to *Jerusalem* **Yeru Shalem**;
and *Jesus went before* **Yah Shua preceded** them:
and they *were amazed* **astonished**;
and as they followed, they were *afraid* **awestricken**.
And he took again the twelve,
and began to *tell* **word to** them
what *things should* **is about to** happen unto him,
33 *Saying*, Behold,
we *go up* **ascend** to *Jerusalem* **Yeru Shalem**;
and the Son of *man* **humanity** shall
be *delivered* **betrayed**
unto the *chief priests,* **archpriests** and unto the scribes;
and they shall condemn him to death,

and shall *deliver* **betray** him to the *Gentiles* **goyim**:

34 And they shall mock him,
and shall scourge him,
and shall spit upon him, and shall *kill* **slaughter** him:
and the third day he shall rise *again*.

THE SELFISH WILL OF YAAQOVOS AND YAHN

35 And *James* **Yaaqovos** and *John* **Yahn**,
the sons of *Zebedee* **Zabdi**,
come unto him, *saying* **wording**, *Master*, **Doctor**,
we *would* **will** that thou shouldest do for us
whatsoever we shall *desire* **ask**.

36 And he said unto them,
What *would* **will** ye that I should do for you?

37 They said unto him,
Grant **Give** unto us that we may sit,
one *on* **at** thy right *hand*,
and *the other on* **one at** thy left *hand*, in thy glory.

38 But *Jesus* **Yah Shua** said unto them,
Ye know not what ye ask:
can ye drink of the cup that I drink *of*?
and be baptized
with the baptism that I am baptized *with*?

39 And they said unto him, We can.
And *Jesus* **Yah Shua** said unto them,
Ye shall indeed drink of the cup that I drink of;
and *with* the baptism that I am baptized *withal*
shall ye be baptized:

40 But to sit *on* **at** my right
hand and *on* **at** my left *hand*
is not mine to give;
but it shall be given to them for whom it is prepared.

41 And when the ten heard it,
they began to *be much displeased* **indignify** with
James **about Yaaqovos** and *Yahn* **Yahn**.

42 But *Jesus* **Yah Shua** called them to him,
and *saith* **wordeth** unto them,
Ye know that they which are *accounted* **thought**
to rule over the *Gentiles* **goyim**
exercise lordship **rule** over them;
and their *great* **mega** ones
exercise authority upon **authorize over** them.

43 But *so* **thus** shall it not be among you:
but whosoever *will* **willeth to** be *great* **mega** among you,
shall be your minister:
— wording among themselves,
Who can be saved?

27 And Yah Shua, looking upon them, words,
With humanity it is impossible,
but not with Elohim:

for with Elohim all are possible.

28 And Petros begins to word to him,
Behold, we forsake all, and follow you.

29 And Yah Shua answers, saying,
Amen! I word to you,
no one who forsakes house
or brothers or sisters or father or mother
or woman or children or fields
for my sake, and the evangelism,

30 but he takes a hundredfold now in this season
— houses and brothers and sisters
and mothers and children
and fields with persecutions;
and eternal life in the coming eons.

31 And many first become final;
and the final first.

YAH SHUA PROPHESIES
HIS DEATH AND RESURRECTION

32 And they are in the way
ascending to Yeru Shalem;
and Yah Shua precedes them:
and they astonish;
and as they follow, they are awestricken.
And again he takes the twelve,
and begins to word to them
what is about to happen to him,

33 Behold, we ascend to Yeru Shalem;
that the Son of humanity
be betrayed to the archpriests and to the scribes
— to condemn him to death
and to betray him to the goyim

34 and to mock him and scourge him
and spit upon him and slaughter him
— and the third day he rises.

THE SELFISH WILL OF YAAQOVOS AND YAHN

35 And Yaaqovos and Yahn the sons of Zabdi
come to him, wording, Doctor,
we will that you do for us whatever we ask.

36 And he says to them,
What will you that I do for you?

37 They say to him, Give to us to sit,
one at your right and one at your left
in your glory.

38 But Yah Shua says to them,
You know not what you ask!
Can you drink of the cup I drink?
And be baptized with the baptism I am baptized?

39 And they say to him, We can.

MARK/MAKABI 10, 11

And Yah Shua says to them, Indeed,
of the cup I drink, you drink;
and of the baptism I am baptized, you be baptized:
40 but to sit at my right and at my left
is not mine to give;
but it is given to them for whom it is prepared.
41 And the ten hear,
and begin to indignify about Yaaqovos and Yahn.
42 But Yah Shua calls them
to him and words to them,
You know that they who are thought
to rule over the goyim, rule over them;
and their mega ones authorize over them.
43 But so be it not among you:
but whoever among you wills to be mega,
becomes your minister:
44 And whosoever of you *will* **willeth**
to be *the chiefest* **first**,
shall be servant of all.
45 For even the Son of *man* **humanity** came
not to be ministered unto, but to minister,
and to give his *life* **soul** a *ransom* **redemption** for many.

YAH SHUA RESTORES THE SIGHT OF BAR TAME

46 And they came to *Jericho* **Yericho**:
and as he *went* **departed** out of *Jericho* **Yericho**
with his disciples
and *a great number of people* **an ample multitude**,
blind *Bartimaeus* **Bar Tame**, the son of *Timaeus* **Tame**,
sat by the *highway side* **wayside** begging.
47 And when he heard
that it was *Jesus of Nazareth* **Yah Shua the Nazarene**,
he began to cry out, and *say* **word**,
Jesus **Yah Shua**, thou son of David, *have* mercy *on* me.
48 And many *charged* **rebuked** him
that he should *hold his peace* **hush**:
but he cried the more *a great deal* **vastly**,
Thou son of David, *have* mercy *on* me.
49 And *Jesus* **Yah Shua** stood *still*,
and *commanded him to be called* **said, Voice out to him**.
And they *call* **voiced out to** the blind man,
saying **wording** unto him,
Be of good comfort **Courage**, rise;
he *calleth* **voiceth out to** thee.
50 And he, casting away his garment,
rose, and came to *Jesus* **Yah Shua**.
51 And *Jesus* **Yah Shua** answered
and *said* **worded** unto him,
What *wilt* **willest** thou that I should do unto thee?
The blind man said unto him,
Lord **Rabboni**, that I might *receive my sight* **see**.
52 And *Jesus* **Yah Shua** said unto him, Go thy way;
thy *faith* **trust** hath *made* **saved** thee *whole*.
And *immediately* **straightway** he *received his sight* **saw**,
and followed *Jesus* **Yah Shua** in the way.

THE TRIUMPHANT ENTRY OF YAH SHUA

11 And when they
came nigh to Jerusalem **approached Yeru Shalem**,
unto *Bethphage* **Beth Pag** and *Bethany* **Beth Ania**,
at the mount of Olives,
he *sendeth forth* **apostolizeth** two of his disciples,
2 And *saith* **wordeth** unto them,
Go your way into the village *over against* **in front of** you:
and *as soon* **straightway** as ye be entered into it,
ye shall find a colt tied, whereon never *man* **human** sat;
loose **release** him, and bring him.
3 And *if* **whenever** any *man* **one** say unto you,
Why do ye this?
say ye that *the Lord* **Adonay** hath need of him;
and straightway he *will send* **shall apostolize** him hither.
4 And they went their way,
and found the colt tied by the *door* **portal** without
in a place where two ways met;
and they *loose* **release** him.
5 And *certain* **some** of them that stood there
said **worded** unto them,
What do ye, *loosing* **releasing** the colt?
6 And they said unto them
even as *Jesus* **Yah Shua** had *commanded* **misvahed**:
and they *let* **released** them *go*.
7 And they brought the colt to *Jesus* **Yah Shua**,
and cast their garments on him; and he sat upon him.
8 And many spread their garments in the way:
and others
cut down branches **chopped spreadings** off the trees,
and *strawed* **spread** them in the way.
9 And they that *went before*
preceded, and they that followed,
cried, *saying* **wording**, *Hosanna* **Hoshia Na**;
Blessed is **Eulogized**
he that cometh in the name of *the Lord* **Yah Veh**:
10 *Blessed* **Eulogized**
be the kingdom **sovereigndom** of our father David,
that cometh in the name of *the Lord* **Yah Veh**:
Hosanna **Hoshia Na** in the *highest*
highests. Psalm 118:25, 26
44 and whoever of you wills to be first,
becomes servant of all.
45 For even the Son of humanity comes,
not to be ministered to, but to minister;

and to give his soul a redemption for many.

YAH SHUA RESTORES THE SIGHT OF BAR TAME

46 And they come to Yericho:
and as he departs from Yericho
with his disciples and an ample multitude,
blind Bar Tame/Son of Tame,
sits by the wayside begging:
47 and he hears it is Yah Shua the Nazarene,
and he begins to cry out, and word, Yah
Shua, son of David, mercy me!
48 — and many rebuke him that he hush:
But he cries the more vastly,
Son of David, mercy me!
49 And Yah Shua stands, and says,
Voice out to him.
And they voice out to the blind man, wording to him,
Courage! Rise! He voices out to you!
50 — and he casts his garment, rises,
and comes to Yah Shua.
51 And Yah Shua answers him wording,
What will you that I do to you?
The blind man say to him,
Rabboni, that I see!
52 And Yah Shua says to him,
Go! Your trust saves you.
— and straightway he sees,
and follows Yah Shua in the way.

THE TRIUMPHANT ENTRY OF YAH SHUA

11 And they approach Yeru Shalem
to Beth Pag and Beth Ania at the mount of Olives,
and he apostolizes two of his disciples,
2 and words to them,
Go your way into the village in front of you:
and straightway as ye enter,
you find a colt tied, whereon never human sat:
release him and bring him:
3 and whenever anyone says
to you, Why do you this?
you say, Adonay needs him;
and straightway he apostolizes him here.
4 And they go their way and find the colt tied
outside by the portal by the two ways;
and they release him:
5 and some who stand there word to them,
What do you, releasing the colt?
6 And they say to them even
as Yah Shua misvahed:
and they release them:
7 and they bring the colt to Yah Shua
and cast their garments on it; and he sits on it:
8 and many spread their garments in the way:
and others chop spreadings off the trees
and spread them in the way:
9 and they who precede and they who follow
cry, wording, Hoshia Na!
Eulogized — he who comes in the name of Yah Veh:
10 Eulogized
— the coming sovereigndom of our father David
in the name of Yah Veh:
Hoshia Na in the highests.
Psalm 118:25, 26
11 And *Jesus* **Yah Shua** entered
into *Jerusalem* **Yeru Shalem**,
and into the *temple* **priestal precinct**:
and when he had looked round about upon all *things*,
and *now the eventide was come*
already being the evening hour,
he went out unto *Bethany* **Beth Ania** with the twelve.

YAH SHUA CURSES THE BARREN FIG TREE

12 And on the morrow,
when they were come from *Bethany* **Beth Ania**,
he was hungry:
13 And seeing a fig tree afar
off having leaves, he came,
if *haply* **perhaps** he *might* find *any*
thing **somewhat** thereon:
and when he came to it,
he found *nothing but* **naught except** leaves;
for the *time* **season** of figs was not yet.
14 And *Jesus* **Yah Shua** answered and said unto it,
no *man* **one** eat fruit of thee *hereafter* **any more**
for ever **unto the eons**.
And his disciples heard it.

YAH SHUA CLEANSES THE PRIESTAL PRECINCT

15 And they come to *Jerusalem* **Yeru Shalem**:
and *Jesus* **Yah Shua**
went into **entered** the *temple* **priestal precinct**,
and began to cast out them that
sold and *bought* **marketed**
in the *temple* **priestal precinct**,
and overthrew the tables
of the *moneychangers* **coindealers**,
and the *seats* **cathedras** of them that sold doves;
16 And *would not suffer that*
any man **allowed no one**
should carry **to bear** any vessel

	through the *temple* **priestal precinct**.
17	And he *taught* **doctrinated**, *saying* **wording** unto them, Is it not *written* **scribed**, My house shall be called of all *nations* **goyim** the house of prayer? but ye have made it a *den* **grotto** of *thieves* **robbers**. Yesha Yah 56:7, Yirme Yah 7:11
18	And the scribes and *chief* **arch** priests heard it, and sought how they might destroy him: for they *feared* **awed** him, because all the *people* **multitude** was astonished at his doctrine.
19	And *when even was come* **being evening**, he *went* **departed** out of the city.

THE CURSED TREE WITHERED

20	And in the **early** morning, as they passed by, they saw the fig tree dried *up* from the roots.
21	And *Peter calling to remembrance* **Petros remembering**, *saith* **wordeth** unto him, *Master* **Rabbi**, behold, the fig tree which thou cursedst *is* withered *away*.

MOUNTAIN MOVING TRUST

22	And *Jesus* **Yah Shua** answering *saith* **wordeth** unto them, Have *faith* **trust** in *God* **Elohim**.
23	For *verily I say* **Amen! I word** unto you, That whosoever shall say unto this mountain, Be thou removed, and be thou cast into the sea; and shall not doubt in his heart, but shall *believe* **trust** that those *things* which he *saith* **wordeth** shall *come to pass* **become**; he shall have whatsoever he saith.
24	*Therefore* **Because of this** I *say* **word** unto you, What things soever ye desire **All — as much as ever you ask**, when ye pray, *believe* **trust** that ye *receive* **take** them, and ye shall have them.

FORGIVE, FORGIVEN

25	And when ye stand praying, forgive, if ye have ought against any: that your Father also which is in heaven may forgive you your *trespasses* **backslidings**.
26	But if ye do not forgive, neither *will* **shall** your Father which is in heaven forgive your *trespasses* **backslidings**.

THE AUTHORITY OF YAH SHUA CHALLENGED

27	And they come again to *Jerusalem* **Yeru Shalem**: and as he was walking in the *temple* **priestal precinct**,
11	And Yah Shua enters Yeru Shalem and the priestal precinct: and he looks all around: and already being the evening hour, he goes to Beth Ania with the twelve.

YAH SHUA CURSES THE BARREN FIG TREE

12	And on the morrow, they come from Beth Ania, and he famishes:
13	and seeing a fig tree afar having leaves, he comes, if perhaps to find somewhat thereon: and comes to it and finds naught except leaves — for the season of figs is not yet.
14	And Yah Shua answers, saying to it, No one eats your fruit any more unto the eons! — and his disciples hear it.

YAH SHUA CLEANSES THE PRIESTAL PRECINCT

15	And they go to Yeru Shalem: and Yah Shua enters the priestal precinct and begins to cast out them who sell and market in the priestal precinct; and he overthrows the tables of the coindealers and the cathedras of them who sell doves;
16	and allows no one to bear any vessel through the priestal precinct.
17	And he doctrinates them, wording, Is it not scribed, My house is called by all goyim the house of prayer? And you make it a grotto of robbers. Yesha Yah 56:7, Yirme Yah 7:11
18	And the scribes and archpriests hear: and seek how to destroy him: for they awe him because all the multitude astonishes at his doctrine.
19	And being evening, he departs from the city.

THE CURSED TREE WITHERED

20	And in the early morning, as they pass by, they see the fig tree dried from the roots:
21	and remembering, Petros words to him, Rabbi, behold, the fig tree you cursed withered.

Mountain Moving Trust

22 And Yah Shua answers them, wording,
Have trust in Elohim!
23 For Amen! I word to you,
That whoever says to this mountain,
Remove! and, Cast into the sea!
— and not doubt in his heart,
but trusts that what he words becomes
— he has whatever he says.
24 Because of this I word to you,
All — as much as ever you ask,
when you pray, trust that you take them,
and you have them.

Forgive, Forgiven

25 And when you stand praying,
forgive, if you have ought against any:
that your Father in the heavens
also forgives you your backslidings:
26 and if you forgive not,
your Father in the heavens
forgives not your backslidings.

The Authority Of Yah Shua Challenged

27 And again they go to Yeru Shalem:
and as he walks in the priestal precinct
there come to him the *chief* **arch** priests
and the scribes, and the elders,
28 And *say* **word** unto him,
By **In** what authority doest thou these *things*?
and who gave thee this authority to do these *things*?
29 And *Jesus* **Yah Shua** answered
and said unto them,
I *will* **shall** also ask of you one *question* **word**,
and answer me, and I *will tell* **shall say to** you
by **in** what authority I do these *things*.
30 The baptism of *John* **Yahn**,
was it from heaven, or of *men* **humanity**? answer me.
31 And they *reasoned* **reckoned** with themselves,
saying **wording**, *if* **whenever** we shall say,
From *heaven* **the heavens**;
he *will* **shall** say, *So* **Why** *then* did
ye not *believe* **trust** him?
32 But *if* **whenever** we shall say, Of *men* **humanity**;
they *feared* **awed** the people:
for all *men counted John* **regarded Yahn**,
that he was a prophet indeed.
33 And they answered and *said*
worded unto *Jesus* **Yah Shua**,

We *cannot tell* **know not**.
And *Jesus* **Yah Shua** answering
saith **wordeth** unto them,
Neither *do I tell* **word I to** you
by **in** what authority I do these *things*.

The Parable Of The Vineyard

12 And he began to *speak* **word** unto them
by **in** parables.
A *certain man* **human** planted a vineyard,
and set an hedge about it,
and digged a *place for the winefat* **winevat**,
and built a tower,
and *let* **leased** it *out* to *husbandmen* **cultivators**,
and went *into a far country* **abroad**.
2 And at the season
he *sent* **apostolized** to the *husbandmen* **cultivators**
a servant,
that he might *receive* **take**
from the *husbandmen* **cultivators**
of the fruit of the vineyard.
3 And they *caught* **took** him,
and *beat* **flogged** him,
and *sent* **apostolized** him away empty.
4 And again he *sent* **apostolized** unto them
another servant;
and at him they cast stones,
and *wounded* **struck** him in the head,
and *sent* **apostolized** him away
shamefully **dishonourably** handled.
5 And again he *sent* **apostolized** another;
and him they *killed* **slaughtered**, and many others;
beating **indeed flogging** some,
and *killing* **slaughtering** some.
6 *So* Having yet *Therefore*
one son, his wellbeloved,
he *sent* **apostolized** him also *last* **finally** unto them,
saying **wording**,
They *will reverence* **shall respect** my son.
7 But those *husbandmen* **cultivators**
said among themselves,
This is the heir; come, let us *kill* **slaughter** him,
and the inheritance shall be ours.
8 And they took him, and *killed* **slaughtered** him,
and cast him out of the vineyard.
9 *So* What shall *Therefore the*
Lord **Adoni** of the vineyard do?
he *will* **shall** come and destroy the
husbandmen **cultivators**,
and *will* **shall** give the vineyard unto others.

10 And have ye not read this scripture;
The stone which the builders *rejected* **disapproved**
is become the head of the corner:
11 This *was the Lord's doing* **becomes of Yah Veh**,
and it is marvellous in our eyes?
Psalm 118:22, 23

Attempts To Overpower Yah Shua

12 And they sought to *lay hold on* **overpower** him,
but *feared* **awed** the *people* **multitude**:
for they knew
that he had *spoken* **said** the parable against them:
and they *left* **forsook** him, and went their way.
13 And they *send* **apostolized** unto him
certain **some** of the Pharisees and of the Herodians,
to catch him in his words.
the archpriests and the scribes and the elders
come to him,
28 and word to him,
In what authority do you these?
And who gives you this authority to do these?
29 And Yah Shua answers them, saying,
I also ask one word from you, and answer me,
and I say to you in what authority I do these:
30 The baptism of Yahn
— is it from the heavens? Or from humanity?
Answer me!
31 And they reckon with themselves, wording,
Whenever we say, From the heavens;
he says, So why trust you him not?
32 But whenever we say, From humanity;
they awe the people:
for all regard Yahn is a prophet indeed.
33 And they answer Yah Shua, wording,
We know not.
And Yah Shua answers them, wording,
And I word not to you in what authority I do these.

The Parable Of The Vineyard

12 And he begins to word to them in parables:
A human plants a vineyard and sets a hedge around it
and digs a winevat and builds a tower
and leases it to cultivators and goes abroad:
2 and at the season
he apostolizes a servant to the cultivators
to take from the cultivators
of the fruit of the vineyard:
3 and they take him and flog him
and apostolize him away empty.
4 And again he apostolizes
another servant to them:
and they cast stones at him
and strike him in the head;
and apostolize him away dishonorably handled.
5 And again he apostolizes another:
and they slaughter him
— and many others;
indeed flogging some and slaughtering some.
6 So still having one son — his wellbeloved,
he finally also apostolizes him to them,
wording, They respect my son.
7 But those cultivators say among themselves,
This is the heir! Come! Slaughter him!
And the inheritance becomes ours.
8 — and they take him and slaughter him
and cast him from the vineyard.
9 So what does the adoni of the vineyard?
He comes and destroys the cultivators
and gives the vineyard to others.
10 And read you not this scripture;
The stone the builders disapproved
becomes the head of the corner:
11 this becomes of Yah Vah,
and it is marvellous in our eyes?
Psalm 118:22, 23

Attempts To Overpower Yah Shua

12 And they seek to overpower him
but awe the multitude:
for they know he says the parable against them:
and they forsake him, and go their way:
13 and they apostolize
some of the Pharisees and of the Herodians to him,
to catch him in his words.
14 And when they were come,
they *say* **word** unto him,
Master **Doctor**, we know that thou art true,
and *carest for* **concerned about** no *man* **one**:
for thou *regardest* **observest** not
the *person* **face** of *men* **humanity**,
but *teachest* **doctrinatest** the way
of *God* **Elohim** in truth:
Is it *lawful* **allowed**
to give tribute to *Caesar* **the Kaisar**, or not?
15 shall we give, or shall we not give?
But he, knowing their hypocrisy, said unto them,
Why *tempt* **test** ye me?
bring me a *penny* **denarion**, that I may see it.

16	And they brought it. And he *saith* **wordeth** unto them, Whose is this *image* **icon** and *superscription* **epigraph**? And they said unto him, *Caesar's* **The kaisar's**.		and the *God* **Elohim** of *Jacob* **Yaaqov**?
17	And *Jesus* **Yah Shua** answering said unto them, *Render to Caesar the things that are Caesar's* **Give the Kaisar's to the Kaisar,** *and to God the things that are God's* **and Elohim's to Elohim**. And they marvelled at him.	27	He is not the *God* **Elohim** of the dead, but the *God* **Elohim** of the living: *so* ye *therefore do greatly err* **vastly wander**.

The Greatest Misvah

28	And one of the scribes came, and having heard them *reasoning* **disputing** together, and perceiving that he had answered them well, asked him, Which is the first *commandment* **misvah** of all?
29	And *Jesus* **Yah Shua** answered him, The first of all the *commandments* **misvoth** is, Hear, O *Israel* **Yisra El**; *the Lord* **Yah Veh** our *God* **Elohim** is one *Lord* **Yah Veh**:

Yah Shua Asked Concerning The Resurrection

18	*Then* **And** come unto him the *Sadducees* **Sadoqiym**, which *say* **word** there is no resurrection; and they asked him, *saying* **wording**,
19	*Master* **Doctor**, *Moses wrote* **Mosheh scribed** unto us, *If a man's* **Whenever one's** brother die, and leave his *wife behind him* **woman**, and leave no children, that his brother should take his *wife* **woman**, and raise *up seed* **sperma** unto his brother.
20	Now there were seven brethren: and the first took a *wife* **woman**, and dying left no *seed* **sperma**.
21	And the second took her, and died, neither left he any *seed* **sperma**: and the third likewise.
22	And the seven *had* **took** her, and left no *seed* **sperma**: *last of all* **finally** the woman died also.
23	*So* **In** the resurrection *therefore*, when they shall rise, whose *wife* **woman** shall she be of them? for the seven had her to *wife* **woman**.
24	And *Jesus* **Yah Shua** answering said unto them, *So* **Do** ye *not Therefore err* **wander**, because ye know not the scriptures, neither the *power* **dynamis** of *God* **Elohim**?
25	For when they shall rise from the dead, they neither marry, nor are *given* *in marriage* **married off**; but are as the angels which are in heaven.
26	And *as touching* **concerning** the dead, that they rise: have ye not read in the *book* **scroll** of *Moses* **Mosheh**, how in the *bush God spake* **brier Elohim said** unto him, *saying* **wording**, I am the *God* **Elohim** of Abraham, and the *God* **Elohim** of *Isaac* **Yischaq**,

30	And thou shalt love *the Lord* **Yah Veh** thy *God* **Elohim** with all thy heart, and with all thy soul, and with all thy mind, and with all thy strength: this is the first *commandment* **misvah**.
31	And the second is like, *namely this*, Thou shalt love thy neighbour as thyself. There is none other *commandment* **misvah** greater than these. Deuteronomy 6:4, 5, Leviticus 19:8
32	And the scribe said unto him, Well, *Master* **Doctor**, thou hast said the truth:
14	And they come and word to him, Doctor, we know you are true, and concerned about no one: for you observe not the face of humanity, but doctrinate the way of Elohim in truth: Is it allowed to give tribute to the Kaisar? Or not?
15	For us to give? Or for us not to give? And knowing their hypocrisy, he says to them, Why test you me? Bring me a denarion, to see.
16	And they bring it — and he words to them, Whose is this icon and epigraph? And they say to him, Of the kaisar.
17	And Yah Shua answers them, saying, Give that of the Kaisar to the Kaisar, and that of Elohim to Elohim. — and they marvel at him.

Yah Shua Asked Concerning The Resurrection

18	And the Sadoqiym come to him — who word there is no resurrection and they ask him, wording,
19	Doctor, Mosheh scribed to us,

Whenever a brother dies,
and leaves his woman, and leaves no children,
his brother takes his woman
and raises sperma to his brother:
20 there are seven brothers: and the first takes
a woman, and dies leaving no sperma:
21 and the second takes her, and dies,
and leaves no sperma: and the third likewise:
22 and the seven take her, and leave no sperma:
finally the woman also dies:
23 so when they rise in the resurrection,
whose woman is she of them?
for the seven had her to woman.
24 And Yah Shua answers them, saying,
So wander you not?
Neither knowing the scriptures
nor the dynamis of Elohim?
25 For when they rise from the dead,
they neither marry nor are married off;
but are as the angels in the heavens.
26 And concerning the dead, that they rise:
read you not in the scroll of Mosheh, how, in
the brier, Elohim said to him, wording,
I am the Elohim of Abraham
and the Elohim of Yischaq
and the Elohim of Yaaqov?
27 He is not the Elohim of the dead,
but the Elohim of the living:
so you vastly wander.

THE GREATEST MISVAH

28 And one of the scribes comes
and hears them disputing together;
and perceiving that he answers them well,
asks him, Which is the first misvah of all?
29 And Yah Shua answers him,
The first of all the misvoth is,
Hear, O Yisra El;
Yah Veh our Elohim is one Yah Veh:
30 and, Love Yah Veh your Elohim
with all your heart and with all your soul
and with all your mind and with all your strength:
this is the first misvah.
31 And the second is like,
Love your neighbor as yourself.
No other misvah is greater than these.
Deuteronomy 6:4, 5, Leviticus 19:8
32 And the scribe says to him,
Well, Doctor! You say the truth!
for there is one *God* **Elohim**;
and there is none other but he:
33 And to love him with all the heart,
and with all the *understanding* **comprehension**,
and with all the soul, and with all the strength,
and to love his neighbour as himself,
is **much** more than all
whole *burnt offerings* **holocausts** and sacrifices.
34 And *Jesus* **Yah Shua** saw
that he answered *discreetly* **mindfully**,
he said unto him,
Thou art not far
from the *kingdom* **sovereigndom** of *God* **Elohim**.
And no *man* **one** after that durst ask him any question.

YAH SHUA ASKS THE PHARISEES

35 And *Jesus* **Yah Shua** answered and *said* **worded**,
while he *taught* **doctrinated**
in the *temple* **priestal precinct**,
How *say* **word** the scribes
that *Christ* **the Messiah** is the son of David?
36 For David himself said *by* **in**
the *Holy Spirit* **Ruach ha-kodesh**,
the LORD said **An oracle of Yah Veh**
to my *Lord* **Adonay**,
Sit thou *on* **at** my right *hand*,
till I *make* **establish** thine enemies
thy footstool **the stool of thy feet**
37 So David *therefore* himself
calleth **wordeth** him *Lord* **Adonay**;
and whence is he then his son?
And the *common people* **vast
multitude** heard him gladly.
Psalm 110:1
38 And he *said* **worded** unto them in his doctrine,
Beware of **Observe** the scribes,
which *love* **will** to *go* **walk** in *long clothing* **stoles**,
and *love* salutations in the *marketplaces* **markets**,
39 And the *chief seats* **preeminent cathedras**
in the synagogues,
and the *uppermost rooms* **preeminent reposings**
at *feasts* **suppers**:
40 Which devour widows' houses,
and for a *pretence* **pretext** make *long* **far out** prayers:
these shall *receive* **take**
greater damnation **superabundant judgment**.

THE OFFERING OF THE WIDOW

41 And *Jesus* **Yah Shua**
sat *over against* **in front of** the treasury,
and *beheld* **observed** how the *people* **multitude**

	cast *money* **copper** into the treasury:
	and many that were rich cast in much.
42	And there came a *certain* poor widow,
	and she *threw* **put** in two *mites* **leptons**,
	which *make* **be** a *farthing* **quarter**.
43	And he called unto him his disciples,
	and *saith* **wordeth** unto them,
	Verily I say **Amen! I word** unto you,
	That this poor widow hath cast **much** more in,
	than all they which have cast into the treasury:
44	For all they did cast in of
	their *abundance* **surplus**;
	but she of her *want* **lack** did cast in all
	that — **as much as** she had,
	even all her *living* **subsistence**.

The Mount Of Olives Message Of Yah Shua

13	And as he *went* **departed**
	out of the *temple* **priestal precinct**,
	one of his disciples *saith* **wordeth** unto him,
	Master **Doctor**, *see* **behold** what manner of stones
	and what *buildings* **edifices** are here!
2	And *Jesus* **Yah Shua** answering said unto him,
	Seest **Observest** thou these *great*
	buildings **mega edifices**?
	there shall not be *left* **allowed** one stone upon another,
	that shall not be *thrown down* **disintegrated**.
3	And as he sat upon the mount of Olives
	over against **in front of** the *temple* **priestal precinct**,
	Peter **Petros** and *James* **Yaaqovos**
	and *John* **Yahn** and *Andrew* **Andreas**
	asked him privately,
4	*Tell* **Say to** us, when shall these *things* be?
	and what *shall be the* sign when all these
	things shall be fulfilled/**shalamed**?
	For there is one Elohim;
	and there is no other but he.
33	and to love him with all the heart
	and with all the comprehension
	and with all the soul and with all the strength
	and to love his neighbor as himself
	is much more than all whole holocausts and sacrifices.
34	And Yah Shua sees that he answers mindfully,
	and says to him,
	You are not far from the sovereigndom of Elohim.
	— and after that no one dares ask him any question.

Yah Shua Asks The Pharisees

35	And doctrinating in the priestal precinct,

	Yah Shua answers, wording,
	How word the scribes
	that the Messiah is the son of David?
36	For David himself says in the Holy Spirit,
	An oracle of Yah Veh to my Adonay,
	Sit at my right
	until I establish your enemies the stool of your feet.
37	So David himself words him, Adonay;
	and whence is he so his son?
	— and the vast multitude hear him gladly.
	Psalm 110:1
38	And he words to them in his doctrine,
	Observe the scribes who will to walk in stoles
	and salutations in the markets
39	and the preeminent cathedras in the synagogues
	and the preeminent reposings at suppers
	40 — who devour houses of widows and
	for a pretext make far out prayers: these
	take superabundant judgment.

The Offering Of The Widow

41	And Yah Shua sits in front of the treasury
	and observes how the multitude
	casts copper into the treasury
	— and many rich cast in much:
42	and a poor widow comes
	and puts in two leptons — being a quarter.
43	And he calls his disciples to him,
	and words to them,
	Amen! I word to you,
	That this poor widow casts in much more
	than they all cast into the treasury:
44	for they all cast in from their surplus;
	but she from her lack casts in all
	— as much as she has — even all her subsistence.

The Mount Of Olives Message Of Yah Shua

13	And as he departs from the priestal precinct
	one of his disciples words to him, Doctor, Behold!
	What manner of stones! And what edifices!
2	And Yah Shua answering him, says,
	Observe you these mega edifices?
	Not one stone is allowed upon stone,
	that is not disintegrated.
3	And as he sits on the mount of Olives
	in front of the priestal precinct,
	Petros and Yaaqovos and Yahn and Andreas
	ask him privately,
4	Say to us, when become these?

MARK/MAKABI 13

And what sign
when all these are about to be fulfilled/shalamed?
5   And *Jesus* **Yah Shua** answering
them began to *say* **word**,
Take heed **Observe**, lest any *man* *deceive* **one seduce** you:
6   For many shall come in my name,
saying **wording**, *I am Christ* **I AM**;
and shall *deceive* **seduce** many.
7   And when ye shall hear of
wars and rumours of wars,
be **lament** ye not *troubled*: for such *things* must *needs* be;
but the *end* **completion/shalom** shall not be yet.
8   For *nation* **goyim** shall
rise against *nation* **goyim**,
and *kingdom* **sovereigndom**
against *kingdom* **sovereigndom**:
and there shall be *earthquakes* **quakes** in divers places,
and there shall be famines and troubles:
these are the beginnings of *sorrows* **travails**.
9   But *take heed* **observe** to yourselves:
for they shall *deliver* **betray** you *up*
to *councils* **sanhedrim**;
and in the synagogues ye shall be *beaten* **flogged**:
and ye shall be *brought* **set**
before rulers **in front of governors** and *kings* **sovereigns**
for my sake,
for a *testimony* **witness** against them.
10   And the *gospel* **evangelism**
must first be *published* **preached**
among all *nations* **goyim**.
11   But when they shall lead you,
and *deliver* **betray** you *up*,
take no thought beforehand **have no preanxiety**
what ye shall speak,
neither *do ye premeditate* **preanticipate**:
but whatsoever shall be given you in that hour,
that speak ye:
for it is not ye that speak, but the *Holy
Spirit* **Ruach ha-kodesh**.
12   *Now* **And** the brother shall
betray the brother to death,
and the father the *son* **child**;
and children shall rise *up* against their parents,
and shall cause them to be *put to death* **deathified**.
13   And ye shall be hated of all
men for my name's sake:
but he that shall *endure* **abide**
unto the *end* **completion/shalom**,
the **this** same shall be saved.

TRIBULATION

14   But when ye shall see the
abomination of desolation,
spoken of **rhetorized** by *Daniel* **Dani El** the
prophet, standing where it *ought* **must** not,
(let him that readeth *understand* **comprehend**,)
then let them that be in *Judaea* **Yah Hudah**
flee to the mountains:
15   And let him that is on the housetop
not go down into the house,
neither enter *therein*, to take *any*
thing **aught** out of his house:
16   And let him that is in the field
not turn back again for to take *up* his garment.
17   But woe to them that *are*
with child **have in womb**,
and to them that *give suck* **nipple** in those days!
18   And pray ye that your flight
be not in the *winter* **downpour**.
19   For in those days shall be *affliction* **tribulation**,
such as *was* **became** not from the beginning
of the creation which *God* **Elohim** created
unto *this time* **now**, neither shall be.
20   And *except* **unless**
that *the Lord* **Adonay** had shortened those days,
no flesh should be saved:
but for the *elect's* **select's** sake,
whom he hath *chosen* **selected**,
he hath shortened the days.
21   And then *if* **whenever** any
man **one** shall say to you,
Lo **Behold**, here *is Christ* **the Messiah**;
or, *lo* **Behold**, *he is* there;
believe **trust** him not:
22   For *false Christs* **pseudo messiahs**
and *false* **pseudo** prophets shall rise,
and shall *shew* **give** signs and *wonders* **omens**,
to seduce, if it were possible, even the *elect* **select**.
23   But *take ye heed* **observe**: behold,
I have foretold you all *things*.

POST—TRIBULATION

24   But in those days, after that tribulation,
the sun shall *be darkened* **darken**,
and the moon shall not give her *light* **brilliance**,
5   And answering them, Yah Shua begins to word,
Observe, lest anyone seduce you:
6   For many come in my name, wording, I AM;
and seduce many:
7   and when you hear of wars and rumours of wars

	lament not; for such must become:
	but the completion/shalom is not yet:
8	for goyim rises against goyim
	and sovereigndom against sovereigndom:
	and quakes become in divers places
	and famines and troubles become:
	these are the beginnings of travails.
9	But observe to yourselves:
	for they betray you to sanhedrim;
	and flog you in the synagogues:
	and set you in front of governors and sovereigns
	for my sake — for a witness against them:
10	and the evangelism
	must first be preached among all goyim.
11	But when they lead you and betray you,
	neither have preanxiety of what to speak,
	nor preanticipate:
	but whatever is given you in that hour, speak:
	for it is not you who speaks, but the Holy Spirit.
12	And brother betrays brother to death,
	and father, child;
	and children rise against parents
	and have them deathified:
13	and you become hated of
	all for sake of my name:
	but whoever abides to the completion/shalom is saved.

Tribulation

14	But when you see the abomination of desolation
	rhetorized by Dani El the prophet
	standing where it must not
	— whoever reads, comprehend:
	to them in Yah Hudah, flee to the mountains:
15	and to him on the housetop,
	neither descend to the house
	nor enter to take aught from his house:
16	and to him in the field,
	turn not back to take his garment:
17	and woe to them who have in womb
	and to them who nipple in those days:
18	and pray that your flight
	be not in the downpour.
19	For in those days tribulation becomes
	— such as become not
	from the beginning of the creation Elohim created
	to now
	— nor ever becomes.
20	And unless Yah Vah shortens those days
	no flesh is ever saved:
	but for sake of the select whom he selects,
	he shortens the days.

21	And then whenever anyone says to you,
	Behold, here the Messiah! or, Behold, there!
	trust not:
22	for pseudo messiahs and pseudo prophets rise
	and give signs and omens
	to seduce, if possible, even the select.
23	But observe! Behold! I foretell all.

Post-Tribulation

24	But in those days, after that tribulation,
	the sun darkens
	and the moon gives not her brilliance
25	And the stars of *the* heaven shall fall,
	and the *powers* **dynamis** that are in heaven
	shall be shaken.
26	And then shall they see
	the Son of *man* **humanity**
	coming in the clouds
	with *great power* **vast dynamis** and glory.
27	And then shall he *send* **apostolize** his angels,
	and shall gather together his *elect* **select**
	from the four winds,
	from the *uttermost part* **extremity** of the earth
	to the *uttermost part* **extremity** of heaven.

The Parable Of The Fig Tree

28	*Now* **But** learn a parable of the fig tree;
	When her branch *is yet* **becometh already** tender,
	and *putteth forth* **sprouteth** leaves,
	ye know that summer is near:
29	*So* **Thus also** ye *in like manner*,
	when ye shall see these *things come to pass* **become**,
	know that it is nigh, even at the *doors* **portals**.
30	*Verily I say* **Amen! I word** unto you,
	that this generation shall not pass, till
	all these *things be done* **become**.
31	Heaven and earth shall pass *away*:
	but my words shall not pass.
32	But *of* **concerning** that day and that hour
	knoweth no *man* **one**,
	no, not the angels which are in heaven, neither the Son,
	but **except** the Father.

Observe, Watch, Pray

33	*Take ye heed* **Observe**, watch and pray:
	for ye know not when the *time* **season** is.
34	For *the Son of man is* as a *man* **human**
	taking a far journey **having gone abroad**,
	who *left* **forsook** his house,
	and gave authority to his servants,
	and to *every man* **each** his work,

and *commanded* **misvahed** the *porter* **portalguard** to watch.

35 **So** Watch ye *therefore*:
for ye know not when the *master*
adoni of the house cometh,
at even, or at midnight,
or at the *cockcrowing* **roostervoice**,
or in the *early* morning:

36 Lest coming suddenly he find you sleeping.

37 And what I *say* **word** unto you
I *say* **word** unto all, Watch.

14 After two days was the *feast*
of the *passover* **pasach**,
and *of unleavened bread* **the matsah**:
and the *chief priests* **archpriests** and the scribes sought
how they might *take* **overpower** him by *craft* **deception**,
and *put him to death* **slaughter him**.

2 But they *said* **worded**, Not
on the *feast day* **celebration**,
lest *ever* there be *an uproar* **a tumult** of the people.

Yah Shua Anointed

3 And being in *Bethany* **Beth Ania**
in the house of *Simon* **Shimon** the leper,
as he *sat at meat* **reposed**,
there came a woman having an alabaster *box*
of *ointment* **myrrh** of *spikenard* **nard**,
very precious **vastly trustworthy**;
and she *brake* **crushed** the *box* **alabaster**,
and poured it on his head.

4 And there were some
that *had indignation* **indignified** within themselves,
and *said* **worded**,
Why was this *waste* **destruction**
of the *ointment made* **myrrh**?

5 For it might have been sold
for more than three hundred *pence* **denarion**,
and have been given to the poor.
And they *murmured* **sighed** against her.

6 And *Jesus* **Yah Shua** said,
Let **Allow** her *alone*; why *trouble* **embarrass** ye her?
she hath *wrought* **worked** a good work on me.

7 For ye have the poor with you always,
and whensoever ye will ye may do them *good* **well**:
but me ye have not always.

8 She hath done what she could:
she *is come aforehand* **hath anticipated**
to *anoint* **myrrh** my body to the *burying* **embalming**.

25 And the stars of the heavens fall,
and the dynamis in the heavens shake;

26 and then they see the Son of
humanity come in the clouds
with vast dynamis and glory.

27 And then he apostolizes his angels
and gathers his select from the four winds
— from the extremity of the earth
to the extremity of the heavens.

The Parable Of The Fig Tree

28 But learn a parable from the fig tree;
When her branch becomes already tender
and sprouts leaves,
you know summer is near:

29 thus also you,
when you see these become
you know it is near — even at the portals.

30 Amen! I word to you,
that this generation passes not until all these become:

31 the heavens and earth pass
but my words pass not:

32 but concerning that day and that hour,
no one knows
— no, neither the angels in the heavens, nor the Son
— except the Father.

Observe, Watch, Pray

33 Observe, watch and pray:
for you know not when the season is.

34 For as a human who goes abroad
— who forsakes his house
and gives his servants authority
— to each his work
and also misvahs the portalguard to watch.

35 So you watch:
for you know not when the adoni of the house comes
— at evening or at midnight
or at the rooster voice or in the morning:

36 lest coming suddenly he finds you sleeping:

37 and what I word to you I word to all, Watch!

14 And the pasach and the
matsah are two days after:
and the archpriests and the scribes seek
how to overpower him by deception,
and slaughter him:

2 but they word, Not on the celebration,
lest ever there be a tumult of the people.

Yah Shua Anointed

3 And being in Beth Ania in
the house of Shimon the leper,

as he reposes, a woman comes
having an alabaster of myrrh of nard
— vastly trustworthy;
and she crushes the alabaster
and pours it on his head.

4 And some are indignified within themselves,
and word,
Why is this destruction of the myrrh?
5 — for it could have been sold
for more than three hundred denarion
and given to the poor.
— and they sigh against her.
6 And Yah Shua says,
Allow her! Why embarrass her?
She works a good work on me.
7 For the poor you have with you always,
and whenever you will, ye do them well:
but me you have not always:
8 she did what she could:
she anticipated to myrrh my body to the embalming.
9 *Verily ! say* **Amen! I word** unto you,
Wheresoever this *gospel* **evangelism** shall be preached
throughout the whole *world* **cosmos**,
this also that she hath done
shall be spoken of for a memorial of her.

Yah Hudah Plans To Betray Yah Shua

10 And *Judas !scariot* **Yah Hudah the urbanite**,
one of the twelve,
went unto the *chief* **arch** priests
to betray him unto them.
11 And when they heard it, they *were glad* **cheered**,
and *promised* **pre—evangelized**
to give him *money* **silver**.
And he sought how
he might *conveniently* **opportunely** betray him.

Pasach Preparation

12 And the first day of *unleavened bread* **matsah**,
when they *killed* **sacrificed** the *passover* **pasach**,
his disciples *said* **worded** unto him,
Where wilt thou that we go and prepare
that thou mayest eat the *passover* **pasach**?
13 And he *sendeth forth*
apostolizeth two of his disciples,
and *saith* **wordeth** unto them, Go ye into the city,
and there shall meet you
a *man* **human** bearing a pitcher of water: follow him.
14 And wheresoever he shall *go in* **enter**,
say ye to the *goodman of the house* **housedespotes**,

The *Master saith* **Doctor wordeth**,
Where is the *guestchamber* **lodge**,
where I shall eat the *passover* **pasach** with my disciples?
15 And he *will* **shall** shew you
a *large* **mega** upper room
furnished **spread** and prepared:
there *make ready* **prepare** for us.
16 And his disciples went forth,
and came into the city,
and found **exactly** as he had said unto them:
and they *made ready* **prepared** the *passover* **pasach**.

Yah Shua Prophesies His Betrayal

17 And *in the* **being** evening
he cometh with the twelve.
18 And as they *sat* **reposed** and did eat,
Jesus **Yah Shua** said,
Verily ! say **Amen! I word** unto you,
One of you which eateth with me shall betray me.
19 And they began to be sorrowful,
and to *say* **word** unto him one by one, *!s it* I?
and another said, *!s it* I?
20 And he answered and said unto them,
It is one of the twelve,
that *dippeth* **baptizeth** with me in the dish.
21 The Son of *man* **humanity** indeed goeth,
exactly as it is *written of* **scribed concerning** him:
but woe to that *man* **human**
by whom the Son of *man* **humanity** is betrayed!
good were it for that *man* **human**
if he had never been *born* **birthed**.

The Final Pasach Of Yah Shua

22 And as they did eat, *Jesus* **Yah Shua** took bread,
and *blessed* **eulogized**, and brake it, and gave to them,
and said, Take, eat: this is my body.
23 And he took the cup,
and when he had *given thanks* **eucharistized**,
he gave it to them:
and they all drank of it.
24 And he said unto them,
This is my blood of the new *testament* **covenant**,
which is *shed* **poured** for many.
25 *Verily ! say* **Amen! I word** unto you,
I *will* **shall** drink no more of the
fruit **produce** of the vine,
until that day that I drink it new
in the *kingdom* **sovereigndom** of *God* **Elohim**.
26 And when they had *sung an hymn* **hymned**,
they went out into the mount of Olives.

9   Amen! I word to you,
Wherever this evangelism is preached
throughout the whole cosmos,
this also what she did
is spoken of in a memorial of her.

Yah Hudah Plans To Betray Yah Shua

10   And Yah Hudah the urbanite, one of the twelve,
goes to the archpriests to betray him to them.
11   And they hear and cheer;
and pre—evangelize to give him silver:
and he seeks how to opportunely betray him.

Pasach Preparation

12   And the first day of matsah,
when they sacrifice the pasach,
his disciples word to him,
Where will you,
that we go and prepare for you to eat the pasach?
13   And he apostolizes two of his disciples,
and words to them, Go to the city;
and there meet a human bearing a pitcher of water:
follow him.
14   And wherever he enters,
say to the housedespotes,
The Doctor words,
Where is the lodge
to eat the pasach with my disciples?
15   — and he shows you a mega upper room
spread and prepared:
and there prepare for us.
16   — and his disciples go, and come to the city;
and find exactly as he said to them:
and they prepare the pasach.

Yah Shua Prophesies His Betrayal

17   And being evening,
he comes with the twelve:
18   and as they repose and eat, Yah Shua says,
Amen! I word to you,
One of you who eats with me betrays me.
19   And they begin to sorrow
and to word to him one by one, I?
— and another says, I?
20   And he answers them, saying,
It is one of the twelve,
who baptizes with me in the dish.
21   The Son of humanity indeed goes,
exactly as scribed concerning him:
but woe to that human
by whom the Son of humanity is betrayed!
Good for that human
if he had never been birthed.

The Final Pasach Of Yah Shua

22   And as they eat, Yah Shua takes bread,
and eulogizes and breaks and gives them,
and says, Take! Eat! This is my body.
23   And he takes the cup and eucharistizes;
and gives them:
and they all drink thereof.
24   And he says to them,
This is my blood of the new covenant,
poured for many.
25   Amen! I word to you,
I drink no more of the produce of the vine,
until that day
I drink it anew in the sovereigndom of Elohim.
26   — and they hymn and go
to the mount of Olives.

Yah Shua Prophesies Scandalizing

27   And *Jesus saith* **Yah Shua wordeth** unto them,
All ye shall be *offended* **scandalized**
because of **in** me this night:
for it is *written* **scribed**,
I *will* **shall** smite the shepherd,
and the sheep shall be scattered.
28   But after that I am risen,
I *will* **shall** go before you into *Galilee* **Galiyl**.
Zechar Yah 13:7

Yah Shua Prophesies The Denials Of Petros

29   But *Peter* **Petros** said unto him,
Although all shall be *offended* **scandalized**,
yet *will* **shall** not I.
30   And *Jesus saith* **Yah Shua wordeth** unto him,
Verily ! say **Amen! I word** unto thee,
That this day, even in this night,
before **ere** the *cock crow* **rooster voiceth** twice,
thou shalt deny me thrice.
31   But he *spake* **worded**
the more *vehemently* **superabundantly**, *If*
Whenever I *should* **must** die with thee,
I *will not* **shall never ever no way** deny thee *in any wise*.
Likewise also *said* **worded** they all.

Yah Shua In Gath Shemen

32   And they came to a *place* **parcel**

which was named *Gethsemane* **Geth Shemen**:
and he *saith* **wordeth** to his disciples,
Sit ye here, while I shall pray.

33 And he taketh with him *Peter* **Petros**
and *James* **Yaaqovos** and *John* **Yahn**,
and began to *be sore amazed* **utterly astonish**,
and to *be very heavy* **distress**;

34 And *saith* **wordeth** unto them,
My soul is exceeding sorrowful unto death:
tarry **abide** ye here, and watch.

The First Gath Shemen Prayer Of Yah Shua

35 And he *went forward* **proceeded** a little,
and fell on the *ground* **soil**, and prayed that,
if it were possible, the hour might pass from him.

36 And he *said* **worded**, Abba, Father,
all *things* are possible unto thee;
take away this cup from me:
nevertheless **yet** not what I will, but what thou *wilt*.

37 And he cometh, and findeth them sleeping,
and *saith* **wordeth** unto *Peter* **Petros**,
Simon **Shimon**, sleepest thou?
couldest not thou watch one hour?

38 Watch ye and pray,
lest ye enter into *temptation* **testing**.
The spirit *truly* **indeed** is *ready* **eager**,
but the flesh is *weak* **frail**.

The Second Gath Shemen Prayer Of Yah Shua

39 And again he went away, and prayed,
and *spake* **said** the same words.

40 And when he returned, he
found them asleep again,
(for their eyes were heavy,)
neither *wist* **knew** they what to answer him.

The Third Gath Shemen Prayer Of Yah Shua

41 And he cometh the third time,
and *saith* **wordeth** unto them,
Sleep *on now* **finally**, and *take your* rest:
it is enough, the hour is come;
behold, the Son of *man* **humanity**
is betrayed into the hands of sinners.

42 Rise *up*, let us go; *lo* **behold**,
he that betrayeth me *is at hand* **approacheth**.

Yah Hudah Betrays Yah Shua

43 And *immediately* **straightway**,
while he yet spake,
cometh *Judas* **Yah Hudah**, **being** one of the twelve,
and with him
a *great* **vast** multitude with swords and staves,
from the *chief* **arch** priests and the scribes
and the elders.

44 And he that betrayed him
had given them a *token* **signal**, *saying* **wording**,
Whomsoever I shall kiss, that same is he;
take **overpower** him, and lead him away *safely* **securely**.

45 And as soon as he was come,

Yah Shua Prophesies Scandalizing

27 And Yah Shua words to them,
All you scandalize in me this night:
for it is scribed,
I smite the shepherd, and scatter the sheep.

28 But after I rise, I precede you into Galiyl.
Zechar Yah 13:7

Yah Shua Prophesies The Denials Of Petros

29 And Petros says to him,
Although all scandalize, yet not I.

30 And Yah Shua words to him,
Amen! I word to you,
That this day, even in this night,
ere the rooster voices twice,
you deny me thrice.

31 But he words the more superabundantly,
If I must die with you, I never ever no way deny you.
— likewise they all also word.

Yah Shua In Gath Shemen

32 And they come to a parcel named Geth Shemen:
and he words to his disciples,
Sit here while I pray.

33 And he takes
Petros and Yaaqovos and Yahn with him,
and begins to utterly astonish and to distress;

34 and words to them,
My soul is exceeding sorrowful to death:
abide here, and watch.

The First Gath Shemen Prayer Of Yah Shua

35 And he proceeds a little,

and falls on the soil, and prays,
that if possible, the hour pass from him.
36 And he words, Abba, Father,
all are possible with you; take this cup from me:
yet not what I will, but what you.
37 And he comes, and finds them sleeping,
and words to Petros,
Shimon, are you sleeping?
Can you not watch one hour?
38 Watch and pray lest you enter into testing.
The spirit indeed is eager, but the flesh is frail.

THE SECOND GATH SHEMEN PRAYER OF YAH SHUA

39 And he goes again, and prays,
and says the same words:
40 and he returns, and again
he finds them sleeping,
— for their eyes are heavy,
and they know not what to answer him.

THE THIRD GATH SHEMEN PRAYER OF YAH SHUA

41 And he comes the third
time, and words to them,
Sleep, finally! and, Rest! Enough!
The hour is come!
Behold!
The Son of humanity is betrayed
into the hands of sinners.
42 Rise! We go! Behold!
he who betrays me approaches.

YAH HUDAH BETRAYS YAH SHUA

43 And straightway, while he yet speaks,
Yah Hudah comes, being one of the twelve,
and with him a vast multitude with swords and staves
of the archpriests and the scribes and the elders.
44 And he who betrays him, gives them a signal,
wording, Whomever I kiss, is he;
overpower him, and lead him away securely.
45 And as soon as he comes,
he goeth straightway to him,
and *saith* **speaketh**, *Master, master* **Rabbi, rabbi**;
and **ardently** kissed him.
46 And they laid their hands on him,
and *took* **overpowered** him.
47 And one of them *that stood
by* **present** drew a sword,
and smote a servant of the *high* **arch** priest

and *cut off* **removed** his ear **lobe**.
48 And *Jesus* **Yah Shua** answered
and said unto them,
Are ye come out, as against a *thief* **robber**,
with swords and with staves to take me?
49 I was daily with you in the
temple **priestal precinct**
teaching **doctrinating**, and ye *took* **overpowered** me
not: but the scriptures must be fulfilled/**shalamed**.
50 And they all forsook him, and fled.
51 And there followed him a
certain young man **youth**,
having a linen cloth cast about his naked body
who arrayed his nakedness in linen;
and the *young men* **youths**
laid hold on **overpowered** him:
52 And he left the linen *cloth*,
and fled from them naked.
53 And they led *Jesus* **Yah Shua** away
to the *high* **arch** priest
and with him were *assembled* **come together**
all the *chief* **arch** priests and the elders
and the scribes.
54 And *Peter* **Petros** followed him afar off,
even into the *palace* **courtyard** of the *high* **arch** priest
and he sat with the *servants* **attendants**,
and warmed himself at the fire.
55 And the *chief* **arch** priests
and all the *council* **sanhedrim**
sought for witness against *Jesus* **Yah Shua**
to *put* **deathify** him *to death*; and found none.

THE TRIAL OF YAH SHUA

56 For many
bare false witness **pseudo—witnessed** against him,
but their witness *agreed not together* **was not equal**.
57 And there arose *certain* **some**,
and *bare false witness* **pseudo—witnessed** against him,
saying **wording**,
58 We heard him *say* **word**,
I *will destroy* **shall disintegrate**
this *temple that is made with hands* **handmade nave**,
and *within* **by** three days I *will* **shall** build another
made without hands **not handmade**.
59 But neither *so* **thus**
did **was** their witness *agree together* **equal**.
60 And the *high* **arch** priest stood *up* in the midst,
and asked *Jesus* **Yah Shua**, *saying* **wording**,
Answerest thou *nothing* **naught**?
what is it which these witness against thee?

61	But he *held his peace* **hushed**,		and flees from them naked.
	and answered *nothing* **naught**.	53	And they lead Yah Shua to the archpriest:
	Again the *high* **arch** priest asked him,		and all the archpriests and the elders and the scribes
	and *said* **worded** unto him,		come together with him:
	Art thou the *Christ* **Messiah**, the Son	54	and Petros follows him afar off
	of the *Blessed* **Eulogized**?		even into the courtyard of the archpriest;

Yah Shua Affirms His Deity

			and he sits with the attendants
			and warms himself at the fire:
62	And *Jesus* **Yah Shua** said, *I am* **I AM**:	55	and the archpriests and all the sanhedrim
	and ye shall see the Son of *man* **humanity**		seek witness against Yah Shua to deathify him;
	sitting *on* **at** the right *hand* of *power* **the dynamis**,		and find none.
	and coming in the clouds of heaven.		

The Trial Of Yah Shua

63	*Then* **And** the *high* **arch** priest		
	rent **ripped** his *clothes* **tunic**,	56	For many pseudo witness against him,
	and *saith* **wordeth**, What need we any further witnesses?		but their witness is not equal:
64	Ye have heard the blasphemy:	57	and some rise and pseudo witness against him,
	what *think* **manifesteth to** ye?		wording,
	And they all condemned him to be	58	We heard him word,
	guilty of **subject to** death.		I disintegrate this handmade nave,
65	And some began to spit on him,		and by three days I build another not handmade.
	and to cover his face, and to *buffet* **punch** him,	59	— but neither thus is their witness equal.
	and to *say* **word** unto him, Prophesy:	60	And the archpriest stands in their midst
	and the *servants* **attendants**		and asks Yah Shua, wording,
	did strike him with the palms of their hands **slapped him**.		Answer you naught?
			What witness these against you?
		61	— but he hushes and answers naught.
			Again the archpriest asks him, and words to him,
			Are you the Messiah, the Son of the Eulogized?

The First Denial Of Petros

Yah Shua Affirms His Deity

66	And as *Peter* **Petros** was beneath	62	And Yah Shua says, I AM:
	in the *palace* **courtyard**,		and you see the Son of humanity
	there cometh		sitting at the right of the dynamis,
	one of the *maids* **lasses** of the *high* **arch** priest:		and coming in the clouds of the heavens.
	he goes straightway to him,	63	And the archpriest rips his tunic, and words,
	and speaks, Rabbi! Rabbi!		What need have we of any further witnesses?
	— and ardently kisses him.	64	You hear the blasphemy!
46	And they lay their hands on him,		What manifests to you?
	and overpower him:		— and they all condemn him to be subject to death:
47	and one of them present draws a sword,	65	— and some begin to spit on him
	and smites a servant of the archpriest		and to cover his face and to punch him,
	and removes his ear lobe.		and word to him, Prophesy!
48	And Yah Shua answers them, saying,		— and the attendants slap him.
	Come you out, as against a robber,		
	with swords and with staves to take me?		

The First Denial Of Petros

49	I doctrinated with you daily		
	in the priestal precinct	66	And as Petros is below in the courtyard
	and you overpowered me not		one of the lasses of the archpriest comes;
	— except to fulfill/shalam the scriptures.	67	And when she saw *Peter*
50	— and they all forsake him, and flee.		**Petros** warming himself,
51	And a youth follows him,		she looked upon him, and *said* **worded**,
	who arrays his nakedness in linen;		
	and the youths overpower him:		
52	and he leaves the linen,		

MARK/MAKABI 14, 15

And thou also
wast with *Jesus of Nazareth* **Yah Shua the Nazarene**.
68 But he denied, *saying* **wording**,
I know not,
neither understand I what thou *sayest* **wordest**.
And he went out into the *porch* **forecourt**;
and the *cock called* **rooster voiced**.

THE SECOND DENIAL OF PETROS

69 And a *maid* **lass** saw him again,
and began to *say* **word** to them *that stood by* **present**,
This is one of them.
70 And he denied it again.

THE THIRD DENIAL OF PETROS

And a little after,
they that stood by **those present**
said **worded** again to *Peter* **Petros**,
Surely **Truly** thou art one of them:
for thou art a *Galilaean* **Galiliy**,
and thy speech *agreeth* **homologizeth** thereto.
71 But he began to *curse* **anathemetize**
and to *swear* **oath**, saying,
I know not this *man* **human** of whom ye *speak* **word**.
72 And the second time the
cock crew **rooster voiced**.
And *Peter called to mind* **Petros remembered**
the *word* **rhema** that *Jesus* **Yah Shua** said unto him,
Before the *cock crow* **rooster voiceth** twice,
thou shalt *utterly* deny me thrice.
And when he thought thereon, he wept.

YAH SHUA BETRAYED TO PILATOS

15 And straightway in the **early** morning
the *chief* **arch** priests *held* **made** a consultation
with the elders and scribes
and the whole *council* **sanhedrim**,
and bound *Jesus* **Yah Shua**, and *carried* **bore** him away,
and delivered him to *Pilate* **Pilatos**.
2 And *Pilate* **Pilatos** asked him,
Art thou the *King* **Sovereign** of the *Jews* **Yah Hudiym**?
And he answering said unto them,
Thou *sayest* **wordest** it.
3 And the *chief* **arch** priests
accused him of *many things* **much**:
but he answered *nothing* **naught**.
4 And *Pilate* **Pilatos** asked
him again, *saying* **wording**,
Answerest thou *nothing* **naught**? behold,
how *many things* **much** they witness against thee.

5 But *Jesus* **Yah Shua** yet
answered *nothing* **naught**;
so that *Pilate* **Pilatos** marvelled.
6 Now at that *feast* **celebration**
he released unto them one prisoner,
whomsoever they *desired* **asked**.
7 And there was one *named*
Barabbas **worded Bar Abbas**,
which lay bound with them
that had *made insurrection* **co—rioted** with him,
who had *committed* **done** murder
in the *insurrection* **riot**.
8 And the multitude crying
aloud began to *desire* **ask** him
to do **exactly** as he had even done unto them.
9 But *Pilate* **Pilatos** answered
them, *saying* **wording**,
will ye that I release unto you
the *King* **Sovereign** of the *Jews* **Yah Hudiym**?
10 For he knew that the *chief* **arch** priests
had *delivered* **betrayed** him for envy.
11 But the *chief* **arch** priests
moved **excited** the *people* **multitude**,
that he should rather release *Barabbas* **Bar Abbas**
unto them.
12 And *Pilate* **Pilatos** answered
and said again unto them,
What will ye then that I shall do unto him
whom ye *call* **word**
the *king* **sovereign** of the *Jews* **Yah Hudiym**?
13 And they cried out again, *Crucify him.* **Stake!**
14 *Then Pilate said* **And**
Pilatos worded unto them,
and she sees Petros warming himself,
and she looks on him, and words,
And you also were with Yah Shua the Nazarene.
68 But he denies, wording,
I neither know nor understand what you word.
— and he enters the forecourt;
and the rooster voices.

THE SECOND DENIAL OF PETROS

69 And again a lass sees him
and begins to word to those present,
This is one of them.
70 — and again he denies.

THE THIRD DENIAL OF PETROS

And a little after,
those present again word to Petros,

	Truly you are one of them:
	for you are a Galiliy and your speech homologizes.
71	And he begins to anathemetize and to oath,
	I know not this human of whom you word.
72	— and the rooster voices the second time.
	And Petros remembers
	the rhema Yah Shua said to him,
	Ere the rooster voices twice,
	you utterly deny me thrice.
	— and he thinks thereon, and weeps.

Yah Shua Betrayed To Pilatos

15	And straightway in the early morning
	the archpriests make a consultation
	with the elders and scribes and the whole sanhedrim;
	and bind Yah Shua and bear him away
	and deliver him to Pilatos.
2	And Pilatos asks him,
	Are you the Sovereign of the Yah Hudiym?
	And he answers them, saying,
	You have worded.
3	And the archpriests accuse him of much:
	but he answers naught.
4	And again Pilatos asks him, wording,
	Answer you naught? Behold!
	How much they witness against you.
5	And Yah Shua still answers naught;
	so that Pilatos marvels.
6	Now at every celebration
	he releases one prisoner to them
	— whomever they ask.
7	And someone worded Bar Abbas,
	lies bound with them, who co—rioted with him
	who did murder in the riot.
8	— and crying out, the
	multitude begins to ask him
	to do exactly as he had even done to them.
9	And Pilatos answers them, wording,
	will ye that I release to you
	the Sovereign of the Yah Hudiym?
10	— for he knows that the archpriests
	betray him for envy.
11	And the archpriests excite the multitude
	that he rather release Bar Abbas to them.
12	And again Pilatos answers them, saying,
	So what will you have me do to him
	whom you word the sovereign of the Yah Hudiym?
13	And again they cry out, Stake!
14	And Pilatos words to them,
	Why **Indeed**, what evil hath he done?
	And they cried out the more
	exceedingly **superabundantly**,
	Crucify him. **Stake!**
15	And *so Pilate* **Pilatos**,
	willing to *content* **satisfy** the *people* **multitude**,
	released *Barabbas* **Bar Abbas** unto them,
	and delivered *Jesus* **Yah Shua**,
	when he had *scourged* **whipped** him,
	to be *crucified* **staked**.
16	And the *soldiers* **warriors** led him away
	into the *hall* **courtyard**, *called* **the** Praetorium;
	and they call together the whole *band* **squad**.
17	And they *clothed* **endued** him with purple,
	and *platted* **braided** a *crown* **wreath** of thorns,
	and put it about his head,
18	And began to salute him,
	Hail **Cheers**, *King* **Sovereign** of the *Jews* **Yah Hudiym**!
19	And they *smote* **struck** him
	on the head with a reed,
	and *did* spit upon him,
	and *bowing* **placing** their knees worshipped him.
20	And when they had mocked him,
	they *took off* **stripped** the purple from him,
	and *put* **endued** his own clothes on him,
	and led him out to *crucify* **stake** him.
21	And they compel one
	Simon **Shimon** a Cyrenian,
	who passed by, coming out of the *country* **field**,
	the father of Alexander and Rufus,
	to bear his *cross* **stake**.
22	And they bring him
	unto the place *Golgotha* **Gulgoleth**,
	which is, *being interpreted* **translated**,
	The place of a skull **Cranium Place**.
23	And they gave him to drink
	wine *mingled* with **tincture of** myrrh:
	but he *received* **took** it not.

Yah Shua Staked

24	And when they had *crucified* **staked** him,
	they *parted* **divided** his garments,
	casting lots upon them, what every man should take.
25	And it was the third hour,
	and they *crucified* **staked** him.
26	And the *superscription*
	epigraph of his accusation
	was *written over* **epigraphed**,
	THE *KING* **SOVEREIGN** OF THE
	JEWS **YAH HUDIYM**.

27 And with him they *crucify* **stake** two *thieves* **robbers**;
the one *on* **at** his right *hand*,
and the *other on* **one at** his left.
28 And the scripture was fulfilled/**shalamed**,
which *saith* **wordeth**,
And he was *numbered* **reckoned**
with the *transgressors* **torah violators**.
Yesha Yah 53:9, 12
29 And they that passed by
railed on **blasphemed** him,
wagging their heads, and *saying* **wording**, *Ah* **Aha**,
thou that *destroyest* **disintegratest** the *temple* **nave**,
and buildest it in three days,
30 Save thyself, and come
down from the *cross* **stake**.
31 Likewise also the *chief* **arch** priests mocking
said **worded** among *themselves* **one another**
with the scribes,
He saved others; himself he cannot save.
32 *Let Christ* **The Messiah!**
the *King* **Sovereign** of *Israel* **Yisra El!**
descend now from the *cross* **stake**,
that we may see and *believe* **trust**.
And they that were *crucified* **staked** with him
reviled **reproached** him.
33 And *when* **being** the sixth hour *was come*,
there was darkness **became** over the whole *land* **earth**
until the ninth hour.
34 And at the ninth hour
Jesus **Yah Shua** cried with a *loud* **mega** voice,
saying **wording**, Eloi, Eloi, lama sabachthani?
which is, *being interpreted* **translated**,
My *God* **Elohim**, my *God* **Elohim**,
why hast thou forsaken me?
Psalm 22:1
35 And some of them *that stood by* **present**,
when they heard it, *said* **worded**, Behold,
he *calleth Elias* **voiceth to Eli Yah**.
Indeed, what evil did he?
And they cry out the more superabundantly, Stake!
15 And Pilatos, willing to satisfy the multitude,
releases Bar Abbas to them,
and delivers Yah Shua, to whip and to stake.
16 And the warriors lead him away
into the courtyard — the Praetorium;
and they call the whole squad together:
17 and they endue him with purple and braid a
wreath of thorns and put it around his head.
18 And they begin to salute him,
Cheers! Sovereign of the Yah Hudiym!
19 — and they strike him on the head with a reed
and spit on him;
and placing their knees they worship him:
20 and as they mock him
they strip the purple from him; and endue his own
clothes on him and lead him out to stake him:
21 and they compel one Shimon a Cyrenian,
who passes by, coming from the field,
the father of Alexander and Rufus, to bear his stake.
22 And they bring him to the place Gulgoleth,
which translates, Cranium Place.
23 And they give him wine with tincture of myrrh
to drink:
but he takes it not.

Yah Shua Staked

24 And they stake him, and divide his garments,
casting lots upon them, whatevery man takes.
25 And it is the third hour, and they stake him:
26 and the epigraph of his
accusation is epigraphed,

The Sovereign Of The Yah Hudiym.

27 And they stake two robbers with him
— the one at his right and the one at his left.
28 to fulfill/shalam the scripture that words,
And he is reckoned with the torah
violators. Yesha Yah 53:9,12
29 And all who pass by blaspheme him,
wagging their heads, and wording, Aha,
you who disintegrates the nave
and builds it in three days:
30 Save yourself! and, Come down from the stake!
31 Likewise also the archpriests with the scribes
mock words among one another;
He saved others! Himself he cannot save!
32 The Messiah! The Sovereign of Yisra El!
Descend now from the stake,
so that we see and trust.
— and those staked with him, reproach him.
33 And being the sixth hour;
darkness becomes over the whole earth
until the ninth hour.
34 And at the ninth hour
Yah Shua cries with a mega voice,
wording, Eloi, Eloi, lama sabachthani?
which translates,
My Elohim, my Elohim, why forsake you me?
Psalm 22:1

35	And some of them present hear,
	and word, Behold! He voices to Eli Yah.
36	And one ran and filled a spunge full of vinegar,
	and put it on a reed, and gave him to drink,
	saying **wording**, *Let alone* **Allow**;
	let us see whether *Elias will* **Eli Yah shall** come
	to take him down.
37	And *Jesus* **Yah Shua**
	cried with a loud **released a mega** voice,
	and *gave up the ghost* **expired**.

REACTIONS: MATERIAL AND PHYSICAL

38	And the veil of the *temple*
	nave was *rent* **split** in twain
	from *the top* **above** to *the bottom* **below**.
39	And when the centurion,
	which *stood over against* **was present opposite** him,
	saw that he *so* **thus** cried out,
	and *gave up the ghost* **expired**, he said,
	Truly this *man* **human** was the Son of *God* **Elohim**.
40	There were also women
	looking on **observing** afar off:
	among whom was *Mary* **Miryam the** Magdalene,
	and *Mary* **Miryam**
	the mother of *James* **Yaaqovos** the
	less and of *Joses* **Yoses**,
	and *Salome* **Shalome**;
41	(Who also, when he was in *Galilee* **Galiyl**,
	followed him, and ministered unto him;)
	and many other women
	which *came up* **ascended** with him
	unto *Jerusalem* **Yeru Shalem**.

YAH SHUA ENTOMBED

42	And *now when the even was*
	come **already being evening**,
	because it was the preparation,
	that is, the *day before the sabbath* **foreshabbath**,
43	*Joseph* **Yoseph** of *Arimathaea* **Rahmah**,
	an honourable **a respected** counsellor,
	which also *waited for* **awaited**
	the *kingdom* **sovereigndom** of *God* **Elohim**,
	came, and *went in boldly* **dared go in** unto *Pilate* **Pilatos**,
	and *craved* **asked for** the body of *Jesus* **Yah Shua**.
44	And *Pilate* **Pilatos** marvelled
	if he were already dead:
	and calling unto him the centurion,
	he asked him whether he had been *any while* **long** dead.
45	And when he knew it of the centurion,
	he *gave* **granted** the body to *Joseph* **Yoseph**.
46	And he bought *fine* linen, and took him down,
	and wrapped him in the linen,
	and laid him in a *sepulchre* **tomb**
	which was hewn out of a rock,
	and rolled a stone
	unto the *door* **portal** of the *sepulchre* **tomb**.
47	And *Mary* **Miryam the** Magdalene
	and *Mary* **Miryam** the mother of *Joses* **Yoses**
	beheld **observed** where he was *laid* **placed**.

YAH SHUA RESURRECTED

16	And when the *sabbath* **shabbath** was past,
	Mary **Miryam the** Magdalene,
	and *Mary* **Miryam** the mother of *James* **Yaaqovos**,
	and *Salome* **Shalome**,
	had bought *sweet spices* **aromatics**,
	that they might come and anoint him.
2	And very early in the morning
	the first *day* of the *week* **shabbaths**, they
	came unto the *sepulchre* **tomb**
	at the rising of the sun.
3	And they *said* **worded** among themselves,
	Who shall roll us away the stone
	from the *door* **portal** of the *sepulchre* **tomb**?
4	And when they looked,
	they *saw* **observed** that the stone was rolled away:
	for it was *very great* **extremely mega**.
5	And entering into the *sepulchre* **tomb**,
	they saw a *young man* **youth** sitting *on* **at** the right side,
	clothed **arrayed** in a *long* white *garment* **stole**;
	and they were *affrighted* **utterly astonished**.
6	And he *saith* **wordeth** unto them,
	Be not *affrighted* **utterly astonished**:
	Ye seek *Jesus of Nazareth* **Yah Shua the Nazarene**,
	which was *crucified* **staked**:
	he is risen; he is not here:
	behold, the place where they *laid* **placed** him.
7	But go your way,
	tell **say to** his disciples and *Peter* **Petros**
36	And one runs and fills a spunge full of vinegar,
	and puts it on a reed, and gives him to drink,
	wording, Allow!
	We see whether Eli Yah comes to take him down.
37	And Yah Shua releases a
	mega voice, and expires.

REACTIONS: MATERIAL AND PHYSICAL

38	And the veil of the nave splits in two
	from above to below.
39	And the centurion who is present opposite him,
	sees that he thus cries out, and expires,
	he says, Truly this human is the Son of Elohim.

40 There are also women observing afar off:
among whom is Miryam the Magdalene,
and Miryam
the mother of Yaaqovos the less and of Yoses,
and Shalome;
41 — who also, when he was in Galiyl,
followed him, and ministered to him
and many other women
who ascended with him to Yeru Shalem.

Yah Shua Entombed

42 And already, being evening;
and because it is the preparation
— that is, the foreshabbath,
43 Yoseph of Rahmah, a respected counsellor,
who also awaits the sovereigndom of Elohim,
comes, and dares to go to Pilatos,
and asks for the body of Yah Shua.
44 And Pilatos marvels if he is already dead:
and calling the centurion to him,
he asks whether he had long died:
45 and knowing from the centurion,
he grants the body to Yoseph.
46 And he buys linen, and takes him down,
and wraps him in the linen;
and lays him in a tomb hewn from a rock,
and rolls a stone to the portal of the tomb.
47 And Miryam the Magdalene
and Miryam the mother of Yoses
observe where he is placed.

Yah Shua Resurrected

16 And the shabbath passes,
and Miryam the Magdalene
and Miryam the mother of Yaaqovos and Shalome
buy aromatics to go and anoint him:
2 and very early in the morning
on the first of the shabbaths,
they go to the tomb at the rising of the sun.
3 And they word among themselves,
Who rolls away the stone
from the portal of the tomb for us?
4 And they look
and observe the stone is rolled away:
for it is extremely mega.
5 And entering the tomb
they see a youth arrayed in a white stole
sitting at the right;
and they are utterly astonished.
6 And he words to them,
Be not utterly astonished:
You seek Yah Shua the Nazarene who was staked:
He is risen! He is not here!
Behold! The place where they placed him!
7 But go your way,
say to his disciples and Petros
that he *goeth before* **precedes** you into *Galilee* **Galiyl**:
there shall ye see him, **exactly** as he said unto you.
8 And they went out quickly,
and fled from the *sepulchre* **tomb**;
for they trembled
and *were amazed* **ecstasis overtook them**:
neither said they *any thing* **aught** to any *man* **one**;
for they were *afraid* **awestricken**.
9 *Now when Jesus was* **Having** risen early
the morning of the first *day* of the *week* **shabbaths**,
he *appeared* **manifested** first to *Mary*
Miryam the Magdalene,
out of whom he had cast seven *devils* **demons**.
10 And she went
and *told* **evangelized** them that had been with him,
as they mourned and wept.
11 And they, when they had
heard that he was alive,
and had been *seen* **observed** of her,
believed not **distrusted**.
12 After that he appeared in another form
unto two of them,
as they walked, and went into the *country* **field**.
13 And they went and *told* **evangelized** it
unto *the residue* **those remaining**: neither
believed **trusted** they them.
14 Afterward he appeared unto the eleven
as they *sat at meat* **reposed**,
and *upbraided them with* **reproached**
their *unbelief* **trustlessness**
and *hardness of heart* **hard—heartness**,
because they *believed* **trusted** not them
which had *seen* **observed** him after he was risen.

Yah Shua Apostolizes The Trusting

15 And he said unto them,
Go ye into all the *world* **cosmos**,
and preach the *gospel* **evangelism**
to *every creature* **all creation**.
16 He that *believeth* **trusteth** and is baptized
shall be saved;
but **and** he that *believeth not* **distrusteth**
shall be *damned* **condemned**.

SIGNS FOLLOW THE TRUSTERS

17 And these signs shall follow
them that *believe* **trust**;
In my name shall they cast out *devils* **demons**;
they shall speak with new tongues;

18 They shall take *up* serpents;
and if they drink *any* **aught** deadly *thing*,
it shall not *hurt* **injure** them;
they shall lay hands on the sick,
and they shall *recover* **become well**.
Loukas 10:19, 20

YAH SHUA TAKEN

19 **But** So **indeed** *then*
after *the Lord* **Adonay** had spoken unto them,
he was *received* **taken** up into heaven,
and sat *on* **at** the right *hand* of *God* **Elohim**.

SIGNS CONFIRM THE WORD

20 And they went forth, and preached every where,
the Lord working with them **Adonay co—working**,
and confirming the word *with* **by** signs following.
Amen.
that he precedes you into Galiyl:
there you see him, exactly as he said to you.

8 And they go quickly and flee the tomb;
for they tremble and ecstasis overtakes them:
and they say naught to anyone;
for they are awestricken.

9 Having risen early the
morning of the first shabbaths,
he first manifests himself to Miryam the Magdalene
from whom he had cast seven demons.

10 And she goes
and evangelizes them who had been with him,
— mourning and weeping.

11 And they, when they hear he is alive,
and that she observed him, distrust.

12 And after these,
he appears in another form to two of them,
as they walk and go into the field:

13 and they go and evangelize to those remaining:
and they trust them not.

14 Afterward he appears to
the eleven as they repose,
and reproaches their trustlessness
and hard—heartedness
because they trusted not them
who observed him after he rose.

YAH SHUA APOSTOLIZES THE TRUSTING

15 And he says to them,
Go into all the cosmos
and preach the evangelism to all creation.

16 Whoever trusts and is baptized is saved;
and whoever distrusts is condemned.

SIGNS FOLLOW THE TRUSTERS

17 And these signs follow them who trust:
In my name they cast out demons;
they speak with new tongues;

18 they take serpents;
and if they drink aught deadly, it injures
them not; they lay hands on the sick, and
they become well. Loukas 10:19, 20

YAH SHUA TAKEN

19 And so indeed, after Adonay speaks to them,
he is taken into the heavens,
and sits at the right of Elohim.

SIGNS CONFIRM THE WORD

20 And they go and preach every where
— Adonay co—working
and confirming the word by signs following.
Amen.

LUKE/UR 1

INTRODUCTION

1 *Forasmuch as* **Since indeed**
many have taken in hand to set forth in order
a declaration *of* **about** those *things* **matters**
which are *most surely believed* **fully borne** among us,

2 Even as they delivered them unto us,
which from the beginning
were eyewitnesses **saw for ourselves**,
and *ministers* **became attendants** of the word;

3 *It seemed good to me* **I thought** also,
having *had perfect understanding* **followed precisely**
of all *things* from *the very first* **above**,
to *write* **scribe** unto thee in *order* **sequence**,
most *excellent Theophilus* **powerful Theo Philus**,

4 That thou mightest know
the certainty of those *things* **words**,
wherein **about which**
thou hast been *instructed* **catechized**.

THE BIRTH OF YAHN THE BAPTIZER FORETOLD

5 There *was* **became** in the days of Herod,
the *king* **sovereign** of *Judaea* **Yah Hudah**,
a *certain* priest named *Zacharias* **Zechar Yah**,
of the course of *Abia* **Abi Yah**:
and his *wife* **woman**
was of the daughters of *Aaron* **Aharon**,
and her name was *Elisabeth* **Eli Sheba**.

6 And they were both *righteous* **just**
before God **in the sight of Elohim**,
walking in all
the *commandments* **misvoth** and *ordinances* **judgments**
of *the Lord* **Yah Veh** blameless.

7 And they had no child,
because that *Elisabeth* **as Eli Sheba** was *barren* **sterile**,
and they both were
now well stricken in years **advanced in days**.

8 And it *came to pass* **became**,
that while he
executed the priest's office **priested**
before God **at the face of Elohim**
in the order of his course,

9 According to the custom of
the *priest's office* **priesthood**,
his lot was to *burn* incense
when he *went* **entered**
into the *temple* **nave** of *the Lord* **Yah Veh**.

10 And the whole multitude of the people
were praying without at the *time* **hour** of incense.

11 And there appeared unto him
an angel of *the Lord* **Yah Veh**
standing *on* **at** the right *side* of the
sacrifice altar of incense.

12 And when *Zacharias* **Zechar Yah** saw him,
he was troubled, and *fear* **awe** fell upon him.

13 But the angel said unto him,
Fear **Awe** not, *Zacharias* **Zechar Yah**:
for thy *prayer* **petition** is heard;
and thy *wife Elisabeth* **woman Eli Sheba**
shall *bear* **birth** thee a son,
and thou shalt call his name *John* **Yahn**.

14 And *thou shalt have joy* **he shall be thy cheer**
and *gladness* **thy jumping for joy**;
and many shall *rejoice* **cheer** at his birth.

15 For he shall be *great* **mega** in
the sight of *the Lord* **Yah Veh**,
and shall not *no way* drink
neither wine nor *strong drink* **intoxicants**;
and he shall be filled/**shalamed** with the
Holy Spirit **Ruach ha-kodesh**,
even from his mother's womb.

16 And many of the *children* **sons** of *Israel* **Yisra El**
shall he turn to *the Lord* **Yah Veh** their *God* **Elohim**.

17 And he shall *go before* **precede** him
in the spirit and *power* **dynamis** of *Elias* **Eli Yah**
to turn the hearts of the fathers to the children,
and the *disobedient* **distrusting**
to the *wisdom* **thought** of the just;
to *make ready* **prepare** a people
prepared for *the Lord* **Yah Veh**.

18 And *Zacharias* **Zechar Yah** said unto the angel,
Whereby shall I know this? for I am *an old man* **elderly**,
and my *wife* **woman**
well stricken **advanced** in *years* **days**.

INTRODUCTION

1 Since indeed
many took in hand to set forth in order
a declaration about those matters
which are fully borne among us

2 — even as they delivered to us;
who from the beginning saw for ourselves
and became attendants of the word;

3 I thought also,
having precisely followed all from above,
to scribe to you in sequence,
most powerful Theo Philus,

4 that you know the certainty of those words
about which you have been catechized.

THE BIRTH OF YAHN
THE BAPTIZER FORETOLD

5 And so be it,
in the days of Herod the sovereign of Yah Hudah
there was a priest named Zechar Yah,
of the course of Abi Yah:
and his woman of the daughters of Aharon;
and her name, Eli Sheba:

6 and both are just in the sight of Elohim,
and walk blameless
in all the misvoth and judgments of Yah Veh:

7 and they have no child, as Eli Sheba is sterile;
and they both are advanced in days.

8 And so be it,
as he priests at the face of Elohim
in the order of his course

9 according to the custom of the priesthood,
his lot is to incense
as he enters the nave of Yah Veh:

10 and outside, the whole multitude of the people
is praying at the hour of incense.

11 And an angel of Yah Veh appears to him
standing at the right of the sacrifice altar of incense:

12 and Zechar Yah sees him
and he is troubled and awe befalls him.

13 But the angel says to him, Awe not, Zechar Yah:
for your petition is heard;
and your woman Eli Sheba births you a son:
and call his name Yahn:

14 and he becomes your cheer
and your jumping for joy;
and many cheer at his birth:

15 for he becomes mega in the sight of Yah Veh,
and no way drinks wine or intoxicants;
and he is fills full/shalams with the Holy Spirit
even from the womb of his mother:

16 and he turns many of the sons of Yisra El
to Yah Veh their Elohim:

17 and he precedes him
in the spirit and dynamis of Eli Yah
to turn the hearts of the fathers to the children,
and the distrusting to the thought of the just;
to prepare a people — prepared for Yah Veh.

18 And Zechar Yah says to the angel,
By what know I this?
For I am elderly, and my woman advanced in days.

19 And the angel answering said unto him,
I am *Gabriel* **Gabri El**,
that stand in the *presence* **sight** of *God* **Elohim**;
and am *sent* **apostolized** to speak unto thee,
and to *shew* **evangelize** thee *these glad tidings*.

20 And, behold,
thou shalt be *dumb* **hushed**, and not able to speak,
until the day that these *things* shall be *performed*,
because thou *believest* **trustest** not my words,
which shall be *fulfilled*/**shalamed** in their season.

21 And the people
waited for Zacharias **awaited Zechar Yah**,
and marvelled that he *tarried so long* **took his time**
in the *temple* **nave**.

22 And when he came out, he
could not speak unto them:
and they *perceived* **knew**
that he had seen a vision in the *temple* **nave**:
for he *beckoned* **nodded** unto them,
and *remained speechless* **continually abode mute**.

23 And *so be* it *came to pass*, that,
as soon as the days of his *ministration* **liturgy**
were *accomplished*/**shalamed**,
he departed to his own house.

24 And after those days
his *wife Elisabeth* **woman Eli Sheba** conceived,
and *hid* **concealed** herself five months, *saying* **wording**,

25 Thus hath *the Lord dealt* **Yah Veh done** with me
in the days wherein he *looked on* **regarded** me,
to *take away* **remove** my reproach
among *men* **humanity**.

THE BIRTH OF YAH SHUA FORETOLD

26 And in the sixth month
the angel *Gabriel* **Gabri El**
was *sent* **apostolized** from *God* **Elohim**
unto a city of *Galilee* **Galiyl**, named Nazareth,

27 To a virgin
espoused to a man whose name was *Joseph* **Yoseph**,
of the house of David;
and the virgin's name was *Mary* **Miryam**.

28 And the angel came in unto her, and said,
Hail **Cheers**,
thou that art *highly favoured* **O charised* one**:
the Lord is **Yah Veh be** with thee:
blessed **eulogized** art thou among women.

29 And when she saw him,
she was troubled at his *saying* **word**,
and *cast in her mind* **reasoned**
what manner of salutation this should be.
*verb of charis

30 And the angel said unto her,
Fear **Awe** not, *Mary* **Miryam**:
for thou hast found *favour* **charism** with *God* **Elohim**.

LUKE/UR 1

31   And, behold, thou shalt conceive in thy womb,
and *bring forth* **birth** a son,
and shalt call his name *Jesus* **Yah Shua**.
32   He shall be *great* **mega**,
and shall be called the Son of *the Highest* **Elyon**:
and *the Lord God* **Yah Veh Elohim**
shall give unto him the throne of his father David:
33   And he shall reign over
the house of *Jacob* **Yaaqov**
for ever **unto the eons**;
and of his *kingdom* **sovereigndom**
there shall be no *end* **finality**.
34   Then said *Mary* **Miryam** unto the angel,
How shall this be, *seeing* **since** I know not a man?
35 And the angel answered and said unto her, The
Holy Spirit **Ruach ha-kodesh** shall come upon thee,
and the *power* **dynamis** of *the Highest* **Elyon**
shall overshadow thee:
therefore **so** also that holy *thing*
which *shall be born of thee* **thou shalt birth**
shall be called the Son of *God* **Elohim**.
36   And, behold, thy cousin *Elisabeth* **Eli Sheba**,
she hath also conceived a son in her *old age* **senescence**:
and this is the sixth month with her,
who was called *barren* **sterile**.
37   For with *God* **Elohim** nothing
no rhema shall be impossible.
38   And *Mary* **Miryam** said,
Behold the *handmaid* **maiden** of *the Lord* **Yah Veh**;
be it unto me according to thy *word* **rhema**.
And the angel departed from her.
19   And the angel answers him, saying,
I am Gabri El who stands in the sight of Elohim;
and am apostolized to speak to you
and to evangelize you:
20   and behold, you become hushed
and not able to speak
until the day these become
— because you trust not
my words to fulfill/shalam in their season.
21   And the people await Zechar Yah
and marvel that he takes his time in the nave:
22   and he comes out and cannot speak to them:
and they know he saw a vision in the nave
— for he nods to them and continually abides mute.
23   And so be it,
as soon as he fulfills/shalams the days of his liturgy,
he departs to his own house.
24   And after those days
his woman Eli Sheba conceives
and conceals herself five months, wording,

25   Thus Yah Veh does with me
in the days wherein he regards me
to remove my reproach among humanity.

THE BIRTH OF YAH SHUA FORETOLD

26   And in the sixth month
Elohim apostolizes the angel Gabri El to
a city of Galiyl named Nazareth
27   — to a virgin espoused to a man
whose name is Yoseph of the house of David;
and the name of the virgin is Miryam.
28   And the angel comes to her, and says,
Cheers, O charised* one:
Yah Veh *be* with you:
eulogized *are* you among women.
29   — and she sees him, and is troubled at his word;
and reasons what manner of salutation this is.
*verb of charis
30   And the angel says to her, Awe not, Miryam:
for you find charism with Elohim.
31   And behold, you conceive in your womb
and birth a son: and call his name Yah Shua.
32   He becomes mega
and is called the Son of Elyon:
and Yah Veh Elohim
gives him the throne of his father David:
33   and he reigns over the house of Yaaqov
to the eons;
and there is no finality of his sovereigndom.
34   So Miryam says to the angel,
How becomes this, since I know not a man?
35   And the angel answers her, saying,
The Holy Spirit comes upon you
and the dynamis of Elyon overshadows you:
so also that holy *one* birthed of you
is called the Son of Elohim.
36   And behold, your cousin Eli Sheba
also conceives a son in her senescence:
and this is her sixth month — who is called sterile:
37   for with Elohim no rhema is impossible.
38   And Miryam says,
Behold the maiden of Yah Veh;
so be it to me according to your rhema.
— and the angel departs from her.

MIRYAM VISITS ELI SHEBA

39   And *Mary* **Miryam** arose in those days,
and went into the *hill country* **mountains**
with *haste* **diligence**,
into a city of *Juda* **Yah Hudah**;
40   And entered into the house
of *Zacharias* **Zechar Yah**,
and saluted *Elisabeth* **Eli Sheba**.

The Song Of Eli Sheba

41 And *so be* it *came to pass*, that,
when *Elisabeth* **Eli Sheba**
heard the salutation of *Mary* **Miryam**,
the *babe* **infant** leaped in her womb;
and *Elisabeth* **Eli Sheba** was *filled*/**shalamed**
with the *Holy Spirit* **Ruach ha-kodesh**:
42 And she *spake out* **exclaimed**
with a *loud* **mega** voice,
and said,
Blessed **Eulogized** art thou among women,
and *blessed* **eulogized** is the fruit of thy womb.
43 And whence is this to me,
that the mother of my *Lord* **Adonay** should come to me?
44 For, *lo* **behold**,
as soon as the voice of thy salutation
sounded **became** in mine ears,
the *babe* **infant** leaped in my womb **and jumped** for joy.
45 And blessed is she that *believed* **trusted**:
for there shall be a *performance* **fulfilling/shalam**
of those *things* which were *told* **spoken to** her
from *the Lord* **Yah Veh**.

The Song Of Miryam

46 And *Mary* **Miryam** said,
My soul *doth magnify the Lord* **magnifieth Yah Veh**,
47 And my spirit *hath rejoiced* **jumpeth for joy**
in *God* **Elohim** my Saviour.
48 For he hath *regarded* **looked upon**
the *low estate* **humiliation** of his *handmaiden* **maiden**:
for, behold,
from *henceforth* **now on** all generations
shall call me blessed.
49 For he that is *mighty* **able**
hath *done to* **dealt with** me *great things* **magnificently**;
and holy is his name.
50 And his mercy *is* on them that *fear* **awe** him
from generation to generation.
51 He hath *shewed strength*
dealt power with his arm;
he hath scattered the proud
in the *imagination* **mind** of their hearts.
52 He hath put down the *mighty* **dynasties**
from their *seats* **thrones**,
and exalted *them of low degree* **the humble**.
53 He hath *filled*/**shalamed** the
hungry with good *things*;
and the rich he hath *sent* **apostolized forth** empty *away*.
54 He hath *holpen* **supported**
his *servant Israel* **lad Yisra El**,
in remembrance of his **to remember** mercy;
55 **Exactly** As he spake to our fathers,
to Abraham,
and to his *seed for ever* **sperma unto the eons**.
56 And *Mary* **Miryam** abode
with her about three months,
and returned to her own house.

The Birth Of Yahn The Baptizer

57 Now *Elisabeth's full* **Eli Sheba's** time
came/**was shalamed**
that she should *be delivered* **birth**;
and she *brought forth* **birthed** a son.
58 And her *neighbours* **fellow**
settlers and her *cousins* **kindred**
heard how *the Lord* **Yah Veh**
had *shewed great mercy upon* **magnified** her;
and they rejoiced with her.
59 And *so be* it *came to pass*,
that on the eighth day they came to circumcise the child;
and they called him *Zacharias* **Zechar Yah**,
after the name of his father.
60 And his mother answered
and said, *Not so* **Indeed not**;
but he shall be called *John* **Yahn**.
61 And they said unto her,
There is none of thy kindred that is called by this name.
62 And they *made signs* **nodded** to his father,
how he *would* **willed** to have him called.
63 And he asked for a *writing table* **tablet**,
and *wrote* **scribed**, *saying* **wording**,

Miryam Visits Eli Sheba

39 And in those days,
Miryam rises with diligence
and goes to the mountains to a city of Yah Hudah;
40 and enters the house of Zechar Yah
and salutes Eli Sheba.

The Song Of Eli Sheba

41 And so be it,
when Eli Sheba hears the salutation of Miryam,
the infant leaps in her womb;
and Eli Sheba fullfills/shalams with the Holy Spirit.
42 And with a mega voice, she exclaims and says,
Eulogized — you among women!
And eulogized — the fruit of your womb!
43 And whence *is* this to me,
that the mother of my Adonay comes to me?
44 For behold,

as soon as the voice of your salutation
became in my ears,
the infant leaped in my womb and jumped for joy:
45   and blessed is she who trusts:
for there becomes a fulfilling/shalaming
of those spoken to her by Yah Veh.

THE SONG OF MIRYAM

46   And Miryam says, My soul magnifies Yah Veh,
47   and my spirit jumps for
joy in Elohim my Saviour:
48   for he looked upon the
humiliation of his maiden:
for behold,
from now on all generations call me blessed:
49   for he who is able does magnificently with me
and holy *is* his name.
50   And his mercy *is* on them who awe him
from generation to generation.
51   He deals power with his arm;
he scatters the proud in the mind of their hearts;
52   he puts down the dynasties from their thrones
and exalts the humble:
53   he fills/shalams the famished with good
and the rich he apostolizes forth empty:
54   he supports his lad Yisra El to remember mercy;
55   exactly as he spoke to our fathers,
to Abraham, and to his sperma to the eons.
56   — and Miryam abides with
her about three months
and returns to her own house.

THE BIRTH OF YAHN THE BAPTIZER

57   And the time for Eli Sheba
to birth fulfills/shalams;
and she births a son:
58   and her fellow settlers and her kindred
hear how Yah Veh magnifies her;
and they rejoice with her.
59   And so be it,
on the eighth day they come to circumcise the child;
and they call him Zechar Yah
after the name of his father.
60   And his mother answers, saying,
Indeed not! But he is called Yahn.
61   And they say to her,
None of your kindred is called by this name.
62   And they nod to his father,
how he wills to call him:
63   and he asks for a tablet, and scribes, wording,
His name is *John* **Yahn**.
And they marvelled all.
64   And his mouth was opened immediately,
and his tongue loosed, and he spake,
and *praised God* **eulogized Elohim**.
65   And *fear came* **awe became** on all
that *dwelt* **settled** round about them:
and all these *sayings* **rhema**
were *noised abroad* **thoroughly told** throughout
all the *hill country* **mountains** of *Judaea* **Yah Hudah**.
66   And all they that heard them
laid **placed** them *up* in their hearts, *saying* **wording**,
What *manner of child* **then** shall this **child** be!
And the hand of *the Lord* **Yah Veh** was with him.

THE PROPHECY OF ZECHAR YAH

67   And his father *Zacharias* **Zechar Yah**
was filled/shalamed with the *Holy
Spirit* **Ruach ha-kodesh**,
and prophesied, *saying* **wording**,
68   *Blessed* **Eulogized**
be the *Lord God* **Yah Veh Elohim** of *Israel* **Yisra El**;
for he hath visited
and *redeemed* **dealt redemption to** his people,
69   And hath raised *up* an horn of salvation for us
in the house of his *servant* **lad** David;
70   **Exactly** As he spake
by **through** the mouth of his holy prophets,
which have been *since* **from** the *world began* **eons**:
71   That we should *be saved* **have salvation**
from our enemies,
and from the hand of all that hate us;
72   To *perform the* **deal** mercy
promised to **with our** fathers,
and to remember his holy covenant;
73   The oath which he *sware*
oathed to our father Abraham,
74   That he *would grant* **should give** unto us,
that we being *delivered* **rescued**
out of the hand of our enemies
might *serve* **liturgize** him *without fear* **fearlessly**,
75   In *holiness* **mercy** and *righteousness* **justness**
before him **in his sight**, all the days of our life.
76   And thou, child,
shalt be called the prophet of *the Highest* **Elyon**:
for thou shalt *go before* **precede** the
face of *the Lord* **Adonay**
to prepare his ways;
77   To give knowledge of salvation unto his people
by **in** the *remission* **forgiveness** of their sins,

78 Through the *tender* **spleen**
of mercy of our *God* **Elohim**;
whereby the *dayspring* **rising** from on high
hath visited us,
79 To *give light to* **appear upon**
them that sit in darkness
and in the shadow of death,
to *guide* **direct** our feet into the way of *peace* **shalom**.
80 And the child grew, and *waxed*
strong empowered in spirit,
and was in the *deserts* **wildernesses**
till the day of his *shewing* **exhibiting** unto *Israel* **Yisra El**.

The Birth Of Yah Shua

2 And *so be* it *came to pass* in those days,
that there went out a *decree* **dogma**
from *Caesar* **Kaisar** Augustus
that all the world should be *taxed* **registered**.
2 (And this *taxing was*
registration first *made* **became**
when Cyrenius was governor of Syria.)
3 And all went to *be taxed* **register**,
every one **each** into his own city.
4 And *Joseph* **Yoseph** also *went up* **ascended**
from *Galilee* **Galiyl**, out of the city of Nazareth,
into *Judaea* **Yah Hudah**, unto the city of David,
which is called *Bethlehem* **Beth Lechem**;
(because he was
of the house and *lineage* **patriarchy** of David:)
5 To *be taxed* **register** with *Mary* **Miryam**
his espoused *wife* **woman**,
being great with child **swelling within**.
6 And so *be* it *was*, that, while they were there,
His name is Yahn.
— and they all marvel.
64 And immediately his mouth opens
and his tongue loosens and he speaks
and he eulogizes Elohim.
65 And awe becomes on all
who settle around them:
and they thoroughly tell all these rhema
throughout all the mountains of Yah Hudah.
66 And all who hear them
place them in their hearts, wording,
What them becomes of this child!
— and the hand of Yah Veh is with him.

The Prophecy Of Zechar Yah

67 And his father Zechar Yah,
filled full/shalamed with the Holy Spirit,
prophesies, wording,
68 Eulogized — Yah Veh Elohim of Yisra El:
for he visits and deals redemption to his people
69 and raises a horn of salvation for us
in the house of his lad David;
70 exactly as he spoke
through the mouth of his holy prophets,
being from the eons:
71 to have salvation from our enemies,
and from the hand of all who hate us;
72 to deal mercy with our fathers
and to remember his holy covenant;
73 the oath he oathed to our father Abraham
74 to fearlessly give us,
being rescued from the hand of our enemies,
to liturgize him,
75 in mercy and justness in his sight,
all the days of our life.
76 And you, child, are called the prophet of Elyon:
for you precede the face of Adonay
to prepare his ways;
77 to give knowledge of salvation to his people
in the forgiveness of their sins,
78 through the spleen of mercy of our Elohim;
whereby the rising from on high visits us;
79 to appear on them who sit in darkness
and in the shadow of death;
to direct our feet in the way of shalom.
80 And the child grows — empowered in spirit
and is in the wildernesses
until the day of his exhibiting to Yisra El.

The Birth Of Yah Shua

2 And so be it, in those days,
a dogma comes from Kaisar Augustus
to register all the world:
2 this registration first becomes
when Cyrenius is governor of Syria;
3 and all go to register — each to his own city.
4 And Yoseph also ascends from Galiyl
from the city of Nazareth to Yah Hudah
to the city of David, called Beth Lechem
— because he is of the house and patriarchy of David:
5 to register with Miryam his espoused woman
who is swelling within.
6 And so be it, in being there,
the days were *accomplished* **fulfilled/shalamed**
that she should *be delivered* **birth**.
7 And she *brought forth* **birthed**
her *firstborn* **firstbirthed** son,

and *wrapped* **swathed** him *in swaddling clothes*,
and *laid* **reclined** him in a manger;
because there was no *room* **place** for them
in the *inn* **lodge**.

8   And there were in the same *country* **region**
shepherds abiding in the field,
keeping watch **guarding the guard**
over their *flock* **shepherddom** by night.

9   And, *lo* **behold**, the angel of *the Lord* **Yah Veh**
came upon **stood over** them,
and the glory of *the Lord* **Yah Veh**
shone round about **haloed** them:
and they *were sore afraid* **awed a mega awe**.

10 And the angel said unto them, *Fear* **Awe** not:
for, behold,
I *bring you good tidings* **evangelize to you**
of *great joy* **mega cheer**,
which shall be to all people.

11 For unto you is born this
day in the city of David
a Saviour,
which is *Christ the Lord* **Messiah Adonay**.

12 And this shall be a sign unto you;
Ye shall find the *babe* **infant**
wrapped in swaddling clothes **swathed**,
lying in a manger.

13 And suddenly there *was* **became** with the angel
a multitude of the heavenly host
praising God **halaling Elohim**, and *saying* **wording**,

14 Glory to *God* **Elohim** in the *highest* **highests**,
and on earth *peace* **shalom**,
good will **well—approval** toward *men* **humanity**.

15 And **so be** it *came to pass*,
as the angels were gone *away* from them into heaven,
the humans — the shepherds said one to another,
Let us now *go* **pass through**
even unto Bethlehem **as far as Beth Lechem**,
and see this *thing* **rhema**
which *is come to pass* **hath become**,
which *the Lord* **Yah Veh** hath made known unto us.

16 And they came with haste,
and found *Mary* **Miryam**, and *Joseph* **Yoseph**,
and the *babe* **infant** lying in a manger.

17 And when they had seen it,
they *made known abroad* **broadcasted** the *saying* **rhema**
which was *told* **spoken to** them concerning this child.

18 And all they that heard it
wondered at **marvelled about** those *things*
which were *told* **spoken to** them by the shepherds.

19 But *Mary* **Miryam**
kept **preserved** all these *things* **rhema**,
and *pondered* **considered** them in her heart.

20 And the shepherds returned,
glorifying and *praising God* **halaling Elohim**
for all *the things* **those**
that they had heard and seen,
exactly as it was *told* **spoken** unto them.

THE PRESENTATION OF YAH SHUA

21 And when eight days were
accomplished **fulfilled/shalamed**
for the circumcising of the child,
his name was called *Jesus* **Yah Shua**,
which was so *named* **called** of the angel
before **ere** he was conceived in the womb.

22 And when the days of her *purification* **purifying**
according to the *law* **torah** of *Moses* **Mosheh**
were *accomplished* **fulfilled/shalamed**,
they brought him to *Jerusalem* **Yeru Shalem**,
to present him to *the Lord* **Yah Veh**;

23 (**Exactly** As *it is written* **scribed**
in the *law* **torah** of *the Lord* **Yah Veh**,
Every male that openeth the *womb* **matrix**
shall be called holy *to the Lord* **unto Yah Veh**;)

24 And to *offer* **give** a sacrifice
according to that which is said
in the *law* **torah** of *the Lord* **Yah Veh**,
A *pair* **yoke** of turtledoves,
or two *young pigeons* **youngling doves**.

she fulfills/shalams the days for her to birth:

7   and she births her firstbirthed son
and swathes him and reclines him in a manger;
because there is no place for them in the lodge.

8   And in the same region
shepherds abide in the field,
guarding the guard over their shepherddom by night:

9   and behold, the angel of
Yah Veh stands over them
and the glory of Yah Veh haloes them:
and they awe a mega awe.

10 And the angel says to them, Awe not:
for behold, I evangelize to you of mega cheer
which becomes to all people:

11 for to you is birthed this day in the city of David
a Saviour who is Messiah Adonay:

12 and this is your sign;
You find the infant swathed, and lying in a manger.

13 And suddenly with the angel
there becomes a multitude of the heavenly host
halaling Elohim, and wording,

14 Glory to Elohim in the highests
and on earth shalom
and well—approval toward humanity.
15 And so be it,
as the angels go from them into the heavens,
the humans — the shepherds say one to another,
We pass through as far as Beth Lechem
and see this rhema which becomes
— which Yah Veh makes known to us.
16 And they come with haste
and find Miryam and Yoseph
and the infant lying in a manger:
17 and they see,
and they broadcast the rhema spoken to them
concerning this child:
18 and all who hear
marvel about what the shepherds speak to them.
19 — but Miryam preserves all these rhema
and considers them in her heart.
20 And the shepherds return
glorifying and halaling Elohim
for all they heard and saw
— exactly as spoken to them.

THE PRESENTATION OF YAH SHUA

21 And when eight days fulfill/shalam
to circumcise the child,
his name is called Yah Shua
— being so called by the angel
ere he was conceived in the womb.
22 And when she fulfills/shalams
the days of her purifying
according to the torah of Mosheh,
they bring him to Yeru Shalem
to present him to Yah Veh
23 — exactly as scribed in the torah of Yah Veh:
Every male opening the matrix
is called holy to Yah Veh:
24 and give a sacrifice
according to that said in the torah of Yah Veh,
A yoke of turtledoves or two youngling doves.
25 And, behold,
there was a *man* **human** in *Jerusalem* **Yeru Shalem**,
whose name was *Simeon* **Shimon**;
and *the same man* **this human**
was just and *devout* **well—received**,
waiting for **awaiting** the consolation of *Israel* **Yisra El**:
and the *Holy Spirit* **Ruach ha-kodesh** was upon him.
26 And it was *revealed* **oracled** unto him
by the *Holy Spirit* **Ruach ha-kodesh**,
that he should not see death,
before **ere** he had seen *the Lord's*
Christ **Yah Veh's Messiah**.
27 And he came *by* **in** the Spirit
into the *temple* **priestal precinct**:
and when the parents
brought in **introduced** the child *Jesus* **Yah Shua**,
to do for him
after the custom **as accustomed** of the *law* **torah**,
28 *Then took* **And received** he him *up* in his arms,
and *blessed God* **eulogized Elohim**, and said,
29 *Lord* **Despotes**,
now *lettest* **release** thou thy servant *depart*
in *peace* **shalom**,
according to thy *word* **rhema**:
30 For mine eyes have seen thy salvation,
31 Which thou hast prepared
before **in front of** the face of all people;
32 A light *to lighten* **of apocalypse**
to the *Gentiles* **goyim**,
and the glory of thy people *Israel* **Yisra El**.
33 And *Joseph* **Yoseph** and his mother
marvelled at those *things*
which were spoken *of* **concerning** him.
34 And *Simeon blessed* **Shimon eulogized** them,
and said unto *Mary* **Miryam** his mother,
Behold, this *child* is set
for the *fall* **downfall** and *rising again* **resurrection**
of many in *Israel* **Yisra El**;
and for a sign
which shall be *spoken against* **contradicted**;
35 (Yea, a *sword* **sabre**
shall *pierce* **pass** through thy own soul also,)
that the *thoughts* **reasonings** of many hearts
may be *revealed* **unveiled**.
36 And there was one *Anna* **Hannah**, a prophetess,
the daughter of *Phanuel* **Peni El**,
of the *tribe* **scion** of *Aser* **Asher**:
she was *of great age* **advanced in many days**,
and had lived with *an husband* **a man**
seven years from her virginity;
37 And she *was* a widow
of about *fourscore* **eighty** and four years,
which departed not from the *temple* **priestal precinct**,
but *served God* **liturgized Elohim**
with fastings and *prayers* **petitions** night and day.
38 And she *coming in* **standing**
by that *instant* **hour**
gave thanks **homologized** likewise
unto *the Lord* **Adonay**,

and spake *of* **concerning** him to all them
that *looked for* **awaited** redemption
in *Jerusalem* **Yeru Shalem**.

39 And when they had *performed*
completed/shalamed
all *things*
according to the *law* **torah** of *the Lord* **Yah Veh**,
they returned into *Galilee* **Galiyl**,
to their own city Nazareth.

40 And the child grew,
and *waxed strong* **empowered** in
spirit, filled with wisdom:
and the *grace* **charism** of *God* **Elohim** was upon him.

THE LADHOOD MINISTRY OF YAH SHUA

41 *Now* **And** his parents
went to *Jerusalem* **Yeru Shalem** every year
at the *feast* **celebration** of the *passover* **pasach**.

42 And when he *was* **became** twelve years *old*,
they *went up* **ascended** to *Jerusalem* **Yeru Shalem**
after the custom of the *feast* **celebration**.

43 And when they had fulfilled/**shalamed** the days,
as they returned,
the *child Jesus* **lad Yah Shua**
tarried **abode** behind in *Jerusalem* **Yeru Shalem**;
and *Joseph* **Yoseph** and his mother knew not of it.

25 And behold, in Yeru Shalem,
a human whose name *is* Shimon;
and this human is just and well—received,
awaiting the consolation of Yisra El:
and the Holy Spirit is upon him.

26 And the Holy Spirit oracles to him
that he not see death
ere he sees the Messiah of Yah Veh.

27 And he comes in the Spirit
into the priestal precinct:
and the parents introduce the child Yah Shua,
to do for him as accustomed by the torah.

28 And he receives him in his arms
and eulogizes Elohim and says

29 Despotes, now release your servant in shalom,
according to your rhema:

30 for my eyes see your salvation,

31 whom you prepared
in front of the face of all people;

32 a light of apocalypse to the goyim
and the glory of your people Yisra El.

33 — and Yoseph and his mother
marvel at what is spoken concerning him.

34 And Shimon eulogizes them,
and says to Miryam his mother, Behold,
this is set for the downfall and resurrection
of many in Yisra El;
and for a sign to contradict.

35 Yes, a sabre also passes through your own soul
to unveil the reasonings of many hearts.

36 And there is Hannah, a prophetess
the daughter of Peni El of the scion of Asher
— she is advanced in many days:
who lived with a man seven years from her virginity;

37 and she *is* a widow of about eighty—four years
who departs not from the priestal precinct,
but liturgizes Elohim with fastings and petitions
night and day.

38 And standing by that hour
she homologizes likewise to Adonay,
and speaks concerning him
to all in Yeru Shalem who await redemption.

39 And when they complete/shalam all
according to the torah of Yah Veh,
they return to Galiyl, to their own city Nazareth.

40 And the child grows,
empowered in spirit, filled with wisdom:
and the charism of Elohim is upon him.

THE LADHOOD MINISTRY OF YAH SHUA

41 And his parents go to Yeru Shalem every year
at the celebration of the pasach:

42 and when he becomes twelve years,
they ascend to Yeru Shalem
after the custom of the celebration

43 — and they fulfill/shalam the days.
And as they return,
the lad Yah Shua abides behind in Yeru Shalem;
and Yoseph and his mother know it not:

44 But they, *supposing* **presuming** him
to have been in the *company* **caravan**,
went **had come** a day's journey;
and they sought him
among their *kinsfolk* **kin** and acquaintance.

45 And when they found him not,
they *turned back again* **returned**
to *Jerusalem* **Yeru Shalem**, seeking him.

46 And *so be* it *came to pass*, that after three days
they found him in the *temple* **priestal precinct**,
sitting in the midst of the doctors,
both hearing them, and asking them *questions*.

47 And all that heard him
were astonished **astounded**
at his *understanding* **comprehension** and answers.

48	And when they saw him, they *were amazed* **astonished**: and his mother said unto him, *Son* **Child**, why hast thou thus dealt with us? behold, thy father and I have sought thee *sorrowing* **grieving**.
49	And he said unto them, How is it that ye sought me? *wist* **knew** ye not that I must be about my Father's business?
50	And they *understood* **comprehended** not the *saying* **rhema** which he spake unto them.
51	And he *went down* **descended** with them, and came to Nazareth, and *was subject* **subjugated** unto them: *but* **and** his mother **thoroughly** kept all these *sayings* **rhemas** in her heart.
52	And *Jesus increased* **Yah Shua advanced** in wisdom and *stature* **maturity**, and in *favour* **charism** with *God* **Elohim** and *man* **humanity**.

Yahn The Baptizer Fulfills/ Shalams Prophecy

3	Now in the fifteenth year of the *reign* **governing** of *Tiberius Caesar* **Kaisar Tiberius**, Pontius *Pilate* **Pilatos** being governor of *Judaea* **Yah Hudah**, and Herod being tetrarch of *Galilee* **Galiyl**, and his brother *Philip* **Phillipos** **being** tetrarch of *Ituraea* **Yetur** and of the region of Trachonitis, and Lysanias the tetrarch of Abilene,
2	*Annas* **Hanan Yah** and Caiaphas being the *high priests* **archpriests**, the *word* **rhema** of *God* **Elohim** *came* **became** unto *John* **Yahn** the son of *Zacharias* **Zechar Yah** in the wilderness.
3	And he came into all the *country* **region** round about *Jordan* **Yarden**, preaching the baptism of repentance for the *remission* **forgiveness** of sins;
4	As *it is written* **scribed** in the *book* **scroll** of the words of *Esaias* **Yesha Yah** the prophet, *saying* **wording**, The voice of one crying in the wilderness, Prepare ye the way of *the Lord* **Yah Veh**, make his paths straight.
5	Every valley shall be filled, and every mountain and hill shall be *brought low* **humbled**; and the crooked shall be made into straight, and the *rough* **jagged** ways shall be made **into** smooth;
6	And all flesh shall see the salvation of *God* **Elohim**. Yesha Yah 40:3—5
7	*Then said* **So** he **worded** to the multitude that *came forth* **proceeded** to be baptized of him, O *generation* **progeny** of vipers, who hath *warned* **exemplified** you to flee from the wrath *to come* **about to be**?
8	*Bring forth therefore* **So produce** fruits worthy of repentance, and begin not to *say* **word** within yourselves, We have Abraham to our father: for I *say* **word** unto you, That *God* **Elohim** is able of these stones to raise *up* children unto Abraham.
9	And *now* **already** also the axe is laid unto the root of the trees:
44	and they, presuming he is in the caravan, go a journey of a day; and they seek him among their kin and acquaintances:
45	and when they find him not they return to Yeru Shalem, seeking him.
46	And so be it, after three days, they find him in the priestal precinct sitting midst the doctors — both hearing them and asking them:
47	and all who hear him astound at his comprehension and answers.
48	And they see him and astonish: and his mother says to him, Child, why deal you thus with us? Behold, your father and I seek you grieving.
49	And he says to them, Why seek me? Know you not I must be about the business of my Father?
50	— and they comprehend not the rhema he speaks to them.
51	And he descends with them and they go to Nazareth; and he subjugates to them: and his mother thoroughly keeps all these rhemas in her heart:
52	and Yah Shua advances in wisdom and maturity and in charism with Elohim and humanity.

Yahn The Baptizer Fulfills/ Shalams Prophecy

3 Now in the fifteenth year
of the governing of Kaisar Tiberius,
Pontius Pilatos being governor of Yah Hudah,
and Herod tetrarch of Galiyl,
and his brother Phillipos tetrarch of Yetur
and of the region of Trachonitis,
and Lysanias the tetrarch of Abilene,

2 Hanan Yah and Caiaphas being the archpriests;
the rhema of Elohim
becomes to Yahn the son of Zechar
Yah in the wilderness:

3 and he goes to all the region around Yarden
preaching the baptism of repentance
for the forgiveness of sins

4 — as scribed in the scroll
of the words of Yesha Yah the prophet, wording,
The voice of one crying in the wilderness,
Prepare the way of Yah Veh,
make his paths straight.

5 Every valley *is* filled,
and every mountain and hill humbled; and the crooked
made into straight, and the jagged ways made smooth;

6 and all flesh sees the salvation of Elohim.
Yesha Yah 40:3—5

7 So he words to the multitude
who proceed to be baptized by him,
O progeny of vipers,
who exemplifies you to flee the wrath about to be?

8 So produce fruits worthy of repentance:
and begin not to word within yourselves,
We have Abraham to our father.
For I word to you,
that Elohim is able, from these stones,
to raise children to Abraham.

9 And also
the axe is already laid to the root of the trees:
so every tree *therefore*
which *bringeth* **produceth** not *forth* good fruit
is *hewn down* **exscinded**, and cast into the fire.

10 And the *people* **multitude**
asked him, *saying* **wording**,
So What shall we do *then*?

11 He answereth and *saith* **wordeth** unto them,
He that hath two *coats* **tunics**,
let him impart to him that hath none;
and he that hath *meat* **food**, let him do likewise.

12 *Then* **And** came also *publicans* **customs agents**
to be baptized,
and said unto him, *Master* **Doctor**, what shall we do?

13 And he said unto them,
Exact no more
than that which is *appointed* **ordained** you.

14 And the *soldiers* **warriors** likewise
demanded **asked** of him,
saying **wording**, And what shall we do?
And he said unto them,
Do violence to **Intimidate** no *man* **one**,
neither *accuse any falsely* **sycophant**;
and be *content* **satisfied** with your wages.

15 And as the people *were in expectation* **awaited**,
and all men *mused* **reasoned** in their hearts
of John **about Yahn**,
whether *lest ever* he *were* **be** the *Christ* **Messiah**, or not;

16 *John* **Yahn** answered, *saying*
wording unto them all,
I indeed baptize you *with* **in** water;
but one mightier than I cometh,
the latchet of whose shoes
I am not *worthy* **adequate** to unloose:
he shall baptize you *with the* **in** Holy
Spirit **Ruach ha-kodesh**
and *with* **in** fire:

17 Whose **winnowing** fan is in his hand,
and he *will* **shall** throughly purge his **threshing** floor,
and *will* **shall** gather the *wheat* **grain**
into his *garner* **granary**;
but the chaff he *will* **shall** burn with fire unquenchable.

18 And *many* **much** other *things* **indeed**
in his *exhortation* **beseeching**
preached **evangelized** he unto the people.

19 But Herod the tetrarch,
being *reproved* **rebuked** by him *for* **concerning** Herodias
his brother *Philip's wife* **Phillipos' woman**,
and *for* **concerning** all the evils which Herod had done,

20 Added yet this above all,
that he *shut up John* **locked Yahn**
in *prison* **the guardhouse**.

The Baptism Of Yah Shua

21 *Now* **And so be it,** when all
the people were baptized,
it came to pass,
that *Jesus* **Yah Shua** also being baptized, and praying,
the heaven was opened,

22 And the *Holy Spirit* **Ruach
ha-kodesh** descended
in a bodily *shape* **semblance** *like* **as** a dove upon him,

and a voice *came* **became** from heaven,
which *said* **worded**,
Thou art my beloved Son;
in thee I *am well pleased* **well—approve**.

THE GENEALOGY OF YAH SHUA

23   And *Jesus* **Yah Shua** himself
began to be about thirty years *of age*,
being (as was *supposed* **presumed**)
the son of *Joseph* **Yoseph**,
which was the son of *Heli* **of Eli**,

24   Which was the son of Matthat,
which was the son of Levi,
which was the son of *Melchi* **of Melech**,
which was the son of *Janna* **of Yanah**,
which was the son of *Joseph* **of Yoseph**,

25   Which was the son of
Mattathias **of Mattith Yah**,
which was the son of Amos,
which was the son of *Naum* **of Nachum**,
which was the son of Esli,
which was the son of *Nagge* **of Nogah**,

26   Which was the son of Maath,
which was the son of *Mattathias* **of Mattith Yah**,
which was the son of *Semei* **of Shimi**,
which was the son of *Joseph* **of Yoseph**,
so that every tree not producing good fruit
is exscinded, and cast into the fire.

10   And the multitude ask him, wording,
So what do we?

11   He answers them, wording,
Whoever has two tunics,
impart to him who has none:
and whoever has food, do likewise.

12   And customs agents also come to be baptized,
and say to him, Doctor, what do we?

13   And he says to them,
Exact no more than that ordained of you.

14   And the warriors likewise ask of him, wording,
And what do we?
And he says to them,
Intimidate no one! Sycophant not!
And be satisfied with your wages!

15   And as the people await
and all men reason in their hearts about Yahn
— lest ever he is the Messiah.

16   Yahn answers them all, wording,
I indeed baptize you in water;
but one mightier than I comes,
the latchet of whose shoes
I am not adequate to unloose:
he baptizes you in Holy Spirit and in fire:

17   whose winnowing fan is in his hand
and he throughly purges his threshing floor;
and gathers the grain into his granary;
but burns the chaff with fire unquenchable.

18   — and indeed, in his beseeching,
he evangelizes much other to the people.

19   And Herod the tetrarch,
being rebuked by him concerning Herodias
the woman of his brother Phillipos,
and concerning all the evils Herod did

20   still adds this above all:
he locks Yahn in the guardhouse.

THE BAPTISM OF YAH SHUA

21   And so be it, all the people are baptized,
and also Yah Shua, being baptized, prays;
and the heavens open,

22   and the Holy Spirit descends on him
in a bodily semblance as a dove;
and a voice becomes from the heavens, wording,
You are my beloved Son; in you I well—approve.

THE GENEALOGY OF YAH SHUA

23   And Yah Shua himself begins
to be about thirty years
— being, as is presumed:
the son of Yoseph,
of Eli,

24   of Matthat,
of Levi,
of Melech,
of Yanah,
of Yoseph,

25   of Mattith Yah,
of Amos,
of Nachum,
of Esli,
of Nogah,

26   of Maath,
of Mattith Yah,
of Shimi,
of Yoseph,
which was the son of *Juda* **of Yah Hudah**,

27   Which was the son of *Joanna* **of Yah Hanna**,
which was the son of *Rhesa* **of Rapha Yah**,
which was the son of *Zorobabel* **of Zerbub Babel**,
which was the son of *Salathiel* **of Shealti El**,
which was the son of *Neri* **of Neri Yah**,

28 Which was the son of Melchi **of Melech**,
which was the son of Addi,
which was the son of Cosam **of Qesem**,
which was the son of Elmodam **of Almodad**,
which was the son of Er,
29 Which was the son of Jose **of Yoses**,
which was the son of Eliezer **of Eli Ezer**,
which was the son of Jorim **of Yorim**,
which was the son of Matthat,
which was the son of Levi,
30 Which was the son of Simeon **of Shimon**,
which was the son of Juda **of Yah Hudah**,
which was the son of Joseph **of Yoseph**,
which was the son of Jonan,
which was the son of Eliakim **of El Yaqim**,
31 Which was the son of Melea,
which was the son of Menan **of Maina**,
which was the son of Mattatha,
which was the son of Nathan,
which was the son of David,
32 Which was the son of Jesse **of Yishay**,
which was the son of Obed,
which was the son of Booz,
which was the son of Salmon,
which was the son of Naasson **of Nachshon**,
33 Which was the son of Aminadab **of Ammi Nadab**,
which was the son of Aram **of Ram**,
which was the son of Esrom **of Hesron**,
which was the son of Phares **of Peres**,
which was the son of Juda **of Yah Hudah**,
34 Which was the son of Jacob **of Yaaqov**,
which was the son of Isaac **of Yischaq**,
which was the son of Abraham,
which was the son of Thara **of Terach**,
which was the son of Nachor,
35 Which was the son of Saruch **of Serug**, which was the son of Ragau **of Reu**, which was the son of Phalec **of Peleg**, which was the son of Heber **of Eber**, which was the son of Sala **of Shalach**,
36 Which was the son of Cainan **of Qeynan**,
which was the son of Arphaxad **of Arpachshad**,
which was the son of Sem **of Shem**,
which was the son of Noe **of Noach**,
which was the son of Lamech **of Lemech**,
37 Which was the son of Mathusala **of Methu Shelach**,
which was the son of Enoch **of Hanoch**,
which was the son of Jared **of Yered**,
which was the son of Maleleel **of Ma Halal El**,

which was the son of Cainan **of Qayin**,
38 Which was the son of Enos **of Enosh**,
which was the son of Seth **of Sheth**,
which was the son of Adam,
which was the son of God **of Elohim**.

THE TESTING OF YAH SHUA

4 And *Jesus* **Yah Shua**
being full of the *Holy Spirit* **Ruach ha-kodesh**
returned from *Jordan* **Yarden**,
and was led by the Spirit into the wilderness,
2 Being forty days *tempted* **tested** of the devil **Diabolos**.
And in those days he *did eat nothing* **ate naught**:
and when they were *ended* **complete**,
he afterward hungered.
3 And *the devil* **Diabolos** said unto him,
If thou be the Son of *God* **Elohim**,
command **say** this stone that it *be made* **become** bread.
4 And *Jesus* **Yah Shua** answered him, *saying* **wording**,
It is *written* **scribed**,
That *man* **humanity** shall not live by bread alone, but by every *word* **rhema** of *God* **Yah Veh**. Deuteronomy 8:3

of Yah Hudah,
27 of Yah Hanna,
of Rapha Yah,
of Zerbub Babel,
of Shealti El,
of Neri Yah,
28 of Melech,
of Addi,
of Qesem,
of Almodad,
of Er,
29 of Yoses,
of Eli Ezer, of Yorim, of Matthat, of Levi,
30 of Shimon,
of Yah Hudah,
of Yoseph,
of Jonan,
of El Yaqim,
31 of Melea,
of Maina,
of Mattatha,
of Nathan,
of David,
32 of Yishay,
of Obed,
of Booz,

of Salmon,
of Nachshon,
33 of Ammi Nadab,
of Ram,
of Hesron,
of Peres,
of Yah Hudah,
34 of Yaaqov, of Yischaq, of Abraham,
of Terach, of Nachor,
35 of Serug,
of Reu,
of Peleg,
of Eber,
of Shalach,
36 of Qeynan,
of Arpachshad,
of Shem,
of Noach,
of Lemech,
37 of Methu Shelach,
of Hanoch, of Yered,
of Ma Halal El,
of Qayin,
38 of Enosh,
of Sheth,
of Adam,
of Elohim.

The Testing Of Yah Shua

4 And Yah Shua, full of the Holy Spirit,
returns from Yarden
and is led in the Spirit into the wilderness;
2 being tested forty days by Diabolos:
and in those days he eats naught: and
after they complete, he famishes.
3 And Diabolos says to him,
If you are the Son of Elohim,
say that this stone become bread.
4 And Yah Shua answers him, wording,
It is scribed,
Humanity lives not by bread alone,
but by every rhema of Yah Veh.
Deuteronomy 8:3
5 And *the devil* **Diabolos**,
taking **bringing** him *up* into an high mountain,
shewed unto him
all the *kingdoms* **sovereigndoms** of the world
in a moment of time.
6 And *the devil* **Diabolos** said unto him,
All this *power will* **authority shall** I give thee,
and the glory of them:
for that is delivered unto me;
and to whomsoever I *will* **shall** I give it.
7 *If* **So whenever** thou *therefore*
wilt **shalt** worship *me* **in my sight**,
all shall be thine.
8 And *Jesus* **Yah Shua**
answered and said unto him,
Get thee behind me, Satan:
for it is *written* **scribed**,
Thou shalt worship *the Lord* **Yah Veh** thy *God* **Elohim**,
and him only shalt thou *serve* **liturgize**.
Deuteronomy 6:13, 10:20
9 And he brought him to *Jerusalem* **Yeru Shalem**,
and *set* **stood** him
on a *pinnacle* **wing** of the *temple* **priestal precinct**,
and said unto him,
If thou be the Son of *God* **Elohim**,
cast thyself *down* from hence:
10 For it is *written* **scribed**,
He shall *give* **misvah** his angels
charge over **concerning** thee,
to *keep* **thoroughly guard** thee:
11 And in their hands they shall *bear* **lift** thee *up*,
lest *at any time* **ever** thou dash thy foot against a stone.
Psalm 91:11, 12
12 And *Jesus* **Yah Shua** answering said unto him,
It is said,
Thou shalt not *tempt* **test** *the Lord* **Yah Veh**
thy *God* **Elohim**. Deuteronomy 6:16
13 And when *the devil* **Diabolos**
had *ended* **completed** all the *temptation* **testing**,
he departed from him for a season.

The Ministry Of Yah Shua

14 And *Jesus* **Yah Shua** returned
in the *power* **dynamis** of the Spirit into *Galilee* **Galiyl**:
and there went out a fame *of* **concerning** him
through all the region round about.
15 And he *taught* **doctrinated** in their synagogues,
being glorified of all.
16 And he came to Nazareth,
where he had been *brought up* **nurtured**:
and, as his custom was, he *went*
entered into the synagogue
on the *sabbath* day **of the shabbaths**,
and *stood up for* **rose** to read.
17 And there was *delivered* **given** unto him
the *book* **scroll** of the prophet *Esaias* **Yesha Yah**.
And when he had *opened* **unfurled** the *book* **scroll**,

he found the place where it was *written* **scribed**,
18 *The* Spirit of *the Lord* **Yah Veh** is upon me,
because he hath anointed me
to *preach the gospel to* **evangelize** the poor;
he hath *sent* **apostolized** me
to heal the *brokenhearted* **crushed in heart**,
to preach *deliverance* **forgiveness** to the captives,
and *recovering of* sight to the blind,
to set at liberty **apostolize** them that are *bruised* **crushed in forgiveness**,
19 To preach the acceptable
year of *the Lord* **Yah Veh**.
Yesha Yah 61:1, 2
20 And he *closed* **furled** the *book* **scroll**,
and he gave it *again* **back** to the *minister* **attendant**,
and sat down.
And the eyes of all them that were in the synagogue
were fastened on **stared at** him.
21 And he began to *say* **word** unto them,
This day is this scripture **fulfilled/shalamed** in your ears.
22 And all *bare him witness* **witnessed**,
and *wondered* **marvelled** at the
gracious words **of charism**
which proceeded out of his mouth.
And they *said* **worded**, Is not this *Joseph's* **Yoseph's** son?
23 And he said unto them,
5 And Diabolos brings him to a high mountain
and in a moment of time
shows him all the sovereigndoms of the world:
6 and Diabolos says to him,
I give you all this authority and all their glory
— for that is delivered to me
and to whomever I give it:
7 so whenever you worship in my sight,
all becomes yours.
8 And Yah Shua answers him, saying,
You, Go behind me, Satan:
for it is scribed,
Worship Yah Veh your Elohim;
and him only liturgize.
Deuteronomy 6:13, 10:20
9 And he brings him to Yeru Shalem
and stands him on a wing of the priestal precinct,
and says to him,
If you are the Son of Elohim
cast yourself from hence:
10 for it is scribed,
He misvahs his angels concerning you
to thoroughly guard you;

11 and they lift you in their hands
lest ever you dash your foot against a stone.
Psalm 91:11, 12
12 And Yah Shua answers him, saying,
It says,
Test not Yah Veh your Elohim.
Deuteronomy 6:16
13 — and Diabolos completes all the testing
and departs from him for a season.

The Ministry Of Yah Shua

14 And Yah Shua returns to Galiyl in the
dynamis of the Spirit: and a fame concerning
him goes all around the region:
15 and he doctrinates in their synagogues,
being glorified by all.
16 And he goes to Nazareth
where he was nurtured:
and as his custom,
he enters the synagogue on the day of the shabbaths
and rises to read:
17 and he is given the scroll
of the prophet Yesha Yah:
and he unfurls the scroll,
and finds the place where it is scribed,
18 Spirit of Yah Veh is upon me,
because he anoints me to evangelize the poor;
he apostolizes me to heal the crushed in heart;
to preach forgiveness to the captives
and sight to the blind;
to apostolize the crushed in forgiveness;
19 to preach the acceptable year of Yah Veh.
Yesha Yah 61:1, 2
20 And he furls the scroll,
and gives it to the attendant and sits:
and the eyes of all in the synagogue stare at him.
21 And he begins to word to them,
This day this scripture fulfills/shalams in your ears.
22 — and all witness and marvel
at the words of charism
which proceed from his mouth:
and they word, Is not this the son of Yoseph?
23 And he says to them,
Ye *will surely* **shall most certainly** say unto me
this *proverb* **parable**,
Physician **Healer**, *heal* **cure** thyself:
whatsoever **as much as** we have heard
done **become** in *Capernaum* **Kaphar Nachum**,
do also here in thy *country* **fatherland**.
24 And he said, *Verily I say*
Amen! I word unto you,

No prophet is *accepted* **acceptable**
in his own *country* **fatherland**.
25 But I *tell* **word** you of a truth,
many widows were in *Israel* **Yisra El**
in the days of *Elias* **Eli Yah**,
when the heaven was shut *up* three years and six months,
when *great* **mega** famine
was **became** throughout all the land;
26 But unto none of them was *Elias* **Eli Yah** sent,
save **except** unto *Sarepta* **Sarephath**, a city of
Sidon, unto a woman that was a widow.
27 And many lepers were in *Israel* **Yisra El**
in the time of Eliseus **with Eli Shua** the prophet;
and none of them was *cleansed* **purified**,
saving **except** Naaman the *Syrian* **Syriaiy**.
28 And all they in the synagogue,
when they heard these *things*,
were filled **full** with *wrath* **fury**,
29 And rose *up*, and *thrust* **cast** him out of the city,
and led him unto the brow of the *hill* **mountain**
whereon their city was built,
that they might cast him down *headlong*.
30 But he passing through the midst of them
went his way,
31 And came down to
Capernaum **Kaphar Nachum**,
a city of *Galilee* **Galiyl**,
and *taught* **doctrinated** them
on the *sabbath days* **shabbaths**.
32 And they *were* astonished at his doctrine:
for his word was *with power* **in authority**.

YAH SHUA ORDERS AN IMPURE DEMON

33 And in the synagogue there was a *man* **human**,
which had a spirit of an *unclean devil* **impure demon**,
and *cried out* **screamed** with a *loud* **mega** voice,
34 *saying* **wording**, Let us alone; **Aha!**
what have we to do with thee,
thou *Jesus of Nazareth* **Yah Shua — Nazarene**?
art thou come to destroy us?
I know thee who thou art; the Holy *One* of *God* **Elohim**.
35 And *Jesus* **Yah Shua** rebuked
him, *saying* **wording**,
Hold thy peace **Be muzzled**, and come out
of him. And when the *devil* **demon**
had *thrown* **tossed** him in the midst,
he came out of him, and hurt him not.
36 And **so be it,** they *were* all *amazed* **astonish**,
and *spake* **talked** among *themselves* **one another**,
saying **wording**, What a word is this!

for *with* **in** authority and *power* **dynamis**
he *commandeth* **ordereth** the *unclean* **impure** spirits,
and they come out.
37 And the *fame of* **echo concerning** him
went out **proceeded** into every place of
the *country* **region** round about.

YAH SHUA CURES THE MOTHER IN LAW OF SHIMON

38 And he arose out of the synagogue,
and entered into *Simon's* **Shimon's** house.
And *Simon's wife's* **Shimon's** mother **in law**
was *taken with* **overtaken by** a *great* **mega** fever;
and they *besought* **asked** him *for* **concerning** her.
39 And he stood over her, and rebuked the fever;
and it *left* **forsook** her:
and immediately she arose and ministered unto them.
40 *Now* **And** when the sun was *setting* **lowering**,
all *they that* — **as many as** had any *sick* **frail**
with divers diseases
brought them unto him;
and he *laid* **put** his hands on *every* **each** one of them,
and *healed* **cured** them.
41 And *devils* **demons** also came out of many,
crying out, and *saying* **wording**,
Thou art *Christ* **the Messiah** the Son of *God* **Elohim**.
Most certainly you say this parable to me,
Healer, cure yourself:
as much as we hear that became in Kaphar Nachum,
do also here in your fatherland.
24 And he says,
Amen! I word to you,
No prophet is acceptable in his own fatherland:
25 but of a truth, I word you,
many widows were in Yisra El in the days of Eli Yah
when the heavens shut for three years and six months,
when mega famine became throughout all the land:
26 and Eli Yah was sent to none of them
except to Sarephath of Sidon — to a widow woman:
27 and many lepers were in Yisra El
with Eli Shua the prophet;
and none of them was purified
except Naaman the Syriaiy.
28 And all in the synagogue hear these
and fill full with fury;
29 and they rise and cast him from the city
and lead him to the brow of the mountain
on which their city is built
— to cast him down:
30 and he passes through among them

and goes his way:
31 and goes down to Kaphar Nachum
a city of Galiyl,
and he doctrinates them on the shabbaths:
32 and they astonish at his doctrine:
for his word is in authority.

YAH SHUA ORDERS AN IMPURE DEMON

33 And in the synagogue there is a human
with a spirit of an impure demon;
screaming with a mega voice,
34 wording, Aha!
What have we to do with you,
Yah Shua — Nazarene?
Come you to destroy us?
I know you who you are — the Holy of Elohim.
35 And Yah Shua rebukes him, wording,
Muzzle! and, Come from him!
— and the demon, tossing him among them,
comes from him and hurts him not.
36 And so be it, all astonish
and they talk among one another,
wording, What a word this is!
For he orders the impure spirits
in authority and dynamis,
and out they come.
37 — and the echo concerning him
proceeds into every place all around the region.

YAH SHUA CURES THE MOTHER IN LAW OF SHIMON

38 And he rises from the synagogue
and enters the house of Shimon:
and the mother in law of Shimon
is overtaken by a mega fever;
and they ask him concerning her:
39 and he stands over her and rebukes the fever;
and it forsakes her:
and immediately she rises and ministers to them.
40 And as the sun lowers,
all — as many as have any frail with divers diseases
bring them to him;
and he puts his hands on each one of them
and cures them:
41 and demons also come from many
crying out and wording,
You are the Messiah the Son of Elohim.
And he rebuking them
suffered **allowed** them not to speak:
for they knew that he was *Christ* **the Messiah**.

42 And *when it was* **being** day,
he departed and went into a *desert* **desolate** place:
and the *people* **multitude** sought him,
and came unto him, and *stayed* **held** him,
that he should not depart from them.
43 And he said unto them,
I must *preach* **evangelize**
the *kingdom* **sovereigndom** of *God* **Elohim**
to other cities also:
for *therefore* **because of this** am I *sent* **apostolized**.
44 And he preached in the
synagogues of *Galilee* **Galiyl**.

THE FIRST DISCIPLES OF YAH SHUA

5 And *so be* it *came to pass*, that,
as the *people pressed* **multitude imposed** upon him
to hear the word of *God* **Elohim**,
he stood by the lake of *Gennesaret* **Kinneroth**,
2 And saw two *ships* **sailers** standing by the lake:
but the *fishermen* **fishers**
were gone out of **had turned from** them,
and were rinsing their nets.
3 And he *entered* **embarked**
into one of the *ships* **sailers**,
which was *Simon's* **Shimon's**,
and *prayed* **asked** him
that he *would thrust* **should launch**
out a little from the land.
And he sat *down*,
and *taught* **doctrinated** the *people* **multitude**
out of the *ship* **sailer**.
4 Now when he had *left* **paused** speaking,
he said unto *Simon* **Shimon**,
Launch out into the *deep* **depths**,
and *let down* **lower** your nets for a *draught* **catch**.
5 And *Simon* **Shimon** answering said unto him,
Master **Rabbi**,
we have *toiled* **laboured through** all the night,
and have taken *nothing* **naught**:
nevertheless at thy *word* **rhema**
I *will let down* **shall lower** the net.
6 And when they had this done,
they inclosed a *great* **vast** multitude of fishes:
and their net *brake* **ripped**.
7 And they *beckoned* **nodded** unto their partners,
which were in the other *ship* **sailer**,
that they should come and *help* **take** them.
And they came, and filled **full** both the *ships* **sailers**,
so that they began to sink.
8 When *Simon Peter* **Shimon Petros** saw it,

	he *fell down* **prostrated** at *Jesus'* **Yah Shua's** knees,
	saying **wording**, Depart from me;
	for I am a sinful man, O *Lord* **Adonay**.
9	For *he was astonished*
	astonishment enveloped him,
	and all that were with him,
	at the *draught* **catch** of the fishes which they had taken:
10	And *so was* **likewise** also
	James **Yaaqovos**, and *John* **Yahn**,
	the sons of *Zebedee* **Zabdi**,
	which were *partners* **partakers** with *Simon* **Shimon**.
	And *Jesus* **Yah Shua** said unto *Simon* **Shimon**,
	Fear **Awe** not;
	from *henceforth* **now on**
	thou shalt *catch men* **capture live humans**.
11	And when they had
	brought **moored** their *ships* **sailers** to land,
	they forsook all, and followed him.

YAH SHUA PURIFIES A LEPER

12	And **so be** it *came to pass*,
	when he was in a *certain* city, behold,
	a man full of leprosy:
	who seeing *Jesus* **Yah Shua** fell on his face,
	and *besought* **petitioned** him, *saying*, **wording**,
	Lord **Adonay**, *if* **whenever** thou *wilt* **willest**,
	thou canst *make* **purify** me *clean*.
13	And he *put forth* **spread** his
	hand, and touched him,
	saying, I will: be thou *clean* **purified**.
	And *immediately* **straightway** the
	leprosy departed from him.
	— and he rebukes them and allows them not to speak
	for they know he is the Messiah.
42	And being day;
	he departs and goes to a desolate place:
	and the multitude seeks him
	and comes to him and holds him
	that he not depart from them.
43	And he says to them,
	I must evangelize the sovereigndom of Elohim
	to other cities also:
	for because of this I am apostolized.
44	— and he preaches in the synagogues of Galiyl.

THE FIRST DISCIPLES OF YAH SHUA

5	And so be it,
	as the multitude imposes on him
	to hear the word of Elohim,
	he stands by the lake of Kinneroth
2	and sees two sailers standing by the lake:
	but the fishers had turned from them,
	rinsing their nets:
3	and he embarks into one of the sailers
	which is to Shimon,
	and asks him to launch out a little from the land:
	and he sits and doctrinates the multitude
	from the sailer.
4	And he pauses speaking, and says to Shimon,
	Launch out into the depths
	and lower your nets for a catch.
5	And Shimon answers him, saying,
	Rabbi, we labored all through the night,
	and took naught:
	nevertheless at your rhema, I lower the net.
6	And they do this,
	and enclose a vast multitude of fishes
	and their net rips:
7	and they nod to their
	partners in the other sailer,
	to come and take them:
	and they come, and fill full both the sailers
	so that they begin to sink.
8	And Shimon Petros sees
	and prostrates at the knees of Yah Shua, wording,
	Depart from me;
	for I am a sinful man, O Adonay.
9	— for astonishment envelopes him
	and all who are with him
	at the catch of the fishes they took:
10	and likewise also
	Yaaqovos and Yahn, the sons of Zabdi,
	who are partakers with Shimon.
	And Yah Shua says to Shimon, Awe not!
	From now on you capture live humans.
11	— and they moore their sailers to land;
	and forsake all and follow him.

YAH SHUA PURIFIES A LEPER

12	And so be it, he is in a city, and behold,
	a man full of leprosy sees Yah Shua
	and falls on his face and petitions him,
	wording, Adonay,
	whenever you will, you can purify me.
13	And he spreads his hand, and touches him,
	saying, I will: Purify!
	— and straightway the leprosy departs from him.
14	And he *charged* **evangelized** him
	to *tell* **say to** no *man* **one**:
	but go, and shew thyself to the priest,

and offer for thy *cleansing* **purifying**,
according **exactly** as *Moses commanded* **Mosheh ordered**,
for a *testimony* **witness** unto them.
15 But so much the more
went there a fame abroad of him **word about him passed through**:
and *great* **vast** multitudes came together to hear,
and to be *healed* **cured** by him
of their *infirmities* **frailties**.
16 And he withdrew himself into the wilderness,
and prayed.

Yah Shua Heals A Paralytic

17 And **so be** it *came to pass on a certain* **one** day,
as he was *teaching* **doctrinating**,
that there were Pharisees and doctors of the *law* **torah**
sitting *by*,
which were come out
of every *town* **village** of *Galilee* **Galiyl**,
and *Judaea* **Yah Hudah**, and *Jerusalem* **Yeru Shalem**:
and the *power* **dynamis** of *the Lord* **Adonay**
was *present* to heal them.
18 And, behold, men brought in a bed
a *man* **human** which was *taken with a palsy* **a paralytic**:
and they sought *means* to bring him in,
and to *lay* **place** him *before him* **in his sight**.
19 And when they could not find
by **through** what way they might bring him in
because of the multitude,
they *went up* **ascended** on the housetop,
and let him down through the tiling
with his *couch* **recliner**
into the midst *before Jesus* **in front of Yah Shua**.
20 And when he saw their *faith*
trust, he said unto him,
man **human**, thy sins are forgiven thee.
21 And the scribes and the
Pharisees began to reason,
saying **wording**,
Who is this which speaketh blasphemies?
Who can forgive sins, *but God* **except Elohim** alone?
22 But *when Jesus* **Yah Shua**,
perceived **knowing** their *thoughts* **reasonings**,
he answering said unto them,
What reason ye in your hearts?
23 Whether is easier, to say,
Thy sins be forgiven thee;
or to say, Rise *up* and walk?
24 But that ye may know that
the Son of *man* **humanity**
hath *power* **authority** upon earth to forgive sins,
(he said unto the *sick of the palsy* **a paralytic**,)
I *say* **word** unto thee, Arise,
and take *up* thy *couch* **recliner**, and go into thine house.
25 And immediately he rose *up*
before them **in their sight**,
and took *up* that whereon he lay,
and departed to his own house, glorifying *God* **Elohim**.
26 And they were all *amazed*
overtaken by ecstasis,
and they glorified *God* **Elohim**,
and were filled **full** with *fear* **awe**, *saying* **wording**,
We have seen *strange things* **paradoxes** to day.

Yah Shua Calls Levi

27 And after these *things* he went *forth*,
and saw a *publican* **customs agent**, named Levi,
sitting at the *receipt of custom* **customs**:
and he said unto him, Follow me.
28 And he left all, rose *up*, and followed him.
29 And Levi made him a *great* **mega** feast
in his own house:
and there was a *great company* **vast multitude**
of *publicans* **customs agents** and of others
that *sat down* **reposed** with them.
30 But **And** their scribes and Pharisees
murmured against his disciples, *saying*
wording, Why do ye eat and drink
with *publicans* **customs agents** and sinners?
31 And *Jesus* **Yah Shua** answering said unto them,
They that are whole need not a *physician* **healer**;
but they that are *sick* **ill**.
32 I came not to call the *righteous* **just**,
but sinners to repentance.
14 And he evangelizes him to say to no one:
But go and show yourself to the priest;
and offer for your purifying
exactly as Mosheh ordered,
for a witness to them.
15 But so much the more,
word about him passes through:
and vast multitudes come together to hear
and to be cured by him of their frailties.
16 And he withdraws himself into the wilderness
and prays.

Yah Shua Heals A Paralytic

17 And so be it, one day as he doctrinates,
Pharisees and doctors of the torah sit
— who come from every village of Galiyl

and Yah Hudah and Yeru Shalem:
and the dynamis of Adonay is to heal them.
18 And behold,
men bring in a paralyzed human on a bed:
and they seek to bring him in,
and to place him in his sight:
19 and they cannot find the way to bring him in
because of the multitude;
and they ascend on the housetop
and let him down through the tiling with his recliner
midst them in front of Yah Shua.
20 And he sees their trust, and says to him,
Human, your sins are forgiven you.
21 And the scribes and the
Pharisees begin to reason,
wording, Who is this speaking blasphemies?
Who can forgive sins, except Elohim alone?
22 But Yah Shua, knowing their reasonings,
answers them, saying,
What reason you in your hearts?
23 Which is easier to say,
Your sins be forgiven you?
or to say, Rise and walk?
24 But so that you know that the Son of humanity
has authority on earth to forgive sins
— he says to the paralyzed,
I word to you, Rise!
And take your recliner, and go to your house!
25 — and immediately he rises in their sight
and takes that on which he lies
and departs to his own house, glorifying Elohim.
26 And ecstasis overtakes them;
and they glorify Elohim,
and fill full with awe, wording,
We see paradoxes today.

YAH SHUA CALLS LEVI

27 And after these,
he goes and sees a customs agent named Levi
sitting at the customs:
and he says to him, Follow me.
28 — and he leaves all, rises, and follows him.
29 And Levi makes him a mega feast
in his own house:
and there is a vast multitude
of customs agents and of others reposing with them.
30 And their scribes and Pharisees
murmur against his disciples, wording,
Why eat and drink with customs agents and sinners?
31 And Yah Shua answers them, saying,

They who are whole need not a healer;
but they who are ill.
32 I come not to call the just,
but sinners to repentance.

YAH SHUA ON FASTING

33 And they said unto him,
Why do the disciples of *John* **Yahn**
fast *often* **frequently**, and make *prayers* **petitions**,
and likewise *the disciples of* the Pharisees;
but thine eat and drink?
34 And he said unto them,
Can ye make the *children* **sons** of the bridechamber fast,
while the bridegroom is with them?
35 But the days *will* **shall** come,
when *ever* the bridegroom
shall be *taken away* **removed** from them,
and then shall they fast in those days.
36 And he *spake* **worded** also a parable unto them;
no *man* **one** putteth a *piece* **patch** of a new garment
upon an old;
if otherwise **but if not**,
then both the new *maketh a rent* **splitteth**,
and the *piece that was taken* **patch** out of the new
agreeth **symphonizeth** not with the old.
37 And no *man* **one** putteth new
wine into old *bottles* **skins**;
else **but if not**
the new wine *will* **shall** burst the *bottles* **skins**,
and *be spilled* **poureth**,
and the *bottles* **skins** shall *perish* **destruct**.
38 But new wine must be put
into new *bottles* **skins**;
and both are preserved.
39 No *man* **one** also having drunk old *wine*
straightway desireth **willeth** new:
for he *saith* **wordeth**, The old is *better* **useful**.

YAH SHUA, ADONAY OF THE SHABBATH

6 And **so be** it *came to pass*
on the second *sabbath after the first* **first shabbath**,
that he went through the *corn fields* **spores**;
and his disciples plucked the *ears of corn* **kernels**,
and did eat, rubbing them in their hands.
2 And *certain* **some** of the
Pharisees said unto them,
Why do ye that which is not *lawful* **allowed**
to do on the *sabbath days* **shabbaths**?
3 And *Jesus* **Yah Shua** answering them said,
Have ye not read so much as this, what David did,

	when himself *was an hungered* **famished**,
	and they which were with him;
4	How he *went* **entered** into
	the house of *God* **Elohim**,
	and did take and eat the *shewbread* **prothesis bread**,
	and gave also to them that were with him;
	which it is not *lawful* **allowed** to eat
	but **except** for the priests alone?
	1 Shemu El 21:6

Yah Shua Restores A Withered Hand

5	And he *said* **worded** unto them,
	That the Son of *man* **humanity**
	is *Lord* **Adonay** also of the *sabbath* **shabbath**.
6	And **so be** it *came to pass*
	also on another *sabbath* **shabbath**,
	that he entered into the synagogue
	and *taught* **doctrinated**:
	and there was a *man* **human** whose
	right hand was withered.
7	And the scribes and Pharisees
	watched **observed** him,
	whether he *would heal* **should cure**
	on the *sabbath day* **shabbath**;
	that they might find an accusation against him.
8	But he knew their *thoughts* **reasonings**,
	and said to the *man* **human**
	which had the withered hand,
	Rise *up*, and stand *forth* in the midst.
	And he arose and stood *forth*.
9	*Then* **So** said *Jesus* **Yah Shua** unto them,
	I *will* **shall** ask you one *thing*;
	Is it *lawful* **allowed** on the *sabbath days* **shabbaths**
	to do good, or to do evil?
	to save *life* **soul**, or to destroy *it*?
10	And looking round about upon them all,
	he said unto the *man* **human**,
	Stretch forth **Spread** thy hand.
	And he did *so* **thus**:
	and his hand was restored whole as the other.

Yah Shua On Fasting

33	And they say to him,
	Why fast the disciples of Yahn frequently
	and make petitions
	— and likewise the Pharisees;
	but yours eat and drink?
34	And he says to them,
	Can you make the sons of the bridechamber fast,
	while the bridegroom is with them?
35	But days come,
	whenever the bridegroom removes from them,
	and then they fast in those days.
36	And he also words them a parable;
	No one puts a patch of a new garment on an old;
	but if not, both split:
	and the patch of the new symphonizes not with the old.
37	And no one puts new wine in old skins;
	but if not, the new wine bursts the skins and pours,
	and the skins destruct.
38	But new wine must be put into new skins;
	and both are preserved.
39	Also no one who drinks the old wills the new:
	for, he words, The old is useful.

Yah Shua, Adonay Of The Shabbath

6	And so be it, on the second first shabbath,
	he goes through the spores;
	and his disciples pluck the kernels and eat
	rubbing them in their hands.
2	And some of the Pharisees say to them,
	Why do you what is not allowed to do
	on the shabbaths?
3	And Yah Shua answers them, saying,
	Read you not even this
	— what David and those with him did
	when he famished?
4	How he entered the house of Elohim
	and took and ate the prothesis bread;
	and also gave to them with him
	— which is not allowed to eat
	except for the priests alone?
	1 Shemu El 21:6

Yah Shua Restores A Withered Hand

5	And he words to them,
	The Son of humanity is also Adonay of the shabbath.
6	And so be it, also on another shabbath,
	he enters the synagogue and doctrinates:
	and there is a human with a withered right hand:
7	and the scribes and Pharisees observe him
	whether he cures on the shabbath
	— to find an accusation against him.
8	But he knows their reasonings,
	and says to the human with the withered hand,
	Rise, and stand in the midst.
	— and he rises and stands.
9	So Yah Shua says to them,
	I ask you one:
	Is it allowed on the shabbaths to do good?

	Or to do evil?
	To save soul? Or to destroy?
10	And looking all round on them all,
	he says to the human, Spread your hand.
	— and he does thus:
	and his hand restores whole as the other.
11	And they were filled **full**
	with *madness* **mindlessness**;
	and *communed* **talked thoroughly** one with another
	what they might do to *Jesus* **Yah Shua**.

Yah Shua Selects Twelve Apostles

12	And **so be** it *came to pass* in those days,
	that he went out into a mountain to pray,
	and continued all night in prayer to *God* **Elohim**.
13	And *when it was* **being** day,
	he called unto him his disciples:
	and of them he *chose* **selected** twelve,
	whom also he named apostles;
14	*Simon* **Shimon**, (whom he
	also named *Peter* **Petros**,)
	and *Andrew* **Andreas** his brother,
	James **Yaaqovos** and *John* **Yahn**,
	Philip **Phillipos** and *Bartholomew* **Bar Talmay**,
15	*Matthew* **Matthaios** and *Thomas* **Taom**,
	James **Yaaqovos** the son of *Alphaeus* **Heleph**,
	and *Simon* **Shimon** called *Zelotes* **the Zealot**,
16	And *Judas* **Yah Hudah** the
	brother of *James* **Yaaqovos**,
	and *Judas Iscariot* **Yah Hudah the urbanite**,
	which also *was* **became** the traitor.
17	And he *came down* **descended** with them,
	and stood *in the plain* **on a level place**,
	and the *company* **multitude** of his disciples,
	and a *great* **vast** multitude of people
	out of all *Judaea* **Yah Hudah** and
	Jerusalem **Yeru Shalem**,
	and from the sea coast of *Tyre* **Sor** and Sidon,
	which came to hear him,
	and to be healed of their diseases;
18	And they that were *vexed with*
	unclean **by impure** spirits:
	and they were *healed* **cured**.
19	And the whole multitude sought to touch him:
	for there went *virtue* **dynamis** out of him,
	and healed them all.

The Beatitudes

20	And he lifted *up* his eyes on his disciples,
	and *said* **worded**,
	Blessed, *be ye* **the** poor:
	for yours is the *kingdom* **sovereigndom** of *God* **Elohim**.
21	Blessed, *are ye* that *hunger* **famish** now:
	for ye shall be filled.
	Blessed, *are ye* that weep now: for ye shall laugh.
22	Blessed *are* ye,
	when **ever** *men* **humanity** shall hate you,
	and when **ever** they shall *separate* **set** you **apart**
	from their company,
	and shall reproach you, and cast out your name as evil,
	for the Son of *man's* **humanity's** sake.
23	*Rejoice* **Cheer** ye in that day, and leap for joy:
	for, behold, your reward is *great* **vast** in heaven:
	for in the like manner did their
	fathers unto the prophets.

The Woes

24	But woe unto you that are rich!
	for ye have received your consolation **in full**.
25	Woe unto you that are full!
	for ye shall *hunger* **famish**.
	Woe unto you that laugh now!
	for ye shall mourn and weep.
26	Woe unto you,
	when **ever** all *men* **humanity** shall *speak* **say** well of you!
	for *so* **in like manner**
	did their fathers to the *false* **pseudo** prophets.

Yah Shua On Loving Enemies

27	But I *say* **word** unto you which hear,
	Love your enemies,
	do *good* **well** to them which hate you,
28	*Bless* **Eulogize** them that curse you,
	and pray for them which *despitefully use* **threaten** you.
29	And unto him
	that *smiteth* **striketh** thee on the *one* cheek
	offer **present** also the other;
	and him that taketh away thy *cloak* **garment**
	forbid not *to take* thy *coat* **tunic** also.
30	Give to every man that asketh of thee;
	and of him that taketh away thy goods
	ask them **demand** not *again*.
31	And **exactly** as ye *would* **will**
	that *men* **humanity** should do to you,
	do ye also to them likewise.
32	For if ye love them which love you,
11	And they fill full with mindlessness;
	and talk thoroughly one with another
	of what to do to Yah Shua.

Yah Shua Selects Twelve Apostles

12 And so be it, in those days,
he goes to a mountain to pray,
and continues all night in prayer to Elohim.
13 And being day, he calls his disciples to him:
and he selects twelve of them
whom also he names apostles:
14 Shimon, whom he also named Petros
and Andreas his brother,
Yaaqovos and Yahn,
Phillipos and Bar Talmay,
15 Matthaios and Taom,
Yaaqovos of Heleph
and Shimon called the Zealot
16 and Yah Hudah of Yaaqovos and Yah Hudah
the urbanite — who also becomes traitor.
17 And he descends with them
and stands on a level place:
and the multitude of his disciples
and a vast multitude of people
from all Yah Hudah and Yeru Shalem
and from the sea coast of Sor and Sidon
come to hear him
and to be healed of their diseases:
18 and those vexed by impure spirits are cured:
19 and the whole multitude seeks to touch him:
for dynamis comes from him and heals them all.

The Beatitudes

20 And he lifts his eyes on his disciples, and words,
Blessed — the poor:
for yours is the sovereigndom of Elohim.
21 Blessed — who now famish: for you fill.
Blessed — who now weep: for you laugh.
22 Blessed — you, whenever humanity hates you
and whenever they set you apart and reproach
you and cast out your name as evil
for sake of the Son of humanity.
23 Cheer in that day and leap for joy!
For behold, your reward in the heavens is vast:
for in the like manner their fathers did to the prophets.

The Woes

24 But woe to you, the rich:
for you received your consolation in full;
25 woe to you the filled:
for you famish;
woe to you who now laugh:
for you mourn and weep;
26 woe to you
whenever all humanity says well of you:
for in like manner
their fathers did to the pseudo prophets.

Yah Shua On Loving Enemies

27 But I word to you who hear:
Love your enemies;
do well to them who hate you;
28 eulogize them who curse you;
and pray for them who threaten you;
29 and to whoever strikes you on the cheek,
present also the other:
and to whoever takes away your garment,
forbid not also your tunic;
30 give to everyone who asks of you;
and of him who takes away your goods
demand not;
31 and exactly as you will that humanity do to you,
do you also to them likewise.
32 For if you love them who love you,
what *thank have ye* **charism is yours**?
for sinners also love those that love them.
33 And *if* **whenever** ye do good to them
which do good to you,
what *thank have ye* **charism is yours**?
for sinners also do even the same.
34 And *if* **whenever** ye lend *to them*
of whom ye hope to *receive* **take**,
what *thank have ye* **charism is yours**?
for sinners also lend to sinners,
to *receive as much again* **take equal**.
35 But love ye your enemies,
and do good, and lend,
hoping for *nothing* **naught** again;
and your reward shall be *great* **vast**,
and ye shall be the *children* **sons** of *the Highest* **Elyon**:
for he is kind unto the *unthankful* **uneucharistic**
and to the evil.
36 So Be ye *therefore merciful* **compassionate**
exactly as your Father also is *merciful* **compassionate**.

Yah Shua On Judging Others

37 Judge not, and ye shall *not*
never no way be judged:
condemn not, and ye shall *not* **never**
no way be condemned:
forgive, and ye shall be forgiven:
38 Give, and it shall be given unto you;
good measure, *pressed down* **packed**,
and shaken *together*, and *running over* **overflowing**,

	shall men give into your bosom.
	For with the same measure that ye *mete withal* **measure**
	it shall be *measured* **remeasured** to you *again*.
39	And he *spake* **said** a parable unto them,
	Can the blind *lead* **guide** the blind?
	shall they not **indeed** both fall into the *ditch* **cistern**?
40	The disciple is not above his *master* **doctor**:
	but every one that is *perfect* **prepared**
	shall be as his *master* **doctor**.
41	And why *beholdest* **seest** thou the *mote* **twig**
	that is in thy brother's eye,
	but perceivest not the beam that is in thine own eye?
42	Either how canst thou *say* **word** to thy brother,
	Brother, *let* **allow** me
	pull **cast** out the *mote* **twig** that is in thine eye,
	when thou thyself
	beholdest **seest** not the beam that is in thine own eye?
	Thou hypocrite,
	cast out first the beam out of thine own eye,
	and then shalt thou see clearly
	to *pull* **cast** out the *mote* **twig** that is in thy brother's eye.

Yah Shua On Trees And Fruit

43	For a good tree
	bringeth **produceth** not *forth corrupt* **putrefied** fruit;
	neither doth a *corrupt* **putrefied** tree
	bring forth **produce** good fruit.
44	For *every* **each** tree is known by his own fruit.
	For of thorns men do not gather figs,
	nor of a *bramble bush* **brier** *gather* **dry** they grapes.
45	A good *man* **human**
	out of the good treasure of his heart
	bringeth forth **produceth** that which is good;
	and an evil *man* **human**
	out of the evil treasure of his heart
	bringeth forth **produceth** that which is evil:
	for of the **super** abundance of the heart
	his mouth speaketh.
46	And why call ye me, *Lord*
	Adonay, *Lord* **Adonay**,
	and do not *the things* **that** which I *say* **word**?

Yah Shua On Foundations

47	Whosoever cometh to me,
	and heareth my *sayings* **words**, and doeth them,
	I *will shew* **shall exemplify** you to whom he is like:
48	He is like a *man* **human** which built an house,
	and digged deep,
	and *laid* **placed** the foundation on a rock:
	and when the flood *arose* **became**,

	the stream *beat vehemently* **burst** upon that house,
	and could not shake it: for it was founded upon a rock.
49	But he that heareth, and doeth not,
	is like a *man* **human**
	that *without* **apart from** a foundation
	built an house upon the earth;
	what charism is yours?
	— for sinners also love those who love them:
33	and whenever you do good
	to them who do good to you,
	what charism is yours?
	— for even sinners also do the same:
34	and whenever you lend from
	whom you hope to take,
	what charism is yours?
	— for sinners also lend to sinners to take equal.
35	But love your enemies and do good and lend,
	hoping for naught again;
	and vast is your reward
	and you become the sons of Elyon:
	— for he is kind to the uneucharistic and to the evil.
36	So be compassionate
	exactly as your Father also is compassionate.

Yah Shua On Judging Others

37	Judge not; that you never no way be judged:
	condemn not; that you never no way be
	condemned: forgive; and be forgiven:
38	give; and be given:
	good measure, packed and shaken, and overflowing,
	men give into your bosom:
	for the measure you measure is remeasured to you.
39	And he says a parable to them,
	Can the blind guide the blind?
	Indeed fall they not both into the cistern?
40	The disciple is not above his doctor:
	but everyone who prepares is as his doctor.
41	And why see you the twig
	in the eye of your brother
	but perceive not the beam in your own eye?
42	Or, how can you word to your brother,
	Brother, allow me to cast out the twig in your eye
	when you yourself see not the beam in your own eye?
	Hypocrite!
	First cast the beam from your own eye;
	and then you see clearly
	to cast the twig in the eye of your brother.

Yah Shua On Trees And Fruit

43	For neither a good tree produces putrefied fruit;

LUKE/UR 6, 7

nor a putrefied tree produces good fruit:
44 for each tree is known by its own fruit.
For men neither gather figs of thorns,
nor dry grapes of a brier.
45 A good human
from the good treasure of his heart
produces good;
and an evil human
from the evil treasure of his heart
produces evil:
for his mouth speaks
from the super abundance of the heart.
46 And why call you me, Adonay, Adonay,
and do not what I word?

YAH SHUA ON FOUNDATIONS

47 Whoever comes to me
and hears my words and does them
— I exemplify you to whom he is likened:
48 he is likened to a human who builds a house
and digs deep and places the foundation on a rock:
and a flood becomes
and the stream bursts on that house
and cannot shake it for it is founded on a rock.
49 And whoever hears, and does not,
is likened to a human
who builds a house on the earth
apart from a foundation
against **upon** which the stream *did*
beat vehemently **burst**,
and *immediately* **straightway** it fell;
and the *ruin* **fragmentation** of that house
was great **became mega**.

YAH SHUA HEALS THE SERVANT OF THE CENTURION

7 *Now* **And** when he had
ended **fulfilled/shalamed** all his *sayings* **rhema**
in the *audience* **hearing** of the people,
he entered into *Capernaum* **Kaphar Nachum**.
2 And a *certain* centurion's servant, who
was *dear* **honourable** unto him, was
sick **ill**, and *ready* **about** to die.
3 And when he heard *of Jesus*
concerning Yah Shua,
he *sent* **apostolized** unto him
the elders of the *Jews* **Yah Hudiym**,
beseeching **asking** him
that he *would* **should** come and *heal* **save** his servant.

4 And when they came to *Jesus* **Yah Shua**,
they besought him *instantly* **diligently**, *saying* **wording**,
That he was worthy for whom he should *do* **cause** this:
5 For he loveth our *nation* **goyim**,
and he hath built us a synagogue.
6 Then *Jesus* **Yah Shua** went with them.
And when he was *now* **already** not far from the house,
the centurion sent friends to him,
saying **wording** unto him,
Lord **Adonay**, *trouble* **harass** not thyself
for I am not *worthy* **adequate**
that thou shouldest enter under my *roof* **thatch**:
7 *Wherefore* **So** neither *thought*
deemed I myself worthy
to come unto thee:
but say in a word, and my *servant* **lad** shall be healed.
8 For I also am a *man* **human**
set **ordained** under authority,
having under me *soldiers* **warriors**,
and I *say* **word** unto this one, Go, and he goeth;
and to another, Come, and he cometh;
and to my servant, Do this, and he doeth *it*.
9 When *Jesus* **Yah Shua** heard these *things*,
he marvelled at him,
and turned him about,
and said unto the *people* **multitude** that followed him,
I *say* **word** unto you,
I have not found so *great faith* **much trust**,
no, not **even** in *Israel* **Yisra El**.
10 And they that were sent, returning to the house,
found the servant whole that had been *sick* **frail**.

YAH SHUA RAISES THE SON OF A WIDOW

11 And *so be* it *came to pass the day after* **next**,
that he went into a city called Nain;
and *many* **enough** of his disciples went with him,
and much *people* **multitude**.
12 *Now* **And** when he
came nigh to **approached** the gate of the city, behold,
there was a dead man carried out,
the only **birthed** son of his mother,
and she was a widow:
and *much people* **sufficient multitude** of the city
was with her.
13 And when *the Lord* **Adonay** saw her,
he had *compassion* **a sympathetic spleen** on her,
and said unto her, Weep not.
14 And he came and touched the *bier* **coffin**:
and they that bare him stood *still*.
And he said, *Young man* **Youth**,

	I *say* **word** unto thee, Arise.
15	And he that was dead sat
	up, and began to speak.
	And he *delivered* **gave** him to his mother.
16	And *there came a fear on* **an awe overtook** all:
	and they glorified *God* **Elohim**, *saying* **wording**,
	That a *great* **mega** prophet is risen *up* among us;
	and, That *God* **Elohim** hath visited his people.
17	And this *rumour of* **word concerning** him
	went forth throughout all *Judaea* **Yah Hudah**,
	and throughout all the region round about.

BAPTIZER YAHN ENQUIRES OF YAH SHUA

18	And the disciples of *John* **Yahn**
	shewed **evangelized** him *of* **about** all these *things*.
19	And *John* **Yahn** calling unto
	him two of his disciples
	— upon which the stream bursts
	and straightway it falls;
	and the fragmentation of that house becomes mega.

YAH SHUA HEALS THE SERVANT OF THE CENTURION

7	And when he fulfills/shalams all his rhema
	in the hearing of the people,
	he enters Kaphar Nachum:
2	and a servant of a centurion
	who is honorable to him
	is ill and about to die:
3	and he hears concerning Yah Shua,
	and apostolizes the elders of the Yah Hudiym to him,
	asking him to come and save his servant.
4	And they come to Yah Shua,
	and beseech him diligently, wording,
	He is worthy, for whom you cause this:
5	for he loves our goyim and
	he built us a synagogue.
6	And Yah Shua goes with them:
	and when he is already not far from the house
	the centurion sends friends to him, wording to him,
	Adonay, harass not yourself
	for I am not adequate that you enter under my thatch:
7	so I deem myself not worthy
	to come to you:
	but say in a word, and my lad is healed.
8	— for I also am a human
	ordained under authority
	having warriors under me:
	and I word to this one, Go! — and he goes;
	and to another, Come! — and he comes;
	and to my servant, Do this! — and he does.

9	And Yah Shua hears these and marvels at him
	and turns around
	and says to the multitude following him,
	I word to you,
	I find not so much trust — not even in Yisra El.
10	— and they who were sent, return to the house
	and find the servant who had been frail, whole.

YAH SHUA RAISES THE SON OF A WIDOW

11	And so be it,
	next he goes to a city called Nain;
	and enough of his disciples and a vast multitude
	go with him:
12	and he approaches the gate of the city,
	and behold, a dead man being carried out
	— the only birthed son of his mother;
	and she is a widow:
	and a sufficient multitude of the city is with her.
13	And Adonay sees her,
	and has a sympathetic spleen on her,
	and says to her, Weep not!
14	— and he comes and touches the coffin
	and they who bear him stand.
	And he says, Youth, I word to you, Rise!
15	— and the dead sits, and begins to speak:
	and he gives him to his mother.
16	And awe overtakes them all:
	and they glorify Elohim, wording,
	A mega prophet rises among us!
	and, Elohim visits his people!
17	— and this word concerning him
	goes in all Yah Hudah
	and throughout the region all around.

BAPTIZER YAHN ENQUIRES OF YAH SHUA

18	And the disciples of Yahn
	evangelize him about all these.
19	And Yahn calls two of his disciples to him
	sent them to *Jesus* **Yah Shua**, *saying* **wording**,
	Art thou he that should come? or
	look **await** we *for* another?
20	When the men were come unto him, they said,
	John Baptist **Yahn the baptizer**
	hath *sent* **apostolized** us unto thee, *saying* **wording**,
	Art thou he that should come? or
	look **await** we *for* another?
21	And in that same hour he cured many
	of their *infirmities* **diseases** and *plagues* **scourges**,
	and of evil spirits;
	and unto many *that were* blind

he *gave sight* **granted charism to see**.
22 Then *Jesus* **Yah Shua** answering said unto them,
Go *your way*, and *tell John* **evangelize Yahn**
what *things* ye have seen and heard;
how that the blind see, the lame walk,
the lepers *are cleansed* **purified**, the *deaf* **mute** hear,
the dead *are* raised,
to **and** the poor *the gospel is preached* **evangelized**.
23 And blessed *is* he, whosoever
shall not be offended — **unless you
be scandalized** in me.
24 And when the *messengers* **angels** of *John* **Yahn**
were departed,
he began to *speak* **word** unto the *people* **multitude**
concerning *John* **Yahn**,
What went ye out into the wilderness for to see?
A reed shaken *with* **by** the wind?
25 But what went ye out for to see?
A *man* **human** clothed in *soft raiment*
effeminate garment?
Behold, they which are
gorgeously apparelled **gloriously garmented**,
and *live delicately* **indulgent**,
are in *kings' courts* **sovereign's palaces**.
26 But what went ye out for to see? A prophet?
Yea, I *say* **word** unto you,
and *much* **superabundantly** more than a prophet.
27 This is he, *of* **concerning**
whom it is *written* **scribed**,
Behold,
I *send* **apostolize** my *messenger* **angel**
before **in front of** thy face,
which shall prepare thy way *before* **in front of** thee.
28 For I *say* **word** unto you,
Among those that are *born* **birthed** of women
there is not a greater prophet
than *John* **Yahn** the *Baptist* **Baptizer**:
but he that is least
in the *kingdom* **sovereigndom** of *God* **Elohim**
is greater than he.
29 And all the people that heard him,
and the *publicans* **customs agents**, justified *God* **Elohim**,
being baptized with the baptism of *John* **Yahn**.
30 But the Pharisees and *lawyers* **torahists**
rejected **set aside** the counsel of *God* **Elohim**
against themselves,
being not baptized of him.
31 And *the Lord* **Adonay** said,
Whereunto then
shall I liken *the men* **humanity** of this generation?
and to what are they like?
32 They are like unto children
sitting in the *marketplace* **market**,
and calling one to another, and *saying* **wording**,
We have *piped* **fluted** unto you,
and ye have not danced;
we have *mourned* **lamented** to you,
and ye have not wept.
33 For *John* **Yahn** the *Baptist* **Baptizer** came
neither eating bread nor drinking wine;
and ye *say* **word**, He hath a *devil* **demon**.
34 The Son of *man* **humanity**
is come eating and drinking;
and ye *say* **word**, Behold,
a gluttonous *man* **human**, and a winebibber,
a friend of *publicans* **customs agents** and sinners!
35 But wisdom is justified of all her children.

A WOMAN SINNER ANOINTS YAH SHUA

36 And one of the Pharisees
desired **asked** him that he *would* **should** eat with him.
and sends them to Yah Shua, wording,
Are you he who comes? Or await we another?
20 And the men come to him, and say,
Yahn the baptizer apostolizes us to you, wording,
Are you he who comes? Or await we another?
21 — and in that same hour he cures many
of their diseases and of scourges and of evil spirits;
and to many blind he grants charism to see.
22 And Yah Shua answers them, saying,
Go, and evangelize Yahn what you see and hear:
the blind see; the lame walk;
the lepers purify; the mute hear;
the dead rise; and the poor *are* evangelized.
23 And blessed — he, whoever,
— unless you scandalize in me.
24 And the angels of Yahn depart,
and he begins to word to the multitude
concerning Yahn:
What went you out to the wilderness to see?
A reed shaken by the wind?
25 But what went you out to see?
A human clothed in effeminate garment?
Behold, the gloriously garmented and indulgent
are in palaces of sovereigns.
26 But what went you out to see? A prophet?
Yes, I word to you,
and superabundantly more than a prophet.
27 This is he, concerning whom it is scribed,
Behold, I apostolize my angel in front of your
face, to prepare your way in front of you.

28 For I word to you,
Among those birthed of women,
there is not a greater prophet than Yahn the Baptizer:
but the least in the sovereigndom of Elohim
is greater than he.
29 And all the people who hear him
and the customs agents justify Elohim,
being baptized with the baptism of Yahn:
30 but the Pharisees and torahists
set aside the counsel of Elohim against themselves
not being baptized by him.
31 And Adonay says,
So to what liken I humanity of this generation?
And to what liken they?
32 They are likened to children
sitting in the market
and calling one to another, and wording,
We flute to you, and you dance not;
we lament to you, and you weep not:
33 for Yahn the Baptizer comes,
neither eating bread nor drinking wine;
and you word, He has a demon:
34 the Son of humanity comes
eating and drinking;
and you word,
Behold, a human glutton and a winebibber
a friend of customs agents and sinners!
35 — and wisdom is justified of all her children.

A Woman Sinner Anoints Yah Shua

36 And one of the Pharisees
asks him to eat with him:
And he *went into* **entered** the Pharisee's house,
and *sat down to meat* **reclined**.
37 And, behold, a woman in
the city, which was a sinner,
when she knew that *Jesus* **Yah Shua**
sat at meat **reposed** in the Pharisee's house,
brought **provided** an alabaster *box* of *ointment* **myrrh**,
38 And stood at his feet behind him weeping,
and began to *wash* **moisten** his feet with tears,
and *did wipe* **squeezedried** them
with the hairs of her head,
and **ardently** kissed his feet,
and anointed them with the *ointment* **myrrh**.
39 *Now* **But** when the Pharisee
which had *bidden* **called** him
saw it,
he spake within himself, *saying* **wording**,
This *man*, if he were a prophet,
would **should** have known who
and what manner of woman this is that toucheth him:
for she is a sinner.

Yah Shua On Lenders

40 And *Jesus* **Yah Shua** answering said unto him,
Simon **Shimon**, I have somewhat to say unto
thee. And he saith, *Master* **Doctor**, say on.
41 There was a *certain creditor* **lender**
which had two debtors:
the one *owed* **was indebted**
five hundred *pence* **denarion**,
and the other fifty.
42 And when they had *nothing*
naught to *pay* **give back**,
he *frankly forgave* **granted** them both **charism**.
Tell me therefore **So say**,
which of them *will* **shall** love him most?
43 *Simon* **Shimon** answered and said,
I *suppose* **perceive** that he,
to whom he *forgave* **granted** most **charism**.
And he said unto him,
Thou hast *rightly* **straightforwardly** judged.
44 And he turned to the woman,
and said unto *Simon* **Shimon**,
Seest thou this woman?
I entered into thine house,
thou gavest me no water for my feet:
but she hath *washed* **moistened** my feet with tears,
and *wiped them* **squeezedried** with the hairs of her head.
45 Thou gavest me no kiss:
but this *woman* **one** since *the time I came in* **I entered**
hath not ceased to **ardently** kiss my feet.
46 My head with *olive* oil thou didst not anoint:
but this *woman* **one**
hath anointed my feet with *ointment* **myrrh**.
47 *Wherefore* **For this cause** I *say* **word** unto thee,
Her sins, which are many, are forgiven;
for she loved much:
but to whom little is forgiven, *the same* loveth little.
48 And he said unto her, Thy sins are forgiven.
49 And they that *sat at meat* **reposed** with him
began to *say* **word** within themselves,
Who is this that forgiveth sins also?
50 And he said to the woman,
Thy *faith* **trust** hath saved thee; go in *peace* **shalom**.
8 And **so be** it *came to pass*
afterward **in sequence**,
that he *went throughout* **passed through**
every city and village,

preaching and *shewing the glad tidings of* **evangelizing**
the *kingdom* **sovereigndom** of *God* **Elohim**:
and the twelve were with him,
2 And *certain* **some** women,
which had been *healed* **cured**
of evil spirits and *infirmities* **frailties**,
Mary **Miryam** called Magdalene,
out of whom went seven *devils* **demons**,
3 And *Joanna* **Yah Hanna**
the *wife* **woman** of Chuza
Herod's *steward* **manager**,
and *Susanna* **Shoshanna**, and many others,
which ministered unto him of their *substance* **holdings**.

Yah Shua On The Sporer

4 And when much *people* **multitude**
were gathered together,
and *were come* **journeyed** to him out of every city,
and he enters the house of the Pharisee and reclines:
37 and behold, a woman in the city — a sinner
knowing that Yah Shua reposes in the house of
the Pharisee: provides an alabaster of myrrh;
38 and stands at his feet behind him weeping
and begins to moisten his feet with tears;
and squeezedries them with the hairs of her head
and ardently kisses his feet
and anoints them with the myrrh.
39 But the Pharisee who called him, sees,
and speaks within himself, wording,
This — if he is a prophet,
knows who and what manner of woman this is
who touches him
— for she is a sinner.

Yah Shua On Lenders

40 And Yah Shua answers him, saying,
Shimon, I have somewhat to say to you.
And he says, Doctor, say on.
41 A lender has two debtors:
the one is indebted five hundred denarion
and the other fifty:
42 and they having naught to give
he grants them both charism.
So say, which of them loves him most?
43 Shimon answers, saying,
I perceive him to whom he granted most charism.
And he says to him,
You judge straightforwardly.
44 And he turns to the woman,
and says to Shimon,

See this woman?
I entered your house,
you gave me no water for my feet;
but she has moistens my feet with tears,
and squeezedries with the hairs of her head:
45 you gave me no kiss;
but this one — since I entered
ceases not to ardently kiss my feet:
46 you anointed not my head with olive oil;
but this one anoints my feet with myrrh:
47 for this cause, I word to you,
Her many sins are forgiven; for she loves much:
but to whom little is forgiven, loves little.
48 And he says to her, Your sins are forgiven.
49 — and they who repose with him begin to word
within themselves, Who is this who also forgives sins?
50 And he says to the woman,
Your trust saves you! Go in shalom!

8 And so be it, in sequence,
he passes through every city and village
preaching and evangelizing the sovereigndom of Elohim:
and the twelve are with him;
2 with some women
who were cured of evil spirits and frailties
— Miryam called Magdalene
from whom came seven demons,
3 and Yah Hanna the woman of Chuza
manager of Herod,
and Shoshanna, and many others
who ministered to him from their holdings.

Yah Shua On The Sporer

4 And a vast multitude gathers together,
and journeys to him from every city:
he *spake by* **said through** a parable:
5 A *sower* **sporer** went out to
sow **spore** his *seed* **sperma**:
and as he *sowed* **spored**, some
indeed fell by the way side;
and it was *trodden down* **trampled**,
and the *fowls* **flyers** of the *air* **heavens** devoured it.
6 And *some* **others** fell upon a rock;
and as soon as it *was sprung up* **sprouted**,
it withered *away*, because it *lacked* **had no** moisture.
7 And *some* **others** fell among thorns;
and the thorns *sprang up* **sprouted** with it, and choked it.
8 And other fell on good *ground* **earth**,
and *sprang up* **sprouted**
and *bare* **produced** fruit an hundredfold.
And when he had *said* **worded** these *things*,

he *cried* **voiced** out,
He that hath ears to hear, let him hear.
9 And his disciples asked him, *saying* **wording**,
What might this parable be?
10 And he said,
Unto you it is given to know the mysteries
of the *kingdom* **sovereigndom** of *God* **Elohim**:
but to *others* **the rest** in parables;
that seeing they might not see,
and hearing they might not *understand* **comprehend**.
11 Now the parable is this:
The *seed* **sperma** is the word of *God* **Elohim**.
12 Those by the way side are they that hear;
then cometh *the devil* **Diabolos**,
and taketh away the word out of their hearts,
lest they should *believe* **trust** and be saved.
13 They on the rock *are they*,
which, when *ever* they hear,
receive the word with *joy* **cheer**;
and these have no root,
which for a *while believe* **season trust**,
and in *time* **season** of *temptation* **testing** fall away.
14 And that which fell among thorns are they,
which, when they have heard, go forth,
and are *choked* **strangled**
with cares **by anxieties** and riches and pleasures
of *this life* **existence**,
and bring no fruit to *perfection* **completion/shalom**.
15 *But* **And** that on the *good*
ground **beautiful earth** are they,
which in *an honest* **a beautiful** and good heart,
having heard the word, *keep it* **hold on**,
and *bring forth* **bear** fruit *with patience* **by endurance**.

Yah Shua On Candles

16 No *man* **one**, when he hath lighted a candle,
covereth **veileth** it with a vessel,
or putteth it under a bed;
but *setteth* **putteth** it on a *candlestick* **menorah**,
that they which enter in may see the light.
17 For *nothing* **naught** is *secret* **secreted**,
that shall not be *made* manifest;
neither *any thing hid* **secreted**,
that shall not be known
and *come abroad* **be manifest**.
18 *Take heed therefore* **So see** how ye hear:
for whosoever hath, to him shall be given;
and whosoever hath not, from him shall be taken
even that which he *seemeth to have* **thinketh he hath**.
19 *Then* **And** came to him his
mother and his brethren,
and could not *come* **get** at him for the *press* **multitude**.
20 And it was *told* **evangelized** him
by certain which said **wording**,
Thy mother and thy brethren stand without,
desiring **willing** to see thee.
21 And he answered and said unto them,
My mother and my brethren
are these which hear the word of *God* **Elohim**, and do it.

Yah Shua Rebukes The Wind

22 *Now it came to pass on a*
certain **And so be it one** day,
that he *went* **embarked** into a *ship* **sailer**
with his disciples:
and he said unto them, Let us *go over* **pass through**
unto the other side of the lake.
And they *launched forth* **embarked**.
23 But as they sailed he fell asleep:
and through a parable, he says,
5 A sporer goes to spore his sperma:
and as he spores
some indeed falls by the way side and it is trampled;
and the flyers of the heavens devour it:
6 and others fall on a rock;
and as soon as it sprouts
it withers because it has no moisture:
7 and others fall among thorns;
and the thorns sprout with it, and choke it:
8 and others fall on good earth;
and sprout and produce fruit a hundredfold.
— and he words these and voices out,
Whoever has ears to hear, hear!
9 And his disciples ask him, wording,
What is this parable?
10 And he says,
To you it is given to know the mysteries
of the sovereigndom of Elohim:
but to the rest in parables;
that seeing, they see not,
and hearing, they comprehend not.
11 Now this is the parable:
The sperma is the word of Elohim;
12 those by the way side are they who hear;
then Diabolos comes
and takes the word from their hearts,
lest they trust and be saved.
13 They on the rock, who, whenever they hear,
receive the word with cheer;
and they have no root
— who for a season trust

14 And that falling among thorns
are they who hear and go;
and are strangled by anxieties
and riches and pleasures of existence
and bring no fruit to completion/shalom.
15 And that on the beautiful earth
are they who, in a beautiful and good heart,
hear the word, hold on, and bear fruit by endurance.

Yah Shua On Candles

16 No one lights a candle and veils it with a vessel,
or puts it under a bed;
but puts it on a menorah,
that whoever enters sees the light.
17 For naught is secreted,
that becomes not manifest;
and naught is secreted,
that is not known and manifest.
18 So see how you hear:
for whoever has, to him is given;
and whoever has not, from him is taken
even what he thinks he has.
19 And his mother and his brothers come to him,
and cannot get at him for the multitude.
20 And they evangelize him, wording,
Your mother and your brothers stand outside;
they will to see you.
21 And he answers them, saying,
My mother and my brothers
are these who hear the word of Elohim, and do it.

Yah Shua Rebukes The Wind

22 And so be it, one day,
he embarks in a sailer with his disciples:
and he says to them,
Pass through across the lake.
— and they embark.
23 And as they sail he falls asleep:
and there *came down* **descended**
a *storm of wind* **whirlwind** on the lake;
and they were filled **full** with water,
and were in *jeopardy* **peril**.
24 And they came to him, and *awoke* **roused** him,
saying **wording**, *Master, master* **Rabbi, rabbi**,
we *perish* **destruct**.
Then he arose,
and rebuked the wind and the
raging **surging** of the water:
and they *ceased* **paused**, and there *was* **became** a calm.
25 And he said unto them,
Where is your *faith* **trust**?
And they *being afraid wondered* **awing, marvelled**,
saying **wording** one to another,
What manner of man **Who then** is this!
for he *commandeth* **ordereth** even the winds and water,
and they obey him.

Yah Shua Evangelizes Impure Spirits

26 And they *arrived* **sailed**
at **down to** the *country* **region** of the Gadarenes,
which is *over against Galilee* **opposite Galiyl**.
27 And when he went forth to land,
there met him out of the city a *certain* man,
which had *devils long* **demons enough** time,
and *ware no clothes* **not clothed in a garment**,
neither abode in any house, but in the tombs.
28 When he saw *Jesus* **Yah
Shua**, he *cried out* **screamed**,
and *fell down before* **prostrated in front of** him,
and with a *loud* **mega** voice said,
What have I to do with thee, *Jesus* **Yah Shua**,
thou Son of *God most high* **El Elyon**?
I *beseech* **petition** thee, *torment* **torture** me not.
29 (For he had *commanded* **evangelized**
the *unclean* **impure** spirit to come
out of the *man* **human**.
For oftentimes it had caught him:
and he was *kept* **guarded**
bound with *chains* **fetters** and in *fetters* **shackles**;
and he *brake* **ripped** the *bands* **bonds**,
and was driven of the *devil* **demon** into the wilderness.)
30 And *Jesus* **Yah Shua** asked him, *saying* **wording**,
What is thy name?
And he said, Legion:
because many *devils* **demons** were entered into him.
31 And they besought him
that he *would* **should** not *command* **order** them
to go out into the *deep* **abyss**.
32 And there was there *an herd*
a drove of *many* **ample** swine
feeding **grazing** on the mountain:
and they besought him
that he *would suffer* **should allow**
them to enter into them.
And he *suffered* **allowed** them.
33 *Then* **And** went the *devils*
demons out of the *man* **human**,
and entered into the swine:
and the *herd* **drove** ran violently down a *steep place* **cliff**

	into the lake, and were choked.	29	— for he had evangelized
34	When they that *fed* **grazed** them		the impure spirit to come from the human:
	saw what *was done* **had become**,		for oftentimes it catches him:
	they fled, and went and *told* **evangelized** it		and they guard him,
	in the city and in the *country* **field**.		bind with fetters and in shackles;
35	Then they went out to see		and he rips the bonds,
	what *was done* **had become**;		and the demon drives him into the wilderness.
	and came to *Jesus* **Yah Shua**,	30	And Yah Shua asks him, wording,
	and found the *man* **human**,		What is your name?
	out of whom the *devils* **demons** were departed,		And he says, Legion!
	sitting at the feet of *Jesus* **Yah Shua**,		— because many demons entered him:
	clothed, and *in his right mind* **sound minded**:	31	and they beseech him
	and they were *afraid* **awestricken**.		to not order them to go into the abyss.
36	They also which saw it *told* **evangelized** them	32	And there is an ample drove of swine
	by what means **how**		grazing on the mountain:
	he that was *possessed of the devils* **demonized**		and they beseech him to allow them to enter them.
	was *healed* **saved**.		— and he allows them.
37	*Then* **And** the whole multitude	33	And the demons come from the human
	of the *country* **region** of the Gadarenes round about		and enter the swine:
	besought **asked** him to depart from them;		and violently the drove runs down a cliff into the lake
	for they were *taken* **held** with *great fear* **mega awe**:		and choke.
	and he *went up* **embarked** into the *ship* **sailer**,	34	And they who graze them see what becomes,
	and returned *back again*.		and they flee,
	and a whirlwind descends on the lake		and go and evangelize in the city and in the field.
	and they fill full and *are* in peril:	35	And they go to see what became;
24	and they come to him, and rouse him, wording,		and come to Yah Shua
	Rabbi! Rabbi! We destruct!		and find the human from whom the demons departed
	And he rises,		sitting at the feet of Yah Shua,
	and rebukes the wind and the surging of the water:		clothed, and sound minded:
	and they pause, and a calm beomes:		and they are awestricken:
25	and he says to them, Where is your trust?	36	and they who see
	And awing, they marvel, wording one to another,		also evangelize them how the demonized was saved.
	Who then is this?	37	And the whole multitude
	Who even orders the winds and water		around the region of the Gadarenes
	and they obey him?		ask him to depart from them;
			for they are held with mega awe:
	YAH SHUA EVANGELIZES IMPURE SPIRITS		and he embarks in the sailer and returns.
26	And they sail to the region of the Gadarenes	38	And the man
	opposite Galiyl:		out of whom the *devils* **demons** were departed
27	and he comes to land,		*besought* **petitioned** him that he might be with him:
	and a man from the city meets him		but *Jesus sent* **Yah Shua released** him *away*,
	who has demons time enough:		*saying* **wording**,
	he neither clothes in a garment,	39	Return to thine own house,
	nor abides in any house, but in the tombs:		and *shew how great things* **declare as much as**
28	and seeing Yah Shua, he screams,		*God* **Elohim** hath done unto thee.
	and prostrates in front of him:		And he went his way,
	and with a mega voice, says,		and *published* **preached** throughout the whole city
	What have I to do with you,		*how great things Jesus* **as much as Yah Shua**
	Yah Shua, you Son of El Elyon?		had done unto him.
	I petition you, torture me not.	40	And *so be* it *came to pass*, that,

when *Jesus* **Yah Shua** *was* returned,
the *people gladly* **multitude** received him:
for they were all *waiting for* **awaiting** him.

THE DYING DAUGHTER OF YAIR

41 And, behold, there came
a man named *Jairus* **Yair**,
and he was *a ruler* **an arch** of the synagogue:
and he fell down at *Jesus'* **Yah Shua's** feet,
and besought him
that he *would come into* **should enter** his house:

42 For he had one only *begotten* daughter,
about twelve years *of age*, and she *lay a* **was** dying.
But as he went
the *people thronged* **multitude strangled** him.

WOMAN TOUCHES YAH SHUA

43 And a woman
having *an issue* **a flux** of blood twelve years,
which had spent all her *living* **subsistence**
upon *physicians* **healers**,
neither could be *healed* **cured** of any,

44 Came behind him,
and touched the *border* **edge** of his garment:
and immediately her *issue* **flux** of blood *stanched* **stood**.

45 And *Jesus* **Yah Shua** said, Who touched me?
When all denied,
Peter **Petros** and they that were with him said,
Master **Rabbi**,
the multitude *throng* **hold** thee and press thee,
and *sayest* **wordest** thou, Who touched me?

46 And *Jesus* **Yah Shua** said,
Somebody **Someone** hath touched me:
for I *perceive* **know**
that *virtue* **dynamis** is gone out of me.

47 And when the woman saw that she was not hid,
she came trembling,
and *falling down before* **prostrating in front of** him,
she *declared* **evangelized** unto him
before **in sight of** all the people
for what cause she had touched him,
and how she was healed immediately.

48 And he said unto her, Daughter,
be of good comfort **Courage**:
thy *faith* **trust** hath *made* **saved** thee *whole*;
go in *peace* **shalom**.

THE DAUGHTER OF YAIR DIES

49 While he yet spake, there cometh one
from the *ruler of the synagogue's house* **synagogue arch**,
saying **wording** to him, Thy daughter is dead;
trouble **harass** not the *Master* **Doctor**.

50 But when *Jesus* **Yah Shua** heard *it*,
he answered him, *saying* **wording**, *Fear* **Awe** not:
believe **trust** only, and she shall be *made whole* **saved**.

51 And when he *came* **entered** into the house,
he *suffered* **allowed** no *man* **one** to *go in* **enter**,
save *Peter* **except Petros**, and *James*
Yaaqovos, and *John* **Yahn**,
and the father and the mother of the *maiden* **lass**.

52 And all wept, and *bewailed* **chopped over** her:
but he said, Weep not; she is not dead, but sleepeth.

53 And they *laughed* **ridiculed** him *to scorn*,
knowing that she was dead.

YAH SHUA RAISES THE DAUGHTER OF YAIR

54 And he *put* **cast** them all out,
and *took* **overpowered** her by the hand,
and *called* **voiced out**, *saying* **wording**, *Maid* **Lass**, arise.

55 And her spirit *came again* **returned**,
and she arose straightway:
and he *commanded* **ordained** to give her *meat* **eats**.

38 And the man from whom the demons departed
petitions him to be with him:
and Yah Shua releases him, wording,

39 Return to your own house,
and declare as much as Elohim did to you.
— and he goes his way
and preaches throughout the whole city
as much as Yah Shua did to him.

40 And so be it, as Yah Shua returns,
the multitude receives him:
for they all await him.

THE DYING DAUGHTER OF YAIR

41 And behold, a man named Yair comes;
and he is an arch of the synagogue:
and he falls down at the feet of Yah Shua
and beseeches him to enter his house:

42 for he has one only daughter
about twelve years and she is dying:
but as he goes, the multitude strangles him.

WOMAN TOUCHES YAH SHUA

43 And a woman having a
flux of blood twelve years;
who spent all her subsistence on healers
and could not be cured by any,

44 comes behind him
and touches the edge of his garment:

	and immediately her flux of blood stands.
45	And Yah Shua says, Who touched me?
	When all deny,
	Petros and those with him say, Rabbi,
	the multitude holds you and presses you
	— and word you, Who touched me?
46	And Yah Shua says, Someone touched me:
	for I know dynamis is gone from me.
47	And the woman, seeing she is not hid,
	comes trembling and prostrates in front of him;
	she evangelizes to him in sight of all the people
	why she touched him
	and how she is immediately healed.
48	And he says to her, Daughter, Courage!
	Your trust saves you! Go in shalom!

The Daughter Of Yair Dies

49	While he yet speaks,
	someone comes from the synagogue arch,
	wording to him, Your daughter is dead;
	harass not the Doctor.
50	But Yah Shua hears,
	and answers him, wording, Awe not!
	Only trust, and she is saved!
51	And he enters the house,
	and allows no one to enter
	except Petros and Yaaqovos and Yahn
	and the father and the mother of the lass:
52	and all weep and chop over her.
	But he says, Weep not! She is not dead, but sleeps!
53	— and they ridicule him, knowing she is dead.

Yah Shua Raises The Daughter Of Yair

54	And he casts them all out
	and overpowers her by the hand
	and voices out, wording, Lass, rise!
55	— and her spirit returns
	and straightway she rises.
	And he ordains to give her eats:
56	And her parents were *astonished* **astounded**:
	but he *charged* **evangelized** them
	that they should *tell* **say to** no *man* **one**
	what *was done* **had become**.

Yah Shua Apostolizes The Twelve

9	*Then* **And** he called his twelve disciples together,
	and gave them *power* **dynamis** and authority
	over all *devils* **demons**, and to cure diseases.
2	And he *sent* **apostolized** them

to preach the *kingdom* **sovereigndom** of *God* **Elohim**,
and to heal the *sick* **frail**.

3	And he said unto them,
	Take *nothing* **naught** for your journey,
	neither *staves* **rod**, nor *scrip* **wallet**,
	neither bread, neither *money* **silver**;
	neither have two *coats apiece* **tunics each**.
4	And whatsoever house ye enter into,
	there abide, and thence depart.
5	And *whosoever will* **as many**
	as ever not receive you,
	when ye go out of that city,
	shake off the very dust from your feet
	for a *testimony* **witness** against them.
6	And they departed,
	and *went* **passed** through the *towns* **villages**,
	preaching the gospel **evangelizing**,
	and healing every where.
7	Now Herod the tetrarch
	heard of all that *was done* **had become** by him:
	and he was **thoroughly** perplexed,
	because that it was *said* **worded** of some,
	that *John* **Yahn** was risen from the dead;
8	And of some, that *Elias* **Eli**
	Yah had *appeared*; **manifested**
	and of others,
	that one of the *old* **ancient** prophets was risen *again*.
9	And Herod said, *John* **Yahn** have I beheaded:
	but who is this, *of* **concerning** whom I hear such *things*?
	And he *desired* **sought** to see him.

Yah Shua Feeds Five Thousand

10	And the apostles, when they were returned,
	told **declared** to him *all that* **as much as** they had done.
	And he took them,
	and *went aside* **withdrew** privately
	into a *desert* **desolate** place
	belonging to the city called *Bethsaida* **Beth Sayad**.
11	And the *people* **multitude**,
	when they knew it, followed him:
	and he received them,
	and spake unto them
	of **concerning** the *kingdom*
	sovereigndom of *God* **Elohim**,
	and healed them that had need of *healing* **therapy**.
12	And when the day began to *wear away* **recline**,
	then **and** came the twelve, and said unto him,
	Send **Release** the multitude *away*,
	that they may go
	into the *towns* **villages** and *country* **fields** round about,

    and lodge, and *get victuals* **find food**:
for we are here in a *desert* **desolate** place.
13   But he said unto them, Give ye them to eat.
And they said,
We have no more but five *loaves* **breads** and two fishes;
except **unless** we should go
and buy *meat* **food** for all this people.
14   For they were about five thousand men.
And he said to his disciples,
Make **Have** them *sit down* **recline** by fifties
in a company.
15   And they did so, and *made*
had them all *sit down* **recline**.
16   *Then* **And** he took
the five *loaves* **breads** and the two fishes,
and looking *up* to heaven,
he *blessed* **eulogized** them, and brake,
and gave to the disciples to set *before* **by** the multitude.
17   And they did eat, and were all filled:
and there was taken *up*
of fragments that *remained* **superabounded** to them
twelve baskets.

The Profession Of Petros Of Yah Shua

18   And *so be* it *came to pass*,
as he was alone praying,
his disciples were with him:
56   and her parents are astounded:
but he evangelizes them to say to no one
what became.

Yah Shua Apostolizes The Twelve

9   And he calls his twelve disciples together
and gives them dynamis and authority over all demons,
and to cure diseases.
2   And he apostolizes them
to preach the sovereigndom of Elohim
and to heal the frail.
3   And he says to them,
Take naught for your journey
— neither rod nor wallet nor bread nor silver;
nor have two tunics each:
4   and whatever house you enter,
there abide and there depart:
5   and as many as ever receive you not
when you go from that city
shake off the very dust from your feet
for a witness against them.
6   — and they depart and pass through the villages
evangelizing and healing everywhere.

7   And Herod the tetrarch
hears of all that becomes by him
and he is thoroughly perplexed:
because some word that Yahn is risen from the dead;
8   and some, that Eli Yah is manifested;
and others, that one of the ancient prophets is risen.
9   And Herod says, Yahn I beheaded:
but who is this, concerning whom I hear such?
— and he seeks to see him.

Yah Shua Feeds Five Thousand

10   And the apostles return
and declare to him as much as they do.
And he takes them
and withdraws privately to a desolate place
belonging to the city called Beth Sayad.
11   And the multitude knows and follows him:
and he receives them and speaks to them
concerning the sovereigndom of Elohim;
and heals those in need of therapy.
12   And the day begins to recline,
and the twelve come to him and say,
Release the multitude
to go into the villages and around the fields
and lodge and find food:
for we are here in a desolate place.
13   But he says to them, You give them to eat.
And they say,
We have no more but five breads and two fishes
— unless we go and buy food for all this people.
14   — for they are about five thousand men.
And he says to his disciples,
Recline them by fifties in a company.
15   — and thus they do and recline them all.
16   And he takes the five breads and the two fishes
and looks to the heavens;
he eulogizes them and breaks;
and gives to the disciples to set by the multitude:
17   and they eat and all fill up:
and they take twelve baskets of the fragments
that superabound to them.

The Profession Of Petros Of Yah Shua

18   And so be it, as he is alone praying,
his disciples are with him:
and he asked them, *saying* **wording**,
Whom say the *people* **multitude** that I am?
19   They answering said, *John*
Yahn the *Baptist* **baptizer**;
but *some say* **others**, *Elias* **Eli Yah**;

and others *say*,
that one of the *old* **ancient** prophets is risen *again*.

20 He said unto them, But
whom *say* **word** ye that I am?
Peter **Petros** answering said,
The *Christ* **Messiah** of *God* **Elohim**.

21 And he straitly *charged* **admonished** them,
and *commanded* **evangelized** them
to *tell no man that thing* **say that to no one**;

22 Saying,
The Son of *man* **humanity** must
suffer *many things* **much**,
and be *rejected* **disapproved** of the elders
and *chief* **arch** priests and scribes,
and be *slain* **slaughtered**, and be raised the third day.

23 And he *said* **worded** to them all,
If any *man will* **one willeth to** come after me,
let him deny himself,
and take *up* his *cross* **stake** daily, and follow me.

24 For whosoever *will* **willeth to** save his *life* **soul**
shall lose it:
but whosoever *will* **shall** lose his *life* **soul** for my sake,
the same shall save it.

25 For what is a *man advantaged*
human benefited,
if he gain the whole *world* **cosmos**,
and lose himself, or be *cast away* **lost**?

26 For whosoever
shall be ashamed of me and of my words,
of him shall the Son of *man* **humanity** be ashamed,
when *ever* he shall come in his own glory,
and in his Father's, and of the holy angels.

27 But I *tell* **word to** you *of a truth* **truly**,
there be some standing here,
which shall *not* **never no way** taste of death,
till they see the *kingdom* **sovereigndom** of *God* **Elohim**.

THE METAMORPHOSIS OF YAH SHUA

28 And **so be** it *came to pass*
about *an* eight days after these *sayings* **words**,
he took *Peter* **Petros** and *John* **Yahn**
and *James* **Yaaqovos**,
and *went up* **ascended** into a mountain to pray.

29 And as he prayed,
the *fashion* **semblance** of his *countenance* **face**
was altered **became another**,
and his *raiment* **garment**
was white and *glistering* **effulgent**. see
Matthaios 17:2, Markos 9:2

30 And, behold, there talked with him two men,

which were *Moses* **Mosheh** and *Elias* **Eli Yah**:

31 Who appeared in glory,
and *spake* **worded** of his *decease* **exodus**
which he *should accomplish* **was about to fulfill/shalam**
at *Jerusalem* **Yeru Shalem**.

32 But *Peter* **Petros** and they that were with him
were *heavy* **burdened** with sleep:
and when they were **thoroughly** awake,
they saw his glory, and the two men that stood with him.

33 And **so be** it *came to pass*,
as they departed from him,
Peter **Petros** said unto *Jesus* **Yah Shua**,
Master **Rabbi**, it is good for us to be here:
and let us make three tabernacles;
one for thee,
and one for *Moses* **Mosheh**, and one for *Elias* **Eli Yah**:
not knowing what he *said* **worded**.

34 While he *thus spake* **worded these**,
there *came* **became** a cloud, and overshadowed them:
and they *feared* **awed** as they entered into the cloud.

35 And there *came* **became** a voice out of the cloud,
saying **wording**, This is my beloved Son: hear him.

36 And when the voice *was past* **had become**,
Jesus **Yah Shua** was found alone.
And they *kept it close* **hushed**,
and *told* **evangelized to** no *man* **one** in those days
any of those *things* which they had seen.

YAH SHUA REBUKES AN IMPURE SPIRIT

37 And **so be** it *came to pass*, that on the next day,
when they were come down from the *hill*
mountain, much *people* **multitude** met him.
and he asks them, wording,
Whom say the multitude me to be?

19 They answer, saying, Yahn the baptizer;
but others, Eli Yah;
and others, One of the ancient prophets is risen.

20 He says to them, But whom word you me to be?
Petros answers, saying, The Messiah of Elohim.

21 And he straitly admonishes them
and evangelizes them to say that to no one;

22 saying, The Son of humanity must suffer much,
and be disapproved by the elders
and archpriests and scribes;
and slaughtered; and the third day rise.

23 And he words to them all,
If anyone wills to come after me,
have him deny himself
and take his stake daily and follow me.

24 For whoever wills to save his soul, loses it:

and whoever loses his soul for my sake, saves it.
25 For what is a human benefited
having gained the whole cosmos
and lose himself — or be lost?
26 For whoever shames of me and of my words,
of him the Son of humanity shames
— whenever he comes in his own glory,
and of his Father, and of the holy angels.
27 But I word to you truly,
some standing here, never no way taste of death,
until they see the sovereigndom of Elohim.

The Metamorphosis Of Yah Shua

28 And so be it, about eight days after these words,
he takes Petros and Yahn and Yaaqovos
and ascends a mountain to pray:
29 and as he prays
the semblance of his face becomes another;
and his garment is white and effulgent:
see Matthaois 17:2, Markos 9:2
30 and behold, two men talk with him
— Mosheh and Eli Yah:
31 who appear in glory,
and word of the exodus
he is about to fulfill/shalam at Yeru Shalem.
32 But Petros and those with him
are burdened with sleep:
and when they thoroughly waken,
they see his glory and the two men standing with him.
33 And so be it, as they depart from him,
Petros says to Yah Shua,
Rabbi, it is good for us to be here:
and to make three tabernacles
— one for you
and one for Mosheh and one for Eli Yah.
— not knowing what he words.
34 And as he words these,
a cloud becomes and overshadows them:
and they awe as they enter the cloud:
35 and a voice becomes from the cloud, wording,
This is my beloved Son! Hear him!
36 And when this voice becomes,
Yah Shua is found alone:
and they hush and evangelize to no one in those days
any of what they saw.

Yah Shua Rebukes An Impure Spirit

37 And so be it, the next day,
they descend the mountain
and a vast multitude meets him.

38 And, behold, a man of the
company **multitude** cried out,
saying **wording**, *Master* **Doctor**, I *beseech* **petition** thee,
look upon my son: for he is mine only *child* **birthed**.
39 And, *lo* **behold**,
a spirit taketh him, and he suddenly crieth out;
and it *teareth* **convulseth** him
that he foameth again **with frothing**,
and *bruising* **crushing** him hardly departeth from him.
40 And I *besought* **petitioned** thy disciples
to cast him out; and they could not.
41 And *Jesus* **Yah Shua** answering said,
O *faithless* **trustless**
and *perverse* **thoroughly perverted** generation,
how long **until when** shall I be with you,
and *suffer* **tolerate** you?
Bring thy son hither.
42 And as he was yet a coming,
the *devil threw* **demon burst** him *down*,
and *tare* **convulsed** him.
And *Jesus* **Yah Shua** rebuked the *unclean* **impure** spirit,
and healed the *child* **lad**,
and *delivered* **gave** him *again* **back** to his father.
43 *And* **But** they were all *amazed* **astonished**
at the *mighty power* **majesty** of *God* **Elohim**.
But while they *wondered* **marvelled** every one
at all *things* which *Jesus* **Yah Shua** did,
he said unto his disciples,
44 *Let* **Place** these *sayings sink*
down **words** into your ears:
for the Son of *man* **humanity**
shall be delivered **is about to be betrayed**
into the hands of *men* **humanity**.
45 But they *understood* **knew**
not this *saying* **rhema**,
and it was hid from them, that they perceived it not:
and they *feared* **awed** to ask him *of*
about that *saying* **rhema**.

Being The Greatest

46 Then there *arose* **entered**
a reasoning among them,
which **ever** of them should be greatest.
47 And *Jesus* **Yah Shua**,
perceiving the *thought* **reasoning** of their heart,
took **hold of** a child, and *set* **stood** him by him,
48 And said unto them,
Whosoever shall receive this child in my name
receiveth me:
and whosoever shall receive me

	receiveth him that *sent* **apostolized** me: for he that is least among you all, the same shall be *great* **mega**.		the demon bursts him and convulses him: and Yah Shua rebukes the impure spirit and heals the lad and gives him back to his father.
49	And *John* **Yahn** answered and said, *Master* **Rabbi**, we saw one casting out *devils* **demons** in thy name; and we forbad him, because he followeth not with us.	43	— and they all astonish at the majesty of Elohim. And while everyone marvels at all that Yah Shua does, he say to his disciples,
50	And *Jesus* **Yah Shua** said unto him, Forbid him not: for he that is not against us is for us.	44	Place these words in your ears: for the Son of humanity is about to be betrayed into the hands of humanity.
	SHOMERONIYM RECEIVE NOT YAH SHUA	45	— but they know not this rhema, and it is hid from them, so that they perceive not: and they awe to ask him about that rhema.
51	And **so be** it *came to pass*, when the *time was come* **day fulfilled/shalamed** that he should be *received up* **taken**, he *stedfastly set* **established** his face to go to *Jerusalem* **Yeru Shalem**,		BEING THE GREATEST
52	And *sent messengers* **apostolized angels** *before* **in front of** his face: and they went, and entered into a village of the *Samaritans* **Shomeroniym** so as to *make ready* **prepare** for him.	46	But a reasoning enters among them, whoever of them is greatest.
		47	And Yah Shua, perceiving the reasoning of their heart, takes hold of a child and stands him by him,
53	And they did not receive him, because his face was as though he *would* **should** go to *Jerusalem* **Yeru Shalem**.	48	and says to them, Whoever receives this child in my name receives me: and whoever receives me receives him who apostolized me: for whoever is least among you all, the same becomes mega.
54	And when his disciples *James* **Yaaqovos** and *John* **Yahn** saw this, they said, *Lord* **Adonay**, *wilt* **willest** thou that we *command* **tell** fire to *come down* **descend** from heaven, and consume them, even as *Elias* **Eli Yah** did?	49	And Yahn answers, saying, Rabbi, we saw one casting out demons in your name; and we forbad him because he follows not with us.
55	But he turned, and rebuked them, and said, Ye know not what manner of spirit ye are of.	50	And Yah Shua says to him, Forbid him not: for whoever is not against us is for us.
56	For the Son of *man* **humanity** is not come to destroy *men's lives* **the souls of humanity**, but to save them. And they went to another village.		SHOMERONIYM RECEIVE NOT YAH SHUA
		51	And so be it, when the day fulfills/shalams to take him, he establishes his face to go to Yeru Shalem;
38	And behold, a man of the multitude cries out, wording, Doctor, I petition you; look upon my son; for he is my only birthed:	52	and apostolizes angels in front of his face: and they go and enter a village of the Shomeroniym so as to prepare for him:
39	and behold, a spirit takes him and he suddenly cries out; and it convulses him with frothing and crushes him hardly and departs from him:	53	and they receive him not, because his face is as though he goes to Yeru Shalem.
40	and I petitioned your disciples to cast him out; and they cannot.	54	And his disciples Yaaqovos and Yahn see this, and say, Adonay, will you that we tell fire to descend from the heavens, and consume them — even as Eli Yah did?
41	And Yah Shua answers, saying, O trustless and thoroughly perverted generation, until when am I with you, and tolerate you? Bring your son here.	55	But he turns and rebukes them, and says, You know not of what manner of spirit you are:
42	And as he is still coming,	56	for the Son of humanity comes not

to destroy the souls of humanity
but to save them.
— and they go to another village.

PRIORITIES

57 And *so be* it *came to pass*,
that, as they went in the way,
a certain man **one** said unto him, *Lord* **Adonay**,
I *will* **shall** follow thee whithersoever thou goest.
58 And *Jesus* **Yah Shua** said unto him,
Foxes have *holes* **burrows**,
and *birds* **flyers** of the *air* **heavens** have nests;
but the Son of *man* **humanity**
hath not where to *lay* **recline** his head.
59 And he said unto another, Follow me.
But he said, *Lord* **Adonay**,
suffer **allow** me first to go and *bury* **entomb** my father.
60 *Jesus* **Yah Shua** said unto him,
Let **Allow** the dead *bury* **to entomb** their dead:
but go thou and *preach* **evangelize**
the *kingdom* **sovereigndom** of *God* **Elohim**.
61 And another also said, *Lord* **Adonay**,
I *will* **shall** follow thee;
but *let* **allow** me first go bid them *farewell* **bye bye**,
which are at home at my house.
62 And *Jesus* **Yah Shua** said unto him, no *man* **one**,
having put his hand to the plough, and looking back,
is **well** fit for the *kingdom* **sovereigndom** of *God* **Elohim**.

YAH SHUA APOSTOLIZES THE SEVENTY:
THE FIRST EVANGELISTIC ADVANCE TEAM

10 **Now** After these *things*
the Lord appointed **Adonay designated**
other seventy also,
and *sent* **apostolized** them *two and two* **by twos**
before **in front of** his face into every city and place,
whither he himself *would* **was about to** come.
2 *Therefore said* **So worded** he unto them,
The harvest *truly* **indeed** is *great* **vast**,
but the *labourers are* **workers** few:
pray **so petition** ye therefore the
Lord **Adonay** of the harvest,
that he *would* **should**
send forth labourers **cast workers** into his harvest.
3 Go *your ways*: behold,
I *send* **apostolize** you *forth* as lambs among wolves.
4 *Carry* **Bear** neither *purse* **pouch**,
nor *scrip* **wallet**, nor shoes:
and salute no *man* **one** by the way.
5 And into whatsoever house ye enter,
first *say* **word**, *Peace be* **Shalom** to this house.
6 And *if* **whenever indeed** the
son of *peace* **shalom** be there,
your *peace* **shalom** shall *rest* **repose** upon it:
but if not, it shall *turn* **return** to you *again*.
7 And in the same house *remain* **abide**,
eating and drinking such *things* as they give:
for the *labourer* **worker** is worthy of his hire.
Go **Depart** not from house to house.
8 And into whatsoever city ye
enter, and they receive you,
eat such *things* as are set *before* **by** you:
9 And *heal* **cure** the *sick* **frail** that are therein,
and *say* **word** unto them,
The *kingdom* **sovereigndom** of *God* **Elohim**
is come nigh unto **approacheth** you.
10 But into whatsoever city ye enter,
and they receive you not,
go your ways out into the *streets* **broadways** of the same,
and say,
11 Even the very dust of your city,
which *cleaveth on* **adhereth to** us,
we *do wipe* **scrape** off against you:
notwithstanding be ye sure of **however know** this,
that the *kingdom* **sovereigndom** of *God* **Elohim**
is come nigh unto **hath approached** you.
12 *But* **And** I *say* **word** unto you,
that it shall be more tolerable in that day
for *Sodom* **Sedom**, than for that city.
13 Woe unto thee, Chorazin!
woe unto thee, *Bethsaida* **Beth Sayad**!
for if the *mighty works* **dynamis**
had *been done* **become** in *Tyre* **Sor** and Sidon,
which have *been done* **become** in you,
they had *a great while* **long** ago repented,
sitting in *sackcloth* **saq** and ashes.

PRIORITIES

57 And so be it, as they go in the way,
one says to him, Adonay,
I follow you wherever you go.
58 And Yah Shua says to him,
Foxes have burrows
and flyers of the heavens have nests;
but the Son of humanity
has nowhere to recline his head.
59 And he says to another, Follow me.
But he says, Adonay,
allow me first to go and entomb my father.
60 Yah Shua says to him,

Allow the dead to entomb their dead:
but you go
and evangelize the sovereigndom of Elohim.
61 And also another says, Adonay,
I follow you;
but allow me first go bid bye bye,
to them at home at my house.
62 And Yah Shua says to him,
No one, having put his hand on the plough,
and looking back,
is well fit for the sovereigndom of Elohim.

Yah Shua Apostolizes The Seventy: The First Evangelistic Advance Team

10 Now after these,
Adonay also designates seventy others;
and apostolizes them by twos in front of his face
to every city and place he is about to go:
2 so he words to them,
The harvest indeed is vast, but the workers few:
so petition Adonay of the harvest,
to cast forth workers into his harvest.
3 Go! Behold,
I apostolize you as lambs among wolves:
4 Bear neither pouch nor wallet nor shoes;
and salute no one by the way:
5 and whatever house you enter,
first word, Shalom to this house!
6 And indeed whenever the
son of shalom is there,
your shalom reposes thereon:
but if not, it returns to you:
7 and abide in the same house
eating and drinking such as they give:
for the worker is worthy of his hire:
depart not from house to house.
8 And whatever city you
enter, and they receive you,
eat such as is set by you:
9 and cure the frail therein,
and word to them,
The sovereigndom of Elohim approaches you.
10 But whatever city you enter
and they receive you not:
go your ways out into the broadways of the same,
and say,
11 Even the very dust of your
city which adheres to us
we scrape off against you:
however know this,
the sovereigndom of Elohim approached you:
12 and I word to you,
that in that day it becomes more tolerable for Sedom
than for that city.
13 Woe to you, Chorazin! Woe to you, Beth Sayad!
For if the dynamis that became in you
had become in Sor and Sidon,
they had long ago repented
— sitting in saq and ashes.
14 But it shall be more tolerable
for *Tyre* **Sor** and Sidon at the judgment, than for you.
15 And thou, *Capernaum* **Kaphar Nachum**,
which art exalted to heaven,
shalt be *thrust* **brought** down to *hell*
sheol/hades. Yesha Yah 14:12—15
16 He that heareth you heareth me;
and he that *despiseth* **setteth** you **aside**
despiseth **setteth** me **aside**;
and he that *despiseth* **setteth** me **aside**
despiseth **setteth aside** him that *sent* **apostolized** me.

The Seventy Report To Yah Shua

17 And the seventy returned again with *joy* **cheer**,
saying **wording**, *Lord* **Adonay**,
even the *devils are subject* **demons subjugate** unto us
through **by** thy name.
18 And he said unto them,
I *beheld* **observed** Satan as lightning fall from
heaven. Yahn 12:31, 32, Apocalypse 12:9
19 Behold, I give unto you *power* **authority**
to *tread* **trample** on serpents and scorpions,
and over all the *power* **dynamis** of the enemy:
and *nothing* **naught** shall *by any*
means hurt **no way injure** you.
20 *Notwithstanding* **However**
in this *rejoice* **cheer** not,
that the spirits *are subject* **subjugate**
unto you; but rather *rejoice* **cheer**,
because your names are *written* **scribed** in heaven.
21 In that hour
Jesus rejoiced **Yah Shua jumped for joy** in spirit,
and said, I *thank* **avow** thee, O Father,
Lord **Adonay** of heaven and earth,
that thou hast *hid* **secreted** these *things*
from the wise and *prudent* **comprehending**,
and hast *revealed* **unveiled** them unto babes:
even so **yea**, Father;
for *so* **thus** it *seemed good* **became well—approved**
in *thy sight* **front of thee**.
22 All *things* are delivered to me of my Father:

and no *man* **one** knoweth who the Son is,
but **except** the Father;
and who the Father is, *but* **except** the Son,
and he to *whom* **whomever**
the Son *will* **willeth** to *reveal* **unveil** him.
23 And he turned him unto his disciples,
and said privately,
Blessed are the eyes which see *the*
things **those** that ye see:
24 For I *tell* **word** *unto* you,
that many prophets and *kings* **sovereigns**
have *desired* **willed** to see those *things* which ye see,
and have not seen *them*;
and to hear those *things* which ye hear,
and have not heard *them*.

Yah Shua On True Neighbourship

25 And, behold, a *certain lawyer*
stood up **torahist rose**,
and *tempted* **tested** him, *saying* **wording**, *Master*
Doctor, what shall I do to inherit eternal life?
26 He said unto him,
What is *written* **scribed** in the *law*
torah? how readest thou?
27 And he answering said,
Thou shalt love *the Lord* **Yah Veh** thy *God* **Elohim**
with all thy heart, and with all thy soul,
and with all thy *strength* **might**, and with all thy mind;
and thy neighbour as thyself.
28 And he said unto him,
Thou hast answered *right* **straightforwardly**:
this do, and thou shalt live.
29 But he, *willing* **having willed** to justify himself,
said unto *Jesus* **Yah Shua**, And who is my neighbour?
30 And *Jesus answering* **Yah Shua perceiving** said,
A *certain man went down* **human descended**
from *Jerusalem* **Yeru Shalem** to *Jericho* **Yericho**,
and fell among *thieves* **robbers**,
which stripped him of his raiment,
and *wounded* **plagued** him,
and departed, *leaving* **forsaking** him half dead.
31 And by *chance* **coincidence**,
there *came down* **descended** a *certain* priest that way:
and when he saw him,
he passed by *on the other side* **opposite**.
14 But it is more tolerable
for Sor and Sidon at the judgment, than for you.
15 And you, Kaphar Nachum,
exalted to the heavens,
you descend to sheol/hades.

Yesha Yah 14:12—15
16 Whoever hears you, hears me;
and whoever sets you aside, sets me aside;
and whoever sets me aside
sets him aside who apostolized me.

The Seventy Report To Yah Shua

17 And the seventy return with cheer, wording,
Adonay,
even the demons subjugate to us by your name.
18 And he says to them,
I observed Satan as lightning falls from the
heavens. Yahn 12:31, 32, Apocalypse 12:9
19 Behold, I give you authority
to trample on serpents and scorpions;
and over all the dynamis of the enemy:
and naught no way injures you.
20 However cheer not in this,
that the spirits subjugate to you;
but cheer rather,
because your names are scribed in the heavens.
21 In that hour Yah Shua jumps for joy in spirit,
and says, I avow you, O Father,
Adonay of the heavens and earth,
that you secrete these
from the wise and comprehending,
and unveil them to babes:
yes, Father;
and thus it becomes well—approved in front of you.
22 All are delivered to me by my Father:
and no one knows who the Son is, except the Father;
and who the Father is, except the Son;
and to whomever the Son wills to unveil him.
23 And he turns to his disciples, and says privately,
Blessed — the eyes that see what you see:
24 for I word to you,
that many prophets and sovereigns
willed to see what you see, and saw not;
and to hear what you hear, and heard not.

Yah Shua On True Neighborship

25 And behold, a torahist rises, and tests him,
wording, Doctor, what do I to inherit eternal life?
26 He says to him,
What is scribed in the torah? How read you?
27 And he answers, saying,
Love Yah Veh your Elohim
with all your heart and with all your soul
and with all your might and with all your mind
— and your neighbor as yourself.

28   And he says to him,
You answer straightforwardly:
this do, and you live.
29   But he wills to justify himself,
and says to Yah Shua, And who is my neighbor?
30   And perceiving, Yah Shua says,
A human descends from Yeru Shalem to Yericho
and falls among robbers
who strip him of his raiment and plague him;
and depart, forsaking him half dead.
31   And by coincidence, a priest descends that way:
and he sees him and passes by opposite.
32   And likewise a *Levite* **Leviy**,
when he was **being** at the place,
came and *looked on him* **saw**,
and passed by *on the other side* **opposite**.
33   But a *certain* Samaritan
Shomeroniy, as he journeyed,
came where he was: and when he saw him,
he had *compassion* **a sympathetic spleen** on him,
34   And went to him, and bound
up his *wounds* **trauma**,
pouring in **olive** oil and wine,
and *set* **mounted** him on his own *beast* **animal**,
and brought him to an inn, and took care of him.
35   And on the morrow when he departed,
he *took out* **cast** two *pence* **denarion**,
and gave them to the *host* **innkeeper**, and said unto him,
Take care of him; and whatsoever thou spendest more,
when I come again, *I will repay* **shall give to** thee.
36   Which now of these three, thinkest thou,
was **became** neighbour
unto him that fell among the *thieves* **robbers**?
37   And he said, He that *shewed*
dealt mercy *on* **with** him.
Then **So** said *Jesus* **Yah Shua** unto him,
Go, and do thou likewise.

Yah Shua On Ministry vs Worship

38   *Now it came to pass* **And so be it**, as they went,
that he entered into a *certain* village:
and a *certain* woman named Martha
received him into her house.
39   And she had a sister called *Mary* **Miryam**,
which also sat at *Jesus'* **Yah Shua's** feet,
and heard his word.
40   But Martha was cumbered
about much *serving* **ministry**,
and *came to* **stood by** him, and said,
Lord **Adonay**, dost *art* thou not *care* **concerned**
that my sister hath left me to *serve* **minister** alone?
bid her therefore **so say** that she help me.
41   And *Jesus* **Yah Shua**
answered and said unto her,
Martha, Martha, thou art *careful* **anxious**
and troubled about *many things* **much**:
42   But one *thing* is needful:
and *Mary* **Miryam** hath *chosen* **selected** that good part,
which shall not be *taken away* **removed** from her.

The Pattern For Prayer Of Yah Shua

11   And **so be** it *came to pass*, that,
as he was praying in a *certain* place,
when he ceased, one of his disciples said unto him,
Lord **Adonay**, *teach* **doctrinate** us to pray,
exactly as *John* **Yahn** also *taught*
doctrinated his disciples.
2   And he said unto them,
when **ever** ye pray, *say* **word**,
Our Father which art in heaven,
Hallowed be thy name.
Thy *kingdom* **sovereigndom** come.
Thy will *be done* **become**,
as in *heaven* **the heavens**, so in earth.
3   Give us *day by day* **daily**
our *daily* **subsistence** bread.
4   And forgive us our sins;
for we also forgive every one that is indebted to us.
And *lead* **bear** us not into *temptation* **testing**;
but *deliver* **rescue** us from evil.

Yah Shua On Persistence

5   And he said unto them,
Which of you shall have a friend,
and shall go unto him at midnight, and say unto him,
Friend, lend me three *loaves* **breads**;
6   *For* **Since** a friend of mine
in his journey is come to me,
and I have *nothing* **naught** to set *before* **by** him?
7   And he from within shall answer and say,
Trouble **Embarrass** me not:
the *door* **portal** is *now* **already** shut,
and my children are **lying** with me *in* bed;
I cannot rise and give thee.
8   I *say* **word** unto you,
Though he *will* **shall** not rise and give him,
because he is his friend,
yet **indeed** because of his *importunity* **impudence**
he *will* **shall** rise and give him as many as he needeth.
9   And I *say* **word** unto you,
32   And likewise a Leviy, being at the place,

33 comes and sees and passes by opposite.
Some Shomeroniy, as he journeys,
comes where he is and sees him and has
a sympathetic spleen on him:
34 and goes to him and binds his trauma
— pouring in olive oil and wine
and mounts him on his own animal
and brings him to an inn and takes care of him:
35 and on the morrow as he departs,
he casts two denarion
and gives them to the innkeeper, and says to him,
Take care of him; and whatever you spend more,
when I come again, I give to you.
36 Who of these three, think you,
became neighbor to him who fell among the robbers?
37 And he says, He who dealt mercy with him.
So Yah Shua says to him, Go, and do likewise.

Yah Shua On Ministry vs Worship

38 And so be it, as they go, he enters a village:
and a woman named Martha
receives him into her house:
39 and she has a sister called Miryam,
who also sits at the feet of Yah Shua
and hears his word:
40 but Martha is much encumbered about ministry
and stands by him, and says,
Adonay, are you not concerned
that my sister leaves me to minister alone?
So say that she help me.
41 And Yah Shua answers her, saying,
Martha, Martha,
you are anxious and troubled about much:
42 but one is needful:
and Miryam selects that good part,
not to be removed from her.

The Pattern For Prayer Of Yah Shua

11 And so be it, as he prays in a place,
when he ceases, one of his disciples say to him,
Adonay, doctrinate us to pray
exactly as Yahn also doctrinated his disciples.
2 And he says to them, whenever you pray, word,
Our Father in the heavens,
Hallowed be your name:
your sovereigndom come:
your will become —
as in the heavens, thus in earth.
3 Give us daily our subsistence bread:
4 and forgive us our sins;
for we also forgive everyone indebted to us.
And bear us not into testing
but rescue us from evil.

Yah Shua On Persistence

5 And he says to them,
Who of you has a friend
and goes to him at midnight, and says to him,
Friend, lend me three breads;
6 since a friend of mine in
his journey comes to me
and I have naught to set by him?
7 — and he answers from inside, saying,
Embarrass me not:
the portal is already shut
and my children lie down with me;
I cannot rise and give you.
8 I word to you,
Though he not rise and give him
because he is his friend,
yet indeed because of his impudence
he rises and gives him as much as he needs.
9 And I word to you,
Ask, and it shall be given you;
seek, and ye shall find;
knock, and it shall be opened unto you.
10 For every one that asketh *receiveth* **taketh**;
and he that seeketh findeth;
and to him that knocketh it shall be opened.
11 *If* a son shall ask bread of
any of you that is a father,
will **shall** he give a stone?
or if *he ask* a fish,
will **shall** he for a fish give him a serpent?
12 Or *if* **whenever** he shall ask an egg,
will **shall** he *offer* **give** him a scorpion?
13 If ye then, being evil,
know how to give good gifts unto your children:
how much more shall your heavenly Father
give the Holy Spirit to them that ask him?
Yah Shua Casts Out A Demon
14 And he was casting *out* a *devil* **demon**,
and it was *dumb* **mute**.
And **so be** it *came to pass*,
when the *devil* **demon** was gone out,
the *dumb* **mute** spake;
and the *people wondered* **multitude marvelled**.

Yah Shua Accused Of Blasphemy

15 But some of them said,

	He casteth out *devils* **demons**		a *certain* woman of the *company* **multitude**
	through Beelzebub **by Baal Zebub** the		lifted *up* her voice, and said unto him,
	chief **arch** of the *devils* **demons**.		Blessed *is* the womb that *bare* **birthed** thee,
16	And others, *tempting* **testing** him,		and the *paps* **breasts** which thou hast *sucked* **nippled**.
	sought of him a sign from heaven.	28	But he said, *Yea* **Yet then** rather,
17	But he, knowing their thoughts, said unto them,		blessed *are* they that hear the word of *God* **Elohim**,
	Every *kingdom* **sovereigndom** divided against itself		and *keep* **guard** it.
	is brought to desolation **desolateth**;		Ask, and it is given you: seek, and ~~you~~ you
	and a house *divided* against a house falleth.		find: knock, and it opens to you.
18	If Satan also *be divided*	10	For everyone who asks, takes;
	divideth against himself,		and whoever seeks, finds; and knocks, and it opens.
	how shall his *kingdom* **sovereigndom** stand?	11	And what father, if a son asks bread of you,
	because ye *say* **word** that I cast out *devils* **demons**		gives him a stone?
	through Beelzebub **by Baal Zebub**.		Or if a fish, for a fish gives a serpent?
19	And if I by *Beelzebub* **Baal Zebub**	12	Or whenever he asks an
	cast out *devils* **demons**,		egg, gives him a scorpion?
	by whom do your sons cast them *out*?	13	So if you, being evil,
	therefore **because of this** shall they be your judges.		know how to give good gifts to your children:
20	But if I *with* **by** the finger of *God* **Elohim**		how much more your Father in the heavenlies
	cast out *devils* **demons**,		gives the Holy Spirit to them who ask him?
	no doubt **then** the *kingdom*		
	sovereigndom of *God* **Elohim**		YAH SHUA CASTS OUT A DEMON
	is come **hath approached** upon you.		
21	When **ever** *a strong man* **the mighty** armed	14	And he casts a demon, and it is mute:
	keepeth **guardeth** his *palace* **courtyard**, his		and so be it,
	goods **holdings** are in *peace* **shalom**:		the demon goes and the mute speaks.
22	But when a *stronger* **mightier** than he		— and the multitude marvels.
	shall come upon him,		
	and *overcome* **triumph over** him,		YAH SHUA ACCUSED OF BLASPHEMY
	he taketh from him all his *armour* **panoply**		
	wherein he *trusted* **confided**,	15	And some of them say, He casts out demons
	and *divideth* **distributeth** his *spoils* **booty**.		by Baal Zebub the arch of the demons.
23	He that is not with me is against me:	16	And others, testing him,
	and he that gathereth not with me scattereth.		seek a sign from the heavens from him.
24	When **ever** the *unclean* **impure** spirit	17	But he, knowing their thoughts, says to them,
	is gone out of a *man* **human**,		Every sovereigndom divided against itself desolates;
	he *walketh* **passeth** through *dry* **waterless** places,		and a house against a house falls.
	seeking *rest* **repose**;	18	And also, if Satan divides against himself,
	and finding none, he *saith* **wordeth**,		how stands his sovereigndom?
	I *will* **shall** return unto my house whence I came *out*.		— because you word that I cast out demons
25	And when he cometh,		by Baal Zebub.
	he findeth it swept and *garnished* **adorned**.	19	And if I by Baal Zebub cast demons,
26	Then goeth he, and taketh		by whom do your sons cast them?
	to him seven other spirits		because of this they become your judges.
	more *wicked* **evil** than himself;	20	But if by the finger of Elohim I cast out demons,
	and they enter *in*, and *dwell* **settle** there:		then the sovereigndom of Elohim approaches you.
	and the *last state* **finality** of that *man* **human**	21	Whenever the mighty armed
	is **becometh** worse than the first.		guards his courtyard,
27	And *so be* it *came to pass*,		his holdings are in shalom:
	as he *spake* **worded** these *things*,	22	but when a mightier than he comes upon him
			and triumphs over him,
			he takes from him

LUKE/UR 11

all his panoply wherein he confided
and distributes his booty.
23 Whoever is not with me is against me:
and whoever gathers not with me scatters.
24 Whenever the impure spirit goes from a human
he passes through waterless places seeking repose:
and finding none, he words,
I return to my house whence I come.
25 And when he comes,
he finds it swept and adorned.
26 Then he goes,
and takes seven other spirits more evil than himself;
and they enter and settle there:
and the finality of that human
becomes worse than the first.
27 And so be it, as he words these,
a woman of the multitude lifts her voice
and says to him,
Blessed — the womb that birthed you,
and the breasts you nippled.
28 But he says, Still rather,
blessed — whoever hear the word of Elohim
and guard it.

The Sign Of Yonah

29 And when the *people* **multitude**
were gathered thick together **thronged**,
he began to *say* **word**, This is an evil generation:
they seek a sign; and there shall no sign be given it,
but **except** the sign of *Jonas* **Yonah** the prophet.
30 For *exactly* as *Jonas* **Yonah**
was **became** a sign unto the *Ninevites* **Neviym**,
so **thus** shall also the Son of *man* **humanity**
be to this generation.
31 *The queen* **A sovereigness** of the south
shall rise *up* in the judgment
with the men of this generation,
and condemn them:
for she came from the *utmost parts*
extremities of the earth
to hear the wisdom of *Solomon* **Sholomoh**;
and, behold,
a greater **much more** than *Solomon* **Sholomoh** is here.
32 The men of *Nineve* **Nineveh**
shall rise *up* in the judgment with this generation,
and shall condemn it:
for they repented at the preaching of *Jonas* **Yonah**;
and, behold,
a greater **much more** than *Jonas* **Yonah** is here.

Yah Shua On Candles And Menorah

33 No *man* **one**, when he hath lighted a candle,
putteth it in a secret place,
neither under a *bushel* **measure**,
but on a *candlestick* **menorah**,
that they which *come in* **enter** may
see the *light* **brilliance**.
34 The *light* **candle** of the body is the eye:
therefore **so** when *ever* thine eye is *single* **clear**,
thy whole body also is *full of light* **brightly lighted**;
but when *thine eye is* evil,
thy body also is *full of darkness* **dark**.
35 *Take heed therefore* **So scope out**
that the light which is in thee be not darkness.
36 **So** If thy whole body *therefore*
be *full of light* **brightly lighted**, having no part dark,
the whole shall be *full of light* **brightly lighted**,
as when **ever** the *bright shining* **lightning** of a candle
doth give **lighteth** thee *light*.

Yah Shua On The Six Woes

37 And as he spake,
a *certain* Pharisee *besought* **asked** him to dine with him:
and he *went in* **entered**, and *sat down to meat* **reposed**.
38 And when the Pharisee saw it, he marvelled
that he had not first *washed* **baptized** before dinner.
39 And *the Lord* **Adonay** said unto him,
Now *do* ye Pharisees
make clean the outside of **purify outward**
the cup and the platter;
but your inward *part*
is full of *ravening* **plunder** and wickedness.
40 *Ye fools* **Thoughtless**,
did not he that made that which is *without* **outward**
make that which is *within* **inward** also?
41 But rather give *alms* **mercies**
of *such things as ye have* **your inner self**;
and, behold, all *things* are *clean* **pure** unto you.
42 But woe unto you, Pharisees!
for ye tithe mint and rue and all *manner of* herbs,
and pass over judgment and the love of *God* **Elohim**:
these *ought* **must** ye to have done,
and not to *leave* **forsake** the other *undone*.
43 Woe unto you, Pharisees!
for ye love the *uppermost seats* **preeminent cathedras**
in the synagogues,
and *greetings* **salutations** in the markets.
44 Woe unto you, scribes and
Pharisees, hypocrites!
for ye are as *graves which appear not* **covered tombs**,

and the *men* **humans** that walk over *them*
are not aware of them **know it not**.
45   Then answered one of the *lawyers* **torahists**,
and *said* **worded** unto him, *Master* **Doctor**,
thus *saying* **wording**, thou *reproachest* **insultest** us also.
46   And he said, Woe unto you
also, ye *lawyers* **torahists**!
for ye *lade men* **overburden humanity**

The Sign Of Yonah

29   And the multitude throngs,
and he begins to word,
This is an evil generation:
they seek a sign; and no sign is given
except the sign of Yonah the prophet:
30   for exactly as Yonah
became a sign to the Nineviym
thus also the Son of humanity to this generation.
31   A sovereigness of the south
rises in the judgment with the men of this generation,
to condemn them:
for she came from the extremities of the earth
to hear the wisdom of Sholomoh;
and behold, much more than Sholomoh is here.
32   The men of Nineveh
rise in the judgment with this generation
to condemn it:
for they repented at the preaching of Yonah;
and behold, much more than Yonah is here.

Yah Shua On Candles And Menorah

33   No one lights a candle and
puts it in a secret place
neither under a measure;
but on a menorah
that whoever enters sees the brilliance.
34   The candle of the body is the eye:
so whenever your eye is clear,
your whole body also is brightly lighted;
but when evil, your body also is dark.
35   So scope out;
that the light within you be not darkness.
36   So if your whole body is brightly lighted
having no part dark,
the whole is brightly lighted,
as whenever the lightning of a candle lights you.

Yah Shua On The Six Woes

37   And as he speaks,
a Pharisee asks him to dine with him:
and he enters, and reposes:
38   and the Pharisee sees, and marvels
that he not first baptizes preceding dinner.
39   And Adonay says to him,
Now you Pharisees
purify the cup and the platter outward;
but your inward is full of plunder and wickedness.
40   Thoughtless!
He who made the outward
made he not also the inward?
41   But rather give mercies of your inward self;
and behold, all are pure to you.
42   But woe to you, Pharisees!
For you tithe mint and rue and all herbs;
and pass over judgment and the love of Elohim:
these you must do, and not forsake the other.
43   Woe to you, Pharisees!
for you love the preeminent cathedras in the synagogues
and salutations in the markets.
44   Woe to you, scribes and Pharisees! Hypocrites!
for you are as covered tombs,
and the humans who walk over know it not.
45   And one of the torahists answers,
wording, Doctor,
Thus wording, you also insult us.
46   And he says, Woe to you also, you torahists!
For you overburden humanity
with **oppressive** burdens *grievous to be borne*,
and ye yourselves touch not the burdens
with one of your fingers.
47   Woe unto you!
for ye build the *sepulchres* **tombs** of the prophets,
and your fathers *killed* **slaughtered** them.
48   *Truly* **Then** ye *bear* witness
that ye *allow* **well—approve**
the *deeds* **works** of your fathers:
for they indeed *killed* **slaughtered** them,
and ye build their *sepulchres* **tombs**.
49   *Therefore* **Because of this**
also said the wisdom of *God* **Elohim**,
I *will send* **shall apostolize** them prophets and apostles,
and *some* of them they shall *slay*
slaughter and persecute:
50   That the blood of all the prophets,
which was shed **poured**
from the foundation of the *world* **cosmos**,
may be required of this generation;
51   From the blood of Abel
unto the blood of *Zacharias* **Zechar Yah**
which *perished* **destructed**

between the **sacrifice** altar and the *temple* **house**:
Verily I say **Yea I word** unto you,
It shall be required of this generation.

52 Woe unto you, *lawyers* **torahists**!
for ye have taken away the key of knowledge:
ye entered not in yourselves,
and them that were entering in ye *hindered* **forbad**.

53 And as he *said* **worded** these *things* unto them,
the scribes and the Pharisees
began to *urge* **begrudge** him *vehemently* **excessively**,
and to provoke him
to *speak of many things* **instruct about much**:

54 *Laying wait* **Lurking** for him,
and seeking to *catch* **hunt** something out of his mouth,
that they might accuse him.

YAH SHUA ON HYPOCRISY

12 In the mean time,
when there were gathered together
an innumerable **a** multitude of *people* **myriads**,
insomuch that they *trode* **trampled** one upon another,
he began to *say* **word** unto his disciples first of all,
Beware **Heed** ye **yourselves**
of the *leaven* **fermentation** of the Pharisees
which is hypocrisy.

2 For there is *nothing covered*
naught altogether concealed,
that shall not be *revealed* **unveiled**;
neither *hid* **secreted**, that shall not be known.

3 *Therefore* **So**
whatsoever **as much as** ye have spoken in darkness
shall be heard in the light;
and that which ye have spoken in
the ear in *closets* **pantries**
shall be *proclaimed* **preached** upon the housetops.

4 And I *say* **word** unto you my friends,
Be **Awe** not *afraid* of them that *kill* **slaughter** the body,
and after that have no more **superabundantly**
that they can do.

5 But I *will forewarn* **shall exemplify** you
whom ye shall *fear* **awe**:
Fear **Awe** him, which after he hath *killed* **slaughtered**,
hath *power* **authority**
to cast into *hell* **Gay Hinnom/the valley of burning**;
yea, I *say* **word** unto you, *Fear* **Awe** him.

6 Are not **indeed** five sparrows
sold for two *farthings* **assarions**,
and not one of them is forgotten
before God **in the sight of Elohim**?

7 But even the very hairs of
your head are all numbered.
Fear **So awe** not *therefore*:
ye *are of more value than* **thoroughly
surpass** many sparrows.

8 Also I *say* **word** unto you,
Whosoever shall *confess* **profess** me
before men **in front of humanity**,
him shall the Son of *man* **humanity** also *confess* **profess**
before **in front of** the angels of *God* **Elohim**:

9 But he that denieth me *before*
men **in sight of humanity**
with oppressive burdens;
and you yourselves touch not the burdens
with one of your fingers.

47 Woe to you!
For you build the tombs of the prophets,
and your fathers slaughtered them:

48 then you witness that you well—approve
the works of your fathers:
for they indeed slaughtered them,
and you build their tombs.

49 Because of this also the wisdom of Elohim says,
I apostolize them prophets and apostles,
and of them, they slaughter and persecute:

50 that the blood of all the prophets,
poured from the foundation of the cosmos,
is required of this generation

51 — from the blood of Abel
to the blood of Zechar Yah
— who destructed
between the sacrifice altar and the house:
yes, I word to you,
It is required of this generation.

52 Woe to you, torahists!
For you take the key of knowledge:
and you yourselves enter not;
and them entering, you forbid.

53 And as he words these to them,
the scribes and the Pharisees
begin to begrudge him excessively
and to provoke him to instruct about much

54 — lurking for him,
and seeking to hunt something from his mouth,
to accuse him.

YAH SHUA ON HYPOCRISY

12 In the mean time,
a multitude of myriads gathers together
so that they trample on one another:

and he begins to word to his disciples first,
Heed yourselves of the fermentation of the Pharisees
which is hypocrisy:
2 for naught is altogether concealed,
that is not unveiled;
and secreted, that is not known:
3 so as much as you speak in darkness
is heard in the light;
and what you speak in the ear in pantries
is preached on the housetops.
4 And I word to you my friends,
Awe not them who slaughter the body,
and after can do no more superabundantly:
5 but I exemplify you whom to awe;
awe him, who after he slaughters,
has authority
to cast into Gay Hinnom/the Valley of Burning;
yes, I word to you, awe him.
6 Are not indeed
five sparrows sold for two assarions?
— and not one is forgotten in the sight of Elohim.
7 But even the hairs of your
head are all numbered.
So awe not:
you thoroughly surpass many sparrows.
8 Also I word to you,
whoever professes me in front of humanity,
the Son of humanity also professes
in front of the angels of Elohim:
9 but whoever denies me in sight of humanity
shall be denied *before* **in sight of**
the angels of *God* **Elohim**.
10 And whosoever shall *speak* **say** a word
against the Son of *man* **humanity**,
it shall be forgiven him:
but unto him
that blasphemeth against the *Holy
Spirit* **Ruach ha-kodesh**
it shall not be forgiven.
11 And when **ever** they *bring* **offer** you
unto the synagogues,
and unto *magistrates* **hierarchies**,
and *powers* **authorities**,
take ye no thought **be ye not anxious**
how or what *thing* ye shall answer,
or what ye shall *say* **plead**:
12 For the *Holy Spirit* **Ruach ha-kodesh** shall *teach* **doctrinate** you
in the same hour what ye *ought to* **must** say.

YAH SHUA ON AVARICE

13 And one of the *company* **multitude** said unto him,
Master **Doctor**, *speak* **say** to my brother,
that he divide the inheritance with me.
14 And he said unto him, *man* **human**,
who *made* **seated** me a judge or a divider over you?
15 And he said unto them,
Take heed **See**,
and *beware of covetousness* **guard against avarice**:
for *a man's* **one's** life
consisteth **be** not in the **super** abundance
of *the things which he possesseth* **his holdings**.
16 And he *spake* **worded** a parable unto them,
saying **speaking**,
The *ground* **region** of a *certain* rich *man* **human**
brought forth plentifully **bore well**:
17 And he *thought* **reasoned** within himself,
saying **wording**, What shall I do,
because I have no room
where to *bestow* **gather** my fruits?
18 And he said, This *will* **shall** I do:
I *will* **shall** pull down my *barns* **granaries**,
and build greater;
and there *will* **shall** I *bestow* **gather**
all my *fruits* **produce** and my goods.
19 And I *will* **shall** say to my soul,
Soul, thou hast much goods laid *up* for many years;
take thine ease **rest**, eat, drink, and *be merry* **rejoice**.
20 But *God* **Elohim** said unto
him, *Thou fool* **Thoughtless**,
this night thy soul shall be required of thee:
then whose shall those *things* be,
which thou hast *provided* **prepared**?
21 *So* **Thus** is he
that *layeth up treasure* **treasureth** for himself,
and is not rich toward *God* **Elohim**.

YAH SHUA ON ANXIETY FOR THE SOUL

22 And he said unto his disciples,
Therefore **Because of this** I *say* **word** unto you,
Take no thought **Be not anxious** for your *life* **soul**,
what ye shall eat;
neither for the body, what ye shall *put on* **endue**.
23 The *life* **soul** is more than *meat* **nourishment**,
and the body *is more* than *raiment* **enduement**.
24 *Consider* **Perceive** the ravens:
for they neither *sow* **spore** nor *reap* **harvest**;
which neither have *storehouse* **pantry** nor *barn* **granary**;
and *God feedeth* **Elohim nourisheth** them:

how much more
are ye better than ye **thoroughly
surpass** the fowls **flyers**?

25 And which of you with
taking thought **by anxiety**
can add to his stature one cubit?

26 **So** If ye then be not able to
do that thing which is least,
why take **be** ye thought **anxious** for the rest?

27 Consider **Perceive** the lilies how they grow:
they toil **labour** not, they spin not;
and yet I say **word** unto you,
that Solomon **Sholomoh** in all his glory
was not arrayed like one of these.

28 **But** If then God so **Elohim
thus** clothe the grass **herbage**,
which is to day in the field,
and to morrow is cast into the oven;
how much more will he clothe you,
O ye of little faith **trust**?

is denied in sight of the angels of Elohim.

10 And whoever says a word
to the Son of humanity,
is forgiven:
but whoever blasphemes to the Holy Spirit
is not forgiven.

11 And whenever they offer you to the synagogues
and to hierarchies and authorities,
be not anxious how or what you answer
or what you plead:

12 for in that same hour
the Holy Spirit doctrinates you what you must say.

Yah Shua On Avarice

13 And one of the multitude says to him,
Doctor, say to my brother
to divide the inheritance with me.

14 And he says to him, human,
who seated me a judge or a divider over you?

15 And he says to them,
See, and guard against avarice:
for the life of one
is not in the super abundance of his holdings.

16 And he words a parable to them, speaking,
The region of a rich human bears well:

17 and he reasons within himself,
wording, What do I?
— because I have no room to gather my fruits.

18 And he says, I do this:
I pull down my granaries and build greater;
and there gather all my produce and my goods:

19 and say to my soul,
Soul, you have vast goods laid for many years;
Rest! Eat! Drink! Rejoice!

20 And Elohim says to him, Thoughtless!
This night your soul is required of you:
so whose are those that you prepared?

21 Thus is he who treasures for himself,
and is not rich toward Elohim.

Yah Shua On Anxiety For The Soul

22 And he says to his disciples,
Because of this I word to you,
be anxious, neither for your soul — what you eat;
nor for the body — what you endue:

23 the soul is more than nourishment
and the body than enduement.

24 Perceive the ravens:
for they neither spore nor harvest
— neither have pantry nor granary;
and Elohim nourishes them.
How much more thoroughly surpass you the flyers?

25 And who of you by anxiety
can add one cubit to his stature?

26 So if you are not able to do what is least,
why be anxious for the rest?

27 Perceive the lilies how they grow:
they neither labor, nor spin;
and yet I word to you,
that Sholomoh in all his glory
arrayed not as one of these.

28 But if Elohim thus clothes the herbage
— which today is in the field
and tomorrow is cast into the oven;
how much more you, O you of little trust?

29 And seek not ye what ye shall eat,
or what ye shall drink,
neither be ye of doubtful mind **in suspense**.

30 For all these things
do the nations **goyim** of the world **cosmos** seek after:
and your Father knoweth that ye
have need of these things.

31 But rather
seek ye the kingdom **sovereigndom** of God **Elohim**;
and all these things shall be added unto you.

32 Fear **Awe** not, little flock **shepherddom**;
for it is your Father's good pleasure
your Father well—approveth
to give you the kingdom **sovereigndom**.

33 Sell that ye have **your holdings**,

and give *alms* **mercies**;
provide **make** yourselves *bags* **pouches**
which *wax* **antiquate** not *old*,
a treasure in the heavens *that faileth not* **inexhaustible**,
where no thief approacheth, neither moth corrupteth.

34   For where your treasure is,
there *will* **shall** your heart be also.

YAH SHUA ON PREPAREDNESS

35   Let your loins be girded about,
and *your lights* **candles** burning;
36   And **liken** ye yourselves
like unto *men* **humanity**
that *wait for* **await** their *Lord* **Adonay**,
when he *will return* **shall depart**
from the *wedding* **marriage**;
that when he cometh and knocketh,
they may open unto him *immediately* **straightway**.
37   Blessed *are* those servants,
whom *the Lord* **Adonay**
when he cometh shall find watching:
Verily ! say **Amen! I word** unto you,
that he shall gird himself,
and *make* **recline** them *to sit down to meat*,
and *will come forth* **shall pass by**
and *serve* **minister to** them.
38   And *if* **whenever** he shall come
— in the second *watch* **guard**,
or come in the third *watch* **guard**,
and find them *so* **thus**, blessed *are* those servants.
39   And this know,
that if the *goodman of the house* **housedespotes**
had known what hour the thief *would* **should** come,
he *would* **should** have watched,
and not have *suffered* **allowed**
his house to be broken through.
40   *So* **Be** ye *therefore ready* **prepared** also:
for the Son of *man* **humanity**
cometh at an hour when ye think not.
41   *Then Peter* **And Petros** said
unto him, *Lord* **Adonay**,
speakest **wordest** thou this parable unto us,
or even to all?
42   And *the Lord* **Adonay** said,
Who then is that *faithful* **trustworthy**
and *wise steward* **thoughtful administrator**,
whom his *lord* **adoni**
shall *make ruler* **seat** over his *household* **therapy**,
to give them their *portion* **measure** of *meat* **grain**
in due season?

43   Blessed *is* that servant,
whom his *lord* **adoni** when he cometh
shall find *so* **thus** doing.
44   *Of a truth ! say* **Truly I word** unto you,
that he *will make* **shall seat** him *ruler*
over all *that he hath* **his holdings**.
45   But *and if* **whenever** that
servant say in his heart,
My *lord delayeth* **adoni taketh** his **time in** coming;
and shall begin to *beat* **strike**
the *menservants* **lads** and *maidens* **lasses**,
and to eat and drink, and to *be drunken* **intoxicate**;
46   The *lord* **adoni** of that servant
will **shall** come in a day
when he *looketh not for* **awaiteth** him **not**,
and at an hour *when* **which** he *is not aware* **knoweth not**,
and *will cut him in sunder* **shall dichotomize him**,
and *will a*ppoint him **shall place** his portion
with the *unbelievers* **trustless**.
47   And that servant, which
knew his *lord's* **adoni's** will,
29   And neither seek what to eat or what to drink;
nor be in suspense:
30   for all these the goyim of the cosmos seek after:
and your Father knows you need these:
31   but rather seek the sovereigndom of Elohim;
and all these add to you.
32   Awe not, little shepherddom;
for your Father well—approves
to give you the sovereigndom.
33   Sell your holdings and give mercies;
make yourselves pouches which antiquate not
— an inexhaustible treasure in the heavens
where neither thief approaches nor moth corrupts:
34   for where your treasure is,
there also your heart is.

YAH SHUA ON PREPAREDNESS

35   Gird your loins all around
with candles burning:
36   and liken yourselves to humanity
who await their Adonay
as he departs from the marriage;
so that when he comes and knocks,
they straightway open to him.
37   Blessed — those servants,
whom when Adonay comes, finds watching:
Amen! I word to you,
that he girds himself and recline them,
and passes by and ministers to them:

38   and whenever he comes
— in the second guard,
or comes in the third guard,
and find them thus, blessed — those servants.
39   And know this,
that if the housedespotes
knows what hour the thief comes
he watches;
and allows not his house to be broken through.
40   So you also, be prepared:
for the Son of humanity
comes at an hour when you think not.
41   And Petros says to him, Adonay,
word you this parable to us — or even to all?
42   And Adonay says,
Who then is that trustworthy
and thoughtful administrator
whom his adoni seats over his therapy
to give their measure of grain in due season?
43   Blessed — that servant,
whom, when his adoni comes, finds doing thus.
44   Truly I word to you,
that he seats him over all his holdings.
45   But whenever that servant says in his heart,
My adoni takes his time in coming;
and he begins to strike the lads and lasses;
and to eat and drink and to intoxicate;
46   the adoni of that servant comes
in a day he awaits him not
and at an hour he knows not;
and dichotomizes him,
and places his portion with the trustless.
47   And that servant, who
knows the will of his adoni,
and prepared not *himself*,
neither did according to his will,
shall be *beaten with many stripes* **flogged often**.
48   But he that knew not,
and *did commit things* **dealt** worthy of *stripes* **plagues**,
shall be *beaten with few stripes* **flogged little**.
For unto whomsoever much is given,
of him shall be much *required* **sought**:
and to whom men have *committed* **set forth** much,
of him they *will* **shall** ask *the more* **superabundantly**.

Yah Shua On Unity Vs Division

49   I am come to *send* **cast** fire on the earth;
and what will I, if it be already *kindled* **lit**?
50   But I have a baptism to be baptized with;
and how am I *straitened* **held**
till it be *accomplished* **completed/shalamed**!
51   *Suppose* **Think** ye
that I am come to give *peace* **shalom** on earth?
I *tell* **word** unto you, *Nay* **Indeed
not**; but rather division:
52   For from henceforth
there shall be five in one house divided,
three against two, and two against three.
53   The father shall be divided against the son,
and the son against the father;
the mother against the daughter,
and the daughter against the mother;
the mother in law against her *daughter in law* **bride**,
and the *daughter in law* **bride** against her mother in law.

Yah Shua On Proofing The Season

54   And he *said* **worded** also
to the *people* **multitude**,
when **ever** ye see a cloud rise out of the *west*
lowering, straightway ye *say* **word**,
There cometh a *shower* **thunderstorm**;
and **so be** it *is*.
55   And when **ever**
ye see the south wind blow **the southerly puffeth**,
ye *say* **word**, There *will* **shall** be *heat* **a scorch**;
and **so be** it *cometh to pass*.
56   Ye hypocrites, ye *can discern* **know to proof**
the face of the *sky* **heavens** and of the earth;
but how is it
that ye *do not discern* **proof not** this *time* **season**?
57   Yea, and why even of yourselves
judge ye not what is *right* **just**?
58   *When* **Indeed as** thou
goest with thine adversary
to the *magistrate* **arch**,
as thou art *in* **on** the way,
give *diligence* **work**
that thou mayest be *delivered* **released** from him;
lest **ever** he *hale* **drag** thee to the judge,
and the judge deliver thee to the officer,
and the officer cast thee into *prison* **the guardhouse**.
59   I *tell* **word** unto thee,
thou shalt *not* **never no way** depart thence,
till thou hast *paid* **given back** the
very last mite **final flake**.

Yah Shua On Repentance

13   There were present at that season
some that *told* **evangelized** him
of **about** the *Galilaeans* **Galiliym**,

whose blood *Pilate* **Pilatos** had
mingled with their sacrifices.
2 And *Jesus* **Yah Shua** answering said unto them,
Suppose **Think** ye that these *Galilaeans* **Galiliym**
were **became** sinners above all the *Galilaeans* **Galiliym**,
because they suffered such *things*?
3 I *tell* **word** unto you, *Nay* **Indeed not**:
but, *except* **unless** ye repent,
ye shall all likewise *perish* **destruct**.
4 Or those eighteen,
upon whom the tower in *Siloam* **Shiloach** fell,
and *slew* **slaughtered** them,
think ye that they *were sinners* **became indebted**
above all *men* **humanity**
that *dwelt* **settled** in *Jerusalem* **Yeru Shalem**?
5 I *tell* **word** unto you, *Nay* **Indeed not**:
but *except* **unless** ye repent,
ye shall all likewise *perish* **destruct**.
who neither prepares nor does according to his will
is flogged often.
48 But whoever knows not
whose doings are worthy of plagues
is flogged little.
For to whomever much is given,
of him much is sought:
and to whom men set forth much,
of him they ask superabundantly.

Yah Shua On Unity vs Division

49 I come to cast fire on the earth;
and what will I, if it be already lit?
50 But I have a baptism to be baptized with;
and how I am held until it is completed/shalamed!
51 Think you that I come to give shalom on earth?
I word to you, Indeed not; but rather division:
52 for from henceforth
five in one house divide
— three against two and two against three
53 — the father divides against the son
and the son against the father;
the mother against the daughter
and the daughter against the mother;
the mother in law against her bride,
and the bride against her mother in law.

Yah Shua On Proofing The Season

54 And he also words to the multitude,
whenever you see a cloud rise from the lowering
straightway you word,
A thunderstorm comes; — and so be it.

55 And whenever the southerly puffs,
you word, A scorch becomes — and so be it.
56 Hypocrites!
You know how to proof
the face of the heavens and of the earth;
but how is it you proof not this season?
57 Yes, and even of yourselves,
why judge you not what is just?
58 Indeed as you and your adversary
go to the arch,
as you are on the way
give work to be released from him;
lest ever he drag you to the judge
and the judge deliver you to the officer
and the officer cast you into the guardhouse.
59 I word to you,
that you never no way depart there,
until you give the final flake.

Yah Shua On Repentance

13 And present at that season
are some who evangelize him about the Galiliym,
whose blood Pilatos mingled with their sacrifices.
2 And Yah Shua answers them, saying,
Think you that these Galiliym
became sinners above all the Galiliym
because they suffered such?
3 I word to you, Indeed not:
but unless you repent, you all likewise destruct.
4 Or those eighteen
upon whom the tower in Shiloach fell
and slaughtered them:
think you that they became indebted
above all humanity who settle in Yeru Shalem?
5 I word to you, Indeed not:
but unless you repent, you all likewise destruct.

Yah Shua On The Fig Tree

6 **And** He *spake* **worded** also this parable;
A certain man **Someone** had a fig tree
planted in his vineyard;
and he came and sought fruit thereon, and found none.
7 *Then* **And** said he unto the
dresser of his vineyard, Behold,
these three years I come seeking fruit on this fig tree,
and find none:
cut *exscind* it *down*;
why *cumbereth* it **inactivate** the *ground* **earth**?
8 And he answering *said* **worded** unto him,
Lord **Adoni**, *let* **allow** it *alone* this year also,

till I shall dig about it, and *dung it* **cast in manure**:
9 And if it *bear* **indeed produce** fruit, *well*:
and if not,
then after that thou shalt cut it down
be about to exscind it.

Yah Shua Cures On The Shabbath

10 And he was *teaching* **doctrinating**
in one of the synagogues on the *sabbath* **shabbaths**.
11 And, behold, there was a woman
which had a spirit of *infirmity* **frailty** eighteen years,
and was *bowed* **bent** together,
and *could in no wise* **was completely unable**
lift up **to unbend** herself.
12 And when *Jesus* **Yah Shua** saw her,
he called *her to him*, and said unto her,
Woman, thou art *loosed* **released**
from thine *infirmity* **frailty**.
13 And he *laid* **put** his hands on her:
and immediately she *was made straight* **straightened**,
and glorified *God* **Elohim**.
14 And the *ruler of the* synagogue **arch**
answered *with indignation* **indignifying**,
because that *Jesus* **Yah Shua**
had *healed* **cured** on the *sabbath day* **shabbath**,
and *said* **worded** unto the *people* **multitude**,
There are six days in which men *ought to* **must** work:
so in them *therefore* come and be *healed* **cured**,
and not on the *sabbath day* **shabbath**.
15 *The Lord then* **So Adonay**
answered him, and said,
Thou hypocrite,
doth not each one of you on the *sabbath* **shabbath**
loose his ox or his *ass* **burro** from the *stall* **manger**,
and lead him away to *watering* **moisten**?
16 And *ought* **must** not this woman,
being a daughter of Abraham, whom Satan hath bound,
lo **behold**, these eighteen years,
be loosed from this bond on the *sabbath* **shabbath** day?
17 And when he had *said* **worded** these *things*,
all his adversaries *were ashamed* **shamed**:
and all the *people rejoiced* **multitude cheered**
for all the *glorious things* **glories**
that *were done* **became** by him.

Yah Shua On The Sovereigndom Of Elohim: The Mustard Kernel

18 Then *said* **worded** he,
Unto what is the *kingdom* **sovereigndom**
of *God* **Elohim** like?
and whereunto shall I *resemble* **liken** it?
19 It is like a *grain of* mustard *seed* **kernel**,
which a *man* **human** took, and cast into his garden;
and it grew, and *waxed* **became** a *great* **mega** tree;
and the *fowls* **flyers** of the *air* **heavens**
lodged **nested** in the branches of it.

The Fermentation

20 And again he said, Whereunto shall I liken
the *kingdom* **sovereigndom** of *God* **Elohim**?
21 It is like *leaven* **fermentation**,
which a woman took
and hid in three *measures* **seahs** of *meal* **flour**,
till the whole *was leavened* **fermented**.
22 And he went through the cities and villages,
teaching **doctrinating**,
and *journeying* **making his way** toward
Jerusalem **Yeru Shalem**.

The Narrow Gate

23 *Then* **And** said one unto him,
Lord **Adonay**, are there few that be saved?
And he said unto them,
24 *Strive* **Agonize** to enter *in at*
through the *strait* **narrow** gate:

Yah Shua On The Fig Tree

6 And he words this parable:
Someone has a fig tree planted in his vineyard;
and he comes and seeks fruit, and finds none:
7 and he says to the dresser
of his vineyard, Behold,
these three years I come seeking fruit on this fig tree
and find none:
Exscind! Why inactivate the earth?
8 And he answers him, wording,
Adoni, allow it this year also,
until I dig all around and cast in manure:
9 and if indeed it produces fruit —
and if not, be about to exscind it.

Yah Shua Cures On The Shabbath

10 And he doctrinates
in one of the synagogues on the shabbaths:
11 and behold,
a woman having a spirit of frailty eighteen years,
and is bent together,
and is completely unable to unbend:
12 and Yah Shua sees her and calls and says to her,
Woman, you are released from your frailty.

13 — and he puts his hands on her:
and immediately she straightens and glorifies Elohim.
14 And answering, the
synagogue arch is indignified
because Yah Shua cures on the shabbath;
so he words to the multitude,
There are six days in which men must work:
so come and be cured in them
and not on the shabbath.
15 So Adonay answers him, saying,
Hypocrite! Does not each one of you on the shabbath
loose his ox or his burro from the manger
and lead him away to moisten?
16 And must not this woman,
being a daughter of Abraham, whom Satan bound,
behold, these eighteen years,
be loosed from this bond on the shabbath day?
17 — and he words these
and all his adversaries shame:
and all the multitude cheers
for all the glories that become by him.

Yah Shua On The Sovereigndom Of Elohim: The Mustard Kernel

18 Then he words,
To what is the sovereigndom of Elohim likened?
And to what liken I it?
19 It is likened to a mustard kernel
a human takes and casts into his garden;
and it grows and becomes a mega tree:
and the flyers of the heavens nest in the branches.

The Fermentation

20 And again he says,
Whereto liken I the sovereigndom of Elohim?
21 It is likened to fermentation
a woman takes and hides in three seahs of flour
until the whole ferments.
22 And he goes through the cities and villages
doctrinating,
and makes his way toward Yeru Shalem.

The Narrow Gate

23 And someone says to him,
Adonay, are there few that be saved?
And he says to them,
24 Agonize to enter through the narrow gate:
for many, I *say* **word** unto you, *will* **shall** seek to enter in,
and shall not be able.
25 *When once the master of the house is risen up*
From whenever the housedespotes riseth,
and hath *shut to* **locked** the *door* **portal**,
and ye begin to stand without,
and to knock at the *door* **portal**, *saying* **wording**,
Lord **Adonay**, *Lord* **Adonay**, open unto us;
and he shall answer and say unto you,
I know you not whence ye are:
26 Then shall ye begin to *say* **word**,
We have eaten and drunk in thy *presence* **sight**,
and thou hast *taught* **doctrinated**
in our *streets* **broadways**.
27 But he shall say, I *tell* **word unto** you,
I know you not whence ye are;
depart from me, all ye workers of *iniquity* **injustice**.
28 There shall be weeping and gnashing of teeth,
when **ever** ye shall see
Abraham, and *Isaac* **Yischaq**, and *Jacob* **Yaaqov**,
and all the prophets,
in the *kingdom* **sovereigndom** of *God* **Elohim**,
and you yourselves thrust out.
29 And they shall come
from the *east* **rising**, and *from* the *west* **lowering**,
and from the north, and *from* the south,
and shall *sit down* **recline**
in the *kingdom* **sovereigndom** of *God* **Elohim**.
30 And, behold,
there are *last* **final** which shall be first,
and there are first which shall be *last* **final**.

The Response Of Yah Shua To Herod

31 The same day there came
certain **some** of the Pharisees,
saying **wording** unto him,
Get thee out, and depart hence:
for Herod *will kill* **willeth to slaughter** thee.
32 And he said unto them, Go
ye, and *tell* **say to** that fox,
Behold, I cast *out devils* **demons**,
and I *do cures* **fully complete/shalam healings**
to day and to morrow,
and the third *day* I shall be *perfected*
completed/shalamed.
33 *Nevertheless* **However** I must walk
to day, and to morrow, and *the day following* **after**:
for it *cannot* be **not acceptable** that a prophet
perish **destruct** out of *Jerusalem* **Yeru Shalem**.

The Concern Of Yah Shua Over Yeru Shalem

34 O *Jerusalem, Jerusalem*
Yeru Shalem, Yeru Shalem,
which *killest* **slaughterest** the prophets,
and stonest them that are *sent* **apostolized** unto thee;
how often *would* I **willed**
to have gathered thy children together,
in manner as a hen *doth gather*
her *brood* **young** under *her* wings,
and ye *would* **willed** not!

35 Behold, your house is *left*
forsaken unto you desolate:
and *Verily I say* **Amen! I word** unto you,
Ye shall *not* **never no way** see me,
until *the time* **it** come when ye shall say,
Blessed **Eulogized** is he
that cometh in the name of *the Lord* **Yah Veh**.

Yah Shua Heals On The Shabbath

14 And **so be it** *came to pass*,
as he *went* **came** into the house
of one of the *chief* **arch** Pharisees
to eat bread on the *sabbath day* **shabbath**,
that they *watched* **observed** him.

2 And, behold,
there was a *certain man before* **human in front of** him
which had the dropsy — **dropsical**.

3 And *Jesus* **Yah Shua** answering
spake **said** unto the *lawyers* **torahists** and Pharisees,
saying **wording**, Is it *lawful* **allowed**
to *heal* **cure** on the *sabbath day* **shabbath**?

4 And they *held their peace* **quieted**.
And he took **hold of** him,
and healed him, and *let* **released** him *go*;

5 And answered them, saying,
Which of you
shall have *an ass* **a burro** or an ox fallen into a pit,

for many, I word to you, seek to enter,
and are not able;

25 for from whenever the housedespotes rises
and locks the portal;
and you begin to stand outside
and to knock at the portal, wording,
Adonay, Adonay, open to us;
— and he answers you, saying,
I know not whence you are:

26 — then you begin to word,
We ate and drank in your sight,
and you doctrinated in our broadways.

27 And he says, I word to you,
I know not whence you are;
depart from me, all you workers of injustice.

28 There becomes weeping and gnashing of teeth
whenever you see
Abraham and Yischaq and Yaaqov and all the prophets
in the sovereigndom of Elohim
— and you yourselves thrust out.

29 — and they come
from the rising and the lowering
and from the north and the south
and recline in the sovereigndom of Elohim:

30 — and behold,
the final become first,
and the first become final.

The Response Of Yah Shua To Herod

31 The same day, some of the Pharisees come,
and word to him,
Go! and, Depart hence!
— for Herod wills to slaughter you.

32 And he says to them, You go and say to that fox,
Behold, I cast demons,
and I fully complete/shalam healings
today and tomorrow;
and on the third I am completed/shalamed:

33 however I must walk
today and tomorrow and after:
for it is not acceptable that a prophet
destruct from Yeru Shalem.

The Concern Of Yah Shua Over Yeru Shalem

34 O, Yeru Shalem, Yeru Shalem,
who slaughters the prophets,
and stones them who apostolize to you;
how often I willed to gather your children together
in manner as a hen her young under her wings:
and you will not!

35 Behold, your house is forsaken to you desolate!
— and, Amen! I word to you,
You never no way see me until it comes when you say,
Eulogized — he who comes in the name of Yah Veh.

Yah Shua Heals On The Shabbath

14 And so be it,
as he goes in the house of one of the arch Pharisees
to eat bread on the shabbath,
they observe him:

2	and behold, there is a human in front of him — dropsical:
3	and Yah Shua answers, saying to the torahists and Pharisees, wording, Is it allowed to cure on the shabbath?
4	— and they quiet. And he takes hold of him and heals him and releases him;
5	— and answers them, saying, Which of you has a burro or an ox fallen into a pit and *will* **shall** not straightway *pull* **draw** him *out* on the *sabbath* **shabbath** day?
6	And they could not *answer* **contradict** him *again* **as** to these *things*.

Yah Shua On Position

7	And he *put forth* **worded** a parable to those which were *bidden* **called**, when he *marked* **heeding** how they *chose out* **selected** the *chief rooms* **preeminent recliners**; *saying* **wording** unto them,
8	when **ever** thou art *bidden* **called** of any *man* **one** to a *wedding* **marriage**, *sit* **recline** not *down* in the highest room; lest **ever** a more honourable *man* than thou be *bidden* **called** of him;
9	And he that *bade* **called** thee and him come and say to thee, Give this *man* **one** place; and thou begin with shame to *take* **hold on to** the *lowest room* **final place**.
10	But thou art *bidden* **called**, go and *sit down* **repose** in the *lowest room* **final place**; that when **ever** he that *bade* **called** thee cometh, he may say unto thee, Friend, *go up* **ascend** higher: then shalt thou have *worship* **glory** in the *presence* **sight** of them that *sit* *at meat* **repose** with thee.
11	For whosoever exalteth himself shall be *abased* **humbled**; and he that humbleth himself shall be exalted.
12	*Then said* **And worded** he also to him that *bade* **called** him, when **ever** thou makest a dinner or a supper, *call* **voice** not *out* **to** thy friends, nor thy brethren, neither thy *kinsmen* **kin**, nor thy rich neighbours; lest **ever** they also *bid* **call** thee *again* **back**, and a recompence *be made* **become** thee.
13	But when **ever** thou makest a feast, call the poor, the maimed, the lame, the blind:
14	And thou shalt be blessed; for they cannot recompense thee: for thou shalt be recompensed at the resurrection of the just.

Yah Shua On The Mega Supper

15	And when one of them that *sat at meat* **reposed** with him heard these *things*, he said unto him, Blessed *is* he that shall eat bread in the *kingdom* **sovereigndom** of *God* **Elohim**.
16	*Then* **But** said he unto him, A *certain man* **human** made a *great* **mega** supper, and *bade* **called** many:
17	And *sent* **apostolized** his servant at supper *time* **hour** to say to them that were *bidden* **called**, Come; for all *things* are *now ready* **already prepared**.
18	And they all *with one consent* began to *make excuse* **beg off**. The first said unto him, I have bought a *piece of ground* **field**, and I *must needs* **need** go and see it: I *pray* **ask** thee have me *excused* **beg off**.
19	And another said, I have bought five yoke of oxen, and I go to prove them: I *pray* **ask** thee have me *excused* **beg off**.
20	And another said, I have married a *wife* **woman**, and *therefore* **because of this** I cannot come.
21	So that servant came, and *shewed* **evangelized** his *lord* **adoni** these *things*. Then the *master of the house* **housedespotes** being *angry* **wroth** said to his servant, Go out quickly into the *streets* **broadways** and *lanes* **streets** of the city, and bring in hither the poor, and the maimed, and the *halt* **lame**, and the blind.
22	And the servant said, *Lord* **Adoni**, *so be* it is *done* as thou hast *commanded* **ordered**, and yet there is *room* **place**.
23	And the *lord* **adoni** said unto the servant,

and not straightway draws him on the shabbath day?

6	— and they cannot contradict him as to these.

Yah Shua On Position

7	And he words a parable to those called — heeding how they select the preeminent recliners;

wording to them,
8 Whenever anyone calls you to a marriage
recline not in the highest room;
lest ever he calls a more honorable than you:
9 and he who called you comes and says to you,
Give this one the place:
and you begin to shame to hold on to the final place.
10 But when you are called,
go and repose in the final place;
so that whenever he who called you comes,
he says to you, Friend, ascend higher!
— then you have glory
in the sight of them who repose with you.
11 For whoever exalts himself is humbled;
and whoever humbles himself is exalted.
12 And he also words to him who called him,
Whenever you make a dinner or a supper,
voice out, neither to your friends nor your brothers,
nor your kin nor your rich neighbors;
lest ever they also call you back
and a recompence becomes you:
13 but whenever you make a feast,
call the poor, the maimed, the lame, the blind:
14 and you are blessed;
for they cannot recompense you:
for you are recompensed
at the resurrection of the just.

Yah Shua On The Mega Supper

15 And one of them reposing with him hears these,
and says to him,
Blessed — whoever eats bread
in the sovereigndom of Elohim.
16 But he says to him,
A human made a mega supper and called many:
17 and apostolized his servant at supper hour
to say to the called, Come!
For all are already prepared.
18 — and they all begin to beg off.
The first says to him,
I bought a field, and I need go and see it:
I ask you that I beg off.
19 And another says,
I bought five yoke of oxen, and I go to prove them:
I ask you that I beg off.
20 And another says,
I married a woman, and because of this
I cannot come.
21 So that servant comes,
and evangelizes these to his adoni.

So, being wroth,
the housedespotes says to his servant,
Go quickly into the broadways and streets of the city
and bring in the poor and the maimed
and the lame and the blind!
22 And the servant says, Adoni,
so be it as you ordered,
and still there is place.
23 And the adoni says to the servant,
Go out into the *highways* **ways** and hedges,
and compel them to *come in* **enter**,
that my house may be filled.
24 For I *say* **word** unto you,
That none of those men which were *bidden* **called**
shall taste of my supper.

Yah Shua On Discipleship

25 And there went *great* **vast** multitudes with him:
and he turned, and said unto them,
26 If any *man* come to me,
and hate not his father, and mother, and *wife* **woman**,
and children, and brethren, and sisters,
yea, and **even** his own *life* **soul** *also*,
he cannot be my disciple.
27 And whosoever *doth* **shall**
not bear his *cross* **stake**,
and come after me, cannot be my disciple.

The Tower

28 For which of you,
intending **having willed** to build a tower,
indeed sitteth not down first,
and *counteth* **computeth** the *cost* **expense**,
whether he have *sufficient to finish it* **for the finishing**?
29 Lest *haply* **ever**,
after he hath *laid* **placed** the foundation,
and is not able to *finish* **fully complete** it,
all that *behold* **observe** it begin to mock him,
30 *saying* **wording**, This *man*
human began to build,
and was not able to *finish* **fully complete/shalam**.

Treaty Of Shalom

31 Or what *king* **sovereign**,
going to *make* **encounter** war against
another *king* **sovereign**,
indeed sitteth not down first,
and *consulteth* **counseleth**
whether he be able *with* **by** ten thousand
to meet him that cometh against him

	with twenty thousand?
32	Or else **But if not**,
	while the other is yet *a great way* **afar** off,
	he *sendeth an ambassage* **apostolizeth a presbytry**
	and *desireth conditions of peace* **asketh for shalom**.
33	So *likewise* **then**, whosoever he be of you
	that *forsaketh* **biddeth** not **bye bye**
	all that he hath **to all his holdings**,
	he cannot be my disciple.

Yah Shua On Insipid Salt

34	Salt is good:
	but *if* the salt have *lost his savour* **become insipid**,
	wherewith shall it be seasoned?
35	It is neither *well* **fit** for the *land* **earth**,
	nor yet for *the dunghill* **manure**; but men cast it *out*.
	He that hath ears to hear, let him hear.

Yah Shua On The Lost Sheep

15	*Then drew near* **And approached** unto him
	all the *publicans* **customs agents** and sinners
	for to hear him.
2	And the Pharisees and scribes murmured,
	saying **wording**,
	This *man receiveth* **one awaiteth** sinners,
	and eateth with them.
3	And he *spake* **worded** this parable unto them,
	saying **speaking**,
4	What *man* **human** of you,
	having an hundred sheep,
	if he lose one of them,
	doth not leave the ninety and nine in the wilderness,
	and go after that which is lost, until he find it?
5	And when he hath found it,
	he *layeth* **putteth** it on his shoulders, *rejoicing* **cheering**.
6	And when he cometh home,
	he calleth together his friends and neighbours,
	saying **wording** unto them, Rejoice with me;
	for I have found my sheep which was lost.
7	I *say* **word** unto you,
	that likewise *joy* **cheer** shall be in heaven
	over one sinner that repenteth,
	more than over ninety and nine just persons,
	which need no repentance.

Yah Shua On The Lost Drachma

8	*Either* **Or** what woman having
	ten *pieces of silver* **drachmas**,
	Go into the ways and hedges and compel them to enter,
	to fill my house.

24	For I word to you,
	That none of those men who are called
	taste of my supper.

Yah Shua On Discipleship

25	And vast multitudes go with him:
	and he turns, and says to them,
26	If anyone comes to me,
	and hates not his father and mother and woman
	and children and brothers and sisters
	— yes, and even his own soul,
	he cannot be my disciple.
27	And whoever bears not his stake,
	and comes after me, cannot be my disciple.

The Tower

28	For who of you, who wills to build a tower,
	indeed sits not down first and computes the expense,
	whether he has *enough* for the finishing?
29	Lest ever, after he places the foundation
	and is not able to fully complete,
	all who observe begin to mock him,
30	wording, This human began to build,
	and is not able to fully complete/shalam.

Treaty Of Shalom

31	Or what sovereign,
	going to encounter war against another sovereign,
	indeed sits not down first,
	and counsels
	whether he is able by ten thousand
	to meet him who comes against him
	with twenty thousand?
32	But if not, while the other is yet afar off,
	he apostolizes a presbytry and asks for shalom.
33	So then, everyone of you
	who bids not bye bye to all his holdings
	cannot be my disciple.

Yah Shua On Insipid Salt

34	Salt is good:
	but the salt being insipid, how is it to season?
35	It is neither well fit for the earth,
	nor yet for manure; but for men to cast.
	Whoever has ears to hear, hear.

Yah Shua On The Lost Sheep

15	And all the customs agents and sinners
	approach to hear him:

2	and the Pharisees and scribes murmur, wording, This one awaits sinners and eats with them.
3	And he words this parable to them, speaking,
4	What human of you, having a hundred sheep, and loses one of them, leaves not the ninety—nine in the wilderness and goes after the lost, until he finds it?
5	And when he finds it, he puts it on his shoulders, cheering:
6	and when he comes home, he calls together his friends and neighbors, wording to them, Rejoice with me; for I found my sheep — the lost.
7	I word to you, that likewise cheer becomes in the heavens over one sinner who repents — more than over ninety—nine just persons who need no repentance.

Yah Shua On The Lost Drachma

8	Or what woman, having ten drachmas, *if* **whenever** she lose one *piece* **drachma**, doth not **indeed** light a candle, and sweep the house, and seek *diligently* **carefully** till she find it?
9	And when she hath found it, she calleth her friends and her neighbours together, *saying* **wording**, Rejoice with me; for I have found the *piece* **drachma** which I had lost.
10	Likewise, I *say* **word** unto you, there *is joy* **shall be cheer** in the *presence* **sight** of the angels of *God* **Elohim** over one sinner that repenteth.

Yah Shua On The Lost Son

11	And he said, A *certain man* **human** had two sons:
12	And the younger of them said to his father, Father, give me the portion of *goods* **substance** that *falleth to* **is laid up for** me. And he *divided* **distributed** unto them his *living* **subsistence**.
13	And not many days after the younger son gathered all together, and *took his journey* **went abroad** into a *far country* **distant region**, and there *wasted* **squandered** his substance with *riotous* **dissipative** living.
14	And when he had spent all, there *arose* **became** a mighty famine in that *land* **region**; and he began to *be in want* **lack**.
15	And he went and joined himself to a citizen of that *country* **region**; and he sent him into his fields to *feed* **graze** swine.
16	And he *would fain have filled* **panted to fill** his belly with the *husks* **pods** that the swine did eat: and no *man* **one** gave unto him.
17	And when he came to himself, he said, How many *hired servants* **hirelings** of my father's have bread *enough and to spare* **super abundant**, and I *perish* **destruct** with *hunger* **famine**!
18	I *will* **shall** arise and go to my father, and *will* **shall** say unto him, Father, I have sinned against heaven, and *before thee* **in thy sight**,
19	And am no more worthy to be called thy son: make me as one of thy *hired servants* **hirelings**.
20	And he arose, and came to his father. But when he was yet *a great way* **afar** off, his father saw him, and had *compassion* **a sympathetic spleen**, and ran, and fell on his neck, and **ardently** kissed him.
21	And the son said unto him, Father, I have sinned against heaven, and in thy sight, and am no more worthy to be called thy son.
22	But the father said to his servants, Bring *forth* the *best robe* **preeminent stole**, and *put it on* **endue** him; and *put* **give** a *finger* ring on his hand, and shoes on his feet:
23	And bring hither the fatted calf, and *kill it* **sacrifice**; and let us eat, and *be merry* **rejoice**:
24	For this my son was dead, and *is alive again* **reliveth**; he was lost, and is found. And they began to *be merry* **rejoice**.
25	*Now* **And** his elder son was in the field: and as he came and *drew nigh to* **approached** the house, he heard *musick* **symphony** and *dancing* **chorus**.
26	And he called one of the *servants* **lads**, and asked what these *things meant* **be**.
27	And he said unto him, Thy brother is come; and thy father hath *killed* **sacrificed** the fatted calf, because he hath *received* **taken** him safe and sound.
28	And he was *angry* **wroth**, and *would* **willed to** not *go in* **enter**: *therefore* **so** came his father out, and *intreated* **consoled** him.
29	And he answering said to his father,

Lo **Behold**, *these* **so** many years do I serve thee,
neither transgressed I at any time
never ever have I passed over
thy *commandment* **misvah**:
and yet thou never **ever** gavest me a *kid* **goat**,
that I might *make merry* **rejoice** with my friends:
whenever she loses one drachma,
does not indeed light a candle and sweep the house
and seeks carefully until she finds it?

9 And when she finds it,
she calls her friends and her neighbors together,
wording, Rejoice with me;
for I found the drachma I lost.

10 Likewise, I word to you,
cheer becomes in the sight of the angels of Elohim
over one sinner who repents.

Yah Shua On The Lost Son

11 And he says, A human has two sons:
12 and the younger of them says to his father,
Father, give me the portion of substance laid up.
— and he distributes his subsistence to them.
13 And not many days after
the younger son gathers all together and goes abroad
to a distant region; and there squanders his substance
with dissipative living
14 and he spends it all:
and a mighty famine becomes in that region;
and he begins to lack:
15 and he goes and joins himself
to a citizen of that region:
and he sends him into his fields to graze swine:
16 and he pants to fill his belly
with the pods the swine eat:
and no one gives him.
17 And he comes to himself, and says,
How many hirelings of my father
have super abundant bread,
and I destruct with famine!
18 I rise and go to my father, and say to him,
Father, I sinned against the heavens and in your sight;
19 and am no more worthy to be called your son:
make me as one of your hirelings.
20 And he rises, and comes to his father.
and still being afar,
his father sees him and has a sympathetic spleen
and runs and falls on his neck
and ardently kisses him:
21 — and the son says to him, Father,
I sinned against the heavens and in your sight
and am no more worthy to be called your son.
22 But the father says to his servants,
Bring the preeminent stole and endue him;
and give a finger ring on his hand
and shoes on his feet;
23 and bring the fatted calf and sacrifice;
and eat, and rejoice:
24 for this my son was dead, and relives;
he was lost, and is found.
— and they begin to rejoice.
25 And his elder son is in the field:
and as he comes and approaches the house
he hears symphony and chorus:
26 and he calls one of the lads,
and asks what these be.
27 And he says to him, Your brother is come;
and your father sacrifices the fatted calf
because he takes him safe and sound.
28 — and he is wroth and wills to not enter.
So his father comes out to console him:
29 and he answers his father, saying,
Behold, so many years I serve you,
never ever passed I over your misvah:
and yet you never ever gave me a goat
to rejoice with my friends:
30 But as soon as this thy son was come,
which hath devoured thy *living* **subsistence**
with *harlots* **whores**,
thou hast *killed* **sacrificed** for him the fatted calf.
31 And he said unto him, *Son* **Child**,
thou art ever with me, and all that I have is thine.
32 It was *meet* **necessary**
that we should *make merry* **rejoice**, and *be glad* **cheer**:
for this thy brother was dead, and *is alive again* **reliveth**;
and was lost, and is found.

Yah Shua On The Thoughtful Administrator

16 And he *said* **worded** also unto his disciples,
There was a *certain* rich *man* **human**,
which had *a steward* **an administrator**;
and *the same* **this one** was accused unto him
that he had *wasted* **squandered** his *goods* **holdings**.
2 And he *called* **voiced out**
to him, and said unto him,
How **What** is it that I hear this *of* **concerning** thee?
give *an account* **word**
of thy *stewardship* **administration**;
for thou mayest *not still* be *no longer*
steward **administrator**.

3   Then **And** the *steward*
administrator said within himself,
What shall I do?
for my *lord taketh away* **adoni removeth** from me
the *stewardship* **administration**:
I cannot dig; to beg I am ashamed.
4   I *am resolved* **know** what to do,
that, when **ever** I am
put out of **removed from** the
stewardship **administration**,
they may receive me into their houses.
5   So **And** he called *every* **each** one
of his *lord's* **adoni's** debtors unto him,
and *said* **worded** unto the first,
How much *owest* **art** thou **indebted** unto my *lord* **adoni**?
6   And he said, An hundred
measures **baths** of *olive* oil.
And he said unto him, *Take* **Receive** thy *bill* **scribing**,
and sit down quickly, and *write* **scribe** fifty.
7   Then said he to another,
And how much *owest* **art** thou **indebted**?
And he said, An hundred *measures* **kors** of *wheat* **grain**.
And he *said* **worded** unto him,
Take **Receive** thy *bill* **scribing**,
and *write fourscore* **scribe eighty**.
8   And *the Lord* **Adonay**
commended **halaled** the unjust *steward* **administrator**,
because he had done *wisely* **thoughtfully**:
for the *children* **sons** of this *world* **eon** are
in their generation
wiser **more thoughtful** than the *children* **sons** of light.
9   And I *say* **word** unto you,
Make to yourselves
friends of the mammon of *unrighteousness* **injustice**;
that, when **ever** ye fail,
they may receive you
into *everlasting habitations* **eternal tabernacles**.
10   He that is *faithful* **trustworthy**
in that which is least
is *faithful* **trustworthy** also in much:
and he that is unjust in the least
is unjust also in much.
11   **So** If *therefore*
ye have not *been faithful* **become trustworthy**
in the *unrighteous* **unjust** mammon,
who *will commit to your trust* **shall entrust you**
to **with** the true?
12   And if ye have not *been*
faithful **become trustworthy**
in that which is *another man's* **another's**, who
shall give you that which is your own?
13   No *servant* **housekeeper**
can serve two *masters* **adonim**:
for either he *will* **shall** hate the one,
and love the other;
or else he *will hold to* **shall uphold** the one,
and *despise* **disesteem** the other.
Ye cannot serve *God* **Elohim** and mammon.
14   And the Pharisees also,
who *were covetous* **befriended silver**,
heard all these *things*:
and they *derided* **sneered at** him.
30   but as soon as this — your son comes
— who devoured your subsistence with whores,
for him you sacrifice the fatted calf.
31   And he says to him,
Child, you are ever with me; and all I have is yours.
32   It is necessary to rejoice, and cheer:
for this your brother was dead and relives;
and was lost, and is found.

Yah Shua On The Thoughtful Administrator

16   And he also words to his disciples,
A rich human has an administrator;
who is accused of squandering his holdings:
2   and he voices out to him, and says to him,
What hear I concerning you?
Give word of your administration;
for you are not still my administrator.
3   And the administrator says within himself,
What do I?
— for my adoni removes the administration from me:
I cannot dig; I am ashamed to beg:
4   I know what to do:
whenever I am removed from the administration,
that they receive me into their houses.
5   And he calls
each one of the debtors of his adoni to him;
and words to the first,
How much are you indebted to my adoni?
6   And he says, A hundred baths of olive oil.
And he says to him, Receive your scribing,
and sit down quickly and scribe fifty.
7   Then he says to another,
And how much are you indebted?
And he says, A hundred kors of grain.
And he words to him,
Receive your scribing and scribe eighty.

8	And Adonay halals the unjust administrator
	because he did thoughtfully:
	for the sons of this eon in their generation
	are more thoughtful than the sons of light.
9	And I word to you,
	Make yourselves friends of the mammon of injustice;
	so that, whenever you fail,
	they receive you into eternal tabernacles.
10	Whoever is trustworthy in the least
	is also trustworthy in much:
	and whoever is unjust in the least
	is also unjust in much.
11	So if you are not trustworthy
	in the unjust mammon,
	who entrusts you with the true?
12	And if you are not trustworthy
	in that of another,
	who gives you that which is your own?
13	No housekeeper can serve two adonim:
	for either he hates the one and loves the other;
	or else he upholds the one and disesteems the other.
	You cannot serve Elohim and mammon.
14	And the Pharisees who befriend silver
	also hear all these:
	and they sneer at him.
15	And he said unto them,
	Ye are they which justify yourselves
	before men **in the sight of humanity**;
	but *God* **Elohim** knoweth your hearts:
	for that which is *highly esteemed*
	high among *men* **humanity**
	is abomination in the sight of *God* **Elohim**.

Yah Shua On The Torah And The Prophets

16	The *law* **torah** and the
	prophets were until *John* **Yahn**:
	since *that time* **then**
	the *kingdom* **sovereigndom** of *God* **Elohim**
	is *preached* **evangelized**,
	and every *man presseth* **one forceth** into it.
17	And it is easier for heaven and earth to pass,
	than one tittle of the *law* **torah** to *fail* **fall**.
18	Whosoever *putteth away*
	releaseth his *wife* **woman**,
	and marrieth another, *committeth adultery*
	adulterizeth: and whosoever marrieth her
	that is *put away* **released** from her *husband* **man**
	committed adultery **adulterizeth**.

Yah Shua On The Rich Human And El Azar

19	There was a *certain* rich *man* **human**,
	which was clothed in purple and *fine* **white** linen,
	and *fared sumptuously every day*
	rejoiced radiantly daily:
20	And there was a *certain* beggar
	named *Lazarus* **El Azar**,
	which was *laid* **cast** at his gate, *full of sores* **ulcerous**,
21	And *desiring* **panting** to be
	fed **filled** with the crumbs
	which fell from the rich man's table:
	moreover **but even** the dogs came
	and licked his *sores* **ulcers**.
22	And **so be** it *came to pass*, that the beggar died,
	and was *carried* **borne** by the angels
	into Abraham's bosom:
	the rich man also died, and was *buried* **entombed**;
23	And in *hell* **sheol/hades** he lift *up* his eyes,
	being in torments,
	and seeth Abraham afar off,
	and *Lazarus* **El Azar** in his bosom.
24	And he *cried* **voiced out**
	and said, Father Abraham,
	have mercy *on* me, and send *Lazarus* **El Azar**,
	that he may *dip* **baptize** the tip of his finger in water,
	and cool my tongue;
	for I am *tormented* **grieved** in this flame.
25	But Abraham said, *Son* **Child**,
	remember that thou in thy life *time*
	receivedst **took** thy good *things*,
	and likewise *Lazarus* **El Azar** evil *things*:
	but now he is *comforted* **consoled**,
	and thou art *tormented* **grieved**.
26	And beside all this, between us and you
	there is a *great gulf fixed* **mega chasm established**:
	so that they which *would* **will to** pass **through**
	from hence to you cannot;
	neither can they pass **through** to us,
	that would come from thence.
27	*Then* **And** he said, *So* I *pray*
	ask thee *therefore*, father,
	that thou *wouldest* **shouldest** send him
	to my father's house:
28	For I have five brethren;
	that he may *testify* **throroughly witness** unto them,
	lest they also come into this place of torment.
29	Abraham *saith* **wordeth** unto him,
	They have *Moses* **Mosheh** and the prophets;
	let them hear them.
30	And he said, *Nay* **Indeed not**, father Abraham:

LUKE/UR 17

but *if* **whenever** one went unto them from the dead,
they *will* **shall** repent.
31   And he said unto him,
If they hear not *Moses* **Mosheh** and the prophets,
neither *will* **shall** they be *persuaded* **convinced**,
though *if* **not even whenever** one rose from the dead.

YAH SHUA ON SCANDALS

17   *Then* **And** said he unto the disciples,
It is impossible
but that offences will **that scandals shall not** come:
but woe *unto him,* through whom they come!
2   It were *better* **more advantageous** for him
that if a millstone **turned by a burro**
15   And he says to them,
You justify yourselves in the sight of humanity;
but Elohim knows your hearts:
for what is high among humanity
is abomination in the sight of Elohim.

YAH SHUA ON THE TORAH AND THE PROPHETS

16   The torah and the prophets *were* until Yahn:
since then, the sovereigndom of Elohim is evangelized,
and everyone forces into it:
17   and it is easier for the heavens and earth to pass
than one tittle of the torah to fall:
18   whoever releases his woman
and marries another
adulterizes:
and whoever marries her
who is released from her man
adulterizes.

YAH SHUA ON THE RICH HUMAN AND EL AZAR

19   A rich human clothed in purple and white linen
rejoices radiantly daily:
20   and a beggar named El Azar is cast at his gate
— ulcerous;
21   and panting to be filled with the crumbs
which fall from the table of the rich man:
but even the dogs come and lick his ulcers.
22   And so be it, the beggar dies,
and is borne by the angels to the bosom of Abraham:
the rich man also dies and is entombed;
23   and in sheol/hades, being in torments,
he lifts his eyes,
and sees Abraham afar off and El Azar in his bosom.

24   And he voices out and says, Father Abraham,
mercy me, and send El Azar
to baptize the tip of his finger in water
and cool my tongue;
for I grieve in this flame.
25   But Abraham says, Child,
remember that you in your life took your good;
and El Azar likewise evil:
and now he consoles and you grieve:
26   and beside all this, between us and you,
a mega chasm is established:
so that whoever wills
neither can pass through from hence to you;
nor can they pass through to us from there.
27   And he says, So I ask you, father,
to send him to the house of my father:
28   for I have five brothers
— to throroughly witness to them
lest they also come into this place of torment.
29   Abraham words to him,
They have Mosheh and the prophets;
have them hear them.
30   And he says, Indeed not, father Abraham:
but whenever one from the dead goes to them,
they repent.
31   And he says to him,
If they hear not Mosheh and the prophets,
they are not convinced
even whenever one rises from the dead.

YAH SHUA ON SCANDALS

17   And he says to the disciples,
It is impossible that scandals not come:
but woe through whom they come!
2   It is more advantageous for him
if a millstone turned by a burro
were hanged about his neck,
and he *cast* **tossed** into the sea,
than that he should *offend* **scandalize**
one of these little ones.
3   *Take* heed to yourselves:
if **whenever** thy brother *trespass* **sin**
against thee, rebuke him;
and *if* **whenever** he repent, forgive him.
4   And *if* **whenever** he *trespass* **sin** against thee
seven times in a day,
and seven times in a day turn again to thee,
saying **wording**, I repent;
thou shalt forgive him.
5   And the apostles said unto *the Lord* **Adonay**,

	Increase **Add to** our *faith* **trust**.
6	And *the Lord* **Adonay** said,

If ye had *faith* **trust** as a *grain of* mustard *seed* **kernel**,
ye might *say* **word** unto this sycamine *tree*,
Be thou *plucked up by the root* **uprooted**,
and be thou planted in the sea; and it should obey you.

7	But which of you,

having a servant plowing or *feeding cattle* **shepherding**,
will **shall** say unto him *by and by* **straightway**,
when he *is come* **entereth** from the field,
Go, *and sit down to meat* **pass near and repose**?

8	*And will* **But indeed, shall**

he not *rather* say unto him,
Make ready **Prepare** wherewith I may sup,
and gird thyself,
and *serve* **minister to** me, till I have eaten and drunken;
and *afterward* **after these** thou shalt eat and drink?

9	*Doth he thank* **Hath he charism for** that servant

because he did *the things* **those**
that were *commanded* **ordained** of him?
I *trow* **think** not.

10	So likewise ye,

when *ever* ye shall have done all those *things*
which are *commanded* **ordained** you,
say **word**, We are *unprofitable* **useless** servants:
we have done that
which *was our duty* **we were indebted** to do.

Yah Shua Heals Ten Lepers

11	And **so be** it *came to pass*,

as he went to *Jerusalem* **Yeru Shalem**,
that he passed through
the midst of *Samaria* **Shomeron** and *Galilee* **Galiyl**.

12	And as he entered into a *certain* village,

there met him ten men that were lepers,
which stood afar off:

13	And they lifted *up* their

voices, and *said* **worded**,
Jesus **Yah Shua**, *Master* **Rabbi**, *have* mercy *on* us.

14	And when he saw them, he said unto them,

Go shew yourselves unto the priests.
And **so be** it *came to pass*, that,
as they went, they were *cleansed* **purified**.

15	And one of them, when he

saw that he was healed,
turned back **returned**,
and with a *loud* **mega** voice glorified *God* **Elohim**,

16	And fell down on his face at his feet,

giving **eucharistizing** him *thanks*:
and he was a *Samaritan* **Shomeroniy**.

17	And *Jesus* **Yah Shua** answering said,

Were there not **indeed** ten *cleansed* **purified**?
but where are the nine?

18	There are not found

that returned to give glory to *God* **Elohim**,
save **except** this *stranger* **alien**.

19	And he said unto him, Arise, go thy way:

thy *faith* **trust** hath *made* **saved** thee *whole*.

Yah Shua On The Sovereigndom Of Elohim

20	And when he was *demanded*

asked of the Pharisees,
when the *kingdom* **sovereigndom** of *God* **Elohim**
should come,
he answered them and said,
The *kingdom* **sovereigndom** of *God* **Elohim**
cometh not with observation:

21	Neither shall they say,

Lo **Behold** here! or, *Lo* **Behold** there! for, behold,
the *kingdom* **sovereigndom** of *God*
Elohim is within you.

22	And he said unto the disciples,

The days *will* **shall** come,
hangs around his neck,
and he is tossed into the sea,
than that he scandalize one of these little ones.

3	Heed yourselves:

Whenever your brother sins against you, rebuke him;
and whenever he repents, forgive him:

4	and whenever he sins against

you seven times a day
and seven times a day turns again to you,
wording, I repent;
forgive him.

5	And the apostles say to Adonay,

Add to our trust.

6	And Adonay says,

If you had trust as a mustard kernel,
you ever word to this sycamine,
Uproot! Plant in the sea!
— and it obeys you.

7	But who of you,

having a servant plowing or shepherding,
says to him straightway as he enters from the field,
Come and repose?

8	But indeed, says he not to him,

Prepare somewhat to sup,
and gird yourself
and minister to me until I eat and drink
— and after these you eat and drink?

9 Has he charism for that servant
because he did what is ordained of him?
I think not.
10 So likewise you,
whenever you do all you are ordained,
word, We are useless servants:
we do what we are indebted to do.

Yah Shua Heals Ten Lepers

11 And so be it, as he goes to Yeru Shalem,
he passes through midst Shomeron and Galiyl:
12 and as he enters a village,
ten men — lepers meet him, standing afar:
13 and they lift their voices, and word,
Yah Shua, Rabbi, mercy us.
14 And he sees them and says,
Go show yourselves to the priests.
— and so be it, as they go, they are purified.
15 And one of them seeing he is healed, returns,
and with a mega voice glorifies Elohim;
16 and falls on his face at his feet
and eucharistizes him
— and he is a Shomeroniy.
17 And Yah Shua answers, saying,
Were there not indeed ten purified?
but the nine — where?
18 None are found who return
to give glory to Elohim
except this alien:
19 and he says to him, Rise, go your way:
your trust saves you.

Yah Shua On The Sovereigndom Of Elohim

20 And the Pharisees ask
when the sovereigndom of Elohim is coming;
and he answers them, saying,
The sovereigndom of Elohim comes
neither with observation:
21 nor say they,
Behold here! or, Behold there!
for, behold,
the sovereigndom of Elohim is within you.
22 And he says to the disciples, Days come,
when ye shall *desire* **pant**
to see one of the days of the Son of *man* **humanity**,
and ye shall not see it.
23 And they shall say to you,
See **Behold** here; or, *see* **behold** there:
go not after them, nor *follow* **pursue** them.
24 For **exactly** as the lightning,
that *lighteneth* **lightningeth**
out of the one part under heaven,
shineth **radiateth** unto the other part under heaven;
so shall also the Son of *man* **humanity** be in his day.
25 But first must he suffer *many things* **much**,
and be *rejected* **dissapproved** of this generation.
26 And **exactly** as it *was* **became**
in the days of *Noe* **Noach**,
so shall it be also
in the days of the Son of *man* **humanity**.
27 They did eat, they drank, they married *wives*,
they *were given in marriage* **married off**,
until the day that *Noe* **Noach** entered into the ark,
and the *flood* **cataclysm** came, and destroyed them all.
28 Likewise also as it *was*
became in the days of Lot;
they *did eat* **ate**, they drank,
they bought, they sold, they planted, they builded;
29 But the same day that Lot
went out of *Sodom* **Sedom**
it rained fire and *brimstone* **sulphur** from
heaven, and destroyed them all.
30 *Even thus* **In like manner**
shall it be in the day
when the Son of *man* **humanity** is *revealed* **unveiled**.
31 In that day,
he which shall be upon the housetop,
and his *stuff* **vessels** in the house,
let him not *come down* **descend** to take it away:
and he that is in the field,
let him likewise not return *back*.
32 Remember Lot's *wife* **woman**.
33 Whosoever shall seek to save his *life* **soul**
shall lose it;
and whosoever shall lose *his life* **it**
shall preserve it.
34 I *tell* **word to** you, in that night
there shall be two *men* in one bed;
the one shall be taken,
and the other shall be *left* **forsaken**.
35 Two *women* shall be grinding together;
the one shall be taken, and the other *left* **forsaken**.
36 Two *men* shall be in the field;
the one shall be taken, and the other *left* **forsaken**.
37 And they answered and *said* **worded** unto him,
Where, *Lord* **Adonay**?
And he said unto them, Wheresoever the body is,
thither will **there shall** the eagles be gathered together.

Yah Shua On The Judge And The Widow

18 And he *spake* **worded** a parable unto them
to this end,
that men *ought always to* **must ever** pray,
and not *to faint* **weary**;

2 *Saying* **Wording**,
There was in a city a judge,
which *feared* **awed** not *God* **Elohim**,
neither *regarded man* **respected humanity**:

3 And there was a widow in that city;
and she came unto him, *saying* **wording**,
Avenge me of mine adversary.

4 And he *would* **willed** not *to* **for a** *while* **time**:
but *afterward* **after these** he said within himself,
Though I *fear* **awe** not *God* **Elohim**,
nor *regard man* **respect humanity**;

5 Yet **indeed**
because this widow *troubleth* **embarrasseth** me,
I *will* **shall** avenge her,
lest by her *continual* coming **unto**
the completion/shalom
she *weary* **subdue** me.

6 And *the Lord* **Adonay** said,
Hear what the unjust judge *saith* **wordeth**.

7 And shall not *God* **Elohim**
avenge his own *elect* **select**,
which cry day and night unto him,
when you pant
to see one of the days of the Son of humanity,
and you see it not:

23 and they say to you,
Behold here! or, Behold there!
neither go after, nor pursue them:

24 for exactly as the lightning
lightnings from the one part under the heavens,
radiating to the other part under the heavens,
so also becomes the Son of humanity in his day.

25 But first he must suffer much
and be dissapproved by this generation.

26 And exactly as it became in the days of Noach,
so it also becomes
in the days of the Son of humanity:

27 they ate, they drank, they
married, they married off
until the day Noach entered the ark,
and the cataclysm came and destroyed them all.

28 Likewise also, so it became in the days of Lot;
they ate, they drank,
they bought, they sold, they planted, they built:

29 but the same day Lot came from Sedom
fire and sulphur rained from the heavens
and destroyed all.

30 In like manner, it becomes
in the day the Son of humanity is unveiled:

31 In that day,
whoever is on the housetop
and his vessels in the house,
descend not to take it away:
and likewise whoever is in the field,
return not.

32 Remember the woman of Lot.

33 Whoever seeks to save his soul, loses it;
and whoever loses it, preserves it.

34 I word to you, in that night,
two are in one bed;
the one *is* taken and the other forsaken:

35 two are grinding together;
the one *is* taken and the other forsaken:

36 two are in the field;
the one *is* taken, and the other forsaken.

37 And they answer him, wording,
Where, Adonay?
And he says to them, Wherever the body is,
the eagles gather together.

Yah Shua On The Judge And The Widow

18 And he words a parable to them, to this end,
that men must ever pray and not weary:

2 wording, There is a judge in a city,
who neither awes Elohim nor respects humanity:

3 and there is a widow in that city;
and she comes to him, wording,
Avenge me of mine adversary.

4 And for a time, he wills not:
but after these he says within himself,
Though I neither awe Elohim nor respect humanity;

5 yet indeed, because this widow embarrasses me,
I avenge her;
lest by her coming to the completion/shalom,
she subdues me.

6 And Adonay says,
Hear what the unjust judge words:

7 avenges not Elohim his own select
who cry day and night to him
though he *bear long* **be patient** with them?

8 I *tell* **word unto** you
that he *will* **shall** avenge them *speedily* **with quickness**.
Nevertheless **However**
when the Son of *man* **humanity** cometh,

shall he find *faith* **trust** on the earth?

9 And he *spake* **said** this
parable unto *certain* **some**
which *trusted* **confided** in themselves
that they were *righteous* **just**,
and *despised others* **belittled the rest**:

YAH SHUA ON THE PHARISEE AND THE CUSTOMS AGENT

10 Two *men went up* **humans ascended**
into the *temple* **priestal precinct** to pray;
the one a Pharisee,
and the other a *publican* **customs agent**.
11 The Pharisee stood
and prayed *thus* **these** with himself,
God **Elohim**, I *thank* **eucharistize** thee,
that I am not **exactly**
as *other men are* **the rest of humanity**,
extortioners **plunderers**, unjust, adulterers,
or even as this *publican* **customs agent**.
12 I fast twice *in* **on** the *week* **shabbath**,
I *give tithes of* **tithe** all *that —* **as much as** I possess.
13 And the *publican* **customs agent**, standing afar off,
would **willed to** not **even** lift *up* so much as his eyes
unto heaven,
but *smote* **struck** upon his *breast* **chest**, *saying* **wording**,
God be merciful to **Elohim, kapur/atone for** me a sinner.
14 I *tell* **word** unto you,
this *man went down* **one descended**
to his house justified
rather than the other:
for every one that exalteth himself
shall be *abased* **humbled**;
and he that humbleth himself
shall be exalted.

YAH SHUA ON INFANTS

15 And they *brought unto* **offered** him also infants,
that he *would* **should** touch them:
but when his disciples saw it, they rebuked them.
16 But *Jesus* **Yah Shua** called
them *unto him*, and said,
Suffer **Allow** little children to come unto me,
and forbid them not:
for of such is the *kingdom* **sovereigndom** of *God* **Elohim**.
17 *Verily I say* **Amen! I word** unto you,
Whosoever *shall not —* **unless you**
receive the *kingdom* **sovereigndom** of *God* **Elohim**
as a little child

shall *in no wise enter* **no way entereth** therein.

YAH SHUA ON ETERNAL LIFE

18 And *a certain ruler* **an arch** asked him,
saying **wording**, Good *Master* **Doctor**,
what shall I do to inherit eternal life?
19 And *Jesus* **Yah Shua** said unto him,
Why *callest* **wordest** thou me good?
none is good, *save* **except** one, *that is*, *God* **Elohim**.
20 Thou knowest the *commandments* **misvoth**,
Do not commit adultery **adulterize not**,
Do not kill **murder not**,
Do not steal **not**,
Do not bear false **pseudo** witness **not**,
Honour thy father and thy mother.
21 And he said,
All these have I *kept* **guarded** from my youth up.
22 Now when *Jesus* **Yah Shua** heard these *things*,
he said unto him, Yet lackest thou one *thing*:
sell all *that —* **as much as** thou hast,
and distribute unto the poor,
and thou shalt have treasure in heaven:
and come, follow me.
23 And when he heard *this* **these**,
he *was very* **became exceeding** sorrowful:
for he was *very* **extremely** rich.
24 And when *Jesus* **Yah Shua** saw
that he *was very* **became exceeding** sorrowful, he said,
How *hardly* shall **difficultly** they that have riches
enter into the *kingdom* **sovereigndom** of *God* **Elohim**!
— though he is patient with them?
8 I word to you
that he avenges them with quickness.
However when the Son of humanity comes,
finds he trust on the earth?
9 — and he says this parable to some
who confide in themselves that they are just
and belittle the rest:

YAH SHUA ON THE PHARISEE AND THE CUSTOMS AGENT

10 Two humans
ascend into the priestal precinct to pray;
the one a Pharisee and the other a customs agent.
11 The Pharisee stands and
prays these with himself,
Elohim, I eucharistize you,
that I am not exactly as the rest of humanity
— plunderers, unjust, adulterers,
or even as this customs agent:

12	I fast twice on the shabbath, I tithe all — as much as I possess.		and he says, How difficultly they who have riches enter the sovereigndom of Elohim!
13	And the customs agent, stands afar off, and wills not even so much as to lift his eyes to the heavens; but strikes on his chest, wording, Elohim, kapur/atone for me a sinner.	25	For it is easier for a *camel* **rope*** to *go* **enter** through a needle's eye, than for *a* **the** rich *man* to enter into the *kingdom* **sovereigndom** of *God* **Elohim**. *see Lamsa
14	I word to you, this one descends to his house justified rather than the other: for everyone who exalts himself, is humbled; and whoever humbles himself, is exalted.	26	And they that heard it said, Who then can be saved?
		27	And he said, *The things* **Those** which are impossible with *men* **humanity** are possible with *God* **Elohim**.

YAH SHUA ON INFANTS

15 And they also offer him infants to touch:
but his disciples see, and rebuke them.
16 But Yah Shua calls them, and says,
Allow little children to come to me
and forbid them not:
for of such is the sovereigndom of Elohim.
17 Amen! I word to you,
Whoever
— unless you receive the sovereigndom of Elohim
as a little child
you no way enter therein.

28 Then *Peter* **And Petros** said,
Lo **Behold**, we have *left* **forsaken** all, and followed thee.
29 And he said unto them,
Verily I say **Amen! I word** unto you,
There is no *man* **one** that hath *left* **forsaken** house,
or parents, or brethren, or *wife* **woman**, or children,
for the *kingdom* **sovereigndom** of *God's* **Elohim's** sake,
30 Who shall not **no way**
receive manifold **take much** more
in this present *time* **season**,
and in the *world* **eon** to come life *everlasting* **eternal**.

YAH SHUA ON ETERNAL LIFE

18 And an arch asks him, wording, Good Doctor,
What do I to inherit eternal life?
19 And Yah Shua says to him,
Why word you me good?
None is good, except one — Elohim.
20 You know the misvoth:
Adulterize not!
Murder not!
Steal not!
Pseudo witness not!
Honor your father and your mother!
21 And he says, I guarded all these from my youth.
22 And Yah Shua hears these, and says to him,
Yet you lack one:
sell all — as much as you have
and distribute to the poor
and have treasure in the heavens:
and come, follow me.
23 — and hearing these
he becomes exceeding sorrowful:
for he is extremely rich.
24 And Yah Shua sees
that he becomes exceeding sorrowful;

YAH SHUA PROPHECIES HIS DEATH AND RESURRECTION

31 Then he took unto him the
twelve, and said unto them,
Behold, we *go up* **ascend** to *Jerusalem* **Yeru Shalem**,
and all *things* that are *written* **scribed**
by **through** the prophets
concerning the Son of *man* **humanity**
shall be *accomplished* **completed/shalamed**.
32 For he shall be *delivered* **betrayed**
unto the *Gentiles* **goyim**,
and shall be mocked, and *spitefully entreated* **insulted**,
and spitted on:
33 And they shall scourge him,
and *put* **slaughter** him *to death*:
and the third day he shall rise *again*.
34 And they *understood* **comprehended**
none of these *things*:
and this *saying* **rhema** was *hid* **secreted** from them,
neither knew they
the things **those** which were *spoken* **worded**.

YAH SHUA HEALS SOMEONE BLIND

35 And **so be** it *came to pass*,

that as he *was come nigh* **approached**
unto *Jericho* **Yericho**,
a certain **someone** blind *man* sat
by the way side begging:
36 And hearing the multitude
pass by **going through**,
he asked what it meant.
37 And they *told* **evangelized** him,
that *Jesus of Nazareth* **Yah Shua the Nazarene**
passeth by.
38 And he cried, *saying* **wording**,
Jesus **Yah Shua**, *thou* son of David, *have* mercy *on* me.
39 And they which *went before*
preceded rebuked him,
that he should *hold his peace* **hush**:
but he cried so much the more,
Thou son of David, *have* mercy *on* me.
40 And *Jesus* **Yah Shua** stood,
and *commanded* **summoned** him
to be brought unto him:
and when he *was come near* **approached**, he asked him,
41 *Saying* **Wording**,
What *wilt* **willest** thou that I shall do unto thee?
And he said, *Lord* **Adonay**,
that I may *receive my sight* **see**.
42 And *Jesus* **Yah Shua** said unto him,
Receive thy sight **See**: thy *faith* **trust** hath saved thee.
43 And immediately he *received his sight* **saw**,
and followed him, glorifying *God* **Elohim**:
and all the people, when they saw it,
gave *praise* **halal** unto *God* **Elohim**.

Salvation Comes To House Of Zakkay

19 And *Jesus* **Yah Shua**
entered and passed through *Jericho* **Yericho**.
2 And, behold, *there was* a man
named Zacchaeus **by name called Zakkay**,
which was the
chief among the publicans **arch customs agent**,
and he was rich.
3 And he sought to see *Jesus*
Yah Shua who he was;
and could not for the *press* **multitude**,
because he was little of stature.
25 For it is easier for a rope*
to enter through the eye of a needle,
than for the rich
to enter the sovereigndom of Elohim.
*see Lamsa

26 And they who hear, say, So who can be saved?
27 And he says,
Those which are impossible with humanity
are possible with Elohim.
28 And Petros says,
Behold, we forsake all, and follow you.
29 And he says to them,
Amen! I word to you,
No one forsakes house
or parents or brothers or woman or children
for sake of the sovereigndom of Elohim,
30 who no way takes much more
in this present season;
and in the coming eon, life eternal.

Yah Shua Prophecies His Death And Resurrection

31 And he takes the twelve
to him, and says to them,
Behold, we ascend to Yeru Shalem,
to complete/shalam
all those scribed through the prophets
concerning the Son of humanity
32 — to betray him to the goyim
and to mock and insult and spit on:
33 and to scourge and slaughter him:
and the third day he rises.
34 And they comprehend none of these:
and this rhema is secreted from them,
and they know not what was worded.

Yah Shua Heals Someone Blind

35 And so be it, as he approaches Yericho,
someone blind sits by the way side begging:
36 and hearing the multitude going through,
he asks what it means:
37 and they evangelize him
that Yah Shua the Nazarene passes by:
38 — and he cries, wording,
Yah Shua, son of David, mercy me!
39 And they who precede, rebuke him to hush:
but he cries so much the more,
Son of David, mercy me!
40 And Yah Shua stands,
and summons to bring him:
and when he approaches, he asks him,
41 wording, What will you that I do to you?
And he says, Adonay, that I see!
42 And Yah Shua says to him,
See! Your trust saves you.

43	— and immediately he sees, and follows him, glorifying Elohim: — and all the people see it and give halal to Elohim.

SALVATION COMES TO HOUSE OF ZAKKAY

19	And Yah Shua enters and passes through Yericho.
2	And behold, a man by name called Zakkay; and he is the arch customs agent; and he is rich:
3	and he seeks to see Yah Shua, who he is; and cannot because of the multitude because he is little of stature.
4	And he ran *before* **in front**, and *climbed up* **ascended** into a sycomore *tree* to see him: for he was *about* to pass *that way* **through**.
5	And when *Jesus* **Yah Shua** came to the place, he looked *up*, and saw him, and said unto him, *Zacchaeus* **Zakkay**, *make haste* **hasten**, and *come down* **descend**; for to day I must abide at thy house.
6	And he *made haste* **hastened**, and *came down* **descended**, and received him *joyfully* **cheerfully**.
7	And when they saw it, they all murmured, *saying* **wording**, That he *was gone* **entered** to *be guest* **lodge** with a man that is a sinner.
8	And *Zacchaeus* **Zakkay** stood, and said unto *the Lord* **Adonay**: Behold, *Lord* **Adonay**, the half of my *goods* **holdings** I give to the poor; and if I have *taken any thing* **sycophanted ought** from any *man* **one** *by false accusation*, I *restore* **give** him fourfold.
9	And *Jesus* **Yah Shua** said unto him, This day is salvation *come to* **become** this house, *forsomuch* as he also is a son of Abraham.
10	For the Son of *man* **humanity** is come to seek and to save that which was lost.

YAH SHUA ON THE TEN MINAS

11	And as they heard these *things*, he added and *spake* **said** a parable, because he was nigh to *Jerusalem* **Yeru Shalem**, and because they thought that the *kingdom* **sovereigndom** of *God* **Elohim** should *immediately* **was about to** appear.
12	*So* He said *therefore*,
	A *certain nobleman* **well birthed human** went into a far *country* **region** to *receive* **take** for himself a *kingdom* **sovereigndom**, and to return.
13	And he called his ten servants, and *delivered* **gave** them ten *pounds* **minas**, and said unto them, *Occupy* **Barter** till I come.
14	But his citizens hated him, and *sent* **apostolized** a *message* **presbytery** after him, *saying* **wording**, We will not *have* **that** this *man* to reign over us.
15	And *so be* it *came to pass*, that when he *was returned* **came back**, having *received* **taken** the *kingdom* **sovereigndom**, then he *commanded* **said to voice out** these servants to be called unto him, to whom he had given the *money* **silver**, that he might know how much *every man* **each** had *gained by trading* **thoroughly applied himself**.
16	*Then* **And** came the first, *saying* **wording**, *Lord* **Adoni**, thy *pound* **mina** hath *gained* **acquired** ten *pounds* **minas**.
17	And he said unto him, Well done, thou good servant: because thou hast *been faithful* **become trustworthy** in *very little* **the least**, have thou authority over ten cities.
18	And the second came, *saying* **wording**, *Lord* **Adoni**, thy *pound* **mina** hath *gained* **produced** five *pounds* **minas**.
19	And he said likewise to him, Be thou also over five cities.
20	And another came, *saying* **wording**, *Lord* **Adoni**, behold, *here is* thy *pound* **mina**, which I have *kept* **laid** *up* in a *napkin* **sudarium**:
21	For I *feared* **awed** thee, because thou art an austere *man* **human**: thou takest *up* that thou *layedst* **placedst** not *down*, and *reapest* **harvestest** that thou *didst* **sporest** not *sow*.
22	And he *saith* **wordeth** unto him, Out of thine own mouth *will* **shall** I judge thee, thou *wicked* **evil** servant. Thou knewest that I was an austere *man* **human**,
4	And he runs in front, and ascends into a sycomore to see him: for he is about to pass through.
5	And as Yah Shua comes to the place,

he looks, and sees him, and says to him,
Zakkay, hasten, and descend;
for today I must abide at your house.
6 — and he hastens and descends
and receives him cheerfully.
7 And they see, and they all murmur, wording,
He enters to lodge with a man — a sinner.
8 And Zakkay stands, and says to Adonay:
Behold, Adonay,
the half of my holdings I give to the poor;
and if I have sycophanted ought from anyone,
I give fourfold.
9 And Yah Shua says to him,
This day salvation becomes to this house.
— he also is a son of Abraham.
10 For the Son of humanity
comes to seek and to save the lost.

Yah Shua On The Ten Minas

11 And as they hear these, he
adds and says a parable,
because he is near Yeru Shalem;
and because they think
the sovereigndom of Elohim is about to appear.
12 So he says,
A well birthed human goes to a far region
to take a sovereigndom for himself and to return.
13 And he calls his ten servants
and gives them ten minas;
and says to them, Barter until I come.
14 But his citizens hate him
and apostolize a presbytery after him, wording,
We will that this *one* not reign over us.
15 And so be it, when he comes back,
having taken the sovereigndom,
he says to voice out to call these servants to him
— to whom he had given the silver,
to know how much each thoroughly applied himself.
16 And the first comes, wording,
Adoni, your mina acquired ten minas.
17 And he says to him, Well
done, you good servant:
because you became trustworthy in the least,
have authority over ten cities.
18 And the second comes, wording,
Adoni, your mina produced five minas.
19 And likewise he says to him,
You also be over five cities.
20 And another comes, wording,
Adoni, behold, your mina,

which I laid in a sudarium:
21 for I awe you,
because you are an austere human:
you take what you place not,
and harvest what you spore not.
22 And he words to him,
From your own mouth I judge you, evil servant:
you know I am an austere human,
taking *up* that I *laid* **placed** not *down*,
and *reaping* **harvesting** that I *did* **spored** not *sow*:
23 *Wherefore then* **And why**
gavest not thou my *money* **silver** into the *bank* **table**,
that at my coming
I might have *required* **exacted** mine
own with *usury* **interest**?
24 And he said unto them that stood by,
Take from him the *pound* **mina**,
and give it to him that hath ten *pounds* **minas**.
25 (And they said unto him, *Lord* **Adoni**,
he hath ten *pounds* **minas**.)
26 For I *say* **word** unto you,
That unto every one which hath
shall be given;
and from him that hath not,
even that he hath shall be taken away from him.
27 But those mine enemies,
which *would* **willed** not that I should reign over them,
bring hither,
and *slay* **slaughter** them *before* **in front of** me.

Yah Shua Enters Yeru Shalem

28 And when he had *thus spoken* **said these**,
he went *before* **ahead**,
ascending *up* to *Jerusalem* **Yeru Shalem**.
29 And *so be* it *came to pass*,
when he *was come nigh* **approached**
to *Bethpage* **Beth Pag** and *Bethany* **Beth Ania**,
at the mount called *the mount* of Olives,
he *sent* **apostolized** two of his disciples,
30 Saying,
Go ye into the village *over against* **opposite** you;
in the which at your entering ye shall find a colt tied,
whereon yet never *man* **human** ever sat:
loose *him*, and bring him *hither*.
31 And *if* **whenever** any *man* **one** ask you,
Why do ye loose *him*?
thus shall *ye* say unto him,
Because *the Lord* **Adonay** hath need of him.
32 And they that were *sent*
apostolized went their way,

	and found even as he had said unto them.
33	And as they were loosing the colt, the *owners thereof* **adonim** said unto them, Why loose ye the colt?
34	And they said, *the Lord* **Adonay** hath need of him.
35	And they brought him to *Jesus* **Yah Shua**: and they *cast* **tossed** their garments upon the colt, and they *set Jesus* **mounted Yah Shua** thereon.
36	And as he went, they spread their *clothes* **garments** in the way.
37	And when he *was come nigh* **approached**, *even* **already** at the descent of the mount of Olives, the whole multitude of the disciples began to *rejoice* **cheer** and *praise God* **halal Elohim** with a *loud* **mega** voice for all the *mighty works* **dynamis** that they had seen;
38	*saying* **wording**, *Blessed* **Eulogized** be the *King* **Sovereign** that cometh in the name of *the Lord* **Yah Veh**: *peace* **shalom** in heaven, and glory in the *highest* **highests**. Psalm 118:25, 26
39	And some of the Pharisees from *among* the multitude said unto him, *Master* **Doctor**, rebuke thy disciples.
40	And he answered and said unto them, I *tell* **word** unto you that, *if* **whenever** these should *hold their peace* **hush**, the stones *would* **should** immediately cry out.
41	And when he *was come near* **approached**, he *beheld* **saw** the city, and wept over it,
42	*Saying* **Wording**, If thou hadst known, even thou, *at least* **yet indeed** in this thy day, *the things* **these** which *belong unto* **shall be for** thy *peace* **shalom**! but now they are *hid* **secreted** from thine eyes.
43	For the days shall come upon thee, that thine enemies shall *cast* **envelop** a *trench* **palisade** about thee, and *compass* **surround** thee *round*, and *keep* **hold** thee in on every side, taking what I place not, and harvest what I spore not:
23	And why gave you not my silver to the table, so that at my coming I had ever exacted my own with interest?
24	And he says to them who stand by, Take the mina from him and give to him having ten minas.
25	— and they say to him, Adoni, he has ten minas.
26	For I word to you, To everyone who has, *is given*; and from him who has not, even what he has, is taken from him:
27	but those, my enemies, who will that I not reign over them, bring them here and slaughter in front of me.

YAH SHUA ENTERS YERU SHALEM

28	And he says these, and he goes ahead and ascends to Yeru Shalem.
29	And so be it, as he approaches Beth Pag and Beth Ania at the mount called, Of Olives, he apostolizes two of his disciples,
30	Saying, Go into the village opposite you; wherein, as you enter, you find a colt tied, whereon no human yet ever sat; loose and bring him:
31	and whenever anyone asks you, Why loose you it? say thus to him, Because Adonay has need of him.
32	— and the apostolized go their way and find even as he said to them.
33	And as they loose the colt, the adonim say to them, Why loose you the colt?
34	And they say, Adonay has need of him.
35	And they bring him to Yah Shua: and they toss their garments on the colt and they mount Yah Shua thereon:
36	and as he goes, they spread their garments in the way.
37	And as he approaches, already at the descent of the mount of Olives, the whole multitude of the disciples begins to cheer and halal Elohim with a mega voice for all the dynamis they had seen;
38	wording, Eulogized — the Sovereign who comes in the name of Yah Veh: shalom in the heavens and glory in the highests. Psalm 118:25, 26
39	And some of the Pharisees from the multitude say to him, Doctor, rebuke your disciples.
40	And he answers them, saying, I word to you that whenever these hush, the stones immediately cry out.
41	And as he approaches

	he sees the city and weeps over it,
42	wording, If you had known, even you,
	yet indeed in this, your day,
	all these that be for your shalom!
	But now they are secreted from your eyes.
43	For days come upon you,
	that your enemies envelop a palisade around you,
	and surround you and hold you in on every side,
44	And shall *lay* **raze** thee *even with the ground*,
	and thy children within thee;
	and they shall not *leave* **allow** in thee
	one stone upon *another* **stone**;
	because thou knewest not
	the *time* **season** of thy visitation.

Yah Shua Enters The Priestal Precinct

45	And he *went* **entered** into
	the *temple* **priestal precinct**,
	and began to cast *out* them that sold therein,
	and them that bought;
46	*Saying* **Wording** unto them,
	It is *written* **scribed**, My house is the house of prayer:
	but ye have made it a *den* **grotto** of *thieves* **robbers**.
47	And he *taught* **doctrinated** daily
	in the *temple* **priestal precinct**.
	But the *chief* **arch** priests and the scribes
	and the *chief* **preeminent** of the people
	sought to destroy him,
48	And could not find what they might do:
	for all the people
	were very attentive to hear him
	heard him with suspense.

The Authority Of Yah Shua Questioned

20	And *so be* it *came to pass*,
	that on one of those days,
	as he *taught* **doctrinated** the people
	in the *temple* **priestal precinct**,
	and *preached the gospel* **evangelized**,
	the *chief* **arch** priests and the scribes
	came upon **stood by** him with the elders,
2	And *spake* **said** unto him, *saying* **wording**,
	Tell **Say to** us, by what authority doest thou these *things*?
	or who is he that gave thee this authority?
3	And he answered and said unto them,
	I *will* **shall** also ask you one *thing* **word**;
	and *answer* **say to** me:
4	The baptism of *John* **Yahn**,
	was it from heaven, or of *men* **humanity**?
5	And they *reasoned* **reckoned** with themselves,

	saying **wording**, *if* **whenever** we shall say, From heaven;
	he *will* **shall** say, Why then *believed* **trusted** ye him not?
6	But and *if* **whenever** we say, Of *men* **humanity**;
	all the people *will* **shall** stone us:
	for they be *persuaded* **convinced**
	that *John* **Yahn** was a prophet.
7	And they answered,
	that they *could* **knew** not *tell* whence it was.
8	And *Jesus* **Yah Shua** said unto them,
	Neither *tell* **word** I you
	by what authority I do these *things*.

Yah Shua On The Cultivators

9	*Then* **And** began he to *speak* **word** to the people
	this parable;
	A *certain man* **human** planted a vineyard,
	and *let* **leased** it *forth* to *husbandmen* **cultivators**,
	and went *into a far country* **abroad**
	for *a long* **an ample** time.
10	And at the season he *sent* **apostolized** a servant
	to the *husbandmen* **cultivators**,
	that they should give him of the fruit of the vineyard:
	but the *husbandmen beat* **cultivators flogged** him,
	and *sent* **apostolized** him *away* empty.
11	And again he *sent* **added**
	to send another servant:
	and they *beat* **flogged** him also,
	and *entreated* **dishonoured** him *shamefully*,
	and *sent* **apostolized** him *away* empty.
12	And again he *sent* **added to send** a third:
	and they *wounded* **traumatized** him also,
	and cast him *out*.
13	Then said the *lord* **adoni** of the vineyard,
	What shall I do?
	I *will* **shall** send my beloved son:
	it may be **perhaps** they *will reverence* **shall respect** him
	when they see him.
14	But when the *husbandmen* **cultivators** saw him,
	they reasoned among themselves, *saying* **wording**,
	This is the heir: come, let us *kill* **slaughter** him,
	that the inheritance may be ours.
15	So they cast him out of the vineyard,
	and *killed* **slaughtered** him.
44	and raze you and your children within you;
	and they allow not stone upon stone in you;
	because you know not the season of your visitation.

Yah Shua Enters The Priestal Precinct

45	And he enters the priestal precinct,
	and begins to cast them who sell therein

	and them who buy;
46	wording to them,
	It is scribed, My house is the house of prayer:
	but you make it a grotto of robbers.
47	And he doctrinates daily in the priestal precinct:
	but the archpriests and the scribes
	and the preeminent of the people
	seek to destroy him,
48	and cannot find what to do:
	for all the people hear him with suspense.

THE AUTHORITY OF YAH SHUA QUESTIONED

20	And so be it, on one of those days,
	as he doctrinates the people in the priestal precinct
	and evangelizes,
	the archpriests and the scribes
	stand by him with the elders,
2	and say to him, wording,
	Say to us, By what authority do you these?
	Or who gave you this authority?
3	And he answers them, saying,
	I also ask you one word; and you say to me:
4	The baptism of Yahn
	— is it from the heavens, or of humanity?
5	And they reckon with themselves, wording,
	Whenever we say, From the heavens;
	he says, So why trust you him not?
6	But when ever we say, Of humanity;
	all the people stone us:
	for they are convinced that Yahn is a prophet.
7	— and they answer that
	they know not whence it is.
8	And Yah Shua says to them,
	Neither word I you by what authority I do these.

YAH SHUA ON THE CULTIVATORS

9	And he begins to word
	this parable to the people;
	A human plants a vineyard
	and leases it to cultivators
	and goes abroad for an ample time:
10	and at the season
	he apostolizes a servant to the cultivators
	to give him of the fruit of the vineyard;
	but the cultivators flog him
	and apostolize him forth empty:
11	and again he adds to send another servant;
	and they also flog him and dishonor him
	and apostolize him empty:
12	and again he adds to send a third;

	and they also traumatize him and cast him.
13	And the adoni of the vineyard says,
	What do I? I send my beloved son:
	perhaps they respect him when they see him.
14	But the cultivators see him,
	and they reason among themselves,
	wording, This is the heir: come, we slaughter him,
	that the inheritance be ours.
15	— so they cast him from the vineyard
	and slaughter him.
	So What *therefore*
	shall the *lord* **adoni** of the vineyard do unto them?
16	He shall come
	and destroy these *husbandmen* **cultivators**,
	and shall give the vineyard to others.
	And when they heard it, they said,
	God forbid **So be it not**.
17	And he *beheld* **looked at** them, and said,
	So what is this *then* that is *written* **scribed**,
	The stone which the builders *rejected* **dissapproved**,
	the same **this** is become the head of the corner?
18	Whosoever shall fall upon that stone
	shall be *broken* **crushed**;
	but on whomsoever it shall fall,
	it will grind him to powder **shall be**
	pulverized. Psalm 118:22, 23
19	And the *chief* **arch** priests and the scribes
	the same hour sought to lay hands on him;
	and they *feared* **awed** the people:
	for they *perceived* **knew**
	that he had *spoken* **said** this parable against them.

YAH SHUA ON TRIBUTE

20	And they *watched* **observed** him,
	and *sent forth spies* **apostolized liars in waiting**,
	which should *feign* **hypocrize** themselves just men,
	that they might take hold of his words,
	that so they might *deliver* **betray** him
	unto the *power* **hierarchy** and authority of the governor.
21	And they asked him, *saying* **wording**,
	Master **Doctor**, we know that thou *sayest* **wordest**
	and *teachest rightly* **doctrinatest straightforwardly**,
	neither *acceptest* **takest** thou the *person of any* **face**,
	but *teachest* **doctrinatest** the way of
	God truly **Elohim in truth**:
22	Is it *lawful* **allowed** for us
	to give tribute unto *Caesar* **the Kaisar**, or no?
23	But he perceived their *craftiness* **cunning**,
	and said unto them, Why *tempt* **test** ye me?
24	Shew me a *penny* **denarion**.

Whose *image* **icon** and *superscription* **epigraph** hath it?
They answered and said, *Caesar's* **The Kaisar's**.
25 And he said unto them,
Render therefore unto Caesar the things which be Caesar's
So give the Kaisar's to the Kaisar,
and unto God the things which be God's
and Elohim's to Elohim.
26 And they could not
take hold of his *words before* **rhema**
in front of the people:
and they marvelled at his answer,
and *held their peace* **hushed**.

YAH SHUA ON MARRIAGE
IN THE RESURRECTION

27 *Then* **And** came *to him*
certain **some** of the *Sadducees* **Sadoqiym**,
which *deny* **contradict** that there is any resurrection;
and they asked him,
28 *Saying* **Wording**, *Master* **Doctor**,
Moses wrote **Mosheh scribed** unto us,
If **Whenever** any *man's* **one's** brother die,
having a *wife* **woman**,
and he die *without children* **childless**,
that his brother should take his *wife* **woman**,
and raise *up seed* **sperma** unto his brother.
29 **So** There were *therefore* seven brethren:
and the first took a *wife* **woman**, and
died *without children* **childless**.
30 And the second took her to *wife* **woman**,
and he died childless.
31 And the third took her;
and in like manner the seven also:
and they left no children, and died.
32 *Last of all* **Afterward** the woman died also.
33 *Therefore* **So** in the resurrection
whose *wife of them is* **woman becometh**
she? for seven had her to *wife* **woman**.
34 And *Jesus* **Yah Shua** answering said unto them,
The *children* **sons** of this *world* **eon** marry,
and are *given in marriage* **married off**:
35 But they which shall be accounted worthy
to obtain that *world* **eon**,

So what *is* the adoni of the vineyard to do to them?
16 He comes and destroys these cultivators
and gives the vineyard to others.
— and they hear; and they say, So be it not.
17 And he looks at them, and says,
So what is this that is scribed,
The stone the builders dissapproved,

this becomes the head of the corner?
18 Whoever falls upon that stone *is* crushed;
and on whomever it falls *is* pulverized. Psalm 118:22, 23
19 And the same hour
the archpriests and the scribes seek to lay hands on him;
and they awe the people:
for they know he says this parable against them.

YAH SHUA ON TRIBUTE

20 And they observe him,
and apostolize liars in waiting
who hypocrize themselves as just men;
to take hold of his words
and to betray him
to the hierarchy and authority of the governor.
21 And they ask him, wording,
Doctor, we know that you word
and doctrinate straightforwardly,
and you take not the face,
but doctrinate the way of Elohim in truth:
22 Are we allowed to give tribute to the Kaisar?
Or no?
23 But he perceives their cunning and says to them,
Why test you me?
24 Show me a denarion.
Whose icon and epigraph has it?
They answer, saying, Of the Kaisar.
25 And he says to them,
So give that of the Kaisar to the Kaisar
and that of Elohim to Elohim.
26 And they cannot
take hold of his rhema in front of the people:
and they marvel at his answer and hush.

YAH SHUA ON MARRIAGE
IN THE RESURRECTION

27 And some of the Sadoqiym come
— who contradict that there is any resurrection;
and they ask him,
28 wording, Doctor,
Mosheh scribed to us,
Whenever the brother of anyone dies,
having a woman, and he dies childless,
his brother takes his woman,
and raises sperma to his brother:
29 so there are seven brothers:
and the first takes a woman,
and dies childless:
30 and the second takes her to woman,
and he dies childless:

31	and the third takes her
	— and in like manner, also the seven: and
	they leave no children, and die:
32	afterward the woman also dies:
33	so in the resurrection,
	whose woman becomes she
	— for seven had her to woman?
34	And Yah Shua answers them, saying,
	The sons of this eon marry and *are* married off:
35	but they who are accounted worthy
	to obtain that eon,
	and the resurrection from the dead,
	neither marry, nor are *given in marriage* **married off**:
36	Neither **indeed** can they **even** die *any more*:
	for they are equal unto the angels;
	and are the *children* **sons** of *God* **Elohim**,
	being the *children* **sons** of the resurrection.
37	*Now* **But** that the dead are raised,
	even *Moses shewed* **Mosheh disclosed** at the *bush* **brier**,
	when he *calleth the Lord* **wordeth Yah Veh**
	the *God* **Elohim** of Abraham,
	and the *God* **Elohim** of *Isaac* **Yischaq**, and
	the *God* **Elohim** of *Jacob* **Yaaqov**.
	Exodus 3:1— 6
38	For he is not *a God* **Elohim** of the dead,
	but of the living: for all live unto him.
39	*Then certain* **Some** of the
	scribes answering said,
	Master **Doctor**, thou hast well said.
40	And *after that* **yet**
	they durst not ask him any question at all.

Yah Shua On The Messiah

41	And he said unto them,
	How *say* **word** they that *Christ* **the**
	Messiah is David's son?
42	And David himself
	saith **wordeth** in the *book* **scroll** of Psalms,
	the LORD said **an oracle of Yah**
	Veh unto my *Lord* **Adonay**,
	Sit thou *on* **at** my right *hand*,
43	Till I *make* **place** thine enemies thy footstool.
	Psalm 110:1
44	*So* David *therefore* calleth him *Lord* **Adonay**,
	how is he then his son?
45	Then in the *audience* **hearing** of all the people
	he said unto his disciples,
46	*Beware of* **Heed** the scribes,
	which *desire* **will** to walk in *long robes* **stoles**,
	and *love greetings* **befriend salutations** in the markets,

	and the *highest seats* **preeminent cathedras**
	in the synagogues,
	and the *chief rooms* **preeminent**
	recliners at *feasts* **suppers**;
47	Which devour widows' houses,
	and for a *shew* **pretext** make *long* **far out** prayers:
	the same **these** shall *receive* **take**
	greater damnation **more superabundant judgment**.

Yah Shua On The Two Flakes Of The Widow

21	And he looked *up*, and saw the rich *men*
	casting their *gifts* **oblations** into the treasury.
2	And he saw also a *certain* **needy** poor widow
	casting in thither two *mites* **flakes**.
3	And he said, Of a truth I
	say **Truly I word** unto you,
	that this poor widow hath cast in more than they all:
4	For all these have of their **super** abundance
	cast in unto the *offerings* **oblations** of *God*
	Elohim: but she of her *penury* **lack**
	hath cast in all the *living* **subsistence** that she had.

Yah Shua On The Completion Of The Eon

5	And as some *spake* **worded**
	of **about** the *temple* **priestal precinct**,
	how it was adorned with goodly stones and *gifts* **votives**,
	he said,
6	As for these *things* which ye *behold* **observe**,
	the days *will* **shall** come,
	in the which there shall not be *left* **allowed**
	one stone upon *another* **stone**,
	that shall not be *thrown down* **disintegrated**.
7	And they asked him, *Saying*
	Wording, *Master* **Doctor**,
	but **so** when shall these *things* be?
	and what sign *will* **shall** there be
	when *ever* these *things* shall *come to pass* **become**?
8	And he said,
	Take heed **See** that ye be not *deceived* **seduced**:
	for many shall come in my name, *saying* **wording**,
	I am Christ **I AM**;
	and the *time draweth near* **season approacheth**:
	so go ye not *therefore* after them.
9	But when **ever** ye shall hear
	of wars and *commotions* **instabilities**,
	be not terrified:
	for these *things* must first *come to pass* **become**;
	but the *end* **completion/shalom** is
	not *by and by* **straightway**.

	and the resurrection from the dead,
	neither marry, nor *are* married off:
36	neither indeed can they even die:
	for they are equal to the angels
	— and are the sons of Elohim,
	being the sons of the resurrection.
37	But that the dead are raised,
	even Mosheh disclosed at the brier,
	when he worded Yah Veh *is* the Elohim of Abraham
	and the Elohim of Yischaq
	and the Elohim of Yaaqov.
	Exodus 3:1— 6
38	For he is not Elohim of the dead,
	but of the living: for all live to him.
39	Some of the scribes answer, saying,
	Doctor, you say well.
40	— and yet they dare no more
	to ask him any question at all.

Yah Shua On The Messiah

41	And he says to them,
	How word they that the Messiah is the son of David?
42	And David himself words
	in the scroll of Psalms,
	An oracle of Yah Veh to my Adonay,
	Sit you at my right
43	until I place your enemies the stool of your feet.
	Psalm 110:1
44	So David called him Adonay:
	So how is he his son?
45	And in the hearing of all the people
	he says to his disciples,
46	Heed the scribes who will to walk in stoles
	and befriend salutations in the markets
	and the preeminent cathedras in the synagogues
	and the preeminent recliners at suppers;
47	who devour houses of widows
	and for a pretext make far out prayers:
	these take more superabundant judgment.

Yah Shua On The Two Flakes Of The Widow

21	And he looks and sees the rich
	cast their oblations into the treasury:
2	and he also sees a needy poor widow
	cast in two flakes.
3	And he says, Truly I word to you,
	that this poor widow casts in more than they all:
4	for all these from their super abundance
	cast in to the oblations of Elohim:

	but she of her lack
	casts in all her subsistence.

Yah Shua On The Completion Of The Eon

5	And as some word about the priestal precinct
	— how it is adorned with goodly stones and votives,
	he says,
6	As for these which you observe,
	the days come,
	in which there is not allowed stone upon stone,
	that is not disintegrated.
7	And they ask him, Wording, Doctor,
	so when become these?
	and what *is* the sign whenever these become?
8	And he says,
	See that you *be* not seduced:
	for many come in my name, wording, I AM;
	and the season approaches:
	So you, go not after them.
9	But whenever you hear of wars and instabilities,
	be not terrified:
	for these must first be;
	but the completion/shalom is not straightway.
10	Then *said* **worded** he unto them,
	Nation **Goyim** shall rise against *nation* **goyim**,
	and *kingdom* **sovereigndom**
	against *kingdom* **sovereigndom**:
11	And *great earthquakes* **mega quakes**
	shall be in divers places,
	and famines, and pestilences;
	and *fearful sights* **awesomenesses** and *great* **mega** signs
	shall there be from heaven.
12	*But before* **And ere** all these,
	they shall lay their hands on you, and persecute you,
	delivering **betraying** you *up* to the synagogues,
	and into *prisons* **guardhouses**,
	being brought *before* **in front of**
	kings **sovereigns** and *rulers* **governors**
	for my name's sake.
13	And it shall turn to you for a *testimony* **witness**.
14	*Settle* **So place** it *therefore* in your hearts,
	not to *meditate before* **premeditate**
	what ye shall *answer* **plead**:
15	For I *will* **shall** give you a mouth and wisdom,
	which all your adversaries
	shall not be able to *gainsay* **refute** nor *resist* **withstand**.
16	And ye shall be betrayed both by parents,
	and brethren, and *kinsfolks* **kin**, and friends;
	and some of you shall they *cause to*
	be put to death **deathify**.

17	And ye shall be hated of all men for my name's sake.	28	And when these *things* begin to *come to pass* **become**, then *look up* **unbend**, and lift *up* your heads; for your redemption draweth nigh.
18	But there shall *not* **never no way** an hair of your head *perish* **destruct**.	29	And he *spake* **said** to them a parable; *Behold* **See** the fig tree, and all the trees;
19	In your *patience* **endurance** possess ye your souls.	30	when **ever** they now *shoot* **put** forth, ye see and know of your own selves that *summer* **warmth** is *now* **already** nigh *at hand*.
20	And when **ever** ye shall see *Jerusalem* **Yeru Shalem** *compassed with armies* **surrounded by warriors**, then know that the desolation thereof *is nigh* **approacheth**.	31	So likewise ye, when **ever** ye see these *things come to pass* **become**, know ye that the *kingdom* **sovereigndom** of *God* **Elohim** is nigh *at hand*.
21	Then let them which are in *Judaea* **Yah Hudah** flee to the mountains; and let them which are in the midst of it depart *out*; and let not them that are in the *countries* **regions** enter *thereinto*.	10	Then he words to them, Goyim rises against goyim and sovereigndom against sovereigndom:
22	For these be the days of vengeance, that all *things* which are *written* **scribed** may be fulfilled/**shalamed**.	11	and mega quakes in divers places and famines and pestilences and awesomenesses and mega signs become from the heavens.
23	But woe unto them that *are with child* **have in womb**, and to them that *give suck* **nipple**, in those days! for there shall be *great distress* **mega need** *in* **upon** the *land* **earth**, and wrath upon this people.	12	And ere all these, they lay their hands on you and persecute you betraying you to the synagogues and into guardhouses and bring you in front of sovereigns and governors for sake of my name:
24	And they shall fall by the edge of the sword, and shall be *led away captive* **captured** into all *nations* **goyim**: and *Jerusalem* **Yeru Shalem** shall be *trodden down* **trampled** of the *Gentiles* **goyim**, until the *times* **seasons** of the *Gentiles* **goyim** be fulfilled/**shalamed**.	13	and it turns to you for a witness.
		14	So place in your hearts, to not premeditate what you plead:
25	And there shall be signs in the sun, and in the moon, and in the stars; and upon the earth *distress* **oppression** of *nations* **goyim**, with perplexity; the sea **surging** and *the waves roaring* **echoing**;	15	for I give you a mouth and wisdom, which all your adversaries can neither refute nor withstand:
26	Men's hearts failing them **Humanity breathing cold** for *fear* **awe**, and for *looking after* **awaiting** those *things* which are coming on the *earth* **world**: for the *powers* **dynamis** of heaven shall be shaken. Yesha Yah 13:9—13	16	— and you are betrayed — both by parents and brothers and kin and friends; and some of you, they deathify:
		17	and you become hated of all men for sake of my name:
		18	but a hair of your head never no way destructs.
		19	In your endurance you possess your souls.
	Yah Shua On The Parousia Of The Son Of Humanity	20	And whenever you see Yeru Shalem surrounded by warriors, then know that the desolation thereof approaches:
27	And then shall they see the Son of *man* **humanity** coming in a cloud with *power* **dynamis** and *great* **vast** glory.	21	Then they in Yah Hudah, flee to the mountains; and they in her midst, depart; and they in the regions, enter not.
		22	For these are the days of vengeance, to fulfill/shalam all that *is* scribed.
		23	And woe to them who have in womb and to them who nipple in those days! for mega need becomes upon the earth

	and wrath upon this people:	37	And in the day *time* he
24	and they fall by the mouth of the sword,		was *teaching* **doctrinating**
	and are captured into all goyim:		in the *temple* **priestal precinct**;
	and Yeru Shalem becomes trampled by the goyim,		and at night he went out, and *abode* **camped**
	until the seasons of the goyim fulfill/shalam.		in the mount that is called *the mount* of Olives.
25	And signs become in the sun	38	And all the people came
	and in the moon and in the stars:		*early in the morning* **at dawn** to him
	and upon the earth,		in the *temple* **priestal precinct**, for to hear him.

Satan Enters Yah Hudah The Urbanite

	oppression by goyim with perplexity,		
	the sea surging and echoing,	22	*Now* **And** the *feast* **celebration** of
26	humanity breathing cold for awe,		*unleavened bread* **matsah** *drew nigh* **approached**,
	and awaiting those coming on the world:		which is *called* **worded** the *Passover* **pasach**.
	for the dynamis of the heavens become	2	And the *chief* **arch** priests and scribes
	shaken. Yesha Yah 13:9—13		sought how they might *kill* **take** him **out**;
			for they *feared* **awed** the people.
		3	*Then* **And** entered Satan into

Yah Shua On The Parousia Of The Son Of Humanity

			Judas surnamed Iscariot **Yah Hudah**
			called the urbanite,
27	And then they see the Son of humanity		being of the number of the twelve.
	coming in a cloud with dynamis and vast glory.	4	And he went his way,
28	And when these begin to become, then unbend		and *communed* **talked**
	and lift your heads; for your redemption draws near.		with the *chief* **arch** priests and *captains* **strategoi**,
29	And he says a parable to them;		how he might betray him unto them.
	See the fig tree and all the trees;	5	And they *were glad* **cheered**,
30	whenever they now put forth		and covenanted to give him *money* **silver**.
	you see and know of your own selves	6	And he *promised* **avowed**,
	that warmth is already near:		and sought opportunity to betray him unto them
31	so likewise you,		*in the absence of* **away from** the multitude.
	whenever you see these become,		
	you know that the sovereigndom of Elohim is near.		

The Final Pasach Of Yah Shua

32	*Verily I say* **Amen! I word** unto you,		
	This generation shall *not* **never no way** pass away,	7	*Then* **And** came the day of
	till all *be fulfilled* **becometh**.		*unleavened bread* **matsah**,
33	Heaven and earth shall pass away:		when the *passover* **pasach** must be *killed* **sacrificed**.
	but my words shall *not* **never no way** pass away.	8	And he *sent Peter* **apostolized**
34	And *take* heed to yourselves,		**Petros** and *John* **Yahn**,
	lest *at any time* **ever**		saying,
	your hearts be *overcharged* **burdened**		Go and prepare us the *passover* **pasach**, that we may eat.
	with *surfeiting* **hangovers**, and	9	And they said unto him,
	drunkenness **intoxication**,		Where *wilt* **willest** thou that we prepare?
	and *cares* **anxieties** of *this life* **existence**,	10	And he said unto them, Behold,
	and so that day *come upon* **stand by** you unawares.		when ye are entered into the city,
35	For as a snare shall it come on all them		there shall a *man* **human** meet you,
	that *dwell* **sit** on the face of the whole earth.		bearing a pitcher of water;
36	*Watch ye therefore* **So stay awake**,		follow him into the house where he entereth *in*.
	and *pray always* **petition in every season**,	11	And ye shall say
	that ye may be accounted worthy		unto the *goodman of the house* **housedespotes**,
	to escape all these *things*		The *Master saith* **Doctor wordeth** unto thee,
	that shall *come* **are about** to *pass* **become**,		Where is the *guestchamber* **lodge**,
	and to stand *before* **in front of** the		where I shall eat the *passover* **pasach** with my disciples?
	Son of *man* **humanity**.		

12	And he shall shew you
	a *large* **mega** upper room *furnished* **spread**:
	there *make ready* **prepare**.
13	And they went,
	and found *exactly* as he had said unto them:
	and they *made ready* **prepared** the *passover* **pasach**.
14	And when the hour *was come* **had become**,
	he *sat down* **reposed**, and the twelve apostles with him.
15	And he said unto them,
	With *desire* **panting** I have *desired* **panted**
	to eat this *passover* **pasach** with you *before* **ere** I suffer:
16	For I *say* **word** unto you,
	I *will not any more* **shall never no way** eat thereof,
	until it be fulfilled/**shalamed**
	in the *kingdom* **sovereigndom** of *God* **Elohim**.
32	Amen! I word to you,
	This generation never no way passes away
	until all becomes.
33	The heavens and earth pass away:
	but my words never no way pass away.
34	And heed to yourselves,
	lest ever your hearts burden with hangovers
	and intoxication and anxieties of existence,
	so that day stands by you unawares.
35	For it comes as a snare
	on all who sit on the face of the whole earth.
36	So stay awake
	and petition in every season
	that you be accounted worthy
	to escape all these that are about to become;
	and to stand in front of the Son of humanity.
37	And at day
	he doctrinates in the priestal precinct;
	and at night he goes out
	and camps in the mount called, Of Olives:
38	and at dawn all the people come to him
	in the priestal precinct to hear him.

Satan Enters Yah Hudah The Urbanite

22	And the celebration of matsah approaches,
	which is worded, pasach.
2	And the archpriests and scribes
	seek how to take him out; for they awe the people.
3	And Satan enters Yah Hudah called the urbanite
	— being of the number of the twelve:
4	and he goes his way
	and talks with the archpriests and strategoi
	on how to betray him to them:
5	and they cheer and covenant to give him silver:
6	and he avows
	and seeks opportunity to betray him to them
	away from the multitude.

The Final Pasach Of Yah Shua

7	And the day of matsah comes,
	to sacrifice the pasach:
8	and he apostolizes Petros and Yahn, saying,
	Go and prepare us the pasach to eat.
9	And they say to him,
	Where will you that we prepare?
10	And he says to them, Behold,
	when you enter the city,
	there you meet a human bearing a pitcher of water;
	follow him to the house he enters:
11	and say to the housedespotes,
	The Doctor words to you,
	Where is the lodge,
	where I eat the pasach with my disciples?
12	— and he shows you a mega upper room spread:
	there you prepare.
13	And they go and find exactly as he said to them:
	and they prepare the pasach.
14	And when the hour becomes, he reposes,
	and the twelve apostles with him.
15	And he says to them,
	With panting
	I pant to eat this pasach with you ere I suffer:
16	for I word to you,
	I never no way eat thereof,
	until it is fulfilled/shalamed
	in the sovereigndom of Elohim.
17	And he *took* **received** the cup,
	and *gave thanks* **eucharistized**, and said,
	Take this, and divide it among yourselves:
18	For I *say* **word** unto you,
	I *will not* **shall never no way**
	drink of the *fruit* **produce** of the vine,
	until the *kingdom* **sovereigndom** of *God* **Elohim**
	shall come.
19	And he took bread, and
	gave thanks **eucharistized**,
	and brake it, and gave unto them, *saying* **wording**,
	This is my body which is given for you:
	this do in remembrance of me.
20	Likewise also the cup after *supper* **supping**,
	saying **wording**,
	This cup is the new *testament* **covenant** in my blood,
	which is *shed* **poured** for you.
21	But, behold,
	the hand of him that betrayeth me

is with me on the table.
22   And *truly* **indeed** the Son
of *man* **humanity** goeth,
as *it was determined* **decreed**:
but woe unto that *man* **human**
by **through** whom he is betrayed!
23   And they began to *enquire*
dispute among themselves,
which of them it was
that should *do* **be about to transact** this *thing*.
24   And there *was* **became**
also a strife among them,
which of them should be *accounted* **thought** the greatest.
25   And he said unto them,
The *kings* **Sovereigns** of the *Gentiles* **goyim**
exercise lordship **rule over** them;
and they
that *exercise authority upon* **authorize over** them
are called *benefactors* **well—workers**.
26   But ye shall not be so:
but he that is greatest among you,
let him be as the younger;
and he that *is chief* **governeth**,
as he that *doth serve* **ministereth**.
27   For whether is greater,
he that sitteth at meat reposeth, or
he that serveth ministereth?
is not **indeed** he that *sitteth at meat* **reposeth**?
but I am among you as he that *serveth* **ministereth**.
28   Ye are they which have
continued **to abide** with me
in my *temptations* **testings**.
29   And I *appoint* **covenant** unto
you a *kingdom* **sovereigndom**,
exactly as my Father hath *appointed*
covenanted unto me;
30   That ye may eat and drink at my table
in my *kingdom* **sovereigndom**,
and sit on thrones
judging the twelve *tribes* **scions** of *Israel* **Yisra El**.
31   And *the Lord* **Adonay** said,
Simon, Simon **Shimon, Shimon**, behold,
Satan hath *desired to have* **demanded** you,
that he may sift you as *wheat* **grain**:
32   But I have *prayed* **petitioned** for thee,
that thy *faith* **trust** fail not:
and *when* **once** thou art *converted* **turned around**,
strengthen **establish** thy brethren.
33   And he said unto him, *Lord* **Adonay**,
I am *ready* **prepared** to go with thee,
both into *prison* **the guardhouse**, and to death.

34   And he said, I *tell* **word** unto thee, *Peter* **Petros**,
the *cock* **rooster** shall *not* **never no way**
crow **voice out** this day,
before that ere thou shalt thrice
deny that thou knowest me.
35   And he said unto them,
When I *sent* **apostolized** you without *purse* **pouch**,
and *scrip* **wallet**, and shoes,
lacked ye *any thing* **aught**?
And they said, *nothing* **naught**.
36   *Then* **So** said he unto them, But now,
he that hath a *purse* **pouch**, let him take it,
and likewise his *scrip* **wallet**:
and he that hath no sword,
let him sell his garment, and buy one.
17   And he receives the cup and eucharistizes,
and says, Take this and divide it among yourselves:
18   for I word to you,
I never no way drink of the produce of the vine
until the sovereigndom of Elohim comes.
19   And he takes bread and eucharistizes,
and breaks and gives to them, wording,
This is my body which is given for you:
do this in remembrance of me.
20   Likewise also the cup after supping, wording,
This cup is the new covenant in my blood,
which is poured for you.
21   But behold,
the hand of him who betrays me
is with me on the table:
22   and indeed the Son of
humanity goes as decreed:
but woe to that human through whom he is betrayed!
23   And they begin to dispute among themselves,
which of them is about to transact this:
24   and also a strife becomes among them,
which of them is thought to be the greatest.
25   And he says to them,
The sovereigns of the goyim rule over them;
and they who authorize over them
are called well—workers:
26   but not you:
but he who is greatest among you,
becomes as the younger;
and he who governs as he who ministers.
27   For which is greater
— he who reposes or he who ministers?
Is not indeed he who reposes?
But I — I am among you as he who ministers.
28   You are they

who continue to abide with me in my testings:
29 and I covenant to you a sovereigndom,
exactly as my Father covenanted to me;
30 that you eat and drink at my table
in my sovereigndom,
and sit on thrones
judging the twelve scions of Yisra El.
31 And Adonay says, Shimon, Shimon,
behold, Satan demands you, to sift you as grain:
32 but I petitioned for you, that your trust not fail:
and once you turn, establish your brothers.
33 And he says to him, Adonay,
I am prepared to go with you,
both into the guardhouse, and to death.
34 And he says, I word to you, Petros,
the rooster never no way voices out this day
ere you thrice deny that you know me.
35 And he says to them,
When I apostolized you
without pouch and wallet and shoes,
lacked you aught?
And they say, Naught.
36 So he says to them, But now,
whoever has a pouch, take it,
and likewise his wallet:
and whoever has no sword,
sell his garment, and buy one.
37 For I *say* **word** unto you,
that *is written* **scribed**
must yet be *accomplished* **completed/shalamed** in me,
And he was reckoned
among **with** the *transgressors* **untorahed**:
for *the things* **those** concerning me
have *an end* **a completion/shalom**.
Yesha Yah 53:2
38 And they said, *Lord* **Adonay**,
behold, here are two swords.
And he said unto them, It is enough.

The Prayers Of Yah Shua On The Mount Of Olives

39 And he came out, and went,
as *he was wont* **his custom**, to the mount of Olives;
and his disciples also followed him.
40 And when he *was* **became** at the place,
he said unto them,
Pray that ye enter not into *temptation* **testing**.
41 And he was withdrawn from
them about a stone's cast,
and *kneeled down* **placed his knees**, and prayed,

42 *Saying* **Wording**, Father,
if thou *be willing* **willest**, remove this cup from me:
nevertheless **however** not my will,
but thine, *be done* **become**.
43 And there appeared an angel
unto him from heaven,
strengthening **invigorating** him.
44 And being in an agony
he prayed more *earnestly* **intently**:
and his sweat *was* **became** as *it were*
great *drops* **clots** of blood
falling down to **descending upon** the *ground* **earth**.
45 And when he rose *up* from prayer,
and was come to his disciples, he found
them sleeping for sorrow,
46 And said unto them, Why sleep ye?
rise and pray, lest ye enter into *temptation* **testing**.

The Arrest Of Yah Shua

47 And while he yet spake, behold a multitude,
and he that was *called Judas* **worded Yah Hudah**,
one of the twelve, *went before* **preceded** them,
and *drew near* **approached** unto
Jesus **Yah Shua** to kiss him.
48 But *Jesus* **Yah Shua** said
unto him, *Judas* **Yah Hudah**,
betrayest thou the Son of *man* **humanity** with a kiss?
49 When they which were about him
saw what *would follow* **should become**,
they said unto him, *Lord* **Adonay**,
shall *we* smite with the sword?
50 And one of them
smote the servant of the *high* **arch** priest,
and *cut off* **removed** his right ear.
51 And *Jesus* **Yah Shua** answered and said,
Suffer **Allow** ye thus far.
And he touched his ear **lobe**, and healed him.
52 Then *Jesus* **Yah Shua** said
unto the *chief* **arch** priests,
and *captains* **strategoi** of the *temple* **priestal precinct**,
and the elders, which were come to him,
Be ye come out,
as against a *thief* **robber**, with swords and staves?
53 When I was daily with you
in the *temple* **priestal precinct**,
ye *stretched forth* **spread** no hands against me:
but this is your hour,
and the *power* **authority** of darkness.

The Three Denials Of Petros

54 Then took they him, and led him,
and brought him into the *high* **arch** priest's house.
And *Peter* **Petros** followed afar off.
55 And when they had *kindled* **lighted** a fire
in the midst of the *hall* **courtyard**,
and were set down together,
Peter **Petros** sat down among them.

The First Denial Of Petros

56 But a *certain maid beheld* **lass saw** him
as he sat by the *fire* **light**,
and *earnestly looked upon* **stared at** him, and said,
This *man* **one** was also with him.
37 For I word to you,
what is scribed
must yet be completed/shalamed in me,
And he is reckoned with the torahed:
for those concerning me have a completion/
shalom. Yesha Yah 53:2
38 And they say, Adonay,
behold, here are two swords.
And he says to them, It is enough.

The Prayers Of Yah Shua On The Mount Of Olives

39 And he comes and goes, as *is* his custom,
to the mount, Of Olives;
and his disciples also follow him.
40 And being at the place, he says to them,
Pray that you enter not into testing.
41 And he withdraws from them about a stone cast,
and places his knees, and prays,
42 wording, Father,
if you will, remove this cup from me:
however not my will, but yours, become.
43 And an angel from the heavens appears to him
and invigorates him.
44 And being in an agony he prays more intently:
and his sweat becomes as great clots of blood
descending on the earth.
45 And he rises from prayer
and comes to his disciples;
and he finds them sleeping for sorrow,
46 and says to them, Why sleep you?
Rise and pray, lest you enter into testing.

The Arrest Of Yah Shua

47 And as he yet speaks, behold a multitude:
and he who is worded Yah Hudah,
one of the twelve, precedes them,
and approaches Yah Shua to kiss him.
48 But Yah Shua says to him, Yah Hudah,
betray you the Son of humanity with a kiss?
49 And those around him seeing what became,
say to him, Adonay, smite we with the sword?
50 And one of them
smites the servant of the archpriest,
and removes his right ear.
51 And Yah Shua answers, saying,
Allow you thus.
— and he touches his ear lobe and heals him.
52 And Yah Shua says to the archpriests
and strategoi of the priestal precinct,
and the elders who come to him,
Come you with swords and staves
as against a robber?
53 Being with you daily in the priestal precinct
you spread no hands against me:
but this is your hour and the authority of darkness.

The Three Denials Of Petros

54 And they take him and lead him
and bring him into the house of the archpriest:
and Petros follows afar.
55 And they light a fire midst the courtyard
and sit down together;
and Petros sits down in their midst.

The First Denial Of Petros

56 And a lass sees him as he sits by the light
and stares at him,
and says, This one is also with him.
57 And he denied him, *saying* **wording**,
Woman, I know him not.

The Second Denial Of Petros

58 And after a little *while*
another saw him, and said,
Thou art also of them.
And *Peter* **Petros** said, *man* **human**, *I am not* **Not I**.

The Third Denial Of Petros

59 And *about the space of* one
hour *after* **having passed**
another *confidently* **thoroughly**
affirmed, *saying* **wording**,
Of a truth this *fellow* **one** also was with him:
for he is a *Galilaean* **Galiliy**.

60	And *Peter* **Petros** said, *Man* **Human**, I know not what thou *sayest* **wordest**. And immediately, while he yet spake, the *cock crew* **rooster voiced out**.
61	And *the Lord* **Adonay** turned, and looked upon *Peter* **Petros**. And *Peter* **Petros** remembered the word of *the Lord* **Adonay**, how he had said unto him, *Before* **Ere** the *cock crow* **rooster voice out**, thou shalt deny me thrice.
62	And *Peter* **Petros** went *out*, and wept bitterly.

Yah Shua Blasphemed

63	And the men that held *Jesus* **Yah Shua** mocked him, and *smote* **flogged** him.
64	And when they had *blindfolded* **entirely covered** him, they struck him on the face, and asked him, *saying* **wording**, Prophesy, who is it that smote thee?
65	And *many other things* **much more** blasphemously *spake* **worded** they against him.

Yah Shua In Front Of The Sanhedrim

66	And *as soon as it was* **being** day, the elders of the people and the *chief* **arch** priests and the scribes *came* **gathered** together, and *led* **brought** him into their *council* **sanhedrim**, *saying* **wording**,
67	*Art thou the Christ?* **If thou be the Messiah** *Tell* **Say** to us. And he said unto them, *if* **whenever** I *tell* **say to** you, ye *will* **shall** not **no way** *believe* **trust**:
68	And *if* **whenever** I also ask you, ye *will not* **shall never no way** answer me, nor *let* **release** me go.
69	*Hereafter shall* **From now on** the Son of *man sit on* **humanity** **shall sit at** the right *hand* of the *power* **dynamis** of *God* **Elohim**.
70	*Then* **And** said they all, **So** Art thou *then* the Son of *God* **Elohim**? And he said unto them, Ye *say* **word** that *I am* **I AM**.
71	And they said, What need we *any further* **still** witness? for we ourselves have heard of his own mouth.

Yah Shua In Front Of Pilatos

23	And the whole multitude of them arose, and led him unto *Pilate* **Pilatos**.
2	And they began to accuse him, *saying* **wording**, We found this *fellow* perverting the *nation* **goyim**, and forbidding to give tribute to *Caesar* **the Kaisar**, *saying* **wording** that he himself is *Christ a King* **Messiah Sovereign**.
3	And *Pilate* **Pilatos** asked him, *saying* **wording**, Art thou the *King* **Sovereign** of the *Jews* **Yah Hudiym**? And he answered him and said, Thou *sayest it* **hast worded**.
4	*Then* **And** said *Pilate* **Pilatos** to the *chief* **arch** priests and to the *people* **multitude**, I find no *fault* **cause** in this *man* **human**.
5	And they were the more *fierce* **insistent**, *saying* **wording**, He stirreth up the people, *teaching* **doctrinating** throughout all *Jewry* **Yah Hudah**,
57	And he denies him, wording, Woman, I know him not.

The Second Denial Of Petros

58	And after a little, another sees him, and says, You are also of them. And Petros says, Human, Not I.

The Third Denial Of Petros

59	And one hour passes and another thoroughly affirms, wording, Of a truth this one also is with him: for he is a Galiliy.
60	And Petros says, Human, I know not what you word. And immediately, while he yet speaks, the rooster voices:
61	and Adonay turns and looks on Petros: and Petros remembers the word of Adonay — how he said to him, Ere the rooster voices, you deny me thrice.
62	— and Petros goes out, and weeps bitterly.

Yah Shua Blasphemed

63	And the men holding Yah Shua mock him and flog him:
64	and they entirely cover him, and strike him on the face, and ask him, wording, Prophesy, who smote you?
65	And they word

much more blasphemously against him.

Yah Shua In Front Of The Sanhedrim

66 And being day,
the elders of the people and the archpriests
and the scribes gather together,
and bring him into their sanhedrim, wording,
67 If you are the Messiah, say to us.
And he says to them, Whenever I say to you,
you never no way trust:
68 and also, whenever I ask you,
you no way neither answer me nor release me.
69 From now on the Son of humanity
sits at the right of the dynamis of Elohim.
70 And they all say,
So are you the Son of Elohim?
And he says to them, You word that I AM.
71 And they say, Why need we still witness?
For we ourselves hear from his own mouth.

Yah Shua In Front Of Pilatos

23 And rising;
the whole multitude leads him to Pilatos.
2 And they begin accusing him, wording,
We find this *one* perverting the goyim,
and forbidding to give tribute to the Kaisar,
wording that he himself is Messiah Sovereign.
3 And Pilatos asks him, wording,
Are you the Sovereign of the Yah Hudiym?
And he answers him, saying,
You worded.
4 And Pilatos says to the archpriests
and to the multitude,
I find no cause in this human.
5 And they are the more insistent,
wording, He stirs the people,
doctrinating throughout all Yah Hudah
beginning from *Galilee* **Galiyl** to *this place* **here**.
6 When *Pilate* **Pilatos** heard of *Galilee* **Galiyl**,
he asked whether the *man* **human**
were be a *Galilaean* **Galiliy**.

Yah Shua In Front Of Herod

7 And as soon as he knew
that he *belonged unto* **is from** Herod's
jurisdiction **authority**,
he *sent* **resent** him to Herod,
who himself also was at *Jerusalem* **Yeru Shalem**
at that time **in those days**.
8 And when Herod saw *Jesus* **Yah Shua**,
he was *exceeding glad* **extremely cheerful**:
for he *was desirous* **had willed** to see him
of **for** a long *season*,
because he had heard *many things of* **much about** him;
and he hoped to have seen some *miracle* **sign**
done **become** by him.
9 *Then* **And** he *questioned with* **asked** him
in *many* **enough** words;
but he answered him *nothing* **naught**.
10 And the *chief* **arch** priests and scribes stood
and *vehemently* **vigorously** accused him.
11 And Herod with his *men of war* **warriors**
set **belittled** him *at nought*, and mocked him,
and arrayed him in *a gorgeous robe* **radiant apparel**,
and *sent* **resent** him *again* to *Pilate* **Pilatos**.
12 And the same day *Pilate* **Pilatos** and Herod
were made **became** friends *together* **with one another**:
for *before* **previously**
they were at enmity between themselves.

Pilatos Wills To Release Yah Shua

13 And *Pilate* **Pilatos**,
when he had called together the *chief* **arch** priests
and the *rulers* **archs** and the people,
14 Said unto them,
Ye have *brought* **offered** this *man* **human** unto me,
as one that *perverteth* **turneth away** the people:
and, behold, I,
having examined him *before you* **in your sight**,
have found no *fault* **cause** in this *man* **human**
touching **of** those *things* whereof ye accuse him:
15 *No*, nor *yet* **even** Herod:
for I *sent* **resent** you to him; and, *lo* **behold**,
nothing **naught** worthy of death
is *done unto* **transacted by** him.
16 **So** I *will therefore chastise* **shall discipline** him,
and release *him*.
17 (For of necessity
he must release one unto them at the *feast* **celebration**.)
18 And *they* **the whole multitude**
cried out all at once **screamed simultaneously**,
saying **wording**, Away with **Take** this *man* **one**,
and release unto us *Barabbas* **Bar Abbas**:
19 (Who for a *certain sedition* **riot**
made **having become** in the city, and for murder,
was cast into *prison* **the guardhouse**.)
20 *Pilate therefore* **So Pilatos**,
willing **having willed** to release *Jesus* **Yah Shua**,
spake again to them.
21 But they *cried* **shouted**, *saying* **wording**,

Crucify him, crucify him. **Stake! Stake him!**

22 And he said unto them the third time,
Why **Indeed**, what evil hath he done?
I have found no cause of death in him:
So I *will therefore chastise* **shall discipline** him
and *let* **release** him *go*.

23 And they *were instant* **imposed**
with *loud* **mega** voices,
requiring **asking** that he might be *crucified* **staked**.
And the voices of them
and of the *chief* **arch** priests *prevailed* **overpowered**.

24 And *Pilate gave sentence* **Pilatos adjudged**
that it should be as they required.

25 And he released unto them
him that for *sedition* **riot** and murder
was cast into *prison* **the guardhouse**,
whom they had *desired* **asked**;
but he *delivered Jesus* **betrayed Yah Shua**
to their will **as they willed**.

beginning from Galiyl to here.

6 When Pilatos hears of Galiyl,
he asks whether the human be a Galiliy.

YAH SHUA IN FRONT OF HEROD

7 And as soon as he knows
that he is from the authority of Herod,
he resends him to Herod,
who himself is also at Yeru Shalem in those days.

8 And Herod sees Yah Shua,
and is extremely cheerful:
for he had willed to see him for long,
because he heard much about him;
and he hoped to see some sign become by him.

9 And he asks him enough words;
but he answers him naught:

10 and the archpriests and scribes stand
and vigorously accuse him:

11 and Herod with his warriors
belittle him and mock him
and array him in radiant apparel
and resend him to Pilatos.

12 And the same day Pilatos and Herod
become friends with one another:
for previously
they were at enmity between themselves.

PILATOS WILLS TO RELEASE YAH SHUA

13 And Pilatos calls together
the archpriests and the archs and the people,

14 and says to them,

You offer this human to me
as one who turns the people:
and behold, I, examining him in your sight,
find no cause in this human
of those whereof you accuse him:

15 nor even Herod:
for I resent you to him; and behold, he
transacted naught worthy of death:

16 so I discipline him and release.

17 — for of necessity
he releases one to them at the celebration.

18 And the whole multitude
screams simultaneously,
wording, Take this one,
and release to us Bar Abbas:

19 — who for a riot being in
the city and for murder,
was cast in the guardhouse.

20 So Pilatos, wills to release Yah Shua,
and speaks to them again:

21 but they shout, wording, Stake! Stake him!

22 And he says to them the third time,
Indeed, what evil did he?
I find no cause of death in him:
so I discipline him and release him.

23 And they impose with mega voices,
asking to stake him:
and the voices of them
and of the archpriests overpowered.

24 And Pilatos adjudges that it be as they require:

25 and he releases to them
him who for riot and murder
was cast into the guardhouse,
whom they had asked;
but he betrays Yah Shua as they willed.

SHIMON BEARS THE STAKE OF YAH SHUA

26 And as they led him away,
they *laid* **took** hold upon *one Simon*
Shimon, a Cyrenian,
coming out of the *country* **field**,
and on him they *laid* **put** the *cross* **stake**,
that he might bear it after *Jesus* **Yah Shua**.

27 And there followed him
a *great company* **vast multitude** of people,
and of women,
which also *bewailed* **chopped** and lamented him.

28 But *Jesus* **Yah Shua** turning unto them said,
Daughters of *Jerusalem* **Yeru Shalem**, weep not for me,
but **however** weep for yourselves, and for your children.

29 For, behold, the days are coming,
in the which they shall say, Blessed *are* the *barren* **sterile**,
and the wombs that never *bare* **birthed**,
and the *paps* **breasts** which never *gave suck* **nippled**.
30 Then shall they begin to
say **word** to the mountains,
Fall on us;
and to the hills, *Cover* **Vail** us.
31 For if they do these *things*
in a *green tree* **watered staff**,
what shall *be done* **become** in the dry?
32 And there were also two other,
malefactors **evilworkers**,
led with him to be *put to death* **taken out**.

YAH SHUA STAKED

33 And when they were come to the place,
which is called *Calvary* **Cranium**, there
they *crucified* **staked** him,
and the *malefactors* **evilworkers**, one
on **indeed at** the right *hand*,
and the other *on* **at** the left.
34 Then *said Jesus* **worded Yah Shua**,
Father, forgive them; for they know not what they do.
And they *parted* **divided** his *raiment* **garment**,
and cast lots.
35 And the people stood *beholding* **observing**.
And the *rulers* **archs** also with
them *derided him* **sneered**,
saying **wording**, He saved others; let him save himself,
if he be *Christ* **the Messiah**,
the *chosen* **selected** of *God* **Elohim**.
36 And the *soldiers* **warriors** also mocked him,
coming to him, and offering him vinegar,
37 And *saying* **wording**,
If thou be the *King* **Sovereign** of the *Jews* **Yah Hudiym**,
save thyself.
38 And *a superscription* **an epigraph**
also was *written* **scribed** over him
in *letters* **scribings** of *Greek* **Hellenic**,
and *Latin* **Romaic**, and *Hebrew* **Hebraic**,
THIS IS THE *KING* **SOVEREIGN**
OF THE *JEWS* **YAH HUDIYM**.
39 And one of the *malefactors* **evilworkers**
which were hanged
railed on **blasphemed** him, *saying* **wording**,
If thou be *Christ* **the Messiah**, save thyself and us.
40 But the other answering rebuked him,
saying **wording**, Dost not thou *fear God* **awe Elohim**,
seeing thou art in the same *condemnation* **judgment**?
41 And we indeed justly;
for we *receive the due reward* **take that worthy**
of our *deeds* **transactions**:
but this *man* **one**
hath *done nothing amiss* **transacted naught inordinate**.
42 And he *said* **worded** unto *Jesus* **Yah Shua**,
Lord **Adonay**, remember me
when *ever* thou comest into thy *kingdom* **sovereigndom**.
43 And *Jesus* **Yah Shua** said unto him,
Verily I say **Amen! I word** unto thee,
To day shalt thou be with me in paradise.

YAH SHUA EXPIRES

44 And it was about the sixth hour,
and there *was* **became** a darkness over all the earth
until the ninth hour.
45 And the sun was darkened,
and the veil of the *temple* **nave**
was *rent* **split** in the midst.

SHIMON BEARS THE STAKE OF YAH SHUA

26 And as they lead him away,
they take hold on Shimon, a Cyrenian,
coming from the field;
and they put the stake on him
to bear it after Yah Shua.
27 And a vast multitude of people follow him,
and also of women who chop and lament him.
28 And Yah Shua turns to them and says,
Daughters of Yeru Shalem, weep not for me:
however weep for yourselves and for your children.
29 For, behold, the days come in which they say,
Blessed — the sterile
and the wombs that never birthed
and the breasts that never nippled.
30 Then they begin to word to the mountains,
Fall on us;
and to the hills, Veil us.
31 For if they do these in a watered staff,
what becomes in the dry?
32 And also two others — evilworkers
are led to be taken out with him.

YAH SHUA STAKED

33 And they come to the place called Cranium,
and there they stake him and the evilworkers,
one indeed at the right and one at the left.
34 And Yah Shua words, Father, forgive them;
for they know not what they do.
— and they divide his garment and cast lots.

35 and the people stand observing.
and also the archs with them sneer, wording,
He saved others; *let* him save himself,
if he be the Messiah, the select of Elohim.
36 And the warriors also mock him,
coming to him, and offering him vinegar,
37 and wording,
If you are the Sovereign of the Yah Hudiym,
save yourself.
38 And also an epigraph is scribed over him
in scribings of Hellenic and Romaic and Hebraic,

This Is The Sovereign Of The Yah Hudiym.

39 And one of the evilworkers who is staked
blasphemes him, wording,
If you are the Messiah, save yourself and us.
40 But the other answers rebuking him, wording,
Awe you not Elohim,
seeing you are in the same judgment?
41 And we indeed justly;
for we take that worthy of our transactions:
but this *one* transacted naught inordinate.
42 And he words to Yah Shua,
Adonay, remember me
whenever you come into your sovereigndom.
43 And Yah Shua says to him,
Amen! I word to you,
Today you are with me in paradise.

Yah Shua Expires

44 And being about the sixth hour,
a darkness becomes over all the earth
until the ninth hour:
45 and the sun darkens,
and the veil of the nave splits in the middle.
46 And when *Jesus* **Yah Shua**
had *cried* **voiced** with a *loud* **mega** voice, he said,
Father, into thy hands I *commend* **set forth** my spirit:
and having said thus, he *gave up the ghost* **expired**.
47 Now when the centurion
saw what *was done* **had become**,
he glorified *God* **Elohim**, *saying* **wording**,
Certainly **Indeed** this was a *righteous man* **just human**.
48 And all the *people* **multitude**
that *came* **convened** together to that *sight* **observation**,
beholding the things **observing these**
which *were done* **had become**,
smote **struck** their *breasts* **chests**, and returned.
49 And all his acquaintance,
and the women that followed him from *Galilee* **Galiyl**,
stood afar off, *beholding* **seeing** these *things*.

Yah Shua Entombed

50 And, behold, there was a
man named *Joseph* **Yoseph**,
being a counsellor; *and he was* a good man, and *a* just:
51 (The same had not *consented* **agreed**
to the counsel and *deed* **acts** of them;)
he was of *Arimathaea* **Rahmah**,
a city of the *Jews* **Yah Hudiym**:
who also himself *waited for* **awaited**
the *kingdom* **sovereigndom** of *God* **Elohim**.
52 This *man* **one** went unto *Pilate* **Pilatos**,
and *begged* **asked** the body of *Jesus* **Yah Shua**.
53 And he took it down, and wrapped it in linen,
and *laid* **placed** it in a *sepulchre* **tomb**
that was *hewn in stone* **quarried from rock**,
wherein *never man before was* **no one yet had** laid.
54 And that day was the preparation,
and the *sabbath drew on* **shabbath dawned**.
55 And the women also,
which came with him from *Galilee* **Galiyl**,
followed after, and *beheld* **saw** the *sepulchre* **tomb**,
and how his body was *laid* **placed**.
56 And they returned,
and prepared *spices* **aromatics** and *ointments* **myrrh**;
and *rested* **indeed quieted on** the *sabbath day* **shabbath**
according to the *commandment* **misvah**.

The Resurrection Of Yah Shua

24 Now upon the first *day* of the *week* **shabbaths**,
very early **deep** in the morning,
they came unto the *sepulchre* **tomb**,
bringing the *spices* **aromatics** which they had prepared,
and *certain others* **some** with them.
2 And they found the stone
rolled away from the *sepulchre* **tomb**.
3 And they entered *in*,
and found not the body
of *the Lord Jesus* **Adonay Yah Shua**.
4 And *so be it* *came to pass*,
as they were *much* **thoroughly** perplexed thereabout,
behold, two men stood by them
in *shining garments* **flashing apparel**:
5 And *as they were afraid* **being awestricken**
and *bowed down* **reclined** their faces to the earth,
they said unto them,
Why seek ye the living *among* **with** the dead?
6 He is not here, but is risen:

remember how he spake unto you when
he was yet in *Galilee* **Galiyl**,
7 *Saying* **Wording**,
The Son of *man* **humanity** must be *delivered* **betrayed**
into the hands of sinful *men* **humanity**,
and be *crucified* **staked**, and the third day rise *again*.
8 And they remembered his *words* **rhema**,
9 And returned from the *sepulchre* **tomb**,
and *told* **evangelized** all these *things* unto the eleven,
and to all the rest.
10 It was *Mary* **Miryam** the Magdalene
and *Joanna* **Yah Hanna**,
and *Mary* **Miryam** *the mother* of *James* **Yaaqovos**,
and *other women* **the rest** that were with them,
which *told* **worded** these *things* unto the apostles.
11 And their *words* **rhema**
seemed to them **manifested in their**
sight as *idle tales* **gab**,
and they *believed* **distrusted** them *not*.
46 And Yah Shua voices with a mega voice, saying,
Father, into your hands I set forth my spirit:
— and saying thus, he expires.
47 Now the centurion seeing what becomes,
glorifies Elohim, wording,
Indeed this is a just human.
48 And all the multitude
convening together to that observation,
observing these that become,
strike their chests, and return:
49 and all his acquaintances
and the women who followed him from Galiyl
stand afar off, seeing these.

YAH SHUA ENTOMBED

50 And behold, a man named Yoseph,
being a counsellor; a good man and just:
51 — who agreed not to their counsel and acts
— of Rahmah, a city of the Yah Hudiym:
who himself also
awaited the sovereigndom of Elohim:
52 this one goes to Pilatos,
and asks the body of Yah Shua:
53 and he takes it down and wraps it in linen
and places it in a tomb quarried from
rock — wherein no one had yet laid:
54 and that day is the preparation
and the shabbath dawns.
55 And also the women
who came with him from Galiyl,
follow after, and see the tomb,
and how his body is placed:
56 and they return and prepare
aromatics and myrrh;
and indeed quiet on the shabbath
according to the misvah.

THE RESURRECTION OF YAH SHUA

24 And on the first of the shabbaths,
deep in the morning, they come to the tomb,
bringing the aromatics they prepared,
and some with them:
2 and they find the stone
rolled away from the tomb:
3 and they enter
and find not the body of Adonay Yah Shua.
4 And so be it,
they are thoroughly perplexed about this,
that behold,
two men in flashing apparel stand by them.
5 — and being awestricken,
they recline their faces to the earth.
And they say to them,
Why seek you the living with the dead?
6 He is not here, but is risen:
remember how he spoke to you
when he *was* still in Galiyl,
7 wording, The Son of humanity must be betrayed
into the hands of sinful humanity,
and be staked, and the third day rise.
8 And they remember his rhema;
9 and return from the tomb
and evangelize all these to the eleven
and to all the rest:
10 it is Miryam the Magdalene and Yah Hanna
and Miryam of Yaaqovos and the rest with them
word these to the apostles:
11 and their rhema manifests in their sight as gab;
and they distrust them.
12 *Then* **But** arose *Peter* **Petros**,
and ran unto the *sepulchre* **tomb**;
and stooping down,
he *behold* **saw** the linen clothes laid *by themselves* **alone**,
and departed, *wondering* **marvelling** in himself
at that which *was come to pass* **had become**.

ON THE WAY TO EMMAUS

13 And, behold, two of them went that same day
to a village *called* **named** Emmaus,
which was from *Jerusalem* **Yeru Shalem**
about *threescore furlongs* **sixty stadia**.

14	And they *talked* **homologized** together *of* **about** all these *things* which had happened.
15	And *so be* it *came to pass*, that, while they *communed* **homologized** *together* **with one another** and *reasoned* **disputed**, *Jesus* **Yah Shua** himself *drew near* **approached**, and went with them.
16	But their eyes were *holden* **overpowered** that they should not know him.
17	And he said unto them, What manner of *communications* **words** are these that ye *have one to* **cast one against** another, as ye walk, and are *sad* **sullen**?
18	And the one of them, whose name was Cleopas, answering said unto him, *Art* **Hast** thou only *a stranger* **settled** in *Jerusalem* **Yeru Shalem**, and hast not known *the things* **those** which *are come to pass* **have become** there in these days?
19	And he said unto them, What *things*? And they said unto him, Concerning *Jesus of Nazareth* **Yah Shua the Nazarene**, which**,** *was* **being a man** — a prophet *mighty* **able** in *deed* **work** and word *before God* **in front of Elohim** and all the people:
20	And how the *chief* **arch** priests and our **arch** rulers delivered him to be *condemned* **judged** to death, and have *crucified* **staked** him.
21	But we *trusted* **hoped** that it had been he which *should have redeemed Israel* **was about to redeem Yisra El**: *and beside all this* **but yet indeed**, to day is the third day since these *things were done* **have become**.
22	*Yea, and certain* **Yet some** women also of our company *made* **astounded** us *astonished*, which were *early* **at dawn** at the *sepulchre* **tomb**;
23	And when they found not his body, they came, *saying* **wording**, that they had also seen a vision of angels, which *said* **worded** that he was alive.
24	And *certain* **some** of them which were with us went to the *sepulchre* **tomb**, and found it even so as the women had said: but him they saw not.
25	*Then* **And** he said unto them, O *fools* **mindless**, and slow of heart to *believe* **trust** all that the prophets have spoken:
26	**Indeed,** *Ought* **needed** not *Christ* **the Messiah** to have suffered these *things*, and to enter into his glory?
27	And beginning at *Moses* **Mosheh** and all the prophets, he *expounded* **translated** unto them in all the scriptures *the things* **of those** concerning himself.
28	And they *drew nigh* **approached** unto the village, whither they went: and he *made as though* **had preplanned** he would have gone **to go** further.
29	*But* **And** they constrained him, *saying* **wording**, Abide with us: for it is toward evening, and the day *is far spent* **reclineth**. And he *went in* **entered** to *tarry* **abide** with them.

THE INTERRUPTED EUCHARIST

30	And *so be* it *came to pass*, as he *sat at meat* **reclined** with them, he took bread, and *blessed* **eulogized** it,
12	But Petros rises and runs to the tomb; and stooping down he sees the linen clothes laid alone; and departs, marvelling in himself at what had become.

ON THE WAY TO EMMAUS

13	And behold, that same day, two of them go to a village named Emmaus — about sixty stadia from Yeru Shalem:
14	and they homologize together about all these that happened.
15	And so be it, as they homologize with one another and dispute, Yah Shua himself approaches and goes with them:
16	but their eyes are overpowered so that they know him not.
17	And he says to them, What manner of words are these that you cast one against another as you walk — and are sullen?
18	And one, whose name is Cleopas, answers him, saying, Have you only settled in Yeru Shalem, and know not those that became there in these days?
19	And he says to them, What? And they say to him, Concerning Yah Shua the Nazarene, who, being a man

    — a prophet able in work and word in
    front of Elohim and all the people:
20   and how the archpriests and our arch rulers
    delivered him to judgment of death,
    and staked him:
21   but we had hoped
  it was he who is about to redeem Yisra El:
    but yet indeed,
  today is the third day since these became:
22 yet some women of our company astounded us
    being at the tomb at dawn;
23 and they found not his body; and they come,
   wording that they also saw a vision of
   angels, who worded that he is alive:
24 and some of them with us went to the tomb
   and found it even as the women said:
    but they saw him not.
25   And he says to them,
    O mindless and slow of heart
   to trust all the prophets have spoken:
26   Indeed,
  needed not the Messiah to suffer these
    and to enter his glory?
27   —and beginning at Mosheh
    and all the prophets,
    he translates to them
of all the scriptures of those concerning himself.
28 And they approach the village where they go:
    and he preplans to go further:
29   and they constrain him, wording,
   Abide with us: for it is toward evening,
    and the day reclines.
  — and he enters to abide with them.

THE INTERRUPTED EUCHARIST

30 And so be it, as he reclines with them,
    he takes bread and eulogizes
    and brake, and gave to them.
31   And their eyes were opened,
     and they knew him;
and he *vanished out of their sight* **became invisible**.
32   And they said one to another,
   Did not **indeed** our heart burn within us,
   while he *talked* **spoke** with us by the way,
  and while he opened to us the scriptures?
33   And they rose *up* the same hour,
  and returned to *Jerusalem* **Yeru Shalem**, and
   found the eleven gathered together,
    and them that were with them,

34   *Saying* **Wording**, *the Lord*
    Adonay is risen indeed,
  and hath appeared to *Simon* **Shimon**.
35   And they *told* **declared**
 what things were done *of those in the way*,
and how he was known of them in breaking of bread.

YAH SHUA STANDS MIDST THE DISCIPLES

36   And as they thus spake,
Jesus **Yah Shua** himself stood in the midst of them,
   and *saith* **wordeth** unto them,
   Peace **Shalom** be unto you.
37   But they *were* **became** terrified
   and *affrighted* **awestricken**,
   and *supposed* **thought** that they
   had *seen* **observed** a spirit.
38 And he said unto them, Why are ye troubled?
and why do thoughts *arise* **ascend** in your hearts?
39   *Behold* **See** my hands and my
   feet, *that it is I myself* **I AM**:
   handle **touch** me, and see;
  for a spirit hath not flesh and bones,
  exactly as ye *see* **observe** me have.
40   And when he had thus *spoken* **said**,
  he shewed them his hands and his feet.
41 And while they yet *believed not* **distrusted**
    for *joy* **cheer**,
   and *wondered* **marvelled**,
he said unto them, Have ye here any *meat* **food**?
42   And they gave him a *piece*
   portion of a broiled fish,
    and of an honeycomb.
43   And he took it, and did eat
   before them **in their sight**.
44   And he said unto them,
These are the words which I spake unto you,
   while I was yet with you,
that all *things* must be fulfilled/**shalamed**,
   which were *written* **scribed**
  in the *law* **torah** of *Moses* **Mosheh**,
and in the prophets, and in the psalms, concerning me.
45 Then opened he their *understanding* **mind**,
that they might *understand* **comprehend** the scriptures,
46 And said unto them, Thus it is *written* **scribed**,
    and thus it
behoved Christ **was necessary for the Messiah** to suffer,
  and to rise from the dead the third day:
47   And that repentance and
  remission **forgiveness** of sins

should be preached in his name among all *nations* **goyim**, beginning at *Jerusalem* **Yeru Shalem**.
48 And ye are witnesses of these *things*.
49 And, behold,
I *send* **apostolize**
the *promise* **pre—evangelism** of my Father upon you:
but *tarry* **sit** ye in the city of *Jerusalem* **Yeru Shalem**,
until ye be endued with *power* **dynamis** from on high.

Yah Shua Borne Into The Heavens

50 And he led them out as far
as to *Bethany* **Beth Ania**,
and he lifted *up* his hands, and *blessed* **eulogized** them.
51 And *so be* it *came to pass*,
while he *blessed* **in his eulogizing** them,
he *was parted* **passed** from them,
and *carried up* **was borne** into heaven.
52 And they worshipped him,
and returned to *Jerusalem* **Yeru Shalem**
with *great joy* **mega cheer**:
53 And were continually in the
temple **priestal precinct**,
praising **halaling** and *blessing God* **eulogizing Elohim**.
Amen.

and breaks and gives to them.
31 And their eyes open and they know him
— and he becomes invisible.
32 And they say one to another,
Burned not indeed our heart within us,
as he spoke with us by the way
and as he opened the scriptures to us?
33 And the same hour
they rise and return to Yeru Shalem;
and find the eleven gathered together
— and those with them,
34 wording, Adonay is risen indeed,
and appeared to Shimon.
35 And they declare of those in the way
and how he *was* known by them in breaking of bread.

Yah Shua Stands Midst The Disciples

36 And as they thus speak,
Yah Shua himself stands in their midst;
and words to them, Shalom to you.
37 But being terrified and awestricken,
they think they observe a spirit.
38 And he says to them, Why are you troubled?
And why ascend thoughts in your hearts?
39 See my hands and my feet, I AM!
Touch me and see;
for a spirit has not flesh and bones,
exactly as you observe me have.
40 And he says thus,
and shows them his hands and his feet:
41 and while they yet distrust
for cheer, and marvel,
he says to them, Have you any food here?
42 And they give him a portion of a broiled fish
and of a honeycomb:
43 and he takes it, and eats in their sight.
44 And he says to them,
These are the words I spoke to you
while yet with you,
that all must fulfill/shalam
which are scribed in the torah of Mosheh
and in the prophets and in the psalms concerning me.
45 Then he opens their mind
to comprehend the scriptures:
46 and he says to them, Thus it is scribed,
and thus it is necessary for the Messiah to suffer,
and to rise from the dead the third day:
47 and that repentance and forgiveness of sins
be preached in his name among all goyim
beginning at Yeru Shalem.
48 — and you are witnesses of these.
49 And behold,
I apostolize the pre—evangelism of my Father
upon you:
but you, sit in the city of Yeru Shalem,
until you be endued with dynamis from on high.

Yah Shua Borne Into The Heavens

50 And he leads them out as far as Beth Ania;
and he lifts his hands and eulogizes them.
51 And so be it, in his eulogizing them,
he passes from them and is borne into the heavens:
52 and they worship him,
and return to Yeru Shalem with mega cheer:
53 and are continually in the priestal precinct,
halaling and eulogizing Elohim.
Amen.

Introduction

1 Indeed, The *former treatise* **first word** have I made, O *Theophilus* **Theo Philos**, *of* **concerning** all that *Jesus* **Yah Shua** began both to do and *teach* **doctrinate**,

2 Until the day in which he was taken *up*, after that he through the *Holy Spirit* **Ruach ha-kodesh** had *given commandments* **misvahed** unto the apostles whom he had *chosen* **selected**:

3 To whom also he *shewed* **presented** himself alive after his *passion* **suffering** by many *infallible* proofs, being seen of them **through** forty days, and *speaking of the things* **wording about those** *pertaining to* **of** the *kingdom* **sovereigndom** of *God* **Elohim**:

4 And, being *assembled* **thronged** together with them, *commanded* **evangelized** them that they should not *depart* **separate** from *Jerusalem* **Yeru Shalem**, but *wait for* **await** the *promise* **pre—evangelism** of the Father, which, saith he, ye have heard of me.

5 For *John truly* **Yahn indeed** baptized *with* **in** water; but ye shall be baptized *with* **in** the *Holy Spirit* **Ruach ha-kodesh** not many days *hence* **after this**.

6 When **So indeed** they *therefore* were come together, **and** they asked of him, *saying* **wording**, *Lord* **Adonay**, *wilt* **shalt** thou at this time restore *again* the *kingdom* **sovereigndom** to *Israel* **Yisra El**?

7 And he said unto them, It is not for you to know the times or the seasons, which the Father hath put in his own *power* **authority**.

8 But ye shall *receive power* **take dynamis**, after that the *Holy Spirit* **Ruach ha-kodesh** is come upon you: and *ye* shall be witnesses unto me both in *Jerusalem* **Yeru Shalem**, and in all *Judaea* **Yah Hudah**, and in *Samaria* **Shomeron**, and unto the *uttermost part* **finality** of the earth.

The Ascension Of Yah Shua

9 And when he had *spoken* **said** these *things*, while they *beheld* **looked**, he was *taken up* **lifted**; and a cloud *received* **took** him out of their *sight* **eyes**.

Prophecy Of The Parousia

10 And *while* **as** they *looked stedfastly* **stared** *toward* **into** heaven as he went *up*, behold, two men stood by them in white apparel;

11 Which also said, Ye men *of Galilee* — **Galiliym**, why stand ye *gazing* **looking** up into heaven? this same *Jesus* **Yah Shua**, which is taken *up* from you into heaven, shall *so* **thus** come in like manner as ye have *seen* **observed** him go into heaven.

The Upper Loft

12 Then returned they unto *Jerusalem* **Yeru Shalem** from the mount called *Olivet* **Olive Orchard**, which is *from Jerusalem* **near Yeru Shalem** a *sabbath day's* **shabbath** journey.

13 And when they *were come in* **entered**, they *went up* **ascended** into an upper *room* **loft**, where abode both *Peter* **Petros**, and *James* **Yaaqovos**, and *John* **Yahn** and *Andrew* **Andreas**, *Philip* **Philippos**, and *Thomas* **Taom**, *Bartholomew* **Bar Talmay**, and *Matthew* **Matthaios**, and *James* **Yaaqovos** the son of *Alphaeus* **Heleph**, and *Simon Zelotes* **Shimon the Zealot**, and *Judas* **Yah Hudah** the brother of *James* **Yaaqovos**.

14 These all continued with *one accord* **in unanimity** in prayer and *supplication* **petition**, with the women, and *Mary* **Miryam** the mother of *Jesus* **Yah Shua**, and with his brethren.

Matthias Replaces Yah Hudah

15 And in those days *Peter stood up* **Petros rose** in the midst of the disciples, and said, (the *number* **multitude** of names *together* **of them** were about an hundred and twenty,)

16 Men and brethren,

Introduction

1 Indeed, I do this first word, O Theo Philos, concerning all Yah Shua began both to do and doctrinate

2 until the day he *was* taken — after he, through the Holy Spirit, misvahed to the apostles whom he selected:

3 to whom also he presented himself alive after his suffering by many proofs;

being seen by them through forty days,
and wording about those
of the sovereigndom of Elohim:
4 and being thronged together with them,
evangelized them to not separate from Yeru Shalem,
but to await the pre—evangelism of the Father,
which, says he, you heard of me.
5 For Yahn indeed baptized in water;
but you, baptized in Holy Spirit
not many days after this.
6 So indeed they come together,
and ask him, wording, Adonay,
restore you the sovereigndom to Yisra El at this time?
7 And he says to them,
It is not yours to know the times or the seasons
the Father put in his own authority:
8 but you take dynamis,
at the coming of the Holy Spirit upon you;
and you become my witnesses
— both in Yeru Shalem and in all Yah Hudah
and in Shomeron and to the finality of the earth.

The Ascension Of Yah Shua

9 And having said these, and as they look,
he is lifted; and a cloud takes him from their eyes.

Prophecy Of The Parousia

10 And as they stare into the heavens as he goes,
behold, two men stand by them in white apparel;
11 who also say, You men — Galiliym,
why stand you looking into the heavens?
This same Yah Shua,
taken from you into the heavens
comes thus in like manner
as you observed him go into the heavens.

The Upper Loft

12 Then they return to Yeru Shalem
from the mount called Olive Orchard, near
Yeru Shalem — a shabbath journey.
13 And they enter and ascend to an upper loft,
where both Petros and Yaaqovos
and Yahn and Andreas
Philippos and Taom
Bar Talmay and Matthaios
and Yaaqovos of Heleph and Shimon the Zealot
and Yah Hudah of Yaaqovos abide.
14 These all continue in unanimity
in prayer and petition with the women
and Mary Miryam the mother of Yah Shua
and with his brothers.

Matthias Replaces Yah Hudah

15 And in those days
Petros rises midst the disciples, and says,
— the multitude of their names
is about a hundred and twenty,
16 Men and brothers,
this scripture must *needs have been*
be fulfilled/**shalamed**,
which the *Holy Spirit* **Ruach ha-kodesh**
by **through** the mouth of David
spake before **foretold** concerning
Judas **about Yah Hudah**,
which was **being** guide
to them that took *Jesus* **Yah Shua**.
17 For he was *numbered* **reckoned** with us,
and *had obtained part* **was allotted**
his lot of this ministry.
18 *Now* **So indeed**
this *man purchased* **one acquired** a *field* **parcel**
with **from** the reward of iniquity;
and *falling* **being** headlong,
he *burst asunder* **cracked open** in the **midst**,
and all his *bowels gushed out* **spleen
poured**. Zechar Yah 11:12
19 And *so be* it *was* known
unto all *the dwellers* **who settled** at
Jerusalem **Yeru Shalem**;
insomuch as **so** that field is called
in their *proper tongue* **own dialect**,
Aceldama, **Heleq Dam**,
that is to say, The *field* **parcel** of blood.
20 For it is *written* **scribed** in
the *book* **scroll** of Psalms,
Let his *habitation be* **hut become** desolate,
and let no *man dwell* **one settle** therein:
and his *bishoprick* **episcopate** let another take.
Psalm 69:25
21 *Wherefore* **So**
of these men which have *companied* **come** with us
all the time that *the Lord Jesus* **Adonay Yah Shua**
went in **entered** and *out* **exited** among us,
22 Beginning from the baptism of *John* **Yahn**,
unto that same day that he was taken *up* from us,
must one *be ordained to be* **become** a witness with us
of his resurrection.
23 And they *appointed* **set** two,
Joseph **Yoseph** called *Barsabas* **Bar Sabah**,
who was *surnamed* **called** Justus,

and Matthias.

24 And they prayed, and said, Thou, *Lord* **Adonay**, *which knowest the hearts of all men* **all heart—knowing**, shew whether of these two **the one** thou hast *chosen* **selected**,

25 That he may take *part* **his lot** of this ministry and apostleship, from which *Judas* **Yah Hudah** *by transgression fell* **transgressed**, that he might go to his own place.

26 And they gave forth their lots; and the lot fell upon Matthias; and he was *numbered* **enrolled** with the eleven apostles.

THE DAY OF PENTECOST

2 And *when* **in** the day of Pentecost *was fully come* **being fulfilled/shalamed**, they were all *with one accord* **in unanimity** in one place.

2 And **so be it,** suddenly *there came a sound —* **an echo** from heaven as of a *rushing mighty wind* **bearing forceful puff**, and it filled **full** all the house where they were sitting.

3 And there appeared unto them *cloven* **divided** tongues like as of fire, and it sat upon each *one* of them.

4 And they were all filled **full** with the *Holy Spirit* **Ruach ha-kodesh**, and began to speak with other tongues, **exactly** as the Spirit gave them utterance.

5 And there were *dwelling* **settling** at *Jerusalem* **Yeru Shalem** *Jews* **Yah Hudiym**, *devout* **well—received** men, out of every *nation* **goyim** under heaven.

6 Now when **And so be it,** this *was noised abroad* **voice** , the multitude came together, and were *confounded* **confused**, because that *every man* **each** heard them speak in his own *language* **dialect**.

7 And they *were* all *amazed* **astounded** and marvelled, *saying* **wording** one to another, Behold, are not all these which speak *Galilaeans* **Galiliym**?

8 And how hear we *every man* **each** in our own *tongue* **dialect**, wherein we were *born* **birthed**?

this scripture must fulfill/shalam, that the Holy Spirit through the mouth of David foretold about Yah Hudah, being guide to them who took Yah Shua:

17 because he was reckoned with us, and *was* allotted his lot of this ministry.

18 So indeed, this one acquired a parcel from the reward of iniquity; and being headlong, he cracked open in the middle and all his spleen poured forth.
Zechar Yah 11:12

19 And so be it known to all who settle at Yeru Shalem; so that field, in their own dialect, is called, Heleq Dam, that is to say, The Parcel of Blood.

20 For it is scribed in the scroll of Psalms, His hut becomes desolate, and no one settles therein: and another takes his episcopate.
Psalm 69:25

21 So, of these men who came with us all the time Adonay Yah Shua entered and exited among us,

22 beginning from the baptism of Yahn, to that same day he taken from us, one must, with us, become a witness of his resurrection.

23 And they set two, Yoseph called Bar Sabah who is called Justus, and Matthias:

24 and they pray, and say, You, Adonay, all heart—knowing, of these two, show the one you select

25 to take his lot of this ministry and apostleship from which Yah Hudah transgressed to go to his own place.

26 And they give their lots; and the lot falls upon Matthias; and he is enrolled with the eleven apostles.

THE DAY OF PENTECOST

2 And the day of Pentecost being fulfilled/shalamed, they are all in unanimity in one place.

2 And so be it, suddenly — an echo from the heavens, as of a bearing forceful puff: and it fills full the whole house where they sit:

3 and divided tongues as of fire appear to them, and sit on each of them:

4 and they all fill full with the Holy Spirit and begin to speak with other tongues — exactly as the Spirit gives them utterance.

5 And settling at Yeru Shalem,
are Yah Hudiym — well—received men
from every goyim under the heavens:
6 and so be it, this voice;
and the multitude comes together and is confused
because each hears them speak in his own dialect.
7 And they all astound and marvel,
wording one to another, Behold,
are not all these who speak Galiliym?
8 And how hear we each in our own dialect
wherein we are birthed?
9 Parthians, and *Medes* **Maday**,
and *Elamites* **Elamiym**,
and *the dwellers* **they who settled** in Mesopotamia,
and in *Judaea* **Yah Hudah**, and Cappadocia,
in Pontus, and Asia,
10 Phrygia, and Pamphylia, in *Egypt* **Misrayim**,
and in the parts of Libya about Cyrene,
and *strangers of Rome* **the Romans residing there**,
Jews **Yah Hudiym** and proselytes,
11 Cretes and *Arabians* **Arabs**,
we do hear them speak in our tongues
the *wonderful works* **magnificence** of *God* **Elohim**.
12 And they were all *amazed* **astounded**,
and were *in doubt* **thoroughly perplexed**,
saying **wording** one to another,
What *meaneth* **willeth** this *to be*?
13 Others *mocking said* **jeering worded**,
These men are full of new sweet wine.

The First Message Of Petros

14 But *Peter* **Petros**, standing *up* with the eleven,
lifted *up* his voice, and *said* **uttered** unto them,
Ye men of Judaea **Men — Yah Hudiym**,
and all ye that *dwell* **settle** at *Jerusalem* **Yeru Shalem**,
be this known unto you,
and hearken to my *words* **rhema**:

The Prophecy Of Yah El Fulfilled/Shalamed

15 For these are not *drunken* **intoxicated**,
as ye *suppose* **perceive**,
seeing **indeed** it is but the third hour of the day.
16 But this is that which was *spoken* **said**
by **through** the prophet *Joel* **Yah El**;
17 And it shall *come to pass*
become in the *last* **final** days,
saith God **wordeth Elohim**,
I *will* **shall** pour *out* of my Spirit upon all flesh:
and your sons and your daughters shall prophesy,
and your *young men* **youths** shall see visions,
and your *old men* **elders** shall dream dreams:
18 And **yet indeed**
on my servants and on my *hand maidens* **maids**
I *will* **shall** pour *out* in those days of my Spirit;
and they shall prophesy:
19 And I *will shew* **shall give**
wonders **omens** in *the* heaven above,
and signs in the earth *beneath* **below**;
blood, and fire, and vapour of smoke:
20 The sun shall be turned into darkness,
and the moon into blood,
before **ere** the *great* **mega** and *notable* **epiphanous**
day of *the Lord* **Yah Veh** come:
21 And **so be it** *shall come to pass*,
that **everyone** — whosoever
shall call on the name of *the Lord* **Yah Veh**
shall be saved.
Yah El 2:31, 32

Yah Shua Is Adonay And Messiah

22 *Ye men of Israel* **Men — Yisra Eliym**, hear these words;
Jesus of Nazareth **Yah Shua the Nazarene**,
a man *approved* of *God* **Elohim, shown** among you
by *miracles* **dynamis** and *wonders* **omens** and signs,
which *God* **Elohim** did *by* **through** him
in the midst of you,
exactly as ye yourselves also know:
23 Him, being *delivered* **given over**
by the *determinate* **decreed** counsel
and *foreknowledge* **prognosis** of *God* **Elohim**,
ye have taken,
and *by wicked* **through untorahed** hands
have *crucified* **staked** and *slain* **taken out**:
24 Whom *God* **Elohim** hath raised *up*,
having loosed the *pains* **travail** of death:
because **as** it was not possible
that he should be *holden of* **overpowered by** it.

The Prophecy Of David Fulfilled/Shalamed

25 For David *speaketh concerning*
wordeth unto him,
I foresaw *the Lord always* **Yah Veh through all time**
before **in sight of** my face,
for he is *on* **at** my right *hand*,
that I should not be *moved* **shaken**:
26 *Therefore* **Because of this** did my heart rejoice,
and my tongue *was glad* **jumped for joy**;

9 — Parthians and Maday and Elamiym
and they who settle in Mesopotamia
and in Yah Hudah and Cappadocia,
in Pontus and Asia,
10 Phrygia and Pamphylia, in Misrayim
and in the parts of Libya around Cyrene
and the Romans residing there,
Yah Hudiym and proselytes,
11 Cretes and Arabs
— we hear them speak the magnificence of Elohim
in our tongues.
12 And they are all astounded
and thoroughly perplexed,
wording one to another, Whatever will this be?
13 Others jeering, word,
These men are full of new sweet wine.

The First Message Of Petros

14 But Petros, standing with the eleven,
lifts his voice, and utters to them,
Men — Yah Hudiym
and all you settling at Yeru Shalem,
Know this, and hearken to my rhema.

The Prophecy Of Yah El Fulfilled/Shalamed

15 For these are not intoxicated, as you perceive;
indeed it is but the third hour of the day:
16 but this is that said through the prophet Yah El:
17 And it becomes, in the
final days, words Elohim,
I pour of my Spirit on all flesh:
and your sons and your daughters prophesy,
and your youths see visions,
and your elders dream dreams:
18 and yet indeed, in those days,
I pour of my Spirit;
on my servants and on my maids,
and they prophesy:
19 and I give omens in the heavens above
and signs in the earth below
— blood and fire and vapour of smoke:
20 the sun turns to darkness
and the moon to blood
ere the mega and epiphanous day of Yah Veh comes:
21 and so be it, everyone
— whoever calls on the name of Yah
Veh is saved. Yah El 2:31, 32

Yah Shua Is Adonay And Messiah

22 Men — Yisra Eliym, hear these words,
Yah Shua the Nazarene, a man of Elohim,
shown to you by dynamis and omens and signs,
which Elohim did through him in your midst
— exactly as you yourselves also know:
23 this one, being given over
by the decreed counsel and prognosis of Elohim,
you took,
and through untorahed hands, staked and took out:
24 whom Elohim raised
— having loosed the travail of death:
as it is not possible
for him to be overpowered thereby.

The Prophecy Of David Fulfilled/Shalamed

25 For David words to him,
I foresaw Yah Veh through all time
in sight of my face;
for he is at my right that I not be shaken:
26 because of this my heart rejoices
and my tongue jumps for joy;
moreover **yet** also my flesh shall *rest* **nest** in hope:
27 Because thou
wilt **shalt** not leave my soul in *hell* **sheol/hades**,
neither *wilt* **shalt** thou
suffer thine Holy One **give thy Merciful**
to see corruption.
28 Thou hast made known to me the ways of life;
thou shalt *make me full of joy* **shalam me with rejoicing**
with thy *countenance* **face**.
Psalm 16:8—11
29 Men and brethren,
let **allow** me *freely speak* **to boldly say** unto you
of **concerning** the patriarch David,
that he is both dead and *buried* **entombed**,
and his *sepulchre* **tomb** is with us unto this day.
30 *Therefore* **So** being a prophet,
and knowing that *God* **Elohim**
had *sworn with* **oathed** an oath to him,
that of the fruit of his loins, according to the flesh,
he *would* **should** raise *up Christ* **the Messiah**
to sit on his throne;
31 He *seeing* **foreseeing** this *before*
spake of the resurrection of *Christ* **the Messiah**,
that his soul was not left in *hell* **sheol/hades**,
neither his flesh did see corruption.

32   This *Jesus* **Yah Shua** hath
God **Elohim** raised *up*,
whereof we all are witnesses.

33   *Therefore* **So**
being *by* **at** the right hand of *God* **Elohim** exalted,
and having *received* **taken** of the Father
the *promise* **pre—evangelism** of the
Holy Spirit **Ruach ha-kodesh**,
he hath *shed forth* **poured** this,
which ye now see and hear.

34   For David is not ascended into the heavens:
but he *saith* himself **wordeth**,
the LORD said **An oracle of Yah
Veh** unto my *Lord* **Adonay**,
Sit thou *on* **at** my right *hand*,

35   Until I *make* **place** thy *foes* **enemies**
thy footstool **the stool of they feet**.
Psalm 110:1

36   *Therefore* **So** let all the house of *Israel* **Yisra El**
know *assuredly* **certainly**,
that *God* **Elohim** hath made the same *Jesus* **Yah Shua**,
whom ye have *crucified* **staked**,
both *Lord* **Adonay** and *Christ* **Messiah**.

Taking The Gratuity Of The Holy Spirit

37   Now when they heard this,
they were *pricked* **pierced** in their heart,
and said unto *Peter* **Petros** and to the rest of the apostles,
Men and brethren, what shall we do?

38   Then *Peter* **Petros** said unto them,
Repent, and be baptized *every one* **each** of you
in the name of *Jesus Christ* **Yah Shua Messiah**
for **unto** the *remission* **forgiveness** of sins,
and ye shall *receive* **take**
the *gift* **gratuity** of the *Holy Spirit* **Ruach ha-kodesh**.

39   For the *promise* **pre—evangelism** is unto you,
and to your children, and to all that are afar off,
even as many
as *the Lord* **Yah Veh** our *God* **Elohim** shall call.
Yah El 2:32

40   And with many other words
did he *testify* **witness** and *exhort* **beseech**,
saying **wording**,
Save yourselves **Be ye saved**
from this *untoward* **crooked** generation.

The First Ecclesia

41   *Then* **So indeed**
they that *gladly* **with pleasure** received his word
were baptized:

and *the same* **that** day there were added *unto them*
about three thousand souls.

42   And they continued stedfastly
in the apostles' doctrine and *fellowship* **communion**,
and in breaking of bread, and in prayers.

43   And *fear came* **awe became** upon every soul:
and many *wonders* **omens** and signs *were*
done by **became through** the apostles.
yet also my flesh nests in hope:

27   because you neither leave
my soul in sheol/hades
nor give your Merciful to see corruption:

28   You make known to me the ways of life;
you fill full/shalam me with rejoicing
with your face. Psalm 16:8—11

29   Men and brothers,
allow me to boldly say to you
concerning the patriarch David
— that he is both dead and entombed
and his tomb is with us to this day.

30   So being a prophet
and knowing that Elohim oathed an oath to him
that, of the fruit of his loins, according to the flesh,
he raises the Messiah to sit on his throne:

31   foreseeing this,
he speaks of the resurrection of the Messiah,
that neither his soul is left in sheol/hades,
nor his flesh sees corruption:

32   this Yah Shua Elohim raised
whereof we all are witnesses.

33   So, being exalted at the right of Elohim,
and having taken
the pre—evangelism of the Holy Spirit
from the Father,
he poured this, which you now see and hear.

34   For David ascended not into the heavens:
but he himself words,
An oracle of Yah Veh to my Adonay,
You, sit at my right

35   until I place your enemies the stool of your feet.
Psalm 110:1

36   So all the house of Yisra El certainly knows
that Elohim made the same Yah Shua
— whom you staked
both Adonay and Messiah.

Taking The Gratuity Of The Holy Spirit

37   And hearing this,
they are pierced in their heart
and say to Petros and to the rest of the apostles,

Men and brothers, What do we?
38 And Petros says to them,
Repent and be baptized — each of you
in the name of Yah Shua Messiah
to the forgiveness of sins,
and take the gratuity of the Holy Spirit:
39 for the pre—evangelism is to you
and to your children and to all who are afar
— even as many as Yah Veh our Elohim calls.
Yah El 2:32
40 And he witnesses and beseeches
with many other words, wording,
You, be saved from this crooked generation.

THE FIRST ECCLESIA

41 So indeed
they who receive his word with pleasure
are baptized;
and about three thousand souls are added that day:
42 and they continue stedfastly
in the doctrine and communion of the apostles
and in breaking of bread and in prayers:
43 and awe becomes upon every soul:
and many omens and signs
become through the apostles.
44 And all that *believed* **trusted**
were *together* **in one**,
and had all *things* common;
45 And sold their possessions and goods,
and *parted* **divided** them to all *men*,
as every *man* **one** had need.
46 And they,
continuing daily *with one accord* **in unanimity**
in the *temple* **priestal precinct**,
and breaking bread from house to house
did eat **partook** their *meat* **nourishment**
with gladness **in jumping for joy**
and *singleness* **simplicity** of heart,
47 *Praising God* **Halaling Elohim**,
and having *favour* **charism** with all the people.
And *the Lord* **Adonay** added to the *church* **ecclesia** daily
such as should be saved.

THE DAY OF PENTECOST:
THE FIRST SIGN OF PETROS

3 Now *Peter* **Petros** and *John* **Yahn**
went up together **ascended themselves**
into the *temple* **priestal precinct** at the hour of prayer,
being the ninth *hour*.
2 And a *certain* man
being lame from his mother's womb was *carried* **borne**,
whom they *laid* **placed** daily
at the *gate* **portal** of the *temple* **priestal precinct**
which is *called* **worded** Beautiful,
to ask *alms* **mercies** of them
that entered into the *temple* **priestal precinct**;
3 Who seeing *Peter* **Petros** and *John* **Yahn**
about to *go* **enter** into the *temple* **priestal precinct**
asked *an alms* **mercies**.
4 And *Peter* **Petros**,
fastening **staring** his eyes upon him with *John* **Yahn**,
said, Look on us.
5 And he *gave heed unto* **heeded** them,
expecting **awaiting** to *receive* **take** something of them.
6 *Then Peter* **But Petros** said,
Silver and gold have I none;
but such as I have give I thee:
In the name of
Jesus Christ of Nazareth **Yah Shua**
Messiah the Nazarene
rise *up* and walk.
7 And he *took* **seized** him by the right hand,
and *lifted* **raised** him *up*:
and immediately his feet and *ancle bones* **sockets**
received strength **solidified**.
8 And he leaping *up* stood, and walked,
and entered with them into the *temple* **priestal precinct**,
walking, and leaping, and *praising God* **halaling Elohim**.
9 And all the people saw him walking
and *praising God* **halaling Elohim**:
10 And they knew that it was
he which sat for *alms* **mercies**
at the Beautiful gate of the *temple* **priestal precinct**:
and they were filled **full**
with *wonder* **astonishment** and *amazement* **ecstasis**
at that which had happened unto him.
11 And as the lame *man* which was healed
held Peter **overpowered Petros** and *John* **Yahn**,
all the people *ran* **rushed** together unto them
in the *porch* **portico** that is called *Solomon's* **Sholomoh's**,
greatly wondering **utterly astonished**.

THE SECOND MESSAGE OF PETROS

12 And when *Peter* **Petros** saw it,
he answered unto the people,
Ye men of Israel **Men — Yisra Eliym**,
why marvel ye at this?
or why *look ye so earnestly on* **stare at** us,
as though by our own

power **dynamis** or *holiness* **reverence**
we had *made this man* **caused him** to walk?

13   The *God* **Elohim** of Abraham,
and of *Isaac* **Yischaq**, and of *Jacob* **Yaaqov**,
the *God* **Elohim** of our fathers,
hath glorified his *Son Jesus* **Lad Yah Shua**;
whom ye delivered *up*,
and denied him in the *presence* **face** of *Pilate* **Pilatos**,
when he *was determined* **had judged**
to *let* **release** him *go*.

14   But ye denied the Holy *One* and the Just,
and *desired* **asked a man** — a murderer

44   And all who trust are in one,
and have all in common;

45   and sell their possessions and goods
and divide them to all as everyone has need.

46   And continuing daily in unanimity
in the priestal precinct,
and breaking bread from house to house,
they partake their nourishment
in jumping for joy and simplicity of heart,

47   halaling Elohim
and having charism with all the people:
and Adonay adds those being saved
to the ecclesia daily.

The Day Of Pentecost: The First Sign Of Petros

3   And Petros and Yahn
ascend into the priestal precinct
at the hour of prayer — the ninth:

2   and a man, lame from the womb of his mother,
is being carried
— whom they place daily
at the portal of the priestal precinct, worded Beautiful,
to ask mercies of them entering the priestal precinct:

3   who, seeing Petros and Yahn
about to enter the priestal precinct,
asks mercies.

4   And Petros,
staring his eyes on him with Yahn, says,
Look on us.

5   And he heeds them,
awaiting to take somewhat from them.

6   But Petros says, Silver and gold I have none;
but such as I have I give you:
In the name of Yah Shua Messiah the Nazarene,
rise and walk!

7   — and he seizes his right hand and raises him:
and immediately his feet and sockets solidify:

8   and leaping, he stands and walks
and enters the priestal precinct with them
— walking and leaping and halaling Elohim.

9   And all the people
see him walking and halaling Elohim:

10   and they know it is he who sat for mercies
at the gate Beautiful of the priestal precinct:
and they fill full with astonishment and ecstasis
at what happened to him:

11   and as the healed lame man
overpowers Petros and Yahn,
all the people
rush toward them in the portico called Of Sholomoh
utterly astonished.

The Second Message Of Petros

12   And Petros sees,
and he answers the people,
Men — Yisra Eliym, why marvel at this?
Or why stare at us
— as though by our own dynamis or reverence
we caused him to walk?

13   The Elohim of Abraham and
of Yischaq and of Yaaqov
— the Elohim of our fathers
glorified his lad Yah Shua
— whom you delivered
and denied at the face of Pilatos
when he judged to release him:

14   but you denied the Holy and the Just,
and asked that a man — a murderer
to be granted **charism** unto you;

15   And *killed* **slaughtered** the
Prince **Hierarch** of life,
whom *God* **Elohim** hath raised from the dead;
whereof we are witnesses.

16   And his name *through*
faith **by trust** in his name*
hath *made* **solidified** this man *strong*,
whom ye *see* **observe** and know:
yea, the *faith* **trust** which is *by* **through** him
the name* hath given him
this *perfect soundness* **complete wholeness**
in the presence of you all.
*the name: see 4:10—12

17   And now, brethren,
I *wot* **perceive** that through *ignorance* **unknowingness**
ye *did* **transacted** it,
exactly as *did* also your *rulers* **archs**.

18   But those *things*,

ACTS 3, 4

which *God before* **Elohim** had *shewed* **pre—evangelized**
by **through** the mouth of all his prophets,
that *Christ* **the Messiah** should suffer,
he hath *so* **thus** fulfilled/**shalamed**.

19 *So* Repent ye *therefore*, and
be converted **turn around**,
that **unto wiping out** your sins *may be blotted out*,
when the *times* **seasons** of refreshing shall come
from the *presence* **face** of *the Lord* **Yah Veh**.

20 And he shall
send Jesus Christ **apostolize Yah Shua Messiah**,
which *before* **previously** was preached unto you:

21 Whom indeed the heaven must receive
until the times of *restitution* **restoration** of all *things*,
which *God* **Elohim** hath spoken
by **through** the mouth of all his holy prophets
since **from** the *world began* **eons**.

22 For *Moses truly* **Mosheh**
indeed said unto the fathers,
A prophet shall *the Lord* **Yah Veh** your *God* **Elohim**
raise *up* unto you of your brethren, like unto me;
him shall ye hear in all *things*
whatsoever — **as much as** he shall *say* **speak**
unto you. Deuteronomy 18:15, 19

23 And *so be* it shall *come to pass*, that every soul,
which *will* **shall** not hear that prophet,
shall be **utterly** destroyed from *among* the people.

24 Yea, and all the prophets from *Samuel* **Shemu El**
and those that follow *after* **in sequence**,
as many as have spoken,
have likewise *foretold* **pre—evangelized** of these days.

25 Ye are the *children* **sons** of the prophets,
and of the covenant
which *God made* **Elohim covenanted** with our fathers,
saying **wording** unto Abraham,
And in thy *seed* **sperma**
shall all the *kindreds* **patriarchies** of the earth
be *blessed* **eulogized**.

26 Unto you first,
God **Elohim**, having raised *up* his
Son Jesus **Lad Yah Shua**,
sent apostolized him to *bless* **eulogize** you,
in turning away *every one* **each** of you
from his *iniquities* **evils**.

THE FIRST PERSECUTION

4 And as they spake unto the people,
the priests, and the *captain* **strategos**
of the *temple* **priestal precinct**,
and the *Sadducees* **Sadoqiym**, *came upon* **stood by** them,

2 Being grieved
that **because** they *taught* **doctrinated** the people,
and *preached through Jesus* **evangelized in Yah Shua**
the resurrection from the dead.

3 And they laid hands on them,
and put them in *hold* **guard** unto the *next day* **morrow**:
for it was now *eventide* **being already evening**.

4 Howbeit
many of them which heard the word *believed* **trusted**;
and the number of the men
was **became** about five thousand.

THE THIRD MESSAGE OF PETROS

5 And *it came to pass on* **being** the morrow,
that their *rulers* **archs**, and elders, and scribes,

6 And *Annas* **Hanan Yah** the *high* **arch** priest,
and Caiaphas, and *John* **Yahn**, and Alexander,
be granted charism unto you;

15 and slaughtered the Hierarch of life
whom Elohim raised from the dead
— whereof we are witnesses.

16 And by the trust in the name*,
solidified this one whom you observe and know:
yes, the trust that is through him
the name* gives him complete wholeness
in your presence.
*the name: see 4:10—12

17 And now, brothers,
I perceive that you transacted this
through unknowingness
— exactly as also your archs.

18 But those which Elohim pre—evangelized
through the mouth of all his prophets
— that the Messiah suffer, he thus fulfilled/shalamed.

19 So repent and restore, to wipe out your sins,
when the seasons of refreshing come
from the face of Yah Veh.

20 And he apostolized Yah Shua Messiah,
who was previously preached to you:

21 whom indeed the heavens must receive
until the times of restoration of all,
of which Elohim spoke
through the mouth of all his holy prophets
from the eons.

22 For Mosheh indeed said to the fathers,
Yah Veh your Elohim
raises a prophet to you of your brothers, like to me;
You, hear him in all
— as much as he speaks to you. Deuteronomy 18:15, 19

23 And so be it,

every soul who hears not that prophet,
is utterly destroyed from the people.
24 Yes, and all the prophets from Shemu El
and those who follow in sequence,
as many as spoke,
likewise pre—evangelized of these days.
25 You are the sons of the prophets
and of the covenant
which Elohim covenanted with your fathers;
wording to Abraham,
And in your sperma
all the patriarchies of the earth eulogize.
26 To you first,
Elohim raised his lad Yah Shua,
apostolized him to eulogize you,
in turning each of you away from his evils.

THE FIRST PERSECUTION

4 And as they speak to the people,
the priests and the strategos of the priestal precinct
and the Sadoqiym stand by them,
2 grieved — because they doctrinate the people
and evangelize that the resurrection from the dead
is in Yah Shua:
3 and they lay hands on them
and put them in guard to the morrow
— already being evening.
4 Howbeit many of them who hear the word trust
— the number of the men being about five thousand.

THE THIRD MESSAGE OF PETROS

5 And being the morrow,
their archs and elders and scribes
6 and Hanan Yah the archpriest
and Caiaphas and Yahn and Alexander
and as many as were of the *kindred* **genos**
of the *high* **arch** priest,
were gathered together at *Jerusalem* **Yeru Shalem**.
7 And when they had set them
in the midst, they asked,
By **In** what *power* **dynamis**, or *by* **in** what name,
have ye done this?
8 Then *Peter* **Petros**,
filled/shalamed with the *Holy Spirit* **Ruach ha-kodesh**,
said unto them,
Ye *rulers* **archs** of the people, and
elders of *Israel* **Yisra El**,
9 If we this day be examined
of the good *deed* **work**
done to the *impotent man* **frail human**,

by what *means he* **this one** is *made whole* **saved**;
10 Be it known unto you all,
and to all the people of *Israel* **Yisra El**,
that *by* **in** the name of
Jesus Christ of Nazareth **Yah Shua
Messiah the Nazarene**,
whom ye *crucified* **staked**,
whom *God* **Elohim** raised from the dead,
even by him doth *in his name* this *man* **one** stand
here before you *in your sight* whole.
11 This is the stone
which was *set at nought* **belittled** of you builders,
which is become **unto** the head of the corner.
12 Neither is there salvation in any other:
for there is none other name under heaven
given *among men* **by humanity**,
whereby we must be saved.
13 Now when they *saw* **observed**
the boldness of *Peter* **Petros** and *John* **Yahn**,
and *perceived* **overtook** that they were
unlearned **unlettered** and *ignorant* **unlearned**
men **humans**,
they marvelled;
and they *took knowledge of them* **knew**,
that they had been with *Jesus* **Yah Shua**.
14 And *beholding* **seeing** the *man* **human**
which was *healed* **cured** standing with them,
they could *say nothing against* **not refute** it.
15 But when they had
commanded **summoned** them
to *go aside get* **out of** the *council* **sanhedrim**,
they *conferred* **considered** among
themselves **one another**,
16 *Saying* **Wording**,
What shall we do to these *men* **humans**?
for that indeed a *notable miracle* **known sign**
hath *been done by* **become through** them
is manifest to all them
that *dwell* **settle** in *Jerusalem* **Yeru Shalem**;
and we cannot deny it.
17 But that it spread no *further*
more among the people,
let us *straitly* **threateningly** threaten them,
that they speak *henceforth* **no more** to no *man* **human**
in this name.
18 And they called them,
and *commanded* **evangelized** them
not to *speak* **utter** at all
nor *teach* **doctrinate** in the name of *Jesus* **Yah Shua**.
19 But *Peter* **Petros** and *John* **Yahn**

answered and said unto them,
Whether it be *right* **just** in the sight of *God* **Elohim**
to hearken unto you *more* **rather** than unto *God* **Elohim**,
judge ye.
20   For we cannot but speak
the things **those** which we have seen and heard.
21   *So* **But** when they had further threatened them,
they *let* **released** them *go*,
finding *nothing* **naught** how they might punish them,
because of the people:
for all *men* glorified *God* **Elohim**
for **over** that which *was done* **became**.
22   For the *man* **human**
was *above* **more than** forty years *old*,
on whom this *miracle* **sign** of healing
was shewed **had become**.

MESSIANISTS FILL/SHALAM WITH THE HOLY SPIRIT

23   And being *let go* **released**,
they *went* **came** to their own *company*,
and *reported all that* **evangelized as much as**
the *chief* **arch** priests and elders had said unto them.
and as many as are of the genos of the archpriest
gather together at Yeru Shalem.
7   And they set them among them, and ask,
In what dynamis or in what name do you this?
8   So Petros, filled/shalamed with the Holy Spirit,
says to them,
You archs of the people and elders of Yisra El,
9   If this day we *are* examined on the good work
done to the frail human,
by what/whom this *one* is saved;
10   so be it known to you all
and to all the people of Yisra El,
that in the name of Yah Shua Messiah the Nazarene
— whom you staked
— whom Elohim raised from the dead
— in whom this *one* stands whole in your sight.
11   This is the stone belittled by you builders
which became the head of the corner:
12   and salvation is in no other:
for there is no other name under the heavens
given by humanity,
whereby we must be saved.
13   But they observe the
boldness of Petros and Yahn,
and overtaking
that they are unlettered and unlearned humans,
they marvel;
and they know that they were with Yah Shua.
14   And seeing the cured
human standing with them,
they cannot refute it.
15   But they summon them to
go from the sanhedrim,
and they consider among one another,
16   wording, What do we to these humans?
For indeed a known sign became through them
— manifest to all who settle in Yeru Shalem;
and we cannot deny it.
17   But so it spreads no more among the people,
threateningly we threaten them
to speak no more to no human in this name.
18   — and they call them and evangelize them
to neither utter at all
nor doctrinate in the name of Yah Shua.
19   But Petros and Yahn answer them, saying,
Whether it be just in the sight of Elohim
to hearken to you rather than to Elohim,
you judge.
20   For we cannot but speak
what we saw and heard.
21   But they threaten them further and release them
finding naught how to punish them
because of the people:
for all glorify Elohim over what became;
22   for the human on whom
this sign of healing became
was more than forty years.

MESSIANISTS FILL/SHALAM WITH THE HOLY SPIRIT

23   And being released, they come to their own,
and evangelize
as much as the archpriests and elders said to them:
24   And when they heard that,
they lifted *up* their voice to *God* **Elohim**
with one accord **in unanimity**, and said,
Lord **Despotes**, thou art *God* **Elohim**,
which hast made heaven **the heavens**,
and earth, and the sea,
and all that in them is:
25   Who *by* **through** the mouth
of thy *servant* **lad** David
hast said, Why did the *heathen rage* **goyim snort**
and the people *imagine* **premeditate in** vain *things*?
26   The *kings* **sovereigns** of the earth stood *up*,
and the *rulers* **archs** were gathered together

	against *the Lord* **Yah Veh**, and against
	his *Christ* **Messiah**. Psalm 2:1, 2
27	For of a truth,
	against thy holy *child Jesus* **lad Yah Shua**,
	whom thou hast anointed,
	both Herod, and Pontius *Pilate* **Pilatos**,
	with the *Gentiles* **goyim**, and the
	people of *Israel* **Yisra El**,
	were gathered together,
28	For to do
	whatsoever **as much as** thy hand and thy counsel
	determined before **predetermined** to *be done* **become**.
29	And now, Lord **Yah Veh**, *behold*
	regard their threatenings:
	and *grant* **give** unto thy servants,
	that with all boldness they may speak thy word,
30	By *stretching forth* **spreading** thine hand to heal;
	and that signs and *wonders* **omens** may *be done* **become**
	by **through** the name
	of thy holy *child Jesus* **lad Yah Shua**.
31	And when they had *prayed* **petitioned**,
	the place was shaken
	where they were assembled together;
	and they were all filled/**shalamed**
	with the *Holy Spirit* **Ruach ha-kodesh**,
	and they spake the word of *God* **Elohim** with boldness.

TRUSTERS SHARE THEIR HOLDINGS

32	And the multitude of them that *believed* **trusted**
	were of one heart and of one soul:
	neither *said* **worded** any of them
	that ought of *the things which he possessed* **his holdings**
	was his own;
	but they had all *things* common.
33	And with *great power* **mega dynamis**
	gave the apostles witness
	of the resurrection of *the Lord Jesus* **Adonay Yah Shua**:
	and *great grace* **mega charism** was upon them all.
34	**Indeed** Neither was there
	any among them that lacked:
	for as many as were possessors of *lands* **parcels** or houses
	sold them,
	and brought the prices of *the things* **those** that were sold,
35	And *laid* **placed** them *down* at the apostles' feet:
	and *distribution was made* **distributed**
	unto *every man* **each**
	according as he had need **as any needed**.
36	And *Joses* **Yoses**,
	who by the apostles was *surnamed*
	Barnabas **called Bar Nabi**,

	(which *is, being interpreted* **translates**
	The son of consolation,)
	a *Levite* **Leviy**,
	and *of the country of Cyprus* **by genos, a Cypriy**,
37	Having *land* **a field**, sold it,
	and brought the *money* **riches**,
	and *laid* **placed** it at the apostles' feet.

HANAN YAH AND SAPPHIRA
LIE TO THE HOLY SPIRIT

5	But a *certain* man named *Ananias* **Hanan Yah**,
	with Sapphira his *wife* **woman**, sold a possession,
2	And kept back *part* of the price,
	his *wife* **woman** also being *privy to it* **aware**,
	and brought a *certain* part,
	and *laid* **placed** it at the apostles' feet.
3	But *Peter* **Petros** said, *Ananias* **Hanan Yah**,
	why hath Satan filled/**shalamed** thine heart
	to lie to the *Holy Spirit* **Ruach ha-kodesh**,
	and to keep back *part* of the price of the *land* **parcel**?
4	*Whiles it remained* **In abiding**,
	was **abode** it not *indeed* thine *own*?
	and after it was sold,
	was it not in thine own *power* **authority**?
24	and when they hear,
	they lift their voice to Elohim in unanimity, and say,
	Despotes, you are Elohim,
	who made the heavens and earth and the sea
	and all therein:
25	who through the mouth of your lad David said,
	Why do the goyim snort
	and the people premeditate in vain?
26	The sovereigns of the earth stand,
	and the archs gather together
	against Yah Veh and against his Messiah.
	Psalm 2:1, 2
27	For of a truth,
	against your holy lad Yah Shua whom you anointed,
	both Herod and Pontius Pilatos
	with the goyim and the people of Yisra El
	gathered together,
28	to do as much as your hand and your counsel
	predetermined to become.
29	And now, Yah Veh, regard their threatenings:
	and give to your servants
	to speak your word with all boldness,
30	by spreading your hand to heal;
	and that signs and omens become
	through the name of your holy lad Yah Shua.
31	And having petitioned,

the place where they assemble together shakes;
and they all fill/shalam with the Holy Spirit,
and they speak the word of Elohim with boldness.

TRUSTERS SHARE THEIR HOLDINGS

32 And the multitude of them who trust
are of one heart and of one soul:
not any of them
word that aught of his holdings is his own;
but they have all *in* common:
33 and with mega dynamis
the apostles give witness
of the resurrection of Adonay Yah Shua:
and mega charism is on them all.
34 Indeed not any among them lack:
for as many as possess parcels or houses, sell
them, and bring the prices of those sold,
35 and place them at the feet of the apostles:
and distribute to each as any needed.
36 And Yoses,
whom the apostles call Bar Nabi,
which translates, Son of Consolation
— a Leviy, and by genos, a Cypriy,
37 having a field, sells it, and brings the riches,
and places them at the feet of the apostles.

HANAN YAH AND SAPPHIRA
LIE TO THE HOLY SPIRIT

5 But a man named Hanan Yah,
with Sapphira his woman, sell a possession;
2 and keep back of the price
— his woman also being aware;
and brings a part
and places it at the feet of the apostles.
3 But Petros says, Hanan Yah,
why has Satan filled/shalamed your heart
to lie to the Holy Spirit,
to keep back of the price of the parcel?
4 In abiding, abode it not indeed yours?
And, being sold, was it in your own authority?
why hast thou *conceived* **placed** this *thing* **matter**
in thine heart?
thou hast not lied unto *men* **humanity**,
but unto *God* **Elohim**.
5 And *Ananias* **Hanan Yah**
hearing these words fell down,
and *gave up the ghost* **expired**:
and *so be it*, *great fear* **a mega awe**
came on all them that heard these *things*.
6 And the *young men* **youths** arose,
wound **enshrouded** him *up*,
and *carried* **brought** him *out* **forth**,
and *buried* **entombed** him.
7 And *so be* it *was*
about the *space* **interval** of three hours after,
when his *wife* **woman**,
not knowing what *was done* **had become**,
came in **entered**.
8 And *Peter* **Petros** answered
unto her, *Tell* **Say** to me
whether ye *sold* **gave** up the *land* **parcel** for so much?
And she said, Yea, for so much.
9 *Then Peter* **And Petros** said unto her,
How is it that ye have *agreed together* **symphonized**
to *tempt* **test** the Spirit of *the Lord* **Yah Veh**?
behold, the feet of them
which have *buried* **entombed** thy *husband* **man**
are at the *door* **portal**,
and shall *carry* **bring** thee *out* **forth**.
10 *Then* **And** fell she *down*
straightway **immediately**
at his feet,
and *yielded up the ghost* **expired**:
and the *young men came in* **youths entered**,
and found her dead, and, *carrying* **bringing** her forth,
buried **entombed** her by her *husband* **man**.
11 And *so be it*, *great fear* **a mega awe**
came upon all the *church* **ecclesia**,
and upon *as many as* **all who** heard these *things*.

SIGNS AND OMENS

12 And *by* **through** the hands of the apostles
were many signs and *wonders* **omens**
wrought **become** among the people;
(and they were all *with one accord* **in unanimity**
in *Solomon's porch* **Sholomoh's portico**.
13 And of the rest durst no *man*
one join himself to them:
but the people magnified them.
14 And *believers* **they who trusted**
were the more added to *the Lord* **Adonay**,
multitudes both of men and women.)
15 *Insomuch* **So** that they
brought forth the *sick* **frail**
into the *streets* **broadways**,
and *laid* **placed** them on beds and *couches* **pads**,
that *at the least* **even** the shadow of Peter
passing by **coming** might overshadow some of them.
16 There came also a multitude
out of the cities round about

unto *Jerusalem* **Yeru Shalem**,
bringing *sick* **frail** folks,
and them which were vexed *with*
unclean **by impure** spirits:
and they were *healed every one* **all cured**.

THE SECOND PERSECUTION

17   *Then* **And** the *high* **arch** priest rose *up*,
and all they that were with him,
(which is the *sect* **heresy** of the *Sadducees* **Sadoqiym**,)
and were *filled*/**shalamed** with *indignation* **zeal**,
18   And laid their hands on the apostles,
and put them in the *common* **public** prison.
19   But the angel of *the Lord* **Yah Veh**
by **through the** night
opened the *prison doors* **guardhouse portals**,
and *brought* **led** them *forth*, and said,
20   Go, stand and speak in the
temple **priestal precinct**
to the people,
all the *words* **rhema** of this life.
21   And when they heard that,
they entered into the *temple early* **priestal precinct**
in the morning **by dawn**, and *taught* **doctrinated**.
But the *high* **arch** priest came,
and they that were with him,
and called the *council* **sanhedrim** together,
Why place you this matter in your heart?
You lie, not to humanity, but to Elohim.
5   And hearing these words,
Hanan Yah falls down and expires:
and so be it, a mega awe on all who hear these:
6   and the youths rise and enshroud him
and bring him forth and entomb him.
7   And so be it,
about the interval of three hours after,
his woman, not knowing what had become, enters.
8   And Petros answers her, Say to me,
whether you gave the parcel for so much?
And she says, Yes, for so much.
9   And Petros says to her,
Why symphonized you to test the Spirit of Yah Veh?
Behold, the feet of them who entombed your man
are at the portal, and bring you forth.
10   And immediately,
she falls at his feet and expires:
and the youths enter and find her dead;
and bring her and entomb her by her man.
11   And so be it, a mega awe on all the ecclesia,
and on all who hear these.

SIGNS AND OMENS

12   And through the hands of the apostles
many signs and omens become among the people;
and they are all in unanimity
in the portico of Sholomoh.
13   And of the rest,
no one dares join himself to them;
but the people magnify them:
14   and all the more
they who trust are added to Adonay
— multitudes both of men and women
15   — so that they bring the
frail into the broadways
and place them on beds and pads
— so that if even the shadow of the coming of Peter
overshadow some of them.
16   And also a multitude from
the surrounding cities
comes to Yeru Shalem,
bringing frail folks and those vexed by impure spirits
— and they are all cured.

THE SECOND PERSECUTION

17   And the archpriest and all with him rise
— which is of the heresy of the Sadoqiym
and they fill/shalam with zeal;
18   and they lay their hands on the apostles
and put them in the public prison.
19   But through the night,
the angel of Yah Veh opens the guardhouse portals
and leads them, and says,
20   Go, stand in the priestal precinct
and speak to the people of all the rhema of this life.
21   — and when they hear that,
they enter the priestal precinct by dawn
and doctrinate.
But the archpriest and those with him come,
and call together the sanhedrim
and all the *senate* **ancients**
of the *children* **sons** of *Israel* **Yisra El**,
and *sent* **apostolized** to the prison to have them brought.
22   But when the *officers* **attendants** came,
and found them not in the *prison* **guardhouse**,
they returned and *told* **evangelized**,
23   *Saying* **Wording**,
The prison *truly* **indeed** found we shut
with all safety **in security**,
and the *keepers* **guards** standing *without* **outside**
before **in front of** the *doors* **portals**:

ACTS 5

but when we had opened, we found no *man* one within.
24 *Now* **And** when the *high* priest
and the *captain* **strategos**
of the *temple* **priestal precinct**
and the *chief* **arch** priests heard these *things* **words**,
they *doubted of* **were thoroughly perplexed about** them
whereunto **whatever** this *would grow* **should be**.
25 *Then* **But** came one and *told* **evangelized** them,
saying **wording**,
Behold, the men whom ye put in *prison* **guardhouse**
are standing in the *temple* **priestal precinct**,
teaching **doctrinating** the people.
26 Then went
the *captain* **strategos** with the *officers* **attendants**,
and brought them without violence:
for they *feared* **awed** the people,
lest **that** they should *have been* **not be** stoned.
27 And when they had brought them,
they set them *before* **in** the *council* **sanhedrim**:
and the *high* **arch** priest asked them,
28 *Saying*, **Wording, In evanglizing**,
Did not we *straitly command* **evangelize** you
that ye should not *teach* **doctrinate** in this name?
and, behold,
ye have filled/**shalamed** *Jerusalem* **Yeru Shalem**
with your doctrine,
and *intend* **will** to bring
this *man's* **human's** blood upon us.
29 *Then Peter* **But Petros** and the other apostles
answered and said,
We *ought to* **must first** obey *God* **Elohim**
rather than *men* **humanity**.
30 The *God* **Elohim** of our fathers
raised *up Jesus* **Yah Shua**,
whom ye *slew* **thoroughly handled**
and hanged on a *tree* **staff**.
31 Him hath *God* **Elohim**
exalted *with* **at** his right *hand*
to be a *Prince* **I-lierarch** and *a* Savior,
for to give repentance to *Israel* **Yisra El**,
and forgiveness of sins.
32 And we are his witnesses of these *things* **rhema**;
and so is also the *Holy Spirit* **Ruach ha-kodesh**,
whom *God* **Elohim** hath given to them
that *first* obey him.
33 When they heard *that*,
they *were* cut* *to the heart*,
and *took counsel* **counseled** to *slay* **take** them
out. *as in cutting an oath or a covenant
34 *Then stood there up* **But** one **rose**
in the *council* **sanhedrim**, a Pharisee,
named *Gamaliel* **Gamli El**, a doctor of the *law* **torah**,
had in reputation **honoured** among all the people,
and *commanded* **summoned**
to *put* **make** the apostles *forth* **out** a little space;
35 And said unto them, *Ye men*
of Israel **Men — Yisra Eliym**,
take heed to yourselves
what ye *intend* **are about** to *do* **transact**
as *touching* **to** these *men* **humans**.
36 For *before* **ere** these days rose *up* Theudas,
boasting **wording** himself to be *somebody* **someone**;
to whom a number of men, about four hundred,
joined themselves:
who was *slain* **taken out**;
and all, as many as obeyed him,
were *scattered* **dissolved**, and *brought to* **became** nought.
37 After this man
rose *up Judas of Galilee* **Yah I-ludah — a Galiliy**
in the days of the *taxing* **registration**,
and all the ancients of the sons of Yisra El,
and apostolize to the prison to have them brought.
22 But the attendants come
and find them not in the guardhouse;
and they return and evangelize,
23 wording,
We indeed found the prison shut in security,
and the guards standing outside in front of the portals:
but when we opened, we found no one inside.
24 And when the priest
and the strategos of the priestal precinct
and the archpriests hear these words,
they are thoroughly perplexed about them
— whatever this be.
25 But one comes and evangelizes them, wording,
Behold, the men you put in the guardhouse
are standing in the priestal precinct,
doctrinating the people.
26 Then the strategoi goes with the attendants
and brings them without violence:
that they not be stoned; for they awed the people.
27 And they bring them
and set them in the sanhedrim:
and the archpriest asks them,
28 wording, In evanglizing,
evangelized we not to not doctrinate in this name?
And behold,
you fill/shalam Yeru Shalem with your doctrine
and will to bring the blood of this human upon us.

29 But Petros and the other
apostles answer, saying,
We must first obey Elohim rather than humanity.
30 The Elohim of our fathers raised Yah Shua
whom you thoroughly handled and hanged on a staff:
31 Elohim exalted him at his right
— a Hierarch and Savior
to give Yisra El repentance and forgiveness of sins:
32 and we are his witnesses of these rhema;
and so also the Holy Spirit,
whom Elohim gave to them who first obeyed him.
33 When they hear, they cut*,
and counsel to take them out.
*as in cutting an oath or a covenant
34 But one rises in the sanhedrim
— a Pharisee named Gamli El — a doctor of the torah
honored among all the people:
and he summons
to make a little space for the apostles;
35 and says to them, Men — Yisra Eliym,
heed to yourselves what you are about to transact
as to these humans.
36 For ere these days,
rose Theudas, wording himself to be someone;
to whom a number of men, about four hundred,
joined themselves; who was taken out:
and all, as many as obeyed him,
dissolved, and became to naught.
37 After this one, rose Yah Hudah — a Galiliy
in the days of the registration,
and drew away much people after him:
he also *perished* **destructed**;
and all, *even* as many as obeyed him,
were dispersed **scattered**.
38 And now I *say* **word** unto you,
Refrain **Depart** from these *men* **humans**,
and let them alone:
for *if* **whenever** this counsel or this work
be of *men* **humanity**,
it *will come to nought* **shall disintegrate**:
39 But if it be of *God* **Elohim**,
ye cannot *overthrow* **disintegrate** it;
lest *haply* **ever** ye be found
even to *fight against God* **be Elohim—opponents**.
40 And *to him they agreed* **he convinced them**:
and when they had called the apostles,
and *beaten* **flogged** them,
they *commanded* **evangelized**
that they should not speak in the
name of *Jesus* **Yah Shua**,

and *let* **released** them *go*.
41 *And therefore* **So indeed** they departed
from the *presence* **face** of the *council* **sanhedrim**,
rejoicing **cheering** that they were counted worthy
to *suffer shame* **be dishonoured** for his name.
42 And daily in the *temple* **priestal precinct**,
and in every house,
they *ceased* **paused** not
to *teach* **doctrinate** and *preach* **evangelize**
Jesus Christ **Yah Shua the Messiah**.

THE MINISTRY OF TABLES

6 And in those days,
when the number of the disciples was multiplied,
there *arose* **became** a murmuring
of the *Grecians* **Hellenists**
against the Hebrews,
because their widows were *neglected* **overlooked**
in the daily *ministration* **ministry**.
2 *Then* **And** the twelve
called the multitude of the disciples unto them,
and said, It is not *reason* **pleasing**
that we should leave the word of *God* **Elohim**,
and *serve* **minister** tables.
3 *Wherefore* **So**, brethren,
look ye **scope** out *among you*
seven men of *honest report* **witness**,
full of the *Holy Spirit* **Ruach ha-kodesh** and wisdom,
whom we may *appoint* **seat** over this *business* **need**.
4 But we
will give ourselves continually to **shall continue in** prayer,
and to the ministry of the word.
5 And the *saying* **word** pleased
in sight of the whole multitude:
and they *chose Stephan* **selected Stephanos**,
a man full of *faith* **trust** and of the
Holy Spirit **Ruach ha-kodesh**,
and *Philip* **Philippos**, and Prochorus, and Nicanor,
and Timon, and Parmenas,
and Nicolas a proselyte *of Antioch* — **an Antiochan**:
6 Whom they set *before* **in**
the sight of the apostles:
and when they had prayed,
they *laid* **put** their hands on them.
7 And the word of *God increased* **Elohim grew**;
and the number of the disciples multiplied
in *Jerusalem greatly* **Yeru Shalem extremely**;
and a *great company* **vast multitude** of the priests
were obedient to the faith **obeyed the trust**.

ACTS 6

Third Persecution

8 And *Stephen* **Stephanos**,
full of *faith* **trust** and *power* **dynamis**,
did *great wonders* **mega omens** and *miracles* **signs**
among the people.
9 *Then* **And** there arose *certain*
some of the synagogue,
which is *called the synagogue of the* **worded** Libertines,
and Cyrenians, and Alexandrians,
and of them of Cilicia and of Asia,
disputing with *Stephen* **Stephanos**.
10 And they were not able to *resist* **withstand**
the wisdom and the spirit by which he spake.
11 Then they *suborned* **instigated** men,
which *said* **worded**, We have heard him speak
blasphemous *words* **rhema** against Moses
unto Mosheh, and *against God* **Elohim**.
and drew many people after him; and he destructed:
and all, as many as obeyed him, scattered.
38 And now I word to you,
Depart from these humans, and let them alone:
for whenever this counsel or this work is of humanity,
it disintegrates:
39 but if it is of Elohim, you cannot disintegrate it;
lest ever
you are even found to be Elohim—opponents.
40 — and he convinces them.
And they call the apostles, and flog them,
and evangelize them
to not speak in the name of Yah Shua;
and release them.
41 So indeed
they depart from the face of the sanhedrim
— cheering that they are counted worthy
to be dishonored for his name:
42 and daily,
in the priestal precinct and in every house,
they pause not
to doctrinate and evangelize Yah Shua the Messiah.

The Ministry Of Tables

6 And in these days,
as the number of the disciples multiplies,
there becomes a murmuring of the Hellenists
against the Hebrews,
because they overlook the widows
in the daily ministry.
2 And the twelve
call the multitude of the disciples to them,
and say, It is not pleasing to leave the word of Elohim,
and minister tables:
3 so, brothers,
scope out seven men of witness
full of the Holy Spirit and wisdom
to seat over this need:
4 but we continue in prayer
and to the ministry of the word.
5 And the word pleases
in sight of the whole multitude:
and they select Stephanos,
a man full of trust and of the Holy Spirit,
and Philippos and Prochorus and Nicanor
and Timon and Parmenas
and Nicolas a proselyte — an Antiochan:
6 whom they set in the sight of the apostles:
and as they pray, they put their hands on them.
7 And the word of Elohim grows;
and the number of the disciples in Yeru Shalem
multiplies extremely;
and a vast multitude of the priests obey the trust.

Third Persecution

8 And Stephanos, full of trust and dynamis,
does mega omens and signs among the people:
9 and some of the synagogue rise
— worded, Libertines
and Cyrenians and Alexandrians
and of them of Cilicia and of Asia;
and they dispute with Stephanos:
10 and they are not able to withstand
the wisdom and the spirit by which he speaks.
11 So they instigate men, who word,
We heard him speak
blasphemous rhema as to Mosheh and Elohim!
12 And they *stirred up* **excited** the people,
and the elders, and the scribes,
and *came upon* **stood by** him,
and caught him, and brought him
to the *council* **sanhedrim**,
13 And set *up false* **pseudo**
witnesses, which *said* **worded**,
This *man ceaseth* **human pauseth** not
to speak blasphemous *words* **rhema**
against this holy place, and the *law* **torah**:
14 For we have heard him *say* **word**,
that this *Jesus of Nazareth* **Yah Shua the Nazarene**
shall *destroy* **disintegrate** this place,
and shall change the customs
which *Moses* **Mosheh** delivered us.

15 And all that sat in the *council* **sanhedrim**,
looking stedfastly on **staring unto** him,
saw his face as it had been the face of an angel.

THE MESSAGE OF STEPHANOS

7 Then said the *high* **arch** priest,
Are **If** these *things so* **be thus**?
2 And he said, Men, brethren,
and fathers, hearken;
The *God* **Elohim** of glory
appeared unto our father Abraham,
when he was in Mesopotamia,
before **ere** he *dwelt* **settled** in Haran,
3 And said unto him,
Get thee out of thy *country* **land**, and from thy kindred,
and come into the land which I shall shew thee.
4 Then came he
out of the land of the *Chaldaeans* **Kesediym**,
and *dwelt* **settled** in Haran:
and from thence, *when* **after** his father was dead,
he *removed* **exiled** him into this land,
wherein ye now *dwell* **settle**.
5 And he gave him none inheritance in it,
no, not *so much as to set his foot on* **even a foot bamah**:
yet he *promised* **pre—evangelized**
that he *would* **should** give it to him
for **unto** a possession,
and to his *seed* **sperma** after him,
when *as* yet he had no child.
6 And *God* **Elohim** spake *on this wise* **thus**,
That his *seed* **sperma** should *sojourn* **be a settler**
in *a strange* **another's** land;
and that they should bring them into *bondage* **servitude**,
and *entreat* **vilify** them *evil* four hundred years.
7 And the *nation* **goyim**
to whom *ever* they shall be *in bondage* **servient**
will **shall** I judge, said *God* **Elohim**:
and after that shall they come *forth*,
and *serve* **liturgize** me in this place.
8 And he gave him the covenant of circumcision:
and *so Abraham begat Isaac* **thus birthed Yischaq**,
and circumcised him the eighth day;
and *Isaac* **Yischaq**, *begat Jacob* **Yaaqov**;
and *Jacob* **Yaaqov**, *begat* the twelve patriarchs.
9 And the patriarchs, *moved with envy* **zeal**,
sold Joseph **gave Yoseph** into *Egypt* **Misrayim**:
but *God* **and Elohim** was with him,
10 And *delivered* **released** him
out of all his *afflictions* **tribulations**,
and gave him *favour* **charism** and wisdom

in the sight of *Pharaoh* **Paroh**
king **sovereign** of *Egypt* **Misrayim**;
and he *made* **seated** him governor
over *Egypt* **Misrayim** and all his house.
11 *Now* **But** there came a *dearth* **famine**
over all the land
of *Egypt* **Misrayim** and *Chanaan* **Kenaan**,
and *great affliction* **mega tribulation**:
and our fathers found no *sustenance* **forage**.
12 But when *Jacob* **Yaaqov** heard
that there was *corn* **grain** in *Egypt* **Misrayim**, he
sent out **apostolized forth** our fathers first.
13 And at the second *time*
Joseph was made **Yoseph became** known to his brethren;
and *Joseph's kindred* **Yoseph's genos**
was *made known* **manifest** unto *Pharaoh* **Paroh**.
14 Then *sent Joseph* **apostolized Yoseph**,
12 — and they excite the people
and the elders and the scribes.
And those standing by
catch him and bring him to the sanhedrim;
13 and set pseudo witnesses, who word,
This human pauses not
to speak blasphemous rhema
against this holy place and the torah:
14 for we heard him word,
that this Yah Shua the Nazarene
disintegrates this place,
and changes the customs Mosheh delivered us.
15 — and all who sit in the sanhedrim stare to him,
and see his face as the face of an angel.

THE MESSAGE OF STEPHANOS

7 And the archpriest says, If these be thus?
2 And he says, Men, brothers
and fathers, hearken;
the Elohim of glory
appeared to our father Abraham
being in Mesopotamia, ere he settled in Haran,
3 and said to him,
You, go from your land and from your kindred;
and come to the land I show you.
4 Then he comes from the land of the Kesediym
and settles in Haran:
and from there, after his father dies,
he exiles him to this land wherein you now settle:
5 and he gave him no inheritance therein
— no, not even a foot bamah:
yet he pre—evangelized
to give it to him for a possession,

ACTS 7

     and to his sperma after him
     — he having no child.
6   And Elohim spoke thus,
     that his sperma becomes a settler
     in the land of another;
     and to bring them into servitude and
     vilify them four hundred years.
7   And the goyim to whomever they be servient,
     I judge, says Elohim:
     and after that,
     they come and liturgize me in this place.
8   And he gives him the covenant of circumcision:
     and thus births Yischaq,
     and circumcises him the eighth day;
     and Yischaq, Yaaqov;
     and Yaaqov, the twelve patriarchs.
9   And with zeal
     the patriarchs give Yoseph into Misrayim:
     and Elohim is with him
10   and releases him from all his tribulations,
     and gives him charism and wisdom
     in the sight of Paroh sovereign of Misrayim;
     and he seats him governor
     over Misrayim and all his house.
11   But a famine
     comes over all the land of Misrayim and Kenaan
     — and mega tribulation:
     and our fathers find no forage:
12   but Yaaqov hears there is grain in Misrayim,
     and apostolizes our fathers first:
13   and at the second
     Yoseph becomes known to his brothers;
     and the genos of Yoseph manifests to Paroh.
14   So Yoseph apostolizes,
     and called his father *Jacob* **Yaaqov** to him,
     and all his kindred,
     threescore and fifteen **seventy and five** souls.
15   *So Jacob* **And Yaaqov**
     went down **descended** into *Egypt* **Misrayim**, and died,
     he, and our fathers,
16   And were *carried over* **transplaced**
     into *Sychem* **Shechem**
     and *laid* **placed** in the *sepulchre* **tomb**
     that Abraham bought for a *sum* **price** of *money* **silver**
     of the sons of *Emmor* **Hamor**
     the father of *Sychem* **Shechem**.
17   But *when* **exactly as** the time
     of the *promise drew nigh* **pre—evangelism approached**,
     which *God* **Elohim** had *sworn* **oathed** to Abraham,
     the people grew and multiplied in *Egypt* **Misrayim**,
18   Till another *king* **sovereign** arose,
     which knew not *Joseph* **Yoseph**.
19   *The same dealt subtilly* **This one sophisticated**
     with our *kindred* **genos**,
     and *evil entreated* **vilified** our fathers,
     so that they *cast out* **exposed** their
     young children **infants**,
     to the end that they might not live.
20   In which *time Moses* **season**
     Mosheh was *born* **birthed**,
     and was exceeding *fair* **urbane** to *God* **Elohim**,
     and *nourished up* **nurtured** in his father's house
     three months:
21   And when he was *cast out* **exposed**,
     Pharaoh's **Paroh's** daughter took him *up*,
     and *nourished* **nurtured** him *for* **as** her own son.
22   And *Moses* **Mosheh** was *learned* **disciplined**
     in all the wisdom of the *Egyptians* **Misrayim**,
     and was mighty able in words and in *deeds* **works**.
23   And when *he was full*
     forty years old **time was fulfilled/shalamed**,
     it *came into* **ascended upon** his heart
     to visit his brethren the *children* **sons** of *Israel* **Yisra El**.
24   And seeing one of them *suffer wrong* **injured**,
     he defended him,
     and *avenged* **dealt vengeance for** him
     that was *oppressed* **worn**,
     and smote the *Egyptian* **Misrayim**:
25   For he *supposed* **presumed** his brethren
     would **should** have *understood* **comprehended**
     how that *God by* **Elohim through** his hand
     would deliver **should give** them **salvation**:
     but they *understood* **comprehended** not.
26   And the next day
     he *shewed himself* **appeared** unto them as they strove,
     and *would* **should** have set them at *one* **shalom** again,
     saying, *Sirs* **Men**, ye are brethren;
     why *do* **injure** ye *wrong* one to another?
27   But he that *did* **injured** his neighbour *wrong*
     thrust **shoved** him away, saying,
     Who *made* **seated** thee
     a ruler **an arch** and *a* judge over us?
28   *Wilt* **Willest** thou *kill me* **to take me out**
     as **in the manner** thou *diddest* **tookest out**
     the *Egyptian* **Misrayim** yesterday?
29   Then fled *Moses* **Mosheh** at this *saying* **word**,
     and *was* **became** a *stranger* **settler**
     in the land of *Madian* **Midyan**,
     where he *begat* **birthed** two sons.

30   And when forty years were
expired **fulfilled/shalamed**,
there appeared to him
in the wilderness of mount *Sina* **Sinay**
an angel of *the Lord* **Yah Veh**
in a flame of fire in a *bush* **brier**.

31   When *Moses* **Mosheh** saw it,
he *wondered* **marvelled** at the *sight* **vision**:
and as he drew near to *behold* **perceive** it,
the voice of *the Lord came* **Yah Veh became** unto him,

32   *Saying, I am the God* **I — Elohim** of thy fathers,
the God **Elohim** of Abraham,
and *the God* **Elohim** of *Isaac* **Yischaq**,
and *the God* **Elohim** of *Jacob* **Yaaqov**.
Then *Moses trembled* **Mosheh became trembling**,
and durst not *behold* **perceive**.

and calls his father Yaaqov and all his kindred to him
— seventy—five souls.

15   And Yaaqov descends into Misrayim and dies
— he, and our fathers,

16   and are transplaced to Shechem
and placed in the tomb Abraham bought
for a price of silver
from the sons of Hamor of Shechem.

17   But exactly at the time
the pre—evangelism approaches
— which Elohim had oathed to Abraham,
the people grow and multiply in Misrayim

18   — until another sovereign rises
who knows not Yoseph.

19   This one sophisticates with our genos
and vilifies our fathers;
so that they expose their infants to not live:

20   in which season Mosheh is birthed,
and is exceedingly urbane to Elohim,
and he is nurtured in the house of his father
three months:

21   and being exposed,
the daughter of Paroh takes him
and nurtures him as her own son:

22   and Mosheh is disciplined
in all the wisdom of the Misrayim,
capable in words and in works.

23   And forty years time fulfills/shalams,
and it ascends on his heart
to visit his brothers, the sons of Yisra El:

24   and seeing one of them injured,
he defends him,
and deals vengeance for him who was worn;
and smites the Misrayim:

25   for he presumes his brothers comprehend
how Elohim, through his hand, gives them salvation:
and they comprehend not.

26   And the next day
he appears to them as they strive,
to set them at shalom again, saying,
Men, You, brothers, why injure one another?

27   But he who injures his neighbor
shoves him away, saying,
Who seated you an arch and judge over us?

28   Will you to take me out
in the manner you took out the Misrayim yesterday?

29   — and at this word, Mosheh flees
and becomes a settler in the land of Midyan,
where he births two sons.

30   And forty years fulfill/shalam,
and an angel of Yah Veh appears to him
in a flame of fire in a brier
in the wilderness of mount Sinay.

31   And Mosheh sees, and marvels at the vision:
and as he draws near to perceive it,
the voice of Yah Veh becomes to him,

32   I — Elohim of your fathers;
Elohim of Abraham and Elohim of
Yischaq and Elohim of Yaaqov.
— so Mosheh trembles, and dares not perceive.

33   *Then* **And** said *the Lord* **Yah Veh** to him,
Put off **Loose** thy shoes from thy feet:
for the place *where* **whereon** thou standest
is holy *ground* **land**.

34   *I have seen* **In seeing**,
I have seen the *affliction* **vilification** of my people
which is in *Egypt* **Misrayim**,
and I have heard their *groaning* **sighing**,
and am *come down* **descended** to *deliver* **release** them.
And now come,
I *will send* **shall apostolize** thee into *Egypt* **Misrayim**.

35   This *Moses* **Mosheh** whom they *refused* **denied**,
saying,
Who *made* **seated** thee *a ruler* **an arch** and *a* judge?
the same did *God send* **Elohim apostolize**
to be a ruler **arch** and *a deliverer* **redeemer**
by the hand of the angel
which appeared to him in the *bush* **brier**.
Exodus 3:2—6

36   *He brought* **This one led** them out,
after that he had *shewed wonders* **made omens** and signs
in the land of *Egypt* **Misrayim**, and in the *Red* **Reed** sea,
and in the wilderness forty years.

37   This is that *Moses* **Mosheh**,

which said unto the children sons of Israel Yisra El,
A prophet shall the Lord Yah Veh your God Elohim
raise *up* unto you of your brethren, like unto me;
him shall ye hear ye him.
Deuteronomy 18:15, 18, 19
38   This is he,
that *was* **became** in the *church* **ecclesia** in the wilderness
with the angel which spake to him
in the mount *Sina* **Sinay**, and with our fathers:
who received the *lively* **living** oracles to give unto us:
39   To whom our fathers *would* **willed**
to not *obey* **become obedient**,
but *thrust* **shoved** him **away** from them,
and in their hearts
turned back again **returned** into *Egypt* **Misrayim**,
40   Saying unto *Aaron* **Aharon**,
Make us *gods* **elohim** to *go before* **precede** us:
for *as for* this *Moses* **Mosheh**,
which *brought* **led** us out of the land of *Egypt* **Misrayim**,
we *wot* **know** not what is become of him.
41   And they made a calf in those days,
and *offered* **brought** sacrifice unto the idol,
and rejoiced in the works of their own hands.
42   *Then God* **But Elohim** turned,
and *gave* **surrendered** them *up*
to *worship* **liturgize** the host of heaven;
exactly as it is *written* **scribed**
in the *book* **scroll** of the prophets,
O ye house of *Israel* **Yisra El**,
have ye offered to me
slain beasts **slaughters** and sacrifices
by the space of forty years in the wilderness?
43   Yea, ye took *up* the tabernacle
of *Moloch* **Molech**,
and the star of your god *Remphan* **Kiyun**,
figures **types** which ye made to worship them:
and I *will carry* **shall exile** you *away*
beyond *Babylon* **Babel**.
44   Our fathers
had the tabernacle of witness in the wilderness,
exactly as he had *appointed* **ordained**,
speaking unto *Moses* **Mosheh**, that he should make it
according to the *fashion* **type** that he had seen.
45   Which also our fathers
that came after **having in succession received**
brought in with *Jesus* **Yah Shua***
into the possession of the *Gentiles* **goyim**,
whom *God drave out* **Elohim expelled**
before **from** the face of our fathers,
unto the days of David;

46   Who found *favour* **charism**
before God **in the sight of Elohim**,
and *desired* **asked** to find a tabernacle
for the *God* **Elohim** of *Jacob* **Yaaqov**.
*Yah Shua: successor of Mosheh
33   And Yah Veh says to him,
Loose your shoes from your feet:
for the place whereon you stand is holy land.
34   In seeing,
I see the vilification of my people in Misrayim
and I hear their sighing;
and descend to release them.
And now come, I apostolize you to Misrayim.
35   This Mosheh whom they denied, saying,
Who seated you an arch and judge?
this same one Elohim apostolized arch and redeemer
by the hand of the angel
who appeared to him in the brier.
Exodus 3:2—6
36   This one led them out,
after he made omens and signs
in the land of Misrayim and in the Reed sea,
and in the wilderness forty years:
37   this is that Mosheh,
who said to the sons of Yisra El,
Yah Veh your Elohim raises a prophet to you
of your brothers, like to me;
You, hear him.
Deuteronomy 18:15, 18, 19
38   This is he,
who became in the ecclesia in the wilderness
with the angel who spoke to him in the mount Sinay;
and with our fathers:
who received the living oracles to give to us:
39   to whom our fathers willed
to not become obedient
but shoved him away from them,
and in their hearts returned to Misrayim,
40   saying to Aharon,
Make us elohim to precede us:
for this Mosheh,
who leads us from the land of Misrayim,
we know not what became of him.
41   And in those days, they make a calf
and bring sacrifice to the idol
and rejoice in the works of their own hands.
42   But Elohim turns,
and surrenders them
to liturgize the host of the heavens;
exactly as scribed in the scroll of the prophets,

You, house of Yisra El,
offer you slaughters and sacrifices to me
by the space of forty years in the wilderness?
43 Yes, you took the tabernacle of Molech
and the star of Kiyun, your el;
— types you made to worship:
and I exiled you beyond Babel.
44 Our fathers
had the tabernacle of witness in the wilderness,
exactly as he ordained,
speaking to Mosheh
to make it according to the type he saw:
45 which also our fathers,
having received in succession,
brought in with Yah Shua*
into the possession of the goyim
— whom Elohim expelled
from the face of our fathers
to the days of David;
46 who found charism in the sight of Elohim,
and asked to find a tabernacle
for the Elohim of Yaaqov. *Yah
Shua: successor of Mosheh
47 But *Solomon* **Sholomoh** built him an house.
48 *Howbeit the most High*
dwelleth **Yet Elyon settleth** not
in *temples made with hands* **handmade naves**;
exactly as *saith* **wordeth** the prophet,
49 Heaven is my throne, and earth is my footstool:
what house *will* **shall** ye build me?
saith the Lord **wordeth Yah Veh**:
or what is the place of my *rest* **shabbath**?
Yesha Yah 66:1, 2
50 Hath not **indeed** my hand made all these *things*?
51 Ye *stiffnecked* **hardnaped**
and *uncircumcised* **noncircumcised** in heart and ears,
ye *do always resist* **ever oppose** the
Holy Spirit **Ruach ha-kodesh**:
as your fathers *did*, so do ye.
52 Which of the prophets
have not your fathers persecuted? and
they have *slain* **slaughtered** them which
shewed before **pre—evangelized**
of **concerning** the coming of the Just *One*;
of whom ye have *been* **become** now
the *betrayers* **traitors** and murderers:
53 Who have *received* **taken** the *law* **torah**
by **unto** the *disposition* **ordinance** of angels,
and have not *kept* **guarded** it.

Stephanos Is Stoned

54 When they heard these *things*,
they were cut to the heart,
and they gnashed on him with their teeth.
55 But he, being full of the *Holy*
Spirit **Ruach ha-kodesh**,
looked up stedfastly **stared** into heaven,
and saw the glory of *God* **Elohim**,
and *Jesus* **Yah Shua**
standing *on* **at** the right *hand* of *God* **Elohim**,
56 And said, Behold, I *see*
observe the heavens opened,
and the Son of *man* **humanity**
standing *on* **at** the right *hand* of *God* **Elohim**.
57 *Then* **And** they cried out
with a *loud* **mega** voice,
and *stopped* **held** their ears,
and ran *violently* upon him
with one accord **in unanimity**,
58 And cast him out of the city, and stoned him:
and the witnesses *laid* **put** down their *clothes* **garments**
at *a young man's feet* **the feet of a youth**,
whose name was *Saul* **called Shaul**.
59 And they stoned *Stephen* **Stephanos**,
calling upon *God* **Elohim**, and *saying* **wording**,
Lord Jesus **Adonay Yah Shua**, receive my spirit.
60 And he *kneeled down* **placed his knees**,
and cried with a *loud* **mega** voice,
Lord **Adonay**, *lay* **set** not this sin to their charge.
And when he had said this, he fell asleep.
8 And *Saul* **Shaul** was
consenting **well—approving**
unto his *death* **his taking out**.

Fourth Persecution

And **so be it,** at that *time* **day**
there was *a great* **a mega** persecution
against **upon** the *church* **ecclesia**
which was at *Jerusalem* **in Yeru Shalem**;
and they were all *scattered abroad* **thoroughly dispersed**
throughout the regions
of *Judaea* **Yah Hudah** and *Samaria* **Shomeron**,
except the apostles.
2 And *devout* **well—received** men
carried *Stephen* **Stephanos** to his burial,
and made *great lamentation* **mega chopping** over him.
3 As for *Saul* **Shaul**,
he *made havock of* **ravaged** the *church* **ecclesia**,
entering into every house,

and *haling* **dragging** men and women
committed **delivered** them to *prison* **the guardhouse**.
4   *Therefore* **So indeed**
they that were *scattered abroad* **thoroughly dispersed**
went every where **passed through**
preaching **evangelizing** the word.

PHILIPPOS DOES SIGNS

5   *Then Philip* **And Philippos**
went down to the city of *Samaria* **Shomeron**,
and preached *Christ* **the Messiah** unto them.

47   But Sholomoh builds himself a house.
48   Elyon still settles not in handmade naves;
exactly as the prophet words,
49   The heavens are my throne
and earth is the stool of my feet!
What house build you *for* me?
words Yah Veh:
Or what is the place of my shabbath?
Yesha Yah 66:1, 2
50   Has not indeed my hand made all these?
51   You hardnaped and noncircumcised
in heart and ears,
you ever oppose the Holy Spirit.
As your fathers, also you.
52   Which of the prophets
have your fathers not persecuted?
And they slaughtered them
who pre—evangelized concerning the coming of the Just
— of whom you now become traitors and murderers:
53   who take the torah by the ordinance of angels,
and guard it not.

STEPHANOS IS STONED

54   They hear these and are cut to the heart;
and they gnash on him with their teeth:
55   but being full of the Holy Spirit,
he stares into the heavens
and sees the glory of Elohim;
and Yah Shua standing at the right of Elohim,
56   and says, Behold, I observe the heavens open,
and the Son of humanity
standing at the right of Elohim.
57   And they cry out with a mega voice
and hold their ears,
and run violently upon him in unanimity,
58   and cast him from the city, and stone him:
and the witnesses put down their garments
at the feet of a youth called Shaul:
59   and they stone Stephanos:
calling on Elohim, wording,
Adonay Yah Shua, receive my spirit.
60   And he places his knees
and cries with a mega voice,
Adonay, set not this sin to their charge.
— and saying this, he falls asleep.

8
— and Shaul well—approves his taking out.

FOURTH PERSECUTION

And so be it, in that day,
a mega persecution on the ecclesia in Yeru Shalem;
and they all thoroughly disperse
throughout the regions of Yah Hudah and Shomeron
— except the apostles.
2   And well—received men carry Stephanos
and make a mega chopping over him.
3   As for Shaul, he ravages the ecclesia
— entering every house,
and dragging men and women
and delivering them to the guardhouse.
4   So indeed, they thoroughly disperse
and pass through evangelizing the word.

PHILIPPOS DOES SIGNS

5   And Philippos goes down
to the city of Shomeron
and preaches the Messiah to them:
6   And the *people with one accord*
multitude in unanimity
gave heed unto **heeded** those *things*
which *Philip spake* **Philippos worded**,
hearing and seeing the *miracles* **signs** which he did.
7   For *unclean* **impure** spirits,
crying with *loud* **mega** voice,
came out of many that were possessed with them:
and many *taken with palsies* **a paralytic**,
and *that were* lame, were *healed* **cured**.
8   And **so be it**,
there was great joy **a mega cheer** in that city.
9   But there was a *certain* man,
called Simon **named Shimon**,
which *beforetime* **previously** in the
same city used sorcery,
and *bewitched* **astounded**
the *people* **goyim** of *Samaria* **Shomeron**,
giving out **wording** that himself
was some *great* **mega** one:
10   To whom they all *gave heed* **heeded**,
from the least to the *greatest* **mega**, *saying* **wording**,
This *man* **one**

	is the *great power* **mega dynamis** of *God* **Elohim**.		in the sight of *God* **Elohim**.
11	And to him they *had regard* **heeded**,	22	So Repent *therefore* of this
	because that of long time		thy *wickedness* **malice**,
	he had *bewitched* **astounded** them		and *pray God* **petition Elohim**,
	with *sorceries* **magicing**.		if *perhaps* **indeed** the *thought* **mind** of thine heart
12	But when they *believed Philip* **trusted Philippos**		may be forgiven thee.
	preaching the things **evangelizing those**	23	For I *perceive* **see**
	concerning the *kingdom* **sovereigndom** of *God* **Elohim**,		that thou art in the *gall* **choler** of bitterness,
	and the name of *Jesus Christ* **Yah Shua Messiah**,		and in the bond of iniquity.
	they were baptized, both men and women.	24	Then answered *Simon* **Shimon**, and said,
13	Then *Simon* **Shimon** himself		*Pray* **Petition** ye to *the Lord* **Adonay** for me,
	believed **trusted** also:	6	and in unanimity
	and when he was baptized,		the multitude heeds what Philippos words
	he continued with *Philip* **Philippos**,		— hearing and seeing the signs he does.
	and *wondered* **was astounded**,	7	For impure spirits, crying with mega voice,
	beholding **observing**		come from many of the possessed:
	the *miracles* **dynamis** and **mega** signs		and many paralyzed and lame are cured;
	which *were done* **became**.	8	and so be it, a mega cheer in that city.
14	*Now* **And** when the apostles	9	But some man named Shimon,
	which were at *Jerusalem* **Yeru Shalem**		who previously used sorcery in the same city,
	heard that *Samaria* **Shomeron**		who astounded the goyim of Shomeron;
	had received the word of *God* **Elohim**,		wording that *he* himself is some mega one:
	they *sent* **apostolized** unto them	10	whom they all heed,
	Peter **Petros** and *John* **Yahn**:		from the least to the mega, wording,
15	Who, when they *were come down* **descended**,		This *one* is the mega dynamis of Elohim.
	prayed *for* **concerning** them,	11	— and they heed him,
	that they might *receive* **take** the *Holy*		because he astounded them with magicing
	Spirit **Ruach ha-kodesh**:		for a long time.
16	(For as yet he was fallen upon none of them:	12	But when they trust Philippos
	only they were baptized		evangelizing those
	in the name of *the Lord Jesus* **Adonay Yah Shua**.)		concerning the sovereigndom of Elohim
17	Then *laid* **put** they their hands on them,		and the name of Yah Shua Messiah,
	and they *received* **took** the *Holy Spirit* **Ruach ha-kodesh**.		they are baptized — both men and women:
18	And when *Simon saw* **Shimon observed**	13	and Shimon himself also trusts:
	that through laying on of the apostles' hands		and being baptized, he continues with Philippos;
	the *Holy Spirit* **Ruach ha-kodesh** was given,		and is astounded,
	he offered them *money* **riches**,		observing the dynamis and mega signs that become.
19	*Saying* **Wording**, Give me	14	And the apostles at Yeru Shalem hear
	also this *power* **authority**,		that a Shomeron receives the word of Elohim,
	that on whomsoever I *lay* **put** hands,		they apostolize Petros and Yahn to them:
	he may *receive* **take** the *Holy Spirit* **Ruach ha-kodesh**.	15	who, having descended,
20	But *Peter* **Petros** said unto him,		pray concerning them to take the Holy Spirit:
	Thy *money* **silver**	16	— for as yet he had fallen on none of them
	perish with thee **be unto thy destruction**,		— only being baptized
	because thou hast *thought* **presumed**		in the name of Adonay Yah Shua.
	that the *gift* **gratuity** of *God* **Elohim**	17	Then they put their hands on them,
	may be *purchased with money* **acquired through riches**.		and they take the Holy Spirit.
21	Thou hast neither part nor	18	And when Shimon observes
	lot in this *matter* **word**:		that the Holy Spirit is given
	for thy heart is not *right* **straight**		through laying on of the hands of the apostles,

he offers them riches,
19 wording, Give me also this authority,
that on whomever I put hands,
he takes the Holy Spirit.
20 But Petros says to him,
Your silver be to your destruction!
— because you presume that the gratuity of Elohim
is acquired through riches.
21 You have neither part nor lot in this word:
for your heart is not straight in the sight of Elohim.
22 So repent of this your malice;
and petition Elohim,
if indeed the mind of your heart be forgiven you:
23 for I see you are in the choler of bitterness
and in the bond of iniquity.
24 And Shimon answers, saying,
You, petition Adonay for me,
that none of these *things* which ye have *spoken* **said**
come upon me.
25 *And therefore* **So indeed** they,
when they had *testified* **witnessed**
and *preached* **spoken** the word of *the Lord* **Adonay**,
returned to *Jerusalem* **Yeru Shalem**,
and *preached the gospel* **evangelized**
in many villages of the *Samaritans* **Shomeroniym**.

PHILIPPOS AND THE ETHIOPIAN

26 And the angel of *the Lord* **Yah Veh**
spake unto *Philip* **Philippos**, *saying* **wording**,
Arise, and go toward the *south* **midday**
unto the way
that *goeth down* **descendeth** from
Jerusalem **Yeru Shalem**
unto *Gaza* **Azzah**, which is *desert* **desolate**.
27 And he arose and went: and, behold, a man
of Ethiopia — **an Ethiopian**,
an eunuch *of great authority* — **a dynast** under Candace
queen **sovereigness** of the Ethiopians,
who had the charge of all her treasure,
and had come to *Jerusalem* **Yeru Shalem** for to worship,
28 Was returning, and sitting *in* **upon** his chariot
read *Esaias* **Yesha Yah** the prophet.
29 Then the Spirit said unto *Philip* **Philippos**,
Go near, and join thyself to this chariot.
30 And *Philip* **Philippos** ran *thither to him*,
and heard him read the prophet *Esaias* **Yesha Yah**,
and said, **Yet indeed,**
Understandest **Knowest** thou *then* what thou readest?
31 And he said, **Indeed,** How can I,
except **unless** some *man* **one** should guide me?

And he *desired Philip* **besought Philippos**
that he *would come up* **should ascend** and sit with him.
32 The *place* **passage** of the scripture which he read was this,
He was led as a sheep to the slaughter;
and *like* **as** a lamb
dumb before **voiceless in front of** his shearer,
so **thus** opened he not his mouth:
33 In his humiliation his judgment was taken away:
and who shall declare his generation?
for his life is taken from the earth.
Yesha Yah 53:7, 8
34 And the eunuch answered *Philip* **Philippos**,
and said, I *pray* **petition** thee,
of **concerning** whom *speaketh* **wordeth** the prophet this?
of **concerning** himself, or *of*
concerning some other *man*?
35 Then *Philip* **And Philippos** opened his mouth,
and began *at* **from** the same scripture, and
preached unto him *Jesus* **Yah Shua**.
36 And as they went on their way,
they came unto a *certain* water:
and the eunuch said, *See* **Behold**, *here is* water;
what *doth hinder* **forbiddeth** me to be baptized?
37 And *Philip* **Philippos** said,
If thou *believest with* **trustest from** all thine heart,
thou *mayest* **art allowed**.
And he answered and said,
I *believe* **trust** that *Jesus Christ* **Yah Shua Messiah**
is the Son of *God* **Elohim**.
38 And he *commanded* **summoned** the chariot
to stand *still*:
and they *went down* **descended** both into the water,
both *Philip* **Philippos** and the eunuch;
and he baptized him.
39 And when they *were come up* **ascended**
out of the water,
the Spirit of *the Lord* **Yah Veh**
caught away Philip **seized Philippos**,
that the eunuch saw him no more:
and **indeed** he went on his way *rejoicing* **cheering**.
40 But *Philip* **Philippos** was
found at *Azotus* **Ashdod**:
and passing through
he *preached* **evangelized** in all the cities,
till he came to *Caesarea* **Kaisaria**.

YAH SHUA CONFRONTS SHAUL

9 And *Saul* **Shaul**,
yet breathing out threatenings and *slaughter* **murder**

that none of these that you say come upon me.
25 So indeed,
having witnessed and spoken the word of Adonay,
they return to Yeru Shalem,
and evangelize in many villages of the Shomeroniym.

PHILIPPOS AND THE ETHIOPIAN

26 And the angel of Yah Veh
speaks to Philippos, wording,
Rise, and go toward the midday
to the way that descends from Yeru Shalem
— to Azzah — this is desolate.
27 And he rises and goes: and behold, a man
— an Ethiopian eunuch — a dynast under Candace
sovereigness of the Ethiopians
who has the charge of all her treasure,
and he comes to Yeru Shalem to worship;
28 and in returning;
sits on his chariot reading Yesha Yah the prophet.
29 And the Spirit says to Philippos,
Go near, and join yourself to this chariot.
30 And Philippos runs,
and hears him read the prophet Yesha Yah,
and says, Yet indeed, know you then what you read?
31 And he says, Indeed, how can I,
unless someone guides me?
— and he beseeches Philippos to
ascend and sit with him.
32 The passage of the scripture he reads is this:
He is led as a sheep to the slaughter;
and as a lamb voiceless in front of his shearer,
thus he opens not his mouth:
33 in his humiliation his judgment is taken away:
And who declares his generation? — for
his life is taken from the earth.
Yesha Yah 53:7, 8
34 And the eunuch answers Philippos,
saying, I petition you,
concerning whom words the prophet this?
Concerning himself? Or concerning some other?
35 And Philippos opens his mouth
and begins from the same scripture
and preaches Yah Shua to him:
36 and as they go their way, they come to a water:
and the eunuch says, Behold, water!
What forbids me to be baptized?
37 And Philippos says,
If you trust from all your heart, you are allowed.
And he answers, saying,
I trust that Yah Shua Messiah is the Son of Elohim.
38 And he summons the chariot to stand:
and they both descend into the water
— both Philippos and the eunuch;
and he baptizes him.
39 And when they ascend from the water
the Spirit of Yah Veh seizes Philippos
so that the eunuch sees him no more:
and indeed he goes on his way cheering.
40 But Philippos is found at Ashdod:
and passing through
he evangelizes in all the cities
until he comes to Kaisaria.

YAH SHUA CONFRONTS SHAUL

9 And Shaul,
still breathing out threatenings and murder

against **unto** the disciples of *the Lord* **Adonay**,
went unto the *high* **arch** priest,
2 And *desired* **asked** of him *letters* **epistles**
to *Damascus* **Dammeseq** to the synagogues,
that *if* **whenever** he found any **being** of this way,
whether they were men or women,
he might bring them bound unto
Jerusalem **Yeru Shalem**.
3 And as he *journeyed* **went**, *so be it,*
he *came near Damascus* **approached Dammeseq**:
and suddenly
there shined round about him **he was enveloped**
in a light from heaven:
4 And he fell to the earth,
and heard a voice *saying* **wording** unto him,
Saul, Saul **Shaul, Shaul**, why persecutest thou me?
5 And he said, Who art thou, *Lord* **Adonay**?
And *the Lord* **Adonay** said,
I am Jesus **I AM Yah Shua** whom thou persecutest:
it is hard for thee to *kick* **heel** against the *pricks* **stings**.
6 And he trembling and
astonished said, *Lord* **Adonay**,
what *wilt* **willest** thou have me to do?
And *the Lord* **Adonay** *said* unto him,
Arise, and *go into* **enter** the city,
and it shall be *told* **spoken** thee what thou must do.
7 And the men which journeyed with him
stood *speechless* **nodding**,
indeed hearing a voice, but *seeing*
observing no *man* **one**.
8 And *Saul* **Shaul** arose from the earth;
and when his eyes were opened, he saw no *man* **one**:
but they **hand** led him *by the hand*,

	and brought him into *Damascus* **Dammeseq**.
9	And he was three days *without sight* **not seeing**, and neither did eat nor drink.
10	And there was a *certain* disciple at *Damascus* **Dammeseq**, named *Ananias* **Hanan Yah**; and to him said *the Lord* **Adonay** in a vision, *Ananias* **Hanan Yah**. And he said, Behold, *I am here, Lord* **I — Adonay**.
11	And *the Lord* **Adonay** said unto him, Arise, and go into the street which is called Straight, and *enquire* **seek** in the house of *Judas* **Yah Hudah** for one *called Saul* **named Shaul**, *of Tarsus* **— a Tarsiy**: for, behold, he prayeth,
12	And hath seen in a vision a man named *Ananias coming in* **Hanan Yah entering**, and putting his hand on him, that he might *receive his sight* **see**.
13	*Then Ananias* **And Hanan Yah** answered, *Lord* **Adonay**, I have heard by many *of* **concerning** this man, *how much evil* **as many evils as** he hath done to thy *saints* **holy** at *Jerusalem* **Yeru Shalem**:
14	And here he hath authority from the *chief* **arch** priests to bind all that call on thy name.
15	*But the Lord* **And Adonay** said unto him, Go thy way: for he is a *chosen* **selected** vessel unto me, to bear my name *before* **in the sight of** the *Gentiles* **goyim**, and *kings* **sovereigns**, and the *children* **sons** of *Israel* **Yisra El**:
16	For I *will shew* **shall exemplify** him *how great things* **as much as** he must suffer for my name's sake.

SHAUL FILLS/SHALAMS WITH THE HOLY SPIRIT

17	And *Ananias* **Hanan Yah** went *his way*, and entered into the house; and putting his hands on him said, Brother *Saul* **Shaul**, *the Lord* **Adonay**, even *Jesus* **Yah Shua**, that appeared unto thee in the way as thou camest, hath *sent* **apostolized** me, that thou mightest *receive thy sight* **see**, and be filled/**shalamed** with the *Holy Spirit* **Ruach ha-kodesh**.
18	And *immediately* **straightway** there fell from his eyes as it *had been scales* **were leperous flakes**: and **immediately** he *received sight forthwith* **saw**, and arose, and was baptized. to the disciples of Adonay, goes to the archpriest,
2	and asks him for epistles to Dammeseq — to the synagogues; that whenever he finds any being of this way, whether men or women, to bring them bound to Yeru Shalem.
3	And as he goes, so be it, he approaches Dammeseq: and suddenly he is enveloped in a light from the heavens
4	and he falls to the earth: and he hears a voice wording to him, Shaul, Shaul, why persecute you me?
5	And he says, Who are you, Adonay? And Adonay says, I AM Yah Shua whom you persecute: it is hard for you to heel against the stings.
6	And trembling and astonished, he says, Adonay, what will you that I do? And Adonay *says* to him, Rise and enter the city, to be spoken to as to what to do.
7	— and the men journeying with him stand nodding — indeed hearing a voice but observing no one.
8	And Shaul rises from the earth; — his eyes are open but he sees no one: but they hand lead him and bring him to Dammeseq:
9	and he is three days not seeing, and neither eats nor drinks.
10	And there is a disciple at Dammeseq named Hanan Yah; and Adonay says to him in a vision, Hanan Yah! And he says, Behold, I — Adonay.
11	And Adonay says to him, Rise, and go to the street called Straight, and in the house of Yah Hudah seek for one named Shaul — a Tarsiy: for, behold, he prays:
12	and in a vision he sees a man named Hanan Yah entering, and putting his hand on him, to see.
13	And Hanan Yah answers, Adonay, I hear from many concerning this man, as many evils as he does to your holy at Yeru Shalem:
14	and here he has authority from the archpriests

to bind all who call on your name.
15 And Adonay says to him, Go your way:
for he is a selected vessel to me
to bear my name in the sight of the goyim
and sovereigns and the sons of Yisra El:
16 for I exemplify to him
as much as he must suffer for sake of my name.

SHAUL FILLS/SHALAMS WITH THE HOLY SPIRIT

17 And Hanan Yah goes and enters the house;
and putting his hands on him, says, Brother Shaul,
Adonay, even Yah Shua,
who appeared to you in the way as you came,
apostolized me
so that you see and fill/shalam with the Holy Spirit.
18 And straightway,
as leperous flakes fall from his eyes:
and immediately he sees and rises and is baptized:
19 And when he had *received meat* **taken nourishment**,
he was *strengthened* **invigorated**.
Then was *Saul certain* **Shaul some** days
with the disciples which were at *Damascus* **Dammeseq**.

SHAUL PREACHES THE MESSIAH

20 And straightway
he preached *Christ* **the Messiah** in the synagogues,
that he is the Son of *God* **Elohim**.
21 *But* **And** all that heard him
were *amazed* **astounded**,
and *said* **worded**;
Is not this he that *destroyed* **ravaged** them
which called on this name in *Jerusalem* **Yeru Shalem**,
and came hither *for that intent*,
that he might bring them bound
unto the *chief* **arch** priests?
22 But *Saul* **Shaul**
increased the more in strength **dynamized much**,
and *confounded* **confused** the *Jews* **Yah Hudiym**
which *dwelt at Damascus* **settled in Dammeseq**,
proving **concluding** that this is *very Christ* **the Messiah**.
23 And after that many days
were *fulfilled*/**shalamed**,
the *Jews took counsel* **Yah Hudiym counseled**
to *kill* **take** him **out**:
24 But their *laying await* **plotting**
was known of *Saul* **Shaul**.
And they *watched* **observed** the gates day and night
to *kill* **take** him **out**.
25 *Then* **But** the disciples took him by night,
and *let* **lowered** him *down by* **through** the wall
in a basket.

SHAUL IN YERU SHALEM

26 And when *Saul* **Shaul**
was come to *Jerusalem* **Yeru Shalem**,
he *assayed* **tried** to join himself to the disciples:
but **and** they were all *afraid of* **awed** him,
and *believed* **trusted** not that he was a disciple.
27 But *Barnabas* **Bar Nabi** took him,
and brought him to the apostles,
and declared unto them
how he had seen *the Lord* **Adonay** in the way,
and that he had spoken to him,
and how he had *preached boldly* **emboldened**
at *Damascus* **Dammeseq**
in the name of *Jesus* **Yah Shua**.
28 And he was with them
coming in **entering** and *going out* **departing**
at *Jerusalem* **Yeru Shalem**.
29 And he spake *boldly* **emboldened**
in the name of the Lord Jesus,
and disputed against the *Grecians* **Hellenists**:
but they *went about* **took in hand**
to *slay him* **take him out**.

SHAUL IN TARSUS

30 *Which* when the brethren knew,
they brought him down to *Caesarea* **Kaisaria**,
and *sent* **apostolized** him forth to Tarsus.
31 *Then* **So indeed**
had the *churches rest* **ecclesiae shalom**
throughout all *Judaea* **Yah Hudah**
and *Galilee* **Galiyl** and *Samaria* **Shomeron**,
and were *edified* **built** up;
and walking in the *fear* **awe** of *the Lord* **Yah Veh**,
and in the *comfort* **consolation** of the
Holy Spirit **Ruach ha-kodesh**,
were multiplied.

PETROS HEALS A PARALYTIC

32 And **so be** it *came to pass*,
as *Peter* **Petros** passed throughout *all quarters*,
he came down also to the *saints* **holy**
which *dwelt* **settled** at *Lydda* **Lod**.
33 And there he found a *certain*
man **human** named Aeneas,
which had *kept* **lain upon** his *bed* **pad** eight
years, and was *sick of the palsy* **a paralytic**.

34   And *Peter* **Petros** said unto him, Aeneas,
Jesus Christ **Yah Shua the Messiah**
maketh **healeth** thee *whole*:
arise, and *make thy bed* **spread**.
And he arose *immediately* **straightway**.
19   and he takes nourishment and invigorates.
and for some days
Shaul is with the disciples at Dammeseq.

Shaul Preaches The Messiah

20   And straightway, in the synagogues,
he preaches that the Messiah is the Son of Elohim.
21   And all who hear him are astounded,
and word; Is not this he who ravages those
who call on this name in Yeru Shalem,
and comes here
to bring them bound to the archpriests?
22   But Shaul, much dynamized,
confuses the Yah Hudiym who settle in Dammeseq,
concluding that this is the Messiah.
23   And after many days fulfill/shalam,
the Yah Hudiym counsel to take him out:
24   but Shaul knows of their plotting:
and they observe the gates day and night
to take him out:
25   but the disciples take him by night
and lower him through the wall in a basket.

Shaul In Yeru Shalem

26   And Shaul comes to Yeru Shalem,
and tries to join himself to the disciples:
and they all awe him
and trust not that he is a disciple.
27   But Bar Nabi takes him,
and brings him to the apostles,
and declares to them
how he saw Adonay in the way, and spoke to him;
and how he emboldened at Dammeseq
in the name of Yah Shua.
28   And he is with them at Yeru Shalem
— entering and departing:
29   and emboldened,
he speaks and disputes against the Hellenists:
and they take in hand to take him out.

Shaul In Tarsus

30   But the brothers know,
and descend him to Kaisaria, and
apostolize him to Tarsus.
31   So indeed the ecclesiae has shalom
throughout all Yah Hudah and Galiyl and Shomeron;
and being built
and walking in the awe of Yah Veh
and in the consolation of the Holy Spirit
they multiply.

Petros Heals A Paralytic

32   And so be it, as Petros passes through,
he also comes down to the holy who settle at Lod:
33   and there he finds a human named Aeneas
who lays on his pad eight years paralyzed.
34   And Petros says to him, Aeneas,
Yah Shua the Messiah heals you!
Rise, and spread!
— and straightway he rises:
35   And all that *dwelt* **settled**
at *Lydda* **Lod** and *Saron* **Sharon** saw him,
and turned to *the Lord* **Adonay**.

Petros Raises One Dead

36   *Now* **And** there was at *Joppa* **Yapho**
a *certain* disciple* named Tabitha,
which *by interpretation* **translates**
is called Dorcas **worded, Gazelle**:
this *woman* **one**
was full of good works and *almsdeeds* **mercies**
which she did.
*feminine: a female disciple.
37   And **so be** it *came to pass* in those days,
that she was *sick* **frail**, and died:
whom when they had *washed* **bathed**,
they *laid* **placed** her in an upper *chamber* **loft**.
38   And *forasmuch as Lydda* **Lod**
was nigh to *Joppa* **Yapho**,
and the disciples had heard that *Peter* **Petros** was there,
they *sent* **apostolized** unto him two men,
desiring **beseeching** him
that he *would* **should** not *delay* **hesitate**
to *come* **pass through** to them.
39   Then *Peter* **Petros** arose and went with them.
When he was come,
they brought him into the upper *chamber* **loft**:
and all the widows stood by him weeping,
and shewing the *coats* **tunics** and garments
which Dorcas — **as many as Gazelle** made,
while she was with them.
40   But *Peter put* **Petros cast** them all *forth* **out**,
and *kneeled down* **placed his knees**, and prayed;
and turning him to the body said, Tabitha, arise.
And she opened her eyes:

and when she saw *Peter* **Petros**, she sat *up*.
41 And he gave her his hand,
and *lifted* **raised** her *up*,
and when he had called the *saints* **holy** and widows,
presented her alive.
42 And it *was* **became** known
throughout all *Joppa* **Yapho**;
and many *believed* **trusted** in *the Lord* **Adonay**.
43 And **so be** it *came to pass*,
that he *tarried* **abode** many days in *Joppa* **Yapho**
with one *Simon* **Shimon** a tanner.

THE VISION OF CORNELIUS

10 **But** There was a *certain*
man in *Caesarea* **Kaisaria**
called **named** Cornelius,
a centurion of the *band* **squad** called *the* Italian *band*,
2 A *devout man* **well revered**,
and one that *feared God* **awed Elohim** with all his house,
which *gave much alms* **did many mercies** to the people,
and *prayed* **petitioned** to *God alway* **Elohim continually**.
3 He saw in a vision *evidently* **manifestly**
about the ninth hour of the day
an angel of *God* **Elohim** *coming in* **entering** to him,
and saying unto him, Cornelius.
4 And when he *looked on* **stared at** him,
he *was afraid* **became awestricken**, and said,
What is it, *Lord* **Adonay**?
And he said unto him,
Thy prayers and *thine alms* **thy mercies**
are *come up for* **ascended unto** a memorial
before God **in the sight of Elohim**.
5 And now send men to *Joppa* **Yapho**,
and *call for one Simon* **summon Shimon**,
whose surname is Peter **who is called Petros**:
6 He lodgeth with one *Simon* **Shimon** a tanner,
whose house is by the sea side:
he shall *tell* **speak to** thee what thou *oughtest to* **must** do.
7 And when the angel which
spake unto Cornelius
was departed,
he called two of his *household servants* **housekeepers**,
and a *devout soldier* **well—revered warrior**
of them that waited on him *continually*;
8 And when he had declared
all these *things* unto them,
he *sent* **apostolized** them to *Joppa* **Yapho**.

THE VISION OF PETROS

9 On the morrow,

35 and all who settle at Lod and Sharon see him
and turn to Adonay.

PETROS RAISES ONE DEAD

36 And there is a disciple* at
Yapho named Tabitha,
which translates worded, Gazelle:
this one is full of good works and mercies
which she does.
*feminine: a female disciple.
37 And so be it, in those days, she is frail, and dies:
and they bathe her and place her in an upper loft.
38 And so be it, Lod is near Yapho,
and the disciples hear that Petros is there,
and they apostolize two men to him,
beseeching him to not hesitate
to pass through to them;
39 — and Petros rises and goes with them.
And he comes,
and they bring him into the upper loft:
and all the widows stand by him weeping
and showing the tunics and garments
— as many as Gazelle made, being with them.
40 But Petros casts them all out,
and places his knees and prays;
and turning to the body, he says, Tabitha, Rise!
And she opens her eyes;
and seeing Petros, she sits:
41 and he gives her *his* hand and raises her;
and calls the holy and widows
and presents her alive.
42 And it became known throughout all Yapho;
and many trust in Adonay.
43 And so be it,
he abides in Yapho many days
with one Shimon a tanner.

THE VISION OF CORNELIUS

10 But there is a man in Kaisaria named Cornelius
— a centurion of the squad called Italian;
2 well revered,
and one who awes Elohim with all his house;
who does many mercies to the people;
and petitions to Elohim continually.
3 About the ninth hour of the day
he sees manifest in a vision
an angel of Elohim entering to him,
and saying to him, Cornelius!
4 And he stares at him, and becomes awestricken,
and says, What is it, Adonay?

And he says to him,
Your prayers and your mercies
ascend to a memorial in the sight of Elohim:

5 and now send men to Yapho,
and summon Shimon who is called Petros:

6 he lodges with one Shimon a tanner
whose house is by the sea side: he
speaks to you what you must do.

7 And the angel who speaks to Cornelius departs:
and he calls two of his housekeepers,
and a well—revered warrior
of those who wait on him;

8 and he declares all these to them
and apostolizes them to Yapho.

THE VISION OF PETROS

9 On the morrow,
as they *went on their journey* **journeyed**,
and *drew nigh unto* **approached** the city,
Peter **Petros**
went up **ascended** upon the housetop to pray
about the sixth hour:

10 And he became *very* **intensely** hungry,
and *would* **willed to** have *eaten* **tasted**:
but while they *made ready* **prepared**,
he fell into a trance **an ecstasis fell upon him**,

11 And *saw* **observed** heaven opened,
and a *certain* vessel descending upon him,
as *it had been a great sheet* — **a mega linen**
knit **bound** at the four *corners* **beginnings**,
and let down to the earth:

12 Wherein were all *manner*
of fourfooted beasts **quadrepeds** of the earth,
and *wild* beasts, and *creeping things* **creepers**,
and *fowls* **flyers** of the *air* **heavens**.

13 And *so be it, there came* a voice to him,
Rise, *Peter* **Petros**; *kill* **sacrifice**, and eat.

14 But *Peter* **Petros** said, *Not
so* **No way**, *Lord* **Adonay**;
for I have never *ever* eaten *any thing* **ought**
that is *common* **profane** or *unclean* **impure**.

15 And *the voice spake unto
him again the second time*
a second voice to him,
What *God* **Elohim** hath *cleansed* **purified**,
that call not thou common **thou shalt not profane**.

16 And This *was done* **became** thrice:
and the vessel was *received up* **taken again** into heaven.

17 *Now* **And** while *Peter* **Petros**
doubted **was thoroughly perplexed** in himself
what this vision which he had seen should mean ever be,
behold,
the men which were *sent* **apostolized** from Cornelius
had *made enquiry* **thoroughly interrogated**
for *Simon's* **Shimon's** house,
and stood *before* **by** the gate,

18 And called, and asked whether *Simon* **Shimon**,
which was *surnamed Peter* **called Petros**,
were lodged there.

19 *While Peter thought* **But as Petros pondered**
on **about** the vision,
the Spirit said unto him, Behold, three men seek thee.

20 **But** Arise *therefore*, and *get thee down* **descend**,
and go with them, doubting *nothing* **naught**:
for **because** I have *sent* **apostolized** them.

21 *Then Peter went down* **And
Petros descended** to the men
which were sent apostolized unto him from Cornelius;
and said, Behold, I am he whom ye seek:
what is the cause wherefore ye are *come* **present**?

22 And they said, Cornelius the centurion,
a just man, and one that *feareth God* **aweth Elohim**,
and *of good report* **well—witnessed**
among *by* all the nation *goyim* of the *Jews* **Yah I-ludiym**,
was *warned from God* **oracled** by an holy angel
to *send for* **summon** thee into his house,
and to hear *words* **rhema** of thee.

23 *Then called* **So** he **invited**
them *in*, and lodged them.
And on the morrow *Peter* **Petros** went away with them,
and *certain* **some** brethren from *Joppa* **Yapho**
accompanied **came with** him.

24 And the morrow after
they entered into *Caesarea* **Kaisaria**.
And Cornelius *waited for* **awaited** them,
and he had called together
his kinsmen and *near* **dependant** friends.

25 And as *Peter was coming in* **Petros entered**,
Cornelius met him,
and fell *down* at his feet, and worshipped him.

26 But *Peter took* **Petros raised**
him *up*, *saying* **wording**,
Stand up **Arise**; I myself also am a *man* **human**.

27 And as he *talked* **conversed** with him,
he *went in* **entered**,
and found many that were come together.

28 And he said unto them,
Ye *know* **understand** how that it is
an *unlawful thing* **illicit**
for a man *that is a Jew* — **a Yah I-ludiy**

	to *keep company* **join**,	24	and on the morrow after, they enter Kaisaria.
	or come unto one of another *nation* **scion**;		And Cornelius awaits them,
	as they journey and approach the city,		and he calls together
	Petros ascends on the housetop to pray		his kinsmen and dependant friends:
	at about the sixth hour;	25	and as Petros enters, Cornelius meets him,
10	and he becomes intensely famished		and falls at his feet, and worships him.
	and wills to taste:	26	And Petros raises him, wording,
	but as they prepare, an ecstasis falls on him;		Rise! I myself also am a human!
11	and he observes the heavens open;	27	And as he converses with him, he enters,
	and a vessel descends on him		and finds many come together:
	as a mega linen bound at the four beginnings,	28	and he says to them,
	and lowers to the earth:		You understand how that it is illicit for a man
12	wherein are all quadrepeds of the earth		— a Yah Hudiy to join
	and beasts and creepers		or come to one of another scion;
	and flyers of the heavens:		*but God* **But Elohim** hath shewed me
13	and so be it, a voice to him,		that I should not *call* **word** any *man* **human**
	Rise, Petros! Sacrifice, and eat!		*common* **profane** or *unclean* **impure**.
14	But Petros says, No way, Adonay;	29	*Therefore* **So** came I *unto you*
	for I never ever ate aught profane or impure.		*without gainsaying* **unquestioningly**,
15	And a second voice to him,		as soon as I was *sent for* **summoned**:
	What Elohim purifies, you profane not!		So I ask *therefore*
16	And this becomes thrice:		for what *intent* **word** ye have *sent for* **summoned** me?
	and the vessel is taken again into the heavens.	30	And Cornelius said,
17	And as Petros		**For** Four days *ago* I was fasting until this hour;
	is thoroughly perplexed in himself		and at the ninth hour I prayed in my house, and, behold,
	whatever this vision he sees, be,		a man stood *before me* **in my sight**
	behold, the men apostolized from Cornelius		in *bright clothing* **radiant apparel**,
	thoroughly interrogate for the house of Shimon,	31	And said, Cornelius, thy prayer is heard,
	and stand by the gate,		and *thine alms* **thy mercies**
18	and call, and ask whether Shimon called Petros,		are *had in remembrance* **remembered**
	lodges there.		in the sight of *God* **Elohim**.
19	But as Petros ponders about the vision;	32	So Send *therefore* to *Joppa* **Yapho**,
	the Spirit says to him,		and call *hither* *Simon* **Shimon**,
	Behold, three men seek you!		whose surname is *Peter* **called Petros**;
20	But rise and descend		he is lodged in the house of *one Simon* **Shimon**
	and go with them — doubting naught:		a tanner by the sea side:
	because I apostolized them.		who, when he cometh, shall speak unto thee.
21	And Petros descends to the men	33	So Immediately *therefore* I sent to thee;
	apostolized to him from Cornelius;		and thou hast well done that thou art come.
	and says, Behold, I am whom you seek:		So Now *therefore* are we all here present
	for what cause you are present?		*before God* **in the sight of Elohim**,
22	And they say, Cornelius the centurion,		to hear all *things* **those**
	a just man, and one who awes Elohim,		that are commanded thee of *God* **Elohim**.

THE FOURTH MESSAGE OF PETROS

	and well—witnessed
	by all the goyim of the Yah Hudiym,
	was oracled by a holy angel to summon you to his house,
	and to hear rhema of you.
23	So he invites them, and lodges them:
	and on the morrow Petros goes with them,
	and some brothers from Yapho come with him:

34	Then *Peter* **Petros** opened his mouth, and said,
	Of a truth I *perceive* **overtake**
	that *God* **Elohim** is *no respecter of persons* **not partial**:
35	But in every *nation* **goyim**,
	he that *feareth* **aweth** him,

ACTS 10

and worketh *righteousness* **justness**,
is *accepted* **acceptable** with him.
36 The word which *God sent* **Elohim apostolized**
unto the *children* **sons** of *Israel* **Yisra El**,
preaching peace **evangelizing shalom**
by Jesus Christ **through Yah Shua Messiah**:
(he is *Lord* **Adonay** of all:)
37 That *word* **rhema**, *I say*, ye know,
which *was published* **became**
throughout all *Judaea* **Yah Hudah**,
and began from *Galilee* **Galiyl**,
after the baptism which *John* **Yahn** preached;
38 How *God* **Elohim**
anointed *Jesus of Nazareth* **Yah Shua the Nazarene**
with the *Holy Spirit* **Ruach ha-kodesh**
and with *power* **dynamis**:
who *went about* **passed through**
doing good **working well**,
and healing all
that were *oppressed* **overpowered** of *the devil* **Diabolos**;
for *God* **Elohim** was with him.
39 And we are witnesses of all *things* which he did
both in the *land* **region** of the *Jews* **Yah Hudiym**,
and in *Jerusalem* **Yeru Shalem**;
whom they *slew* **took out** and hanged on a *tree* **staff**:
40 Him *God* **Elohim** raised *up* the third day,
and *shewed* **gave** him *openly* **to become manifest**;
41 Not to all the people,
but unto witnesses
chosen before **preselected** of *God* **Elohim**,
even to us,
who did eat and drink with him
after he rose from the dead.
42 And he *commanded* **evangelized** us
to preach unto the people,
and to *testify* **witness** that it is he
which was *ordained* **decreed** of *God* **Elohim**
to be the Judge of *quick* **living** and dead.
43 To him give all the prophets witness,
that through his name
whosoever *believeth* **trusteth** in him
shall *receive remission* **take forgiveness** of sins.

HOLY SPIRIT POURED ON THE GOYIM

44 While *Peter* **Petros** yet
spake these *words* **rhema**,
the *Holy Spirit* **Ruach ha-kodesh** fell on
all them which heard the word.
and Elohim showed me
that I not word any human profane or impure:

29 so I come unquestioningly
as soon as summoned:
So I ask, for what word summon you me?
30 And Cornelius says,
I fasted four days until this hour;
and at the ninth hour I prayed in my house,
and behold,
a man standing in my sight in radiant apparel,
31 and says, Cornelius, your prayer is heard,
and your mercies are remembered
in the sight of Elohim:
32 so send to Yapho,
and call Shimon called Petros;
he lodges in the house of Shimon
a tanner by the sea side:
who, when he comes, speaks to you.
33 So immediately I sent to you;
and you do well in coming.
So now we are all here present in the sight of Elohim,
to hear all those Elohim commanded you.

THE FOURTH MESSAGE OF PETROS

34 And Petros opens his mouth, and says,
Of a truth I overtake that Elohim is not partial:
35 but in every goyim,
whoever awes him and works justness
is acceptable with him.
36 The word Elohim apostolized
to the sons of Yisra El,
evangelizing shalom through Yah Shua Messiah:
— he is Adonay of all:
37 that rhema, you know,
became throughout all Yah Hudah,
beginning from Galiyl,
as to the baptism Yahn preached:
38 how Elohim anointed Yah Shua the Nazarene
with the Holy Spirit and with dynamis:
who passed through working well,
and healing all who were overpowered by Diabolos
— for Elohim was with him.
39 And we are witnesses of all he did
both in the region of the Yah Hudiym
and in Yeru Shalem;
whom they took out and hanged on a staff:
40 whom Elohim raised the third day
and gave him to become manifest
41 — not to all the people,
but to witnesses preselected by Elohim
— to us who ate and drank with him
after he rose from the dead:

42 and he evangelized us to preach to the people,
and to witness that it is he who is decreed of
Elohim to be the Judge of living and dead:
43 to whom all the prophets witness,
that through his name
whoever trusts in him takes forgiveness of sins.

Holy Spirit Poured On The Goyim

44 While Petros still speaks these rhema,
the Holy Spirit falls on all who hear the word:
45 And they of the circumcision
which *believed* **trusted**
were *astonished* **astounded**,
as many as came with *Peter* **Petros**,
because that on the *Gentiles* **goyim** also
was poured out the *gift* **gratuity** of the
Holy Spirit **Ruach ha-kodesh**.
46 For they heard them speak with tongues,
and magnify *God* **Elohim**.
Then answered *Peter* **Petros**,
47 Can any *man* **one** forbid water,
that these should not be baptized,
which have *received* **taken** the *Holy
Spirit* **Ruach ha-kodesh**
exactly as well as we?
48 And he commanded them to be baptized
in the name of *the Lord* **Adonay**.
Then *prayed* **asked** they him
to *tarry certain* **abide some** days.

The Vision Of Cornelius: Petros Relates His Vision

11 And the apostles and brethren
that were in *Judaea* **Yah Hudah**
heard that the *Gentiles* **goyim**
had also received the word of *God* **Elohim**.
2 And when *Peter* **Petros**
was come up **ascended** to *Jerusalem* **Yeru Shalem**,
they that were of the circumcision contended with him,
3 *Saying* **Wording**,
Thou *wentest in* **enterest** to men uncircumcised,
and didst eat with them.
4 But *Peter* **Petros**
rehearsed the matter from the beginning **began**,
and expounded it *by order* **in sequence** unto them,
saying **wording**,
5 I was in the city of *Joppa* **Yapho** praying:
and in *a trance* **an ecstasis** I saw a vision,
A *certain* vessel descend,
as *it had been a great sheet* **a mega linen**,

let down from heaven by four *corners* **beginnings**;
and it came *even* to me:
6 *Upon* **Unto** the which
when I had *fastened mine eyes* **stared**,
I *considered* **perceived**,
and saw *fourfooted beasts* **quadrepeds** of the earth,
and *wild* beasts, and *creeping things* **creepers**,
and *fowls* **flyers** of the *air* **heavens**.
7 And I heard a voice *saying* **wording** unto me,
Arise, *Peter* **Petros**; *slay* **sacrifice** and eat.
8 But I said, Not so **No way**, Lord **Adonay**:
for *nothing common* **naught profane** or *unclean* **impure**
hath *at any time* **ever** entered into my mouth.
9 But the voice answered me
again **twice** from heaven,
What *God* **Elohim** hath *cleansed* **purified**,
that *call not* common **profane thou not**.
10 And this *was done three times* **became thrice**:
and all were drawn *up* again into heaven.
11 And, behold, immediately there were three men
already *come unto* **standing by** the house
where **wherein** I was,
sent **apostolized** from *Caesarea* **Kaisaria** unto me.
12 And the Spirit *bade* **said for**
me *go* **to come** with them,
nothing **naught** doubting.
Moreover
these six brethren *accompanied* **came with** me,
and we entered into the man's house:
13 And he *shewed* **evangelized** us
how he had seen an angel in his house,
which stood and said unto him,
Send **Apostolize** men to *Joppa* **Yapho**,
and *call for Simon* **summon Shimon**,
whose surname is *Peter* **called Petros**;
14 Who shall *tell speak rhemas to* thee *words*,
whereby thou and all thy house shall be saved.
15 And as I began to speak,
the *Holy Spirit* **Ruach ha-kodesh** fell on
them, **exactly** as on us at the beginning.
16 *Then* **And** remembered I
the *words* **rhema** of *the Lord* **Adonay**,
how that he *said* **worded**,
John **Yahn** indeed baptized *with* **in** water;
but ye shall be baptized *with* **in** the
Holy Spirit **Ruach ha-kodesh**.
45 and they of the circumcision who trust
are astounded — as many as come with Petros,
because the gratuity of the Holy Spirit
is also poured on the goyim:

46 for they hear them speak with tongues,
and magnify Elohim.
Then Petros answers,
47 Can anyone forbid water,
that these not be baptized,
who took the Holy Spirit exactly as well as we?
48 — and he commands them to be baptized
in the name of Adonay.
Then they ask him to abide some days.

THE VISION OF CORNELIUS:
PETROS RELATES HIS VISION

11 And the apostles and brothers in Yah Hudah
hear that the goyim also receive the word of Elohim.
2 And when Petros ascends to Yeru Shalem
they of the circumcision contend with him,
3 wording, You entered to uncircumcised men
and ate with them.
4 But Petros begins
and expounds to them in sequence, wording,
5 I was in the city of Yapho praying:
and in an ecstasis I saw a vision
— a vessel descending as a mega linen
lowered from the heavens by four beginnings;
and it came to me:
6 to which, when I stared, I perceived,
and saw quadrepeds of the earth
and beasts and creepers and flyers of the heavens:
7 and I heard a voice wording to me,
Rise, Petros! Sacrifice and eat!
8 And I said, No way, Adonay:
for naught profane or impure ever entered my mouth.
9 But a voice answers me twice from the heavens,
What Elohim purifies, profane not.
10 — and this became thrice:
and all were drawn into the heavens.
11 And behold, immediately there were three men
already standing by the house where I was,
apostolized from Kaisaria to me:
12 and the Spirit said for me to come with them,
naught doubting:
moreover these six brothers came with me
and we entered the house of this man.
13 And he evangelized us
how he saw an angel in his house,
which stood and said to him,
Apostolize men to Yapho
and summon Shimon called Petros;
14 who speaks rhemas to you,
whereby you and all your house become saved.

15 And as I began to speak,
the Holy Spirit fell on them,
exactly as on us at the beginning:
16 and I remembered the rhema of Adonay,
that he worded,
Yahn indeed baptizes in water;
but you, baptized in Holy Spirit.
17 *Forasmuch then as* **So if**
God **Elohim** gave them the *like gift* **equal gratuity**
as he did unto us, who *believed* **trusted**
on *the Lord Jesus Christ* **Adonay Yah Shua Messiah**;
what was I, that I could *withstand God* **forbid Elohim**?
18 When they heard these *things*,
they *held their peace* **quieted**,
and glorified *God* **Elohim**, *saying* **wording**,
Then **And yet indeed**
hath *God* **Elohim** also to the *Gentiles* **goyim**
granted **given** repentance unto life.

FIRST MESSIANISTS

19 *Now therefore* **So indeed**
they which were *scattered abroad* **thoroughly dispersed**
upon **by** the *persecution* **tribulation**
that *arose about Stephen* **became after Stephanos**
travelled as far as Phenice **passed through unto Phoinix**,
and Cyprus, and Antioch,
preaching **speaking** the word to none
but **except** unto the *Jews* **Yah Hudiym** only.
20 And some of them
were men of *Cyprus* — **Cypriots** and *Cyrene* **Cyrenians**,
which, when they *were come to* **entered** Antioch,
spake unto the *Grecians* **Hellenists**,
preaching the Lord Jesus **evangelizing Adonay Yah Shua**.
21 And the hand of *the Lord*
Adonay was with them:
and a *great* **vast** number *believed* **trusted**,
and turned unto *the Lord* **Adonay**.
22 *Then tidings of* **And word about** these *things*
came **was heard** unto the ears of the *church* **ecclesia**
which was in *Jerusalem* **Yeru Shalem**:
and they *sent forth Barnabas* **apostolized Bar Nabi**,
that he should *go as far as* **pass through unto** Antioch.
23 Who, when he came,
and had seen the *grace* **charism** of *God* **Elohim**,
was glad **cheered**, and *exhorted* **besought** them all,
that with *purpose* **prothesis** of heart
they *would cleave unto the Lord* **should abide in Adonay**.
24 For he was a good man,
and full of the *Holy Spirit* **Ruach ha-kodesh** and of *faith* **trust**:

and *much people* **a vast multitude**
was added unto *the Lord* **Adonay**.

25 Then departed *Barnabas* **Bar Nabi** to Tarsus,
for to seek *Saul* **Shaul**:

26 And when he had found him,
he brought him unto Antioch.
And *so be* it *came to pass*, that a whole year
they assembled themselves *with* **in** the *church* **ecclesia**,
and *taught* **doctrinated** much *people* **multitude**.
And the disciples were *called Christians*
oracled Messianists
first in Antioch.

27 And in these days came prophets
from *Jerusalem* **Yeru Shalem** unto Antioch.

28 And there *stood up* **rose** one of them
named *Agabus* **Hagab**,
and signified *by* **through** the Spirit
that there *should* **was about to** be
great dearth **a mega** throughout
famine upon all the world:
which *came to pass* **became**
in the days of *Claudius Caesar* **under Kaisar Claudius**.

29 *Then* **And** the disciples, *every man* **each one**
according to his ability **exactly as each prospered**,
determined **decreed for ministry**
to send *relief* unto the brethren
which *dwelt* **settled** in *Judaea* **Yah Hudah**:

30 Which also they did,
and *sent it* **apostolized** to the elders
by **through** the hands
of *Barnabas* **Bar Nabi** and *Saul* **Shaul**.

FIFTH PERSECUTION

12 *Now* **And** about that *time* **season**
Herod the *king stretched forth*
sovereign laid on his hands
to *vex certain* **vilify some** of the *church* **ecclesia**.

2 And he *killed James* **took out Yaaqovos**
the brother of *John* **Yahn** with the sword.

3 And because he saw it pleased the *Jews* **Yah Hudiym**,
he *proceeded further* **added** to take *Peter* **Petros** also.
(Then were the days of *unleavened bread* **matsah**.)

17 So if Elohim gives them the equal gratuity
as he does us
who trust on Adonay Yah Shua Messiah;
and I — who am I to forbid Elohim?

18 When they hear these,
they quiet and glorify Elohim, wording,
Then indeed
Elohim also gives the goyim repentance to life.

FIRST MESSIANISTS

19 So indeed,
those thoroughly dispersed
by the tribulation that became after Stephanos,
pass through to Phoinix and Cyprus and Antioch,
speaking the word to none
except only to the Yah Hudiym.

20 And some of them — Cypriots and Cyrenians,
enter Antioch, and speak to the Hellenists,
evangelizing Adonay Yah Shua:

21 and the hand of Adonay is with them:
and a vast number trust and turn to Adonay.

22 And the ears of the ecclesia in Yeru Shalem
hear about these words; and they apostolize
Bar Nabi to pass through to Antioch

23 — who, when he comes
and sees the charism of Elohim, cheers,
and beseeches them all,
that with prothesis of heart, they abide in Adonay.

24 For he is a good man,
and full of Holy Spirit and of trust:
and a vast multitude is added to Adonay.

25 And Bar Nabi departs to Tarsus to seek Shaul:

26 and he finds him, and brings him to Antioch.
And so be it, that for a whole year,
they assemble themselves in the ecclesia
and doctrinate a vast multitude:
and they oracle the disciples as Messianists
first in Antioch.

27 And in these days
prophets come from Yeru Shalem to Antioch:

28 and one of them named Hagab
rises and signifies through the Spirit
that there is about to be
a mega famine on all the world
— which becomes under Kaisar Claudius.

29 And the disciples,
each one exactly as each prospers,
decrees for ministry
to send to the brothers settled in Yah Hudah:

30 which they also do,
and apostolize to the elders
through the hands of Bar Nabi and Shaul.

FIFTH PERSECUTION

12 And about that season
Herod the sovereign lays on his hands
to vilify some of the ecclesia:

2 and he takes out Yaaqovos the brother of Yahn

ACTS 12

with the sword:
3 and because he sees it pleases the Yah Hudiym,
he adds to also take out Petros
— these are the days of matsah:
4 And when he had *apprehended* **seized** him,
he put him in *prison* **the guardhouse**,
and delivered him
to four quaternions of *soldiers* **warriors**
to *keep* **guard** him;
intending **having willed** after *Easter* **pasach**
to bring him forth to the people.
5 *Peter therefore* **So Petros indeed**
was *kept* **guarded** in *prison* **the guardhouse**:
but prayer *was made without ceasing* **became intense**
of the *church* **ecclesia** unto *God* **Elohim** for him.
6 And when Herod
would have brought **was about to bring** him *forth*,
the *same* night
Peter **Petros** was sleeping between two *soldiers* **warriors**,
bound with two *chains* **fetters**:
and the *keepers before* **guards in front of** the *door* **portal**
kept **guarded** the *prison* **guardhouse**.
7 And, behold,
the **an** angel of *the Lord came upon*
him **Yah Veh stood by**,
and a light *shined* **radiated** in the *prison* **dwelling**:
and he smote *Peter* **Petros** on the side,
and raised him *up, saying* **wording**, Arise up quickly.
And his *chains* **fetters** fell *off* from his hands.
8 And the angel said unto him,
Gird thyself, and bind on thy sandals.
And *so* **thus** he did.
And he *saith* **wordeth** unto him,
Cast **Array** thy garment *about thee*, and follow me.
9 And he went *out*, and followed him;
and *wist* **knew** not that it was true
which *was done by* **became through** the angel;
but thought he saw a vision.
10 When they *were past* **had passed through**
the first and the second *ward* **guardhouse**,
they came unto the iron gate
that *leadeth* **beareth** unto the city;
which opened to them *of his own accord* **automatically**:
and they went *out*,
and *passed on* **proceeded** through one street;
and *forthwith* **straightway** the angel departed from him.
11 And when *Peter was come*
Petros became to himself,
he said, Now I know *of a surety* **truly**,
that the Lord Yah Veh hath sent apostolized his angel,
and hath *delivered* **released** me out of the hand of Herod,
and from all the expectation
of the people of the *Jews* **Yah Hudiym**.
12 And when he had *considered the thing* **awared**,
he came to the house of *Mary* **Miryam**
the mother of *John* **Yahn**,
whose *surname was Mark* **who was called Markos**;
where many were gathered together praying.
13 And as *Peter* **Petros**
knocked at the *door* **portal** of the gate,
a *damsel* **lass** came to *hearken* **obey**, named Rhoda.
14 And when she knew *Peter's* **Petros'** voice,
she opened not the gate for *gladness* **cheer**,
but *ran in* **hastened**,
and *told* **evangelized**
how *Peter that* **Petros** stood before the gate.
15 And they *said* **worded** unto
her, Thou *art mad* **ravest**.
But she *constantly* **thoroughly** affirmed
that it was *even so* **thus**.
Then **And** said they, It is his angel.
16 But *Peter continued* **Petros abode** knocking:
and when they had opened *the door*, and saw him,
they were *astonished* **astounded**.
17 But he, *beckoning* **signaling**
unto them with the hand
to *hold their peace* **hush**,
declared unto them how *the Lord* **Yah Veh**
had *brought* **led** him out of the *prison* **guardhouse**.
And he said,
Go *shew* **evangelize** these *things* unto *James* **Yaaqovos**,
and to the brethren.
And he departed, and went into another place.
18 *Now as soon as it was* **And being** day,
there was no small *stir* **trouble**
among the *soldiers* **warriors**,
what was become of *Peter* **Petros**.
4 and he seizes him and puts
him in the guardhouse
and delivers him to four quaternions of warriors
to guard him;
and wills to bring him to the people after pasach.
5 So indeed Petros is guarded in the guardhouse:
and the prayer of the ecclesia to Elohim
for him becomes intense:
6 and when Herod is about to bring him
— that night Petros sleeps between two warriors
bound with two fetters:
and guards in front of the portal
guard the guardhouse:

7 and behold, an angel of Yah Veh stands by,
and a light radiates in the dwelling:
and he smites Petros on the side,
and raises him, wording, Rise quickly!
— and his fetters fall from his hands.

8 And the angel says to him,
Gird yourself and bind your sandals.
— and thus he does.
And he words to him,
Array your garment and follow me.

9 And he goes out, and follows him;
and knows not
that what becomes through the angel is true;
but thinks he sees a vision.

10 When they pass through
the first and the second guardhouse,
they come to the iron gate that bears to the city;
which opens to them automatically:
and they go and proceed through one street;
and straightway the angel departs from him.

11 And Petros, being by himself, says,
Now I know truly
that Yah Veh apostolized his angel
to release me from the hand of Herod
and from all the expectation
of the people of the Yah Hudiym.

12 And being aware,
he comes to the house of Miryam the mother of Yahn
who is called Markos
— where many gather together praying.

13 And as Petros knocks at the portal of the gate,
a lass named Rhoda comes to obey:

14 and she knows the voice of Petros:
and for cheer, she opens not the gate,
but hastens and evangelizes
that Petros stands in front of the gate.

15 And they word to her, You rave!
— but she thoroughly affirms that it is so.
And they say, It is his angel.

16 But Petros abides knocking:
and they open, and see him,
and they are astounded.

17 And he signals with the hand for them to hush,
and declares to them how Yah Veh
led him from the guardhouse.
And he says,
Go evangelize these to Yaaqovos and to the brothers.
— and he departs and goes to another place.

18 And being day,
there is no small trouble among the warriors
about what became of Petros:

19 And when Herod had sought for him,
and found him not,
he examined the *keepers* **guards**,
and *commanded* **summoned** that they
should be *put to death* **led away**.
And he went down from *Judaea* **Yah Hudah**
to *Caesarea* **Kaisaria**, and there *abode* **tarried**.

Herod Is Maggot Eaten

20 And Herod was *highly displeased* **exasperated**
with *them of Tyre* **the Soriym** and *Sidon* **the Sidoniym**:
but they *came* **presented themselves**
with one accord **in unanimity** to him,
and, having *made* **convinced** Blastus
the king's chamberlain their friend
who was over the sovereign's bedchamber,
desired peace **asked for shalom**;
because their *country* **region**
was nourished by the *king's* **sovereign's** country.

21 And upon *a set* **an ordered** day Herod,
arrayed **endued** in *royal* **sovereign**
apparel, sat upon his *throne* **bamah**,
and *made an oration unto* **addressed** them.

22 And the *people gave a shout*
public shouted, saying,
It is the voice of a god, and not of a *man* **human**.

23 And immediately
the **an** angel of *the Lord* **Yah Veh** smote him,
because he gave not *God* **Elohim** the glory:
and he *was* **became** eaten of *worms* **maggots**,
and *gave up the ghost* **expired**.

24 But the word of *God* **Elohim**
grew and multiplied.

25 And *Barnabas* **Bar Nabi** and *Saul* **Shaul**
returned from *Jerusalem* **Yeru Shalem**,
when they had fulfilled/**shalamed** their ministry,
and took with them *John* **Yahn**,
whose surname was Mark **who was called Markos**.

Shaul And Bar Nabi Are Set Apart

13 Now there were in the *church* **ecclesia**
that was at Antioch
certain **some** prophets and *teachers* **doctors**;
as *Barnabas* **Bar Nabi** and *Simeon* **Shimon**
that was called Niger,
and *Lucius of Cyrene* — **Loukios a
Cyrenian**, and Manaen,
which had been *brought up* **nursed**
with Herod the tetrarch,

and *Saul* **Shaul**.
2 As they *ministered* **liturgized**
to *the Lord* **Adonay**,
and fasted,
the *Holy Spirit* **Ruach ha-kodesh** said,
Separate me **Now set apart**
Barnabas **Bar Nabi** and *Saul* **Shaul**
for **unto** the work whereunto I have called them.

The First Journey Of Shaul And Bar Nabi

3 *And when they had* **Then**
having fasted and prayed,
and *laid* **put** their hands on them,
they *sent* **released** them *away*.
4 **So indeed** they,
being *sent forth* **dispatched** by the
Holy Spirit **Ruach ha-kodesh**,
departed **went down** unto Seleucia;
and from thence they sailed to Cyprus.
5 And *when they were* **being** at Salamis,
they *preached* **evangelized** the word of *God* **Elohim**
in the synagogues of the *Jews* **Yah Hudiym**:
and they had also *John* **Yahn** *to* **as**
their *minister* **attendant**.
6 And when they had *gone* **passed** through the isle
unto Paphos,
they found a *certain sorcerer* **magi**,
a *false* **pseudo** prophet, a *Jew* **Yah Hudiy**,
whose name was *Bar—Jesus* **Bar Yah Shua**:
7 Which was with the *deputy*
proconsul of the country,
Sergius *Paulus* **Paulos**,
a *prudent* man **of comprehension**;
who called for *Barnabas* **Bar Nabi** and *Saul* **Shaul**,
and *desired* **sought** to hear the word of *God* **Elohim**.
8 But Elymas the *sorcerer* **magi**
(for *so is* **thus** his name *by interpretation* **translates**)
withstood them,
seeking to *turn away* **thoroughly pervert**
the *deputy* **proconsul** from the *faith* **trust**.
19 and when Herod seeks for
him, and finds him not,
he examines the guards
and summons that they be led away:
and he goes down from Yah Hudah to Kaisaria
and tarries there.

Herod Is Maggot Eaten

20 And Herod is exasperated
with the Soriym and the Sidoniym:
but they present themselves to him in unanimity;
and convince Blastus
who is over the bedchamber of the sovereign;
and ask for shalom;
because their region is nourished
by the country of the sovereign.
21 And on an ordered day,
Herod, endued in sovereign apparel, sits
on his bamah and addresses them.
22 And the public shouts,
The voice of an el and not of a human!
23 And immediately
an angel of Yah Veh smites him
because he gives not Elohim the glory:
and he becomes eaten of maggots and expires:
24 but the word of Elohim grows and multiplies.
25 And they fulfill/shalam their ministry,
and Bar Nabi and Shaul return from Yeru Shalem,
and take Yahn, who is called Markos with them.

Shaul And Bar Nabi Are Set Apart

13 Now there in the ecclesia at Antioch
are some prophets and doctors;
as Bar Nabi and Shimon who is called Niger
and Loukios a Cyrenian and Manaen,
who was nursed with Herod the tetrarch, and Shaul.
2 And as they liturgize to Adonay and fast,
the Holy Spirit says,
Now set apart Bar Nabi and Shaul
to the work I called them.

The First Journey Of Shaul And Bar Nabi

3 Then having fasted and prayed,
they put their hands on them and release them.
4 So indeed, being dispatched by the Holy Spirit,
they go down to Seleucia;
and from there they sail to Cyprus:
5 and being at Salamis,
they evangelize the word of Elohim
in the synagogues of the Yah Hudiym
— and they also have Yahn as their attendant.
6 And they pass through the isle to Paphos
and find a magi — a pseudo prophet — a Yah Hudiy
whose name is Bar Yah Shua:
7 who is with Sergius Paulos the proconsul
— a man of comprehension;
who calls for Bar Nabi and Shaul,
and seeks to hear the word of Elohim.

8 But Elymas the magi
— thus his name translates
withstands them,
seeking to thoroughly pervert the proconsul
from the trust.

SHAUL IS PAULOS

9 Then *Saul* **Shaul**, (who
also is called *Paul* **Paulos**,)
filled/**shalamed** with the *Holy Spirit* **Ruach ha-kodesh**, *set his eyes on* **stared unto** him.
10 And said,
O full of all *subtilty* **deceit** and all *mischief* **malignity**,
thou *child* **son** of *the devil* **Diabolos**,
thou enemy of all *righteousness* **justness**,
wilt **shalt** thou not *cease* **pause**
to pervert **from thoroughly perverting**
the *right* **straight** ways of *the Lord* **Yah Veh**?
11 And now, behold,
the hand of *the Lord is* **Adonay** upon thee,
and thou shalt be blind,
not seeing the sun *for* **until** a season.
And immediately
there fell on him a *mist* **dimness** and a darkness;
and he went about seeking some
to **hand** lead him *by the hand*.
12 Then the *deputy* **proconsul**,
when he saw what *was done* **became**, *believed* **trusted**,
being astonished at the doctrine of *the Lord* **Adonay**.
13 *Now* **And** when *Paul* **Paulos**
and *his company* **those around him**
loosed **embarked** from Paphos,
they came to Perga in Pamphylia:
and *John* **Yahn** departing from them
returned to *Jerusalem* **Jeru Shalem**.

THE SYNAGOGUE MESSAGE OF PAULOS

14 But when they *departed*
passed through from Perga,
they came to Antioch in Pisidia,
and *went* **entered** into the synagogue
on the *sabbath* **shabbath** day, and sat *down*.
15 And after
the reading of the *law* **torah** and the prophets
the *rulers of the* synagogue **archs**
sent **apostolized** unto them, *saying* **wording**,
Ye men and brethren,
if ye have any word of *exhortation*
consolation for the people,
say **word on**.

16 *Then Paul stood up* **And Paulos arose**
and *beckoning* **signaling** with his hand said,
Men *of Israel* — **Yisra Eliym**,
and ye that *fear God* **awe Elohim**,
give audience **hearken**.
17 The *God* **Elohim** of this people of *Israel* **Yisra El**
chose **selected** our fathers,
and exalted the people
when they dwelt as strangers **in their settling**
in the land of *Egypt* **Misrayim**,
and with an high arm *brought* **led** he them out of it.
18 And about the time of forty years
suffered **endured** he their manners in the wilderness.
19 And when he had
destroyed **taken out** seven *nations* **goyim**
in the land of *Chanaan* **Kenaan**,
he *divided* **allotted** their land to them *by lot*.
20 And after that he gave unto them judges
about the space of four hundred and fifty
years, until *Samuel* **Shemu El** the prophet.
21 And *afterward* **from thence**
they *desired* **asked** a *king* **sovereign**:
and *God* **Elohim** gave unto them *Saul* **Shaul**
the son of *Cis* **Qish**,
a man of the *tribe* **scion** of *Benjamin* **Ben Yamin**,
by the space of forty years.
22 And when he had removed him,
he raised *up* unto them David to be their *king* **sovereign**;
to whom also he *gave their testimony* **witnessed**,
and said, I have found David *the son* of *Jesse* **Yishay**,
a man after mine own heart,
which shall *fulfil* **do** all my will.
23 Of this man's *seed* **sperma** hath *God* **Elohim**
according to his *promise* **pre—evangelism** raised
unto *Israel* **Yisra El** a Saviour, *Jesus* **Yah Shua**:
24 When *John* **Yahn** had *first* **previously** preached
before **preceding the face of** his *coming* **entrance**
the baptism of repentance
to all the people of *Israel* **Yisra El**.

SHAUL IS PAULOS

9 So Shaul — also called Paulos,
fills/shalams with the Holy Spirit, stares at him,
10 and says, O full of all deceit and all malignity,
you son of Diabolos,
you enemy of all justness,
pause you not from thoroughly perverting
the straight ways of Yah Veh?
11 And now, behold,
the hand of Adonay upon you,

and you become blind
not seeing the sun until a season.
— and immediately
a dimness and a darkness falls on him;
and he goes around
seeking someone to hand lead him.
12 Then the proconsul
sees what becomes and trusts,
being astonished at the doctrine of Adonay.
13 And Paulos and those around
him embark from Paphos,
and come to Perga in Pamphylia:
and Yahn departs from them and
returns to Jeru Shalem.

THE SYNAGOGUE MESSAGE OF PAULOS

14 But they pass through from Perga
and come to Antioch in Pisidia;
and on the shabbath day
enter the synagogue and sit.
15 And after the reading of
the torah and the prophets,
the synagogue archs apostolize to them, wording,
Men and brothers,
if you have any word of consolation for the people,
word on.
16 And Paulos rises, signals with his hand,
and says, Men — Yisra Eliym,
and you who awe Elohim, hearken!
17 The Elohim of this people of Yisra El
selected our fathers,
and exalted the people
in their settling in the land of Misrayim,
and with a high arm he led them from it:
18 and about the time of forty years
he endured their manners in the wilderness:
19 and he took out seven goyim
in the land of Kenaan,
and allotted them their land:
20 and after that, he gave them judges
about the space of four hundred and fifty
years — until Shemu El the prophet:
21 and from there, they asked a sovereign:
and Elohim gave them Shaul the son of Qish
— a man of the scion of Ben Yamin
by the space of forty years:
22 and he removed him,
and raised David to be their sovereign:
to whom also he witnessed, and said,
I find David of Yishay a man after my own heart,
who does all my will.
23 Of the *sperma* of this man,
according to his pre—evangelism,
Elohim raises to Yisra El a Saviour, Yah Shua
24 when Yahn previously preached
the baptism of repentance
preceding the face of his entrance,
to all the people of Yisra El.
25 And as *John* **Yahn** fulfilled/
shalamed his *course* **race**,
he *said* **worded**,
Whom *think* **surmise** ye that I am? I am not *he*.
But, behold, *there* **he** cometh *one* after me,
whose shoes of his feet I am not worthy to loose.
26 Men and brethren,
children **sons** of the *stock* **genos** of Abraham,
and whosoever among you *feareth God* **aweth Elohim**,
to you is the word of this salvation *sent* **apostolized**.
27 For they that *dwell* **settle**
at *Jerusalem* **Yeru Shalem**,
and their *rulers* **archs**, *because* they knew him not,
nor yet the voices of the prophets
which are read every *sabbath day* **shabbath**,
they have fulfilled/**shalamed**
them in condemning him **by judging**.
28 And though they found
no cause of death *in him*,
yet *desired* **asked** they *Pilate* **Pilatos**
that he should be *slain* **taken out**.
29 And when they had fulfilled/**shalamed** all
that was *written of* **scribed concerning** him,
they took him down from the *tree* **staff**,
and *laid* **placed** him in a *sepulchre* **tomb**.
30 But *God* **Elohim** raised him from the dead:
31 And he was seen many days of them
which *came up* **ascended together** with him
from *Galilee* **Galiyl** to *Jerusalem* **Yeru Shalem**,
who are his witnesses unto the people.
32 And we *declare* **evangelize**
unto you *glad tidings*,
how that the *promise* **pre—evangelism** which
was made **became** unto the fathers,
33 *God* **Elohim** hath fulfilled/
shalamed *the same* **this**
unto us their children,
in that he hath raised *up Jesus again* **Yah Shua**;
as it is also *written* **scribed** in the second psalm,
Thou art my Son, this day have I *begotten* **birthed** thee.
Psalm 2:7

34	And as concerning that he raised him *up* from the dead, now *no more* **not about** to return to corruption, he said *on this wise* **thus**, I *will* **shall** give you the *sure mercies* **trustworthy mercifuls** of David. Yesha Yah 55:3		Whom surmise you that I am? I am not *he*. But, behold, he comes after me, whose shoes of his feet I am not worthy to loose.
35	Wherefore he *saith* **wordeth** also in another *psalm*, Thou shalt not *suffer thine Holy One* **give thy Merciful** to see corruption. Psalm 16:10	26	Men and brothers, sons of the genos of Abraham, and whoever among you awes Elohim, the word of this salvation is apostolized o you.
36	For **indeed** David, after he had *served* **tended** his own generation by the *will* **counsel** of *God* **Elohim**, fell on sleep, and was *laid* **added** unto his fathers, and saw corruption:	27	For they who settle at Yeru Shalem, and their archs, neither know this one, nor the voices of the prophets read every shabbath — who in judging, they fulfill/shalam.
37	But he, whom *God* **Elohim** raised *again*, saw no corruption.	28	And though they found no cause of death, they still asked Pilatos to take him out:
38	*So* Be it known unto you *therefore*, men and brethren, that through this man is *preached* **evangelized** unto you the forgiveness of sins:	29	and when they fulfilled/shalamed all that is scribed concerning him, they took him down from the staff and placed him in a tomb:
39	And *at* **in** him all that *believe* **trust** are justified from all *things*, from which ye could not be justified *at* **in** the *law* **torah** of *Moses* **Mosheh**.	30	but Elohim raised him from the dead:
		31	and he was seen many days by them who ascended together with him from Galiyl to Yeru Shalem — who are his witnesses to the people.
40	*Beware therefore* **So look**, lest that come upon you, which is *spoken of* **said** in the prophets;	32	And we evangelize to you, how that the pre—evangelism which became the fathers,
41	*Behold* **See**, ye despisers, and *wonder* **marvel**, and *perish* **disappear**: for I work a work in your days, a work which ye shall in no wise *believe* **no way never trust**, *though a man if* **even though one** declare it unto you.	33	Elohim fulfills/shalams to us their children, in that he raised Yah Shua; as also scribed in the second psalm, You are my Son, this day I birthed you. Psalm 2:7
42	And when the *Jews* **Yah I-ludiym** *were gone* **departed** out of the synagogue, the *Gentiles besought* **goyim entreated** that these words rhema might be *preached* **spoken** to them the next *sabbath* **shabbath**.	34	And that he raised him from the dead, no more to return to corruption, he says thus, I give you the trustworthy mercifuls of David. Yesha Yah 55:3
		35	Wherefore he also words in another, You give not your Merciful to see corruption. Psalm 16:10
43	Now when the *congregation* **synagogue** was *broken up* **released**, many of the *Jews* **Yah I-ludiym** and *religious* **venerating** proselytes followed *Paul* **Paulos** and *Barnabas* **Bar Nabi**: who, speaking to them, *persuaded* **convinced** them to *continue* **abide** in the *grace* **charism** of *God* **Elohim**.	36	For David indeed, after he tended his own generation by the counsel of Elohim, fell on sleep; and was added to his fathers and saw corruption:
		37	but he, whom Elohim raised, saw no corruption.
		38	So be it known to you, men and brothers, that through this man the forgiveness of sins is evangelized to you:
25	And as Yahn fulfills/shalams his race, he words,	39	and all who trust in him are justified from all — from which you could not be justified

in the torah of Mosheh.
40 So look, lest that come upon you,
which is said in the prophets;
41 See, you despisers; and marvel, and disappear:
for I work a work in your days,
a work which you no way never trust,
even though one declare it to you.
42 And the Yah Hudiym
depart from the synagogue,
and the goyim entreat them
to speak these rhema to them the next shabbath.
43 And they release the synagogue,
and many of the Yah Hudiym
and venerating proselytes
follow Paulos and Bar Nabi:
who, speaking to them,
convince them to abide in the charism of Elohim:
44 And the *next sabbath day* **coming shabbath**
came almost **nearly** the whole city **gathered** together
to hear the word of *God* **Elohim**.
45 But when the *Jews* **Yah Hudiym** saw the multitudes,
they were filled/**shalamed** with *envy* **zeal**,
and *spake against* **contradicted** those *things*
which were *spoken* **worded** by *Paul* **Paulos**,
by contradicting and blaspheming.

PAULOS AND BAR NABI TURN TO THE GOYIM

46 Then *Paul* **Paulos** and *Barnabas* **Bar Nabi**
waxed bold **emboldened**, and said,
It was necessary that the word of *God* **Elohim**
should first *have been* **be** spoken to you:
but *seeing* **since** ye *put* **shove** it from you,
and judge yourselves unworthy of *everlasting* **eternal** life,
lo **behold**, we turn to the *Gentiles* **goyim**.
47 For *so* **thus**
hath *the Lord commanded* **Yah Veh misvahed** us, *saying*,
I have *set* **placed** thee to be a light of the *Gentiles* **goyim**,
that thou shouldest be *for* **unto** salvation
unto the *ends* **finality** of the earth.
Yesha Yah 42:6,7
48 And when the *Gentiles* **goyim** heard this,
they *were glad* **cheered**,
and glorified the word of *the Lord* **Adonay**:
and as many as were ordained to eternal life
believed **trusted**.
49 And the word of *the Lord* **Adonay**
was *published* **borne** throughout all the region.
50 But the *Jews stirred up* **Yah Hudiym enraged**
the *devout* **venerating** and *honourable* **well—respected** women,
and the *chief* **preeminent** men of the city,
and *raised* **roused** up persecution
against Paul **upon Paulos** and *Barnabas* **Bar Nabi**,
and *expelled* **cast** them out of their *coasts* **boundaries**.
51 But they shook off the dust of
their feet *against* **upon** them,
and came unto Iconium.
52 And the disciples were filled/
shalamed with *joy* **cheer**,
and with the *Holy Spirit* **Ruach ha-kodesh**.

MINISTRY IN THE ICONIUM SYNAGOGUE

14 And it *came to pass* **became** in Iconium,
that they *went* **entered** both together
into the synagogue of the *Jews* **Yah Hudiym**,
and *so* **thus** spake, *so* that a *great* **vast** multitude
both of the *Jews* **Yah Hudiym**
and also of the *Greeks believed* **Hellenists trusted**.
2 But the *unbelieving Jews*
distrusting Yah Hudiym
stirred up **roused** the *Gentiles* **goyim**,
and *made* **vilified** their *minds evil affected* **souls**
against the brethren.
3 **So indeed** Long time
therefore abode **tarried** they
speaking boldly **emboldened** in *the Lord* **Adonay**,
which *gave testimony* **witnessed**
unto the word of his *grace* **charism**,
and *granted* **gave** signs and *wonders* **omens**
to *be done by* **become through** their hands.
4 *But* **And** the multitude of the
city was *divided* **schismed**:
and **indeed** part held with the *Jews* **Yah Hudiym**, and part with the apostles.

MINISTRY IN LYCAONIA

5 And when
there *was an assault made* **became a violent impulse**
both of the *Gentiles* **goyim**,
and also of the *Jews* **Yah Hudiym** with their *rulers* **archs**,
to *use* **insult** them *despitefully*, and to stone them,
6 They were ware of it, and
fled unto Lystra and Derbe,
cities of Lycaonia,
and unto the region *that lieth* round about:
7 And there they *preached the gospel* **evangelized**.

Paulos Heals One Lame

8 And there sat a *certain* man at Lystra,
impotent in his feet,
being *a cripple* **lame** from his mother's womb,
who never **ever** had walked:
9 *The same* **This one** heard *Paul* **Paulos** speak:
who *stedfastly beholding* **staring at** him,
and perceiving that he had *faith* **trust** to be *healed* **saved**,
10 Said with a *loud* **mega** voice,
44 and the coming shabbath
nearly the whole city gathers together
to hear the word of Elohim:
45 and the Yah Hudiym see the multitudes,
and fill/shalam with zeal,
and contradict those worded by Paulos,
by contradicting and blaspheming.

Paulos And Bar Nabi Turn To The Goyim

46 And Paulos and Bar Nabi embolden, and say,
It is necessary that the word of Elohim
be spoken to you first:
but since you shove it from you,
and judge yourselves unworthy of eternal life,
behold, we turn to the goyim:
47 for thus Yah Veh misvahed us:
I place you, a light of the goyim,
to be to salvation to the finality of
the earth. Yesha Yah 42:6,7
48 And the goyim hear this
and they cheer and glorify the word of Adonay:
and as many as are ordained to eternal life, trust:
49 and the word of Adonay
is borne throughout all the region:
50 but the Yah Hudiym enrage
the venerating and well—respected women
and the preeminent men of the city;
and rouse persecution on Paulos and Bar Nabi
and cast them from their boundaries:
51 but they shake the dust
from their feet upon them,
and come to Iconium:
52 and the disciples fill/shalam
with cheer and Holy Spirit.

Ministry In The Iconium Synagogue

14 And so be it, in Iconium,
they enter the synagogue of the Yah Hudiym together,
and thus speak;
so that a vast multitude
both of the Yah Hudiym and of the Hellenists trust:
2 and the distrusting Yah
Hudiym rouse the goyim
and vilify their souls against the brothers.
3 So indeed they tarry a long time;
embolden in Adonay
and witness to the word of his charism
and give signs and omens to become
through their hands.
4 And the multitude of the city schisms:
and indeed, part hold with the Yah
Hudiym, and part with the apostles.

Ministry In Lycaonia

5 And when a violent impulse
— both of the goyim
and of the Yah Hudiym with their archs;
to insult them and to stone them:
6 and being aware,
they flee to Lystra and Derbe — cities of Lycaonia,
and to the surrounding region:
7 and there they evangelize.

Paulos Heals One Lame

8 And at Lystra, a man sits, impotent in his feet;
being lame from the womb of his mother;
who never ever walked:
9 this *one* hears Paulos speak:
who stares at him,
and perceives he has trust to be saved,
10 and he says with a mega voice,
Stand upright **Arise straight** on thy feet.
And he leaped and walked.
11 And when the *people* **multitude** saw
what *Paul* **Paulos** had done,
they lifted *up* their voices,
saying **wording** in *the speech of Lycaonia* **Lycaoniy**,
The *gods* **elohim** are *come down* **descended** to us
in the likeness of *men* **humanity**.
12 And **indeed**
they called *Barnabas* **Bar Nabi**, *Jupiter* **Zeus**;
and *Paul* **Paulos**, *Mercurius* **Hermes**,
because **since** he was
the *chief speaker* **governnor of words**.
13 *Then* **And** the priest of *Jupiter* **Zeus**,
which was *before* **in front of** their city,
brought *oxen* **bulls** and *garlands* **wreaths** unto the gates,
and *would have done* **willed to** sacrifice
with the *people* **multitude**.

ACTS 14

14 Which when the apostles,
Barnabas **Bar Nabi** and Paul **Paulos**, heard of,
they *rent* **ripped** their *clothes* **garments**,
and *ran in among* **leaped unto** the *people* **multitude**,
crying out,

15 And *saying* **wording**,
Sirs **Men**, why do ye these *things*?
We also are *men* **humans** of like passions with you,
and *preach* **evangelize** unto you
that ye should turn from these vanities
unto the living *God* **Elohim**,
which made heaven, and earth, and the sea,
and all *things* that are therein:

16 Who in *times past* **generations departed**
suffered **allowed** all *nations* **goyim**
to walk in their own ways.

17 *Nevertheless* **Though** he left not himself
without witness **unwitnessed**,
in that he did good,
and gave us rain from heaven, and fruitful seasons,
filling our hearts
with *food* **nourishment** and *gladness* **rejoicing**.

18 And *with* **wording** these *sayings*
scarce **with difficulty**
restrained **shabbathized** they the *people* **multitude**,
that they had not *done sacrifice* **sacrificed** unto them.

Paulos Stoned

19 And there came *thither* certain
Jews **some Yah Hudiym**
from Antioch and Iconium,
who *persuaded* **convinced** the *people* **multitude**,
and having stoned *Paul* **Paulos**,
drew **dragged** him out of the city,
supposing **presuming** he had *been dead* **died**.
See: 2 Corinthians 12:1—3

20 *Howbeit*,
as the disciples *stood round about* **surrounded** him,
he rose *up*, and *came* **entered** into the city:
and *on* the *next day* **morrow**
he departed with *Barnabas* **Bar Nabi** to Derbe.

21 And when they had *preached*
the gospel **evangelized**
to that city,
and had *taught* **discipled** many,
they returned *again* to Lystra,
and to Iconium, and Antioch,

22 *Confirming* **Establishing**
the souls of the disciples,
and *exhorting* **beseeching** them
to *continue* **remain** in the *faith* **trust**,
and that we must through much tribulation
enter into the *kingdom* **sovereigndom** of *God* **Elohim**.

Ecclesia Elders

23 And when they had *ordained* **voted** them elders
in every *church* **ecclesia**,
and had prayed with fasting,
they *commended* **set** them to *the Lord* **Adonay**,
on **in** whom they *believed* **trusted**.

24 And after they had passed throughout Pisidia,
they came to Pamphylia.

25 And when they had *preached* **spoken** the word
in Perga,
they *went down* **descended** into Attalia:

26 And thence sailed to Antioch,
Rise straight on your feet!
— and he leaps and walks.

11 And the multitude sees what Paulos does,
and they lift their voices, wording in Lycaoniy,
The elohim descend to us in the likeness of humanity!

12 — and indeed, they call Bar Nabi, Zeus;
and Paulos, Hermes,
since he is the governnor of words.

13 And the priest of Zeus,
who is in front of their city,
brings bulls and wreaths to the gates,
and wills to sacrifice with the multitude:

14 and the apostles Bar Nabi and Paulos hear,
and they rip their garments and leap at the multitude,
crying out,

15 and wording,
Men, why do these?
We also are humans of like passions with you,
and evangelize to you
to turn from these vanities to the living Elohim
who made the heavens and earth and the sea
and all therein:

16 who in departed generations,
allowed all goyim to walk in their own ways:

17 though he left not himself unwitnessed,
in that he did good;
and gave us rain from the heavens
and fruitful seasons;
filling our hearts with nourishment and rejoicing.

18 — and wording these,
difficultly they shabbathize the multitude
to not sacrifice to them.

PAULOS STONED

19   And some Yah Hudiym
come from Antioch and Iconium,
who convince the multitude;
and they stone Paulos and drag him from the city,
presuming he died:
See: 2 Corinthians 12:1—3

20   and the disciples surround him;
and he rises and enters the city:
and on the morrow
he departs with Bar Nabi to Derbe.

21   And they evangelize to that
city and disciple many;
and return to Lystra and Iconium and Antioch,

22   establishing the souls of the disciples,
and beseeching them to remain in the trust;
and that we must through much tribulation
enter the sovereigndom of Elohim.

ECCLESIA ELDERS

23   And they vote elders in every ecclesia,
and pray with fasting;
and they set them to Adonay,
in whom they trust.

24   And after they pass throughout Pisidia
they come to Pamphylia;

25   and they speak the word in Perga
and descend to Attalia;

26   and there sail to Antioch;
from whence they had been *recommended* **delivered**
to the *grace* **charism** of *God* **Elohim**
for **unto** the work which they fulfilled/shalamed.

27   And when they were come,
and had gathered the *church* **ecclesia** together,
they *rehearsed* **evangelized**
all that *God* **as much as Elohim** had done with them,
and how he had opened the *door* **portal** of *faith* **trust**
unto the *Gentiles* **goyim**.

28   And there they *abode long* **tarried no little** time
with the disciples.

YAH HUDIYM DOCTRINATE CUSTOM OF MOSHEH

15   And *certain* **some** men
which came down from *Judaea* **Yah Hudah**
taught **doctrinated** the brethren, and said,
Except **Unless** ye be circumcised
after the *manner* **custom** of *Moses* **Mosheh**,
ye cannot be saved.

PAULOS AND BAR NABI ASCEND TO YERU SHALEM

2   *When therefore Paul* **So be it,
Paulos** and *Barnabas* **Bar Nabi**
had no small *dissension* **riot** and disputation
with them, they *determined* **ordained**
that *Paul* **Paulos** and *Barnabas* **Bar Nabi**,
and *certain* **some** other *of them*
should *go up* **ascend** to *Jerusalem* **Yeru Shalem**
unto the apostles and elders about this question.

3   And *therefore* **so indeed**
being *brought on their way* **forwarded**
by the *church* **ecclesia**,
they passed through
Phenice **Phoinix** and *Samaria* **Shomeron**,
declaring
the *conversion* **turning around** of the *Gentiles* **goyim**:
and they caused *great joy* **mega cheer**
unto all the brethren.

4   And when they were come
to *Jerusalem* **Yeru Shalem**,
they were received of the *church* **ecclesia**,
and of the apostles and elders,
and they *declared* **evangelized**
all things that God **as much as
Elohim** had done with them.

5   *But* **And** there rose *up*
certain **some** of the *sect* **heresy** of the Pharisees
which *believed* **trusted**, *saying* **wording**,
That it was *needful* **necessary** to circumcise them,
and to *command* **evangelize** them
to *keep* **guard** the *law* **torah** of *Moses* **Mosheh**.

6   And the apostles and elders
came **assembled** together
for to *consider of* **know about** this *matter* **word**.

THE MESSAGE OF PETROS

7   And when there had been
much *disputing* **disputation**,
Peter **Petros** rose *up*, and said unto them,
Men and brethren,
ye *know* **understand** how
that *a good while ago* **from ancient days**
God made choice **Elohim selected** among us,
that the *Gentiles by* **goyim through** my mouth
should hear the word of the *gospel* **evangelism**,
and *believe* **trust**.

8   And *God* **Elohim**,
which *knoweth the hearts* **all heart—knowing**,

ACTS 15

bare them witness,
giving them the *Holy Spirit* **Ruach ha-kodesh**,
even **exactly** as *he did* unto us;

9 And *put no difference* **distinguished not**
between us and them,
purifying their hearts by *faith* **trust**.

10 **So** Now *therefore* why
tempt **test** ye *God* **Elohim**,
to put a yoke upon the neck of the disciples,
which neither our fathers nor we were able to bear?

11 But we *believe* **trust**
that through the *grace* **charism**
of *the Lord Jesus Christ* **Adonay Yah Shua Messiah**
we shall be saved, *even* **in manner** as they.

THE WITNESS OF PAULOS AND BAR NABI

12 Then all the multitude *kept silence* **hushed**,
from whence they are delivered
to the charism of Elohim
to fulfill/shalam the work.

27 And they come and gather the ecclesia together;
and they evangelize
as much as Elohim does with them;
and how he opens the portal of trust to the goyim:

28 and there they tarry no little
time with the disciples.

YAH HUDIYM DOCTRINATE CUSTOM OF MOSHEH

15 And some men come down from Yah Hudah
and doctrinate the brothers, and say,
Unless you circumcise after the custom of Mosheh,
you cannot be saved.

PAULOS AND BAR NABI ASCEND TO YERU SHALEM

2 So be it, there is no small riot and disputation
with Paulos and Bar Nabi,
they ordain Paulos and Bar Nabi and some others
to ascend to Yeru Shalem
to the apostles and elders about this question.

3 And so indeed,
being forwarded by the ecclesia,
they pass through Phoinix and Shomeron,
declaring the turning around of the goyim:
and they cause mega cheer to all the brothers.

4 And coming to Yeru Shalem,
the ecclesia and the apostles and elders receive them;
and they evangelize
as much as Elohim does with them.

5 And some of the heresy of
the Pharisees who trust,
rise, wording,
It is necessary to circumcise them,
and to evangelize them to guard the torah of Mosheh.

6 — and the apostles and elders assemble together
to know what this word is about.

THE MESSAGE OF PETROS

7 And there being much disputation,
Petros rises, and says to them,
Men and brothers,
you understand how that from ancient days
Elohim selected among us,
that through my mouth
the goyim hear the word of the evangelism,
and trust:

8 and Elohim, all heart—
knowing, bore them witness,
giving them the Holy Spirit, even exactly as to us;

9 and distinguished not between us and them,
purifying their hearts by trust:

10 so now, why test you Elohim,
to put a yoke upon the neck of the disciples,
which neither our fathers nor we were able to bear?

11 But through the charism
of Adonay Yah Shua Messiah
we trust to be saved, in manner as they.

THE WITNESS OF PAULOS AND BAR NABI

12 And all the multitude hushes,
and *gave audience* **hearkened**
to *Barnabas* **Bar Nabi** and *Paul* **Paulos**,
declaring
what *miracles* **as many signs** and *wonders* **omens**
God **Elohim** had *wrought* **done**
among the *Gentiles by* **goyim through** them.

THE WITNESS OF YAAQOVOS

13 And after they had *held their peace* **hushed**,
James **Yaaqovos** answered, *saying* **wording**,
Men and brethren, hearken unto me:

14 *Simeon* **Shimon** hath declared
exactly how *God* **Elohim** at the first
did visit the *Gentiles* **goyim**,
to take out of them a people *for* **unto** his name.

15 And to this
agree **symphonize** the words of the prophets;
exactly as *it is written* **scribed**,

16	After this I *will* **shall** return,		being *assembled with one accord* **in unanimity**,
	and *will build again* **shall rebuild**		to send *chosen* **select** men unto you
	the tabernacle of David,		with our beloved *Barnabas* **Bar Nabi** and *Paul* **Paulos**,
	which is fallen *down*;	26	*Men* **Humans**
	and I *will build again* **shall rebuild**		that have *hazarded* **surrendered** their *lives* **souls**
	the *ruins* **diggings** thereof,		for the name
	and I *will* **shall** set it *up*:		of our *Lord Jesus Christ* **Adonay Yah Shua Messiah**.
17	That the *residue* **rest** of *men* **humanity**	27	**So** We have *sent* **apostolized** therefore
	might seek after *the Lord* **Yah Veh**,		*Judas* **Yah Hudah** and Silas,
	and all the *Gentiles* **goyim**, upon		who shall also *tell* **evangelize** you the same *things*
	whom my name is called,		*by mouth* **through word**.

16 After this I *will* **shall** return,
and *will build again* **shall rebuild**
the tabernacle of David,
which is fallen *down*;
and I *will build again* **shall rebuild**
the *ruins* **diggings** thereof,
and I *will* **shall** set it *up*:

17 That the *residue* **rest** of *men* **humanity**
might seek after *the Lord* **Yah Veh**,
and all the *Gentiles* **goyim**, upon
whom my name is called,
saith the Lord **wordeth Yah Veh**,
who doeth all these *things*.
Amos 9:11, 12

18 Known unto *God* **Elohim**
are all his works from the *beginning of the world* **eons**.

19 *Wherefore my sentence is* **So I judge**,
that we *trouble not* **harrass** them **no further**,
which from among the *Gentiles* **goyim**
are turned to *God* **Elohim**:

20 But that we *write* **epistolize** unto them,
that they abstain from pollutions of idols,
and from *fornication* **whoredom**,
and from *things* **strangled**, and from blood.

21 For *Moses* **Mosheh**
of old time **from ancient generations**
hath in every city them that preach him,
being read in the synagogues every
sabbath day **shabbath**.

22 Then *pleased it* the apostles
and elders **thought well**
with the whole *church* **ecclesia**,
to send *chosen* **select** men of their own company
to Antioch
with *Paul* **Paulos** and *Barnabas* **Bar Nabi**; *namely*,
Juda surnamed Barsabas **Yah Hudah called Bar Sabah**,
and Silas, *chief* **governing** men among the brethren:

23 And they *wrote letters by* **scribed through** them
after this manner **thus**;
The apostles and elders and brethren *send greeting*
unto the brethren which are of the *Gentiles* **goyim**
in Antioch and Syria and Cilicia, **Cheers**.

24 *Forasmuch* **Since** as we have heard,
that *certain* **some** which went out from
us have troubled you with words,
subverting **upsetting** your souls, *saying* **wording**,
Ye must be circumcised,
and, *keep* **Guard** the *law:* **torah!**
to whom we gave no such *commandment* **charge**:

25 *It seemed good unto us* **We thought well**,
being *assembled with one accord* **in unanimity**,
to send *chosen* **select** men unto you
with our beloved *Barnabas* **Bar Nabi** and *Paul* **Paulos**,

26 *Men* **Humans**
that have *hazarded* **surrendered** their *lives* **souls**
for the name
of our *Lord Jesus Christ* **Adonay Yah Shua Messiah**.

27 **So** We have *sent* **apostolized** therefore
Judas **Yah Hudah** and Silas,
who shall also *tell* **evangelize** you the same *things*
by mouth **through word**.
and hearkens to Bar Nabi and Paulos,
declaring as many signs and omens
Elohim did through them among the goyim.

THE WITNESS OF YAAQOVOS

13 And after they hush,
Yaaqovos answers, wording,
Men and brothers, hearken to me!

14 Shimon declared exactly
how Elohim at the first visited the goyim, to
take from them a people to his name.

15 And to this
the words of the prophets symphonize;
exactly as scribed,

16 After this,
I return and rebuild the tabernacle of David that fell;
and I rebuild the diggings, and I set it:

17 *so* that the rest of humanity seeks after Yah Veh,
and all the goyim upon whom my name is called,
words Yah Veh, who does all these.
Amos 9:11, 12

18 Known to Elohim
are all his works from the eons:

19 so I judge that we harrass them no further,
who from among the goyim, turn to Elohim:

20 but that we epistolize them
to abstain from pollutions of idols
and from whoredom
and from strangled
and from blood.

21 For from ancient generations and in every city
Mosheh has them who preach of him;
being read in the synagogues every shabbath.

22 Then the apostles and elders
with the whole ecclesia
think well to send select men of their own company
to Antioch with Paulos and Bar Nabi
— Yah Hudah called Bar Sabah and Silas
— governing men among the brothers.

23 And through them, they scribe thus:
The apostles and elders and brothers
to the brothers of the goyim
in Antioch and Syria and Cilicia:
Cheers!
24 Since we hear that some who go out from us
trouble you with words; upsetting your souls;
wording to circumcise and guard the torah
— to whom we gave no such charge:
25 we think well, being in unanimity,
to send select men to you
with our beloved Bar Nabi and Paulos
26 — humans who surrender their souls
for the name of our Adonay Yah Shua Messiah.
27 So we apostolize Yah Hudah and Silas,
who also evangelize you the same through word.
28 For *it seemed good to*
the *Holy Spirit* **Ruach ha-kodesh**,
and *to us*, **we thought well**
to *lay* **put** upon you no *greater* **more** burden
than *except* these necessary *things*;
29 That ye abstain
from *meats offered to idols* **idol sacrifices**,
and from blood, and from *things* strangled,
and from *fornication* **whoredom**:
from which *if* ye keep yourselves,
ye shall *do* **transact** well.
Fare ye well.
30 So **indeed**, when they were *dismissed* **released**,
they came to Antioch:
and when they had gathered the multitude together,
they *delivered* **gave over** the epistle:
31 Which when they had read,
they *rejoiced for* **cheered over** the consolation.
32 And *Judas* **Yah Hudah** and Silas,
being prophets also themselves,
exhorted **besought** the brethren
with **through** many words,
and *confirmed* **established** them.
33 And after they *tarried there*
a space **had done time**,
they were *let go* **released** in *peace* **shalom**
from the brethren unto the apostles.
34 Notwithstanding
it pleased Silas **thought well** to abide there still.

THE SECOND JOURNEY OF PAULOS

35 *Paul* **Paulos** also and *Barnabas* **Bar Nabi**
continued **tarried** in Antioch,
teaching **doctrinating** and *preaching* **evangelizing**
the word of *the Lord* **Adonay**, with many others also.
36 And some days after
Paul **Paulos** said unto *Barnabas* **Bar Nabi**,
Let us *go again* **now turn around**
and visit our brethren in every city
where **wherein** we have *preached* **evangelized**
the word of *the Lord* **Adonay**,
and see — how they do.
37 And *Barnabas determined* **Bar Nabi counseled**
to take with them *John* **Yahn**,
whose surname was Mark **who was called Markos**.

PAULOS AND BAR NABI SEPARATE

38 But *Paul thought not good*
Paulos deemed unworthy
to take him with them,
who departed from them from Pamphylia,
and *went* **came** not with them to the work.
39 And **so be it**,
the contention was so sharp **an agitation** between them,
so that they *departed asunder*
separated one from the other:
and so *Barnabas* **Bar Nabi** took *Mark* **Markos**,
and sailed unto Cyprus;
40 And *Paul chose* **Paulos**
selected Silas, and departed,
being *recommended* **surrendered** by the brethren
unto the *grace* **charism** of *God* **Elohim**.
41 And he *went* **passed** through Syria and Cilicia,
confirming the *churches* **ecclesiae**.

TIMO THEOS JOINS PAULOS

16 Then *came* **arrived** he *to* **in** Derbe and Lystra:
and, behold, a *certain* disciple was there,
named *Timotheus* **Timo Theos**,
the son of a *certain* woman,
which was a Jewess, and believed
a trustworthy Yah Hudiy;
but his father was *a Greek* **Hellene**:
2 Which was *well reported* **witnessed** of
by the brethren that were at Lystra and Iconium.
3 *Him would Paul have* **Paulos willed him**
to go forth with him;
and took and circumcised him
because of the *Jews* **Yah Hudiym**
which were in those *quarters* **places**:
for they knew all that his father was a *Greek* **Hellene**.
4 And as they went through the cities,
they delivered them the *decrees* **dogmas**
for to *keep* **guard**,

that were *ordained* **judged** of the apostles and elders
28 For the Holy Spirit and we
think well to put no more burden upon you
— except these necessary:
29 that you abstain from idol sacrifices
and from blood
and from strangled
and from whoredom;
from which, keeping yourselves, you transact well.
Fare you well!
30 So indeed,
they are released, and they go to Antioch:
and they gather the multitude together,
and they give over the epistle:
31 which, having read,
they cheer over the consolation.
32 And Yah Hudah and Silas, also being prophets,
beseech the brothers through many words
and establish them.
33 And after they do time,
they are released from the brothers to the apostles
in shalom.
34 Notwithstanding
Silas thinks well to abide there still.

The Second Journey Of Paulos

35 Paulos and Bar Nabi also tarry in Antioch;
doctrinating and evangelizing the word of Adonay
with many others also.
36 And some days after, Paulos says to Bar Nabi,
Now we turn around and visit our brothers
in every city
wherein we evangelized the word of Adonay,
— how they do.
37 And Bar Nabi counsels to take Yahn,
who is called Markos with them.

Paulos And Bar Nabi Separate

38 And Paulos deems him
unworthy to take with them
— who had departed from them from Pamphylia,
and came not to the work with them.
39 And so be it,
there is an agitation between them,
so that they separate one from the other:
and so Bar Nabi takes Markos and sails to Cyprus;
40 and Paulos selects Silas, and departs
— being surrendered by the brothers
to the charism of Elohim.
41 And he passes through Syria and Cilicia,
confirming the ecclesiae.

Timo Theos Joins Paulos

16 And he arrives in Derbe and Lystra:
and behold, a disciple is there named Timo Theos,
the son of a woman — a trustworthy Yah Hudiy;
but of a father — a Hellene:
2 and the brothers at Lystra and Iconium
witness of him.
3 Paulos wills him to go with him;
and takes and circumcises him
because of the Yah Hudiym in those places:
for they all know his father is a Hellene.
4 And as they go through the cities,
they deliver them the dogmas to guard, that
are judged by the apostles and elders
which were at *Jerusalem* **Yeru Shalem**.
5 And so **indeed** were the *churches* **ecclesiae**
established **solidified** in the *faith* **trust**,
and *increased* **superabounded** in number daily.

The Vision Of Paulos

6 *Now* when they had gone throughout Phrygia
and the **Galatian** region *of Galatia*,
and were forbidden of the *Holy Spirit* **Ruach ha-kodesh**
to *preach* **speak** the word in Asia,
7 After they were come to Mysia,
they *assayed* **tested** to go into Bithynia:
but **and** the Spirit *suffered* **allowed** them not.
8 And they passing by Mysia
came down **descended** to Troas.
9 And a vision appeared to *Paul* **Paulos**
in **through** the night;
There stood a man *of Macedonia* — **a Macedonian**
and prayed **who besought** him, *saying* **wording**,
Come over **Pass through** into Macedonia, and help us.
10 And after he had seen the vision,
immediately **straightway**
we *endeavoured* **sought** to go into Macedonia,
assuredly gathering **concluding**
that *the Lord* **Adonay** had called us
for to *preach the gospel* **evangelize** unto them.
11 *Therefore loosing* **So, embarking** from Troas,
we came *with a straight course*
straightly to Samothracia,
and *the* next *day* to Neapolis;

On To Philippi

12 And from thence to Philippi,
which is the *chief* **preeminent** city

of that part of Macedonia, and a colony:
and we were in that city
abiding certain **tarrying some** days.
13 And on the *sabbath* **day of the shabbaths**
we went out of the city by a *river* **stream** side,
where prayer was *wont* **presumed** to be made;
and we sat *down*, and spake unto the women
which *resorted thither* **came together**.
14 And a *certain* woman named Lydia,
a seller of purple, of the city of Thyatira,
which *worshipped God* **venerated Elohim**, heard us:
whose heart *the Lord* **Adonay** opened,
that she *attended* **heeded** unto the *things* **those**
which were spoken of by *Paul* **Paulos**.
15 And when she was baptized, and her household,
she *besought* **entreated** us, *saying* **wording**,
If ye have judged me
to be *faithful* **trustworthy** to *the Lord* **Adonay**,
come **enter** into my house, and abide *there*.
And she constrained us.

Paulos Evangelizes Out A Spirit Of Python

16 And **so be** it *came to pass*, as we went to prayer,
a *certain damsel* **lass**
possessed with **having** a spirit of
divination **Python** met us,
which *brought* **presented** her *masters* **adonim**
much *gain* **work** by soothsaying:
17 The same followed *Paul* **Paulos** and us,
and cried, *saying* **wording**,
These *men* **humans**
are the servants of *the most high God* **El Elyon**,
which *shew* **evangelize** unto us the way of salvation.
18 And this did she many days.
But *Paul* **Paulos**, being grieved,
turned and said to the spirit,
I *command* **evangelize** thee
in the name of *Jesus Christ* **Yah Shua Messiah**
to come out of her.
And he came out the same hour.
19 And when her *masters* **adonim** saw
that the *hope* **hopes** of their *gains* was **work were** gone,
they *caught Paul* **took Paulos** and Silas,
and drew them into the *marketplace* **market**
unto the *rulers* **archs**,
20 And brought them to the
magistrates **strategoi**, saying,
These *men, being Jews* **humans — Yah Hudiym**,
do exceedingly trouble **utterly disturb** our city,

21 And *teach* **evangelize** customs,
at Yeru Shalem.
5 So indeed the ecclesiae solidify in the trust,
and superabound in number daily.

The Vision Of Paulos

6 And going throughout Phrygia
and the Galatian region,
— forbidden by the Holy Spirit to
speak the word in Asia;
7 and coming to Mysia, they
test to go into Bithynia:
and the Spirit allows them not:
8 and passing by Mysia they descend to Troas.
9 And through the night, a
vision appears to Paulos;
a man standing — a Macedonian
who beseeches him, wording,
Pass through to Macedonia, and help us.
10 And after he sees the vision,
straightway we seek to go to Macedonia,
concluding that Adonay calls us
to evangelize to them.
11 So embarking from Troas,
we come straightly to Samothracia,
and next to Neapolis.

On To Philippi

12 And from there to Philippi
— the preeminent city of that part of Macedonia
— a colony;
and we tarry in that city some days:
13 and on the day of the shabbaths
we go from the city by a stream side,
where prayer is presumed to be made;
and we sit and speak to the women who come together.
14 And a woman named Lydia,
a seller of purple, of the city of Thyatira,
who venerates Elohim, hears us:
whose heart Adonay opens,
to heed to those spoken by Paulos:
15 and when she and her household are baptized,
she entreats us, wording,
If you judge me trustworthy to Adonay,
enter my house, and abide.
— and she constrains us.

Paulos Evangelizes Out A Spirit Of Python

16 And so be it, as we go to prayer,

a lass having a spirit of Python meets us,
who presents her adonim much work by soothsaying:

17 who follows Paulos and us, and cries, wording,
These humans are the servants of El Elyon
who evangelize the way of salvation to us.

18 — and she does this many days.
But Paulos, being grieved,
turns to the spirit, and says,
I evangelize you in the name of Yah Shua Messiah
to come from her.
— and he comes out the same hour.

19 And when her adonim see
that the hopes of their work are gone,
they take Paulos and Silas,
and draw them into the market to the archs;

20 and bring them to the strategoi, saying,
These humans — Yah Hudiym
utterly disturb our city,

21 and evangelize customs
which are not *lawful* **allowed** for us to receive,
neither to *observe* **do**, being Romans.

22 And the multitude *rose up*
stood together against them:
and the *magistrates* **strategoi**
rent off **rip** their *clothes* **garments**,
and *commanded* **summoned** to *beat* **bastinado** them.

Paulos And Silas Under Guard

23 And when they had
laid **put** many *stripes* **plagues** upon them,
they cast them into *prison* **the guardhouse**,
charging **evangelizing** the *jailor* **prison guard**
to *keep* **guard** them *safely* **securely**:

24 Who, having *received* **taken**
such *a charge* **an evangelism**,
thrust **cast** them into the inner *prison* **guardhouse**,
and *made* **secured** their feet *fast* in the *stocks* **staves**.

25 And at midnight *Paul* **Paulos** and Silas prayed,
and *sang praises* **hymned** unto *God* **Elohim**:
and the prisoners heard them.

A Mega Quake Shakes The Prison

26 And suddenly
there *was* **became** a *great earthquake* **mega quake**,
so that the foundations of the prison were shaken:
and immediately all the *doors* **portals** were opened,
and every one's bands were loosed.

27 And the *keeper* **guard** of the prison
awaking out of his sleep **being awakened**,
and seeing the *prison doors* **guardhouse portals** open,
he drew *out* his sword,
and *would have killed* **was about to take** himself **out**,
supposing **presuming** that the prisoners
had *been fled* **escaped**.

28 But *Paul cried* **Paulos called**
with a *loud* **mega** voice
saying **wording**, Do **Transact** thyself no *harm* **evil**:
for we are all here.

29 *Then* **And** he *called* **asked** for a light,
and *sprang in* **leaped**, and *came* **became** trembling,
and *fell down* **prostrated**
before Paul **in front of Paulos** and Silas,

30 And brought them out, and said,
Sirs **Adonim**, what must I do to be saved?

31 And they said, *Believe* **Trust**
on *the Lord Jesus Christ* **Adonay Yah Shua Messiah**,
and thou shalt be saved, and thy house.

32 And they spake unto him
the word of *the Lord* **Adonay**,
and to all that were in his house.

33 And he took them *in* the same hour of the night,
and *washed* **bathed** their *stripes* **plagues**;
and was baptized, he and all his,
straightway **immediately**.

34 And when he had brought them into his house,
he set *meat before them* **a table**, and
rejoiced **jumped for joy**,
believing **trusting** in *God* **Elohim** with all his house.

35 And *when it was* **being** day,
the *magistrates* **strategoi**
sent **apostolized** the *serjeants* **staff bearers**,
saying **wording**, Let **Release** those *men* go **humans**.

36 And the *keeper of the prison* **prison guard**
told **evangelized** this *saying* **word** to *Paul* **Paulos**,
The *magistrates* **strategoi** have sent to *let* **release** you *go*:
so *now* **therefore** depart, and go in *peace* **shalom**.

37 But *Paul* **Paulos** said unto them,
They have *beaten* **flogged** us *openly* **publicly**
uncondemned **unsentenced**,
being *Romans* **Roman humans**,
and have cast us into *prison* **the guardhouse**;
and now do they *thrust* **cast** us out *privily* **secretly**?
nay *verily* **indeed**;
but let them come themselves and *fetch* **lead** us out.

38 And the *serjeants* **staff bearers**
told **evangelized** these *words* **rhema**
unto the *magistrates* **strategoi**:
and they *feared* **awed**,
when they heard that they were Romans.

39 And they came and *besought* **entreated** them,

and led them out,
and *desired* **asked** them to depart out of the city.
40 And they went out of the *prison* **guardhouse**,
neither allowed for us to receive,
nor, being Romans, to do.
22 And the multitude stands
together against them:
and the strategoi rip their garments
and summon to bastinado them.

Paulos And Silas Under Guard

23 And they put many plagues on them
and cast them into the guardhouse,
evangelizing the prison guard to guard them securely:
24 who, having taken such an evangelism,
casts them into the inner guardhouse,
and secures their feet in the staves.
25 And at midnight,
Paulos and Silas pray and hymn to Elohim:
and the prisoners hear them.

A Mega Quake Shakes The Prison

26 And suddenly, there becomes a mega quake
so that the foundations of the prison shake:
and immediately all the portals open
and the bands of everyone loosen:
27 and being wakened,
the guard of the prison
seeing the guardhouse portals open,
he draws his sword
and is about to take himself out
— presuming the prisoners escaped.
28 But Paulos calls out with a mega voice,
wording, Transact yourself no evil: for we are all here.
29 And he asks for a light,
and leaps and becomes trembling
and prostrates in front of Paulos and Silas;
30 and brings them out, and says,
Adonim, what must I do to be saved?
31 And they say, Trust on
Adonay Yah Shua Messiah,
and you are saved — and your house.
32 And they speak the word of Adonay
to him and to all in his house:
33 and in the same hour of the night,
he takes them and bathes their plagues;
and immediately is baptized — he and all his:
34 and he brings them to his house
and sets a table and jumps for joy
— trusting in Elohim with all his house.

35 And being day,
the strategoi apostolize the staff bearers,
wording, Release those humans.
36 And the prison guard
evangelizes this word to Paulos,
The strategoi sends to release you:
so now depart, and go in shalom.
37 But Paulos says to them,
They flogged us publicly — unsentenced,
being Roman humans,
and cast us into the guardhouse!
And now cast they us out secretly?
Indeed not!
But have them come themselves and lead us out.
38 And the staff bearers
evangelizes these rhema to the strategoi:
and they awe when they hear they are Romans:
39 and they come and entreat
them and lead them out
and ask them to depart from the city.
40 And they go from the guardhouse
and *entered into the house of* **come unto** Lydia:
and when they had seen the brethren,
they *comforted* **consoled** them, and departed.

On To Thessalonikee

17 Now when they had passed through
Amphipolis and Apollonia,
they came to *Thessalonica* **Thessalonikee**,
where was a synagogue of the *Jews* **Yah Hudiym**:
2 And *Paul* **Paulos**, as his *manner* **custom** was,
went in unto them,
and three *sabbath days* **shabbaths**
reasoned with them out of the scriptures,
3 Opening and *alleging* **setting forth**,
that *Christ* **the Messiah** must needs have suffered,
and risen *again* from the dead;
and that this *Jesus* **Yah Shua**,
whom I *preach* **evangelize** unto you,
is *Christ* **the Messiah**.
4 And some of them *believed* **confided**,
and *consorted* **associated** with *Paul* **Paulos** and Silas;
and of the *devout Greeks* **venerating Hellenes**
a *great* **vast** multitude,
and of the *chief* **preeminent** women not a few.
5 But the *Jews which believed
not* **distrusting Yah Hudiym**,
moved with envy **being zealous**,
took unto them *certain lewd fellows* **some evil men**
of the baser sort — **forum debaters**,

and *gathered* **assembled** a *company* **multitude**,
and *set all* **tumulted** the city *on an uproar*,
and *assaulted* **stood by** the house of Jason,
and sought to bring them out to the *people* **public**.

6 And when they found them not,
they *drew* **dragged** Jason and *certain* **some** brethren
unto the *rulers of the city* **politarchees**, crying,
These that have *turned* **roused** the world *upside down*
are *come hither* **present** also; Whom Jason hath received:
and these all *do* **transact** contrary
to the *decrees* **dogmas** of *Caesar* **the Kaisar**,
saying **wording** that there is another *king* **sovereign**,
one *Jesus* **Yah Shua**.

8 And they *troubled* **agitated**
the *people* **multitude**
and the *rulers of the city* **politarchees**,
when they heard these *things*.

9 And when they had taken
security **sufficient** of Jason,
and of the *other* **rest**, they *let them go* **released them**.

On To Berea

10 And the brethren *immediately* **straightway**
sent away Paul **dispatched Paulos** and
Silas *by* **through** night unto Berea:
who coming *thither*
went into the synagogue of the *Jews* **Yah Hudiym**.

11 These were more *noble* **well—birthed**
than those in *Thessalonica* **Thessalonikee**,
in that they received the word
with all *readiness of mind* **eagerness**,
and *searched* **examined** the scriptures daily,
whether those *things were so* **be thus**.

12 *Therefore* **So indeed** many
of them *believed* **trusted**;
also of *honourable* **well—respected** women which
were *Greeks* **Hellenists**, and of men, not a few.

13 But when
the *Jews* **Yah Hudiym** of *Thessalonica* **Thessalonikee**
had knowledge that the word of *God* **Elohim**
was *preached* **evangelized** of *Paul* **Paulos** at Berea,
they came *thither* **there** also,
and *stirred* **shook** up the *people* **multitude**.

14 And then *immediately* **straightway**
the brethren *sent away Paul* **apostolized Paulos forth**
to go as *it were to* **upon** the sea:
but Silas and *Timotheus* **Timo Theos** abode there still.

On To Athens

15 And they that *conducted Paul* **seated Paulos**
brought him unto Athens:
and *receiving* **taking** a *commandment* **misvah**
unto Silas and *Timotheus* **Timo Theos**
for to come to him *with all speed* **most quickly**,
they departed.
and come to Lydia:
and when they see the brothers,
they console them and depart.

On To Thessalonikee

17 And passing through Amphipolis and Apollonia
they come to Thessalonikee;
where there is a synagogue of the Yah Hudiym:

2 and as his custom, Paulos comes to them,
and for three shabbaths
reasons with them from the scriptures

3 — opening and setting forth
that the Messiah needed to suffer
and rise from the dead;
and that this Yah Shua whom I evangelize to you,
is the Messiah.

4 And some of them confide
and associate with Paulos and Silas
— with a vast multitude of the venerating Hellenes
and of the preeminent women not a few:

5 but the distrusting Yah Hudiym, being zealous,
take some evil men to them — forum debaters,
and assemble a multitude and tumult the city;
and stand by the house of Jason
and seek to bring them out to the public.

6 And when they find them not,
they drag Jason and some brothers to the politarchees,
crying, These who rouse the world are present also
— whom Jason received:
and these all transact contrary
to the dogmas of the Kaisar
— wording that there is another sovereign, Yah Shua.

8 And when they hear these
they agitate the multitude and the politarchees:

9 And taking sufficient from
Jason and from the rest,
they release them.

On To Berea

10 And straightway through the night
the brothers dispatch Paulos and Silas to Berea:
who come and enter
the synagogue of the Yah Hudiym

11 — these are more well—birthed
than those in Thessalonikee

— in that they receive the word with all eagerness
and examine the scriptures daily
— whether they be thus.
12. So indeed many of them trust;
also of well—respected women Hellenists;
and of men not a few.
13. But when the Yah Hudiym of Thessalonikee
know that the word of Elohim
is evangelized by Paulos at Berea,
they come there and shake the multitude:
14. and straightway
the brothers apostolize Paulos to go, as upon the sea:
and Silas and Timo Theos still abide there.

ON TO ATHENS

15. And they who seat Paulos bring him to Athens:
and take a misvah to Silas and Timo Theos
to come to him most quickly,
and they depart.
16. *Now* **But** while *Paul* **Paulos**
waited for **awaited** them at Athens,
his spirit *was stirred* **agitated** in him,
when he *saw* **observed** the city
wholly given to idolatry **being downright idolatrous**.
17. *Therefore* **So indeed**
disputed **reasoned** he in the synagogue
with the *Jews* **Yah Hudiym**,
and with the *devout* **venerating** persons,
and in the market daily with them that met with him.
18. *Then certain* **But some**
philosophers of the Epicureans,
and of the Stoicks, encountered him.
And some *said* **spake**,
What *will* **willeth** this *babbler say*
spermalogist to word?
other some, He *seemeth* **thinketh well**
to be *a setter forth* **an evangelizer**
of strange *gods* **demons**:
because he *preached* **evangelized** unto them
Jesus **Yah Shua**, and the resurrection.
19. And they took him, and
brought him unto Areopagus,
saying **wording**,
May **Can** we know what this new doctrine,
whereof thou speakest, is?
20. For thou *bringest* **bearest**
certain **somewhat** strange *things* to our *ears* **hearing**:
so we *would* **will to** know *therefore*
what these *things* will **to** mean.
21. (For all the Athenians and strangers
which *were* **residing** there
spent their time **leisured** in *nothing else* **none other**,
but either to *tell* **word**, or to hear some new *thing*.)

THE AREOPAGUS MESSAGE OF PAULOS

22. *Then Paul* **And Paulos**
stood in the midst of *Mars' hill* **Areopagus**,
and said, *Ye men of Athens* **Men — Athenians**,
I *perceive* **observe** that in all *things*
ye are *too superstitious* **demon—dreaders**.
23. For as I passed *by* **through**,
and *beheld* **considered**
your *devotions* **objects of reverence**,
I found *an altar with this inscription*
a bamah epigraphed,

TO THE UNKNOWN GOD EL

So Whom *therefore*
ye *ignorantly worship* **unknowingly revere**,
him *declare* **evangelize** I unto you.
24. *God* **Elohim** that made the *world* **cosmos**
and all *things* therein,
seeing that he is Lord **this one being Adonay**
of heaven and earth,
dwelleth **settleth** not
in *temples made with hands* **handmade naves**;
25. Neither is *worshipped* **cured**
with men's **by human hands**
as though he needed *any thing* **aught**,
seeing he giveth to all life,
and *breath* **puffing**, and all *things*;
26. And hath made of one blood
all *nations* **goyim** of *men* **humanity**
for to *dwell* **settle** on all the face of the earth,
and hath *determined* **decreed** the times
before appointed **and prearranged the seasons**,
and the *bounds* **boundaries** of their
habitation **settlement**;
27. That they should seek *the Lord* **Yah Veh**,
if *haply* **then indeed** they might *feel after* **touch** him,
and find him,
though he be not far from *every* **each**
one of us: Yesha Yah 55:6
28. For in him we live, and *move* **stir**,
and *have our being* **be**;
as *certain* **some** also of your own poets have said,
For we are also his *offspring* **genos**.
29. *Forasmuch* then *as we are*
So being the *offspring* **genos** of *God* **Elohim**,
we *ought* **are indebted** not to *think* **presume**

that the *Godhead* **Elohimness**
is **be** like unto gold, or silver, or stone,
graven **etched** by *art* **techniques**
and *man's device* **human deliberation**.
16 But Paulos awaits them at Athens;
and his spirit agitates within him
when he observes the city
being downright idolatrous:
17 so indeed he reasons in the synagogue
with the Yah Hudiym and with the venerating persons
and daily in the market with those meeting with him.
18 But some philosophers of the Epicureans
and of the Stoicks encounter him:
and some speak,
What wills this spermalogist to word?
and some others, He thinks well
to be an evangelizer of strange demons
— because he evangelizes
Yah Shua and the resurrection to them.
19 And they take him and bring him to Areopagus,
wording, Can we know this new doctrine
whereof you speak?
20 For you bear somewhat strange to our hearing:
so we will to know what these will to mean.
21 — for all the Asoians and
strangers residing there
leisure in none other,
than either to word, or to hear somewhat new.

The Areopagus Message Of Paulos

22 And Paulos stands midst Areopagus,
and says, Men — Asoians,
I observe that in all you are demon—dreaders.
23 For as I passed through
and considered your objects of reverence,
I found a bamah epigraphed,

To The Unknown El

— so whom you unknowingly revere,
I evangelize to you.
24 Elohim, who made the cosmos and all therein,
this one being Adonay of the heavens and earth,
neither settles in handmade naves
25 nor is cured by human hands
— as though he needed aught;
seeing he gives life and puffing and all to all;
26 and also made of one blood
all goyim of humanity
to settle on all the face of the earth;
and decreed the times and prearranged the seasons
and the boundaries of their settlement;
27 to seek Yah Veh
— if then indeed, to touch him and to find him
— though he is not far from each one of us:
Yesha Yah 55:6
28 for in him we live and stir and be;
as some also of your own poets say,
For we are also his genos.
29 So, being of the genos of Elohim,
we are indebted to not presume
that the likeness of Elohim
is likened to gold or silver or stone
etched by human techniques and deliberations.
30 *And therefore* **So indeed**
the times of this *ignorance* **unknowingness**
God winked at **Elohim overlooked**;
but now *commandeth* **evangelizeth** all *men* **humanity**
every where to repent:
31 Because he hath *appointed* **set** a day,
in the which he *will* **shall be about to** judge the world
in *righteousness* **justness**
by *that* **a** man whom he hath *ordained* **decreed**;
whereof he hath given assurance **having presented trust**
unto all *men*,
in that he hath raised him from the dead.
32 And when they heard of the
resurrection of the dead,
some *mocked* **indeed jeered**: and others said,
We *will* **shall** hear thee again *of* **concerning** this *matter*.
33 *So Paul* **Thus Paulos**
departed from among them.
34 Howbeit *certain* **some** men
clave unto **joined** him,
and *believed* **trusted**:
among the which was
Dionysius the *Areopagite* **Areopagiy**,
and a woman named Damaris, and others with them.

On To Corinth

18 After these *things*
Paul departed **Paulos separated** from Athens,
and came to Corinth;
2 And found a *certain Jew*
Yah Hudiy named Aquila,
born in Pontos **a Pontican by genos**,
lately **recently** come from Italy,
with his *wife* **woman** Priscilla;
(because that Claudius had *commanded* **ordained**
all *Jews* **Yah Hudiym** to *depart* **separate** from Rome):
and came unto them.

3 And because he was *of the same craft* **a fellow artisan**, he abode with them, and *wrought* **worked**: for by their *occupation* **art** they were *tentmakers* **tabernaclemakers**.
4 And he reasoned in the synagogue every *sabbath* **shabbath**, and *persuaded* **convinced** the *Jews* **Yah Hudiym** and the *Greeks* **Hellenes**.
5 And when Silas and *Timotheus* **Timo Theos** were come **down** from Macedonia, *Paul* **Paulos** was *pressed* **held** in the spirit, and *testified* **witnessed** to the *Jews* **Yah Hudiym** that *Jesus* **Yah Shua** was *Christ* **the Messiah**.
6 And when they opposed themselves, and blasphemed, he shook his *raiment* **garment**, and said unto them, Your blood be upon your own heads; I am *clean* **pure**; from *henceforth* **now on** I *will* **shall** go unto the *Gentiles* **goyim**.
7 And he departed thence, and *entered into* **came to** *a certain man's* **someone's** house, named Justus, one that *worshipped God* **venerated Elohim**, whose house joined *hard to* the synagogue.
8 And Crispus, the *chief ruler* **arch** of the synagogue, *believed* **trusted** on *the Lord* **Adonay** with all his house; and many of the Corinthians hearing *believed* **trusted**, and were baptized.
9 *Then spake the Lord* **And Adonay said** to *Paul* **Paulos** in the night *by* **through** a vision, Be **Awe** not *afraid*, but speak, and *hold* **hush** not *thy peace*:
10 *For I am* **Because I AM** with thee, and no *man* **one** shall *set* **put** on thee to *hurt* **vilify** thee: *for* **because** I have much people in this city.
11 And he *continued* **sat** there a year and six months, *teaching* **doctrinating** the word of *God* **Elohim** among them.
12 And when Gallio was the *deputy* **proconsul** of Achaia, the *Jews made insurrection* **Yah Hudiym rushed** *with one accord* **in unanimity** against *Paul* **Paulos**, and brought him to the *judgment seat* **bamah**.
13 *Saying* **Wording**, This *fellow* **one** persuadeth men to *worship God* **venerate Elohim** contrary to the *law* **torah**.
14 And when *Paul* **Paulos** was now about to open his mouth, Gallio said unto the *Jews* **Yah Hudiym**,
30 So indeed Elohim overlooked the times of this unknowingness; but now evangelizes all humanity every where to repent:
31 because he set a day, in which he is about to judge the world in justness by a man whom he decreed; having presented trust to all, in that he raised him from the dead.
32 And they hear of the resurrection of the dead, and indeed, some jeer: and others say, We hear you again concerning this.
33 And thus Paulos departs from among them:
34 howbeit some men join him, and trust: among whom is Dionysius the Areopagiy and a woman named Damaris and others with them.

On To Corinth

18 After these, Paulos separates from Athens and comes to Corinth;
2 and finds a Yah Hudiy named Aquila — a Pontican by genos, recently come from Italy with his woman Priscilla — because Claudius ordained that all Yah Hudiym separate from Rome: and he comes to them:
3 and because he is a fellow artisan, he abides with them and works for by art, they are tabernaclemakers.
4 And he reasons in the synagogue every shabbath, and convinces the Yah Hudiym and the Hellenes.
5 And when both Silas and Timo Theos come down from Macedonia, Paulos is held in the spirit, and witnesses to the Yah Hudiym that Yah Shua is the Messiah.
6 And when they oppose and blaspheme, he shakes his garment, and says to them, Your blood be upon your own heads; I am pure; from now on I go to the goyim.
7 — and he departs thence. And he comes to the house of one named Justus — who venerates Elohim,

whose house joins the synagogue.
8 And Crispus, the arch of the synagogue,
trusts on Adonay with all his house;
and many of the Corinthians who hear
trust and are baptized.
9 And through a vision in the night
Adonay says to Paulos,
Awe not, but speak, and hush not:
10 because I AM with you:
and no one puts on you to vilify you
because I have much people in this city.
11 — and he sits there a year and six months
doctrinating the word of Elohim among them.
12 And while Gallio is the proconsul of Achaia,
the Yah Hudiym rush in unanimity against Paulos
and bring him to the bamah,
13 wording,
This *one* persuades men to venerate Elohim
contrary to the torah.
14 And as Paulos is now about to open his mouth,
Gallio says to the Yah Hudiym,
Therefore **So indeed,**
If it were *a* **some** matter of *wrong* **injustice**
or *wicked lewdness* **evil villany**, O ye *Jews* **Yah Hudiym**,
reason would **according to word,**
that I should *bear with* **tolerate** you:
15 But if it be a question *of*
concerning words and names,
and of your *law* **torah**, look ye to it;
for I will *be no* **to not be** judge of *such matters* **these.**
16 And he *drave* **dismissed** them
from the *judgment seat* **bamah.**
17 *Then* all the *Greeks* **Hellenes** took Sosthenes,
the *chief ruler* **arch** of the synagogue,
and *beat* **struck** him
before **in front of** the *judgment seat* **bamah.**
And Gallio *cared* **concerned** himself
for none of those *things.*

THE VOW OF PAULOS

18 And *Paul after this tarried*
there **Paulos abode** yet
a *good while* **long day,**
and *then took his leave of* **bade bye bye to** the brethren,
and sailed thence into Syria,
and with him Priscilla and Aquila;
having shorn his head in Cenchrea: for he had a vow.
19 And he *came to* **arrived in** Ephesus,
and left them there:
but he himself entered into the synagogue,
and reasoned with the *Jews* **Yah Hudiym.**
20 *When* **And** they *desired* **asked** him
to *tarry longer* **abide more** time with them,
he consented not;
21 But bade them *farewell* **bye bye,** saying,
I must *by all means* **most certainly**
keep **do** this *feast* **celebration**
that cometh in *Jerusalem* **Yeru Shalem**:
but I *will* **shall** return again unto you,
if God will **Elohim willing.**
And he *sailed* **embarked** from Ephesus.
22 And when he had
landed **descended** at *Caesarea* **Kaisaria,**
and *gone up* **ascended,** and saluted the *church* **ecclesia,**
he *went down* **descended** to Antioch.
23 And after he had *spent* **done** some time there,
he departed,
and *went over* **passed through**
all the *country of Galatia* **Galatian region** and Phrygia
in *order* **sequence,**
strengthening **establishing** all the disciples.

APOLLOS IN EPHESUS

24 And a *certain Jew* **Yah Hudiy** named Apollos,
born at Alexandria — **an Alexandrian by genos,**
an eloquent **a** man — **an orator,**
and *mighty* **able** in the scriptures,
came to **arrived in** Ephesus.
25 This *man* **one** was *instructed* **catechized**
in the way of *the Lord* **Adonay;**
and being *fervent* **zealous** in *the* spirit,
he spake and *taught diligently* **doctrinated exactly**
the things of the Lord **concerning Adonay,**
knowing **understanding** only the baptism of *John* **Yahn.**
26 And he began *to speak boldly* **emboldened**
in the synagogue:
whom when Aquila and Priscilla had heard,
they took him *unto them,* and expounded unto him
the way of *God* **Elohim** more *perfectly* **exactly.**
27 And when he *was disposed* **had willed**
to pass **through** into Achaia,
the brethren *wrote* **scribed,**
exhorting **encouraging** the disciples to receive him:
who, when he was come, *helped* **considered** them much
which had *believed* **trusted** through *grace* **charism**:
28 For he *mightily* **vigorously**
convinced **overwhelmed** the *Jews* **Yah Hudiym,**
and that publickly,
shewing *by* **through** the scriptures
that *Jesus* **Yah Shua** was *Christ* **the Messiah.**

Paulos At Ephesus

19 And so be it *came to pass*, that,
while Apollos was at Corinth,
Paul **Paulos** having passed through
the upper *coasts* **parts**
So indeed,
If it is some matter of injustice or evil villany,
O you Yah Hudiym,
according to word, I tolerate you:

15 but if it be a question
concerning words and names,
and of your torah, you look to it;
for I will to not be judge of these.

16 — and he dismisses them from the bamah.

17 All the Hellenes
take Sosthenes the arch of the synagogue,
and strike him in front of the bamah:
and Gallio concerns himself for none of those.

The Vow Of Paulos

18 And Paulos still abides a long day;
and bids bye bye to the brothers
and sails to Syria with Priscilla and Aquila;
and in Cenchrea he shears his head: for he has a vow:

19 and he arrives in Ephesus and leaves them there:
but he himself enters the synagogue,
and reasons with the Yah Hudiym.

20 And they ask him to abide
more time with them;
and he consents not

21 but bids them bye bye, saying,
I most certainly must do the coming celebration
in Yeru Shalem:
and Elohim willing, I return again to you.
— and he embarks from Ephesus.

22 And he descends to Kaisaria,
and ascends and salutes the ecclesia:
and he descends to Antioch:

23 and after he does some time there,
he departs and passes through
all the Galatian region and Phrygia in sequence
— establishing all the disciples.

Apollos In Ephesus

24 And a Yah Hudiy named Apollos
— an Alexandrian by genos
a man — an orator and able in the scriptures,
arrives in Ephesus.

25 This *one* is catechized in the way of Adonay;
and being zealous in spirit,
he speaks and doctrinates exactly concerning Adonay
— understanding only the baptism of Yahn:

26 and he begins emboldened in the synagogue:
whom when Aquila and Priscilla hear,
they take him and expound to him
the way of Elohim more exactly.

27 And he wills to pass through into Achaia,
and the brothers scribe
to encourage the disciples to receive him:
who, when he comes, to consider them much,
who had the trust through charism:

28 for he vigorously overwhelms the Yah Hudiym
— and that publicly,
showing through the scriptures
that Yah Shua is the Messiah.

Paulos At Ephesus

19 And so be it, while Apollos is at Corinth,
Paulos passes through the upper parts
came to Ephesus:
and finding *certain* **some** disciples,

2 He said unto them,
Have ye *received* **taken** the *Holy Spirit* **Ruach ha-kodesh**
since ye *believed* **trusted**?
And they said unto him,
We have not *so much as* **even** heard
whether **if** there be any *Holy Spirit* **Ruach ha-kodesh**.

3 And he said unto them,
Unto what then were ye baptized?
And they said, Unto *John*'s **Yahn**'s baptism.

4 *Then* **And** said *Paul* **Paulos**,
John verily **Yahn indeed**
baptized *with* the baptism of repentance,
saying **wording** unto the people,
that they should *believe on* **trust in** him
which should come after him,
that is, *on Christ Jesus* **in the Messiah Yah Shua**.

5 When they heard *this*,
they were baptized
in the name of *the Lord Jesus* **Adonay Yah Shua**.

6 And when *Paul* **Paulos**
had *laid* **put** his hands upon them,
the *Holy Spirit* **Ruach ha-kodesh** came on them;
and they spake with tongues, and prophesied.

7 And all the men were about twelve.

8 And he *went* **entered** into the synagogue,
and spake boldly **emboldened**
for the space of **unto** three months,
disputing **reasoning** and *persuading* **convincing**

	the things
	concerning the *kingdom* **sovereigndom** of *God* **Elohim**.
9	But when *divers* **some** were hardened,
	and *believed not* **distrusted**,
	but *spake evil of* **vilified** that way
	before **in the sight of** the multitude,
	he departed from them,
	and *separated* **set apart** the disciples,
	disputing **dialoguing** daily in the
	school of one Tyrannus.
10	And this *continued* **became**
	by the space of **unto** two years;
	so that all they which *dwelt* **settled** in Asia
	heard the word of *the Lord Jesus* **Adonay Yah Shua**,
	both *Jews* **Yah Hudiym** and *Greeks* **Hellenes**.

THE DYNAMIS OF ELOHIM THROUGH PAULOS

11	And *God* **Elohim**
	wrought special miracles **did no ordinary dynamis**
	by **through** the hands of *Paul* **Paulos**:
12	So that from his *body* **skin**
	were brought unto the *sick* **frail**
	handkerchiefs **sudarium** or aprons,
	and the diseases *departed* **released** from them,
	and the evil spirits went out of them.
13	Then *certain* **some** of the
	vagabond Jews **wandering Yah Hudiym** — exorcists,
	took *upon them* **in hand**
	to *call* **name** over them which had evil spirits
	the name of *the Lord Jesus* **Adonay Yah Shua**,
	saying **wording**, We *adjure* **oath** you by *Jesus* **Yah Shua**
	whom *Paul* **Paulos** preacheth.
14	And there were **some** seven sons of *one* Sceva,
	a *Jew* **Yah Hudiy**, and *chief of the priests* **archpriest**,
	which did so.
15	And the evil spirit answered and said,
	Jesus **Yah Shua** I know,
	and *Paul* **Paulos** I *know* **understand**;
	but who are ye?
16	And the *man* **human** in
	whom the evil spirit was
	leaped on them,
	and *overcame* **rule over** them,
	and prevailed against them,
	so that they *fled* **escaped** out of that house
	naked and *wounded* **traumatized**.
17	And this *was* **became** known
	to all the *Jews* **Yah Hudiym** and *Greeks* **Hellenes**
	also *dwelling* **settling** at Ephesus;
	and *fear* **awe** fell on them all,

	and the name of *the Lord Jesus* **Adonay Yah Shua**
	was magnified.
	and comes to Ephesus:
	and finding some disciples,
2	he says to them,
	Having trusted, have you taken the Holy Spirit?
	And they say to him,
	We have not even heard
	if there be any Holy Spirit.
3	And he says to them,
	To what then were you baptized?
	And they say, To the baptism of Yahn.
4	And Paulos says,
	Yahn indeed baptized the baptism of repentance,
	wording to the people
	to trust in him who comes after him —
	that is, in the Messiah Yah Shua.
5	When they hear,
	they are baptized in the name of Adonay Yah Shua:
6	and when Paulos puts his hands on them,
	the Holy Spirit comes upon them;
	and they speak with tongues and prophesy.
7	— and in all, there are about twelve men.
8	And for three months
	he enters the synagogue emboldened
	— reasoning and convincing
	concerning the sovereigndom of Elohim:
9	but when some harden and distrust,
	and vilify that way in the sight of the multitude
	he departs from them;
	and sets apart the disciples,
	dialoguing daily in the school of one Tyrannus:
10	and these become for two years,
	so that all who settle in Asia
	hear the word of Adonay Yah Shua
	— both Yah Hudiym and Hellenes.

THE DYNAMIS OF ELOHIM THROUGH PAULOS

11	And it is no ordinary dynamis
	that Elohim does through the hands of Paulos:
12	so that, from his skin,
	they bring sudarium or aprons to the frail;
	and the diseases release from them
	and the evil spirits go from them.
13	And some of the wandering
	Yah Hudiym — exorcists
	take in hand to name the name of Adonay Yah Shua
	over those having evil spirits,
	wording, We oath you by Yah Shua
	whom Paulos preaches.

14 And there are some seven sons of Sceva
— a Yah Hudiy and archpriest, who do thus.
15 And the evil spirit answers, saying,
Yah Shua I know
and Paulos I understand!
But who are you?
16 And the human in whom the evil spirit is
leaps on them and rules over them
and prevails against them
— so that they escape from that house
naked and traumatized.
17 And this becomes known
to all the Yah Hudiym and Hellenes
also settling at Ephesus;
and awe falls on them all;
and the name of Adonay Yah Shua is magnified.
18 And many that *believed* **trusted** came,
and *confessed* **avowed**,
and *shewed* **evangelized** their *deeds* **acts**.
19 Many of them also
which *used curious arts* **transacted magic**
brought their *books* **scrolls** together,
and burned them *before* **in the sight of** all *men*:
and they *counted* **reckoned** the price of them,
and found it *fifty thousand pieces* **five myriads** of silver.
20 *So mightily* **Thus powerfully**
grew the word of *God* **Elohim** and prevailed.
21 After these *things* were
ended **fulfilled/shalamed**,
Paul purposed **Paulos placed** in the spirit,
when he had passed through Macedonia and Achaia,
to go to *Jerusalem* **Yeru Shalem**, saying,
After I have been there, I must also see Rome.
22 *So* **And** he *sent* **apostolized** into Macedonia
two of them that ministered unto him,
Timotheus **Timo Theos** and Erastus;
but he himself stayed in Asia for a *season* **time**.

TROUBLE OF THE SILVERSMITHS

23 And *the same time* **at that season**
there *arose* **became** no small *stir* **trouble**
about **concerning** that way.
24 For *a certain man* **someone** named Demetrius,
a silversmith,
which made silver *shrines* **naves** for *Diana* **Artemis**,
brought **presented** no small *gain* **work**
unto the *craftsmen* **technicians**;
25 Whom he *called* **gathered** together
with the *workmen* **workers**
of *like* **such** occupation, and said,
Sirs **Men**, ye *know* **understand** that by this *craft* **work**
we *have our wealth* **prosper**.
26 Moreover ye *see* **observe** and hear,
that not alone at Ephesus,
but *almost* **throughout** nearly all Asia,
this *Paul* **Paulos** hath *persuaded* **convinced**
and *turned away* **removed** much *people* **multitude**,
saying **wording** that they be no *gods* **elohim**,
which *are made with* **become through** hands:
27 So that not only this our *craft* **part**
is *come* in *danger* **peril**
to *be set at nought* **come to disrepute**;
but also that the *temple* **priestal precinct**
of the *great* **mega** goddess *Diana* **Artemis**
should be *despised* **reckoned unto naught**,
and her *magnificence* **majesty**
should be *destroyed* **is about to be taken down**,
whom all Asia and the world *worshippeth* **venerateth**.
28 And when they heard these *sayings*,
they *were* **became** full of *wrath* **fury**,
and cried out, *saying* **wording**,
Great is Diana **Mega** — **Artemis** of the Ephesians.
29 And the whole city was
filled **full** with confusion:
and having caught Gaius and Aristarchus,
men *of Macedonia* — **Macedonians**,
Paul's companions in travel **Paulos' co—travellers**,
they *rushed with one accord* **ran violently in unanimity**
into the theatre.
30 And when *Paul would have* **Paulos had willed**
entered **to enter** in unto the *people* **public**,
the disciples *suffered* **allowed** him not.
31 And *certain* **some** of the chief of Asia **Asiarchs**,
which were his friends, sent unto him,
desiring **entreating** him
that he *would* **should** not *adventure* **give** himself
into the theatre.
32 *Some therefore* **So others indeed** cried one *thing*,
and some another:
for the *assembly* **ecclesia** was confused:
and the *more part* **most** knew not
wherefore **for what cause** they were come together.
33 And they *drew* **having
previously instigated** Alexander
out of the multitude,
the *Jews* **Yah Hudiym** putting him forward.
And Alexander *beckoned* **signaled** with the hand,
and *would* **willed** to *have made his defence* **pleaded**
unto the *people* **public**.
18 And many who trust, come and avow

19 and evangelize of their acts.
19 Many of them also who transacted magic
bring their scrolls together
and burn them in the sight of all:
and they reckon the price of them
and find it five myriads of silver.
20 Thus powerfully
the word of Elohim grows and prevails.
21 After these fulfill/shalam,
Paulos places in the spirit,
when he passes through Macedonia and Achaia,
to go to Yeru Shalem, saying,
After my being there, I must also see Rome.
22 And he apostolizes two who minister to him
to Macedonia
— Timo Theos and Erastus;
he himself stays in Asia for a time.

TROUBLE OF THE SILVERSMITHS

23 And at that season,
there being no small trouble concerning that way,
24 someone named Demetrius — a silversmith
who makes silver naves for Artemis, presents
no small work to the technicians;
25 whom he gathers together
with the workers of such occupation, and says,
Men, you understand that by this work we prosper:
26 moreover you observe and hear,
that not alone at Ephesus,
but throughout nearly all Asia,
this Paulos convinces and removes a vast multitude;
wording that no elohim becomes through hands:
27 so that not only this our part
comes in peril to disrepute;
but also that the priestal precinct
of the mega goddess Artemis
is reckoned as naught,
and her majesty is about to be taken down
— whom all Asia and the world venerates.
28 And hearing these, they become full of fury,
they cry out, wording,
Mega! Artemis of the Ephesians!
29 And the whole city fills/shalams with confusion:
and catching Gaius and Aristarchus,
men — Macedonians, co—travellers of Paulos,
they run violently in unanimity into the theatre.
30 And Paulos wills to enter to the public,
and the disciples allow him not:
31 and some of the Asiarchs — his friends,
send to him,
entreating him to not give himself into the theatre.
32 So others indeed cry out one, and some another;
for the ecclesia is confused:
and most of them know not
for what cause they come together.
33 And having previously instigated Alexander
from the multitude,
the Yah Hudiym put him forward:
and Alexander signals with the hand,
and wills to plead to the public:
34 But when they knew that
he was *a Jew* **Yah I-ludiy**,
all with one voice **there became one cry from all**
*about the space of two hours cried
out* **for about two hours**,
Great is Diana **Mega — Artemis** of the Ephesians.
35 And when the *townclerk* **scribe**
had *appeased* **quieted** the *people* **multitude**,
he said, Ye men *of Ephesus* — **Ephesians**, indeed,
what *man* **human** is there that knoweth not
how that the city of the Ephesians
is a *worshipper* **nave sweeper**
of the *great* **mega** goddess *Diana* **Artemis**,
and of the *image which fell down from Jupiter* **meteorite**?
36 *So* Seeing *then* that these *things
cannot be spoken against* **being unquestionable**,
ye *ought to* **must** be quiet,
and to *do nothing rashly* **transact naught precipitously**.
37 For ye have brought hither these men,
which are neither
robbers **strippers** of *churches* **priestal precincts**,
nor yet blasphemers of your goddess.
38 *Wherefore* **So indeed,** if Demetrius,
and the *technicians* **artisans** which are with him,
have a *matter* **word** against any man,
the law is open **have them lead a forum debate**,
and there are *deputies* **proconsuls**:
let them *implead* **accuse** one another.
39 But if ye *enquire any thing* **seek aught**
concerning any other matters,
it shall be *determined* **resolved**
in a lawful assembly **by the ecclesia under the torah**.
40 For we are in *danger* **peril**
to be *called in question* **accused**
for **about** this day's *uproar* **riot**,
there being no cause *whereby* **concerning which**
we *may* **can** give *an account* **word**
of this *concourse* **coalition**.
41 And when he had *thus spoken* **said these**
he *dismissed* **released** the *assembly* **ecclesia**.

ON TO MACEDONIA AND I-LELLAS

20 And after the *uproar was ceased* **tumult paused**,
Paul **Paulos** called unto him the disciples,
and *embraced* **saluted** them,
and departed for to go into Macedonia.
2 And when he had
gone over **passed through** those parts,
and had *given* **besought** them
much exhortation **with many words**,
he came into *Greece* **I-lellas**,
3 And *there abode* **did** three months.
And **so be it**,
when *the Jews laid wait* **the Yah
I-ludiym plotted** for him,
as he was about to *sail* **embark** into Syria,
he purposed **his decision became**
to return through Macedonia.
4 And there *accompanied* **followed** him into Asia
Sopater *of Berea* — **a Berean**;
and of the *Thessalonians* **Thessalonikeus**,
Aristarchus and Secundus;
and Gaius *of Derbe* **a Derbean**,
and *Timotheus* **Timo Theos**;
and *of Asia* **Asians**, Tychicus and Trophimus.
5 These *going before* **who preceded**,
tarried **abode** for us at Troas.

ON TO TROAS

6 And we sailed away from Philippi
after the days of *unleavened bread* **matsah**,
and came unto them to Troas in five days;
where we *abode* **tarried** seven days.
7 And upon the first *day* of the *week* **shabbath**,
when the disciples *came* **assembled** together
to break bread,
Paul preached **Paulos reasoned** unto them,
ready **about** to depart on the morrow;
and *continued* **stretched** his *speech* **words**
until midnight.
8 And there were many *lights* **lamps**
in the upper *chamber* **loft**,
34 but knowing he is Yah Hudiy,
there becomes as one cry from all for about two hours,
Mega — Artemis of the Ephesians!
35 And the scribe, quieting the multitude,
says, Men — Ephesians, indeed,
what human is there who knows not
that the city of the Ephesians
is a nave sweeper of the mega goddess Artemis,
and of the meteorite?
36 So seeing,
and being unquestionable,
you must be quiet
and transact naught precipitously.
37 For you bring these men here,
who are neither strippers of priestal precincts,
nor yet blasphemers of your goddess.
38 So indeed, if Demetrius
and the artisans with him
have a word against any man,
have them lead a forum debate;
and there are proconsuls:
have them accuse one another.
39 But if you seek aught
concerning any other matters,
resolve it by the ecclesia under the torah.
40 For we are in peril
of being accused about the riot of this day,
there being no cause concerning which
we can give word of this coalition.
41 — and he says these, and releases the ecclesia.

ON TO MACEDONIA AND I-LELLAS

20 And after the tumult pauses,
Paulos calls the disciples to him,
and salutes and departs to go into Macedonia:
2 and he passes through those parts,
and beseeches them with many words;
and he comes into Hellas
3 and does three months.
And so be it, the Yah Hudiym plot for him
as he is about to embark to Syria;
and his decision becomes to return through Macedonia:
4 and following him into Asia,
Sopater a Berean,
and Aristarchus and Secundus of the Thessalonikeus,
and Gaius a Derbean,
and Timo Theos,
and Tychicus and Trophimus, Asians:
5 these who precede, abide for us at Troas.

ON TO TROAS

6 And after the days of matsah
we sail from Philippi;
and in five days, come to them to Troas;
where we tarry seven days:
7 and on the first of the shabbath,
as the disciples assemble together to break bread,
Paulos reasons to them

	— about to depart on the morrow;
	and stretches his words until midnight.
8	And there are many lamps in the upper loft
	where they were gathered together.
9	And there sat in a window
	a *certain young man* **youth** named Eutychus,
	being fallen **brought down** into a deep sleep:
	and as *Paul was long preaching* **Paulos reasoned much**,
	he *sunk* **was brought** down *with* **by** sleep,
	and fell down from the third loft,
	and was taken *up* dead.
10	And *Paul went down* **Paulos descended**,
	and fell on him,
	and embracing him said,
	Trouble **Tumult** not yourselves; for his *life* **soul** is in him.
11	When he *therefore was come up* **ascended** again,
	and had broken bread, and *eaten* **tasted**,
	and *talked a long while* **homologized at length**,
	even till *break of day* **dawn**, *so* **thus** he departed.
12	And they brought the *young man* **lad** alive,
	and were not a *little comforted* **slight measure consoled**.

ON TO MILETUS

13	And we *went before* **proceeded** to *ship* **the sailer**,
	and *sailed* **embarked** unto Assos,
	there *intending* **thence about** to take in *Paul* **Paulos**:
	for *so* **thus** had he *appointed* **ordained**,
	minding himself to go afoot.
14	And when he *met with* **encountered** us at Assos,
	we took him in, and came to Mitylene.
15	And we sailed thence, and
	came **the arrived** next *day*
	over against **cast along side opposite** Hios;
	and *the next day* **regarding another**,
	we arrived at Samos,
	and *tarried* **abode** at Trogyllium;
	and *the* next *day* we came to Miletus.
16	For *Paul* **Paulos** had *determined*
	judged to sail by Ephesus,
	because he would **that it** not *become*
	spend the **that he waste** time in Asia:
	for he hasted, if it were possible for him,
	to be at *Jerusalem* **Yeru Shalem** the day of Pentecost.

PAULOS AND THE EPHESIAN ELDERS

17	And from Miletus he sent to Ephesus,
	and called the elders of the *church* **ecclesia**.
18	And when they were come
	to him, he said unto them,
	Ye *know* **understand**,
	from the first day
	that I came **from which I embarked** into Asia,
	after what manner I have *been* **become** with you
	at all *seasons* **times**,
19	Serving *the Lord* **Adonay**
	with all *humility of mind* **humblemindedness**,
	and with many tears, and *temptations* **testings**,
	which *befell* **happened** to me
	by the *lying in wait* **plotting** of the *Jews* **Yah Hudiym**:
20	And how I *kept back nothing* **withheld naught**
	that was *profitable unto you* **beneficial**,
	but have shewed **that I have not evangelized unto** you,
	and have *taught* **doctrinated** you publickly,
	and from house to house,
21	*Testifying* **Witnessing** both
	to the *Jews* **Yah Hudiym**,
	and also to the *Greeks* **Hellenes**,
	repentance toward *God* **unto Elohim**,
	and *faith* **trust**
	toward **unto** our *Lord Jesus Christ*
	Adonay Yah Shua Messiah.
22	And now, behold,
	I go bound in the spirit unto *Jerusalem* **Yeru Shalem**,
	not knowing *the things* **those**
	that shall *befall* **meet** me there:
23	*Save* **Except** that the *Holy*
	Spirit **Ruach ha-kodesh**
	witnesseth in every city,
	saying **wording** that bonds and *afflictions* **tribulations**
	abide me.
24	But none of these *things* **words** move me,
	neither *count* **regard** I my *life* **soul**
	dear **precious** unto myself,
	so that I might *finish* **complete/shalam** my *course* **race**
	with *joy* **cheer**,
	and the ministry, which I have *received* **taken**
	of *the Lord Jesus* **Adonay Yah Shua**,
	to *testify* **witness** the *gospel* **evangelism**
	of the *grace* **charism** of *God* **Elohim**.
25	And now, behold, I know that ye all,
	among whom I have *gone* **passed through**
	where they gather together:
9	and sitting in a window,
	a youth named Eutychus
	is brought down into a deep sleep:
	and as Paulos reasons much,
	he *is* brought down by sleep,
	and falls from the third loft, and is taken for dead.
10	And Paulos descends, and falls on him,
	and embracing him, says,

Tumult not yourselves; for his soul is in him.
11 And he ascends and breaks bread and tastes;
and homologizes at length — even until dawn,
thus he departs:
12 and they bring the lad alive,
and are consoled not a slight measure.

ON TO MILETUS

13 And we proceed to the sailer
and embark to Assos to take in Paulos there:
for thus he ordains, to go afoot.
14 And he encounters us at Assos,
and we take him in and come to Mitylene.
15 And there we sail;
and arrive next, cast along side opposite Hios;
and regarding another,
we arrive at Samos and abide at Trogyllium;
and next we come to Miletus.
16 For Paulos judges to sail past Ephesus,
that it be that he not waste time in Asia:
for he hastens, if possible,
to be at Yeru Shalem the day of Pentecost.

PAULOS AND THE EPHESIAN ELDERS

17 And from Miletus he sends to Ephesus
and calls the elders of the ecclesia:
18 and when they come to him, he says to them,
You understand,
from the first day I embarked into Asia,
after what manner I became with you at all times:
19 serving Adonay with all humblemindedness
and with many tears and testings
which happened to me
by the plotting of the Yah Hudiym:
20 and how I withheld naught beneficial,
that I evangelized not to you;
and doctrinated you publicly
and from house to house
21 — witnessing
both to the Yah Hudiym and to the Hellenes
repentance to Elohim,
and trust to our Adonay Yah Shua Messiah.
22 And now, behold,
I go bound in the Spirit to Yeru Shalem, not
knowing those that meet me there:
23 except that the Holy Spirit
witnesses in every city,
wording that bonds and tribulations abide me.
24 But none of these words move me
nor regard I my soul precious to myself

— so as to complete/shalam my race with cheer,
and the ministry I took of Adonay Yah Shua,
to witness the evangelism of the charism of Elohim.
25 And now, behold, I know that you all,
among whom I pass through
preaching the *kingdom* **sovereigndom** of *God* **Elohim**,
shall see my face no more.
26 *Wherefore* **So**
I *take you to record* **witness to you in** this day,
that I am pure from the blood of all *men*.
27 For I have not *shunned* **withheld**
to *declare* **evangelize** unto you
all the **whole** counsel of *God* **Elohim**.
28 *Take* **So** heed *therefore* unto yourselves,
and to all the *flock* **shepherddom**,
over the which the *Holy Spirit* **Ruach ha-kodesh**
hath *made* **placed** you *overseers* **episcopates**,
to *feed* **shepherd** the *church* **ecclesia** of *God* **Elohim**,
which he hath *purchased* **acquired**
with **through** his own blood.
29 For I know this, that after my departing
shall *grievous* **burdenous** wolves
enter in *among* **unto** you,
not sparing the *flock* **shepherddom**.
30 Also of your own selves shall men arise,
speaking *perverse things* **thorough perversions**,
to draw away disciples after them.
31 *Therefore* **So** watch, and remember,
that *by the space of* **for** three years I *ceased* **paused** not to
warn every **remind each** one night and day with tears.
32 And now, brethren,
I *commend you* **set you forth** to *God* **Elohim**,
and to the word of his *grace* **charism**,
which is able to build you *up*,
and to give you an inheritance
among all *them which are sanctified* **the hallowed**.
33 I have *coveted* **panted**
after no *man's* **one's** silver,
or gold, or *apparel* **garment**.
34 Yea, ye yourselves know,
that these hands
have *ministered* **tended** unto my necessities,
and to them that were with me.
35 I have *shewed you* **exemplified** all *things*,
how that *so* **thus** labouring
ye ought to support the *weak* **frail**,
and to remember
the words of *the Lord Jesus* **Adonay Yah Shua**,
how he said,
It is more blessed to give than to *receive* **take**.

36	And when he had *thus spoken* **said these**, he *kneeled down* **placed his knees**, and prayed with them all.		which he acquired through his own blood.
37	And *they all wept sore* **there became much weeping**, and fell on *Paul's* **Paulos'** neck, and **ardently** kissed him,	29	For I know this, that after my departing, burdenous wolves enter to you, not sparing the shepherddom.
38	*Sorrowing most of all* **Grieving especially** *for* **over** the words which he *spake* **said**, that they *should see* **were about to observe** his face no more. And they *accompanied* **forwarded** him unto the *ship* **sailer**.	30	And of your own selves, men rise, speaking thorough perversions, to draw disciples after them.
		31	So watch, and remember, that for three years I paused not to remind each one night and day with tears.

ON TO SOR

21 And **so be** it *came to pass*, that after we *were gotten* **withdrew** from them, and had *launched* **embarked**, we came *with a straight course* **straightly** unto Coos, and *the day following* **next** unto Rhodes, and from thence unto Patara:

2 And finding a *ship* **sailer** *sailing over* **passing through** unto *Phenicia* **Phoinix**, *we went aboard, and set forth* **in embarking, we embarked**.

3 *Now* **And** when *we had discovered* Cyprus **appeared**, we left it on the left *hand*, and sailed into Syria, and *landed* **moored** at *Tyre* **Sor**: for there the *ship* **sailer** was to unlade her burden.

DISCIPLES WARN PAULOS

4 And finding disciples, we *tarried* **abode** there seven days: who *said* **worded** to *Paul* **Paulos** through the Spirit, that he should not *go up* **ascend** to *Jerusalem* **Yeru Shalem**.

5 And **so be it**, when we had *accomplished* **completed/ shalamed** those days, we departed and went our way;

preaching the sovereigndom of Elohim, see my face no more.

26 So I witness to you in this day, that I am pure from the blood of all:

27 for I withhold naught to evangelize the whole counsel of Elohim to you.

28 So heed to yourselves and to all the shepherddom, over which the Holy Spirit placed you episcopates — to shepherd the ecclesia of Elohim

32 And now, brothers, I set you forth to Elohim, and to the word of his charism, which is able to build you, and to give you an inheritance among all the hallowed.

33 I panted after silver or gold or garment from no one.

34 Yes, you yourselves know that these hands tended to my necessities — and to them with me.

35 I exemplified all, how that thus laboring, you ought to support the frail, and to remember the words of Adonay Yah Shua, how he says, It is more blessed to give than to take.

36 — and saying these, he places his knees and prays with them all.

37 And there becomes much weeping; they fall on the neck of Paulos and ardently kiss him,

38 grieving especially over the words he says, that they are about to observe his face no more. — and they forward him to the sailer.

ON TO SOR

21 And so be it, we withdraw from them and embark; and we come straightly to Coos and next to Rhodes; and from there to Patara:

2 and finding a sailer, we pass through to Phoinix; in embarking, we embark

3 and Cyprus appears: we leave it on the left and sail into Syria and moore at Sor: for there the sailer unburdens her burden.

DISCIPLES WARN PAULOS

4 We abide there seven days: and find disciples who, through the Spirit, word to Paulos to not ascend to Yeru Shalem.

5 And so be it, we complete/shalam those days, and depart and go our way; and they all *brought* **forwarded** us *on our way*,

ACTS 21

with *wives* **women** and children,
till we were out of the city:
and we *kneeled down* **placed our knees** on the shore,
and prayed.
6   And when we had
taken our leave **saluted** one *of* another,
we *took ship* **embarked into a sailer**;
and they returned *home* **to their own** again.
7   And when we had *finished* **accomplished**
our *course* **sailing** from *Tyre* **Sor**,
we *came to* **arrived at** Ptolemais,
and saluted the brethren, and abode with them one day.
8   And *the* next *day*
we that were *of Paul's company* **around Paulos** departed,
and came unto *Caesarea* **Kaisaria**:
and we entered
into the house of *Philip* **Philippos** the evangelist,
which was one **being** of the seven; and abode with him.
9   And *the same man* **this one** had four daughters,
virgins, which did prophesy.

Hagab Warns Paulos

10 And as we *tarried there* **abode** many days,
there came down from *Judaea* **Yah Hudah** a
certain prophet, named *Agabus* **Hagab**.
11   And when he was come unto us,
he took *Paul's* **Paulos'** girdle,
and bound his own hands and feet, and said,
Thus *saith* **wordeth** the *Holy Spirit* **Ruach ha-kodesh**.
So **Thus** shall the *Jews* **Yah Hudiym**
at *Jerusalem* **Yeru Shalem**
bind the man that owneth this girdle,
and shall *deliver* **betray** him
into the hands of the *Gentiles* **goyim**.
12   And when we heard these *things*,
both we, and they of that place,
besought **entreated** him
not to *go up* **ascend** to *Jerusalem* **Yeru Shalem**.

On To Yeru Shalem

13   Then *Paul* **But Paulos** answered,
What *mean* **do** ye to weep
and to *break* **crumble** mine heart?
for I am *ready* **prepared** not to be bound only,
but also to die at *Jerusalem* **Yeru Shalem**
for the name of *the Lord Jesus* **Adonay Yah Shua**.
14   And *when he,*
would not be persuaded **not being convinced**,
we *ceased* **quieted**, saying,
So be The will of *the Lord be done* **Adonay**.

15   And after those days we *took*
up our carriages **packed**,
and *went up* **ascended** to *Jerusalem* **Yeru Shalem**.
16   There went with us also
certain **some** of the disciples of *Caesarea* **Kaisaria**,
and brought with them one Mnason of Cyprus,
an *old* **ancient** disciple, with whom we should lodge.
17   And *when we*
were come to Jerusalem **being at Yeru Shalem**,
the brethren received us *gladly* **with pleasure**.

The Vow Of Paulos

18   And *the day following* **next**
Paul went **Paulos entered in** with us
unto *James* **Yaaqovos**;
and all the elders were *present* **come**.
19   And when he had saluted them,
he declared *particularly* **each, one by one**
what *things God* **Elohim** had *wrought* **done**
among the *Gentiles by* **goyim through** his ministry.
20   And when they heard it,
they glorified *the Lord* **Adonay**,
and said unto him, Thou *seest* **observest**, brother,
how many *thousands* **myriads** of *Jews* **Yah Hudiym**
there are which *believe* **trust**;
and they are all *zealous* **zealots** of the *law* **torah**:
21   And they are *informed of* **catechized about** thee,
that thou *teachest* **doctrinatest** all the *Jews* **Yah Hudiym**
which are among the *Gentiles* **goyim**
to *forsake Moses* **apostatize from Mosheh**,
saying **wording**
that they ought not to circumcise their children,
neither to walk after the customs.

and they all, with women and children,
forward us until we are out of the city:
and we place our knees on the shore and pray:
6   and saluting one another,
we embark into a sailer;
and they return to their own again.
7   And when we accomplish our sailing from Sor
we arrive at Ptolemais and salute the brothers;
and abide with them one day.
8   And on the morrow,
we who are around Paulos depart
and come to Kaisaria:
and we enter the house of Philippos the evangelist
— being of the seven; and abide with him.
9   And this *one* has four daughters
— virgins, who prophesy.

Hagab Warns Paulos

10 And abiding many days,
a prophet named Hagab comes down from Yah Hudah
11 and comes to us:
and he takes the girdle of Paulos,
and binds his own hands and feet, and says,
Thus words the Holy Spirit:
Thus the Yah Hudiym at Yeru Shalem
bind the man who owns this girdle;
and betray him into the hands of the goyim.
12 And when we hear these,
both we and they of that place
entreat him to not ascend to Yeru Shalem.

On To Yeru Shalem

13 But Paulos answers,
What do you, weeping and crumbling my heart?
For I am prepared, not only to be bound,
but also to die at Yeru Shalem
for the name of Adonay Yah Shua.
14 And he, not being convinced,
we quiet, saying, So be the will of Adonay.
15 And after those days,
we pack and ascend to Yeru Shalem:
16 and some of the disciples of Kaisaria
also come with us
and bring one Mnason of Cyprus with them
— an ancient disciple, with whom we are to lodge.
17 And being at Yeru Shalem,
the brothers receive us with pleasure.

The Vow Of Paulos

18 And next, Paulos enters with us to Yaaqovos;
and all the elders come:
19 and he salutes them,
and declares to each, one by one,
what Elohim did among the goyim
through his ministry.
20 — and they hear it and glorify Adonay.
And they say to him, You observe, brother,
how many myriads of Yah Hudiym
there are who trust;
and they are all zealots of the torah:
21 and they catechize about you,
that you doctrinate
all the Yah Hudiym among the goyim
to apostatize from Mosheh,
wording that they ought
neither to circumcise their children,
nor to walk after the customs.
22 So What is it *therefore*?
the multitude must *needs* **most certainly** come together:
for they *will* **shall** hear that thou art come.
23 So Do *therefore* this that we *say* **word** to thee:
We have four men which have a vow on them;
24 Them take, and *purify* **hallow** thyself with them,
and be *at charges with* **spent by** them,
that they may shave their heads:
and all may know that those *things*,
whereof they were *informed* **catechized**
concerning **about** thee,
are *nothing* **naught**;
but that thou thyself also *walkest orderly* **marchest**,
and *keepest* **guardest** the *law* **torah**.
25 *As touching* **Concerning** the *Gentiles* **goyim**
which *believe* **trust**,
we have *written* **epistolized** and *concluded* **judged**
that they *observe no* **guard none** such *thing*,
save only **except** that they *keep* **guard** themselves
from *things offered to idols* **idol sacrifices**,
and from blood, and from strangled,
and from *fornication* **whoredom**.
26 Then *Paul* **Paulos** took the men,
and the *next* day **after**
purifying **hallowing** himself with them
entered into the *temple* **priestal precinct**,
to *signify* **evangelize** the *accomplishment*
fulfillment/shalom
of the days of *purification* **hallowing**,
until that an offering should be offered
for *every* **each** one of them.

Yah Hudiym Seize Paulos

27 And when the seven days
were *almost ended* **about to be completed/shalamed**,
the *Jews* **Yah Hudiym** which were of Asia,
when they *saw* **observed** him
in the *temple* **priestal precinct**,
stirred up all **confused** the *people* **whole multitude**,
and laid hands on him,
28 Crying out, Men *of Israel* — **Yisra Eliym**, help:
This is the *man* **human**,
that *teacheth all men* **doctrinateth everyone** every where
against the people, and the *law* **torah**, and this place:
and *further* **even** brought *Greeks* **Hellenes**
also into the *temple* **priestal precinct**,
and hath *polluted* **profaned** this holy place.
29 (For they had seen *before* **previously**
with him in the city Trophimus an Ephesian,

whom they *supposed* **presumed** that *Paul* **Paulos**
had brought into the *temple* **priestal precinct**.)
30   And all the city was *moved* **stirred**,
and the people *ran* **became rushing** together:
and they took *Paul* **Paulos**,
and drew him out of the *temple* **priestal precinct**:
and *forthwith* **straightway** the *doors* **portals** were shut.
31   And as they *went about*
sought to *kill* **slaughter** him,
tidings came **reports ascended**
unto the *chief captain* **chiliarch** of the *band* **squad**,
that all *Jerusalem* **Yeru Shalem** was
in an uproar **confused**.
32   Who immediately
took *soldiers* **warriors** and centurions,
and ran down unto them:
and when they saw
the *chief captain* **chiliarch** and the *soldiers* **warriors**,
they *left beating of Paul* **paused from striking Paulos**.
33   Then the *chief captain* **chiliarch**
came near **approached**, and took him,
and *commanded* **summoned** him
to be bound with two *chains* **fetters**;
and *demanded* **asked** who he was,
and what he had done.
34   And *some* **others** cried one *thing*,
some another, among the multitude:
and when he could not know the certainty
for **because** of the tumult,
he *commanded* **summoned** him
to be *carried* **brought** into the *castle* **encampment**.
35   And when he *came* **became** upon the stairs,
so it was **it so happened**,
22   So what is it?
The multitude must most certainly come together:
for they hear that you have come.
23   So do this, what we word to you:
We have four men who have a vow on them;
24   take them, and hallow yourself with them,
and be spent by them, to shave the head:
that all know that those,
whereof they are catechized about you, are naught;
but that you yourself also march and guard the torah.
25   And concerning the goyim who trust,
we epistolize and judge them to not guard such
— except to guard themselves from idol sacrifices
and from blood
and from strangled
and from whoredom.
26   Then Paulos takes the men,
and the day after, hallows himself with them;
and enters the priestal precinct
to evangelize the fulfillment/shalom
of the days of hallowing,
until an offering is offered for each one of them.

Yah Hudiym Seize Paulos

27   And as the seven days
are about to be completed/shalamed,
the Yah Hudiym of Asia,
when they observe him in the priestal precinct,
confuse the whole multitude and lay hands on him,
28   crying out, Men — Yisra Eliym, help!
This is the human
who doctrinates everyone every where
against the people and the torah and this place:
and even brings Hellenes into the priestal precinct
and profanes this holy place.
29   — for previously
they saw Trophimus an Ephesian
with him in the city
— whom they presumed that Paulos
brought into the priestal precinct.
30   And all the city stirs and
the people rush together:
and they take Paulos
and draw him from the priestal precinct:
and straightway shut the portals.
31   And as they seek to slaughter him,
reports ascend to the chiliarch of the squad
that all Yeru Shalem is confused:
32   who immediately takes warriors and centurions
and runs down to them:
and seeing the chiliarch and the warriors
they pause from striking Paulos.
33   Then the chiliarch approaches and takes him;
and summons to bind him with two fetters;
and asks who he is and what he did.
34   And some among the multitude cry one,
and some another:
and as he cannot know the certainty
because of the tumult,
he summons to bring him into the encampment.
35   And being on the stairs, it so happens,
that he was borne of the *soldiers* **warriors**
for the violence of the *people* **multitude**.
36   For the multitude of the people followed after,
crying, Away with him.

Paulos Pleads To Speak

37 And as *Paul* **Paulos**
was *about* to be *led* **brought** into
the *castle* **encampment**,
he *said* **worded** unto the *chief captain* **chiliarch**,
may I *Am I allowed to* speak *somewhat* unto thee?
Who said, *Canst* **Knowest** thou *speak Greek* **Hellenic**?

38 *So* Art not thou that *Egyptian* **Misrayim**,
which *before* **ere** these days *madest an uproar* **roused**,
and leddest out into the wilderness
four thousand men that were *murderers* **assassins**?

39 But *Paul* **Paulos** said,
I am *indeed* a *man* **human**
which am a Jew — **a Yah Hudiy**
of Tarsus, a city in — **a Tarsiy of** Cilicia,
a citizen of no *mean* **ignoble** city:
and, I *beseech* **petition** thee,
suffer **allow** me to speak unto the people.

Paulos Pleads To The People

40 And when he had *given* **allowed** him *licence*,
Paul **Paulos** stood on the stairs,
and *beckoned* **signaled** with the hand unto the people.
And when there *was made* **became**
a *great silence* **vast hush**,
he *spake unto* **addressed** them
in the Hebrew *tongue* **dialect**, *saying* **wording**,

22 Men, brethren, and fathers,
hear ye my *defence which I make* **pleading**
now unto you.

2 (And when they heard that he *spake* **addressed**
in the Hebrew *tongue* **dialect** to them,
they *kept* **presented** the more *silence* **quiet**: and he saith,)

3 I am *verily* **indeed** a man
which am a Jew — **a Yah Hudiy**,
born **birthed** in Tarsus, *a city in* Cilicia,
yet *brought up* **nurtured** in this city
at the feet of *Gamaliel* **Gamli El**,
and *taught* **disciplined**
according to the *perfect manner* **exactness**
of the *law* **torah** of the fathers,
and *was zealous* **being a zealot** toward *God* **Elohim**,
exactly as ye all are this day.

4 And I persecuted this way unto the death,
binding and *delivering* **betraying** into prisons
both men and women.

5 As also the *high* **arch** priest
doth *bear me* witness **me**,
and all the *estate of the elders* **presbytry**:

from whom also
I received *letters* **epistles** unto the brethren,
and went to *Damascus* **Dammeseq**
to bring them which were there bound
unto *Jerusalem* **Yeru Shalem**,
for to be *punished* **dishonoured**.

6 And *so be* it *came to pass*, that,
as I *made my journey* **went**,
and *was come nigh* **approached** *unto Damascus*
Dammeseq about *noon* **midday**, suddenly
there shone from heaven a great light round about me
a vast light from the heavens enveloped me.

7 And I fell unto the ground,
and heard a voice *saying* **wording** unto me,
Saul, Saul **Shaul, Shaul**, why persecutest thou me?

8 And I answered, Who art thou, *Lord* **Adonay**?
And he said unto me,
I am Jesus of Nazareth **I AM Yah Shua the Nazarene**,
whom thou persecutest.

9 And they that were with me
saw **observed** indeed the light,
and *were afraid* **became awestricken**;
but they heard not the voice of him that spake to me.

10 And I said, What shall I do, *Lord* **Adonay**?
And *the Lord* **Adonay** said unto me, Arise,
and go into *Damascus* **Dammeseq**;
and there it shall be *told* **spoken to** thee
of **concerning** all *things* which are *appointed* **ordained**
for thee to do.

he is borne by the warriors
because of the violence of the multitude
36 — for the multitude of the people follow after,
crying, Away with him!

Paulos Pleads To Speak

37 And as they are about to bring Paulos
into the encampment,
he words to the chiliarch,
Am I allowed to speak somewhat to you?
Who say, Know you Hellenic?

38 So are you not that Misrayim
who ere these days
roused and led out four thousand men
— assassins into the wilderness?

39 But Paulos says, I indeed am a human
— a Yah Hudiy — a Tarsiy of Cilicia
— a citizen of no ignoble city:
and, I petition you, allow me to speak to the people.

40 — and he allows him.

PAULOS PLEADS TO THE PEOPLE
PAULOS STANDS ON THE STAIRS,

and signals with the hand to the people:
and there becomes a vast hush;
he addresses them in the Hebrew dialect,
wording,

22 Men, brothers, and fathers,
hear now my pleading to you.

2 And when they hear him address them
in the Hebrew dialect,
they present the more quiet.
And he says,

3 I indeed am a man
— a Yah Hudiy birthed in Tarsus, Cilicia,
yet nurtured in this city at the feet of Gamli El;
and disciplined
according to the exactness of the torah of the fathers,
and being a zealot toward Elohim
— exactly as all of you this day:

4 and I persecuted this way to the death,
binding and betraying
both men and women into prisons:

5 as also the archpriest and all the presbytry
witness of me:
from whom I also received epistles to the brothers,
and went to Dammeseq
to bring the bound to Yeru Shalem
to dishonor them.

6 And so be it, about midday,
as I went and approached Dammeseq,
suddenly a vast light from the heavens enveloped me

7 and I fell to the ground:
and I heard a voice wording to me, Shaul,
Shaul, why persecute you me?

8 And I answer, Who are you, Adonay?
And he said to me,
I AM Yah Shua the Nazarene whom you persecute.

9 And those with me indeed observed the light
and became awestricken;
but they heard not the voice of him who speaks to me.

10 And I said, What do I, Adonay?
And Adonay said to me,
Rise and go into Dammeseq;
and there be spoken to
concerning all you are ordained to do.

11 And when I could not *see* **look**
for the glory of that light,
being hand led by the hand of them that were with me,
I came into *Damascus* **Dammeseq**.

12 And one *Ananias* **Hanan Yah**,
a *devout* **well—revered** man according to the *law* **torah**,
having a good report **well—witnessed**
of all the *Jews* **Yah Hudiym**
which *dwelt* **settled** there,

13 Came unto me, and stood **by**, and said unto me,
Brother *Saul* **Shaul**, *receive thy sight* **see**.
And the same hour I *looked up upon* **saw unto** him.

14 And he said,
The *God* **Elohim** of our fathers
hath *chosen* **preselected** thee,
that thou shouldest know his will,
and see *that* **the** Just One,
and shouldest hear the voice of his mouth.

15 For thou shalt be his witness
unto all *men* **humanity**
of what thou hast seen and heard.

16 And now *why tarriest thou*
what art thou about to do?
arise, and be baptized, and *wash away* **bathe** thy sins,
calling on the name of *the Lord* **Adonay**.

17 And *so be it* **came to pass**, that,
when I *was come again* **returned**
to *Jerusalem* **Yeru Shalem**,
even while I prayed in the *temple* **priestal precinct**,
I *was* **became** in *a trance* **an ecstasis**;

18 And saw him *saying* **wording** unto me,
Make haste **Hasten**,
and get thee quickly out of *Jerusalem* **Yeru Shalem**:
for **because** they *will* **shall** not receive
thy *testimony* **witness** concerning me.

19 And I said, *Lord* **Adonay**,
they *know* **understand** that I
imprisoned and *beat* **flogged**
in every synagogue
them that *believed* **trusted** on thee:

20 And when the blood of thy *martyr* **witness**
Stephen **Stephanos** was *shed* **poured forth**,
I also was standing by,
and consenting unto his *death* **taking out**,
and *kept* **guarded** the *raiment* **garment**
of them that *slew* **took** him **out**.

21 And he said unto me, Depart:
for I *will send* **shall apostolize** thee
far hence unto the *Gentiles* **goyim**.

22 And they *gave him audience*
unto heard this word,
and then lifted *up* their voices, and *said* **worded**,
Away with such *a fellow* from the earth:
for it is not *fit* **becoming** that he should live.

23	And as they cried out, and *cast off* **tossed** their *clothes* **garments**, and *threw* **cast** dust into the air,	17	And so be it, when I returned to Yeru Shalem, even as I prayed in the priestal precinct, I became in an ecstasis;
24	The *chief captain* **chiliarch** *commanded* **summoned** him to be brought into the *castle* **encampment**, and *bade that he should be examined* **said to test him** by scourging; that he might know *wherefore* **for what cause** they *cried so* **shouted thus** against him.	18	and saw him wording to me, Hasten, and quickly go from Yeru Shalem: because they receive not your witness concerning me.
		19	And I said, Adonay, they understand that in every synagogue I imprisoned and flogged them who trust on you:
25	And as they *bound* **stretched** him with thongs, Paul **Paulos** said unto the centurion that stood by, *Is it lawful for you* **Are you allowed** to scourge a *man that is* **human** — a Roman, and *uncondemned* **unsentenced**?	20	and when they poured the blood of your witness Stephanos, I also stood by, and consented to taking him out, and guarded the garment of them who took him out.
26	When the centurion heard that, he went and *told* **evangelized** the *chief captain* **chiliarch**, *saying* **wording**, *Take heed* **See** what thou *doest* **art about to do**: for this *man* **human** is a Roman.	21	And he said to me, Depart: for I apostolize you far hence to the goyim.
		22	And they hear this word, and they lift their voice, and word, Away with such from the earth! For it is not becoming for him to live!
27	*Then* **And** the *chief captain* **chiliarch** came, and said unto him, *Tell* **Word unto** me, art thou a Roman? He said, Yea.	23	And as they cry out, and toss their garments and cast dust into the air,
28	And the *chief captain* **chiliarch** answered, With a *great* **vast** sum *obtained* **acquired** I this *freedom* **citizenship**. And Paul **Paulos** said, But I *was free born* — **birthed**.	24	the chiliarch summons to bring him into the encampment, and says to test him by scourging; to know for what cause they shout thus against him.
29	*Then* **So** straightway they departed from him which *should have examined* **were about to test** him:	25	And as they stretch him with thongs, Paulos says to the centurion who stands by, Are you allowed to scourge a human — a Roman and unsentenced?
11	And I looked not, because of the glory of that light; and those with me, hand led me, and I came to Dammeseq.	26	And the centurion hears that, and he goes and evangelizes the chiliarch, wording, See what you are about to do: for this human is a Roman.
12	And one Hanan Yah, a well—revered man according to the torah, well—witnessed by all the Yah Hudiym who settle there,	27	And the chiliarch comes and says to him, Word to me, are you a Roman? He says, Yes.
13	came to me, and stood by, and said to me, Brother Shaul, see! — and the same hour I saw him.	28	And the chiliarch answers, I acquired this citizenship with a vast sum. And Paulos says, But I — birthed.
14	And he said, The Elohim of our fathers preselected you to know his will and see the Just One, and to hear the voice of his mouth:	29	So straightway, they who are about to test him depart from him: and the *chief captain* **chiliarch** also was *afraid* **awestricken**, *after he knew* **knowing** that he was a Roman, and because he had bound him.
15	because you become his witness to all humanity of what you saw and heard.		
16	And now what are you about to do? Rise and be baptized and bathe your sins — calling on the name of Adonay.		PAULOS PLEADS TO THE SANHEDRIM
		30	On the morrow,

because he *would* **willed**
to have known **the certainty**
wherefore he was accused of the *Jews* **Yah Hudiym**,
he loosed him from his *bands* **bonds**,
and *commanded* **summoned** the *chief* **arch** priests
and all their *council* **sanhedrim** to *appear* **come**,
and brought *Paul* **Paulos** down,
and set him *before* **unto** them.

23 And *Paul* **Paulos**,
earnestly beholding **staring at** the *council* **sanhedrim**,
said, Men and brethren,
I have *lived* **citizenized** in all good conscience
before *God* **Elohim** until this day.

2 And the *high* **arch** priest *Ananias* **Hanan Yah**
commanded **ordered** them that stood by
him to *smite* **strike** him on the mouth.

3 Then said *Paul* **Paulos** unto him,
God shall smite **Elohim is about to strike** thee,
thou *whited* **whitewashed** wall:
for sittest thou to judge me after the *law* **torah**,
and *commandest* **summonest** me to be *smitten* **stricken**
contrary to the *law* **torah**?

4 And they that stood by said,
Revilest **Abusest** thou *God's high* **Elohim's arch** priest?

5 Then said *Paul* **Paulos**, I
wist **knew** not, brethren,
that he was the *high* **arch** priest:
for it is *written* **scribed**,
Thou shalt not *speak* **say** evil
of the *ruler* **arch** of thy people.

6 But when *Paul perceived* **Paulos knew**
that the one part were *Sadducees* **Sadoqiym**,
and the other Pharisees,
he cried out in the *council* **sanhedrim**,
Men and brethren, I am a Pharisee, the son of a Pharisee:
of **concerning** the hope and resurrection of the dead
I am *called in question* **judged**.

7 And when he had so *said* **spoken**,
there arose a dissension **so be it, a riot**
between the Pharisees and the *Sadducees* **Sadoqiym**:
and the multitude was *divided* **schismed**.

8 For the *Sadducees say* **Sadoqiym indeed word**
that there is no resurrection, neither angel, nor
spirit: but the Pharisees *confess* **profess** both.

9 And *so be it*, there arose a great **a mega** cry:
and the scribes that were of the Pharisees' part arose,
and *strove* **fought fiercely**, *saying* **wording**,
We find no evil in this *man* **human**:
but **and** if a spirit or an angel hath spoken to him,
let us not *fight against God* **be Elohim—resisters**.

10 And *when there arose a great
dissension* **so be it, a vast riot**,
the *chief captain* **chiliarch**,
fearing lest *Paul* **Paulos** should *have been* **be**
pulled in pieces **thoroughly drawn apart** of them,
commanded **summoned** the *soldiers* **warriors**
to *go down* **descend**,
and to *take* **seize** him *by force* from among them,
and to bring him into the *castle* **encampment**.

ADONAY ENCOURAGES PAULOS

11 And the **next** night *following*
the *Lord* **Adonay** stood by him,
and said, *Be of good cheer* **Courage**, *Paul* **Paulos**:
for as thou hast *testified of* **witnessed about** me
in *Jerusalem* **Yeru Shalem**,
so **thus** must thou bear witness also at Rome.

THE COALITION OF THE YAH HUDIYM

12 And *when it was* **being** day,
certain **some** of the *Jews* **Yah Hudiym**
banded together **made a coalition**,
and *bound* **anathematized** themselves *under a curse*,
saying **wording**
that they *would* **should** neither eat nor drink
till they had *killed Paul* **slaughtered Paulos**.
and the chiliarch is also awestricken
— knowing he is a Roman,
and because he had bound him.

PAULOS PLEADS TO THE SANHEDRIM

30 On the morrow,
because he wills to know the certainty
whereof he is accused of the Yah Hudiym,
he looses him from his bonds;
and summons the archpriests
and all their sanhedrim to come;
and brings Paulos down and sets him to them.

23 And staring at the sanhedrim,
Paulos says, Men and brothers,
in all good conscience
I citizenize in front of Elohim until this day.
2 — and the archpriest Hanan Yah orders those
standing by him to strike him on the mouth.
3 Then Paulos says to him,
Elohim is about to strike you, you whitewashed wall:
for sit you to judge me after the torah,
and summon me to be stricken contrary to the torah?
4 And they who stand by say,
Abuse you the archpriest of Elohim?

5 So Paulos says, I knew not, brothers,
that he is the archpriest.
— for it is scribed,
You, say no evil of the arch of your people.
6 But Paulos,
knowing that the one part are Sadoqiym
and the other Phariseess,
he cries out in the sanhedrim,
Men and brothers,
I am a Pharisee, the son of a Pharisee:
concerning the hope and resurrection of the dead
I am judged.
7 And when he thus speaks, so be it,
a riot between the Phariseess and the Sadoqiym:
and the multitude schisms:
8 for the Sadoqiym indeed word
that there is neither resurrection nor angel nor spirit:
but the Phariseess profess both.
9 And so be it, a mega cry:
and the scribes of the part of the Pharisees
rise and fight fiercely,
wording, We find no evil in this human:
and if a spirit or an angel has spoken to him,
that we not resist Elohim.
10 And so be it, a vast riot,
and the chiliarch fearing,
lest Paulos be thoroughly drawn apart by them,
summons the warriors to descend
and to seize him from among them;
and to bring him into the encampment.

Adonay Encourages Paulos

11 And the next night Adonay stands by him,
and says, Courage, Paulos!
For as you witnessed about me in Yeru Shalem,
thus you must also witness at Rome.

The Coalition Of The Yah Hudiym

12 And being day,
some of the Yah Hudiym make a coalition
and anathematize themselves,
wording to neither eat nor drink
until they slaughter Paulos:
13 And they were more than forty
which had made this conspiracy.
14 And they came to the *chief*
arch priests and elders,
and said, We have *bound* **anathematized** ourselves
under a great *curse* **anathema**,
that we *will eat nothing* **shall taste naught**
until we have *slain Paul* **slaughtered Paulos**.
15 *So* **Now therefore** ye with the *council* **sanhedrim**
signify **manifest** to the *chief captain* **chiliarch**
that he bring him down unto you to morrow,
as though ye *would enquire something* **should know**
more *perfectly concerning* **exactly about** him:
and we, *or ever he come near* **ere he approacheth**,
are *ready* **prepared** to *kill* **take** him **out**.
16 And when *Paul's* **Paulos'** sister's son
heard of their *lying in wait* **lurking**,
he *went* **came** and entered into the *castle* **encampment**,
and *told Paul* **evangelized to Paulos**.
17 *Then Paul* **And Paulos**
called one of the centurions unto him, and said,
Bring this *young man* **youth** unto
the *chief captain* **chiliarch**:
for he hath *a certain thing* **somewhat**
to *tell* **evangelize** to him.
18 *So* **indeed** he took him,
and brought him to the *chief captain* **chiliarch**, and said,
Paul **Paulos** the prisoner called me unto him,
and *prayed* **asked** me
to bring this *young man* **youth** unto thee,
who hath *something* **somewhat** to *say* **speak** to thee.
19 *Then* **And** the *chief captain*
chiliarch took him by the hand,
and *went with him aside* **withdrew** privately,
and asked him,
What is that thou hast to *tell* **evangelize** to me?
20 And he said, The *Jews* **Yah I-ludiym**
have *agreed* **covenanted** to *desire* **ask** thee
that thou *wouldest* **shouldest** bring down *Paul* **Paulos**
to morrow into the *council* **sanhedrim**,
as though they *would* **should** enquire somewhat of him
more *perfectly* **exactly**.
21 *But do not thou yield unto them*
So let them not convince you:
for there *lie in wait* **lurk** for him
of them more than forty men,
which have *bound* **anathematized**
themselves *with an oath*,
that they *will* **shall** neither eat nor drink
till they have *killed* **taken** him **out**:
and now are they *ready* **prepared**,
looking for a promise **awaiting a pre—evangelism**
from thee.
22 *So* **indeed** the *chief captain* **chiliarch**
then *let* **released** the *young man depart* **youth**,
and *charged* **evangelized him**,
See thou *tell* **divulge** to no *man* **one**

that thou hast *shewed* **manifested** these *things* to me.

ON TO KAISARIA

23 And he called *unto him* two centurions, saying,
Make ready **Prepare** two hundred *soldiers* **warriors**
to go to *Caesarea* **Kaisaria**,
and horsemen *threescore and ten* **seventy**,
and *spearmen* **right receivers** two hundred,
at **from** the third hour of the night;
24 And *provide* **present** them *beasts* **animals**,
that they may *set Paul on* **mount Paulos**,
and bring him safe unto *Felix* **Phelix** the governor.
25 And he *wrote a letter* **scribed an epistle**
after this manner **containing this type**:
26 Claudius Lysias
unto the most *excellent* **powerful** governor *Felix* **Phelix**;
sendeth greeting **Cheers**:
27 This man was taken of the *Jews* **Yah I-ludiym**,
and *should have been killed* **was about to be taken out**
of them:
then *came I* **stood by** with *an army* **warriors**,
and *rescued* **released** him,
having *understood* **learned** that he was a Roman.
28 And when I *would* **willed**
to have known the cause
wherefore they accused him,
13 and more than forty make this conspiracy.
14 And they come to the archpriests and elders,
and say, We anathematized ourselves
under a great anathema,
to taste naught until we slaughter Paulos:
15 so now you and the sanhedrim
manifest to the chiliarch
to bring him down to you tomorrow
— as though to know more exactly about him:
and ere he approaches,
we are prepared to take him out.
16 And the son of the sister of Paulos
hears of their lurking,
and he comes and enters the encampment
and evangelizes to Paulos.
17 And Paulos calls one of the centurions to him,
and says, Bring this youth to the chiliarch:
for he has somewhat to evangelize to him.
18 So indeed he takes him,
and brings him to the chiliarch, and says, Paulos the
prisoner called me to him, and asked me to bring this
youth to you — who has somewhat to speak to you.
19 And the chiliarch takes him by the hand,
and withdraws privately, and asks him,

What have you to evangelize to me?
20 And he says,
The Yah Hudiym covenanted to ask you
to bring Paulos down to the sanhedrim tomorrow,
as though to enquire somewhat more exactly of him:
21 so let them not convince you:
for more than forty of their men lurk for him,
who anathematized themselves
to neither eat nor drink until they take him out:
and now they are prepared
— awaiting a pre—evangelism from you.
22 So indeed, the chiliarch releases the youth,
and evangelizes him,
You, divulge to no one that you manifest these to me.

ON TO KAISARIA

23 And he calls two centurions, saying,
Prepare two hundred warriors to go to Kaisaria
and seventy horsemen
and two hundred right receivers from
the third hour of the night;
24 and present animals for Paulos to mount
to bring him safe to Phelix the governor.
25 And he scribes an epistle containing this type:
26 Claudius Lysias:
To the most powerful governor Phelix:
Cheers.
27 This man was taken by the Yah Hudiym,
and they were about to take him out:
and having learned he is a Roman
I stood by with warriors and released him:
28 and when I willed to know the cause
for which they accused him,
I brought him *forth* into their *council* **sanhedrim**:
29 Whom I *perceived* **found**
to be accused of questions
of **about** their *law* **torah**,
but to have *nothing laid to his charge* **no accusation**
worthy of death or of bonds.
30 And when it was *told me* **disclosed**
how that the *Jews* **Yah Hudiym**
laid wait **plotted** for the man,
I sent *straightway* **immediately** to thee,
and *gave commandment* **evangelized** to his accusers
also to *say before* **word unto** thee
what they had against him.
Farewell.
31 *Then* **So indeed** the *soldiers* **warriors**,
as it was *commanded* **ordained** them, took *Paul* **Paulos**,
and brought him *by* **through** night to Antipatris.

32   **And** On the morrow
they *left* **allowed** the *horsemen* **cavalry** to go with him,
and returned to the *castle* **encampment**:
33   Who, when they *came to*
Caesarea **entered Kaisaria**,
and *delivered* **gave over** the epistle to the governor,
presented *Paul* **Paulos** also *before* **in front of** him.
34   And when the governor had read *the letter*,
he asked of what province he was.
And when he *understood that he was* **asked,** of Cilicia;
35   I *will* **shall** hear thee **patiently**, said he,
when thine accusers are also come.
And he *commanded* **summoned** him to be *kept* **guarded**
in Herod's *judgment hall* **praetorium**.

The Accusation Of Tertullus Against Paulos

24   And after five days
Ananias **Hanan Yah** the *high* **arch** priest
descended with the elders,
and with *a certain* **some** orator named Tertullus,
who *informed* **manifested to** the governor
against *Paul* **Paulos**.
2   And when he was called *forth*,
Tertullus began to accuse him, *saying* **wording**,
Seeing that *by* **through** thee
we *enjoy great quietness* **have obtained vast shalom**,
and that very worthy deeds
are *done* **become** unto this *nation* **goyim**
by thy *providence* **provision**,
3   We *accept* **receive** it *always* **every way**,
and *in all places* **everywhere**,
most *noble Felix* **powerful Phelix**,
with all *thankfulness* **eucharist**.
4   *Notwithstanding* **But**,
that I *be not further tedious unto* **hinder** thee **no more**,
I *pray* **beseech** thee
that thou *wouldest* **shouldest** hear us
of thy *clemency a few words* **gentleness concisely**.
5   For we have found this man *a pestilent fellow*,
and *a mover of sedition* **stirring riot**
among all the *Jews* **Yah Hudiym** throughout the world,
and a *ringleader* **prime officer**
of the *sect* **heresy** of the Nazarenes:
6   Who also hath *gone about* **tested**
to profane the *temple* **priestal precinct**:
whom we *took* **overpowered**,
and *would* **willed to** have judged
according to our *law* **torah**.
7   But the *chief captain* **chiliarch**
Lysias *came upon us* **passed by**,
and with *great* **much** violence
took him away out of our hands,
8   *commanding* **summoning** his accusers
to come unto thee:
by examining of whom thyself
mayest take knowledge of **canst
know about** all these *things*,
whereof we accuse him.
9   And the *Jews* **Yah Hudiym**
also *assented* **covenanted**,
saying **professing** that these *things* were *so* **thus**.

Paulos Pleads To Phelix

10   Then *Paul* **Paulos**,
after that the governor had *beckoned* **nodded** unto him
to *speak* **word**, answered,
I brought him to their sanhedrim:
29   and I found him
to be accused of questions about their torah;
but to have no accusation
worthy of death or of bonds:
30   and when it was disclosed
how the Yah Hudiym plotted for the man,
I immediately sent to you,
and also evangelized to his accusers to word to you
what they have against him.
Farewell.
31   So indeed the warriors,
as they were ordained, take Paulos,
and bring him through the night to Antipatris:
32   and on the morrow,
they allow the cavalry to go with him
and return to the encampment:
33   who, when they enter Kaisaria,
and give the epistle to the governor,
they also present Paulos in front of him.
34   And the governor reads,
and he asks of what province he is.
And when he asks, *he says,* Of Cilicia.
35   And he says, I hear you patiently
when your accusers also come.
— and he summons him
to be guarded in the praetorium of Herod.

The Accusation Of Tertullus Against Paulos

24   And after five days
Hanan Yah the archpriest descends with the elders

and with some orator named Tertullus
who manifests to the governor against Paulos.

2 And when he is called,
Tertullus begins to accuse him, wording,
Seeing that through you we obtain vast shalom,
and that by your provision
very worthy deeds become this goyim,
3 we receive it every way and everywhere,
most powerful Phelix, with all eucharist.
4 But so that I hinder you no more,
I beseech you, in your gentleness,
to hear us concisely.
5 For we find this man pestilent and stirring riot
among all the Yah Hudiym throughout the world,
and a prime officer of the heresy of the Nazarenes:
6 who also tested to profane the priestal precinct:
whom we overpowered
and willed to judge according to our torah.
7 But chiliarch Lysias passed by,
and with much violence, took him from our hands,
8 summoning his accusers to come to you:
who, by your examining,
can know about all these whereof we accuse him.
9 — and the Yah Hudiym also covenant,
professing that these are thus.

Paulos Pleads To Phelix

10 And after the governor nods to him to word,
Paulos answers,
Forasmuch as I *know* **understand** that thou
hast been of many years a judge unto this *nation* **goyim**,
I do the more cheerfully *answer* **plead**
for **concerning** myself:
11 Because that thou *mayest*
understand **canst know**,
that there are yet *but* **no more than** twelve days
since *I went up* **from my ascending**
to *Jerusalem* **Yeru Shalem** for to worship.
12 And they neither
found me in the *temple* **priestal precinct**
disputing **reasoning** with any *man* **one**,
neither *raising up* **making** the
people **multitude conspire**,
neither in the synagogues, nor in the city:
13 Neither can they *prove the things* **present those**
whereof **about which** they now accuse me.
14 But this I *confess* **profess** unto thee,
that after the way which they *call* **word** heresy,
so *worship* **thus liturgize** I the *God*
Elohim of my fathers,
believing **trusting** all *things* which are *written* **scribed**
in the *law* **torah** and in the prophets:
15 And have hope *toward God* **in Elohim**,
which they themselves also *allow* **await**,
that there *shall* **is about to** be a resurrection of the dead,
both of the just and unjust.
16 And *herein do* **in this** I exercise myself,
to have *always* **continually** a conscience void to offence
toward *God* **Elohim**, and *toward men* **humanity**.
17 *Now after* **And through** many years
I came to *bring alms* **do mercies** to my *nation* **goyim**,
and offerings.
18 Whereupon *certain Jews*
some Yah Hudiym from Asia
found me *purified* **hallowed**
in the *temple* **priestal precinct**,
neither with multitude, nor with tumult.
19 Who *ought* **need** to have been here
before **present by** thee,
and *object* **accuse**, if *ever* they had ought against me.
20 Or else let these same here say,
if they have found any *evil doing* **injustice** in me,
while I stood *before* **by** the *council* **sanhedrim**,
21 *Except it be for* **Other than about** this one voice,
that I cried standing among them, *Touching*
Concerning the resurrection of the dead
I am *called in question* **judged** by you this day.
22 And when *Felix* **Phelix** heard these *things*,
having more *perfect* **exact** knowledge
of **concerning** that way,
he *deferred* **delayed** them, and said,
When Lysias the *chief captain* **chiliarch**
shall *come down* **descend**,
I *will* **shall** know
the uttermost of your matter **exactly as to you**.
23 And he *commanded* **ordained** a centurion
to *keep Paul* **guard Paulos**,
and to let him have *liberty* **relaxation**,
and that he should forbid none of his *acquaintance* **own**
to *minister* **tend** or come unto him.

The Witness Of Paulos To Phelix

24 And after *certain* **some** days,
when *Felix* **Phelix** came with his *wife* **woman** Drusilla,
which was being a *Jewess* **Yah Hudiy**,
he *sent for Paul* **summoned Paulos**,
and heard him
concerning the *faith* **trust** in *Christ* **the Messiah**.
25 And as he reasoned
of righteousness **concerning justness**,

temperance **self—control**,
and **the** judgment *to come* **about to be**,
Felix trembled **Phelix became awestricken**
and answered,
Go thy way for *this time* **now**;
when I *have a convenient* **partake a** season,
I *will* **shall** call for thee.

26 He hoped *also* **simultaneously**
that *money* **riches**
should *have been* **be** given him of *Paul* **Paulos**,
that he might loose him:
wherefore **so** he *sent for* **summoned** him the oftener,
and *communed* **homologized** with him.
I understand that for many years
you have been a judge to this goyim,
I plead the more cheerfully concerning myself:

11 because you can know
that there are yet no more than twelve days
from my ascending to Yeru Shalem to worship:

12 and they neither found me
in the priestal precinct
reasoning with anyone,
nor making the multitude conspire
— neither in the synagogues nor in the city:

13 neither can they present those
about which they now accuse me.

14 But this I profess to you,
that after the way they word, heresy,
thus liturgize I the Elohim of my fathers,
trusting all which are scribed
in the torah and in the prophets:

15 and have hope in Elohim
— whom they themselves also await:
that there is about to be a resurrection of the dead
— both of the just and unjust.

16 And in this I exercise myself,
to continually have a conscience void of offence
toward Elohim and humanity.

17 And through many years
I come to do mercies and offerings to my goyim:
18 whereupon some Yah Hudiym from Asia
found me hallowed in the priestal precinct —
neither with multitude nor with tumult:

19 who need to be here, present by you,
and accuse, if they have aught against me.

20 Or else have these same here say,
if they find any injustice in me,
while I stand in front of the sanhedrim;

21 — other than about this one voice,
that I cried standing among them.

Concerning the resurrection of the dead
I am judged by you this day.

22 And hearing these, Phelix delays them,
to have more exact knowledge concerning that way;
and says, When Lysias the chiliarch descends,
I know exactly as to you.

23 And he ordains a centurion to guard Paulos
and that he have relaxation; and to forbid none
of his own to tend him or come to him.

The Witness Of Paulos To Phelix

24 And after some days,
Phelix comes with his woman Drusilla
— being a Yah Hudiy,
he summons Paulos,
and hears him concerning the trust in the Messiah:

25 and as he reasons concerning justness,
self—control, and the judgment about to be,
Phelix becomes awestricken, and answers,
Go your way for now;
when I partake a season, I call for you.

26 He hopes simultaneously
that Paulos gives him riches, so as to loose him:
so he summons him the oftener,
and homologizes with him.

27 But after two years **being fulfilled/shalamed**
Porcius Festus **Porkios Phestus**
came into Felix' room **succeeded Phelix**:
and *Felix* **Phelix**,
willing **having willed**
to *shew the Jews* **lay on the Yah Hudiym**
a *pleasure* **charism**,
left *Paul* **Paulos** bound.

Yah Hudiym Seek To Summon Paulos

25 *Now* **So** when *Festus* **Phestus**
was come **embarked** into the province,
after three days
he ascended from *Caesarea* **Kaisaria**
to *Jerusalem* **Yeru Shalem**.

2 *Then* **And** the *high* **arch** priest
and the *chief* **preeminent** of the *Jews* **Yah Hudiym**
informed **manifested** him against *Paul* **Paulos**,
and *besought* **entreated** him,

3 And *desired favour* **asked charism** against him,
that he *would send for* **should summon** him
to *Jerusalem* **Yeru Shalem**,
laying wait **lurking** in the way to *kill* **take** him **out**.

4 But *Festus* **So indeed Phestus** answered,
that *Paul* **Paulos** should be *kept* **guarded**

at *Caesarea* **Kaisaria**,
and that he himself
would **was about to** depart *shortly* **quickly** thither.

5   *So* Let them **therefore**, said
he, which among you are able,
go down with me, and accuse this man,
if there be any wickedness in him.

6   And when he had tarried among them
more than ten days,
he *went down* **descended** unto *Caesarea* **Kaisaria**;
and *the next day* **on the morrow** sitting
on the *judgment seat* **bamah**
commanded Paul **summoned Paulos** to be brought.

7   And when he was come,
the *Jews* **Yah Hudiym** which *came down* **descended**
from *Jerusalem* **Yeru Shalem** stood round about,
and *laid* **brought** many
and *grievous complaints* **burdenous accusations**
against *Paul* **Paulos**,
which they could not *prove* **show**.

8   *While* he *answered* **pleaded** for himself,
Neither *against* **unto** the *law* **torah**
of the *Jews* **Yah Hudiym**,
neither *against* **unto** the *temple* **priestal precinct**,
nor yet *against Caesar* **unto the Kaisar**
have I *offended any thing at all* **sinned somewhat**.

9   But *Festus* **Phestus**,
willing **having willed**
to *do* **lay** the *Jews* **Yah Hudiym** a *pleasure* **charism**,
answered *Paul* **Paulos**, and said,
Wilt **Willest** thou
go up **ascend** to *Jerusalem* **Yeru Shalem**,
and there be judged
of **concerning** these *things before* **by** me?

Paulos Calls On The Kaisar

10   *Then* **But** said *Paul* **Paulos**,
I stand at *Caesar's judgment seat* **the Kaisar's bamah**,
where I *ought to* **must** be judged:
to the *Jews* **Yah Hudiym**
have I *done no wrong* **not injured**,
as thou very well knowest.

11   For **indeed** if I *be an offender* **have injured**,
or have *committed any thing* **transacted somewhat**
worthy of death,
I *refuse* **shun** not to die:
but if there be none of these *things*
whereof these accuse me,
no *man may deliver* **one can grant charism of** me
unto them.

I *appeal unto Caesar* **call upon the Kaisar**.

12   Then *Festus* **Phestus**,
when he had *conferred* **talked** with the council,
answered,
Hast thou appealed unto *Caesar* **the Kaisar**?
unto *Caesar* **the Kaisar** shalt thou go.

13   And *after certain* **some** days **having past**,

27   But fulfilling/shalaming two years
Porkios Phestus succeeds Phelix:
and Phelix wills to lay a charism on the Yah Hudiym
and leaves Paulos bound.

Yah Hudiym Seek To Summon Paulos

25   So Phestus embarks to the province;
and after three days
he ascends from Kaisaria to Yeru Shalem.

2   And the archpriest
and the preeminent of the Yah Hudiym
manifest him against Paulos, and entreat him,

3   and ask charism against him
to summon him to Yeru Shalem
— lurking in the way to take him out.

4   So indeed Phestus answers,
to guard Paulos at Kaisaria,
and that he himself is about to depart quickly.

5   So have those among you, says he,
who are able,
go down with me and accuse this man —
if there be any wickedness in him.

6   And he tarries among them more than ten days,
and descends to Kaisaria;
and on the morrow, sitting on the bamah,
summons to bring Paulos:

7   and when he comes,
the Yah Hudiym who descended from Yeru Shalem
stand all around,
and bring many and burdenous accusations
against Paulos
which they cannot show.

8   And he pleads for himself,
Neither to the torah of the Yah Hudiym
nor to the priestal precinct
nor yet to the Kaisar have I sinned somewhat.

9   But Phestus
wills to lay a charism on the Yah Hudiym,
and answers Paulos, saying,
Will you to ascend to Yeru Shalem,
and there be judged by me concerning these?

Paulos Calls On The Kaisar

10 But Paulos says,
I stand at the bamah of the Kaisar
where I must be judged:
I injured not the Yah Hudiym,
as you very well know.

11 For indeed, if I injured
or transacted somewhat worthy of death,
I shun not to die:
and if there be none of these
whereof these accuse me,
no one can give me as a charism to them:
I call upon the Kaisar.

12 Then Phestus, having talked with the council, answers,
Appeal to the Kaisar? To the Kaisar you go!

13 And some days having passed,
king **sovereign** Agrippa and Bernice
came unto Caesarea **arrived in Kaisaria**
to salute *Festus* **Phestus**.

14 And when they had *been*
tarried there many days,
Festus declared Paul's **Phestus
propounded Paulos'** cause
unto the *king* **sovereign**, *saying* **wording**,
There is *a certain* **some** man
left *in bonds* **prisoner** by *Felix* **Phelix**:

15 About whom,
when I *was at Jerusalem* **became in Yeru Shalem**,
the *chief* **arch** priests and the elders
of the *Jews informed me* **Yah I-ludiym manifested**,
desiring **asking** to have judgment against him.

16 To whom I answered,
It is not the *manner* **custom** of the Romans
to *deliver* **grant charism** over any *man* **human**
to die **unto destruction**,
before **ere** that he which is accused
have the accusers face to face,
and *have licence to answer for himself* **take his pleading**
concerning *the crime laid against him* **his accusation**.

17 *Therefore* **So**, when they were come hither,
without any **making no** delay
on the morrow I sat on the *judgment seat* **bamah**,
and *commanded* **summoned** the
man to be brought forth.

18 *Against* **Concerning** whom
when the accusers stood *up*,
they brought none accusation
of such *things* as I *supposed* **surmised**:

19 But had *certain* **some** questions against him
of concerning their own superstition demon—dreading,
and of about one Jesus Yah Shua, which was dead,
whom *Paul affirmed* **Paulos professed** to be alive.

20 And *because I doubted* **being perplexed**
of such manner of **about these** questions,
I *asked him* **worded**,
whether he *would* **willed to** go to
Jerusalem **Yeru Shalem**,
and there be judged *of* **concerning** these matters.

21 But when *Paul* **Paulos**
had *appealed* **called** to be *reserved* **guarded**
unto the *hearing* **diagnosis** of *Augustus* **Sebastos**,
I *commanded* **summoned** him to be kept
till I might send him to *Caesar* **the Kaisar**.

22 *Then* **And** Agrippa said unto *Festus* **Phestus**,
I *would* also **will to** hear the *man* **human** myself.
To morrow, said he, thou shalt hear him.

23 *And* **So** on the morrow,
when Agrippa was come, and Bernice,
with *great pomp* **much fantasy**,
and was entered into the place of hearing,
with the *chief captains* **chiliarchs**,
and *principal* **eminent** men of the city,
at *Festus' commandment* **Phestus' summons**
Paul **Paulos** was brought forth.

24 And *Festus* **Phestus** said,
King **Sovereign** Agrippa,
and all men which are *here* present *with us* **together**,
ye *see* **observe** this man,
about whom all the multitude of the *Jews* **Yah I-ludiym**
have *dealt* **interceded** with me,
both at *Jerusalem* **Yeru Shalem**, and also here,
crying that he *ought* **must** not *to* live any longer.

25 But when I *found* **overtook**
that he had *committed nothing* **transacted naught**
worthy of death,
and that he himself
hath *appealed* **called** to *Augustus* **Sebastos**,
I have *determined* **judged** to send him.

26 *Of* **About** whom
I have *no certain thing* **nought** to *write* **scribe**
unto my *lord* **adoni**.
Wherefore **So** I have brought him forth *before* **by** you,
and specially *before* **by** thee, O *king* **sovereign** Agrippa,
that, after examination *had* **having become**,
I might have somewhat to *write* **scribe**.

27 For *it seemeth to me unreasonable*
I thought it irrational to send a prisoner,
and not withal to signify the *crimes* **accusations**
laid against him.

	sovereign Agrippa and Bernice
	arrive in Kaisaria to salute Phestus.
14	And tarrying there many days,
	Phestus propounds the cause of Paulos
	to the sovereign, wording,
	There is some man left prisoner by Phelix:
15	about whom, when I became in Yeru Shalem,
	the archpriests and the elders
	of the Yah Hudiym manifested,
	asking to have judgment against him:
16	to whom I answered,
	It is not the custom of the Romans
	to give any human as a charism for destruction,
	ere the accused has the accusers face to face,
	and take his pleading concerning his accusation.
17	So, they came here,
	and I, making no delay,
	on the morrow I sat on the bamah,
	and summoned to bring the man forth
18	— concerning whom, when the accusers stood,
	they brought no accusation of such as I surmised:
19	but had some questions against him
	concerning their own demon—dreading,
	and about one Yah Shua, who is dead
	— whom Paulos professes to be alive.
20	And being perplexed about these questions,
	I worded whether he willed to go to Yeru Shalem,
	and there be judged concerning these matters.
21	But Paulos called
	to be guarded to the diagnosis of Sebastos;
	and I summoned to keep him
	until I send him to the Kaisar.
22	And Agrippa says to Phestus,
	I also will to hear this human myself.
	Tomorrow, says he, you hear him.
23	So on the morrow, with much fantasy,
	Agrippa and Bernice come
	and enter the auditorium,
	with the chiliarchs and eminent men of the city;
	and at the summons of Phestus, Paulos is brought.
24	And Phestus says, Sovereign Agrippa,
	and all men present together,
	observe this man,
	about whom all the multitude of the Yah Hudiym
	interceded with me
	— both at Yeru Shalem and also here,
	crying that he must not live any longer.
25	But I overtake
	that he transacted naught worthy of death,
	and that he himself calls to Sebastos,
	I judge to send him
26	— about whom
	I have naught to scribe to my adoni.
	So I bring him by you
	— and especially by you, sovereign Agrippa,
	that examination having become,
	I have somewhat to scribe.
27	For I thought it irrational to send a prisoner,
	and not to signify the accusations laid against him.

PAULOS PLEADS TO AGRIPPA

26	Then Agrippa said unto *Paul* **Paulos**,
	Thou art *permitted* **allowed** to *speak* **word** for thyself.
	Then *Paul stretched forth* **Paulos spread** the hand,
	and *answered* **pleaded** for himself:
2	I *think* **deem** myself *happy* **blessed**,
	king **Sovereign** Agrippa,
	because I *shall answer* **am about to plead** for myself this day
	before **by** thee *touching* **concerning** all *the things*
	whereof I am accused of the *Jews* **Yah I-ludiym**:
3	Especially because I know thee
	to be *expert* **knowledgeable** in all customs and questions
	which are among the *Jews* **Yah I-ludiym**:
	wherefore *so* I *beseech* **petition** thee to hear me patiently.
4	**So indeed**
	My *manner of life* **existence** from my youth,
	which was *at the first* **being from the beginning**
	among mine own *nation* **goyim** at
	Jerusalem **Yeru Shalem**,
	know all the *Jews* **Yah I-ludiym**;
5	Which *knew* **foreknew** me
	from *the beginning* **above**,
	if **whenever** they *would testify* **willed to witness**,
	that after the most *straitest sect* **exact heresy**
	of our *religion* **ceremonials** I lived a Pharisee.
6	And now I stand and am judged
	for **unto** the hope of the *promise* **pre—evangelism**
	made of God **that became by Elohim**, unto our fathers:
7	Unto which *promise* our twelve *tribes* **scions**,
	instantly serving God **intently liturgizing** day and night,
	hope to *come* **arrive**.
	For **Concerning** which *hope's sake* **hope**,
	king **Sovereign** Agrippa,
	I am accused of the *Jews* **Yah I-ludiym**.
8	Why should it be *thought* **judged**
	a thing incredible **trustless** with you,
	that God **if Elohim** should raise the dead?
9	So I *verily* **indeed** thought with myself,
	that I *ought to do many things* **must transact much**

contrary to the name
of *Jesus of Nazareth* **Yah Shua the Nazarene**.
10   Which *thing* I also did in
Jerusalem **Yeru Shalem**:
and many of the *saints* **holy**
did I *shut up* **lock down** in *prison* **the guardhouse**,
having *received* **taken** authority
from the *chief* **arch** priests;
and when they were *put to death* **taken out**,
I *gave my voice* **brought down my pebble** against them.
11   And I *punished* **dishonoured** them oft
in every synagogue,
and compelled them to blaspheme;
and *being exceedingly mad* **raving superabundantly**
against them,
I persecuted them even unto *strange* **outlying** cities.
12   *Whereupon* **Wherein** as I
went to *Damascus* **Dammeseq**
with authority and *commission* **permisssion**
from the *chief* **arch** priests,
13   At midday, O *king* **sovereign**,
I saw in the way a light from heaven,
above the *brightness* **radiance** of the sun,
shining round about **haloing** me
and them which *journeyed* **went** with me.
14   And when we were all fallen **down** to the earth,
I heard a voice speaking unto me,
and *saying* **wording** in the Hebrew *tongue* **dialect**,
Saul, Saul **Shaul, Shaul**, why persecutest thou me?
it is hard for thee to *kick* **heel** against the *pricks* **stings**.
15   And I said, Who art thou, *Lord* **Adonay**?
And he said,
I am Jesus **I AM Yah Shua** whom thou persecutest.
16   But rise, and stand upon thy feet:
for I have appeared unto thee *for this purpose* **unto this**,
to *make* **preselect** thee
a minister **an attendant** and a witness
both of these *things* which thou hast seen,
and of those *things*
in the which I *will* **shall** appear unto thee;
17   *Delivering* **Releasing** thee from the people,
and from the *Gentiles* **goyim**,

PAULOS PLEADS TO AGRIPPA

26   So Agrippa says to Paulos,
You are allowed to word for yourself.
So Paulos spreads the hand and pleads for himself:
2   I deem myself blessed, Sovereign Agrippa,
because this day
I am about to plead for myself by you
concerning all
whereof I am accused by the Yah Hudiym:
3   especially because I know you
to be knowledgeable in all customs and questions
among the Yah Hudiym:
so I petition you to hear me patiently.
4   So indeed, my existence from my youth,
being from the beginning
among my own goyim at Yeru Shalem,
all the Yah Hudiym know;
5   who foreknew me from above,
whenever they will to witness,
that after the most exact heresy of our ceremonials
I lived a Pharisee:
6   and now I stand,
judged for the hope of the pre—evangelism
that became to our fathers by Elohim:
7   to which our twelve scions,
intently liturgizing day and night, hope to arrive:
concerning which hope, Sovereign Agrippa,
I am accused by the Yah Hudiym.
8   Why be it judged trustless with you,
if Elohim raises the dead?
9   So I indeed thought with myself,
that I must transact much
contrary to the name of Yah Shua the Nazarene.
10   Which I also did in Yeru Shalem:
and I locked many of the holy in the guardhouse,
taking authority from the archpriests:
and when they were taken out,
I brought my pebble against them:
11   and I dishonored them
often in every synagogue,
and compelled them to blaspheme:
and raving superabundantly against them,
I persecuted them even to outlying cities.
12   Wherein as I went to Dammeseq
with authority and permisssion from the archpriests,
13   at midday, O sovereign,
I see in the way a light from the heavens,
above the radiance of the sun,
haloing me and them who went with me:
14   and we all fell to the earth,
and I heard a voice speaking to me, and wording in the
Hebrew dialect, Shaul, Shaul, why persecute you me?
It is hard for you to heel against the stings.
15   And I said, Who are you, Adonay?
And he said,
I AM Yah Shua whom you persecute.
16   But rise and stand on your feet;

and for this I appear to you:
to preselect you, an attendant and a witness
both of these which you have seen,
and of those in which I am to appear to you;
17 releasing you from the
people and from the goyim
unto whom now I *send* **apostolize** thee,
18 To open their eyes,
and to turn them from darkness to light,
and *from* the *power* **authority** of Satan
unto *God* **Elohim**,
that they may *receive* **take** forgiveness of sins,
and *inheritance* **their lot** among them
which are *sanctified* **hallowed** by *faith* **trust** that is in me.
19 Whereupon, O *king* **Sovereign** Agrippa,
I *was* **became** not *disobedient* **distrusting**
unto the heavenly vision:
20 But *shewed* **evangelized** first
unto them of *Damascus* **Dammeseq**,
and at *Jerusalem* **Yeru Shalem**,
and *throughout* **to** all the *coasts*
regions of *Judaea* **Yah I-ludah**,
and *then* to the *Gentiles* **goyim**,
that they should repent and turn to *God* **Elohim**,
and *do* **transact** works *meet for* **worthy of** repentance.
21 For these causes the *Jews*
caught **Yah I-ludiym took** me
in the *temple* **priestal precinct**,
and *went about* **tried** to *kill* **thoroughly handle** me.
22 So Having *therefore* obtained
help of *God* **Elohim**,
I *continue* **stand** unto this day,
witnessing both to *small* **little** and *great* **mega**,
saying **wording** none other *things*
than *except* those which the prophets
and *Moses* **Mosheh**
did *say* **should come spoke of are about to become**:
23 That *Christ* **Whether the Messiah** should suffer,
and *that* **whether** he should be the first
that should rise from **the resurrection of** the dead,
and *should shew* **about to evangelize** light
unto the people, and to the *Gentiles* **goyim**.
24 And as he *thus spake* **pleaded these** for himself,
Festus **Phestus** said with a *loud* **mega** voice,
Paul **Paulos**, thou *art beside thyself* **ravest**;
much *learning* **scribing** doth make thee *mad* **maniacal**.
25 But he said, I am not *mad* **raving**,
most *noble Festus* **powerful Phestus**;
but *speak forth* **utter** the *words* **rhema** of truth
and *soberness* **soundmindedness**.

26 For the *king* **sovereign**
knoweth of **understandeth about** these *things*,
before whom also I speak *freely* **emboldened**:
for I am *persuaded* **convinced**
that none of these *things* are hidden from him;
for this *thing* was not *done* **transacted** in a corner.
27 *King* **Sovereign** Agrippa,
believest **trustest** thou the prophets? I
know that thou *believest* **trustest**.
28 *Then* **And** Agrippa said unto *Paul* **Paulos**,
Almost **In a little** thou *persuadest* **convincest**
me to *be* **become** a *Christian* **Messianist**.
29 And *Paul* **Paulos** said,
I *would* **should vow** to *God* **Elohim**,
that not only thou, but also all that hear me this day,
were both *almost* **become**
both in little, and *altogether* **in much**
such as **what sort** I am, except these bonds.
30 And when he had *thus spoken* **said these**,
the *king* **sovereign** rose *up*,
and the governor, and Bernice,
and they that sat with them:
31 And when they *were gone aside* **had withdrawn**,
they *talked between themselves* **spake to one another**,
saying **wording**,
This *man doeth nothing* **human transacteth naught**
worthy of death or of bonds.
32 Then said Agrippa unto *Festus* **Phestus**,
This *man might* **human could** have been
set at liberty **released**,
if he had not appealed **except that he called**
unto *Caesar* **the Kaisar**.

ON TO ROME

27 And when it was *determined* **judged**
that we should sail into Italy,
they delivered *Paul* **Paulos**
and *certain* **some** other prisoners unto one named Julius,
a centurion of *Augustus' band* **the venerable squad**.
— to whom I now apostolize you
18 to open their eyes
and to turn them from darkness to light;
and the authority of Satan to Elohim,
that they take forgiveness of sins:
and their lot
among them who are hallowed by their trust in me.
19 Whereupon, O Sovereign Agrippa,
I became not distrusting to the heavenly vision:
20 but evangelized first to them of Dammeseq
and at Yeru Shalem

and to all the regions of Yah Hudah
and to the goyim
— to repent and turn to Elohim
and transact works worthy of repentance.
21 For these causes
the Yah Hudiym took me in the priestal precinct
and tried to thoroughly handle me.
22 So having obtained help from Elohim,
I stand to this day
witnessing both to little and mega;
wording none other except those
of which the prophets and Mosheh spoke
which are about to become:
23 — whether the Messiah suffer
and whether he be the first
to rise from the resurrection of the dead;
and about to evangelize light
to the people and to the goyim.
24 And as he pleads these for himself,
Phestus says with a mega voice,
Paulos, you rave!
Much scribing makes you maniacal.
25 But he says, I rave not, most powerful Phestus;
but utter the rhema of truth and soundmindedness.
26 For the sovereign understands about these,
in front of whom I also speak emboldnened:
for I am convinced
that none of these are hidden from him;
for this is not transacted in a corner.
27 Sovereign Agrippa, trust you the prophets?
I know you trust!
28 And Agrippa says to Paulos,
In a little you convince me to become a Messianist.
29 And Paulos says,
I vow to Elohim,
that not only you, but also all who hear me this day,
become both, in little and in much,
what sort I am, except for these bonds.
30 And when he says these,
the sovereign and the governor and Bernice
and they who sit with them rise:
31 and they withdraw,
and speak to one another, wording,
This human transacted naught
worthy of death or of bonds.
32 And Agrippa says to Phestus,
This human could have been released,
except that he called to the Kaisar.

ON TO ROME

27 And when they judge us to sail to Italy,
they deliver Paulos and some other prisoners
to one named Julius
— a centurion of the venerable squad.
2 And *entering* **embarking**
into a *ship* **sailer** of Adramyttium,
we *launched* **embarked**,
meaning **about** to sail by the *coasts* **places** of Asia;
one Aristarchus,
a Macedonian of *Thessalonica* — **Thessalonikee**
being with us.
3 And *the next day* **on another**
we *touched at* **moored in** Sidon.
And Julius
courteously entreated Paul **supplied
philantrophy to Paulos**,
and *gave him liberty* **allowed him** to go unto his friends
to *refresh himself* **obtain their care**.
4 And when we had *launched*
embarked from thence,
we sailed under Cyprus,
because the winds were contrary.
5 And when we had sailed
over **through** the *sea* **deep** of Cilicia and Pamphylia,
we *came* **descended** to Myra, *a city* of *Lycia* **Loukia**.
6 And there the centurion
found a *ship* **sailer** of Alexandria sailing into Italy;
and he *put* **embarked** us *therein*.
7 And when we had sailed slowly many days,
and *scarce* **difficultly**
were come **being** over against Cnidus,
the wind not *suffering* **allowing** us,
we sailed under Crete, over against Salmone;
8 And, *hardly passing it* **difficultly sailing by**,
came unto a place which is called
The fair havens **Good Harbor**;
nigh whereunto was the city of Lasea.
9 *Now when* **And** much time
was spent **being past**,
and *when* sailing *was now* **already being** dangerous,
because the fast *was now* **being** already past,
Paul admonished **Paulos advised** them,
10 And *said* **worded** unto them, *Sirs* **Men**,
I *perceive* **observe** that this *voyage* **sailing**
will **is about to** be
with *hurt* **hubris** and much *damage* **loss**,
not only of the lading and *ship* **sailer**,
but also of our *lives* **souls**.

11   *Nevertheless* **But** the centurion
believed the master **had confidence of the pilot**
and the *owner of the* ship **captain**,
more **rather** than those *things*
which were *spoken* **worded** by *Paul* **Paulos**.
12   And *because* the *haven* **harbor**
was not commodious **being inconvenient** to winter in,
the more part **most of them**
advised to depart **placed counsel to embark** thence *also*,
if *by any means* **somehow**
they *might attain to Phenice* **could arrive in Phoinix**,
and there to winter;
which *is an haven* — **a harbor** of Crete,
and *lieth* **looketh**
toward the south west and north west.
13   And when the *south wind* **southerly**
blew softly **puffed gently**,
supposing **thinking** that they had
obtained **empowered** their *purpose* **prothesis**,
loosing thence, they sailed close by Crete.

The Storm On The Way

14   But not *long* **much** after
there *arose* **cast** against it a tempestuous wind,
called Euroclydon.
15   And when the *ship* **sailer** was caught,
and could not *bear up into* **eye against** the wind,
we *let her drive* **gave her up and were borne away**.
16   And *running under a certain*
sailing past some island
which is called Clauda,
we *had much work to come by the boat*
were difficultly able to become masters of the skiff:
17   Which when they had taken *up*,
they used helps, undergirding the *ship* **sailer**;
and, *fearing* **awing**
lest they should fall into the quicksands,
strake **lowered** sail, and *so* **thus** were *driven* **borne**.
18   And we being *exceedingly*
extremely tempest tossed
with a tempest,
2   And embarking in a sailer of Adramyttium,
we embark, about to sail by the places of Asia;
one Aristarchus — a Macedonian — a Thessalonikee
being with us.
3   And on another we moor in Sidon.
And Julius supplies philantrophy to Paulos
and allows him to go to his friends to obtain their care.
4   And embarking from there,
we sail under Cyprus,
because the winds are contrary:
5   and sailing through the deep
of Cilicia and Pamphylia,
we descend to Myra, of Loukia:
6   and there the centurion
finds a sailer of Alexandria sailing to Italy;
and he embarks us.
7   And sailing slowly many days, and difficultly,
being over against Cnidus
— the wind not allowing us,
we sail under Crete, over against Salmone;
8   and, difficultly sailing by,
come to a place called Good Harbor;
near the city of Lasea.
9   And much time being past,
and sailing already being dangerous,
because of the fast already being past,
Paulos advises them,
10   and words to them, Men,
I observe that this sailing
is about to be with hubris and much loss
— not only of the lading and sailer,
but also of our souls.
11   But the centurion
had the confidence of the pilot and the ship captain,
rather than those worded by Paulos.
12   And the harbor, being inconvenient to winter in,
most of them placed counsel to embark there,
if somehow they can arrive in Phoinix
— a harbor of Crete
that looks toward the south west and north west.
and to winter there.
13   And the southerly puffs gently;
and thinking they empower their prothesis,
loosing there, they sail close by Crete.

The Storm On The Way

14   But not much after
a tempestuous wind called Euroclydon
casts against it:
15   and the sailer is caught
and cannot eye against the wind;
and we give her up and are borne away.
16   And sailing past some island called Clauda,
we are able, difficultly,
to become masters of the skiff:
17   which, they take,
and using helps, undergird the sailer;
and awing, lest they fall into the quicksands,
lower sail, and thus are borne.

18 And we, being extremely tempest tossed,
the next *day* they *lightened the ship* **made an ejection**;
19 And the third *day*
we *cast* **tossed** out with our own hands
the tackling of the *ship* **sailer**.
20 And when neither sun nor stars
in many days appeared,
and no small *tempest* **downpour** lay on us,
all hope that we should be saved
was *then* **finally** taken away.
21 *But after long abstinence* **And there being much fasting**
Paul **Paulos then** stood *forth* in the midst of them,
and said, *Sirs* **O Men**,
ye **indeed**
should **needed to** have *hearkened unto* **first obeyed** me,
and not have *loosed* **embarked** from Crete,
and to have gained this *harm* **hubris** and loss.
22 And now I *exhort* **advise** you
to *be of good cheer* **cheer up**:
for there shall be no loss
of *any man's life among* **soul of** you,
but *except* of the *ship* **sailer**.
23 For there stood by me this night
the **an** angel of *God* **Elohim**,
whose I am, and whom I *serve* **liturgize**,
24 *Saying* **Wording**, *Fear* **Awe** not, *Paul* **Paulos**;
thou must be *brought* **presented**
before *Caesar* **in front of the Kaisar**:
and, *lo* **behold**,
God **Elohim** hath *given* **granted** thee **charism**
of all them that sail with thee.
25 *Wherefore* **So**, *sirs* **men**,
be *of good cheer* **cheer up**:
for I *believe God* **trust Elohim**,
that it shall be *even* **thus**
as it was told **in the manner it was spoken unto** me.
26 Howbeit
we must be *cast upon a certain island* **fall unto some isle**.
27 *But when* **And being** the
fourteenth night *was come*,
as we were *driven up and down* **borne** in Adria,
about midnight
the *shipmen deemed* **sailer crew surmised**
that they drew near to some *country* **region**;
28 And sounded, and found it twenty fathoms:
and when they had *gone* **passed through** a little further,
they sounded again, and found it fifteen fathoms.
29 *Then fearing* **And awing** lest somehow
we should have fallen *upon rocks* **unto jagged places**,
they *cast* **tossed** four anchors out of the stern,
and *wished for the* **vowed that it become** day.
30 And as the *shipmen* **sailer crew**
were about to flee out of the *ship* **sailer**,
when they had *let down* **lowered**
the *boat* **skiff** into the sea,
under *colour* **pretext** as though
they *would have cast* **were about to spread** anchors
out of the *foreship* **prow**,
31 *Paul* **Paulos**
said to the centurion and to the *soldiers* **warriors**,
Except **Unless** these abide in the *ship* **sailer**,
ye cannot be saved.
32 Then the *soldiers* **warriors**
cut off the ropes of the *boat* **skiff**,
and let her fall off.
33 And *while* **until** the day *was coming on* **became**,
Paul besought **Paulos entreated** them all
to *take meat* **partake nourishment**, *saying* **wording**,
This day is the fourteenth day that
ye have *tarried* **awaited**
and *continued* **thoroughy completed/shalamed** fasting,
having taken *nothing* **naught**.
34 *Wherefore* **So** I *pray* **beseech** you
to take *some meat* **nourishment**:
for this is for your *health* **salvation**:
for there shall not an hair fall from
the head of any of you.
35 And when he had *thus spoken* **said these**,
he took bread,
and *gave thanks* **eucharistized** to *God* **Elohim**
in *presence* **sight** of them all:
and when he had broken it, he began to eat.
they next make an ejection;
19 and third,
we toss out the tackling of the sailer
with our own hands.
20 And neither sun nor stars appear in many days,
and no small downpour lies on us,
and all hope to be saved is finally taken away.
21 And there being much fasting;
then Paulos stands in their midst, and says,
O Men, you indeed needed to have first obeyed me,
to not embark from Crete,
and to gain this hubris and loss:
22 and now I advise you to cheer up:
for there is no loss of your soul, except of the sailer.
23 For an angel of Elohim stood by me this night
— whose I am and whom I liturgize,
24 wording, Awe not, Paulos;

you must be presented in front of the Kaisar:
and behold, Elohim grants you charism
of all who sail with you.
25 So men, cheer up!
For I trust Elohim,
that so be it in the manner spoken to me.
26 However, we must fall to some isle.
27 And being the fourteenth night,
as we are borne in Adria, about midnight,
the sailer crew surmises
that they draw near to some region;
28 and sound; and find it twenty fathoms:
and when they pass through a little further, they
sound again; and find it fifteen fathoms.
29 And awing, lest somehow
we fall to jagged places,
they toss four anchors from the stern,
and vow that it become day.
30 And as the sailer crew is
about to flee from the sailer,
they lower the skiff into the sea,
under pretext
as though they are about to spread anchors
from the prow,
31 Paulos says to the centurion and to the warriors,
Unless these abide in the sailer, you cannot be saved.
32 So the warriors cut off the ropes of the skiff
and let her fall off.
33 And until day becomes,
Paulos entreats them all to partake nourishment,
wording, This day is the fourteenth day you await
and thoroughly complete/shalam fasting, taking naught.
34 So I beseech you to take nourishment:
for this is for your salvation:
for not a hair falls from the head of any of you.
35 And saying these,
he takes bread and eucharistizes to Elohim
in sight of them all:
and breaks and begins to eat.
36 *Then were* **And** they all *of*
good cheer **became cheered**,
and they also took *some meat* **nourishment**.
37 And we were in all in the *ship* **sailer**
two hundred
threescore and sixteen **and seventy and six** souls.
38 And when they had
eaten enough **gluttonized nourishment**,
they lightened the *ship* **sailer**,
and cast out the *wheat* **grain** into the sea.

39 And *when it was* **being** day,
they knew not the land:
but they *discovered a certain creek* **perceived some bay**
with a shore,
into the which they *were minded* **had counseled**,
if it were possible, to *thrust in* **propel** the *ship* **sailer**.
40 And when they had taken *up* the anchors,
they *committed themselves* **release** unto the sea,
and **simultaneously** loosed the rudder *bands* **tiller**,
and *hoised up* **lifted** the *mainsail* **foresail**
to the *wind* **puffing**,
and *made toward* **held unto** shore.
41 And falling into a place
where *of the* two seas *met*,
they ran the ship aground;
and the *forepart* **prow** *indeed* stuck *fast* **tight**,
and *remained* **abode** unmoveable,
but the *hinder part* **stern** was *broken* **loosed**
with **by** the violence of the waves.
42 And the *soldiers'* **warriors'** counsel
was **became** to *kill* **slaughter** the prisoners,
lest any of them should swim out, and *escape* **flee**.
43 But the centurion,
willing **having willed** to save *Paul* **Paulos**,
kept **forbad** them from their *purpose* **counsel**;
and *commanded* **summoned** that they which could swim
should cast *themselves* first *into the sea*,
and *get* **depart** to land:
44 And the rest, some **indeed** on boards,
and some on *broken pieces* **some** of the *ship* **sailer**.
And so **be** it *came to pass*,
that they *escaped all safe* **were saved** to land.

SAVED AT MELITA ISLAND

28 And *when they were escaped* **being saved**,
then they knew that the island was called Melita.
2 And the *barbarous people* **barbarians**
shewed **presented** us no *little* kindness
ordinary philantrophy:
for they *kindled* **lit** a fire, and received us every one,
because of the *present* rain **standing by**,
and because of the cold.

VIPER SEIZES THE HAND OF PAULOS

3 And when *Paul* **Paulos**
had *gathered* **tied** a *bundle* **multitude** of *sticks* **kindling**,
and *laid* **put** them on the fire,
there came a viper out of the heat,
and *fastened on* **seized** his hand.
4 And when the barbarians

saw the *venomous* beast hang *on* **from** his hand,
they *said* **worded** among *themselves* **one another**,
No doubt **Most certainly** this *man* **human** is a murderer,
whom, though he *hath escaped* **be saved from** the sea,
yet *vengeance suffereth* **judgment alloweth** not to live.

5   *And therefore* **So indeed**
he shook off the beast into the fire,
and *felt* **suffered** no *harm* **evil**.

6   Howbeit they *looked* **watched**
when he should *have swollen* **ought to be inflamed**,
or fallen down dead suddenly:
but after they had *looked a great while* **awaited much**,
and *saw no harm* **observed nought inordinate**
come to **become** him,
they changed their minds,
and *said* **worded** that he was *a god* **an El**.

Paulos Heals The Father Of Publius

7   *In the same quarters* **Around those places**
were *possessions* **parcels**
of the *chief* **preeminent** man of the island,
whose name was Publius; who *received* **entertained** us,
and lodged us three days courteously.

36   And they all become cheered
and they also take nourishment.

37   And we in the sailer
are two hundred and seventy—six souls in all.

38   And they gluttonize nourishment,
and they lighten the sailer
and cast the grain in the sea.

39   And being day, they know not the land:
and they perceive some bay with a shore,
into which, they counsel, if possible,
to propel the sailer.

40   And they take the anchors
and release to the sea;
and simultaneously loose the rudder tiller
and lift the foresail to the puffing
and hold toward shore.

41   And falling into a place of the two seas,
they run the ship aground;
and indeed the prow sticks tight
and abides unmoveable;
but the stern is loosed by the violence of the waves.

42   And the counsel of the warriors
is to slaughter the prisoners,
lest any of them swim out and flee.

43   But the centurion wills to save Paulos,
and forbids their counsel;
and summons those who can swim

44   to cast first and depart to land:
and the rest — some indeed on boards
and some on some of the sailer. And
so be it, they are saved to land.

Saved At Melita Island

28   And being saved,
they know the island is called Melita.

2   And the barbarians present us
no ordinary philantrophy:
for they light a fire and receive everyone of us
— because of the rain standing by
and because of the cold.

Viper Seizes The Hand Of Paulos

3   And Paulos ties a a multitude of kindling,
and puts them on the fire;
and a viper comes from the heat and seizes his hand.

4   And when the barbarians
see the beast hang from his hand,
they word among one another,
Most certainly this human is a murderer,
whom, though being saved from the sea,
yet judgment allows not to live.

5   So indeed he shakes off the beast into the fire
and suffers no evil.

6   But they watch for when he ought to inflame,
or suddenly fall down dead:
but after they await much
and observe nought inordinate become him,
they change their minds, and word that he is an El.

Paulos Heals The Father Of Publius

7   Around those places
are parcels of the preeminent man of the island,
whose name is Publius;
who entertains us,
and courteously lodges us three days.

8   And **so be** it *came to pass*,
that the father of Publius *lay sick of* **was held by** a fever
and of *a bloody flux* **dysentery**:
to whom *Paul* **Paulos** entered *in*, and prayed,
and *laid* **put** his hands on him, and healed him.

9   So when this *was done* **became**,
others also **the rest**,
which had *diseases* **frailties** in the island,
came, and were *healed* **cured**:

10   Who also honoured us with many honours;
and when we *departed* **embarked**,
they *laded* **put** us with such *things*

as were *necessary* **needed**.
11 And after three months
we *departed* **embarked** in a *ship* **sailer** of Alexandria,
which had wintered in the isle,
whose sign was *Castor and Pollux* **Dioscuri**.
12 And *landing* **mooring** at Syracuse,
we *tarried* **abode** there three days.
13 And from thence
we *fetched a compass* **wandered around**,
and *came to* **arrived in** Rhegium:
and after one day
the *south wind blew up* **southerly sprung**,
and we came *the next day* to Puteoli:
14 Where we found brethren,
and were *desired* **besought**
to *tarry with* **abide among** them seven days:
and *so* **thus** we went *toward* **unto** Rome.
15 And from thence,
when the brethren heard *of* **concerning** us,
they came to meet us
as far as Appii forum, and The three taverns:
whom when *Paul* **Paulos** saw,
he *thanked God* **eucharistized
Elohim**, and took courage.

Paulos Comes To Rome

16 And when we came to Rome,
the centurion delivered the prisoners
to the *captain of the guard* **arch warrior**:
but *Paul* **Paulos**
was *suffered* **allowed** to *dwell* **abide** by himself
with a *soldier* **warrior** that *kept* **guarded** him.

Paulos Witnesses To The Yah Hudiym

17 And *so be* it *came to pass*, that after three days
Paul **Paulos** called the *chief* **preeminent**
of the *Jews* **Yah Hudiym** together:
and when they were come together,
he *said* **worded** unto them, Men and brethren,
though I have *committed nothing* **done naught**
against the people, or customs of our fathers,
yet was I delivered prisoner from *Jerusalem* **Yeru Shalem**
into the hands of the Romans.
18 Who, when they had examined me,
would have let me go **had willed to release me**,
because there was no cause of death in me.
19 But when the *Jews* **Yah Hudiym**
spake against it **contradicted**,
I was *constrained* **compelled**
to *appeal* **call** unto *Caesar* **the Kaisar**;

not that I had *ought* **somewhat** to
accuse my *nation of* **goyim**.
20 *For* **So for** this cause *therefore*
have I *called for* **besought** you,
to see you, and to speak with you:
because **indeed**,
that for **sake of** the hope of *Israel* **Yisra El**
I am bound with this chain **this fetter hangs around me**.
21 And they said unto him,
We neither received *letters* **scribings**
out of *Judaea* **Yah Hudah** concerning thee,
neither any of the brethren that
came *shewed* **evangelized**
or spake any *harm of* **evil concerning** thee.
22 But we desire to hear of thee what thou thinkest:
for **indeed** as concerning this *sect*
heresy, we know that every where
it is *spoken against* **contradicted**.
23 And when they had *appointed*
ordained him a day,
8 And so be it,
the father of Publius is held by a fever and dysentery
— to whom Paulos enters and prays
and puts his hands on him and heals him.
9 So when this becomes,
the rest in the island, who have frailties,
come and are cured;
10 who also honor us with many honors:
and when we embark,
they put us with such as are needed.
11 And after three months
we embark in a sailer of Alexandria
which wintered in the isle
— whose sign is Dioscuri:
12 and mooring at Syracuse,
we abide there three days:
13 and from there, we wander around,
and arrive in Rhegium:
and after one day, the southerly springs forth,
and next we come to Puteoli:
14 where we find brothers,
who beseech us to abide among them seven days:
and thus we go to Rome:
15 and from there,
when the brothers hear concerning us,
they come to meet us
as far as Appii Forum and The Three Taverns
— whom when Paulos sees,
he eucharistizes Elohim and takes courage.

Paulos Comes To Rome

16 And when we come to Rome,
the centurion delivers the prisoners
to the arch warrior:
but allows Paulos to abide by himself
with a warrior to guard him.

Paulos Witnesses To The Yah Hudiym

17 And so be it, after three days,
Paulos calls together
the preeminent of the Yah Hudiym:
and when they come together,
he words to them, Men and brothers,
though I have done naught against the people
or customs of our fathers,
yet I am delivered — a prisoner from Yeru Shalem
into the hands of the Romans:
18 who, when they examined me,
willed to release me,
because there is no cause of death in me.
19 And when the Yah Hudiym contradicted,
I was compelled to call to the Kaisar
— not that I had somewhat to accuse my goyim.
20 So for this cause I beseech you,
to see you and to speak with you:
indeed, that for sake of the hope of Yisra El,
this fetter hangs around me.
21 And they say to him,
We neither received scribings
from Yah Hudah concerning you;
nor any of the brothers who came
evangelized or spoke any evil concerning you.
22 But we desire to hear from you, what you think:
for indeed as concerning this heresy,
we know it is contradicted every where.
23 And they ordain him a day;
there came many to him into his lodging;
to whom he expounded and *testified* **witnessed**
the *kingdom* **sovereigndom** of *God* **Elohim**,
persuading **convincing** them concerning *Jesus* **Yah Shua**,
both out of the *law* **torah** of *Moses* **Mosheh**,
and out of the prophets, from **early** morning till evening.
24 And some *believed* **indeed confided**
the things **in those** which were *spoken* **worded**,
and some *believed not* **distrusted**.

Paulos Turns From The Yah Hudiym

25 And *when they agreed not* **disagreeing**
among themselves **with one another**,
they *departed* **released**,
after that *Paul* **Paulos** had spoken one *word* **rhema**,
Well spake the *Holy Spirit* **Ruach ha-kodesh**
by Esaias **through Yesha Yah** the prophet
unto our fathers,
26 *Saying* **Wording**, Go unto this people, and say,
Hearing ye shall hear,
and shall not *understand* **no way comprehend**;
and seeing ye shall see, and not *perceive* **no way see**:
27 For the heart of this people
is *waxed gross* **calloused**,
and their ears *are dull* **burdensome** of hearing,
and their eyes have they *closed* **shut**;
lest *ever* they should see with their eyes,
and hear with their ears,
and *understand* **comprehend** with their heart,
and should *be converted* **turn around**,
and I should heal them.
Yesha Yah 6:9,10

The Salvation Of Elohim Is Apostolized To The Goyim

28 So Be it known *therefore* unto you,
that the salvation of *God* **Elohim**
is *sent* **apostolized** unto the *Gentiles* **goyim**,
and that they *will* **shall** hear it.
29 And when he had said these words,
the *Jews* **Yah Hudiym** departed,
and had *great reasoning* **much disputation**
among themselves.

Paulos Preaches And Doctrinates The Sovereigndom Of Elohim And Adonay Yah Shua Messiah

30 And *Paul dwelt* **Paulos abode** two whole years
in his own *hired house* **rental**,
and received all that *came in* **entered** unto him,
31 Preaching the *kingdom*
sovereigndom of *God* **Elohim**,
and *teaching* **doctrinating** those *things*
which concern
the *Lord Jesus Christ* **Adonay Yah Shua Messiah**,
with all *confidence* **boldness**,
no man forbidding him **unhindered**.
and many come to him into his lodging;
to whom he expounds and witnesses
the sovereigndom of Elohim,
convincing them concerning Yah Shua,
both from the torah of Mosheh and from the prophets
from early morning until evening.

ACTS 28

24   And some indeed confide
in those that are worded
— and some distrust.

Paulos Turns From The Yah Hudiym

25   And disagreeing with one another,
they release after Paulos speaks one rhema,
Well spoke the Holy Spirit
through Yesha Yah the prophet,
to our fathers,
26   wording, Go to this people, and say,
Hearing you hear, and no way comprehend;
and seeing you see, and no way see:
27   for the heart of this people calloused,
and their ears burdensome of hearing,
and they shut their eyes;
lest ever they see with their eyes
and hear with their ears
and comprehend with their heart
and turn around
— and I heal them.
Yesha Yah 6:9,10

The Salvation Of Elohim Is Apostolized To The Goyim

28   So be it known to you,
that the salvation of Elohim is apostolized to the goyim;
and they hear it.
29   And saying these words,
the Yah Hudiym depart,
having much disputation among themselves.

Paulos Preaches And Doctrinates The Sovereigndom Of Elohim And Adonay Yah Shua Messiah

30   And Paulos abides two whole years
in his own rental,
and receives all who enter to him,
31   preaching the sovereigndom of Elohim,
and doctrinating those
concerning Adonay Yah Shua Messiah
with all boldness — unhindered.

VOLUME SIX
EPISTLES

ROMANS 1

SALUTATION

1 *Paul* **Paulos**,
a servant of *Jesus Christ* **Yah Shua Messiah**,
a called *to be an* apostle,
separated **set apart**
unto the *gospel* **evangelism** of *God* **Elohim**,

2 (Which he had *promised*
afore **pre—evangelized**
by **through** his prophets in the holy scriptures,)

3 Concerning his Son *Jesus Christ* **Yah Shua Messiah**
our *Lord* **Adonay**,
which *was made* **became** of the *seed* **sperma** of David
according to the flesh;

4 And *declared to be* **decreed**
the Son of *God* **Elohim**
with power **in dynamis**,
according to the spirit of holiness,
by the resurrection from the dead:

5 *By* **Through** whom
we have *received grace* **taken charism** and apostleship,
for **unto** obedience *to* **of** the *faith* **trust**
among all *nations* **goyim**, for his name:

6 Among whom are ye also
the called of *Jesus Christ* **Yah Shua Messiah**:

7 To all that be in Rome,
beloved of *God* **Elohim**, called *to be saints* **holy**:
Grace **Charism** to you and *peace* **shalom**
from *God* **Elohim** our Father,
and *the Lord Jesus Christ* **Adonay Yah Shua Messiah**.

8 First **indeed**, I *thank*
eucharistize my *God* **Elohim**
through *Jesus Christ* **Yah Shua Messiah** for you all,
that your *faith* **trust** is *spoken of* **evangelized**
throughout **in** the whole *world* **cosmos**.

PAULOS DESIRES TO VISIT ROME

9 For *God* **Elohim** is my witness,
whom I *serve with* **liturgize in** my spirit
in the *gospel* **evangelism** of his Son,
that without ceasing **as unceasingly**
I make *mention* **remembrance** of you
always in my prayers;

10 *Making request* **Petitioning**,
if *by any means now at length* **somehow ever**
I might *have a prosperous journey* **prosper**
by **in** the will of *God* **Elohim** to come unto you.

SPIRITUAL CHARISMA

11 For I *long* **yearn** to see you,
that I may impart unto you some spiritual *gift* **charisma**,
to *the end ye may be established* **establish you**;

12 That is, that I may be
comforted **consoled** together
with **in** you
by **through** the *mutual faith* **trust in one another**
both of you and me — **yours and mine**.

13 Now I *would* **will**
not have you ignorant **that you not
be unknowing**, brethren,
that *oftentimes* **often**
I *purposed* **predetermined** to come unto you,
(but was *let* **forbidden** hitherto,)
that I might have some fruit among you also,
even **exactly** as among *other Gentiles*
the rest of the goyim.

14 I am debtor
both to the *Greeks* **Hellenes**, and to the Barbarians;
both to the wise, and to the *unwise* **mindless**.

15 *So* **Thus**, as much as in me is,
I am *ready* **eager** to *preach the gospel* **evangelize**
to you that are at Rome also.

THE DYNAMIS OF THE EVANGELISM

16 For I am not ashamed
of the *gospel* **evangelism** of *Christ* **Messiah**:
for it is the *power* **dynamis** of *God*
Elohim unto salvation
to every one that *believeth* **trusteth**;
both to the *Jew* **Yah Hudiy** first,
and also to the *Greek* **Hellene**.

17 For therein
is the *righteousness* **justness** of *God*
revealed **Elohim unveiled**
from *faith* **trust** to *faith* **trust**:
exactly as *it is written* **scribed**,
The just shall live by *faith* **trust**.
Habakkuk 2:4

IRREVERENCE AND INJUSTICE

18 For the wrath of *God* **Elohim**
is *revealed* **unveiled** from *heaven* **the heavens**

SALUTATION

1 Paulos, a servant of Yah Shua Messiah;
a called apostle
set apart to the evangelism of Elohim;

2 which he pre—evangelized
through his prophets in the holy scriptures;
3 concerning his Son Yah
Shua Messiah our Adonay;
who, as to flesh,
became of the sperma of David;
4 and, as to spirit, of holiness
the decreed the Son of Elohim in dynamis
by the resurrection from the dead:
5 through whom we take charism and apostleship
to obedience of the trust
among all goyim for his name:
6 among whom you are also
the called of Yah Shua Messiah:
7 To all in Rome,
beloved of Elohim, called holy:
charism and shalom to you
from Elohim our Father
and Adonay Yah Shua Messiah.
8 First indeed, I eucharistize my Elohim
through Yah Shua Messiah for you all,
that your trust is evangelized in the whole cosmos.

Paulos Desires To Visit Rome

9 For Elohim is my witness
— whom I liturgize in my spirit
in the evangelism of his Son;
as unceasingly
I make remembrance of you always in my prayers;
10 petitioning,
whenever I prosper in the will of Elohim
to come unto you.

Spiritual Charisma

11 For I yearn to see you,
to impart some spiritual charisma to you
to establish you;
12 that is, to be consoled together in you
through the trust in one another — yours and mine.
13 And I will that you not be unknowing, brothers,
that I often predetermined to come to you;
— but was forbidden until now
that I also have some fruit among you,
exactly as among the rest of the goyim.
14 I am debtor
both to the Hellenes and to the Barbarians;
both to the wise and to the mindless.
15 Thus, as much as in me is,
I am also eager to evangelize to you
who are at Rome.

The Dynamis Of The Evangelism

16 For I am not ashamed
of the evangelism of Messiah:
for it is the dynamis of Elohim to salvation
to everyone who trusts
— both to the Yah Hudiy first and also to the Hellene.
17 For therein is the justness of Elohim unveiled
from trust to trust:
exactly as scribed,
The just live by trust.
Habakkuk 2:4

Irreverence And Injustice

18 For the wrath of Elohim
is unveiled from the heavens

against all *ungodliness* **irreverence**
and *unrighteousness* **injustice** of *men* **humanity**,
who hold the truth in *unrighteousness* **injustice**;
19 Because that which may
be known of *God* **Elohim**
is manifest in them;
for *God* **Elohim** hath *shewed* **manifested** it unto them.
20 For *the invisible things of him* **his invisibles**
from the creation of the *world* **cosmos** are clearly seen,
being *understood* **comprehended**
by *the things that are made* **his doings**,
even **both** his eternal *power* **dynamis**
and *Godhead* **Divinity**;
so that they are *without excuse* **inexcusable**:
21 Because that, when they knew *God* **Elohim**,
they glorified him not as *God* **Elohim**,
neither *were thankful* **eucharistized**;
but became vain in their *imaginations* **reasonings**,
and their *foolish* **uncomprehending** heart was darkened.
22 Professing themselves to be wise,
they became fools,
23 And changed the glory
of the uncorruptible *God* **Elohim**
into an *image* **icon**
made like **likened** to corruptible *man* **humanity**,
and to *birds* **flyers**, and *fourfooted beasts* **quadrupeds**,
and *creeping things* **creepers**.
24 Wherefore *God* **Elohim** also
gave **surrendered** them *up* to *uncleanness* **impurity**
through **in** the *lusts* **pantings** of their own hearts,
to dishonour their own bodies
between **among** themselves:

ROMANS 1

25   Who *changed* **exchanged**
the truth of *God* **Elohim**
into a lie,
and *worshipped* **venerated** and *served* **liturgized**
the creature *more than* **beyond** the Creator,
who is *blessed for ever* **eulogized unto the eons**.
Amen.

HOMOSEXUALITY

26   For this cause
God gave **Elohim surrendered** them *up*
unto *vile affections* **dishonourable passions**:
for *even* **both** their *women* **females**
did change **exchanged** the *natural use* **physical function**
into that which is against nature:
27   And likewise also the *men* **males**,
leaving **forsaking** the *natural use* **physical function**
of the *woman* **female**,
burned **inflamed** in their *lust*
craving one toward another;
men with men **males among males**
working *that which is unseemly* **misbehaviour**,
and *receiving in* **taking unto** themselves
that *recompence* **retribution** of their *error* **seduction**
which was *meet* **necessary**.
28   And *even* **exactly** as they did not *like* **approve**
to *retain God* **regard Elohim** in *their* knowledge,
God gave **Elohim surrendered** them *over*
to a *reprobate* **disapproved** mind,
to do those *things* which are not *convenient* **becoming**;
29   Being filled with all *unrighteousness* **injustice**,
fornication **whoredom**, *wickedness* **evil**,
covetousness **avarice**, maliciousness;
full of envy, murder, *debate* **contention**,
deceit, *malignity* **mischievousness**; whisperers,
30   *Backbiters* **Slanderers**, *haters
of God* **Elohim—haters**,
despiteful **insulters**, proud, *boasters*
braggarts, inventors of evil *things*,
disobedient **distrusting** to parents,
31   *Without understanding* **Uncomprehending**,
covenantbreakers **uncovenanted**,
without natural affection **selfish**,
implacable **disagreeable**, unmerciful:
32   Who knowing the judgment of *God* **Elohim**,
that they which *commit* **transact** such *things*
are worthy of death,
not only do the same,
but *have pleasure in* **think well of** them
that *do* **transact** them.

against all irreverence and injustice of humanity
who hold the truth in injustice;
19   because what is known of Elohim
is manifest in them;
for Elohim manifests to them.
20   For his invisibles
from the creation of the cosmos are clearly seen
being comprehended by his doings
— both his eternal dynamis and divinity;
so that they are inexcusable:
21   because when they knew Elohim
they neither glorified him as Elohim,
nor eucharistized;
but became vain in their reasonings
and darkened their uncomprehending heart:
22   professing themselves to be wise
they became fools;
23   and changed the glory of
the uncorruptible Elohim
into an icon likened to corruptible humanity
and to flyers and quadrupeds and creepers.
24   So Elohim also surrendered them to impurity
in the pantings of their own hearts,
to dishonor their own bodies among themselves:
25   who exchanged the truth of Elohim into a lie
and venerated and liturgized the creature
beyond the Creator — who is eulogized to the eons.
Amen.

HOMOSEXUALITY

26   For this cause
Elohim surrendered them to dishonorable passions:
for both their females
exchanged the physical function
to that against nature:
27   and likewise also the males
forsaking the physical function of the female;
inflamed in their craving one toward another;
males among males working misbehavior;
and taking to themselves
that retribution of their seduction which is necessary.
28   And exactly as they approve
to not regard Elohim in knowledge,
Elohim surrenders them to a disapproved mind,
to do what is not becoming;
29   being filled with all injustice,
whoredom,
evil,
avarice,
maliciousness;

full of envy,
murder,
contention,
deceit,
mischievousness,
whisperers,
30 slanderers,
Elohim—haters,
insulters,
proud,
braggarts,
inventors of evil,
distrusting to parents,
31 uncomprehending,
uncovenanted,
selfish,
disagreeable,
unmercied:
32 who, knowing the judgment of Elohim,
that they, who transact such are worthy of death,
not only do the same
but think well of them who transact them.

THE JUST JUDGMENT OF ELOHIM THE JUST JUDGMENT

2 Therefore thou art inexcusable,
O *man* **humanity**,
whosoever thou art that judgest:
for wherein thou judgest another,
thou condemnest thyself;
for thou that judgest *doest* **transactest** the same *things*.
2 But we *are sure* **perceive**
that the judgment of *God* **Elohim** is according to truth
against them which *commit* **transact** such *things*.
3 And *thinkest* **reckonest**
thou this, O *man* **humanity**,
that judgest them which *do* **transact** such *things*,
and doest the same,
that thou shalt escape the judgment of *God* **Elohim**?
4 Or *despisest* **disesteemest** thou
the riches of his *goodness* **kindness**
and *forbearance* **tolerance** and *longsuffering* **patience**;
not knowing that the *goodness* **kindness** of *God* **Elohim**
leadeth thee to repentance?
5 But after thy hardness and
impenitent **unrepentant** heart
treasurest up unto thyself wrath
against **in** the day of wrath and *revelation* **apocalypse**
of the *righteous* **just** judgment of *God* **Elohim**;

6 Who *will render* **shall give**
back to *every man* **each**
according to his *deeds* **works**:
7 To them who **indeed**
by *patient continuance* **endurance**
in *well doing* **good works**
seek for glory and honour
and *immortality* **incorruptibility**, eternal life:
8 But unto them that are *contentious* **rivalrous**,
and *do not obey* **indeed distrust** the truth,
but obey *unrighteousness* **injustice**,
indignation **fury**, and wrath,
9 Tribulation and *anguish* **distress**,
upon every soul of *man doeth* **humanity**
that worketh evil,
both of the *Jew* **Yah Hudiy** first,
and also of the *Gentile* **Hellene**;
10 But glory, honour, and *peace* **shalom**,
to every *man* **one** that worketh good,
both to the *Jew* **Yah Hudiy** first,
and also to the *Gentile* **Hellene**:
11 For there is no *respect of persons* **partiality**
with *God* **Elohim**.
12 For as many as have sinned without *law* **torah**
shall also *perish* **destruct** without *law* **torah**:
and as many as have sinned in *the law* **torah**
shall be judged *by the law* **through torah**;
13 (For not the hearers of the *law* **torah**
are just *before God* **with Elohim**,
but the doers of the *law* **torah** shall be justified.
14 For when the *Gentiles* **goyim**,
which have not the *law* **torah**,
do by nature *the things* **those** contained in the *law* **torah**,
these, having not the *law* **torah**,
are a *law* **torah** unto themselves:
15 Which *shew* **indicate** the work of the *law* **torah**
written **scribed** in their hearts,
their conscience also *bearing witness* **co—witnessing**,
and their *thoughts* **logic** *the mean while* accusing
or else *excusing* **pleading between** one another;)
16 In the day when *God* **Elohim**
shall judge the secrets of *men* **humanity**
by Jesus Christ **through Yah Shua Messiah**
according to my *gospel* **evangelism**.

THE YAH HUDIY AND THE TORAH

17 Behold, thou art *called a Jew* **named Yah Hudiy**,
and *restest* **reposest** in the *law* **torah**,
and makest thy boast *of God* **in Elohim**,
18 And knowest his will,

        and approvest *the things* **those**
        that *are more excellent* **thoroughly surpass**,
        being *instructed* **catechized** out of the *law* **torah**;

19   And art confident
        that thou thyself art a guide of the blind, a
        light of them which are in darkness,

20   *An instructor* **A pedagogue**
        of the *foolish* **thoughtless**,
        a *teacher* **doctor** of babes,
        which hast the form of knowledge
        and of the truth in the *law* **torah**.

2   So you are inexcusable, O humanity
        — all who judge:
        for wherein you judge another,
        you condemn yourself;
        for you who judge transact the same.

2   And we perceive
        that the judgment of Elohim is according to truth
        against them who transact such.

3   And reckon this, O humanity,
        who judges them who transact such
        and do the same,
        that you escape the judgment of Elohim?

4   Or disesteem you the riches of his kindness
        and tolerance and patience;
        not knowing that the kindness of Elohim
        leads you to repentance?

5   But according to your hardness
        and unrepentant heart
        you treasure to yourself wrath
        in the day of wrath and apocalypse
        of the just judgment of Elohim;

6   who gives back to each according to his works:

7   to them indeed, who by
        endurance in good works,
        seek for glory and honor
        and incorruptibility — eternal life:

8   but to the rivalrous
        who indeed distrust the truth
        but obey injustice, fury and wrath,

9   tribulation and distress
        upon every soul of humanity who works evil
  — both of the Yah Hudiy first and also of the Hellene;

10   and glory, honor and shalom,
        to everyone who works good
  — both to the Yah Hudiy first and also to the Hellene:

11   for there is no partiality with Elohim.

12   For as many as sin without torah
        also destruct without torah: and as many as
        sin in torah are judged through torah;

13   for not the hearers of the
        torah are just with Elohim,
        but the doers of the torah are justified.

14   For when the goyim who have not the torah
        do by nature those contained in the torah,
        these, not having the torah, are a torah to themselves:

15   which indicates the work of the torah
        scribed in their hearts;
        their conscience also co—witnessing
        and their logic accusing
        or else pleading between one another;

16   in the day Elohim judges
        the secrets of humanity
        through Yah Shua Messiah
        according to my evangelism.

The Yah Hudiy And The Torah

17   Behold, you are named Yah Hudiy
        and repose in the torah
        and make your boast in Elohim,

18   and know his will
        and approve those that thoroughly surpass,
        being catechized from the torah;

19   and are confident
        that you yourself are a guide of the blind
        — a light of them in darkness,

20   a pedagogue of the thoughtless,
        a doctor of babes
        having the form of knowledge
        and of the truth in the torah.

21   Thou therefore which
        teachest **doctrinatest** another,
        teachest **doctrinatest** thou not thyself?
  thou that preachest, *a man should not steal* **Steal not**,
        dost thou steal **stealest thou**?

22   Thou that *sayest* **wordest**,
        a man should not commit adultery
        Thou shalt not adulterize,
        dost thou *commit adultery* **adulterize**?
        thou that abhorrest idols,
  dost thou *commit sacrilege* **strip priestal precincts**?

23   Thou that makest thy boast *of the law* **in torah**,
        through *breaking* **transgressing** the *law*
        torah dishonourest thou *God* **Elohim**?

24   For the name of *God* **Elohim**
  is blasphemed among the *Gentiles* **goyim** through you,
        exactly as *it is written* **scribed**.

25   For circumcision *verily*
        profiteth **indeed benefiteth**,
    if **whenever** thou *keep* **transact** the *law* **torah**:

but *if* whenever thou *be a breaker of*
transgress the *law* **torah**,
thy circumcision is *made* **become** uncircumcision.

26 Therefore *if* **whenever** the uncircumcision
keep **guard** the *righteousness* **judgment** of the *law* **torah**,
shall not *indeed* his uncircumcision
be *counted for* **reckoned unto** circumcision?

27 And *shall not* uncircumcision
which is by nature,
if it fulfill **fulfilling/shalaming**
the *law* **torah**, judge thee,
who *by* **through** the *letter* **scribing** and circumcision
dost transgress the *law* **torah**?

28 For he is not *a Jew* **Yah Hudiy**,
which is one *outwardly* **in manifestation**;
neither *is that* circumcision,
which is *outward* **in manifestation** in the flesh:

29 But he is *a Jew* **Yah Hudiy**,
which is one *inwardly* **in the secrets**;
and circumcision is that of the heart, in the spirit,
and not in the *letter* **scribing**;
whose *praise* **halal** is not of *men* **humanity**,
but of *God* **Elohim**.

THE SUPERABUNDANCE OF THE YAH HUDIY

3 What *advantage* **superabundance** then
hath the *Jew* **Yah Hudiy**?
or what *profit* **benefit** *is there* of circumcision?

2 Much every *way* **manner**: *chiefly* **first** indeed,
because that unto them
were *committed* **entrusted** the oracles of *God* **Elohim**.

3 For what if some *did not believe* **distrusted**?
shall their *unbelief* **distrust**
make the faith of God without effect
inactivate the trust of Elohim?

4 *God forbid* **So be it not**:
yea, let *God* **Elohim** be true, but
every *man* **human** a liar;
exactly as *it is written* **scribed**,
That *ever* thou mightest be justified
in thy *sayings* **words**,
and mightest *overcome* **triumph**
when thou art **in being** judged.
Psalm 51:4

OUR UNJUSTNESS

5 But if our *unrighteousness* **unjustness**
commend the *righteousness* **justness** of *God* **Elohim**,
what shall we say?
Is *God unrighteous* **Elohim unjust**
who *taketh vengeance* **bringeth wrath**?
(I *speak* **word** as a *man* **human**)

6 *God forbid* **So be it not**:
for then **otherwise**
how shall *God* **Elohim** judge the *world* **cosmos**?

7 For if the truth of *God* **Elohim**
hath more abounded through **superaboundeth in** my lie
unto his glory;
why yet am I also judged as a sinner?

8 And not *rather*,
(**exactly** as we be *slanderously reported* **blasphemed**,
and **exactly** as some *affirm* **say** that we *say* **word**,)
Let us do evil, that good may come?
whose *damnation* **judgment** is just.

9 What then? *are* **excel** we *better than they*?
No, *in no wise* **most certainly not**:
for we have *before proved* **previously accused**
both *Jews* **Yah Hudiym** and *Gentiles* **Hellenes**,
that they are all under sin;

21 So you who doctrinate another,
doctrinate you not yourself?
You who preach, Steal not, you — steal?

22 You who word, Adulterize
not, you — adulterize?
You who abhor idols, you — strip priestal precincts?

23 You who boast in torah,
through transgressing the torah
dishonor you Elohim?

24 For through you
the name of Elohim is blasphemed among the goyim
exactly as scribed.

25 For circumcision indeed benefits,
whenever you transact the torah:
but whenever you transgress the torah,
your circumcision becomes uncircumcision.

26 So whenever the uncircumcision
guards the judgment of the torah,
is not indeed his uncircumcision
reckoned to circumcision?

27 And uncircumcision,
by nature fulfilling/shalaming the torah,
judges you,
who through the scribing and circumcision
transgress the torah.

28 For he is not a Yah Hudiy, manifestly;
nor circumcision in the flesh, manifestly:

29 But he is a Yah Hudiy, in the secrets;
and circumcision is of heart
— in spirit and not in scribing;
whose halal is not of humanity, but of Elohim.

ROMANS 3

The Superabundance Of The Yah Hudiy

3 So what superabundance has the Yah Hudiy?
Or what *is the* benefit of circumcision?
2 Much every manner:
first indeed,
because the oracles of Elohim were entrusted to them.
3 So what if some distrusted?
does their distrust inactivate the trust of Elohim?
4 So be it not:
yes — so be it: Elohim is true and every human a liar;
exactly as scribed,
That you ever be justified in your words
and triumph in being judged.
Psalm 51:4

Our Unjustness

5 But if our unjustness
commends the justness of Elohim,
what say we?
Is Elohim, who brings wrath, unjust?
I word as a human.
6 So be it not:
otherwise how judges Elohim the cosmos?
7 For if the truth of Elohim
superabounds to his glory
in my lie;
why am I yet also judged as a sinner?
8 And not, exactly as we are blasphemed,
and exactly as some say that we word,
Do evil, so that good comes?
— whose judgment is just.
9 So what? Excel we?
No, most certainly not:
for we previously accused
both Yah Hudiym and Hellenes,
that they are all under sin;
10 **Exactly** As *it is written* **scribed**,
There is none *righteous* **just**, *no,* not **even** one:
11 There is none that
understandeth **comprehendeth**,
there is none that seeketh after *God* **Elohim**.
12 They are all *gone out of the way* **deviated**,
they are *together* **simultaneously**
become unprofitable **useless**;
there is none that doeth *good* **kindness**,
no, not **even** one. Psalm 14:1–3
13 Their *throat* **larynx** is an open *sepulchre* **tomb**;
with their tongues they have *used deceit* **deceived**;
the *poison* **venom** of asps is under their lips:
14 Whose mouth is full of cursing and bitterness:
15 Their feet are *swift* **sharp** to *shed* **pour** blood:
16 *Destruction* **Crushing** and
misery are in their ways:
17 And the way of *peace* **shalom**
have they not known:
18 There is no *fear* **awe** of *God* **Elohim**
before **in front of** their eyes.
Psalms 5:9, 10:7, 36:1, 140:3, Yesha Yah 59:7,8
19 Now we know that
what things soever **as much as** the
law saith **torah wordeth**,
it *saith* **speaketh** to them who are
under **in** the *law* **torah**:
that every mouth may be *stopped* **sealed**,
and all the *world* **cosmos**
may become *guilty* **under judgment**
before God **in front of Elohim**.
20 *Therefore* **Because** by the
deeds **works** of the *law* **torah**
there shall *no* **not any** flesh be justified in his sight:
for *by* **through** the *law* **torah** is the knowledge of sin.

Justness Through Trust

21 But now the *righteousness* **justness** of *God* **Elohim**
without **apart from** the *law* **torah** is manifested,
being witnessed by the *law* **torah** and the prophets;
22 Even the *righteousness* **justness** of *God* **Elohim**
which is *by faith* **through trust**
of *Jesus Christ* **Yah Shua Messiah**
unto all and upon all them that *believe* **trust**:
for there is no *difference* **distinction**:
23 For all have sinned,
and *come short of* **failed** the glory of *God* **Elohim**;
24 Being justified *freely*
gratuitously by his *grace* **charism**
through the redemption
that is in *Christ Jesus* **Messiah Yah Shua**:
25 Whom *God* **Elohim** hath
set forth **predetermined**
to be *a propitiation* **a kapporeth/an atonement**
through *faith* **trust** in his blood,
to *declare* **indicate** his *righteousness* **justness**
for the *remission* **passing over** of sins
that *are past* **have previously transpired**,
through **in** the *forbearance* **tolerance** of *God* **Elohim**;
26 To *declare, I say* **indicate**,
at this time **in this present season**
unto his *righteousness* **justness**:
that he might be just,

and *the justifier of* **justifying** him
which believeth **by trust** in *Jesus* **Yah Shua**.
27 Where is boasting then? It is excluded.
By **Through** what *law* **torah**? of works?
Nay **indeed**: but *by* **through** the *law* **torah** of *faith* **trust**.
28 Therefore we *conclude* **reckon**
that a *man* **human** is justified by *faith* **trust**
without **apart from** the *deeds* **works** of the *law* **torah**.
29 *Or* Is he the *God* **Elohim**
of the *Jews* **Yah Hudiym** only?
is he **indeed** not also of the *Gentiles* **goyim**?
Yes, of the *Gentiles* **goyim** also:
30 *Seeing* **Since** it is one *God* **Elohim**,
which shall justify the circumcision by *faith* **trust**,
and uncircumcision through *faith* **trust**.
31 Do we then *make void* **inactivate** the *law* **torah**
through *faith* **trust**?
God forbid **So be it not**:
yea **rather**, we *establish* **set** the *law* **torah**.

The Justness Of Abraham

4 What shall we say then
that Abraham our father,
as pertaining to the flesh, hath found?
2 For if Abraham were justified by works,
he hath whereof to *glory* **boast**;
but not *before God* **toward Elohim**.
10 Exactly as scribed,
None is just — not even one:
11 none comprehend — none seek after Elohim.
12 They all deviate — simultaneously useless;
none doing kindness — not even one.
Psalm 14:1—3
13 Their larynx is an open tomb;
they deceive with their tongues;
the venom of asps is under their lips;
14 whose mouth is full of cursing and bitterness;
15 whose feet are sharp to pour blood;
16 crushing and misery are in their ways;
17 and the way of shalom they have not known;
18 there is no awe of Elohim in front of their eyes.
Psalms 5:9, 10:7, 36:1, 140:3, Yesha Yah 59:7,8
19 Now we know, as much as the torah words,
it speaks to those in the torah:
that every mouth be sealed
and all the cosmos become under judgment
in front of Elohim.
20 Because by the works of the torah
no flesh is justified in his sight:
for through the torah is the knowledge of sin.

Justness Through Trust

21 But now the justness of Elohim
manifests apart from the torah,
being witnessed by the torah and the prophets;
22 even the justness of Elohim
through trust of Yah Shua Messiah
to all and on all who trust
— for there is no distinction:
23 for all have sinned and
failed the glory of Elohim;
24 being justified gratuitously by his charism
through the redemption in Messiah Yah Shua:
25 whom Elohim predetermined
to be a kapporeth/an atonement
through trust in his blood,
to indicate his justness for the passing over of sins
that previously transpired,
in the tolerance of Elohim;
26 to indicate in this present season to his justness:
for his being just
and justifies them who trust in Yah Shua.
27 So where is boasting? It is excluded.
Through what torah? Of works?
Indeed not — but through the torah of trust.
28 So we reckon that a human is justified by trust
apart from the works of the torah.
29 Or is he the Elohim of the Yah Hudiym only?
Is he indeed not also of the goyim?
Yes, also of the goyim:
30 Since one Elohim justifies
the circumcision by trust
and uncircumcision through trust.
31 So inactivate we the torah through trust?
So be it not:
yes rather, we set torah.

The Justness Of Abraham

4 So what say we?
That Abraham our father found, as to flesh?
2 For if Abraham were justified by works
he has whereof to boast; but not toward Elohim.
3 For what *saith* **wordeth** the scripture?
Abraham *believed God* **trusted Elohim**,
and it was *counted* **reckoned** unto him
for righteousness **unto justness**.
Genesis 15:6
4 Now to him that worketh
is the reward not reckoned of *grace* **charism**, but of debt.
5 But to him that worketh not,
but *believeth* **trusteth** on him

ROMANS 3

that justifieth the *ungodly* **irreverent**,
his *faith* **trust**
is *counted for righteousness* **reckoned unto justness**.

6 Even **Exactly** as David also *describeth* **wordeth**
the blessedness of *the man* **humanity**,
unto whom
God imputeth righteousness **Elohim reckoneth justness**
without **apart from** works,

7 Saying, Blessed are they
whose *iniquities* **torah violations** are forgiven,
and whose sins are covered.

8 Blessed is the man to whom
the Lord will **Adonay shall** not **no**
way *impute* **reckon** sin.
Psalm 32:1, 2

Justness Vs Ordinances

9 Cometh this blessedness then
upon the circumcision only,
or upon the uncircumcision also?
for we *say* **word** that *faith* **trust**
was reckoned to Abraham
for righteousness **unto justness**.

10 How was it then reckoned?
when he was **being** in circumcision,
or in uncircumcision?
Not in circumcision, but in uncircumcision.

11 And he *received* **took** the sign of circumcision,
a seal of the *righteousness* **justness**
of the *faith* **trust** which he had
yet **through** being uncircumcised **in uncircumcision**:
that he might be **unto his being** the father
of all them that *believe* **trust**,
though *they be not circumcised*
being in uncircumcision;
that *righteousness* **unto justness**
might be imputed **being reckoned** unto them also:

12 And the father of circumcision
to them who are not of the circumcision only,
but who also *walk* **march** in the *steps* **tracks**
of that *faith* **trust** of our father Abraham,
which he had being yet uncircumcised
in uncircumcision.

Justification Vs The Torah

13 For the *promise* **pre—evangelism**,
that he should be the heir of the *world* **cosmos**,
was not to Abraham, or to his *seed* **sperma**,
through the *law* **torah**,
but through the *righteousness* **justness** of *faith* **trust**.

14 For if they which are of the *law* **torah** be heirs,
faith **trust** is *made void* **voided**,
and the *promise* **pre—evangelism**
made of none effect **inactivated**:

15 Because **Indeed** the *law* **torah** worketh wrath:
for where no *law* **torah** is, there is no transgression.

Justness Through Trust By Charism

16 Therefore it is *of faith* **through trust**,
that it might be by *grace* **charism**;
to the end **unto** the *promise* **pre—evangelism**
might be sure **being stedfast** to all the *seed* **sperma**;
not to that only which is of the *law* **torah**,
but to that also which is of the *faith* **trust** of Abraham;
who is the father of us all,

17 (**Exactly** As *it is written* **scribed**,
I have *made* **placed** thee a father
of many *nations* **goyim**,)
before **in front of** him whom he *believed* **trusted**,
even *God* **Elohim**,
who *quickeneth* **enliveneth** the dead,
and calleth those *things which be not* **not being**
as *though they were* **being**.

18 Who against hope *believed* **trusted** in hope,
that he might become the father of many *nations* **goyim**;
according to that which was *spoken* **said**, *So* **Thus**
shall thy *seed* **sperma** be. Genesis 15:5, 17:5

3 For what words the scripture?
Abraham trusted Elohim
and it reckoned to him to justness.
Genesis 15:6

4 And to him who works,
the reward is not reckoned as to charism,
but as to debt:

5 and to him who works not
but trusts on him who justifies the irreverent,
his trust is reckoned to justness.

6 Exactly as David also words
of the blessedness of humanity,
to whom Elohim reckons justness apart from works,

7 Blessed — they whose torah
violations are forgiven
and whose sins are covered.

8 Blessed — the man
to whom Adonay no way reckons sin.
Psalm 32:1, 2

Justness Vs Ordinances

9 So this blessedness, *is* it on the circumcised?
Or also on the uncircumcised?

For we word
that trust was reckoned to Abraham to justness.
10 So how was it reckoned?
Being in circumcision?
Or in uncircumcision?
Not in circumcision but in uncircumcision.
11 And he took the sign of circumcision
— a seal of the justness of the trust he had
through being in uncircumcision:
to his being the father of all who trust,
though being in uncircumcision;
to justness also being reckoned to them:
12 and the father of circumcision to them,
not only of the circumcision,
but also to them who march in the tracks of the trust
of our father Abraham, being in uncircumcision.

Justification Vs The Torah

13 For the pre—evangelism he had,
being the heir of the cosmos,
was not to Abraham or his sperma through the torah,
but through the justness of trust.
14 For if they of the torah are heirs
trust is voided;
and the pre—evangelism inactivated:
15 indeed the torah works wrath:
for where no torah is, no transgression *is*.

Justness Through Trust By Charism

16 So as through trust, thus as to charism;
to the pre—evangelism
being steadfast to all the sperma;
not only to them of the torah,
but also to them of the trust of Abraham
— who is the father of us all:
17 exactly as scribed,
I placed you a father of many goyim,
in front of him whom he trusted — Elohim,
who enlivens the dead
and calls those not being, as being:
18 who against hope trusted in hope,
being the father of many goyim;
according to what was said,
Thus be your sperma.
Genesis 15:5, 17:5
19 And being not *weak* **frail** in *faith* **the trust**,
he considered not his own body
now dead **already deadened**,
when he was about an **being some** hundred years old,
neither yet

the *deadness* **necrosis** of Sarah's *womb* **matrix**:
20 He *staggered* **doubted** not
at **unto** the *promise* **pre—evangelism** of *God* **Elohim**
through *unbelief* **trustlessness**;
but was *strong* **dynamized** in *faith* **trust**,
giving glory to *God* **Elohim**;
21 And being fully *persuaded* **assured** that,
what he had *promised* **pre—evangelized**,
he was able also to *perform* **do**.
22 And therefore it was *imputed* **reckoned** to him
for righteousness **unto justness**.
23 Now it was not *written*
scribed for his sake alone,
that it was *imputed* **reckoned** to him;
24 But for us also,
to whom it shall be *imputed* **reckoned**,
if we *believe* **trust** on him
that raised up *Jesus* **Yah Shua** our *Lord* **Adonay**
from the dead;
25 Who was delivered for our *offences* **downfalls**,
and was raised again for our justification.

The Result Of Justness

5 Therefore being justified by *faith* **trust**,
we have *peace* **shalom** with *God* **Elohim**
through our *Lord Jesus Christ*
Adonay Yah Shua Messiah:
2 *By* **Through** whom also we have access
by *trust* faith into this *grace* **charism** wherein we stand,
and *rejoice* **boast** in hope of the glory of *God* **Elohim**.
3 And not only *so*, but we *glory*
boast in tribulations also:
knowing that tribulation worketh *patience* **endurance**;
4 And *patience* **endurance**, *experience* **proof**;
and *experience* **proof**, hope:
5 And hope *maketh* **shameth** not *ashamed*;
because the love of *God* **Elohim**
is *shed abroad* **poured** in our hearts
by **through** the *Holy Spirit* **Ruach ha-
kodesh** which is given unto us.
6 For *when we were yet without
strength* **we being frail**,
in *due time* **season**
Christ **Messiah** died for the *ungodly* **irreverent**.
7 For *scarcely* **difficultly**
for *a righteous man will one* **the just shall some** die:
yet peradventure **indeed perhaps**
for *a good man* **the good**
some *would* **should** even dare to die.

8	But *God* **Elohim** commendeth his love *toward* **unto** us, in that, *while* we *were* **being** yet sinners, *Christ* **Messiah** died for us.	24	but also for us, to whom it is about to be reckoned — to us who trust on him who raised Yah Shua our Adonay from the dead:
9	Much more then, *being* now **having been** justified *by* **in** his blood, we shall be saved from wrath through him.	25	who was delivered for our downfalls and raised again for our justification.

THE RESULT OF JUSTNESS

10	For if, *when we were* **being** enemies, we were reconciled to *God* **Elohim** *by* **through** the death of his Son, much more, being reconciled, we shall be saved *by* **in** his life.
11	And not only *so*, but we also *joy* **boast** in *God* **Elohim** through our *Lord Jesus Christ* **Adonay Yah Shua Messiah**, *by* **through** whom we have now *received* **taken** the *atonement* **reconciliation**.

THE ORIGIN OF SIN

12	Wherefore, **exactly** as *by* **through** one *man* **human** sin entered into the *world* **cosmos**, and death *by* **through** sin; and *so* **thus** death passed *upon* **unto** all *men* **humanity**, for that all have sinned:
13	(For until the *law* **torah** sin was in the *world* **cosmos**: but sin is not *imputed* **reckoned** when there *is* **being** no *law* **torah**.
14	*Nevertheless* **Rather** death reigned from Adam to *Moses* **Mosheh**, even over them that had not sinned after the *similitude* **likeness** of Adam's transgression, who is the *figure* **type** of *him* **the one** that *was* **about** to *come* **be**.
19	And not being frail in the trust, he neither considered his own body — already necreotized — being some hundred years old, nor yet the necrosis of the matrix of Sarah:
20	nor doubted he the pre—evangelism of Elohim through trustlessness; but dynamized in trust, giving glory to Elohim;
21	and being fully assured that what he pre—evangelized he was also able to do:
22	and so it was reckoned to him to justness.
23	And it was not scribed for his sake alone that it was reckoned to him;

5

1	So being justified by trust, we have shalom with Elohim through our Adonay Yah Shua Messiah:
2	through whom we also have access by trust into this charism wherein we stand and boast in hope of the glory of Elohim.
3	And not only, but we also boast in tribulations: knowing that tribulation works endurance;
4	and endurance, proof; and proof, hope:
5	and hope never shames; because the love of Elohim pours in our hearts through the Holy Spirit who is given to us.
6	For in our frailty, in season, Messiah died for the irreverent.
7	For difficultly, for the just some die: indeed perhaps, for the good, some even dare to die.
8	And Elohim commends his love to us, in that we, still being sinners, Messiah died for us.
9	So much more, being justified in his blood, through him we are saved from wrath.
10	For if, being enemies, we are reconciled to Elohim through the death of his Son, much more, being reconciled, we are saved in his life.
11	And not only, but we also boast in Elohim through our Adonay Yah Shua Messiah, through whom we now take the reconciliation.

THE ORIGIN OF SIN

12	So, exactly as through one human, sin entered into the cosmos, and death through sin, and thus death passed to all humanity — for all sinned:
13	for until the torah, sin was in the cosmos: but there being no torah, sin reckoned not.
14	Rather death reigned from Adam to Mosheh, even over them who sinned not

after the likeness of the transgression of Adam
— who is the type of the one about to be.

JUSTIFICATION AND LIFE THROUGH YAH SHUA MESSIAH

15 But not as the *offence* **downfall**,
so **thus** also is the *free gift* **charisma**.
For if through the *offence* **downfall** of one many be dead,
much more the *grace* **charism** of *God* **Elohim**,
and the *gift by grace* **gratuity in charism**,
which is by one *man* **human**,
Jesus Christ **Yah Shua Messiah**
hath *abounded* **superabounded** unto many.

16 And not as *it was by* **through** one that sinned,
so is the *gift* **gratuity**:
for the judgment **indeed** was by one
to condemnation,
but the *free gift* **charisma** is of many *offences* **downfalls**
unto justification.

17 For if by one man's *offence* **downfall**
death reigned *by* **through** one;
much more they which *receive* **take**
abundance **a superabundance** of *grace* **charism**
and of the *gift* **gratuity** of *righteousness* **justness**
shall reign in life *by* **through** one,
Jesus Christ **Yah Shua Messiah**.)

18 Therefore as *by the offence of* **through** one
judgment came upon **downfall to** all *men* **humanity**
is to condemnation;
even *so* **thus** *by the righteousness of* **through** one
the free gift **justification**
came upon all men **to all humanity**
is unto justification of life.

19 For **exactly** as
by **through** one *man's* **human's** disobedience
many were *made* **seated** sinners,
so by **thus through** the obedience of one
shall many be *made righteous* **seated just**.

20 Moreover the *law* **torah** surreptitiously entered,
that the *offence* **downfall** might *abound* **superabound**.
But where sin *abounded* **superabounded**,
grace **charism**
did much more abound **exceedingly superabounded**:

21 That **exactly** as sin hath reigned *unto* **in** death,
even *so* **thus** might *grace* **charism** reign
through *righteousness* **justness** unto eternal life
by Jesus Christ **through Yah Shua**
Messiah our *Lord* **Adonay**.

DEAD TO SIN, ALIVE IN THE MESSIAH

6 What shall we say then?
shall we *continue* **abide** in sin,
that *grace* **charism** may *abound* **superabound**?

2 *God forbid* **So be it not**.
How shall we that are dead to sin,
still live *any longer* therein?

3 **Or** Know ye not, that so many of us
as were baptized into *Jesus Christ* **Yah Shua Messiah**
were baptized into his death?

4 Therefore we are *buried* **co—buried** with him
by **through** baptism into death:
that *like* **exactly** as *Christ* **Messiah**
was raised *up* from the dead
by **through** the glory of the Father,
even *so* **thus** we also should walk in newness of life.

5 For if we have been *planted*
together **co—planted**
in the likeness of his death,
we shall be also
in the likeness **rather** of his resurrection:

6 Knowing this,
that our old *man* **humanity** is *crucified*
with him **co—staked**,
that the body of sin might be *destroyed* **inactivated**,
so that *henceforth* we should *not* **no longer** serve sin.

7 For he that is dead is *freed* **justified** from sin.

8 Now if we be dead with *Christ* **Messiah**,
we *believe* **trust** that we shall also *live* **co—live** with him:

9 Knowing that *Christ* **Messiah**
being raised from the dead
dieth *no more* **not still**;
death *hath no more dominion over*
shall not still overlord him.

10 For in that he died, he died unto sin once:
but in that he liveth, he liveth unto *God* **Elohim**.

11 *Likewise* **Thus** reckon ye also yourselves
to be dead indeed unto sin, but alive unto *God* **Elohim**
through **in** *Jesus Christ* **Yah Shua**
Messiah our *Lord* **Adonay**.

JUSTIFICATION AND LIFE THROUGH YAH SHUA MESSIAH

15 But not as the downfall, thus also the charisma.
For if through the downfall of one many die,
much more the charism of Elohim
and the gratuity in charism
of one human, Yah Shua Messiah
superabounds to many.

16	And not as through one who sinned,
	thus the gratuity:
	for the judgment indeed was by one
	to condemnation,
	but the charisma *is of many downfalls*
	to justification.
17	For if by the downfall of one
	death reigns through one;
	much more they
	who take a superabundance of charism
	and of the gratuity of justness
	reign in life through one, Yah Shua Messiah.
18	Thus as through one downfall
	all humanity is unto condemnation;
	even thus through one justification
	all humanity is unto justification of life.
19	For exactly
	as through the disobedience of one human
	many were seated sinners,
	thus through the obedience of one
	many are seated just.
20	And the torah entered surreptitiously,
	so that the downfall superabound:
	and where sin superabounded,
	charism exceedingly superabounded:
21	so that exactly as sin reigned in death,
	even thus charism reigns through justness
	unto eternal life
	through Yah Shua Messiah our Adonay.

Dead To Sin, Alive In The Messiah

6	So what say we?
	Abide we in sin that charism superabound?
2	So be it not!
	We who died to sin, how live we still therein?
3	Or Know you not,
	as many of us
	as are baptized into Yah Shua Messiah
	are baptized to his death?
4	So we are co—buried with him
	through baptism into death:
	so that, exactly as Messiah rose from the dead
	through the glory of the Father,
	even thus we also walk in newness of life.
5	For if we become co—planted
	in the likeness of his death,
	thus we also become
	rather of his resurrection:
6	Knowing this,
	that our old humanity is co—staked
	to inactivate the body of sin
	so that we no longer serve sin.
7	For whoever dies is justified from the sin.
8	And if we die with Messiah,
	we trust to also co—live with him:
9	knowing that Messiah, raised from the dead,
	dies no more;
	death overlords him no more.
10	For in that he died, he died to sin once:
	but in that he lives, he lives to Elohim.
11	Thus indeed, also reckon yourselves dead to sin,
	and living to Elohim
	in Yah Shua Messiah our Adonay.

Present Your Members As Weapons Of Justness

12	Let not sin therefore reign in your mortal body,
	that ye should obey it in the *lusts* **pantings** *thereof*.
13	Neither *yield* **present** ye your members
	as *instruments* **weapons** of *unrighteousness* **injustice**
	unto sin:
	but yield yourselves unto *God* **Elohim**,
	as *those that are* alive from the dead,
	and your members
	as *instruments* **weapons** of *righteousness* **justness**
	unto *God* **Elohim**.
14	For sin shall not *have*
	dominion over **overlord** you:
	for ye are not under the *law* **torah**,
	but under *grace* **charism**.
15	What then? shall we sin,
	because we are not under the *law* **torah**,
	but under *grace* **charism**?
	God forbid **So be it not**.
16	Know ye not, that to whom ye yield yourselves
	servants *to obey* **to obedience**,
	his servants ye are to whom ye obey;
	whether **either indeed** of sin unto death,
	or of obedience unto *righteousness* **justness**?
17	But *God be thanked* **charism to Elohim**,
	that ye were the servants of sin,
	but ye have obeyed from the heart
	that *form* **type** of doctrine
	which *was* **wherein ye were** delivered *you*.
18	Being then *made free* **liberated** from sin,
	ye became *the servants of righteousness*
	subservient to justness.
19	I *speak after the manner*
	of men **word as a human**
	because of the *infirmity* **frailty** of your flesh:

for **exactly** as ye have *yielded* **presented** your members
servants to *uncleanness* **impurity**
and to *iniquity* **torah violations**
unto *iniquity* **torah violations**;
even *so* **thus** now *yield* **present** your members
servants to *righteousness* **justness** unto holiness.
20 For when ye were the servants of sin,
ye were *free* **liberated** from *righteousness* **justness**.
21 What fruit had ye then
in those *things* whereof ye are now ashamed?
for the *end* **completion/shalom** of those *things* is death.
22 But now being *made free* **liberated** from sin,
and become *servants* **subservient** to *God* **Elohim**, ye have your fruit unto holiness,
and the *end* **completion/shalom**, *everlasting* **eternal** life.
23 For the wages of sin is death;
but the *gift* **charisma** of *God* **Elohim** is eternal life
through Jesus **in Yah Shua Messiah** our *Lord* **Adonay**.

ANALOGY OF MARRIAGE

7 **Or** Know ye not, brethren,
(for I speak to them that know the *law* **torah**,)
how that the *law* **torah**
hath dominion over a man **overlordeth a human**
as long *time* as he liveth?
2 For the woman *which hath
an husband* **under man**
is bound by the *law* **torah** to her *husband* **man**
so long as he liveth;
but *if* **whenever** the *husband* **man** be dead,
she is *loosed* **inactivated**
from the *law* **torah** of her *husband* **man**.
3 So *then if* **whenever**,
while her *husband* **man** liveth
she *be married to another man*
becometh another man's,
she shall be *called* **oracled as** an adulteress:
but *if her husband* **whenever her man** be dead,
she is *free* **liberated** from that *law* **torah**;
so that she is no adulteress,
though she *be married to* **become** another *man* **man's**.
4 *Wherefore* **So**, my brethren,
ye also are *become dead* **deathified** to the *law* **torah**
by **through** the body of *Christ* **the Messiah**;
that ye should be *married to another* **another's**,
even to him who is raised from the dead,
that we should *bring forth* **bear** fruit unto *God* **Elohim**.
5 For when we were in the flesh,
the *motions* **sufferings** of sins,
which were *by* **through** the *law* **torah**,

PRESENT YOUR MEMBERS AS WEAPONS OF JUSTNESS

12 So neither let sin reign in your mortal body
to obey its pantings:
13 nor present your members
as weapons of injustice to sin:
but yield yourselves to Elohim,
as living from the dead
and your members as weapons of justness to Elohim.
14 For sin overlords you not:
for you are not under the torah, but under charism.
15 So what?
Sin we, because we are not under the torah,
but under charism?
So be it not.
16 Know you not,
that to whomever you yield yourselves
as servants to obedience,
you are servants to whomever you obey
— indeed either of sin to death
or of obedience to justness?
17 And charism to Elohim,
that you, having been the servants of sin,
and from the heart
you obeyed that type of doctrine
wherein you were delivered.
18 And so being liberated from sin,
you became subservient to justness.
19 I word as a human
because of the frailty of your flesh:
for exactly as you presented your members
as servants to impurity
and to torah violations to torah violations;
thus even now
present your members servants to justness
— to holiness.
20 For when you were servants of sin,
you were liberated from justness.
21 So what fruit had you
in those whereof you are now ashamed?
For the completion/shalom of those is death.
22 And now, being liberated from sin
and being subservient to Elohim,
you have your fruit to holiness
and the completion/shalom — eternal life.
23 For the wages of the sin is death;
but the charisma of Elohim is eternal life
in Yah Shua Messiah our Adonay.

ANALOGY OF MARRIAGE

7 Or know you not, brothers,
for I speak to them who know the torah,
how that the torah overlords a human
as long time as he lives?

2 For the woman under man
is bound to her man by the torah;
but whenever the man dies,
she is inactivated from the torah of her man.

3 So whenever,
while her man lives she becomes to another man,
she is oracled as an adulteress:
and whenever her man dies,
she is liberated from that torah;
so that she is no adulteress,
though she becomes to another man.

4 So my brothers,
you also are deathified to the torah
through the body of the Messiah;
to become to another
— to him who rose from the dead,
so that we bear fruit to Elohim.

5 For when we were in the flesh,
the sufferings of sins, through the torah,
did work **energized** in our members
to *bring forth* **bear** fruit unto death.

6 But now
we are *delivered* **inactivated** from the *law* **torah**,
that being dead wherein we were held;
so that we should serve in newness of spirit,
and not in the *oldness* **antiquity** of the *letter* **scribing**.

7 What shall we say then?
Is the *law* **torah** sin?
God forbid **So be it not**.
Nay **Rather**, I had not known sin,
but by **except through** the *law* **torah**:
for I had not known *lust* **panting**,
except the *law* **torah** had *said* **worded**,
Thou shalt not *covet* **pant**.

8 But sin, taking *occasion* **opportunity**
by **through** the *commandment* **misvah**,
wrought **worked** in me
all *manner of concupiscence* **panting**.
For *without* **apart from** the *law* **torah**
sin was dead.

9 For I was alive
without **apart from** the *law once* **torah formerly**:
but when the *commandment* **misvah** came,
sin *revived* **relived**, and I died.

10 And the *commandment* **misvah**,
which was ordained to unto life,
I found *to be* **this** unto death.

11 For sin, taking *occasion* **opportunity**
by **through** the *commandment* **misvah**,
deceived **seduced** me,
and *by* **through** it *slew* **slaughtered** me.

12 *Wherefore* **So indeed** the *law* **torah** is holy,
and the *commandment* **misvah** holy, and just, and good.

TWO NATURES UNDER THE TORAH

13 Was then that which is good
made **become** death unto me?
God forbid **So be it not**.
But sin, that it might *appear* **be manifest as** sin,
working death in me *by* **through** that which is good;
that sin *by* **through** the *commandment* **misvah**
might become exceeding sinful.

14 For we know that the *law* **torah** is spiritual:
but I am *carnal* **fleshly**, sold under sin.

15 For that which I *do* **work**, I *allow* **know** not:
for what I *would* **will**, that *do* **transact** I not;
but what I hate, that do I.

16 If then I do that which I *would* not **will**,
I *consent unto* **assent with** the *law* **torah** that it is good.

17 Now then it is *no more* **not still** I that *do* **work** it,
but sin that dwelleth in me.

18 For I know that in me (that is, in my flesh,)
dwelleth no good *thing*:
for to will is present with me;
but *how to perform* **to work** that which is good
I find not.

19 For the good that I *would* **will**, I do not:
but the evil which I *would* not **will**, that I *do* **transact**.

20 Now if I do that I *would* not will,
it is *no more* **not still** I that *do* **work** it,
but sin that dwelleth in me.

21 I find then *a law* **the torah**, that,
when I *would* **will to** do good, evil is present with me.

22 For I delight in the *law* **torah** of *God* **Elohim**
after the inward *man* **human**:

23 But I see another *law* **torah** in my members,
warring against the *law* **torah** of my mind,
and *bringing* **capturing** me *into captivity*
to the *law* **torah** of sin *which is* **being** in my members.

24 O wretched man that I am
Miserable human — I!
who shall *deliver* **rescue** me from the body of this death?

25 I *thank God* **eucharistize Elohim**

through *Jesus Christ* **Yah Shua Messiah** our *Lord* **Adonay**.
So **Therefore** then with the mind
I myself **indeed** serve the *law* **torah** of *God* **Elohim**;
but with the flesh the *law* **torah** of sin.
energized in our members to bear fruit to death.

6 But now we are inactivated from the torah,
being dead wherein we were held;
to serve in newness of spirit
and not in the antiquity of the scribing.

7 So what say we? Is the torah sin?
So be it not.
Rather, I knew not sin, except through the torah:
nor knew I panting, except the torah worded,
Pant not.

8 And the sin, taking opportunity
through the misvah,
worked all panting in me.
For apart from the torah, sin is dead.

9 For formerly apart from the torah, I lived:
but when the misvah came, sin relived and I died.

10 And the misvah for life, I found for death.

11 For sin, taking opportunity through the misvah,
seduced me
and thereby slaughtered me.

12 So indeed the torah is holy
and the misvah holy and just and good.

Two Natures Under The Torah

13 So has the good become my death?
So be it not.
But sin, manifest as sin,
to work death in me through the good;
so that through the misvah
sin becomes exceeding sinful.

14 For we know the torah is spiritual:
and I am fleshly, sold under sin.

15 For what I work, I know not:
for what I will, I transact not;
but what I hate, I do.

16 So if I do what I not will,
I assent with the torah that it is good.

17 So now it is not still I who work it,
but the sin dwelling in me.

18 For I know that in me, that is, in my flesh,
dwells no good:
for to will is present with me;
but to work good, I find not.

19 For the good I will, I do not:
but the evil I do not will, I transact.

20 And if I do what I not will, it is not still I
who works, but sin that dwells in me.

21 So I find the torah, that,
when I will to do good, evil is present with me.

22 For I delight in the torah of Elohim
after the inward human:

23 and I see another torah in my members,
warring against the torah of my mind
and capturing me to the torah of sin
being in my members.

24 Miserable human — I!
Who rescues me from the body of this death?

25 I eucharistize Elohim
through Yah Shua Messiah our Adonay.
So indeed with the mind I serve the torah of Elohim;
and with the flesh, the torah of sin.

The Torah Of The Spirit; Life In The Messiah

8 There is therefore now no
condemnation to them
which are in *Christ Jesus* **Messiah Yah Shua**, *who walk not after the flesh, but after the Spirit**. *not in mss; but see 8:4

2 For the *law* **torah** of the Spirit of life
in *Christ Jesus* **Messiah Yah Shua**
hath *made* **liberated** me *free*
from the *law* **torah** of sin and death.

3 For *what the law could not do*
the torah, in being incapable,
in that it *was weak* **frail** through the flesh,
God **Elohim** sending his own Son
in the likeness of *sinful flesh* **the flesh of sin**, and for sin,
condemned sin in the flesh:

4 That the *righteousness*
judgment of the *law* **torah**
might be fulfilled/**shalamed** in us,
who walk not after the flesh, but after the Spirit.

In Flesh vs In Spirit

5 For they *that are* **being** after the flesh
do mind the things **think** of the flesh;
but they that are after the Spirit
the things of the Spirit.

6 For *to be carnally minded*
the thought of the flesh
is death;
but *to be spiritually minded* **the thought of the spirit**
is life and *peace* **shalom**.

7	Because the *carnal mind* **thought of the flesh**	
	is enmity *against God* **unto Elohim**:	
	for it is not *subject* **subjugated**	
	to the *law* **torah** of *God* **Elohim**,	
	neither indeed can be.	
8	So then they *that are in the* **being in** flesh	
	cannot please *God* **Elohim**.	
9	But ye are not in *the* flesh, but in *the* Spirit,	
	if so be that **whenever** the Spirit of	
	God **Elohim** dwell in you.	
	Now if *any man* **one**	
	have not the Spirit of *Christ* **Messiah**,	
	he is none of his.	
10	And if *Christ* **Messiah** *be* in you,	
	the body is **indeed** dead because of sin;	
	but the Spirit *is* life because of *righteousness* **justness**.	
11	But if the Spirit of him	
	that raised up *Jesus* **Yah Shua** from the dead	
	dwell in you,	
	he that raised up *Christ* **Messiah** from the dead	
	shall also *quicken* **enliven** your mortal bodies	
	by **through** his Spirit that dwelleth in you.	
12	*Therefore*, **So then**, brethren, we are debtors,	
	not to the flesh, to live after the flesh.	
13	For if ye live after the flesh,	
	ye shall **be about to** die:	
	but if ye through *the* Spirit	
	do mortify **deathify** the *deeds* **functions** of the body,	
	ye shall live.	
14	For as many as are led by	
	the Spirit of *God* **Elohim**,	
	they are the sons of *God* **Elohim**.	

The Spirit Of Sonship

15	For ye have not *received* **taken**	
	the spirit of *bondage* **servitude** again to *fear* **awe**;	
	but ye have *received* **taken** the Spirit of *adoption* **sonship**,	
	whereby **wherein** we cry, Abba, Father.	
16	The *Spirit itself* **selfsame Spirit**	
	beareth witness **co—witnesseth** with our spirit,	
	that we are the children of *God* **Elohim**:	
17	And if children, then heirs;	
	heirs of *God* **Elohim**,	
	and *joint—heirs* **co—heirs indeed** with *Christ* **Messiah**;	
	if so be that **whenever** we *suffer with him* **co—suffer**,	
	that we may be also *glorified together* **co—glorified**.	
18	For I reckon	
	that the sufferings of this present *time* **season**	
	are not worthy *to be compared* with the glory	
	which shall **about to** be *revealed* **unveiled***	
	in us. *verb of apocalypse	
19	For the *earnest expectation* **intense anticipation**	
	of the creature	
	waiteth for **awaiteth** the *manifestation* **apocalypse**	
	of the sons of *God* **Elohim**.	
20	For the creature was *made*	
	subject **subjugated** to vanity,	
	not *willingly* **voluntarily**,	

The Torah Of The Spirit; Life In The Messiah

8	So there is now no condemnation to them	
	who are in Messiah Yah Shua.	
	*not in mss; but see 8:4	
2	For the torah of the Spirit	
	of life in Messiah Yah Shua	
	liberates me from the torah of sin and death.	
3	For the torah, being incapable,	
	— frail through the flesh,	
	Elohim sending his own Son	
	in the likeness of the flesh of sin;	
	and for sin, condemned the sin in the flesh:	
4	to fulfill/shalam the judgment of the torah in us,	
	who walk not after flesh, but after Spirit.	

In Flesh Vs In Spirit

5	For they being after flesh, think of the flesh;	
	and they after Spirit, of the Spirit.	
6	For the thought of the flesh, *is* death;	
	but the thought of the spirit, life and shalom.	
7	Because the thought of the	
	flesh is enmity to Elohim:	
	for it neither subjugates to the torah of Elohim	
	nor indeed can.	
8	So they who are in flesh, cannot please Elohim.	
9	And you are not in flesh, but in Spirit	
	whenever the Spirit of Elohim dwell in you.	
	and if one has not the Spirit of Messiah,	
	he is none of his.	
10	And if Messiah *is* in you,	
	the body *is* indeed dead because of sin;	
	and the Spirit *is* life because of justness.	
11	But if the Spirit of him	
	who raised Yah Shua from the dead dwells in you,	
	he who raised Messiah from the dead	
	also enlivens your mortal bodies	
	through his Spirit dwelling in you.	
12	So then brothers, we are debtors,	
	not to the flesh — to live after the flesh.	

ROMANS 8

13   For if you live after flesh, you are about to die:
but if you, through Spirit,
deathify the functions of the body, you live.
14   For as many as are led by Spirit of Elohim,
are the sons of Elohim.

The Spirit Of Sonship

15   For you take not
the spirit of servitude again to awe;
but you take the Spirit of sonship,
wherein we cry, Abba, Father.
16   The self—same Spirit
co—witnesses with our spirit,
that we are the children of Elohim:
17   and if children, then heirs
— heirs of Elohim
— and indeed co—heirs with Messiah;
whenever we co—suffer to also co—glorify.
18   For I reckon
that the sufferings of this present season
are not worthy
of the glory about to be unveiled* in us.
*verb of apocalypse
19   For the intense anticipation of the creature
awaits the apocalypse of the sons of Elohim.
20   For the creature subjugated to vanity
— not voluntarily
but *by reason of* **through** him
who *hath subjected the same* **subjugated** in hope,
21   Because the creature itself also
shall be *delivered* **liberated**
from the *bondage* **servitude** of corruption
into the *glorious* liberty **of the glory**
of the children of *God* **Elohim**.
22   For we know that the whole creation
groaneth **co—sigheth** and *travaileth* **co—travaileth**
in pain *together* until now.
23   And not only *they*, but ourselves also,
which have the *firstfruits* **firstlings** of the Spirit,
even we ourselves *groan within* **sigh among** ourselves,
waiting for **awaiting** the *adoption* **sonship**,
to wit, the redemption of our body.
24   For we are saved by hope:
but hope that is seen is not hope:
for what *a man* **one** seeth,
why *doth* **shall** he yet hope *for*?
25   But if we hope for that we see not,
then *do* we
with patience wait for it **through endurance await**.

The Intercessory Ministry Of The Holy Spirit

26   Likewise the Spirit also *helpeth* **co—helpeth**
our *infirmities* **frailties**:
for we know not what *we* should pray for
according as we *ought* **must**:
but the Spirit *itself*
maketh intercession **intercedeth exceedingly** for us
with *groanings which cannot be*
uttered **unutterable sighs**.
27   And he that searcheth the hearts
knoweth what is the *mind* **thought** of the Spirit,
because he *maketh intercession* **intercedeth**
for the *saints* **holy**
according to the will of *God* **Elohim**.
28   And we know that all *things*
work together for **co—work unto** good
to them that love *God* **Elohim**,
to them *who are* **being** the called
according to his *purpose* **prothesis**.

The Sequence Of The Protection Of Elohim

29   For whom he *did foreknow* **foreknew**,
he also *did predestinate* **predetermined**
to be conformed to the *image* **icon** of his Son,
that he might *be* **unto his being**
the firstborn among many brethren.
30   Moreover
whom he *did predestinate* **predetermined**,
them he also called:
and whom he called, them he also justified: and
whom he justified, them he also glorified.

Nine Questions, Direct And Rhetorical

31   What shall we then say to these *things*?
If *God* **Elohim** be for us, who *can be* against us?
32   He that *yet* **indeed** spared not his own Son,
but delivered him up for us all,
how **indeed** shall he not with him also
freely give us all things **grant us charism with all**?
33   Who shall *lay any thing to the charge of* **accuse**
God's elect **Elohim's select**?
It is God that justifieth. **Elohim that justifieth?**
34   Who is he that condemneth?
It is Christ **Messiah** that died,
yea rather, that is risen again,
who is even at the right *hand* of *God* **Elohim**,
who also *maketh intercession for us.* **intercedeth for us?**

35 Who shall separate us
from the love of *Christ* **the Messiah**?
shall tribulation, or distress, or persecution,
or famine, or nakedness, or peril, or sword?
36 **Exactly** As *it is written* **scribed**,
For thy sake we are *killed* **deathified** all the day long;
we are *accounted* **reckoned** as sheep for the slaughter.
37 *Nay* **Rather**, in all these *things*
we are *more than conquerors* **exceedingly triumphant**
through him that loved us.
but through him who subjugated in hope,
21 so that the creature itself also liberates
from the servitude of corruption
into the liberty of the glory of the children of Elohim.
22 For we know that all creation
co—sighs and co—travails in pain until now:
23 and not only *they*, but we also,
who have the firstlings of the Spirit,
even we also sigh among ourselves,
awaiting the sonship — the redemption of our body.
24 For we are saved by hope:
but hope seen is not hope:
for why still hope for what one sees?
25 And if we hope for what we see not,
thus we, through endurance, await.

The Intercessory Ministry Of The Holy Spirit

26 Likewise the Spirit also co—helps our frailties:
for we know not what to pray for
according as we must:
but the Spirit intercedes exceedingly for us
with unutterable sighs.
27 And he who searches the hearts
knows the thought of the Spirit,
because he intercedes for the holy
according to the will of Elohim.
28 And we know that all co—works to good
to them who love Elohim,
to them being the called according to his prothesis.

The Sequence Of The Protection Of Elohim

29 For whom he foreknew, he also predetermined
— conformed to the icon of his Son,
to his being the firstborn among many brothers.
30 And whom he predetermined, he also called:
and whom he called, he also justified:
and whom he justified, he also glorified.

Nine Questions, Direct And Rhetorical

31 So what say we to these?
If Elohim *is* for us, who *is* against us?
32 — Who indeed spared not his own Son,
but delivered him up for us all,
how indeed, with him,
grants he us not also charism with all?
33 Who accuses the select of Elohim?
Elohim who justifies?
34 Who condemns?
Messiah who died, yes rather, who rose
— who is even at the right of Elohim
— who also intercedes for us?
35 Who separates us from the love of the Messiah?
— Tribulation or distress or persecution or
famine or nakedness or peril or sword?
36 Exactly as scribed,
For your sake we are deathified all the day long
— reckoned as sheep for the slaughter.
37 Rather, in all these we are
exceedingly triumphant
through him who loved us.
Psalm 44:22
38 For I am *persuaded* **convinced**,
that neither death, nor life, nor angels,
nor *principalities* **hierarchies**, nor *powers* **dynamis**,
nor *things* **the** present,
nor *things to come* **the about to be**,
39 Nor height, nor depth, nor
any other *creature* **creation**,
shall be able to separate us from the love of *God* **Elohim**,
which is in
Christ Jesus **Messiah Yah Shua** our *Lord* **Adonay**.

The Selection Of Yisra El By Elohim

9 I *say* **word** the truth in *Christ* **Messiah**, I lie not,
my conscience also *bearing me witness* **co—witnessing**
in the *Holy Spirit* **Ruach ha-kodesh**,
2 That I have *great heaviness* **mega sorrow**
and *continual sorrow* **unceasing grief** in my heart.
3 For I *could wish* **vowed** that
myself were *accursed* **anathema** from *Christ* **the Messiah**
for my brethren, my *kinsmen* **kin** according to the flesh:
4 Who are *Israelites* **Yisra Elym**;
to whom pertaineth **whose is** the *adoption* **sonship**,
and the glory, and the covenants,
and the *giving* **setting** of the *law* **torah**,
and the *service of God* **liturgy**,
and the *promises* **pre—evangelisms**;

5 Whose are the fathers,
and of whom as concerning the flesh
Christ **the Messiah** came, *who is* **being** over all,
God blessed for ever **Elohim eulogized unto the eons**.
Amen.

6 Not *such* as though the word of *God* **Elohim**
hath *taken none effect* **failed**.
For they are not all *Israel* **Yisra El**,
which are of *Israel* **Yisra El**:

7 Neither, because they are the
seed **sperma** of Abraham,
are they all children:
but, In *Isaac* **Yischaq** shall thy *seed*
sperma be called. Genesis 21:12

8 That is, They which are the children of the flesh,
these are not the children of *God* **Elohim**:
but the children of the *promise* **pre—evangelism**
are *counted for* **reckoned unto** the *seed* **sperma**.

9 For this is the word of
promise **pre—evangelism**,
At this *time will* **season shall** I come,
and Sarah shall have a son.
Genesis 18:10

10 And not only *this*;
but when *Rebecca* **Rebekah**
also had *conceived* **coition** by one,
even by our father *Isaac* **Yischaq**;

11 (For *the children* being not yet born,
neither having *done* **transacted** any good or evil,
that the *purpose* **prothesis** of *God* **Elohim**
according to *election* **selection** might *stand* **abide**,
not of works, but of him that calleth;)

12 It was *said* **rhetorized** unto her,
The *elder* **greater** shall serve the *younger* **lesser**.
Genesis 25:23

13 **Exactly** As *it is written* **scribed**,
Jacob **Yaaqov** have I loved, but *Esau*
Esav have I hated. Malachi 1:2, 3

14 What shall we say then?
Is there unrighteousness **Injustice** with *God* **Elohim**?
God forbid **So be it not**.

15 For he *saith* **wordeth** to *Moses* **Mosheh**,
I will have mercy on whom I will have mercy
I shall mercy whomever I shall mercy,
*and I will have compassion
on whom I will have compassion.*
and I shall compassion whomever I shall compassion.

16 So then it is not of him that willeth,
nor of him that runneth,
but of *God* **Elohim** that *sheweth mercy* **mercieth**.

17 For the scripture *saith*
wordeth unto *Pharaoh* **Paroh**,
Even *for* **unto** this *same purpose* have I raised thee up,
that I might *shew* **indicate** my *power* **dynamis** in thee,
and that my name might be *declared* **evangelized**
throughout **in** all the earth.

38 For I am convinced
that neither death nor life nor angels
nor hierarchies nor dynamis
nor the present nor the about to be

39 nor height nor depth nor any other creation
can separate us from the love of Elohim
in Messiah Yah Shua our Adonay.

THE SELECTION OF YISRA EL BY ELOHIM

9 I word the truth in Messiah; I lie not;
my conscience also co—witnesses in the Holy Spirit;

2 that I have mega sorrow
and unceasing grief in my heart.

3 For I vowed
— I myself to be anathema from the Messiah
for my brothers — my kin according to the flesh:

4 who are Yisra Eliym;
to whom are the sonship and the glory
and the covenants and the setting of the torah
and the liturgy and the pre—evangelisms;

5 whose *are* the fathers
and of whom as concerning the flesh
the Messiah came, being over all
— Elohim eulogized to the eons.
Amen.

6 Not such as though the word of Elohim failed.
For neither are they of Yisra El,
all Yisra Eliym:

7 nor because they are the sperma of Abraham,
all children:
but, In Yischaq *is* your sperma called.
Genesis 21:12

8 That is, the children of the flesh,
are not the children of Elohim:
but the children of the pre—evangelism
are reckoned to the sperma.

9 For this is the word of pre—evangelism,
At this season I come, and Sarah has a son. Genesis 18:10

10 And not only *so*;
but also Rebekah having coition by one,
even by our father Yischaq;

11 neither being yet birthed,
nor having transacted any good or evil,
that the prothesis of Elohim

ROMANS 9

according to selection abide,
not of works, but of him who calls;
12 It was rhetorized to her,
The greater serves the lesser.
Genesis 25:23
13 Exactly as scribed,
Yaaqov I loved, and Esav I hated.
Malachi 1:2, 3
14 So what say we?
Injustice with Elohim?
So be it not.
15 For he words to Mosheh,
I mercy whomever I mercy
and I compassion whomever I compassion.
16 — so it is neither of him who wills,
nor of him who runs,
but of Elohim who mercies.
17 For the scripture words to Paroh,
Even to this I raised you,
to indicate my dynamis in you
and to evangelize my name in all the earth.
Hoshea 1:10
18 *Therefore* **So then,**
hath he mercy on whom he will have mercy
he mercieth whom he willeth,
and whom he *will* **willeth** he hardeneth.
19 Thou *wilt* **shalt** say then unto me,
Why doth he yet *find fault* **blame**?
For who hath *resisted* **withstood** his *will* **counsel**?
20 *Nay but* **Yet so,** O *man* **humanity**,
who art thou
that *repliest against God* **contradictest Elohim**?
shall the *thing formed it* **molded**
say to him that *formed* **molded** ,
Why hast thou made me thus?
21 **Or** Hath not the potter *power*
authority over the clay,
of the same lump
to make one vessel **indeed** unto honour,
and another unto dishonour?
22 *What* **And** if *God* **Elohim**,
willing **willeth** to *shew* **indicate** his wrath,
and to make his *power* **ability** known,
endured with **bore in** much *longsuffering* **patience**
the vessels of wrath *fitted to* **prepared unto** destruction:
23 And that he might make
known the riches of his glory
on the vessels of mercy,
which he had *afore* **previously** prepared unto glory,

24 Even us, whom he hath called, not of the *Jews*
Yah Hudiym only, but also of the *Gentiles* **goyim**?
25 As he *saith* **wordeth** also in *Osee* **Hoshea**,
I *will* **shall** call them my people,
which were not my people;
and her beloved,
which was not beloved.
26 And it shall *come to pass* **become**,
that in the place where it was *said* **rhetorized** unto them,
Ye are not my people;
there shall they be called
the *children* **sons** of the living *God* **Elohim**.
Hoshea 1:10
27 *Esaias* **Yesha Yah** also crieth
concerning Israel **in behalf of Yisra El**,
Though **Whenever** the number
of the *children* **sons** of *Israel* **Yisra El**
be as the sand of the sea,
a remnant shall be saved:
28 For he *will finish* **shall complete/
shalam** the *work* **word**,
and cut it short in *righteousness* **justness**:
because a short *work* **word**
will the *Lord* **shall Yah Veh** make upon
the earth. Yesha Yah 10:22, 23
29 And **exactly** as *Esaias said*
before **Yesha Yah foretold**,
Except the Lord of **Unless Yah Veh** Sabaoth
had left *us* **behind** a *seed* **sperma**,
we had *been* **ever become** as *Sodoma* **Sedom**,
and *been made like* **ever likened**
unto Gomorrha **as Amorah**.

JUSTNESS BY TRUST

30 What shall we say then?
That the *Gentiles* **goyim**,
which *followed* **pursued** not *after righteousness* **justness**,
have *attained to righteousness* **overtaken justness**,
even the *righteousness* **justness** which is *of faith* **by trust**.
31 But *Israel* **Yisra El**, which
followed after **pursued**
the *law* **torah** of *righteousness* **justness**,
hath not attained
to the *law* **torah** of *righteousness* **justness**.
32 *Wherefore* **Why**?
Because *they sought it* not by *faith* **trust**,
but as *it were* by the works of the *law* **torah**.
For they stumbled at that stumblingstone;
33 **Exactly** As *it is written* **scribed**,
Behold, I *lay* **place** in *Sion* **Siyon** a stumblingstone

and rock of *offence* **scandal**:
and whosoever *believeth* **trusteth** on him
shall not *be ashamed* **shame**.
Psalm 118:22, Yesha Yah 8:14, 28:16

18 So, whomever he wills, he mercies;
and whomever he wills, he hardens.
19 So you say to me, Why blames he still?
For who withstands his counsel?
20 Yet so, O humanity,
who are you to contradict Elohim?
Says the molded to the molder,
Why made you me thus?
21 Or has not the potter authority over the clay
— to make of the same lump
one vessel indeed to honor
and another to dishonor?
22 And if Elohim wills to indicate his wrath
and to make known his ability,
bears in much patience
the vessels of wrath prepared for destruction:
23 and to make known the riches of his glory
on the vessels of mercy,
whom he previously prepared for glory,
24 — us, whom he called,
not of the Yah Hudiym only, but also of the goyim?
25 As he also words in Hoshea,
I call the Not my people, My people;
and the Not beloved, Beloved.
26 And so be it,
that in the place they rhetorized,
You, Not my people;
there they call them, Sons of the living Elohim.
Hoshea 1:10
27 Yesha Yah also cries in behalf of Yisra El,
Whenever the number of the sons of Yisra El
become as the sand of the sea,
only the remnant is saved:
28 for he completes/shalams the word
and cuts it short in justness:
because Yah Veh makes a short word
upon the earth. Yesha Yah 10:22, 23
29 And exactly as Yesha Yah foretold,
Unless Yah Veh Sabaoth had left behind a sperma,
we had ever become as Sedom
and ever likened as Amorah.

Justness By Trust

30 So what?
Say we that the goyim who pursued not justness
overtook justness — even the justness of trust?
31 And Yisra El, who pursued the torah of justness,
attained not to the torah of justness?
32 Why?
Because — not by trust,
but as by the works of the torah.
For they stumbled at that stumblingstone;
33 exactly as scribed,
Behold, I place in Siyon
a stumblingstone and a rock of scandal: and
whoever trusts thereon, shames not.
Psalm 118:22, Yesha Yah 8:14, 28:16

Yisra El Lacking Trust

10 Brethren, **indeed**,
my heart's desire **the well approving of my heart**
and *prayer* **petition** to *God* **Elohim** for *Israel* **Yisra El** is,
that they might be saved **unto their salvation**.
2 For I *bear them record* **witness**
that they have a zeal of *God* **Elohim**,
but not according to knowledge.
3 For they being *ignorant* **unknowing**
of *God's righteousness* **Elohim's justness**,
and *going about* **seeking**
to *establish* **set** their own *righteousness* **justness**,
have not *submitted* **subjugated** themselves
unto the *righteousness* **justness** of *God* **Elohim**.
4 For *Christ* **Messiah**
is the *end* **completion/shalom** of the *law* **torah**
for righteousness **unto justness**
to every one that *believeth* **trusteth**.
5 For *Moses describeth* **Mosheh scribes**
the righteousness **of the justness**
which is of the *law* **torah**,
That the *man* **human** which doeth those *things*
shall live *by* **in** them.
Leviticus 18:5
6 But the *righteousness* **justness**
which is of *faith* **trust**
speaketh on this wise **wordeth thus**,
Say not in thine heart,
Who shall ascend into *heaven* **the heavens**?
(that is, to bring *Christ* **Messiah** *down from above*:)
7 Or, Who shall descend into the *deep* **abyss**?
(that is, to bring *up Christ* **Messiah** *again* from the dead.)
8 But what *saith* **wordeth** it?
The *word* **rhema** is nigh thee,
even in thy mouth, and in thy heart:
that is, the *word* **rhema** of *faith* **trust**, which
we preach; Deuteronomy 30:12—14

ROMANS 10

9 That *if* **whenever** thou shalt
confess with **profess in** thy mouth
the Lord Jesus **Adonay Yah Shua**,
and shalt *believe* **trust** in thine heart
that *God* **Elohim** hath raised him from the dead,
thou shalt be saved.

10 For with the heart
man believeth **trust is** unto *righteousness* **justness**;
and with the mouth
confession **profession** is *made* unto salvation.

11 For the scripture *saith* **wordeth**,
Whosoever *believeth* **trusteth** on him
shall not *be ashamed* **shame**.
Yesha Yah 29:16, 49:23

12 For there is no *difference* **distinction**
between the Jew **both Yah Hudiy** and *the Greek* **Hellene**:
for the same *Lord* **Adonay** over all
is rich unto all that call upon him.

13 For whosoever
shall call upon the name of *the Lord* **Yah Veh**
shall be saved.
Yah El 2:32

14 **So** How then shall they call on him
in whom they have not *believed* **trusted**?
and how shall they *believe* **trust** in him
of whom they have not heard?
and how shall they hear *without* **apart from** a preacher?

15 And how shall they preach,
except **unless** they be *sent* **apostolized**?
exactly as *it is written* **scribed**,
How beautiful are the feet of them
that *preach the gospel of peace* **evangelize shalom**,
and *bring glad tidings of* **evangelize** good
things! Yesha Yah 52:7, Nachum 1:15

16 But they have not all obeyed
the *gospel* **evangelism**.
For *Esaias saith* **Yesha Yah wordeth**, *Lord* **Yah Veh**,
who *hath believed* **trusted** our *report* **hearing**?
Yesha Yah 53:1

17 So then *faith* **trust** *cometh* by hearing,
and hearing by the *word* **rhema** of *God* **Elohim**.

18 But I *say* **word**, Have they not heard?
Yes verily **Yet indeed**, their sound went into all the earth,
and their *words* **rhema**
unto the *ends* **extremities** of the world.

YISRA EL LACKING TRUST

10 Brothers, indeed,
the well approving of my heart
and petition to Elohim for Yisra El is to their salvation.

2 For I witness
that they have a zeal of Elohim
— but not according to knowledge:

3 For, unknowing of the justness of Elohim
and seeking to set their own justness,
subjugate themselves not to the justness of Elohim.

4 For Messiah is the completion/
shalom of the torah
to justness
to everyone who trusts.

5 For Mosheh scribes of the justness of the torah,
That the human doing them, lives
in them. Leviticus 18:5

6 And the justness of trust words thus,
Say not in your heart,
Who ascends to the heavens?
— that is, to bring Messiah:

7 or, Who descends to the abyss?
that is, to bring Messiah from the dead.

8 But what words it?
The rhema is near you
— in your mouth and in your heart: that is, the rhema
of trust, that we preach; Deuteronomy 30:12—14

9 so that whenever you profess Adonay Yah Shua
in your mouth
and trust in your heart
that Elohim raised him from the dead,
you become saved.

10 For with the heart, trust is to justness;
and with the mouth, profession is to salvation.

11 For the scripture words,
Whoever trusts on him shames
not. Yesha Yah 29:16, 49:23

12 For there is no distinction
— Yah Hudiy and Hellene:
for the same Adonay over all
is rich to all who call upon him.

13 For whoever calls upon the name of Yah Veh
becomes saved.
Yah El 2:32

14 So then, how call they on
him in whom they trust not?
And how trust they in him whom they heard not?
And how hear they apart from a preacher?

15 And how preach they
unless they *are* apostolized?
Exactly as scribed,
How beautiful their feet
who evangelize shalom and evangelize
good! Yesha Yah 52:7, Nachum 1:15

16 But not all of them obeyed the evangelism.

For *Yesha Yah* words, **Yah Veh**,
who trusted our hearing?
Yesha Yah 53:1

17 So, trust by hearing
and hearing by the rhema of Elohim.
18 But I word, Heard they not?
Yes indeed, their sound goes to all the earth
and their rhema to the extremities of the world.
Psalm 19:4
19 But I *say* **word**, Did not *Israel* **Yisra El** know?
First *Moses saith* **Mosheh worded**,
I *will provoke* **shall incite** you to jealousy
by *them that are no people* **a nongoyim**,
and by *a foolish nation* **an uncomprehending goyim**
I *will anger* **shall enrage** you.
Deuteronomy 32:21
20 But *Esaias* **Yesha Yah** is very *bold* **courageous**,
and *saith* **wordeth**, I was found of them
that sought me not;
I *was made* **became** manifest unto them
that asked not after me.
21 But to *Israel* **Yisra El** he *saith* **wordeth**,
All day long I have *stretched forth* **spread** my hands
unto a *disobedient* **distrusting**
and *gainsaying* **contradicting** people.
Yesha Yah 42:6, 7, 65:1, 2

The Yisra Eliy Survivors

11 So I *say* **word** *then*,
Hath *God cast* **Elohim shoved** away his people?
God forbid **So be it not**.
For I also am an *Israelite* **Yisra Eliy**,
of the *seed* **sperma** of Abraham,
of the *tribe* **scion** of *Benjamin* **Ben Yamin**.
2 *God* **Elohim** hath not *cast*
shoved away his people
which he foreknew.
Wot **Or perceive** ye not
what the scripture *saith of Elias* **wordeth in Eli Yah**?
how he *maketh intercession* **intercedeth** to *God* **Elohim**
against *Israel saying* **Yisra El wording**,
3 *Lord* **Yah Veh**, they have *killed*
slaughtered thy prophets,
and digged down thine **sacrifice** altars;
and I *also* am *left* **behind** alone,
and they seek my *life* **soul**.
1 Sovereigns 19:10, 14
4 But what *saith* **wordeth**
the *answer of God* **oracle** unto him?
I have *reserved* **left** to myself seven thousand
men, who have not bowed the knee to *the
image of* Baal. 1 Sovereigns 19:18
5 Even *so* **thus** then at this
present *time* **season** also
there is a remnant
according to the *election* **selection** of *grace* **charism**.
6 And if by *grace* **charism**,
then is it *no more* **not still** of works:
otherwise *grace* **charism**
is *no more grace* **not still charism**.
But if *it be* of works,
then it is *no more grace* **not still charism**:
otherwise work is *no more* **not still** work.
7 What then?
Israel **Yisra El** hath not obtained
that which he seeketh for;
but the *election* **selection** hath obtained it,
and the rest were *blinded* **petrified**.
8 (*According* **Exactly** as *it is written* **scribed**,
God **Elohim** hath given them
the spirit of *slumber* **insensitivity**,
eyes that they should not see,
and ears that they should not hear;) unto
this day **today**. Yesha Yah 29:10
9 And David *saith* **wordeth**,
Let their table *be made* **become into** a snare,
and **into** a *trap* **prey**,
and **into** a *stumblingblock* **scandal**,
and **into** a recompence unto them:
10 Let their eyes be darkened,
that they may not see,
and bow down their back *alway*
continually. Psalm 69:22
11 So I *say* **word** *then*,
Have they stumbled that they should fall?
God forbid **So be it not**:
but *rather* through their *fall* **downfall**
salvation is *come* unto the *Gentiles* **goyim**,
for to *provoke* **incite** them to jealousy.
12 Now if the *fall* **downfall** of them
be the riches of the *world* **cosmos**,
and the diminishing of them the
riches of the *Gentiles* **goyim**;
how much more their fulness?
19 But I word, Knows Yisra El not?
that Mosheh first worded,
I incite you to jealousy by a nongoyim
and by an uncomprehending goyim I
enrage you. Deuteronomy 32:21

ROMANS 11

20 And Yesha Yah is very courageous, and words,
I was found by them who sought me not;
I became manifest to them who asked not after me.
21 And to Yisra El he words,
All day long I spread my hands
to a distrusting and contradicting
people. Yesha Yah 42:6, 7, 65:1, 2

THE YISRA ELIY SURVIVORS

11 So I word,
Has Elohim shoved away his people?
So be it not.
For I also am an Yisra Eliy
of the sperma of Abraham, of the scion of Ben Yamin.
2 Elohim shoved not away his people
whom he foreknew.
Or perceive you not
what the scripture words in Eli Yah?
how he interceded to Elohim against Yisra El,
wording,
3 Yah Veh, they slaughtered your prophets
and dug your sacrifice altars!
And also, I am behind alone and they
seek my soul! 1 Sovereigns 19:10, 14
4 But what words the oracle to him?
I leave to myself seven thousand men,
who bow not the knee to Baal.
1 Sovereigns 19:18
5 Thus also at this present season,
there is a remnant
according to the selection by charism:
6 and if by charism, it is not still by works:
otherwise charism is not still by charism: and
if by works, it is not still by charism:
otherwise work is not still by work.
7 So what?
Yisra El obtained not what he seeks;
but the selection obtained, and the rest petrified.
8 Exactly as scribed,
Elohim gives them the spirit of insensitivity,
eyes that they see not and ears that they hear not
— to this day today.
Yesha Yah 29:10
9 And David words,
Let their table become into a snare and into a prey
and into a scandal and into a recompence to them:
10 that their eyes darken, that they see not
and bow their back continually.
Psalm 69:22
11 So I word, Stumble they to fall?
So be it not.
But through their downfall,
there is salvation to the goyim
— to incite them to jealousy:
12 and if their downfall is the riches of the cosmos,
and their diminishing the riches of the goyim,
how much more their fulness/shalom?
13 For I *speak* **word** to you *Gentiles* **goyim**,
inasmuch **indeed**
as I am the apostle of the *Gentiles* **goyim**,
I *magnify mine office* **glorify my ministry**:
14 If *by any means* **somehow** I may *provoke* **incite**
to emulation them which are my flesh **to
jealousy**, and might save some of them.
15 For if the casting away of them
be the reconciling of the *world* **cosmos**,
what shall the *receiving* **reception** of them be,
but **if not** life from the dead?
16 For if the *firstfruit* **firstlings** be holy,
the lump is also *holy*:
and if the root be holy, so are the branches.
17 And if some of the branches
be *broken off* **exscinded**,
and thou, being a wild olive *tree*,
wert graffed in among them **were ingrafted**,
and with them
partakest **becamest co—partaker** of the root
and fatness of the *olive tree* **olives**;
18 *Boast* **Exult** not against the branches.
But if thou *boast* **exult**,
thou bearest not the root, but the root thee.
19 Thou *wilt* **shalt** say then,
The branches were *broken off* **exscinded**,
that I might be *graffed in* **ingrafted**.
20 Well;
because of *unbelief* **trustlessness** they were
broken off **exscinded**, and thou standest by *faith*
trust. Be not highminded, but *fear* **awe**:
21 For if *God* **Elohim** spared
not the natural branches,
take heed lest **somehow** he *also* spare not thee.
22 *Behold therefore* **So perceive**
the *goodness* **kindness** and severity of *God* **Elohim**:
on them which fell, **indeed** severity;
but toward thee, *goodness* **kindness**,
if whenever thou continue abide
in his goodness kindness:
otherwise thou also shalt be *cut off* **exscinded**.
23 And they also,

if **unless ever** they abide *not* **still**
in *unbelief* **trustlessness**,
shall be *graffed in* **ingrafted**:
for *God* **Elohim** is able to *graff* **ingraft** them *in* again.

24 For if thou wert *cut* **exscinded**
out of the olive *tree*
which is wild by nature,
and wert *graffed contrary to* **ingrafted against** nature
into a good olive *tree*:
how much more shall these, which
be the natural *branches*,
be *graffed* **ingrafted** into their own *olive tree* **olives**?

25 For I *would* **will** not, brethren,
that ye should be *ignorant* **unknowing** of this mystery,
lest ye should
be wise in your own conceits **think beyond yourselves**;
that *blindness in* **petrifaction by** part
is happened to Israel **became unto Yisra El**,
until the fulness of the *Gentiles be come in* **goyim enter**.

26 And *so* **thus** all *Israel* **Yisra El** shall be saved:
exactly as *it is written* **scribed**,
There shall come out of *Sion* **Siyon**
the *Deliverer* **Rescuer**,
and shall turn away *ungodliness* **irreverence**
from *Jacob* **Yaaqov**:

27 For this is my covenant unto them,
when I shall *take away* **remove** their
sins. Psalm 14:7, Yesha Yah 59:20

28 **Indeed**, As concerning the *gospel* **evangelism**,
they are enemies for your sakes:
but as touching the *election* **selection**,
they are beloved for the fathers' sakes.

29 For the *gifts* **charismata**
and calling of *God* **Elohim**
are *without repentance* **irrevocable**.

30 For **exactly** as ye *in times past* **formerly**
have not believed God **distrusted Elohim**,
yet *have* now *obtained mercy* **be mercied**
through their *unbelief* **distrust**:

31 Even *so* **thus**
have these also now *not believed* **distrusted**,
that through your mercy
they also may *obtain mercy* **be mercied**.

13 For I word to you — to the goyim:
indeed, inasmuch as I am the apostle of the goyim
I glorify my ministry:

14 if somehow I incite my flesh to jealousy
and save some of them.

15 For if their casting away
be the reconciling of the cosmos,
what a reception
if not life from the dead?

16 For if the firstlings be holy, the lump also:
and if the root be holy, the branches also.

17 And if some of the branches are exscinded
and you, being a wild olive, are ingrafted
and with them become co—partaker of the root
and fatness of the olives;

18 exult not against the branches.
But if you exult,
you bear not the root, but the root you.

19 So you say,
The branches were exscinded, to ingraft me.

20 Well!
Because of trustlessness, they were exscinded
and by trust, you stand.
Be not highminded, but awe:

21 for if Elohim spared not the natural branches,
heed lest somehow he spare not you.

22 So perceive the kindness and severity of Elohim:
on them who fell, indeed severity;
and toward you, kindness
— whenever you abide in his kindness:
otherwise you also become exscinded;

23 and they also become ingrafted,
unless they ever abide in trustlessness: for
Elohim is able to ingraft them again.

24 For if you, by nature,
are exscinded from the wild olive,
and against nature are ingrafted into a good olive:
how much more are these the natural
ingrafted into their own olive?

25 For brothers,
I will not that you be unknowing of this mystery,
lest you think beyond yourselves;
that petrifaction by part became Yisra El,
until the fulness/shalom of the goyim enter.

26 And thus all Yisra El is saved!
Exactly as scribed,
The Rescuer comes from Siyon
and turns irreverence from Yaaqov:

27 for this is my covenant to them
when I remove their sins. Psalm 14:7, Yesha Yah 59:20

28 Indeed, as concerning the evangelism,
enemies for your sakes:
but as touching the selection,
beloved for the sakes of the fathers.

29 For the charismata and calling of Elohim
are irrevocable.

30 For exactly as you formerly distrusted Elohim,

ROMANS 11, 12

      yet are mercied through their distrust:
31   even thus these also now distrust
— that through your mercy, they also are mercied.
32   For *God* **Elohim**
hath *concluded* **locked** them all **together**
in *unbelief* **distrust**,
that he might *have* mercy *upon* **them** all.
33   O the depth of the riches
both of the wisdom and knowledge of *God* **Elohim**!
how *unsearchable* **unexplorable** are his judgments,
and his ways *past finding out* **untraceable**!
34   For who hath known
the *mind* **Spirit** of *the Lord* **Yah Veh**?
or who hath been his counsellor?
35   Or who hath first given to him,
and it shall be recompensed unto him *again*?
36   For of him, and through him, and *to* **unto** him,
are all *things*:
to whom *be* glory *for ever* **unto the eons**.
Amen.
Yesha Yah 40:13

The Holy Metamorphosis

12   So I beseech you *therefore*, brethren,
by **through** the *mercies* **compassions** of *God* **Elohim**,
that ye present your bodies a living sacrifice,
holy, *acceptable* **well—pleasing** unto *God* **Elohim**,
which is your *reasonable service* **logical liturgy**.
2   And be not *conformed*
configured to this *world* **eon**:
but be *ye transformed* **metamorphosed**
by the renewing of your mind,
that ye may prove what is that good,
and *acceptable* **well—pleasing**,
and *perfect* **completed/shalamed**, will of *God* **Elohim**.

The Charismata

3   For I *say* **word**, through the
grace **charism** given unto me,
to every *man that is* **one being** among you,
not to *think of himself* **superexalt**
more *highly* than he *ought to think* **need superexalt**;
but to think *soberly* **unto being soundminded**,
according as *God* **Elohim** hath *dealt* **imparted**
to *every man* **each** the measure of
faith **trust**. Philippians 2:1—8
4   For **exactly** *as* we have
many members in one body,
and all members have not the same *office* **function**:

5   *So* **Thus** we, *being* many, are
one body in *Christ* **Messiah**,
and *every one* **each** members one of another.
6   Having then *gifts* **charismata**
differing **thoroughly excelling**
according to the *grace* **charism** that is given to us,
whether *if also* prophecy,
let us prophesy according to the proportion of *faith* **trust**;
7   Or *if also* ministry,
let us wait on our *ministering* **in ministering**:
or he that teacheth *if also doctrinating*
on *teaching* **in doctrine**;
8   Or he that exhorteth *if also consoling*,
on *exhortation* **in consolation**:
he that giveth **in imparting**,
let him do it *with simplicity* **in liberality**;
he that ruleth **in presiding**,
with **in** diligence;
he that sheweth mercy **in mercying**,
with cheerfulness **in hilarity**.
I Corinthians 12:1—11
9   Let love be *without
dissimulation* **unhypocritical**.
Abhor *that which is* evil;
cleave **adhere** to *that which is* good.
10   *Be kindly* **Cherish**
affectioned **befriending** one to another
with brotherly love **in befriending**;
in honour preferring one another;
11   Not slothful in *business* **diligence**;
fervent **zealous** in spirit;
serving *the Lord* **Adonay in season**;
12   *Rejoicing* **Cheering** in hope;
patient **abiding** in tribulation;
continuing instant in prayer;
13   *Distributing* **Imparting**
to the *necessity* **needs** of *saints* **the holy**;
given to hospitality **pursuing the
befriending of strangers**.
14   *Bless* **Eulogize** them which persecute you:
bless **eulogize**, and curse not.
32   For Elohim locked them all together in distrust
to mercy them all.
33   O the depth of the riches
of both the wisdom and knowledge of Elohim!
How unexplorable his judgments
and his ways untraceable!
34   For who knows the Spirit of Yah Veh?
Or who is his counselor?
35   Or who first gives to him

36	so that it is recompensed to him? For of him and through him and to him, all *is*: to whom *be* glory to the eons. Amen. Yesha Yah 40:13	13 14 15 16	imparting to the needs of the holy; pursuing the befriending of strangers; eulogize them who persecute you — eulogize and curse not; *Rejoice* **Cheer** with them that *do rejoice* **cheer**, and weep with them that weep. Be of the same *mind* **thought** one toward another.

THE HOLY METAMORPHOSIS

12   So I beseech you, brothers,
through the compassions of Elohim,
that you present your bodies a living sacrifice,
holy, well—pleasing to Elohim
— your logical liturgy.

2   And be not configured to this eon:
but metamorphosed by the renewing of your mind,
to prove what that good
and well—pleasing
and completed/shalamed will of Elohim is.

THE CHARISMATA

3   For through the charism given to me
I word to everyone being among you,
to not superexalt more than he need superexalt;
but to think to being soundminded,
as Elohim imparted to each the measure of trust.
Philippians 2:1—8

4   For exactly as we have
many members in one body
and all members have not the same function:

5   thus we many are one body in Messiah
and each members one of another.

6   So having charismata — thoroughly excelling
according to the charism given to us,
if prophecy, according to the proportion of trust;

7   if also ministry, in ministering;
if also doctrinating, in doctrine;

8   if also consoling, in consolation;
if also imparting, in liberality;
if also presiding, in diligence;
if also mercying, in hilarity.
I Corinthians 12:1—11

9   Love, eunhypocritical;
abhor evil;
adhere to good;

10   in befriending one another, cherish befriending;
in honor, preferring one another;

11   not slothful in diligence;
zealous in spirit;
serving Adonay in season;

12   cheering in hope;
abiding in tribulation;
continuing instant in prayer;

16 (cont.) *Mind* **Think** not *high things* **highly**,
but *condescend to men of low estate*
lead with the humble.
Be not wise in your own conceits
Think not beyond yourselves.

17   *Recompense* **Give back** to
no *man* **one** evil for evil.
Provide *things honest* **good**
in the sight of all *men* **humanity**.

18   If it be possible, as much as *lieth in* **is of** you,
live peaceably **shalam** with all *men* **humanity**.

19   Dearly beloved, avenge not yourselves,
but *rather* give place unto wrath:
for it is *written* **scribed**, Vengeance is mine;
I *will repay* **shall recompense**,
saith the Lord **wordeth Yah Veh**.
Deuteronomy 32:35

20   *Therefore if* **So whenever** thine enemy hunger,
force feed him;
if **whenever** he thirst, give him drink:
for in so doing
thou shalt heap coals of fire on his head.

21   *Be not overcome of evil* **Let
not evil triumph over you**,
but *overcome evil with* **triumph over
evil in** good. Proverbs 25:21, 22

ALL AUTHORITY IS ELOHIM—ORDAINED

13   Let every soul *be subject* **subjugate**
unto the *higher powers* **superior authorities**.
For there is no *power* **authority**
but **except** of *God* **Elohim**:
the *powers* **authorities** that be
are ordained of *God* **Elohim**.

2   **So** Whosoever *therefore*
resisteth **withstandeth** the *power* **authority**,
resisteth **opposeth** the ordinance of *God* **Elohim**:
and they that *resist* **withstand**
shall *receive* **take** to themselves *damnation* **judgment**.

3   For *rulers* **archs** are not *a*
terror **an awe** to good works,
but to the evil.

ALL AUTHORITY IS ELOHIM—ORDAINED

13 Every soul,
subjugate to the superior authorities.
For there is no authority except of Elohim:
the authorities that be are ordained of Elohim.

2 So whoever withstands the authority
opposes the ordinance of Elohim:
and whoever withstands
stake judgment to themselves.

3 For archs are not an awe to good works
but to the evil.
So will you, to not be awestricken of the authority?
Do good
and you have halal of the same:

4 for he is your minister of Elohim for good.
But whenever you do evil, awe;
for he bears not the sword in vain:
for he is the minister of Elohim
— the avenger to wrath upon whoever transacts evil.

5 So it is necessary to subjugate,
not only for wrath, but also for sake of conscience.

6 For this cause complete/
shalam your tribute also:
for they are liturgists of Elohim, continuing therein.

7 So give to all their dues:
to whom tribute, tribute;
to whom completion/shalom, completion/shalom;
to whom awe, awe;
to whom honor, honor.

8 Be indebted to no one
except to love one another:
for whoever loves another fulfills/shalams the torah.

9 For:
adulterize not!
murder not!
steal not!
pseudo witness not!

Wilt **Willest** thou then not be *afraid* **awestricken**
of the *power* **authority**?
do that which is good,
and thou shalt have *praise* **halal** of the same:

4 For he is the minister of *God*
Elohim to thee for good.
But *if* **whenever** thou do that which
is evil, be *afraid* **awed**;
for he beareth not the sword in vain:
for he is the minister of *God* **Elohim**,
a revenger to execute **the avenger unto** wrath
upon him that *doeth* **transacteth** evil.

5 Wherefore
ye must *needs be subject* **necessarily subjugate**,
not only for wrath, but also for conscience sake.

6 For for this cause *pay* **complete/
shalam** ye tribute also:
for they are *God's ministers* **Elohim's liturgists**,
attending continually **continuing**
upon **unto** this *very thing*.

7 *Render therefore* **So give** to all their dues:
tribute to whom tribute is due
to whom tribute, tribute;
custom to whom custom
to whom completion/shalom, completion/shalom;
fear to whom fear
to whom awe, awe;
honour to whom honour
to whom honour, honour.

8 *Owe no man any thing* **Be indebted to no one**,
but **except** to love one another:
for he that loveth another hath fulfilled the *law* **torah**.

9 For this,
Thou shalt not *commit adultery* **adulterize**,
Thou shalt not *kill* **murder**,
Thou shalt not steal,
Thou shalt not *bear false* **pseudo** witness,
Thou shalt not *covet* **pant**;
and if *there be* any other *commandment* **misvah**,
it is *briefly comprehended* **summed up**
in this *saying* **word**, namely,
Thou shalt love thy neighbour as thyself.

15 cheer with the cheering
and weep with the weeping;

16 of the same thought one toward another;
think not highly, but lead with the humble;
think not beyond yourselves;

17 give no one evil for evil;
provide good in the sight of all humanity.

18 If possible, as much as is of you,
complete/shalam with all humanity.

19 Dearly beloved, avenge not yourselves,
but give place to wrath:
for it is scribed, Vengeance is mine;
I recompense, words Yah Veh.
Deuteronomy 32:35

20 So whenever your enemy famishes,
force feed him;
whenever he thirsts, give him drink:
for in so doing you heap coals of fire on his head;

21 so that evil triumphs not over you,
but that the good triumphs over evil. Proverbs 25:21, 22

pant not!
— and if *there is* any other misvah
it is summed up in this word,
namely,
Love your neighbour as yourself!
10 Love worketh no *ill* **evil** to his neighbour:
therefore love is the fulfilling of the *law*
torah. Exodus 20:13—17, Leviticus 19:18
11 And that, knowing the *time* **season**,
that *now* **already** it is *high time* **the hour**
to *awake* **rise** out of sleep:
for now is our salvation nearer
than when we *believed* **trusted**.
12 The night is *far spent* **advanced**,
the day *is at hand* **approacheth**:
let us therefore *cast* **put** off the works of darkness,
and let us *put on* **endue** the *armour* **weapon** of light.
13 Let us walk *honestly* **decorously**, as in the day;
not in *rioting* **carousing** and *drunkenness* **intoxication**,
not in *chambering* **coition** and *wantonness* **lechery**,
not in *strife* **contention** and *envying* **zeal**.
14 But *put* **endue** ye *on*
the Lord Jesus Christ **Adonay Yah Shua Messiah**,
and make not provision for the flesh
to *fulfil the lusts thereof* **do its pantings**.

THE FRAIL IN THE TRUST

14 Him that is *weak* **frail** in the *faith* **trust**
receive **take** ye **unto yourselves**,
but not to *doubtful disputations* **discern reasonings**.
2 For **indeed** one *believeth* **trusteth**
that he may eat all *things*:
another, who is *weak* **frail**, eateth herbs.
3 Let not him that eateth
despise **belittle** him that eateth not;
and let not him which eateth not
judge him that eateth:
for *God* **Elohim** hath *received* **taken** him **unto himself**.
4 Who art thou that judgest
another man's servant **another's housekeeper**?
to his own *master* **adoni** he standeth **firm** or falleth.
Yea, he shall *be holden up* **stand**:
for *God* **Elohim** is able to *make him* stand **him**.
5 One man *esteemeth* **judgeth**
one day above another:
another *esteemeth* **judgeth** every day *alike*.
Let *every man* **each** be fully *persuaded* **assured**
in his own mind.
6 He that *regardeth* **thinketh of** the day,
regardeth **thinketh** it unto *the Lord* **Adonay**;

and he that *regardeth* **thinketh** not the day,
to *the Lord* **Adonay** he *doth not regard it* **thinketh not**.
He that eateth, eateth to *the Lord* **Adonay**,
for he *giveth God thanks* **eucharistizeth Elohim**;
and he that eateth not, to *the Lord* **Adonay** he eateth not,
and *giveth God thanks* **eucharistizeth Elohim**.
7 For none of us liveth to himself,
and no *man* **one** dieth to himself.
8 For *whether* **whenever** we live,
we live unto *the Lord* **Adonay**;
and *whether* **whenever** we die,
we die unto *the Lord* **Adonay**:
whether **So whenever** we live *therefore*,
or **whenever** we die, we are *the Lord's* **Adonay's**.
9 For to this end *Christ* **Messiah**
both died, and rose, and *revived* **relived**,
that he might
be Lord both of **overlord** the dead and living.

JUDGING AND JUSTNESS

10 But why dost thou judge thy brother?
or why dost thou *set at nought* **belittle** thy brother?
for we shall all stand
before **by** the *judgment seat* **bamah**
of *Christ* **the Messiah**.
11 For it is *written* **scribed**,
As I live, *saith the Lord* **wordeth Yah Veh**,
every knee shall bow to me,
and every tongue shall *confess* **avow** to *God* **Elohim**.
Yesha Yah 45:23, Philippians 2:10, 12
12 So then *every one* **each** of us
shall give *account of* **word concerning** himself
to *God* **Elohim**.
13 Let us *not* **no longer** therefore
judge one another *any more*:
but judge this rather,
that no *man* **one** put a *stumblingblock* **stumbling**
or *an occasion to fall* **a scandal** in his brother's way.
10 Love works no evil to his neighbour:
so love is the fulness/shalom of the torah.
Exodus 20:13—17, Leviticus 19:18
11 And this:
knowing the season,
that it is already the hour to rise from sleep;
for now our salvation is nearer than when we trusted.
12 The night advances, the day approaches:
so put off the works of darkness
and endue the weapon of light.
13 Walk decorously as in the day;
not in carousing and intoxication;

ROMANS 14, 15

not in coition and lechery;
not in contention and zeal;
14 but endue Adonay Yah Shua Messiah
and make no provision for the flesh to do its pantings.

THE FRAIL IN THE TRUST

14 And take not the frail in the trust
to discern reasonings.
2 For indeed one who trusts, eats all:
another, who is frail, eats herbs.
3 Whoever eats, belittle not whoever eats not;
and whoever eats not, judge not whoever
eats: for Elohim takes them to himself.
4 You
— who are you to judge the housekeeper of another?
unto his own adoni he stands firm or falls.
Yes, he stands:
for Elohim is able to stand him.
5 One judges one day above another;
another judges every day.
Each of you, assure fully in your own mind.
6 Whoever thinks of the day,
thinks it to Adonay;
and whoever thinks not the day,
thinks it not to Adonay;
whoever eats,
eats to Adonay for he eucharistizes Elohim;
and whoever eats not to Adonay,
eats not and eucharistizes Elohim.
7 For none of us lives to self
and no one dies to self.
8 For whenever we live, we live to Adonay;
and whenever we die, we die to Adonay:
so whenever we live, whenever we die,
we are to Adonay.
9 For to this end
Messiah both died and rose and relived
— to overlord the dead and living.

JUDGING AND JUSTNESS

10 And you, why judge your brother?
Or why belittle your brother?
For we all stand by the bamah of the Messiah.
11 For it is scribed, As I live, Yah Veh words,
every knee bows to me
and every tongue avows to Elohim.
Yesha Yah 45:23, Philippians 2:10, 12
12 So each of us gives word
to Elohim concerning self.
13 So judge one another no longer:
but rather judge this,
that no one put a stumbling
or a scandal in the way of his brother.
14 I know, and am *persuaded* **convinced**
by the Lord Jesus **in Adonay Yah Shua**,
that there is *nothing unclean* **naught
profane** *of* **through** itself:
but **except** to him that *esteemeth* **reckoneth**
any thing **somewhat** to be *unclean* **profane**,
to him it is *unclean* **profane**.
15 But if thy brother
be *grieved with thy meat* **sorrowed through food**,
now walkest thou not *charitably* **still longer in love**.
Destroy not him with thy *meat* **food**,
for whom *Christ* **Messiah** died.
16 Let not then your good be
evil spoken of **blasphemed**:
17 For the *kingdom* **sovereigndom** of *God* **Elohim**
is not *meat* **eat** and drink;
but *righteousness* **justness**, and *peace* **shalom**,
and *joy* **cheer** in the *Holy Spirit* **Ruach ha-kodesh**.
18 For he that in these *things*
serveth *Christ* **the Messiah**
is *acceptable* **well—pleasing** to *God* **Elohim**,
and approved of *men* **humanity**.
19 Let us therefore *follow after* **then pursue**
the things **those** which make for *peace* **shalom**,
and *things* **those** wherewith one may edify another.
20 For *meat* **sake of food**
destroy **disintegrate** not the work of *God* **Elohim**.
All *things* indeed are pure;
but it is evil for that *man* **human**
who eateth *with offence* **through stumbling**.
21 It is good neither to eat *flesh*
meat, nor to drink wine,
nor *any thing whereby* **aught wherein**
thy brother stumbleth, or is *offended*
scandalized, or is *made weak* **frailed**.
22 Hast thou *faith* **trust**?
have it to thyself *before God* **in sight of Elohim**.
Happy **Blessed** is he
that *condemneth* **judgeth** not himself
in that *thing* which he *alloweth* **approveth**.
23 And he that doubteth
is *damned if* **condemned whenever** he eat,
because *he eateth* **it is** not of *faith* **trust**:
for whatsoever is not of *faith* **trust** is sin.

PLEASING SELF

15 *So* **We** *then* that are *strong* **able**

ought **are indebted**
to bear the *infirmities* **frailties** of the *weak* **impotent**,
and not to please ourselves.

2 **Indeed** Let *every one* **each**
of us please his neighbour
for **unto** his good to edification.

3 For even *Christ* **the Messiah**
pleased not himself;
but, **exactly** as *it is written* **scribed**,
The reproaches of them that reproached thee fell on me.

4 For *whatsoever things* **as many as**
were *written aforetime* **preinscribed**,
were *written for* **preinscribed unto**
our *learning* **doctrine**,
that we through *patience* **endurance**
and *comfort* **consolation** of the
scriptures might have hope.

5 Now the *God* **Elohim**
of *patience* **endurance** and **the** consolation
grant you to be likeminded **give you like thoughts**
one *toward* **among** another
according to *Christ Jesus* **Messiah Yah Shua**:

6 That ye may with *one mind*
unanimity and one mouth
glorify *God* **Elohim**,
even the Father
of our *Lord Jesus Christ* **Adonay Yah Shua Messiah**.

7 Wherefore *receive ye* **take**
unto yourselves one another,
exactly as *Christ* **the Messiah**
also *received* **took** us to the glory of *God* **Elohim**.

8 Now I *say* **word** that *Jesus*
Christ **Yah Shua Messiah**
was **became** a minister of the circumcision
for the truth of *God* **Elohim**,
to confirm **establishing**
the *promises made* **pre—evangelisms** unto the fathers:

9 And that the *Gentiles* **goyim** might
glorify *God* **Elohim** for his mercy;
exactly as *it is written* **scribed**,
For this cause
I *will confess* **shall avow** to thee
among the *Gentiles* **goyim**,
and *sing* **psalm** unto thy name.
Psalm 18:49

14 I know and am convinced in Adonay Yah Shua
that naught is profane through itself:
except to him who reckons aught profane,
to him it is profane.

15 And if your brother sorrows through food,
you no longer still walk in love. Destroy
not him for whom Messiah died
through your food:

16 so that your good is not blasphemed.

17 For the sovereigndom of Elohim
is not eat and drink;
but justness and shalom
and cheer in the Holy Spirit.

18 For whoever serves the Messiah in these
is well—pleasing to Elohim and approved of humanity.

19 So pursue those that make for shalom
and those that edify one another.

20 Disintegrate not the work of Elohim
for sake of food.
All indeed are pure;
but evil for that human who, through stumbling, eats.

21 It is good neither to eat meat
nor to drink wine
nor aught wherein your brother stumbles
or is scandalized, or is frailed.

22 Have you trust?
Have it to yourself in sight of Elohim.
Blessed
— whoever judges not self by what he approves.

23 And whoever doubts
is condemned whenever he eats
because it is not of trust:
for whatever is not of trust is sin.

Pleasing Self

15 So we who are able
are indebted to bear the frailties of the impotent
and not to please ourselves.

2 Indeed,
each of us is to please his neighbour
for good to edification.

3 For even the Messiah pleased not himself;
but exactly as scribed,
The reproaches of them who reproached you
fell on me:

4 for as many as were preinscribed,
were preinscribed to our doctrine,
so that we, through the endurance
and the consolation of the scriptures
have the hope.

5 And the Elohim
of the endurance and the consolation
give you like thoughts among one another
according to Messiah Yah Shua:

6 so that you,

ROMANS 15

with unanimity and one mouth glorify Elohim
— even the Father of our Adonay Yah Shua Messiah.

7 So take one another to yourselves,
exactly as the Messiah
also took us to the glory of Elohim.

8 And I word that Yah Shua Messiah
became a minister of the circumcision
for the truth of Elohim,
to establish the pre—evangelisms to the fathers:

9 and that the goyim glorify
Elohim for his mercy;
exactly as scribed,
For this cause I avow to you among the goyim
and psalm to your name.
Psalm 18:49

10 And again he *saith* **wordeth**,
Rejoice, ye *Gentiles* **goyim**, with his
people. Deuteronomy 32:43

11 And again,
Praise the Lord **Halalu Yah**, all ye *Gentiles* **goyim**;
and *laud* **halal** him, all ye people.

12 And again, *Esaias saith* **Yesha Yah wordeth**,
There shall be a root of *Jesse* **Yishay**,
and he that shall rise
to *reign* **rule** over the *Gentiles* **goyim**;
in him shall the *Gentiles trust* **goyim hope**.
Psalm 18:49, 117:1, Yesha Yah11:1,10, 42:6, 7

13 Now the *God* **Elohim** of hope fill you **full**
with all *joy* **cheer** and *peace* **shalom**
in *believing* **trusting**,
that ye may *abound* **superabound** in hope,
through **in** the *power* **dynamis** of the
Holy Spirit **Ruach ha-kodesh**.

14 And I myself also
am *persuaded of* **convinced concerning** you,
my brethren, that ye also *are* **be** full of goodness,
filled **full** with all knowledge,
able also to *admonish* **remind** one another.

15 *Nevertheless* **And so**, brethren,
I have *written* **scribed** the more boldly unto you
in some sort **partly**,
as putting you in mind of re—reminding you,
because of the *grace* **charism**
that is given to me of *God* **Elohim**,

16 That I should be the *minister* **liturgist**
of *Jesus Christ* **Yah Shua Messiah** to the *Gentiles* **goyim**,
ministering **priesting**
the *gospel* **evangelism** of *God* **Elohim**,
that the offering *up* of the *Gentiles* **goyim**
might be *acceptable* **wellreceived**,
being *sanctified* **hallowed** by the *Holy
Spirit* **Ruach ha-kodesh**.

17 **So** I have *therefore whereof I may glory* **boasting**
through Jesus Christ **in Yah Shua Messiah**
in those things which pertain to God **toward Elohim**.

18 For I *will* **shall** not dare to
speak of any of those *things*
which *Christ* **Messiah** hath not *wrought* **worked**
by me, to make the *Gentiles* **goyim** obedient,
by word and *deed* **work**,

19 *Through mighty* **In dynamis**
of signs and *wonders* **omens**,
by **in** the *power* **dynamis** of the Spirit of *God* **Elohim**;
so that from *Jerusalem* **Yeru Shalem** and round about
unto Illyricum,
I have *fully preached* **fulfilled/shalamed**
the *gospel* **evangelism** of *Christ* **the Messiah**.

20 Yea, *so* **thus** have I *strived*
befriendingly esteemed
to *preach the gospel* **evangelize**,
not where *Christ* **Messiah** was named,
lest I should build
upon *another man's* **another's** foundation:

21 But *exactly* as it is *written* **scribed**,
To **Concerning** whom
he was **they that were** not *spoken of* **evangelized**,
they shall see:
and they that have not heard
shall *understand* **comprehend**.
Yesha Yah 52:15

THE TRAVEL PLANS OF PAULOS

22 *For which cause* **So** also
I have been much hindered from coming to you.

23 But now having no more
place in these *parts* **climes**,
and having *a great desire* **an intense yearning**
these many years to come unto you;

24 *Whensoever* **Whenever**
I *take my journey* **depart** into *Spain* **Spania**,
I *will* **shall** come to you:
for I *trust* **hope** to *see* **observe** you
in my *journey* **going through**,
and to be
brought on my way thitherward **forwarded** by you,
if **whenever** first
I be *somewhat* **partly** filled *with your company* **by you**.

25 But now I go unto *Jerusalem* **Yeru Shalem**
to minister unto the *saints* **holy**.

10 And again he words,

Rejoice, you goyim, with his people.
Deuteronomy 32:43

11 And again,
Halalu Yah, all you goyim;
and halal him, all you people.

12 And again, Yesha Yah words,
And so be it, a root of Yishay;
and he rises to rule over the goyim:
in him the goyim hope.
Psalm 18:49, 117:1, Yesha Yah 11:1,10, 42:6,7

13 Now the Elohim of the hope
fill you full/shalam you
with all cheer and shalom in trusting;
so that you superabound in hope
in the dynamis of the Holy Spirit.

14 And I am convinced — I myself also
concerning you my brothers,
that you also be full of goodness
filled full/shalamed with all knowledge
also able to remind one another.

15 And so brothers,
I scribe the more boldly to you
partly to re—remind you,
because of the charism given me by Elohim,

16 being the liturgist of Yah Shua Messiah
to the goyim,
priesting the evangelism of Elohim,
so that the offering of the goyim is well—received,
being hallowed by the Holy Spirit.

17 So I boast in Yah Shua Messiah
toward Elohim.

18 For I dare not speak of any of those
that Messiah works not through me,
to make the goyim obedient by word and work

19 in dynamis of signs and omens,
in the dynamis of the Spirit of Elohim;
so that from Yeru Shalem and around to Illyricum,
I fulfilled/shalamed the evangelism of the Messiah.

20 Yes, thus I befriendingly esteemed to evangelize
— not where Messiah was named,
lest I build on the foundation of another:

21 but exactly as scribed,
Concerning those who were not evangelized,
See:
and whoever had not heard
Comprehend.
Yesha Yah 52:15

THE TRAVEL PLANS OF PAULOS

22 So also, I was much hindered to come to you:

23 and now having no more place in these climes
and having an intense yearning these many years
to come to you;

24 whenever I depart to Spania, I come to you:
for I hope to observe you in my going through
and have you forward *me*,
whenever you first partly enrich me.

25 And now I go to Yeru Shalem
to minister to the holy.

26 For it hath *pleased* **well—approved**
them of Macedonia and Achaia
to make a *certain contribution* **communion**
for **unto** the poor *saints* **holy**
which are at Jerusalem **in Yeru Shalem**.

27 *It hath pleased them verily*
They indeed well—approved;
and their debtors they are.
For if the *Gentiles* **goyim**
have *been made partakers* **communed**
of their *spiritual things* **spirituals**,
their duty is also **they are indebted**
to *minister* **liturgize** unto them in *carnal things* **fleshlies**.

28 **So** When *therefore*
I have *performed* **fully completed/shalamed** this,
and have sealed to them this fruit,
I *will come by* **shall depart through** you
into *Spain* **Spania**.

29 And I am sure that, when I come unto you,
I shall come in the fulness of the *blessing* **eulogy**
of the *gospel* **evangelism** of *Christ* **the Messiah**.

30 **But** *Now* I beseech you, brethren,
for the *Lord Jesus Christ's sake*,
sake of our Adonay Yah Shua Messiah
and for the love of the Spirit,
that ye *strive together* **co—strive** with me
in *your* prayers to *God* **Elohim** for me;

31 That I may be *delivered* **rescued** from them
that *do not believe* **distrust** in *Judaea* **Yah Hudah**;
and that my *service* **ministry**
which I have for Jerusalem **unto Yeru Shalem**
may be *accepted* **well—received** of the *saints* **holy**;

32 That I may come unto you *with joy* **in cheer**
by **through** the will of *God* **Elohim**,
and may with you be refreshed.

33 Now the *God* **Elohim** of
peace **shalom** be with you all.
Amen.

PAULOS SALUTES THE HOLY

16 I commend unto you Phebe our sister,

	which is **being** a *servant* **minister**
	of the *church which is at* **ecclesia in** Cenchrea:
2	That ye *receive* **await** her in *the Lord* **Adonay**,
	as becometh saints **worthily of the holy**,
	and that ye *assist* **stand by** her
	in whatsoever *business* **matter** she *ever* hath need of you:
	for she hath *been* **become**
	a *succourer* **patroness** of many,
	and of myself also.
3	*Greet* **Salute** Priscilla and Aquila
	my helpers **co—workers** in *Christ*
	Jesus **Messiah Yah Shua**:
4	Who have for my *life* **soul**
	laid down their own necks:
	unto whom not only I *give thanks* **eucharistize**,
	but also all the *churches* **ecclesiae** of the *Gentiles* **goyim**.
5	Likewise *greet* the *church*
	ecclesia that is in their house.
	Salute my *wellbeloved* **beloved** Epaenetus,
	who is the *firstfruits* **firstlings** of Achaia
	unto *Christ* **Messiah**.
6	*Greet Mary* **Salute Miryam**,
	who *bestowed* **laboured** much *labour on* **unto** us.
7	Salute Andronicus and Junia, my *kinsmen* **kin**,
	and my *fellowprisoners* **co—captives**,
	who are *of note* **eminent** among the apostles,
	who also *were* **became** in *Christ* **Messiah** before me.
8	*Greet* **Salute** Amplias my
	beloved in *the Lord* **Adonay**.
9	Salute *Urbane* **Urbanos**,
	our *helper* **co—worker** in *Christ* **Messiah**,
	and Stachys my beloved.
10	Salute Apelles approved in *Christ* **Messiah**.
	Salute them which are of Aristobulus' **household**.
11	Salute Herodion my *kinsmen* **kindred**.
	Greet **Salute** them *that be of the household* of Narcissus,
	which are in *the Lord* **Adonay**.
12	Salute Tryphena and Tryphosa,
	who labour in *the Lord* **Adonay**.
	Salute the beloved Persis,
	which laboured much in *the Lord* **Adonay**.
13	Salute Rufus *chosen* **selected**
	in *the Lord* **Adonay**,
	and his mother and mine.
14	Salute Asyncritus, Phlegon,
	Hermas, Patrobas, Hermes,
	and the brethren which are with them.
26	For they of Macedonia and Achaia
	well—approved to make a communion
	to the poor holy in Yeru Shalem:
27	— they indeed well—approved;
	and their debtors they are.
	For if the goyim commune of their spirituals,
	they are indebted to liturgize in their fleshlies.
28	So when I fully complete/shalam this
	and seal this fruit to them,
	I depart through you into Spania.
29	And I am sure that, when I come to you,
	I come in the fulness/shalom of the eulogy
	of the evangelism of the Messiah.
30	But I beseech you brothers,
	for sake of our Adonay Yah Shua Messiah
	and for the love of the Spirit,
	that you co—strive in prayers to Elohim for me;
31	to be rescued from them in Yah Hudah
	who distrust;
	and that my ministry to Yeru Shalem
	be well—received by the holy;
32	to come to you in cheer
	through the will of Elohim
	and be refreshed with you.
33	And the Elohim of shalom be with you all.
	Amen.

Paulos Salutes The Holy

16	I commend to you our sister Phebe,
	being a minister of the ecclesia in Cenchrea:
2	that you await her in
	Adonay, worthily of the holy
	and stand by her
	in whatever matter she ever has need of you:
	for she became a patroness of many, and also of me.
3	Salute Priscilla and Aquila
	co—workers in Messiah Yah Shua:
4	who laid down their own necks for my soul:
	to whom, not only I eucharistize,
	but also all the ecclesiae of the goyim:
5	likewise the ecclesia in their house.
	Salute my beloved Epaenetus,
	the firstlings of Achaia to Messiah:
6	salute Miryam who labored much to us:
7	salute Andronicus and Junia
	my kin and my co—captives
	who are eminent among the apostles
	who also became in Messiah preceding me:
8	salute Amplias my beloved in Adonay:
9	salute Urbanos our co—worker in Messiah
	and Stachys my beloved:
10	salute Apelles approved in Messiah:
	salute them of Aristobulus:

11	salute Herodion my kindred:
	salute them of Narcissus, who are in Adonay:
12	salute Tryphena and Tryphosa
	who labor in Adonay:
	salute the beloved Persis
	who labors much in Adonay:
13	salute Rufus the selected in Adonay
	and his mother and mine:
14	salute Asyncritus, Phlegon, Hermas, Patrobas,
	Hermes and the brothers with them:
15	Salute Philologus, and Julia,
	Nereus, and his sister, and Olympas,
	and all the *saints* **holy** which are with them.
16	Salute one another *with* **in** an holy kiss.
	The *churches* **ecclesiae** of *Christ* **the Messiah** salute you.

Paulos Warns The Holy

17 Now I beseech you, brethren,
mark **scope** them
which cause divisions and *offences* **scandals**
contrary to **against** the doctrine which ye have learned;
and *avoid* **deviate from** them.
18 For they that are such serve not
our *Lord Jesus Christ* **Adonay Yah Shua Messiah**,
but their own belly;
and *by good* **through kind** words
and *fair speeches* **eulogy**
deceive **seduce** the hearts of the simple.
19 For your obedience
is *come abroad* **spread** unto all *men*.
I *am glad* **cheer** therefore on your behalf:
but yet **indeed** I *would have* **will that** you **be** wise
unto that which is good,
and *simple concerning* **unadulterated as to** evil.
20 And the *God* **Elohim** of *peace* **shalom**
shall *bruise* **crush** Satan under your feet
shortly **in quickness**.
The *grace* **charism**
of our *Lord Jesus Christ* **Adonay Yah Shua Messiah**
be with you.
Amen.

Salutes Of The Co-Workers

21 *Timotheus* **Timo Theos**
my *workfellow* **co—worker**,
and Lucius, and Jason, and Sosipater,
my *kinsmen* **kindred**, salute you.
22 I Tertius, who *wrote* **scribed** this epistle,
salute you in *the Lord* **Adonay**.
23 Gaius *mine host* **my stranger**,
and of the whole *church* **ecclesia**, saluteth you.
Erastus the *chamberlain* **administrator** of the city
saluteth you,
and Quartus a brother.
24 The *grace* **charism**
of our *Lord Jesus Christ* **Adonay Yah Shua Messiah**
be with you all.
Amen.

Doxology

25 Now to him that is *of power* **able** to stablish you
according to my *gospel* **evangelism**,
and the preaching of *Jesus Christ* **Yah Shua Messiah**,
according to the *revelation* **apocalypse** of the mystery,
which was *kept secret* **hushed**
since *the world began* **eternal time**,
26 But now is *made manifest* **manifested**,
and *by the* **through prophetic** scriptures *of the prophets*,
according to the *commandment* **order**
of the *everlasting God* **eternal Elohim**,
made known to all *nations* **goyim**
for **unto** the obedience of *faith* **trust**:
27 To *God* **Elohim** only wise,
be glory through *Jesus Christ* **Yah Shua Messiah**
for ever **unto the eons**.
Amen.

15 salute Philologus and Julia,
Nereus and his sister and Olympas
and all the holy with them:
16 salute one another in a holy kiss:
the ecclesiae of the Messiah salute you.

Paulos Warns The Holy

17 And I beseech you brothers,
scope them who cause divisions and scandals
against the doctrine you learned
— and deviate from them.
18 For they who are such
serve not our Adonay Yah Shua Messiah,
but their own belly;
and through kind words and eulogy
seduce the hearts of the simple.
19 For your obedience spreads to all:
so I cheer on your behalf:
but yet indeed, I will that you be wise as to good
and unadulterated as to evil:
20 and that the Elohim of shalom
quickly crush Satan under your feet.
The charism of our Adonay Yah Shua Messiah
be with you.

Amen.

Salutes Of The Co-Workers

21 Timo Theos my co—worker
and Lucius and Jason and Sosipater my kindred
salute you:
22 I Tertius, who scribe this epistle,
salute you in Adonay:
23 Gaius my stranger
and of the whole ecclesia, salute you:
Erastus the administrator of the city salutes you
and Quartus a brother.
24 The charism of our Adonay Yah Shua Messiah
be with you all.
Amen.

Doxology

25 And to him who is able to establish you
according to my evangelism
and the preaching of Yah Shua Messiah,
according to the apocalypse of the mystery
having been hushed since eternal time,
26 but now manifested;
and through prophetic scriptures,
according to the order of the eternal Elohim,
made known to all goyim to the obedience of trust.
27 To Elohim, only wise,
be glory through Yah Shua Messiah to the eons.
Amen.

Salutation

1 *Paul* **Paulos**, *called to be an* **a called** apostle
of *Jesus Christ* **Yah Shua Messiah**
through the will of *God* **Elohim**,
and Sosthenes our brother,

2 Unto the *church* **ecclesia** of *God* **Elohim**
which is at **being in** Corinth,
to them that are *sanctified* **hallowed**
in *Christ Jesus* **Messiah Yah Shua**,
called *to be saints* **holy**,
with all that in every place call upon the name
of *Jesus Christ* **Yah Shua Messiah** our *Lord* **Adonay**,
both their's and our's:

3 *Grace be* **Charism** unto you, and *peace* **shalom**,
from *God* **Elohim** our Father,
and *from*
the *Lord Jesus Christ* **Adonay Yah Shua Messiah**.

Charism And Charisma

4 I *thank* **eucharistize** my *God* **Elohim** always
on your behalf **concerning you**,
for the *grace* **charism** of *God* **Elohim** which is given you
by Jesus Christ **in Yah Shua Messiah**;

5 That in *every thing* **all** ye
are enriched *by* **in** him,
in all *utterance* **word**, and *in* all knowledge;

6 *Even* **Exactly** as
the *testimony* **witness** of *Christ* **the Messiah**
was *confirmed* **established** in you:

7 So that ye *come behind* **fail** in no *gift* **charisma**;
waiting for **awaiting** the *coming* **apocalypse**
of our *Lord Jesus Christ* **Adonay Yah Shua Messiah**:

8 Who shall also *confirm* **establish** you
unto the *end* **completion/shalom**,
that ye may be blameless — **unaccusable**
in the day
of our *Lord Jesus Christ* **Adonay Yah Shua Messiah**.

9 *God* **Elohim** is *faithful* **trustworthy**,
by **through** whom ye were called
unto the *fellowship* **communion** of his Son
Jesus Christ **Yah Shua Messiah** our *Lord* **Adonay**.

Schisms In The Ecclesia

10 Now I beseech you, brethren,
by **through** the name
of our *Lord Jesus Christ* **Adonay Yah Shua Messiah**,
that ye all *speak* **word** the same *thing*,
and that there be no *divisions* **schisms** among you;
but that ye be *perfectly joined together* **prepared**
in the same mind and in the same *judgment* **opinion**.

11 For it hath been *declared* **evidenced** unto me
of **concerning** you, my brethren,
by them which are *of the house* of Chloe,
that there are contentions among you.

12 Now this I *say* **word**,
that *every one* **each** of you *saith* **wordeth**,
I am *indeed* of *Paul* **Paulos**; and I of Apollos;
and I of *Cephas* **Kepha**; and I of *Christ* **Messiah**.

13 Is *Christ* **the Messiah** divided?
was *Paul crucified* **Paulos staked** for you?
or were ye baptized in the name of *Paul* **Paulos**?

14 I *thank God* **eucharistize Elohim**
that I baptized none of you,
but **except** Crispus and Gaius;

15 Lest any should say
that I had baptized in *mine own* **my** name.

16 And I baptized also the household of Stephanas:
besides **finally**, I know not *whether*
if I baptized any other.

17 For *Christ sent* **Messiah**
apostolized me not to baptize,
but to *preach the gospel* **evangelize**:
not *with* **in** wisdom of words,
lest the *cross* **stake** of *Christ* **the Messiah**
should be *made of none effect* **voided**.

18 For the *preaching* **word** of the *cross* **stake**
is to them that *perish* **destruct indeed** foolishness;
but unto us which are saved
it is the *power* **dynamis** of *God* **Elohim**.

19 For it is *written* **scribed**,
I *will* **shall** destroy the wisdom of the wise,
and *will bring to nothing* **shall set aside**
the *understanding* **comprehension**
of the *prudent* **comprehending**.
Yesha Yah 29:14

Salutation

1 Paulos, a called apostle of Yah Shua Messiah
through the will of Elohim
and Sossoes our brother:

2 To the ecclesia of Elohim being in Corinth,
hallowed in Messiah Yah Shua — called holy;
with all who in every place
call on the name of Yah Shua Messiah our Adonay
— both theirs and ours:

3 Charism to you
and shalom of Elohim our Father
and Adonay Yah Shua Messiah.

1 CORINTHIANS 1

Charism And Charisma

4 I always eucharistize my
Elohim, concerning you,
for the charism of Elohim
given you in Yah Shua Messiah;
5 that you enrich in him in all
— in all word and all knowledge;
6 exactly as the witness of the Messiah
establishes in you:
7 so that you fail in no charisma;
awaiting the apocalypse
of our Adonay Yah Shua Messiah:
8 who also establishes you to completion/shalom,
— unaccusable
in the day of our Adonay Yah Shua Messiah.
9 Elohim *is* trustworthy,
through whom you were called to the communion
of his Son Yah Shua Messiah our Adonay.

Schisms In The Ecclesia

10 And I beseech you brothers,
through the name of our Adonay Yah Shua Messiah,
that you all word the same
and that there be no schisms among you;
and that you prepare
in the same mind and in the same opinion.
11 For it was evidenced to me
concerning you my brothers,
by them of Chloe,
that there are contentions among you.
12 And I word this — that each of you words,
I am indeed of Paulos; and I of Apollos;
and I of Kepha; and I of Messiah.
13 Is the Messiah divided?
Was Paulos staked for you?
Or were you baptized in the name of Paulos?
14 I eucharistize Elohim that
I baptized none of you,
except Crispus and Gaius;
15 lest any say that I baptized in my name:
16 and I also baptized the house of Stephanas;
finally, I know not if I baptized any other.
17 For Messiah apostolized me
not to baptize but to evangelize:
not in wisdom of words
lest the stake of the Messiah be voided.
18 For the word of the stake
is to them who destruct, foolishness indeed;
and to us, being saved, the dynamis of Elohim.
19 For it is scribed, I destroy
the wisdom of the wise
and set aside the comprehension of the
comprehending. Yesha Yah 29:14
20 Where is the wise? where is the scribe?
where is the disputer of this *world* **eon**?
hath not *God* **Elohim** indeed
made foolish **follied** the wisdom of this *world* **cosmos**?
21 For *after that* **since** in the
wisdom of *God* **Elohim**
the *world by* **cosmos through** wisdom
knew not *God* **Elohim**,
it pleased God **Elohim well—approved**
by **that through** the foolishness of preaching
to save them that *believe* **trust**.
22 *For* **Since** the *Jews require*
Yah Hudiym ask a sign,
and the *Greeks* **Hellenes** seek after wisdom:
23 But we preach *Christ crucified* **Messiah staked**,
unto the *Jews* **Yah Hudiym**
indeed a *stumblingblock* **scandal**,
and unto the *Greeks* **Hellenes** foolishness;
24 But unto them which are called,
both *Jews* **Yah Hudiym** and *Greeks* **Hellenes**,
Christ **Messiah** the *power* **dynamis** of *God* **Elohim**,
and the wisdom of *God* **Elohim**.
25 Because the foolishness of *God* **Elohim**
is wiser than *men* **humanity**;
and the *weakness* **frailty** of *God* **Elohim**
is *stronger* **mightier** than *men* **humanity**.
26 For ye see your calling, brethren,
how that not many wise *men* after the flesh,
not many *mighty* **able**, not many *noble* **well—birthed**,
are called:
27 But *God* **Elohim** hath *chosen* **selected**
the foolish *things* of the *world* **cosmos**
to *confound* **shame** the wise;
and *God* **Elohim** hath *chosen* **selected**
the *weak things* **frailties** of the *world* **cosmos**
to *confound* **shame** the *things which are* mighty;
28 And *base things* **the ignoble**
of the *world* **cosmos**,
and *things which are despised* **the belittled**,
hath *God chosen* **Elohim selected**,
yea, and *things which are not* **those not being**,
to *bring to nought* **inactivate** *things that are* **those being**:
29 That no flesh should *glory*
boast in his *presence* **sight**.
30 But of him are ye in *Christ*
Jesus **Messiah Yah Shua**,

who of *God* **Elohim** *is made* **become** unto us
wisdom, and *righteousness* **justness**,
and *sanctification* **holiness**, and redemption:
31 That, *according* **exactly** as *it is written* **scribed**,
He that *glorieth* **boasteth**,
let him *glory* **boast** in *the Lord* **Yah Veh**. Yirme Yah 9:23, 24

Paulos Evangelizes The Messiah

2 And I **also**, brethren, when I came to you,
came not with excellency of *speech* **word** or of wisdom,
declaring **evangelizing** unto you
the *testimony* **witness** of *God* **Elohim**.

2 For I *determined* **judged**
not to know *any thing* **aught** among you,
save Jesus Christ **except Yah Shua Messiah**,
and him *crucified* **staked**.

3 And I *was* **became** with you in *weakness* **frailty**,
and in *fear* **awe**, and in much trembling.

4 And my *speech* **word** and my preaching
was not *with enticing* **in persuasive** words
of *man's* **human** wisdom,
but in *demonstration* **manifestation** of the Spirit
and of *power* **dynamis**:

5 That your *faith* **trust** should not *stand* **be**
in the wisdom of *men* **humanity**,
but in the *power* **dynamis** of *God* **Elohim**.

6 *Howbeit* **But** we speak wisdom
among them that are *perfect* **completed/shalamed**:
yet not the wisdom of this *world* **eon**,
nor of the *princes* **archs** of this *world* **eon**,
that *come to nought* **inactivate**:

7 But we speak the wisdom of
God **Elohim** in a mystery,
even the hidden wisdom — **the secreted**,
which *God ordained* **Elohim predetermined**
before the *world* **eons** unto our glory:

8 Which none of the *princes*
archs of this *world* **eon** knew:

20 Where is the wise?
Where is the scribe?
Where is the disputer of this eon?
Elohim indeed,
follies he not the wisdom of this cosmos?

21 For since in the wisdom of Elohim
the cosmos knew not Elohim through wisdom,
Elohim well—approved
that through the foolishness of preaching
to save them who trust.

22 Since the Yah Hudiym ask a sign
and the Hellenes seek after wisdom:

23 we also — we preach Messiah staked
— to the Yah Hudiym, indeed a scandal
and to the Hellenes foolishness;

24 and to the called
— both Yah Hudiym and Hellenes,
Messiah
— the dynamis of Elohim and the wisdom of Elohim.

25 Because the foolishness of Elohim
is wiser than humanity;
and the frailty of Elohim
mightier than humanity.

26 For you see your calling brothers,
how that not many wise after the flesh,
not many able, not many well—birthed:

27 But Elohim selects the foolish of the cosmos
to shame the wise;
and Elohim selects the frailties of the cosmos
to shame the mighty;

28 and the ignoble of the cosmos and the belittled
Elohim selects;
yes, and those not being to inactivate those being:

29 so that no flesh boasts in his sight.

30 And you of him — you are in Messiah Yah Shua,
who of Elohim becomes our wisdom and
justness and holiness and redemption:

31 that, exactly as scribed,
Whoever boasts, boast in the Yah Veh.
Yirme Yah 9:23, 24

Paulos Evangelizes The Messiah

2 And I also, brothers, when I came to you
I came not with excellency of word or of wisdom,
evangelizing to you the witness of Elohim.

2 For I judged to know naught among you,
except Yah Shua Messiah and him staked.

3 And I became with you in frailty
and in awe and in much trembling:

4 and my word and my preaching
was not in persuasive words of human wisdom
— but in manifestation of the Spirit and of dynamis:

5 that your trust not be in human wisdom
but in the dynamis of Elohim.

6 But we speak wisdom
among the completed/shalamed:
— yet neither the wisdom of this eon
nor of the archs of this eon who inactivate:

7 but we speak the wisdom
of Elohim in a mystery,
— the secreted

which Elohim predetermined to our glory
preceding the eons:
8   which none of the archs of this eon knew:
for **if** — had they known *it*, they *would* **should** not **ever**
have *crucified* **staked** the *Lord* **Adonay** of glory.

THE SECRETED MYSTERY SECRETED

9   But **exactly** as *it is written* **scribed**,
Eye hath not seen, nor ear heard,
neither have *entered* **ascended**
into the heart of *man* **humanity**,
the things **those** which *God* **Elohim** hath prepared
for them that love him.
Yesha Yah 64:4

THE SECRETED MYSTERY UNVEILED

10   But *God* **Elohim** hath *revealed*
unveiled them unto us
by **through** his Spirit:
for the Spirit searcheth all *things*,
yea, the *deep things* **depths** of *God* **Elohim**.
11   For what *man* **human**
knoweth *the things* **those** of a *man* **human**,
save **except** the spirit of *man* **humanity** which is in him?
even *so the things* **thus those** of *God* **Elohim**
knoweth no *man* **one**,
but **except** the Spirit of *God* **Elohim**.
12   Now we have *received* **taken**,
not the spirit of the *world* **cosmos**,
but the spirit which is of *God* **Elohim**; that
we might know *the things* **those**
that are *freely given* **granted charism**
to us of *God* **Elohim**.
13   Which *things* also we speak, not in the words
which *man's* **human** wisdom *teacheth* **doctrinateth**,
but **in** which the *Holy Spirit* **Ruach ha-
kodesh** *teacheth* **doctrinateth**;
comparing **co—judging** spiritual *things* with spiritual.
14   But the *natural man* **soulical human**
receiveth not *the things* **those** of
the Spirit of *God* **Elohim**:
for they are foolishness unto him:
neither can he know *them*,
because they are spiritually *discerned* **judged**.
15   But he that is spiritual **indeed** judgeth all *things*,
yet he himself is judged of no *man* **one**.
16   For who hath known the
mind of *the Lord* **Adonay**,
that he may *instruct* **coalesce** him?
But we have the mind of *Christ* **Messiah**.

SPIRITUAL VS FLESHLY

3   And I, brethren,
could not speak unto you as unto spiritual,
but as unto *carnal* **fleshly**,
even as unto babes in *Christ* **Messiah**.
2   I have *fed* **given** you *with* milk **to drink**,
and not *with meat* **food**:
for *hitherto* ye were not *yet* able *to bear it*,
but neither yet now are ye able.
3   For ye are yet *carnal* **fleshly**:
for whereas there is among you *envying* **zeal**,
and *strife* **contention**, and divisions,
are ye not *carnal* **indeed fleshly**
and walk as *men* **humanity**?
4   For while one *saith* **wordeth**,
I **indeed** *am* of *Paul* **Paulos**; and
another, I *am* of Apollos;
are ye not *carnal* **indeed fleshly**?
5   Who then is *Paul* **Paulos**, and who is Apollos,
but ministers *by* **through** whom ye *believed* **trusted**,
even as the *Lord* **Adonay** gave to *every man* **each**?
6   I have planted, Apollos *watered* **irrigated**;
but *God gave the increase* **Elohim grew**.
7   So then neither is he that
planteth *any thing* **aught**,
neither he that *watereth* **irrigateth**;
but *God* **Elohim** that *giveth the increase* **groweth**.
8   Now he that planteth and
he that *watereth* **irrigateth**
are one:
and *every man* **each** shall *receive* **take** his own reward
according to his own labour.
9   For we are *labourers together*
co—workers with *God* **Elohim**:
ye are *God's husbandry* — **Elohim's cultivation**,
ye are *God's building* — **Elohim's edifice**.
10   According to the *grace* **charism** of *God* **Elohim**
which is given unto me,
as a wise *masterbuilder* **architect**,
I have *laid* **placed** the foundation,
and another buildeth thereon.
But let *every man take heed* **each see**
how he buildeth thereupon.
for if they had known,
they had never staked Adonay of glory.

THE SECRETED MYSTERY SECRETED

9   But exactly as scribed,
Neither eye saw

nor ear heard
nor ascended to the human heart
what Elohim prepared for them who love him.
Yesha Yah 64:4

THE SECRETED MYSTERY UNVEILED

10 But Elohim unveils to us through his Spirit:
for the Spirit searches all — yes, the depths of Elohim.
11 For what human knows those of a human,
except the spirit of humanity within him?
Even thus, those of Elohim, no one knows,
except the Spirit of Elohim.
12 And we take not the spirit of the cosmos
but the spirit of Elohim
— so that we know those who granted charism to us
by Elohim:
13 which also we speak
not in the words that human wisdom doctrinates,
but in that which the Holy Spirit doctrinates;
co—judging spiritual with spiritual.
14 And the soulical human
receives not those of the Spirit of Elohim:
for they are foolishness to him:
nor can he know,
because they are spiritually judged.
15 But whoever is spiritual, indeed judges all;
yet he himself is judged by no one.
16 For who knows the mind of Adonay,
to coalesce him?
And we — we have the mind of Messiah.

SPIRITUAL VS FLESHLY

3 And brothers,
I was not able to speak to you as to spiritual
but as to fleshly — as to babes in Messiah.
2 I gave you milk to drink and not food:
for you were not yet able,
but not even now are you yet able:
3 for you are yet fleshly:
for among you
there are zeal and contention and divisions:
are you not indeed fleshly and walk as humanity?
4 For while one words,
I indeed of Paulos; and another, I of Apollos;
are you not indeed fleshly?
5 So who is Paulos and who is Apollos
but ministers through whom you trusted
— even as Adonay gave each to all?
6 I plant, Apollos irrigates;
but Elohim grows.

7 So neither is whoever plants aught
nor whoever irrigates;
but Elohim who grows.
8 And whoever plants and
whoever irrigates are one:
and each takes his own reward
according to his own labor.
9 For we are co—workers with Elohim:
— the cultivation of Elohim — the edifice of Elohim.
10 According to the charism Elohim gives me,
as a wise architect,
I place the foundation, and another builds:
and each sees how he builds.
11 For other foundation can no *man* lay **one place**
than that is laid,
which is *Jesus Christ* **Yah Shua Messiah**.
12 Now if any *man* **one** build upon this foundation
gold, silver, precious stones,
wood **timber**, *hay* **herbage**, stubble;
13 *Every man's* **Each one's** work
shall be *made* manifest:
for the day shall *declare* **evidence** it,
because it shall be *revealed by* **unveiled in** fire;
and the fire shall *try every man's* **proof each one's** work
of what sort *it is*.
14 If any *man's* **one's** work abide
which he hath built thereupon,
he shall *receive* **take** a reward.
15 If any *man's* **one's** work shall be burned,
he shall *suffer* **have** loss:
but he himself shall be saved; yet
so **thus** as *by* **through** fire.

THE HOLY NAVE OF ELOHIM

16 Know ye not
that ye are the *temple* **nave** of *God* **Elohim**,
and that the Spirit of *God* **Elohim** dwelleth in you?
17 If any *man defile* **one corrupts**
the *temple* **nave** of *God* **Elohim**,
him shall *God* **Elohim** destroy;
for the *temple* **nave** of *God* **Elohim** is holy,
which *temple* ye are.
18 Let no *man deceive* **one seduce** himself.
If any *man* **one** among you
seemeth **thinketh** to be wise in this *world* **eon**,
let him become a fool, that he may *be* **become** wise.
19 For the wisdom of this *world* **cosmos**
is foolishness with *God* **Elohim**.
For it is *written* **scribed**,
He *taketh* **graspeth** the wise

20	in their own *craftiness* **cunning**. And again, *The Lord* **Yah Veh** knoweth the *thoughts* **reasonings** of the wise, that they are vain. Iyob 5:13, Psalm 94:11, 20
21	*Therefore* **So** let no *man glory* **one boast** in *men* **humanity**. For all *things* are your's;
22	Whether *Paul* **Paulos**, *or whether* Apollos, *or Cephas* **whether Kepha**, *or whether* the *world* **cosmos**, *or whether* life, *or whether* death, *or things* **whether the** present, *or things to come* **whether the about to be**; all are your's;
23	And ye are *Christ's* **Messiah's**; and *Christ* **Messiah** is *God's* **Elohim's**.

The Ministry

4	Let *a man so account of us* **humanity reckon us thus**, as *of the ministers* **attendants** of *Christ* **Messiah**, and *stewards* **administrators** of the mysteries of God Elohim.
2	*Moreover* **Finally** it is *required* **sought** in *stewards* **administrators**, that *a man* **each** be found *faithful* **trustworthy**.
3	But with me it is *a very small thing* **insignificant** that I should be judged of you, or of *man's judgment* **humanity's day**: *yea* **yet**, I judge not mine *own* self.
4	For *I know nothing by myself* **am aware of naught**; yet am I not *hereby* **herein** justified: but he that judgeth me is the Lord Adonay.
5	*Therefore* **So then** judge *nothing* **naught** before the *time* **season**, until *ever* the *Lord* **Adonay** come, who both *will bring to* **shall** light up the *hidden things* **secrets** of darkness, and *will make* **shall** manifest the counsels of the hearts: and then shall *every man* **each** have praise become the halal of God Elohim.
6	And these *things*, brethren, I have *in a figure transferred* **transfigured** to myself and to Apollos for your sakes; that ye might learn in us not to think *of men* above **beyond** that which is *written* **scribed**, *that no* **lest** one of you be puffed up for one against another.
11	For no one can place another foundation than the *one laid* — Yah Shua Messiah:
12	and if anyone build on this foundation gold, silver, precious stones, timber, herbage, stubble;
13	the work of each becomes manifest: for the day evidences it because it unveils in fire; and the fire proofs the work of each — of what sort.
14	If anyone builds a work that abides he takes a reward:
15	if the work of anyone burns he has loss — but he himself is saved — yet thus as through fire.

The Holy Nave Of Elohim

16	Know you not that you are the nave of Elohim and that the Spirit of Elohim dwells in you?
17	If anyone corrupts the nave of Elohim, him Elohim destroys; for the nave of Elohim, which you are, is holy.
18	Seduce not yourselves. If anyone among you thinks to be wise in this eon, may he become a fool, that he becomes wise.
19	For the wisdom of this cosmos is foolishness with Elohim. For it is scribed, He grasps the wise in their own cunning.
20	And again, Yah Veh knows the reasonings of the wise, that they are vain. Iyob 5:13, Psalm 94:11, 20
21	So boast not in humanity: for all are yours;
22	whether Paulos, whether Apollos, whether Kepha, whether the cosmos, whether life, whether death, whether the present, whether the about to be — all are to you;
23	and you are to Messiah; and Messiah is to Elohim.

The Ministry

4	Humanity, reckon us thus: as attendants of Messiah and administrators of the mysteries of Elohim.
2	Finally it is sought in administrators,

to find each trustworthy.

3 And for me,
it is insignificant to be judged by you,
or of the day of humanity:
yet, I judge not myself.

4 For I am aware of naught;
yet I am not justified herein:
but he who judges me is Adonay.

5 So judge naught preceding the season,
until ever Adonay comes,
who both lights the secrets of darkness
and manifests the counsels of the hearts:
and then each becomes the halal of Elohim.

6 And these, brothers,
I transfigure to me and to Apollos for your sakes;
that in us,
you learn to not think beyond what is scribed,
lest one of you puff one against another.

7 For who *maketh* **distinguisheth** thee
to differ from another?
and what hast thou
that thou *didst* **hast** not *receive* **taken**? now if thou
didst receive it **hast taken**, why *dost thou glory*
boastest thou, as if thou hadst not *received it* **taken**?

8 *Now* **Already** ye *are full* **have gluttonized**,
now **already** ye *are rich* **have enriched**,
ye have reigned as *kings* **sovereigns**
without **apart from** us:
and **yet indeed**,
I would to God **O that** ye *did reign* **had reigned**,
that we also might *reign* **co—reign** with you.

9 For I think that *God* **Elohim**
hath *set forth* **manifested** us the apostles last,
as *it were appointed* **doomed** to death:
for we *are made* **become** a spectacle
unto the *world* **cosmos**,
and to angels, and to *men* **humanity**.

10 We are fools for *Christ's* **Messiah's** sake,
but ye *are wise* **thoughtful** in *Christ* **Messiah**;
we *are weak* **frail**, but ye *are strong* **mighty**;
ye *are honourable* **glorious**,
but we *are despised* **dishonoured**.

11 Even unto this present hour
we both hunger, and thirst,
and are naked, and are *buffeted* **punched**,
and *have no certain dwellingplace* **unsettled**;
12 And labour, working with our own hands:
being reviled **abused**, we *bless* **eulogize**;
being persecuted, we *suffer* **tolerate** it:

13 *Being defamed* **Blasphemed**, we **comfort**:
we are *made* **become**
as the *filth* **offscouring** of the *world* **cosmos**,
and are the *offscouring* **offscrapings** of all *things*
unto this day **until now**.

14 I *write* **scribe** not these *things* to shame you,
but as my beloved *sons* **children**, I *warn* **remind** you.

15 For *though* **even if** ye have
ten thousand instructers **a myriad pedagogues**
in *Christ* **Messiah**,
yet *have ye* not many fathers:
for in *Christ Jesus* **Messiah Yah Shua**
I have begotten you through the *gospel* **evangelism**.

16 *Wherefore* **So** I beseech you,
be ye *followers* **mimickers** of me.

17 For this cause
have I sent unto you *Timotheus* **Timo Theos**,
who is my beloved *son* **child**,
and *faithful* **trustworthy** in *the Lord* **Adonay**,
who shall *bring* **remind** you
into remembrance of my ways
which be in *Christ* **Messiah**,
exactly as I *teach* **doctrinate** every where
in every *church* **ecclesia**.

18 Now some are puffed *up*,
as though I *would* **should** not come to you.

19 But I *will* **shall** come to you *shortly* **quickly**,
if *the Lord will* **ever Adonay willeth**,
and *will* **shall** know,
not the *speech* **word** of them which are puffed up,
but the *power* **dynamis**.

20 For the *kingdom* **sovereigndom** of *God* **Elohim**
is not in word, but in *power* **dynamis**.

21 What will ye?
shall I come unto you with a rod,
or in love, and *in the* **a** spirit of meekness?

Paulos Rebukes Whoredom

5 *It is reported commonly* **I actually hear**
that there is fornication **of whoredom** among you,
and such *fornication* **whoredom**
as is not *so much as* **even** named
among the *Gentiles* **goyim**,
that one should have his father's *wife* **woman**.

2 And ye are puffed up,
and have not **indeed** rather mourned,
that he that hath done this *deed* **work**
might be taken away from among you.

3 For I *verily* **indeed**,

7 For who distinguishes you?
And what have you that you have not taken?

and if you have taken,
why boast as if you had not taken?
8 Already you gluttonize;
already you enrich;
— reign as sovereigns apart from us:
and yet indeed, O that you reign;
so that we also co—reign.
9 For I think that Elohim
manifests us the apostles last
as doomed to death:
for we become a spectacle
to the cosmos and to angels and to humanity:
10 We are fools for sake of the Messiah
— and you thoughtful in Messiah;
we are frail — and you mighty;
you glorious — and we dishonored.
11 Even to this present hour
we both famish and thirst
— naked and punched and unsettled;
12 and labor, working with our own hands:
abused, we eulogize;
persecuted, we tolerate;
13 blasphemed, we comfort;
we become as the offscouring of the cosmos,
the offscrapings of all until now.
14 I scribe these not to shame you,
but as my beloved children, I remind you.
15 For even if you have
a myriad pedagogues in Messiah,
yet not many fathers:
for in Messiah Yah Shua
I birthed you through the evangelism.
16 So I beseech you, become mimickers of me.
17 For this cause I sent you Timo Theos,
my beloved child and trustworthy in Adonay,
to remind you of my ways in Messiah,
exactly as I doctrinate every where in every ecclesia.
18 Now some are puffed as
though I not come to you.
19 But I come to you quickly
whenever Adonay wills
— and know not the word of them who are puffed,
but the dynamis.
20 For the sovereigndom of Elohim is not in word
but in dynamis.
21 What will you?
That I come to you with a rod?
Or in love and a spirit of meekness?

Paulos Rebukes Whoredom

5 I actually hear of whoredom among you;
and such whoredom
as is not even named among the goyim;
that one has the woman of his father.
2 And you puff up, and indeed rather not mourn,
than take away from among you
whoever does this work.
3 For I indeed,
as absent in body, but present in spirit,
have judged already, as though I were present,
concerning him that hath *so done this deed* **thus worked**,
4 In the name
of our *Lord Jesus Christ* **Adonay Yah Shua Messiah**,
when ye are gathered together, and my spirit,
with the *power* **dynamis**
of our *Lord Jesus Christ* **Adonay Yah Shua Messiah**,
5 To deliver such an one unto Satan
for **unto** the *destruction* **ruin** of the flesh,
that the spirit may be saved
in the day of the *Lord Jesus* **Adonay Yah Shua**.
6 Your *glorying* **boasting** is not good.
Know ye not that a little *leaven* **fermentation**
leaveneth **fermenteth** the whole lump?
7 **So** Purge out *therefore* the
old *leaven* **fermentation**,
that ye may be a new lump,
exactly as ye are *unleavened* **as matsah**.
For even *Christ* **Messiah** our *passover* **pasach**
is sacrificed for us:
8 *Therefore* **So** let us *keep the feast* **celebrate**,
not *with* **in** old *leaven* **fermentation**,
neither *with* **in** the *leaven* **fermentation**
of malice and *wickedness* **evil**;
but *with* **in** the *unleavened bread* **matsah**
of sincerity and truth.
9 I *wrote* **scribed** unto you in an epistle
not to *company* **co—mingle**
with *fornicators* **whoremongers**:
10 Yet **most certainly** not *altogether*
with the *fornicators* **whoremongers**
of this *world* **cosmos**,
or with the *covetous* **avaricious**,
or *extortioners* **plunderers**, or with idolaters;
for then must ye needs **otherwise be ye indebted**
to go out of the *world* **cosmos**.
11 But now I have *written* **scribed** unto you
not to *keep company* **co—mingle**,
if **whenever** any *man* **one** that is *called a* **named** brother

	be *either* a *fornicator* **whoremonger**,
	or *covetous* **avaricious**, or an idolater,
	or *a railer* **an abuser**, or *a drunkard* **an intoxicator**,
	or *an extortioner* **a plunderer**;
	with such an one *no not* **never** to eat.
12	For what have I to do
	to judge them also that are without?
	do not ye **indeed** judge them that are within?
13	But them that are without *God* **Elohim** judgeth.
	Therefore put **So take** away from among
	yourselves that *wicked person* **evil**.

The Holy Suing The Holy

6	Dare any of you,
	having a matter *against* **toward** another,
	go to law before **be judged by** the unjust,
	and not **indeed** *before* **by** the *saints* **holy**?
2	*Do* **Know** ye not *know*
	that the *saints* **holy** shall judge the *world* **cosmos**?
	and if the *world* **cosmos** shall be judged *by* **in** you,
	are ye unworthy to judge the *smallest matters* **lesser**?
3	Know ye not that we shall judge angels?
	how much more
	things that pertain to **those of** this *life* **existence**?
4	*if then* **so indeed, whenever** ye have judgments
	of *things pertaining to this life* **this existence**,
	set them to judge
	who are *least esteemed* **belittled** in the *church* **ecclesia**.
5	I *speak* **word** to *your* shame **you**.
	Is it *so* **thus**,
	that there *is not a* **be no** wise *man* among you?
	no, not **even** one that shall be able to *judge* **discern**
	between **among** his brethren?
6	But brother *goeth to law with* **judges** brother,
	and that *before* **by** the *unbelievers* **trustless**.
7	*Now therefore* **So already indeed**
	there is *utterly* **actually** a fault among you,
	because ye *go to law one* **have judgments**
	with *another* **your own**.
	Why *do* **be** ye not rather *take wrong* **injured**?
	why *do* **indeed be** ye not rather
	suffer yourselves to be defrauded **cheated**?
	as being absent in body and being present in spirit
	— as being present,
	I already judged him who thus works.
4	In the name of our Adonay Yah Shua Messiah
	when you co—gather with my spirit
	and with the dynamis
	of our Adonay Yah Shua Messiah,
5	to deliver such an one to Satan

	— to ruin the flesh — to save the spirit
	in the day of Adonay Yah Shua.
6	Your boasting is not good.
	Know you not that a little fermentation
	ferments the whole lump?
7	So purge out the old fermentation
	to be a new lump exactly as matsah.
	For even Messiah our pasach is sacrificed for us:
	8 so celebrate — neither in old fermentation
	nor in the fermentation of malice and evil;
	but in the matsah of sincerity and truth.
9	I scribed to you in an epistle
	to not co—mingle with whoremongers:
10	yet most certainly not
	with the whoremongers of this cosmos
	or with the avaricious or plunderers or with idolaters;
	otherwise you are indebted to go from the cosmos.
11	And now I scribe you to not co—mingle;
	whenever anyone named brother
	— either a whoremonger or avaricious or an idolater
	or an abuser or an intoxicator or a plunderer;
	never ever eat with such a one.
12	For what have I to do
	to also judge those who are outside?
	And not indeed judge those who are inside?
13	And those who are outside Elohim judges.
	So take away that evil from among yourselves.

The Holy Suing The Holy

6	Dare any of you, having
	a matter toward another,
	be judged by the unjust?
	And not indeed by the holy?
2	Know you not that the holy
	are to judge the cosmos?
	and if the cosmos judges you
	are you unworthy to judge the lesser?
3	Know you not that we are to judge angels?
	How much more those of this existence?
4	So indeed
	whenever you have judgments of this existence,
	set the belittled in the ecclesia to judge.
5	I word to shame you.
	Is it thus, that there are no wise among you?
	— not even one able to discern among his brothers?
6	But brother judges brother
	— and that by the trustless.
7	So indeed already
	there is actually a fault among you
	because you have judgments with your own.

1 CORINTHIANS 6, 7

Why not rather be injured?
Why indeed not rather be cheated?
8 *Nay* **Rather**, ye *do wrong* **injure**, and *defraud* **cheat**,
and that your brethren.
9 **Or** Know ye not
that the *unrighteous* **unjust** shall not inherit
the *kingdom* **sovereigndom** of *God* **Elohim**?
Be not *deceived* **seduced**:
neither *fornicators* **whoremongers**, nor idolaters,
nor adulterers, nor effeminate,
nor *abusers of themselves with mankind* **homosexuals**,
10 Nor thieves, nor *covetous* **avaricious**,
nor *drunkards* **intoxicators**, nor *revilers* **abusers**,
nor *extortioners* **plunderers**,
shall inherit the *kingdom* **sovereigndom** of *God* **Elohim**.
11 And *such* **these** were some of you:
but ye are *washed* **bathed**,
but ye are *sanctified* **hallowed**,
but ye are justified
in the name of *the Lord Jesus* **Adonay Yah Shua**,
and *by* **in** the Spirit of our *God* **Elohim**.
12 All *things* are *lawful unto* **allowed** me,
but all *things* are not *expedient* **beneficial**:
all *things* are *lawful for* **allowed** me,
but I *will* **shall** not be *brought*
under the *power* **authority** of any.
13 *Meats* **Food** for the belly,
and the belly for *meats* **food**:
but *God* **Elohim** shall *destroy* **inactivate** both
it **these** and *them* **those**.
Now the body is not for *fornication* **whoredom**,
but for *the Lord* **Adonay**;
and *the Lord* **Adonay** for the body.
14 And *God* **Elohim** hath both
raised up *the Lord* **Adonay**,
and *will* **shall** also raise *up* us
by **through** his *own power* **dynamis**.
15 Know ye not
that your bodies are the members of *Christ* **Messiah**?
so shall I *then* take the members of *Christ* **the Messiah**,
and make them the members of *an harlot* **a whore**?
God forbid **So be it not**.
16 **What? Or** know ye not
that he which is joined to *an harlot* **a whore** is one body?
for two, saith he, shall be **into** one flesh.
Genesis 2:24
17 But he that is joined unto *the Lord* **Adonay**
is one spirit.
18 Flee *fornication* **whoredom**.

Every sin *that a man if* **whenever a human** doeth
is without the body;
but he that *committeth fornication* **whoreth**
sinneth *against* **unto** his own body.
19 **What? Or** know ye not that your body
is the *temple* **nave** of the *Holy Spirit* **Ruach ha-kodesh**
which is in you,
which ye have of *God* **Elohim**, and ye are not your own?
20 For ye are bought with a price:
therefore **so** glorify *God* **Elohim** in your body,
and in your spirit, which are *God's* **Elohim's**.

INTIMATE RELATIONSHIPS

7 Now concerning *the things* **those**
whereof **about which** ye *wrote* **scribed** unto me:
It is good for a *man* **human** not to touch a woman.
2 *Nevertheless,* **And**
to avoid fornication **because of whoredom**,
let *every man* **each** have his own *wife* **woman**,
and let *every woman* **each** have her own *husband* **man**.
3 *Let the husband render*
The man is indebted to give
unto the *wife due benevolence*
woman well—mindedness:
and likewise also the *wife* **woman**
unto the *husband* **man**.
4 The *wife* **woman**
hath not *power* **authority** of her own body,
but the *husband* **man**:
and likewise also the *husband* **man**
hath not *power* **authority** of his own body,
but the *wife* **woman**.
8 But you
— you rather injure and cheat your brothers.
9 Or know you not
the unjust inherit not the sovereigndom of Elohim?
be not seduced:
neither whoremongers
nor idolaters
nor adulterers
nor effeminate
nor homosexuals
10 nor thieves
nor avaricious
nor intoxicators
nor abusers
nor plunderers
inherit the sovereigndom of Elohim.
11 And some of you were these:
but you are bathed

	but you are hallowed
	but you are justified
	in the name of Adonay Yah Shua
	and in the Spirit of our Elohim.
12	I am allowed all;
	but all are not beneficial:
	I am allowed all
	but I am not under the authority of any.
13	Food for the belly and the belly for food:
	but Elohim inactivates both these and those.
	And the body is not for whoredom,
	but for Adonay;
	and Adonay for the body:
14	and Elohim both
	raised Adonay and raises us through his dynamis.
15	Know you not
	that your bodies are the members of Messiah?
	So take I the members of the Messiah
	and make them the members of a whore?
	So be it not.
16	Or know you not
	that whoever joins a whore is one body?
	For two, says he, become one flesh.
	Genesis 2:24
17	And whoever joins Adonay is one spirit.
18	Flee whoredom.
	Every sin a human ever does is outside the body;
	and whoever whores, sins against his own body.
19	Or know you not
	that your body is the nave of the Holy Spirit in you
	which you have of Elohim
	— and you are not your own?
20	For you are bought with a price:
	so glorify Elohim in your body
	and in your spirit, which are of Elohim.

INTIMATE RELATIONSHIPS

7	Now concerning those
	about which you scribed me:
	It is good for a human to not touch a woman.
2	And because of whoredom
	each is to hold his own woman
	and each her own man.
3	The man is indebted
	to give well—mindedness to the woman:
	and likewise also the woman to the man.
4	The woman has not authority of her own body
	— but the man:
	and likewise also the man
	has not authority of his own body
	— but the woman.
5	*Defraud* **Cheat** ye not one the other,
	except *it be* **somehow** *ever*
	with consent **by symphonizing** for a *time* **season**,
	that ye may *give yourselves* **have leisure**
	to **for** fasting and prayer; and come together again,
	that **lest** Satan *tempt* **test** you *not*
	for your *incontinency* **restraint**.
6	But I *speak* **word** this by *permission* **experience**,
	and not *of commandment* **by order**.
7	For I *would* **will**
	that all *men were* **humanity be** even as I myself.
	But *every man* **each**
	hath his *proper gift* **own charisma** of *God* **Elohim**,
	one *after this manner* **indeed thus**,
	and another *after that* **thus**.
8	So I *say* **word** *therefore* to
	the unmarried and widows,
	It is good for them *if* **whenever** they abide even as I.
9	But if they cannot *contain* **control themselves**,
	let them marry:
	for it is better to marry than *to burn* **be fiery**.
10	And unto the married I *command* **evangelize**,
	yet not I, but *the Lord* **Adonay**,
	Let not the *wife depart* **woman separate**
	from her *husband* **man**:
11	But and *if and* **whenever** she *depart* **separate**,
	let her *remain* **abide** unmarried
	or be reconciled to her *husband* **man**:
	and let not the *husband* **man**
	put away **forsake** his *wife* **woman**.
12	But to the rest *speak* **word**
	I, not *the Lord* **Adonay**:
	If any brother hath a *wife* **woman**
	that believeth not — **trustless**,
	and she *be pleased* **thinks well** to dwell with him,
	let him not *put her away* **forsake her**.
13	And the woman which hath *an husband* **a man**
	that believeth not — **trustless**,
	and if he *be pleased* **thinks well** to dwell with her,
	let her not *leave* **forsake** him.
14	For the *unbelieving husband* **trustless man**
	is *sanctified by* **hallowed in** the *wife* **woman**,
	and the *unbelieving wife* **trustless woman**
	is *sanctified by* **hallowed in** the *husband* **man**:
	else **then** were your children *unclean* **impure**;
	but now are they holy.
15	But if the *unbelieving depart* **trustless separate**,
	let him *depart* **separate**.
	A brother or a sister is not *under bondage* **subservient**

in such *cases*:
but *God* **Elohim** hath called us *to peace* **in shalom**.

16 For what knowest thou, O *wife* **woman**,
whether thou shalt save thy *husband* **man**? or how knowest thou, O man,
whether thou shalt save thy *wife* **woman**?

17 *But* **Except** as *God* **Elohim**
hath *distributed* **imparted** to *every man* **each**,
as *the Lord* **Adonay** hath called *every one* **to each**,
so **thus** let him walk.
And *so* **thus** ordain I in all *churches* **ecclesiae**.

Circumcision, Decircumcision, Uncircumcision

18 Is any *man* called being circumcised?
let him not *become uncircumcised* **decircumcise**.
Is any called in uncircumcision?
let him not *be circumcised* **circumcise**.

19 Circumcision is *nothing* **naught**,
and uncircumcision is *nothing* **naught**,
but the *keeping* **guarding**
of the *commandments* **misvoth** of *God* **Elohim**.

20 Let *every man* **each** abide
in *the same* **that** calling
wherein he was called.

21 Art thou called *being* a servant?
care **concern** not *for it*:
but if thou mayest be *made free* **able to be liberated**,
use it rather.

22 For he that is called in *the Lord* **Adonay**,
being a servant,
is *the Lord's freeman* **Adonay's liberated**:
likewise also he that is called,
being free **liberated**, is *Christ's* **Messiah's** servant.

23 Ye are bought with a price;

5 Cheat not one another,
except somehow ever by symphonizing for a season,
that you have leisure for fasting and prayer;
and come together again
— lest Satan test you for your restraint.

6 — and I word this by
experience and not by order.

7 For I will that all humanity be even as I myself:
but each has his own charisma of Elohim,
indeed one thus and one thus.

8 So I word to the unmarried and widows,
It is good for them whenever they abide even as I:

9 and if they cannot control themselves,
have them marry:
for it is better to marry than *be* fiery.

10 And to the married, I evangelize
— not I but Adonay,
that the woman not separate from her man:

11 but and whenever she separates,
she is to abide unmarried or reconcile to her man:
the man is not to forsake his woman.

12 And to the rest, I word — not Adonay:
if any brother has a woman — trustless
and she thinks well to dwell with him
he is not to forsake her.

13 And the woman has a man — trustless
and he thinks well to dwell with her
she is not to forsake him.

14 For the trustless man is hallowed in the woman
and the trustless woman is hallowed in the man:
else then your children are impure;
but now they are holy.

15 And if the trustless separate, separate.
A brother or a sister is not subservient in such:
and Elohim calls us in shalom.

16 For what know you, O woman,
whether you save your man?
Or how know you, O man,
whether you save your woman?

17 Except as Elohim imparts to each,
as Adonay calls to each,
thus walk:
and thus I ordain in all ecclesiae.

Circumcision, Decircumcision, Uncircumcision

18 Is any called being circumcised?
Decircumcise not.
Is any called in uncircumcision?
Circumcise not.

19 Circumcision is naught
and uncircumcision is naught
but the guarding of the misvoth of Elohim.

20 Each of you,
abide in that calling wherein you are called.

21 Are you called a servant?
Concern not:
but if you are able to be liberated, use it rather.

22 For whoever in Adonay is called, Servant,
is the liberated of Adonay:
likewise also he that is called, Liberated,
is the servant of Messiah.

23 You are bought with a price;
be not ye the servants of *men* **humanity**.

24 Brethren, let *every man* **each**, wherein he is called,
therein abide with *God* **Elohim**.

VIRGINS

25 Now concerning virgins
I have no *commandment of the Lord* **order from Adonay**:
yet I give my *judgment* **opinion**,
as one that hath *obtained mercy* **been mercied**
of *the Lord* **Adonay** to be *faithful* **trustworthy**.
26 *So* I *suppose therefore* **presume**
that this is good for the present *distress* **necessity**,
I say, that it is good for a *man so* **human thus** to be.
27 Art thou bound unto a *wife* **woman**?
seek not to be loosed.
Art thou loosed from a *wife* **woman**?
seek not a *wife* **woman**.
28 But and *if* **whenever** thou
marry, thou hast not sinned;
and *if* **whenever** a virgin marry, she hath not sinned.
Nevertheless
such shall have *trouble* **tribulation** in the flesh:
but I spare you.
29 But this I say, brethren,
the *time* **season** is *short* **shortened**:
it remaineth **finally**,
that both they that have *wives* **women**
be as though they had none;
30 And they that weep, as though they wept not;
and they that *rejoice* **cheer**,
as though they *rejoiced* **cheered** not;
and they that buy, as though they *possessed* **held** not;
31 And they that use this *world* **cosmos**,
as not abusing *it*:
for the *fashion* **configuration** of this *world* **cosmos**
passeth away.
32 But I *would* **will**
have you without carefulness **that you be unanxious**.
He that is unmarried *careth* **is anxious**
for *the things that belong to the Lord* **that of Adonay**,
how he may please *the Lord* **Adonay**:
33 But he that is married *careth* **is anxious**
for *the things that are* **that** of the *world* **cosmos**,
how he may please his *wife* **woman**.
34 There is difference *also*
between a *wife* **woman** and a virgin. The
unmarried woman *careth* **is anxious** for
the things that of the *Lord* **Adonay**,
that she may be holy both in body and in spirit:
but she that is married *careth* **is anxious**
for *the things that* of the *world* **cosmos**,
how she may please her *husband* **man**.
35 And this I *speak* **word** for
your own *profit* **benefit**;
not that I may *cast a snare* **lay a noose** upon you,
but for that which is *comely* **honourable**,
and that ye may attend with a view
upon the Lord Adonay
without distraction **to undistracted devotion**.
36 But if any *man think* **one presume**
that he *behaveth himself uncomely* **misbehaveth**
toward his virgin,
if whenever she pass the flower of
her age is beyond her acme,
and *need so require* **thus becometh indebted**,
let him do what he *will* **willeth**, he sinneth not:
let them marry.
37 *Nevertheless* **nd**
he that standeth *stedfast* **grounded** in his heart,
having no *necessity* **distress**,
but hath *power over* **authority concerning** his own will,
and hath *so decreed* **thus judged** in his heart
that he *will keep* **shall guard** his virgin, doeth well.
38 So then he that *giveth her in
marriage* **marrieth her off**
doeth well;
but he that *giveth her not in marriage*
marrieth her not off
doeth better.
39 The *wife* **woman** is bound by the *law* **torah**
as long *time* as her *husband* **man** liveth;
but *if* **whenever** her *husband be dead* **man sleeps**,
she is *at liberty* **liberated** to be
married to whom she will;
only in the *Lord* **Adonay**.
be not the servants of humanity.
24 Brothers — each, wherein you are called,
abide therein with Elohim.
25 Now concerning virgins
I have no order from Adonay;
still I give my opinion:
as one mercied by Adonay, to be trustworthy.
26 So I presume
that this is good for the present necessity
— that this is good for a human thus to be.
27 Are you bound to a woman?
Seek not to be loosed.
Are you loosed from a woman?
Seek not a woman.
28 But and whenever you marry, you sin not;

and whenever a virgin marries, she sins not:
and such have tribulation in the flesh:
and I spare you.
29 And I say this, brothers, the season is shortened:
finally,
that both whoever have women
be as not having;
30 and whoever weeps
as not weeping;
and whoever cheers
as not cheering;
and whoever buys
as not holding;
31 and whoever uses this cosmos
as not abusing:
for the configuration of this cosmos passes away.
32 But I will that you be unanxious.
whoever is unmarried
is anxious for that of Adonay
— how to please Adonay:
33 but whoever is married
is anxious for that of the cosmos —
how to please his woman.
34 There is difference between
a woman and a virgin.
The unmarried woman
is anxious for that of Adonay
— to be holy, both in body and in spirit:
but whoever is married
is anxious for that of the cosmos
— how to please her man.
35 And I word this for your own benefit
— not to lay a noose upon you;
but for what is honorable
with a view upon Adonay to undistracted devotion.
36 And if anyone presumes
to misbehave toward his virgin,
whenever she is beyond her acme
and thus becomes indebted,
to do as he wills, he sins not — have them marry.
37 And whoever stands grounded in his heart,
not distressed,
and has authority concerning his own will
and thus judges in his heart to guard his virgin
does well.
38 So whoever marries her off does well;
and whoever marries her not off does better.
39 The woman is bound by the torah
as long time as her man lives;
but whenever her man sleeps,
she is liberated to marry whom she so wills
— only in Adonay.
40 But *she is happier* **blessed be she**
if **whenever** she *so* **thus** abide, after
my *judgment* **opinion**:
and I think also that I have the Spirit of *God* **Elohim**.

Idol Sacrifices

8 Now *as touching* **concerning**
things offered unto idols **idol sacrifices**,
we know that we all have knowledge.
Knowledge puffeth *up*, but *charity* **love** edifieth.
2 And if any *man* **one** think,
that he knoweth *any thing* **aught**,
he knoweth *nothing* **naught** yet
exactly as he *ought* **needeth** to know.
3 But if any *man* **one** love *God* **Elohim**,
the same **this** is known of him.
4 *As* **So** concerning *therefore*
the eating of *those things*
that are offered in sacrifice unto idols **idol sacrifices**,
we know that an idol
is *nothing* **naught** in the *world* **cosmos**,
and that there is none other *God but* **Elohim except** one.
5 For *though* if **even** there be *those*
that are *called gods* **worded elohim**,
whether in *heaven* **the heavens** or in earth,
(**exactly** as there be *gods* **elohim** many,
and *lords* **adoniym** many,)
6 But to us, *there is but* one
God **Elohim**, the Father,
of whom *are* all *things* **is**, and we in him;
and one *Lord Jesus Christ* **Adonay Yah Shua Messiah**,
by **through** whom *are* all *things* **is**,
and we *by* **through** him.
7 *Howbeit* **Yet**
there is not in every *man* **one** that knowledge:
for some with conscience of the idol
unto this hour **until now** eat it
as *a thing offered unto* an idol **sacrifice**;
and their conscience being *weak* **frail** is *defiled* **stained**.
8 But *meat* **food**
commendeth **presenteth** us not to *God* **Elohim**:
for neither, *if* **whenever** we eat,
are we the better **do we superabound**;
neither, *if* **whenever** we eat not, *are*
we the worse **do we lack**.
9 But *take heed* **see**,
lest *by any means* **somehow**
this *liberty* **authority** of your's

become a *stumblingblock* **stumbling**
to them that are *weak* **frail**.
10 For *if* **whenever** any *man* **one**
see thee which hast knowledge
sit at meat **repose** in *the idol's temple* **an idolion**,
shall not **indeed** the conscience of him
which is weak **being frail**
be *emboldened* **edified** to eat
those things which are offered to idols **idol sacrifices**;
11 And through thy knowledge
shall the *weak* **frail** brother *perish* **destruct**,
for whom *Christ* **Messiah** died?
12 But when ye sin *so against*
thus unto the brethren,
and *wound* **strike** their *weak* **frail** conscience,
ye sin *against Christ* **unto Messiah**.
13 *Wherefore* **So**,
if *meat make* **food scandalize** my brother *to offend*,
I *will* **shall no way** eat no *flesh* **meat**
while **unto** the *world standeth* **eons**,
lest I *make* **scandalize** my brother *to offend*.

THE AUTHORITY OF THE HOLY

9 Am I not an apostle? am I not *free* **liberated**?
have I not **indeed** seen
Jesus Christ **Yah Shua Messiah** our *Lord* **Adonay**?
are not ye my work in *the Lord* **Adonay**?
2 If I be not an apostle unto others,
yet *doubtless* **indeed** I am to you:
for the seal of mine apostleship
are ye in *the Lord* **Adonay**.
3 *Mine answer* **My pleading**
to them that *do examine* **judge** me is this,
4 Have we not *power* **authority**
to eat and to drink?
5 Have we not *power* **authority**
to lead about a sister,
a *wife* **woman**, as well as *other* **the rest of the** apostles,
and *as* the brethren of the *Lord* **Adonay**,
and *Cephas* **Kepha**?
40 But blessed — whenever she thus abides,
after my opinion:
and I also think I have the Spirit of Elohim.

IDOL SACRIFICES

8 And concerning idol sacrifices:
We know that we all have knowledge.
Knowledge puffs, but love edifies.
2 And if anyone thinks he knows aught,
still he knows naught, exactly as he needs to know.
3 And if anyone loves Elohim, he knows this .
4 So, concerning the eating of idol sacrifices, we
know that an idol is naught in the cosmos and
that there is no other Elohim except one.
5 For even if there are those
who are worded, elohim,
whether in the heavens or in earth,
exactly as there are many elohim and many adoniym
6 — yet to us, one Elohim the Father,
by whom all is, and we in him;
— and one Adonay Yah Shua Messiah,
through whom all is and we through him.
7 Yet that knowledge is not in everyone:
for until now some with conscience of the idol
eat as an idol sacrifice;
and their conscience being frail is stained.
8 But food presents us not to Elohim:
for whenever we eat, we superabound not;
and whenever we eat not, we lack not.
9 But see — lest somehow your authority
becomes a stumbling to the frail.
10 For whenever anyone has knowledge,
and sees you repose in an idolion,
is not indeed the conscience of the frail
edified to eat idol sacrifices
11 — and through your knowledge,
the frail brother, for whom Messiah died, destructs?
12 And when you sin thus to the brothers
and strike their frail conscience
you sin to Messiah.
13 So if food scandalizes my brother,
I no way eat meat to the eons,
lest I scandalize my brother.

THE AUTHORITY OF THE HOLY

9 Am I not an apostle?
Am I not liberated?
Saw I not indeed Yah Shua Messiah our Adonay?
Are you not my work in Adonay?
2 If I am not an apostle to others,
yet indeed, I am to you:
for you are the seal of my apostleship in Adonay.
3 My pleading to them who judge me is this:
4 Have we not authority to eat and to drink?
5 Have we not authority
to lead about a sister, a woman,
as well as the rest of the apostles
and as the brothers of Adonay and Kepha?
6 Or I only and *Barnabas* **Bar Nabi**,

1 CORINTHIANS 9

      have not we *power* **authority**
      to *forbear working* **not work**?
7   Who *goeth a warfare any time* **ever warreth**
      at his own *charges* **wages**?
      who planteth a vineyard,
      and eateth not of the fruit thereof?
or who *feedeth* **shepherdeth** a *flock* **shepherddom**,
and eateth not of the milk of the *flock* **shepherddom**?
8   *Say* **Speak** I these *things* as a *man* **human**?
      or *saith* **indeed wordeth** not the
      law **torah** the same also?
9   For it is *written* **scribed**
      in the *law* **torah** of *Moses* **Mosheh**,
      Thou shalt not muzzle the mouth of the ox
      that treadeth *out* the corn.
      Doth God take care for **Concerneth Elohim**
      with oxen? Deuteronomy 25:4
10   Or *saith* **wordeth** he it
      altogether **most certainly** for our sakes?
      For our sakes, *no doubt* **indeed**,
      this is *written* **scribed**:
that he that ploweth *should* **is indebt to** plow in hope;
      and that he that thresheth in hope
      should *be partaker* **partake** of his hope.
11   If we have sown unto you
      spiritual things **spirituals**,
      is it *a great thing* **so mega**
      if we shall *reap* **harvest** your *carnal things* **fleshlies**?
12   If others
      be partakers **partake** of this *power* **authority** over you,
      are not we rather?
Nevertheless **Yet** we have not used this *power* **authority**;
      but *suffer* **endure** all *things*,
      lest we should **somehow** hinder
      the *gospel* **evangelism** of *Christ* **the Messiah**.
13   *Do* **Know** ye not *know* that they
which *minister about holy things* **work the priestal**
live **eat** of the *things of the temple* **priestal precinct**?
      and they which wait *at* **on** the *sacrifice* **altar**
      are *partakers* **co—partakers** with the *sacrifice* **altar**?
14   Even *so* **thus** hath the *Lord* **Adonay** ordained
that they which *preach* **evangelize** the *gospel* **evangelism**
      should live of the *gospel* **evangelism**.
15   But I have used none of these *things*:
      neither have I *written* **scribed** these *things*,
      that it should *thus* be *so done unto* **in** me:
      for it were *better* **good** for me to die,
      rather than that any *man* **one**
      should *make my glorying* void **my boasting**.
16   For *though I preach the gospel*
      whenever I evangelize,

      I have *nothing* **naught** to *glory of* **boast**:
for necessity is laid upon me; yea, woe *is* unto me,
      if **whenever** I *preach* **evangelize** not *the gospel*!
17   For if I *do* **transact** this
      thing willingly **voluntarily**,
      I have a reward:
      but if *against my will* **involuntarily**,
      a *dispensation of the gospel* **an administration**
      is *committed* **entrusted** unto me.

THE REWARD OF THE HOLY

18   **So** What is my reward *then*?
Verily that, when I *preach the gospel* **evangelize**,
      I may *make* **place**
      the *gospel* **evangelism** of *Christ* **the Messiah**
      without charge,
      that I abuse not my *power* **authority**
      in the *gospel* **evangelism**.
19   For though I be *free* **liberated** from all *men*,
yet *have I made myself servant* **I am subservient** unto all,
      that I might gain the more.
20   And unto the *Jews* **Yah Hudiym**,
      I became as a *Jew* **Yah Hudiy**,
      that I might gain the *Jews* **Yah Hudiym**;
      to them that are under *the law* **torah**,
      as under *the law* **torah**,
that I might gain them that are under *the law* **torah**;
21   To them that are *without law* **untorahed**,
      as *without law* **untorahed**,
      (being not *without law* **untorahed** to *God* **Elohim**,
      but *under the law* **entorahed** to *Christ* **Messiah**,)
that I might gain them that are *without law* **untorahed**.
6   Or only I and Bar Nabi,
      have we not authority to not work?
7   Who wars at his own wages?
      Who plants a vineyard and eats not of the fruit?
      Or who shepherds a shepherddom
      and eats not of the milk of the shepherddom?
8   Speak I these as a human?
      Or indeed words not the torah the same also?
9   For it is scribed in the torah of Mosheh,
      Muzzle not the mouth of the ox
      that treads the corn.
      Deuteronomy 25:4
      Is Elohim concerned with oxen?
10   Or words he most certainly for our sakes?
      Indeed, for our sakes, this is scribed:
      that whoever plows
      is indebted to plow in hope;
      and whoever threshes in hope

11	If we spore spirituals to you,
	is it so mega if we harvest your fleshlies?
12	If others partake of this authority over you,
	— not rather we?
	Yet we use not this authority, but endure all;
	lest somehow
	we hinder the evangelism of the Messiah.
13	Know you not that whoever works the priestal
	eats of the priestal precinct?
	and whoever waits on the sacrifice altar
	are co—partakers with the sacrifice altar?
14	Even thus has Adonay ordained
	that whoever evangelizes the evangelism
	lives by the evangelism.
15	And I neither use these:
	nor scribe I these to be thus in me:
	for it is good for me to die,
	rather than anyone void my boasting.
16	For whenever I evangelize,
	I have naught to boast:
	for necessity is laid upon me;
	yes, woe to me, whenever I evangelize not!
17	For if I transact this voluntarily,
	I have a reward:
	but if involuntarily,
	an administration is entrusted to me.

The Reward Of The Holy

18	What so is my reward?
	That when I evangelize,
	I place the evangelism of the Messiah without charge,
	that I abuse not my authority in the evangelism.
19	For though I am liberated from all
	yet I am subservient to all
	— to gain the more.
20	And to the Yah Hudiym
	I become as a Yah Hudiy
	to gain the Yah Hudiym;
	to them under torah, as under torah,
	to gain them under torah;
21	to them untorahed, as untorahed,
	not being untorahed to Elohim,
	but entorahed to Messiah,
	to gain the untorahed.
22	To the *weak* **frail** became I as *weak* **frail**,
	that I might gain the *weak* **frail**:
	I am *made all things to all men* **become all to all**,
	that I might *by all means* **most certainly** save some.
23	And this I do for the *gospel's* **evangelism's** sake,

	that I might be *partaker thereof with you* **a co—partaker**.
24	Know ye not that they
	which run in a *race* **stadium**
	indeed run all,
	but one *receiveth* **taketh** the *prize* **umpirage**?
	So run **Run thus**, that ye may *obtain* **overtake**.
25	And *every man* **everyone**
	that *striveth* **agonizeth** for the mastery
	is *temperate* **self—controlled** in all *things*.
	Now **So** they *do it* **indeed**,
	to *obtain* **take** a corruptible *crown* **wreath**;
	but we an incorruptible.
26	**So** I *therefore so* run **thus**, not as uncertainly;
	so fight **thus** I **fistfight**,
	not as one that *beateth* **floggeth** the air:
27	But I *keep under* **subdue** my body,
	and bring it into *subjection* **servitude**:
	lest *that by any means* **somehow**,
	when I have preached to others,
	I myself should *be a castaway* **become disapproved**.

Warnings Against Idolatry

10	Moreover, brethren,
	I *would* **will** not that ye should be *ignorant* **unknowing**,
	how that all our fathers were under the cloud,
	and all passed through the sea;
2	And were all baptized unto *Moses* **Mosheh**
	in the cloud and in the sea;
3	And did all eat the same spiritual *meat* **food**;
4	And did all drink the same spiritual drink:
	for they drank of that spiritual Rock that followed them:
	and that Rock was *Christ* **the Messiah**.
5	But *with* **in** many of them
	God was not well pleased **Elohim well—approved not**:
	for they were *overthrown* **scattered** in the wilderness.
6	Now these *things were*
	became our *examples* **types**,
	to the intent **that** we should not
	lust **pant** after evil *things*,
	exactly as they *also lusted* **panted**.
7	Neither be ye idolaters,
	exactly as were some of them;
	as *it is written* **scribed**,
	The people sat down to eat and drink,
	and rose up to *play* **ridicule**.
	Exodus 32:6
8	Neither let us *commit fornication* **whore**,
	exactly as some of them *committed* **whored**, and
	fell in one day three and twenty thousand.
9	Neither let us *tempt Christ* **test the Messiah**,

1 CORINTHIANS 10

    exactly as some of them also *tempted* **tested**,
    and were destroyed of serpents.
10   Neither murmur ye,
    exactly as some of them also murmured,
    and were destroyed of the destroyer.
11   Now all these *things* happened unto them
    for *ensamples* **types**:
    and they are *written* **scribed**
    for our *admonition* **reminding**,
    upon **unto** whom
    the *ends* **completion/shalom** of the *world* **eons**
    are come **has arrived**.
12   *Wherefore* **So then** let him
    that thinketh he standeth
    take heed **see** lest he fall.

TESTING

13   There hath no *temptation* **testing** taken you
    but **except** such as is *common to man* **human**:
    but *God* **Elohim** is *faithful* **trustworthy**,
    who *will* **shall** not *suffer* **allow** you to be *tempted* **tested**
    above that ye are able **beyond your ability**;
    but *will* **shall** with the *temptation* **testing**
    also make *a way to escape* **an exit**,
    that ye may be able to *bear* **endure** it.
14   *Wherefore* **So**, my *dearly*
    beloved, flee from idolatry.
15   I *speak* **word** as *to wise*
    men **unto the thoughtful**;
    judge ye what I say.
22   To the frail I become as frail,
    to gain the frail:
    I become all to all,
    to most certainly save some.
23   And this I do for sake of the evangelism,
    to become a co—partaker.
24   Know you not, that whoever runs in a stadium,
    indeed all run, but one takes the umpirage?
    Run thus — to overtake.
25   And everyone who agonizes for the mastery
    is self—controlled in all:
    they indeed, to take a corruptible wreath;
    but we an incorruptible.
26   So thus I run — not as uncertainly;
    thus I fistfight — not as one flogging the air:
27   but I subdue my body and bring it to servitude:
    lest somehow, having preached to others,
    I myself become disapproved.

WARNINGS AGAINST IDOLATRY

10   And brothers,
    I will that you not be unknowing,
    how that all our fathers were under the cloud
    and all passed through the sea;
2   and all to Mosheh
    were baptized in the cloud and in the sea;
3   and all ate the same spiritual food;
4   and all drank the same spiritual drink:
    for they drank of a spiritual Rock following them:
    and the Rock was the Messiah.
5   But in many of them
    Elohim well—approved not;
    for they scattered in the wilderness:
6   and these became our types,
    to not pant after evil, exactly as they panted.
7   Neither be idolaters, exactly as some of them:
    as scribed,
    The people sat down to eat and drink
    and rose up to ridicule.
    Exodus 32:6
8   Whore not,
    exactly as some of them whored
    and twenty—three thousand fell in one day:
9   nor test the Messiah,
    exactly as some of them also tested and
    were destroyed by serpents:
10   nor murmur,
    exactly as some of them also murmured
    and were destroyed by the destroyer.
11   And all these happened to them for types:
    and they are scribed to remind us,
    to whom the completion/shalom of the eons arrives.
12   So, whoever thinks he stands,
    see lest he fall.

TESTING

13   No testing overtakes you
    except such as is human:
    but Elohim is trustworthy
    who allows you to not
    to be tested beyond your ability;
    but with the testing also makes an exit
    so that you are able to endure.
14   So my beloved, flee from idolatry.
15   I word as to the thoughtful,
    judge what I say.

1 CORINTHIANS 10, 11

COMMUNION

16 The cup of *blessing* **eulogy**
which we *bless* **eulogize**,
is it not **indeed**
the communion of the blood of *Christ* **the Messiah**?
The bread which we break,
is it not **indeed**
the communion of the body of *Christ* **the Messiah**?

17 For we being many are one bread, *and* one body:
for we *are* all *partakers* **partake** of that one bread.

18 *Behold Israel* **See Yisra El** after the flesh:
indeed, are not they which eat of the sacrifices
partakers **communicants** of the *sacrifice* altar?

19 **So** What say I *then*?
that the idol is *any thing* **somewhat**,
or that
which is offered in sacrifice to idols **an idol sacrifice**
is *any thing* **somewhat**?

20 But *I say*,
that *the things* **those** which the *Gentiles* **goyim** sacrifice,
they sacrifice to *devils* **demons**, and not to *God* **Elohim**:
and I *would* **will** not that ye
should have fellowships **become communicants**
with *devils* **demons**.

21 Ye cannot drink the cup of *the Lord* **Adonay**,
and the cup of *devils* **demons**:
ye cannot *be partakers* **partake** of
the *Lord's* table **of Yah Veh**,
and of the table of *devils* **demons**.
Malachi 1:7

CONSCIENCE

22 *Do* **Or, incite** we *provoke* the
Lord **Adonay** to jealousy?
are we *stronger* **mightier** than he?

23 All *things* are *lawful for* **allowed** me,
but all *things* are not *expedient* **beneficial**:
all *things* are *lawful for* **allowed** me,
but all *things* edify not.

24 Let no *man* **one** seek his own,
but *every man* **each** another's *wealth*.

25 Whatsoever is sold in the shambles, *that* eat,
asking no question **not judging** for conscience sake:

26 For the earth is *the Lord's* **Yah Veh's**,
and the fulness/**shalom** thereof. Psalm 24:1

27 If any of *them that believe not* **the trustless**
bid **call** you *to a feast*,
and ye *be disposed* **will** to go;
whatsoever is set *before* **by** you, eat,
asking no question **not judging** for conscience sake.

28 But *if* **whenever** any *man* **one** say unto you,
This is *offered in sacrifice unto idols* **an idol sacrifice**,
eat not for his sake that *shewed* **disclosed** it,
and for conscience sake:
for the earth is *the Lord* **Yah Veh's**,
and the *fulness* **shalom** thereof:
Psalm 24:1

29 Conscience, I *say* **word**,
not **indeed** thine own, but of the other:
for why is my liberty judged
of *another man's* **another's** conscience?

30 For if I by *grace* be *a partaker* **charism partake**,
why am I *evil spoken of* **blasphemed**
for that for which I *give thanks* **eucharistize**?

31 **So** Whether *therefore* ye
eat, *or* **whether ye** drink,
or **whether** whatsoever ye do,
do all to the glory of *God* **Elohim**.

32 *Give none offence* **Become inoffensive**,
neither to the *Jews* **Yah Hudiym**,
nor to the *Gentiles* **Hellene**,
nor **and** to the *church* **ecclesia** of *God* **Elohim**:

33 Even as I please all *men* in all *things*,
not seeking mine own *profit* **benefit**,
but *the profit* of many, that they may be saved.

RELATIONSHIPS

11 Be ye *followers* **mimickers** of me,
even **exactly** as I also *am* of *Christ* **Messiah**.

2 Now I *praise* **halal** you, brethren,
that ye remember me in all *things*,
and *keep* **hold** the *ordinances* **traditions**,
exactly as I delivered them to you.

COMMUNION

16 The cup of eulogy we eulogize,
is it not indeed
the communion of the blood of the Messiah?
The bread we break,
is it not indeed
the communion of the body of the Messiah?

17 For we, being many, are one bread — one body:
for we all partake of that one bread.

18 See Yisra El after the flesh:
indeed, are not they who eat of the sacrifices,
communicants of the sacrifice altar?

19 So what say I?
That the idol is somewhat?
Or that an idol sacrifice is somewhat?

20 But those that the goyim sacrifice,

455

1 CORINTHIANS 11

they sacrifice to demons and not to Elohim:
and I will
that you not become communicants with demons.
21 You cannot drink the cup of Adonay
and the cup of demons:
you cannot partake of the table of Yah Veh
and of the table of demons.
Malachi 1:7

CONSCIENCE

22 Or, incite we Adonay to jealousy?
Are we mightier than he?
23 I am allowed all, but all is not beneficial:
I am allowed all, but all edifies not.
24 Seek not *for* your own,
but each *for* the other.
25 Whatever is sold in the shambles
eat for sake of conscience — not judging:
26 For the earth is to Yah Vah
and the fulness/shalom thereof.
Psalm 24:1
27 If any of the trustless call you and you will to go;
eat whatever is set by you
for sake of conscience — not judging.
28 But whenever anyone says to you,
This is an idol sacrifice!
eat not for sake of him who disclosed it
and for sake of conscience:
for the earth is to Yah Vah
and the fulness/shalom thereof:
Psalm 24:1
29 Conscience, I word,
indeed not of your own, but of the other:
for why is my liberty judged
by the conscience of another?
30 And if I, by charism partake,
why blaspheme me for what I eucharistize?
31 So, whether you eat
whether you drink
whether whatever you do
— do all to the glory of Elohim.
32 Become inoffensive,
both to the Yah Hudiym and to the Hellene
and to the ecclesia of Elohim:
33 even as I please all in all, not seeking my
own benefit but of many — to be saved.

RELATIONSHIPS

11 Become mimickers of me
exactly as I also of Messiah.

2 And I halal you brothers,
that you remember me in all
— and hold the traditions,
exactly as I delivered them to you.

TRESSES

3 But I *would have* **will that** you know,
that the head of every man is *Christ* **the Messiah**;
and the head of the woman is the man;
and the head of *Christ* **Messiah** is *God* **Elohim**.
4 Every man praying or prophesying, having his head
covered **veiled**, *dishonoureth* **shameth** his head.
5 But every woman that prayeth or prophesieth
with her head *uncovered* **unveiled**
dishonoureth **shameth** her head:
for that is even all one as if she were shaven.
6 For if the woman be not *covered* **veiled**,
let her also be shorn:
but if it be a shame for a woman to be shorn or shaven,
let her be *covered* **veiled**.
7 For a man indeed
ought **is indebted** not to *cover* **veil** his head,
forasmuch **being** as he is the *image* **icon**
and glory of *God* **Elohim**:
but the woman is the glory of the man.
8 For the man is not of the woman:
but the woman of the man.
9 Neither **indeed** was the
man created for the woman;
but the woman for the man.
10 For this cause *ought* the woman **is indebted**
to have *power* **authority** on her head
because of the angels.
11 *Nevertheless* **However**
neither is the man *without* **apart from** the woman,
neither the woman *without* **apart from** the man,
in *the Lord* **Adonay**.
12 For *exactly* as the woman is of the man,
even *so* **thus** is the man also *by* **through** the woman;
but all *things* of *God* **Elohim**.
13 Judge in yourselves: is it *comely* **befitting**
that a woman pray unto *God* **Elohim**
uncovered **unveiled**?
14 **Or** Doth not even nature
itself *teach* **doctrinate** you,
3 But I will you to know,
that the head of every man is the Messiah;
and the head of the woman is the man;
and the head of Messiah is Elohim.
4 Every man praying or prophesying

	having his head veiled
	shames his head:
5	and every woman praying or prophesying
	having her head unveiled
	shames her head
	— for all that is even as one shaven.
6	For if the woman veils not,
	have her also shear:
	but if it is a shame for a woman to shear or shave,
	have her veil.
7	For indeed a man is indebted
	to not veil his head,
	being the icon and glory of Elohim;
	but woman is the glory of man:
8	For man is not of woman;
	but woman of man:
9	indeed man was not created for the woman;
	but woman for the man.
10	For this cause the woman is indebted
	to have authority on her head because of the angels.
11	However, in Adonay,
	neither is man apart from woman
	nor woman apart from man.
12	For exactly as the woman is of the man
	even thus is the man also through the woman
	— but all of Elohim.

TRESSES

that, *if* **whenever** a man have *long hair* **tresses**,
it is a *shame* **dishonour** unto him?
15 But *if* **whenever** a woman have *long hair* **tresses**,
it is a glory to her:
for *her hair is* **tresses are** given her for a *covering* **mantle**.
16 But if any *man* **one**
seem **thinketh** to be *contentious* **quarrelsome**,
we have no such custom,
neither the *churches* **ecclesiae** of *God* **Elohim**.

EUCHARIST

17 Now in this that I *declare unto you* **evangelize**,
I *praise* **halal** you not,
that ye come together not *for* **to** the better,
but *for* **unto** the worse.
18 For **indeed** first of all,
when ye come together in the *church* **ecclesia**,
I hear that there be *divisions* **schisms** among you;
and I *partly believe* **somewhat trust** it.
19 For there must be also heresies among you,
that they which are approved

may *be made* **become** manifest among you.
20 **So** When ye come together
therefore into one place,
this is not to eat *the Lord's* **Adonay's** supper.
21 For in eating
every one taketh before other **each anticipateth**
his own supper:
and **indeed** one is hungry,
and another is *drunken* **intoxicated**.
22 *What*? **Indeed!**
have ye not houses to eat and to drink in?
or *despise* **disesteem** ye
the *church* **ecclesia** of *God* **Elohim**,
and shame them that have not?
What shall I say to you? shall I *praise* **halal** you in this?
I *praise* **halal** you not.
13 Judge in yourselves:
Is it befitting that a woman pray to Elohim unveiled?
14 Or does not even nature itself doctrinate you,
that whenever a man has tresses
it is a dishonor to him?
15 And whenever a woman has tresses,
it is a glory to her
— for tresses are given her for a mantle.
16 And if anyone thinks to be quarrelsome,
neither we nor the ecclesiae of Elohim
have such custom.

EUCHARIST

17 And in evangelizing, I halal you not,
in that you come together
not to the better but to the worse.
18 For indeed first of all,
when you come together in the ecclesia,
I hear that there are schisms among you;
and I somewhat trust it.
19 For there must also be heresies among you,
so that those approved become manifest among you.
20 So you are coming together into one place,
not to eat the supper of Adonay:
21 for in eating,
each anticipates his own supper
— indeed one is famished and another is intoxicated.
22 Indeed, have you not houses to eat and to drink?
Or disesteem you the ecclesia of Elohim?
And shame them who have not?
What say I to you?
Halal I you in this?
I halal you not.

1 CORINTHIANS 11, 12

THE SEQUENCE OF THE EUCHARIST: PRECEDING SUPPER

23 For I have *received* **taken** of *the Lord* **Adonay**
that which also I delivered unto you,
That *the Lord Jesus* **Adonay Yah Shua**
in the *same* night in which he was betrayed
took bread:
24 And when he had *given thanks* **eucharistized**,
he brake it, and said,
Take, eat: this is my body, which is broken for you:
this do in remembrance of me.

AFTER SUPPER

25 After the same manner also *he took* the cup,
when he had *supped* **after supping**, *saying* **wording**,
This cup is the new *testament* **covenant** in my blood:
this do ye, as oft as **ever** ye drink it,
in remembrance of me.
26 For as often as **ever** ye eat this bread,
and drink this cup,
ye do *shew the Lord's* **evangelize Adonay's** death
till **ever** he come.
27 *Wherefore* **So** whosoever shall eat this bread,
and **or** drink this cup of *the Lord* **Adonay**, unworthily,
shall be *guilty of* **subject**
to the body and blood of *the Lord* **Adonay**.
28 But let a *man examine* **human proof** himself,
and *so* **thus** let him eat of that bread,
and drink of that cup.
29 For he that eateth and drinketh unworthily,
eateth and drinketh *damnation* **judgment** to himself,
not discerning *the Lord's* **Adonay's** body.
30 For this cause
many are *weak* **frail** and *sickly* **infirm** among you,
and many sleep.
31 For if we *would judge* **should discern** ourselves,
we should not **ever** be judged.
32 But when we are judged,
we are *chastened* **disciplined** of *the Lord* **Adonay**,
that we should not be condemned
with the *world* **cosmos**.
33 *Wherefore* **So** my brethren,
when ye come together to eat,
tarry **await** one *for* another.
34 And if any *man* hunger, let him eat at home;
that ye come not together unto *condemnation* **judgment**.
And the rest *will* **shall** I *set in order* **ordain**
when **as ever** I come.

SPIRITUALS

12 Now concerning *spiritual gifts* **spirituals**, brethren,
I *would* **will** not have you *ignorant* **unknowing**.
2 Ye know that ye were *Gentiles* **goyim**,
carried away **led** unto these *dumb* **voiceless** idols,
even as ye were **ever** led.
3 *Wherefore I give* **So I make**
known to you *to understand*,
that no *man* **one** speaking *by* **in** the Spirit of *God* **Elohim**
calleth Jesus accursed **wordeth, Yah Shua anathema**:
and that no *man* **one** can say,
that Jesus is the Lord **Adonay Yah Shua**,
but by **except in** the *Holy Spirit* **Ruach ha-kodesh**.

DISTINCTIONS OF CHARISMATA MINISTRIES, AND ENERGIZINGS

4 Now there are *diversities* **distinctions**
of *gifts* **charismata**,
but the same Spirit.
5 And there are *differences* **distinctions**
of *administrations* **ministries**,
but the same *Lord* **Adonay**.
6 And there are *diversities* **distinctions**
of *operations* **energizings**,
but it is the same *God* **Elohim**
which *worketh* **energizeth** all in all.

THE SEQUENCE OF THE EUCHARIST: PRECEDING SUPPER

23 For I — I took from Adonay
what I also delivered to you,
that Adonay Yah Shua
in the night he was betrayed, took bread:
24 and when he eucharistized,
he broke, and said, Take — eat:
this is my body, broken for you:
this do to the remembrance of me.

AFTER SUPPER

25 After the same manner also the cup,
after supping, wording,
This cup is the new covenant in my blood:
this do, as often as ever you drink,
in remembrance of me.
26 For as often as ever
you eat this bread and drink this cup,
you evangelize the death of Adonay
until ever he comes.

27	So whoever eats this bread,		*by* **in** the same Spirit;
	or drinks this cup of Adonay — unworthily,		to another the *gifts* **charismata** of *healing* **healings**
	is subject to the body and blood of Adonay:		*by* **in** the same Spirit;
28	and each human is to proof himself	10	To another
	and thus eat of that bread and drink of that cup.		the *working* **energizings** of *miracles* **dynamis**;
	29 For whoever eats and drinks unworthily		to another prophecy;
	eats and drinks judgment to himself —		to another *discerning* **discernments** of spirits;
	not discerning the body of Adonay.		to another *divers kinds* **genos** of tongues;
30	For this cause many among		to another the *interpretation* **translation** of tongues:
	you are frail and infirm	11	But all these
	and many sleep.		*worketh* **energizeth** that one and the selfsame Spirit,
31	For if we discern ourselves,		*dividing* **distributing** to *every man* **each his own**
	we are never ever judged:		*severally* **exactly** as he *will* **willeth**.
32	and being judged,		Romans 12:3—8

The Body Of The Messiah

	we are disciplined by Adonay,	12	For **exactly** as the body is one,
	to not be condemned with the cosmos.		and hath many members,
33	So my brothers,		and all the members of that one body,
	when you come together to eat, await one another.		being many, are one body:
34	And if any famish, eat at home;		*so* **thus** also *is Christ* **the Messiah**.
	that you not come together to judgment.	13	For *by* **in** one Spirit are we
	And the rest I ordain as ever I come.		all baptized into one body,

Spirituals

12	Now concerning spirituals, brothers,		whether *we be Jews* **Yah Hudiym**,
	I will that you not be unknowing.		*or Gentiles* **whether Hellenes**,
2	You know that you were goyim,		whether *we be bond or free* **servant, whether liberated**;
	led to these voiceless idols — as ever you were led.		and have been all made to drink into one Spirit.
3	So I make known to you,		

One Body, Many Members

	that no one speaking in Spirit of Elohim	14	For the body is not one member, but many.
	words, Yah Shua anathema:	15	*If* **Whenever** the foot shall say,
	and that no one can say, Adonay Yah Shua,		Because I am not the hand, I am not of the body;
	except in Holy Spirit.		is it therefore not of the body?

Distinctions Of Charismata, Ministries, And Energizings

		16	And *if* **whenever** the ear shall say,
			Because I am not the eye, I am not of the body;
4	And there are distinctions of charismata		*so* is it *therefore* not of the body?
	and the same Spirit:	17	If the whole body were an eye,
5	and there are distinctions of ministries		where were the hearing?
	and the same Adonay:		If the whole were hearing,
6	and there are distinctions of energizings		where were the smelling?
	and the same Elohim who energizes all in all.	18	But now hath *God* **Elohim** set the members
			every one **each** of them in the body,

Distributions Of Spirituals

			exactly as *it hath pleased him* **he willed**.
7	But the manifestation of the Spirit	19	And if they were all one member,
	is given to *every man* **each** to *profit withal* **benefit**.		where were the body?
8	For **indeed** to one is given *by* **through** the Spirit	20	But now **indeed** are they many members,
	the word of wisdom;		yet but one body.
	to another the word of knowledge	21	And the eye cannot say unto the hand,
	by **in** the same Spirit;		I have no need of thee:
9	To another *faith* **trust**		nor again the head to the feet,

1 CORINTHIANS 12

THE BODY OF THE MESSIAH

12 For exactly as the body is one
and has many members;
and all the members of that one body
being many, are one body;
thus also the Messiah.
13 For in one Spirit we all are
baptized into one body,
whether Yah Hudiym, whether Hellenes,
whether servants, whether liberated;
and have all to drink into one Spirit.

ONE BODY, MANY MEMBERS

14 For the body is not one member, but many.
15 Whenever the foot says,
Because I am not the hand, I am not of the body;
so is it not of the body?
16 And whenever the ear says,
Because I am not the eye, I am not of the body;
so is it not of the body?
17 If the whole body were an eye,
where the hearing?
If the whole were hearing,
where the smelling?
18 And now Elohim sets the members
— each in the body — exactly as he wills.
19 And if they all were one member,
where the body?
20 And now indeed,
many members, yet but one body.
21 And the eye cannot say to the hand,
I have no need of you:
nor again the head to the feet,
I have no need of you.
22 Rather, much more,
those members of the body we think to be frail
are necessary;
23 and on those of the body
we think of as dishonorable,
we place superabundant honor;
and on our misbehavors, superabundant honor.
24 For our honorables have no need:
but Elohim co—mingles the body
giving superabundant honor to what lacked;
25 that there be no schism in the body;
but that the members
have the same anxiety one for another.
26 And whether one member suffers,
all the members co—suffer;

I have no need of you.
22 *Nay* **Rather**, much more
those members of the body,
which *seem* **we think** to be *more feeble* **frail**,
are necessary:
23 And those *members* of the body,
which we think to be *less honourable* **dishonourable**,
upon these
we *bestow more abundant* **place superabundant** honour;
and our *uncomely parts* **misbehavors**
have *more abundant comeliness* **superabundant honour**.
24 For our *comely parts* **honourables** have no need:
but *God* **Elohim** hath *tempered* **co—mingled** the body
together,
having given *more abundant* **superabundant** honour
to that *part* which lacked.
25 That there should be no schism in the body;
but that the members
should have the same *care* **anxiety** one for another.
26 And whether one member suffer,
all the members *suffer with it* **co—suffer**;
or **whether** one member be *honoured* **glorified**,
all the members *rejoice with it* **co—rejoice**.
27 Now ye are the body of *Christ* **Messiah**,
and members in particular.

DISTRIBUTIONS OF SPIRITUALS

7 And the manifestation of the Spirit
is given to each to benefit:
8 for indeed to one is given through the Spirit
the word of wisdom;
to another the word of knowledge
in the same Spirit;
9 to another trust
in the same Spirit;
to another the charismata of healings
in the same Spirit;
10 to another
the energizings of dynamis;
to another prophecy;
to another discernments of spirits;
to another genos of tongues;
to another the translation of tongues.
11 But all these
energize the one and the selfsame Spirit,
distributing to each his own,
exactly as he wills.
Romans 12:3—8

or whether one member is glorified,
all the members co—rejoice:

27 and you are the body of Messiah
and members in particular.

The Charismata In The Ecclesia

28 And **indeed**
God **Elohim** hath set some in the *church* **ecclesia**,
first apostles,
secondarily prophets, thirdly *teachers* **doctors**,
after that miracles **then dynamis**,
then *gifts* **charismata** of healings,
helps **supports**, *governments* **pilots**,
diversities **genos** of tongues.

29 Are all apostles? are all prophets?
are all *teachers* **doctors**?
are **have** all *workers of miracles* **dynamis**?

30 Have all the *gifts* **charismata**
of *healing* **healings**?
do all speak with tongues? do all *interpret* **translate**?

31 But *covet earnestly* **be zealous**
for the *best gifts* **better charismata**:
and yet shew I unto you a more excellent way.

THE WAY OF LOVE

13 *Though* **Whenever** I speak
with the tongues of *men* **humans** and of angels,
and have not *charity* **love**,
I am become *as sounding brass* **echoing copper**,
or a *tinkling* **hallooing** cymbal.

2 And *though* **whenever** I
have *the gift of* prophecy,
and *understand* **perceive** all mysteries,
and all knowledge;
and *though* **whenever** I have all *faith* **trust**,
so that I *could* remove mountains,
and have not *charity* **love**, I am *nothing* **naught**.

3 And *though* **whenever**
I *bestow* **force feed** all my *goods* **holdings**
to feed the poor **upon others**,
and *though* **whenever**
I *give* **surrender** my body to be burned,
and have not *charity* **love**,
it *profiteth* **benefiteth** me *nothing* **naught**.

4 *Charity suffereth long* **Love
is patient**, and is kind;
charity envieth not **love is never jealous**;
charity vaunteth not itself **love never brags**,
is not puffed up **never puffs**,

5 *Doth not behave itself
unseemly* **Never misbehaves**,
seeketh not her own **never self—seeking**,
is not easily provoked **never easily agitated**,
thinketh no **never reckoneth** evil;

6 *Rejoiceth not in iniquity*
Never cheereth in injustice,
but *rejoiceth* **co—cheereth** in the truth;

7 *Beareth* **Endureth** all *things*,
believeth **trusteth** all *things*,
hopeth all *things*,
endureth **abideth** all *things*.

8 *Charity* **Love** never **ever** faileth:
but whether *there be* prophecies,
they shall *fail* **inactivate**;
whether *there be* tongues,
they shall *cease* **pause**;
whether *there be* knowledge,
it shall *vanish away* **inactivate**.

9 For we know *in* **by** part,
and we prophesy *in* **by** part.

10 But when *that which is perfect*
the completed/shalamed
is come,
then that which is *in* **by** part
shall be *done away* **inactivated**.

11 When I was a *child* **baby**,
I spake as a *child* **baby**,
I *understood* **thought** as a *child* **baby**,
I *thought* **reckoned** as a *child* **baby**:
but when I became a man,
I *put away childish things* **inactivated the babyish**.

12 For now we see through a *glass* **mirror**,
darkly **obscurely**;
but then face to face:
now I know *in* **by** part;
but then shall I know *even* **exactly** as also I am known.

13 And now abideth *faith* **trust**, hope, *charity* **love**,
these three;
but the greatest of these is *charity* **love**.

The Charismata In The Ecclesia

28 And indeed Elohim set some in the ecclesia:
first apostles,
secondly prophets,
thirdly doctors,
then dynamis,
then charismata of healings,
supports,
pilots,
genos of tongues.

29 All apostles?

1 CORINTHIANS 13, 14

All prophets?
All doctors?
All dynamis?
30 All the charismata of healings?
All speak with tongues?
All translate?
31 But be zealous for the better charismata:
and I show you a still more excellent way.

THE WAY OF LOVE

13 Whenever I speak
with the tongues of humans and of angels
and have not love,
I become an echoing copper or a hallooing cymbal.
2 And whenever I have prophecy
and perceive all mysteries and all knowledge,
and whenever I have all trust to remove mountains
and have not love, I am naught.
3 And whenever I force feed
all my holdings on others
and whenever I surrender my body to burn,
and have not love
it benefits me naught.
4 Love is patient and is kind,
love is never jealous,
love never brags,
never puffs,
5 never misbehaves,
never self—seeking,
never easily agitated,
never reckons evil,
6 never cheers in injustice
but co—cheers in the truth,
7 endures all,
trusts all,
hopes all,
abides all:
8 love never ever fails.
And whether prophecies, they inactivate;
whether tongues, they pause;
whether knowledge, it inactivates.
9 For by part we know; and by part we prophesy:
10 But when the completed/shalamed comes
then the by part becomes inactivated.
11 When I was a baby
I spoke as a baby
I thought as a baby
I reckoned as a baby:
and when I became a man
I inactivated the babyish.

12 For now we see obscurely as through a mirror;
but then, face to face:
now I know by part;
but then I know exactly as also I am known.
13 And now abide trust, hope, love
— these three:
and the greatest of these is love.

PROPHECY, TONGUES, AND TRANSLATION

14 *Follow after charity* **Pursue love**,
and *desire spiritual gifts* **be zealous for spirituals**,
but rather that ye may prophesy.
2 For he that speaketh in *an unknown** **a** tongue
speaketh not unto *men* **humanity**, but unto *God* **Elohim**:
for no *man understandeth* **one heareth** him;
howbeit **for** in the spirit he speaketh mysteries.
*unknown tongues are unknown in Scripture
3 But he that prophesieth
speaketh unto *men* **humanity** to edification,
and *exhortation* **beseeching**, and *comfort* **consolation**.
4 He that speaketh in *an unknown*
a tongue edifieth himself;
but he that prophesieth edifieth the *church* **ecclesia**.
5 I *would* **will** that ye all spake with tongues
but rather that ye prophesied:
for greater is he that prophesieth
than he that speaketh with tongues,
except **unless** he *interpret* **translate**,
that the *church* **ecclesia** may *receive* **take** edifying.
6 Now, brethren,
even if I come unto you speaking with tongues,
what shall I *profit* **benefit** you,
except **unless** I shall speak to you
either *by revelation* **in apocalypse**, or *by* **in** knowledge,
or *by* **in** prophesying, or *by* **in** doctrine?
7 *And even* **Yet still**,
things without life **the soulless** giving *sound* **voice**,
whether *pipe* **flute** or *harp* **cither**,
except **unless** they give a distinction in the sounds,
how shall it be known
what is *piped* **fluted** or *harped* **cithered**?
8 For *if* **whenever** the trumpet
give an uncertain *sound* **voice**,
who shall prepare himself to *the battle* **war**?
9 *So* **Thus** likewise ye,
except **unless** ye *utter by* **give through** the tongue
words *easy to be* **well** understood,
how shall it be known what is spoken?
for ye shall speak into the air.
10 There are, *it may be* **if perhaps**,

so many *kinds* **genos** of voices in the *world* **cosmos**,
and none of them is *without signification* **voiceless**.
11 Therefore *if* **unless ever** I know *not*
the *meaning* **dynamis** of the voice,
I shall be unto him that speaketh a barbarian,
and he that speaketh shall be a barbarian unto me.
12 Even *so ye* **thus**,
forasmuch as **since** ye are zealous of *spiritual gifts* **spirits**,
seek that ye may *excel* **superabound**
to the edifying of the *church* **ecclesia**.
13 *Wherefore* **So** let him that
speaketh in *an unknown* **a** tongue
pray that he may *interpret* **translate**.
14 For *if* **whenever** I pray in *an unknown* **a** tongue,
my spirit prayeth,
but my *understanding* **mind** is unfruitful.
15 **So** What *is it then*?
I *will* **shall** pray with the spirit,
and I *will* **shall** pray with the *understanding* **mind** also:
I *will sing* **shall psalm** with the spirit,
and I *will sing* **shall psalm**
with the *understanding* **mind** also.
16 *Else when* **Unless if**
thou shalt *bless* **eulogize** with the spirit,
how shall he
that *occupieth* **filleth** the *room*
place of the unlearned say
Amen at thy *giving of thanks* **eucharist**,
seeing **since** he *understandeth* **perceiveth** not
what thou *sayest* **wordest**?
17 For thou *verily* **indeed**
givest thanks **eucharistizest** well,
but the other is not edified.
18 I *thank* **eucharistize** my *God* **Elohim**,
I speak with tongues more than ye all:
19 Yet in the *church* **ecclesia**
I *had rather* **will to** speak five words
with **through** my *understanding* **mind**,
that *by my voice* I might *teach* **catechize** others also,
than *ten thousand* **a myriad** words
in *an unknown* **a** tongue.

Prophecy, Tongues, And Translation

14 Pursue love
and be zealous for spirituals
— but rather to prophesy.
2 For whoever speaks in a tongue
speaks not to humanity
but to Elohim;
for no one hearkens;
for in spirit, he speaks mysteries.
3 And whoever prophesies to humanity
speaks to edification and beseeching and consolation:
4 whoever speaks in a tongue edifies himself;
and whoever prophesies edifies the ecclesia.
5 I will that you all speak with tongues
but rather that you prophesy:
for whoever prophesies
is greater than whoever speaks with tongues,
— unless he translates to edify the ecclesia.
6 And now brothers,
whenever I come to you speaking with tongues,
what benefit I you
— unless I speak to you
either in apocalypse or in knowledge?
Or in prophesying or in doctrine?
7 Still the soulless, giving voice,
whether flute or cither,
unless they give a distinction in the sounds,
how know we what is fluted or cithered?
8 And whenever the trumpet
gives an uncertain voice,
who prepares himself to war?
9 Thus likewise you, unless through the tongue,
you give words well understood,
how know we what is spoken?
— for you speak to air.
10 There are, if perhaps,
so many genos of voices in the cosmos
and none of them is voiceless.
11 So unless ever I know the dynamis of the voice
I am as a barbarian to him who speaks
and whoever speaks as a barbarian to me.
12 Even thus, since you are zealous of spirits,
seek that you superabound to edify the ecclesia.
13 So whoever speaks in a tongue,
pray that he translate.
14 For whenever I pray in a tongue, my spirit prays,
but my mind is unfruitful.
15 So what?
I pray with the spirit
and I pray with the mind also:
I psalm with the spirit
and I psalm with the mind also.
16 Unless if you eulogize with the spirit, he
who fills the place of the unlearned, how
says he, upon your eucharist, Amen! —
since he perceives not what you word?
17 For indeed you eucharistize well
but the other is not edified.

1 CORINTHIANS 14

18 I eucharistize my Elohim
— I speak with tongues more than you all:
19 yet in the ecclesia
I will to speak five words through my mind,
to catechize others also,
than a myriad words in a tongue.
20 Brethren, be not children
in *understanding* **thought**:
howbeit **rather** in malice be ye *children* **babies**,
but in *understanding* **thought** be
men **completed/shalamed**.
21 In the *law* **torah** it is *written* **scribed**,
With men of **In** other tongues and **in** other lips
will I speak unto this people;
and yet *for all that will* **thus shall** they not hear me,
saith the Lord **wordeth Yah Veh**.
Yesha Yah 28:11, 12, Deuteronomy 28:49
22 *Wherefore* **So** tongues are *for* **unto** a sign,
not to them that *believe* **trust**,
but to *them that believe not* **the trustless**:
but prophesying
serveth **is** not for *them that believe not* **the trustless**,
but for them which *believe* **trust**.
23 *therefore if* **So whenever**
the whole *church* **ecclesia**
be come together into one place,
and all speak with tongues,
and there *come in those that are* **enter the** unlearned,
or *unbelievers* **trustless**,
will **shall** they not say that ye *are mad* **rave**?
24 But *if* **whenever** all prophesy,
and there *come in* **enter**
one that believeth not **a trustless**, or *one* **an** unlearned,
he is *convinced* **reproved** of all, he is judged of all:
25 And thus are the secrets of his heart
made **become** manifest;
and *so* **thus** falling down on his face
he *will* **shall** worship *God* **Elohim**,
and *report* **evangelize**
that *God* **Elohim** is in you *of a truth* **indeed**.
26 *So* How is it *then*, brethren?
when ye come together,
every one **each** of you hath a psalm, hath a doctrine,
hath a tongue, hath *a revelation* **an apocalypse**,
hath *an interpretation* **a translation**.
Let all *things* be *done* unto edifying.

RULES FOR SPEAKING IN A TONGUE

27 If *also* any *man* **one** speak
in *an unknown* **a** tongue,
let it be by two, or at the most by three,
and that by *course* **part**; and let one *interpret* **translate**.
28 But *if there* **whenever there**
be no *interpreter* **translator**,
let him *keep silence* **hush** in the *church* **ecclesia**;
and let him speak to himself, and to *God* **Elohim**.

RULES FOR PROPHETS AND DISCERNERS

29 Let the prophets speak two or three,
and let the other *judge* **discern**.
30 *If any thing* **Whenever**
aught be *revealed* **unveiled**
to another that sitteth by,
let the first *hold his peace* **hush**.
31 For ye *may* **can** all prophesy one by one,
that all may learn, and all may be *comforted* **consoled**.
32 And the spirits of the prophets
are *subject* **subjugate** to the prophets.
33 For *God* **Elohim** is not *the*
author of *confusion* **instability**,
but of *peace* **shalom**,
as in all *churches* **ecclesiae** of the *saints* **holy**.
34 Let your women *keep silence* **hush**
in the *churches* **ecclesiae**:
for it is not *permitted* **allowed** unto them to speak;
but they are *commanded*
to *be under obedience* **subjugate**,
exactly as also *saith* **wordeth** the *law* **torah**.
35 And if they will to learn *any thing* **somewhat**,
let them ask their *husbands* **own men** at home:
for it is a shame
for women to speak in the *church* **ecclesia**.
36 *What?* **Or** came the word of
God **Elohim** *out* from you?
or *came it* **has it arrived** unto you only?
37 If any *man* **one** think himself
to be a prophet, or spiritual,
let him acknowledge that
the things **those** that I *write* **scribe** unto you
are the *commandments* **misvoth** of the *Lord* **Adonay**.
38 But if any *man* **one** be *ignorant* **unknowing**,
let him be *ignorant* **unknowing**.
39 *Wherefore* **So**, brethren,
covet **be zealous** to prophesy,
and forbid not to speak with tongues.
40 Let all *things be done decently* **become decorous**
and in order.
20 Brothers, be not children in thought:
rather be babies in malice
and completed/shalamed in thought.

21   In the torah it is scribed,
With men in other tongues and in other lips
I will to speak to this people;
and thus they still hear me not,
words Yah Veh.
Yesha Yah 28:11, 12, Deuteronomy 28:49

22   So tongues are not a sign to the trusting
but to the trustless:
and prophesying is not for the trustless
but for the trusting.

23   So whenever the whole ecclesia
comes together to one place
and all speak with tongues
— and an unlearned or a trustless enter,
say they not that you rave?

24   And whenever all prophesy
and a trustless or an unlearned enters,
he is reproved by all; he is judged by all:
25 And thus the secrets of his heart become manifest;
and thus falling on his face he worships Elohim
and evangelizes that Elohim is in you indeed.

26   So how is it, brothers, when you come together,
each of you has a psalm?
Has a doctrine?
Has a tongue?
Has an apocalypse?
Has a translation?
Have all to edify.

Rules For Speaking In A Tongue

27   Also, if anyone speaks in a tongue,
by two, or at the most by three;
and that by part — and let one translate.

28   And whenever there is no translator,
have him hush in the ecclesia; and
speak to himself and to Elohim.

Rules For Prophets And Discerners

29   Have the prophets speak two or three,
and the others discern:

30   and whenever aught is unveiled
to another sitting by,
have the first hush.

31   For you can all prophesy one by one,
so that all learn and all *be* consoled.

32   And the spirits of the prophets
are subjugate to the prophets.

33   For Elohim is not of instability — but of shalom,
as in all ecclesiae of the holy.

34   Hush your women in the ecclesiae:
allow them not to speak;
but they are to subjugate,
exactly as the torah also words.

35   And if they will to learn somewhat,
have them ask their own men at home:
for it is a shame for women to speak in the ecclesia.

36   Or comes the word of Elohim from you?
Or arrives it only to you?

37   If anyone thinks himself
to be a prophet, or spiritual,
have him acknowledge that those I scribe to you
are the misvoth of Adonay.

38   And if anyone is unknowing,
have him be unknowing.

39   So, brothers, be zealous to prophesy
and forbid not to speak with tongues.

40   Have all become decorous and in order.

The Evangelism Defined

15   Moreover, brethren,
I *declare* **make known** unto you *the gospel* **evangelism**
which I *preached* **evangelized** unto you,
which also ye have *received* **taken**,
and wherein ye stand;

2   *By* **Through** which also ye are saved,
if ye *keep in memory what* **hold the word**
I *preached* **evangelized** unto you,
unless **except lest** ye have *believed* **trusted** in vain.

3   For I delivered unto you **in the** first
of all that which I also *received* **had taken**,
how that *Christ* **Messiah** died for our sins
according to the scriptures;

4   And that he was buried,
and that he rose *again* the third day
according to the scriptures:

5   And that he was seen of *Cephas* **Kepha**,
then of the twelve:

6   *After that* **Then**,
he was seen of above five hundred brethren at once;
of whom the *greater part remain* **most abide**
unto *this present* **now**,
but some are fallen asleep.

7   *After that* **Then**, he was seen of *James* **Yaaqovos**;
then of all the apostles.

8   And last of all he was seen of me also,
just as though *as of one born out of due time* **miscarried**.

9   For I am the least of the apostles,
that am not *meet* **adequate** to be called an apostle,
because I persecuted the *church* **ecclesia** of *God* **Elohim**.

10   But by the *grace* **charism** of *God* **Elohim**

I am what I am:
and his *grace* **charism**
which was bestowed upon **unto** me
was **became** not in vain;
but I laboured
more *abundantly* **superabundantly** than they all:
yet not I,
but the *grace* **charism** of *God* **Elohim**
which was with me.

11 *Therefore* **So** whether *it were* I, *or* **whether** they,
so **thus** we preach, and *so* **thus** ye *believed* **trusted**.

The Resurrection, Essential To The Trust

12 Now if *Christ* **Messiah** be preached
that he rose from the dead,
how *say* **word** some among you
that there is no resurrection of the dead?

13 But if there be no resurrection of the dead,
then is *Christ* **Messiah** not risen:

14 And if *Christ* **Messiah** be not risen,
then is our preaching vain,
and your *faith* **trust** is also vain.

15 *Yea* **Yes**,
and we are found *false* **pseudo** witnesses of *God* **Elohim**;
because we have *testified* **witnessed** of *God* **Elohim**
that he raised *up Christ* **the Messiah**:
whom he raised not *up*,
if *so be that* **indeed** the dead rise not.

16 For if the dead rise not,
then is not *Christ* **Messiah** raised:

17 And if *Christ* **Messiah** be not raised,
your *faith* **trust** is vain; ye are yet in your sins.

18 Then they also
which are fallen asleep in *Christ* **Messiah**
are *perished* **destroyed**.

19 If in this life only we have
hope in *Christ* **Messiah**,
we are of all *men* **humanity** most
miserable **least mercied**.

The Sequence Of The Resurrection

20 But now is *Christ* **Messiah** risen from the dead,
and become the *firstfruits* **firstlings** of them that slept.

21 For since *by man* **through humanity**,
came death,
by man **through humanity**,
came also the resurrection of the dead.

22 For **exactly** as in Adam all die,
even *so* **thus** in *Christ* **the Messiah** shall
all be *made alive* **enlivened**.

The Evangelism Defined

15 And brothers,
I make known to you
the evangelism I evangelized to you
— which you also took, wherein you also stand;

2 through which also you are saved
if you hold the word I evangelized to you;
except lest you trust in vain.

3 For I first delivered to you of all I also took
— that Messiah died for our sins
according to the scriptures;

4 and that he was buried;
and that he rose the third day
according to the scriptures:

5 and that Kepha saw him, then the twelve:

6 then over five hundred
brothers saw him at once,
most of whom abide to now;
but some fell asleep;

7 then Yaaqovos saw him;
then all the apostles;

8 and last of all I saw him,
just as thoughas one miscarried:

9 for I am the least of the apostles
— who am not adequate to be called an apostle:
because I persecuted the ecclesia of Elohim.

10 And by the charism of Elohim, I am what I am:
and his charism to me became not in vain;
but I labored more superabundantly than they all:
yet not I — but the charism of Elohim within me.

11 So whether I, whether they,
thus we preached, and thus you trusted.

The Resurrection, Essential To The Trust

12 Now if we preach that
Messiah rose from the dead,
how word some among you
that there is no resurrection of the dead?

13 And if there is no resurrection of the dead
Messiah rose not:

14 and if Messiah rose not,
then our preaching is vain
and also your trust is vain.

15 Yes, and we are found
pseudo witnesses of Elohim;
because we witnessed that Elohim raised the Messiah:
whom he raised not — if indeed the dead rise not.

16 For if the dead rise not, Messiah rose not:

17 And if Messiah rose not,

your trust is vain — you are still in your sins.
18 Then also
they who fell asleep in Messiah are destroyed.
19 If in this life only we have hope in Messiah,
we are least mercied of all humanity.

THE SEQUENCE OF THE RESURRECTION

20 And now, Messiah rose from the dead
and became the firstlings of them who slept.
21 For since through humanity, death,
also through humanity, the resurrection of the dead.
22 For exactly as in Adam all die,
even thus in the Messiah all enliven:
23 But *every man* **each** in his own order:
Christ **Messiah** the *firstfruits* **firstlings**;
afterward **then** they that are *Christ's* **Messiah's**
at his *coming* **parousia**.
24 Then *cometh* the end **completion/shalom**,
when he shall have delivered *up*
the *kingdom* **sovereigndom** to *God* **Elohim**,
even the Father;
when he shall have *put down* **inactivated**
all *rule* **hierarchies** and all authority
and *power* **dynamis**.
25 For he must reign,
till **whenever** he hath put all enemies under his feet.
26 The *last* **final** enemy
that shall be *destroyed* **inactivated**
is death.
27 For he hath *put* **subjugated**
all *things* under his feet.
But when he saith
all *things* are *put under him* **subjugated**,
it is *manifest* **evident** that he is excepted,
which *did put* **subjugated** all *things* under him.
28 And when all *things*
shall be *subdued* **subjugated** unto him,
then shall the Son also himself
be *subject* **subjugated** unto him
that *put* **subjugated** all *things* under him,
that *God* **Elohim** may be all in all.
29 Else what shall they do
which are baptized for the dead,
if the dead rise not at all?
why are they then baptized for the dead?
30 And why stand we in *jeopardy* **peril** every hour?
31 *I protest by your rejoicing*
which I have in Christ Jesus our Lord,
I die daily
boasting in what I have
in Messiah Yah Shua our Adonay.
32 If after the manner of *men* **humanity**
I *have fought* **strove** with beasts at Ephesus,
what *advantageth* **benefiteth** it me, if the dead rise not?
let us eat and drink; for to morrow we die.
33 Be not *deceived* **seduced**:
evil *communications* **homilies**
corrupt *good manners* **kind habits**.
34 *Awake to righteousness*
Sober up justly, and sin not;
for some *have not the knowledge* **are unknowing**
of *God* **Elohim**:
I *speak* **word** this to *your* shame **you**.

THE MANNER OF THE RESURRECTION

35 But some *man will* **shall** say,
How are the dead raised *up*?
and, with what body do they come?
36 Thou *fool* **thoughtless**,
that which thou *sowest* **sporest** is
not *quickened* **enlivened**,
except **unless** it die:
37 And that which thou *sowest* **sporest**,
thou *sowest* **sporest** not that body that shall be,
but *bare grain* **naked kernel**,
it may chance **if perhaps** of *wheat* **grain**,
or of some other *grain*:
38 But *God* **Elohim** giveth it a body
exactly as *it hath pleased him* **he hath willed**,
and to *every seed* **each sperma** his own body.
39 All flesh is not the same flesh:
but there is **indeed** one *kind of* flesh of *men* **humanity**,
another flesh of *beasts* **animals**,
another of fishes,
and another of *birds* **flyers**.
40 *There are* also *celestial* bodies **heavenlies**,
and bodies *terrestrial* **earthly**:
but the glory of the *celestial* **heavenlies**
is *one* **indeed another,**
and the *glory of the terrestrial* **earthly**
is another.
41 *There is* one glory of the sun,
and another glory of the moon,
and another glory of the stars:
for *one* star
differeth from another **thoroughly**
surpasseth star in glory.
23 and each in his own order:
Messiah the firstlings;
then whoever are of the Messiah at his parousia.

1 CORINTHIANS 15

24 Then the completion/shalom
when he delivers the sovereigndom to Elohim
— even the Father;
when he inactivates
all hierarchies and all authority and dynamis.
25 For he must reign,
until whenever he puts all enemies under his feet.
26 The final enemy to inactivate is death.
27 For he subjugates all under his feet.
and when he says, All are subjugated,
it is evident that he is excepted,
who subjugated all under him.
28 And when all subjugates to him
then the Son himself also subjugates to him
who subjugated all under him
that Elohim be all in all.
29 Else what do they who are baptized for the dead
if the dead rise not at all?
Why then are they baptized for the dead?
30 And why stand we in peril every hour?
31 I die daily,
boasting in what I have
in Messiah Yah Shua our Adonay.
32 If after the manner of humanity
I strove with beasts at Ephesus,
what benefit I, if the dead rise not?
Eat and drink — for tomorrow we die.
33 Be not seduced;
evil homilies corrupt kind habits.
34 Sober up justly and sin not;
for some are unknowing of Elohim:
I word this to shame you.

THE MANNER OF THE RESURRECTION

35 But some say, How are the dead raised?
And with what body come they?
36 You thoughtless!
What you spore enlivens not unless it die:
37 and what you spore,
you spore not the body to be,
but a naked kernel,
if perhaps of grain or of some other:
38 and Elohim gives a body exactly as he wills
and to each sperma its own body.
39 All flesh is not the same flesh:
but indeed there is one flesh of humanity
another flesh of animals
another of fishes
another of flyers;
40 also bodies of the heavenlies
and bodies of the earthly:
but indeed the glory of the heavenlies is another
and of the earthly is another:
41 one glory of the sun
and another glory of the moon
and another glory of the stars:
for star thoroughly surpasses star in glory.
42 So **Thus** also is the resurrection of the dead.
It is sown **spored** in corruption;
it is raised in incorruption:
43 *It is sown* **spored** in dishonour;
it is raised in glory:
it is sown **spored** in *weakness* **frailty**;
it is raised in *power* **dynamis**:
44 *It is sown* **spored** a *natural* **soulical** body;
it is raised a spiritual body.
There is a *natural* **soulical** body,
and there is a spiritual body.
45 And *so* **thus** it is *written* **scribed**,
The first *man* **human** Adam
was made **became into** a living soul;
the *last* **final** Adam
was made a quickening **into an enlivening** spirit.
46 *Howbeit* **Rather** that was
not first which is spiritual,
but that which is *natural* **soulical**;
and *afterward* **then** that which is spiritual.
47 The first *man* **human** is
of the earth, *earthy* **dust**;
the second *man* **human**
is *the Lord* **Adonay** from *heaven* **the heavens**.
48 *Such* **As** is the *earthy* **dust**,
such are they also that are *earthy* **dust**:
and **such** as is the *heavenly* **heavenlies**,
such are they also that are *heavenly* **heavenlies**.
49 And **exactly**
as we have borne the *image* **icon** of the *earthy* **dust**,
we shall also
bear the *image* **icon** of the *heavenly* **heavenlies**.
50 Now this I say, brethren, that flesh and blood
cannot inherit the *kingdom*
sovereigndom of *God* **Elohim**;
neither doth *corruption* **corruptibility**
inherit *incorruption* **incorruptibility**.

THE MYSTERY OF THE RESURRECTION

51 Behold, I *shew* **word** you a mystery;
Indeed, We shall not all sleep,
but we shall all be changed,
52 In a moment, in the *twinkling* **atom** of an eye,

1 CORINTHIANS 15, 16

<table>
<tr><td>

at **in** the *last trump* **final trumpet**:
for *the trumpet* **indeed it** shall *sound* **trump**,
and the dead shall be raised incorruptible,
and we shall be changed.

53   For this corruptible
must *put on incorruption* **endue incorruptibility**,
and this mortal must *put on*
immortality **endue athanasia**.

54   So when this corruptible
shall have *put on incorruption* **endued incorruptibility**,
and this mortal
shall have *put on immortality* **endued athanasia**,
then shall be *brought to pass* the *saying* **word**
that is *written* **scribed**,
Death is swallowed *up* in *victory* **triumph**.
Yesha Yah 25:8

55   O death, where is thy sting?
O *grave* **hades**, where is thy *victory* **triumph**?

56   The sting of death is sin;
and the *strength* **dynamis** of sin is the *law* **torah**.

57   But *thanks* **charism** be to *God* **Elohim**,
which giveth us the *victory* **triumph**
through our *Lord Jesus Christ*
Adonay Yah Shua Messiah.

58   *Therefore* **So**, my beloved brethren,
be ye *stedfast* **grounded**, unmoveable,
always *abounding* **superabounding**
in the work of *the Lord* **Adonay**,
forasmuch as ye know **knowing**
that your labour is not in vain in *the Lord* **Adonay**.

CONTRIBUTIONS

16   Now concerning the *collection* **contribution**
for **to** the *saints* **holy**,
exactly as I have *given order* **ordained**
to the *churches* **ecclesiae** of Galatia, even *so* **thus** do ye.

2   Upon the first *day* of the *week* **shabbaths**
let *every one* **each** of you *lay* **place** by him *in store*,
as God hath **treasuring up as ever he** prospered *him*,
that there be no *gatherings* **contributions** when I come.

3   And when I come,
whomsoever ye shall approve *by*
through your *letters* **epistles**,

42   Thus also the resurrection of the dead:
spored in corruption;
raised in incorruption:

43   spored in dishonor;
raised in glory:
spored in frailty;

</td><td>

raised in dynamis:

44   spored a soulical body;
raised a spiritual body.
There is a soulical body
and there is a spiritual body.

45   And thus it is scribed,
The first human Adam became into a living soul;
the final Adam into an enlivening spirit.

46   Rather the spiritual is not first;
but the soulical — and then the spiritual.

47   The first human is dust from the earth;
the second human is Adonay from the heavens.

48   Such as the dust,
such also those of dust:
and such as the heavenlies,
such also those of the heavenlies.

49   And exactly as we bear the icon of the dust
we also bear the icon of the heavenlies.

50   And this I say brothers,
that flesh and blood
cannot inherit the sovereigndom of Elohim;
corruptibility inherits not incorruptibility.

THE MYSTERY OF THE RESURRECTION

51   Behold, I word you a mystery;
indeed, we all sleep not, and we all change;

52   in a moment — in the atom of an eye
— in the final trumpet:
for indeed it trumps;
and the dead rise incorruptible
and we all change.

53   For this corruptible must endue athanasia;
and this mortal must endue immortality.

54   So when this corruptible endues incorruptibility
and this mortal endues athanasia
— then becomes the word that is scribed,
Death is swallowed in triumph.
Yesha Yah 25:8

55   O death, where is your sting?
O hades/sheol, where is your triumph?

56   The sting of death is sin;
and the dynamis of sin is the torah.

57   And to Elohim
— charism to him who gives us the triumph
through our Adonay Yah Shua Messiah.

58   So my beloved brothers,
become grounded; unmoveable;
always superabounding in the work of Adonay
knowing that your labor in Adonay is not in vain.

</td></tr>
</table>

1 CORINTHIANS 16

CONTRIBUTIONS

16 And concerning the contribution to the holy;
exactly as I ordained the ecclesiae of Galatia
even thus you also do.

2 On the first of the shabbaths
each of you place by him;
treasuring up as ever he prospered;
that there be no contributions when I come.

3 And when I come,
whomever you approve through your epistles,
them *will* **shall** I send
to *bring* **bear away** your *liberality* **charism**
unto *Jerusalem* **Yeru Shalem**.

4 And *if* **whenever** it be *meet* **worthy** that I go also,
they shall go with me.

THE TRAVEL PLANS OF PAULOS

5 Now I *will* **shall** come unto you,
when I shall pass through Macedonia:
for I *do* pass through Macedonia.

6 And *it* may *be that* **perhaps**
I *will* **shall** abide **nearby**,
yea, and winter with you,
that ye may *bring* **forward** me *on my journey*
whithersoever I go.

7 For I *will* **have willed to** not
see you now *by* **in** the way;
but I *trust* **hope** to *tarry a while*
abide some time with you,
if *the Lord permit* **ever Adonay allow**.

8 But I *will tarry at* **shall abide**
in Ephesus until Pentecost.

9 For a *great door* **mega portal**
and *effectual* **energized**
is opened unto me,
and *there are* many adversaries.

10 Now *if* **whenever** Timotheus come,
see that he may be with you *without fear* **fearless**:
for he worketh the work of *the Lord* **Adonay**, as I also *do*.

11 Let no *man* **one** therefore *despise* **belittle** him:
but *conduct* **forward** him *forth* in *peace* **shalom**,
that he may come unto me:
for I *look for* **await** him with the brethren.

12 As *touching* **Concerning** our brother Apollos,
I *greatly desired* **besought** him *much*
to come unto you with the brethren:
but *his will was* **he willed most certainly**
not *at all* to come *at this time* **now**;
but he *will* **shall** come
when he shall have *convenient time* **opportunity**.

ADMONITIONS AND SALUTES

13 Watch ye, stand *fast* **firm** in the *faith* **trust**,
quit you like men **manly**, be *strong* **powerful**.

14 Let all *your things be done*
with charity **be in love**.

15 I beseech you, brethren,
(ye know the house of Stephanas,
that it is the *firstfruits* **firstlings** of Achaia,
and that they have *addicted* **ordained** themselves
to the ministry of the *saints* **holy**,)

16 That ye *submit* **subjugate**
yourselves *unto* **under** such,
and to every one that *helpeth with us* **co—worketh**,
and laboureth.

17 I *am glad of* **cheer over** the *coming* **appearing**
of Stephanas and *Fortunatus* **Phortunatos** and Achaicus:
for that which was lacking on your part
they have *supplied* **fulfilled**.

18 For they have refreshed my spirit and your's:
therefore **so** acknowledge ye them that are such.

19 The *churches* **ecclesiae** of Asia salute you.
Aquila and Priscilla salute you
much in *the Lord* **Adonay**,
with the *church* **ecclesia** that is in their house.

20 All the brethren *greet* **salute** you.
Greet ye one another *with* **in** an holy kiss.

21 The salutation of *me Paul*
Paulos with mine own hand.

22 If any *man love* **one befriend** not
the Lord Jesus Christ **Adonay Yah Shua Messiah**,
let him be Anathema.Maranatha.

23 The *grace* **charism**
of our *Lord Jesus Christ* **Adonay Yah Shua Messiah**
be with you.

24 My love be with you all
in *Christ Jesus* **Messiah Yah Shua**.
Amen.

I send to bear away your charism to Yeru Shalem.

4 And whenever it is worthy that I also go,
they go with me.

THE TRAVEL PLANS OF PAULOS

5 And I come to you when I
pass through Macedonia:
for I pass through Macedonia;

6 and perhaps I abide nearby
— yes, and winter with you;
and that you forward me wherever I go.

7 For I will to not see you now in the way;
but I hope to abide some time with you
whenever Adonay allows.
8 And I abide in Ephesus until Pentecost:
9 for a mega and energized portal opens to me
— and many adversaries.
10 And whenever Timotheus comes,
see that he becomes fearless with you:
for he works the work of Adonay, as also I.
11 no one of you is to belittle him:
but forward him in shalom to come to me:
for I await him with the brothers.
12 Concerning our brother Apollos,
I besought him much
to come to you with the brothers:
and he most certainly willed to not come now;
but he comes when he has opportunity.

ADMONITIONS AND SALUTES

13 Watch! Stand firm in the trust!
Manly! Powerful!
14 Have all become in love!
15 I beseech you brothers,
that you know the house of Stephanas
— that it is the firstlings of Achaia
and that they ordained themselves
to the ministry of the holy:
16 that you subjugate yourselves under such
and to everyone co—working and laboring.
17 I cheer over the appearing
of Stephanas and Phortunatos and Achaicus:
for they fulfilled/shalamed your lack;
18 for they refreshed my spirit and yours:
so acknowledge them who are such.
19 The ecclesiae of Asia salute you;
Aquila and Priscilla salute you much in Adonay,
with the ecclesia in their house;
20 all the brothers salute you.
Greet one another in an holy kiss.
21 The salutation of Paulos with my own hand.
22 If anyone befriends not
Adonay Yah Shua Messiah,
have him be anathema.
Maranatha!
23 The charism of our Adonay Yah Shua Messiah
be with you:
24 my love *be* with you all in Messiah Yah Shua.
Amen.

2 CORINTHIANS 1

SALUTATION

1 *Paul* **Paulos**, an apostle of
Jesus Christ **Yah Shua Messiah**
by **through** the will of *God* **Elohim**,
and *Timothy* **Timo Theos** our brother,
unto the *church* **ecclesia** of *God* **Elohim**
which is at **in** Corinth,
with all the *saints which are* **holy** in all Achaia:

2 *Grace be* **Charism** to you and *peace* **shalom**
from *God* **Elohim** our Father,
and *from the Lord Jesus Christ*
Adonay Yah Shua Messiah.

3 *Blessed* **Eulogized** be *God*
Elohim, even the Father
of our *Lord Jesus Christ* **Adonay Yah Shua Messiah**,
the Father of *mercies* **compassions**,
and the *God* **Elohim** of all *comfort* **consolation**;

4 Who *comforteth* **consoleth**
us in all our tribulation,
that we may be able to *comfort* **console** them
which are in any *trouble* **tribulation**,
by **through** the *comfort* **consolation** wherewith
we ourselves are *comforted* **consoled** of *God* **Elohim**.

5 For **exactly** as the sufferings
of *Christ* **the Messiah**
abound **superabound** in us,
so **thus** our consolation also
aboundeth by Christ **superaboundeth through Messiah**.

6 And whether we be *afflicted* **tribulated**,
it is for your consolation and salvation,
which *is effectual* **energizeth** in the enduring
of the same sufferings which we also suffer:
or whether we be *comforted* **consoled**,
it is for your consolation and salvation.

7 And our hope of you is stedfast,
knowing, that
exactly as ye are *partakers*
communicants of the sufferings,
so **thus** shall ye be also of the consolation.

8 For we *would* **will** not, brethren,
have you *ignorant* **unknowing** of our *trouble* **tribulation**
which *came to* **became** us in Asia,
that we were
pressed out of measure **excessively burdened**,
above strength **beyond dynamis**,
insomuch that we despaired even of *life* **living**:

9 But we had the sentence of death in ourselves,
that we should not *trust* **confide** in ourselves,
but in *God* **Elohim** which raiseth the dead:

10 Who *delivered* **rescued** us from so great a death,
and *doth deliver* **rescueth**:
in whom we *trust* **hope**
that he *will* **shall** yet *deliver* **rescue** us;

11 Ye also *helping together* **co—working**
by *prayer* **petition** for us,
that for the *gift bestowed upon* **charisma unto** us
by *the means of* many *persons* **faces**
thanks may be *given by* **eucharistized through** many
on our behalf.

12 For our *rejoicing* **boasting** is this,
the *testimony* **witness** of our conscience,
that *in simplicity* **with liberality**
and *Godly* sincerity **of Elohim**,
not *with* **in** fleshly wisdom,
but *by* **in** the *grace* **charism** of *God* **Elohim**,
we have had our *conversation* **behaviour**
in the *world* **cosmos**,
and more *abundantly* **superabundantly**
to you—ward **toward you**.

13 For we *write* **scribe** none other *things* unto you,
than **rather** what ye read or acknowledge;
and I *trust* **hope** ye shall acknowledge
even to the *end* **completion/shalom**;

14 **Exactly** As also ye have
acknowledged us *in* **by** part,
that we are your *rejoicing* **boasting**,
even **exactly** as ye also are our's
in the day of *the Lord Jesus* **Adonay Yah Shua**.

THE ALTERED TRAVEL PLANS OF PAULOS

15 And in this confidence
I *was minded* **had willed** to come unto you before,
that ye might have a second *benefit* **charism**;

16 And to pass *by* **through** you into Macedonia,
and to come again out of Macedonia unto you,
and of you to be *brought on my way* **forwarded**
toward *Judaea* **unto Yah Hudah**.

SALUTATION

1 Paulos, an apostle of Yah Shua Messiah
through the will of Elohim
and Timo Theos the brother:
To the ecclesia of Elohim in Corinth;
with all the holy in all Achaia:

2 Charism to you and shalom
from Elohim our Father
and Adonay Yah Shua Messiah.

3 Eulogized be Elohim
even the Father of our Adonay Yah Shua Messiah

	— the Father of compassions
	and the Elohim of all consolation:
4	who consoles us in all our tribulation;
	so that we can console those in any tribulation;
	through the consolation
	whereby we ourselves are consoled of Elohim.
5	For exactly as the sufferings of the Messiah
	superabound in us,
	thus our consolation
	also superabounds through Messiah.
6	And whether we be tribulated,
	it is for your consolation and salvation,
	which energizes in the enduring
	of the same sufferings we also suffer:
	whether we are consoled,
	it is for your consolation and salvation.
7	And our hope for you is steadfast,
	knowing that
	exactly as you are communicants of the sufferings,
	thus also of the consolation.
8	For we will not, brothers,
	that you be unknowing of our tribulation
	which became us in Asia;
	that we were excessively burdened beyond dynamis
	insomuch that we even despaired of living:
9	but we ourselves
	had the sentence of death in ourselves
	so that we confided not in ourselves
	— but in Elohim who raised the dead:
10	who rescued us from so great a death
	— and rescues;
	in whom we hope to still rescue:
11	you also co—working for us by your petitions,
	for the charisma to us by many faces,
	and through many be eucharistized for us.
12	For this is our boasting:
	the witness of our conscience:
	that with liberality and sincerity of Elohim
	— not in fleshly wisdom but in the charism of Elohim
	we have our behavior in the cosmos
	and more superabundantly toward you.
13	For we scribe none other to you
	than rather what you read or acknowledge;
	and I hope that you acknowledge
	even to the completion/shalom;
14	exactly as also you acknowledged us by part
	— that we are your boasting
	exactly as you also are ours
	in the day of Adonay Yah Shua.

THE ALTERED TRAVEL PLANS OF PAULOS

15	And in this confidence
	I willed to come to you previously, so
	that you have a second charism;
	16 and to pass through you into Macedonia
	and to come again to you from Macedonia and
	to be forwarded by you to Yah Hudah.

THE YES OF ELOHIM

17	So When I *therefore* was
	thus *minded* **counseled**,
	did I **then** use *lightness* **levity**?
	or *the things* **those** that I *purpose* **counsel**,
	do I *purpose* **counsel** according to the flesh,
	that with me there should be yea yea, and nay nay?
18	But as *God* **Elohim** is *true* **trustworthy**,
	our word toward you *was* **became** not yea and nay.
19	For the Son of *God* **Elohim**,
	Jesus Christ **Yah Shua Messiah**,
	who was preached among you *by* **through** us,
	even by **through** me
	and Silvanus and *Timotheus* **Timo Theos**,
	was **became** not yea and nay,
	but in him *was* **became** yea.
20	For *all* **as many as** the
	promises **pre—evangelisms**
	of *God* **Elohim** in him are yea, and in him Amen,
	unto the glory of *God by* **Elohim through** us.
21	Now he which stablisheth us with you
	in *Christ* **Messiah**,
	and hath anointed us, is *God* **Elohim**;
22	Who hath also sealed us,
	and given the *earnest* **pledge** of the Spirit in our hearts.
23	Moreover I call *God* **Elohim**
	for a *record* **witness** upon my soul,
	that to spare you I came *not as yet*
	no more unto Corinth.
24	Not for that we
	have dominion over **overlord** your *faith* **trust**,
	but are *helpers* **co—workers** of your *joy* **cheer**:
	for by *faith* **trust** ye stand.
2	But I *determined* **judged** this with myself,
	that I *would* **should** not come again to you
	in *heaviness* **sorrow**.
2	For if I *make you sorry* **sorrow you**,
	who is he then that *maketh* **rejoiceth** me *glad*,
	but the same **except that**
	which is *made sorry* **sorrowed** by me?
3	And I *wrote* **scribed** this same unto you,

2 CORINTHIANS 2

lest, when I came,
I should have sorrow *from them*
of whom I *ought to* rejoice **need cheer**;
having confidence in you all,
that my *joy is the joy* **cheer is** of you all.
4   For out of much *affliction* **tribulation**
and *anguish* **oppression** of heart
I *wrote* **scribed** unto you *with* **through** many tears;
not that ye should *be grieved* **sorrow**,
but that ye might know the love which I have
more *abundantly* **superabundantly** unto you.

FORGIVING THE OFFENDER

5   But if any have *caused grief* **sorrowed**,
he hath not *grieved* **sorrowed** me, but *in* **by** part:
that I may not *overcharge* **overburden** you all.
6 Sufficient to such a *man* **one** is this *punishment*
disesteeming, which was *inflicted* of many.
7   So that contrariwise ye *ought* rather
to forgive him **grant charism**, and *comfort* **console** him,
lest *perhaps* **somehow** such a one
should be swallowed *up*
with *overmuch* **superabundant** sorrow.
8   *Wherefore* **So** I beseech you
that ye *would* **should** confirm your
love *toward* **unto** him.
9 For to this *end* also did I *write* **scribe**,
that I might know the proof of you,
whether ye be obedient in all *things*.
10   To whom ye
forgive any thing **somewhat grant charism**,
I *forgive* also:
for if I *forgave any thing* **somewhat granted charism**,
to whom I *forgave it* **granted charism**,
for your sakes *forgave I it*
in the *person* **face** of *Christ* **Messiah**;
11   Lest Satan should *get an*
advantage of **defraud** us:
for we are not *ignorant* **unknowing**
of his *devices* **comprehensions**.
12   *Furthermore,* **And** when I came to Troas
to *preach Christ's gospel* **evangelize the Messiah**,
and a *door* **portal** was opened unto me
of the Lord **in Adonay**,

THE YES OF ELOHIM

17   So counseling thus, use I levity?
Or those I counsel,
counsel I according to the flesh
— so that with me there is Yes yes and No no?

18   And *as* Elohim *is* trustworthy,
our word toward you became not Yes and No.
19   For the Son of Elohim, Yah Shua Messiah,
being preached among you through us
— through me and Silvanus and Timo Theos
became not Yes and No;
but in him became Yes.
20   For as many as the pre—evangelisms of Elohim
in him are Yes and in him Amen,
to the glory of Elohim through us.
21   Now he who established us with you in Messiah
and who anointed us, is Elohim;
22   who also sealed us
and gave the pledge of the Spirit in our hearts.
23   And I call Elohim for a witness upon my soul,
so as to spare you, I came no more to Corinth.
24   Not that we overlord your trust,
but are co—workers of your cheer:
for by trust you stand.
2   And I judged this with myself,
to not come again to you in sorrow.
2   For if I sorrow you, who then rejoices me
— except whomever I sorrowed?
3   And I scribe this same to you,
lest, when I come,
I have sorrow from whom I needed cheer;
having confidence in you all,
that my cheer is of you all.
4   For from much tribulation
and oppression of heart
I scribed to you through many tears;
not to sorrow you
— but that you know the love I have
more superabundantly to you.

FORGIVING THE OFFENDER

5   And if anyone sorrows
he sorrows not me — except partly:
that I not overburden you all.
6   Sufficient to such a one
is this disesteeming by many.
7   So that contrariwise
rather grant him charism and console him;
lest somehow
such a one is swallowed with superabundant sorrow.
8   So I beseech you to confirm your love to him.
9   For this I also scribe, to know the proof of you
— whether you be obedient in all.
10   To whom you somewhat grant charism
— I also:

for if I somewhat grant charism
I grant charism for your sakes in the face of Messiah;
11 lest Satan defraud us:
for we are not unknowing of his comprehensions.
12 And when I came to Troas
to evangelize the Messiah
and a portal was opened to me in Adonay,
13 I had no *rest* **relaxation** in my spirit,
because I found not Titus my brother:
but *taking my leave of* **bidding** them **bye bye**,
I went from thence into Macedonia.

The Triumphant In The Messiah

14 *Now thanks* **And charism** be unto *God* **Elohim**,
which always causeth us
to triumph in *Christ* **the Messiah**,
and *maketh manifest* **manifesteth** the *savour* **fragrance**
of his knowledge *by* **through** us in every place.
15 For we are unto *God* **Elohim**
a *sweet savour* **good fragrance** of *Christ* **Messiah**,
in them that are saved, and in them that *perish* **destruct**:
16 To the one **indeed**
we are the *savour* **fragrance** of death unto death;
and to the other the *savour* **fragrance** of life unto life.
And who is *sufficient* **adequate** for these *things*?
17 For we are not as many,
which *corrupt* **huckster** the word of *God* **Elohim**:
but as of sincerity, but as of *God* **Elohim**,
in the sight of *God* **Elohim** speak we in *Christ* **Messiah**.

Scribings Of The Heart

3 Do we begin again to commend ourselves?
or need we **unless** as some *others*,
need we epistles of commendation to you,
or *letters of* commendation from you?
2 Ye are our epistle *written*
inscribed in our hearts,
known and read of all *men* **humanity**:
3 *Forasmuch as ye are manifestly*
declared **Manifested**
to be the epistle of *Christ* **Messiah** ministered
by us, *written* **inscribed** not with ink,
but with the Spirit of the living *God* **Elohim**;
not in *tables* **slabs** of stone,
but in fleshy *tables* **slabs** of the heart.
4 And such *trust* **confidence** have we
through *Christ to God—ward* **the**
Messiah toward Elohim:
5 Not that we are *sufficient* **adequate** of ourselves
to *think any thing* **reckon somewhat** as of ourselves;
but our *sufficiency* **adequacy** is of *God* **Elohim**;
6 Who also hath *made* **enabled** us *able* ministers of the
new *testament* **covenant**; not of *the letter* **scribing**, but
of *the* spirit: for the *letter killeth* **scribing slaughtereth**,
but the spirit *giveth life* **enliveneth**.
7 But if the *ministration* **ministry** of death,
written and **inscribings** engraven in stones,
was glorious **became in glory**,
so that the *children* **sons** of *Israel* **Yisra El**
could not *stedfastly behold* **stare**
unto the face of *Moses* **Mosheh**
for the glory of his *countenance* **face**;
which *glory* was to be *done away* **inactivated**:
8 How **indeed**
shall not the *ministration* **ministry** of the spirit
be rather *glorious* **in glory**?
9 For if the *ministration*
ministry of condemnation
be glory,
much more *doth*
the *ministration* **ministry** of *righteousness* **justness**
exceed **superaboundeth** in glory.
10 For even that which was *made glorious* **glorified**
had no glory in this *respect* **part**,
by reason **because** of the glory that excelleth.
11 For if that which is *done away* **inactivated**
was *glorious* **through glory**,
much more that which *remaineth* **abideth**
is glorious **be in glory**.

The Inactivated Covenant

12 Seeing then that we have such hope,
we use *great plainness* **much boldness** of speech:
13 And not *exactly* as *Moses* **Mosheh**,
which put a vail over his face,
that the *children* **sons** of *Israel* **Yisra El**
could not *stedfastly look* **stare** to the
end **completion/shalom**
of that which is *abolished* **inactivated**:
14 But their *minds* **comprehensions**
were *blinded* **petrified**:
for until this day *remaineth* **abideth** the same
vail untaken away — **not unveiled**
13 I had no relaxation in my spirit;
because I found not Titus my brother:
but bidding them bye bye,
I went from there into Macedonia.

The Triumphant In The Messiah

14 And charism be to Elohim,
who always causes us to triumph in the Messiah
and manifests the fragrance of his knowledge
through us in every place.
15 For to Elohim
we are a good fragrance of Messiah
— in them who are saved and in them who destruct:
16 indeed to the one the
fragrance of death to death;
and to the other the fragrance of life to
life. And who is adequate for these?
17 For we are not as many
who huckster the word of Elohim:
but as of sincerity — but as of Elohim,
in the sight of Elohim we speak in Messiah.

Scribings Of The Heart

3 Begin we again to commend ourselves?
Unless, as some,
need we epistles of commendation to you?
Or commendation from you?
2 You are our epistle inscribed in our hearts,
known and read of all humanity:
3 manifested to be the epistle of Messiah
ministered by us;
inscribed, not with ink,
but with the Spirit of the living Elohim;
not in slabs of stone,
but in fleshy slabs of the heart.
4 And we have such confidence
through the Messiah toward Elohim:
5 not that we are adequate of ourselves
to reckon somewhat as of ourselves;
but our adequacy is of Elohim
6 who also enables us
— ministers of the new covenant;
not of scribing but of spirit:
for the scribing slaughters, and the spirit enlivens.
7 And if the ministry of death
— inscribings engraved in stones
became in glory
— so that the sons of Yisra El
could not stare to the face of Mosheh
for the glory of his face
— which *inscribings* were being inactivated:
8 how indeed not rather
the ministry of the spirit be in glory?
9 For if the ministry of condemnation *be in* glory,
much more rather
the ministry of justness superabounds in glory.
10 For even that which was glorified
has no glory in this part
because of the glory that excels:
11 for if that which is inactivated
was through glory,
much more that which abides *be* in glory.

The Inactivated Covenant

12 So seeing that we have such hope
we use much boldness of speech:
13 and not exactly as Mosheh
— who put a veil over his face
so the sons of Yisra El could not stare
to the completion/shalom of what is inactivated:
14 but their comprehensions petrified:
for until this day the same abides — not unveiled
in the reading of the old *testament* **covenant**;
which *vail* is *done away* **inactivated** in *Christ* **Messiah**.
15 But even unto this day,
when *Moses* **Mosheh** is read,
the vail is **laid** upon their heart.
16 Nevertheless
when **ever** it shall turn to *the Lord* **Yah Veh**,
the vail shall be taken away.
Exodus 34:34
17 Now *the Lord* **Adonay** is that Spirit:
and where the Spirit of *the Lord* **Yah Veh** is,
there is liberty.
18 But we all, with *open* **unveiled** face
beholding as in a glass **reflecting**
the glory of *the Lord* **Yah Veh**,
are *changed* **metamorphosed** into the same *image* **icon**
from glory to glory,
even **exactly** as by the Spirit of *the Lord* **Yah Veh**.
Exodus 16:7

The Light From The Dark

4 *Therefore seeing we have*
So having this ministry,
exactly as we have *received mercy* **been mercied**,
we *faint* **weary** not;
2 But have *renounced* **disowned**
the *hidden things* **secrets** of *dishonesty* **shame**,
not walking in *craftiness* **cunningness**,
nor handling the word of *God* **Elohim** deceitfully;
but by manifestation of the truth commending ourselves
to every *man's* **human's** conscience
in the sight of *God* **Elohim**.

3	*But* **And also,** if our *gospel* **evangelism** be *hid* **veiled**, it is *hid to* **veiled among** them that are lost:	14	Knowing that he which raised *up* the Lord Jesus **Adonay Yah Shua** shall raise *up* us also by *Jesus* **Yah Shua**, and shall present us with you.
4	In whom the *God* **Elohim** of this *world* **eon** hath blinded the *minds* **comprehensions** of *them which believe not* **the trustless**, lest the light of the *glorious gospel* **evangelism of the glory** of *Christ* **the Messiah**, who is the *image* **icon** of *God* **Elohim**, should *shine* **radiate** unto them.	15	For all *things* **these** are for your sakes, in the reading of the old covenant; which is inactivated in Messiah.
		15	But even to this day when Mosheh is read, the veil lies on their heart.
		16	Nevertheless whenever they turn to Yah Veh, the veil is taken away. Exodus 34:34
5	For we preach not ourselves, but *Christ Jesus the Lord* **Messiah Yah Shua Adonay**; and ourselves your servants for *Jesus'* **Yah Shua's** sake.	17	And Adonay is that Spirit: and where the Spirit of Yah Veh is there is liberty.
6	For *God* **Elohim**, who *commanded* **said** the light *to shine* **radiate** out of darkness, hath *shined* **radiated** in our hearts, *to give the light* **for the radiancy** of the knowledge of the glory of *God* **Elohim** in the face of *Jesus Christ* **Yah Shua Messiah**.	18	And we all, with unveiled face, reflecting the glory Yah Veh, are metamorphosed into the same icon from glory to glory exactly as by the Spirit of Yah Veh. Exodus 16:7

Clay Vessels

The Light From The Dark

7	But we have this treasure in *earthen* **clay** vessels, that the excellency of the *power* **dynamis** may be of *God* **Elohim**, and not of us.	4	So having this ministry, exactly as we are mercied, we weary not;
8	We are *troubled on every side* **tribulated in all**, yet not distressed; *we are* perplexed, but not in despair;	2	but disown the secrets of shame; neither walking in cunningness nor handling the word of Elohim deceitfully; but by manifestation of the truth commending ourselves to the conscience of every human in the sight of Elohim.
9	Persecuted, but not forsaken; cast down, but not destroyed;		
10	Always *bearing about* **carrying** in the body the *dying* **death** of *the Lord Jesus* **Adonay Yah Shua**, that the life also of *Jesus* **Yah Shua** might be *made* manifest in our body.	3	And also, if our evangelism is veiled, it is veiled among the lost:
11	For we which live are *alway* **ever** delivered unto death for *Jesus'* **Yah Shua's** sake, that the life also of *Jesus* **Yah Shua** might be *made* manifest in our mortal flesh.	4	in whom the elohim of this eon blinds the comprehensions of the trustless, lest the light of the evangelism of the glory of the Messiah — being the icon of Elohim radiate to them.
12	So then **indeed** death *worketh* **energizeth** in us, but life in you.	5	For we preach not ourselves but Messiah Yah Shua Adonay; and ourselves your servants for sake of Yah Shua.

The Spirit Of The Trust

13	We having the same spirit of *faith* **the trust**, according as *it is written* **scribed**, I *believed* **trusted**, and therefore have I spoken; we also *believe* **trust**, and therefore speak; Psalm 116:10
6	For Elohim, who said, Light, radiate from darkness! radiates in our hearts for the radiancy of the knowledge of the glory of Elohim in the face of Yah Shua Messiah.

Clay Vessels

7 And we have this treasure in clay vessels;
that the excellency of the dynamis be of Elohim
and not of us.
8 We are tribulated in all, yet not distressed;
we are perplexed, but not in despair;
9 persecuted, but not forsaken;
cast down, but not destroyed:
10 Always carrying in the body
the death of Adonay Yah Shua,
so that the life of Yah Shua
also manifests in our body.
11 For we who live are ever delivered to death
for sake of Yah Shua,
so that the life of Yah Shua
also manifests in our mortal flesh.
12 So thus indeed,
the death energizes in us, and the life in you.

The Spirit Of The Trust

13 We, having the same spirit of the trust,
according as scribed,
I trusted and thus I spoke;
we also trust and thus speak;
Psalm 116:10
14 knowing that he who raised Adonay Yah Shua,
through Yah Shua, also raises us
— and presents us with you.
15 For all these are for your sakes
that the *abundant grace* **superabundant charism**
might through the *thanksgiving* **eucharist** of many
redound **superabound** to the glory of *God* **Elohim**.
16 *For which cause* **So**, we *faint* **weary** not;
but though our outward *man perish* **humanity corrupt**,
yet the inward *man* is renewed day by day.
17 For our light *affliction* **tribulation**,
which is *but for a moment* **momentary**,
worketh for us
a far more **an exceeding unto** exceeding
and eternal *weight* **burden** of glory;
18 While we *look* **scope** not at
the *things which are* seen,
but at the *things which are* not seen:
for the *things which are* seen are temporal; but
the *things which are* not seen are eternal.

Houses, Tents, And Edifices

5 For we know
that *if* **whenever** our earthly house of this tabernacle
were dissolved **disintegrate**,
we have *a building* **an edifice** of *God* **Elohim**,
an house not *made with hands* **handmade**,
eternal in the heavens.
2 For in this we *groan* **sigh**,
earnestly desiring **yearning** to be *clothed upon* **endued**
with our house which is from *heaven* **the heavens**:
3 If *so be that* **indeed** being *clothed* **endued**
we shall not be found naked.

At Home Vs Away From Home

4 For we *that are* **being** in this
tabernacle *do groan* **sigh**,
being burdened:
not for that we would **since we will to not**
be *unclothed* **stripped**,
but *clothed upon* **endued**,
that *mortality* **the mortal** might be swallowed *up* of life.
5 Now he that hath *wrought* **worked** us
for the selfsame *thing* is *God* **Elohim**,
who also hath given unto us
the *earnest* **pledge** of the Spirit.
6 *Therefore* **So** we are always
confident **encouraged**,
knowing that, whilst we are at home in the body, we
are *absent* **away from home** from *the Lord* **Adonay**:
7 (For we walk *by faith* **through trust**,
not *by sight* **through semblance**:)
8 We are *confident* **encouraged**, *I say*,
and *willing* **well—approve** rather
to be *absent* **away from home** from the body,
and to be *present* **at home** with *the Lord* **Adonay**.
9 *Wherefore* **So** we *labour*
befriendingly esteem, that,
whether *present* **at home**,
or *absent* **whether away from home**,
we may be *accepted of* **well—pleasing unto** him.
10 For we must all *appear* **manifest**
before the *judgment seat* **in front of the bamah**
of *Christ* **the Messiah**;
that *every one* **each** may receive
the things done *in* **through** his body,
according to **toward** that he hath *done* **transacted**,
whether *it be* good, *or bad* **whether evil**.

All Died

11 **So** Knowing *therefore* the
terror **awe** of *the Lord* **Adonay**,
we *persuade men* **convince humanity**;
but we are *made* manifest unto *God* **Elohim**;
and I *trust* **hope** also

are *made* manifest in your consciences.
12 For we commend not ourselves again unto you,
but give you *occasion* **opportunity**
to *glory* **boast** on our behalf,
that ye may have somewhat *to answer* **toward** them
which *glory* **boast** in *appearance* **face**, and not in heart.
13 For whether *we be beside ourselves* **astounded**,
it is to *God* **Elohim**:
or whether *we be sober* **soundminded**,
it is for your cause.
14 For the love of *Christ* **the Messiah**
constraineth **holdeth** us **together**;
because we thus judge,
that if one died for all, then were all dead:
15 And *that* he died for all,
— that the superabundant charism
through the eucharist of many,
superabound to the glory of Elohim.
16 So we weary not;
but if indeed our outward humanity corrupts,
yet the inward renews day by day.
17 For our momentary light
tribulation works for us
an exceeding to exceeding eternal burden of glory;
18 while we scope not at the
seen, but at the not seen:
for the seen are temporal; but the not seen are eternal.

Houses, Tents, And Edifices

5 For we know
that whenever our earthly house of this tabernacle
disintegrates,
we have an edifice of Elohim
— a house not handmade — eternal in the heavens.
2 For in this we sigh,
yearning to be endued
with our house from the heavens:
3 If indeed being endued we not be found naked.

At Home Vs Away From Home

4 For we sigh
— being in this tabernacle — being burdened:
since we will to not be stripped, but endued,
that the mortal be swallowed by life.
5 Now he who works the same for us is Elohim
who also gives us the pledge of the Spirit.
6 So we are always encouraged, knowing that,
while we are at home in the body,
we are away from home from Adonay:

7 For we walk through trust,
not through semblance:
8 we are encouraged and well—approve
rather to be away from home from the
body and to be at home with Adonay.
9 So we befriendingly esteem that
— whether at home — whether away from home,
we be well—pleasing to him.
10 For we must all manifest
in front of the bamah of the Messiah;
that each, through his body,
receives according to what he transacted
— whether good — whether evil.

All Died

11 So knowing the awe of Adonay,
we convince humanity; and manifest to Elohim;
and I hope also, manifest in your consciences.
12 For we commend not ourselves again to you,
but give you opportunity to boast on our behalf,
to have somewhat toward them who
boast in face and not in heart.
13 For whether astounded, it is to Elohim;
or whether soundminded, it is to you.
14 For the love of the Messiah holds us together;
because we judge thus:
that if one died for all, thus all are dead:
15 and he died for all,
that they which live
should *not henceforth* **no longer** live unto themselves,
but unto him which died for them, and rose *again*.

The Ministry Of Reconciliation

16 *Wherefore* **So**
henceforth know we no *man* **one** after the flesh:
yea, though we have known *Christ* **Messiah**
after the flesh,
yet **from** now *henceforth* **on**
know we him *no more* **not still**.
17 *Therefore* **So then** if any *man*
one be in *Christ* **Messiah**,
he is a new *creature* **creation**:
old things are **the archaic has** passed *away*;
behold, all *things are* become new.
18 And all *things* are of *God* **Elohim**,
who hath reconciled us to himself
by Jesus Christ **through Yah Shua Messiah**,
and hath given to us the ministry of reconciliation;
19 *To wit* **How**, that *God* **Elohim**
was in *Christ* **Messiah**,

reconciling the *world* **cosmos** unto himself,
not *imputing* **reckoning**
their *trespasses* **backslidings** unto them;
and hath *committed unto* **placed in** us
the word of reconciliation.

20   *Now then* **So**
we are *ambassadors* **presbyters** for *Christ* **Messiah**,
as *though God* **Elohim**
did beseech you by **beseeching through** us:
we *pray* **petition** you in *Christ's* **Messiah's** stead,
be ye reconciled to *God* **Elohim**.

21   For he hath made him
to be sin for us **sin in our behalf**,
who knew no sin;
that we might *be made* **become**
the *righteousness* **justness** of *God* **Elohim** in him.

The Day Of Salvation Is Now!

6   **So** We *then, as workers together*
with him **co—working**,
beseech you also
that ye receive not the *grace* **charism** of *God* **Elohim**
in vain.

2   (For he *saith* **wordeth**,
I have heard thee
in *a time accepted* **an acceptable season**,
and in the day of salvation
have I *succoured* **helped** thee:
behold, now is the *accepted* **well—received** time;
behold, now is the day of salvation.)

3   Giving no *offence* **stumbling** in *any thing* **aught**,
that the ministry be not *blamed* **blemished**:

4   But in all *things approving*
commending ourselves
as the ministers of *God* **Elohim**,
in *much patience* **many endurances**,
in *afflictions* **tribulations**,
in *necessities* **compulsions**, in distresses,

5   In stripes, in *imprisonments* **guardhouses**,
in *tumults* **instabilities**, in labours,
in watchings, in fastings;

6   *By pureness* **In holiness**, *by* **in** knowledge,
by longsuffering **in patience**, *by* **in** kindness,
by **in** the *Holy Spirit* **Ruach ha-kodesh**,
by **in** love *unfeigned* **unpretentious**,

7   *By* **In** the word of truth,
by **in** the *power* **dynamis** of *God* **Elohim**,
by **through** the *armour* **weapon** of *righteousness* **justness**
on **at** the right *hand* and *on* **at** the left,

8   *By honour* **Through glory** and dishonour,

by evil report **through defamation**
and *good report* **euphony**:
as *deceivers* **seducers**, and *yet* true;

9   As unknown, and *yet* well known;
as dying, and, behold, we live;
as *chastened* **disciplined**, and not *killed* **deathified**;

10   As *sorrowful* **sorrowed**,
yet *alway rejoicing* **ever cheering**;
as poor, yet *making* **enriching** many *rich*;
as having *nothing* **naught**,
and *yet possessing* **holding** all *things*.

11   O ye Corinthians, our mouth is open unto you,
our heart is *enlarged* **broadened**.
that whoever lives, lives no longer to themselves,
but to him who died for them and rose.

The Ministry Of Reconciliation

16   So henceforth we know no one after the flesh:
yes, though we knew Messiah after the flesh,
yet from now on we still know not.

17   So anyone in Messiah is a new creation:
the archaic passed; behold, all becomes new.

18   And all are of Elohim,
who reconciles us to himself
through Yah Shua Messiah
and gives us the ministry of reconciliation;

19   — how that Elohim was in Messiah,
reconciling the cosmos to himself
— not reckoning their backslidings to them;
and places the word of reconciliation in us.

20   So we are presbyters for Messiah,
as Elohim beseeching through us:
we petition in the stead of Messiah,
be reconciled to Elohim.

21   For him, who knew no sin,
he made him sin in our behalf;
so that we become the justness of Elohim in him.

The Day Of Salvation Is Now!

6   So co—working, we also beseech you
to not receive the charism of Elohim in vain.

2   For he words,
In an acceptable season, I heard you;
and in the day of salvation, I helped you:
behold, now is the well—received time;
behold, now is the day of salvation.
Yesha yah 49:8

3   Give no stumbling in aught,
to not blemish the ministry:

4   but commend ourselves in
all as the ministers of Elohim,
in many endurances,
in tribulations,
in compulsions,
in distresses,

5   in stripes,
in guardhouses,
in instabilities,
in labors,
in watchings,
in fastings;

6   in holiness,
in knowledge,
in patience,
in kindness,
in the Holy Spirit,
in love unpretentious,

7   in the word of truth,
in the dynamis of Elohim;
through the weapon of justness
at the right and at the left,

8   through glory and dishonor,
through defamation and euphony;
as seducers and true,

9 as unknown and well known, as dying and
behold, we live, as disciplined and not deathified,

10   as sorrowed yet ever cheering,
as poor yet enriching many,
as having naught and holding all.

11   O you Corinthians, our mouth opens to you,
our heart broadens.

12   Ye are not *straitened* **distressed** in us,
but ye are straitened distressed
in your own bowels spleens.

13   Now for a *recompence* **retribution** in the same,
(I *speak* **word** as unto *my* children,)
be ye also *enlarged* **broadened**.

Unequal Yokes

14   Be ye not unequally yoked *together*
with *unbelievers* **the trustless**:
for what *fellowship* **partaking** hath
righteousness **justness**
with *unrighteousness* **torah violations**?
and what communion hath light with darkness?

15   And what *concord* **symphony**
hath *Christ* **Messiah** with *Belial* **Beli Yaal**?
or what part hath *he that believeth* **the trusting**
with *an infidel* **the trustless**?

16   And what *agreement* **togetherness**
hath the *temple* **nave** of *God* **Elohim** with idols?
for ye are the *temple* **nave** of the living *God* **Elohim**;
exactly as *God* **Elohim** hath said,
I *will dwell in* **shall indwell** them,
and walk *in* **among** them;
and I *will* **shall** be their *God* **Elohim**,
and they shall be my people. Leviticus
26:12, Yirme Yah 31:33,
Yechezq El 36:28, Zechar Yah 13:9

The Call To Be Set Apart

17   *Wherefore* **So** come out from among them,
and be ye *separate* **set apart**,
saith the Lord **wordeth Yah Veh**,
and touch not the *unclean thing* **impure**;
and I *will* **shall** also receive you,

18   And *will* **shall** be
a Father unto you, **Father,**
and ye shall be *my* **unto me,** sons and daughters,
saith the Lord Almighty **wordeth Yah Veh
Sabaoth.** Yesha Yah 52:11, Yirme Yah 31:9

The Call To Purify

7   **So** Having *therefore* these
promises **pre—evangelisms**,
dearly beloved, let us *cleanse* **purify** ourselves
from all *filthiness* **staining** of the flesh and spirit,
perfecting **fully completing/shalaming** holiness
in the *fear* **awe** of *God* **Elohim**.

2   *Receive* **Accept** us;
we have *wronged* **injured** no *man* **one**,
we have corrupted no *man* **one**,
we have defrauded no *man* **one**.

3   I *speak* **word** not this
to condemn you **for condemnation**:
for I have *said before* **foretold**,
that ye are in our hearts
to *die* **co—die** and *live with you* **co—live**.

4   *Great* **Much** is my boldness
of speech toward you,
great **much** is my *glorying* **boasting** of you:
I am filled **full** with *comfort* **consolation**,
I am *exceeding* **exceedingly**
joyful **superabundantly cheerful** in all our tribulation.

5   For, when we were come into Macedonia,
our flesh had no *rest* **relaxation**,
but we were *troubled on every side* **tribulated in all**;
without *were fightings* **strifes**, within *were fears* **awes**.

2 CORINTHIANS 7

6 *Nevertheless God* **Yet Elohim**,
that *comforteth* **consoleth**
those that are cast down **the humbled**,
comforted **consoled** us
by **in** the *coming* **appearing** of Titus;
7 And not *by* **in** his *coming* **appearing** only,
but *by* **in** the consolation
wherewith he was *comforted* **consoled** in you,
when he *told* **evangelized** us
your *earnest desire* **yearning**,
your *mourning* **grieving**,
your *fervent mind* **zeal** toward me;
so that I *rejoiced* **cheered** the more.

SORROW TOWARD ELOHIM, REPENTANCE TO SALVATION

8 For though I *made* **sorrowed** you *sorry*
with a letter **in an epistle**,
I *do not repent* **regret not**, though I did *repent* **regret**:
12 You are not distressed in us,
but you are distressed in your *own* spleens.
13 and as a retribution in the same,
I word as to children, that you also broaden.

UNEQUAL YOKES

14 Yoke not unequally with the trustless!
For what partaking has justness with torah violations?
And what communion has light with darkness?
15 And what symphony has
Messiah with Beli Yaal?
Or what part has the trusting with the trustless?
16 And what togetherness
has the nave of Elohim with idols?
For you are the nave of the living Elohim;
exactly as Elohim says,
I indwell them and walk among them;
and I become their Elohim;
and they become my people.
Leviticus 26:12, Yirme Yah 31:33,
Yechezq El 36:28, Zechar Yah 13:9

THE CALL TO SET APART

17 So come out from among them,
and be set apart, words Yah Veh,
and touch not the impure;
and I also receive you,
18 and become to you, Father
and you become to me, sons and daughters,
words Yah Veh Sabaoth.
Yesha Yah 52:11, Yirme Yah 31:9

THE CALL TO PURIFY

7 So beloved,
having these pre—evangelisms,
we purify ourselves
from all staining of the flesh and spirit,
fully completing/shalaming holiness
in the awe of Elohim.
2 Accept us:
we injured no one;
we corrupted no one;
we defrauded no one.
3 I word this not for condemnation:
for I foretold
that you are in our hearts to co—die and co—live.
4 Much *is* my boldness of speech toward you,
much *is* my boasting of you:
I am filled full with consolation;
I am exceedingly superabundantly cheerful
in all our tribulation.
5 For when we came into Macedonia
our flesh had no relaxation;
but we were tribulated in all
— outward strifes — inward awes.
6 Yet Elohim who consoles the humbled
consoled us in the appearing of Titus;
7 and not only in his appearing;
but in the consolation
wherewith he was consoled in you
— when he evangelized us of your yearning,
your grieving, your zeal toward me;
so that I cheered the more.

SORROW TOWARD ELOHIM, REPENTANCE TO SALVATION

8 For though I sorrowed you in an epistle,
I regret not — though I regretted:
for I *perceive* **see** that *the same* **this** epistle
hath *made* **sorrowed** you *sorry*,
though *it were* but for *a season* **an hour**.
9 Now I *rejoice* **cheer**,
not that ye were *made sorry* **sorrowed**,
but that ye sorrowed *to* **unto** repentance:
for ye *were made sorry* **sorrowed**
after a Godly manner **toward Elohim**,
that ye might *receive damage* **have no loss** by us
in nothing.
10 For *Godly* sorrow **toward Elohim**
worketh repentance to salvation
not to be repented of **unrequitable**:

but the sorrow of the *world* **cosmos** worketh death.
11 For behold this *selfsame thing,*
that ye sorrowed *after a Godly sort* **toward Elohim**,
what carefulness **how much diligence**
it *wrought* **worked** in you,
yea, *what clearing of yourselves* **rather, pleading**,
yea, what **rather,** indignation,
yea, what *fear* **rather, awe**,
yea, what *vehement desire* **rather, yearning**,
yea, what **rather,** zeal,
yea, what *revenge* **rather, vengeance**!
In all *things* **these**
ye have *approved* **commended** yourselves
to be *clear* **hallowed** in this matter.
12 *Wherefore* **So**,
though I *wrote* **scribed** unto you,
I did it not for his *cause* **sake**
that had *done the wrong* **injured**,
nor for his *cause* **sake**
that *suffered wrong* **was injured**,
but **for sake** that our *care* **diligence** for you
in the sight of *God* **Elohim**
might *appear* **manifest** unto you.
13 *Therefore* **So** we were
comforted **consoled** in your *comfort* **consolation**:
yea, and *exceedingly* the more **superabundantly**
joyed **cheered** we for the *joy* **cheer** of Titus,
because his spirit was refreshed by you all.
14 For if I have boasted *any thing* **somewhat** to him
of you,
I am not ashamed;
but as we spake all *things* to you in truth,
even *so* **thus** our boasting, *which I made* before Titus,
is found **becometh** a truth.
15 And his *inward affection* **spleen**
is more *abundant toward* **superabundant unto** you,
whilst he remembereth the obedience of you all,
how with *fear* **awe** and trembling ye received him.
16 **So** I *rejoice* **cheer** *therefore*
that I *have confidence* **be encouraged**
in you in all *things*.

Contributions

8 *Moreover*, brethren,
we *do you to wit* **make known to you**
of the *grace* **charism** of *God* **Elohim**
bestowed **given**
on **in** the *churches* **ecclesiae** of Macedonia;
2 How that in
a great trial **much proofing** of *affliction* **tribulation**

the *abundance* **superabundance** of their *joy* **cheer**
and their deep poverty
abounded **superabounded**
unto the riches of their liberality.
3 For to their *power* **dynamis**,
I *bear record* **witness**,
yea, and beyond their *power* **dynamis**,
they *were willing* **volunteered** of themselves.
4 *Praying* **Petitioning** us with
much *intreaty* **beseeching**
that we *would* **should** receive the *gift* **charism**,
and *take upon us* the *fellowship* **communion**
of the ministering **and ministry** to the *saints* **holy**.
5 And *this they did,* not **exactly** as we hoped,
but first gave their own selves to the *Lord* **Adonay**,
and unto us *by* **through** the will of *God* **Elohim**.
6 *Insomuch that we desired*
Unto my beseeching Titus,
that **exactly** as he had begun **previously**,
for I see that this epistle sorrowed you
though but for an hour.
9 Now I cheer — not that you were sorrowed;
but that you sorrowed to repentance:
for you sorrowed toward Elohim
so that you have no loss by us.
10 For sorrow toward Elohim
works repentance to salvation — unrequitable:
but the sorrow of the cosmos works death.
11 For behold this,
that you sorrowed toward Elohim,
how much diligence it worked in you
rather, pleading;
yes, rather indignation;
yes, rather awe;
yes, rather yearning;
yes, rather zeal;
yes, rather vengeance.
In all these you commend yourselves
to be hallowed in this matter.
12 So, though I scribe to you
— neither for sake of the injurer
nor for sake of the injured;
but for sake that in the sight of Elohim
our diligence for you be manifest to you.
13 So we consoled in your consolation:
yes and the more superabundantly
we cheered for the cheer of Titus
because you all refreshed his spirit.
14 For if I boasted to him somewhat of you,
I shame not;

but as we spoke to you all in truth,
even thus our boasting in front of Titus
becomes a truth.
15 And his spleen is more superabundant to you
while he remembers all your obedience
— how with awe and trembling you received him.
16 So I cheer that I am encouraged in you in all.

Contributions

8 Brothers,
we have you know the charism of Elohim
given in the ecclesiae of Macedonia;
2 how that in much proofing by tribulation
the superabundance of their cheer
and their deep poverty
superabounds to the riches of their liberality.
3 For I witness to their dynamis — yes and beyond
their dynamis that they volunteer of themselves;
4 petitioning us with much beseeching
to receive the charism
and the communion and ministry to the holy.
5 And not exactly as we hoped,
but first they gave their own selves to Adonay
and to us through the will of Elohim.
6 To my beseeching Titus,
that exactly as he previously began,
so **thus** he *would* **should** also
finish **fully complete/shalam** in you
the same grace **this charism** also.
7 *Therefore* **Rather**,
exactly as ye *abound* **superabound** in *every thing* **all**,
in *faith* **trust**, and *utterance* **word**, and knowledge,
and in all diligence, and in your love to us,
see that ye *abound* **superabound**
in this *grace* **charism** also.
8 *I speak* **word,** not by *commandment* **order**,
but *by occasion of* **through** the
forwardness **diligence** of others,
and to prove the *sincerity* **genuineness** of your love.
9 For ye know the *grace* **charism**
of our *Lord Jesus Christ* **Adonay Yah Shua Messiah**,
that, *though he was* **being** rich,
yet for your sakes he *became poor* **impoverished**,
that ye through his poverty might be *rich* **enriched**.
10 And herein I give *my advice* **opinion**:
for this is *expedient* **beneficial** for you,
who have begun *before* **previously**, not only to do,
but also to *be forward* **will,** *from* a year *ago*.
11 Now therefore *perform* **fully complete/shalam**
the doing of it;
that **exactly** as there was *a readiness*
an eagerness to will,
so there may be a performance
thus to fully complete/shalam also
out of that which ye have.
12 For if there be *first a willing*
mind **set forth an eagerness**,
it is *accepted* **wellreceived**
according to *that a man* **whatever anyone** hath,
and not according to that he hath not.
13 *For I mean* not that *other*
men **others** be *eased* **relaxed**,
and ye *burdened* **tribulated**:
14 But by an equality,
that *now at* **in** this *time* **present season**
your abundance
may be *a supply for* **unto** their *want* **lack**,
that their *abundance* **superabundance** also
may be *a supply for* **unto** your want:
that there may be equality:
15 **Exactly** As *it is written* **scribed**,
He that had *gathered* much
had nothing over **superabounded not**;
and he that had *gathered* little had no *lack* **less**.
Exodus 16:18
16 But *thanks* **charism** be to *God* **Elohim**,
which *put* **gave** the same *earnest care* **diligence**
into the heart of Titus for you.
17 For indeed
he *accepted* **received** the *exhortation* **consolation**;
but being more *forward* **diligent**,
of his own accord he **he voluntarily** went unto you.
18 And we have sent with him the brother,
whose *praise* **halal** is in the *gospel* **evangelism**
throughout all the *churches* **ecclesiae**;
19 And not that only,
but who was also *chosen* **voted** of the *churches* **ecclesiae**
to travel with us with this *grace* **charism**,
which is *administered* **ministered** by us
to the glory of the same *Lord* **Adonay**,
and *declaration* of your *ready mind* **eagerness**:
20 *Avoiding* **Abstaining** this,
that *no man* **lest anyone** should *blame* **blemish** us
in this *abundance* **stoutness**
which is *administered in this* **ministered** by us:
21 Providing for *honest things* **good**,
not only in the sight of *the Lord* **Adonay**,
but also in the sight of *men* **humanity**.
22 And we have sent with them our brother,
whom we have *oftentimes* **often** proved

        being diligent in *many things* **much**,
        but now much more diligent,
        upon *the great* **much** confidence
        which I have in **unto** you.

23   Whether *any do enquire* of Titus,
        he is my *partner* **communicant** and
        fellowhelper **co—worker**
        concerning **unto** you:
        thus he also fully completes/shalams
        this charism in you.

7   Rather, exactly as you superabound in all
        — in trust and word and knowledge
        and in all diligence and in your love to us,
        see that you superabound in this charism also.

8   I word, not by order,
        but through the diligence of others,
        and to prove the genuineness of your love.

9   For you know the charism
        of our Adonay Yah Shua Messiah:
        that, being rich, for your sakes he impoverished:
        that through his poverty, you enrich.

10   And herein I give opinion:
        for this is beneficial for you,
        who previously began,
        not only to do, but also to will, from a year *ago*.

11   So now fully complete/shalam the doing thereof;
        that exactly as there was an eagerness to will,
        thus also to fully complete/shalam
        from what you have.

12   For if you set forth an eagerness,
        it is well—received
        — according to whatever anyone has
        and not according to whatever he has not

13   — not that others relax and you tribulate:
14   but by an equality,
        that in this present season
        your abundance becomes to their lack,
        and also their superabundance becomes to your want
        so that equality becomes:

15   exactly as scribed,
        Whoever had much, superabounded not;
        and whoever had little, lessened not.
        Exodus 16:18

16   And charism to Elohim
        who gives the same diligence into the heart of Titus
        for you.

17   For he indeed received the consolation;
        but being more diligent, he voluntarily went to you.

18   And with him,
        we sent the brother whose halal is in the evangelism
        throughout all the ecclesiae;

19   And not only that,
        but who was also voted of the ecclesiae
        to travel with us with this charism,
        ministered by us
        to the glory of the same Adonay
        and of your eagerness:

20   abstaining from this,
        lest anyone blemish us in this stoutness
        ministered by us:

21   providing for good
        — not only in the sight of Adonay
        but also in the sight of humanity.

22   And with them, we sent our brother
        whom we often proofed to be diligent in much,
        — but now much more diligent
        upon much confidence to you;

23   whether of Titus
        my communicant and co—worker to you:
        or **whether** our brethren *be enquired of*,
        they are the *messengers* **apostles**
        of the *churches* **ecclesiae**,
        and the glory of *Christ* **Messiah**.

24   *Wherefore shew* **So indicate** ye to them,
        and *before* **unto the face of** the *churches* **ecclesiae**,
        unto the *proof* **indication** of your love,
        and of our boasting on your behalf.

THE ZEAL OF GIVING

9   *For as* **Indeed**, *touching* **concerning**
        the *ministering* **ministry** to the *saints* **holy**,
        it is superfluous for me to *write* **scribe** to you:

2   For I know *the forwardness*
        of your *mind* **eagerness**,
        for which I boast of you
        to *them of Macedonia* **the Macedonians**,
        that Achaia was *ready* **prepared** a year ago;
        and your zeal hath provoked *very* many.

3   Yet have I sent the brethren,
        lest our boasting of you should be
        in vain in this *behalf* **part**;
        that, **exactly** as I *said* **worded**, ye may be *ready* **prepared**:

4   Lest *haply* **somehow**
        if they of Macedonia **whenever the Macedonians**
        come with me,
        and find you unprepared,
        we (that we *say* **word** not, ye)
        should be ashamed in this same confident boasting.

5   *Therefore I thought* **So I deemed** it necessary
        to *exhort* **beseech** the brethren,

2 CORINTHIANS 9

that they *would go before* **should precede** unto you,
and *make up beforehand* **pre—
prepare** your *bounty* **eulogy**,
whereof ye had *notice before* **been pre—evangelized**,
that the same might be *ready* **prepared thus**,
as a *matter of bounty* **eulogy**,
and not **exactly** as of *covetousness* **avarice**.

6 But this *I say*, He which
soweth **sporeth** sparingly
shall *reap* **harvest** also sparingly;
and he which *soweth* **sporeth** bountifully **unto eulogy**
shall *reap* also bountifully **harvest unto eulogy**.

7 *Every man according* **Each exactly**
as he *purposeth* **prefereth** in his heart, *so let him give*;
not *grudgingly* **of sorrow**, or of *necessity* **compulsion**:
for *God* **Elohim** loveth a *cheerful* **hilarious** giver.

8 And *God* **Elohim** is able
to make all *grace* **charism**
abound toward **superabound unto** you;
that ye, always having all *sufficiency* **self—contentment**
in all *things*,
may *abound to* **superabound unto** every good work:

9 (**Exactly** As *it is written* **scribed**,
He hath *dispersed* **scattered** abroad;
he hath given to the *poor* **toiling**:
his *righteousness* **justness**
remaineth for ever **abideth unto the eons**.
Psalm 112:9

10 Now he
that *ministereth seed* **contributeth sperma** to the sower
both *minister* **supply** bread *for your food* **to eat**,
and multiply your *seed sown* **spores**,
and *increase* **groweth** the *fruits* **produce**
of your *righteousness* **justness**;)

11 Being enriched
in every thing *to* **unto** all *bountifulness* **liberality**,
which *causeth* **worketh** through us
thanksgiving **eucharist** to *God* **Elohim**.

12 For the *administration*
ministry of this *service* **liturgy**
not only *supplieth* **fully furnisheth**
the *want* **lack** of the *saints* **holy**,
but is *abundant* **superabundant** also
by **through** many *thanksgivings* **eucharists**
unto *God* **Elohim**;

13 Whiles *by* **through** the *experiment* **proofing**
of this *ministration* **ministry**
they glorify *God* **Elohim** for your professed subjection
unto the *gospel* **evangelism** of *Christ* **the Messiah**,
and for your liberal *distribution* **communion** unto them,
and unto all *men*;

14 And by their *prayer* **petition** for you,
which *long* **yearn** after you
for the exceeding *grace* **charism** of *God* **Elohim** in you.

15 *Thanks* **Charism** be unto *God* **Elohim**
for his *unspeakable gift* **indescribable gratuity**.

whether of our brothers
the apostles of the ecclesiae, the glory of Messiah.

24 So indicate to them
and to the face of the ecclesiae,
the indication of your love
and of our boasting on your behalf.

THE ZEAL OF GIVING

9 Indeed, concerning the ministry to the holy,
it is superfluous for me to scribe to you:

2 for I know your eagerness
of which I boast to the Macedonians
— that Achaia prepared a year ago;
and your zeal provokes many.

3 Yet I sent the brothers,
lest our boasting of you be in vain in this part;
that, exactly as I worded, Be prepared:

4 Lest somehow
whenever the Macedonians come with me
and find you unprepared,
we — we word not, you
— we be shamed in this same confident boasting.

5 So I deemed it necessary
to beseech the brothers to precede to you
and pre—prepare your eulogy,
whereof you were pre—evangelized
— to prepare the same thus, as a eulogy
— and not exactly as of avarice.

6 And this, whoever spores sparingly
also harvests sparingly;
and whoever spores to eulogy
harvests to eulogy:

7 each exactly as he prefers in his heart
— not of sorrow or of compulsion:
for Elohim loves a hilarious giver.

8 And Elohim is able
to superabound all charism to you;
that you, always having all self—contentment in all,
superabound to every good work:

9 exactly as scribed,
He scatters abroad;
he gives to the toiling:
his justness abides to the eons.
Psalm 112:9

10　　　　Now whoever contributes sperma to the sower
　　　　　both supplies bread to eat
　　　　　and multiplies your spores
　　　　　and grows the produce of your justness;
11　　　　being enriched to all liberality,
　　　which, through us, works eucharist to Elohim.
12　　　　For the ministry of this liturgy
　　　not only fully furnishes the lack of the holy,
　　　　　but also is superabundant
　　　　through many eucharists to Elohim;
13　　　while through the proofing of this ministry
　　　they glorify Elohim for your professed subjection
　　　　　to the evangelism of the Messiah
　　　and for your liberal communion to them and to all;
14　　　　And by their petition in your behalf
　　　　　　yearn after you
　　　because of the exceeding charism of Elohim in you.
15　　　　　　Charism to Elohim
　　　　　for his indescribable gratuity.

THE WITNESS OF PAULOS TO HIS MINISTRY

10　　　Now I *Paul* **Paulos** myself beseech you
　　　　　by **through** the meekness and gentleness
　　　　　　　of *Christ* **the Messiah**,
　　　　　who *indeed* in *presence* **face**
　　　　　　am *base* **humble** among you,
　　　　　　but being absent
　　　　am *bold toward* **courageous unto** you:
2　　　　But I *beseech* **petition** you,
　　that I may not be *bold* **courageous** when I am present
　　　　　　with that confidence,
　　wherewith I *think* **reckon** to be bold against some,
　　　　　which *think of* **reckon** us
　　　　as if we walked according to *the* flesh.
3　　　　　For though we walk in *the* flesh,
　　　　we do not war after *the* flesh:
4　　　　　(For the weapons of our
　　　　　warfare are not *carnal* **fleshly**,
　　　but *mighty* **able** through *God* **Elohim**
　　to the pulling down of *strong holds* **fortresses**;)
5　　　　Casting down *imaginations* **logic**,
　　　　and every *high thing* **exaltation**
　that exalteth itself against the knowledge of *God* **Elohim**,
　　　　and *bringing into captivity* **capturing**
　　　　　every *thought* **comprehension**
　　　　to the obedience of *Christ* **the Messiah**;
　6 And having in *a readiness* **preparedness**
　　　　to *revenge* **avenge** all disobedience,
　　　　when your obedience is fulfilled.
7　　　　　　Do ye look *on things*
　　　　after the outward appearance **according to face**?
　　If any *man trust to* **one confides in** himself
　　　　　that he is *Christ's* **Messiah's**,
　　let him of himself *think* **reckon** this again,
　　　that, **exactly** as he is *Christ's* **Messiah's**,
　　　even *so* **thus** are we *Christ's* **Messiah's**.
8　　　　For *though* **even whenever** I should boast
　　　　somewhat more **superabundantly**
　　　　　of **concerning** our authority,
　　　which the *Lord* **Adonay** hath given us
　　　　　　for **unto** edification,
　　and not *for your destruction* **to pull you down**,
　　　　I should not *be ashamed* **shame**:
9　　　　That I may not *seem* **be thought of**
　as *if I would terrify* **ever I should utterly frighten** you
　　　　　by letters **through epistles**.
10　　　For his *letters* **epistles indeed**, say they,
　　　are *weighty* **burdenous** and *powerful* **mighty**;
　but his *bodily presence* **body appearance** is *weak* **frail**,
　　　and his *speech contemptible* **word belittling**.
11　　　Let such an one *think* **reckon** this, that,
　　such as we are in word *by letters* **through epistles**
　　　　　when we are absent,
　　　such *will* **shall** we be also in *deed* **work**
　　　　　when we are present.
12　　　　　For we dare not
　　　make **compare** ourselves *of the number*,
　　　　　or *compare* **co—judge** ourselves
　　　with some that commend themselves:
　　but they measuring themselves *by* **in** themselves,
　　　　and *comparing* **co—judging**
　　　　themselves among themselves,
　　　　are **comprehend** not *wise*.
13　　　But we *will* **shall indeed** not boast
　　of things without our measure **immeasurably**,
　　but according to the measure of the *rule* **canon**
　which *God* **Elohim** hath *distributed* **imparted** to us,
　　　a measure to reach even unto you.
14　　　For we *stretch* **overspread** not ourselves
　　　　　beyond our measure,
　　　as though we reached not unto you:
　for we *are come as far as* **have arrived** to you also
　　　　in *preaching* the *gospel* **evangelism**
　　　　　　of *Christ* **the Messiah**:
15　　　　　Not boasting *of things*
　　　without our measure **immeasurably**,
　　that is, of *other men's* **in other's** labours;
　　　　　but having hope,
　　when your *faith* **trust** is *increased* **grown**,
　　that we shall be *enlarged* **magnified** by you

2 CORINTHIANS 10, 11

according to our *rule* **canon**
abundantly **unto superabundance**,

THE WITNESS OF PAULOS TO HIS MINISTRY

10 And I myself — Paulos beseech you
through the meekness and gentleness of the Messiah
— who indeed in face *am* humble among you
but in absentia, courageous to you:

2 and I petition,
to not be courageous when I am present
with that confidence,
wherewith I reckon to be bold against some
— who reckon us as walking according to flesh.

3 For though we walk in flesh,
we war not according to flesh:

4 for the weapons of our warfare are not fleshly,
but able through Elohim to pulling down fortresses;

5 and casting down logic
and every exaltation that exalts itself against
the knowledge of Elohim; and capturing every
comprehension to the obedience of the Messiah;

6 and prepared to avenge all disobedience
when you fulfill your obedience.

7 Look you according to face?
If anyone confides in himself to be of Messiah,
have him reckon himself again;
that, exactly as he is of Messiah,
even thus we are of Messiah.

8 For even whenever I boast
somewhat more superabundantly
concerning our authority,
that Adonay gave us to edify, and not to pull down,
I shame not:

9 That I not be thought of
as ever utterly frightening you through epistles.

10 For his epistles indeed, they say,
are burdenous and mighty;
and his body appearance is frail
and his word belittling.

11 Have such a one reckon this,
such as we are in word through epistles
when we are absent,
such also we are in work
when we are present.

12 For we dare not compare ourselves
or co—judge ourselves
with some who commend themselves:
but whoever measure themselves in themselves
and co—judge themselves among themselves,
comprehend not.

13 And indeed, we boast not immeasurably,
but according to the canon Elohim imparted to us,
a measure to reach even to you.

14 For we overspread ourselves not
as not reaching you:
for in the evangelism of the Messiah
we also arrived to you:

15 not boasting immeasurably
in the labors of others;
but having hope, that as your trust grows,
that you magnify us according to our canon
to superabundance,

16 To *preach the gospel* **evangelize**
in the regions beyond you,
and not **prepare** to boast in *another man's* **another's**
line of things made ready to our hand **canon**.

17 But he that *glorieth* **boasteth**,
let him *glory* **boast** in *the Lord* **Yah Veh**.
Yirme Yah 9:24

18 For not he that commendeth
himself is approved,
but whom *the Lord* **Yah Veh** commendeth.

11 *Would to God* **O that** ye
could bear with **tolerate me**
a little in my *folly* **thoughtlessness**:
and *indeed bear with* **yet tolerate** me.

2 For I am *jealous* **zealous** over you
with *Godly jealousy* **the zeal of Elohim**:
for I have *espoused* **betrothed** you to one *husband* **man**,
that I may present *you as* a *chaste* **hallowed** virgin
to *Christ* **the Messiah**.

3 But I *fear* **awe**, lest *by any means* **somehow**,
as the serpent *beguiled Eve* **seduced Havvah**
through **in** his *subtilty* **cunning**,
so **thus** your *minds* **comprehensions**
should be corrupted
from the *simplicity* **liberality** that
is in *Christ* **the Messiah**.

4 For **indeed** if he that cometh
preacheth another *Jesus* **Yah Shua**,
whom we have not preached,
or if ye *receive* **take** another spirit,
which ye have not *received* **taken**,
or another *gospel* **evangelism**,
which ye have not *accepted* **received**,
ye might *well bear with him* **have tolerated well**.

5 For I *suppose* **reckon** I *was*
not a whit **failed in naught**
behind **beyond**
the *very chiefest* **extremely superior** apostles.

6	But though I be *rude* **unlearned** in *speech* **word**, yet not in knowledge; but **in all** we have been *throughly made* manifest *among* **unto** you in all *things*.	17	And whoever boasts, boast in Yah Veh. Yirme Yah 9:24
7	*Or* Have I *committed an offence* **sinned** in *abasing* **humbling** myself that ye might be exalted, because I have *preached* **evangelized** to you the *gospel* **evangelism** of *God freely* **Elohim gratuitously**?	18	For not he who commends himself is approved, but whom Yah Veh commends.
8	I *robbed* **stripped** other *churches* **ecclesiae**, taking wages *of them*, *to do you service* **for your ministry**.	**11**	O that you tolerate me a little in my thoughtlessness — and still tolerate me:
		2	for I am zealous over you with the zeal of Elohim: for I betrothed you to one man a hallowed virgin, to present to the Messiah.
9	And when I was present with you, and wanted, I was *chargeable* **insensitive** to no *man* **one**: for that which was lacking to me the brethren which came from Macedonia *supplied* **fully furnished**: and in all *things* I have *kept* **guarded** myself *from being burdensome* **burdenless** unto you, and *so will* **thus shall** I *keep* **guard** myself.	3	And I awe, lest somehow, as the serpent seduced Havvah in his cunning, that thus you corrupt your comprehensions from the liberality in the Messiah.
		4	For indeed if whoever comes preaches another Yah Shua whom we preach not, or if you take another spirit you had not taken, or another evangelism you had not received, you tolerate it well.
10	As the truth of *Christ* **Messiah** is in me, no man shall *stop* **seal** me *of* **unto** this boasting in the *regions* **climes** of Achaia.	5	For I reckon that I failed in naught beyond the extremely superior apostles.
11	*Wherefore* **Why**? because I love you not? *God* **Elohim** knoweth.	6	But though I am unlearned in word, yet not in knowledge; but in all we manifested all to you.
12	But what I do, *that I will do* **I do**, that I may *cut off occasion* **exscind opportunity** from them which *desire occasion* **will for opportunity**; that wherein they *glory* **boast**, they may be found *even* **exactly** as we.	7	Or sin I in humbling myself to exalt you — because I evangelize to you the evangelism of Elohim gratuitously?
		8	I stripped other ecclesiae taking wages for your ministry.
	PSEUDO APOSTLES	9	And when I was present with you and wanted I was insensitive to no one: for whatever I lacked, the brothers who came from Macedonia fully furnished: and in all I guarded myself burdenless to you: and thus I guard myself.
13	For such are *false* **pseudo** apostles, deceitful workers, *transforming* **transfiguring** themselves into the apostles of *Christ* **Messiah**.
14	And no marvel; for Satan himself is *transformed* **transfigured** into an angel of light.
15	Therefore it is *no great thing* **not mega** if his ministers also be *transformed* **transfigured** as the ministers of *righteousness* **justness**; whose *end* **completion/shalom** shall be according to their works.	10	As the truth of Messiah is in me, my boasting is not sealed in the climes of Achaia.
		11	Why? Because I love you not? Elohim knows.
	THE SUFFERINGS OF PAULOS	12	And I do what I do, to exscind opportunity from them who will for opportunity; that wherein they boast, they be found exactly as we.
16	I *say* **word** again, Let no *man* **one** think me *a fool* **to be thoughtless**; if *otherwise*, yet as a fool *even as* **thoughtless** receive me, that I *also* may boast myself a little.
16	to evangelize beyond you and not prepare to boast in the canon of others.		PSEUDO APOSTLES
		13	For such are pseudo apostles — deceitful workers,

2 CORINTHIANS 11, 12

transfiguring themselves to the apostles of Messiah:
14 and no marvel;
for Satan transfigures himself into an angel of light.
15 So it is not mega if his ministers also
transfigure as the ministers of justness;
whose completion/shalom is according to their works.

THE SUFFERINGS OF PAULOS

16 I word again
that no one think I am thoughtless;
and if otherwise, even receive me as thoughtless
so that I also boast a little.
17 That which I speak,
I speak it not after the *Lord* **Adonay**,
but as *it were foolishly* **in thoughtlessness**,
in this confidence of boasting.
18 *Seeing that* **Since** many
glory **boast** after the flesh,
I *will glory* **shall boast** also.
19 For ye *suffer fools* **tolerate the thoughtless**
gladly **with pleasure**,
seeing ye yourselves are *wise* **being thoughtful**.
20 For ye *suffer* **tolerate**,
if *a man bring* **anyone enslave** you *into bondage*,
if *a man* **anyone** devour *you*,
if *a man* **anyone** take *of you*,
if *a man* **anyone** exalt himself,
if *a man smite* **anyone flog** you on the face.
21 I *speak as* **word** concerning *reproach* **dishonour**,
as though we had been *weak* **frail**. Howbeit
But whereinsoever any is bold,
(I *speak foolishly* **word in thoughtlessness**,)
I am bold also.

APOSTLES VS PSEUDO APOSTLES

22 Are they Hebrews? *so am* I **also**.
Are they *Israelites* **Yisra Elym**? *so am* I **also**.
Are they the *seed* **sperma** of Abraham? *so am* I **also**.
23 Are they ministers of *Christ* **Messiah**?
(I speak *as a fool* **insanely**) I *am* more;
in labours more *abundant* **superabundant**,
in stripes *above measure* **excessively**,
in prisons *more frequent* **guardhouses superabundant**,
in deaths oft.
24 Of the *Jews* **Yah Hudiym**
five times *received* **took** I forty *stripes* save one.
25 Thrice *was I beaten with rods* **bastinadoed**,
once *was I* stoned,
thrice *I suffered shipwreck* **shipwrecked**,
a night and a day *I have been* **done** in the deep;

26 *In* journeyings often, *in* perils of *waters* **streams**,
in perils of robbers,
in perils by *mine own countrymen* **my genos**,
in perils by the *heathen* **goyim**, *in* perils in the city,
in perils in the wilderness, *in* perils in the sea,
in perils *among false* **of pseudo** brethren;
27 In *weariness* **labours** and *painfulness* **toil**,
in watchings often, in *hunger* **famine** and thirst,
in fastings often, in cold and nakedness.
28 *Beside* **Except apart from**
those *things that are without*
that which *cometh* **conspireth** upon me daily,
the *care* **anxieties** of all the *churches* **ecclesiae**.
29 Who is *weak* **frail**, and I am not *weak* **frail**?
who is *offended* **scandalized**, and I *burn* not **fiery**?
30 If I must *needs glory* **boast**,
I *will glory* **shall boast** of *the things* **those**
which concern *mine infirmities* **my frailties**.
31 The *God* **Elohim** and Father
of our *Lord Jesus Christ* **Adonay Yah Shua Messiah**,
which is *blessed* **being eulogized**
for evermore **unto the eons**,
knoweth that I lie not.
32 In *Damascus* **Dammeseq**
the *governor* **ethnarch** under Aretas the *king* **sovereign**
kept the city of the *Damascenes* **Dammeseqim**
with a garrison,
desirous **having willed** to *apprehend* **seize** me:
33 And through a window in a *basket* **wicker**
was I *let down by* **lowered through** the wall,
and escaped his hands.

PAULOS IN PARADISE

12 It is not *expedient* **beneficial** for me
doubtless **now** to *glory* **boast**.
I **indeed** will come to visions and
revelations **apocalypses**
of *the Lord* **Adonay**.
2 I knew a *man* **human** in *Christ* **Messiah**
above fourteen years ago,
(whether in *the* body, I *cannot tell* **know not**;
or whether out of the body, I *cannot tell* **know not**:
God **Elohim** knoweth;)
such an one
caught up to **seized unto** the third *heaven* **heavens**.
17 What I speak, I speak not after Adonay,
but as in thoughtlessness, in this confidence of boasting,
18 since many boast after the flesh, I also boast.
19 For with pleasure, you tolerate the thoughtless,
you yourselves being thoughtful.

20	For you tolerate
	if anyone enslaves you,
	if anyone devours,
	if anyone takes,
	if anyone exalts himself,
	if anyone flogs you on the face.
21	I word concerning dishonor, as being frail.
	But wherever any is bold
	— I word in thoughtlessness — I also am bold.

APOSTLES VS PSEUDO APOSTLES

22	Are they Hebrews? I also.
	Are they Yisra Eliym? I also.
	Are they the sperma of Abraham? I also.
23	Are they ministers of Messiah?
	— I speak insanely — I more;
	in labors, more superabundant;
	in stripes, superexcessively;
	in guardhouses, superabundant;
	in deaths, often.
24	Of the Yah Hudiym
	five times I took forty save one;
25	thrice bastinadoed;
	once stoned;
	thrice shipwrecked;
	a night and a day done in the deep;
26	journeyings often;
	perils of streams;
	perils of robbers;
	perils by my genos;
	perils by the goyim;
	perils in the city;
	perils in the wilderness;
	perils in the sea;
	perils of pseudo brothers;
27	in labors and toil;
	in watchings often,
	in famine and thirst;
	in fastings often,
	in cold and nakedness:
28	except apart from those
	that conspire upon me daily;
	the anxieties of all the ecclesiae.
29	Who is frail and I not frail?
	Who is scandalized and I not fiery?
30	If I must boast,
	I boast of those that concern my frailties.
31	The Elohim and Father
	of our Adonay Yah Shua Messiah
	who is eulogized to the eons,
	knows that I lie not.
32	In Dammeseq
	the ethnarch under Aretas the sovereign
	kept the city of the Dammeseqim with a garrison,
	having willed to seize me:
33	and through a window in a wicker
	I was lowered through the wall
	and escaped his hands.

PAULOS IN PARADISE

12	It is not beneficial for me to boast:
	indeed I come to visions and apocalypses of Adonay.
2	I knew a human in Messiah fourteen years ago;
	whether in body, I know not;
	whether out of the body, I know not:
	Elohim knows;
	such an one seized to the third heavens.
3	And I knew such a *man* **human**,
	(whether in *the* body, *or* **whether** out of the body,
	I *cannot tell* **know not**: *God* **Elohim** knoweth;)
4	How that he was *caught up* **seized** into paradise,
	and heard *unspeakable words* **inexpressable**
	rhema, which it is not *lawful* **allowed**
	for a *man* **human** to *utter* **speak**.
5	Of such an one *will I glory* **shall I boast**:
	yet of myself I *will* **shall** not *glory* **boast**,
	but **except** in *mine infirmities* **my frailties**.
6	For *though* **whenever** I would
	desire **willed** to *glory* **boast**,
	I shall not be *a fool* **thoughtless**;
	for I *will* **shall** say the truth: but *now I forbear* **I spare**,
	lest any *man* **one** should *think of* **reckon unto** me
	above that which he seeth me *to be*,
	or that he heareth **somewhat** of me.

THE THORN OF PAULOS

7	And lest I should be **superciliously** exalted
	above measure
	through the *abundance* **excellence**
	of the *revelations* **apocalypses**,
	there was given to me a thorn in the flesh,
	the messenger **an angel** of Satan to *buffet* **punch** me,
	lest I should be **superciliously** exalted *above measure*.
	Numbers 33:55, Yah Shua 23:13, Judges 2:3,
	Yechezq El 28:24, Nachum 1:10
8	For this *thing* I besought
	the *Lord* **Adonay** thrice,
	that it might depart from me.
9	And he said unto me,
	My *grace* **charism** is sufficient for thee:

2 CORINTHIANS 12

for my *strength* **dynamis**
is *made perfect* **completed/shalamed** in *weakness* **frailty**.
Most gladly **So with pleasure** *therefore*
will **shall** I rather *glory* **boast** in my *infirmities* **frailties**,
that the *power* **dynamis** of *Christ* **the Messiah**
may *rest* **tabernacle** upon me.

10 Therefore I *take pleasure* **well—approve**
in *infirmities* **frailties**, in *reproaches* **hubris**,
in *necessities* **compulsions**, in persecutions,
in distresses for *Christ's* **Messiah's** sake:
for when I am *weak* **frail**, then am I *strong* **able**.

11 I am become *a fool* **thoughtless**
in *glorying* **boasting**;
ye have compelled me:
for I *ought to have been commended of you* **was indebted**:
for in *nothing* **naught** am I behind
the *very chiefest* **extremely superior** apostles,
though I be *nothing* **naught**.

12 *Truly* **Indeed** the signs of an apostle
were *wrought among* **worked in** you
in all *patience* **endurance**,
in signs, and *wonders* **omens**, and
mighty deeds **dynamis**.

13 For what is it wherein ye were *inferior* **slighted**
to *other churches* **the rest of the ecclesiae**,
except it be
that I myself was not *burdensome* **insensitive** to you?
forgive me this wrong
grant me charism for this injustice.

PAULOS PREPARES A THIRD VISIT

14 Behold,
the third time I *am ready* **have prepared** to come to you;
and *I will* **shall** not be *burdensome* **insensitive** to you:
for I seek not your's but you:
for the children *ought not* **are not indebted**
to *lay* **treasure** up for the parents,
but the parents for the children.

15 And I *will very gladly* **shall with pleasure** spend
and be *spent for you* **expended for your souls**;
though the more *abundantly*
superabundantly I love you,
the less I be loved.

16 But be it so, I did not *burden* **load** you **down**:
nevertheless **rather**, being *crafty* **cunning**,
I *caught* **took** you with *guile* **deceit**.

17 Did I *make a gain of* **defraud** you
by **through** any of them whom I
sent **apostolized** unto you?

18 I *desired* **besought** Titus,
and with him I *sent* **apostolized** a brother.

Did Titus *make a gain of* **defraud** you?
walked we not in the same spirit?
walked we — not in the same *steps* **tracks**?

3 And I knew such a human,
whether in body, whether out of the body,
I know not; Elohim knows:
4 that he was seized into paradise and heard
inexpressable rhemas not allowed for a human to speak.

5 Of such an one I boast:
yet of myself I boast not — except in my frailties.

6 For whenever I will to boast,
I become not thoughtless;
for I say the truth; but I spare:
lest anyone reckon me above what he sees me,
or somewhat hears of me.

THE THORN OF PAULOS

7 And lest I be superciliously exalted
through the excellence of the apocalypses,
I was given a thorn in the flesh
— an angel of Satan to punch me,
lest I be superciliously exalted.
Numbers 33:55, Yah Shua 23:13, Judges
2:3, Yechezq El 28:24, Nachum 1:10

8 For this I besought Adonay thrice
that it depart from me.

9 And he said to me,
My charism is sufficient for you:
for my dynamis is completed/shalamed in frailty.
So rather, with pleasure I boast in my frailties,
that the dynamis of the Messiah tabernacle upon me.

10 So I well—approve
in frailties,
in hubris,
in compulsions,
in persecutions,
in distresses for sake of Messiah:
for when I am frail, then I am able.

11 I become thoughtless in boasting;
you compel me — for I am indebted:
for I am behind in naught
of the extremely superior apostles
— though I am naught.

12 Indeed the signs of an
apostle were worked in you
in all endurance
— in signs and omens and dynamis.

13 For wherein were you belittled
beyond the rest of the ecclesiae?
— unless I myself was not insensitive to you?
Grant me charism for this injustice.

Paulos Prepares A Third Visit

14 Behold, I prepare to come to you a third time;
and I am not insensitive to you;
for I seek not yours — but you: for
the children are not indebted
to treasure for the parents,
but the parents for the children.
15 And with pleasure
I spend and expend for your souls;
though the more superabundantly I love you,
the less I am loved.
16 And so be it, I overloaded you not:
rather, being cunning, I took you with deceit.
17 Defrauded I you through any of them
whom I apostolized to you?
18 I besought Titus
and I apostolized a brother with him.
Defrauded Titus you?
Walked we not in the same spirit?
— Not in the same tracks?

Paulos Warns The Ecclesia

19 Again,
think ye that we *excuse ourselves* **plead** unto you?
we speak
before God **in sight of Elohim** in *Christ* **Messiah**:
but *we* do all *things*, dearly beloved, for your edifying.
20 For I *fear* **awe**, lest *somehow*, when I come,
I shall not find you such as I *would* **had willed**,
and that I shall be found unto you
such as ye *would* **had** not **willed**:
lest *somehow* there be *debates* **contentions**,
envyings **zeals**, *wraths* **furies**, *strifes* **rivalries**,
backbitings **slanders**, whisperings,
swellings **puffings**, tumults, **instabilities**:
21 And lest, when I come again,
my *God will* **Elohim shall** humble me *among* **unto** you,
and that I shall *bewail* **mourn** many
which have sinned *already* **previously**,
and have not repented of the *uncleanness* **impurity**
and *fornication* **whoredom** and *lasciviousness* **lechery**
which they have *committed* **transacted**.

13 This is the third *time* I am coming to you.
In the mouth of two or three witnesses
shall every *word be established* **rhema stand**.
2 I *told you before* **foresaid**,
and *foretell you* **forespeak**,
as if I were present, the second time;
and being absent now:
I *write* **scribe** to them
which *heretofore* **previously** have sinned,
and to all *other* **the rest**,
that, *if* **whenever** I come again, I *will* **shall** not spare:
3 Since ye seek a proof of *Christ*
Messiah speaking in me,
which *to you—ward* **unto you** is not *weak*
frail, but is *mighty* **dynamic** in you.
4 For *though* **if indeed**
he was *crucified through weakness* **staked by frailty**,
yet he liveth by the *power* **dynamis** of *God* **Elohim**.
For we also are *weak* **frail** in him,
but we shall live with him
by the *power* **dynamis** of *God toward* **Elohim unto** you.
5 *Examine* **Test** yourselves,
whether ye be in the *faith* **trust**; prove your own selves.
Or Know ye not your own selves,
how that *Jesus Christ* **Yah Shua Messiah** is in you,
except **somehow**
ye be *reprobates* **somewhat disapproved**?
6 But I *trust* **hope** that ye shall know
that we are not *reprobates* **disapproved**.
7 Now I *pray* **vow** to God
Elohim that ye do no evil;
not that we should *appear* **manifest** approved,
but that ye should do that which is *honest* **good**,
though we be as *reprobates* **disapproved**.
8 For we can do *nothing* **naught** against the truth,
but for the truth.
9 For we *are glad* **cheer**,
when we are *weak* **frail**, and ye are *strong* **able**:
and this also we *wish* **vow**, even your perfection.
10 Therefore I *write* **scribe**
these *things* being absent,
lest being present I should use *sharpness* **severity**,
according to the *power* **authority**
which *the Lord* **Adonay** hath given me to edification,
and not to *destruction* **pull you down**.

Salute And Doxology

11 Finally, brethren, *farewell* **Cheers**.
Be *perfect* **prepared**, be of good comfort,
be of one mind **think the same**,
live in peace **completed/shalamed**;
and the *God* **Elohim** of love and *peace* **shalom**
shall be with you.
12 *Greet* **Salute** one another *with* **in** an holy kiss.
13 All the *saints* **holy** salute you.
14 The *grace* **charism**
of *the Lord Jesus Christ* **Adonay Yah Shua Messiah**,

and the love of *God* **Elohim**,
and the communion of the *Holy Spirit* **Ruach ha-kodesh**,
be with you all.
Amen.

PAULOS WARNS THE ECCLESIA

19   Again, think you that we plead to you?
We speak in sight of Elohim in Messiah:
and beloved, all are to edify you.
20   For I awe, lest somehow, when I come,
I find you not such as I willed
and that you find me such as you had not willed:
lest somehow there be contentions,
zeals,
furies,
rivalries, slanders, whisperings, puffings, instabilities:
21   lest, when I come again,
my Elohim humble me to you
and that I mourn many who previously sinned
and repented not of the impurity
and whoredom and lechery they transacted.

13   This is my third coming to you.
In the mouth of two or three witnesses
every rhema stands.
2   I foresaid and forespeak,
as being present, the second time;
and now being absent:
I scribe to them who previously sinned
and to all the rest,
that, whenever I come again, I spare not:
3   Since you seek a proof of
Messiah speaking in me,
who to you is not frail but in you is dynamic.
4   For indeed if he was staked by frailty,
yet he lives by the dynamis of Elohim.
For we also are frail in him,
but we live with him
by the dynamis of Elohim unto you.

5   Test yourselves — whether you are in the trust;
prove your own selves.
Or know you not your own selves,
how that Yah Shua Messiah is in you,
except somehow you become disapproved?
6   And I hope you know
that we are not disapproved.
7   And I vow to Elohim that you do no evil
— not that we be manifest approved,
but that you do what is good,
though we be as disapproved.
8   For we can do naught against the truth
— but for the truth.
9   For we cheer when we are frail
and you are able:
and this also we vow — your perfection.
10   So being absent, I scribe these;
lest being present, I use severity,
according to the authority
Adonay gave me to edify
— and not to pull you down.

SALUTE AND DOXOLOGY

11   Finally brothers, Cheers.
be prepared;
of good comfort;
think the same;
completed/shalamed:
and the Elohim of love and shalom be with you.
12   Salute one another in a holy kiss.
13   All the holy salute you.
14   The charism of Adonay Yah Shua Messiah
and the love of Elohim
and the communion of the Holy Spirit,
be with you all.
Amen.

Salutation

1 *Paul* **Paulos**, an apostle,
(not of men humanity, neither by
man through humanity,
but *by Jesus Christ* **through Yah Shua Messiah**,
and *God* **Elohim** the Father,
who raised him from the dead;)

2 And all the brethren which are with me,
unto the churches ecclesiae of Galatia:

3 *Grace be* **Charism** to you and *peace* **shalom**
from God Elohim the Father,
and from our Lord Jesus Christ
Adonay Yah Shua Messiah,

4 Who gave himself for our sins,
that he might *deliver* **release** us
from this present evil *world* **eon**,
according to the will of *God* **Elohim** and our Father:

5 To whom be glory
for ever and ever unto the eons of the eons.
Amen.

One Evangelism

6 I marvel that ye are
so soon removed **thus quickly transplaced**
from him that called you
into the *grace* **charism** of *Christ* **Messiah**
unto another *gospel* **evangelism**:

7 Which is not another;
but **except** there be some that trouble you,
and *would pervert* **will to overturn**
the *gospel* **evangelism** of *Christ* **the Messiah**.

8 But *though* **whenever** we,
or an angel from heaven,
preach **evangelize** any other *gospel* unto you
than that which we have *preached* **evangelized** unto you,
let him be *accursed* **anathema**.

9 As we *said before* **foretold**,
so *say* **word** I now again,
If any *man preach* **one evangelize** any other *gospel*
unto you than that ye have *received* **taken**,
let him be *accursed* **anathema**.

10 For do I now *persuade men* **convince humanity**,
or *God* **Elohim**?
or do I seek to please *men* **humanity**?
for if I yet pleased *men* **humanity**,
I should not *ever* be the servant of *Christ* **Messiah**.

The Apocalypse Of Paulos

11 But I *certify you* **have you know**, brethren,
that the *gospel* **evangelism**
which was *preached of* **evangelized by** me
is not after *man* **humanity**.

12 For I neither *received* **took** it of *man* **humanity**,
neither was I *taught it* **doctrinated**,
but *by* **through** the *revelation* **apocalypse**
of *Jesus Christ* **Yah Shua Messiah**.

13 For ye have heard of my
conversation in time past **former behaviour**
in *the Jews' religion* **Yah Hudahism**,
how that *beyond measure* **excessively**
I persecuted the *church* **ecclesia** of *God* **Elohim**,
and *wasted* **ravaged** it:

14 And *profited* **advanced**
in *the Jews' religion* **Yah Hudahism**
above many my *equals* **contemporaries**
in mine own *nation* **genos**,
being more *exceedingly* **superabundantly**
zealous **a zealot** of the traditions
of my *fathers* **patriarchs**.

15 But when *it pleased God*
Elohim well—approved,
who *separated me* **set me apart** from my mother's
womb, and called me *by* **through** his *grace* **charism**,

16 To *reveal* **unveil** his Son in me,
that I might *preach* **evangelize** him
among the *heathen* **goyim**;
immediately **straightway** I *conferred* **counselled**
not with flesh and blood:

17 Neither *went* **ascended** I *up*
to *Jerusalem* **Yeru Shalem**
to them which were apostles *before* **preceding** me;
but I *went* **departed** into Arabia,
and returned again unto *Damascus* **Dammeseq**.

18 Then after three years
I *went up* **ascended** to *Jerusalem* **Yeru Shalem**
to *see Peter* **inquire of Petros**,
and abode with him fifteen days.

Salutation

1 Paulos, an apostle
neither of humanity nor through humanity
— but through Yah Shua Messiah
and Elohim the Father who raised him from the dead;

2 and all the brothers with me:
To the ecclesiae of Galatia:

3 Charism to you and shalom
from Elohim the Father
and our Adonay Yah Shua Messiah,

4 who gave himself for our sins,

GALATIANS 1, 2

to release us from this present evil eon,
according to the will of Elohim and our Father:
5   to whom be glory to the eons of the eons.
Amen.

ONE EVANGELISM

6   I marvel that you are so quickly transplaced
from him who called you into the charism
of Messiah to another evangelism:
7   which is not another;
except that some who trouble you,
will to overturn the evangelism of the Messiah.
8   But whenever we, or an angel from the heavens
evangelize any other to you
than what we evangelized to you,
he becomes anathema.
9   As we foretold, and now word again,
If anyone evangelizes any other to you
than what you took,
he becomes anathema.
10   For now, convince I humanity? Or Elohim?
Or seek I to please humanity?
For if I yet please humanity,
I am never ever the servant of Messiah.

THE APOCALYPSE OF PAULOS

11   But I have you know, brothers,
that the evangelism evangelized by me
is not after humanity.
12   For I neither took it from humanity
nor was I doctrinated;
but through the apocalypse of Yah Shua Messiah.
13   For you heard
of my former behavior in Yah Hudahism,
how I excessively
persecuted and ravaged the ecclesia of Elohim:
14   and advanced in Yah Hudahism
above my many contemporaries in my own genos
— being more superabundantly
a zealot of the traditions of my patriarchs.
15   And when Elohim well—approved
— who set me apart from the womb of my mother
and through his charism, called me
16   to unveil his Son in me
to evangelize him among the goyim;
I neither straightway counseled with flesh and blood:
17   nor ascended to Yeru Shalem
to them who were apostles preceding me;
but I departed to Arabia and returned to Dammeseq.
18   Then after three years
I ascended to Yeru Shalem to inquire of Petros
and abode with him fifteen days.
19   But other of the apostles saw I none,
save James the Lord's **except Yaaqovos Adonay's** brother.
20   Now *the things* **that** which
I *write* **scribe** unto you,
behold, *before God* **in sight of Elohim**, I lie not.
21   *Afterwards* **Then**
I came into the *regions* **climes** of Syria and Cilicia;
22   And was unknown by face
unto the *churches* **ecclesiae** of *Judaea* **Yah Hudah**
which were in *Christ* **Messiah**:
23   But they had heard only,
That he which persecuted us *in times past* **formerly**
now *preacheth* **evangelizeth** the *faith* **trust**
which once he *destroyed* **ravaged**.
24   And they glorified *God* **Elohim** in me.

THE BROTHERS APPROVE PAULOS

2   Then **through** fourteen years *after*
I *went up* **ascended** again to *Jerusalem* **Yeru Shalem**
with *Barnabas* **Bar Nabi**, and took Titus with me also.
2   And I *went up* **ascended**
by *revelation* **apocalypse**,
and *communicated* **propounded** unto them
that *gospel* **evangelism**
which I preach among the *Gentiles* **goyim**,
but privately to them
which were *of reputation* **well—thought of**,
lest *by any means* **somehow** I should run, or had run,
in vain.
3   But neither Titus, who was with me,
being a *Greek* **Hellene**,
was compelled to be circumcised:
4   And that because of *false* **pseudo** brethren
unawares brought **surreptitiously smuggled** in,
who *came in privily* **surreptitiously entered**
to spy out our liberty
which we have in *Christ Jesus* **Messiah Yah Shua**,
that they might *bring* **enslave** us *into bondage*:
5   To whom we *gave place* **yielded** by subjection,
no, not for an hour;
that the truth of the *gospel* **evangelism**
might *continue* **continually abide** with you.
6   But of these
who *seemed* **were thought** to be somewhat,
(*whatsoever* **what sort** they **formerly** were,
it *maketh no matter* **mattereth not** to me:
God **Elohim**
accepteth **taketh** no *man's person* **human's face**:)

for they who *seemed* **were thought**
to be *somewhat in conference* **counsellors**
added *nothing* **naught** to me:
7 But contrariwise,
when they saw that *the gospel of* the uncircumcision
was *committed* **entrusted** unto me,
exactly as *the gospel of* the circumcision
was unto *Peter* **Petros**;
8 (For he that *wrought effectually* **energized**
in *Peter* **Petros** to the apostleship of the circumcision,
the same *was mighty* **energized**
in me *toward* **unto** the *Gentiles* **goyim**:)
9 And when *James* **Yaaqovos**,
Cephas **Kepha**, and *John* **Yahn**,
who *seemed* **were thought** to be pillars,
perceived **knew** the *grace* **charism**
that was given unto me,
they gave to me and *Barnabas* **Bar Nabi**
the *right hands* **rights** of *fellowship* **communion**;
that we should go unto the heathen
— we unto the goyim,
and they unto the circumcision.
10 Only *they would* that we
should remember the poor;
the same which I also was *forward* **diligent** to do.

Paulos Withstands Petros

11 But when *Peter* **Petros** was come to Antioch,
I withstood him to the face,
because he was to be *blamed* **condemned**.
12 For *before that* **prior to**
certain **some** came from *James* **Yaaqovos**,
he did eat with the *Gentiles* **goyim**:
but when they were come,
he withdrew and *separated* **set** himself **apart**,
fearing **awestricken of** them
which were of the circumcision.
19 But I saw none of the other apostles,
except Yaaqovos, the brother of Adonay.
20 Now what I scribe to you,
behold, in sight of Elohim, I lie not.
21 Then I came to the climes of Syria and Cilicia;
22 and I was unknown by face
to the ecclesiae of the Yah Hudiym in Messiah:
23 but they only heard,
He who formerly persecuted us
now evangelizes the trust he once ravaged.
24 — and they glorified Elohim in me.

GALATIANS 2

The Brothers Approve Paulos

2 So through fourteen years
I ascended again to Yeru Shalem with Bar Nabi
— and also took Titus with me.
2 And I ascended by apocalypse
and propounded to them
the evangelism I preach among the goyim
— but privately to them who were well—thought of,
lest somehow I run — or had run in vain.
3 But not even Titus, who was with me,
being Hellene,
was compelled to be circumcised:
4 and that because of pseudo brothers
surreptitiously smuggled in,
who surreptitiously entered to spy out the liberty
we have in Messiah Yah Shua,
to enslave us:
5 to whom we yielded by subjection
no — not for an hour;
that the truth of the evangelism
continually abide with you.
6 But of these who were thought to be somewhat
— whatever sort they formerly were
— it matters not to me
— Elohim takes no human by face
for those thought to be counselors
added naught;
7 but contrariwise,
when they saw
that the uncircumcised were entrusted to me,
exactly as the circumcised to Petros
8 — for he who energized in Petros
to the apostleship of the circumcision,
energized in me to the goyim:
9 and when Yaaqovos and Kepha and Yahn,
thought to be pillars,
knew the charism given me,
they gave the right of communion
to me and Bar Nabi;
— we to the goyim and they to the circumcision:
10 only that we remember the poor;
which I also was diligent to do.

Paulos Withstands Petros

11 And when Petros came to Antioch,
I withstood him to the face,
because he was to be condemned.
12 For prior to some coming from Yaaqovos
he ate with the goyim:
and when they came

GALATIANS 2, 3

he withdrew and set himself apart
— awestricken of them of the circumcision.
13 And the *other* Jews **rest of the Yah Hudiym**
dissembled **hypocrized** likewise with him;
insomuch **so** as that *Barnabas* **Bar Nabi** also
was *carried* **led** away with their *dissimulation* **hypocrisy**.
14 But when I saw that they
walked **were** not *uprightly* **straightfooted**
according to **unto** the truth of the *gospel* **evangelism**,
I said unto *Peter before* **Petros in front of** them all,
If thou, being *a* Jew **Yah Hudiy**,
livest *after the manner of Gentiles* **goyishly**,
and not *as do the Jews* **Yah Hudaically**,
why compellest thou the *Gentiles* **goyim**
to *live as do the Jews* **Yah Hudahize**?
15 We who are *Jews* **Yah Hudiym** by nature,
and not sinners of the *Gentiles* **goyim**,
16 Knowing that *a man* **humanity** is not justified
by the works of the *law* **torah**,
but *by the faith* **only through trust**
of Jesus Christ **from Yah Shua Messiah**,
even we have *believed* **trusted**
in *Jesus Christ* **Yah Shua Messiah**
that we might be justified
by the *faith of Christ* **trust of Messiah**,
and not by the works of the *law* **torah**:
for **because** by the works of the *law* **torah**
shall no flesh be justified.
17 But if, while we seek to be
justified *by Christ* **in Messiah**,
we ourselves also are found sinners,
is *therefore Christ* **then Messiah** the minister of sin?
God forbid **So be it not**.
18 For if I build again
the things **those** which I *destroyed* **disintegrated**,
I *make* **constitute** myself a transgressor.
19 For I through the *law* **torah**
am dead to the *law* **torah**,
that I might live unto *God* **Elohim**.
20 I am *crucified* **co—staked** with *Christ* **Messiah**:
nevertheless I live;
yet not **no longer** I, but *Christ* **Messiah** liveth in me:
and the life which I now live in the flesh
I live *by* **in** the *faith* **trust** of the Son of *God* **Elohim**,
who loved me, and *gave* **surrendered** himself for me.
21 I do not *frustrate* **set aside**
the *grace* **charism** of *God* **Elohim**:
for if *righteousness* **justness**
come by **is through** the *law* **torah**,
then *Christ* **Messiah** is dead *in vain* **for naught**.

TAKING THE HOLY SPIRIT

3 O *foolish* **mindless** Galatians,
who hath *bewitched* **fascinated** you,
that ye should not obey the truth,
before **in front of** whose eyes *Jesus
Christ* **Yah Shua Messiah**
hath been *evidently set forth* **preinscribed**,
crucified **staked** among you?
2 This only *would* **will** I *to* learn of you,
Received **Took** ye the Spirit
by the works of the *law* **torah**,
or by the hearing of *faith* **trust**?
3 Are ye *so foolish* **thus mindless**?
having begun in the Spirit,
are ye now *made perfect* **completed/
shalamed** by the flesh?
4 Have ye suffered so *many things* **much** in vain?
if *it be yet* **indeed** in vain.
5 **So** He *therefore* that *ministereth
supplieth* to you the Spirit,
and *worketh miracles* **energizeth dynamis** among you,
doeth he it by the works of the *law* **torah**,
or by the hearing of *faith* **trust**?

THE COVENANT OF ELOHIM WITH ABRAHAM

6 Even as Abraham *believed God* **trusted Elohim**,
and it was *accounted* **reckoned** to him
for righteousness **unto justness**.
7 Know ye therefore that they
which are of *faith* **trust**,
the same are the *children* **sons** of Abraham.
8 And the scripture, foreseeing that *God* **Elohim**
would **should** justify the *heathen* **goyim**
through faith **by trust**,
preached before the gospel **pre—evangelized**
unto Abraham, *saying*,
In thee shall all *nations* **goyim** be *blessed* **eulogized**.
13 And likewise
the rest of the Yah Hudiym hypocrized with him;
so that also Bar Nabi was led away by their hypocrisy.
14 But when I saw that they were not straightfooted
to the truth of the evangelism,
I said to Petros in front of them all,
If you, being Yah Hudiy,
live goyishly and not Yah Hudaically,
why compel you the goyim to Yah Hudahize?
15 We who are Yah Hudiym by nature
and not sinners of the goyim,
16 knowing that humanity is not justified

by the works of the torah,
but only through trust from Yah Shua Messiah,
even we trust in Yah Shua Messiah
to be justified by the trust of Messiah
and not by the works of the torah:
because no flesh is justified by the works of the torah.

17 But if, while we seek to be justified in Messiah,
we ourselves also are found sinners,
is Messiah the minister of sin?
So be it not.

18 For if I build again what I disintegrated,
I constitute myself a transgressor.

19 For through the torah I died to the torah
to live to Elohim.

20 I am co—staked with Messiah:
nevertheless I live;
— no longer I, but Messiah lives in me:
and the life I now live in the flesh
I live in the trust of the Son of Elohim,
who loved me and surrendered himself for me.

21 I set not aside the charism of Elohim:
for if justness is through the torah,
then Messiah died for naught.

Taking The Holy Spirit

3 O mindless Galatians,
who fascinated you to not obey the truth
— in front of whose eyes Yah Shua Messiah
was preinscribed among you — staked?

2 I will to learn only this of you:
Took you the Spirit by the works of the torah?
Or by the hearing of trust?

3 Are you thus mindless?
Having begun in Spirit,
complete/shalam you now in flesh?

4 Suffer you so much in vain — if indeed in vain?

5 So he who supplies the Spirit to you
and energizes dynamis among you
— is it by the works of the torah
or by the hearing of trust?

The Covenant Of Elohim With Abraham

6 Even as Abraham trusted Elohim
and it was reckoned to him to justness

7 — so you know that whoever are of trust
are the sons of Abraham.

8 And the scripture,
foreseeing that Elohim justifies the goyim by trust
pre—evangelized to Abraham,
In you all the goyim are eulogized.

9 So then they which be of *faith* **trust**
are blessed with *faithful* **trustworthy** Abraham.
Genesis 12:1—3

The Works Of The Torah vs The Curse Of The Torah

10 For as many as are of the works of the *law* **torah**
are under the curse:
for it is *written* **scribed**,
Cursed is every one
that *continueth* **abideth** not in all *things*
which are *written* **scribed**
in the *book* **scroll** of the *law* **torah** to do them.

11 But that no *man* **one** is justified
by **in** the *law* **torah** *in the sight of God* **by Elohim**,
it is evident:
for, The just shall live by *faith* **trust**.

12 And the *law* **torah** is not of *faith* **trust**:
but, The *man* **human** that doeth them shall live in them.
Deuteronomy 27:6, Habakkuk 2:4, Leviticus 18:5

The Marketing Of The Messiah From The Curse Of The Torah

13 *Christ* **Messiah** hath *redeemed* **marketed** us
from the curse of the *law* **torah**,
being made **having become** a curse for us:
for it is *written* **scribed**,
Cursed is every one that hangeth on a *tree* **staff**:

14 That the blessing of Abraham
might *come on* **become unto** the *Gentiles* **goyim**
through Jesus Christ **in Yah Shua Messiah**;
that we might *receive* **take**
the *promise* **pre—evangelism** of the Spirit
through *faith* **trust**.
Deuteronomy 21:23

15 Brethren, I *speak* **word** after
the manner of *men* **humanity**;
Though it be but a man's **Yet still, a human** covenant,
yet if it be *being* confirmed,
no *man disannulleth* **one setteth aside**, or addeth thereto.

16 Now to Abraham and his *seed* **sperma**
were the *promises made* **pre—evangelisms rhetorized**.
He *saith* **wordeth** not, And to *seeds* **spermas**, as of many;
but as of one, And to thy *seed* **sperma**,
which is *Christ* **Messiah**.
Genesis 13:15, 25:5, 6

17 And this I *say* **word**, *that* the covenant,
that was *confirmed before of God*
pre—ratified by Elohim

GALATIANS 3

in *Christ* **Messiah**,
the *law* **torah**,
which *was* **became** four hundred and thirty years after,
cannot *disannul* **invalidate**,
that it should
make the promise of none effect
inactivate the pre—evangelism.

18 For if the inheritance be *of the law* **by torah**,
it is *no more of promise* **not still by pre—evangelism**:
but *God gave it* **Elohim granted charism** to Abraham
by promise **through pre—evangelism**.

19 *Wherefore then serveth the*
law **So why the torah**?
It was added because of transgressions,
till the *seed* **sperma** should come
to whom the *promise* **pre—evangelism** was made;
and it was ordained *by* **through** angels
in the hand of a mediator.

20 Now a mediator is not *a mediator* of one,
but *God* **Elohim** is one.

21 So Is the *law* **torah** then
against the *promises* **pre—evangelisms** of *God* **Elohim**?
God forbid **So be it not**:
for if there had been a *law* **torah** given
which *could have given life* **was able to enliven**,
verily righteousness **indeed justness**
should have been by the *law* **torah**.

22 But the scripture
hath *concluded* **locked** all **together** under sin,
that the *promise* **pre—evangelism**
by *faith of Jesus Christ* **trust from Yah Shua Messiah**
might be given to them that *believe* **trust**.

23 But *before faith* **ere the trust** came,
we were *kept* **garrisoned** under the *law* **torah**,
shut up **locked together** unto the *faith* **trust**
which should afterwards be *revealed* **unveiled**.

9 So they of trust
are blessed with trustworthy Abraham.
Genesis 12:1—3

THE WORKS OF THE TORAH
VS THE CURSE OF THE TORAH

10 For as many as are of the works of the torah
are under the curse:
for it is scribed,
Cursed is everyone who abides not in all
which are scribed in the scroll of the torah
— to do them.

11 And it is evident
that no one is justified by Elohim in the torah:
for, The just live by trust.

12 — and the torah is not of trust:
but, The human who does them, lives in them.
Deuteronomy 27:6, Habakkuk 2:4, Leviticus 18:5

THE MARKETING OF THE MESSIAH
FROM THE CURSE OF THE TORAH

13 Messiah marketed us from
the curse of the torah
— becoming a curse for us:
for it is scribed,
Cursed is everyone who hangs on a staff:

14 that the blessing of Abraham
becomes to the goyim
in Yah Shua Messiah;
to take the pre—evangelism of the Spirit through trust.
Deuteronomy 21:23

15 Brothers, I word after the manner of humanity;
Yet still, a human covenant, being confirmed,
no one sets aside, or adds thereto.

16 And the pre—evangelisms were rhetorized
to Abraham and his sperma.
He words not, And to spermas — as of
many; but as of one, And to your sperma,
who is Messiah. Genesis 13:15, 25:5, 6

17 And this I word, the covenant — the torah
which was pre—ratified by Elohim in Messiah,
which became four hundred and thirty years after,
cannot invalidate to inactivate the pre—evangelism.

18 For if the inheritance is by torah
it is not still by pre—evangelism:
but Elohim granted charism to Abraham
through pre—evangelism.

19 So why the torah?
It was added because of transgressions,
until the sperma come
— to whom the pre—evangelism was made
ordained through angels in the hand of a mediator.

20 And a mediator is not of one,
but Elohim is one.

21 So is the torah
against the pre—evangelisms of Elohim?
So be it not:
for if a torah had been given
which was able to enliven,
then indeed justness had been by the torah.

22 But the scripture locked all together under sin
— so that the pre—evangelism by trust
from Yah Shua Messiah
be given to them who trust.

23 But ere the trust came,
we were garrisoned under the torah
— locked together to the trust
to be unveiled afterwards.
24 *Wherefore* **So** the *law* **torah**
was **became** our *schoolmaster* **pedagogue**
to bring us unto Christ **unto Messiah**,
that we might be justified by *faith* **trust**.
25 But after that *faith* **the trust** is come,
we are *no longer* **not still**
under a *schoolmaster* **pedagogue**.
26 For ye are all the *children* **sons** of *God* **Elohim**
by faith **through the trust**
in *Christ Jesus* **Messiah Yah Shua**.
27 For as many of you
as have been baptized into *Christ* **Messiah**
have *put on Christ* **endued Messiah**.
28 There is neither *Jew* **Yah Hudiy** nor *Greek* **Hellene**,
there is neither bond nor *free* **liberated**,
there is neither male nor female:
for ye are all one in *Christ Jesus* **Messiah Yah Shua**.
29 And if ye be *Christ's* **Messiah's**,
then are ye Abraham's *seed* **sperma**,
and heirs according to the *promise* **pre—evangelism**.

From Servant To Sonship

4 Now I *say* **word**, That the heir,
as long *time* as he is a *child* **baby**,
differeth nothing from **surpasseth not** a servant,
though he be lord **being adoni** of all;
2 But is under
tutors **managers** and *governors* **administrators**
until the *time appointed* **preappointment** of the father.
3 Even *so* **thus** we, when we were *children* **babies**,
were *in bondage* **subservient**
under the elements of the *world* **cosmos**:
4 But when the fulness of the time was come,
God sent forth **Elohim apostolized** his Son,
made **become** of a woman,
made **become** under the *law* **torah**,
5 To *redeem* **market** them that
were under the *law* **torah**,
that we might *receive* **take** the *adoption of sons* **sonship**.
6 And because ye are sons,
God **Elohim**
hath *sent forth* **apostolized** the Spirit of his Son
into your hearts, crying, Abba, Father.
7 *Wherefore* **So then** thou art
no more **not still** a servant,
but a son;
and if a son,
then an heir of *God* **Elohim** through *Christ* **Messiah**.

Concerning Servitude

8 *Howbeit* **But indeed** then,
when ye knew not *God* **Elohim**,
ye *did service* **were in servitude** unto them
which by nature are no *gods* **elohim**.
9 But now, after that ye have known *God* **Elohim**,
or rather are known of *God* **Elohim**,
how turn ye **around** again
to the *weak* **frail** and *beggarly* **poor** elements,
whereunto ye *desire again* **uppermostly** will
to be in *bondage* **servitude**?
10 Ye observe days, and months,
and *times* **seasons**, and years.
11 I am *afraid* **awestricken** of you,
lest **somehow** I have
bestowed upon you labour **laboured unto you** in vain.
12 Brethren, I *beseech* **petition**
you, *be* **become** as I *am*;
for I *am* **also** as ye *are*:
ye have not injured me at all.
13 Ye know how through
infirmity **frailty** of the flesh
I *preached the gospel* **pre—evangelized** unto you
at the first.
14 And my *temptation* **testing**
which was in my flesh
ye *despised* **belittled** not, nor *rejected* **spit out**;
but received me as an angel of *God* **Elohim**,
even as *Christ Jesus* **Messiah Yah Shua**.

The Galatians Perplex Paulos

15 **So** Where is *then* the blessedness ye spake of?
for I *bear you record* **witness**, that, if *it had been* possible,
ye *would have plucked out* **had extracted**
your own eyes,
and *have* **had ever** given them to me.
16 **So then,** Am I *therefore* become your enemy,
because I *tell you the truth* **be true**?
24 So the torah became our pedagogue to Messiah,
that we be justified by trust.
25 And the trust, having come,
we are not still under a pedagogue.
26 For you are all the sons of Elohim
through the trust in Messiah Yah Shua.
27 For as many of you, being
baptized into Messiah,

GALATIANS 4

endued Messiah.
28 There is neither Yah Hudiy nor Hellene;
there is neither bond nor liberated;
there is neither male nor female:
for you are all one in Messiah Yah Shua;
29 and if you are of Messiah
then you of the sperma of Abraham
and heirs according to the pre—evangelism.

From Servant To Sonship

4 And I word,
as long time as the heir is a baby,
he surpasses not a servant — being adoni of all;
2 but is under managers and administrators
until the pre—appointment of the father.
3 Even so thus we, when we were babies,
were subservient under the elements of the cosmos:
4 but when the fulness/shalom of the time came
Elohim apostolized his Son
— become of a woman — become under the torah
5 to market them who were under the torah
so that we take the sonship.
6 And because you are sons,
Elohim apostolized the Spirit of his Son
into your hearts, crying, Abba Father.
7 So then, you are not still a servant, but a son;
and if a son, then an heir of Elohim through Messiah.

Concerning Servitude

8 But then indeed,
when you knew not Elohim, you were in servitude
to them, who by nature, are no elohim.
9 But now, knowing Elohim
— or rather Elohim knowing us,
how return you to the frail and poor elements,
to which you uppermostly will to be in servitude?
10 You observe days and months
and seasons and years.
11 I am awstricken of you,
lest somehow I labored to you in vain.
12 Brothers, I petition you,
become as I; for I am also as you:
you injured me not at all.
13 You know how through frailty of the flesh
I pre—evangelized to you:
14 and my testing in my flesh
you neither belittled, nor spit out;
but received me as an angel of Elohim
— as Messiah Yah Shua.

The Galatians Perplex Paulos

15 So where is the blessedness of which you speak?
For I witness, that if possible,
you had extracted your own eyes
and had ever given them to me.
16 So, become I your enemy
because I am true?
17 They *zealously affect* are
zealous over you, but not well;
yea **rather**, they *would* **will to** exclude you,
that ye might *affect* **be zealous over** them.
18 But it is good to be *zealously affected* **zealous**
always *in a* **over** good *thing*,
and not only *when I am* **in my being** present with you.
19 My little children, of whom
I travail in birth again
until *Christ* **Messiah** be formed in you,
20 I *desire* **will** to be present with you now,
and to change my voice;
for I *stand in doubt of* **am perplexed in** you.

Allegory Of Hagar And Sarah

21 *Tell* **Word to** me,
ye that *desire* **will** to be under the *law* **torah**,
do ye not hear the *law* **torah**?
22 For it is *written* **scribed**,
that Abraham had two sons,
the one by *a bondmaid* **the lass**,
the other by *a freewoman* **the liberated**.
23 But **indeed** he *who was* of the *bondwoman* **lass**
was *born* **birthed** after the flesh;
but he of the *freewoman* **liberated**
was by promise **through pre—evangelism**.
24 Which *things are an allegory* **are allegorized**:
for these are the two covenants;
the one **indeed** from the mount *Sinai* **Sinay**,
which *gendereth* **birtheth** to *bondage* **servitude**,
which is *Agar* **Hagar**.
25 For this *Agar* **Hagar** is
mount *Sinai* **Sinay** in Arabia,
and *answereth* **correspondeth**
to Jerusalem **with Yeru Shalem** which now is,
and is in *bondage* **servitude** with her children.
26 But *Jerusalem which is* **the Yeru Shalem** above
is *free* **liberated**,
which is the mother of us all.
27 For it is *written* **scribed**,
Rejoice, thou *barren* **sterile** that *bearest* **birthest** not;
break forth and cry, thou that travailest not:

for *the desolate hath many more children* **many are the children of the desolate rather** than she which hath *an husband* **a man**. Yesha Yah 54:1

28 Now we, brethren, as *Isaac* **Yischaq** was, are the children of *promise* **pre—evangelism**.

29 But **exactly** as then he that was *born after the* **birthed** according to flesh persecuted him *that was born after the* **according to** Spirit, even *so it is* **thus** now.

30 *Nevertheless* **Rather**, what *saith* **wordeth** the scripture? Cast *out* the *bondwoman* **lass** and her son: for the son of the *bondwoman* **lass** shall not *be heir* **no way inherit** with the son of the *freewoman* **liberated**. Genesis 21:9, 10

31 So then, brethren, we are not children of the *bondwoman* **lass**, but of the *free* **liberated**.

THE LIBERTY OF THE LIBERATED

5 Stand *fast* **firm** therefore in the liberty wherewith *Christ* **Messiah** hath *made us free* **liberated us**, and be not *entangled* **begrudged** again with the yoke of *bondage* **servitude**.

THE SERVITUDE OF SERVANTS

2 Behold, I *Paul say* **Paulos word** unto you, that *if* **whenever** ye be circumcised, *Christ* **Messiah** shall *profit* **benefit** you *nothing* **naught**.

3 For I *testify* **witness** again to every *man* **human** that is circumcised, that he is a debtor to do the whole *law* **torah**.

4 *Christ is become of no effect unto you* **Ye are inactivated from the Messiah**, whosoever of you are justified *by* **in** the *law* **torah**; ye are fallen from *grace* **charism**.

THE HOPE OF THE HOLY

5 For we through the Spirit *wait for* **await** the hope of *righteousness* **justness** by *faith* **trust**.

6 For in *Jesus Christ* **Yah Shua Messiah** neither circumcision *availeth any thing* **is of any ability**, nor uncircumcision; but *faith* **trust** which *worketh by* **energizeth through** love.

17 They are zealous over you, but not well; yes rather, they will to exclude you; so that you be zealous over them.

18 And it is always good to be zealous over good and not only in my being present with you.

19 My little children, of whom I travail in birth again until Messiah forms in you,

20 I will to be present with you now and to change my voice; for I am perplexed in you.

ALLEGORY OF HAGAR AND SARAH

21 Word to me — you who will to be under the torah, Hear you not the torah?

22 For it is scribed, that Abraham had two sons, the one by the lass, the other by the liberated.

23 But indeed he of the lass was birthed after the flesh; and he of the liberated, through pre—evangelism;

24 which are allegorized: for these are the two covenants; the one indeed from the Mount Sinay — which births to servitude — which is Hagar.

25 For this Hagar is Mount Sinay in Arabia and corresponds with Yeru Shalem — which now is and is in servitude with her children.

26 But the Yeru Shalem above is liberated — the mother of us all.

27 For it is scribed, Rejoice, you sterile who birth not; break forth and cry, you who travail not: for many are the children of the desolate rather than she who has a man. Yesha Yah 54:1

28 And brothers, as Yischaq, we are the children of pre—evangelism.

29 But so exactly as he who was birthed according to flesh persecuted him according to Spirit; even thus now.

30 Rather, what words the scripture? Cast out the lass and her son: for the son of the lass no way inherits with the son of the liberated. Genesis 21:9, 10

31 So then brothers, we are not children of the lass, but of the liberated.

GALATIANS 5

The Liberty Of The Liberated

5 So stand firm in the liberty
Messiah liberated us;
and begrudge not again
with the yoke of servitude.

The Servitude Of Servants

2 Behold, I Paulos word to you,
whenever you circumcise
Messiah benefits you naught.
3 For I witness again to every circumcised human,
that he is a debtor to do the whole torah.
4 You — you who justify in torah
inactivate *yourselves* from the Messiah
— you are fallen from the charism.

The Hope Of The Holy

5 For by Spirit,
we await the hope of justness by trust.
6 For in Yah Shua Messiah
neither is circumcision of any ability,
nor uncircumcision;
but trust, that energizes through love.

The Torah Fulfilled In Love

7 Ye did run well;
who did hinder you that ye should not obey the truth?
8 This *persuasion* **confidence**
cometh **is** not of him that calleth you.
9 A little *leaven* **fermentation**
leaveneth **fermenteth** the whole lump.
10 I have confidence in you
through the Lord **in Adonay**,
that ye *will be none* **shall not think** otherwise *minded*:
but he that troubleth you shall bear his judgment,
whosoever he be.
11 And I, brethren, if I yet preach circumcision,
why do I yet suffer persecution?
then is the *offence* **scandal** of the *cross* **stake**
ceased **inactivated**.
12 *I would* **O that** they were even *cut off* **amputated**
which *trouble* **rouse you**.
13 For, brethren, ye have been called unto liberty;
only *use* not liberty
for an occasion **unto an opportunity** to the flesh,
but *by* **through** love serve one another.
14 For *all* the *law* **whole torah**
is fulfilled/**shalamed** in one word,
even in this; Thou shalt love thy neighbour
as thyself. Leviticus 19:18

15 But if ye bite and devour one another,
take heed see that ye be not consumed one of another.

The In Spirit Walk

16 This I *say* **word** then, Walk in *the* Spirit,
and ye shall not **no way**
fulfil **complete/shalam** the *lust* **panting** of the flesh.
17 For the flesh *lusteth* **panteth** against the Spirit,
and the Spirit against the flesh:
and these are contrary
the one to the other **to one another**:
so that ye cannot do *the things* **those**
that ye *would* **ever will**.
18 But if ye be led of the Spirit,
ye are not under the *law* **torah**.

The Many Works Of The Flesh

19 Now the works of the flesh are manifest,
which are *these*;
Adultery, *fornication* **whoredom**,
uncleanness **impurity**, *lasciviousness* **lechery**,
20 Idolatry, *witchcraft* **pharmacy**, *hatred* **enmity**,
variance **contention**, *emulations* **zeals**, *wrath* **fury**,
strife **rivalry**, *seditions* **divisions**, heresies,
21 Envyings, murders, *drunkenness* **intoxication**,
revellings **carousings**, and such like:
of the which I *tell you before* **forespeak**,
exactly as I have also *told you in time past* **foretold**,
that they which *do* **transact** such *things*
shall not inherit
the *kingdom* **sovereigndom** of *God* **Elohim**.

The Singular Fruit Of The Spirit

22 But the fruit of the Spirit is love, *joy* **cheer**,
peace **shalom**, *longsuffering* **patience**,
gentleness **kindness**, goodness, *faith* **trust**,
23 Meekness, *temperance* **self—control**:
against such there is no *law* **torah**.
24 And they that *are Christ's* **be the Messiah's**
have *crucified* **staked** the flesh
with the *affections* **passions** and *lusts* **pantings**.
25 If we live in *the* Spirit,
let us also *walk* **march** in *the* Spirit.
26 Let us not be *desirous of vain glory* **vainglorious**,
provoking **irritating** one another, envying one another.

The Torah Fulfilled In Love

7 You run well;
who hinders you to not obey the truth?
8 This confidence is not of him who calls you.

9	A little fermentation ferments the whole lump.
10	I have confidence in you in Adonay, that you not think otherwise: but whoever troubles you — whoever bears his judgment.
11	And I, brothers, if I still preach circumcision, why suffer I still persecution? Then the scandal of the stake is inactivated.
12	O that whoever rouses you, even amputate.
13	For brothers, you are called to liberty — only not liberty to an opportunity of the flesh but through love to serve one another.
14	For the whole torah fulfills/shalams in one word, — in this; Love your neighbour as yourself. Leviticus 19:18
15	And if you bite and devour one another, see that you not consume one another.

The In Spirit Walk

16	So I word this, Walk in Spirit and you never no way complete/shalam the panting of the flesh.
17	For the flesh pants against the Spirit and the Spirit against the flesh — and these are contrary to one another: so that you cannot ever do those that you ever will.
18	But if you are led by the Spirit, you are not under the torah.

The Many Works Of The Flesh

19	Now the works of the flesh are manifest, which are: Adultery, whoredom, impurity, lechery,
20	idolatry, pharmacy, enmity, contention, zeals, fury, rivalry, divisions, heresies,
21	envyings, murders, intoxication, carousings and such like: of which I forespeak exactly as I also foretold, that whoever transacts such inherit not the sovereigndom of Elohim.

The Singular Fruit Of The Spirit

22	And the fruit of the Spirit: love, cheer, shalom, patience, kindness, goodness, trust,
23	meekness, self—control: against such there is no torah.
24	And whoever are of the Messiah stake the flesh with the passions and pantings.
25	If we live in Spirit, we also march in Spirit
26	— not being vainglorious, irritating one another, envying one another.

The Ministry Of Restoration

6	Brethren, *if* **whenever** a *man* **human** be overtaken in *a fault* **backsliding**, ye which are spiritual, *restore* **prepare** such an one in the spirit of meekness; *considering* **scoping** thyself, lest thou also be *tempted* **tested**.
2	Bear ye one another's burdens, and *so* **thus** fulfil the *law* **torah** of *Christ* **the Messiah**.
3	For if *a man* **some one** think himself to be *something* **somewhat**, *when he is nothing* **being no one**, he *deceiveth* **deludeth** himself.
4	But let *every man* **each** prove his own work, and then shall he have *rejoicing* **boasting** in himself alone, and not in another.
5	For *every man* **each** shall bear his own burden.
6	Let him that is *taught* **catechized** in the word *communicate* **impart** unto him that *teacheth* **catechizeth** in all good *things*.
7	Be not *deceived* **seduced**; *God* **Elohim** is not *mocked* **snubbed**: for whatsoever a *man* **human** *soweth* **sporeth**, that shall he also *reap* **harvest**.
8	For he that *soweth* **sporeth** to his flesh shall of the flesh *reap* **harvest** corruption; but he that *soweth* **sporeth** to the Spirit shall of the Spirit *reap* **harvest** life *everlasting* **eternal**.
9	And let us not be weary in *well* doing **good**: for in *due* **our own** season we shall *reap* **harvest**, if we *faint* **weaken** not.
10	*So* **As** we have *therefore opportunity* **season**,

GALATIANS 5, 6

let us *do* **work** good unto all *men*,
especially unto them
who are of the household of *faith* **the trust**.

THE BOASTING OF PAULOS

11 Ye see how *large a letter* **great a scribing**
I have *written* **scribed** unto you with mine own hand.
12 As many as *desire* **will** to
make a fair shew in the flesh,
they *constrain* **compel** you to be circumcised;
only lest they should suffer persecution
for the *cross* **stake** of *Christ* **the Messiah**.
13 For neither they themselves
who are circumcised
keep **guard** the *law* **torah**;
but *desire* **will** to have you circumcised,
that they may *glory* **boast** in your flesh.
14 But *God forbid* **So be it not**
that I should *glory* **boast**,
save **except** in the *cross* **stake**
of our *Lord Jesus Christ* **Adonay Yah Shua Messiah**,
by **through** whom
the *world* **cosmos** is *crucified* **staked** unto me,
and I *also* unto the *world* **cosmos**.
15 For in *Christ Jesus* **Messiah Yah Shua**
neither circumcision *availeth any thing* **is of any ability**,
nor uncircumcision,
but a new *creature* **creation**.
16 And as many as *walk* **march**
according to **by** this *rule* **canon**,
peace **shalom** be on them, and mercy,
and upon the *Israel* **Yisra El** of *God* **Elohim**.
17 From henceforth
let no *man trouble* **one belabour to embarrass** me:
for I bear in my body
the *marks* **stigmas** of the *Lord Jesus* **Adonay Yah Shua**.
18 Brethren, the *grace* **charism**
of our *Lord Jesus Christ* **Adonay Yah Shua Messiah**
be with your spirit.
Amen.

THE MINISTRY OF RESTORATION

6 Brothers,
whenever a human is overtaken in backsliding,
you who are spiritual,
prepare such a one in the spirit of meekness;
scoping yourself, lest you also are tested.
2 Bear the burdens of one another
and thus fulfil the torah of the Messiah.
3 For if someone thinks he is somewhat,
being no one, he deludes himself:
4 and each proofs his own work
and then he boasts in himself alone
and not in another:
5 for each bears his own burden.
6 Whoever catechizes in the word,
impart to him who catechizes in all good.
7 be not seduced: Elohim is not snubbed:
for whatever a human spores
he also harvests;
8 because whoever spores to his flesh
of the flesh harvests corruption;
and whoever spores to the Spirit
of the Spirit harvests life eternal.
9 And let us not weary in doing good:
for in our own season we harvest
— if we weaken not.
10 So as we have season, work good to all,
especially to the household of the trust.

THE BOASTING OF PAULOS

11 You see how great a scribing
I scribe to you with my own hand.
12 As many as will to make a fair show in the flesh,
compel you to circumcise;
only lest they suffer persecution
for the stake of the Messiah.
13 For neither they who circumcises
guard the torah;
but they will to have you circumcised,
so as to boast in your flesh.
14 So be it not that I boast,
except in the stake of our Adonay Yah Shua Messiah
— through whom the cosmos is staked to me
and also I to the cosmos.
15 For in Messiah Yah Shua
neither is circumcision of any ability
nor uncircumcision
— but a new creation.
16 And as many as march by this canon,
shalom and mercy on them
and on the Yisra El of Elohim.
17 From henceforth
belabor not to embarrass me:
for I bear in my body
the stigmas of Adonay Yah Shua.
18 Brothers,
the charism of our Adonay Yah Shua Messiah
be with your spirit.
Amen.

SALUTATION

1 *Paul* **Paulos**,
an apostle of *Jesus Christ* **Yah Shua Messiah**
by **through** the will of *God* **Elohim**,
to the *saints which are at* **holy being in** Ephesus,
and *to the faithful* **trustworthy**
in *Christ Jesus* **Messiah Yah Shua**:

2 *Grace be* **Charism** to you, and *peace* **shalom**,
from *God* **Elohim** our Father,
and *from*
the *Lord Jesus Christ* **Adonay Yah Shua Messiah**.

3 Blessed be the *God* **Elohim** and Father
of our *Lord Jesus Christ* **Adonay Yah Shua Messiah**,
who hath blessed us *with* **in** all spiritual blessings
in *heavenly places* **the heavenlies** in *Christ* **Messiah**:

4 *According* **Exactly** as he hath
chosen **selected** us in him
before **ere** the foundation of the *world* **cosmos**,
that we should be holy and *without blame* **unblemished**
before him **in his sight** in love:

5 Having *predestinated* **predetermined** us
unto *the adoption of children* **sonship**
by Jesus Christ **through Yah Shua Messiah** to himself,
according to the *good pleasure*
well—approval of his will,

6 To the *praise* **halal** of the
glory of his *grace* **charism**,
wherein he hath
made us accepted **endued us with charism**
in the beloved.

7 In whom we have redemption
through his blood,
the forgiveness of *sins* **backslidings**,
according to the riches of his *grace* **charism**;

8 Wherein
he hath *abounded toward* **superabounded unto** us
in all wisdom and *prudence* **thought**;

9 Having made known unto
us the mystery of his will,
according to his *good pleasure* **well—approval**
which he hath *purposed* **predetermined** in himself:

10 That in the *dispensation* **administration**
of the fulness /**shalom**of *times* **seasons**
he might *gather together in one* **sum up** all *things*
in *Christ* **the Messiah**,
both which are in *heaven* **the heavens**,
and which are on earth; *even* in him:

11 In whom also
we have *obtained an inheritance* **inherited**,
being *predestinated* **predetermined**
according to the *purpose* **prothesis**
of him who *worketh* **energizeth** all *things*
after the counsel of his own will:

12 *That we should be* **Unto our being**
to the *praise* **halal** of his glory,
who *first trusted* **forehoped** in *Christ* **the Messiah**.

13 In whom ye also *trusted*,
after that ye heard the word of truth,
the *gospel* **evangelism** of your salvation:
in whom also, *after that ye believed* **having trusted**,
ye were sealed
with that holy Spirit of *promise* **pre—evangelism**,

14 Which is the *earnest* **pledge** of our inheritance
until **unto** the redemption
of the *purchased possession* **acquisition**,
unto the *praise* **halal** of his glory.

THE SPIRIT OF WISDOM AND APOCALYPSE

15 *Wherefore* **So** I also, after
I heard of your *faith* **trust**
in the *Lord Jesus* **Adonay Yah Shua**,
and love unto all the *saints* **holy**,

16 *Cease* **Pause** not to *give*
thanks **eucharistize** for you,
making *mention* **rememberance** of you in my prayers;

17 That the *God* **Elohim**
of our *Lord Jesus Christ* **Adonay Yah Shua Messiah**,
the Father of glory,
may give unto you
the spirit of wisdom and *revelation* **apocalypse**
in the knowledge of him:

18 The eyes of your *understanding* **mind**
being enlightened;
that ye may know **unto knowing**
what is the hope of his calling,
and what the riches of the glory of his inheritance
in the *saints* **holy**,

SALUTATION

1 Paulos, an apostle of Yah Shua Messiah
through the will of Elohim:
To the holy in Ephesus
and trustworthy in Messiah Yah Shua:

2 Charism to you and shalom,
from Elohim our Father
and Adonay Yah Shua Messiah.

3 Blessed be the Elohim and Father
of our Adonay Yah Shua Messiah,
who blessed us in all spiritual blessings

EPHESIANS 1, 2

      in the heavenlies in Messiah:
4   exactly as he selected us in him
      ere the foundation of the cosmos,
      to be holy and unblemished in his sight in love:
5   having predetermined us to sonship
      through Yah Shua Messiah to himself,
      according to the well—approval of his will,
6   to the halal of the glory of his charism,
      wherein he charised us in the beloved:
7   in whom we have redemption through his blood
      — the forgiveness of backslidings according
      to the riches of his charism;
8   wherein he superabounds us
      in all wisdom and thought;
9   having us know the mystery of his will
      — according to his well—approval
      which he pre—determined in himself:
10   that in the administration
      of the fulness/shalom of seasons
      he sum up all in the Messiah
      — both in the heavens and on earth
      — in him:
11   in whom we also inherit,
being pre—determined according to the prothesis
      of him who energizes all
      after the counsel of his own will:
12   to our being to the halal of his glory,
      who fore—hoped in the Messiah:
13   in whom you also, having
      heard the word of truth
      — the evangelism of your salvation:
      in whom also, having trusted,
      you were sealed
      with that holy Spirit of pre—evangelism,
14   who is the pledge of our inheritance
      to the redemption of the acquisition,
      to the halal of his glory.

THE SPIRIT OF WISDOM AND APOCALYPSE

15   So I also,
      after I heard of your trust in Adonay Yah Shua
      and love to all the holy,
16   pause not to eucharistize for you,
      making remembrance of you in my prayers;
17   that the Elohim of our
      Adonay Yah Shua Messiah
      the Father of glory,
      give you the spirit of wisdom and apocalypse
      in the knowledge of him:
18   the eyes of your mind being enlightened;
      to know the hope of his calling,
      and the riches of the glory of his inheritance
      in the holy,
19   And what is the exceeding *greatness* **magnitude**
      of his *power* **dynamis**
      to us—ward **unto us** who *believe* **trust**,
      according to the *working* **energizing**
      of his mighty *power* **might**,
20   Which he *wrought* **energized**
      in *Christ* **the Messiah**,
      when he raised him from the dead,
      and *set* **sat** him *at* **at** his *own* right *hand*
      in the *heavenly places* **heavenlies**,
21   Far above
      all *principality* **hierarchies**, and *power* **authority**,
      and *might* **dynamis**, and *dominion* **lordship**,
      and every name that is named,
      not only in this *world* **eon**,
      but also in that which is to come:
22   And hath *put* **subjugated**
      all *things* under his feet,
      and gave him *to be* the head over all *things*
      to the *church* **ecclesia**,
23   Which is his body,
      the *fulness*/**shalom** of him that
      filleth/**shalameth** all in all.

SALVATION BY CHARISM THROUGH THE TRUST

2   And you *hath he quickened*,
who were *being* dead in *trespasses* **backslidings** and sins;
2   Wherein *in time past ye* **you formerly** walked
      according to the *course* **eon** of this *world*
      cosmos, according to the *prince* **arch**
      of the *power* **authority** of the air,
      the spirit that now *worketh* **energizeth**
      in the *children* **sons** of *disobedience* **distrust**:
3   Among whom also
      we all had our *conversation* **behaviour**
in times past **ever** in the *lusts* **pantings** of our flesh,
      fulfilling **doing** the *desires* **will**
      of the flesh and of the mind;
      and were by nature the children of wrath,
      even as *others* **the rest**.
4   But *God* **Elohim**, *who is* **being** rich in mercy,
      for his *great* **vast** love wherewith he loved us,
5   Even *when we were* **being**
      dead in *sins* **backslidings**,
      hath *quickened us together* **co—enlivened**
      us with *Christ* **the Messiah**,
      (by *grace* **charism** ye are saved;)

6	And hath *raised* **co—raised** us *up together*, *and made us sit together* **co—seated us** in *heavenly places* **the heavenlies** in *Christ Jesus* **Messiah Yah Shua**:	23	— his body, the fulness/shalom of him who fills full/shalams all in all.

SALVATION BY CHARISM THROUGH THE TRUST

7	That in the *ages* **eons** to come he might *shew* **indicate** the exceeding riches of his *grace* **charism** in his kindness toward us *through Christ Jesus* **in Messiah Yah Shua**.
8	For by *grace* **charism** are ye saved through *faith* **the trust**; and that not of yourselves: it is the *gift* **oblation** of *God* **Elohim**:
9	Not of works, lest any *man* **one** should boast.
10	For we are his *workmanship* **doing**, created in *Christ Jesus* **Messiah Yah Shua** unto good works, which *God* **Elohim** hath *before ordained* **previously prepared** that we should walk in them.

SHALOM THROUGH THE BLOOD OF MESSIAH

11	*Wherefore* **So** remember, that ye *being in time past* **ever** *Gentiles* **goyim** in the flesh, who are *called* **worded** Uncircumcision by that which is *called the* **worded** Circumcision in *the* flesh *made by hands* **handmade**;
12	That at that *time* **season** ye were *without Christ* **apart from Messiah**, being *aliens* **alienated** from the *commonwealth* **citizenship** of *Israel* **Yisra El**, and strangers from the covenants of *promise* **the pre—evangelism**, having no hope, and *without God* **atheist** in the *world* **cosmos**:
13	But now in *Christ Jesus* **Messiah Yah Shua**
19	and the exceeding magnitude of his dynamis to us who trust, according to the energizing of his mighty might,
20	which he energized in the Messiah when he raised him from the dead and sat him at his right in the heavenlies,
21	far above all hierarchies and authority and dynamis and lordship and every name that is named — not only in this eon but also in the coming:
22	and subjugated all under his feet and gave him head over all to the ecclesia

2	And you — being dead in backslidings and sins
2	wherein you formerly walked according to the eon of this cosmos, according to the arch of the authority of the air, the spirit that now energizes in the sons of distrust:
3	among whom also we all had our behavior ever in the pantings of our flesh, doing the will of the flesh and of the mind; and by nature being the children of wrath even as the rest:
4	and Elohim, being rich in mercy, for his vast love wherewith he loved us,
5	even being dead in backslidings, co—enlivened us with the Messiah — by charism you are saved;
6	and co—raised and co—seated us in the heavenlies in Messiah Yah Shua:
7	so that in the eons to come he indicates the exceeding riches of his charism in his kindness toward us in Messiah Yah Shua
8	— for you are saved by the charism through the trust; and that not of yourselves: it is the oblation of Elohim:
9	not of works, lest anyone boast.
10	For we are his doing, created in Messiah Yah Shua to good works, which Elohim previously prepared that we walk in them.

SHALOM THROUGH THE BLOOD OF MESSIAH

11	So remember that you, ever goyim in the flesh, who are worded, Uncircumcision by those worded, Circumcision — in the flesh — handmade;
12	that at that season you, being apart from Messiah, being alienated from the citizenship of Yisra El; strangers from the covenants of the pre—evangelism having no hope and atheist in the cosmos:
13	and now in Messiah Yah Shua ye *who sometimes were* **formerly being** far off *are made* **have become** nigh by the blood of *Christ* **the Messiah**.

EPHESIANS 2, 3

14 For he is our *peace* **shalom**,
who hath made both one,
and hath *broken down* **loosed**
the middle *wall* **hedge** of partition *between us*;
15 Having *abolished* **inactivated**
in his flesh the enmity,
even the *law* **torah** of *commandments* **misvoth**
contained in *ordinances* **dogmas**;
for to make in **that through** himself
of twain **created the two** into one new *man* **human**,
so making *peace* **shalom**;
16 And that he might *fully* reconcile
both unto *God* **Elohim**
in one body *by* **through** the *cross* **stake**,
having *slain* **slaughtered** the enmity *thereby* **therein**:
17 And came and *preached*
peace **evangelized shalom**
to you which were afar off,
and to them that were nigh.
18 For through him we both
have access *by* **in** one Spirit
unto the Father.

THE NEW HOLY NAVE

19 *So* **Now therefore**
ye are no more strangers and *foreigners* **settlers**,
but *fellowcitizens* **co—citizens** with the *saints* **holy**,
and of the household of *God* **Elohim**;
20 And are built upon the foundation
of the apostles and prophets,
Jesus Christ **Yah Shua Messiah** himself
being the chief corner *stone*;
21 In whom all the
building fitly framed together **co—joined edifice**
groweth unto an holy *temple* **nave** in *the Lord* **Adonay**:
22 In whom ye also are *builded*
together **co—settled**
for an habitation **unto a settlement** of *God* **Elohim**
through the **in** Spirit.

THE APOCALYPSE OF
THE MYSTERY OF THE ECCLESIA

3 For this cause I *Paul* **Paulos**,
the prisoner of *Jesus Christ* **Yah Shua Messiah**
for you *Gentiles* **goyim**,
2 If **indeed** ye have heard
of the *dispensation* **administration**
of the *grace* **charism** of *God* **Elohim**
which is given me *to you—ward* **unto you**:
3 How that by *revelation* **apocalypse**
he made known unto me the mystery;
(**exactly** as I *wrote afore* **preinscribed** in few words,
4 *Whereby* **Whereunto**, when ye read,
ye may *understand* **be able to comprehend**
my *knowledge* **comprehension**
in the mystery of *Christ* **the Messiah**)
5 Which in other *ages* **generations**
was not made known unto the sons of *men* **humanity**,
as it is now *revealed* **unveiled**
unto his holy apostles and prophets *by the* **in** Spirit;
6 That the *Gentiles* **goyim**
should be *fellowheirs* **co—heirs**,
and *of the same body* **co—bodied**,
and *partakers* **co—partakers** of his
promise **pre—evangelism**
in *Christ by* **the Messiah through** the *gospel* **evangelism**:
7 Whereof I *was made* **became** a minister,
according to the *gift* **gratuity**
of the *grace* **charism** of *God* **Elohim**
given unto me
by the *effectual working* **energizing**
of his *power* **dynamis**.
8 Unto me,
who am less than the least of all *saints* **the holy**,
is this *grace* **charism** given,
that I should *preach* **evangelize**
among the *Gentiles* **goyim**
the *unsearchable* **untraceable** riches
of *Christ* **the Messiah**;
9 And to *make* **enlighten** all *men* **to see**
what is the *fellowship* **communion** of the mystery,
which from the *beginning of the world* **eons**
hath been *hid* **secreted** in *God* **Elohim**,
who created all *things*
by Jesus Christ **through Yah Shua Messiah**:
— being formerly afar
you became near by the blood of the Messiah.
14 For he is our shalom — who made both one
and loosed the middle hedge of partition;
15 inactivating the enmity in his flesh,
even the torah, misvoth in dogmas;
that through himself
he created the two into one new human,
making shalom;
16 and that he fully reconciled both to Elohim
in one body through the stake,
having slaughtered the enmity therein:
17 and came and evangelized shalom
— to you who were afar off and to them who were near.
18 For through him, in one Spirit,
we both have access to the Father.

THE NEW HOLY NAVE

19 So now you are no more strangers and settlers
— but co—citizens with the holy
and of the household of Elohim;
20 built upon the foundation
of the apostles and prophets,
Yah Shua Messiah himself being the chief corner;
21 in whom all the co—joined edifice
grows to a holy nave in Adonay:
22 in whom you also are co—settled
for a settlement of Elohim in Spirit.

THE APOCALYPSE OF THE MYSTERY OF THE ECCLESIA

3 For this cause I Paulos
the prisoner of Yah Shua Messiah for you goyim,
2 if indeed you heard
of the administration of the charism of Elohim
given me regarding you:
3 how that by apocalypse
he had me know the mystery;
exactly as I pre—inscribed in few words,
4 whereto, when you read,
you can comprehend my comprehension
in the mystery of the Messiah;
5 which in other generations
was not known to the sons of humanity,
as it is now unveiled
to his holy apostles and prophets in Spirit;
6 that the goyim be co—heirs and co—bodied
and co—partakers of his pre—evangelism in
the Messiah through the evangelism:
7 whereof I became a minister,
according to the gratuity of the charism of Elohim
given me by the energizing of his dynamis:
8 to me — less than the least of all the holy
this charism is given
— to evangelize among the goyim
the untraceable riches of the Messiah;
9 and to enlighten so that all see
the communion of the mystery
— which from the eons was secreted in Elohim
who created all through Yah Shua Messiah:
10 *To the intent* **so that** now
unto the *principalities* **hierarchies**
and *powers* **authorities**
in *heavenly places* **the heavenlies**
might be known *by* **through** the *church* **ecclesia**
the *manifold* **multifarious** wisdom of *God* **Elohim**,
11 According to the *eternal*
purpose **prothesis of the eons**
which he *purposed* **made**
in *Christ Jesus* **Messiah Yah Shua** our *Lord* **Adonay**:
12 In whom we have boldness and access
with **in** confidence
by **through** the *faith* **trust** of him.
13 *Wherefore* **So** I *desire* **ask** that ye *faint* **weary** not
at my tribulations for you, which is your glory.

THE PRAYER OF PAULOS FOR LOVE

14 For this cause I bow my knees unto the Father
of our *Lord Jesus Christ* **Adonay Yah Shua Messiah**,
15 Of whom the whole *family* **patriarchy**
in *heaven* **the heavens** and earth is named,
16 That he *would grant* **should give** you,
according to the riches of his glory,
to be *strengthened* **empowered** with *might* **dynamis**
by **through** his Spirit in the inner *man* **human**;
17 That *Christ* **the Messiah**
may dwell in your hearts
by faith **through the trust**;
that ye, being rooted and *grounded* **founded** in love,
18 May be able to comprehend
with all *saints* **the holy**
what is the breadth, and length, and depth, and height;
19 And to know the love of *Christ* **the Messiah**,
which *passeth* **exceedeth** knowledge,
that ye might be filled/**shalamed**
with **unto** all the fulness/**shalom** of *God* **Elohim**.

DOXOLOGY

20 Now unto him
that is able to do *exceeding abundantly* **superabundantly**
above all that we ask or *think* **comprehend**,
according to the *power* **dynamis**
that *worketh* **energizeth** in us,
21 Unto him be glory in the *church* **ecclesia**
by *Christ Jesus* **Messiah Yah Shua**
throughout **unto** all *ages* **generations**,
world without end **eon of the eons.**
Amen.

THE UNITY OF THE SPIRIT

4 So I *therefore*, the prisoner
of the Lord **in Adonay**,
beseech you that ye walk worthy
of the *vocation* **calling** wherewith ye are called,
2 With all *lowliness*
humblemindedness and meekness,

EPHESIANS 4

     with *longsuffering* **patience**,
     forbearing **tolerating** one another in love;
3   *Endeavouring* **Diligent**
     to *keep* **guard** the unity of the Spirit
     in the bond of *peace* **shalom**.
4   *There is* one body, and one Spirit,
even **exactly** as ye are called in one hope of your calling;
5   One *Lord* **Adonay**, one *faith* **trust**, one baptism,
6   One *God* **Elohim** and Father of all,
who is above all, and through all, and in you all.

THE DESCENSION AND ASCENSION OF THE MESSIAH

7   But unto *every* **each** one of
us is given *grace* **charism**
according to the measure of the *gift* **gratuity**
of *Christ* **the Messiah**.
8   *Wherefore* **So** he *saith* **wordeth**,
When he ascended *up* on high,
he led captivity captive,
and gave gifts unto *men* **humanity**.
Psalm 68:18
9   (Now that he ascended,
what is it *but* **except** that he also descended first
into the *lower* **substrata** parts of the earth?
10   He that descended
is the same also that ascended *up* far above all heavens,
that he might *fill* **fulfill/shalam** all *things*.)

THE FOURFOLD MINISTRY

11   And he gave some **indeed**, apostles;
and some, prophets; and some, evangelists;
and some, *pastors* **shepherds** and *teachers* **doctors**;
12   For the perfecting of the *saints* **holy**,
for **unto** the work of the ministry,
for **unto** the edifying of the body of *Christ* **the Messiah**:
10   so that now
through the ecclesia
the hierarchies and authorities in the heavenlies
know the multifarious wisdom of Elohim,
11   according to the prothesis of the eons
which he made in Messiah Yah Shua our Adonay:
12   in whom we have boldness and access
in confidence through the trust of him.
13   So I ask that you weary not
at my tribulations for you, which is your glory.

THE PRAYER OF PAULOS FOR LOVE

14   For this cause I bow my knees to the Father
of our Adonay Yah Shua Messiah,
15   of whom the whole patriarchy
in the heavens and earth is named;
16   that he give you
— according to the riches of his glory
to be empowered with dynamis
through his Spirit in the inner human;
17   that through the trust
the Messiah dwell in your hearts;
that you, being rooted and founded in love,
18   can comprehend with all the holy
the breadth and length and depth and height;
19   and to know the love of the Messiah,
which exceeds knowledge, to fill you full/shalam you
to all the fulness/shalom of Elohim.

DOXOLOGY

20   And to him who is able to do superabundantly
above all we ask or comprehend,
according to the dynamis energizing in us,
21   to him be glory in the ecclesia
by Messiah Yah Shua
to all generations — eon of the eons.
Amen.

THE UNITY OF THE SPIRIT

4   So I, the prisoner in Adonay,
beseech you to walk worthily
of the calling wherewith you are called,
2   with all humblemindedness and meekness,
with patience, tolerating one another in love;
3   diligent to guard the unity of the Spirit
in the bond of shalom:
4   — one body and one Spirit,
even exactly as you are called
in one hope of your calling;
5   — one Adonay, one trust, one baptism,
6   one Elohim and Father of all,
who *is* above all and through all and in you all.

THE DESCENSION AND ASCENSION OF THE MESSIAH

7   And charism is given to each one of us
according to the measure
of the gratuity of the Messiah.
8   So he words,
Having ascended on high,
he captured the captives and gave gifts to humanity.
Psalm 68:18
9   Now that he ascended,
what is it except that he also first descended

into the substrata parts of the earth?
10 He who descended
is the same who also ascended
far above all the heavens to fulfill/shalam all.

THE FOURFOLD MINISTRY

11 And indeed, he gave some, apostles;
and some, prophets;
and some, evangelists;
and some, shepherds and doctors;
12 for the perfecting of the holy
— to the work of the ministry
— to the edifying of the body of the Messiah:
13 Till we all *come* **attain**
in **unto** the unity of the *faith* **trust**,
and of the knowledge of the Son of *God* **Elohim**,
unto a *perfect man* **man of shalom**,
unto the measure of the *stature* **maturity**
of the fulness of *Christ* **the Messiah**:
14 That we *henceforth*
be no *more children* **longer babies**,
tossed to and fro **surging**, and carried about
with every wind of doctrine,
by **in** the *sleight* **dice** of men, and *in* cunning *craftiness*,
whereby they lie in wait to deceive
with their methods of seduction;
15 But *speaking the truth* **being true** in love,
may grow up into him in all *things*, which
is the head, *even Christ* **the Messiah**:
16 From whom the whole body
fitly joined together **co—joined** and *compacted* **coalesced**
by **through** that which every joint
supplieth **contributeth**,
according to the *effectual working* **energizing**
in the measure of *every* **each single** part,
maketh *increase* **growth** of the body
unto the edifying of itself in love.

THE UNHOLY LIFE

17 *This I say therefore* **So I word**,
and *testify* **witness** in *the Lord* **Adonay**,
that ye *henceforth* walk *not* **no longer**
exactly as *other Gentiles* walk **the rest of the goyim**,
in the vanity of their mind,
18 Having the *understanding* **mind** darkened,
being alienated from the life of *God* **Elohim**
through the *ignorance* **unknowingness**
that is in them,
because of **through** the *blindness*
petrifaction of their heart:

19 Who being *past feeling* **apathetic**
have *given* **surrendered** themselves *over*
unto *lasciviousness* **lechery**,
to work **unto working** all *uncleanness* **impurity**
with greediness **in avarice**.

THE HOLY LIFE

20 But ye have not *so* **thus**
learned *Christ* **the Messiah**;
21 If *so be that* **indeed** ye have heard him,
and have been *taught by* **doctrinated in** him,
exactly as the truth is in *Jesus* **Yah Shua**:
22 That ye put off
concerning the *former conversation* **previous behaviour**
the old *man* **humanity**,
which is corrupt
according to the *deceitful lusts* **pantings of delusion**;
23 And be renewed in the spirit of your mind;
24 And that ye *put on* **endue**
the new *man* **humanity**,
which after *God* **Elohim**
is created in *righteousness* **justness**
and true *holiness* **mercy**.
25 *Wherefore* **So** putting away lying,
let each speak *every man* truth with his neighbour:
for we are members one of another.

ADMONITIONS TO THE HOLY

26 Be ye *angry* **wroth**, and sin not:
let not the sun go down upon your *wrath* **rage**:
27 Neither give place to *the devil* **Diabolos**.
28 Let him that stole steal no more:
but rather let him labour,
working with his hands *the thing* **that** which is good,
that he may have
to *give* **impart** to him that *needeth* **hath need**.
29 Let no *corrupt communication* **putrefied word**
proceed out of your mouth,
but *that which is* **if there be any** good
to the *use of* edifying **of that which is needed**,
that it may *minister grace* **give charism** unto the hearers.
30 And *grieve* **sorrow** not the
holy Spirit of *God* **Elohim**,
whereby **in whom** ye are sealed
unto the day of redemption.
31 Let all bitterness, and *wrath* **fury**, and anger,
and *clamour* **crying out**, and *evil speaking* **blasphemy**,
be *put* **taken** away from you, with all malice:
32 And be ye kind one to another,
tenderhearted **tenderspleened**,

13 until we all attain to the unity of the trust
and the knowledge of the Son of Elohim
to a man of shalom;
to the measure of the maturity
of the fulness/shalom of the Messiah:
14 that we no longer be babies
surging and carried about with every wind of doctrine
in the dice of men and in cunning
with their methods of seduction;
15 but being true in love, grow up in him in all,
who is the head, the Messiah:
16 from whom the whole body
co—joined and coalesced
through what every joint contributes,
according to the energizing
in the measure of each single part,
makes growth of the body to edify itself in love.

THE UNHOLY LIFE

17 So I word this, and witness in Adonay,
to no longer walk exactly as the rest of the goyim
in the vanity of their mind;
18 darkened in mind
— alienated from the life of Elohim
through the unknowingness in them
through the petrifaction of their heart:
19 who being apathetic
surrender themselves to lechery;
working all impurity in avarice.

THE HOLY LIFE

20 And you learned not the Messiah thus;
21 if indeed you hear him
and being doctrinated in him
exactly as the truth is in Yah Shua:
22 that concerning your previous behavior
you put off the old humanity,
which according to the pantings of delusion
is corrupt;
23 and renew the spirit of your mind;
24 and endue the new humanity as to Elohim
— created in justness and true mercy.
25 So put away lying
— each speaking truth with your neighbour:
for we are members of one another.

ADMONITIONS TO THE HOLY

26 Be wroth and sin not:
neither have the sun go down upon your rage:
27 nor give place to Diabolos.

28 Whoever stole, steal no more:
but rather labor,
working good with the hands,
so as to impart to him who needs.
29 Have no putrefied word
proceed from your mouth;
but if there be any good to the edifying of what is needed
that it give charism to the hearers.
30 And sorrow not the holy Spirit of Elohim,
in whom you are sealed to the day of redemption.
31 Take from you all bitterness and fury and anger
and crying out and blasphemy with all malice:
32 and be kind one to another,
tenderspleened,
forgiving one another **granting charism to yourselves**,
even **exactly** as *God for Christ's sake* **Elohim in Messiah**
hath *forgiven* **granted charism to** you.

WALKING HOLY

5 **So** Be ye *therefore followers*
mimickers of *God* **Elohim**,
as *dear* **beloved** children;
2 And walk in love,
exactly as *Christ* **Messiah** also hath loved us,
and hath *given* **surrendered** himself for us
an offering and a sacrifice to *God* **Elohim**
for **unto** a
sweetsmelling savour **well—fragranced fragrance**.
3 But *fornication* **whoredom**,
and all *uncleanness* **impurity**, or *covetousness* **avarice**,
let it not **no way** be *once* named among you,
exactly as *becometh saints* **befitteth the holy**;
4 Neither *filthiness* **shamefulness**,
nor *foolish talking* **morology**, nor *jesting* **repartee**,
which are not *convenient* **proper**:
but rather *giving of thanks* **eucharistize**.
5 For this ye know,
that no whoremonger, nor *unclean* **impure** person,
nor *covetous man* **avaricious**, who is an idolater, hath
any inheritance in the *kingdom* **sovereigndom**
of *Christ* **the Messiah** and of *God* **Elohim**.
6 Let no *man deceive one*
delude you with vain words:
for *because of* **through** these *things*
cometh the wrath of *God* **Elohim**
upon the *children* **sons** of *disobedience* **distrust**.
7 **So** Be not ye *therefore*
partakers with them **co—partakers**.
8 For ye were *sometimes* **formerly** darkness,
but now are *ye* light in *the Lord* **Adonay**:

EPHESIANS 5

walk as children of light:
9 (For the fruit of the Spirit is in all goodness
and *righteousness* **justness** and truth;)
10 Proving what is *acceptable* **well—pleasing**
unto *the Lord* **Adonay**.
11 And *have no fellowship* **co—partake not**
with the unfruitful works of darkness,
but rather reprove them.
12 For it is a shame even to
speak **word** of those *things*
which *are done of* **become by** them in secret.
13 But all *things* that are reproved
are *made* manifest by the light:
for whatsoever doth *make* manifest is light.
14 *Wherefore* **So** he *saith* **wordeth**,
Awake **Arise** thou that sleepest, and arise from the dead,
and *Christ* **the Messiah** shall *give* **illuminate**
thee *light*. Yesha Yah 60:1,2
15 See then *that* **how precisely**
ye walk *circumspectly*,
not as *fools* **unwise**, but as wise,
16 *Redeeming* **Marketing** the *time* **season**,
because the days are evil.
17 *Wherefore* **So** be ye not *unwise* **thoughtless**,
but *understanding* **comprehending** what
the will of *the Lord* **Adonay** is.
18 And be not *drunk* **intoxicated** with wine,
wherein is *excess* **dissipation**;
but be *filled with the* **shalamed in** Spirit;
19 Speaking to yourselves in psalms and hymns
and spiritual *songs* **odes**,
singing and *making melody* **psalming** in your heart
to *the Lord* **Adonay**;
20 *Giving thanks* **Eucharistizing**
always for all *things*
unto *God* **Elohim** and the Father in the name
of our *Lord Jesus Christ* **Adonay Yah Shua Messiah**;
21 *Submitting* **Subjugate** yourselves one to another
in the *fear* **awe** of *God* **Elohim**.

SUBJUGATING

22 *Wives* **Women**,
submit **subjugate** yourselves unto
your own *husbands* **men**,
as unto *the Lord* **Adonay**.
23 For the *husband* **man** is the
head of the *wife* **woman**,
even *exactly* as *Christ* **the Messiah**
is the head of the *church* **ecclesia**: and
he is the saviour of the body.

granting charism to yourselves,
even exactly as Elohim in Messiah
grants you charism.

WALKING HOLY

5 So as beloved children,
be mimickers of Elohim;
2 and walk in love,
exactly as Messiah also loved us
and surrendered himself for us
— an offering and a sacrifice to Elohim
to a well—fragranced fragrance.
3 And whoredom and all impurity or avarice
— never no way name it among you
exactly as befits the holy;
4 neither shamefulness
nor morology
nor repartee
which are not proper:
but rather eucharistize.
5 For you know this,
that every whoremonger or impure person
or avaricious who is an idolater,
has no inheritance
in the sovereigndom of the Messiah and of Elohim.
6 Be not deluded with vain words:
for through these
the wrath of Elohim comes upon the sons of distrust.
7 So be not co—partakers.
8 For formerly you were darkness
and now light in Adonay:
walk as children of light:
9 for the fruit of the Spirit is in all goodness
and justness and truth;
10 proving what is well—pleasing to Adonay.
11 And co—partake not
with the unfruitful works of darkness
— but rather reprove them.
12 For it is a shame even to word of those
which become by them in secret.
13 And all who are reproved are manifested by
the light: for whatever manifests is light.
14 So he words,
Rise you who sleep, and rise from the dead; and
the Messiah illuminates you. Yesha Yah 60:1,2
15 So see that you walk precisely
— not as unwise, but as wise,
16 marketing the season because the days are evil.
17 So be not thoughtless,
but comprehend the will of Adonay.

EPHESIANS 5, 6

18 And be not intoxicated with wine
wherein is dissipation;
but be filled full/shalamed in Spirit;
19 speaking to yourselves in psalms and hymns
and spiritual odes,
singing and psalming in your heart to Adonay;
20 eucharistizing always for
all to Elohim and Father
in the name of our Adonay Yah Shua Messiah;
21 subjugating yourselves to one another
in the awe of Elohim.

Subjugating

22 Women,
subjugate yourselves to your own men as to Adonay.
23 For the man is the head of the woman,
exactly as the Messiah is the head of the ecclesia;
and he is the saviour of the body:
24 *Therefore* **Rather**,
exactly as the *church* **ecclesia**
is *subject* **subjugated** unto *Christ* **the Messiah**,
so let the wives be **even thus the women**
to their own *husbands* **men** in *every thing* **all**.
25 *Husbands* **Men**,
love your *wives* **women**,
even **exactly** as *Christ* **the Messiah**
also loved the *church* **ecclesia**,
and *gave* **surrendered** himself for it;
26 That he might *sanctify*
hallow and *cleanse* **purify** it
with the *washing* **bathing** of water *by* **in** the *word* **rhema**,
27 That he might present it to himself
a glorious *church* **ecclesia**,
not having *spot* **stain**, or wrinkle, or any such *thing*;
but that it should be holy
and *without blemish* **unblemished**.
28 So *ought* **Thus** men *are* **indebted**
to love their *wives* **women** as their own bodies.
He that loveth his *wife* **woman** loveth himself.
29 For no *man* **one** ever yet hated his own flesh;
but *nourisheth* **nurtureth** and cherisheth it,
even **exactly** as *the Lord* **Adonay** the *church* **ecclesia**:
30 For we are members of his body,
of his flesh, and of his bones.
31 For this cause
shall a *man* **human** leave his father and mother,
and shall *be joined* **adhere** unto his *wife* **woman**,
and they two shall be **into** one flesh.
32 This is a *great* **mega** mystery:
but I *speak* **word**
concerning *Christ* **as to Messiah** and the *church* **ecclesia**.

33 *Nevertheless* **Moreover**,
let *every one* **each** of you *in particular so* **one by one**
thus love his *wife* **woman** even as himself;
and the *wife* **woman** see
that she *reverence* **awe** her *husband* **man**.

6 Children,
obey your parents in *the Lord* **Adonay**:
for this is *right* **just**.
2 Honour thy father and mother;
which is the first *commandment* **misvah**
with promise **in pre—evangelism**;
3 That it may be well with thee,
and thou *mayest live long* **shall be long lived**
on the earth.
Exodus 20:12
4 And, ye fathers,
provoke **enrage** not your children *to wrath*:
but *bring* **nurture** them *up* in the *nurture* **discipline**
and admonition of *the Lord* **Adonay**.
5 Servants,
be obedient to **obey** them that are *your masters* **adonim**
according to the flesh,
with *fear* **awe** and trembling,
in *singleness* **liberality** of your heart,
as unto *Christ* **the Messiah**;
6 Not with eyeservice, as
menpleasers **humanitypleasers**;
but as the servants of *Christ* **the Messiah**,
doing the will of *God* **Elohim** from the *heart* **soul**;
7 With good will *doing service* **in servitude**,
as to *the Lord* **Adonay**, and not to *men* **humanity**:
8 Knowing that whatsoever good *thing*
any man **each** doeth,
the same shall he receive of *the Lord* **Adonay**,
whether *he be* bond **servant**, *or* free **whether liberated**.
9 And, ye *masters* **adoniym**,
do the same *things* unto them,
forbearing **leaving off** threatening:
knowing that your *Master* **Adonay**
also is in *heaven* **the heavens**;
neither is there *respect of persons* **partiality** with him.
10 Finally, my brethren,
be *strong* **dynamized** in *the Lord* **Adonay**,
and in the power of his might.

The Panoply Of Elohim

11 *Put on* **Endue** the whole
armour **panoply** of *God* **Elohim**,
that ye may be able to stand
against the *wiles* **methods** of *the devil* **Diabolos**.

24	Rather,
	exactly as the ecclesia subjugates to the Messiah,
	even thus the women to their own men in all.
25	Men,
	love your women,
	even exactly as the Messiah also loved the ecclesia
	and surrendered himself for it;
26	to hallow and purify it
	with the bathing of water in the rhema,
27	to present to himself a glorious ecclesia
	— not having stain or wrinkle or any such;
	but that it be holy and unblemished.
28	Thus the men are indebted
	to love their women as their own bodies.
	Whoever loves his woman loves himself.
29	For no one ever yet hates his own flesh;
	but nurtures and cherishes it,
	even exactly as Adonay the ecclesia:
30	for we are members of his body
	— of his flesh and of his bones.
31	For this cause
	a human leaves his father and mother
	and adheres to his woman;
	and the two become into one flesh.
32	This is a mega mystery:
	but I word as to Messiah and the ecclesia.
33	Moreover — each of you — one by one
	thus love his woman even as himself; and
	the woman see that she awes her man.
6	Children,
	obey your parents in Adonay:
	for this is just.
2	Honor your father and mother;
	which is the first misvah in pre—evangelism;
3	that it be well with you
	and you be long lived on the earth.
	Exodus 20:12
4	And you, fathers,
	enrage not your children:
	but nurture them
	in the discipline and admonition of Adonay.
5	Servants,
	obey your adonim according to the flesh
	with awe and trembling;
	in liberality of your heart as to the Messiah:
6	not with eyeservice, as humanitypleasers;
	but as the servants of the Messiah doing
	the will of Elohim from the soul;
7	with good will in servitude,
	as to Adonay, and not as to humanity:
8	knowing that whatever good each does,
	he receives the same of Adonay
	— whether servant, whether liberated.
9	And you, adoniym,
	do the same to them, leaving off threatening:
	knowing also that your Adonay
	is in the heavens;
	and there is no partiality with him.
10	Finally, my brothers,
	be dynamized in Adonay
	and in the power of his might.

THE PANOPLY OF ELOHIM

11	Endue the whole panoply of Elohim,
	to be able to stand against the methods of Diabolos.
12	For we *wrestle* **quiver** not
	against flesh and blood,
	but against *principalities* **hierarchies**,
	against *powers* **authorities**,
	against the *rulers* **cosmic powers**
	of the darkness of this *world* **eon**,
	against spiritual *wickedness* **evil**
	in *high places* **the heavenlies**.
13	*Wherefore* **So** take unto you
	the whole *armour* **panoply** of *God* **Elohim**,
	that ye may be able to withstand in the evil day,
	and having *done* **worked** all, to stand.
14	Stand therefore,
	having your loins girt about *with* **in** truth,
	and having *on* **endued**
	the breastplate of *righteousness* **justness**;
15	And your feet *shod with*
	bound in the preparation
	of the *gospel* **evangelism** of *peace* **shalom**;
16	Above all, taking the shield of *faith* **the trust**,
	wherewith **wherein** ye shall be able to quench all
	the fiery *darts* **missiles** of the *wicked* **evil**.
17	And *take* **receive** the helmet of salvation,
	and the sword of the Spirit,
	which is the *word* **rhema** of *God* **Elohim**:
18	Praying *always with* **in all seasons**
	through all prayer and *supplication*
	petition in *the* Spirit,
	and watching thereunto *with* **in** all perseverance
	and *supplication* **petition** for all *saints* **the holy**;
19	And for me,
	that *utterance* **word** may be given unto me,
	that I may **to open** my mouth *boldly* **in boldness**,
	to make known the mystery of the *gospel* **evangelism**,
20	For which I am

EPHESIANS 6, 6

an *ambassador* **a presbyter** in *bonds* **fetters**:
that therein I may *speak boldly* **be bold**,
as *I ought to* **and** speak **as I must**.
21 *But* **And so** that ye also may know my affairs,
and how I *do* **transact**,
Tychicus, a beloved brother
and *faithful* **trustworthy** minister in *the Lord* **Adonay**,
shall make known to you all *things*:
22 Whom I have sent unto you
for **unto** the same purpose,
that ye might know **about** our affairs,
and that he might *comfort* **console** your hearts.

BENEDICTION

23 *Peace* **Shalom** be to the brethren,
and love with *faith* **trust**,
from *God* **Elohim** the Father
and *the Lord Jesus Christ* **Adonay Yah Shua Messiah**.
24 *Grace* **Charism** be with all them
that love our *Lord Jesus Christ*
Adonay Yah Shua Messiah
in *sincerity* **incorruptibility**.
Amen.
12 For we quiver not against flesh and blood,
but against hierarchies,
against authorities,
against the cosmic powers of the darkness of this eon,
against spiritual evil in the heavenlies.
13 So take to yourselves
the whole panoply of Elohim,
to be able to withstand in the evil day
and having worked all, stand.
14 So stand;
gird your loins in truth
and endue the breastplate of justness:

15 and bind your feet in the preparation
of the evangelism of shalom:
16 above all, take the shield of the trust,
whereby you can quench
all the fiery missiles of the evil:
17 and receive the helmet of salvation
and the sword of the Spirit,
which is the rhema of Elohim:
18 praying in all seasons
through all prayer and petition in Spirit
and watching thereto in all perseverance
and petition for all the holy;
19 and in my behalf,
— that I be given a word
to open my mouth in boldness,
to make known the mystery of the evangelism,
20 for which I am a presbyter in fetters:
that therein I be bold and speak as I must:
21 and so that you know my affairs — you also
and how I transact,
Tychicus, a beloved brother
and trustworthy minister in Adonay,
so that you know all,
22 I send to you for this same purpose,
so that you know about our affairs
and to console your hearts.

BENEDICTION

23 Shalom to the brothers and love with trust
from Elohim the Father
and Adonay Yah Shua Messiah.
24 Charism be with all those
who love our Adonay Yah Shua Messiah
in incorruptibility.
Amen.

SALUTATION

1 Paul *Paulos* and Timotheus *Timo Theos*,
the servants of *Jesus Christ* **Yah Shua Messiah**,
to all the *saints* **holy** in *Christ Jesus* **Messiah Yah Shua**
which are at **being in** Philippi,
with the *bishops* **episcopates** and *deacons* **ministers**:

2 *Grace* **Charism** *be* unto you, and *peace* **shalom**,
from *God* **Elohim** our Father,
and *from*
the Lord *Jesus Christ* **Adonay Yah Shua Messiah**.

THE EUCHARIST OF PAULOS FOR THE HOLY

3 I *thank* **eucharistize** my *God* **Elohim**
upon every remembrance of you,

4 Always in every *prayer* **petition** of mine for you
all *making request* **petitioning** with *joy* **cheer**,

5 For your *fellowship* **communion**
in the *gospel* **evangelism**
from the first day until now;

6 *Being* confident of this *very thing*,
that he which hath begun a good work in you
will perform **complete/shalam** it
until the day of *Jesus Christ* **Yah Shua Messiah**:

7 *Even* **Exactly** as it is *meet* **just**
for me to think this of you all,
because I have you in my heart;
inasmuch as **being** both in my bonds,
and in the
defence **pleading** and *confirmation* **establishment**
of the *gospel* **evangelism**,
ye all are *partakers* **co—partakers** of my *grace* **charism**.

8 For *God* **Elohim** is my *record* **witness**,
how *greatly I long* **I yearn** after you all
in the *bowels* **spleen** of *Jesus Christ* **Yah Shua Messiah**.

9 And this I pray,
that your love may *abound* **superabound**
yet more and more
in knowledge and in all *judgment* **perception**;

10 That ye may approve *things*
those that are excellent;
that ye may be sincere and *without offence*
inoffensive *till* **unto** the day of *Christ* **Messiah**;

11 Being filled/**shalamed**
with the fruits of *righteousness* **justness**,
which are *by Jesus Christ* **through Yah Shua Messiah**,
unto the glory and *praise* **halal** of *God* **Elohim**.

LIFE IN MESSIAH

12 But I *would ye should*
understand **will that ye know**,
brethren,
that *the things which happened*
unto **those concerning** me
have *fallen out rather* **come**
unto the *furtherance* **advancement**
of the *gospel* **evangelism**;

13 So that my bonds in *Christ* **Messiah**
are *become* manifest in all the *palace* **praetorium**,
and *in* **to** all *other places* **the rest**;

14 And many of the brethren in *the Lord* **Adonay**,
waxing confident **convinced** by my bonds,
are *much more* **superabundantly** bold
to speak the word *without fear* **fearlessly**.

15 Some indeed preach *Christ* **the Messiah**
even *of* **through** envy and *strife* **contention**;
and some also *of good will* **through well—approval**:

16 The one *preach Christ*
indeed evangelizes Messiah
of contention **from rivalry**, not *sincerely* **holily**,
supposing to *add affliction* **bring**
tribulation to my bonds:

17 But the other of love, knowing that I am set
for the defence **unto the pleading**
of the *gospel* **evangelism**.

18 What *then* **indeed**?
notwithstanding **moreover**, every *way* **manner**,
whether in *pretence* **pretext**, *or whether* in truth,
Christ **Messiah** is *preached* **evangelized**;
and I therein *do rejoice* **rather cheer**,
yea, and *will rejoice* **shall cheer on**.

19 For I know that this shall turn to my salvation
through your *prayer* **petition**,
and the *supply* **contribution**
of the Spirit of *Jesus Christ* **Yah Shua Messiah**,

SALUTATION

1 Paulos and Timo Theos
— the servants of Yah Shua Messiah:
To all the holy in Messiah Yah Shua in Philippi,
with the episcopates and ministers:

2 Charism to you and shalom
from Elohim our Father
and Adonay Yah Shua Messiah.

THE EUCHARIST OF PAULOS FOR THE HOLY

3 I eucharistize my Elohim
on every remembrance of you,

4 always in my every petition for you all,
petitioning with cheer,

5 for your communion in the evangelism

	from the first day until now;
6	confident of this
	— that he who began a good work in you
	completes/shalams it
	until the day of Yah Shua Messiah:
7	exactly as it is just for me to think this of you all
	because I have you in my heart;
	being both in my bonds
	and in the pleading and establishment
	of the evangelism,
	you all are co—partakers of my charism.
8	For Elohim is my witness
	how I yearn after you all
	in the spleen of Yah Shua Messiah.
9	And this I pray:
	that your love superabound still more and more
	in knowledge and in all perception;
10	to approve what is excellent;
	to be sincere and inoffensive to the day of Messiah;
11	to be filled full/shalamed
	with the fruits of justness
	through Yah Shua Messiah
	to the glory and halal of Elohim.

Life In Messiah

12	And I will you to know, brothers,
	that those concerning me
	come to the advancement of the evangelism;
13	to manifest my bonds in Messiah
	in all the praetorium and to all the rest:
14	and many of the brothers in Adonay
	convinced by my bonds
	are superabundantly bold to speak the word fearlessly.
15	Indeed some even preach the Messiah
	through envy and contention;
	and some also through well—approval:
16	The one indeed evangelizes
	Messiah from rivalry,
	not holily,
	supposing to bring tribulation to my bonds:
17	and the other from love,
	knowing that I am set
	to the pleading of the evangelism.
18	How indeed?
	moreover in every manner!
	— whether in pretext — whether in truth
	Messiah is evangelized;
	and therein I rather cheer — and cheer on.
19	For I know that through your petition,
	this turns to my salvation
	and the contribution of the Spirit of Yah Shua Messiah,
20	According
	to my *earnest expectation* **intense anticipation**
	and *my* hope,
	that in *nothing* **naught** I shall be ashamed,
	but that *with* **in** all boldness, as always,
	thus now also
	Christ **Messiah** shall be magnified in my body,
	whether *it be by* **through** life,
	or by **whether through** death.
21	For to me to live is *Christ* **Messiah**,
	and to die is gain.
22	But if I live in *the* flesh,
	this is the fruit of my *labour* **work**:
	yet what I shall choose I *wot* **know** not.
23	For I am *in a strait betwixt* **overtaken by** two,
	having a *desire* **panting** to depart,
	and to be with *Christ* **Messiah**;
	which is *far* **rather much** better:
24	*Nevertheless* **And** to abide in the flesh
	is *more needful* **necessary** for you.
25	And having this confidence,
	I know that I shall abide and *continue*
	remain with you all
	for **unto** your *furtherance* **advancement**
	and *joy* **cheer** of *faith* **the trust**;
26	That your *rejoicing* **boasting**
	may *be more abundant* **superabound**
	in *Jesus Christ for* **Yah Shua Messiah in** me
	by **through** my coming to you again.
27	Only *let your conversation be* **citizenize**
	as *it becometh* **worthy**
	of the *gospel* **evangelism** of *Christ* **the Messiah**:
	that whether I come and see you,
	or else be **whether** absent,
	I may hear *of* **about** your affairs,
	that ye stand *fast* **firm** in one spirit, with one *mind* **soul**,
	striving together **co—striving**
	for the *faith* **trust** of the *gospel* **evangelism**;
28	And in *nothing* **naught**
	terrified by your adversaries:
	which **indeed** is to them
	an *evident token* **indication** of *perdition* **destruction**,
	but to you of salvation, and that of *God* **Elohim**.
29	For unto you *it is given* **is charism granted**
	in the behalf of *Christ* **Messiah**,
	not only to *believe* **trust** on him,
	but also to suffer for his sake;
30	Having the same *conflict* **agony**
	which **such as** ye saw in me, and now hear to be in me.

Humbling Of Self

2 So If there be *therefore* any
consolation in *Christ* **Messiah**,
if any *comfort* **consolation** of love,
if any *fellowship* **communion** of the Spirit,
if any *bowels* **spleens** and *mercies* **compassions**,

2 Fulfil/**Shalam** ye my *joy* **cheer**,
that ye be likeminded **of the same thought**,
having the same love,
being of one accord **co—souled**,
of one *mind* **thought**.

3 Let *nothing* **naught** be done
through *strife* **rivalry** or vainglory;
but in *lowliness of mind* **humblemindedness**
let each esteem other *better than* **superior to** themselves.

4 *Look* **Scope** not *every man* **each**
on **of** his own *things* **self**,
but *every man* **each** also on *the things* **those** of others.

The Self—Humbling Of Messiah

5 **Indeed** Let this *mind* **thought** be in you,
which was also in *Christ Jesus* **Messiah Yah Shua**:

6 Who, being in the form of *God* **Elohim**,
thought **deemed** it not *robbery* **usurpation**
to be equal with *God* **Elohim**:

7 But *made* **voided** himself *of no reputation*,
and took *upon him* the form of a servant,
and *was made* **became** in the likeness of *men* **humanity**:

8 And being found in *fashion* **configuration**
as a *man* **human**,
he humbled himself,
and became obedient unto death,
even the death of the *cross* **stake**.

20 according to my intense anticipation and hope,
that I be ashamed in naught,
but that in all boldness, as always,
thus now also Messiah is magnified in my body,
— whether through life
— whether through death.

21 For to me, to live *is* Messiah;
and to die is gain.

22 And if to live in flesh, this
is the fruit of my work:
still I know not what to choose.

23 For I am overtaken by two,
having a panting to depart and to be with Messiah;
which is rather much better:

24 and to abide in the flesh *is* necessary for you.

25 And confiding in this,
I know that I abide and remain with you all
to your advancement and cheer of the trust;

26 to superabound your boasting
in Yah Shua Messiah
in me
through my coming to you again.

27 Only citizenize
worthily of the evangelism of the Messiah:
— whether I come and see you — whether absent
that I hear about your affairs,
that you stand firm in one spirit, with one soul,
co—striving for the trust of the evangelism;

28 and terrify in naught of your adversaries:
which indeed is to them an indication of destruction,
but to you of salvation and of Elohim.

29 For charism is granted you in behalf of Messiah,
not only to trust on him, but also to suffer for his sake;

30 having the same agony
such as you saw in me and now hear of in me.

Humbling Of Self

2 So if there is any consolation in Messiah,
if any consolation of love,
if any communion of the Spirit,
if any spleens and compassions,
2 fulfil/shalam my cheer — of the same
thought, having the same love,
co—souled, of one thought,

3 naught through rivalry or vainglory;
but in humblemindedness
esteem each other superior to self:

4 each not scoping for ones own self,
but each also on those of others.

The Self—Humbling Of Messiah

5 Indeed have this thought in you,
which is also in Messiah Yah Shua:

6 who, being in the form of Elohim,
deemed it not usurpation to be equal with Elohim:

7 but voided himself
and took the form of a servant
and became in the likeness of humanity:

8 and being found in configuration as a human,
he humbled himself
and became obedient to death
— even the death of the stake.

The Exaltation Of Messiah

9 *Wherefore* **So**,
God **Elohim** also hath *highly* **supremely** exalted him,
and *given* **granted** him **charism**

PHILIPPIANS 2

— a name *which is* above every name:
10 That *at* **in** the name of *Jesus* **Yah Shua**
every knee should bow,
of *things in heaven* **the heavenlies**,
and *things in earth* **earthly**,
and *things under the earth* **subterranean**;
11 And that every tongue should *confess* **avow**
that *Jesus Christ* **Yah Shua Messiah** is *Lord*
Adonay, to the glory of *God* **Elohim** the Father.
Yesha Yah 45:22,23

Working Out Salvation

12 *Wherefore* **So then**, my beloved,
exactly as ye have always obeyed,
not as in my presence only,
but now much more in my *absence* **being away**,
work out your own salvation with *fear* **awe**
and trembling. Ephesians 2:8—10
13 For it is *God* **Elohim** which
worketh **energizeth** in you
both to will and to *do* **energize**
of his *good pleasure* **well—approval**.
14 Do all *things without* **apart from** murmurings
and *disputings* **reasonings**:
15 That ye may be blameless
and *harmless* **unadulterated**,
the *sons* **children** of *God* **Elohim**,
without rebuke **unblemished**,
in the midst
of a crooked and *perverse nation* **perverted generation**,
among whom ye *shine* **manifest** as
lights in the *world* **cosmos**;
16 Holding forth the word of life;
that I may rejoice **unto my boasting**
in **unto** the day of *Christ* **Messiah**,
that I have not run in vain, neither laboured in vain.
17 *Yea* **Rather**, and if I be *offered* **libated**
upon the sacrifice and service of your *faith* **trust**,
I *joy* **cheer**, and *rejoice* **co—rejoice** with you all.
18 For the same cause also do ye *joy* **cheer**,
and *rejoice with me* **co—rejoice**.

Paulos Sends Timo Theos And Epaphroditus

19 But I *trust* **hope** in the *Lord*
Jesus **Adonay Yah Shua**
to send *Timotheus shortly* **Timo Theos quickly** unto you,
that I also may be *of good comfort* **well—souled**,
when I know **about** your state.
20 For I have no *man likeminded* **one like—souled**,
who *will naturally care* **is genuinely concerned**
for **about** your state.
21 For all seek their own,
not *the things* **those**
which are *Jesus Christ's* **Yah Shua Messiah's**.
22 But ye know the proof of him,
that, as a *son* **child** with the father,
he hath served with me in the *gospel* **evangelism**.
23 **So** Him **indeed** *therefore*
I hope to send *presently* **immediately**,
so soon as **ever** I shall see
about how it *will* **shall** go with me.
24 But I *trust* **confide** in *the Lord* **Adonay**
that I also myself shall come shortly.
25 Yet I *supposed* **deemed** it necessary
to send to you Epaphroditus,
my brother, and *companion in labour* **co—worker**,
and *fellowsoldier* **co—warrior**,
but your *messenger* **apostle**,
and he that ministered to my *wants* **need**.
26 *For* **Since** he *longed* **yearned** after you all,
and was *full of heaviness* **distressed**,
because that ye had heard that he had been *sick* **frail**.
27 For indeed he was *sick nigh*
unto **frail close by** death:
but *God had mercy on* **Elohim mercied** him;
and not on him only, but on me also,
lest I should have sorrow upon sorrow.
28 **So** I sent him *therefore the more carefully* **diligently**,
so that, when ye see him again, ye may *rejoice* **cheer**,
and that I **also** may be *the less sorrowful* **ungrieving**.

The Exaltation Of Messiah

9 So Elohim also supremely exalted him
and granted him charism
— a name above every name:
10 that in the name of Yah Shua every knee bows
— of the heavenlies
and earthly
and subterranean;
11 and that every tongue avow
that Yah Shua Messiah is Adonay,
to the glory of Elohim the Father.
Yesha Yah 45:22,23

Working Out Salvation

12 So my beloved, exactly as you always obeyed,
not as in my presence only,
but now much more in my being away,
work out your own salvation with awe and trembling.

Ephesians 2:8—10

13 For it is Elohim who energizes in you
both to will and to energize his well—approval.
14 Do all apart from murmurings and reasonings:
15 that you be blameless and unadulterated
— the children of Elohim — unblemished
midst a crooked and perverted generation;
in whom you manifest as lights in the cosmos:
16 holding forth the word of life,
to boasting to the day of Messiah,
that I neither ran in vain nor labored in vain.
17 Rather, if I am libated
on the sacrifice and service of your trust,
I cheer and co—rejoice:
18 and for the same cause
you also cheer and co—rejoice with me.

Paulos Sends Timo Theos and Epaphroditus

19 And I hope in Adonay Yah Shua
to quickly send Timo Theos to you,
that I also be well—souled
when I know about your state:
20 for I have no one like—souled,
who is genuinely concerned about your state.
21 For all seek their own
— not those of Yah Shua Messiah.
22 But you know the proof of him,
who, as a child with the father,
he served with me in the evangelism.
23 So indeed, I hope to send him immediately,
as soon as ever I see how it goes with me.
24 And I confide in Adonay
that I myself also come shortly.
25 Yet I deemed it necessary
to send you Epaphroditus,
my brother and co—worker and co—warrior
— and your apostle and minister to my need.
26 Since he yearned after you all
and was distressed,
because you heard he had been frail.
27 For indeed he was frail — close by death:
but Elohim mercied him;
and not only him, but also me,
lest I have sorrow upon sorrow.
28 So I send him diligently,
so that when you see him again, you cheer
and that I also be ungrieving.
29 **So** Receive him *therefore* in the Lord **Adonay**
with all *gladness* **cheer**;

and hold such *in reputation* **honourable**:
30 Because for the work of *Christ*
Messiah he *was nigh* **approached** unto death,
not regarding **hazarding** his *life* **soul**,
to *supply* **fill full/shalam** your lack of *service* **liturgy**
toward me.

Warnings

3 Finally, my brethren, *rejoice*
cheer in the Lord **Adonay**.
To *write* **scribe** the same *things* to you,
to me indeed is not *grievous* **slothful**,
but for you it is *safe* **certain**.
2 *Beware of* **See to the** dogs,
beware of **see to the** evil workers,
beware of the concision **see to the incisors**.
3 For we are the circumcision,
which *worship God* **liturgize Elohim** in *the* spirit,
and *rejoice* **boast** in *Christ Jesus* **Messiah Yah Shua**,
and have no confidence in *the* flesh.
4 Though I might also have
confidence in the flesh.
If any other man thinketh that he hath whereof
he might *trust* **confide** in *the* flesh, I more:
5 Circumcised the eighth day,
of the *stock* **genos** of *Israel* **Yisra El**,
of the *tribe* **scion** of *Benjamin* **Ben Yamin**,
an Hebrew of the Hebrews;
as touching the *law* **torah**, a Pharisee;
6 Concerning zeal, persecuting
the *church* **ecclesia**;
touching the *righteousness* **justness**
which is in the *law* **in torah**, **become** blameless.
7 But *what things* **those that** were gain to me,
those I *counted* **deemed** loss for *Christ* **the Messiah**.
8 *Yea doubtless* **Rather yet then**,
and I *count* **deem** all *things but* loss
for the *excellency* **superiority** of the knowledge
of *Christ Jesus* **Messiah Yah Shua** my *Lord* **Adonay**:
for whom I have *suffered the loss of* **lost** all *things*,
and *do count* **deem** them
but dung **to be hound dog droppings**,
that I may *win Christ* **gain Messiah**,
9 And be found in him,
not having mine own *righteousness* **justness**,
which is of the *law* **torah**,
but that which is through *the faith* **trust**
of *Christ* **Messiah**,
the *righteousness* **justness** which is *of God* **from Elohim**
by *faith* **the trust**:

PHILIPPIANS 3

10 That I may know him,
and the *power* **dynamis** of his resurrection,
and the *fellowship* **communion** of his sufferings,
being *made conformable* **conformed** unto his death;
11 If *by any means* **somehow**
I might attain unto the resurrection of the dead.
12 Not *as though* **that** I had already *attained* **taken**,
either **or** were already *perfect* **completed/
shalamed**: but I *follow* **pursue** after,
if that I may apprehend
that for which also I am apprehended
of *Christ Jesus* **the Messiah Yah Shua**.
13 Brethren, I *count* **reckon** not
myself to have apprehended:
but this one *thing I do*,
forgetting those *things indeed* which are behind,
and reaching *forth*
unto those *things* which are *before* **ahead**,
14 I *press* **pursue** toward the *mark* **scope**
for **unto** the *prize* **umpirage** of the *high* **upper** calling
of *God* **Elohim** in *Christ Jesus* **Messiah Yah Shua**.
15 Let us therefore, as many as be *perfect* **complete**,
be **think** thus *minded*:
and if in *any thing* **aught** ye *be* **think** otherwise *minded*,
God **Elohim** shall *reveal* **unveil** even this unto you.
16 *Nevertheless* **Moreover**,
whereto we have *already* attained,
let us *walk* **march** by the same *rule* **canon**,
let us *mind* **think** the same *thing*.
17 Brethren, be *followers together*
co—mimickers of me,
and *mark* **scope out** them which walk *so* **thus**
exactly as ye have us for *an ensample* **a type**.
29 So receive him in Adonay with all cheer;
and hold such honorable:
30 for, because of the work of Messiah
he approached death, hazarding his soul,
to fill full/shalam your lack of liturgy toward me.

WARNINGS

3 Finally my brothers, cheer in Adonay.
To scribe the same to you,
to me indeed is not slothful, but for you it is certain.
2 See to the dogs;
see to the evil workers;
see to the incisors:
3 for we are the circumcision,
who liturgize Elohim in spirit
and boast in Messiah Yah Shua
and have no confidence in flesh.
4 Though I also have confidence in flesh.
If any other thinks he has whereof to confide in flesh,
I more:
5 circumcised the eighth day;
of the genos of Yisra El;
of the scion of Ben Yamin;
a Hebrew of the Hebrews:
as touching the torah, a Pharisee;
6 concerning zeal, persecuting the ecclesia;
touching the justness in torah, become blameless.
7 But what was gain to me,
I deemed loss for the Messiah.
8 Yes indeed, I still deem all loss
for the superiority of the knowledge
of Messiah Yah Shua my Adonay:
for whom I lost all
and deemed to be hound dog droppings
to gain Messiah
9 and to be found in him
— not having my own justness, of the torah,
but through trust of Messiah,
the justness of Elohim on the trust:
10 to know him
and the dynamis of his resurrection
and the communion of his sufferings
— being conformed to his death;
11 if somehow I attain to the
resurrection of the dead.
12 Not that I had already taken,
or were already completed/shalamed:
but I pursue,
that if also I apprehend
that for which also I am apprehended
of the Messiah Yah Shua.
13 Brothers, I reckon not
myself to have apprehended:
but this one:
indeed forgetting those behind
and reaching to those ahead
14 I pursue toward the scope
to the umpirage of the upper calling
of Elohim in Messiah Yah Shua.
15 So, as many as are complete/
at shalom, think thus:
and if in aught you think otherwise,
Elohim even unveils this to you.
16 Moreover, whereto we attain,
march by the same canon,
think the same.
17 Brothers, become co—mimickers of me

18	and scope them who thus walk exactly as you have us for a type. (For many walk, of whom I have *told* **worded to** you often, and now *tell* **word to** you even weeping, *that they are* the enemies of the *cross* **stake** of *Christ* **the Messiah**:	7	And the *peace* **shalom** of *God* **Elohim**, which *passeth all understanding* **surpasses the mind**, shall *keep* **garrison** your hearts and *minds* **comprehensions** *through Christ Jesus* **in Messiah Yah Shua**.
19	Whose *end* **completion/shalom** is destruction, whose *God* **elohim** is their belly, and whose glory is in their shame, who *mind* **think** earthly *things*.)	8	Finally, brethren, *whatsoever things* **as many as** are true, *whatsoever things* **as many as** are *honest* **venerate**, *whatsoever things* **as many as** are just, *whatsoever things* **as many as** are *pure* **hallowed**, *whatsoever things* **as many as** are *lovely* **friendly**, *whatsoever things* **as many as** are of good report **euphonious**; if *there be* any virtue, and if *there be* any *praise* **halal**, *think on* **reckon** these *things*.

THE CITIZENSHIP OF THE HEAVENS

20	For our *conversation* **citizenship** *is* **exists** in *heaven* **the heavens**; from whence also we *look for* **await** the Saviour, *the Lord Jesus Christ* **Adonay Yah Shua Messiah**:	9	Those *things*, which ye have both learned, and *received* **taken**, and heard, and seen in me, *do* **transact**: and the *God* **Elohim** of *peace* **shalom** shall be with you.
21	Who shall *change* **transfigure** our *vile* body **of humiliation**, that it may *be fashioned* **become conformed** *like unto his glorious* **to the** body **of his glory**, according to the *working* **energizing** whereby he is able even to *subdue* **subjugate** all *things* unto himself.		

PAULOS CHEERS IN ADONAY

		10	But I *rejoiced* **cheered** in the Lord **Adonay** greatly **magnificently**, that now *at the last* **again** your *care* **thought** of me hath *flourished again* **reflourished**; wherein ye were also *careful* **thoughtful**, but *ye lacked opportunity* **inopportune**.

CHEER IN ADONAY ALWAY

4	*Therefore* **So then**, my brethren *dearly* beloved and *longed* **yearned** for, my *joy* **cheer** and *crown* **wreath**, *so* **thus** stand *fast* **firm** in *the* Lord **Adonay**, my *dearly* beloved.	11	Not that I *speak* **word** in respect of *want* **lack**: for I have learned, in whatsoever state I am, therewith to be *content* **selfcontent**.
2	I beseech Euodias, and beseech Syntyche, that they be of the same *mind* **thought** in *the* Lord **Adonay**.	12	I know both how to *be abased* **humble**, and I know how to *abound* **superabound**:
3	And I *intreat* **ask** thee also, *true yokefellow* **genuine colleague**, *help* **uphold** those women which *laboured with me* **co—strived** in the *gospel* **evangelism**, with Clement also, and *with others* **the rest** of my *fellowlabourers* **co—workers**, whose names are in the *book* **scroll** of life.	18	For many walk, of whom I often worded to you and now word to you — even weeping, the enemies of the stake of the Messiah:
		19	whose completion/shalom is destruction, whose elohim is their belly, whose glory is in their shame, who think earthly.

THE CITIZENSHIP OF THE HEAVENS

4	*Rejoice* **Cheer** in *the* Lord **Adonay** alway: and again I say, *Rejoice* **Cheer**.	20	For our citizenship exists in the heavens; from whence also we await the Saviour Adonay Yah Shua Messiah:
5	Let your *moderation* **gentleness** be known unto all *men* **humanity**. The Lord **Adonay** is *at hand* **nigh**.	21	who transfigures our body of humiliation, to become conformed to the body of his glory, according to the energizing whereby he is able even to subjugate all to himself.
6	Be *careful* **anxious** for *nothing* **naught**; but in *every thing* **all** by prayer and *supplication* **petition** with *thanksgiving* **eucharist** let your requests be *made* known unto *God* **Elohim**.		

Cheer In Adonay Alway

4 So my brothers, beloved and yearned for,
my cheer and wreath,
thus stand firm in Adonay, beloved.
2 I beseech Euodias and beseech Syntyche
to be of the same thought in Adonay.
3 And I also ask you, genuine colleague,
uphold those women
who co—strive in the evangelism;
also with Clement
and the rest of my co—workers
whose names are in the scroll of life.
4 Cheer in Adonay alway — again I say, Cheer.
5 Have all humanity know your gentleness.
Adonay is near.
6 Be anxious for naught;
but in all by prayer and petition with eucharist
have Elohim know your requests.
7 And the shalom of Elohim
that surpasses the mind
garrisons your hearts and comprehensions
in Messiah Yah Shua.
8 Finally, brothers,
as many as are true,
as many as *are* venerate,
as many as *are* just,
as many as *are* hallowed,
as many as *are* friendly,
as many as *are* euphonious;
if any virtue and if any halal, reckon these.
9 transact both those that you
learned and took and heard and saw in me:
and the Elohim of shalom be with you.

PAULOS CHEERS IN ADONAY

10 And I cheer in Adonay magnificently,
that now again you reflourish your thought of me;
wherein you also were thoughtful, but inopportune.
11 Not that I word in respect of lack:
for I learned, in whatever state I am,
to be selfcontent.
12 I know both how to humble
and I know how to superabound:
every where and in all *things* **and in all**
I am *instructed* **initiated**
both to be *full* **filled** and to be hungry,
both to *abound* **superabound** and to *suffer need* **lack**.
13 I *can do all things* **am mighty enough**
through *Christ* **in Messiah**
which *strengtheneth* **dynamizeth** me.

14 *Notwithstanding* **Moreover** ye have well done,
that ye *did communicate* **co—partook**
with **of** my *affliction* **tribulation**.
15 Now ye Philippians know also,
that in the beginning of the *gospel* **evangelism**,
when I departed from Macedonia,
no *church communicated with* **ecclesia imparted to** me
as concerning **in the word**
of giving and *receiving* **taking**,
but **except** ye only.
16 For even in *Thessalonica* **Thessalonikee**
ye sent once and *again* **twice** unto my *necessity* **need**.
17 Not because I *desire* **seek** a gift:
but I *desire* **seek** fruit that may *abound* **superabound**
to your *account* **word**.
18 But I have all, and *abound* **superabound**:
I am *full* **fulfilled/shalamed**,
having received of Epaphroditus
the things which were sent **those** from you,
an odour of a sweet smell **a wellfragranced fragrance**,
a sacrifice acceptable, well—pleasing to *God* **Elohim**.
19 But my *God* **Elohim** shall
supply **fill full** all your need
according to his riches in glory
by Christ Jesus **in Messiah Yah Shua**.

SALUTES AND BENEDICTIONS

20 Now unto *God* **Elohim** and our Father be glory
for ever and ever **unto the eons of the eons**.
Amen.
21 Salute *every saint* **all the holy**
in *Christ Jesus* **Messiah Yah Shua**.
The brethren which are with me *greet* **salute** you.
22 All the *saints* **holy** salute you,
chiefly **especially**
they that are of *Caesar's* **the Kaisar's** household.
23 The *grace* **charism**
of our *Lord Jesus Christ* **Adonay Yah Shua Messiah**
be with you all.
Amen.
in all and in all
I am initiated both to fill and to famish;
both to superabound and to lack.
13 I am mighty enough in Messiah
who dynamizes me.
14 Moreover you do well
in co—partaking of my tribulation.
15 And you also know — you Philippians,
that in the beginning of the evangelism
when I departed from Macedonia

no ecclesia imparted to me
in the word of giving and taking
— except you only.
16 For also in Thessalonikee
you sent once and twice to my need.
17 Not that I seek a gift:
but that I seek fruit, superabounding to your word.
18 And I have all and superabound:
I am fulfilled/shalamed
— having received those from you from Epaphroditus,
a well—fragranced fragrance,
a sacrifice acceptable, well—pleasing to Elohim.
19 And my Elohim fulfills/shalams all your need
according to his riches in glory
in Messiah Yah Shua.

SALUTES AND BENEDICTIONS

20 And to Elohim, even our Father
be glory to the eons of the eons.
Amen.
21 Salute all the holy in Messiah Yah Shua:
The brothers with me salute you:
22 All the holy salute you,
especially they of the house of the Kaisar.
23 The charism of our Adonay Yah Shua Messiah
be with you all.
Amen.

COLOSSIANS 1

SALUTATION

1 *Paul* **Paulos**,
an apostle of *Jesus Christ* **Yah Shua Messiah**
by **through** the will of *God* **Elohim**,
and *Timotheus* **Timo Theos** our brother,

2 To the *saints* **holy** and
faithful **trustworthy** brethren
in *Christ* **Messiah** which are at Colosse:
Grace be **Charism** unto you, and *peace* **shalom**,
from *God* **Elohim** our Father
and *the Lord Jesus Christ* **Adonay Yah Shua Messiah**.

EUCHARIST TO ELOHIM

3 We *give thanks to God* **eucharistize Elohim**
and the Father of our
Lord Jesus Christ **Adonay Yah Shua Messiah**,
praying always for you,

4 Since we heard
of your *faith* **trust** in *Christ Jesus* **Messiah Yah Shua**,
and of the love which ye have to all the *saints* **holy**,

5 For the hope which is laid up for you
in *heaven* **the heavens**,
whereof ye heard *before* **previously**
in the word of the truth of the *gospel* **evangelism**;

6 Which is *come* **present** unto you,
exactly as it is in all the *world* **cosmos**;
and *bringeth forth* **beareth** fruit,
exactly as *it doth* also in you,
since **from** the day ye heard *of it*,
and knew the *grace* **charism** of *God* **Elohim** in truth:

7 **Exactly** As ye also learned of Epaphras
our *dear fellowservant* **beloved co—servant**,
who is for you
a *faithful* **trustworthy** minister of *Christ* **the Messiah**;

8 Who also *declared* **evidenced** unto us
your love in *the* Spirit.

PRAYER FOR KNOWLEDGE OF THE WILL OF THE MESSIAH

9 For this cause we also, *since*
from the day we heard *it*,
do **pause** not *cease* to pray for you,
and to *desire* **ask** that ye might be filled/**shalamed**
with the knowledge of his will in all wisdom
and spiritual *understanding* **comprehension**;

10 That ye might walk worthy of *the Lord* **Adonay**
unto all pleasing,
being fruitful **fruitbearing** in every good work,
and *increasing* **growing** in the
knowledge of *God* **Elohim**;

11 *Strengthened with* **Dynamized**
in all *might* **power**,
according to *his glorious* **the power of his glory**,
unto all *patience* **endurance** and *longsuffering* **patience**
with *joyfulness* **cheer**;

12 *Giving thanks* **Eucharistizing** unto the Father,
which hath *made* **enabled** us *meet*
to be partakers **impart**
of the inheritance of the *saints* **holy** in light:

13 Who hath *delivered* **rescued** us
from the *power* **authority** of darkness,
and hath *translated* **removed** us
into the *kingdom* **sovereigndom**
of *his dear* **the Son of his love**:

YAH SHUA, REDEEMER

14 In whom we have redemption
through his blood,
even the forgiveness of sins:

YAH SHUA, ICON OF ELOHIM

15 Who is the *image* **icon** of
the invisible *God* **Elohim**,
the firstborn of *every creature* **all creation**:

YAH SHUA, CREATOR

16 For *by* **in** him were all *things* created,
that are in *heaven* **the heavens**,
and that are *in* **upon the** earth,
visible and invisible,
whether *they be* thrones,
or *dominions* **whether lordships**,
or *principalities* **whether hierarchies**,
or *powers* **whether authorities**:
all *things* were created *by* **through** him,
and *for* **unto** him:

17 And he is before all *things*,
and *by* **in** him all *things* consist.

18 And he is the head of the
body, the *church* **ecclesia**:
who is the beginning, the firstborn from the dead;
that in all *things he might have* **he is** the preeminence.

SALUTATION

1 Paulos, an apostle of Yah Shua Messiah
through the will of Elohim,
and Timo Theos our brother:

2 To the holy and trustworthy
brothers in Messiah
at Colosse:

Charism to you and shalom,
from Elohim our Father
and Adonay Yah Shua Messiah.

EUCHARIST TO ELOHIM

3 We eucharistize Elohim and Father
of our Adonay Yah Shua Messiah
— always praying for you
4 since we heard of your
trust in Messiah Yah Shua
and of your love to all the holy;
5 for the hope laid up for you in the heavens
whereof you previously heard
in the word of the truth of the evangelism;
6 which is present to you
exactly as in all the cosmos;
and bears fruit exactly as also in you,
from the day you heard
and knew the charism of Elohim in truth:
7 exactly as you also learned from Epaphras
our beloved co—servant
who is a trustworthy minister of the Messiah for you;
8 who also evidenced your love in Spirit to us.

PRAYER FOR KNOWLEDGE
OF THE WILL OF THE MESSIAH

9 For this cause, we also, from the day we heard,
pause not to pray for you
— and to ask that you be filled/shalamed
with the knowledge of his will in all wisdom
and spiritual comprehension,
10 that you walk worthy of Adonay,
pleasing to all,
fruitbearing in every good work,
and growing in the knowledge of Elohim;
11 dynamized in all power
according to the power of his glory
to all endurance and patience with cheer;
12 eucharistizing to the Father
who enables us
to impart of the inheritance of the holy in light;
13 who rescued us from the authority of darkness;
and removed us
into the sovereigndom of the Son of his love:

YAH SHUA, REDEEMER

14 in whom we have redemption through his blood
— the forgiveness of sins:

YAH SHUA, ICON OF ELOHIM

15 who is the icon of the invisible Elohim,
the firstborn of all creation:

YAH SHUA, CREATOR

16 For in him all was created
— those in the heavens and those on the earth;
visible and invisible;
whether thrones
whether lordships
whether hierarchies
whether authorities
— all were created through him and to him:
17 and he preceded all, and in him all consists:
18 and he is the head of the body, the ecclesia
— the beginning — the firstborn from the dead;
so that in all he is the preeminence.
19 *For it pleased the Father that*
For in him *should* all fulness **is well—
approved to** dwell; Colossians 2:9
20 And, having *made peace* **completed/shalamed**
through the blood of his *cross* **stake**,
by **through** him to **fully** reconcile
all *things* unto himself;
by **through** him, *I say*,
whether *they be things in* upon the earth,
or things in heaven **whether in the heavens**.
21 And you,
that were sometime **being formerly** alienated
and enemies in *your* mind *by wicked* **in evil** works,
yet now hath he **fully** reconciled
22 In the body of his flesh through death,
to present you holy and *unblameable* **unblemished**
and *unreproveable* **unaccusable** in his sight:
23 If **indeed** ye *continue* **abide** in the *faith* **trust**
grounded **founded** and *settled* **grounded**,
and *be not moved away* **not transported**
from the hope of the *gospel* **evangelism**,
which ye have heard,
and which was preached *to every creature* **in all creation**
which is under heaven;
whereof I *Paul am made* **Paulos became** a minister;
24 Who now *rejoice* **cheer** in my sufferings for you,
and *fill up* **supplement** that which *is behind* **lacketh**
of the *afflictions* **tribulations** of *Christ* **the Messiah**
in my flesh
for his *body's sake* **body**, which is the *church* **ecclesia**:
25 Whereof I *am made* **became** a minister,
according

COLOSSIANS 1, 2

to the *dispensation* **administration** of *God* **Elohim**
which is given to me *for* **unto** you,
to fulfil the word of *God* **Elohim**;
26 *Even* the mystery which hath been *hid* **secreted**
from *ages* **the eons** and from **the** generations,
but now is *made* manifest to his *saints* **holy**:
27 To whom *God would* **Elohim willeth to** make known
what is the riches of the glory of this mystery among the *Gentiles* **goyim**;
which is Christ **Messiah** in you, the hope of glory:
28 Whom we *preach* **evangelize**,
warning every man **reminding all humanity**,
and *teaching every man* **doctrinating all humanity**
in all wisdom;
that we may present *every man* **all humanity**
perfect **completed/shalamed** in *Christ Jesus* **Messiah Yah Shua**:
29 Whereunto I also labour,
striving **agonizing** according to his *working* **energizing**,
which *worketh* **energizeth dynamis** in me *mightily*.

2 For I *would* **will** that ye knew
what great conflict **how much agony** I have for you,
and *for* them at Laodicea,
and *for* as many as have not seen my face in the flesh;
2 That their hearts might be *comforted* **consoled**,
being *knit together* **coalesced** in love,
and unto all riches of the full *assurance* **bearance**
of *understanding* **comprehension**,
to the *acknowledgement* **knowledge**
of the mystery of *God* **Elohim**,
and of the Father, and of *Christ* **the Messiah**;
3 In whom are *hid* **secreted**
all the treasures of wisdom and knowledge.
4 And this I *say* **word**,
lest any *man* **one** should *beguile* **delude** you
with *enticing* **in persuasive** words.
5 For though I be absent in the flesh,
yet am I with you in *the* spirit,
joying **cheering** and *beholding* **seeing** your order,
and the *stedfastness* **solidity**
of your *faith* **trust** in *Christ* **Messiah**.
6 *So* As ye have *therefore received* **taken**
Christ Jesus the Lord **the Messiah Yah Shua Adonay**,
so walk ye in him:
7 Rooted and built *up* in him,
and stablished in the *faith* **trust**,
exactly as ye have been *taught* **doctrinated**,
abounding **superabounding** therein

with *thanksgiving* **in eucharist**.
19 For in him
all fulness/shalom is well—approved to dwell;
Colossians 2:9
20 And having completed/shalamed
through the blood of his stake,
through him to fully reconcile all to himself;
through him
— whether on the earth — whether in the heavens.
21 And you,
being formerly alienated
and enemies in mind in evil works,
yet now he fully reconciles
22 in the body of his flesh through death,
to present you holy and unblemished
and unaccusable in his sight:
23 if indeed you abide in the trust
founded and grounded;
and not transported from the hope of the evangelism
which you heard,
which was preached in all creation under the heavens;
whereof I Paulos became a minister;
24 who now cheer in my sufferings for you
and supplement whatever lacks
of the tribulations of the Messiah in my flesh
for his body, the ecclesia:
25 whereof I became a minister,
according to the administration of Elohim
given to me to you
to fulfill/shalam the word of Elohim
26 — the mystery
secreted from the eons and from the generations,
but now manifested to his holy:
27 to whom Elohim wills to make known
the riches of the glory of this mystery
among the goyim
— Messiah in you, the hope of glory:
28 whom we evangelize,
reminding all humanity
and doctrinating all humanity in all wisdom;
to present all humanity
completed/shalamed in Messiah Yah Shua:
29 whereto I also labor;
agonizing according to his energizing
which energizes dynamis in me.

2 For I will you to know
how much agony I have for you and them at Laodicea
and as many as have not seen my face in the flesh;
2 that their hearts be consoled
— coalesced in love

and to all riches
of the full bearance of comprehension,
to the knowledge of the mystery of Elohim
and of the Father and of the Messiah;
3   in whom all the treasures
of wisdom and knowledge
are secreted.
4   And this I word,
lest anyone delude you in persuasive words.
5   For though I be absent in the flesh,
I am still with you in spirit,
cheering and seeing your order
and the solidity of your trust in Messiah.
6   So, as you took the Messiah Yah Shua Adonay,
walk in him:
7   root and build in him
and establish in the trust,
exactly as you were doctrinated,
superabounding therein in eucharist.
8   *Beware* **See to it** lest any
man spoil **one seduce** you
through philosophy and vain *deceit* **delusion**,
after the tradition of *men* **humanity**,
after the *rudiments* **elements** of the *world* **cosmos**,
and not after *Christ* **Messiah**.

Messiah, The Fulness/Shalom Of Deity

9   For in him
dwelleth all the fulness of *the Godhead*
Deity bodily. Colossians 1:19
10   And ye are complete/**shalamed** in him,
which is the head
of all *principality* **hierarchy** and *power* **authority**:
11   In whom also
ye are circumcised with the circumcision
made without hands **not handmade**,
in *putting off* **stripping** the body of the sins of the flesh
by **in** the circumcision of *Christ* **the Messiah**:
12   *Buried with him* **Co—buried** in baptism,
wherein also
ye are *risen with him* **co—raised** through the *faith* **trust**
of the *operation* **energizing** of *God* **Elohim**,
who hath raised him from the dead.
13   And you, being dead in your *sins* **backslidings**
and the uncircumcision of your flesh,
hath he *quickened together with him* **co—enlivened**,
having *forgiven* **granted** you **charism**
all trespasses **for all your backslidings**;

14   *Blotting* **Wiping** out
the *handwriting* **handscribing** of *ordinances* **dogmas**
that was against us,
which was *contrary* **opposed** to us,
and took it out of the *way* **midst**,
nailing **spiking** it to his *cross* **stake**;
15   And having *spoiled* **stripped**
principalities **hierarchies** and *powers* **authorities**,
he *made a shew of* **exposed** them *openly* **boldly**,
triumphing over them in it.

Warnings

16   Let no *man* **one** therefore judge you
in *meat* **food**, or in drink,
or in *respect of an holyday* **apportioning a celebration**,
or of the new moon, or of the *sabbath days* **shabbaths**:
17   Which are a shadow of *things
to come* **the about to be**;
but the body is of *Christ* **the Messiah**.
18   Let no *man beguile* **one defraud** you
of your reward in a voluntary **of doing his will**
humility **in humblemindedness**
and *worshipping* **ceremonials** of angels,
intruding into those *things* which he hath not seen,
vainly puffed up by *his fleshly* **the mind of his flesh**,
19   And not *holding* **empowering** the Head,
from which *all* **the whole** body
by **through** joints and *bands* **bonds**
having *nourishment ministered* **been supplied**,
and *knit together* **co—alesced**,
increaseth **groweth**
with the *increase* **growth** of *God* **Elohim**.
20   *Wherefore* **So then**
if ye be dead with *Christ* **the Messiah**
from the *rudiments* **elements** of the *world* **cosmos**,
why, as though living in the *world* **cosmos**,
are ye *subject to ordinances* **dogmatized**,
21   (Touch not; taste not; *handle* **finger** not;
22   Which all are to perish
with the *using* **consuming**;)
after the *commandments* **misvoth** and doctrines
of *men* **humanity**?
23   Which *things* have indeed
a *shew* **word** of wisdom
in will *worship* **ceremony**,
and *humility* **humblemindedness**,
and neglecting of the body;
not in any honour to the *satisfying*
gratifying of the flesh.

COLOSSIANS 3

THE HOLY LIFE

3 So *If ye then be* risen **co—raised** with *Christ* **the Messiah**,
seek those *things* which are above,
where *Christ* **the Messiah** sitteth
on **at** the right *hand* of *God* **Elohim**.

2 Set your *affection on things* **thought** above,
not *on things on* **upon** the earth.

8 See to it lest anyone seduce you
through philosophy and vain delusion
— after the tradition of humanity,
— after the elements of the cosmos
and not after Messiah.

MESSIAH, THE FULNESS/SHALOM OF DEITY

9 For in him
dwells all the fulness/shalom of Deity bodily.
Colossians 1:19

10 And you are fulfilled/shalamed in him,
who is the head of all hierarchy and authority:

11 in whom also
you are circumcised with the circumcision
— not handmade,
in stripping the body of the sins of the flesh
in the circumcision of the Messiah;

12 co—buried in baptism,
wherein you are also co—raised through the trust
of the energizing of Elohim,
who raised him from the dead.

13 And you, being dead in your backslidings
and the uncircumcision of your flesh
he co—enlivened,
granting you charism for all your backslidings;

14 wiping the handscribing of dogmas against us
— opposed to us
and taking it from among us, spiking it to his stake;

15 and having stripped hierarchies and authorities,
he exposed them boldly, triumphing over them in it.

WARNINGS

16 So no one is to judge you in food or in drink
or in apportioning a celebration
or of the new moon
or of the shabbaths:

17 which are a shadow of the about to be;
and the body *is* of the Messiah.

18 Be not defrauded
of doing his will in humblemindedness
and ceremonials of angels,
by intruding into the not seen,
vainly puffed up by the mind of his flesh,

19 and not empowering the Head,
from which the whole body through joints and bonds
being supplied and co—alescesd
growing with the growth of Elohim.

20 So if you die with the Messiah
from the elements of the cosmos,
why, as though living in the cosmos,
are you dogmatized

21 — touch not,
taste not,
finger not

22 — which all destruct with the consuming
after the misvoth and doctrines of humanity?

23 Which indeed have a word of wisdom
in will ceremony
and humblemindedness and neglecting of the body
— not in any honor to the gratifying of the flesh.

THE HOLY LIFE

3 So if you co—raised with the Messiah,
seek those which are above,
where the Messiah sits at the right of Elohim.

2 Set your thought above — not on the earth.

3 For *ye are dead* **died**,
and your life is *hid* **secreted** with *Christ* **the Messiah**
in *God* **Elohim**.

4 When *Christ* **ever the Messiah**, *who is* our life,
shall *appear* **be manifested**,
then shall ye also *appear* **be manifested**
with him in glory.

STRIPPING THE OLD HUMANITY

5 *Mortify therefore* **So deaden**
your members which are upon the earth;
fornication **whoredom**, *uncleanness* **impurity**,
inordinate affection **passion**, evil *concupiscence* **panting**,
and *covetousness* **avarice**, which is idolatry:

6 *For* **Through** which *things' sake*
the wrath of *God* **Elohim**
cometh on the *children* **sons** of *disobedience* **distrust**:

7 In the which ye also walked *some time* **formerly**,
when ye lived in them.

8 But now ye also put off all these;
anger **wrath**, *wrath* **fury**, malice, blasphemy,
filthy communication **shameful
words** out of your mouth.

9 Lie not one to another,
seeing that ye have
put off **stripped** the old *man* **humanity**

	with his *deeds* **functions**;
10	And have *put on* **endued** the new *man*,
	which is renewed in knowledge
	after the *image* **icon** of him that created him:
11	Where there is neither
	Greek **Hellene** nor *Jew* **Yah Hudiy**,
	circumcision nor uncircumcision, Barbarian, Scythian,
	bond **servant** nor *free* **liberated**:
	but *Christ* **Messiah** is all, and in all.

ENDUING THE NEW HUMANITY

12	*Put on therefore* **So endue**,
	as the *elect* **select** of *God* **Elohim**, holy and beloved,
	bowels **spleens** of *mercies* **compassions**, kindness,
	humbleness of mind **humblemindedness**,
	meekness, *longsuffering* **patience**;
13	*Forbearing* **Tolerating** one another,
	and *forgiving* **granting** one another **charism**,
	if **whenever** any *man* **one** have *a*
	quarrel **blame** against any:
	even **exactly** as *Christ* **the Messiah**
	forgave you **hath granted you charism**,
	so **thus** also *do* ye.
14	And above all these, *things put on charity* **love**,
	which is the bond of *perfectness* **completion/shalom**.
15	And let the *peace* **shalom** of *God* **Elohim**
	rule **umpire** in your hearts,
	to the which also ye are called in one body;
	and be ye *thankful* **eucharistic**.
16	Let the word of *Christ* **the Messiah**
	dwell in **indwell** you richly in all wisdom;
	teaching **doctrinating** and *admonishing* **reminding**
	one another **yourselves**
	in psalms and hymns and spiritual *songs* **odes**,
	singing *with grace* **in charism** in your hearts
	to *the Lord* **Adonay**.
17	And whatsoever ye **ever** do
	in word or *deed* **in work**,
	do all in the name of *the Lord Jesus* **Adonay Yah Shua**,
	giving thanks **eucharistizing**
	to *God* **Elohim** and the Father *by* **through** him.
18	*Wives* **Women**,
	submit **subjugate** yourselves
	unto your own *husbands* **men**,
	as *it is fit* **proper** in *the Lord* **Adonay**.
19	*Husbands* **Men**,
	love *your wives* **the women**,
	and be not *bitter* **embittered** against them.
20	Children,
	obey *your* **the** parents in all *things*:
	for this is well pleasing unto the *Lord* **Adonay**.
21	Fathers,
	provoke **excite** not your children *to anger*,
	lest they be *discouraged* **apathetic**.
22	Servants,
	obey in all *things*
	your *masters* **adoniym** according to *the* flesh;
3	For you died
	and your life is secreted with the Messiah in Elohim.
4	Whenever the Messiah, our life, manifests,
	then you also manifest with him in glory.

STRIPPING THE OLD HUMANITY

5	So deaden your members on the earth:
	whoredom,
	impurity,
	passion,
	evil panting,
	and avarice — which is idolatry:
6	through which
	the wrath of Elohim comes on the sons of distrust:
7	in which you also formerly walked
	when you lived therein.
8	But now, even you, put all
	these from your mouth;
	wrath,
	fury,
	malice,
	blasphemy,
	shameful words.
9	Lie not one to another
	— seeing that you stripped the old humanity
	with his functions;
10	and endued the new,
	renewed in knowledge
	after the icon of him who created him:
11	where there is neither Hellene nor Yah Hudiy,
	circumcision nor uncircumcision,
	Barbarian, Scythian, servant, liberated:
	— but Messiah is all and in all.

ENDUING THE NEW HUMANITY

12	So endue,
	as the select of Elohim, holy and beloved,
	spleens of compassions,
	kindness,
	humblemindedness,
	meekness,
	patience;
13	tolerate one another

COLOSSIANS 3, 4

and grant one another charism;
whenever anyone has a blame against any:
even exactly as the Messiah grants you charism
thus also you.

14 And above all these, love,
which is the bond of completion/shalom.

15 And the shalom of Elohim
umpire in your hearts,
to which you are also called in one body;
and be eucharistic;

16 that the word of the Messiah
indwell you richly in all wisdom;
doctrinating and reminding yourselves
in psalms and hymns and spiritual odes,
singing in charism in your hearts to Adonay.

17 And whatever you ever do in word or in work,
do all in the name of Adonay Yah Shua,
eucharistizing to Elohim and the Father through him.

18 Women,
subjugate yourselves to your own men
as proper in Adonay.

19 Men,
love your women
and embitter not against them.

20 Children,
obey your parents in all
— for this is well—pleasing to Yah Veh.

21 Fathers,
excite not your children
lest they become apathetic.

22 Servants,
obey your adoniym according to flesh in all;
not *with* **in** eyeservice, as *menpleasers*
humanitypleasers;
but in *singleness* **liberality** of heart,
fearing God **awing Elohim**:

23 And whatsoever ye do,
do it heartily **work from the soul**, as to *the Lord* **Adonay**,
and not unto *men* **humanity**;

24 Knowing that of *the Lord* **Adonay**
ye shall *receive* **take** the *reward* **recompense**
of the inheritance:
for ye serve *the Lord Christ* **Adonay Messiah**.

25 But he that *doeth wrong* **injureth**
shall receive for the *wrong* **injury**
which he hath done:

and there is no *respect of persons* **partiality**.

4 *Masters* **Adoniym**,
give **present** unto *your* servants
that which is just and equal;

knowing that
ye also have *a Master Lord* **an Adonay**
in *heaven* **the heavens**.

2 Continue in prayer,
and watch in the same *with thanksgiving* **in eucharist**;

3 *Withal* **Simultaneously** praying also for us,
that *God would* **Elohim should** open unto us
a door **an opening/a portal** of *utterance* **the word**,
to speak the mystery of *Christ* **the Messiah**,
for which I am also in bonds:

4 That I may *make it* manifest,
as I *ought to* **must** speak.

5 Walk in wisdom toward them that are without,
redeeming **marketing** the *time* **season**.

6 Let your *speech* **word** be
alway *with grace* **in charism**,
seasoned with salt,
that ye may know
how ye *ought to* **must** answer *every man* **each one**.

FINAL SALUTES

7 All my state
shall Tychicus *declare* **maketh known** unto you,
who is a beloved brother,
and a *faithful* **trustworthy** minister
and *fellowservant* **co—servant** in *the Lord* **Adonay**:

8 Whom I have sent unto you
for **unto** the same *purpose*,
that he might know *about* your estate,
and *comfort* **console** your hearts;

9 With Onesimus,
a *faithful* **trustworthy** and beloved brother,
who is *one* of you.
They shall make known unto you
all *things* which are *done* here.

10 Aristarchus my *fellowprisoner*
co—captive saluteth you,
and *Marcus* **Markos**,
sister's son **cousin** to *Barnabas* **Bar Nabi**,
(*touching* **about** whom
ye *received commandments* **took misvoth**: *if*
whenever he come unto you, receive him;)

11 And *Jesus* **Yah Shua**, which
is *called* **worded** Justus,
who are **being** of the circumcision.
These only are my *fellowworkers* **co—workers**
unto the *kingdom* **sovereigndom** of *God* **Elohim**,
which have *been* **become**
a *comfort* **consolation** unto me.

12 Epaphras, who is *one* of you,

a servant of *Christ* **Messiah**, saluteth you,
always *labouring fervently* **agonizing** for you in prayers,
that ye may stand *perfect* **complete/in shalom**
and *complete* **fulfilled/shalamed**
in all the will of *God* **Elohim**.

13 For I *bear* **witness of** him *record*,
that he hath a *great* **vast** zeal for you,
and them *that are* in Laodicea, and them in Hierapolis.

14 *Luke* **Loukas**, the beloved *physician* **healer**,
and Demas, *greet* **salute** you.

15 Salute the brethren which are in Laodicea,
and Nymphas,
and the *church* **ecclesia** which is in his house.

16 And when **ever** this epistle is read among you,
cause that it be read also
in the *church* **ecclesia** of the Laodiceans;
and that ye likewise read *the epistle* **that** from Laodicea.
not in eyeservice, as humanitypleasers; but
in liberality of heart, awing Elohim:

23 and whatever you do, work from the soul,
as to Adonay — and not as to humanity;

24 knowing that of Adonay
you take the recompense of the inheritance:
for you serve Adonay Messiah.

25 And whoever injures, receives for the injury:
and there is no partiality.

4 Adoniym,
present your servants with what is just and equal;
knowing also that you have an Adonay in the heavens.

2 Continue in prayer
and watch in the same in eucharist;

3 also praying simultaneously for us,
that Elohim open an opening/a portal of the word
to speak the mystery of the Messiah;
for whom I am also in bonds:

4 to manifest as I must speak.

5 Walk in wisdom toward those outside,
marketing the season

6 — your word always in
charism seasoned with salt,
so that you know how you must answer each one.

FINAL SALUTES

7 Tychicus, a beloved brother
and a trustworthy minister
and co—servant in Adonay
has you know all my state:

8 whom I send to you to the same,
to know about your estate and console your hearts:

9 with Onesimus,
a trustworthy and beloved brother, who is *one* of you.
They have you know all that are here.

10 Aristarchus my co—captive salutes you
and Markos, cousin to Bar Nabi
— about whom you took misvoth;
whenever he comes to you, receive him:

11 and Yah Shua who is worded Justus,
being of circumcision;
these only are my co—workers
to the sovereigndom of Elohim
who became my consolation.

12 Epaphras, who is *one* of you,
a servant of Messiah, salutes you
— always agonizing for you in prayers,
that you stand complete/in shalom
— fulfilled/shalamed in all the will of Elohim.

13 For I witness of him,
that he has a vast zeal for you
and them in Laodicea and them in Hierapolis.

14 Loukas the beloved healer
and Demas salute you.

15 Salute the brothers in Laodicea and Nymphas
and the ecclesia in his house.

16 And whenever this epistle is read among you,
also have it read in the ecclesia of the Laodiceans;
and that you likewise read that from Laodicea.

17 And say to Archippus, Take
heed **See** to the ministry
which thou hast *received* **taken** in *the Lord* **Adonay**,
that thou fulfil/**shalam** it.

18 The salutation by the hand of me *Paul* **Paulos**.
Remember my bonds.
Grace Charism be with you.
Amen.

17 And say to Archippus,
See to the ministry you took in Adonay,
to fulfil/shalam it.

18 The salutation by my hand — Paulos.
Remember my bonds.
Charism be with you.
Amen.

1 THESSALONIANS 1, 2

SALUTATION

1 Paul *Paulos*, and Silvanus,
and *Timotheus* **Timo Theos**,
unto the *church* **ecclesia**
of *the Thessalonians* **Thessalonikeus**
which is in *God the* **in Elohim** Father
and *in the Lord Jesus Christ* **Adonay Yah Shua Messiah**:
Grace be **Charism** unto you, and *peace* **shalom**,
from *God* **Elohim** our Father,
and *the Lord Jesus Christ* **Adonay Yah Shua Messiah**.

THE EUCHARIST OF PAULOS

2 We *give thanks* **eucharistize** to *God* **Elohim**
always for you all,
making *mention* **rememberance** of you in our prayers;

3 Remembering *without ceasing* **unceasingly**
your work of *faith* **trust**,
and labour of love, and *patience* **endurance** of hope
in our *Lord Jesus Christ* **Adonay Yah Shua Messiah**,
in *the sight* **front** of *God* **Elohim** and our Father;

4 Knowing, brethren beloved,
your *election of God* **selection by Elohim**.

5 For our *gospel came* **evangelism**
became not unto you
in word only,
but also in *power* **dynamis**, and in *the*
Holy Spirit **Ruach ha-kodesh**,
and in much *assurance* **fullbearance**;
exactly as ye know what manner of men
we *were* **became** among you for your sake.

6 And ye became *followers* **mimickers** of us,
and of *the Lord* **Adonay**,
having received the word in much *affliction* **tribulation**,
with *joy* **cheer** of *the* Holy Spirit **Ruach ha-kodesh**.

7 So that ye *were ensamples* **became types**
to all that *believe* **trust** in Macedonia and Achaia.

8 For from you *sounded out* **echoed forth**
the word of *the Lord* **Adonay**
not only in Macedonia and Achaia,
but also in every place
your *faith to God-ward* **trust toward Elohim**
is *spread abroad* **gone**;
so that we need not to speak *any thing* **aught**.

9 For they themselves *shew* **evangelize** of us
what manner of *entering in* **entrance** we had unto you,
and how ye turned to *God* **Elohim** from idols
to serve the living and true *God* **Elohim**;

10 And to *wait for* **await** his Son
from *heaven* **the heavens**,
whom he raised from the dead, *even Jesus* **Yah Shua**,
which *delivered* **rescued** us from the wrath to come.

THE MINISTRY OF THESSALONIKEUS

2 For yourselves, brethren,
know our entrance in unto you,
that it *was* **became** not in vain:

2 But even after that we had
suffered *before* **previously**,
and were *shamefully entreated* **insulted**,
exactly as ye know, at Philippi,
we were bold in our *God* **Elohim** to speak unto you
the *gospel* **evangelism** of *God* **Elohim**
with **in** much *contention* **agony**.

3 For our *exhortation* **consolation**
was not of *deceit* **seduction**,
nor of *uncleanness* **impurity**, nor in *guile* **deceit**:

4 But **exactly** as we were *allowed*
proofed of *God* **Elohim**
to be *put in trust* **entrusted** with the *gospel* **evangelism**,
even so **thus** we speak;
not as pleasing *men* **humanity**,
but *God* **Elohim**, which *trieth* **prooveth** our hearts.

5 For *neither at any time* **never ever**
used **became** we *flattering* **in fawning** words,
exactly as ye know,
nor *in* a *cloke* **pretext** of *covetousness* **avarice**;
God is witness **Elohim witnesseth**:

6 Nor of *men* **humanity** sought we glory,
neither of you, nor *yet* of others,
when we *might* **could** have been burdensome,
as the apostles of *Christ* **Messiah**.

7 But we *were* **became** gentle among you,
even as a nurse *ever* cherisheth her children:

8 *So being affectionately desirous*
Thus yearning of you,
we *were willing* **well—approved**
to have imparted unto you,

SALUTATION

1 Paulos and Silvanus and Timo Theos:
To the ecclesia of Thessalonikeus
in Elohim Father
and Adonay Yah Shua Messiah:
Charism to you and shalom,
from Elohim our Father
and Adonay Yah Shua Messiah.

THE EUCHARIST OF PAULOS

2 We always eucharistize to Elohim for you all

making remembrance of you in our prayers;
3 unceasingly remembering your work of trust
and labor of love and endurance of hope
in our Adonay Yah Shua Messiah
in front of Elohim and our Father,
4 beloved brothers,
knowing your selection by Elohim.
5 For our evangelism to you is not only in word,
but also in dynamis and in Holy Spirit
and in much fullbearance;
exactly as you know
what manner of men we became among you
for your sake:
6 and you became mimickers of us and of Adonay,
receiving the word in much tribulation,
with cheer of Holy Spirit:
7 so that you became types to all who trust
in Macedonia and Achaia:
8 for the word of Adonay echoes from you
— not only in Macedonia and Achaia
but also in every place
your trust toward Elohim goes;
so that we need not speak aught.
9 For they themselves evangelize of us
what manner of entrance we had to you;
and how you turned from idols to Elohim
to serve the living and true Elohim;
10 and to await his Son from the heavens
— Yah Shua — whom he raised from the dead
who rescued us from the wrath to come.

The Ministry Of Thessalonikeus

2 For brothers,
you yourselves know our entrance to you,
that it became not in vain:
2 but even after we previously suffered
and were insulted at Philippi
— exactly as you know
we were bold in our Elohim to speak to you
the evangelism of Elohim in much agony.
3 For our consolation was neither of seduction,
nor of impurity, nor in deceit:
4 but exactly as we were proofed of Elohim
to be entrusted with the evangelism,
thus we speak;
not as pleasing humanity
but Elohim who proofs our hearts.
5 For we never ever became in fawning words
exactly as you know;
nor in a pretext of avarice;

as Elohim witnesses:
6 we sought glory
neither of humanity, nor of you, nor of others,
when as the apostles of Messiah
we could have been burdensome.
7 But we became gentle among you,
even as a nurse ever cherishes her children:
8 thus yearning over you,
we well—approved to impart to you
not the *gospel* **evangelism** of *God* **Elohim** only,
but also our own souls,
because ye *were dear* **became beloved** unto us.
9 For ye remember, brethren,
our labour and *travail* **toil**:
for *labouring* **working** night and day,
because **that** we *would* **should** not
be chargeable unto **overburden** any of you,
we preached unto you
the *gospel* **evangelism** of *God* **Elohim**.
10 Ye are witnesses, and *God* **Elohim** also,
how *holily* **mercifully** and justly and unblameably
we *behaved ourselves* **became** among
you that *believe* **trust**:
11 **Exactly** As ye know
how we *exhorted* **besought** and *comforted* **consoled**,
and *charged every* **witnessed each** one of you,
as a father *doth* his children,
12 That ye *would* **should witness**
to walk worthy of *God* **Elohim**,
who hath called you
unto his *kingdom* **sovereigndom** and glory.
13 For this cause also *thank*
eucharistize we *God* **Elohim**
without ceasing **unceasingly**,
because, when ye *received* **took** the word of *God* **Elohim**
which ye heard of us,
ye received it not as the word of *men* **humanity**,
but **exactly** as it *truly* is *in truth*,
the word of *God* **Elohim**,
which *effectually worketh* **energizeth** also in you
that *believe* **trust**.
14 For ye, brethren, became *followers* **mimickers**
of the *churches* **ecclesiae** of *God* **Elohim**
which **being** in *Judaea* **Yah Hudah**
are in Christ Jesus **being in Messiah Yah Shua**:
for ye also have suffered **in** like **manner** *things*
of **by** your own *countrymen* **co—scions**,
even **exactly** as they have of the *Jews* **Yah Hudiym**:
15 Who both *killed* **slaughtered**

          the Lord Jesus **Adonay Yah Shua**,
          and their own prophets,
          and have persecuted us;
          and they please not *God* **Elohim**,
          and are contrary to all *men* **humanity**:
16   Forbidding us to speak to the *Gentiles* **goyim**
          that they might be saved,
to *fill up* **fill full/shalam** their sins alway:
for the wrath *is come* **arrived** upon them
to *the uttermost* **completion/shalom**.
17   But we, brethren,
being *taken* **orphaned away** from *you* **your face**
for a *short time in presence* **season of an hour**,
          not in heart,
      endeavoured the more abundantly
      being more superabundantly diligent
to see your face *with great desire* **in much panting**.
18   *Wherefore* **So**
we *would have* **had willed to** come unto you,
          even **indeed** I *Paul* **Paulos**,
once and *again* **twice**; but Satan hindered us.
19   For what is our hope, or *joy* **cheer**,
      or *crown* **wreath** of *rejoicing* **boasting**?
Are **Or** not *indeed* even ye in *the presence* **front**
of our *Lord Jesus Christ* **Adonay Yah Shua Messiah**
          at his *coming* **parousia**?
20   For ye are our glory and *joy* **cheer**.

THE HOLINESS OF THE TRUSTERS

3   *Wherefore* **So** when we could
          no longer *forbear* **endure**,
      we *thought it good* **well—approved**
          to be left at Athens alone;
2   And sent *Timotheus* **Timo Theos**,
our brother, and minister of *God* **Elohim**,
      and our *fellowlabourer* **co—worker**
in the *gospel* **evangelism** of *Christ* **the Messiah**,
to establish you, and to *comfort* **console** you
          concerning your *faith* **trust**:
3   That no *man* **one** should be *moved* **shaken**
      by **in** these *afflictions* **tribulations**:
for yourselves know that we are *appointed* **set** thereunto.
4   For verily, when we were with you,
      we *told you before* **forespoke**
that we should *suffer tribulation* **be tribulated**;
even *exactly* as it *came to pass* **became**, and ye know.
      not only the evangelism of Elohim
      but also our own souls;
      because you became beloved to us.
9   For you remember, brothers, our labor and toil

      — working night and day
      to not overburden any of you
we preached to you the evangelism of Elohim.
10   You and Elohim are witnesses,
how mercifully and justly and unblameably
      we became among you who trust:
11   exactly as you know
      how we besought and consoled
      and witnessed each one of you
      as a father his children;
12   that you witness to walk worthy of Elohim
who calls you to his sovereigndom and glory.
13   For this cause also
we eucharistize Elohim unceasingly,
because, when you took the word of Elohim
      which you heard of us,
you received it not as the word of humanity
but exactly as it truly is, the word of Elohim;
      which also energizes in you who trust.
14   For you, brothers,
became mimickers of the ecclesiae of Elohim
being in Yah Hudah — being in Messiah Yah Shua:
      for you also suffered in like manner
      by your own co—scions;
even exactly as they have of the Yah Hudiym:
15   who slaughtered
both Adonay Yah Shua and their own prophets
      and persecuted us;
      and they please not Elohim
and are contrary to all humanity:
16   forbidding us to speak to the goyim to be saved
      — to fill full/shalam their sins alway:
      for the wrath arrives upon them
      to completion/shalom.
17   And we, brothers,
being orphaned away from your face
      for a season of an hour;
      not in heart:
being more superabundantly diligent
to see your face in much panting.
18   So we willed to come to you,
— indeed I Paulos, once and twice;
      and Satan hindered us.
19   For what is our hope? Or cheer?
      Or wreath of boasting?
Or indeed are not even you in front
of our Adonay Yah Shua Messiah at his parousia?
20   For you are our glory and cheer.

The Holiness Of The Trusters

3 So when we could no longer endure,
we *well—approved* **to be left alone** at Asos;

2 and sent *Timo* **Theos**
our brother and minister of Elohim
and our co—worker in the evangelism of the Messiah
to establish you and to console you
concerning your trust:

3 that no one be shaken in these tribulations:
for you yourselves know that we are set thereto.

4 For verily, when we were with you,
we forespoke that we were about to be tribulated
— even *exactly* as it became — as you know.

5 For this cause,
when *even* I could no longer *forbear* **endure**,
I sent to know your *faith* **trust**,
lest *by some means* **somehow**
the *tempter* **tester** have *tempted* **tested** you,
and our labour be *in vain* **void**.

6 But now when *Timotheus* **Timo Theos**
came from you unto us,
and *brought us good tidings* **evangelized**
of your *faith* **trust** and *charity* **love**,
and that ye have good remembrance of us always,
desiring greatly **yearning** to see us,
exactly as we also *to see* you:

7 *Therefore* **Because of this**, brethren,
we were *comforted* **consoled** over you
in all our *affliction* **tribulation** and *distress* **necessity**
by **through** your *faith* **trust**:

8 For now we live,
if **whenever** ye stand *fast* **firm** in *the Lord* **Adonay**.

9 For what *thanks* **eucharist**
can we *render* **recompense** to *God*
Elohim again for you, for all the *joy* **cheer**
wherewith we *joy* **cheer** for your sakes
before **in front of** our *God* **Elohim**;

10 Night and day
praying exceedingly **petitioning superabundantly**
that we might see your face,
and might prepare
that which is lacking in your *faith* **trust**?

11 Now *God* **Elohim** himself and our Father,
and our *Lord Jesus Christ* **Adonay Yah Shua Messiah**,
direct our way unto you.

12 And *the Lord make you to increase*
Adonay superabound you
and *abound* **superabound** in love
one *toward* **unto** another,
and *toward* **unto** all *men*,
even *exactly* as we *do toward* **unto** you:

13 To *the end he may* stablish your hearts
unblameable **unaccusable** in holiness
before God **in front of Elohim**, even our Father,
at the *coming* **parousia**
of our *Lord Jesus Christ* **Adonay Yah Shua Messiah**
with all his *saints* **holy**.

Holiness Over Immorality

4 *Furthermore then* **So finally**
we beseech you, brethren,
and *exhort* **beseech**
you *by the Lord Jesus* **in Adonay Yah Shua**,
that *exactly* as ye have *received* **taken** of us
how ye *ought to* **must** walk and to please *God* **Elohim**,
so that ye *would abound* **should superabound**
more and more.

2 For ye know
what *commandments* **evangelisms** we gave you
by the Lord Jesus **through Adonay Yah Shua**.

3 For this is the will of *God* **Elohim**,
even your *sanctification* **holiness**,
that ye should abstain from *fornication* **whoredom**:

4 That *every* **each** one of you should know
how to *possess* **acquire** his vessel
in *sanctification* **holiness** and honour;

5 Not in the *lust* **passion** of
concupiscence **panting**,
even **exactly** as the *Gentiles* **goyim**
which know not *God* **Elohim**:

6 That no *man go beyond* **one overstep**
and defraud his brother in any matter:
because that *the Lord* **Adonay**
is the avenger *of* **concerning** all such,
exactly as we also have *forewarned* **foretold** you
and *testified* **witnessed**.

7 For *God* **Elohim** hath not called us
unto *uncleanness* **impurity**, but *unto* **in** holiness.

8 So He *therefore* that *despiseth* **setteth aside**,
despiseth **setteth aside** not *man* **humanity**,
but *God* **Elohim**, who hath also
given unto us his holy Spirit.

The Holy Walk

9 But *as touching* **concerning**
brotherly love **befriending brethren**
ye need not that I *write* **scribe** unto you:

1 THESSALONIANS 4

for ye yourselves are *taught of God* **Elohim—doctrinated**
to love one another.

5 For this cause
even when I could no longer endure,
I sent to know of your trust;
lest somehow the tester tests you
and our labor become void.

6 And now, when Timo Theos came from you to us
and evangelized of your trust and love
and that you have good remembrance of us always
— yearning to see us — exactly as we also to see you:

7 because of this, brothers,
we consoled over you
in all our tribulation and necessity
through your trust:

8 for now we live
— whenever you stand firm in Adonay.

9 For what eucharist
can we recompense to Elohim for you,
for all the cheer wherewith we cheer for your sakes
in front of our Elohim

10 — night and day petitioning superabundantly
to see your face
and prepare what is lacking in your trust?

11 And Elohim himself and our Father
and our Adonay Yah Shua Messiah
direct our way to you.

12 And Adonay superabound you
superaboundingly in love to one another and to all
— even exactly as we to you:

13 to establish your hearts unaccusable in holiness
in front of Elohim — even our Father
at the parousia of our Adonay Yah Shua Messiah
with all his holy.

HOLINESS OVER IMMORALITY

4 So finally we beseech you brothers
— beseech you in Adonay Yah Shua,
that exactly as you took from us,
how you must walk and to please Elohim
— to superabound more and more:

2 for you know what evangelisms we gave you
through Adonay Yah Shua.

3 For this is the will of Elohim
— even your holiness;
to abstain from whoredom:

4 that each one of you know
how to acquire his vessel
in holiness and honor;

5 not in the passion of panting
exactly as the goyim who know not Elohim:

6 so that no one oversteps
and defrauds his brother in any matter:
because Adonay is the avenger concerning all such,
exactly as we also foretold you and witness.ed

7 For Elohim calls us not to impurity;
but in holiness.

8 So whoever sets aside,
sets aside not humanity
— but Elohim who also gives us his holy Spirit.

THE HOLY WALK

9 And concerning befriending brothers
you need me not to scribe to you:
for you yourselves are Elohim—doctrinated
to love one another.

10 And indeed ye do it *toward* **unto** all the brethren
which are in all Macedonia:
but we beseech you, brethren,
that ye *increase* **superabound** more and more;

11 And that ye *study* **befriend** **esteeming** to be quiet,
and to *do* **transact** your own business,
and to work with your own hands,
exactly as we *commanded* **evangelized** you;

12 That ye may walk *honestly* **respectably**
toward them that are without,
and that ye may *have lack of nothing* **need naught**.

THE HOPE OF THE RESURRECTION

13 But I *would* **will that you** not
have you to be ignorant **be unknowing**, brethren,
concerning them which are asleep,
that ye sorrow not,
even **exactly** as *others* **the rest** which have no hope.

14 For if we *believe* **trust**
that *Jesus* **Yah Shua** died and rose *again*,
even so **thus** them also
which sleep *in Jesus* **through Yah Shua**
will God **shall Elohim** bring with him.

15 For this we *say* **word** unto you
by **in** the word of *the Lord* **Adonay**,
that we which are alive and *remain* **survive**
unto the coming of *the Lord* **Adonay**
shall *not prevent* **never no way precede** them
which are asleep.

16 For *the Lord* **Adonay** himself

shall descend from heaven
with in a *shout* **summons**,
with in the voice of the archangel,
and *with* **in** the *trump* **trumpet** of *God* **Elohim**:
and the dead in *Christ* **Messiah** shall rise first:

17 Then we which are alive and *remain* **survive**
shall be *caught up together* **seized
simultaneously** with them in the clouds,
to meet *the Lord* **Adonay** in the air:
and *so* **thus** shall we ever be with *the Lord* **Adonay**.

18 *Wherefore* **So then**
comfort one another *with* **in** these words.
1 Corinthians 15:35—38

The Day Of Adonay

5 But *of* **concerning** the times
and the seasons, brethren,
ye have no need that I *write* **scribe** unto you.

2 For yourselves know *perfectly* **precisely**
that the day of *the Lord* **Adonay**
so **thus** cometh as a thief in the night.

3 For when **ever** they shall *say* **word**,
peace **shalom** and *safety* **security**;
then *sudden destruction* **unexpected ruin**
cometh upon **standeth over** them,
exactly as travail upon a woman
with child **having in womb**;
and they shall *not* **never no way** escape.

4 But ye, brethren, are not in darkness,
that that day should overtake you as a thief.

5 Ye are all the *children* **sons** of light,
and the *children* **sons** of the day:
we are not of the night, nor of darkness.

6 *So* **Therefore** let us not
sleep, as *do others* **the rest**;
but let us watch and be sober.

7 For they that sleep sleep in the night;
and they that *be drunken* **intoxicate** are
drunken **intoxicate** in the night.

8 But let us, *who are* **being** of the day, be sober,
putting on **enduing** the breastplate of *faith* **trust** and
love; and for an helmet, the hope of salvation.

9 For *God* **Elohim** hath not
appointed **placed** us to wrath,
but to *obtain* **acquire** salvation
by **through** our *Lord Jesus Christ*
Adonay Yah Shua Messiah,

10 Who died for us,
that, whether we *wake* **watch**,
or **whether we** sleep,

we should live *together* **simultaneously** with him.

11 *Wherefore* **So**
comfort yourselves together **console one another**,
and edify one another, even as also ye do.

10 And indeed
you also do it to all the brothers in all Macedonia:
and we beseech you brothers,
to superabound more and more;

11 and to befriend esteeming quietness and to
transact your own business and to work with your
own hands — exactly as we evangelized you;

12 to walk respectably toward them on the outside:
and that you have need of naught.

The Hope Of The Resurrection

13 And I will that you not be unknowing, brothers,
concerning them who sleep,
that you sorrow not
even exactly as the rest who have no hope.

14 For if we trust that Yah Shua died and rose,
thus they also who sleep through Yah Shua
Elohim brings with him.

15 For we word this to you in the word of Adonay,
that we the living
who survive to the parousia of Adonay
never no way precede them who sleep.

16 For Adonay himself descends from the heavens
— in a summons
in the voice of the archangel
and in the trumpet of Elohim:
and the dead in Messiah rise first:

17 then we the living who survive
are seized simultaneously with them in the clouds
to meet Adonay in the air:
and thus we ever be with Adonay.

18 So comfort one another in these words.
1 Corinthians 15:35—38

The Day Of Adonay

5 And concerning the times
and the seasons, brothers,
you have no need that I scribe to you.

2 For yourselves know precisely
that the day of Adonay comes thus
— as a thief in the night.

3 For whenever they word, Shalom and security;
then unexpected ruin stands over them
— exactly as travail upon a woman having in womb;
and they never no way escape.

4 And you brothers, are not in darkness,

1 THESSALONIANS 5

    that the day overtake you as a thief.
5   You are all the sons of light
    and the sons of the day:
    we are neither of night nor of darkness.
6   So we sleep not as the rest;
    but we watch and are sober.
7   For whoever sleeps, sleeps in the night;
    and whoever intoxicates, intoxicates in the night.
8   And we, being of the day, be sober;
    enduing the breastplate of trust and love;
    and for a helmet, the hope of salvation.
9   For Elohim places us not to wrath,
    but to acquire salvation
    through our Adonay Yah Shua Messiah
10   who died for us;
    so that,
    whether we watch,
    whether we sleep,
    we live simultaneously with him.
11   So console one another
    and edify one another, even as also you do.

FINAL INSTRUCTIONS

12   And we *beseech* **ask** you, brethren,
    to know them which labour among you,
    and *are* **preside** over you in *the Lord* **Adonay**,
    and *admonish* **remind** you;
13   And to esteem them
    very highly **more superabundantly** in love
    for their work's sake.
    And *be at peace* **shalam** among yourselves.
14   Now we *exhort* **beseech** you, brethren,
    warn **remind** them that are *unruly* **disorderly**,
    comfort **console** the *feebleminded* **timidsouled**,
    support the *weak* **frail**, be patient toward all *men*.
15   See that *none* **not any one**
    render **give back** evil for evil unto any *man* **one**;
    but ever *follow* **pursue** that which is good,
    both *among yourselves* **unto one another**,
    and to *all men* **every one**.
16   *Rejoice evermore* **Cheer always**.
17   Pray *without ceasing* **unceasingly**.
18   In *every thing give thanks* **all eucharistize**:
    for this is the will of *God* **Elohim**
    in *Christ Jesus concerning* **Messiah Yah Shua unto** you.
19   Quench not the Spirit.
20   *Despise* **Belittle** not prophesyings.
21   *Prove* **Proof** all *things*; hold
    fast that which is good.
22   Abstain from all *appearance* **semblance** of evil.

TRIUNE HUMANITY

23   And the *very God* **Elohim**
    of *peace* **shalom** himself
    sanctify **hallow** you *wholly* **completely/in shalom**;
    and *I pray God* your whole spirit and soul and body
    be *preserved* **guarded** blameless
    unto **in** the *coming* **parousia**
    of our *Lord Jesus Christ* **Adonay Yah Shua Messiah**.
24   *Faithful* **Trustworthy** is he that calleth you,
    who also *will* **shall** do it.
25   Brethren, pray for us.

FINAL SALUTES AND BENEDICTION

26   *Greet* **Salute** all the brethren
    with **in** an holy kiss.
27   I *charge* **oath** you by *the Lord* **Adonay**
    that this epistle be read unto all the holy brethren.
28   The *grace* **charism**
    of our *Lord Jesus Christ* **Adonay Yah Shua Messiah**
    be with you.
    Amen.

FINAL INSTRUCTIONS

12   And we ask you, brothers,
    to know them who labor among you,
    who preside over you in Adonay and remind you;
13   and to esteem them more
    superabundantly in love
    for sake of their work:
    and shalam among yourselves.
14   And we beseech you brothers;
    remind the disorderly,
    console the timidsouled,
    support the frail,
    be patient toward all.
15   See that no one gives anyone evil for evil;
    but ever pursue the good,
    both to one another and to everyone.
16   Cheer always,
17   pray unceasingly,
18   eucharistize in all;
    — for this is the will of Elohim
    in Messiah Yah Shua to you.
19   Neither quench the Spirit
20   nor belittle prophesyings:
21   proof all,
    hold what is good,
22   abstain from all semblance of evil:

Triune Humanity

23 and the Elohim of shalom himself
hallows you completely/in shalom;
and guards your whole spirit and soul and body
blameless
in the parousia of our Adonay Yah Shua Messiah.
24 Trustworthy is he who
calls you — who also does.
25 Brothers, pray for us.

Final Salutes And Benediction

26 Salute all the brothers in a holy kiss.
27 I oath you by Adonay
to have this epistle read to all the holy brothers.
28 The charism of our Adonay Yah Shua Messiah
be with you.
Amen.

2 THESSALONIANS 1

SALUTATION

1 *Paul* **Paulos**, and Silvanus,
and *Timotheus* **Timo Theos**,
unto the *church* **ecclesia**
of the Thessalonians Thessalonikeus
in *God* **Elohim** our Father
and the Lord Jesus Christ **Adonay Yah Shua Messiah**:
2 *Grace* **Charism** unto you, and *peace* **shalom**,
from *God* **Elohim** our Father
and the Lord Jesus Christ **Adonay Yah Shua Messiah**.

THE EUCHARIST OF PAULOS

3 We are *bound* **indebted**
to *thank God* **eucharistize Elohim** always for you,
brethren,
exactly as it is *meet* **worthy**,
because that your *faith* **trust**
groweth exceedingly **increaseth greatly**,
and the *charity* **love** of *every* **each** one of you all
toward each other *aboundeth* **superaboundeth**;
4 So that we ourselves *glory* **boast** in you
in the *churches* **ecclesiae** of *God* **Elohim**
for your *patience* **endurance** and *faith* **trust**
in all your persecutions and tribulations that ye endure:
5 Which is *a manifest token* **an indication**
of the *righteous* **just** judgment of *God* **Elohim**,
that ye may be counted worthy
of the *kingdom* **sovereigndom** of *God* **Elohim**,
for which ye also suffer:
6 *Seeing it is a righteous thing if* **whenever it is just**
with *God* **Elohim**
to recompense tribulation
to them that *trouble* **tribulate** you;
7 And to you who are *troubled* **tribulated**,
rest **relax** with us,
when the Lord Jesus shall be revealed
in the apocalypse of Adonay Yah Shua from heaven,
with his *mighty* angels **of dynamis**,
8 In flaming fire *taking* **giving** vengeance
on them that know not *God* **Elohim**,
and that obey not the *gospel* **evangelism**
of our *Lord Jesus Christ* **Adonay Yah Shua Messiah**:
9 Who shall be *punished* **penalized in judgment**
with *everlasting destruction* **eternal ruin**
from the *presence* **face** of *the Lord* **Adonay**,
and from the glory of his *power* **might**;
10 *When* **Whenever** he shall come
to be glorified in his *saints* **holy**,
and to be *admired* **marvelled** in
all them that *believe* **trust**
(because our *testimony* **witness** among you
was *believed* **trusted**) in that day.
11 *Wherefore* **Unto which** also
we pray always for you,
that our *God* **Elohim**
would count **should deem** you worthy of this calling,
and fulfill/**shalam** all the *good pleasure* **well—approval**
of *his* goodness,
and the work of *faith with power* **trust in dynamis**:
12 That the name
of our *Lord Jesus Christ* **Adonay Yah Shua Messiah**
may be glorified in you, and ye in him,
according to the *grace* **charism** of our *God* **Elohim**
and *the Lord Jesus Christ* **Adonay Yah Shua Messiah**.

THE TORAH VIOLATOR

2 Now we *beseech* **ask** you, brethren,
by the *coming* **parousia**
of our *Lord Jesus Christ* **Adonay Yah Shua Messiah**,
and by our *gathering* **synagoguing** together unto him,
2 That ye be not *soon* **quickly** shaken *in* **of** mind,
or *be troubled* **lament**,
neither *by* **through** spirit, nor *by* **through** word,
nor *by letter* **through epistle** as from us,
as that the day of *Christ* **the Messiah** is *at hand* **present**.
3 Let no *man deceive* **one seduce** you
by **in** any *means* **manner**:
for that day shall not come **because**,
except **unless** there come
a falling away **an apostatizing** first,
and that *man* **human** of sin be *revealed* **unveiled**,
the son of *perdition* **destruction**;

SALUTATION

1 Paulos and Silvanus and Timo Theos:
To the ecclesia of Thessalonikeus
in Elohim our Father
and Adonay Yah Shua Messiah:
2 Charism to you and shalom
from Elohim our Father
and Adonay Yah Shua Messiah.

THE EUCHARIST OF PAULOS

3 We are always indebted
to eucharistize Elohim for you, brothers,
exactly as is worthy;
that your trust increase greatly
and the love of each one of you all
superabound toward each other;

4 so that we ourselves boast in you
in the ecclesiae of Elohim
for your endurance and trust
in all the persecutions and tribulations you endure:
5 which is an indication of
the just judgment of Elohim
— to count you worthy of the sovereigndom of Elohim
for which you also suffer:
6 whenever it is just with Elohim
to recompense tribulation to them who tribulate you;
7 and you who are tribulated, to relax with us,
in the apocalypse of Adonay Yah Shua
of the heavens,
with his angels of dynamis,
8 in flaming fire giving vengeance
on them who know not Elohim
— who obey not the evangelism
of our Adonay Yah Shua Messiah:
9 to be penalized in judgment with eternal ruin
— from the face of Adonay
and from the glory of his might;
10 whenever he comes to be glorified in his holy
and to be marvelled in all who trust
— because you trust our witness among you in that day:
11 to which also we always pray for you,
that our Elohim deem you worthy of this calling
and fulfill/shalam all the well—approval of goodness
and the work of trust in dynamis:
12 that the name of our Adonay Yah Shua Messiah
be glorified in you — and you in him,
according to the charism
of our Elohim and Adonay Yah Shua Messiah.

The Torah Violator

2 And we ask you, brothers,
by the parousia of our Adonay Yah Shua Messiah
and by our synagoguing together to him,
2 to not quickly shake the mind, or lament
— neither through spirit
nor through word
nor through epistle as *though* from us
— as that the day of the Messiah is present.
3 Be not seduced by anyone in any manner:
— because unless*.
*this sentence is incomplete in the mss
First comes an apostatizing
and the unveiling of the human of sin
— the son of destruction
4 **The adversary,** Who,
opposeth and exalteth **superciliously exalting** himself
above all that is *called God* **worded Elohim**,
or that is *worshipped* **venerated**;
so that he, as *God* **Elohim**,
sitteth in the *temple* **nave** of *God* **Elohim**,
shewing himself that he is *God* **Elohim**.
5 Remember ye not, that, *when*
I was yet **being** with you,
I *told you* **worded** these *things* **unto you**?
6 And now ye know what
withholdeth **holdeth back**
that he might be revealed **unto his being unveiled**
in his *time* **season**.
7 For the mystery of *iniquity* **torah violations**
doth already *work* **energizeth**:
only he *who now letteth will let* **holdeth back**
until he be *taken* out of *the way* **your midst**.
8 And then shall that *Wicked* **torah violator**
be *revealed* **unveiled**,
whom *the Lord* **Adonay** shall consume
with the spirit of his mouth,
and shall *destroy* **inactivate**
with the *brightness* **epiphany** of his *coming* **parousia**:
9 Even him, whose *coming* **parousia**
is after the *working* **energizing** of Satan
with **in** all *power* **dynamis**
and signs and lying *wonders* **omens**,
10 And *with* **in** all *deceivableness* **delusion**
of *unrighteousness* **injustice** in
them that *perish* **destruct**;
because **for** they received not the love of the truth,
that they might be **unto their being** saved.
11 And for this cause *God* **Elohim** shall send them
strong delusion **an energized seduction**,
that they should *believe* **trust** a lie:
12 That they all might be *damned* **judged**
who *believed* **trusted** not the truth,
but *had pleasure* **well—approved**
in *unrighteousness* **injustice**.
13 But we are *bound* **indebted**
to *give thanks* **eucharistize**
alway to *God* **Elohim** for you,
brethren beloved of *the Lord* **Adonay**,
because *God* **Elohim** hath from the beginning
chosen **selected** you to salvation
through sanctification **in holiness** of the Spirit
and *belief* **trust** of the truth:
14 Whereunto he called you
by **through** our *gospel* **evangelism**,
to the *obtaining* **acquiring** of the glory
of our *Lord Jesus Christ* **Adonay Yah Shua Messiah**.

15	*Therefore* **So**, brethren, stand *fast* **firm**, and *hold* **empower** the traditions which ye have been *taught* **doctrinated**, whether *by* **through** word, *or* **whether through** our epistle.		in all dynamis and signs and lying omens,
		10	and in all delusion of injustice in them who destruct: for they receive not the love of the truth to save them.
16	Now our Lord Jesus Christ **Adonay Yah Shua Messiah** himself, and *God* **Elohim**, even our Father, which hath loved us, and hath given us *everlasting* **eternal** consolation and good hope *through grace* **in charism**,	11	And for this cause Elohim sends them an energized seduction so that they trust a lie:
		12	to judge all who trust not the truth, who well–approve injustice.
17	*Comfort* **Console** your hearts, and stablish you in every good word and work.	13	And we we are always indebted to eucharistize to Elohim for you brothers, beloved of Adonay, because from the beginning Elohim selected you to salvation in holiness of the Spirit and trust of the truth:
	THE PETITION OF PAULOS FOR PRAYER	14	whereto he called you through our evangelism, to the acquiring of the glory of our Adonay Yah Shua Messiah.
3	Finally, brethren, pray for us, that the word of *the Lord* **Adonay** may *have free course* **run**, and be glorified, even as *it is* with you:	15	So, brothers, stand firm; and empower the traditions doctrinated to you — whether through word — whether through our epistle.
2	And that we may be *delivered* **rescued** from *unreasonable* **inordinate** and *wicked men* **evil humanity**: for all *men* have not *faith* **trust**.	16	And our Adonay Yah Shua Messiah himself and Elohim our Father who loved us and gave us eternal consolation and good hope in charism,
3	But *the Lord* **Adonay** is *faithful* **trustworthy**, who shall *stablish* **establish** you, and *keep* **guard** you from evil.	17	consoles your hearts and establishes you in every good word and work.
4	And we have confidence in *the Lord* **Adonay** *touching* **toward** you, that ye both do and *will* **shall** do *the things* **that** which we *command* **evangelize** you.		THE PETITION OF PAULOS FOR PRAYER
5	And *the Lord* **Adonay** direct your hearts into the love of *God* **Elohim**, and into the *patient waiting* **endurance** *for Christ* **of the Messiah**.	3	Finally brothers, pray for us that the word of Adonay run and be glorified even as with you:
4	— the adversary who superciliously exalts himself above all that is worded Elohim, or that is venerated — so that he, as Elohim, sits in the nave of Elohim, shewing himself to be Elohim.	2	and rescue us from inordinate and evil humanity: for not all have the trust.
		3	And trustworthy is Adonay, who establishes you and guards you from evil.
5	Remember you not, still being with you, I worded these to you?	4	And we confide in Adonay toward you, to both do and continue doing what we evangelize you:
6	And now you know what holds back his being unveiled in his season.	5	that Adonay direct your hearts to the love of Elohim and to the endurance of the Messiah.
7	For the mystery of torah violations already energizes: he alone holds back until he becomes from your midst.	6	Now we *command* **evangelize** you, brethren, in the name of our *Lord Jesus Christ* **Adonay Yah Shua Messiah**, that ye *withdraw yourselves* **abstain** from every brother that walketh disorderly, and not after the tradition which he *received* **took** of us.
8	And then that torah violator is unveiled, whom Adonay consumes with the spirit of his mouth and inactivates with the epiphany of his parousia		
9	— whose parousia is after the energizing of Satan	7	For yourselves know

how ye *ought to follow* **must mimic** us:
for we behaved not ourselves disorderly among you;
8   Neither did we eat any *man's*
one's bread for naught;
but *wrought* **working**
with **in** labour and *travail* **toil** night and day,
that we might not *be chargeable to* **overburden**
any of you:
9   Not because we have not *power* **authority**,
but to *make* **give** ourselves *an ensample* **a type** unto you
to *follow* **mimic** us.
10   For even when we were with you,
this we *commanded* **evangelized** you,
that if any *would* **willeth to** not work,
neither *should he let him* eat.
11   For we hear
that there are some which walk among you disorderly,
working not at all **not even working**,
but *are busybodies* **overworking**.
12   Now them that are such
we *command* **evangelize** and *exhort* **beseech**
by **through**
our *Lord Jesus Christ* **Adonay Yah Shua Messiah**,
that with quietness they work, and eat their own bread.
13   But ye, brethren, be not
weary in *well* doing **good**.
14   And if any *man* **one**
obey not our word *by* **through** this epistle,
note **signify** that man,
and *have no company* **co—mingle not** with him,
that he may *be ashamed* **shame**.
15   Yet *count him* **deem** not as an enemy,
but *admonish him* **remind** as a brother.

BENEDICTION

16   Now *the Lord* **Adonay** of *peace* **shalom** himself
give you *peace* **shalom**
always by **through** all *means* **in every manner**.
The Lord **Adonay** be with you all.
17   The salutation of *Paul*
Paulos with mine own hand,
which is the *token* **sign** in every epistle:
so **thus** I *write* **scribe**.

18   The *grace* **charism**
of our *Lord Jesus Christ* **Adonay Yah Shua Messiah**
be with you all.
Amen.
6   And we evangelize you brothers,
in the name of our Adonay Yah Shua Messiah,
to abstain from every brother who walks disorderly
and not after the tradition which he took from us.
7   For you know how you must mimic us:
for we neither behave ourselves disorderly among you;
8   nor eat the bread of anyone for nought;
but work in labor and toil night and day
to not overburden any of you:
9   not because we have no authority,
but to give ourselves to you — a type to mimic us.
10   For even being with you,
we evangelized this to you,
that if any wills to not work, that he neither eat.
11   For we hear
that there are some who walk disorderly among you
— not even working, but overworking.
12   Now we evangelize and beseech
through our Adonay Yah Shua Messiah,
whoever are such
to work with quietness and eat their own bread:
13   and you, brothers, weary not in doing good.
14   And if anyone
obeys not our word through this epistle,
signify that man and co—mingle not with him
to shame him.
15   Yet deem him not as an enemy
but remind as a brother.

BENEDICTION

16   And Adonay of shalom himself give you shalom
through all in every manner.
Adonay be with you all.
17   The salutation of Paulos with my own hand,
being the sign in every epistle, thus I scribe.
18   The charism of our Adonay Yah Shua Messiah
be with you all.
Amen.

Salutation

1 *Paul* **Paulos**,
an apostle of *Jesus Christ* **Yah Shua Messiah**
by the *commandment* **order** of *God* **Elohim** our Saviour,
and *Lord Jesus Christ* **Adonay Yah Shua Messiah**,
which is our hope;

2 Unto *Timothy* **Timo Theos**,
my *own son* **genuine child** in *the faith* **trust**:
Grace **Charism**, mercy, and *peace* **shalom**,
from *God* **Elohim** our Father
and *Jesus Christ* **Yah Shua Messiah** our *Lord* **Adonay**.

Paulos Beseeches Timo Theos

3 **Exactly** As I besought thee
to abide still at Ephesus,
when I went into Macedonia,
that thou mightest *charge* **evangelize** some
that they
teach no other doctrine **not doctrinate otherwise**,

4 Neither *give heed to fables* **myths**
and *endless* **unending** genealogies,
which *minister* **cause** questions,
rather than *Godly edifying* **administration of Elohim**
which is in *faith* **trust**: *so do.*

5 Now the *end* **completion/shalom**
of the *commandment* **evangelism**
is *charity* **love** out of a pure heart,
and *of* a good conscience,
and *of faith unfeigned* **trust unhypocritical**:

6 From which some having *swerved* **misaimed**,
have turned aside unto *vain jangling* **mataeology**;

7 *Desiring* **Having willed**
to be *teachers* **doctors** of the *law* **torah**;
understanding **comprehending**
neither what they *say* **word**,
nor *whereof* **about which** they **thoroughly** affirm.

8 But we know that the *law* **torah** is good,
if a man **whenever anyone** use it *lawfully* **torahically**;

9 Knowing this, that the *law* **torah**
is not *made* **set** for *a righteous man* **the just**,
but for the
lawless **torah violator** and *disobedient* **insubordinate**,
for the *ungodly* **irreverent** and for sinners,
for *unholy* **unmerced** and profane,
for *murderers of fathers* **patriciders**
and *murderers of mothers* **matriciders**, for manslayers,

10 For whoremongers,
for *them that defile themselves with*
mankind **homosexuals**,
for *menstealers* **men subduers**,
for liars, for *perjured persons* **perjurers**,
and if there be any other *thing*
that is *contrary* **adverse** to sound doctrine;

11 According to
the *glorious gospel* **evangelism of the glory**
of the blessed *God* **Elohim**,
which was *committed to my trust* **entrusted to me**.

The Personal Witness Of Paulos

12 And I *thank* **have charism**
Christ Jesus **to Messiah Yah Shua** our *Lord* **Adonay**,
who hath *enabled* **dynamized** me,
for that he *counted* **deemed** me *faithful* **trustworthy**,
putting me into the ministry;

13 *Who was before* **Previously being** a blasphemer,
and a persecutor, and *injurious* **insulter**:
but I *obtained mercy* **was mercied**,
because I did it *ignorantly* **unknowingly**
in *unbelief* **trustlessness**.

14 And the *grace* **charism** of our *Lord* **Adonay**
was exceeding abundant **superabounded**
with *faith* **trust** and love
which is in *Christ Jesus* **Messiah Yah Shua**.

15 This is a *faithful saying* **trustworthy word**,
and worthy of all acceptation,
that *Christ Jesus* **Messiah Yah Shua**
came into the *world* **cosmos** to save sinners;
of whom I am *chief* **first**.

16 *Howbeit* **Yet** for this cause
I *obtained mercy* **was mercied**,
that in me first *Jesus Christ* **Yah Shua Messiah**
might *shew forth* **indicate** all *longsuffering* **patience**,

Salutation

1 Paulos, an apostle of Yah Shua Messiah
by the order of Elohim our Saviour
and Adonay Yah Shua Messiah our hope:

2 To Timo Theos, my genuine child in trust:
Charism, mercy and shalom,
from Elohim our Father
and Yah Shua Messiah our Adonay.

Paulos Beseeches Timo Theos

3 Exactly as I besought you
to still abide at Ephesus
when I went into Macedonia,
so that you evangelize some
to neither doctrinate otherwise;

4 nor heed myths and unending genealogies

1 TIMOTHY 1, 2

	— which cause questions
	rather than the administration of Elohim in trust.
5	And the completion/shalom of the evangelism
	is love from a pure heart and a good conscience
	and unhypocritical trust:
6	from which some misaimed,
	and turned aside to mataeology;
7	who willed to be doctors of the torah
	— neither comprehending what they word,
	nor what they thoroughly affirm.
8	And we know the torah is good
	— whenever anyone uses it torahically;
9	knowing this, that the
	torah is not set for the just
	— but for the torah violator and insubordinate,
	for the irreverent and for sinners,
	for unmercied and profane,
	for patriciders and matriciders,
	for manslayers,
10	for whoremongers,
	for homosexuals,
	for men subduers,
	for liars,
	for perjurers;
	and if any other that is adverse to sound doctrine,
11	according to
	the evangelism of the glory of the blessed Elohim
	entrusted to me.

THE PERSONAL WITNESS OF PAULOS

12	And I have charism
	to Messiah Yah Shua our Adonay,
	who dynamized me,
	who deemed me trustworthy,
	putting me into the ministry:
13	previously being a blasphemer
	and a persecutor and insulter:
	but I was mercied
	because I did it unknowingly in trustlessness.
14	And the charism of our Adonay
	superabounded with trust and love
	in Messiah Yah Shua.
15	This word is trustworthy
	and worthy of all acceptation,
	that Messiah Yah Shua
	came into the cosmos to save sinners;
	of whom I am first.
16	Yet for this cause I was mercied,
	that first
	Yah Shua Messiah indicate all patience in me,

	for a *pattern* **prototype** to them
	which should hereafter *believe* **trust** on him
	to life *everlasting* **eternal**.

BENEDICTION

17	Now unto the *King eternal*
	Sovereign of the eons,
	immortal **incorruptible**, invisible,
	the only wise *God* **Elohim**,
	be honour and glory
	for ever and ever **unto the eons of the eons**.
	Amen.

THE MANDATE OF PAULOS

18	This *charge* **evangelism** I
	commit **set forth** unto thee,
	son Timothy **child Timo Theos**,
	according to the prophecies
	which *went before on* **preceded upon** thee,
	that thou *by* **in** them mightest war a good warfare;
19	Holding *faith* **trust**, and a good conscience;
	which some having *put* **shoved** away
	concerning *faith* **the trust**
	have *made shipwreck* **shipwrecked**:
20	Of whom is Hymenaeus and Alexander;
	whom I have delivered unto Satan,
	that they may learn **to discipline them** not to blaspheme.

PETITIONS, PRAYERS, INTERCESSIONS, AND EUCHARISTS

2	So I *exhort therefore* **beseech**, that, first of all,
	supplications **petitions**, prayers, intercessions,
	and *giving of thanks* **eucharists**,
	be made for all *men* **humanity**;
2	For *kings* **sovereigns**,
	and for all *that are* **being** in *authority* **supremacy**;
	that we may *lead* **pass through**
	a *quiet* **tranquil** and *peaceable life* **quiet existence**
	in all *Godliness* **reverence** and *honesty* **veneration**.
3	For this is good and acceptable
	in the sight of *God* **Elohim** our Saviour;
4	Who *will* **willeth**
	have all *men* **humanity** to be saved,
	and to come unto the knowledge of the truth.
5	For there is one *God* **Elohim**, and one mediator
	between *God* **Elohim** and *men* **humanity**, the
	man Christ Jesus **human Messiah Yah Shua**;
6	Who gave himself a *ransom* **redemption** for all,
	to be testified **the witness** in *due* **his own** time.
7	Whereunto I am *ordained* **placed** a preacher,

and an apostle,
(I *speak* **word** the truth in *Christ* **Messiah**, and lie not;)
a *teacher* **doctor** of the *Gentiles* **goyim**
in *faith* **trust** and *verity* **truth**.

Cosmic Manners And Costume

8   I *will* therefore **will**
that men pray *in* every *where* **place**,
lifting *up* holy hands **of mercy**,
without **apart from** wrath and *doubting* **reasoning**.

9   In like manner also, that
women adorn themselves
in *modest apparel* **cosmic costume**,
with *shamefacedness* **awe**
and *sobriety* **soundmindedness**;
not *with broided* **in braided** hair, or gold, or pearls,
or *costly array* **vastly precious garments**;

10   But (which *becometh* **befitteth** women
professing Godliness **pre—evangelizing
Elohim—reverence**)
with **through** good works.

11   Let the woman learn in *silence* **quietness**
with **in** all subjection.

12   But I *suffer* **permit** not a
woman to *teach* **doctrinate**,
nor to *usurp authority over* **dominate** the man,
but to be in *silence* **quietness**.

13   For Adam was first *formed*
molded, then *Eve* **Havvah**.

14   And Adam was not *deceived* **deluded**,
but the woman being *deceived* **deluded**
was **became** in the transgression.

15   *Notwithstanding* **And**
she shall be saved *in* **through** childbearing,
if **whenever** they *continue* **abide** in
faith **trust** and *charity* **love**
and holiness with *sobriety* **soundmindedness**.
for a prototype
to those about to trust on him to life eternal.

Benediction

17   And to the Sovereign of the eons:
incorruptible,
invisible,
the only wise Elohim,
be honor and glory to the eons of the eons.
Amen.

The Mandate Of Paulos

18   Child Timo Theos,
I set forth this evangelism to you,
according to the prophecies that preceded on you,
so that in them, you war a good warfare;

19   holding trust and a good conscience;
which some, concerning the trust,
shoved away and shipwrecked:

20   of whom are Hymenaeus and Alexander;
whom I delivered to Satan
to discipline them to not blaspheme.

Petitions, Prayers, Intercessions, And Eucharists

2   So first of all,
I beseech that petitions, prayers, intercessions
and eucharists be made for all humanity;

2   for sovereigns and for all being in supremacy:
so that we pass through
a tranquil and quiet existence
in all reverence and veneration.

3   For this is good and acceptable
in the sight of Elohim our Saviour;

4   who wills all humanity to be saved
and to come to the knowledge of the truth.

5   For there is one Elohim and one mediator
between Elohim and humanity
— the human Messiah Yah Shua;

6   who gave himself a redemption for all
the witness in his own time:

7   unto whom I am placed a
preacher and an apostle.
I word the truth in Messiah and lie not;
a doctor of the goyim in trust and truth.

Cosmic Manners And Costume

8   So I will that men pray in every place
lifting hands of mercy
apart from wrath and reasoning.

9   In like manner also
that women adorn themselves in cosmic costume
with awe and soundmindedness;
not in braided hair or gold or pearls
or vastly precious garments;

10   but whatever befits women
who pre—evangelize Elohim—reverence
through good works.

11   Have the woman learn in quietness
in all subjection.

12   And I permit a woman
neither to doctrinate nor to dominate the man
but to be in quietness.

13   For Adam was first molded, then Havvah.

14 And Adam was not deluded; but the woman
being deluded became in the transgression:
15 and she is saved through childbearing
— whenever they abide in trust and love and holiness
with soundmindedness.

The Episcopate

3 This is a *true saying* **trustworthy word**,
If *a man* **anyone**
desire **reach for** the *office of a bishop* **episcopate**,
he *desireth* **panteth after** a good work.
2 *A bishop then* **So an episcopate**
must be *blameless* **unapprehendable**,
the *husband* **man** of one *wife* **woman**, *vigilant* **sober**,
sober **soundminded**, *of good behaviour* **cosmic**,
given to hospitality **befriend strangers**,
apt to teach **didactic**;
3 *Not given to wine* **No winesop**, no striker,
not *greedy of filthy lucre* **avaricious**; but *patient* **gentle**,
not *a brawler* **amicable**, not *covetous* **unavaricious**;
4 One that *ruleth* **presideth**
well **over** his own house,
having his children in subjection
with all *gravity* **veneration**;
5 (For if *a man* **one** know not
how to *rule* **preside over** his own house,
how shall he take care
of the *church* **ecclesia** of *God* **Elohim**?)
6 Not a *novice* **neophyte**,
lest being *lifted up with pride* **inflated**
he fall into the *condemnation* **judgment**
of *the devil* **Diabolos**.
7 *Moreover* **And** he must
have a good *report* **witness**
of them which are without;
lest he fall into reproach
and the snare of *the devil* **Diabolos**.

Ministers

8 Likewise *must the deacons*
be grave **ministers venerant**,
not *doubletongued* **doubleworded**,
not *given to* **heeding** much wine,
not *greedy of filthy lucre* **avaricious**;
9 Holding the mystery of the *faith* **trust**
in a pure conscience.
10 And let these also first be proved;
then let them *use the office of a deacon* **minister**,
being *found blameless* **unimpeachable**.
11 *Even so* **Likewise**
must their *wives* **women** be *grave* **venerant**,
not *slanderers* **diabolic**, sober,
faithful **trustworthy** in all *things*.
12 Let the *deacons* **ministers**
be the *husbands* **men** of one *wife* **woman**,
ruling **well—presiding over** their children
and their own houses *well*.
13 For they that
have used the office of a deacon **minister** well
purchase **acquire** to themselves a good degree,
and *great* **vast** boldness in the *faith* **trust**
which is in *Christ Jesus* **Messiah Yah Shua**.
14 These *things write* **scribe** I unto thee,
hoping to come unto thee *shortly* **very quickly**:
15 But *if* **whenever** I *tarry long* **delay**,
that thou mayest know
how thou *oughtest to* **must** behave thyself
in the house of *God* **El**,
which is the *church* **ecclesia** of the living *God* **Elohim**,
the pillar and ground of the truth.

The Mega Profession Of Paulos

16 And *without controversy* **professedly**
great **mega** is the mystery of *Godliness* **reverence**:
God **Elohim** was manifest in *the* flesh,
justified in *the* Spirit, seen of angels,
preached *unto* **in** the *Gentiles* **goyim**,
believed on **trusted** in the *world* **cosmos**,
received up **taken** into glory.

Paulos Prophesies Apostacy

4 Now the Spirit
speaketh expressly **wordeth rhetorically**,
that in the latter *times* **seasons**
some shall depart from the *faith* **trust**,
giving heed to **heeding** seducing spirits,
and doctrines of *devils* **demons**;
2 *Speaking lies* **Pseudologists** in hypocrisy;

The Episcopate

3 Trustworthy the word!
If anyone reaches for the episcopate,
he pants after a good work.
2 So an episcopate must be unapprehendable,
the man of one woman,
sober,
soundminded,
cosmic,
befriend strangers,
didactic,

1 TIMOTHY 4

3   no winesop,
no striker,
not avaricious:
but gentle,
amicable,
unavaricious,
4   one who presides well over his own house
having his children in subjection with all veneration.
5   For if one knows not
how to preside over his own house,
how cares he for the ecclesia of Elohim?
6   Not a neophyte:
lest being inflated
he falls into the judgment of Diabolos:
7   and he must have a good witness
of those outside;
lest he fall into reproach and the snare of Diabolos.

MINISTERS

8   Likewise ministers:
venerant,
not doubleworded,
not heeding much wine,
not avaricious,
9   holding the mystery of the
trust in a pure conscience:
10   and also first be proved, and then minister:
being unimpeachable.
11   Likewise their women:
venerant,
not diabolic,
sober,
trustworthy in all.
12   Ministers:
the men of one woman,
well—presiding over their children
and their own houses.
13   For they who minister well
acquire to themselves a good degree
and vast boldness in the trust in Messiah Yah Shua.
14   I scribe these to you
hoping to come to you very quickly:
15   but whenever I delay,
you know how you must behave yourself
in the house of El
— the ecclesia of the living Elohim the
pillar and ground of the truth.

THE MEGA PROFESSION OF PAULOS

16   And professedly,
mega is the mystery of reverence

— Elohim manifested in flesh,
justified in Spirit,
seen of angels,
preached in the goyim,
trusted in the cosmos,
taken into glory.

PAULOS PROPHESIES APOSTACY

4   And the Spirit words rhetorically,
that in the latter seasons, some depart from the
trust — heeding seducing spirits and doctrines of
demons: 2   pseudologists in hypocrisy
having their conscience
seared with a hot iron **cauterized**;
3   Forbidding to marry,
and commanding to abstain from *meats* **food**,
which *God* **Elohim** hath created
to be *received* **partaken** with *thanksgiving* **eucharist**
of them which believe **by the trustworthy**
and **which** know the truth.
4   For every creature of *God* **Elohim** is good,
and *nothing* **naught** to be *refused* **cast away**,
if it be *received* **taken** with *thanksgiving* **eucharist**:
5   For it is *sanctified* **hallowed**
by **through** the word of *God* **Elohim**
and *prayer* **intercession**.

BEING A GOOD MINISTER

6   *If thou put* **Lay these in front of** the brethren
in remembrance of these things,
thou shalt be a good minister
of *Jesus Christ* **Yah Shua Messiah**,
nourished up **nurtured** in the words of *faith* **the trust**
and of good doctrine,
whereunto thou hast *attained* **closely followed**.
7   But *refuse* **shun**
profane and *old wives' fables* **anile myths**,
and exercise thyself *rather* unto *Godliness* **reverence**.
8   For bodily exercise *profiteth* **benefitteth** little:
but *Godliness is profitable* **reverence is** unto all *things*,
having *promise* **pre—evangelism** of the life that now is,
and of that which is to come.
9   This is a *faithful saying* **trustworthy word**
and worthy of all acceptation.
10   For *therefore* **thereunto**
we both labour and suffer reproach,
because we *trust* **hope** in the living *God* **Elohim**,
who is the Saviour of all *men* **humanity**,
specially of *those that believe* **the trustworthy**.
11   **Evangelize** These *things* command
and *teach* **doctrinate**.

12 Let no *man despise* **one disesteem** thy youth;
but be thou *an example* **a type**
of the *believers* **trustworthy**,
in word, in *conversation* **behaviour**, in *charity* **love**,
in spirit, in *faith* **trust**, in purity.
13 Till I come, *give attendance* **heed** to reading,
to *exhortation* **consolation**, to doctrine.

Disregard Not The Charisma

14 *Neglect* **Disregard** not the
gift **charisma** that is in thee,
which was given thee *by* **through** prophecy, with
the laying on of the hands of the presbytery.
15 Meditate upon these *things*;
give thyself wholly to **be in** them; that
thy *profiting* **advancement**
may *appear to* **be manifest among** all.
16 *Take* heed unto thyself, and unto the doctrine;
continue **abide** in them:
for in doing this thou shalt both save thyself,
and them that hear thee.

Elders And Widows

5 Rebuke not an elder*,
but *intreat him* **beseech** as a father;
and the younger *men* as brethren;
2 The elder** *women* as mothers;
the younger as sisters, *with* **in** all purity.
*masculine, **feminine
3 Honour widows that are widows indeed.
4 But if any widow
have children or *nephews* **descendants**,
let them learn first *to shew piety* **reverence**
at **in** his own home,
and to *requite* **give back recompense**
to their *parents* **progenitors**:
for that is good and acceptable
before God **in sight of Elohim**.
5 Now she that is a widow
indeed, and *desolate* **alone**,
trusteth **hopeth** in *God* **Elohim**,
and *continueth* **abideth**
in *supplications* **petitions** and prayers
night and day.

their conscience cauterized,
3 forbidding to marry,
to abstain from food that Elohim created
— for the trustworthy who know the truth
to partake with eucharist.
4 For every creature of Elohim is good,
and not cast away when taken with eucharist:
5 for it is hallowed
through the word of Elohim and intercession.

Being A Good Minister

6 Lay these in front of the brothers:
to be a good minister of Yah Shua Messiah,
nurtured in the words of the trust
and of good doctrine
which you closely followed:
7 and shun profane and anile myths
and exercise yourself to reverence.
8 For bodily exercise benefits little:
but reverence is to all,
having pre—evangelism of the life that now is,
and is to come.
9 Trustworthy the word
and worthy of all acceptation.
10 For thereto we both labor and suffer reproach;
because we hope in the living Elohim
the Saviour of all humanity
— specially of the trustworthy:
11 evangelize and doctrinate these.
12 Have no one disesteem your youth;
but be a type of the trustworthy
in word, in behavior, in love,
in spirit, in trust, in purity
13 until I come:
heed to reading, to consolation, to doctrine.

Disregard Not The Charisma

14 Disregard not the charisma within you
— given you through prophecy
with the laying on of the hands of the presbytery.
15 Meditate on these:
give yourself wholly to be in them
to manifest your advancement among all.
16 Heed to yourself and to the doctrine;
abide in them:
for in so doing
you save both yourself and whoever hears you.

Elders And Widows

5 Rebuke not an elder*,
but beseech as a father;
the younger as brothers;
2 the elder** as mothers;
the younger as sisters, in all purity.
*masculine; **feminine
3 Honor widows who are widows indeed:

1 TIMOTHY 5, 6

4 and if any widow has children or descendants,
have them first learn reverence in their own house;
and to give recompense to their progenitors:
for that is good and acceptable in sight of Elohim.

5 And she who is a widow indeed, and alone,
hopes in Elohim
and abides in petitions and prayers
night and day:

6 But she that *liveth in pleasure* **luxuriateth**
is dead while she liveth.

7 And **evangelize** these *things give in charge*,
that they may be *blameless* **unapprehendable**.

8 But if any provide not for his own,
and specially for those of his own house,
he hath denied the *faith* **trust**,
and is worse than *an infidel* **the trustless**.

9 Let not a widow be *taken
into the number* **enrolled**
under threescore **at less than sixty** years old, having
been **become** the *wife* **woman** of one man,

10 *Well reported of* **for Witnessed in** good works;
if she have *brought up* **fostered** children,
if she have lodged strangers,
if she have washed the *saints'* feet **of the holy**,
if she have relieved the *afflicted* **tribulated**,
if she have diligently followed every good work.

11 But the younger widows *refuse* **shun**:
for when **ever** they have begun to wax wanton **sensualize**
against *Christ* **Messiah**, they will *to* marry;

12 Having *damnation* **judgment**,
because they have *cast off* **set aside** their first *faith* **trust**.

13 And *withal* **simultaneously**
they learn to be idle,
wandering about *from house to house* **the houses**;
and not only idle,
but *tattlers* **babblers** also and *busybodies* **overworking**,
speaking *things* **that** which they *ought* **must** not.

14 *So* I will **therefore** that the
younger *women* marry,
bear **birth** children, *guide the house* **be
housedespotes**, give none *occasion* **opportunity**
to **cause** the adversary to speak *reproachfully* **abusively**.

15 For some are already turned aside after Satan.

16 If any *man* **trustworthy***
or *woman that believeth* **trustworthy****
have widows, let them relieve them,
and let not the *church* **ecclesia** be *charged* **burdened**;
that it may relieve them that are widows
indeed. *masculine; **feminine

17 Let the elders that *rule* **preside** well
be *counted* **deemed** worthy of double honour,
especially they who labour in the word and doctrine.

18 For the scripture *saith* **wordeth**,
Thou shalt not muzzle the ox that treadeth *out the corn*.
And, The *labourer* **worker** is worthy of his
reward. Deuteronomy 25:4, Loukas 10:7

Resolving Accusations

19 Against an elder receive not an accusation,
but **unless except** before two or three witnesses.

20 Them that sin *rebuke before*
reprove in sight of all,
that *others* **the rest** also may *fear* **awe**.

21 I *charge* **witness** thee *before
God* **in sight of Elohim**,
and *the Lord Jesus Christ* **Adonay Yah Shua
Messiah**, and the *elect* **select** angels,
that thou *observe* **guard** these *things*
without preferring one before another
apart from prejudging,
doing *nothing* **naught** by *partiality* **prejudice**.

22 *Lay* **Place** hands suddenly on no *man* **one**,
neither *be partaker* **partake** of *other men's* **another's**
sins: *keep* **guard** thyself *pure* **hallowed**.

23 Drink no longer water,
but use a little wine for thy stomach's sake
and *thine often infirmities* **thy frequent frailties**.

24 Some *men's* **human's** sins
are *open beforehand* **preevident**,
going before **preceding** to judgment;
and some *men* they follow after.

25 Likewise also the good works *of some*
are *manifest beforehand* **preevidenced**;
and they that are otherwise
cannot be *hid* **secreted**.

6 Let as many servants as are under the yoke
count **deem** their own *masters* **despotes**
worthy of all honour,
that the name of *God* **Elohim** and *his* doctrine
be not blasphemed.

2 And they
that have *believing masters* **trustworthy despotes**,
let them not *despise* **disesteem** them,

6 and she who luxuriates, is dead while she lives:

7 and evangelize these
— that they be unapprehendable.

8 And if anyone provides not for his own
and specially for those of his own house,
he denies the trust
and is worse than the trustless.

9	Enroll not a widow at less than sixty years: having been the woman of one man	24	The sins of some humans are preevident, preceding to judgment: and some follow after.
10	witnessed in good works; if she fostered children, if she lodged strangers, if she washed the feet of the holy, if she relieved the tribulated, if she diligently followed every good work.	25	Likewise also the good works are preevidenced; and those that are otherwise cannot be secreted.

9   Enroll not a widow at less than sixty years:
having been the woman of one man
10   witnessed in good works;
if she fostered children,
if she lodged strangers,
if she washed the feet of the holy,
if she relieved the tribulated,
if she diligently followed every good work.
11   But shun the younger widows:
for whenever they sensualize against Messiah
they will to marry;
12   having judgment,
because they set aside their first trust:
13   and simultaneously they learn to be idle
wandering about the houses:
and not only idle, but also babblers and overworking;
speaking what they must not.
14   So I will that the younger marry,
birth children, be housedespotes;
giving no opportunity
to cause the adversary to speak abusively.
15   For some are already turned aside after Satan.
16   If any trustworthy* or
trustworthy** have widows,
relieve them
and burden not the ecclesia;
that it relieve them who are widows
indeed. *masculine; **feminine
17   Deem the elders who preside well
worthy of double honor,
especially who labor in the word and doctrine.
18   For the scripture words,
Muzzle not the ox that treads.
And, The worker is worthy of his reward.
Deuteronomy 25:4, Loukas 10:7

Resolving Accusations

19   Receive no accusation against an elder
unless except in front of two or three witnesses.
20   Reprove them who sin in sight of all
so that the rest also awe.
21   I witness you in sight of Elohim
and Adonay Yah Shua Messiah and the select angels;
guard these apart from prejudging,
doing naught by prejudice.
22   Place hands suddenly on no one;
partake not of the sins of another;
guard yourself hallowed;
23   drink no longer water
but use a little wine for sake of your stomach
and your frequent frailties.
24   The sins of some humans are preevident,
preceding to judgment: and some follow after.
25   Likewise also the good works are preevidenced;
and those that are otherwise cannot be secreted.

6   As many as are servants under the yoke
deem your own despotes worthy of all honor;
so as not to blaspheme
the name of Elohim and the doctrine
2   And whoever has trustworthy despotes,
disesteem them not;
because they are brethren;
but rather *do them service* **in servitude**,
because they are *faithful* **trustworthy** and beloved,
partakers **supporters** of the *benefit* **good work**.
These *things teach* **doctrinate** and *exhort* **beseech**.

Pseudo Doctrine

3   If any *man teach* **one doctrinate** otherwise,
and *consent* **cometh** not to *wholesome* **sound** words,
even the words
of our *Lord Jesus Christ* **Adonay Yah Shua Messiah**,
and to the doctrine
which is according to *Godliness* **reverence**;
4   He is *proud* **inflated**, knowing *nothing* **naught**,
but *doting* **is diseased** about questions
and *strifes of words* **logomachy**,
whereof *cometh* **becometh** envy, *strife* **contention**,
railings **blasphemies**, evil surmisings,
5   *Perverse disputings of men* **Human diatribes**
of corrupt minds,
and *destitute* **deprived** of the truth,
supposing **presuming**
that gain is *Godliness* **reverence to be gain**:
from such *withdraw thyself* **depart**.
6   But *Godliness* **reverence**
with *contentment* **selfcontentment**
is *great* **mega** gain.
7   For we brought *nothing*
naught into this *world* **cosmos**,
and it is *certain* **evident**
we can *carry nothing out* **bring naught forth**.
8   And having *food* **sustenance**
and *raiment* **covering**
let us be therewith *content* **satisfied**.
9   But they that will to be rich
fall into *temptation* **testing** and a snare,
and into many
foolish **mindless** and *hurtful lusts* **injurious pantings**,
which *drown men* **sink humanity**
in *destruction* **ruin** and *perdition* **destruction**.

1 TIMOTHY 6

10   For *the love of money* **befriending silver**
is the root of all evil:
which while some *coveted after* **reached for**,
they have *erred* **strayed** from the *faith* **trust**,
and pierced themselves through
with many *sorrows* **griefs**.

11   But thou, O *man* **humanity** of *God* **Elohim**,
flee these *things*;
and *follow after righteousness* **pursue justness**,
Godliness **reverence**, *faith* **trust**, love,
patience **endurance**, meekness.

12   *Fight* **Agonize** the good *fight*
agony of *faith* **the trust**,
lay **take** hold on eternal life,
whereunto thou art also called,
and hast professed a good profession
before **in sight of** many witnesses.

13   I *give* **evangelize** thee *charge*
in the sight of *God* **Elohim**,
who *quickeneth* **enliveneth** all *things*, and *before Christ Jesus* **Messiah Yah Shua**, who *before* **in front of** Pontius *Pilate* **Pilatos** witnessed a good *confession* **profession**;

14   That thou *keep* **guard** this
commandment **misvah**
without spot **unstained**,
unrebukeable **unapprehendable**,
until the *appearing* **epiphany**
of our *Lord Jesus Christ* **Adonay Yah Shua Messiah**:

15   Which in his *times* **seasons** he shall shew,
who is the blessed and only *Potentate* **Dynast**,
the *King* **Sovereign** of *kings* **reigners**,
and *Lord* **Adonay** of *lords* **adoniym**;

16   Who only hath *immortality* **athanasia**,
dwelling in the **unapproachable** light
which no man can approach unto;
whom no *man* **human** hath seen, nor can see:
to whom be honour and power *everlasting* **eternal**.
Amen.

WARNING THE RICH

17   *Charge* **Evangelize** them that
are rich in this *world* **eon**,
that they be not highminded,
nor *trust* **hope** in uncertain riches,
but in the living *God* **Elohim**,
because they are brothers:
but rather in servitude
because they are trustworthy and beloved
— supporters of the good work.
Doctrinate these and beseech.

PSEUDO DOCTRINE

3   If anyone doctrinates otherwise
and comes not to sound words,
— the words of our Adonay Yah Shua Messiah
and to the doctrine according to reverence;

4   he is inflated, knowing naught;
but is diseased about questions and logomachy;
whereof becomes envy,
contention,
blasphemies,
evil surmisings,

5   human diatribes of corrupt minds,
deprived of the truth,
presuming reverence to be gain:
depart from such:

6   but reverence with
selfcontentment is mega gain.

7   For we brought naught into this cosmos
and it is evident we can bring naught forth.

8   And having sustenance and covering,
be satisfied.

9   And whoever wills to be rich
falls into testing and a snare;
and into many mindless and injurious pantings,
which sink humanity in ruin and destruction.

10   For befriending silver is the root of all evil:
which, while some reach for,
strayed from the trust
and pierced themselves through with many griefs.

11   And you, O humanity of Elohim, flee these,
and pursue:
justness,
reverence,
trust,
love,
endurance,
meekness:

12   agonize the good agony of the trust,
take hold on eternal life
— to which you were also called,
and professed a good profession
in sight of many witnesses.

13   I evangelize you in the sight of Elohim
who enlivens all:
and Messiah Yah Shua
who witnessed a good profession
in front of Pontius Pilatos:

14   to guard this misvah
— unstained,
unapprehendable

until the epiphany of our Adonay Yah Shua Messiah:
15   which he shows in his seasons
— the blessed and only Dynast
the Sovereign of reigners
and Adonay of adoniym;
16   who alone has athanasia:
dwelling in the unapproachable light
whom no human has seen, nor is able to see:
to whom be honor and eternal power.
Amen.

WARNING THE RICH

17   Evangelize them who are rich in this eon,
that they neither be highminded
nor hope in uncertain riches
— but in the living Elohim
who *giveth* **presenteth** us richly all *things* to enjoy;
18   That they *do* **work** good,
that they be rich in good works,
ready to distribute **to share well**,
willing to communicate **to commune**;
19   *Laying up in store* **Treasuring** for themselves
a good foundation
against the time to come **unto the about to be**,
that they may *lay* **take** hold on eternal life.

FINAL MANDATE AND BENEDICTION

20   O *Timothy* **Timo Theos**,
keep **guard** that
which is *committed to thy trust* **laid by thee**,
avoiding **turning aside**
from profane and vain *babblings* **voices**,
and *oppositions* **the antithesis**
of *science falsely so called* **pseudonymed knowledge**:

21   Which some *professing* **pre—evangelizing**
have *erred* **misaimed** concerning the *faith*
trust. *Grace* **Charism** be with thee.
Amen.
who presents us richly to enjoy all;
18   to work good,
to enrich in good works,
to share well,
to commune;
19   treasuring a good foundation for themselves
to the about to be,
to take hold on eternal life.

FINAL MANDATE AND BENEDICTION

20   O Timo Theos, guard that laid by you,
turning aside from profane and vain voices
and the antithesis of pseudonymed knowledge:
21   which some pre—evangelize,
and misaim concerning the trust.
The charism be with you.
Amen.

2 TIMOTHY 1

SALUTATION

1 *Paul* **Paulos**, an apostle of
Jesus Christ **Yah Shua Messiah**
by **through** the will of *God* **Elohim**,
according to the *promise* **pre—evangelism** of life
which is in *Christ Jesus* **Messiah Yah Shua**,

2 To *Timothy* **Timo Theos**,
my dearly beloved *son* **child**:
Grace **Charism**, mercy, and *peace* **shalom**,
from *God* **Elohim** the Father
and *Christ Jesus* **Messiah Yah Shua** our *Lord* **Adonay**.

3 I *thank God* **have charism to Elohim**,
whom I *serve* **liturgize** from my *forefathers* **progenitors**
with **in** pure conscience,
that *without ceasing* **unceasingly**
I have remembrance *of* **concerning** thee in
my *prayers* **petitions** night and day;

4 *Greatly desiring* **Yearning** to see thee,
being mindful of **remembering** thy tears, that
I may be filled/**shalamed** with *joy* **cheer**;

5 When I *call to* **Taking** remembrance
of the *unfeigned faith* **unhypocritical**
trust that is in thee,
which *dwelt* first *in* **indwelt**
thy *grandmother* **mammy** Lois, and thy mother Eunice;
and I am *persuaded* **convinced** that in thee also.

6 *Wherefore* **For which cause**
I *put* **remind** thee *in remembrance*
that thou *stir up* **refire** the *gift* **charisma** of *God* **Elohim**,
which is in thee
by **through** the *putting* **laying** on of my hands.

7 For *God* **Elohim** hath not given us
the spirit of *fear* **cowardice**;
but of *power* **dynamis**, and of love, and of a sound mind.

8 *So* Be not thou *therefore* ashamed
of the *testimony* **witness** of our *Lord* **Adonay**,
nor of me his prisoner:
but *be thou partaker of the afflictions* **co—suffer**
of **in** the *gospel* **evangelism**
according to the *power* **dynamis** of *God* **Elohim**;

9 Who hath saved us, and
called us with an holy calling,
not according to our works,
but according to his own
purpose **prothesis** and *grace* **charism**,
which was given us in *Christ Jesus* **Messiah Yah Shua**
before *the world began* **eternal time**,

10 But is now *made* manifest
by **through** the *appearing* **epiphany**
of our Saviour *Jesus Christ* **Yah Shua Messiah**,
who hath *abolished* **indeed inactivated** death,
and hath *brought* **enlightened** life
and immortality *to light*
through the *gospel* **evangelism**:

11 Whereunto I am *appointed* **placed**
a preacher, and an apostle,
and a *teacher* **doctor** of the *Gentiles* **goyim**.

12 For the which cause I also suffer these *things*:
nevertheless **yet** I am not ashamed:
for I know whom I have *believed* **trusted**,
and am *persuaded* **convinced** that
he is able to *keep* **guard**
that which I have *committed* **surrendered** unto him
against **unto** that day.

13 Hold fast the *form* **prototype** of sound words,
which thou hast heard of me,
in *faith* **trust** and love
which is in *Christ Jesus* **Messiah Yah Shua**.

14 That good *thing* which was
committed unto **laid by** thee
keep by **guard through** the *Holy Spirit* **Ruach
ha-kodesh** which *dwelleth in* **indwelleth** us.

15 This thou knowest,
that all they which are in Asia be turned *away* from me;
of whom are Phygellus and Hermogenes.

16 The Lord **Adonay** give mercy
unto the house of Onesiphorus;
for he oft refreshed me,
and was not ashamed of my *chain* **fetter**:

17 But, *when he was* **being** in Rome,
he sought me out very diligently, and found me.

18 *The Lord grant* **Adonay give** unto him
that he may find mercy of *the Lord* **Adonay** in that day:
and in *how many things* **as much as**
he ministered unto me at Ephesus,
thou knowest *very well* **better**.

SALUTATION

1 Paulos, an apostle of Yah Shua Messiah
through the will of Elohim,
according to the pre—evangelism of life
in Messiah Yah Shua:

2 To Timo Theos, beloved child:
Charism, mercy and shalom
from Elohim the Father
and Messiah Yah Shua our Adonay.

3 I have charism to Elohim,
whom I liturgize from my progenitors
in pure conscience,
that unceasingly I have remembrance concerning you
in my petitions night and day;

4	yearning to see you, remembering your tears, that I be filled/shalamed with cheer;
5	taking remembrance of the unhypocritical trust within you, which first indwelt your mammy Lois and your mother Eunice: and I am convinced, also in you:
6	for which cause I remind you to refire the charisma of Elohim within you through the laying on of my hands.
7	For Elohim gives us not the spirit of cowardice; but of dynamis and of love and of a sound mind.
8	So neither shame of the witness of our Adonay, nor of me his prisoner: but co—suffer in the evangelism according to the dynamis of Elohim;
9	who saved us and called us with an holy calling — not according to our works but according to his own prothesis and charism given us in Messiah Yah Shua preceding eternal time;
10	and is now manifest through the epiphany of our Saviour Yah Shua Messiah; who indeed inactivated death and enlightened life and immortality through the evangelism:
11	whereto I am placed — a preacher and an apostle and a doctor of the goyim.
12	For which cause I also suffer these: yet I am not ashamed: for I know whom I have trusted and am convinced that he is able to guard what I surrender to him to that day.
13	Hold fast the prototype of sound words, which you heard of me, in trust and love in Messiah Yah Shua.
14	Guard the good laid by you through the Holy Spirit indwelling us.
15	Know this: that all in Asia turned from me; of whom are Phygellus and Hermogenes.
16	Adonay give mercy to the house of Onesiphorus; for he often refreshed me and shamed not of my fetter:
17	But, being in Rome, he sought me out very diligently and found me.
18	Adonay give him to find mercy from Yah Veh in that day: and as much as he ministered to me at Ephesus, you know much better.

Enduring Hardship

2	So Thou *therefore*, my son, be *strong* **dynamized** in the *grace* **charism** that is in *Christ Jesus* **Messiah Yah Shua**.
2	And *the things* **those** that thou hast heard of me *among* **through** many witnesses, *the same commit* **set** thou **forth** to *faithful men* **trustworthy humanity**, who shall be *able* **ample** to *teach* **doctrinate** others also.
3	*So* Thou *therefore* endure *hardness* **hardship**, as a good *soldier* **warrior** of *Jesus Christ* **Yah Shua Messiah**.
4	No *man* **one** that warreth entangleth himself with the *affairs* **transactions** of *this life* **existence**; that he may please him who hath *chosen* **enlisted** him *to be a soldier*.
5	And *if a man* **whenever anyone** *also strive* **contend** for masteries, *yet* is he not *crowned* **wreathed**, *except* **unless** he *strive lawfully* **contend torahically**.
6	The *husbandman that* *laboureth must be first partaker* **cultivator must labor ere he partake** of the fruits.
7	*Consider* **Comprehend** what I *say* **word**; and *the Lord* **indeed Adonay** give thee *understanding* **comprehension** in all *things*.
8	Remember that *Jesus Christ* **Yah Shua Messiah** of the *seed* **sperma** of David was raised from the dead according to my *gospel* **evangelism**:
	9 Wherein I *suffer trouble* **endure hardship**, as an evil *doer* **worker**, *even* unto bonds; but the word of *God* **Elohim** is not bound.
10	*Therefore* **So** I endure all *things* for the *elect's* **select's** sakes, that they may also obtain the salvation which is in *Christ Jesus* **Messiah Yah Shua** with eternal glory.
	11 It is a *faithful saying* **trustworthy word**: For if we *be dead with him* **co—die**, we shall also *live with him* **co—live**:
12	If we *suffer* **endure**, we shall also *reign with him* **co—reign**: if we deny *him*, he also *will* **shall** deny us:
13	If we *believe not* **distrust**, *yet* he abideth *faithful* **trustworthy**: he cannot deny himself.
14	Of these *things put* **remind** them *in remembrance*, *charging* **witnessing**

them before the Lord *in the sight of Adonay*
that they *strive* **logomachize** not
about words to no profit,
but to the *subverting* **catastrophe** of the hearers.

15 *Study* **Be diligent** to *shew* **present** thyself
approved unto *God* **Elohim**,
a *workman* **worker**,
that needeth not to be ashamed **unashamed**,
rightly dividing **straightcutting** the word of truth.

16 But *shun* **stand aloof**
from profane and vain *babblings* **voices**:
for they *will increase* **shall advance**
unto more *ungodliness* **irreverence**.

17 And their word *will eat* **shall pasture**
as *doth* a *canker* **gangrene**:
of whom is Hymenaeus and Philetus;

18 Who concerning the truth
have *erred* **misaimed**,
saying **wording**
that the resurrection *is past* **hath** already **become**;
and *overthrow* **overturn** the *faith* **trust** of some.

19 *Nevertheless* **But yet indeed**
the foundation of *God* **Elohim** standeth *sure* **solid**,
having this seal,
The Lord **Adonay Yah Veh** knoweth them that are his.
And,
Let every one that nameth the name of *Christ* **Messiah**
depart from *iniquity* **injustice**.
Nachum 1:7, Yahn 10:14

20 But in a *great* **mega** house
there are not only vessels of gold and of silver,
but also of wood and of *earth* **clay**;
and some **indeed** to honour, and some to dishonour.

21 If *a man* **ever anyone** therefore
purge himself from these,

Enduring Hardship

2 So my son,
dynamize in the charism in Messiah Yah Shua.

2 And what you hear from me
through many witnesses,
set forth to trustworthy humanity,
who are ample to doctrinate others also.

3 So endure hardship
as a good warrior of Yah Shua Messiah.

4 No one who wars
entangles himself with the transactions of existence;
so as to please him who enlisted him.

5 And whenever anyone contends for masteries
he still is not wreathed unless he contends torahically.

6 The cultivator must labor
ere he partake the fruits.

7 Comprehend what I word;
so that indeed,
Adonay gives you comprehension in all.

8 Remember that Yah Shua Messiah
of the sperma of David
was raised from the dead
according to my evangelism:

9 wherein I endure hardship as an evil worker
— to bonds;
but the word of Elohim is not bound.

10 So I endure all for sake of the select,
so that they also obtain the salvation in
Messiah Yah Shua with eternal glory.

11 Trustworthy the word:
For if we co—die, we also co—live;

12 if we endure, we also co—reign;
if we deny, he also denies us;

13 if we distrust, he abides trustworthy;
he cannot deny himself.

14 Remind them of these,
witnessing in the sight of Adonay
to not logomachize about words that profit not
to the catastrophe of the hearers.

15 Be diligent to present
yourself approved to Elohim,
a worker unashamed
straightcutting the word of truth:

16 and stand aloof from profane and vain voices;
for they advance to more irreverence;

17 and their word pastures as a gangrene:
of whom are Hymenaeus and Philetus;

18 who concerning the truth, misaimed,
wording that the resurrection already became:
and they overturn the trust of some.

19 But yet indeed
the foundation of Elohim still stands solid
— having this seal,
Yah Veh knows who are his.
And, Everyone who names the name of Messiah
departs from injustice.
Nachum 1:7, Yahn 10:14

20 And in a mega house there are vessels
— not only of gold and of silver
but also of wood and of clay;
and some indeed to honor
and some to dishonor:

21 so whenever anyone purges himself from these
he shall be a vessel unto honour,

sanctified **hallowed**,
and *meet for the master's use* **useful to the despotes**,
and prepared unto every good work.

22 Flee also youthful *lusts* **pantings**:
but *follow righteousness* **pursue justness**,
faith **trust**, *charity* **love**, *peace* **shalom**,
with them that call on *the Lord* **Adonay**
out of a pure heart.

23 But foolish and *unlearned* **undisciplined** questions
avoid **shun**,
knowing that they *do gender* **birth** strifes.

24 And the servant of *the Lord* **Adonay** must not strive;
but be gentle unto all *men*,
apt to teach **didactic**, *patient* **enduring evil**,

25 In meekness
instructing **disciplining** those that oppose themselves;
if *God peradventure* **lestever Elohim**
will **shall** give them repentance
to the *acknowledging* **knowledge** of the truth;

26 And that they may *recover themselves* **sober up**
out of the snare of *the devil* **Diabolos**,
who are *taken captive* **captured alive** by him
at **unto** his will.

THE FINAL APOSTACY

3 This know also, that in the *last* **final** days
perilous times **furious seasons** shall
come **become present**.

2 For *men* **humanity** shall *be*
lovers of their own selves **befriending self**,
covetous **befriending silver**, *boasters* **braggarts**, proud,
blasphemers, *disobedient* **distrusting** to parents,
unthankful **uneucharistic**, *unholy* **unmercied**,

3 *Without natural affection* **Selfish**,
trucebreakers **disagreeable**, *false accusers* **diabolic**,
incontinent **uncontrollable**, *fierce* **savage**,
despisers of those that are good **unfriendly**,

4 Traitors, *heady* **precipitous**,
highminded **inflated**,
lovers of **befriending** pleasures
more than *lovers of God* **befriending Elohim**;

5 Having a form of *Godliness* **reverence**,
but denying the *power* **dynamis** thereof:
from such turn away.

6 For of this sort are they
which creep into houses,
and *lead captive silly* **captivate little** women
laden **heaped** with sins,

led away with divers *lusts* **pantings**,

7 *Ever* **Always** learning,
and never able to come to the knowledge of the truth.

8 Now *as* **in the manner**
Jannes and Jambres withstood *Moses* **Mosheh**, *so*
thus do these also *resist* **withstand** the truth:
men **humans** of corrupt minds,
reprobate **disapproved** concerning the *faith* **trust**.

9 But they shall *proceed* **advance** no *further* **more**:
for their *folly* **mindlessness**
shall be *manifest* **exposed** unto all *men*,
as their's also *was* **became**.

THE FINAL MANDATE OF PAULOS

10 But thou hast
fully known **closely followed** my doctrine,
manner of life **the lifestyle**, *purpose* **the prothesis**,
faith **the trust**, *longsuffering* **the patience**,
charity **the love**, *patience* **the endurance**,

11 the Persecutions, *afflictions* **the sufferings**,
which came unto *such as became* me
at Antioch, at Iconium, at Lystra;
what **manner** persecutions I endured:
but out of *them* all
the Lord delivered **Adonay rescued** me.

12 Yea, and all that will **to live** *Godly* **reverently**
in *Christ Jesus* **Messiah Yah Shua**
shall suffer persecution.

he becomes a vessel to honor
— hallowed and useful to the despotes
prepared to every good work.

22 And flee youthful pantings:
and pursue justness,
trust,
love,
and shalom
with them who call on Adonay from a pure heart.

23 And shun foolish and undisciplined questions,
knowing that they birth strifes:

24 and the servant of Adonay never strives;
but is gentle,
didactic,
endures evil to all;

25 and in meekness
disciplines them who oppose themselves;
lestever Elohim gives them repentance
to the knowledge of the truth;

26 and that they sober up
from the snare of Diabolos
— who captures them alive to his will.

The Final Apostacy

3 Know this also
that in the final days furious seasons are present.
2 For there becomes humanity
befriending self,
befriending silver,
braggarts,
proud,
blasphemers,
distrusting to parents,
uneucharistic,
unmercied,
3 selfish,
disagreeable,
diabolic,
uncontrollable,
savage,
unfriendly,
4 traitors,
precipitous,
inflated:
befriending pleasures more than befriending Elohim;
5 having a form of reverence
but denying the dynamis thereof;
— from such turn away.
6 For of this sort are they who creep into houses
and captivate little women heaped with sins
led away with divers pantings;
7 ever learning
and never able to come to the knowledge of the truth.
8 And even as Jannes and
Jambres withstood Mosheh,
thus also these withstand the truth:
humans of corrupt minds
disapproved concerning the trust:
9 but they advance no more:
for their mindlessness is exposed to all
as theirs also became.

The Final Mandate Of Paulos

10 And you — you closely followed my doctrine,
lifestyle, prothesis, the trust, the patience, the love,
the endurance,
11 the persecutions,
the sufferings;
such as became me at Antioch, at Iconium, at Lystra;
what manner persecutions I endured:
and Adonay rescued me from all.
12 Yes and all who will to live reverently
in Messiah Yah Shua suffer persecution:
13 But evil *men* **humanity** and *seducers* **enchanters**
shall *wax worse and* **advance** worse,
deceiving **seducing**, and *being deceiv*d **seduced**.
14 But *continue* **abide** thou in *the things* **those**
which thou hast learned
and hast been *assured of* **entrusted with**,
knowing of whom thou hast learned *them*;
15 And that from *a child* **infancy**
thou hast known the *holy scriptures* **priestal scribings**,
which are able to *make* **enwisen** thee *wise*
unto salvation through *faith* **trust**
which is in *Christ Jesus* **Messiah Yah Shua**.

All Scripture Is Elohim–Spirited

16 All scripture
is *given by inspiration of God* **Elohim—Spirited**,
and is *profitable* **beneficial** for doctrine,
for *reproof* **proof**, for *correction* **setting straight**,
for *instruction* **discipline** in *righteousness* **justness**:
17 That the *man* **human** of *God* **Elohim**
may be *perfect* **equipped**,
thoroughly *furnished* **completed/shalamed**
unto all good works.

4 I *charge thee* **witness** therefore
before God **in sight of Elohim**,
and *the Lord Jesus Christ* **Adonay Yah Shua Messiah**,
who shall judge the *quick* **living** and the dead
at his *appearing* **epiphany**
and his *kingdom* **sovereigndom**;
2 Preach the word;
be instant in season **stand by opportunely**,
out of season **inopportunely**;
reprove, rebuke,
exhort *with* **in** all *longsuffering* **patience** and doctrine.
3 For the *time will come* **season shall be**
when they *will* **shall** not *endure* **tolerate** sound doctrine;
but after their own *lusts* **pantings**
shall they heap to themselves *teachers* **doctors**,
having itching ears **tickling their hearing**;
4 And they shall **indeed**
turn away *their ears* from **hearing** the truth,
and shall *be turned* **turn** unto *fables* **myths**.
5 But *watch* **be** thou **sober** in all *things*,
endure *afflictions* **hardship**, do
the work of an evangelist,
make full proof of **fully bear** thy ministry.

The Departure Of Paulos

6 For I am now ready to be *offered* **libated**,
and the *time* **season** of my departure

	is at hand **standeth by**.		for setting straight,
			for discipline in justness
7	I have *fought* **agonized** a good *fight* **agony**,	17	— to equip the human of Elohim
	I have *finished* **completed/shalamed** my *course* **race**,		— thoroughly complete/at shalom
	I have *kept* **guarded** the *faith* **trust**:		unto all good works.
8	Henceforth there is laid up for me		
	a *crown* **wreath** of *righteousness* **justness**,	**4**	So I witness in sight of Elohim
	which *the Lord* **Adonay**, the *righteous* **just** judge,		and Adonay Yah Shua Messiah,
	shall give me *at* **in** that day:		who judges the living and the dead
	and not to me only,		at his epiphany and his sovereigndom:
	but unto all them also that love his *appearing* **epiphany**.	2	preach the word;
9	*Do thy diligence* **Be diligent**		stand by opportunely and inopportunely;
	to come *shortly* **quickly** unto me:		reprove,
10	For Demas hath forsaken me,		rebuke,
	having loved this present *world* **eon**,		exhort in all patience and doctrine:
	and is departed unto *Thessalonica* **Thessalonikee**;	3	For the season becomes
	Crescens to Galatia, Titus unto Dalmatia.		that they not tolerate sound doctrine;
11	Only *Luke* **Loukas** is with me.		but after their own pantings
	Take *Mark* **Markos**, and bring him with thee:		they heap doctors to themselves
	for he is *profitable* **useful** to me *for* **unto** the ministry.		who tickle their hearing;
12	And Tychicus have I *sent*	4	and indeed, they turn from hearing the truth
	apostolized to Ephesus.		and turn to myths.
13	The cloak that I left at Troas with Carpus,	5	And you,
	when thou comest, bring *with thee*,		be sober in all,
	and the *books* **scrolls**, *but* especially the parchments.		endure hardship,
			do the work of an evangelist,
	BEING ON GUARD		fully bear your ministry.
14	Alexander the coppersmith		THE DEPARTURE OF PAULOS
	did **indicated** me much evil:		
	the Lord reward **Adonay give** him	6	For I am now ready to be libated
	according to his works:		and the season of my departure stands by.
15	Of whom *be guard* thou *ware* also;	7	I agonized a good agony;
	for he hath *greatly* **extremely** withstood our words.		I completed/shalamed my race;
16	*At* **In** my first *answer* **pleading**		I guarded the trust:
	no *man stood* **one convened** with me,	8	henceforth a wreath of justness is laid up for me
	but all *men* forsook me:		which Adonay the just judge gives me in that day
13	and evil humanity and		— and not only to me
	enchanters advance worse		but also to all them who love his epiphany.
	— seducing and seduced.	9	Be diligent to come to me quickly:
14	And you, abide in those you learned	10	for Demas forsook me,
	and are entrusted with,		loving this present eon;
	knowing of whom you learned;		and departed to Thessalonikee;
15	and that from infancy		Crescens to Galatia;
	you have known the priestal scribings		Titus to Dalmatia:
	which are able to enwisen you to salvation	11	only Loukas is with me.
	through trust in Messiah Yah Shua.		Take Markos and bring him with you:
			for he is useful to me to the ministry.
	ALL SCRIPTURE IS ELOHIM—SPIRITED	12	And I apostolized Tychicus to Ephesus.
16	All scripture is Elohim—Spirited and beneficial	13	When you come,
	for doctrine,		bring the cloak I left at Troas with Carpus
	for proof,		and the scrolls — especially the parchments.

Being On Guard

14 Alexander the coppersmith
indicates me much evil;
Adonay give him according to his works:
15 whom also, you guard;
for he extremely withstands our words.
16 In my first pleading
no one convened with me, but all forsook me:
I pray God
that it may *it* not be *laid* **reckoned** to *their charge* **them**.
17 *Notwithstanding the Lord* **And**
Adonay stood *with* **by** me,
and *strengthened* **dynamized** me;
that *by* **through** me
the preaching might be fully *known* **borne**,
and that all the *Gentiles* **goyim** might hear:
and I was *delivered* **rescued** out of the mouth of the lion.
18 And *the Lord* **Adonay** shall *deliver* **rescue** me
from every evil work,
and *will preserve* **shall save** me unto his
heavenly kingdom **sovereigndom of the heavenlies**:
to whom be glory
for ever and ever **unto the eons of the eons**.
Amen.

Salutes And Benediction

19 Salute Prisca and Aquila,
and the household of Onesiphorus.
20 Erastus abode at Corinth:
but Trophimus have I left at *Miletum sick* **Miletus frail**.
21 *Do thy diligence* **Be diligent**
to come *before winter* **ere the downpour**.
Eubulus *greeteth* **saluteth** thee,
and Pudens, and Linus, and Claudia,
and all the brethren.

22 *The Lord Jesus Christ*
Adonay Yah Shua Messiah
be with thy spirit.
Grace **Charism** be with you.
Amen.
so be it not reckoned to them.
17 And Adonay stood by me and dynamized me;
to fully bear the preaching through me;
and that all the goyim hear:
and I was rescued from the mouth of the lion:
18 and Adonay rescues me from every evil work
and saves me to his sovereigndom of the heavenlies:
to whom be glory to the eons of the eons.
Amen.

Salutes And Benediction

19 Salute Prisca and Aquila
and the household of Onesiphorus.
20 Erastus abides at Corinth
and I left Trophimus frail at Miletus.
21 Be diligent to come ere the downpour.
Eubulus salutes you
— and Pudens and Linus and Claudia
and all the brothers.
22 Adonay Yah Shua Messiah be with your spirit.
Charism be with you.
Amen.

TITUS 1

Salutation

1 *Paul* **Paulos**, a servant of *God* **Elohim**,
and an apostle of *Jesus Christ* **Yah Shua Messiah**,
according to the *faith* **trust**
of *God's elect* **Elohim's select**,
and the *acknowledging* **knowledge** of the truth
which is after *Godliness* **reverence**;

2 In hope of eternal life, which *God* **Elohim**,
that cannot lie **the nonpseudo**
promised **pre—evangelized**
before the world began **preceding eternal times**;

3 But hath in *due times* **his own seasons**
manifested his word *through* **in** preaching,
which is *committed* **entrusted** unto me
according to the *commandment* **order**
of *God* **Elohim** our Saviour;

4 To Titus, *mine own son* **genuine child**
after the **according to** common *faith* **trust**:
Grace **Charism**, mercy, and *peace* **shalom**,
from *God* **Elohim** the Father
and *the Lord Jesus Christ* **Adonay Yah Shua Messiah**
our Saviour.

Seating Officers

5 For this cause left I thee in Crete,
that thou shouldest *set in order the things* **arrange those**
that are *wanting* **lacking**,
and *ordain* **seat** elders in every city,
as I had *appointed* **ordained** thee:

6 If any be *blameless* **unaccusable**,
the *husband* **man** of one *wife* **woman**,
having *faithful* **trustworthy** children
not *accused* **under accusation** of *riot* **dissipation**
or *unruly* **insubordination**.

7 For *a bishop* **an episcopate**
must be *blameless* **unaccusable**,
as the *steward* **administrator** of *God* **Elohim**;
not *selfwilled* **selfpleasing**, not *soon angry* **wrathful**,
not given to wine **no winesop**, no striker,
not *given to filthy lucre* **avaricious**;

8 But *a lover of hospitality* **befriending strangers**,
a lover of good men **befriending good**,
sober **soundminded**,
just, *holy* **merciful**, *temperate* **self—controlled**;

9 *Holding fast* **Upholding** the
faithful **trustworthy** word
as he hath been taught **of doctrine**,
that he may be able *by* **in** sound doctrine
both to *exhort* **beseech** and *to convince* **reprove**
the *gainsayers* **contradicters**.

Exposing Insubordinates

10 For there are many
unruly and vain talkers **insubordinate mataeologists**
and *deceivers* **thought deluders**,
specially they of the circumcision:

11 Whose mouths must be stopped,
who *subvert* **overturn** whole houses,
teaching things **doctrinating** which they *ought* **must** not,
for *filthy lucre's sake* **shameful gain**.

12 One of themselves, *even* a
prophet of their own, said,
The Cretians are *alway* **ever** liars,
evil beasts, *slow bellies* **idle wombs**.

13 This witness is true.
Wherefore **For which cause**
rebuke **reprove** them *sharply* **severely**,
that they may be sound in the *faith* **trust**;

14 Not giving heed to *Jewish*
fables **Yah Hudaic myths**,
and *commandments* **misvoth** of *men*
humanity, that turn from the truth.

15 Unto the pure **indeed** all *things* are pure:
but unto them that are defiled and *unbelieving* **trustless**
is *nothing* **naught** pure;
but even their mind and conscience is defiled.

16 They profess that they know *God* **Elohim**;
but in works they deny *him*,
being abominable, and *disobedient* **distrusting**,
and unto every good work *reprobate* **disapproved**.

Salutation

1 Paulos, a servant of Elohim
and an apostle of Yah Shua Messiah,
according to the trust of the select of Elohim;
and the knowledge of the truth
according to reverence

2 in hope of eternal life;
that the non—pseudo Elohim
pre—evangelized preceding eternal times;

3 and in his own seasons
manifests his word in preaching
that which is entrusted to me
according to the order of Elohim our Saviour:

4 To Titus
— genuine child according to common trust:
Charism, mercy and shalom,
from Elohim the Father
and Adonay Yah Shua Messiah our Saviour.

Seating Officers

5 For this cause I left you in Crete
to arrange what lacked;
to seat elders in every city as I ordained you:
6 if any be unaccusable,
the man of one woman,
having trustworthy children,
who are not under accusation
of dissipation or insubordination.
7 For an episcopate, as the
administrator of Elohim,
must be unaccusable,
neither selfpleasing nor wrathful,
nor a winesop,
nor a striker,
nor avaricious;
8 but befriend strangers,
befriend good, soundminded,
just,
merciful,
self—controlled,
9 upholding the trustworthy word of doctrine;
to be capable in sound doctrine
both to beseech and reprove the contradicters.

Exposing Insubordinates

10 For there are many insubordinate mataeologists
and thought deluders
— specially those of the circumcision
11 whose mouths must be stopped;
who overturn whole houses
doctrinating what they must not
for shameful gain.
12 One of them — their own prophet said,
The Cretians are ever liars, evil beasts, idle wombs.
13 This witness is true.
For which cause reprove them severely
to be sound in the trust;
14 not giving heed to Yah Hudaic myths
and misvoth of humanity that turn from the truth.
15 Indeed, to the pure, all are pure:
and to the defiled and trustless, naught is pure;
but even their mind and conscience is defiled.
16 They profess to know Elohim;
but in works they deny:
being abominable and distrusting
and disapproved to every good work.

Sound Doctrine

2 But speak thou *the things* **those**
which *become* **befit** sound doctrine:
2 That the *aged men* **elders***
be sober, *grave* **venerant**,
temperate **soundminded**, sound in *faith* **the trust**, in *charity* **love**, in *patience* **endurance**.
3 The *aged women* **elders**** likewise,
that they be in behaviour as becometh holiness
in priestly demeanor,
not *false accusers* **diabolic**,
not *given* **subservient** to much wine, *teachers of* **doctrinating** good *things*; *masculine; **feminine
4 That *they may teach* the young** women
to may be *sober* **soundminded**,
to love **befriend** their *husbands* **men**,
to love **befriend** their children,
5 To be discreet **Soundminded**, *chaste* **hallowed**,
keepers at home **home guards**, good,
obedient **subjugated** to their own *husbands* **men**,
that the word of *God* **Elohim** be not blasphemed.
6 Young* men likewise
exhort **beseech** to be *sober* **sound** minded.
7 *In* **Concerning** all *things*
shewing **present** thyself a *pattern* **type** of good works:
in doctrine
shewing uncorruptness **presenting incorruption**,
gravity **veneration**, *sincerity* **incorruptibility**,
8 Sound speech **Faultless words**
that cannot be condemned;
that he that is of the contrary part
may be ashamed **shame**,
having no evil *thing* to *say of* **word about**
you. **feminine; *masculine
9 *Exhort* servants to *be obedient* **subjugate**
unto their own *masters* **despotes**,
and to *please* **well—please** them *well* in all *things*;
not *answering again* **contradicting**;
10 Not *purloining* **embezzling**,
but *shewing* **indicating** all good *fidelity* **trust**;
that they may adorn the doctrine
of *God* **Elohim** our Saviour in all *things*.

The Salvational Charism

11 For the *grace of God that bringeth salvation*
salvational charism of Elohim
hath appeared to all *men* **humanity**,
12 *Teaching* **Disciplining** us that,
denying *ungodliness* **irreverence**

and *worldly lusts* **cosmic pantings**,
we should live *soberly* **soundmindedly**, *righteously* **justly**,
and *Godly* **reverently**, in this present *world* **eon**;

13   *Looking for* **Awaiting** that blessed hope,
and the *glorious appearing* **epiphany of the glory**
of the *great God* **mega Elohim**
and our Saviour *Jesus Christ* **Yah Shua Messiah**;

14   Who gave himself for us,
that he might redeem us
from all *iniquity* **torah violations**,
and purify unto himself a peculiar people,
zealous of **zealots in** good works.

15   These *things* speak, and *exhort* **beseech**,
and *rebuke* **reprove** with all *authority* **order**.
Let no *man despise* **one disesteem** thee.

3   *Put* **Remind** them *in mind*
to *be subject* **subjugate**
to *principalities* **hierarchies** and *powers* **authorities**,
to obey magistrates,
to be *ready* **prepared** to every good work,

2   To *speak evil of* **blaspheme** no *man* **one**,
to be *no brawlers* **amicable**, *but* gentle,
shewing **indicating** all meekness unto all *men* **humanity**.

3   For we ourselves also were
sometimes *foolish* **mindless**,
disobedient **distrusting**, *deceived* **seduced**,
serving divers *lusts* **pantings** and pleasures,
living **passing through** in malice and envy,
hateful, *and* hating one another.

4   But *after that* **when** the
kindness and *love* **philanthropy**
of *God* **Elohim** our Saviour *toward man* appeared,

Sound Doctrine

2   And you, speak those that befit sound doctrine:
2   that the elders* be sober,
venerant,
soundminded,
sound in the trust, in love, in endurance.
3   Likewise the elders**:
in priestly demeanor,
not diabolic,
not subservient to much wine,
doctrinating good.
*masculine; **feminine
4   That the young** be soundminded,
befriending their men,
befriending their children,
5   soundminded,
hallowed,
home guards,
good,
subjugate to their own men;
that they not blaspheme the word of Elohim.
6   Likewise beseech the young*
to be sound minded:
7   concerning all,
present yourself a type of good works:
in doctrine: , present:
incorruption,
veneration,
incorruptibility,
8   faultless words;
to shame whoever is of the contrary part,
with no evil to word about you.
**feminine; *masculine
9   Servants:
subjugate to your own despotes
to well—please them in all;
neither contradict,
10   nor embezzel;
but that they indicate all good trust,
to adorn the doctrine of Elohim our Saviour in all.

The Salvational Charism

11   For the salvational charism of Elohim
appeared to all humanity,
12   disciplining us
to deny irreverence and cosmic pantings,
to live soundmindedly,
justly and reverently in this present eon;
13   awaiting that blessed hope
and the epiphany of the glory of the mega Elohim
and our Saviour Yah Shua Messiah;
14   who gave himself for us,
to redeem us from all torah violations
and purify a peculiar people to himself
— zealots in good works.
15   Speak these
and beseech and reprove with all order.
be disesteemed by no one;
3   remind them
to subjugate to hierarchies and authorities.
to obey magistrates.
to be prepared to every good work,
2   to blaspheme no one,
to be amicable, gentle,
to indicate all meekness to all humanity.
3   For we ourselves sometimes also are:
mindless,

distrusting,
seduced,
— serving divers pantings and pleasures,
passing through in malice and envy,
— hateful — hating one another.

4 And when the kindness and philanthropy
of Elohim our Saviour appeared

5 Not by works *of righteousness* **in justness**
which we have done,
but according to his mercy he saved us,
by **through** the *washing* **bathing**
of *regeneration* **regenesis**,
and renewing of the *Holy Spirit* **Ruach ha-kodesh**;

6 Which he *shed* **poured** on us *abundantly* **richly**
through *Jesus Christ* **Yah Shua Messiah** our Saviour;

7 That *being* **having been**
justified by his *grace* **charism**,
we should *be made* **become** heirs
according to the hope of eternal life.

8 This is a *faithful saying* **trustworthy word**,
and these *things* I will
that thou affirm *constantly* **thoroughly**,
that they which have *believed* **trusted** in *God* **Elohim**
might be *careful* **thoughtful**
to *maintain* **preside over** good works.
These *things* are good and *profitable* **beneficial**
unto *men* **humanity**.

9 But *avoid* **stand aloof from** foolish questions,
and genealogies, and contentions,
and *strivings about the law* **strifes of torahists**;
for they are *unprofitable* **unbeneficial** and vain.

10 A *man* **human** that is an heretick
after the first and second admonition *reject* **shun**;

11 Knowing that he that is
such is *subverted* **perverted**,
and sinneth,
being *condemned of himself* **self—condemned**.

Personal Instructions

12 When **ever** I shall send
Artemas unto thee, or Tychicus,
be diligent to come unto me to Nicopolis: for
I have *determined* **judged** there to winter.

13 *Bring* **Forward** Zenas the *lawyer* **torahist**
and Apollos *on their journey* diligently,
that *nothing* **naught** be *wanting* **lacking** unto them.

14 And let our's also learn to *maintain* **preside**
over good works *for* **unto** necessary *uses*
needs, that they be not unfruitful.

Salutes And Benediction

15 All that are with me salute thee.
Greet **Salute** them that *love* **befriend** us in *the faith* **trust**.
Grace **Charism** be with you all.
Amen.

5 — not by works in justness which we did
— but according to his mercy he saved us
through the bathing of regenesis
and renewing of the Holy Spirit;

6 which he richly poured on us
through Yah Shua Messiah our Saviour;

7 being justified by his charism,
to become heirs according to the hope of eternal life.

8 Trustworthy the word:
and I will that you thoroughly affirm these
— so that whoever trusts in Elohim
be thoughtful to preside over good works:
these are good and beneficial to humanity.

9 And stand aloof from foolish questions
and genealogies
and contentions
and strifes of torahists;
for they are unbeneficial and vain.

10 A human — a heretick
after the first and second admonition, shun;

11 knowing that whoever is
such is perverted and sins,
being self—condemned.

Personal Instructions

12 Whenever I send you Artemas or Tychicus,
be diligent to come to me to Nicopolis:
for I judge to winter there.

13 Diligently forward Zenas
the torahist and Apollos,
that they lack naught.

14 And that those of us also learn to preside
over good works to necessary needs
— to not be unfruitful.

Salutes And Benediction

15 All those me salute you.
Salute them who befriend us in trust.
Charism be with you all.
Amen.

Salutation

1 Paulos, a prisoner of Yah Shua Messiah
and Timo Theos our brother:
To Philemon our beloved and co—worker,
2 and to beloved Apphia
and Archippus our co—warrior
and to the ecclesia in your house.
3 Charism to you, and shalom,
from Elohim our Father
and Adonay Yah Shua Messiah.
4 I eucharistize my Elohim,
making remembrance of you always in my prayers,
5 hearing of your love and trust
toward Adonay Yah Shua
and to all the holy;
6 to energize the communion of your trust
by the knowledge of all the good in you
in Messiah Yah Shua.
7 For we have
vast charism and consolation in your love,
because through you, brother,
the spleens of the holy rest.
8 So, though I have much boldness in Messiah
to order you to do what is proper,
9 yet for sake of love, I rather beseech you
— being such a one as Paulos the elder
and now also a prisoner of Yah Shua Messiah.
10 I beseech you concerning my child Onesimus,
whom I birthed in my bonds:
11 who in time past was useless to you,
and now useful to you and to me:
12 whom I send again:
so take him to yourself as my own spleen:
13 whom I had willed to hold back with me,
to minister to me in your stead
in the bonds of the evangelism:
14 and apart from your
decision, I will to do naught;
that your good not be as of necessity, but voluntarily.
15 For perhaps he separated for an hour,
so that you have him eternally
16 — no longer as a servant
but above a servant — a beloved brother,
especially to me — but how much more to you
both in the flesh and in Adonay?
17 So if you regard me a communicant,
take him to you as myself.
18 If he has injured or has indebted aught
reckon that to me;
19 I Paulos scribe with my own hand,
I — I fully satisfy the penalty:
that I word not to you how you are indebted to me
— even your own self.
20 Yes brother, so that I benefit of you in Adonay:
I rest my spleen in Adonay.
21 Being convinced of your obedience
I scribe to you,
knowing that you also do more than I word:

Salutation

1 *Paul* **Paulos**, a prisoner of
Jesus Christ **Yah Shua Messiah**,
and *Timothy* **Timo Theos** our brother,
unto Philemon our *dearly* beloved,
and *fellowlabourer* **co—worker**,
2 And to *our* beloved Apphia,
and Archippus our *fellowsoldier* **co—warrior**,
and to the *church* **ecclesia** in thy house:
3 *Grace* **Charism** to you, and *peace* **shalom**,
from *God* **Elohim** our Father
and *the Lord Jesus Christ* **Adonay Yah Shua Messiah**.
4 I *thank* **eucharistize** my *God* **Elohim**,
making *mention* **remembrance** of thee
always in my prayers,
5 Hearing of thy love and *faith* **trust**,
which thou hast toward *the Lord
Jesus* **Adonay Yah Shua**,
and *toward* **unto** all *saints* **the holy**;
6 That the *communication*
communion of thy *faith* **trust**
may become *effectual* **energized**
by the *acknowledging* **knowledge**
of *every* **all the** good *thing* which is in you
in *Christ Jesus* **Messiah Yah Shua**.
7 For we have
great joy **vast charism** and consolation in thy love,
because the *bowels* **spleens** of the *saints* **holy**
are *refreshed by* **rested through** thee, brother.
8 *Wherefore* **So**,
though I might *be* **have** much *bold*
boldness in *Christ* **Messiah**
to *enjoin* **order** thee
to do that which is *convenient* **proper**,
9 Yet for love's sake I rather beseech *thee*,
being such an one as *Paul* **Paulos** the *aged* **elder**,
and now also a prisoner
of *Jesus Christ* **Yah Shua Messiah**.
10 I beseech thee *for* **concerning**
my *son* **child** Onesimus,

	whom I have *begotten* **birthed** in my bonds:
11	Which in time past was to thee *unprofitable* **useless**, but now *profitable* **useful** to thee and to me:
12	Whom I have sent again: thou therefore *receive* **take** him **unto you**, that is, mine own *bowels* **spleen**:
13	Whom I *would have* **had willed** *retained* **to hold back** with me, that in thy stead he might have ministered unto me in the bonds of the *gospel* **evangelism**:
14	But *without* **apart from** thy *mind* **decision**, would I **will to** do *nothing* **naught**; that thy *benefit* **good** should not be as it were of necessity, but *willingly* **voluntarily**.
15	For perhaps he *therefore departed* **separated** for *a season* **an hour**, that thou shouldest *receive* **have** him *for ever* **eternally**;
16	*Not now* **No longer** as a servant, but above a servant, a brother beloved, specially to me, but how much more unto thee, both in the flesh, and in *the Lord* **Adonay**?
17	*So* If thou *count* **regard** me *therefore* a *partner* **communicant**, *receive* **take** him **unto you** as myself.
18	If he hath *wronged thee* **injured**, or *oweth thee* **is indebted** ought, *put* **reckon** that *on mine account* **to me**;
19	I *Paul* **Paulos** have *written it* **scribed** with mine own hand, I *will repay it* **shall fully satisfy the penalty**: albeit I *do* **word** not *say* to thee how thou *owest* **art indebted** unto me even thine own self *besides*.
20	Yea, brother, let me have *joy* **benefit** of thee in *the Lord* **Adonay**: *refresh* **rest** my *bowels* **spleen** in *the Lord* **Adonay**.
21	*Having confidence* **Being convinced** *in* **of** thy obedience I *wrote* **scribed** unto thee, knowing that thou *wilt* **shalt** also do more than I *say* **word**.
22	But *withal* **simultaneously** prepare me also a lodging: for I *trust* **hope** that through your prayers I shall be *given* **granted charism** unto you.

SALUTE AND BENEDICTION

23	There salute thee Epaphras, my *fellowprisoner* **co—captive** in *Christ Jesus* **Messiah Yah Shua**;
24	*Marcus* **Markos**, Aristarchus, Demas, *Lucas* **Loukas**, my *fellowlabourers* **co—workers**.
25	The *grace* **charism** of our *Lord Jesus Christ* **Adonay Yah Shua Messiah** be with your spirit. Amen.
22	and simultaneously also prepare me a lodging: for I hope that through your prayers you grant me charism.

SALUTE AND BENEDICTION

23	These salute you: Epaphras, my co—captive in Messiah Yah Shua;
24	Markos, Aristarchus, Demas, Loukas, my co—workers.
25	The charism of our Adonay Yah Shua Messiah be with your spirit. Amen.

The Son Of Elohim Is The Essence Of Elohim

1 In many portions and in
many manners, long ago,
Elohim spoke to the fathers in the prophets,

2 and in these final days speaks to us in Son:
whom he placed heir of all;
through whom also he made the eons:

3 who being the effulgence of glory
and the character of his essence
and bearing all by the rhema of his dynamis,
when he, through himself,
made a purifying of our sins,
sat down at the right of the Majesty on high:

4 being so much better than the angels,
as he inherited a more excellent name than they.

The Son, Better Than The Angels

5 For to which of the angels said he ever,
You are my Son, this day I birthed you?
And again,
I become to him, Father, and he becomes to
me, Son? Psalm 2:7, 2 Shemu El 7:14

6 And again,
when he brings the firstbirthed into the world,
he words,
And all angels of Elohim worship
him. Deuteronomy 32:43

7 And indeed to the angels he words,
Who makes his angels spirits and
his liturgists a flame of fire.
Psalm 104:4

8 But to the Son, Your throne, O Elohim,
is to the eons of the eons:
a scion of straightness
is the scion of your sovereigndom.

9 You loved justness and hated torah violations;
so Elohim — your Elohim anointed you
with the olive oil of jumping for joy
above your partners.
Psalm 45:6, 7

10 And in the beginning, O Adonay,
you founded the earth;
and the heavens are the works of your hands:

11 They destruct, and you abide continually;
and they all antiquate as a garment;

12 and as a mantle you coil them and they change:
and you are the same and your years
fail not. Psalm 102:25—27

13 And to which of the angels said he ever,
Sit at my right,
until ever I place your enemies the
stool of your feet? Psalm 110:1

14 Are they not indeed all liturgizing spirits
apostolized to minister
for them who inherit salvation?

2 So we must more superabundantly heed
what we heard
— lest ever we float away.

2 For if the word spoken through angels
became steadfast
and every transgression and disobedience
took a just recompence;

3 how escape we,
neglecting such a vast salvation;
which in the beginning
was taken and told through Adonay
and established to us by them who heard;

4 Elohim also co—witnessing,

The Son Of Elohim Is The Essence Of Elohim

1 *God, who at sundry times* **In many portions**
and in *divers* **many** manners, *spake in time past* long ago,
Elohim spoke unto the fathers *by* **in** the prophets,

2 *Hath* in these *last* **final** days
spoken unto us *by his* **in** Son,
whom he hath *appointed* **placed** heir of all *things*,
by **through** whom also he made the *worlds* **eons**;

3 Who being the *brightness*
effulgence of *his* glory,
and the *express image* **character** of his *person* **essence**,
and *upholding* **bearing** all *things*
by the *word* **rhema** of his *power* **dynamis**,
when he had *by* **through** himself
purged **purified** our sins,
sat down *on* **at** the right *hand* of the Majesty on high;

4 Being *made* so much better than the angels,
inasmuch as he hath *by inheritance obtained* **inherited**
a more excellent name than they.

The Son, Better Than The Angels

5 For unto which of the angels
said he *at any time* **ever**,
Thou art my Son, this day have I *begotten* **birthed** thee?
And again,
I *will* **shall** be to him, *a* Father, and he shall be
to me, *a* Son? Psalm 2:7, 2 Shemu El 7:14

6 And again, when he bringeth *in*
the *firstbegotten* **firstborn** into the world,

HEBREWS 1, 2

he *saith* **wordeth**,
And let all the angels of *God* **Elohim**
worship him. Deuteronomy 32:43

7 And *of* **indeed unto** the angels he *saith* **wordeth**,
Who maketh his angels spirits,
and his *ministers* **liturgists** a flame of fire.
Psalm 104:4

8 But unto the Son *he saith*,
Thy throne, O *God* **Elohim**,
is *for ever and ever* **unto the eons of the eons**:
a *sceptre* **scion** of *righteousness* **straightness**
is the *sceptre* **scion** of thy *kingdom* **sovereigndom**.

9 Thou hast loved *righteousness* **justness**,
and hated *iniquity* **torah violations**;
therefore God **so Elohim**, *even* thy *God* **Elohim**,
hath anointed thee
with the *olive* oil of *gladness* **jumping for joy**
above thy *fellows* **partners**.
Psalm 45:6, 7

10 And, Thou, *Lord* **Adonay**, in the beginning
hast *laid the foundation of* **founded** the earth;
and the heavens are the works of thine hands:

11 They shall *perish* **destruct**;
but thou *remainest* **continually abidest**;
and they all shall *wax old* **antiquate** as doth a garment;

12 And as a *vesture* **mantle**
shalt thou *fold* **coil** them *up*,
and they shall be changed:
but thou art the same, and thy years
shall not fail. Psalm 102:25—27

13 But to which of the angels
said he *at any time* **ever**,
Sit *on* **at** my right *hand*,
until **ever** I *make* **place** thine enemies thy footstool?
Psalm 110:1

14 Are they not all *ministering*
indeed liturgizing spirits,
sent forth **apostolized** to minister for them
who shall *be heirs of* **inherit** salvation?

2 *Therefore* **So** we *ought* **must**
to give the more earnest **more superabundantly** heed
to the things **those** which we have heard,
lest *at any time* **ever** we should *let them slip* **float away**.

2 For if the word spoken *by* **through** angels
was **became** stedfast,
and every transgression and disobedience
received **took** a just recompence *of reward*;

3 How shall we escape,
if we neglect **neglecting** so *great* **vast** salvation;
which *at the first began* **in the beginning was taken**
to be spoken by the Lord **and told through Adonay**,
and was *confirmed* **established** unto us
by them that heard *him*;

4 *God* **Elohim** also *bearing*
them witness **co—witnessing**,
both with signs and *wonders* **omens**,
and with divers *miracles* **dynamis**,
and *gifts* **impartations** of the *Holy*
Spirit **Ruach ha-kodesh**,
according to his own will?

5 For unto the angels hath he not
put in subjection **subjugated** the world to come,
whereof we speak.

The Son Lowered And Wreathed

6 But *one in a certain place* **someone somewhere**
testified **witnessed**, *saying* **wording**,
What is *man* **humanity**,
that thou *art mindful of* **rememberest** him?
or the son of *man* **humanity**, that thou visitest him?

7 Thou *madest* **hast lowered** him
a little lower **somewhat less** than the angels*;
thou *crownedst* **hast wreathed** him
with glory and honour,
and *didst set* **seated** him over the works of thy hands:

8 Thou hast *put* **subjugated** all *things in subjection*
under his feet.
For in that he *put* **subjugated** all
in subjection under him,
he *left nothing* **allowed naught**
that is not put under **unsubjugated to** him.
But now we see not yet
all *things put* **subjugated** under him.

9 But we see *Jesus* **Yah Shua**,
who was *made a little lower* **lowered somewhat less**
than *the angels* **Elohim***
for the suffering of death,
crowned **wreathed** with glory and honour;
that he by the *grace* **charism** of *God* **Elohim**
should taste death for every man.
*see Psalm 8:4—6

10 For it *became* **befitted** him,
for whom *are all things* **the all**,
and *by whom are all things* **through whom the all**,
in bringing many sons unto glory,
to *make* **complete/shalam**
the *captain* **hierarch** of their salvation *perfect*
through sufferings.

11 For both he that *sanctifieth* **halloweth**
and they who are *sanctified* **hallowed** are all of one:

for which cause he is not ashamed to call them brethren,
12 *Saying* **Wording**,
I *will declare* **shall evangelize** thy name
unto my brethren,
in the midst of the *church* **ecclesia**
will I sing praise **shall I hymn** unto thee.
Psalm 22:22
13 And again, I *will put my*
trust **shall confide** in him.
And again, Behold I,
and the children which *God* **Elohim** hath given me.
Yesha Yah 8:17
14 *Forasmuch then* **So since**
as the children are partakers of flesh and blood,
he also himself likewise *took part* **partook** of the same;
so that through death he might *destroy* **inactivate** him
that had the power of death, that is, *the devil* **Diabolos**;
15 And *deliver* **release** them
who **as many as** through *fear* **awe** of death
were **through** all their lifetime
subject to *bondage* **servitude**.
16 For *verily* **doubtless indeed**
he took not *on him the nature* **hold** of angels;
but he took *on him* **hold of** the *seed* **sperma** of Abraham.
Yesha Yah 41:9
17 *Wherefore* **So**
in all *things it behooved him* **he was indebted**
to be *made like* **likened** unto his brethren,
that he might *be* **become**
a merciful and *faithful high* **trustworthy arch** priest
in things pertaining to God **unto Elohim**,
to *make reconciliation* **kapur/atone**
for the sins of the people.
18 For in that he himself hath suffered
being *tempted* **tested**,
he is able to *succour* **help** them
that are *tempted* **tested**.
both with signs and omens and with divers dynamis
and impartations of the Holy Spirit
according to his own will?
5 For he subjugates not the world to come
whereof we speak
to angels.

THE SON LOWERED AND WREATHED

6 But somewhere someone witnessed,
wording, What is humanity, that you remember
him? Or the son of humanity, that you visit him?
7 You lowered him somewhat
less than the angels*;
you wreathed him with glory and honor
and seated him over the works of your hands:
8 you subjugated all under his feet.
For in that he subjugated all under him
he allowed naught unsubjugated to him:
and now we still see not all subjugated under him.
9 And we see Yah Shua,
who was lowered somewhat less than Elohim*
for the suffering of death,
wreathed with glory and honor;
that he by the charism of Elohim
tasted death for every man.
*see Psalm 8:4—6
10 For it befitted him,
for whom the all, and through whom the all,
in bringing many sons to glory
to complete/shalam the hierarch of their salvation
through sufferings.
11 For both the hallower
and the hallowed are all of one:
for which cause
he is not ashamed to call them brothers,
12 wording,
I evangelize your name to my brothers,
midst the ecclesia I hymn to you.
Psalm 22:22
13 And again, I confide in him.
And again, Behold I —
and the children whom Elohim gave me.
Yesha Yah 8:17
14 So since, as the children
partake of flesh and blood,
he also himself likewise partook of the same;
so that through death
he inactivated him who had the power of death
— that is, Diabolos;
15 and released them,
as many as through awe of death
who through all their lifetime
were subject to servitude.
16 For doubtless indeed he took not hold of angels;
but he took hold of the sperma of Abraham.
Yesha Yah 41:9
17 So he was indebted in all
to be likened to his brothers,
to become a merciful and trustworthy archpriest
to Elohim,
to kapur/atone for the sins of the people.
18 For in that he himself
suffered, being tested in all,

he is able to help them who are tested.

THE SON, BETTER THAN MOSHEH

3 *Wherefore* **So**, holy brethren,
partakers of the *heavenly* calling **of the heavenlies**,
consider
the Apostle and *High* **Arch** priest of our profession,
Christ Jesus **Messiah Yah Shua**;

2 Who was *faithful* **Being trustworthy** to him
that *appointed* **dealt with** him,
as also *Moses* **Mosheh** *was faithful* in
all his house. Numbers 12:7

3 For this *man* **one** was *counted* **deemed** worthy
of more glory than *Moses* **Mosheh**,
inasmuch as he who hath *builded* **prepared** the house
hath **the** more honour *than the house*.
Zechar Yah 6:12, 13

4 For every house is *builded*
prepared by some *man* **one**;
but he that *built* **prepared** all *things* is *God* **Elohim**.

5 And *Moses verily* **Mosheh indeed**
was *faithful* **trustworthy** in all his house,
as a *servant* **therapist**,
for **unto** a *testimony* **witness**
of those *things* which were to be spoken *after*;
Numbers 12:7

6 But *Christ* **Messiah** as a son over his own house;
whose house are we,
if **whenever** we hold *fast* **down** the *confidence* **boldness**
and the *rejoicing* **boasting** of the hope
firm **stedfast** unto the *end* **completion**.

7 *Wherefore* **So**
(**exactly** as the *Holy Spirit* **Ruach ha-kodesh** *saith* **wordeth**,
To day *if* **whenever** ye *will* **shall** hear his voice,

8 Harden not your hearts, as in the provocation,
in the day of *temptation* **testing** in the wilderness:

9 *When* **Where** your fathers *tempted* **tested** me,
proved me, and saw my works forty years.

10 *Wherefore* **So**
I was *grieved* **perturbed** with that generation, and said,
They *do alway err* **ever wander** in their heart;
and they have not known my ways.

11 So I *sware* **oathed** in my wrath,
If They shall *not* enter into my *rest* **shabbath**.)
Psalm 95:7—11

12 *Take heed* **See**, brethren,
lest there **ever** be in any of you
an evil heart of *unbelief* **trustlessness**,
in departing from the living *God* **Elohim**.

13 But *exhort one another* **console yourselves**
daily **each day**,
while **as long as** it is called To day;
lest any of you be hardened
through the *deceitfulness* **delusion** of sin.

14 For we are *made* **become**
partakers of *Christ* **the Messiah**,
if **whenever** we hold **down** the
beginning of our confidence
stedfast unto the *end* **completion/shalom**;

15 *While it is said* **In having worded**,
To day *if* **whenever** ye *will* **shall** hear his voice,
harden not your hearts, as in the provocation.
Psalm 95:7,8

16 For some, when they had heard, did provoke:
howbeit **yet** not all
that came out of *Egypt* **Misrayim**
by Moses **through Mosheh**.

17 But with whom was he
grieved **perturbed** forty years?
was it not **indeed** with them that had sinned,
whose carcases fell in the wilderness?

18 And to whom *sware* **oathed** he
that they should not enter into his *rest* **shabbath**,
but **except** to them that *believed not* **distrusted**?

19 So we see that they could not enter in
because of *unbelief* **trustlessness**.

THE SHABBATH OF ELOHIM

4 **So** Let us *therefore fear* **awe**,
lest **ever**, a *promise* **pre—evangelism** being left *us*
of entering into his *rest* **shabbath**,
any of you should *seem* **think**
to *come short of it* **fall behind**.

2 For *unto us was the gospel preached*
we were evangelized, as well as
unto them **exactly as they**:

THE SON, BETTER THAN MOSHEH

3 So holy brothers,
partakers of the calling of the heavenlies,
consider the Apostle and Archpriest of our profession,
Messiah Yah Shua;

2 being trustworthy to him who dealt with him,
as also Mosheh in all his house.
Numbers 12:7

3 For this one was deemed worthy
of more glory than Mosheh,
inasmuch as he who prepares the house

has the more honor.
Zechar Yah 6:12, 13
4 For every house is prepared by someone;
and he who prepares all is Elohim.
5 And indeed,
Mosheh was trustworthy in all his house,
as a therapist,
to witness of those to be spoken of.
Numbers 12:7
6 And Messiah, as a son over his own house:
whose house we are;
whenever we hold down the boldness
and the boasting of the hope
steadfast to the completion/shalom.
7 So, exactly as the Holy Spirit words,
Today whenever you hear his voice,
8 harden not your hearts as in the provocation,
in the day of testing in the wilderness:
9 where your fathers tested me,
proved me,
and saw my works forty years.
10 So I was perturbed with
that generation and said,
They ever wander in their heart;
and they know not my ways.
11 So I oathed in my wrath,
If they enter my shabbath — .
Psalm 95:7—11
12 See, brothers,
lest there ever be in any of you
an evil heart of trustlessness
in departing from the living Elohim;
13 but console yourselves each day,
as long as it is called Today;
lest any of you harden through the delusion of sin.
14 For we become partakers of the Messiah
whenever we hold to the beginning of our confidence
steadfast to the completion/shalom;
15 in wording,
Today, whenever you hear his voice,
harden not your hearts, as in the provocation.
Psalm 95:7,8
16 For some, when they heard, provoked:
yet not all who came from Misrayim through Mosheh.
17 But with whom was he perturbed forty years?
Was it not indeed with them who sinned
— whose carcases fell in the wilderness?
18 And to whom oathed he
that they not enter his shabbath —
except to them who distrusted?
19 So we see that they could not enter in
because of trustlessness.

THE SHABBATH OF ELOHIM

4 So awe, lest ever a pre—evangelism
of entering his shabbath remains, any
of you think you fell behind.
2 For we were evangelized exactly as they:

but the word *preached* **heard** did not *profit* **benefit** them,
not being *mixed* **co—mingled** with *faith* **the trust**
in them that heard it.
3 For we which have *believed* **trusted**
do enter *into rest* **shabbath**,
exactly as he said,
As I have *sworn* **oathed** in my wrath,
if they shall enter into my *rest* **shabbath**:
although the works *were finished* **had been**
from the foundation of the *world* **cosmos**.
Psalm 95:1
4 For he *spake in a certain place* **said somewhere**
of **about** the seventh *day on this wise* **thus**,
And *God* **Elohim**
did rest in **shabbathized** the seventh day
from all his works.
5 And in this *place* again,
If they shall enter into my *rest* **shabbath**.
6 *Seeing therefore* **So since**it remaineth
that some must enter therein,
and they to whom
it was *first preached* **previously evangelized**
entered not in because of *unbelief* **trustlessness**:
7 Again, he *limiteth* **decreed** a *certain* day,
saying **wording** in David, To day, after so long a time;
exactly as it is said,
To day *if* **whenever** ye *will* **shall** hear his voice,
harden not your hearts.
Psalm 95:7, 8
8 For if *Jesus* **Yah Shua***
had *given* **shabbathized** them *rest*,
then *would* **should** he not *afterward* **ever after**
have spoken *of* **about** another day. *Yah
Shua, successor to Mosheh
9 *So* There remaineth *therefore*
a *rest* **shabbatism** to the people of *God* **Elohim**.
10 For he that is entered into his *rest* **shabbath**,
he also hath *ceased* **shabbathized** from his own works,
exactly as *God* **Elohim** *did* from his.
11 *Let us labour therefore* **Be diligent**
to enter into that *rest* **shabbath**,

HEBREWS 4, 5

        lest any *man* **one** fall
after **in** the same example of *unbelief* **trustlessness**.
12   For the word of *God* **Elohim** is *quick* **living**,
and *powerful* **energized**,
and sharper than any *twoedged* **doublemouthed** sword,
piercing even **thoroughly penetrating**
to the *dividing asunder* **parting** of soul and spirit,
and of the joints and marrow,
and is a discerner
of the *thoughts* **deliberation** and *intents* **mind**
of the heart.
Yesha Yah 49:2
13   Neither is there any *creature* **creation**
that is not manifest in his sight:
but all *things* are naked and *opened* **exposed**
unto the eyes of him with whom we
have *to do* **word**. Proverbs 15:11

THE SON, OUR MEGA ARCH PRIEST

14   **So** Seeing *then*
that we have a *great high* **mega arch** priest
that is passed into the heavens,
Jesus **Yah Shua** the Son of *God* **Elohim**,
let us *hold fast* **empower** our profession.
15   For we have not an *high* **arch** priest
which cannot *be touched* **sympathize**
with *the feeling of* our *infirmities* **frailties**;
but was in all points *tempted* **tested**
like as we are **according to our likeness**,
yet without **apart from** sin.
Hoshea 11:8
16   **So** Let us *therefore* come boldly
unto the throne of *grace* **charism**,
that we may *obtain* **take** mercy,
and find *grace* **charism** to *opportunely* help
in time of need.
but the word they heard benefited them not,
not being co—mingled with the trust
by them who heard it.
3   For we who trust, enter shabbath;
exactly as he said,
As I oathed in my wrath,
if they enter my shabbath — :
although the works became
from the foundation of the cosmos.
Psalm 95:1
4   For somewhere, about the seventh, he said thus:
And the seventh day
Elohim shabbathized from all his works.
5   And again in this,

EDC Hebrew / English Bible

If they enter my shabbath — .
6   So since it remains
that some must enter therein
— and they to whom
it was previously evangelized
entered not in because of trustlessness —
7   again, he decrees a day,
wording in David,
Today, after so long a time —
exactly as it is said,
Today whenever you hear his voice,
harden not your hearts.
Psalm 95:7, 8
8   For if Yah Shua* had shabbathized them,
than he had not ever after have spoken about
another day. *Yah Shua, successor to Mosheh
9   So a shabbatism remains
to the people of Elohim.
10   For whoever enters his shabbath
also shabbathizes from his own works
— exactly as Elohim from his.
11   So be diligent to enter that shabbath,
lest anyone fall in the same example of trustlessness.
12   For the word of Elohim is living and energized
and sharper than any double—mouthed sword,
thoroughly penetrating to the parting
of soul and spirit and of the joints and marrow:
and is a discerner
of the deliberation and mind of the heart.
Yesha Yah 49:2
13   And there is no creature
that is not manifest in his sight:
but all *are* naked and exposed to the eyes of him
with whom we word.
Proverbs 15:11

THE SON, OUR MEGA ARCHPRIEST

14   So seeing that we have a mega archpriest
who passed into the heavens
— Yah Shua the Son of Elohim,
we empower our profession.
15   For we have no archpriest
who cannot sympathize with our frailties;
but was in all points tested according to our likeness
— apart from sin.
Hoshea 11:8
16   So come boldly to the throne of charism,
to take mercy and find charism to opportunely help.
5   For every *high* **arch** priest
taken from among *men* **humanity**

	is *ordained* **seated** for *men* **humanity**	
	in *things pertaining to God* **unto Elohim**,	
	that he may offer	
	both *gifts* **offerings** and sacrifices for sins:	
2	Who can *have* compassion	
	on the *ignorant* **unknowing**,	
	and *on them that are out of the way* **the wandering**;	
	for that **since** he himself also	
	is *compassed* **surrounded** with *infirmity* **frailty**.	
3	And *by reason hereof* **through these**	
	he *ought* **was indebted**,	
	exactly as for the people, *so* **thus** also for himself,	
	to offer for sins.	
4	And no *man* **one** taketh	
	this honour unto himself,	
	but **except** he that is called of *God* **Elohim**, **exactly**	
	as *was Aaron* **Aharon**. Exodus 28:1, Numbers 16:40	
5	*So* **Thus** also *Christ* **the**	
	Messiah glorified not himself	
	to *be made* **become** an *high* **arch** priest	
	but he that *said* **spake** unto him,	
	Thou art my Son, to day have I *begotten* **birthed** thee.	
6	**Exactly** As he *saith* **wordeth** also	
	in *another place* **elsewhere**,	
	Thou art a priest *for ever* **unto the eons**	
	after the order of *Melchisedec* **Malki Sedeq**.	
	Psalm 2:7, 110:4	
7	Who in the days of his flesh,	
	when he had offered *up*	
	prayers **petitions** and *supplications* **entreaties**,	
	with *strong* **mighty** crying and tears	
	unto him that was able to save him from death,	
	and was heard *in that he feared* **by his revering**;	
	Psalm 19:9	
8	Though *he were* **being** a Son,	
	yet learned he obedience	
	by *the things* **those** which he suffered;	
9	And being *made perfect* **completed/shalamed**,	
	he became the *author* **causer** of eternal	
	salvation unto all them that obey him;	
10	*Called* **Addressed** of *God* **Elohim**	
	an *high* **arch** priest	
	after the order of *Melchisedec* **Malki Sedeq**.	
11	*Of* **About** whom	
	we have many *things* **words** to *say* **word**,	
	and *hard* **untranslatable** to *be uttered* **speak**,	
	seeing **since** ye *are dull* **be sluggish** of hearing.	

BECOMING DOCTORS

12 For when for the time
ye *ought* **are indebted** to be *teachers* **doctors**,
ye have need that one *teach* **doctrinate** you again
which be the first principles **the beginning elements**
of the oracles of *God* **Elohim**;
and are become such as have need of milk,
and not of *strong meat* **solid nourishment**.

13 For every one that *useth* **partaketh** milk
is *unskilful* **untested**
in the word of *righteousness* **justness**:
for he is a babe.

14 But *strong meat* **solid nourishment**
belongeth to **is for** them
that are *of full age* **completed/shalamed**,
even those who *by reason of use* **through habit**

have their *senses* **perceptions** exercised
to discern both good and evil.

BEARING ON TO COMPLETION/SHALOM

6 *Therefore* **So**
leaving **forsaking** the *principles* **beginnings**
of the *doctrine* **word** of *Christ* **the Messiah**,
let us *go* **bear** on unto *perfection* **completion/shalom**;
not *laying* **casting down** again
the foundation of repentance from dead works,
and of *faith* **trust** toward *God* **Elohim**,

2 Of the doctrine of baptisms,
and of laying on of hands,
and of resurrection of the dead, and of eternal judgment.

3 And this *will* **shall** we do,
if God permit **whenever Elohim alloweth**.

5 For every archpriest taken from humanity
sits in behalf of humanity to Elohim
to offer both offerings and sacrifices for sins:

2 able to compassion
the unknowing and the wandering
— since he himself is also surrounded with frailty.

3 And through these he is indebted
— exactly as for the people, thus also for himself,
to offer for sins.

4 And no one takes this honor to himself
except those called of Elohim exactly as
Aharon. Exodus 28:1, Numbers 16:40

5 Thus also the Messiah glorified not himself
to become an archpriest;
but he who spoke to him,
You are my Son, — today I birthed you.

6 Exactly as he also words elsewhere,
You are a priest to the eons
after the order of Malki Sedeq

Psalm 2:7, 110:4
7 — who in the days of his flesh
when he offered petitions and entreaties,
with mighty crying and tears
to him who was able to save him from death
and was heard by his revering;
Psalm 19:9
8 though being a Son
he still learned obedience by what he suffered;
9 and being completed/shalamed
he became the causer of eternal salvation
to all who obey him;
10 addressed by Elohim,
An archpriest after the order of Malki Sedeq:
11 about whom we have many words to word
and untranslatable to speak
— since you are sluggish of hearing.

Becoming Doctors

12 For at the time
you are indebted to be doctors,
you again need someone to doctrinate you
the beginning elements of the oracles of Elohim;
and become such as have need of milk
and not of solid nourishment.
13 For everyone who partakes of milk
is untested in the word of justness
— he is a babe:
14 and solid nourishment
is for the completed/shalamed
— who through habit exercised their perceptions
to discern both good and evil.

Bearing On To Completion/Shalom

6 So abandoning the beginnings
of the word of the Messiah,
we bear on to completion/shalom;
not casting again
the foundation of repentance from dead works,
and of trust toward Elohim,
2 of the doctrine of baptisms,
and of laying on of hands,
and of resurrection of the dead,
and of eternal judgment:
3 and this we do, whenever Elohim allows.

Falling Away

4 For it is impossible
for those who were once enlightened,
and have tasted
of the *heavenly gift* **gratuity of the heavenlies**,
and *were made* **became** partakers of the
Holy Spirit **Ruach ha-kodesh**,
5 And have tasted the good
word **rhema** of *God* **Elohim**,
and the *powers* **dynamis** of the *world* **eon** to come,
6 If they shall fall away,
to renew them again unto repentance;
seeing they *crucify* **restake** to themselves
the Son of *God* **Elohim** *afresh*,
and *put* **expose** him *to an open shame*.
7 For the earth
which drinketh in the rain that cometh oft upon it,
and bringeth *forth herbs meet* **botany wellfit** for them
by **through** whom it is *dressed* **cultivated**,
receiveth **partaketh** blessing from *God* **Elohim**:
Psalm 65:10
8 But that which *beareth*
bringeth thorns and briers
is *rejected* **disapproved**, and is nigh unto cursing;
whose *end* **completion/shalom** is
to *be burned* **scorching**.
9 But, beloved, we are *persuaded* **convinced**
of better *things of* **concerning** you,
and *things that accompany* **regarding** salvation,
though we thus speak.
10 For *God* **Elohim** is not *unrighteous* **unjust**
to forget your work and labour of love,
which ye have *shewed toward* **indicated unto** his name,
in that ye have ministered to the *saints* **holy**,
and do minister.
11 And we *desire* **pant** that *every* **each** one of you
do shew **indicate** the same diligence
to the full *assurance of hope* **bearance**
unto the *end* **completion/shalom**:
12 That ye be not *slothful* **sluggish**,
but *followers* **mimickers** of them
who through *faith* **trust** and patience
inherit the *promises* **pre—evangelisms**.
13 For when *God* **Elohim**
made promise to **pre—evangelized** Abraham,
because **since** he could *swear* **oath** by no greater,
he *sware* **oathed** by himself,
14 *Saying* **Wording**, Surely
blessing I *will* **shall** bless thee,
and multiplying I *will* **shall** multiply thee.
Genesis 22:16,17
15 And *so* **thus**, after he had
patiently endured **being patient**,
he obtained the *promise* **pre—evangelism**.

16	For *men verily* **humanity indeed** *swear* **oath** by the greater: and an oath *for confirmation is to them* **establisheth** an *end* **finality** of all *strife* **controversy.**		is disapproved and is near cursing — whose completion/shalom is to scorching.
17	Wherein *God* **Elohim**, *willing* **having willed** more *abundantly* **superabundantly** to shew unto the heirs of *promise* **pre—evangelism** the immutability of his counsel, confirmed it by an oath:	9	And beloved, we are convinced of better concerning you and regarding salvation, though we thus speak.
18	That *by* **through** two immutable *things* **matters**, in which it *was* **is** impossible for *God* **Elohim** to lie, we might have a *strong* **mighty** consolation, who have fled for refuge to *lay hold upon* **empower** the hope set *before* **in front of** us:	10	For Elohim is not unjust to forget your work and the labor of love you indicate to his name, ministering to the holy, and ministering.
		11	And we pant that each of you indicate the same diligence to the full bearance to the completion/shalom:
		12	to not be sluggish, but mimickers of them, who through trust and patience, inherit the pre—evangelisms.
19	Which *hope* we have as an anchor of the soul, both *sure* **certain** and stedfast, and which entereth into that within the veil;	13	For when Elohim pre—evangelized to Abraham — since he could oath by no greater he oathed by himself,
		14	wording, Surely in blessing, I bless you and in multiplying I multiply you. Genesis 22:16,17

THE SON, OUR ARCH PRIEST UNTO THE EONS

20	*Whither* **Where** the forerunner is for us entered, *even Jesus* **Yah Shua**, *made* **having become** an *high* **arch** priest *for ever* **unto the eons** after the order of *Melchisedec* **Malki Sedeq**.	15	And thus, being patient, he obtained the pre—evangelism.
		16	For humanity indeed oaths by the greater: and an oath establishes a finality of all controversy.
7	For this *Melchisedec* **Malki Sedeq**, *king* **sovereign** of *Salem* **Shalem**, priest of *the most high God* **El Elyon**, who met *with* Abraham returning from the *slaughter* **chopping** of the *kings* **sovereigns**, and blessed him;	17	Wherein Elohim willed more superabundantly to show the heirs of pre—evangelism the immutability of his counsel, he confirmed it by an oath:
		18	that through two immutable matters, in which it is impossible for Elohim to lie, we who fled for refuge, have a mighty consolation to empower the hope set in front of us:
		19	which we have as an anchor of the soul — both certain and steadfast that enters within the veil;

FALLING AWAY

THE SON, OUR ARCHPRIEST TO THE EONS

4	For it is impossible for those once enlightened, and tasted of the gratuity of the heavenlies, and became partakers of Holy Spirit,	20	where the forerunner — Yah Shua entered for us — Yah Shua — being an archpriest to the eons after the order of Malki Sedeq.
5	and tasted the good rhema of Elohim, and the dynamis of the eon to come,		
6	and fall away, to renew again to repentance: seeing they restake to themselves the Son of Elohim and expose him.	7	For this Malki Sedeq — sovereign of Shalem — priest of El Elyon, met with Abraham returning from the chopping of the sovereigns and blessed him:
7	For the earth that drinks in the rain often coming upon it and brings botany wellfitting for them through whom it is cultivated, partakes blessing from Elohim: Psalm 65:10	2	To whom also Abraham *gave* **imparted** a *tenth part* **tithe** of all;
8	and whoever brings thorns and briers		

first *being by interpretation* **indeed translated**
King **Sovereign** of *righteousness* **justness**,
and *after that* **then** also
King **Sovereign** of *Salem* **Shalem**,
which is, *King* **Sovereign** of *peace* **shalom**;

3 *Without father* **Unfathered**,
without mother **unmothered**,
without descent **ungenealogized**,
having neither beginning of days
nor *end* **completion/shalom** of life;
but *made like* **likenessed** unto the Son of *God* **Elohim**;
abideth a priest *continually* **unto perpetuity**.

4 Now *consider* **observe**
how great this man was **his greatness**,
unto whom even the patriarch Abraham gave
the *tenth* **tithe from the top** of the *spoils* **heap**.

5 And *verily* **indeed** they
that are of the sons of Levi,
who *receive* **take** the office of the priesthood,
have a commandment misvah to take tithes of the people
according to the *law* **torah**, that is, of their brethren,
though they come out of the loins of Abraham:

6 But he
whose descent is not counted from them
who is not genealogized
received tithes of **was tithed by** Abraham,
and blessed him that had the *promises* **pre—
evangelisms**. Genesis 14:20, Numbers 18:21

7 And *without* **apart from** all
contradiction **controversy**
the *less* **lesser** is blessed of the better.

8 And here **indeed**
men **humans** that die *receive* **take** tithes;
but there
he receiveth them, of whom it is witnessed
witness that he liveth.

9 And as *I may so say* **saith the saying**,
Levi also, who *receiveth* **taketh** tithes,
payed tithes in **tithed through** Abraham.

10 For he was yet in the loins of his father,
when *Melchisedec* **Malki Sedeq** met *with* him.

11 **So indeed**, If *therefore*
perfection **completion/shalom**
were *by* **through** the Levitical priesthood,
(for under it the people *received* **set** the *law* **torah**,)
what *further* need was **still** there
that another priest should rise
after the order of *Melchisedec* **Malki Sedeq**,
and not be *called* **worded**
after the order of *Aaron* **Aharon**?

12 For the priesthood being *changed* **transplaced**,
there *is made* **becometh** of necessity
a *change* **transplacing** also of the *law* **torah**.

13 For he of whom these *things* are *spoken* **worded**
pertaineth to another tribe **another scion partaketh**,
of which no *man gave attendance* **one heeded**
at the **sacrifice** altar.

14 For it *is evident* **hath been preevidenced**
that our *Lord sprang* **Adonay rose**
out of *Juda* **Yah Hudah**;
of **unto** which *tribe* **scion**
Moses **Mosheh** spake *nothing* **naught**
concerning priesthood. Genesis 49:8, 10

15 And it is yet *far more* **more
superabundantly** evident:
for that **if** after the *similitude* **likeness**
of *Melchisedec* **Malki Sedeq** there ariseth another priest,

16 Who *is made* **becometh**, not after the *law* **torah**
of a *carnal commandment* **fleshly misvah**, but
after the *power* **dynamis** of an endless life.

17 For he *testifieth* **witnesseth that**,
Thou art a priest *for ever* **unto the eons**
after the order of *Melchisedec* **Malki Sedeq**.
Psalm 110:4

18 For **indeed**
there *is verily* **becometh** a *disannulling* **putting away**
of the *commandment going before* **preceding misvah**
for **because of** the *weakness* **frailty**
and *unprofitableness* **unbeneficialness** thereof.

19 For the *law* **torah**
made nothing perfect **completed naught**,
but the *bringing in* **introduction** of a better hope *did*;

2 to whom Abraham also imparted a tithe of all;
first indeed translated, Sovereign of Justness
and then also, Sovereign of Shalem,
which is, Sovereign of Shalom:

3 unfathered
unmothered
ungenealogized;
neither beginning of days
nor completion/shalom of life;
but likenessed to the Son of Elohim;
abides a priest in perpetuity.

4 And observe his greatness,
to whom even the patriarch Abraham
gave the tithe from the top of the heap.

5 And indeed they of the sons of Levi
who take the office of the priesthood
have a misvah to take tithes of the people
according to the torah

— that is, of their brothers,
though they come from the loins of Abraham:
6 but whoever was not genealogized
was tithed by Abraham
and blessed him who had the pre—evangelisms.
Genesis 14:20, Numbers 18:21
7 And apart from all controversy
the lesser is blessed of the better.
8 And here, indeed, humans who die take tithes;
but there, witness that he lives.
9 And as says the saying,
Levi also, who takes tithes, tithed through Abraham.
10 For he was still in the loins of his father,
when Malki Sedeq met with him.
11 So indeed, if completion/shalom
were through the Levitical priesthood,
— for under it the people set the torah
— what need was still there that another priest rise
after the order of Malki Sedeq
and not worded after the order of Aharon?
12 For the priesthood, being transplaced,
there also becomes a necessity
to transplace the torah.
13 For he, of whom these are worded,
another scion partakes,
whom no one heeds at the sacrifice altar.
14 For it was pre—evidenced
that our Adonay rose from Yah Hudah;
to which scion
Mosheh spake naught concerning
priesthood. Genesis 49:8, 10
15 And it is still more superabundantly evident:
if after the likeness of Malki Sedeq
another priest rises,
16 who becomes,
not after the torah of a fleshly misvah,
but after the dynamis of an endless life.
17 For he witnesses,
You are a priest to the eons
after the order of Malki Sedeq.
Psalm 110:4
18 For indeed there becomes
a putting away of the preceding misvah
because of its frailty and unbeneficialness thereof.
19 For the torah completed/shalamed naught
but the introduction of a better hope
by the **through** which
we *draw nigh unto God* **approach Elohim**.
20 And inasmuch as not
without **apart from** an oath
he was made priest:
21 (For those priests *were*
made **had indeed become**
without **apart from** an oath;
but this with an oath
by **through** him that *said* **worded** unto him,
The Lord sware **Yah Veh oathed**
and *will* **shall** not *repent* **regret**,
Thou art a priest *for ever* **unto the eons**
after the order of *Melchisedec* **Malki Sedeq**:)
Psalm 110:4
22 By so much *was Jesus* **hath Yah Shua**
made a surety **become a pledge**
of a better *testament* **covenant**.
23 And they *truly were* **indeed**
became many priests,
because they were *not suffered* **forbidden**
to *continue* **abide** by reason of death:
24 But this *man* **one**,
because he *continueth ever* **abideth unto the eons**,
hath an *unchangeable* **inviolable** priesthood.
25 *Wherefore* **So** he is able also
to save them *to the uttermost* **completely**
that come unto *God by* **Elohim through** him,
seeing he ever *liveth* **living**
to *make intercession* **intercede** for them.
26 For such an *high priest became*
arch priest befitted us,
who is holy **merciful**, *harmless* **innocent**,
undefiled **unpolluted**, *separate* **separated** from sinners,
and *made* **being** higher than the heavens;
27 Who *needeth not daily* **hath**
no day by day neccessity,
exactly as those *high* , **arch** priests to offer up sacrifice,
first for his own sins, and then for the people's:
for this he did once, when he offered up himself.
28 For the *law maketh men* **torah seateth humans**
high priests which have infirmity
arch priests having frailty;
but the word of the oath,
which was since **after** the *law* **torah**,
maketh the **completeth/shalameth** a Son,
who is consecrated for evermore **unto the eons**.

The Son, Our Arch Priest

8 Now of *the things* **those**
which we have *spoken* **worded,** this is the sum:
We have such an *high* ,**arch** priest
who is *set* **seated** on the right *hand* of the throne
of the Majesty in the heavens;

HEBREWS 8

2   A *minister* **liturgist** of the *sanctuary* **Holies**,
and of the true tabernacle,
which *the Lord pitched* **Yah Veh staked**,
and not *man* **humanity**.

3   For every *high* ,**arch** priest
is *ordained* to offer *gifts* **gratuities** and sacrifices:
Wherefore **So** it is of necessity
that this *man* **one** have somewhat also to offer.

4   For **indeed** if he were on earth,
he should not *be* **ever been** a priest,
seeing that there are **there being** priests
that offer *gifts* **offerings** according to the *law* **torah**:

5   Who *serve* **liturgize** unto
the example and shadow
of *heavenly things* **the heavenlies**,
as Moses was admonished of God
exactly as oracled to Mosheh
when he was about
to *make* **complete/shalam** the tabernacle:
for, See, *saith he*,
that thou make all *things* according to the *pattern* **type**
shewed to thee in the mount.
Exodus 25:40

6   But now
hath he obtained a more excellent *ministry* **liturgy**,
by how much **inasmuch as** also
he is the mediator of a better covenant,
which was established
upon better *promises* **pre—evangelisms**.

7   For if that first *covenant* had
been *faultless* **blameless**,
then should no place have been sought
for the second. Exodus 3:8, 19:5
— through which we approach Elohim.

20   And inasmuch as not apart from an oath:

21   For indeed
they became priests apart from an oath;
but this with an oath
through him who worded to him,
Yah Veh oaths and regrets not,
You are a priest to the eons
after the order of Malki Sedeq.
Psalm 110:4

22   Yah Shua became a pledge
by a much better covenant:

23   and indeed, they became many priests,
because they were forbidden to abide
by reason of death.

24   And this one, because he abides to the eons,
has an inviolable priesthood.

25   So he is also able
to save them to completion/shalom
who come to Elohim through him
— ever living to intercede for them.

26   For such an archpriest befits us
— merciful,
innocent,
unpolluted,
separated from sinners,
and being higher than the heavens;

27   who has no day by day neccessity
exactly as those archpriests
to offer sacrifice
first for his own sins
and then for those of the people:
for he did this once, offering himself.

28   For the torah seats humans
— archpriests having frailty;
but the word of the oath after the torah,
completes/shalams a Son to the eons.

THE SON, OUR ARCHPRIEST

8   And this is the sum of what we worded:
We have such an archpriest
seated at the right of the throne of the Majesty
in the heavens;

2   A liturgist of the Holies
and of the true tabernacle
which Yah Veh staked — and not humanity.

3   For every archpriest offers
gratuities and sacrifices:
so it is necessary
that this one also have somewhat to offer.

4   For indeed if he were on earth,
he had not ever been a priest,
there being priests
who offer offerings according to the torah:

5   who liturgize
to the example and shadow of the heavenlies,
exactly as oracled to Mosheh
when he was about
to complete/shalam the tabernacle:
for,
See that you make all according to the type
shown you in the mount.
Exodus 25:40

6   And now he obtained a more excellent liturgy,
inasmuch as
he is also the mediator of a better covenant
established upon better pre—evangelisms.

7 For if that first had been blameless,
then no place had been sought for
the second. Exodus 3:8, 19:5
8 For *finding fault with* **blaming**
them, he *saith* **wordeth**,
Behold, the days come, *saith the Lord* **wordeth Yah Veh**,
when I *will make* **shall complete/shalam** a new covenant
with the house of *Israel* **Yisra El**
and with the house of *Judah* **Yah Hudah**:
9 Not according to the covenant
that I made with their fathers
in the day when I *took them by the* **held their** hand
to lead them out of the land of *Egypt* **Misrayim**;
because they *continued* **abode** not in my covenant,
and I *regarded* **also disregarded** them *not*,
saith the Lord **wordeth Yah Veh**.
10 For this is the covenant that
I *will make* **shall covenant**
with the house of *Israel* **Yisra El** after those days,
saith the Lord **wordeth Yah Veh**;
I *will put* **shall give** my *laws* **torah** into their mind,
and *write* **epigraph** them in their hearts:
and I *will* **shall** be to them, *a* God **Elohim**,
and they shall be to me, *a* people:
11 And they shall not **no way**
teach every man **doctrinate each** his neighbour,
and *every man* **each** his brother,
saying **wording**, Know *the Lord* **Yah Veh**:
for all shall know me, from the
least to the *greatest* **mega**.
12 For I *will be merciful to* **shall kapur/atone**
their *unrighteousness* **injustice**,
and their sins and their *iniquities* **torah
violations** *will I* **shall I** not **no way** still
remember *no more*. Yirme Yah 31:31—34
13 In that he *saith* **wordeth**, A new *covenant*,
he hath *made the first old* **antiquated the first**.
Now that
which *decayeth* **antiquateth** and *waxeth old* **senesceth**
is *ready* **nigh** to *vanish away* **disappearing**.

The Cosmic Holy Tabernacle

9 *Then verily* **But indeed** the
first *covenant* **tabernacle**
had also
ordinances **judgments** of *divine service* **ministration**,
and a *worldly sanctuary* **cosmic Holies**.
2 For there was a tabernacle *made* **prepared**;
the first, wherein was the *candlestick* **menorah**,
and the table, and the *shewbread* **prothesis bread**;
which is *called* **worded** the *sanctuary* **Holies**.
Exodus 25:30
3 And after the second veil, the tabernacle
which is *called* **worded** the *Holiest of all* **Holy of Holies**;
4 Which had the golden *censer* **incenser**,
and the ark of the covenant
overlaid round **covered** about **on every side** with gold,
wherein was the golden *pot* **jar** that had manna,
and *Aaron's rod* **Aharon's scion** that *budded* **sprouted**,
and the *tables* **slabs** of the covenant;
Exodus 16:33, 25:10, 34:29, Leviticus 16:12,
Numbers 17:10, Deuteronomy 10:2, 5
5 And over it the *cherubims* **cherubim** of glory
shadowing the *mercyseat* **kapporeth**;
of **about** which we cannot now *speak* **word**
particularly **according to its parts**.
6 Now when these *things* were
thus *ordained* **prepared**,
the priests **indeed**
went always into **continually
entered** the first tabernacle,
accomplishing **fully completing**
the *service of God* **liturgy**.
7 But into the second
went the *high* **arch** priest alone once every year,
not *without* **apart from** blood,
which he offered for himself,
and *for* the *errors* **unknowingnesses** of the people:
8 The *Holy Spirit* **Ruach ha-
kodesh** this *signifying* **evidencing**,
that the way into the *holiest of all* **Holies**
was not yet *made* manifest,
while as the first tabernacle was yet standing:
9 Which was a *figure* **parable**
for the time **unto that season** then present,
in which were offered both *gifts* **gratuities** and sacrifices,
that could not *make* **complete/shalam** him
that *did the service perfect* **liturgized**,
as pertaining to the conscience;
10 *Which stood* only *in meats*
upon food and drinks,
8 For blaming them, he worded,
Behold, days come, words Yah Veh,
when I complete/shalam a new covenant
with the house of Yisra El
and with the house of Yah Hudah:
9 not according to the covenant
I made with their fathers
in the day I held their hand
to lead them from the land of Misrayim
— because they abode not in my covenant

HEBREWS 9

and I also disregarded them, words Yah Veh.
10 For this is the covenant
I covenant with the house of Yisra El:
After those days, words Yah Veh;
I give my torah in their mind
and epigraph them in their hearts:
and I become to them — Elohim
and they become to me — people:
11 and they never no way doctrinate
each his neighbour and each his brother,
wording, Know Yah Veh!
— for they all know me — from the least to the mega:
12 for I kapur/atone their injustice;
and their sins and their torah violations
I never no way still remember.
Yirme Yah 31:31—34
13 In that he words, A new,
he antiquates the first:
and whatever antiquates and senesces
is near disappearing.

THE COSMIC HOLY TABERNACLE

9 But indeed the first tabernacle
also had judgments of ministration
and a cosmic Holies:
2 for there they prepared a first tabernacle;
wherein were the menorah
and the table and the prothesis bread;
which is worded, Holies.
Exodus 25:30
3 And after the veil, the second tabernacle
which is worded, Holy of Holies;
4 having the golden incenser
and the ark of the covenant
covered all around on every side with gold,
wherein was the golden jar that had manna
and the scion of Aharon that sprouted
and the slabs of the covenant.
Exodus 16:33, 25:10, 34:29, Leviticus 16:12,
Numbers 17:10, Deuteronomy 10:2, 5
5 And over it,
the cherubim of glory shadowing the kapporeth;
about which we cannot word now about its parts.
6 And these being thus prepared,
the priests indeed
continually entered the first tabernacle,
fully completing the liturgy:
7 and into the second
the archpriest alone once every year
not apart from blood he offered for himself

and the unknowingnesses of the people:
8 — the Holy Spirit evidencing this
— that the way into the Holies was not yet manifest,
while the first tabernacle still stood
9 — a parable to that present season,
in which they offered both gratuities and sacrifices,
that could not complete/shalam him who liturgized,
as pertaining to the conscience
10 — only upon food and drinks

and *divers washings* **more excellent baptisms**,
and *carnal ordinances* **judgments of flesh**,
imposed *on them* until
the *time* **season** of *reformation* **thorough straightening**.
11 But *Christ* **Messiah** being come,
an *high* **arch** priest of **the coming** good *things to come*,
by **through** a greater
and *more perfect* **completed/shalamed** tabernacle,
not *made with hands* **handmade**,
that is *to say*, not of this *building* **creation**;
12 Neither *by* **through** the
blood of goats and calves,
but *by* **through** his own blood
he entered in once into the *holy place* **Holies**,
having *obtained* **found** eternal redemption *for us*.
13 For if the blood of bulls and of goats,
and the ashes of an heifer sprinkling
the *unclean* **profane**,
sanctifieth **halloweth** to the purifying of the flesh:
14 How much more shall the
blood of *Christ* **the Messiah**,
who through the eternal Spirit offered himself
without spot **unblemished** to *God* **Elohim**,
purge **purify** your conscience from dead works
to *serve* **liturgize** the living *God* **Elohim**?
15 And *for this cause* **which**
he is the mediator of the new *testament* **covenant**,
that *by means of* **having become by** death,
for **unto** the redemption of the transgressions
that were under the first *testament* **covenant**,
they which are called
might *receive* **take** the *promise* **pre—evangelism**
of eternal inheritance.
16 For where a *testament* **covenant** is,
there must also of necessity
be **brought** the death of the *testator* **covenantor**.
17 For a *testament* **covenant** is *of force* **stedfast**
after men are dead **upon death**:
otherwise it is *of no strength* **not mighty enough** at all
while the *testator* **covenantor** liveth.

18   *Whereupon* **And so**
neither the first *testament* was *dedicated* **hanukkahed**
without **apart from** blood.
19   For when *Moses* **Mosheh**
had spoken every *precept* **misvah**
to all the people according to the *law* **torah**,
he took the blood of calves and of goats,
with water, and scarlet wool, and hyssop,
and sprinkled both the *book* **scroll**,
and all the people,
20   *Saying* **Wording**,
This is the blood of the *testament* **covenant**
which *God* **Yah Veh** hath *enjoined* **misvahed** unto you.
21   *Moreover* **Likewise** he sprinkled with blood
both the tabernacle,
and all the vessels of the *ministry* **liturgy**.
Exodus 24:8, 29:12, 36, Leviticus 14:16
22   And *almost* **nearly** all *things* are,
by **according to** the *law* **torah**,
purged with **purified in** blood;
and *without shedding* **apart from pouring** of blood
is no remission **becometh no forgiveness**.
23   **So indeed** It was *therefore* necessary
that the *patterns of things* **examples** in the heavens
should be purified with these;
but the *heavenly things* **heavenlies** themselves
with better sacrifices than these.
24   For *Christ* **the Messiah** is not entered
into the *holy places made with hands* **handmade Holies**,
which are the *figures* **antitypes** of the true;
but into heaven itself,
now to *appear* **manifest**
in the *presence* **face** of *God* **Elohim** for us:
25   Nor yet that he should offer himself often,
exactly as the *high* **arch** priest
entereth into the *holy place* **Holies** every year
with **in** blood of others;
26   *For then* **Otherwise** must he often have suffered
since the foundation of the *world* **cosmos**:
but now once in the *end* **completion/
shalom** of the *world* **eon**
hath he *appeared* **been manifest** to put away sin
by **through** the sacrifice of himself.
and more excellent baptisms
and judgments of flesh
— imposed until the season of thorough straightening.
11   And Messiah being come
— an archpriest of the coming good
through a greater and completed/shalamed tabernacle
— neither handmade

— nor of this creation
12   — nor through the blood of goats and calves
— but through his own blood:
he entered the Holies once finding eternal redemption.
13   For if the blood of bulls and of goats
and the ashes of an heifer sprinkling the profane
hallows to the purifying of the flesh:
14   how much more the blood of the Messiah
who through the eternal Spirit
offered himself unblemished to Elohim,
purify your conscience from dead works
to liturgize the living Elohim?
15   And because of this
he is the mediator of the new covenant:
whereas, under the first covenant,
death being the redemption of the transgressions,
the called
take the pre—evangelism of eternal inheritance.
16   For where the covenant *is*,
it is necessary
to bring/bear the death of the covenantor.
17   For a covenant is steadfast upon death:
otherwise it is not mighty enough at all
while the covenantor lives.
18   And so,
the first was not hanukkahed apart from blood.
19 For Mosheh, having spoken every misvah
to all the people according to the torah, he
took the blood of calves and of goats, with
water and scarlet wool and hyssop;
and sprinkled both the scroll and all the people,
20   wording, This is the blood of the covenant
Yah Veh misvahs you.
21   Likewise with blood,
he sprinkled
both the tabernacle and all the vessels of the liturgy.
Exodus 24:8, 29:12, 36, Leviticus 14:16
22   And according to the torah,
nearly all are purified in blood;
and apart from pouring of blood
no forgiveness becomes.
23   So indeed
it was necessary to purify the examples in the heavens
with these;
and the heavenlies themselves
with sacrifices better than these.
24   For the Messiah entered not
the handmade Holies — antitypes of the true;
but the heavens thereof,
to manifest for us now at the face of Elohim:

HEBREWS 9, 10

25 not that he still offers himself often,
exactly as the archpriest enters the Holies every year
in blood of others;
26 otherwise he must have suffered often
from the foundation of the cosmos:
but now in the completion/shalom of the eon
he manifests himself once
to put away sin through the sacrifice of himself.
27 And **inasmuch** as it is *appointed* **laid out**
unto *men* **humanity** once to die,
but after this the judgment:
28 *So Christ* **Thus the Messiah**
was *once* offered **once**
to *bear* **offer** the sins of many;
and unto them that *look for* **await** him
shall he *appear* **be seen** the second *time*
without **apart from** sin unto salvation.

THE YEAR BY YEAR SACRIFICES UNDER THE TORAH

10 For the *law* **torah** having a shadow
of **the coming** good *things to come*,
and not the very *image* **icon** of the *things* **substance**,
can never **ever** with those sacrifices
which they offered year by year
continually **in perpetuity**
make the comers thereunto perfect
complete/shalam them who come.
2 *For then* **Otherwise**
would **should** they not
have *ceased* **ever paused** to be offered?
because that
the *worshippers* **liturgizers** once *purged* **purified**
should **not still** have had *no more* conscience of sins.
3 But in those *sacrifices*
there is a remembrance *again made* of sins every year.
4 For it is *not possible* **impossible**
that the blood of bulls and of goats
should *take away* **remove** sins.
5 *Wherefore* **So** when he cometh
into the *world* **cosmos**,
he *saith* **wordeth**,
Sacrifice and offering thou *wouldest* **willest** not,
but a body hast thou prepared me:
6 In *burnt offerings* **holocausts**
and *sacrifices* for sin
thou hast *had no pleasure* **not thought well**.
7 Then said I, *Lo* **Behold**, I come
(in the *volume* **heading** of the *book* **scroll**
it is *written of* **scribed concerning** me,)
to do thy will, O *God* **Elohim**.
8 Above when he *said* **worded**,
Sacrifice and offering
and *burnt offerings* **holocausts** and *offering* for sin
thou *wouldest* **willest** not,
neither hadst *pleasure therein* **thought well**;
which are offered by the *law* **torah**;
Psalm 40:6—8
9 Then said he, *Lo* **Behold**,
I come to do thy will, O *God* **Elohim**.
He taketh away the first,
that he may *establish* **set** the second.
10 *By the* **In** which will we are *sanctified* **hallowed**
through the offering
of the body of *Jesus Christ* **Yah Shua Messiah**
once *for all*.
11 And every priest **indeed** standeth daily
ministering **liturgizing** and offering
oftentimes the same sacrifices **often**,
which can never **ever** take away sins:

THE SACRIFICE OF THE SON — ONCE

12 But this *man* **one**,
after he had offered one sacrifice for sins
for ever **in perpetuity**,
sat down *on* **at** the right *hand* of *God* **Elohim**;
13 From henceforth *expecting* **awaiting**
till his enemies be *made* **placed** his footstool.
Psalm 110:1
14 For by one offering
he hath *perfected for ever* **completed/
shalamed in perpetuity**
them that are *sanctified* **hallowed**.
15 *Whereof* the *Holy Spirit* **Ruach ha-kodesh** also
is a witness **witnesseth** to us:
for after that he had *said before* **foretold**,
16 This is the covenant
that I *will make* **shall covenant** with them
after those days,
saith the Lord **wordeth Yah Veh**,
I *will put* **shall give** my *laws* **torah** into their hearts,
and in their minds *will I write* **shall I epigraph** them;
17 And their sins and *iniquities* **torah violations**
will I **shall I not no way still** remember
no more. Yirme Yah 31:33, 34
27 And as it is laid out for humanity to die once
and after this the judgment:
28 thus the Messiah was offered once
to offer the sins of many;
and to them who await him

he appears the second — apart from sin to salvation.

THE YEAR BY YEAR SACRIFICES UNDER THE TORAH

10 For the torah
having a shadow of the coming good
and not the very icon of the substance,
can never ever with those sacrifices
which they offered year by year in perpetuity
complete/shalam them who come.

2 Otherwise were they not
to pause in offering them
— because the liturgizers purified once
still had no conscience of sins?

3 — But in them, a remembrance
of sins every year?

4 For it is impossible
for the blood of bulls and of goats to remove sins.

5 So coming into the cosmos, he words,
Sacrifice and offering you willed not,
but a body you prepared me:

6 Of holocausts and for sin you thought not well.

7 Then I said, Behold, I come
— the heading of the scroll scribes concerning me
— to do your will, O Elohim.

8 Wording above,
Sacrifice and offering and holocausts and for sin
you neither willed nor thought well
— which are offered by the torah;
Psalm 40:6—8

9 Then he says,
Behold, I come to do your will, O Elohim.
— he takes away the first to set the second:

10 in whose will we are hallowed
through the offering of the body of Yah Shua Messiah
once.

11 And indeed every priest stands daily
liturgizing and offering the same sacrifices often,
which can never ever take away sins.

THE SACRIFICE OF THE SON — ONCE

12 But this one,
after he offered one sacrifice for sins in perpetuity,
sat down at the right of Elohim;

13 from now on awaiting
until the placing of his enemies for his footstool.
Psalm 110:1

14 For by one offering
he completed/shalamed the hallowed in perpetuity

15 — the Holy Spirit also witnessing to us:
for after he foretold,

16 This is the covenant
I covenant with them after those days,
words Yah Veh,
I give my torah in their hearts
and epigraph them in their minds;

17 and their sins and torah violations
I never no way still remember. Yirme Yah 31:33, 34

18 Now where *remission* **forgiveness** of these is,
there is *no more* **not still** offering for sin.

19 **So** Having *therefore*, brethren,
boldness to enter into the *holiest* **Holies**
by **in** the blood of *Jesus* **Yah Shua**,

20 By a *new* **freshly slaughtered** and living way,
which he hath *consecrated* **hanukkahed** for us,
through the veil, that is *to say*, his flesh;

21 And having *an high* **a mega** priest
over the house of *God* **El**;

22 Let us *draw* **come** near with a true heart
in full *assurance* **bearance** of *faith* **trust**,
having our hearts sprinkled from an evil conscience,
and our bodies *washed* **bathed** with pure water.

23 Let us hold *fast* **down** the
profession of *our faith* **hope**
without wavering **unwaveringly**;
(for he is *faithful* **trustworthy**
that *promised* **pre—evangelized**;)

24 And let us consider one another
to *provoke* **agitate** unto love and to good works:

25 Not forsaking
the *assembling* **synagoguing** of ourselves together,
exactly as the *manner* **custom** of some is;
but *exhorting one another* **consoling**:
and so much the more,
as **long** as ye see the day approaching.

SINNING VOLUNTARILY

26 For if we sin *wilfully* **voluntarily**
after that
we have *received* **taken** the knowledge of the truth,
there remaineth *no more* **not still** sacrifice for sins,

27 But *a certain fearful looking*
for **an awesome expectation**
of judgment and *fiery indignation* **zeal of fire**, which
shall *devour* **consume** the *adversaries* **opposers**.

28 *He* **Anyone** that
despised Moses' law **set aside Mosheh's torah**
died *without mercy* **apart from compassion**
under two or three witnesses:

HEBREWS 10

29 Of how much *sorer* **worse** punishment,
suppose **think** ye,
shall he be *thought* **deemed** worthy,
who hath *trodden under foot* **trampled down**
the Son of *God* **Elohim**,
and hath *counted* **deemed** the blood of the covenant,
wherewith **wherein** he was *sanctified* **hallowed**,
an unholy thing **profane**,
and hath *done despite unto* **insulted**
the Spirit of *grace* **charism**?

30 For we know him that hath said,
Vengeance *belongeth* unto me, I *will* **shall** recompense,
saith the Lord **wordeth Yah Veh**.
And again, *The Lord* **Yah Veh** shall judge
his people. Deuteronomy 32:35, 36

31 *It is a fearful thing* **How awesome**
to fall into the hands of the living *God* **Elohim**.

32 But *call to remembrance* **remember**
the *former* **previous** days, in which,
after ye were illuminated **having been enlightened**,
ye endured
a *great fight* **vast contention** of *afflictions* **sufferings**;

33 Partly **indeed**,
whilst ye were made a gazingstock **being theatricized**
both by reproaches and *afflictions* **tribulations**;
and partly,
whilst ye became *companions* **communicants**
of them that *were so used* **thus behaved**.

34 For ye
had compassion of **sympathized with** me in my bonds,
and *took joyfully* **received with cheer**
the *spoiling* **plunder** of your *goods* **holdings**,
knowing in yourselves that ye have in heaven
a better and *an enduring substance* **abiding holdings**.

35 **So** Cast not away *therefore*
your *confidence* **boldness**,
which hath *great* **mega** recompence *of reward*.

36 For ye have need of *patience* **endurance**, that,
after ye have **having** done the will of *God* **Elohim**,
ye might receive the *promise* **pre—evangelism**.

37 For yet a little *while* — **as much as** — **as long as**,

18 And where there is forgiveness of these,
there is not still offering for sin.

19 So brothers,
having boldness to enter the Holies
in the blood of Yah Shua,

20 by a freshly slaughtered and living way,
that he hanukkahed for us through the veil
— his flesh;

21 and having a mega priest over the house of El;

22 we come near with a true heart
in full bearance of trust,
having our hearts sprinkled from an evil conscience
and our bodies bathed with pure water.

23 Hold down the profession of our hope
unwaveringly;
for he who pre—evangelized is trustworthy.

24 And consider one another
— to agitate to love and to good works:

25 not forsaking to co—synagogue
exactly as the custom of some is
— but consoling:
and so much the more,
as long as you see the day approaching.

Sinning Voluntarily

26 For if we sin voluntarily
after we take the knowledge of the truth,
there remains not still sacrifice for sins;

27 but an awesome expectation
of judgment and zeal of fire to consume the opposers.

28 Anyone who set aside the torah of Mosheh
died apart from compassion
under two or three witnesses:

29 of how much worse punishment, think you,
is he deemed worthy
— who tramples the Son of Elohim?
— and deems profane
the blood of the covenant wherein he was hallowed?
— and insults the Spirit of charism?

30 For we know him who said,
Vengeance is mine — I recompense, words
Yah Veh. And again, Yah Veh judges his
people. Deuteronomy 32:35, 36

31 How awesome
falling into the hands of the living Elohim.

32 And remember the previous days
wherein having been enlightened
you endured a vast contention of sufferings;

33 partly indeed,
being theatricized both by reproaches and tribulations;
and partly,
while you became communicants
of them who thus behaved.

34 For you sympathized with me in my bonds
and with cheer received the plunder of your holdings,
knowing in yourselves that in the heavens
you have a better and abiding holdings.

35 So cast not away your boldness,
which have a *mega* recompence:
36 for you have need of endurance
— that having done the will of *Elohim*,
you receive the *pre—evangelism*.
37 For yet a little while — *as much as* — *as long as*
and he that shall come, *will* **shall** come,
and *will* **shall** not *tarry* **take his time**.
38 Now the just shall live by *faith* **trust**:
but *if* **whenever** any *man draw back* **withdraw**,
my soul shall *have no pleasure* **not think
well** in him. Habakkuk 2:3, 4
39 But we are not of them
who *draw back* **withdraw** unto *perdition* **destruction**;
but of them that *believe* **trust**
to **unto** the *saving* **acquiring** of the soul.

TRUST

11 Now *faith* **trust**
is the substance of *things hoped for* **our hoping**,
the *evidence* **proof** of *things* **those** not seen.
2 For *by* **in** it the elders *obtained
a good report* **witnessed**.
3 Through *faith* **trust** we *understand* **comprehend**
that the *worlds* **eons** were *framed* **prepared**
by the *word* **rhema** of *God* **Elohim**,
so that **unto this**;
things **those** which are seen
were **became** not *made*
of *things* **those** which *do appear* **manifested**.
4 By *faith* **trust** Abel offered unto *God* **Elohim**
a *more excellent* **much better** sacrifice than Cain **Qayin**,
by **through** which he *obtained witness* **witnessed**
that he was righteous **to being just**,
God testifying **Elohim witnessing** of his *gifts* **gratuities**:
and *by* **through** it he being dead yet speaketh.
5 By *faith Enoch* **trust Hanoch**
was *translated* **transplaced**
that he should not see death;
and was not found,
because *God* **Elohim** had *translated* **transplaced** him:
for *before* **ere** his *translation* **transplacing**
he had this *testimony* **witness**,
that he *pleased God* **well—pleased Elohim**.
6 But *without faith* **apart from trust**
it is impossible to *please him* **well—please**:
for he that cometh to *God* **Elohim**
must *believe* **trust** that he is,
and that he *is a rewarder* **becometh a recompenser**
of them that *diligently* seek him.

7 By *faith Noah* **trust Noach**,
being *warned of God* **oracled**
of things **concerning those** not seen as yet,
moved with *fear* **reverence**,
prepared an ark to the *saving* **salvation** of his house;
by the **through** which he condemned the *world* **cosmos**,
and became heir of the *righteousness* **justness**
which is by *faith* **trust**.
8 By *faith* **trust** Abraham,
when he was called to go out into a place
which he *should after receive* **was about to take**
for **unto** an inheritance, obeyed;
and he went *out*, not knowing whither he went.
9 By *faith* **trust**
he *sojourned* **settled**
in the land of *promise* **pre—evangelism**,
as in *a strange country* **another's**,
dwelling **settling** in tabernacles
with *Isaac* **Yischaq** and *Jacob* **Yaaqov**,
the heirs with him **co—heirs**
of the same *promise* **pre—evangelism**:
10 For he *looked for* **awaited** a city
which hath foundations,
whose *builder* **artificer** and *maker* **public worker**
is *God* **Elohim**.
11 Through *faith* **trust** also Sara **herself**
received strength **took dynamis** to conceive *seed* **sperma**,
and *was delivered of a child* **birthed**
when she was
past age **beyond the season of maturescence**,
because **since** she *judged* **deemed** him
faithful **trustworthy** who had
promised **pre—evangelized**.
12 *Therefore sprang there* **So
there birthed**, even of one,
and him as good as dead,
so many **exactly** as the stars of the sky in multitude,
and as the sand which is by the sea shore innumerable.
13 These all died in *faith* **trust**,
not having *received* **taken** the
promises **pre—evangelisms**,
and he who comes, comes
and takes not his time.
38 And the just live by trust:
and whenever anyone withdraws, my
soul thinks not well in him.
Habakkuk 2:3, 4
39 And we are not of them
who withdraw to destruction;
but of them who trust to the acquiring of the soul.

Trust

11 And trust
is the substance of our hoping;
the proof of the unseen.
2 For in this, the elders were witnessed to.
3 By trust
we comprehend that the eons
were prepared by the rhema of Elohim:
in this: the seen became not from those manifested.
4 By trust
Abel offered Elohim a much better sacrifice
than Qayin;
through which he witnessed to being just
— Elohim witnessing of his gratuities:
and through it, being dead, he still speaks.
5 By trust
Hanoch was transplaced to not see death;
and was not found;
because Elohim transplaced him:
for ere his transplacing he had this witness
— that he well—pleased Elohim:
6 and apart from trust
it is impossible to well—please:
for whoever comes to Elohim must trust that he is:
and that he comes a recompenser
to them who seek him.
7 By trust
Noach, being oracled concerning those still unseen,
moved with reverence;
prepared an ark to the salvation of his house;
through which he condemned the cosmos
and became heir of the justness by trust.
8 By trust
Abraham, when called to go to a place
he was about to take to an inheritance, obeyed;
and he went, knowing not where he goes.
9 By trust
he settled in the land of pre—evangelism,
as in anothers,
settling in tabernacles with Yischaq and Yaaqov
— co—heirs of the same pre—evangelism:
10 for he awaited a city having foundations,
whose artificer and public worker *is* Elohim.
11 By trust
Sara also took dynamis to conceive sperma
— and birthed
when she was beyond the season of maturescence;
since she deemed him who had pre—evangelized
trustworthy.
12 So even of one
and him as good as dead
birthed a multitude exactly as the stars of the sky
and innumerable as the sand by the sea shore.
13 These all died in trust
not taking the pre—evangelisms;
but having seen them afar *off*,
and were *persuaded of them* **convinced**,
and *embraced them* **saluted**, and *confessed* **professed**
that they were strangers and pilgrims on the earth.
14 For they that *say word* such *things*
declare plainly **manifest**
that they seek a *country* **fatherland**.
15 And *truly* **indeed**,
if they had *been mindful of that country* **remembered**
from whence they came *out*,
they might have *ever* had *opportunity* **season**
to have returned.
16 But now they *desire* **reach for** a better *country*,
that is, an *heavenly* **heavenlies**:
Wherefore God **So Elohim**
is not ashamed to be called their *God* **Elohim**:
for he hath prepared for them a city.
17 By *faith* **trust** Abraham,
when he was *tried* **tested**, offered *up* Isaac **Yischaq**:
and he that had received the *promises* **pre—evangelisms**
offered *up* his only *begotten son*, **birthed**
18 *Of* **Unto** whom it was *said* **spoken**,
That in *Isaac* **Yischaq** shall thy seed *sperma* be called:
19 *Accounting* **Reckoning** that *God* **Elohim**
was able to raise *him up*, even from the dead;
from whence also he received him in a *figure* **parable**.
20 By *faith* **trust**
Isaac **Yischaq** blessed *Jacob* **Yaaqov** and *Esau* **Esav**
concerning *things* **those** to come.
21 By *faith Jacob* **trust Yaaqov**,
when he was a dying,
blessed *both* **each of** the sons of *Joseph* **Yoseph**;
and worshipped,
leaning upon the *top* **tip** of his *staff* **scion**.
22 By *faith Joseph* **trust Yoseph**, when he died,
made mention **remembered**
of **concerning** the *departing* **exodus**
of the *children* **sons** of *Israel* **Yisra El**;
and *gave commandment* **misvahed**
concerning his bones.
23 By *faith Moses* **trust Mosheh**,
when he was *born* **birthed**,
was *hid* **secreted** three months of his *parents* **fathers**,
because they saw he was *a proper* **an urbane** child;

   and they were not *afraid* **awestricken**
of the king's commandment sovereign's ordinance.
24   By *faith Moses* **trust Mosheh**,
  when he *was come to years* **became mega**,
   refused **denied** to be *called* **worded**,
    the son of *Pharaoh's* **Paroh's** daughter;
25   Choosing rather to *suffer affliction* **co—suffer**
   with the people of *God* **Elohim**,
  than *to enjoy* the *pleasures* **temporal enjoyment**
    of sin *for a season*;
26 Esteeming the reproach of *Christ* **the Messiah**
 greater riches than the treasures in *Egypt* **Misrayim**:
for he *had respect* **looked away** unto the recompence
    of the reward.
27   By *faith* **trust** he forsook *Egypt* **Misrayim**,
    not *fearing* **awestricken**
 by the *wrath* **fury** of the *king* **sovereign**:
   for he *endured* **persevered**,
  as seeing him who is invisible.
28   Through *faith* **trust** he *kept*
   did the *passover* **pasach**,
 and the *sprinkling* **pouring** of blood,
 lest he that destroyed the firstborn
   should *touch* **finger** them.
29   By *faith* **trust**
  they passed through the *Red* **Reed** sea
   as *by* **through** dry *land*:
  which the *Egyptians* **Misrayim**
  assaying to do **taking on to test**
   were *drowned* **swallowed**.
30 By *faith* **trust** the walls of Jericho fell *down*,
after they were *compassed about* **surrounded** seven days.
31   By *faith* **trust Rachab** the *harlot Rahab* **whore**
   perished **co—destructed** not
  with them that *believed not* **distrusted**,
 when she had received the spies with *peace* **shalom**.
32   And what shall I *more say* **still word**?
   but seeing them afar:
 and were convinced and saluted and professed
  that they were strangers and pilgrims on the earth.
14   For whoever words such
  manifest that they seek a fatherland.
15   And indeed,
 if they had remembered from whence they came,
  they had ever had season to return.
16   But now they reach for a better
   — that is, the heavenlies:
 so Elohim shames not to be called their Elohim:
   for he prepared them a city.
17   By trust

  when Abraham was tested, offered Yischaq
   — he who received the pre—evangelisms
   offered his only birthed son,
18   to whom it was spoken,
  In Yischaq your sperma is called:
19   reckoning that Elohim was able to raise
   — even from the dead;
whence also he received him in a parable.
20   By trust
  Yischaq blessed Yaaqov and Esav
   concerning those to come.
21   By trust
    Yaaqov, dying,
  blessed each of the sons of Yoseph;
 and worshipped on the tip of his scion.
22   By trust
    Yoseph, dying,
 remembered concerning the exodus
   of the sons of Yisra El;
  and misvahed concerning his bones.
23   By trust
   Mosheh, being birthed,
 was secreted three months by his fathers,
 because they saw he was an urbane child;
and they awed not by the ordinance of the sovereign.
24   By trust
   Mosheh, becoming mega,
   denied being worded
  the son of the daughter of Paroh;
25   choosing rather
 to co—suffer with the people of Elohim,
  than the temporal enjoyment of sin;
26   esteeming the reproach of the Messiah
 greater riches than the treasures in Misrayim:
  for he looked to the recompence.
27   By trust
   he forsook Misrayim;
not awestricken by the fury of the sovereign:
for he persevered — as seeing him who is invisible.
28   By trust
 he did the pasach and the pouring of blood,
lest he who destroys the firstborn, finger them.
29   By trust
 they passed through the Reed sea as through dry:
  which the Misrayim took to test,
   and were swallowed.
30   By trust
   the walls of Jericho fell,
 after they were surrounded seven days.
31   By trust

HEBREWS 11, 12

Rachab the whore co—destructed not
with them who distrusted,
when she received the spies with shalom.

32 And what word I still?
for the time *would* **should** fail me
to *tell of Gedeon* **declare about Gidon**,
and *of Barak* **Baraq also**, and *of Samson* **Shimshon**,
and *of Jephthae* **Yipthach**; *of* David *also*,
and *Samuel* **Shemu El**, and *of* the prophets:

33 Who through *faith* **trust**
subdued *kingdoms* **sovereigndoms**,
wrought righteousness **worked justness**,
obtained *promises* **pre—evangelisms**,
stopped **sealed** the mouths of lions.

34 Quenched the *violence* **dynamis** of fire,
escaped **fled** the edge of the sword,
out of *weakness* **frailty** were *made strong* **empowered**,
waxed valiant **became mighty** in *fight* **war**,
turned to flight **put down** the *armies* **encampments**
of *the aliens* **others**.

35 Women *received* **took** their dead
raised to life again **by resurrection**:
and others were tortured,
not *accepting deliverance* **receiving redemption**;
that they might obtain a better resurrection:

36 And others *had trial of cruel* **took testings**
of mockings and scourgings, yea,
moreover **yet** of bonds and *imprisonment* **guardhouses**:

37 They were stoned,
they were sawn *asunder* **apart**,
were *tempted* **tested**,
were *slain with* **deathified in murder by** the sword:
they wandered about in sheepskins and goatskins;
being destitute **falling behind**,
afflicted **tribulated**, *tormented* **vilified**;

38 (Of whom the *world* **cosmos** was not worthy:)
they wandered
in *deserts* **wildernesses**, and *in* mountains,
and *in dens* **grottos** and *caves* **caverns** of the earth.

39 And these all,
having *obtained a good report* **witnessed**
through *faith* **the trust**,
received not the *promise* **pre—evangelism**:

40 *God* **Elohim**
having **previously** provided some better *thing* for us,
that they *without* **apart from** us
should not be *made perfect* **completed**.

From The Cloud Of Witnesses To Yah Shua

12 *Wherefore* **So**
seeing we also are *compassed about* **surrounded**
with so *great* **vast** a cloud of witnesses,
let us *lay aside* **put away** every weight,
and the *well—standing* sin *which doth so easily beset us*,
and let us run *with patience* **through endurance**
the *race* **contest** that is set *before* **in front of** us,

2 *Looking* **Considering** unto *Jesus* **Yah Shua**
the *author* **hierarch** and *finisher* **completer**
of *our faith* **the trust**;
who for the *joy* **cheer** that was set before him
endured the *cross* **stake**,
despising **disesteeming** the shame,
and is *set down at* **seated**
at the right *hand* of the throne of *God* **Elohim**.

The Purpose Of The Discipline Of Yah Veh

3 For consider him
that endured such *contradiction* **controversy**
of **by** sinners *against* **unto** himself,
lest ye be wearied and *faint* **weakened**
in your *minds* **souls**.

4 Ye have not yet *resisted* **withstood** unto blood,
striving against **antagonizing with** sin.

5 And ye *have forgotten* **are utterly oblivious**
to the *exhortation* **consolation**
which *speaketh* **reasoneth** unto you
as unto *children* **sons**,
My son, *despise* **disregard** not thou
the *chastening* **discipline** of *the Lord* **Yah Veh**,
nor *faint* **weaken**
when thou art *rebuked of* **reproved by** him:

6 For whom *the Lord* **Yah Veh** loveth
he *chasteneth* **disciplineth**,
and scourgeth every son whom he
receiveth. Proverbs 3:11, 12
for the time fails me to declare about Gidon
and also Baraq and Shimshon and Yipthach;
also David and Shemu El and the prophets

33 — who through trust:
subdued sovereigndoms,
worked justness,
obtained pre—evangelisms,
sealed the mouths of lions,

34 quenched the dynamis of fire,
fled the edge of the sword,

from frailty were empowered,
became mighty in war,
put down the encampments of others,

35 women took their dead by resurrection,
and others were tortured
— not receiving redemption
to obtain a better resurrection,

36 and others
took testings of mockings and scourgings
— yes, still of bonds and guardhouses:

37 they were stoned,
they were sawn apart,
they were tested,
deathified in murder by the sword,
wandered about in sheepskins and goatskins,
falling behind — tribulated — vilified,

38 of whom the cosmos was not worthy:
wandering in wildernesses and mountains
and grottos and caverns of the earth.

39 And these all, witnessing through the trust,
received not the pre—evangelism:

40 Elohim having previously provided
somewhat better for us
— that they not completed/shalamed apart from us.

From The Cloud Of Witnesses To Yah Shua

12 So seeing we also are surrounded
with so vast a cloud of witnesses,
put away every weight and the well—standing sin:
and through endurance,
run the contest set in front of us:

2 considering to Yah Shua
the hierarch and completer/shalamer of the trust
— who for the cheer set in front of him:
endured the stake,
disesteeming the shame,
and is seated at the right of the throne of Elohim.

The Purpose Of The Discipline Of Yah Veh

3 For consider him
who endured such controversy by sinners to himself;
lest you weary and weaken in your souls.

4 You have not yet withstood to blood
antagonizing with sin:

5 and you are utterly oblivious to the consolation
which reasons to you as to sons,
My son,
neither disregard the discipline of Yah Veh,
nor weaken when he reproves you:

6 for Yah Veh disciplines whom he loves
and scourges every son he receives. Proverbs 3:11, 12

7 If ye endure *chastening* **discipline**,
God dealeth with **Elohim offereth** you as with sons;
for what son is he
whom the father *chasteneth* **disciplineth** not?

8 But if ye be *without chastisement*
apart from discipline,
whereof all *are* **become** partakers,
then are ye bastards, and not sons.

9 *Furthermore* **So indeed**
we have had fathers of our flesh which
corrected **disciplined** us,
and we *gave* **respected** them *reverence*:
shall we not much rather
be in subjection **subjugate** unto the Father of spirits,
and live?

10 For they *verily* **indeed** for a few days
chastened us **disciplined**
after their *own pleasure* **well—thinking**;
but he for *our profit* **benefit**,
that we might *be partakers* **partake** of his holiness.

11 Now **indeed** no *chastening*
discipline for the present
seemeth **is thought** to be *joyous* **cheerful**,
but *grievous* **sorrowful**:
nevertheless afterward it *yieldeth* **giveth back**
the *peaceable* **shalom**
of the fruit of *righteousness* **justness**
unto them which are exercised *thereby* **through it**.

12 *Wherefore lift up* **So**
straighten the **limping** hands
which hang down,
and the *feeble* **paralyzed** knees;

13 And make straight *paths* **tracks** for your feet,
lest that which is lame be turned *out of the way* **aside**;
but let it rather be healed.

14 *Follow peace* **Pursue shalom** with all *men*,
and holiness,
without **apart from** which
no *man* **one** shall see *the Lord* **Adonay**:

15 *Looking diligently* **Overseeing**
lest any *man fail* **one fall behind**
of the *grace* **charism** of *God* **Elohim**;
lest any root of bitterness *springing up* **sprouting**,
trouble **harass** you,
and *thereby* **through this** many be defiled;

16 Lest there be any *fornicator* **whoremonger**,
or *profane person* **profaner**,

HEBREWS 12

as *Esau* **Esav**, who for one morsel of *meat* **food**
sold **gave up** his *birthright* **firstrights**.
17 For ye know *how* that *afterward* **thereafter**,
when he *would* **willed to** have inherited the blessing,
he was *rejected* **disapproved**:
for he found no place of repentance,
though he sought it *carefully* with tears.

SINAY VS SIYON

18 For ye are not come
unto the mount *that might be* touched,
and that burned with fire,
nor **and** unto *blackness* **clouds of gloom**,
and darkness, and tempest,
19 And the *sound* **echo** of a trumpet,
and the voice of *words* **rhemas**;
which *voice* they that heard, *intreated* **shunned,**
that the word
should not be *spoken* **added** to them *any more*:
20 (For they could not *endure* **bear**
that which was *commanded* **charged**,
And *if so much as* **whenever**
a beast *touch* **fingers** the mountain,
it shall be stoned,
or *thrust* **pierced** through with a *dart* **missile**:
21 And **thus**
so *terrible* **awesome** was the *sight* **manifestation**,
that *Moses* **Mosheh** said,
I *exceedingly fear* **am utterly frightened**
and *quake* **trembling**:)
Exodus 19:12, 20:18, 19
22 But ye are come unto mount *Sion* **Siyon**,
and unto the city of the living *God* **Elohim**,
the *heavenly Jerusalem* **Yeru Shalem of the heavenlies**,
and to *an innumerable company* **myriads** of angels,

7 If you endure discipline,
Elohim offers you as with sons;
for what son is there whom the father disciplines not?
8 And if you are apart from discipline,
whereof all become partakers, then
you are bastards and not sons.
9 So indeed
we have fathers of our flesh who discipline us
and we respect them:
and not much rather
subjugate to the Father of spirits and live?
10 For they indeed, for a few days,
discipline after their well—thinking;
but he for our benefit
that we partake of his holiness.

11 Now indeed, for the present,
no discipline is thought to be cheerful
— but sorrowful:
nevertheless afterward
it gives the shalom of the fruit of justness
to them who exercise through it.
12 So straighten the limping hands
and the paralyzed knees;
13 and make straight tracks for your feet,
lest whoever is lame turns aside;
but rather be healed.
14 Pursue shalom with all — and holiness
— apart from which no one sees Adonay:
15 overseeing
lest anyone fall behind of the charism of Elohim;
lest any sprouting root of bitterness harass you;
and through this many are defiled;
16 lest there be any whoremonger
or profaner as Esav
— who for one morsel of food gave up his firstrights.
17 For you know that thereafter
when he willed to inherit the blessing
he was disapproved:
for he found no place of repentance,
though he sought it with tears.

SINAY VS SIYON

18 For you come not to the mount
touched and burned with fire
and to clouds of gloom and darkness and tempest
19 and to the echo of a trumpet
and to the voice of rhemas
— which, they who heard, shunned
that the word not be added to them;
20 for they could not bear what was charged: and
whenever a beast fingered the mountain, so be
it stoned or pierced through with a missile:
21 and so awesome was the manifestation,
that Mosheh said, I utterly frighten and
tremble: Exodus 19:12, 20:18, 19
22 But you come to Mount Siyon
to the city of the living Elohim
— the Yeru Shalem of the heavenlies
and to myriads of angels,
23 To the *general assembly* **whole gathering**
and *church* **ecclesia** of the firstborn,
which are *written* **registered** in *heaven* **the heavens**,
and to *God* **Elohim** the Judge of all,
and to the spirits of **the** just *men*
made perfect **having been completed/shalamed,**

24 And to *Jesus* **Yah Shua**
the mediator of the new covenant,
and to the blood of sprinkling,
that speaketh better *things* than *that of* Abel.
25 See that ye *refuse* **shun** not him that speaketh.
For if they *escaped* **fled** not
who *refused* **shunned** him that *spake* **oracled** on earth,
much more shall *not* we *escape*,
if we turn away from him
that speaketh from heaven **of the heavens**:
26 Whose voice then shook the earth:
but now he hath *promised* **pre—evangelized**,
saying **wording**,
Yet once more I *shake* **quake** not the earth only,
but also heaven.
27 And this *word*, Yet once more,
signifieth **evidenceth** the *removing* **transplacing**
of those *things* that are **shaken**,
as of *things* **those** that are made,
that those *things* which cannot be shaken
may *remain* **abide**.
28 *Wherefore* **So** we
receiving **taking** a *kingdom* **sovereigndom**
which cannot be moved **unmovable**,
let us have *grace* **charism**,
whereby **through which** we may *serve* **minister**
God acceptably **to Elohim well—pleasingly**
with *reverence* **awe** and *Godly fear* **reverence**:
29 For our *God* **Elohim** is a consuming fire.

CONCLUSION

13 Let *brotherly love* **befriending the brethren**
continue **abide**.
2 Be not forgetful to *entertain* **befriend** strangers:
for *thereby* **through this**
some have *entertained* **lodged**
angels *unawares* **in hiding**.
3 Remember them that are *in bonds* **bound**,
as *bound with them* **being co—bound**;
and them which *suffer adversity* **are vilified**,
as being yourselves also in the body.
4 Marriage is honourable in all,
and the *bed undefiled* **coition unpolluted**:
but whoremongers and adulterers
God will **Elohim shall** judge.
5 Let your *conversation* **manner**
be *without covetousness* **unavaricious**;
and be *content* **satisfied** with
such things as ye have **the present**:
for he hath said,

I *will* **shall** never **no way** *leave* **let loose of** thee,
nor **no way** forsake thee.
6 So that we may *boldly say* **courageously word**,
The Lord **Yah Veh** is my helper,
and I *will* **shall** not *fear* **awe**
by what *man* **humanity** shall do unto me.
Psalm 118:6
7 Remember them which *have*
the rule over **govern** you,
who have spoken unto you the word of *God* **Elohim**:
whose *faith follow* **trust mimic**,
considering the *end* **outcome** of their
conversation **behaviour**.
8 *Jesus Christ* **Yah Shua**
Messiah the same yesterday,
and to day, and *for ever* **unto the eons**.
9 Be not carried about with
divers and strange doctrines.
For it is *a* good *thing*
that the heart be established with *grace* **charism**;
not with *meats* **foods**,
which have not *profited* **benefited** them
that have *been occupied* **walked** therein.
10 We have *an* **a sacrifice** altar,
whereof they have no *right* **authority** to eat
which *serve* **minister** the tabernacle.
11 For the bodies of those *beasts* **live beings**,
whose blood is brought into the *sanctuary* **Holies**
23 to the whole gathering and
ecclesia of the firstborn
registered in the heavens,
and to Elohim the Judge of all,
and to the spirits of the just
being completed/shalamed,
24 and to Yah Shua the mediator
of the new covenant,
and to the blood of sprinkling
speaking better than Abel.
25 See that you not shun him who speaks.
For if they flee not
— they who shunned him who oracled on earth,
how much more we,
— we who turn from him of the heavens
26 whose voice then shook the earth.
And now he pre—evangelizes, wording,
Still once more I quake, not only the earth,
but also the heavens.
27 And this: Still once more
evidences the transplacing of those that are shaken
as of those that are made;

that those that cannot be shaken still abide.
28 So we, taking an unmovable sovereigndom,
have charism;
through which we minister to Elohim
well—pleasingly with awe and reverence:
29 For our Elohim is a consuming fire.

Conclusion

13 And abide befriending the brothers abides:
2 not forgetful to befriend strangers:
for through this some lodge angels in hiding.
3 Remember the bound as being co—bound;
and the vilified as also being in the body as you.
4 Marriage is honorable in all
and the coition unpolluted:
but Elohim judges whoremongers and adulterers.
5 Your manner, unavaricious;
being satisfied with the present.
For he said,
I neither no way let loose of you
nor no way forsake.
6 So courageously we word,
Yah Veh my helper:
and I awe not what humanity does to me.
Psalm 118:6
7 Remember them who govern you,
who speak the word of Elohim to you:
whose trust mimic,
considering the outcome of their behavior.
8 Yah Shua Messiah the same
— yesterday and today and to the eons.
9 Be not carried about
with divers and strange doctrines.
For it is good to establish the heart with charism;
and not with foods
which benefit not those who walk therein.
10 We have a sacrifice altar,
whereof whoever ministers the tabernacle
has no authority to eat.
11 For the bodies of those live beings,
whose blood is brought into the Holies
by **through** the *high* **arch** priest for sin,
are burned without the *camp* **encampment**.
12 *Wherefore Jesus* **So Yah Shua** also,
that he might *sanctify* **hallow** the people
with **through** his own blood, suffered without the gate.
13 Let us go forth therefore unto him
without the *camp* **encampment**,
bearing his reproach.
14 For here have we no *continuing* **abiding** city,
but we seek one to come.
15 *By* **So through** him *therefore*
let us offer the sacrifice of *praise* **halal** to *God* **Elohim**
continually, that is,
the fruit of *our* lips *giving thanks to* **professing** his name.
16 But to do good and *to*
communicate **communion**
forget not:
for with such sacrifices *God* **Elohim** is well—pleased.
17 Obey them that *have the rule over* **govern** you,
and submit yourselves:
for they watch for your souls,
as they that must give *account* **word**,
that they may do it with *joy* **cheer**,
and not *with grief* **sighing**:
for that is *unprofitable* **disadvantageous** for you.
18 Pray for us:
for we *trust* **are confident**
that we have a good conscience,
in all *things* willing to *live honestly* **behave well**.
19 But I beseech you *the rather* **superabundantly**
to do this,
that I may be restored to you *the sooner* **very quickly**.
20 Now the *God* **Elohim** of *peace* **shalom**,
that brought *again* from the dead
our *Lord Jesus* **Adonay Yah Shua**,
that *great* **mega** shepherd of the sheep,
through **in** the blood of the *everlasting* **eternal** covenant,
21 *Make* **Prepare** you *perfect* in every good work
to do his will,
working **doing** in you
that which is well—pleasing in his sight,
through *Jesus Christ* **Yah Shua Messiah**;
to whom be glory
for ever and ever **unto the eons of the eons**.
Amen.
22 And I beseech you, brethren,
suffer **tolerate** the word of *exhortation* **consolation**:
for I have *written a letter* **epistolized** unto you
in **through** few words.
23 Know ye
that *our* brother *Timothy* **Timo Theos**
is *set at liberty* **released**;
with whom, *if* **whenever** he come *shortly* **very quickly**,
I *will* **shall** see you.

Salutes And Benediction

24 Salute all them that *have*
the rule over **govern** you,
and all the *saints* **holy**.

They of Italy salute you.
25   *Grace* **Charism** be with you all.
Amen.
through the archpriest for sin,
are burned outside the encampment.
12   So Yah Shua also,
to hallow the people through his own blood,
suffered outside the gate.
13   So go forth to him outside the encampment,
bearing his reproach.
14   For we have no abiding city here,
but we seek one to come.
15   So through him
we continually offer the sacrifice of halal to Elohim,
that is, the fruit of our lips, professing his name:
16   and forget not to do good and communion:
for Elohim is well—pleased with such sacrifices.
17   Obey them who govern you
and submit yourselves:
for they watch for your souls
as they that must give word
— to do it with cheer and not with sighing:
for that is disadvantageous for you.
18   Pray for us:
for we are confident that we have a good conscience;
we will to behave well in all.

19   and I superabundantly beseech you to do this:
restore me to you very quickly.
20   And the Elohim of the shalom,
who brought our Adonay Yah Shua from the dead,
that mega shepherd of the sheep
in the blood of the eternal covenant
21   prepare you in every good work to do his will:
doing in you what is well—pleasing in his sight,
through Yah Shua Messiah;
to whom be glory to the eons of the eons.
Amen.
22   And I beseech you, brothers,
tolerate the word of consolation:
for I epistolize you through few words.
23   Know this, that brother Timo Theos is released;
with whom, whenever he comes very quickly,
I see you.

SALUTES AND BENEDICTION

24   Salute all who govern you and all the holy.
They of Italy salute you.
25   Charism be with you all.
Amen.

JAMES/YA'AKOV 1

SALUTATION

1 James **Yaaqovos**,
a servant of God **Elohim**
and of *the Lord Jesus Christ* **Adonay Yah Shua Messiah**,
to the twelve *tribes* **scions**
which are scattered abroad **of the diaspora**,
greeting **Cheers**.

TRUST AND TESTINGS

2 My brethren,
count **deem** it all *joy* **cheer**
when ye fall into divers *temptations* **testings**;

3 Knowing *this*,
that the *trying* **proofing** of your *faith* **trust**
worketh *patience* **endurance**.

4 *But let patience* **And endurance**
have *her perfect* **a work** **of completion/shalom**,
that ye may be *perfect* **complete/
at shalom** and *entire* **whole**,
wanting nothing **lacking naught**.

5 If any of you lack wisdom,
let him ask of *God* **Elohim**,
that giveth to all *men* liberally,
and *upbraideth* **reproacheth** not;
and it shall be given him.

6 But let him ask in *faith* **trust**,
nothing wavering **doubting naught**.
For he that *wavereth* **doubteth**
is like **resembleth** a *wave* **surge** of the sea
driven with the wind **windtossed** and tossed.

7 For let not that *man think* **human suppose**
that he shall *receive any thing* **take aught**
of the *Lord* **Adonay**.

8 A double *minded* **souled** man
is unstable in all his ways.

9 Let the brother of *low degree* **humbleness**
rejoice **boast** in *that he is exalted* **his exaltation**:

10 But the rich,
in *that he is made low* **his humiliation**:
because as the *flower* **blossom** of the *grass* **herbage**
he shall pass *away*.

11 For the sun is no sooner risen
with a *burning heat* **scorch**,
but it withereth the grass,
and the *flower* **blossom** thereof falleth,
and the *grace* **befittingness** of *the fashion of it* **its face**
perisheth **destructeth**:
so **thus** also
shall the rich *man* fade *away* in his ways.

12 Blessed is the man that
endureth *temptation* **testing**:
for when he is tried **because, being approved**,
he shall *receive* **take** the *crown* **wreath** of life,
which *the Lord* **Adonay** hath *promised* **pre—evangelized**
to them that love him.

13 Let no *man say* **one word**
when he is *tempted* **tested**,
Because I am *tempted* **tested** of *God* **Elohim**:
for *God* **Elohim**
cannot **shall not** be *tempted* **tested** with evil,
neither *tempteth* **testeth** he any *man* **one**:

14 But *every man* **each** is *tempted* **tested**,
when he is *drawn away* **enticed** of his own *lust* **panting**,
and *enticed* **entrapped**.

15 Then when *lust* **panting** hath conceived,
it *bringeth forth* **birtheth** sin:
and sin, when it is *finished* **complete/shalamed**,
bringeth forth **breedeth** death.

16 *Do* **Wander** not *err*, my beloved brethren.

17 Every good *gift* **gratuity**
and every *perfect gift* **complete gratuity** is from above,
and *cometh down* **descendeth** from the Father of lights,
with whom is no *variableness* **changeableness**,
neither shadow of turning.

18 Of his own will
begat **bred** he us with the word of truth,
that we should be
a *kind of a firstfruits* **firstlings** of his creatures.

19 *Wherefore* **So then**, my beloved brethren,
let every *man* **human** be *swift* **quick** to
hear, slow to speak, slow to wrath:

20 For the wrath of man
worketh not the *righteousness* **justness** of *God* **Elohim**.

21 *Wherefore lay apart* **So put
away** all *filthiness* **foulness**

SALUTATION

1 Yaaqovos,
a servant of Elohim and of Adonay Yah Shua Messiah:
To the twelve scions of the diaspora:
Cheers.

TRUST AND TESTINGS

2 My brothers,
deem it all cheer when you fall into divers testings;

3 knowing that the proofing of your trust
works endurance:

4 and endurance have a work
of completion/shalom

	so that you are complete/at shalom
	and whole — lacking naught.
5	If any of you lack wisdom, ask of Elohim
	who gives liberally to all and reproaches not
	— and he is given.
6	But ask in trust, doubting naught.
	For whoever doubts resembles a surge of the sea
	windtossed and tossed.
7	For suppose not
	that such a human takes aught of Adonay.
8	A double—souled man is
	unstable in all his ways.
9	But the brother of humbleness
	boasts in his exaltation;
10	and the rich in his humiliation:
	because he passes as the blossom of the herbage.
11	For the sun rises with a scorch
	and withers the grass;
	and the blossom falls
	and destructs the befittingness of its face:
	thus also the rich fades in his ways.
12	Blessed — the man who endures testing:
	because being approved
	he takes the wreath of life
	— which Adonay pre—evangelized
	to them who love him.
13	Word not, when tested,
	Because I am tested of Elohim:
	for Elohim is neither tested with evil
	nor tests anyone:
14	but each is tested
	when he is enticed of his own panting and entrapped.
15	Then when panting conceives, it births sin:
	and when sin completes/shalams, it breeds death.
16	Wander not, my beloved brothers.
17	Every gratuity of good
	and every gratuity of completion/shalom
	is from above;
	and descends from the Father of lights
	— with whom is neither changeableness
	nor shadow of turning.
18	Of his own will
	he bred us with the word of truth
	— to be some firstlings of his creatures.
19	So then, my beloved brothers,
	thus be every human:
	quick to hear,
	slow to speak,
	slow to wrath:
20	For the wrath of man
	works not the justness of Elohim.
21	So put away all foulness
	and *super fluity* **superabundance** of *naughtiness* **malice**,
	and receive *with* **in** meekness the
	engrafted **implanted** word,
	which is able to save your souls.
22	But be ye doers of the word,
	and not hearers only,
	deceiving **deluding** your own selves.
23	*For* **Because** if any be a hearer of the word,
	and not a doer,
	he *is like unto* **resembles** a man
	beholding **perceiving** his *natural* **genetic** face
	in a *glass* **mirror**:
24	For he *beholdeth* **perceiveth** himself,
	and goeth *his way*,
	and straightway forgetteth what manner *of man* he was.
25	But whoso looketh
	into the *perfect law* **torah of**
	completion/shalom of liberty,
	and *continueth* **abideth** therein,
	he being not a forgetful hearer,
	but a doer of the work,
	this *man* **one** shall be blessed in his *deed* **doing**.
26	If any *man* **one** among you
	seem **think** to be *religious* **ceremonious**,
	and bridleth not his tongue,
	but *deceiveth* **deludeth** his own heart,
	this man's *religion* **ceremony** is vain.
27	Pure *religion* **ceremony**
	and *undefiled* **unpolluted**
	before God **with Elohim** and the Father is this,
	To *visit* **scope out** the *fatherless* **orphans** and widows
	in their *affliction* **tribulation**,
	and to *keep* **guard** himself *unspotted* **unstained**
	from the *world* **cosmos**.

THE TEST OF PARTIALITY

2	My brethren,
	have not the *faith* **trust** of our
	Lord Jesus Christ, **Adonay Yah Shua Messiah**
	the Lord of glory
	with respect of persons **in partiality**.
2	For *if* **whenever** there come
	unto your *assembly* **synagogue**
	a man *with a gold ring* **goldringed**,
	in *goodly* **radiant** apparel,
	and there come in also
	a poor man in *vile raiment* **foul apparel**;
3	And ye *have respect to* **look upon** him
	that *weareth* **beareth** the *gay clothing* **radiant apparel**,

JAMES/YA'AKOV 2

and say unto him, Sit thou here *in a good place* **well**;
and say to the poor, Stand thou there,
or sit here under my footstool:

4   Are ye not then *partial* **discerning** in yourselves,
and are become judges of evil *thoughts* **reasonings**?

5   Hearken, my beloved brethren,
Hath not *God* **Elohim**
chosen **selected** the poor of this *world* **cosmos**
rich in *faith* **trust**,
and heirs of the *kingdom* **sovereigndom**
which he hath *promised* **pre—evangelized**
to them that love him?

6   But ye have *despised* **dishonoured** the poor.
Do not **the** rich *men oppress* **overpower** you,
and *draw* **drag** you *before* **unto** the judgment *seats*?

7   Do not they blaspheme that *worthy* **good** name
by the which ye are called?

8   If **yet indeed**
ye *fulfil* **complete/shalam** the *royal law* **sovereign torah**
according to the scripture,
Thou shalt love thy neighbour as thyself,
ye do well:

9   But if ye have *respect to persons* **partiality**,
ye *commit* **work** sin,
and are *convinced* **reproved** of the *law* **torah**
as transgressors.

10   For whosoever shall *keep*
guard the whole *law* **torah**,
and yet *offend* **stumble** in one *point*,
he *is guilty of* **becometh subject to** all.

11   For he that said, Do not
commit adultery **adulterize**,
said also, Do not *kill* **murder**.
Now if thou *commit no adultery* **dost not adulterize**,
yet if thou *kill* **murder**,
thou art become a transgressor of the *law* **torah**.
and superabundance of malice;
and in meekness receive the implanted word
which is able to save your souls:

22   and become doers of the word
and not only hearers — deluding your own selves.

23   Because if any be a hearer of the word
and not a doer,
he resembles a man
perceiving his genetic face in a mirror:

24   for he perceives himself — and goes
— and straightway forgets what manner he is.

25   But whoever
looks into the torah of completion/shalom of liberty
and abides therein,
not being a forgetful hearer but a doer of the work,
this one becomes blessed in his doing.

26   If anyone among you
thinks himself as being ceremonious
and bridles not his tongue
but deludes his own heart
— the ceremony of this man is vain.

27   Pure and unpolluted ceremony
with Elohim and the Father is this:
To scope out the orphans and widows
in their tribulation
and to guard himself unstained from the cosmos.

THE TEST OF PARTIALITY

2   My brothers,
be not partial in the trust
of our Adonay Yah Shua Messiah of glory.

2   For whenever a man comes to your synagogue
— goldringed, in radiant apparel;
and a poor man also comes in foul apparel;

3   and you look on him who
bears the radiant apparel
and say to him, You sit here well!
and say to the poor, You stand there!
or, Sit here under my footstool!

4   discern you not in yourselves
and become judges of evil reasonings?

5   Hearken, my beloved brothers,
Selects not Elohim the poor of this cosmos
rich in trust and heirs of the sovereigndom
which he pre—evangelized to them who love him?

6   But you dishonor the poor.
Is it not the rich who overpower you?
And drag you to the judgment?

7   Blaspheme they not that good name
by which you are called?

8   If indeed
you still complete/shalam the sovereign torah
according to the scripture,
Love your neighbour as yourself,
you do well:

9   But if you are partial, you work sin;
and the torah reproves you as transgressors.

10   For whoever guards the whole torah
and still stumbles in one, becomes subject to all.

11   For he who says, Adulterize not!
also says, Murder not!
And if you adulterize not and still murder,
you become a transgressor of the torah.

12   *So* **Thus** speak ye, and *so* **thus** do,
as they that shall be judged
by **through** the *law* **torah** of liberty.

13	For he shall have judgment
	without mercy **unmercied**,
	that hath *shewed* **dealt** no mercy;
	and mercy *rejoiceth* **exulteth** against judgment.
14	What *doth it profit* **benefit**, my brethren,
	though a man say **whenever one wordeth**
	he hath *faith* **the trust**, and have not works?
	can *faith* **the trust** save him?
15	*if* **whenever** a brother or sister be naked,
	and *destitute of* **lacketh** daily *food* **nourishment**,
16	And one of you say unto them,
	Depart **Go** in *peace* **shalom**, be ye warmed and filled;
	notwithstanding ye give them not
	those *things* which are needful to the body;
	what *doth* **benefiteth** it *profit*?
17	Even *so faith* **thus trust**, *if*
	whenever it hath not works,
	by itself is dead, *being alone*.
18	*Yea, a man* may *say* **Yet one sayeth**,
	Thou hast *faith* **trust**, and I *also* have works:
	shew me thy *faith without* **trust by** thy works,
	and I *will* **shall also** shew thee my
	faith **trust** by my works*.
	*This sentence is a play on emphasis.
19	Thou *believest* **trustest** that
	there is one *God* **Elohim**;
	thou doest well:
	the *devils* **demons** also *believe* **trust**,
	and *tremble* **shudder**.
20	But *wilt* **willest** thou know, O vain *man* **human**,
	that *faith without* **the trust apart from** works is dead?
21	Was not Abraham our father justified by works,
	when he had offered *Isaac* **Yischaq** his son
	upon the **sacrifice** altar?
22	Seest thou *how faith* **that the trust**
	wrought **co—worked** with his works,
	and by works
	was *faith made perfect* **the trust completed/shalamed**?
23	And the scripture was fulfilled/**shalamed**
	which *saith* **wordeth**,
	Abraham *believed God* **trusted Elohim**,
	and it was *imputed* **reckoned** unto him
	for righteousness **unto justness**:
	and he was called the Friend of *God* **Elohim**.
24	*So* Ye see *then how*
	that by works a *man* **human** is justified,
	and not by *faith* **trust** only.
25	Likewise also
	was not *Rahab* **Rachab** the *harlot*
	whore justified by works,
	when she had received the *messengers* **angels**,
	and had sent them *out* another way?
26	For **exactly** as the body
	without **apart from** the spirit
	is dead,
	so faith without **thus the trust apart from** works
	is dead also.

TESTING THE TONGUE

3	My brethren, be not many *masters* **doctors**,
	knowing that
	we shall *receive* **take** the greater condemnation.
2	For *in many things we offend*
	all **we all stumble much**.
	If any *man offend* **one stumble** not in word,
	the same **this one** is a *perfect* **completed/shalamed** man,
	and able also to bridle the whole body.
3	Behold, we put bits in the horses' mouths,
	that they may obey us;
	and we turn *about* their whole body.
4	Behold also the *ships* **sailers**,
	which *though they be* **being** so great,
	and *are* driven of *fierce* **hard** winds,
	yet are they turned *about*
	with **by** a very *small helm* **short rudder**,
	whithersoever the **violent impulse**
	governor listeth **of the straightener willeth**.
5	Even *so* **thus** the tongue is a little member,
	and boasteth *great things* **mega**.
	Behold, how *great a matter* **much forest**
	a little fire *kindleth* **lighteth**!
6	And the tongue is a fire,
	a *world* **cosmos** of *iniquity* **injustice**:
	so **thus** is the tongue **seated** among our members,
12	Thus speak and thus do
	as being judged through the torah of liberty.
13	For whoever deals no mercy
	has unmercied judgment;
	and mercy exults against judgment.
14	What benefit, my brothers,
	whenever one words that he has the trust
	and has not works?
	Can the trust save him?
15	Whenever a brother or sister is naked
	and lacks daily nourishment,
16	and one of you says to them,
	Go in shalom! Be warmed and filled!
	— and not give them those needful to the body;
	what benefit is it?
17	Thus, even trust,

whenever it has not works, by itself is dead.
18 Yet one says,
You have trust and I also have works:
show me your trust by your works
and I also show you my trust by my works*.
*This sentence is a play on emphasis.
19 You — you trust that Elohim is one; you do well:
the demons also trust and shudder.
20 And will you to know, O vain human,
that the trust apart from works is dead?
21 Was not Abraham our father justified by works,
when he offered Yischaq his son
on the sacrifice altar?
22 See how the trust co—worked with his works?
And the trust completed/shalamed by works?
23 And the scripture fulfilled/shalamed, wording,
Abraham trusted Elohim
and it was reckoned to him to justness;
— and he was called the Friend of Elohim.
24 — so you see, a human is justified by works
and not only by trust.
25 Likewise also
was not Rachab the whore justified by works
when she received the angels
and sent them another way?
26 For exactly as the body apart from the spirit
is dead,
thus the trust apart from works
is also dead.

Testing The Tongue

3 My brothers, be not many doctors;
knowing that we take the greater condemnation:
2 for we all stumble much.
If anyone stumbles not in word,
this one is a completed/shalamed man,
also able to bridle the whole body.
3 Behold the horses;
we put bits in their mouths to obey us;
and we turn their whole body.
4 Behold, also the sailers;
being so great and driven of hard winds;
yet are they turned by a very short rudder
wherever the violent impulse of the straightener wills.
5 Thus also the tongue;
a little member that boasts mega.
Behold, how much forest a little fire lights!
6 And the tongue is a fire — a cosmos of injustice:
thus the tongue sits among our members
that it *defileth* **staineth** the whole body,
and *setteth on fire* **inflameth**
the *course* **track** of *nature* **genetics**;
and it is *set on fire* **inflamed**
of hell **by Gay Hinnom/the Valley of Burning**.
7 For *every kind* **all nature**, both of beasts,
and of *birds* **flyers**, *and* both of *serpents* **creepers**,
and of *things* **those** in the sea, is tamed,
and hath been tamed of *mankind* **human nature**:
8 But the tongue can no *man* **human** tame;
it is an *unruly* **unrestrainable** evil
full of *deadly poison* **death bearing venom**.
9 *Therewith bless* **Therein**
eulogize we *God* **Elohim**,
even the Father;
and *therewith* **therein** curse we *men* **humanity**,
which *are made* **became**
after the *similitude* **likeness** of *God* **Elohim**.
10 Out of the same mouth
proceedeth blessing **cometh eulogy** and cursing.
My brethren,
these *things ought not so to* **need not thus** be.
11 Doth a fountain send *forth*
at the same *place* **cavern**
sweet *water* and bitter?
12 Can the fig tree, my brethren,
bear *olive berries* **make olives**?
either a vine, figs?
so can **thus** no fountain
maketh both *yield* salt water and fresh.
13 Who is *a* wise *man*
and *endued with knowledge* **understanding** among you?
let him shew out of a good *conversation* **behaviour**
his works *with* **in** meekness of wisdom.
14 But if ye
have bitter *envying* **zeal** and strife in your hearts,
glory **exult** not, and lie not against the truth.
15 This wisdom descendeth not from above,
but is earthly, *sensual* **soulical**, *devilish* **demonic**.
16 For where *envying* **zeal** and strife is,
there is *confusion* **instability** and every evil *work* **matter**.
17 But the wisdom that is from above
is first *pure* **indeed hallowed**,
then *peaceable* **at shalom**, gentle,
and easy to be intreated **agreeable**,
full of mercy and good fruits,
without partiality **impartial**,
and *without hypocrisy* **unhypocritical**.
18 And the fruit of *righteousness* **justness**
is *sown* **spored** in *peace* **shalom**
of **by** them that make *peace* **shalom**.

SUBJUGATING AND RESISTING

4 *From* whence
come **are** wars and *fightings* **strifes** among you?
come **be they** not hence,
even of your *lust* **pleasures** that war in your members?

2 Ye *lust* **pant**, and have not:
ye *kill* **murder**,
and *desire to have* **are jealous**, and cannot obtain:
ye *fight* **strive** and war,
yet ye have not, because ye ask not.

3 Ye ask, and *receive* **take** not,
because ye ask *amiss* **evily**,
that ye may *consume* **spend** it
upon **in** your *lusts* **pleasures**.

4 Ye adulterers and adulteresses,
know ye not that the friendship of the *world* **cosmos**
is enmity with *God* **Elohim**?
so whosoever *therefore*
will *willeth* to be a friend of the *world* **cosmos**
is *the* **seated an** enemy of *God* **Elohim**.

5 *Do ye* **Or** think **ye**
that the scripture *saith* **wordeth** in vain,
The spirit that dwelleth in us *lusteth* **yearneth** to envy?

6 But he giveth *more grace* **greater charism**.
Wherefore **So** he *saith* **wordeth**,
God resisteth **Elohim opposeth** the proud,
but giveth *grace* **charism** unto the humble.

7 *Submit* **So subjugate** yourselves
therefore to *God* **Elohim**.
Resist *the devil* **Diabolos**, and he *will* **shall** flee from you.

8 *Draw nigh to God* **Approach Elohim**,
and he *will draw nigh to* **shall approach** you.
to stain the whole body
and inflame the track of genetics;
and it is inflamed
by Gay Hinnom/the Valley of Burning.

7 For all nature, both of beasts and of flyers,
both of creepers and of those in the sea,
is tamed — and has been tamed by human nature:

8 but the tongue, no human can tame
— an unrestrainable evil full of death bearing venom:

9 therein we eulogize our Elohim and Father;
and therein we curse humanity
who became after the likeness of Elohim.

10 From the same mouth
comes eulogy and cursing.
My brothers, these need not be thus.

11 A fountain, at the same cavern,
sends it sweet and bitter?

12 Can the fig tree, my brothers, make olives?
Or a vine, figs?
Thus no fountain makes both salt water and fresh.

13 Who among you, is wise and understanding?
Show your works from a good behavior
in meekness of wisdom.

14 But if you have bitter zeal
and strife in your hearts,
neither exult nor lie against the truth.

15 — this wisdom descends not from above
but is earthly, soulical, demonic.

16 For where there are zeal and strife,
there are instability and every evil matter.

17 And indeed,
the wisdom from above is first hallowed,
then at shalom,
gentle,
agreeable,
full of mercy and good fruits,
impartial and unhypocritical:

18 and the fruit of justness spores in shalom
by them who make shalom.

SUBJUGATING AND RESISTING

4 Whence *are* wars and strifes among you?
Are they not
from your pleasures warring in your members?

2 You pant and have not:
you murder and are jealous and unable to obtain:
you strive and war:
and you still have not because you ask not.

3 You ask and take not
because you ask evily to spend it in your pleasures.

4 You adulterers and adulteresses,
know you not that the friendship of the cosmos
is enmity with Elohim?
So whoever wills to be a friend of the cosmos
is seated — an enemy of Elohim.

5 Or think you that the scripture words in vain,
The spirit dwelling in us yearns to envy?

6 But he gives greater charism.
So he words,
Elohim opposes the proud
and gives charism to the humble.

7 So subjugate yourselves to Elohim;
resist Diabolos and he flees from you;

8 approach Elohim and he approaches you;
Cleanse **Purify** your hands, *ye* sinners;
and *purify* **hallow** your hearts, *ye* double *minded* **souled**.

9 Be *afflicted* **miserable**, and mourn, and weep:

let your laughter be *turned* **overturned** to mourning,
and your *joy* **cheer** to *heaviness* **sadness**.
10 Humble yourselves in the
sight of *the Lord* **Yah Veh**,
and he shall *lift* **exalt** you *up*.
11 *Speak* **Slander** not *evil* one *of* another, brethren.
He that *speaketh evil of* **slandereth** his brother,
and judgeth his brother,
speaketh evil of **slandereth** the *law* **torah**,
and judgeth the *law* **torah**:
but if thou judge the *law* **torah**,
thou art not a doer of the *law* **torah**, but a judge.
12 There is one *lawgiver* **torahsetter**, who is able to save
and to destroy: who art thou that judgest another?
13 *Go to* **Come** now, ye that *say* **word**,
To day or to morrow we *will* **shall** go into such a city,
and *continue* **deal** there *a* **one** year,
and *buy and sell* **merchandise**, and get gain:
14 Whereas ye *know* **understand** not
what shall be on the morrow.
For what is your life? It is *even* **indeed** a vapour,
that *appeareth* **manifesteth** for a little *time*,
and then *vanisheth away* **disappeareth**.
15 For that ye ought to *say* **word**,
If the Lord will **Whenever Adonay willeth**,
we shall live, and do this, or that.
16 But now ye *rejoice* **boast** in your boastings:
all such *rejoicing* **boasting** is evil.
17 *Therefore* **So** to him that knoweth to do good,
and doeth *it* not, to him it is sin.

Treasuring Treasures

5 *Go to* **Come** now, ye rich *men*,
weep and howl for your miseries
that shall come upon you.
2 Your riches *are corrupted* **have putrefied**,
and your garments *are* **become** motheaten.
3 Your gold and silver *is cankered* **rusteth**;
and the rust of them
shall be **unto** a witness against you,
and shall eat your flesh as *it were* fire.
Ye have *heaped treasure* **treasured** together
for **in** the *last* **final** days.
4 Behold, the hire of the *labourers* **workers**
who have *reaped down* **ingathered** your *fields* **regions**,
of which *is of* you *kept back by fraud* **cheated**, crieth:
and the cries of them which have *reaped* **harvested**
are entered into the ears
of *the Lord of sabaoth* **Yah Veh Sabaoth**.
5 Ye *have lived in pleasure* **indulged** on the earth,
and *been wanton* **luxuriated**;
ye *have* nourished your hearts, as in a day of slaughter.
6 Ye *have* condemned and
killed **murdered** the just;
and he *doth* *opposeth you* not *resist you*.

The Parousia

7 *So* Be patient *therefore*, brethren,
unto the *coming* **parousia** of *the Lord* **Adonay**.
Behold, the *husbandman* **cultivator**
waiteth for **awaiteth** the precious fruit of the earth,
and hath long patience for it,
until **ever** he *receive* **take**
the *early* **morning** and *latter* **evening** rain.
8 Be ye also patient; stablish your hearts:
for **because** the *coming* **parousia** of *the Lord* **Adonay**
draweth nigh **approacheth**.
9 *Grudge* **Sigh** not one against another, brethren,
lest ye be condemned:
behold, the judge standeth before the *door* **portal**.
10 Take, my brethren, the prophets,
who have spoken in the name of *the Lord* **Yah Veh**,
for an example of *suffering affliction* **injurious hardship**,
and of patience.
11 Behold, we count them
happy **blessed** which endure.
Ye have heard of the *patience* **endurance** of *Job* **Iyob**,
and have seen the *end* **completion/shalom**
of *the Lord* **Yah Veh**;
that *the Lord* **Adonay** is *very pitiful* **large spleened**,
and *of tender mercy* **compassionate**.
purify your hands, sinners;
and hallow your hearts, double souled;
9 be miserable and mourn and weep;
overturn your laughter to mourning
and your cheer to sadness;
10 humble yourselves in the sight of Yah Veh
and he exalts you.
11 Slander not one another, brothers.
whoever slanders his brother and judges his brother
slanders the torah and judges the torah:
but if you judge the torah,
you are not a doer of the torah, but a judge.
12 There is one torahsetter
— able to save and to destroy.
Who are you to judge another?
13 Come now, you who word,
Today or tomorrow we go to such a city
and deal one year and merchandise and gain:
14 whereas you understand not the morrow.

For what is your life?
It is indeed a vapour
— manifests for a little — and then disappears.
15 Instead word thus,
Whenever Adonay wills, we live and do this or that.
16 And now you boast in your boastings:
all such boasting is evil.
17 So, to him who knows to do good, and does not,
to him it is sin.

Treasuring Treasures

5 Come now, you rich,
weep and howl for the miseries coming upon you.
2 Your riches putrefy
and your garments become motheaten:
3 your gold and silver rust;
and their rust becomes a witness against you
to consume your flesh as fire.
You treasured in the final days.
4 Behold, the hire of the workers
who ingathered your regions
— whom you cheated, cries out:
and the cries of them who harvest
enter the ears of Yah Veh Sabaoth.
5 You indulged on the earth and luxuriated;
you nourished your hearts as in a day of slaughter;
6 you condemned and murdered the just;
and he opposes you not.

The Parousia

7 So be patient, brothers,
until the parousia of Adonay.
Behold,
the cultivator awaits the precious fruit of the earth
and has long patience for it
until ever he takes the morning and evening rain.
8 You also, be patient; establish your hearts:
because the parousia of Adonay approaches.
9 Sigh not against one another, brothers,
lest you be condemned:
behold, the judge stands at the portal.
10 My brothers, take the prophets,
who speak in the name of Yah Veh,
for an example of injurious hardship and of patience.
11 Behold, we count them who endure, blessed.
You heard of the endurance of Iyob
and saw the completion/shalom of Yah Veh;
that Adonay is large spleened and compassionate.
12 But *above* **preceding** all *things*, my brethren,
swear **oath** not,
neither by *heaven* **the heavens**,
neither by the earth,
neither by any other oath:
but let your yea be yea; and *your* nay, nay;
lest ye fall into *condemnation* **hypocrisy**.

The Vow Of Trust

13 Is any among you *afflicted* **enduring hardship**?
let him pray.
Is any *merry* **cheerful**? let him *sing psalms* **psalm**.
14 Is any *sick* **frail** among you?
let him call for the elders of the *church* **ecclesia**;
and let them pray over him,
anointing him with **olive** oil
in the name of *the Lord* **Adonay**:
15 And the *prayer* **vow** of *faith* **the trust**
shall save the *sick* **wearied**,
and *the Lord* **Adonay** shall raise him up;
and *if* **whenever** he have *committed* **done** sins,
they shall be forgiven him.
16 Confess your *faults* **backslidings** one to another,
and *pray* **vow** one for another, that ye may be healed.
The *effectual fervent prayer* **energized petition**
of *a righteous man* **the just**
availeth much **is mighty enough**.
17 *Elias* **Eli Yah** was a *man* **human**
subject to like passions **likepassioned** as we *are*,
and he prayed *earnestly* **a prayer** that it might not rain:
and it rained not on the earth
by the space of three years and six months.
18 And he prayed again,
and the *heaven* **heavens** gave rain,
and the earth *brought forth* **sprouted** her fruit.
19 Brethren,
if **whenever** any *of* **among** you *do*
err **wander** from the truth,
and one *convert* **restores** him;
20 Let him know,
that he which *converteth* **turneth** the sinner **around**
from the *error* **wandering** of his way
shall save a soul from death,
and shall *hide* **vail** a multitude of sins.
12 But preceding all, my brothers, oath not:
neither by the heavens,
nor by the earth,
nor by any other oath:
but that your yes be yes; and your no, no;
lest you fall into hypocrisy.

The Vow Of Trust

13 Is any among you enduring hardship?
Pray!
Is any cheerful?
Psalm!
14 Is any frail among you?
Call for the elders of the ecclesia to pray over him;
anointing him with olive oil in the name of Adonay:
15 and the vow of the trust saves the wearied
and Adonay raises him;
and if he does sins, they are forgiven.
16 Confess your backslidings to one another
and vow for one another, to be healed.
The energized petition of the just is mighty enough.
17 Eli Yah was a human,
like—passioned as we;
and he prayed a prayer that it rain not:
and it rained not on the earth
by the space of three years and six months.
18 And he prayed again
and the heavens gave rain
and the earth sprouted her fruit.
19 Brothers,
whenever any among you wanders from the truth
and one restores him;
20 have him know,
whoever restores the sinner from his wandering way
saves a soul from death
and veils a multitude of sins.

Salutation

1 *Peter* **Petros**,
an apostle of *Jesus Christ* **Yah Shua Messiah**,
to the *strangers scattered* **pilgrim diaspora**
throughout Pontus, Galatia,
Cappadocia, Asia, and Bithynia,

2 *Elect* **Select** according to the
foreknowledge **prognosis**
of *God* **Elohim** the Father,
through sanctification of the **in holiness of** Spirit,
unto obedience and sprinkling of the blood
of *Jesus Christ* **Yah Shua Messiah**:
Grace **Charism** unto you,
and *peace* **shalom**, be multiplied.

The Living Hope

3 *Blessed* **Eulogized** be the
God **Elohim** and Father
of our *Lord Jesus Christ* **Adonay Yah Shua Messiah**,
which according to his *abundant* **vast** mercy
hath *begotten* **rebirthed** us *again*
unto a *lively* **living** hope
by the resurrection of *Jesus Christ* **Yah Shua Messiah**
from the dead,

4 To an inheritance
incorruptible, and *undefiled* **unpolluted**,
and that fadeth not away — **amaranthine**,
reserved in heaven for **guarded in the heavens unto** you,

5 Who are *kept* **garrisoned**
by **in** the *power* **dynamis** of *God* **Elohim**
through *faith* **trust** unto salvation
ready **prepared** to be *revealed* **unveiled**
in the *last time* **final season**.

6 Wherein ye *greatly rejoice* **jump for joy**,
though now for a *season* **little**, if need be,
ye are *in heaviness* **sorrowed**
through manifold temptations **in divers testings**:

7 That the *trial* **proofing** of your *faith* **trust**,
being much more precious
than of gold that *perisheth* **destructeth**,
though it be *tried with* **proofed through** fire,
might be found unto *praise* **halal** and honour and glory
at the *appearing* **apocalypse** of *Jesus
Christ* **Yah Shua Messiah**:

8 Whom having not seen, ye love;
in whom, though now ye see him not,
yet *believing* **trusting**, ye *rejoice* **jump for joy**
with *joy unspeakable* **inexpressible cheer**

9 and *full of glory* **glorified**:
Receiving the *end* **completion/
shalom** of your *faith* **trust**,
even the salvation of *your* souls.

10 *Of* **Concerning** which salvation
the prophets have inquired
and *searched diligently* **investigated**,
who prophesied *of* **concerning** the *grace* **charism**
that should come unto you:

11 Searching **unto** what,
or *what manner of time* **which season**
the Spirit of *Christ* **Messiah** which was in them
did signify **evidenced**,
when it *testified beforehand* **prewitnessed**
the sufferings *of Christ* **unto Messiah**,
and the *glory that should follow* **glories after these**.

12 Unto whom it was *revealed* **unveiled**,
that not unto themselves, but unto us
they did minister *the things* **those**,
which are now *reported* **evangelized** unto you
by **through** them that have
preached the gospel **evangelized** unto you
with the **in Holy Spirit** **Ruach ha-kodesh**,
sent down **apostolized** from *heaven* **the heavens**;
which *things* the angels *desire* **pant**
to *look* **stoop** into.

13 *So* **Wherefore** gird up the
loins of your mind, be sober,
and hope to the *end* **completion/shalom**
for the *grace* **charism** that is to be brought unto you
at the *revelation* **apocalypse**
of *Jesus Christ* **Yah Shua Messiah**;

14 As obedient children,
not *fashioning* **configuring** yourselves
according to the *former lusts* **previous pantings**
in your *ignorance* **unknowingness**:

15 But as he which hath called you *is* holy,

Salutation

1 Petros, an apostle of Yah Shua Messiah:
To the pilgrim diaspora throughout Pontus,
Galatia, Cappadocia, Asia and Biyournia,

2 Select
according to the prognosis of Elohim the Father,
in holiness of Spirit,
to obedience
and sprinkling of the blood of Yah Shua Messiah:
Charism to you and shalom be multiplied.

The Living Hope

3 Eulogized be the Elohim and Father

of our Adonay Yah Shua Messiah;
who according to his vast mercy
rebirthed us to a living hope
through the resurrection of Yah Shua Messiah
from the dead:
4 to an inheritance
incorruptible and unpolluted and amaranthine,
guarded in the heavens to you
5 who are garrisoned in the dynamis of Elohim
through trust to salvation
— prepared to be unveiled in the final season:
6 wherein you jump for joy:
though now for a little, if necessary, you
are sorrowed in divers testings
7 that the proofing of your trust:
being much more precious than gold that destructs:
though being proofed through fire
be found unto halal and honor and glory
at the apocalypse of Yah Shua Messiah:
8 whom, not having seen, you love;
in whom, though now you see him not,
yet trusting, you jump for joy
with inexpressible cheer and glorified:
9 receiving the completion/shalom of your trust
— the salvation of your souls:
10 concerning the salvation
of which the prophets inquired and investigated;
who prophesied concerning the charism to you:
11 searching to what or which season
the Spirit of Messiah was evidenced in them,
when it prewitnessed the sufferings to Messiah
and the glories after these:
12 to whom it was unveiled
that they ministered, not to them, but to us
those that are now evangelized to you
through them who evangelized to you
in Holy Spirit apostolized from the heavens
— into which angels pant to stoop into.
13 So gird up the loins of your mind;
be sober and hope to the completion/shalom
for the charism to being brought to you
at the apocalypse of Yah Shua Messiah:
14 as obedient children,
not configuring yourselves to the previous pantings
in your unknowingness:
15 but as he who called you *is* holy,
so be ye holy in all *manner of conversation* **behaviour**;
16 Because it is *written* **scribed**,
Be ye holy; *for* **because** I am holy.
17 And if ye call on the Father,
who without respect of persons
judgeth according to *every man's* **each's** work,
pass **behave** the time of your *sojourning here* **settling**
in *fear* **awe**:
18 *Forasmuch as ye know*
Knowing that ye were not
redeemed with *corruptible things* **corruptibles**,
as silver *and* **or** gold,
from your vain
conversation received by tradition from your fathers
patriarchal traditions;
19 But with the precious blood of *Christ* **Messiah**,
as of a lamb
without blemish **unblemished** and
without spot **unstained**:
20 Who *verily* **indeed** was *foreordained* **foreknown**
before **ere** the foundation of the *world* **cosmos**, but
was manifest in these *last* **final** times for you,
21 Who *by* **through** him *do believe* **trust**
in *God* **Elohim**, that raised him up from the
dead, and gave him glory; *so* that your *faith*
trust and hope might be in *God* **Elohim**.
22 Seeing ye have *purified* **hallowed** your souls
in obeying the truth through the Spirit
unto *unfeigned love* **unhypocritical befriending**
of the brethren,
see that *ye* love one another *with* **from** a pure heart
fervently **intensely**:
23 Being *born again* **rebirthed**,
not of corruptible *seed* **spore**, but of incorruptible,
by **through** the word of *God* **Elohim**,
which liveth and abideth *for ever* **unto the eons**.
24 *For* **Because** all flesh is as *grass* **herbage**,
and all the glory of *man* **humanity**
as the *flower* **blossom** of *grass* **herbage**.
The *grass* **herbage** withereth,
and the *flower* **blossom** thereof falleth away:
25 But the *word* **rhema** of *the Lord* **Yah Veh**
endureth for ever **abideth unto the eons**.
And this is the *word* **rhema**
which by the gospel is *preached* **evangelized** unto you.

As Newborn Infants

2 *Wherefore* **So**
laying aside **putting away** all malice,
and all *guile* **deceit**, and hypocrisies,
and envies, and all *evil speakings* **slanders**,
2 As newborn *babes* **infants**,
desire **yearn** for
the *sincere* **undeceitful** milk of *the word* **logic**,

3	that ye may grow *thereby* **therein**: If *so be* **ever** ye have tasted that *the Lord* **Yah Veh** is *gracious* **kind**. Psalm 34:8		who raised him from the dead and gave him glory; so that your trust and hope be in Elohim.
	AS LIVING STONES	22	Seeing you hallowed your souls in obeying the truth through Spirit to unhypocritical befriending of the brothers
4	To whom coming, *as unto* a living stone, *disallowed* **disapproved** indeed *of men* **by humanity**, but *chosen of God* **select with Elohim**, *and precious* **honourable**,	23	— to love one another intensely from a pure heart; being rebirthed, not of corruptible spore, but of incorruptible,
5	Ye also, as *lively* **living** stones, are built *up* a spiritual house, an holy priesthood, to offer *up* spiritual sacrifices, *acceptable* **well—received** to *God* **Elohim** *by Jesus Christ* **through Yah Shua Messiah**.	24	through the word of Elohim who lives and abides to the eons: because all flesh is as herbage and all the glory of humanity as the blossom of herbage. The herbage withers and the blossom falls:
6	*Wherefore* **So** also it is contained in the scripture, Behold, I *lay* **place** in *Sion* **Siyon** a chief corner stone, *elect* **select**, *precious* **honourable**: and he that *believeth* **trusteth** on him shall not **no way** be *confounded* **shamed**. Yesha Yah 28:16	25	and the rhema of Yah Veh abides to the eons: and this is the rhema evangelized to you.
			AS NEWBORN INFANTS
		2	So putting away all malice and all deceit and hypocrisies and envies and all slanders,
		2	as newborn infants yearn for the undeceitful milk of logic to grow therein:
7	**So** Unto you *therefore* which *believe* **trust,** he is precious: but unto them which *be disobedient* **distrust**, the stone which the builders *disallowed* **disapproved**, *the same* **this one** *is made* **became** the head of the corner,	3	if ever you taste that Yah Veh is kind: Psalm 34:8
			AS LIVING STONES
8	And a stone of stumbling, and a rock of *offence* **scandal**, *even* to them which stumble at the word, *being disobedient* **who distrust**: whereunto also they were *appointed* **set**.	4	coming to him, a living stone; disapproved indeed by humanity but with Elohim, select, honorable;
	thus you be holy in all behavior:	5	and you yourselves, as living stones, are built a spiritual house — a holy priesthood to offer spiritual sacrifices, well—received to Elohim through Yah Shua Messiah.
16	because it is scribed, You, become holy; because I am holy.		
17	And if you call on the Father, who without respect of persons judges according to the work of each, behave this time of your settling in awe:	6	So it is also contained in the scripture, Behold, I place in Siyon a chief corner stone, select, honorable: and whoever trusts on him never no way shames. Yesha Yah 28:16
18	knowing that you were not redeemed with corruptibles as silver or gold of your vain patriarchal traditions;	7	So to you who trust, he is precious: but to them who distrust, the stone the builders disapproved
19	but with the precious blood of Messiah, as of a lamb, unblemished and unstained:	8	this one became the head of the corner, and a stone of stumbling and a rock of scandal to them who stumble at the word — who distrust: to which also they were set.
20	who indeed was foreknown ere the foundation of the cosmos, and manifest in these final times in your behalf;	9	But ye are a *chosen generation* **select genos**, a *royal* **sovereign** priesthood, an holy *nation* **goyim**, a peculiar *people* **acquisition unto himself**;
21	who through him, trust in Elohim		that ye should

1 PETER/PETROS 2, 3

shew forth **evangelize** the *praises* **exultation** of him
who hath called you out of darkness
into his marvellous light;
10 Which in time past were not a people,
but are now the people of *God* **Elohim**:
which had not *obtained mercy* **been mercied**,
but now *have obtained mercy* **be mercied**.
Hoshea 1:6—9
11 *Dearly* beloved,
I beseech you as *strangers* **settlers** and pilgrims,
abstain from fleshly *lusts* **pantings**,
which war against the soul;
12 Having your *conversation*
honest **behaviour good**
among the *Gentiles* **goyim**:
that, *whereas* **in that which**
they *speak against* **slander** you as evildoers,
they may by *your* good works,
which they shall *behold* **observe**,
glorify *God* **Elohim** in the day of visitation.

SUBJUGATING TO GOVERNMENTS

13 *Submit* **So subjugate** yourselves
to every *ordinance of man* **creation of humanity**
for the *Lord's* sake **of Adonay**:
whether it be to the *king* **sovereign**, as supreme;
14 *Or* **Whether** unto governors,
as unto them that are sent *by* **through** him **indeed**
for the punishment of **unto avenging** evildoers, and
for the *praise* **halal** of them that do *well* **good**.
15 *For so* **Because thus** is the will of *God* **Elohim**,
that with *well doing* **doing good**
ye may *put to silence* **muzzle** the
ignorance **unknowingness**
of *foolish men* **thoughtless humanity**:
16 As *free* **liberated**, and not
using your **regarding** liberty
for a cloke **as a covering** of *maliciousness*
malice, but as the servants of *God* **Elohim**.
17 Honour all *men*. Love the brotherhood.
Fear God **Awe Elohim**. Honour the *king* **sovereign**.
18 *Servants* **Housekeepers**,
be subject **subjugate** to *your masters* **despotes**
with *in* all *fear* **awe**;
not only to the good and gentle,
but also to the *froward* **crooked**.
19 For this is *thankworthy* **charism**,
if *a man* **one** for conscience toward *God* **Elohim**
endure *grief* **sorrow**, suffering *wrongfully* **unjustly**.
20 For what *glory* **fame** is it,
if, when ye be *buffeted* **punched** for your *faults* **sinning**,
ye shall *take it patiently* **endure**?
but if, when ye do *well* **good**, and suffer *for it*,
ye *take it patiently* **endure**,
this is *acceptable* **charism** with *God* **Elohim**.
21 For even *hereunto* **unto this** were ye called:
because *Christ* **Messiah** also suffered for
us, leaving **behind** us an example,
that ye should follow his *steps* **tracks**.
22 Who did no sin,
neither was *guile* **deceit** found in his mouth:
23 Who, when he was *reviled* **abused**,
reviled not again **replied unabusively**;
when he suffered, he threatened not;
but *committed* **surrendered** himself to him
that judgeth *righteously* **justly**:
24 Who his own self
bare **took up** our sins in his own body on the *tree* **staff**,
that we, being dead to sins,
should live unto *righteousness* **justness**:
by whose *stripes* **bruises** ye were healed.
25 For ye were as *wandering* sheep *going astray*;
but are now returned
unto the Shepherd and *Bishop* **Episcopate**
of your souls. Yesha Yah 52:14—53:12

SUBJUGATING IN RELATIONSHIPS

3 Likewise, *ye wives* **women**,
be in subjection **subjugate yourselves**
to your own *husbands* **men**;
9 But you *are* a select genos,
a sovereign priesthood,
a holy goyim,
a peculiar acquisition to himself;
to evangelize the exultation
of him who called you from darkness
into his marvellous light:
10 who in time past were, Not a People,
but are now, People of Elohim:
who had been, Not Mercied,
and now, Mercied.
Hoshea 1:6—9
11 Beloved, I beseech you as settlers and pilgrims,
abstain from fleshly pantings
that war against the soul;
12 to have good behavior among the goyim:
so that, wherein they slander you as evildoers,
by observing your good works,
they glorify Elohim in the day of visitation.

SUBJUGATING TO GOVERNMENTS

13 So subjugate yourselves
to every creation of humanity
for the sake of Adonay:
whether to the sovereign as supreme;
14 whether to governors,
as to them who indeed are sent through him
to avenge evildoers,
and for the halal of them doing good.
15 Because thus is the will of Elohim,
that by doing good
you muzzle the unknowingness
of thoughtless humanity:
16 as liberated, and not regarding liberty;
as a covering of malice, but as the servants of Elohim.
17 Honor all.
Love the brotherhood.
Awe Elohim.
Honor the sovereign.
18 Housekeepers:
subjugate to your despotes in all awe
— not only to the good and gentle,
but also to the crooks.
19 For this is charism:
if for sake of conscience toward Elohim
one endures sorrow, suffering unjustly.
20 For what fame is it, if you endure,
when you are punched for your sinning?
But if you endure, when you do good and suffer,
this is charism with Elohim.
21 For even to this, you were called:
because Messiah also suffered for us,
leaving behind an example to follow his tracks
22 — who neither sinned
nor was deceit found in his mouth:
23 who, being abused, replied unabusively;
suffering, threatened not;
and surrendered himself to him who judges justly:
24 who his own self
took our sins in his own body on the staff,
that we, being dead to sins, live to justness:
by whose bruises you are healed.
25 For you were as wandering sheep
— but now you returned
to the Shepherd and Episcopate of your
souls. Yesha Yah 52:14—53:12

SUBJUGATING IN RELATIONSHIPS

3 Likewise, women:
subjugate yourselves to your own men;
that, if any *obey not* **one distrust** the word,
they also may without the word be *won* **gained**
by **through** the *conversation* **behaviour**
of the *wives* **women**;
2 While they *behold* **observe**
your *chaste conversation* **hallowed behaviour**
coupled with fear **in awe**.
3 Whose *adorning* **cosmos**
let it not be
that outward *adorning of plaiting* **braiding** the hair,
and of *wearing* **wrapping around** of gold,
or of *putting on of apparel* **enduing garments**;
4 But *let it be the hidden man* **the secret human**
of the heart,
in that which is *not corruptible* **incorruptible**,
even the ornament — of a meek and quiet spirit,
which is in the sight of *God* **Elohim**
of great price **vastly precious**.
5 For after this manner in the old time
the holy women also,
who *trusted* **hoped** in *God* **Elohim**, adorned themselves,
being in subjection **subjugating** unto
their own *husbands* **men**;
6 Even as *Sara* **Sarah** obeyed Abraham,
calling him *lord* **adoni**:
whose *daughters* **children** ye *are* **became**,
as long as ye do *well* **good**,
and are not *afraid with* **awestricken**
of any *amazement* **terror**.
7 Likewise, *ye husbands* **men**,
dwell with them **co—settle** according to knowledge,
giving **bestowing** honour *unto the wife*,
as unto the *weaker* **frailer** vessel,
and as being *heirs together* **co—heirs**
of the *grace* **charism** of life;
that your prayers be not *hindered* **excsinded**.
8 *Finally* **In completion/shalom**,
be ye all *of one mind* **likeminded**,
having compassion **sympathetic** one of another,
love **befriending** as brethren,
be pitiful **tenderspleened**, *be courteous* **friendly minded**:
9 Not *rendering* **giving** evil for evil,
or *railing* **abuse** for *railing* **abuse**:
but contrariwise *blessing* **eulogize**;
knowing that ye are *thereunto* called **unto this**,
that ye should inherit a *blessing* **eulogy**.
10 For he that *will* **willeth to**
love life, and see good days,
let him *refrain* **pause** his tongue from evil,
and his lips that they speak no *guile* **deceit**:

1 PETER/PETROS 3

11 Let him *eschew* **deviate from** evil, and do good;
let him seek *peace* **shalom**, and *ensue* **pursue** it.
12 *For* **Because** the eyes of *the Lord* **Yah Veh**
are over the *righteous* **just**,
and his ears *are open* unto their *prayers* **petitions**:
but the face of *the Lord* **Yah Veh**
is against them that do evil.
13 And who is he that *will harm* **shall vilify** you,
if **whenever** ye be *followers* **mimickers**
of that which is good?
14 But and if ye suffer for
righteousness' **justness'** sake,
happy are ye **blessed**:
and be not *afraid* **awestricken**
of their *terror* **awesomeness**,
neither be troubled;
15 But *sanctify the Lord God**
hallow Yah Veh Elohim*
in your hearts:
and be *ready always* **ever prepared**
to *give an answer* **plead** to every *man* **one**
that asketh you a *reason* **word**
of **concerning** the hope that is in you
with meekness and *fear* **awe**:
*some mss: Adonay Messiah
16 Having a good conscience; that,
whereas **in that which** they *speak evil of* **slander** you,
as of evildoers, they may *be ashamed* **shame**
that *falsely accuse* **threaten**
your good *conversation* **behaviour** in *Christ* **Messiah**.
17 For it is better,
if *the will of God be* so **Elohim so willeth**,
that ye suffer for *well* doing **good**,
than for *evil* doing **evil**.
that even if any distrust the word,
they also be gained without the word
through the behavior of the women;
2 While in awe,
they observe your hallowed behavior:
3 whose cosmos is not outward
— of braiding the hair
and of wrapping around of gold
or of enduing garments:
4 but that secret human of the heart
in what is incorruptible
— of a meek and quiet spirit
which is vastly precious in the sight of Elohim.
5 For thus also in the old time
the holy women who hoped in Elohim
adorned themselves;
subjugating to their own men
6 — as Sarah obeyed Abraham, calling him adoni:
of whom you became children
— as long as you do good
and are not awestricken of any terror.
7 Likewise men:
co—settle according to knowledge;
bestow honor as to the frailer vessel
and as being co—heirs of the charism of life;
that your prayers be not excsinded.
8 In completion/shalom,
all likeminded,
sympathetic one of another,
befriending as brothers,
tenderspleened,
friendly minded:
9 not giving evil for evil or abuse for abuse
— but contrariwise eulogize;
knowing that you are called to this
— to inherit a eulogy:
10 For whoever wills to love life and see good days,
pause your tongue from evil,
and that your lips not speak deceit,
11 deviate from evil and do good,
seek shalom and pursue it.
12 Because the eyes of Yah Veh are over the just
and his ears to their petitions:
but the face of Yah Veh is against them who do evil.
13 And who *is* he that vilifies you,
whenever you become mimickers of good?
14 But and if you suffer for sake of justness,
Blessed!
And neither awestricken by their awesomeness
nor *be* troubled;
15 but hallow Yah Veh Elohim* in your hearts,
ever prepared to plead to everyone
who asks you a word concerning the hope in you
with meekness and awe:
*some mss: Adonay Messiah
16 having a good conscience;
so that they who slander you as evildoers,
who threaten your good behavior in Messiah,
shame.
17 For it is better, if Elohim thus wills,
that you suffer for doing good, than for doing evil:
18 *For Christ* **Because Messiah**
also hath once suffered for sins,
the just for the unjust,
that he might bring us to *God* **Elohim**,
being put to death **indeed deathified** in *the* flesh,

	but *quickened* **enlivened** by the Spirit:
19	*By* **In** which also he went and preached
	unto the spirits in *prison* **the guardhouse**;
20	Which sometime *were disobedient* **distrusted**,
	when once the *longsuffering* **patience** of *God* **Elohim**
	waited **awaited** in the days of *Noah* **Noach**,
	while the ark was a preparing,
	wherein few, that is,
	eight souls were saved *by* **through** water.
21	The *like figure* **antitype** whereunto *even* baptism
	doth also now *save* **saveth** us
	(not the *putting away* **laying aside**
	of *the* filth of *the* flesh,
	but the *answer* **question** of a good conscience
	toward God **unto Elohim**,)
	by **through** the resurrection of *Jesus*
	Christ **Yah Shua Messiah**:
22	Who is gone into *heaven* **the heavens**,
	and is *on* **in** the right hand of *God* **Elohim**;
	angels and authorities and *powers* **dynamis**
	being made subject **subjugated** unto him.

Subjugating To The Messiah

4	*Forasmuch then* **So**
	as *Christ* **Messiah** hath suffered for us in *the* flesh,
	arm yourselves **be weaponed** likewise
	with the same mind:
	for **because** he that hath suffered in *the* flesh
	hath *ceased* **paused** from sin;
2	That he no longer should *live* **exist**
	the rest of his **remaining** time in *the* flesh
	to the *lusts* **pantings** of *men* **humanity**,
	but to the will of *God* **Elohim**.
3	For the **passing** time *past* of our *life* **existence**
	may suffice us
	to have *wrought* **worked** the will of the *Gentiles* **goyim**,
	when we walked in *lasciviousness* **lechery**,
	lusts **pantings**, *excess of wine* **vinolence**,
	revellings **carousings**, *banquetings* **drinking bouts**,
	and *abominable* **illicit** idolatries:
4	Wherein they think it strange
	that ye *run* **rush** not *with them*
	to *the same excess* **their effusion** of *riot* **dissipation**,
	speaking evil of you **blaspheming**:
5	Who shall give *account* **word** to him
	that is *ready* **prepared**
	to judge the *quick* **living** and the dead.
6	For *for* **unto** this *cause*
	was the gospel preached also to them that are dead
	were the dead evangelized,

	that they might **indeed** be judged
	according to *men* **humanity** in *the* flesh,
	but live according to *God* **Elohim** in *the* spirit.
7	But the *end* **completion/shalom** of all *things*
	is at hand **approacheth**:
	so be ye *therefore sober* **sound**, and watch unto prayer.
8	And *above* **preceding** all *things*
	have *fervent charity among* **intense love unto** yourselves:
	for charity **because love**
	shall *cover* **vail** the multitude of sins.
9	*Use hospitality* **Befriend**
	strangers one to another
	without *grudging* **murmuring**.
10	**Exactly** As *every man* **each**
	hath *received* **taken** the *gift* **charisma**,
	even so minister the same *one to*
	another **unto yourselves**,
	as good *stewards* **administrators**
	of the *manifold grace* **divers charism** of *God* **Elohim**.
11	If any *man* **one** speak,
	let him speak as the oracles of *God* **Elohim**;
	if any *man* **one** minister,
	let him do it as of the *ability* might
	which *God giveth* **Elohim supplieth**:
	that *God* **Elohim** in all *things* may be glorified
	through *Jesus Christ* **Yah Shua Messiah**,
	to whom be *praise* **glory** and dominion
	for ever and ever **unto the eons of the eons**.
	Amen.
18	because Messiah also suffered for sins once
	— the just for the unjust, to bring us to Elohim,
	indeed deathified in flesh
	and enlivened in the Spirit:
19	wherein he also went and preached
	to the spirits in the guardhouse
20	— who sometime distrusted
	when once the patience of Elohim awaited
	in the days of Noach while the ark was a preparing,
	wherein few — that is eight souls
	were saved through water:
21	to which baptism, the
	antitype, now also saves us
	— not the laying aside of filth of flesh
	but the question of a good conscience to Elohim
	through the resurrection of Yah Shua Messiah:
22	who went into the heavens
	— at the right of Elohim
	angels and authorities and dynamis
	being subjugated to him.

Subjugating To The Messiah

4 So as Messiah suffered for us in flesh,
weapon yourselves likewise with the same mind:
because he who suffered in flesh, paused from sin;
2 to no longer exist his remaining time in flesh
to the pantings of humanity
— but to the will of Elohim.
3 Enough of the past time of our existence!
— working the will of the goyim
— walking in lechery,
pantings,
vinolence,
carousings,
drinking bouts,
and illicit idolatries:
4 wherein they think it strange
that you not rush to their effusion of dissipation,
blaspheming:
5 who give word to him
who is prepared to judge the living and the dead.
6 For to this the dead were evangelized,
so that indeed
they be judged according to humanity in flesh,
but live according to Elohim in spirit.
7 But the completion/shalom of all approaches:
so be sound and watch to prayer.
8 And preceding all, have
intense love to yourselves:
because love veils the multitude of sins.
9 Befriend strangers to one another
without murmuring.
10 Exactly as each takes the charisma,
minister the same to yourselves,
as good administrators
of the divers charism of Elohim.
11 If anyone speaks as the oracles of Elohim;
if anyone ministers as of the might that Elohim supplies:
glorify Elohim in all through Yah Shua Messiah,
to whom be glory and dominion
to the eons of the eons.
Amen.

Testings Of Fire

12 Beloved, *think* **is** it not strange
concerning the *fiery trial* **firing in you**
which is to *try* **test** you,
as though *some* **somewhat** strange *thing*
happened unto you:
13 But *rejoice* **cheer**,
inasmuch **according** as ye are partakers
of *Christ's* **Messiah's** sufferings;
that, *when his glory shall be revealed*
at the apocalypse of his glory,
ye may *be glad* also **cheer**,
with *exceeding* **jumping for** joy.
14 If ye be reproached *for* **in**
the name of *Christ* **Messiah**,
happy are ye **blessed**;
for **because** the spirit of glory and of *God* **Elohim**
resteth upon you:
on their part he is *evil spoken of* **indeed blasphemed**,
but on your part he is glorified.
15 *But* **Indeed**
let *none* **not any** of you suffer as a murderer,
or as a thief, or as an evildoer,
or as
a busybody in other men's matters **overseeing others**.
16 Yet if *any man suffer* as a *Christian* **Messianist**,
let him not be ashamed;
but let him glorify *God on* **Elohim in** this *behalf* **part**.
17 *For the time is come* **Because this is the season**
that judgment must begin
at **from** the house of *God* **El**:
and if *it first begin at* **from** us,
what shall the *end* **completion/shalom** be
of them that *obey not* **distrust**
the *gospel* **evangelism** of *God* **Elohim**?
18 And if the *righteous scarcely*
just difficultly be saved,
where shall the *ungodly* **irreverent** and the sinner
appear **be manifest**?
19 *Wherefore* **So**
let them that suffer according to the will of *God* **Elohim**
commit the keeping of **commend** their **own** souls *to him*
in *well* doing **good**,
as unto a *faithful* **trustworthy** Creator.

Shepherding The Shepherddom

5 The elders which are among
you I *exhort* **beseech**,
who am also an elder — **a co—elder**,
and a witness of the sufferings of *Christ* **Messiah**,
and also a partaker of the glory
that shall be *revealed* **unveiled**:
2 *Feed* **Shepherd** the *flock*
shepherddom of *God* **Elohim**
which is among you,
taking the oversight thereof **overseeing**,
not by *constraint* **compulsion**, but *willingly* **voluntarily**;

    not for *filthy lucre* **avarice**, but *of a ready mind* **eagerly**;
3   Neither as *being lords over* **overlording**
God heritage **the inheritance**,
but *being ensamples* **becoming types**
to the *flock* **shepherddom**.
4   And when the *chief* **Arch** Shepherd
shall *appear* **manifest**,
ye shall receive a *crown* **wreath** of glory
that fadeth not away — **amaranthine**.
5   Likewise, *ye* younger,
submit **subjugate** yourselves unto the elder.
Yea, all *of you be subject* **subjugate** one to another,
and be *clothed* **enrobed**
with *humility* **humblemindedness**:
for *God resisteth* **because Elohim opposeth** the proud,
and giveth *grace* **charism** to the humble.
6   **So** Humble yourselves *therefore*
under the *mighty* **powerful** hand of *God* **Elohim**,
that he may exalt you in *due time* **season**:
7   *Casting* **Tossing** all your *care* **anxiety** upon him;
for **because** he *careth for* **is concerned about** you.
8   Be sober, *be vigilant* **watch**;
because your adversary *the devil* **Diabolos**,
as a roaring lion,
walketh about, seeking whom he may *devour* **swallow**:
9   Whom *resist stedfast* **withstand**
solid in the *faith* **trust**,
knowing that the same *afflictions* **sufferings**

TESTINGS OF FIRE

12   Beloved, it is not strange
concerning the firing in you, to test you, as
though somewhat strange becomes you:
13   But cheer,
according as you are partakers
of the sufferings of Messiah;
so that at the apocalypse of his glory
you also cheer with jumping for joy.
14   If you are reproached in the name of Messiah,
Blessed!
— because the spirit of glory and of Elohim
rests upon you:
on their part he is indeed blasphemed,
but on your part he is glorified.
15   Indeed suffer not
as a murderer
or as a thief
or as an evildoer
or as overseeing others.
16   Yet if as a Messianist, shame not;

but glorify Elohim in this part.
17   Because this is the season
that judgment must begin from the house of El:
and if first from us,
what is the completion/shalom of them
who distrust the evangelism of Elohim?
18   And if the just are difficultly saved,
where are the irreverent and the sinner manifested?
19   So whoever suffers according
to the will of Elohim,
commend your own souls in doing good,
as to a trustworthy Creator.

SHEPHERDING THE SHEPHERDDOM

5   I beseech the elders among you
— I a co—elder and a witness
of the sufferings of Messiah,
and also a partaker
of the glory to be unveiled.
2   Shepherd the shepherddom
of Elohim among you,
overseeing — not by compulsion,
but voluntarily;
not for avarice,
but eagerly;
3   not as overlording the inheritance,
but being types to the shepherddom:
4   so that when the Arch Shepherd manifests,
you receive a wreath of glory — amaranthine.
5   Likewise, younger:
subjugate yourselves to the elder. Yes, all
subjugate to one another and enrobe with
humblemindedness: because Elohim opposes
the proud and gives charism to the humble.
6   So humble yourselves
under the powerful hand of Elohim,
so that he exalts you in season:
7   tossing all your anxiety upon him;
because he is concerned about you.
8   Sober! Watch!
— because your adversary, Diabolos,
as a roaring lion,
walks around seeking whom to swallow:
9   whom withstand solid in the trust,
knowing that the same sufferings
are *accomplished* **completed/shalamed**
in your *brethren* **brotherhood**
that are in the *world* **cosmos**.
10   But the *God* **Elohim** of all *grace* **charism**,
who hath called us unto his eternal glory

by Christ Jesus **in Messiah Yah Shua**,
after that ye have suffered a *while* **little**,
make **prepare** you *perfect*, stablish,
strengthen **invigorate**, *settle* **found** you.

11 To him be glory and dominion
for ever and ever **unto the eons of the eons**.
Amen.

Final Salutes

12 *By* **Through** Silvanus,
a *faithful* **trustworthy** brother unto you,
as I *suppose* **reckon**,
I have *written briefly* **scribed through few words**,
exhorting **beseeching**, and *testifying* **witnessing**
that this is the true *grace* **charism** of *God* **Elohim**
wherein ye stand.

13 *The church that is at Babylon* **They in Babel**,
elected together with you **the co—select**, saluteth you;
and *so doth Marcus* **Markos** my son.

14 *Greet* **Salute** ye one another
with a kiss of *charity* **love**.
Peace **Shalom** *be* with you all
that are in *Christ Jesus* **Messiah Yah Shua**.
Amen.
are completed/shalamed
in your brotherhood in the cosmos.

10 And the Elohim of all charism,
who calls us to his eternal glory in Messiah Yah Shua,
after you suffer a little,
prepare you,
establish,
invigorate,
foundation you.

11 To him be glory and dominion
to the eons of the eons.
Amen.

Final Salutes

12 Through Silvanus your trustworthy brother,
I reckon that I scribed through few words,
beseeching and witnessing
that this wherein you stand
is the true charism of Elohim.

13 The co—select in Babel
and Markos my son salute you.

14 Salute one another with a kiss of love.
Shalom with all in Messiah Yah Shua.
Amen.

Salutation

1 *Simon Peter* **Shimon Petros**,
a servant and an apostle of *Jesus
Christ* **Yah Shua Messiah**,
to them that *have obtained* **were allotted**
like **equally** precious *faith* **trust** with us
through **in** the *righteousness* **justness** of *God* **Elohim**
and our Saviour *Jesus Christ* **Yah Shua Messiah**:

2 *Grace* **Charism** and *peace* **shalom**
be multiplied unto you
through **in** the knowledge of *God* **Elohim**,
and of *Jesus* **Yah Shua** our *Lord* **Adonay**,

3 According as his *divine
power* **elohimic dynamis**
hath *given* **granted** unto us all *things*
that pertain unto life and *Godliness* **reverence**,
through the knowledge of him
that hath called us *to* **through** glory and virtue:

4 *Whereby* **Through which** are given unto us
exceeding great **magnificent**
and precious *promises* **pre—evangelisms**:
that *by* **through** these
ye might be partakers of the divine nature,
having escaped the corruption
that is in the *world through lust* **cosmos iin its pantings**.

5 And beside this, *giving* **bringing in** all diligence,
add to **supply in** your *faith* **trust**, virtue;
and *to* **in** virtue, knowledge;

6 And *to* **in** knowledge, *temperance* **self—control**;
and *to temperance* **in self—control**, *patience* **endurance**;
and *to patience* **in endurance**, *Godliness* **reverence**.

7 And *to Godliness* **in reverence**,
brotherly kindness **befriending brethren**;
and *to brotherly kindness* **in befriending brethren**,
charity **love**.

8 For *if these things be* **these being** in you,
and *abound* **superabounding**,
they *make* **seat** you
that ye shall neither be *barren* **idle** nor unfruitful
in the knowledge
of our *Lord Jesus Christ* **Adonay Yah Shua Messiah**.

9 *But* **Indeed** he
that lacketh **to whom** these *things* **are not present**
is blind, and *cannot see afar off* **blinketh**,
and hath *forgotten* **taken forgetfulness**
that he was purged **of the purifying**
from his *old* sins **of long ago**.

10 *Wherefore the* **So** rather, brethren, give diligence
to make your calling and *election sure* **selection stedfast**:
for *if ye do* **doing** these *things*,
ye shall *never fall* **not ever no way stumble**:

11 For *so* **thus** an entrance
shall be *ministered* **supplied** unto you *abundantly* **richly**
into the *everlasting kingdom* **eternal sovereigndom**
of our *Lord* **Adonay** and Saviour
Jesus Christ **Yah Shua Messiah**.

12 *Wherefore I will* **So I shall**
not *be negligent* **disregard**
to *put ever remind* you *always in remembrance*
of **concerning** these *things*,
though ye know *them*,
and be established in the present truth.

The Final Evangelism Of Petros

13 Yea, I *think* **deem** it *meet* **just**,
as long as I am in this tabernacle,
to *stir* **rouse** you *up*
by putting *in reminding* you *in remembrance*;

14 Knowing that *shortly* **quickly**
I must put off this **be the laying aside of** my tabernacle,
even **exactly** as
our *Lord Jesus Christ* **Adonay Yah Shua Messiah**
hath *shewed* **evidenced** me.
Yahn 21:18, 19

15 *Moreover I will endeavour*
And I shall be diligent
that ye may *be able* **regard** after my *decease* **exodus** to
have **do** these *things always* **ever** in remembrance.

16 For we have not followed
cunningly devised fables **sophisticated myths**,
when we made known unto you
the *power* **dynamis** and *coming* **parousia**
of our *Lord Jesus Christ* **Adonay Yah Shua Messiah**,
but *were eyewitnesses* **became spectators** of his majesty.

Salutation

1 Shimon Petros
a servant and an apostle of Yah Shua Messiah:
To them
who were allotted equally precious trust with us
in the justness of Elohim
and our Saviour Yah Shua Messiah:

2 Charism and shalom be multiplied to you
in the knowledge of Elohim
and of Yah Shua our Adonay;

3 as his divine dynamis grants us
all of life and reverence;
through the knowledge of him
who called us through glory and virtue:

4 through which he gives us
magnificent and precious pre—evangelisms:
that through these
you become partakers of the divine nature
— escaping the corruption in the cosmos
in its pantings.
5 And beside this, in bringing you all diligence,
supply in your trust, virtue; and in virtue, knowledge;
6 and in knowledge, self—control; and in self—
control, endurance; and in endurance, reverence;
7 and in reverence, befriending brothers;
and in befriending brothers, love.
8 For these being in you, and superabounding,
they seat you to be neither idle nor unfruitful
in the knowledge of our Adonay Yah Shua Messiah.
9 Indeed he to whom these are not present
is blind and blinks
forgetting the purifying from his sins of long ago.
10 So the rather, brothers,
give diligence
to make your calling and selection steadfast:
for doing these, you never ever no way stumble:
11 for thus you are richly supplied
with an entrance into the eternal sovereigndom
of our Adonay and Saviour Yah Shua Messiah.
12 So I disregard not
to ever remind you concerning these,
though you know
being established in the present truth.

The Final Evangelism Of Petros

13 Yes I deem it just, as long
as I am in this tabernacle,
to rouse you in reminding *you*;
14 knowing how quickly
the laying aside of my tabernacle *is*
— even exactly as our Adonay Yah Shua Messiah
evidenced me.
Yahn 21:18, 19
15 And I also am diligent for you,
so that after my exodus,
you ever regard these in remembrance.
16 For we followed not sophisticated myths
when we had you know
the dynamis and parousia
of our Adonay Yah Shua Messiah;
but became spectators of his majesty.
17 For he *received* **hath taken**
from *God* **Elohim** the Father
honour and glory,
when there *came* **was brought** such a voice to him
from the *excellent* **majestic** glory,
This is my beloved Son,
in **of** whom I *am well pleased* **well—approve**.
18 And this voice
which *came* **was brought** from *heaven*
the heavens we heard,
when we were *being* with him in the holy mount.

Scripture Prophecy

19 We have also a *more sure*
stedfast word of prophecy;
whereunto ye do well that ye take heed,
as unto a light that *shineth* **manifesteth**
in *a dark* **an obscure place**,
until the day *thoroughly* dawn,
and the day *star* **phospherescence** arise in your hearts:
20 Knowing this first,
that *no* **not any** prophecy of the scripture
is **becometh** of
any *private interpretation* **personal explanation**.
21 For the prophecy
came not in old time **was not ever brought**
by the will of *man* **humanity**:
but holy *men* **humans** of *God* **Elohim** spake
as they were moved **borne** by the *Holy
Spirit* **Ruach ha-kodesh**.

Pseudo Prophets And Pseudo Doctors

2 But there *were false* **became pseudo** prophets
also among the people,
even as there shall be *false teachers* **pseudo doctors**
among you,
who *privily* shall *bring in* **surreptitiously introduce**
damnable **destructive** heresies,
even denying the *Lord* **Despotes**
that *bought* **marketed** them,
and bring upon themselves *swift* **quick** destruction.
2 And many
shall follow their *pernicious* **destructive** ways;
by reason of **through** whom the way of truth
shall be *evil spoken of* **blasphemed**.
3 And *through covetousness* **in avarice**
shall they with *feigned* **fabricated** words
make merchandise *of* you:
whose judgment now of *a long time* **old**
lingereth **idleth** not,
and their *damnation* **destruction** slumbereth not.
4 For if *God* **Elohim** spared not the angels that sinned,
but *cast* **incarcerated** them *down to hell* **in Tartaros**,
and delivered them into *chains* **caverns** of darkness,

	to be *reserved* **guarded** unto judgment;	21	becomes by personal explanation: for no prophecy was ever brought by the will of humanity: but holy humans of Elohim spoke — borne by the Holy Spirit.
5	And spared not the *old world* **ancient cosmos**, but *saved Noah* **guarded Noach** the eighth *person*, a preacher of *righteousness* **justness**, bringing in the *flood* **cataclysm** upon the *world* **cosmos** of the *ungodly* **irreverent**;		

Pseudoprophets And Pseudodoctors

6	And *turning* **incinerating** the cities of *Sodom* **Sedom** and *Gomorrha* **Amorah** *into ashes* condemned them with *an overthrow* **a catastrophe**, *making* **setting** them an ensample unto those that *after should* **were about to** live *ungodly* **irreverently**;	2	And so be it also, pseudoprophets among the people — even as pseudodoctors become among you who surreptitiously introduce destructive heresies — even denying the Despotes who marketed them; and bring quick destruction on themselves.
7	And *delivered* **rescued** just Lot, *vexed* **worn down** *with* **by** the *filthy conversation* **lecherous behaviour** of the *wicked* **illicit**:	2	And many follow their destructive ways — who blaspheme the way of truth:
8	(For that *righteous man* **just** *one* dwelling among them, in seeing and hearing, *vexed* **tortured** his *righteous* **just** soul *from* day *to* **by** day with their *unlawful deeds* **untorahed works**;)	3	and in avarice they fabricate words and merchandise of you: whose judgment of old idles not and their destruction slumbers not.
		4	For if Elohim spared not the angels who sinned but incarcerated them in Tartaros; and delivered them into caverns of darkness — guarded unto judgment;
9	*The Lord* **Yah Veh** knoweth how to *deliver* **rescue** the *godly* **well—revering** out of *temptations* **testings**, and to *reserve* **guard** the unjust unto the day of judgment to be punished:	5	and spared not the ancient cosmos; but guarded Noach the eighth — a preacher of justness; bringing in the cataclysm on the cosmos of the irreverent;
10	But *chiefly* **especially** them that walk after the flesh in the *lust* **panting** of *uncleanness* **defilement**, and *despise government* **disesteem lordship**. *Presumptuous are they* **Audacious**, *selfwilled* **selfpleasing**, they *are not afraid* **tremble not** to *speak evil of dignities* **blaspheme glories**.	6	and incinerating the cities of Sedom and Amorah; condemned them with a catastrophe — setting an example to those all around who live irreverently;
17	For having taken honor and glory from Elohim the Father — when such a voice was brought to him from the majestic glory, This is my beloved Son of whom I well—approve.	7	and rescued just Lot worn down by the lecherous behavior of the illicit:
18	— and we heard this voice brought from the heavens being with him in the holy mount.	8	for that just *one* dwelling among them, seeing and hearing, tortured his just soul day by day with their untorahed works;
		9	Yah Veh knows how to rescue the well—revering from testings and to guard the unjust to the day of judgment to punish:

Scripture Prophecy

19	We also have a steadfast word of prophecy; which you do well to heed, as to a light manifesting in an obscure place, until the day thoroughly dawn and the day phospherescence arise in your hearts:	10	and especially those walking after flesh in the panting of defilement, who disesteem lordship, audacious, selfpleasing, who tremble not to blaspheme glories.
20	knowing this first, that not any prophecy of the scripture	11	Whereas angels,

which are **being** greater
in *power* **might** and *might* **dynamis**,
bring *not railing accusation* **no blasphemous judgment**
against them *before the Lord* **with Yah Veh**.
12 But these,
as *natural brute beasts* **physical irrational live beings**,
made **birthed** to be *taken* **captured**
and *destroyed* **corrupted**,
speak evil of the things **blaspheme those**
that they understand not **in which they are unknowing**;
and shall *utterly perish* **corrupt** in their own corruption;
13 And shall receive
the reward of *unrighteousness* **injustice**,
as they that *count* **deem** it pleasure
to *riot* **indulge** in the day time.
Spots they are **Stains** and blemishes,
sporting themselves **reveling**
with **in** their own *deceivings* **delusions**
while they *feast* **revel** with you;
14 Having eyes full of adultery,
and *that cannot cease* **restless** from sin;
beguiling **entrapping** unstable souls:
an heart they have exercised
with *covetous practices* **avarice**;
cursed children **of curse**:
15 Which have forsaken the *right* **straight** way,
and *are gone astray* **wander**,
following the way
of *Balaam* **Bilam** the son of *Bosor* **Beor**,
who loved
the *wages* **rewards** of *unrighteousness* **injustice**;
16 But was *rebuked* **reproofed**
for his *iniquity* **own torah violations**:
the *dumb ass* **voiceless burro**
speaking with man's **uttering in a human** voice
forbad the *madness* **insanity** of the prophet.
17 These are *wells without*
water **waterless fountains**,
clouds
that are *carried with* **driven by** a *tempest* **whirlwind**;
to whom the mist of darkness
is *reserved for ever* **guarded unto the eons**.
18 For when they
speak great swelling words **utter overbulgings** of vanity,
they *allure* **entrap** through the *lusts*
pantings of the flesh,
through much *wantonness* **lechery**,
those that *were clean* **indeed** escaped from them
who *live* **remain** in *error* **seduction**.
19 While they *promise them*
pre—evangelize liberty,

they themselves are the servants of corruption:
for of whom *a man* **anyone** is *overcome* **slighted**,
of the same *by this* is he *brought in bondage* **subservient**.
20 For if after they have escaped
the *pollutions* **defilements** of the *world* **cosmos**
through the knowledge
of *the Lord* **Adonay** and Saviour *Jesus*
Christ **Yah Shua Messiah**,
they are again entangled *therein* **by these**,
and *overcome* **slighted**,
the *latter end is* **their finality**
becometh worse with them
than the *beginning* **first**.
21 For it had been better for them
not to have known the way of *righteousness* **justness**,
than, after they have known it,
to turn from the holy *commandment* **misvah**
delivered unto them.
22 But it is happened unto them
according to the true proverb,
The dog *is turned* **returneth** to his own vomit *again*;
and the *sow* **hog** that *was washed* **bathed**
to her wallowing in the mire.
Proverbs 26:11

THE FINAL DAYS

3 This second epistle, beloved,
I *now write* **scribe** unto you;
in *both* which I *stir up* **rouse** your *pure* **sincere** minds
by way of **in** remembrance:
2 That ye may *be mindful of*
remember the *words* **rhemas**
which were *spoken before* **foresaid** by the holy prophets,
and of the *commandment* **misvah**
of us the apostles of *the Lord* **Adonay** and Saviour:
11 Whereas angels,
being greater in might and dynamis,
brought no blasphemous judgment against them
with Yah Veh.
12 And these, as physical irrational live beings,
birthed to be captured and corrupted,
blaspheme those in which they are unknowing;
and corrupt in their own corruption;
13 and receive the reward of injustice,
as they who deem it pleasure
to indulge in the day time;
— stains and blemishes,
reveling in their own delusions as they revel with you;
14 eyes full of adultery,
and restless from sin;
entrapping unstable souls;

      a heart exercised with avarice;
children of curse
15 who forsake the straight way and wander;
following the way of Bilam of Beor who
loved the rewards of injustice;
16 and was reproofed for his own torah violations:
the voiceless burro uttering in a human voice
forbad the insanity of the prophet.
17 These are waterless fountains
— clouds driven by a whirlwind
to whom the mist of darkness is guarded to the eons.
18 For by uttering overbulgings of vanity,
through the pantings of the flesh, by lechery,
they entrap them,
who indeed escaped from them
who remain in seduction.
19 While they pre—evangelize liberty,
they themselves are the servants of corruption:
for by whom anyone is belittled,
by him is he subservient.
20 For if,
having escaped the defilements of the cosmos
through the knowledge
of Adonay and Saviour Yah Shua Messiah,
and entangled again by these and belittled,
their finality becomes worse than at first.
21 For it had been better for them
to not have known the way of justness,
than having known,
to turn from the holy misvah delivered to them.
22 But it happens to them
according to the true proverb,
The dog returns to his own vomit;
and the hog that bathed to her wallowing
in the mire. Proverbs 26:11

THE FINAL DAYS

3 This second epistle, beloved, I scribe to you;
in which I rouse your sincere minds in remembrance:
2 to remember the rhemas
foresaid by the holy prophets
and the misvah
by us the apostles of Adonay and Saviour:
3 Knowing this first,
that there shall come in the *last* **final** days
scoffers **mockers**,
walking after their own *lusts* **pantings**,
4 And *saying* **wording**,
Where is the *promise* **pre—evangelism**
of his *coming* **parousia**?
for **from** since the fathers fell asleep,
all *things continue as they were* **continually abide thus**
as from the beginning of the creation.
5 *For* **From** this
they *willingly are ignorant of* **will to hide**,
that by the word of *God* **Elohim** the heavens were of old,
and the earth standing out of the water
and *in* **through** the water:
6 *Whereby* **Through which**
the *world* **cosmos** that then was,
being *overflowed* **flooded** with water,
perished **destructed**:
7 But the heavens and the earth, which are now,
by the same word are *kept in store* **treasured**,
reserved **guarded** unto fire
against **unto**
the day of judgment and *perdition* **destruction**
of *ungodly men* **irreverent humanity**.
8 But, beloved,
be not ignorant of this one thing **hide not from this**,
that one day is with *the Lord* **Yah Veh**
as a thousand years,
and a thousand years as one day.
9 *The Lord* **Yah Veh** is not slack
concerning his *promise* **pre—evangelism**,
as some *men count* **deem** slackness;
but is *longsuffering to us—ward* **patient unto us**,
not willing that any should *perish* **destruct**,
but that all should *come* **pass** to repentance.

THE DAY OF YAH VEH

10 But the day of *the Lord will* **Yah Veh shall** come
as a thief in the night;
in the which the heavens
shall pass *away* with a *great noise* **whir**,
and the elements **being causticized**,
shall *melt with fervent heat* **let loose**,
the earth also and the works that are therein
shall be burned *up*.
11 *Seeing then that* **So** all these,
things shall be dissolved **having let loose**,
what manner *of persons ought ye to* **ye must** be
in *all* holy *conversation* **behaviour**
and *godliness* **reverence**,
12 *Looking for* **Awaiting** and hasting
unto the *coming* **parousia** of the day of *God* **Elohim**,
wherein **through which** the heavens being on fire
shall be *dissolved* **loosed**,
and the elements **being causticized**,
shall melt *with fervent heat* **down**?
13 *Nevertheless* **And** we,
according to his *promise* **pre—evangelism**, *look
for* **await** new heavens and a new earth,

wherein dwelleth *righteousness* **justness**.
14   *Wherefore*, **So** beloved,
seeing that ye *look for such things* **await these**,
be diligent that ye may be found of him in *peace* **shalom**,
without spot **unstained**, and *blameless* **unblemished**.
15   And *account* **deem** that
the *longsuffering* **patience**
of our *Lord* **Adonay** is salvation;
even *exactly* as our beloved brother *Paul* **Paulos** also
according to the wisdom given unto him
hath *written* **scribed** unto you;
16   As also in all his epistles,
speaking in them *of* **concerning** these *things*;
in which are some *things*
hard to be understood **incomprehensible**,
which they that are unlearned and unstable *wrest* **twist**,
as *they do* also the *other* **rest of the** scriptures,
unto their own destruction.
3   knowing this first:
that in the final days come mockers
walking after their own pantings;
4   and wording,
Where is the pre—evangelism of his parousia?
From since the fathers fell asleep,
all continually abides thus
as from the beginning of the creation.
5   They will to hide from this:
that by the word of Elohim
the heavens being of old
and the earth standing from the water
and through the water:
6   through which the cosmos then being
flooded with water and destructed:
7   and the heavens and the earth, now being,
by the same word are treasured
— guarded to fire
to the day of judgment
and destruction of irreverent humanity.
8   But beloved, hide not from this:
that one day with Yah Veh is as a thousand years
and a thousand years as one day.
9   Yah Veh is not slack
concerning his pre—evangelism
as some deem slackness;
but is patient to us,
who wills that not any destruct,
but that all pass to repentance.

THE DAY OF YAH VEH

10   But the day of Yah Veh comes
as a thief in the night;
in which the heavens pass with a whir
and the elements, being causticized, let loose;
also the earth and the works therein burn.
11   So all these, having let loose,
what manner must you be
in holy behavior and reverence;
12   awaiting and hastening
to the parousia of the day of Elohim,
through which the heavens being on fire, are loosed;
and the elements being causticized, melt down?
13   And we, according to his pre—evangelism,
await the new heavens and a new earth,
wherein justness dwells.
14   So beloved, seeing that you await these,
be diligent to be found by him in shalom
— unstained and unblemished.
15   And deems the patience of our Adonay,
to be salvation;
even exactly as our beloved brother Paulos also
according to the wisdom given him
scribed to you;
16   as also in all his epistles,
speaking in them concerning these;
in which some are incomprehensible
— which the unlearned and unstable twist
— as also the rest of the scriptures
to their own destruction.
17   **So** Ye *therefore*, beloved,
seeing ye *know* **foreknow** these *things before*,
beware **guard** lest ye also,
being led away
with the *error* **seduction** of the *wicked* **illicit**,
fall from your own stedfastness.
18   But grow in *grace* **charism**,
and in the knowledge of our *Lord* **Adonay** and Saviour
Jesus Christ **Yah Shua Messiah**.
To him be glory
both now and *for ever* **unto the day of the eons**.
Amen.
17   So beloved, seeing you foreknow these,
guard:
lest being led away with the seduction of the illicit
you also fall from your own steadfastness.
18   But grow in charism
and in the knowledge
of our Adonay and Saviour Yah Shua Messiah.
To him be glory
both now and to the day of the eons.
Amen.

Salutation

1 *Jude* **Yah Hudah**,
the servant of *Jesus Christ* **Yah Shua Messiah**,
and brother of *James* **Yaaqovos**,
to them that are *sanctified* **hallowed**
by God **in Elohim** the Father,
and *preserved* **guarded** in *Jesus
Christ* **Yah Shua Messiah**,
and called:

2 Mercy unto you,
and *peace* **shalom**, and love, be multiplied.

Agonizing For The Trust

3 Beloved,
when I *gave* **made** all diligence to *write* **scribe** unto you
of **concerning** the common salvation,
it was needful for me **I needed** to *write* **scribe** unto you,
and *exhort* **beseech** you that ye should earnestly
contend **agonize** for the *faith* **trust**
which was once delivered unto the *saints* **holy**.

4 For *there are certain men* **some humans have**
crept **surreptitiously sneaked** in *unawares*
alongside, who were *before of old* **long ago**
ordained **preinscribed** to this *condemnation* **judgment**,
ungodly men **irreverent**,
turning **transplacing** the *grace*
charism of our *God* **Elohim**
into *lasciviousness* **lechery**,
and denying the only *Lord God* **Despotes Elohim**,
and our *Lord Jesus Christ* **Adonay Yah Shua Messiah**.

Examples Of Past Judgments

5 *I will therefore put you in remembrance*
So I shall remind you,
though ye once knew this,
how that *the Lord* **Yah Veh**,
having saved the people
out of the land of *Egypt* **Misrayim**,
afterward **secondly** destroyed them
that *believed* **trusted** not.

6 And the angels
which *kept* **guarded** not their *first estate* **own hierarchy**,
but left their own *habitation* **house**,
he hath *reserved* **guarded**
in *everlasting chains* **eternal bonds**
under *darkness* **gloom**
unto the judgment of the *great* **mega** day.

7 Even as *Sodom* **Sedom** and *Gomorrha* **Amorah**,
and the cities about them in like manner,
giving themselves over to fornication **whoring**,
and going after *strange* **other** flesh,
are set *forth* for an example,
suffering **enduring** the *vengeance* **judgment**
of eternal fire.

8 *Likewise* **Yet indeed** also these *filthy* dreamers
defile the flesh, *despise dominion* **set aside lordship**,
and *speak evil of dignities* **blaspheme glories**.

9 Yet *Michael* **Michah El** the archangel,
when *contending* **dialoguing** with *the devil* **Diabolos**
he *disputed* **reasoned** about the body of Moses,
durst not bring *up* against him
a *railing accusation* **blasphemy**,
but said, The Lord **Yah Veh** rebuke thee.

10 But **indeed**, these *speak evil* **blaspheme**
of those things which **as much as** they know not:
but *what* **as much as** they *know* **understand**
naturally **physically**,
as *brute beasts* **irrational live beings**,
in those *things* they corrupt themselves.

11 Woe unto them!
for **because** they have gone in the way of *Cain* **Qayin**,
and *ran greedily* **rushed**
after the *error* **seduction** of *Balaam* **Bilam** for reward,
and *perished* **destructed**
in the *gainsaying* **controversy** of *Core* **Korach**.

12 These are *spots* **reefs** in
your *feasts of charity* **love**,
when they *feast* **revel** with you,
feeding **shepherding** themselves *without fear* **fearlessly**:
waterless clouds *they are without water*,
carried about of winds;
autumnal trees *whose fruit withereth*,
without fruit **unfruitful**, twice dead,
plucked up by the roots **uprooted**;

Salutation

1 Yah Hudah,
the servant of Yah Shua Messiah
and brother of Yaaqovos:
To the hallowed in Elohim the Father
and guarded in Yah Shua Messiah — called:

2 Mercy to you
and shalom and love, be multiplied.

Agonizing For The Trust

3 Beloved, scribing to you in all diligence,
concerning the common salvation,
I need to scribe to you and beseech you
to earnestly agonize for the trust

JUDE/Y'HUDAH 1

once delivered to the holy.

4 For some humans
surreptitiously sneaked alongside
— who long ago were preinscribed to this judgment
— irreverent
transplacing the charism of our Elohim into lechery
and denying the only Despotes Elohim
and our Adonay Yah Shua Messiah.

EXAMPLES OF PAST JUDGMENTS

5 So, I remind you,,
though you once knew this,
how that Yah Veh saved the people
from the land of Misrayim;
and secondly destroyed them who trusted not:
6 and the angels who guarded
not their own hierarchy
but left their own house
he guards in eternal bonds under gloom
unto the judgment of the mega day
7 — as Sedom and Amorah
and the surrounding cities in like manner
— whoring and going after other flesh,
are set forth for an example
— enduring the judgment of eternal fire.
8 Yet indeed,
these dreamers still defile the flesh,
set aside lordships,
and blaspheme glories.
9 Yet Michah El the archangel
dialoguing with Diabolos
reasoning about the body of Moses,
dared not bring a blasphemy;
but said, Yah Veh rebuke you!
10 But indeed,
these blaspheme as much as they know not:
but as much as they understand physically,
as irrational live beings,
in those, they corrupt themselves.
11 Woe to them!
because they go in the way of Qayin
and rush for reward
after the seduction of Bilam
and destruct in the controversy of Korach.
12 These are reefs in your
love as they revel with you,
shepherding themselves fearlessly:
waterless clouds carried about by winds,
autumnal trees, unfruitful, twice dead, uprooted,
13 Raging waves of the sea,
foaming out **frothing** their own shame;
wandering **planetary** stars,
to whom is *reserved* **guarded**
the blackness of *darkness* **gloom**
for ever **unto the eons**.
14 And *Enoch* **Hanoch** also,
the seventh from Adam,
prophesied of these, *saying* **wording**,
Behold, *the Lord* **Yah Veh** cometh
with ten thousands of his saints **among his holy myriads**,
15 To *execute* **deal** judgment upon all,
and to *convince* **convict** all
that are *ungodly* **irreverent** among them
of **concerning** all their *ungodly deeds* **irreverent works**
which they have *ungodly committed* **irreverently done**,
and *of* **concerning** all their *hard speeches* **hardnesses**
which *ungodly* **irreverent** sinners
have spoken against him.
Deuteronomy 33:2
16 These are murmurers, *complainers* **fatalists**,
walking after their own *lusts* **pantings**;
and their mouth
speaketh *great swelling words* **overbulgings**,
having men's persons in admiration **marveling over faces**
because of *advantage* **benefit**.

REMEMBERING THE RHEMAS

17 But, beloved, remember ye the *words* **rhemas**
which were *spoken before* **foresaid** of the apostles of
our *Lord Jesus Christ* **Adonay Yah Shua Messiah**;
18 How that they *told* **worded to** you
there should be mockers in the *last* **final** time,
who should walk after their own
ungodly lusts **irreverent pantings**.
19 These be they
who *separate themselves* **set boundaries**,
sensual **soulical**, having not the Spirit.
20 But ye, beloved,
building *up* yourselves on your most holy *faith* **trust**,
praying in *the Holy Spirit* **Ruach ha-kodesh**,
21 *Keep* **Guard** yourselves in
the love of *God* **Elohim**,
looking for **awaiting** the mercy
of our *Lord Jesus Christ* **Adonay Yah Shua Messiah**
unto eternal life.
22 And *of* some *have compassion* **indeed mercy**,
making a difference **discerning**:
23 And others save *with fear* **in awe**,
pulling **seizing** them out of the fire;
hating even the *garment* **tunic**
spotted **stained** by the flesh.

BENEDICTION

24 Now unto him that is able
to *keep* **guard** you *from falling* **unstumbling**,
and to *present* **stand** you *faultless* **unblemished**
before the presence **in sight** of his glory
with exceeding **in jumping for** joy,

25 To the only wise *God* **Elohim** our Saviour,
be glory and majesty,
dominion **power** and *power* **authority**,
both now and *ever* **unto all eons**.
Amen.

13 raging waves of the sea
frothing their own shame,
planetary stars
— to whom is guarded
the blackness of gloom to the eons.

14 And Hanoch also, the seventh from Adam,
prophesied of these, wording,
Behold, Yah Veh comes among his holy myriads,

15 to deal judgment on all
and to convict all who are irreverent among them
concerning all their irreverent works
which they have irreverently done;
and concerning all their hardnesses
which irreverent sinners have spoken
against him. Deuteronomy 33:2

16 These are murmurers
— fatalists walking after their own pantings;
and their mouth speaking overbulgings;
marveling over faces to benefit.

REMEMBERING THE RHEMAS

17 And you, beloved,
remember the rhemas foresaid by the apostles
of our Adonay Yah Shua Messiah;

18 how they worded to you
that there be mockers in the final time,
walking after their own irreverent pantings:

19 who set boundaries;
soulical, not having the Spirit.

20 And you, beloved,
edifying yourselves on your most holy trust,
praying in Holy Spirit,

21 guarding yourselves in the love of Elohim
awaiting the mercy of our Adonay Yah Shua Messiah
to eternal life.

22 And to some indeed, mercy
— discerning thoroughly:

23 and others save in awe,
seizing them from the fire;
hating even the tunic stained by the flesh.

BENEDICTION

24 And to him who is able to
guard you unstumbling
and to stand you unblemished
in sight of his glory — in jumping for joy,

25 to the only wise Elohim our Saviour
be glory and majesty,
power and authority,
both now and to all eons.
Amen.

The Word Of Life

1 That which was from the beginning,
which we have heard,
which we have seen with our eyes,
which we have *looked upon* **observed**,
and our hands have *handled* **touched**,
of **concerning** the Word of life;

2 (For the life was manifested,
and we have seen it, and *bear* witness,
and *shew* **evangelize** unto you that eternal life,
which was with the Father, and was manifested unto us;)

3 That which we have seen and heard
declare **evangelize** we unto you,
that ye also may have *fellowship* **communion** with us:
and truly our *fellowship* **communion** is with the Father,
and with his Son *Jesus Christ* **Yah Shua Messiah**.

4 And these *things write* **scribe** we unto you,
that your *joy* may **cheer** be *full* **fulfilled/shalamed**.

5 This then is the *message* **pre—evangelism**
which we have heard of him,
and *declare* **evangelize** unto you,
that *God* **Elohim** is light, and in
him is no darkness at all.

6 *If* **Whenever** we say that we have
fellowship **communion** with him,
and walk in darkness, we lie, and do not the truth:

7 But *if* **whenever** we walk in
the light, as he is in the light,
we have *fellowship* **communion** one with another,
and the blood of *Jesus Christ* **Yah Shua Messiah** his Son
cleanseth **purifieth** us from all sin.

8 *If* **Whenever** we say that we have no sin,
we *deceive* **seduce** ourselves, and the truth is not in us.

9 *If* **Whenever** we *confess* **profess** our sins,
he is *faithful* **trustworthy** and just to forgive us our sins,
and to *cleanse* **purify** us
from all *unrighteousness* **injustice**.

10 *If* **Whenever** we say that we have not sinned,
we make him a liar, and his word is not in us.

Yah Shua Messiah, The Paraclete

2 My little children,
these *things write* **scribe** I unto you, that ye sin not.
And *if* **whenever** any *man* **one** sin,
we have *an advocate* **a Paraclete** with the Father,
Jesus Christ **Yah Shua Messiah** the *righteous* **just**:

2 And he is the *propitiation*
kopur/atonement for our sins:
and not for ours only,
but also for *the sins of* the whole *world* **cosmos**.

3 And *hereby* **in this** we *do* know
that we *know* **have known** him,
if **whenever** we *keep* **guard** his *commandments* **misvoth**.

4 He that *saith* **wordeth**, I *know* **have known** him,
and *keepeth* **guardeth** not his *commandments*
misvoth, is a liar, and the truth is not in him.

5 But *whoso keepeth* **whoever guardeth** his word,
in him *verily* **truly** is the love of *God* **Elohim**
perfected **completed/shalamed**:
hereby **in this** know we that we are in him.

6 He that *saith* **wordeth** he abideth in him
ought **is indebted** himself also *so* **thus** to
walk, *even* **exactly** as he walked.

7 Brethren,
I *write* **scribe** no new *commandment* **misvah** unto you,
but an old *commandment* **misvah**
which ye had from the beginning.
The old *commandment* **misvah** is the word
which ye have heard from the beginning.

8 Again,
a new *commandment* **misvah** I *write* **scribe** unto you,
which *thing* is true in him and in you:
because the darkness *is past* **passeth away**,
and the true light *now shineth* **already manifesteth**.

9 He that *saith* **wordeth that** he is in the light,
and hateth his brother, is in darkness even until now.

10 He that loveth his brother abideth in the light,
and there is
none occasion of stumbling **no scandal** in him.

11 But he that hateth his brother is in darkness,
and walketh in darkness,
and knoweth not whither he goeth,
because *that* darkness hath blinded his eyes.

The Word Of Life

1 That which was from the beginning,
which we heard,
which our eyes saw,
which we observed and our hands touched
concerning the Word of life;

2 for the life manifested
and we saw and witness
and evangelize to you the eternal life;
being with the Father and manifest to us

3 which we saw and heard:
we evangelize to you,
so that you also have communion with us:
and truly our communion is with the Father
and with his Son Yah Shua Messiah:

4   and we scribe these to you
that your cheer be fulfilled/shalamed.
5   And this is the pre—evangelism
we heard from him and evangelize to you
— that Elohim is light and in him is no darkness at all.
6   Whenever we say we have communion with him
and walk in darkness,
we lie and do not the truth:
7   and whenever we walk in the light,
as he is in the light,
we have communion with one another
— and the blood of Yah Shua Messiah his Son
purifies us from all sin:
8   whenever we say we have no sin
we seduce ourselves and the truth is not in us:
9   whenever we profess our sins,
he is trustworthy and just to forgive our sins
and to purify us from all injustice:
10   whenever we say that we have not sinned
we make him a liar and his word is not in us.

Yah Shua Messiah, The Paraclete

2   My little children,
I scribe these to you that you not sin:
and whenever anyone sins
we have a Paraclete with the Father
— Yah Shua Messiah the just:
2   and he is the kopur/atonement for our sins:
and not for ours only, but also for the whole cosmos.
3   And in this we know that we know him
— whenever we guard his misvoth.
4   Whoever words, I know him!
— and guards not his misvoth,
is a liar and the truth is not in him:
5   and whoever guards his word,
truly in him
the love of Elohim is completed/shalamed:
— in this we know that we are in him.
6   Whoever words that he abides in him
is also indebted to walk thus
— exactly as he walked.
7   Brothers, I scribe you no new misvah,
but an old misvah that you had from the beginning:
the old misvah
is the word you heard from the beginning:
8   again, I scribe you a new misvah
which is true in him and in you:
because the darkness passes away
and the true light already manifests.
9   Whoever words that he is in the light
and hates his brother
is in darkness even until now:
10   whoever loves his brother abides in the light
and there is no scandal in him:
11   but whoever hates his brother
is in darkness and walks in darkness
and knows not where he goes
— because darkness blinds his eyes.
12   I *write* **scribe** unto you, little children,
because your sins are forgiven you for his name's sake.
13   I *write* **scribe** unto you, fathers,
because ye have known him that is from the beginning.
I *write* **scribe** unto you, *young men* **youths**,
because ye have
overcome **triumphed over** the *wicked* **evil** one.
I *write* **scribe** unto you, little children,
because ye have known the Father.
14   I have *written* **scribed** unto you, fathers,
because ye have known him that is from the beginning.
I have *written* **scribed** unto you, *young men* **youths**,
because ye are *strong* **mighty**,
and the word of *God* **Elohim** abideth in you,
and ye have *overcome* **triumphed**
over the *wicked* **evil** one.

Loving The Cosmos

15   Love not the *world* **cosmos**,
neither *the things* **those** that are in the *world* **cosmos**.
If **Whenever** any *man* **one** love the *world* **cosmos**,
the love of the Father is not in him.
16   *For* **Because** all that is in the *world* **cosmos**,
the *lust* **panting** of the flesh,
and the *lust* **panting** of the eyes,
and the pride of *life* **existence**,
is not of the Father, but is of the *world* **cosmos**.
17   And the *world* **cosmos** passeth away,
and the *lust* **panting** thereof:
but he that doeth the will of *God* **Elohim**
abideth *for ever* **unto the eons**.

The Antimessiah

18   Little children, it is the *last time* **final hour**:
and **exactly** as ye have heard
that *antichrist* **the antimessiah** shall come,
even now
are there many *antichrists* **antimessiahs**;
whereby we know that it is the *last time* **final hour**.
2 Yahn 7
19   They went out from us, but they were not of us;
for if they had been of us,

they *would no doubt* **should** have
continued **ever abode** with us:
but *they went out*,
that they might *be made* manifest
that they were not all of us.
20   But ye have an *unction*
anointing from the Holy One,
and ye know all *things*.
21   I have not *written* **scribed** unto you
because ye know not the truth,
but because ye know it,
and that *no* **not any** lie is of the truth.
22   Who is a liar *but* **except** he that denieth
that *Jesus* **Yah Shua** is the *Christ* **Messiah**?
He is antichrist **This one is the antimessiah**,
that denieth the Father and the Son.
2 Yahn 7
23   Whosoever denieth the Son,
the same hath not the Father:
[but] he that acknowledgeth the Son hath the Father also.
24   Let that therefore abide in you,
which ye have heard from the beginning.
If **Whenever** that which ye have
heard from the beginning
shall *remain* **abide** in you,
ye also shall *continue* **abide** in the Son, and in the Father.
25   And this is the *promise* **pre—evangelism**
that he hath *promised* **pre—evangelized** to us,
even — eternal life.
26   These *things* have I *written* **scribed** unto you
concerning them that seduce you.
27   But the anointing which ye
have *received* **taken** of him
abideth in you,
and ye need not that any *man teach* **one doctrinate** you:
but as the same anointing
teacheth **doctrinateth** you *of* **concerning** all *things*,
and is truth, and is no lie,
and *even* **exactly** as it hath *taught* **doctrinated** you,
ye shall abide in him.
12   I scribe to you little children:
because your sins are forgiven for sake of his name.
13   I scribe to you fathers:
because you know him who *is* from beginning.
I scribe to you youths:
because you triumph over the evil one.
I scribe to you little children:
because you know the Father.
14   I scribe to you fathers:
because you know him who *is* from beginning.
I scribe to you youths:
because you are mighty
and the word of Elohim abides in you
and you triumph over the evil one.

Loving The Cosmos

15   Neither love the cosmos,
nor those in the cosmos:
whenever anyone loves the cosmos
the love of the Father is not in him.
16   Because all that is in the cosmos
— the panting of the flesh,
and the panting of the eyes,
and the pride of existence
is not of the Father, but *is* of the cosmos.
17   And the cosmos passes away
and the panting thereof:
and whoever does the will of Elohim
abides to the eons.

The Antimessiah

18   Little children, it is the final hour:
and exactly as you heard
that the antimessiah comes,
even now there are antimessiahs;
whereby we know it is the final hour.
2 Yahn 7
19   They went from us, but they were not of us;
for if they had been of us
they had ever abode with us:
but they manifested they were not all of us.
20   And you have an anointing from the Holy One
and you know all.
21   I scribe not to you
because you know not the truth;
but because you know it, and no lie is of the truth.
22   Who is a liar
except whoever denies that Yah Shua is the Messiah?
This is the antimessiah
— who denies the Father and the Son.
2 Yahn 7
23   Whoever denies the Son has not the Father.
24   So you,
have what you heard from the beginning
abide in you.
Whenever what you heard from the beginning
abides in you,
you also abide in the Son and in the Father.
25   And this is the pre—evangelism
he pre—evangelized to us

26   — eternal life.
26   I scribe these to you
concerning them who seduce you.
27   And you, the anointing you took from him
abides in you
and you need no one to doctrinate you:
but as the same anointing
doctrinates you concerning all
— and is truth and is no lie
— exactly as it doctrinates you,
abide in him.
28   And now, little children, abide in him;
that, when he shall *appear* **manifest**,
we may have *confidence* **boldness**,
and not be ashamed *before* **in front of** him
at his *coming* **parousia**.
29   *If* **Whenever** ye know that he is *righteous* **just**,
ye know that every one that doeth *righteousness* **justness**
is *born* **birthed** of him.

THE LOVE OF THE FATHER

3   *Behold* **Perceive**,
what manner of love
the Father hath *bestowed upon* **given** us,
that we should be called the *sons*
children of *God* **Elohim**:
therefore **because of this** the *world*
cosmos knoweth us not,
because it knew him not.
2   Beloved, now are we the *sons*
children of *God* **Elohim**,
and it *doth* **be** not yet *appear* **manifest**
what we shall be;
but we know that,
when **whenever** he shall *appear* **be manifest**,
we shall be like him;
for **because** we shall see him *exactly* as he is.
3   And every *man* **one** that hath this hope in him
purifieth **halloweth** himself,
even **exactly** as he is *pure* **hallowed**.
4   Whosoever *committeth* **doeth** sin
transgresseth **violateth** also the *law* **torah**:
for sin is the *transgression* **violation** of the *law* **torah**.
5   And ye know that he was manifested
to take away our sins;
and in him is no sin.
6   Whosoever abideth in him sinneth not:
whosoever sinneth hath not seen him,
neither known him.

7   Little children, let no *man*
deceive **one seduce** you:
he that doeth *righteousness* **justness** is *righteous* **just**,
even **exactly** as he is *righteous* **just**.
8   He that *committeth* **doeth**
sin is of *the devil* **Diabolos**;
for the devil **because Diabolos**
sinneth from the beginning.
For **Unto** this *purpose*
the Son of *God* **Elohim** was manifested,
that he might *destroy* **loosen**
the works of *the devil* **Diabolos**.
9   Whosoever is *born* **birthed** of *God* **Elohim**
doth not *commit* sin;
for **because** his *seed remaineth* **sperma abideth** in him:
and he cannot sin, because he is *born*
birthed of *God* **Elohim**.
10   In this the children of *God* **Elohim** are manifest,
and the children of *the devil* **Diabolos**:
whosoever doeth not *righteousness* **justness**
is not of *God* **Elohim**,
neither he that loveth not his brother.

LOVING ONE ANOTHER

11   *For* **Because** this is the *message* **evangelism**
that ye heard from the beginning,
that we should love one another.
12   Not *exactly* as *Cain* **Qayin**,
who was of that *wicked* **evil** one,
and *slew* **slaughtered** his brother.
And *wherefore slew* **for what cause slaughtered** he him?
Because his own works were evil,
and his brother's *righteous* **just**.
13   Marvel not, my brethren,
if the *world* **cosmos** hate you.
14   We know
that we have *passed* **departed** from death unto life,
because we love the brethren.
He that loveth not his brother abideth in death.
15   Whosoever hateth his brother is a murderer:
and ye know that *no* **not any** murderer
hath eternal life abiding in him.
16   *Hereby perceive we* **In this**
we know the love *of God*,
because he *laid down* **placed** his *life* **soul** for us:
and we *ought* **are indebted**
to *lay down* **place** our *lives* **souls** for the brethren.
17   But *whoso* **whoever**
hath this *world's good* **cosmos' subsistence**,
and *seeth* **observeth** his brother have need,

28 And now little children,
abide in him;
so that when he manifests,
we have boldness
and not shame in front of him at his parousia.
29 Whenever you know that he is just,
you know that everyone who does justness
is birthed of him.

THE LOVE OF THE FATHER

3 Perceive!
What manner of love the Father gives us
— to be called the children of Elohim:
because of this, the cosmos knows us not,
because it knew him not.
2 Beloved, we are now the children of Elohim
and it is not yet manifest what we become;
but we know that,
whenever he becomes manifest, we become like him;
because then we see him exactly as he is.
3 And everyone who has this hope in him
hallows himself
— exactly as he is hallowed.
4 Everyone doing sin also violates the torah:
for sin is the violation of the torah.
5 And you know that he was manifested
to take away our sins
— and in him no sin is.
6 Whoever abides in him sins not:
whoever sins neither saw him nor knew him.
7 Little children, be seduced by no one:
whoever does justness is just — exactly as he is just:
8 everyone doing sin is of Diabolos
— because Diabolos sinned from the beginning.
Unto this the Son of Elohim manifested
— to loosen the works of Diabolos.
9 Whoever is birthed of Elohim sins not;
because his sperma abides in him:
and he cannot sin, because he is birthed of Elohim.
10 In this are the children of Elohim
and the children of Diabolos manifest:
whoever does not justness is not of Elohim,
neither whoever loves not his brother.

LOVING ONE ANOTHER

11 Because this is the evangelism
you heard from the beginning
— to love one another.
12 Not exactly as Qayin who was of that evil one,
who slaughtered his brother.
And for what cause slaughtered he him?
Because his own works were evil
and those of his brother, just.
13 Marvel not, my brothers,
if the cosmos hates you.
14 We know that we departed from death to life,
because we love the brothers. Whoever
loves not his brother abides in death:
15 whoever hates his brother is a murderer
— and you know that not any murderer
has eternal life abiding in him.
16 In this we know the love
because he placed his soul for us:
and we are indebted
to place our souls for the brothers.
17 But whoever has the subsistence of this cosmos
and observes his brother has need
and shutteth up his *bowels of
compassion* **spleen** from him,
how *dwelleth* **abideth** the love of *God* **Elohim** in him?
18 My little children, let us not love in word,
neither in tongue; but in *deed* **work** and in truth.
19 And *hereby* **in this** we know
that we are of the truth,
and shall *assure* **confide** our hearts
before **in front of** him.
20 *For if* **Because whenever** our heart condemn us,
God **Elohim** is greater than our heart,
and knoweth all *things*.
21 Beloved, *if* **whenever** our heart condemn us not,
then have we *confidence* **boldness** toward *God* **Elohim**.
22 And *whatsoever* **whenever** we ask,
we *receive* **take** of him,
because we *keep* **guard** his *commandments* **misvoth**,
and do those *things* that are pleasing in his sight.
23 And this is his *commandment* **misvah**,
That we should *believe on* **trust**
the name of his Son *Jesus Christ* **Yah Shua Messiah**,
and love one another,
exactly as he gave us *commandment* **misvah**.
24 And he that *keepeth* **guardeth**
his *commandments* **misvoth**
dwelleth **abideth** in him, and he in him.
And *hereby* **in this** we know that he abideth in us,
by the Spirit which he hath given us.

THE ANTIMESSIAH

4 Beloved, *believe* **trust** not every spirit,
but *try* **proof** the spirits
whether they are of *God* **Elohim**:

because many *false* **pseudo** prophets
are gone out into the *world* **cosmos**.
2   *Hereby* **In this** know ye
the Spirit of *God* **Elohim**:
Every spirit that *confesseth* **professeth**
that *Jesus Christ* **Yah Shua Messiah** is come in the flesh
is of *God* **Elohim**:
3   And every spirit that *confesseth* **professeth** not
that *Jesus Christ* **Yah Shua Messiah** is come in the flesh
is not of *God* **Elohim**:
and this is *that spirit* of *antichrist* **the antimessiah**,
whereof ye have heard that it should come;
and even now already is it in the *world* **cosmos**.
2 Yahn 7
4   Ye are of *God* **Elohim**, little children,
and have *overcome* **triumphed over** them:
because greater is he that is in you,
than he that is in the *world* **cosmos**.
5   They are of the *world* **cosmos**:
therefore **for this** speak they of the *world* **cosmos**,
and the *world* **cosmos** heareth them.
6   We are of *God* **Elohim**:
he that knoweth *God* **Elohim** heareth us;
he that is not of *God* **Elohim** heareth not us.
Hereby **By this** know we the spirit of truth,
and the spirit of *error* **seduction**.

Elohim Is Love

7   Beloved, let us love one another:
for **because** love is of *God* **Elohim**;
and every one that loveth is *born*
birthed of *God* **Elohim**,
and knoweth *God* **Elohim**.
8   He that loveth not
knoweth not God **hath not known Elohim**;
for God **because Elohim** is love.
9   In this was manifested
the love of *God toward* **Elohim in** us,
because that *God* **Elohim**
sent **apostolized** his only *begotten* **birthed** Son
into the *world* **cosmos**,
that we might live through him.
10   *Herein* **In this** is love,
not that we loved *God* **Elohim**, but that he loved us,
and *sent* **apostolized** his Son
to be the *propitiation* **a kopur/an atonement** for our sins.
11   Beloved, if *God so* **Elohim thus** loved us,
we *ought* **are indebted** also to love one another.
12   No *man* **one** hath *seen God* **observed Elohim**
at any time — **not ever**.

If **Whenever** we love one another,
God dwelleth **Elohim abideth** in us,
and his love is *perfected* **completed/shalamed** in us.
and shuts his spleen from him
— how abides the love of Elohim in him?
18   My little children,
love — neither in word nor in tongue;
but in work and in truth.
19   And in this we know we are of the truth
and confide our hearts in front of him.
20   Because whenever our heart condemns us,
Elohim is greater than our heart and knows all.
21   Beloved, whenever our heart condemns us not,
then we have boldness toward Elohim.
22   And whenever we ask, we take of him:
because we guard his misvoth
and do what is pleasing in his sight.
23   And this is his misvah:
that we trust the name of his Son Yah Shua Messiah
and love one another
— exactly as he gave us misvah.
24   And whoever guards his misvoth
abides in him, and he in him.
And in this we know that he abides in us
— by the Spirit he gave us.

The Antimessiah

4   Beloved, trust not every spirit
but proof the spirits whether they are of Elohim:
because many pseudoprophets
have gone into the cosmos.
2   In this you know the Spirit of Elohim:
Every spirit professing
that Yah Shua Messiah is come in the flesh
is of Elohim;
3   and every spirit not professing
that Yah Shua Messiah is come in the flesh
is not of Elohim;
and this is the antimessiah
whom you heard is to come,
and even now already is in the cosmos.
2 Yahn 7
4   You are of Elohim, little children
and triumph over them:
because greater is he who is in you
than he who is in the cosmos.
5   They are of the cosmos:
because they speak of the cosmos
and the cosmos hears them.
6   We are of Elohim:

whoever knows Elohim hears us;
whoever is not of Elohim hears us not.
By this we know the spirit of truth
and the spirit of seduction.

ELOHIM IS LOVE

7 Beloved, love one another:
because love is of Elohim;
and everyone who loves
is birthed of Elohim and knows Elohim.
8 Whoever loves not, knows not Elohim;
because Elohim is love.
9 In this the love of Elohim manifests in us,
because Elohim apostolized his only birthed Son
into the cosmos
— that we, through him, live.
10 In this is the love
— not that we loved Elohim,
but that he loved us and apostolized his Son,
a kopur/an atonement for our sins.
11 Beloved, if Elohim loved us thus,
we also are indebted to love one another.
12 No one ever observed Elohim — not ever.
Whenever we love one another,
Elohim abides in us
and his love is completed/shalamed in us.
13 *Hereby* **In this** know we
that we *dwell* **abide** in him,
and he in us,
because he hath given us of his Spirit.
14 And we have *seen* **observed**
and *do testify* **witness**
that the Father *sent* **apostolized** the Son
to be the Saviour of the *world* **cosmos**.
15 Whosoever shall *confess* **profess**
that *Jesus* **Yah Shua** is the Son of *God* **Elohim**,
God dwelleth **Elohim abideth** in him,
and he in *God* **Elohim**.
16 And we have known and
believed **trusted** the love
that *God* **Elohim** hath *to* **in** us.
God **Elohim** is love;
and he that *dwelleth* **abideth** in love
dwelleth **abideth** in *God* **Elohim**,
and *God* **Elohim** in him.
17 *Herein* **In this** is our love *made perfect*
completed/shalamed, that we may have boldness
in the day of judgment: because *exactly* as
he is, so are we in this *world* **cosmos**.
18 There is no *fear* **awe** in love;
but *perfect* love **of completion/
shalom** casteth out *fear* **awe**:
because *fear* **awe** hath *torment* **punishment**.
He that *feareth* **aweth**
is not *made perfect* **completed/shalamed** in love.
19 We love him, because he first loved us.
20 *If a man* **Whenever one** say,
Because I love *God* **Elohim**,
and hateth his brother, he is a liar:
for he that loveth not his brother whom he hath seen,
how can he love *God* **Elohim** whom he hath not seen?
21 And this *commandment*
misvah have we from him,
That he who loveth *God* **Elohim** love his brother also.

TRIUMPHING OVER THE COSMOS

5 Whosoever *believeth* **trusteth**
that *Jesus* **Yah Shua** is the *Christ* **Messiah**
is *born* **birthed** of *God* **Elohim**:
and every one that loveth him that *begat* **birthed**
loveth him also that is *begotten* **birthed** of him.
2 *By* **In** this we know
that we love the children of *God* **Elohim**,
when we love *God* **Elohim**,
and *keep* **guard** his *commandments* **misvoth**.
3 For this is the love of *God* **Elohim**,
that we *keep* **guard** his *commandments* **misvoth**:
and his *commandments* **misvoth** are not grievous.
4 *For* **Because** whatsoever is
born **birthed** of *God* **Elohim**
overcometh **triumpheth** over the *world*
cosmos: and this is the *victory* **triumph**
that *overcometh* **triumpheth** over the *world* **cosmos**,
even our *faith* **trust**.
5 Who is he
that *overcometh* **triumpheth** over the *world* **cosmos**,
but **except** he that *believeth* **trusteth**
that *Jesus* **Yah Shua** is the Son of *God* **Elohim**?
6 This is he that came *by*
through water and blood,
even *Jesus Christ* — **Yah Shua Messiah**;
not *by* **in** water only, but *by* **in** water and blood.
And *it is* the Spirit *that beareth witness* **witnesseth**,
because the Spirit is truth.
7 *For* **Because** there are three
that *bear record* **witness** in *heaven* **the heavens**,
the Father, the Word, and the *Holy*
Spirit **Ruach ha-kodesh**:
and these three are one.
8 And there are three that *bear* witness in earth,

	the Spirit, and the water, and the blood:
	and these three *agree* **are** in one.
9	If we *receive* **take** the witness of *men* **humanity**,
	the witness of *God* **Elohim** is greater:
	for **because** this is the witness of *God* **Elohim**
	which he hath *testified of* **witnessed concerning** his Son.
10	He that *believeth* **trusteth**
	on the Son of *God* **Elohim**
	hath the witness in himself:
	he that *believeth* **trusteth** not *God* **Elohim**
	hath made him a liar;
	because he *believeth* **trusteth** not *in* the *record* **witness**
	that *God gave of* **Elohim witnessed concerning** his Son.
11	And this is the *record* **witness**,
	that *God* **Elohim** hath given to us eternal life,
	and this life is in his Son.
12	He that hath the Son hath life;
	and he that hath not the Son of
	God **Elohim** hath not life.
13	In this we know that we abide in him
	and he in us:
	because he gave us of his Spirit.
14	and we observed and witness
	that the Father apostolized the Son
	— Saviour of the cosmos.
15	Whoever professes
	that Yah Shua is the Son of Elohim,
	Elohim abides in him, and he in Elohim.
16	And we
	— we know and trust the love Elohim has in us.
	Elohim is love;
	and whoever abides in love
	abides in Elohim — and Elohim in him.
17	In this our love is completed/shalamed,
	that we have boldness in the day of judgment:
	because exactly as he is, so are we in this cosmos.
18	There is no awe in love;
	but love of completion/shalom casts out awe;
	because awe has punishment:
	whoever awes is not completed/shalamed in love.
19	We love him because he first loved us.
20	Whenever one says, Because I love Elohim!
	— and hates his brother, he is a liar:
	for whoever loves not his brother whom he sees,
	how can he love Elohim whom he sees not?
21	And we have this misvah from him,
	whoever loves Elohim also loves his brother.

Triumphing Over The Cosmos

5	Whoever trusts that Yah Shua is the Messiah
	is birthed of Elohim:
	and everyone who loves him who birthed
	also loves him whom he birthed.
2	In this we know we love the children of Elohim
	— when we love Elohim and guard his misvoth.
3	For this is the love of Elohim:
	to guard his misvoth;
	and his misvoth are not grievous.
4	Because everyone birthed of Elohim
	triumphs over the cosmos:
	and this is the triumph that triumphs over the cosmos
	— our trust.
5	Who triumphs over the cosmos
	— except whoever trusts
	that Yah Shua is the Son of Elohim?
6	This is he who came through water and blood
	— Yah Shua Messiah;
	not in water only, but in water and blood:
	and the Spirit witnesses, because the Spirit is truth.
7	Because these three witness in the heavens:
	the Father, the Word and the Holy Spirit:
	and these three are one.
8	And these three witness in earth:
	the Spirit and the water and the blood:
	and these three are in one.
9	If we take the witness of humanity,
	the witness of Elohim is greater:
	because this is the witness of Elohim
	which he witnessed concerning his Son.
10	Whoever trusts on the Son of Elohim
	has the witness in himself: whoever trusts not Elohim
	makes him a liar;
	because he trusts not in the witness
	Elohim witnessed concerning his Son.
11	And this is the witness:
	that Elohim gives us eternal life
	and this life is in his Son.
12	whoever has the Son has life;
	and whoever has not the Son of Elohim has not life.
13	These *things* have I *written* **scribed** unto you
	that *believe on* **trust**
	in the name of the Son of *God* **Elohim**;
	that ye may know that ye have eternal life,
	and that ye may *believe* **trust**
	on **in** the name of the Son of *God* **Elohim**.
14	And this is the *confidence* **boldness**
	that we have *in* **toward** him, that,
	if — whatever we ask any thing according to his will,
	he heareth us:
15	And *if* **whenever** we know that he hear us,

1 JOHN/YOCHANAN 5

    whatsoever we ask,
we know that we have the *petitions* **requests**
that we *desired* **asked** of him.
16   *If* **Whenever** any *man* **one**
see his brother sin a sin which is not unto death,
he shall ask,
and he shall give him life
for them that sin not unto death.
There is a sin unto death:
I do not *say* **word** that he shall *pray* **ask** for it.
17   All *unrighteousness* **injustice** is sin:
and there is a sin not unto death.
18   We know that
whosoever is born **birthed** of *God* **Elohim** sinneth not;
but he that is begotten **birthed** of *God* **Elohim**
keepeth **guardeth** himself,
and that *wicked* **evil** one toucheth him not.
19   And we know that we are of *God* **Elohim**,
and the whole *world* **cosmos**
lieth in *wickedness* **the evil**.
20   And we know that the Son
of *God* **Elohim** is come,
and hath given us *an understanding* **a mind**,
that we may know him that is true,
and we are in him that is true,
even in his Son *Jesus Christ* **Yah Shua Messiah**.
This is the true *God* **Elohim**, and eternal life.
21   Little children, *keep* **guard**
yourselves from idols.
Amen.
13   I scribe these to you
who trust in the name of the Son of Elohim;
so that you know you have eternal life
and that you trust in the name of the Son of Elohim.
14   And this is the boldness we have toward him
that if — whatever we ask according to his will,
he hears us:
15   and whenever we know that he hears us
— whatever we ask
we know we have the requests we ask of him.
16   Whenever anyone sees his brother sin a sin
not to death,
have him ask;
and he gives him life for them who sin
not to death.
There is a sin to death:
I word not that he ask for it.
17   All injustice is sin:
and there is a sin not to death.
18   We know that everyone is birthed of Elohim
sins not;
but everyone birthed of Elohim
guards himself;
and the evil touches him not.
19   And we know we are of Elohim
and the whole cosmos lies in the evil.
20   And we know the Son of Elohim has come
and gives us a mind to know him who is true:
and we are in him who is true
— in his Son Yah Shua Messiah.
This is the true Elohim and eternal life.
21   Little children:
guard yourselves from idols.
Amen.

Salutation

1 The elder unto the *elect* **select** lady* and her children,
whom I love in the truth;
*lady: feminine of adoni
and not I only,
but also all they that have known the truth;

2 *For the truth's sake* **Because of the truth**,
which *dwelleth* **abideth** in us,
and shall be with us *for ever* **unto the eons**.

3 *Grace* **Charism** shall be with you,
mercy, *and peace* **shalom**,
from *God* **Elohim** the Father,
and from
the Lord Jesus Christ **Adonay Yah Shua Messiah**,
the Son of the Father, in truth and love.

4 I *rejoiced greatly* **cheered extremely**
that I found of thy children walking in truth,
exactly as we have *received* **taken**
a *commandment* **misvah** from the Father.

5 And now I beseech thee, lady,
not as though I *wrote* **scribed**
a new *commandment* **misvah** unto thee,
but that which we had from the beginning,
that we love one another.

6 And this is love,
that we walk after his *commandments* **misvoth**.
This is the *commandment* **misvah**,
That, **exactly** as ye have heard from the beginning,
ye should walk in it.

The Antimessiah

7 *For* **Because** many *deceivers* **seducers**
are entered into the *world* **cosmos**,
who *confess* **profess** not
that *Jesus Christ* **Yah Shua Messiah** is come in the flesh.
This is *a deceiver* **the seducer**
and *an antichrist* **the antimessiah**.
1 Yahn 2:18, 22, 4:3

8 Look to yourselves,
that we lose not those *things* which
we have *wrought* **worked**,
but that we *receive* **take** a full reward.

9 Whosoever transgresseth,
and abideth not in the doctrine of *Christ* **the Messiah**,
hath not *God* **Elohim**.
He that abideth in the doctrine of *Christ* **the Messiah**,
he hath both the Father and the Son.

10 If there come any unto you,
and bring not this doctrine,
receive **take** him not into your house,
neither *bid him God speed* **word to him, Cheers!**:

11 For he that *biddeth* **wordeth** to him,
God speed **Cheers!**
is partaker **partaketh** of his evil *deeds* **works**.

Final Salute

12 Having *many things* **much**
to *write* **scribe** unto you,
I *would* **willed** not
write with paper **through sheet** and ink:
but I *trust* **hope** to come unto you,
and speak *face* **mouth** to *face* **mouth**,
that our *joy* **cheer** may be *full* **fulfilled/shalamed**.

13 The children of thy *elect*
select sister *greet* **salute** thee.
Amen. To the select lady* and her children,
whom I love in the truth:
*lady: feminine of adoni
and not I only,

Salutation

1 The elder:
but also all who know the truth;

2 because of the truth abiding in us
being with us to the eons.

3 Charism, mercy and shalom be with you;
from Elohim the Father
and from Adonay Yah Shua Messiah
the Son of the Father
in truth and love.

4 I cheer extremely
to find some of your children walking in truth,
exactly as we took a misvah from the Father.

5 And now I beseech you, lady,
not as though I scribed a new misvah to you,
but what we had from the beginning
— to love one another.

6 And this is love:
to walk after his misvoth.
This is the misvah,
that exactly as you heard from the beginning
— walk in it.

The Antimessiah

7 Because many seducers enter the cosmos,
who profess not
that Yah Shua Messiah is come in the flesh.

This is the seducer and the antimessiah.
1 Yahn 2:18, 22, 4:3

8 Look to yourselves
— that we lose not what we worked
but that we take a full reward.
9 Whoever transgresses
and abides not in the doctrine of the Messiah,
has not Elohim:
whoever abides in the doctrine of the Messiah,
he has both the Father and the Son.
10 If any come to you and bring not this doctrine,
neither take him into your house,
nor word to him, Cheers!:
11 For whoever words him, Cheers!
partakes of his evil works.

FINAL SALUTE

12 Having much to scribe to you,
I will not through sheet and ink:
but I hope to come to you and speak mouth to mouth
to fulfill/shalam our cheer.
13 The children of your select sister salute you.
Amen.

Salutation

1 The elder unto the *wellbeloved* **beloved** Gaius,
whom I love in the truth.
2 Beloved, I *wish above* **vow concerning** all *things*
that thou mayest prosper and be *in health* **whole**,
even **exactly** as thy soul prospereth.
3 For I *rejoiced greatly* **cheered extremely**,
when the brethren came
and *testified* **witnessed** of the truth that is in thee,
even as thou walkest in the truth.
4 I have no greater *joy* **cheer than these,**
than to hear that my children walk in truth.

Being Trustworthy

5 Beloved, thou *doest faithfully*
dealest trustworthily
whatsoever **whenever** thou *doest* **workest**
to the brethren, and to strangers;
6 Which have *borne witness*
witnessed of thy *charity* **love**
before **in the sight of** the *church* **ecclesia**:
whom if thou *bring* forward *on their journey*
after a godly sort **worthily of Elohim**,
thou shalt do well:
7 *Because* **Indeed** that for his
name's sake they went *forth*,
taking *nothing* **naught** of the *Gentiles* **goyim**.
8 *So* We therefore ought **are**
indebted to *receive* **take** such,
that we might *be fellowhelpers* **become co—workers**
to the truth.
9 I *wrote* **scribed** unto the *church* **ecclesia**:
but Diotrephes,
who *loveth* **befriendeth**
to have the preeminence among them,
receiveth us not.
10 *Wherefore, if* **So whenever** I come,
I *will* **shall** remember his *deeds* **works** which he doeth,
prating **babbling** against us with *malicious* **evil** words:
and not *content therewith* **satisfied by these**,
neither doth he himself receive the brethren,
and forbiddeth them that *would* **will**,
and casteth them out of the *church* **ecclesia**.
11 Beloved, *follow* **mimic** not that which is evil,
but that which is good.
He that doeth good is of *God* **Elohim**:
but he that doeth evil hath not seen *God* **Elohim**.
12 Demetrius *hath good report*
is witnessed of all *men*,
and of the truth itself:
yea, and we *also bear record* **witness**;
and ye know that our *record* **witness** is true.

Final Salute

13 I had *many things* **much** to *write* **scribe**,
but I *will* **shall** not *with* **through** ink and *pen* **reed**
write **scribe** unto thee:
14 But I *trust* **hope** I shall
shortly **straightway** see thee,
and we shall speak *face* **mouth** to *face* **mouth**.
Peace **Shalom** be to thee. *Our* friends salute thee.
Greet **Salute** the friends by name.

Salutation

1 The elder:
To the beloved Gaius,
whom I love in the truth:
2 Beloved, I vow concerning all
that you prosper and be whole,
exactly as your soul prospers.
3 For I cheered extremely
when the brothers came
and witnessed of the truth within you;
even as you walk in the truth.
4 I have no greater cheer than these
— than to hear that my children walk in truth.

Being Trustworthy

5 Beloved, deal trustworthily
whenever you work to the brothers and to strangers
6 — who witnessed of your love
in the sight of the ecclesia:
whom, if you forward worthily of Elohim,
you do well:
7 indeed, for sake of his name they went forth
taking naught of the goyim.
8 So we are indebted to take such
to become co—workers to the truth.
9 I scribed to the ecclesia:
but Diotrephes,
who befriends preeminence among them,
receives us not.
10 So, whenever I come,
I remember the works he does,
babbling against us with evil words:
and not satisfied by these
he himself receives not the brothers
and forbids them who so will
— and casts them from the ecclesia.

11   Beloved, mimic not evil, but good.
everyone doing good is of Elohim:
but everyone doing evil has not seen Elohim.
12   Demetrius is witnessed by all,
and of the truth itself:
yes, and we witness;
and you know our witness is true.

Final Salute

13   I have much to scribe,
but I scribe not to you through ink and reed:
14   and I hope to see you straightway
and speak mouth to mouth.
Shalom to you.
The friends salute you.
Salute the friends by name.

Prologue

1 The *Revelation* **Apocalypse**
of *Jesus Christ* **Yah Shua Messiah**,
which *God* **Elohim** gave unto him,
to shew unto his servants *things* **those**
which must *shortly come to pass* **quickly become**;
and he *sent* **apostolized** and signified it
by **through** his angel
unto his servant *John* **Yahn**:

2 Who *bare record* **witnessed**
of the word of *God* **Elohim**,
and of the *testimony* **witness**
of *Jesus Christ* **Yah Shua Messiah**,
and of all *things* that he saw.

The First Beatitude

3 Blessed is he that readeth,
and they that hear the words of this prophecy,
and *keep* **guard** those *things*
which are *written* **scribed** therein:
for the *time* **season** is *at hand* **near**.

Salutation From The Triune Elohim

4 *John* **Yahn** to the seven *churches* **ecclesiae**
which are in Asia:
Grace be **Charism** unto you, and *peace* **shalom**,
from him
which is, and which was, and which is to come
who is, and who was, and who is coming;
and from the seven Spirits
which are *before* **in sight of** his throne;

5 And from *Jesus Christ* **Yah Shua Messiah**,
who is the *faithful* **trustworthy** witness,
and the *first begotten* **firstborn** of the dead,
and the *prince* **arch** of the *kings* **sovereigns** of the earth.
Unto him that loved us,
and *washed* **bathed** us from our sins in his own blood,

6 And hath made us *kings* **sovereigns** and priests
unto *God* **Elohim** and his Father;
to him be glory and *dominion* **power**
for ever and ever **unto the eons of the eons**.
Amen.

7 Behold, he cometh with clouds;
and every eye shall see him,
and they *also* which pierced him:
and all *kindreds* **scions** of the earth
shall *wail* **chop** because of him.
Even so **Yes**, Amen.

8 *I am Alpha and Omega* **I AM the A and the Ù**,
the beginning and the *ending* **completion/shalom**,
saith the Lord **wordeth Yah Veh**,
which is, and which was, and which is to come
who is, and who was, and who is coming,
the Almighty **Sabaoth**.

The Seven Scribings

9 I *John* **Yahn**, who also *am* your brother,
and *companion* **co—partaker** in tribulation,
and in the
kingdom **sovereigndom** and *patience* **endurance**
of *Jesus Christ* **Yah Shua Messiah**,
was **became** in the isle that is called Patmos,
for the word of *God* **Elohim**,
and for the *testimony* **witness**
of *Jesus Christ* **Yah Shua Messiah**.

10 I *was* **became** in *the* Spirit
on the Lord's **in Adonay's** day,
and heard behind me a *great* **mega** voice,
as of a trumpet,

11 *Saying* **Wording**,
I am Alpha and Omega **I AM the A and the Ù**,
the first and the *last* **final**:
and, What thou seest, *write* **scribe** in a *book* **scroll**,
and send it unto the seven *churches* **ecclesiae**
which are in Asia;
unto Ephesus, and unto Smyrna, and unto Pergamos,
and unto Thyatira, and unto Sardis,
and unto Philadelphia, and unto Laodicea.

12 And I turned to see the
voice that spake with me.
And *being turned* **turning**,
I saw seven golden *candlesticks* **menorah**;

13 And in the midst of the
seven *candlesticks* **menorah**

Prologue

1 The Apocalypse of Yah Shua Messiah,
that Elohim gave him
to show his servants what must quickly become;
and he apostolized and signified it through his angel
to his servant Yahn:

2 who witnessed of the word of Elohim
and of the witness of Yah Shua Messiah
and of all he saw.

The First Beatitude

3 Blessed — whoever reads
and whoever hears the words of this prophecy
and guard those scribed therein:
for the season is near.

REVELATION/HAGILU NATAN ELOHIM 1, 2

Salutation From The Triune Elohim

4 Yahn to the seven ecclesiae in Asia:
Charism to you and shalom,
from him who is and who was and who is coming;
and from the seven Spirits in sight of his throne;
5 and from Yah Shua Messiah
the trustworthy witness
and the firstborn from the dead
and the arch of the sovereigns of the earth.
To him who loved us
and bathed us from our sins in his own blood
6 and made us sovereigns and priests
to Elohim and his Father;
to him be glory and power to the eons of the eons.
Amen.
7 Behold, he comes with clouds;
and every eye sees him
and those who pierced him:
and all scions of the earth chop because of him.
Yes, Amen.
8 I AM the A and the Ù,
the beginning and the completion/shalom,
words Yah Veh,
who is and who was and who is coming — Sabaoth.

The Seven Scribings

9 I Yahn
also your brother and co—partaker in tribulation
and in the sovereigndom
and endurance of Yah Shua Messiah,
became in the isle called Patmos
for the word of Elohim
and for the witness of Yah Shua Messiah.
10 I became in Spirit in the day of Adonay;
and heard behind me a mega voice as of a trumpet,
11 wording,
I AM the A and the Ù — the first and the final:
and,
What you see, scribe in a scroll
and send it to the seven ecclesiae in Asia:
to Ephesus
and to Smyrna
and to Pergamos
and to Thyatira
and to Sardis
and to Philadelphia
and to Laodicea.
12 And I turn to see the voice that speaks with me;
and turning, I see seven golden menorah:
13 and midst the seven menorah;
one like unto the Son of *man* **humanity**,
clothed with a garment down **endued** to the foot,
and girt *about* **to** the *paps* **breasts**
with a golden girdle.
14 His head and *his* hairs *were* white *like* **as** wool,
as white as snow;
and his eyes *were* as a flame of fire;
15 And his feet like *unto fine*
brass **brilliant copper**,
as *if they burned* **fired** in a furnace;
and his voice as the *sound* **voice** of many waters.
16 And he had in his right hand seven stars:
and out of his mouth *went* **proceeded**
a sharp *twoedged sword* **double—mouthed sabre**:
and his *countenance* **visage**
was as the sun *shineth* **manifesteth**
in his *strength* **dynamis**.
17 And when I saw him, I fell
at **toward** his feet as dead.
And he *laid* **placed** his right hand upon
me, *saying* **wording** unto me,
Fear **Awe** not; *I am* **I AM** the first and the *last* **final**:
18 I am — he that liveth, and *was* **became** dead;
and, behold, I am alive *for evermore* **unto the eons**,
Amen;
and have the keys of *hell* **Hades/Sheol** and of death.
19 *Write the things* **Scribe**
those which thou hast seen,
and *the things* **those** which are,
and *the things which shall be* **those about to become**
hereafter **after these**;
20 The mystery of the seven stars
which thou sawest *in* **at** my right *hand*,
and the seven golden *candlesticks* **menorah**.
The seven stars
are the angels of the seven *churches* **ecclesiae**:
and the seven *candlesticks* **menorah** which thou sawest
are the seven *churches* **ecclesiae**.

The First Scribing

2 Unto the angel
of the *church* **ecclesia** of *Ephesus* **Ephesians**
write **scribe**;
These *things saith* **wordeth** he
that *holdeth* **empowereth** the seven stars
in his right *hand*,
who walketh in the midst
of the seven golden *candlesticks* **menorah**;
2 I know thy works, and thy labour,
and thy *patience* **endurance**,
and *how* **that** thou canst not bear them which are evil:

	and thou hast *tried* **tested** them	18	— the living who became dead;
	which *say they are* **profess to be** apostles, and are not,		and behold, I am alive to the eons;
	and hast found them *liars* **pseudos**:		Amen:
3	And hast borne, and hast *patience* **endurance**,		and have the keys of Hades/Sheol and of death.
	and for my name's sake	19	Scribe those you saw
	hast laboured, and hast not *fainted* **wearied**.		and those being
4	*Nevertheless* **Yet** I have *somewhat* against thee,		and those to become after these.
	because thou hast *left* **forsaken** thy first love.	20	The mystery of the seven stars
5	*So* Remember *therefore*		you see at my right
	from whence thou art fallen,		and the seven golden menorah:
	and repent, and do the first works;		The seven stars are the angels of the seven ecclesiae:
	or else I will **if not I shall** come unto thee quickly,		and the seven menorah you see
	and *will remove* **shall stir** thy *candlestick* **menorah**		are the seven ecclesiae.

The First Scribing

	out of his place,	**2**	To the angel of the ecclesia of Ephesians,
	except **unless** thou repent.		scribe:
6	But this thou hast,		Thus words he
	that thou hatest the *deeds* **works** of the Nicolaitanes,		who empowers the seven stars in his right;
	which I also hate.		who walks midst the seven golden menorah:
7	He that hath an ear,	2	I know your works
	let him hear what the Spirit *saith* **wordeth**		and your labor and your endurance;
	unto the *churches* **ecclesiae**;		and that you can not bear them who are evil:
	To him that *overcometh* **triumpheth**		and you tested them who profess to be apostles
	will **shall** I give to eat of the *tree* **staff** of life,		and are not;
	which is in the midst of the paradise of *God* **Elohim**.		and found them to be pseudos:
		3	and bear and have endurance;
			and for sake of my name, labor and weary not.
		4	Yet I have against you
			because you forsook your first love.
		5	So remember whence you fell
			and repent and do the first works;
			and if not, I come to you quickly
			and stir your menorah from its place
			unless you repent.
		6	But this you have:
			you hate the works of the Nicolaitanes,
			which I also hate.
		7	Whoever has an ear,
			hear what the Spirit words to the ecclesiae:
			Whoever triumphs
			I give to eat of the staff of life
			midst the paradise of Elohim.

The Second Scribing

8	And unto the angel	8	And to the angel of the ecclesia of Smyrnians,
	of the *church in Smyrna* **ecclesia of Smyrnians**		scribe:
	write **scribe**;		Thus words the first and the final
	These *things saith* **wordeth** the first and the *last* **final**,		who became dead and lives:
	which *was* **became** dead, and is alive;	9	I know your works and tribulation and poverty
9	I know thy works, and tribulation, and poverty,		
	(but thou art rich)		
	one like to the Son of humanity		
	endued to the foot		
	and girt to the breasts with a golden girdle:		
14	his head and hairs		
	— white as wool — as white as snow;		
	and his eyes as a flame of fire;		
15	and his feet like brilliant		
	copper fired in a furnace;		
	and his voice as the voice of many waters.		
16	And having seven stars in his right hand:		
	and a sharp double—mouthed sabre		
	proceeding from his mouth:		
	and his visage manifests as the sun in its dynamis.		
17	And when I see him, I fall		
	toward his feet as dead.		
	And he places his right hand on me,		
	wording to me,		
	Awe not — I AM the first and the final:		

— but you are rich;
and *I know* the blasphemy of them
which *say they* **word themselves**
are Jews **to be Yah Hudiym**,
and are not, but *are* the synagogue of Satan.

10 *Fear* **Awe** none of those *things*
which thou *shalt* **art about to** suffer: behold,
the devil shall **Diabolos is about to** cast *some of* you
into *prison* **the guardhouse**,
that ye may be *tried* **tested**;
and ye shall have tribulation ten days:
be thou *faithful* **trustworthy** unto death,
and I *will* **shall** give thee a *crown* **wreath** of life.

11 He that hath an ear,
let him hear what the Spirit *saith* **wordeth**
unto the *churches* **ecclesiae**;
He that *overcometh* **triumpheth**
shall not **no way** be *hurt* **injured** of the second death.

THE THIRD SCRIBING

12 And to the angel
of the *church* **ecclesia** in Pergamos
write **scribe**;
These *things saith* **wordeth** he
which hath the sharp
sword with two edges **double—mouthed sabre**;

13 I know thy works, and
where thou *dwellest* **settlest**,
even where Satan's *seat* **throne** is:
and thou *holdest fast* **empowerest** my name,
and hast not denied my *faith* **trust**,
even in those days wherein Antipas
was my *faithful martyr* **trustworthy witness**,
who was *slain* **slaughtered** among you,
where Satan *dwelleth* **settleth**.

14 But I have a few *things* against thee,
because thou hast there
them that *hold* **empower** the doctrine of *Balaam* **Bilam**,
who *taught Balac* **doctrinated in Balaq**
to cast a *stumblingblock* **scandal**
before **in the sight of** the *children* **sons** of *Israel* **Yisra El**,
to eat *things sacrificed unto idols* **idol sacrifices**,
and to *commit fornication* **whore**.

15 *So* **Thus** hast thou also them
that *hold* **empower** the doctrine of the Nicolaitanes,
which *thing* I hate.

16 Repent;
or else I will **if not I shall** come unto thee quickly,
and *will fight against* **shall war with** them
with **in** the *sword* **sabre** of my mouth.

17 He that hath an ear,
let him hear what the Spirit *saith* **wordeth**
unto the *churches* **ecclesiae**;
To him that *overcometh* **triumpheth**
will **shall** I give to eat of the *hidden* **secreted** manna,
and *will* **shall** give him a white *stone* **pebble**,
and in the *stone* **pebble** a new name *written* **scribed**,
which no *man* **one** knoweth
saving **except** he that *receiveth* **taketh** it.

THE FOURTH SCRIBING

18 And unto the angel
of the *church* **ecclesia** in Thyatira
write **scribe**;
These *things saith* **wordeth** the Son of *God* **Elohim**,
who hath his eyes *like unto* **as** a flame of fire,
and his feet *are like fine brass* **as brilliant copper**;

19 I know thy works, and *charity* **love**,
and *service* **ministry**, and *faith* **trust**,
and thy *patience* **endurance**, and thy works;
and the *last to be* **final** more than the first.

20 *Notwithstanding* **Still** I have
a few *things* against thee,
because thou *sufferest* **allowest**
that woman *Jezebel* **Iy Zebel**,
which *calleth* **wordeth** herself a prophetess,
to *teach* **doctrinate** and to seduce my servants
to *commit fornication* **whore**,
and to eat *things sacrificed unto idols* **idol sacrifices**.

21 And I gave her *space* **time** to repent
of her *fornication* **whoredom**;
and she repented not.

22 Behold, I *will* **shall** cast her into a bed,
and them that *commit adultery* **adulterize** with her
and the blasphemy of them
who word themselves to be Yah Hudiym
and are naught but the synagogue of Satan.

10 Awe none of those you are about to suffer:
behold,
Diabolos is about to cast you in the guardhouse,
to test;
and you have tribulation ten days:
become trustworthy to death
and I give you a wreath of life.

11 Whoever has an ear,
hear what the Spirit words to the ecclesiae:
Whoever triumphs
is never no way injured of the second death.

THE THIRD SCRIBING

12 And to the angel of the ecclesia in Pergamos,
scribe:

Thus words he
who has the sharp double—mouthed sabre:
13 I know your works and where you settle
— where the throne of Satan is:
and you empower my name
and deny not my trust
— even in those days wherein Antipas
my trustworthy witness was slaughtered among you
— where Satan settles.
14 But I have a few against you,
because you have them
who empower the doctrine of Bilam,
who doctrinated in Balaq
to cast a scandal in the sight of the sons of Yisra El;
to eat idol sacrifices and to whore.
15 Thus you also have them
who empower the doctrine of the Nicolaitanes
— which I hate.
16 Repent:
if not I come to you quickly
and war with them in the sabre of my mouth.
17 Whoever has an ear,
hear what the Spirit words to the ecclesiae:
Whoever triumphs
I give to eat of the secreted manna;
and give him a white pebble;
and in the pebble scribe a new name
that no one knows except whoever takes it.

The Fourth Scribing

18 And to the angel of the ecclesia in Thyatira,
scribe:
Thus words the Son of Elohim
who has his eyes as a flame of fire
and his feet as brilliant copper:
19 I know your works and
love and ministry and trust
and your endurance and your works:
and the final more than the first.
20 Still, I have a few against you,
because you allow that woman Iy Zebel,
who words herself, Prophetess,
to doctrinate and to seduce my servants
to whore and to eat idol sacrifices:
21 and I gave her time to repent of her whoredom
and she repented not.
22 Behold, I cast her into a bed
and whoever adulterizes with her
into great tribulation
— unless they repent of their works:
23 and I slaughter her children in death:

so that all the ecclesiae knows that I AM:
who searches the reins and hearts:
and I give to each of you according to your works.
24 But I word to you and to the rest in Thyatira
— as many as hold not this doctrine
and who know not the depths of Satan,
as they word:
I put no other burden upon you.
25 But empower what you have till ever I come.
26 And whoever triumphs
and guards my works to the completion/shalom,
I give him authority over the goyim:
27 and he shepherds them in a scion of iron,
to shatter as the vessels of a potter:
even as I also took from my Father:
28 and I give him the morning star.
29 Whoever has an ear,
hear what the Spirit words to the ecclesiae.

The Fifth Scribing

3 And to the angel of the ecclesia in Sardis,
scribe:
Thus words he
who has the seven Spirits of Elohim
and the seven stars:
I know your works
— that you have a name that you live, and are dead.
2 Be watchful
and establish the rest who are about to die:
for I have not found your works fulfilled/shalamed
in the sight of Elohim.
3 So remember how you took and heard:
and guard and repent:
so whenever you watch not
I come upon you as a thief; and you never no
way know what hour I come upon you.
4 You have a few names — even in Sardis
who stained not their garments:
and they walk with me in white
because they are worthy.
5 Whoever triumphs arrays in white garments:
and I never no way
erase his name from the scroll of life,
and I confess his name in sight of my Father
and in sight of his angels.
6 Whoever has an ear,
hear what the Spirit words to the ecclesiae.

The Sixth Scribing

7 And to the angel of the ecclesia in Philadelphia,

scribe:
Thus words the holy, the true, who has
the key of David: who opens and no one
shuts and shuts and no one opens:
8   I know your works: behold,
I give an open portal in your sight
and no one can shut it:
because you have a little dynamis
and guard my word
and deny not my name.
into great tribulation,
except **unless** they repent of their *deeds* **works**.
23   And I *will kill* **shall slaughter** her children
with **in** death;
and all the *churches* **ecclesiae** shall know
that *I am he* **I AM**:
which searcheth the reins and hearts:
and I *will* **shall** give unto *every one* **each** of you
according to your works.
24   But unto you I *say* **word**, and
unto the rest in Thyatira,
as many as have not this doctrine,
and which have not known the depths of Satan,
as they *speak* **word**;
I *will* **shall** put upon you none other burden.
25   But that which ye have *already*
hold fast **empower** till **ever** I come.
26   And he that *overcometh* **triumpheth**,
and *keepeth* **guardeth** my works
unto the *end* **completion/shalom**,
to him
will **shall** I give *power* **authority** over the *nations* **goyim**:
27   And he shall *rule* **shepherd** them
with **in** a *rod* **scion** of iron;
as the vessels of a potter
shall they be *broken to shivers* **shattered**:
even as I *received* **also have taken** of my Father.
28   And I *will* **shall** give him the morning star.
29   He that hath an ear,
let him hear what the Spirit *saith* **wordeth**
unto the *churches* **ecclesiae**.

The Fifth Scribing

3   And unto the angel
of the *church* **ecclesia** in Sardis *write* **scribe**;
These *things saith* **wordeth** he
that hath the seven Spirits of *God* **Elohim**,
and the seven stars;
I know thy works,
that thou hast a name that thou livest, and art dead.

2   Be watchful,
and *strengthen* **establish** the *things which remain* **rest**,
that are *ready* **about** to die:
for I have not found thy works
perfect **fulfilled/shalamed**
before God **in the sight of Elohim**.
3   **So** Remember *therefore*
how thou hast *received* **taken** and heard,
and *hold fast* **guard**, and repent.
if therefore **So whenever** thou shalt not watch,
I *will* **shall** come on thee as a thief,
and thou shalt not **no way** know
what hour I *will* **shall** come upon thee.
4   Thou hast a few names even in Sardis
which have not *defiled* **stained** their garments;
and they shall walk with me in white:
for **because** they are worthy.
5   He that *overcometh* **triumpheth**,
the same shall be *clothed* **arrayed**
in white *raiment* **garments**;
and I *will* **shall** not **no way**
blot out **erase** his name
out of the *book* **scroll** of life,
but I *will* **shall** confess his name
before **in sight of** my Father,
and *before* **in sight of** his angels.
6   He that hath an ear,
let him hear what the Spirit *saith* **wordeth**
unto the *churches* **ecclesiae**.

The Sixth Scribing

7   And to the angel
of the *church* **ecclesia** in Philadelphia *write* **scribe**;
These *things saith he that is* **wordeth the** holy,
he that is **the** true, he that hath the key of David,
he that openeth, and no *man* **one** shutteth;
and shutteth, and no *man* **one** openeth;
8   I know thy works: behold,
I have *set before thee* **given in thy sight**
an open *door* **portal**,
and no *man* **one** can shut it:
for **because** thou hast a little *strength* **dynamis**,
and hast *kept* **guarded** my word,
and hast not denied my name.
9   Behold,
I *will make* **shall give** them of the synagogue of Satan,
which *say they* **word themselves**
are Jews **to be Yah Hudiym**,
and are not, but *do* lie;
behold, I *will* **shall** make them to come and worship
before **in sight of** thy feet,

and to know that I have loved thee.
10 Because
thou hast *kept* **guarded** the word of my patience,
I also *will keep* **shall guard** thee
from the hour of *temptation* **testing**,
which shall *about to* come upon all the world,
to *try* **test** them that *dwell* **settle** upon the earth.
11 Behold, I come quickly:
hold **empower** that *fast* which thou hast, that
no *man* **one** take thy *crown* **wreath**.
12 Him that *overcometh* **triumpheth**
will **shall** I make a pillar
in the *temple* **nave** of my *God* **Elohim**,
and he shall *go no more* **not no way still go** out:
and I *will write* **shall scribe** upon him
the name of my *God* **Elohim**,
and the name of the city of my *God* **Elohim**,
which is **the** new *Jerusalem* **Yeru Shalem**,
which *cometh down* **descendeth**
out of *heaven* **the heavens**
from my *God* **Elohim**:
and *I will write upon him* my new name.
13 He that hath an ear,
let him hear what the Spirit *saith* **wordeth**
unto the *churches* **ecclesiae**.

THE SEVENTH SCRIBING

14 And unto the angel
of the *church* **ecclesia** of the Laodiceans
write **scribe**;
These *things saith* **wordeth** the Amen,
the *faithful* **trustworthy** and true witness,
the beginning of the creation of *God* **Elohim**;
15 I know thy works, that thou
art neither cold nor hot:
I would **O that** thou wert cold or hot.
16 So then because thou art lukewarm,
and neither cold nor hot,
I *will spue* **am about to vomit** thee out of my mouth.
17 Because thou *sayest* **wordest**,
Because I am rich,
and *increased with goods* **enriched**,
and have need of *nothing* **naught**;
and knowest not that thou art *wretched* **miserable**,
and *miserable* **least mercied**,
and poor, and blind, and naked:
18 I counsel thee to *buy* **market** of me
gold *tried in* **fired by** the fire,
that thou mayest be *rich* **enriched**;
and white *raiment* **garments**,
that thou mayest be *clothed* **arrayed**,

and that the shame of thy nakedness
do not *appear* **be manifested**;
and anoint thine eyes with *eyesalve* **poultice**,
that thou mayest see.
19 As many as *ever* I *love* **befriend**,
I *rebuke* **reprove** and *chasten* **discipline**:
be zealous therefore, and repent.
20 Behold, I stand at the *door* **portal**, and knock:
if **whenever** any *man* **one** hear my
voice, and open the *door* **portal**,
I *will* **shall** come in to him,
and *will* **shall** sup with him, and he with me.
21 To him that *overcometh* **triumpheth**
will **shall** I *grant* **give** to sit with me in my throne,
even as I also *overcame* **triumphed**,
and am *set down* **seated** with my Father in his throne.
22 He that hath an ear,
let him hear what the Spirit *saith* **wordeth**
unto the *churches* **ecclesiae**.

IN SPIRIT, IN THE HEAVENS

4 After *this I looked* **these I**
perceived, and, behold,
a *door was* **portal** opened in *heaven* **the heavens**:
and the first voice which I heard
was as *it were* of a trumpet *talking* **speaking** with me;
9 Behold, I give them of the synagogue of Satan,
who word themselves to be Yah Hudiym
and are not, but lie:
behold,
I have them come and worship in sight of your feet
so that they know I loved you.
10 Because you guarded the word of my patience
I also guard you from the hour of testing
— about to come on all the world
to test them who settle on the earth.
11 Behold, I come quickly:
empower what you have
so no one takes your wreath.
12 Whoever triumphs
I make a pillar in the nave of my Elohim;
and he never no way still goes out:
and I scribe on him the name of my Elohim
and the name of the city of my Elohim
— the new Yeru Shalem
descending from the heavens from my Elohim
and my new name.
13 Whoever has an ear,
hear what the Spirit words to the ecclesiae.

The Seventh Scribing

14 And to the angel of the
ecclesia of the Laodiceans,
scribe:
These words the Amen,
the trustworthy and true witness,
the beginning of the creation of Elohim:
15 I know your works
— that you are neither cold nor hot:
O that you were cold or hot.
16 So because you are lukewarm
and neither cold nor hot,
I am about to vomit you from my mouth:
17 because you word,
Because I am rich and enriched and need naught!
— and know not that you are miserable
and least mercied and poor and blind and naked:
18 I counsel you to market of
me gold fired by the fire
to enrich you:
and white garments to array you
so that you not manifest
the shame of your nakedness:
and anoint your eyes with poultice
so that you see.
19 As many as ever I befriend
I reprove and discipline:
so be zealous and repent.
20 Behold, I stand at the portal and knock:
whenever anyone hears my voice
and opens the portal,
I come in to him and sup with him
— and he with me.
21 Whoever triumphs,
I give to sit with me in my throne;
even as I also triumphed
and sit with my Father in his throne.
22 Whoever has an ear,
hear what the Spirit words to the ecclesiae.

In Spirit, In The Heavens

4 After these I perceive, and behold,
an opened portal in the heavens:
and the first voice I hear
is as a trumpet speaking with me;
which said **wording**, Come up **Ascend** hither,
and I *will* **shall** shew thee *things*
those which must be *hereafter* **after these***.
*some mss place after these at the beginning of verse 2
2 And **after these*** *immediately* **straightway**
I *was in the* **became in** spirit: and, behold,
a throne *was* set in *heaven* **the heavens**,
and one sat on the throne.
3 And he that sat was *to look upon* **in vision**
like a jasper and a *sardine* **sardius** stone:
and there was a rainbow
round about **surrounding** the throne,
in *sight* **vision** like unto an emerald.
4 And *round about* **surrounding** the throne
were four and twenty *seats* **thrones**:
and upon the *seats* **thrones**
I saw four and twenty elders sitting,
clothed **arrayed** in white *raiment* **garments**;
and they had on their heads *crowns* **wreaths** of gold.
5 And out of the throne
proceeded lightnings and thunderings and voices:
and *there were* seven lamps of fire
burning *before* **in sight of** the throne,
which are the seven Spirits of *God* **Elohim**.
6 And *before* **in sight of** the throne
there was a sea of glass like *unto crystal* **crystaline**:
and in the midst of the throne,
and *round about* **surrounding** the throne,
were four *beasts* **live beings** full of eyes
before **in front** and *behind* **in back**.
7 And the first *beast* **live being** was like a lion,
and the second *beast* **live being** like a
calf, and the third *beast* **live being**
had a face as a *man* **human**,
and the fourth *beast* **live being** was like a flying eagle.
8 And the four *beasts had* **live beings were**
each *of them* **surrounded with** six wings *about him*;
and *they were* full of eyes within:
and they **have no** rest *not* day and night,
saying **wording**, Holy, holy, holy,
Lord God Almighty **Yah Veh El Sabaoth**,
which was, and is, and is to come
who was, and who is, and who is coming.
Yesha Yah 6:3
9 And when those *beasts* **live beings**
give glory and honour and *thanks* **eucharist**
to him that sat on the throne,
who liveth *for ever and ever* **unto the eons of the eons**,
10 The four and twenty elders shall fall *down*
before **in sight of** him that sat on the
throne, and worship him that liveth
for ever and ever **unto the eons of the eons**,
and cast their *crowns before* **wreaths
in sight of** the throne,
saying **wording**,
11 Thou art worthy, O *Lord* **Yah Veh**,

EDC Hebrew / English Bible

to *receive* **take** glory and honour and *power* **dynamis**:
for **because** thou hast created all *things*,
and for thy *pleasure* **will** they are and were created.

THE SEVEN SEALED SCROLL

5   And I saw *in* **on** the right *hand* of him
that sat on the throne
a *book written* **scroll scribed** within
and *on the backside* **in back**,
sealed with seven seals.

2   And I saw a strong angel
proclaiming **preaching** with a *loud* **mega** voice,
Who is worthy to open the *book* **scroll**,
and to loose the seals thereof?

3   And no *man* **one** in *heaven* **the heavens**,
nor in earth, neither under the earth,
was able to open the *book* **scroll**, neither to look thereon.

4   And I wept much,
because no *man* **one** was found worthy
to open and to read the *book* **scroll**,
neither to look thereon.

5   And one of the elders *saith* **wordeth** unto me,
Weep not:
behold, the Lion
wording, Ascend hither,
and I show you
what must be after these*.
*some mss place after these at the beginning of verse 2

2   And after these* straightway I became in spirit:
and behold,
a throne set in the heavens
and one sitting on the throne:

3   and he sitting
is in vision like stone — a jasper and a sardius:
and a rainbow surrounds the throne
in vision like an emerald.

4   And surrounding the throne,
twenty—four thrones:
and on the thrones I see twenty—four elders sitting
— arrayed in white garments;
and wreaths of gold on their heads:

5   and from the throne
proceed lightnings and thunderings and voices:
and seven lamps of fire
burning in sight of the throne
— which are the seven Spirits of Elohim:

6   and in sight of the throne
a sea of glass like crystaline:
and midst the throne and surrounding the throne,
four live beings full of eyes in front and in back.

REVELATION/HAGILU NATAN ELOHIM 5

7   And the first live being, like a lion;
and the second live being, like a calf;
and the third live being has a human face;
and the fourth live being, like a flying eagle.

8   And the four live beings
are each surrounded with six wings
and full of eyes within:
and they have no rest day and night,
wording, Holy, holy, holy, Yah Veh El Sabaoth,
who was and who is and who is coming.
Yesha Yah 6:3

9   And when the live beings
give glory and honor and eucharist
to him sitting on the throne
who lives to the eons of the eons,

10   the twenty—four elders fall
in sight of him sitting on the throne,
and worship him who lives to the eons of the eons
and cast their wreaths in sight of the throne,
wording,

11   You are worthy, O Yah Veh,
to take glory and honor and dynamis:
because you created all
and for your will they are and were created.

THE SEVEN SEALED SCROLL

5   And at the right of him sitting on the throne
I see a scroll scribed inside and backside
sealed with seven seals.

2   And I see a strong angel
preaching with a mega voice,
Who is worthy to open the scroll
and to loose the seals thereof?

3   — and no one is able
neither in the heavens,
nor in earth,
nor under the earth,
to open the scroll,
nor to look thereon.

4   And I weep much,
because no one is found worthy
to open and to read the scroll
nor to look thereon.

5   And one of the elders words to me,
Weep not:
behold, the Lion,
being of the *tribe* **scion** of *Juda* **Yah Hudah**,
the Root of David,
hath *prevailed* **triumphed** to open the *book* **scroll**,
and to loose the seven seals thereof.

647

REVELATION/HAGILU NATAN ELOHIM 5, 6

6 And I *beheld* **perceived**, and, *lo* **behold**,
in the midst of the throne
and of the four *beasts* **live beings**,
and in the midst of the elders,
stood a Lamb **standing**
as *it had* **having** been *slain* **slaughtered**,
having seven horns and seven eyes,
which are the seven Spirits of *God* **Elohim**
sent forth **apostolized** into all the earth.

7 And he came and took the *book* **scroll**
out of the right *hand* of him that sat upon the throne.

8 And when he had taken the *book* **scroll**,
the four *beasts* **live beings** and four and twenty elders
fell *down before* **in sight of** the Lamb,
having *every one* **each** of them *harps* **cithers**,
and golden *vials* **phials** full of *odours* **incense**,
which are the prayers of *saints* **the holy**.

9 And they sung a new *song* **ode**, *saying* **wording**,
Thou art worthy to take the *book* **scroll**,
and to open the seals thereof:
for **because** thou wast *slain* **slaughtered**,
and hast *redeemed* **marketed** us to *God* **Elohim**
by thy blood
out of every *kindred* **scion**, and tongue,
and people, and *nation* **goyim**;

10 And hast made us unto our *God* **Elohim**
kings **sovereigns** and priests:
and we shall reign on the earth.

11 And I *beheld* **perceived**,
and I heard the voice of many angels
round about **surrounding** the throne
and the *beasts* **live beings** and the elders:
and the number of them was
ten thousand **myriads** times *ten thousand* **myriads**,
and thousands of thousands;

12 *Saying* **Wording** with a *loud* **mega** voice,
Worthy is the Lamb that was *slain* **slaughtered**
to *receive power* **take dynamis**, and riches, and wisdom,
and *strength* **might**, and honour,
and glory, and *blessing* **eulogy**.

13 And every creature *which*
is in *heaven* **the heavens**,
and *on* **in** the earth, and under the earth,
and *such as are in* **upon** the sea,
and all *that are* in them,
heard I *saying* **wording**,
Blessing **Eulogy**, and honour, and glory, and power,
be unto him that sitteth upon the throne,
and unto the Lamb
for ever and ever **unto the eons of the eons**.

14 And the four *beasts said* **live beings worded**,
Amen.
And the four and twenty elders
fell *down* and worshipped him that liveth
for ever and ever **unto the eons of the eons**.

THE FIRST SEAL

6 And I saw when the Lamb
opened one of the seals,
and I heard, as *it were* the *noise* **voice** of thunder,
one of the four *beasts saying* **live beings wording**,
Come and see.

2 And I saw, and behold a white horse:
and he that sat on him had a bow;
and a *crown* **wreath** was given unto him:
and he went forth *conquering* **triumphing**,
and to *conquer* **triumph**.

THE SECOND SEAL

3 And when he had opened the second seal,
I heard the second *beast say* **live being wording**,
Come and see.

4 And there went out another horse *that was red*
— **fiery**:
and *power* was given to him that sat thereon
to take *peace* **shalom** from the earth,
and that they should *kill* **slaughter** one another:
and there was given unto him a *great* **mega** sword.
being of the scion of Yah Hudah, the Root of David,
triumphed to open the scroll
and to loose the seven seals thereof.

6 And I perceive, and behold,
midst the throne and the four live beings
and midst the elders
— a Lamb standing — as having been slaughtered
— having seven horns and seven eyes
which are the seven Spirits of Elohim
apostolized into all the earth.

7 And he comes and takes the scroll
from the right of him sitting upon the throne.

8 And when he takes the scroll,
the four live beings and twenty—four elders
fall in sight of the Lamb,
each of them having cithers
and golden phials full of incense
which are the prayers of the holy;

9 and they sing a new ode, wording,
You are worthy to take the scroll
and to open the seals thereof:
because you were slaughtered
and marketed us to Elohim by your blood

from every scion and tongue and people and goyim;
10 and made us sovereigns
and priests to our Elohim
to reign on the earth.
11 And I perceive and I hear
the voice of many angels surrounding the throne
and the live beings and the elders:
and their number is myriads times myriads
and thousands of thousands;
12 wording with a mega voice,
Worthy is the Lamb who was slaughtered
to take dynamis and riches and wisdom
and might and honor and glory and eulogy.
13 And I hear every creature in the heavens
and in the earth and under the earth
and on the sea and all therein,
wording, Eulogy and honor and glory and power,
to him sitting upon the throne
and to the Lamb to the eons of the eons.
14 And the four live beings word, Amen!
And the twenty—four elders fall
and worship him who lives to the eons of the eons.

The First Seal

6 And I see when the Lamb opens one of the seals
and I hear, as the voice of thunder,
one of the four live beings wording,
Come and see.
2 And I see, and behold, a white horse:
and he sitting on him has a bow;
and he is given a wreath:
and he goes triumphing and to triumph.

The Second Seal

3 And when he opens the second seal,
I hear the second live being wording,
Come and see.
4 And another horse goes — fiery:
and he sitting thereon
is given to take shalom from the earth;
and that they slaughter one another:
and he is given a mega sword.

The Third Seal

5 And when he had opened the third seal,
I heard the third *beast say* **live being wording**,
Come and see.
And I *beheld* **perceived**, and *lo* **behold** a black horse;
and he that sat on him
had a *pair of balances* **yoke** in his hand.

6 And I heard a voice
in the midst of the four *beasts say* **live beings wording**,
A *measure* **choinix** of *wheat* **grain**
for a *penny* **denarion**,
and three *measures* **choinixes** of barley
for a *penny* **denarion**;
and *see* thou *hurt* **injure** not the **olive** oil and the wine.

The Fourth Seal

7 And when he had opened the fourth seal,
I heard the voice of the fourth *beast* **live being**
say **wording**,
Come and see.
8 And I *looked* **perceived**, and
behold a *pale* **green** horse:
and his name that sat on him was Death,
and *Hell* **Hades/Sheol** followed with him.
And *power* **authority** was given unto them
over the fourth *part* of the earth,
to *kill with sword* **slaughter in sabre**,
and *with hunger* **in famine**,
and *with* **in** death, and *with* **by** the beasts of the earth.

The Fifth Seal

9 And when he had opened the fifth seal,
I saw under the **sacrifice** altar the souls of them
that were *slain* **slaughtered** for the word of *God* **Elohim**,
and for the *testimony* **witness** which they held:
10 And they cried with a *loud* **mega** voice,
saying **wording**,
How long **Until when**, O *Lord* **Despotes**,
the holy and **the** true,
dost thou not judge and avenge our blood
on **from** them that *dwell* **settle** on the earth?
11 And white *robes* **stoles**
were given unto *every one* **each** of them;
and it was *said* **rhetorized** unto them,
that they should rest yet for a little *season* **time**,
until their *fellowservants* **co—servants** also
and their brethren,
that should be killed **about to be slaughtered**
as they *were*,
should be fulfilled/**shalamed**.

The Sixth Seal

12 And I *beheld* **perceived**
when he had opened the sixth seal,
and, *lo* **behold**,
there *was a great earthquake* **became a mega quake**;
and the sun became black as *sackcloth* **saq** of hair,

and the moon became as blood;
13 And the stars of *heaven* **the heavens** fell
unto the earth, even as a fig tree casteth
her *untimely figs* **unripened**, when she is
shaken **quaked** of a *mighty* **mega** wind.
14 And the *heaven departed* **heavens separated**
as a scroll when it is *rolled together* **coiled**;
and every mountain and island
were *moved* **stirred** out of their places.
15 And the *kings* **sovereigns** of the earth,
and the *great men* **magistrates**, and the rich *men*,
and the *chief captains* **chiliarchs**,
and the *mighty men* **able**,
and every *bondman* **servant**,
and every *free man* **liberated**,
hid **secreted** themselves in the *dens* **grottos**
and in the rocks of the mountains;
16 And *said* **worded** to the mountains and rocks,
Fall on us,
and *hide* **secrete** us
from the face of him that sitteth on the throne,
and from the wrath of the Lamb:
17 *For* **Because** the *great* **mega**
day of his wrath is come;
and who shall be able to stand?

The Third Seal

5 And when he opens the third seal,
I hear the third live being wording,
Come and see.
And I perceive, and behold, a black horse;
and he sitting on him has a yoke in his hand.
6 And I hear a voice midst the four live beings,
wording,
A choinix of grain for a denarion
and three choinixes of barley for a denarion;
and injure not the olive oil and the wine.

The Fourth Seal

7 And when he opens the fourth seal,
I hear the voice of the fourth live being
wording,
Come and see.
8 And I perceive, and behold, a green horse:
and he sitting on him — his name is Death
and Hades/Sheol follows with him.
And they are given authority
over the fourth of the earth
to slaughter in sabre and in famine and in death
and by the beasts of the earth.

The Fifth Seal

9 And when he opens the fifth seal,
I see under the sacrifice altar
the souls of them slaughtered for the word of Elohim
and for the witness they held.
10 And they cry with a mega voice, wording,
Until when, O Despotes, the holy and the true,
judge you not, and avenge our blood
from them who settle on the earth?
11 And each of them is given white stoles;
and they are rhetorized to rest yet for a little time,
until their co—servants and their brothers
about to be slaughtered as they,
also be fulfilled/shalamed.

The Sixth Seal

12 And I perceive, when he opens the sixth seal;
and behold, a mega quake becomes;
and the sun becomes black as saq of hair
and the moon becomes as blood;
13 and the stars of the heavens fall to the earth,
even as a fig tree casts her unripened
when quaked by a mega wind:
14 and the heavens separate
as a scroll when it is coiled;
and every mountain and island
stirs from their places.
15 And the sovereigns of the earth
and the magistrates and the rich
and the chiliarchs and the able
and all the servants and all the liberated
secrete themselves in the grottos
and in the rocks of the mountains:
16 and word to the mountains and rocks,
Fall on us and secrete us
from the face of him sitting on the throne
and from the wrath of the Lamb:
17 because the mega day of his wrath is come;
and who is able to stand?

One Hundred Forty—Four Thousand Sealed

7 And after these *things* I saw four angels
standing on the four corners of the earth,
holding **overpowering** the four winds of the earth,
that the wind should not *blow* **puff** on the earth,
nor on the sea, nor on any tree.
2 And I saw another angel
ascending from the *east* **rising of the sun**,
having the seal of the living *God* **Elohim**:

and he cried with a *loud* **mega** voice to the four angels,
to whom it was given to *hurt* **injure**
the earth and the sea,

3 *Saying* **Wording**, *Hurt* **Injure** not the earth,
neither the sea, nor the trees,
till we have sealed the servants of our *God* **Elohim**
in their foreheads.

4 And I heard the number
of them which were sealed:
and there were — sealed
an hundred *and* forty *and* four thousand
of all the *tribes* **scions**
of the *children* **sons** of *Israel* **Yisra El**.

5 Of the *tribe* **scion** of *Juda* **Yah Hudah**
were sealed twelve thousand.
Of the *tribe* **scion** of *Reuben* **Reu Ben**
were sealed twelve thousand.
Of the *tribe* **scion** of Gad
were sealed twelve thousand.

6 Of the *tribe* **scion** of *Aser* **Asher**
were sealed twelve thousand.
Of the *tribe* **scion** of *Nepthalim* **Naphtali**
were sealed twelve thousand.
Of the *tribe* **scion** of *Manasses* **Menash Sheh**
were sealed twelve thousand.

7 Of the *tribe* **scion** of *Simeon* **Shimon**
were sealed twelve thousand.
Of the *tribe* **scion** of Levi
were sealed twelve thousand.
Of the *tribe* **scion** of *Issachar* **Yissachar**
were sealed twelve thousand.

8 Of the *tribe* **scion** of *Zabulon* **Zebulun**
were sealed twelve thousand.
Of the *tribe* **scion** of *Joseph* **Yoseph**
were sealed twelve thousand.
Of the *tribe* **scion** of *Benjamin* **Ben Yamin**
were sealed twelve thousand.

The Multitude From Mega Tribulation

9 After *this* **these** I *beheld* **perceived**, and, *lo* **behold**,
a *great* **vast** multitude, which no *man* **one** could number,
of all *nations* **goyim**, and *kindreds* **scions**,
and *people* **peoples**, and tongues,
stood before **standing in sight of** the throne,
and *before* **in sight of** the Lamb,
clothed **arrayed** with white *robes* **stoles**,
and *palms* **phoinix** in their hands;

10 And cried with a *loud* **mega**
voice, *saying* **wording**,
Salvation to our *God* **Elohim**
which sitteth upon the throne,
and unto the Lamb.

11 And all the angels stood
round about **surrounding** the throne,
and *about* the elders and the four *beasts* **live beings**,
and fell *before* **in sight of** the throne on their faces,
and worshipped *God* **Elohim**,

12 *Saying* **Wording**, Amen: *Blessing* **Eulogy**,
and glory, and wisdom, and *thanksgiving* **eucharist**,
and honour, and *power* **dynamis**, and might,
be unto our *God* **Elohim**
for ever and ever **unto the eons of the eons**.
Amen.

13 And one of the elders answered,
saying **wording** unto me,
What are these which are arrayed in white *robes* **stoles**?
and whence came they?

14 And I said unto him, *Sir* **Adonay**, thou knowest.
And he said to me,
These are they which came out of *great* **mega** tribulation,
and have *washed* **flowed** their *robes* **stoles**,
and *made them white* **whitened their stoles**
in the blood of the Lamb.

One Hundred Forty–Four Thousand Sealed

7 And after these I see four angels
standing on the four corners of the earth,
overpowering the four winds of the earth,
so that the wind puffs
neither on the earth nor on the sea nor on any tree.

2 And I see another angel
ascend from the rising of the sun,
having the seal of the living Elohim:
and he cries with a mega voice to the four angels,
who are given to injure the earth and the sea,

3 wording,
Injure neither the earth nor the sea nor the trees
until we seal the servants of our Elohim
in their foreheads.

4 And I hear the number sealed:
— sealed one hundred and forty–four thousand
of all the scions of the sons of Yisra El:

5 of the scion of Yah Hudah
twelve thousand sealed;
of the scion of Reu Ben twelve thousand sealed;
of the scion of Gad twelve thousand sealed;

6 of the scion of Asher twelve thousand sealed;
of the scion of Naphtali twelve thousand sealed;
of the scion of Menash Sheh twelve thousand sealed;

7   of the scion of Shimon twelve thousand sealed;
of the scion of Levi twelve thousand sealed; of
the scion of Yissachar twelve thousand sealed;
8 of the scion of Zebulun twelve thousand sealed;
of the scion of Yoseph twelve thousand sealed; of
the scion of Ben Yamin twelve thousand sealed.

THE MULTITUDE FROM MEGA TRIBULATION

9   After these I perceive, and behold,
a vast multitude, which no one could number,
of all goyim and scions and peoples and tongues,
standing in sight of the throne and in sight of the Lamb
arrayed with white stoles and phoinix in their hands;
10   and crying with a mega voice, wording,
Salvation to our Elohim sitting upon the throne
and to the Lamb.
11   And all the angels
and the elders and the four live beings
stand surrounding the throne
and fall on their faces in sight of the throne
and worship Elohim,
12   wording, Amen:
Eulogy and glory and wisdom and eucharist
and honor and dynamis and might
to our Elohim to the eons of the eons.
Amen.
13   And one of the elders answers, wording to me,
Who are these arrayed in white stoles?
And whence came they?
14   And I say to him, Adonay, you know.
And he says to me,
These are they coming from mega tribulation
who flowed their stoles and whitened their stoles
in the blood of the Lamb:
15   *Therefore* **Because of this**
are they *before* **in sight of** the throne of *God* **Elohim**
and *serve* **liturgize** him day and night in his *temple* **nave**:
and he that sitteth on the throne
shall *dwell* **tabernacle** among them.
16   They shall **not still** hunger *no more*,
neither **still** thirst *any more*;
neither shall the sun *light* **fall** on them
nor any *heat* **scorch**.
17   *For* **Because** the Lamb
which is in the midst of the throne
shall *feed* **shepherd** them,
and shall *lead* **guide** them unto
living fountains of waters:
and *God* **Elohim** shall wipe *away*
all tears from their eyes.

THE SEVENTH SEAL

8   And when he had opened the seventh seal,
there *was silence* **became a hush** in *heaven* **the heavens**
about **as** the space of half an hour.

THE SEVEN TRUMPS

2   And I saw the seven angels
which stood *before God* **in sight of Elohim**;
and to them were given seven trumpets.
3   And another angel came and
stood at the **sacrifice** altar,
having a golden *censer* **frankincenser**;
and there was given unto him much incense,
that he should *offer* **give** it
with the prayers of all *saints* **the holy**
upon the golden **sacrifice** altar
which was *before* **in sight of** the throne.
4   And the smoke of the incense,
which came with the prayers of the *saints* **holy**,
ascended *up before God* **in sight of Elohim**
out of the angel's hand.
5   And the angel took the *censer* **frankincenser**,
and filled it *with* **out of the** fire of the **sacrifice** altar,
and cast *it into* **unto** the earth:
and there *were* **became** voices, and thunderings,
and lightnings, and *an earthquake* **a quake**.
6   And the seven angels which
had the seven trumpets
prepared themselves to *sound* **trumpet**.

THE FIRST TRUMP

7   The first angel *sounded* **trumped**,
and there *followed* **became** hail and fire
mingled with blood,
and they were cast *upon* **unto** the earth:
and the third *part* of trees was burnt up,
and all green *grass* **herbage** was burnt up.

THE SECOND TRUMP

8   And the second angel *sounded* **trumped**,
and as *it were a great* **a mega** mountain burning with fire
was cast into the sea:
and the third *part* of the sea became blood;
9   And the third *part* of the creatures
which were in the sea, and had *life* **soul**, died;
and the third *part* of the *ships* **sailers**
were *destroyed* **corrupted**.

THE THIRD TRUMP

10   And the third angel *sounded* **trumped**,
and there fell a *great* **mega** star from *heaven* **the heavens**,

burning as *it were* a lamp,
and it fell upon the third *part* of the *rivers* **streams**,
and upon the fountains of waters:
11 And the name of the star
is *called Wormwood* **worded Absinthe**:
and the third *part* of the waters
became *wormwood* **absinthe**;
and *many men* **much humanity** died of the waters,
because they were *made bitter* **embittered**.

The Fourth Trump

12 And the fourth angel *sounded* **trumped**,
and the third *part* of the sun was *smitten* **deformed**,
and the third *part* of the moon,
and the third *part* of the stars;
so as **that** the third *part* of them was darkened,
and the day *shone* **manifested** not for a third *part* of it,
and the night likewise.
15 because of this
they are in sight of the throne of Elohim
and liturgize in his nave day and night:
and he sitting on the throne tabernacles among them.
16 They neither still famish nor still thirst;
nor falls the sun on them, nor any scorch:
17 because the Lamb midst the throne
shepherds them, and guides them
to living fountains of waters:
and Elohim wipes all tears from their eyes.

The Seventh Seal

8 And when he opens the seventh seal,
a hush becomes in the heavens
as the space of half an hour.

The Seven Trumps

2 And I see the seven angels
stand in sight of Elohim;
and they are given seven trumpets.
3 And another angel came
and stands at the sacrifice altar
having a golden frankincenser;
and he is given much incense,
to give with the prayers of all the holy
on the golden sacrifice altar in sight of the throne.
4 And the smoke of the incense
with the prayers of the holy
ascends from the hand of the angel in sight of Elohim:
5 and the angel takes the frankincenser
and fills it from the fire of the sacrifice altar
and casts it to the earth:

and there become voices and thunderings
and lightnings and a quake.
6 And the seven angels having the seven trumpets
prepare themselves to trump.

The First Trump

7 The first angel trumps
and there becomes hail and fire mingled with blood
and they are cast to the earth:
and the third of trees burns
and all green herbage burns.

The Second Trump

8 And the second angel trumps
and as a mega mountain burning with fire
is cast into the sea:
and the third of the sea becomes blood;
9 and the third of the creatures in the sea
and having a soul, die;
and the third of the sailers corrupt.

The Third Trump

10 And the third angel trumps
and a mega star falls from the heavens
burning as a lamp;
and it falls on the third of the streams
and on the fountains of waters:
11 and the name of the star is worded, Absinthe:
and the third of the waters become absinthe;
and much humanity dies from the waters,
because they embittered.

The Fourth Trump

12 And the fourth angel trumps
and the third of the sun deforms
and the third of the moon
and the third of the stars;
so that the third of them darkens
and the day manifests not for the third thereof
and likewise the night.

The Three Woes

13 And I *beheld* **perceived**, and heard *an* **one** angel
flying *through the midst of heaven* **in the midheavens**,
saying **wording** with a *loud* **mega** voice,
Woe, woe, woe,
to *the inhabiters of* **them who settle on** the earth
by *reason of the other* **the rest of the** voices
of the trumpet of the three angels,
which are *yet to sound* **about to trump**!

The Fifth Trump

9 And the fifth angel *sounded* **trumped**,
and I saw a star fall from *heaven* **the heavens** unto the earth:
and to him was given
the key of the *bottomless* pit **of the abyss**.

2 And he opened the *bottomless* pit **of the abyss**;
and there *arose* **ascended** a smoke out of the pit,
as the smoke of a *great* **mega** furnace;
and the sun and the air were darkened
by reason of **from** the smoke of the pit.

3 And there came out of the smoke
locusts *upon* **unto** the earth:
and unto them was given *power* **authority**,
as the scorpions of the earth have *power* **authority**.

4 And it was *commanded* **rhetorized to** them
that they should not *hurt* **injure**
the *grass* **herbage** of the earth,
neither any green *thing*, neither any tree;
but **except** only those *men* **humans** which have not
the seal of *God* **Elohim** in their foreheads.

5 And to them it was given
that they should not *kill* **slaughter** them,
but that they should be *tormented* **tortured** five months:
and their *torment* **torture**
was as the *torment* **torture** of a scorpion,
when he *striketh* **smiteth** a *man* **human**.

6 And in those days shall
men **humanity** seek death,
and shall not find it;
and shall *desire* **pant** to die, and
death shall flee from them.

7 And the *shapes* **likenesses** of the locusts
were like unto horses prepared unto *battle* **war**;
and on their heads
were *as it were crowns* **wreaths** like gold,
and their faces *were* as the faces of *men* **humans**.

8 And they had hair as the hair of women,
and their teeth *were as the teeth of* **as** lions.

9 And they had breastplates,
as *it were* breastplates of iron;
and the *sound* **voice** of their wings
was as the *sound* **voice** of chariots of many horses
running to *battle* **war**.

10 And they had tails like unto scorpions,
and there were stings in their tails:
and their *power* **authority**
was to *hurt men* **injure humanity** five months.

11 And they had a *king* **sovereign** over them,
which is — the angel of the *bottomless* **abyss** pit,
whose name in *the Hebrew tongue* **Hebraic**
is Abaddon,
but in *the Greek tongue* **Hellenic**
hath his name Apollyon.

12 One woe is *past* **gone**; *and*, behold,
there come two woes *more hereafter* **yet after these**.

The Sixth Trump

13 And the sixth angel *sounded* **trumped**,
and I heard *a* **one** voice
from the four horns of the golden *sacrifice* **altar**
which is *before God* **in sight of Elohim**,

14 *Saying* **Wording** to the sixth angel
which had the trumpet,
Loose the four angels which are bound
in the *great river* **mega stream** Euphrates.

15 And the four angels were loosed,
which were prepared
for **unto** an hour, and a day, and a month, and a year,
for to *slay* **slaughter** the third *part* of *men* **humanity**.

16 And the number
of the *army* **warriors** of the horsemen were
two *hundred thousand thousand* **myriads of myriads**:
and I heard the number of them.

The Three Woes

13 And I perceive,
and hear one angel flying in the midheavens,
wording with a mega voice,
Woe, woe, woe, to them who settle on the earth
because of the rest of the voices
of the trumpet of the three angels
about to trump!

The Fifth Trump

9 And the fifth angel trumps
and I see a star fallen from the heavens to the earth:
and he is given the key of the pit of the abyss.

2 And he opens the pit of the abyss;
and a smoke ascends from the pit
as the smoke of a mega furnace;
and the sun and the air darken
from the smoke of the pit.

3 And from the smoke, locusts come to the earth:
and they are given authority
as the scorpions of the earth have authority.

4 And they are rhetorized to injure
neither the herbage of the earth
nor any green nor any tree;
except only those humans

REVELATION/HAGILU NATAN ELOHIM 9, 10

who have not the seal of Elohim in their foreheads.
5 And they are given
— not to slaughter but to torture them five months:
and their torture is as the torture
of a scorpion smiting a human.
6 And in those days humanity seeks death
and finds not;
and pants to die
and death flees from them.
7 And the likenesses of the locusts
— likens to horses prepared to war;
and on their heads as gold—like wreaths
and their faces as faces: of humans
8 and they have hair as hair of women
and their teeth as lions:
9 and they have breastplates
as breastplates of iron;
and the voice of their wings as the voice of chariots
— of many horses running to war;
10 and their tails like scorpions
and stings in their tails:
and their authority *is* to injure humanity five months.
11 And they have a sovereign over them,
— the angel of the abyss,
his name in Hebraic, Abaddon,
and in Hellenic has the name, Apollyon.
12 The first woe is gone:
and behold, still two woes come after these.

THE SIXTH TRUMP

13 And the sixth angel trumps
and I hear one voice
from the four horns of the golden sacrifice altar
in sight of Elohim,
14 wording to the sixth angel who has the trumpet,
Loose the four angels
bound in the mega stream Euphrates.
15 And the four angels are loosed,
who are prepared
to an hour and a day and a month and a year
to slaughter the third of humanity:
16 and the number of the warriors of the horsemen
is two myriads of myriads:
and I hear their number.
17 And thus I saw the horses in the vision,
and them that sat on them,
having breastplates of *fire* **fiery**,
and *of jacinth* **jacinthine**,
and *brimstone* **sulphurous**:
and the heads of the horses *were* as the heads of lions;
and out of their mouths *issued* **proceeded** fire
and smoke and *brimstone* **sulphur**.
18 By these three
was the third *part* of *men killed* **humanity slaughtered**,
by the fire, and by the smoke,
and by the *brimstone* **sulphur**,
which *issued* **proceeded** out of their mouths.
19 For their *power* **authority** is in their mouth,
and in their tails:
for their tails *were* like unto serpents, and had heads,
and *with* **in** them they do *hurt* **injure**.
cp Apocalypse 16:12—14
20 And the rest of the *men* **humanity**
which were not *killed by* **slaughtered in** these plagues
yet repented not of the works of their hands,
that they should not worship *devils* **demons**,
and idols of gold, and silver, and *brass* **copper**,
and stone, and of wood:
which neither can see, nor hear, nor walk:
21 Neither repented they of their murders,
nor of their *sorceries* **pharmacies**,
nor of their *fornication* **whoredoms**,
nor of their *thefts* **thieveries**.

THE OPEN SCROLLETTE

10 And I saw another mighty angel
come down **descend** from *heaven* **the heavens**,
clothed **arrayed** with a cloud:
and a rainbow *was* upon his head,
and his face *was* as *it were* the sun,
and his feet as pillars of fire:
2 And he had in his hand a
little book **scrollette** open:
and he set his right foot upon the sea,
and his left *foot* on the earth,
3 And cried with a *loud* **mega** voice,
exactly as *when* a lion roareth:
and when he had cried,
seven thunders *uttered* **spake in** their **own** voices.
4 And when the seven thunders
had uttered **spake in** their **own** voices,
I was about to *write* **scribe**:
and I heard a voice from *heaven* **the heavens**
saying **wording** unto me,
Seal up those *things* which the seven
thunders *uttered* **spake**,
and *write* **scribe** them not.
5 And the angel
which I saw stand upon the sea and upon the earth
lifted *up* his hand to *heaven* **the heavens**,
6 And *sware by* **oathed in** him that liveth
for ever and ever **unto the eons of the eons**,

REVELATION/HAGILU NATAN ELOHIM 10

who created *heaven* **the heavens**,
and *the things that* **those** therein *are*,
and the earth, and *the things that* **those** therein *are*,
and the sea, and *the things which are* **those** therein,
that there should be time* *no longer*
not still: *Hellene: chronos

7 But in the days of the voice of the seventh angel,
when he shall *begin to sound* **trump**,
the mystery of *God* **Elohim**
should be *finished* **completed/shalamed**,
as he hath *declared* **evangelized**
to his **own** servants the prophets.

8 And the voice which I heard
from *heaven* **the heavens**
spake *unto* **with** me again, and *said* **worded**,
Go *and* take the *little book* **scrollette**
which is open in the hand of the angel
which standeth upon the sea and upon the earth.

9 And I went unto the angel,
and *said* **worded** unto him,
Give me the *little book* **scrollette**.
And he *said* **worded** unto me, Take it, and eat it *up*;
and it shall *make* **embitter** thy belly *bitter*,
but it shall be in thy mouth sweet as honey.

10 And I took the *little book* **scrollette**
out of the angel's hand,
and ate it *up*;

17 And thus I see the horses in the vision
and those sitting on them have breastplates
fiery and jacinthine and sulphurous:
and the heads of the horses as the heads of lions;
and fire and smoke and sulphur
proceeds from their mouths.

18 By these three
— by the fire and by the smoke and by the sulphur
proceeding from their mouths
the third of humanity is slaughtered:

19 for their authorities
are in their mouth and in their tails:
for their tails are like serpents having heads,
and in them they injure.
cp Apocalypse 16:12—14

20 And the rest of humanity
— not slaughtered in these plagues
repent not of the works of their hands
— to not worship demons
and idols of gold and silver and copper
and of stone and of wood:
which can neither see nor hear nor walk:

21 neither repent they of their murders
nor of their pharmacies
nor of their whoredoms
nor of their thieveries.

THE OPEN SCROLLETTE

10 And I see another mighty angel
descend from the heavens
arrayed with a cloud and a rainbow on his head:
and his face as the sun and his feet as pillars of fire:

2 and in his hand he has an open scrollette:
and he sets his right foot on the sea
and his left on the earth;

3 and cries with a mega voice
exactly as a lion roars:
and when he cries,
seven thunders speak in their own voices.

4 And when the seven thunders
speak in their own voices,
I am about to scribe:
and I hear a voice from the heavens wording to me,
Seal what the seven thunders spoke
and scribe them not.

5 And the angel
I see standing on the sea and on the earth
lifts his hand to the heavens,

6 and oaths in him who lives
to the eons of the eons
— who created the heavens and those therein
and the earth and those therein
and the sea and those therein,
that time* is not still:
*Hellene: chronos

7 But in the days of the voice of the seventh angel,
when he is about to trump,
to complete/shalam the mystery of Elohim,
as he evangelized to his own servants the prophets.

8 And again I hear a voice from the heavens
speaking with me and wording,
Go take the open scrollette
in the hand of the angel
standing on the sea and on the earth.

9 And I go to the angel and word to him,
Give me the scrollette.
And he words to me, Take and eat;
and it embitters your belly,
but it is sweet as honey in your mouth.

10 And I take the scrollette from hand of the angel
and eat it;
and it was in my mouth sweet as honey:
and as soon as I had eaten it, my
belly *was bitter* **embittered**.

11 And he *said* **worded** unto me,
Thou must prophesy again *before*
in front of many peoples,
and *nations* **goyim**, and tongues, and *kings* **sovereigns**.

THE NAVE MEASURED

11 And there was given me a
reed like unto a *rod* **scion**:
and the angel stood, *saying* **wording**,
Rise, and measure the *temple* **nave** of *God* **Elohim**,
and the **sacrifice** altar, and them that worship therein.
2 But the *court* **courtyard**
which is *without* **outside** the *temple* **nave**
leave **cast** out, and measure it not;
for **because** it is given unto the *Gentiles* **goyim**:
and the holy city shall they *tread under foot* **trample**
forty *and* two months.

THE TWO WITNESSES

3 And I *will* **shall** give *power*
unto my two witnesses,
and they shall prophesy
a thousand two hundred *and threescore* **sixty** days,
clothed **arrayed** in *sackcloth* **saq**.
4 These are the two *olive trees* **olives**,
and the two *candlesticks* **menorah**
standing *before* **in sight of** the *God* **Elohim**
of the earth. Zechar Yah 4:2—6, 11—14
5 And if any *man will hurt*
one willeth to injure them,
fire proceedeth out of their mouth,
and *devoureth* **consumeth** their enemies:
and if any *man will hurt* **one willeth to injure** them,
he must *in this manner* **thus** be *killed* **slaughtered**.
cp 11:13
6 These have *power* **authority**
to shut *heaven* **the heavens**,
that *it rain not* **the rain not rain**
in the days of their prophecy:
and have *power* **authority** over waters
to turn them to blood,
and to smite the earth with all plagues,
as often as *ever* they will.
7 And when they shall have
finished **completed/shalamed** their *testimony* **witness**,
the beast that ascendeth out of the *bottomless pit* **abyss**
shall make war *against* **with** them,
and shall *overcome* **triumph over** them,
and *kill* **slaughter** them.
8 And their *dead bodies* **carcasses**
shall *lie in* **be on** the *street* **broadway**
of the *great city* **megalopolis**,
which spiritually is called *Sodom*
Sedom and *Egypt* **Misrayim**,
where also our *Lord* **Adonay** was *crucified* **staked**.
9 And they of the people and *kindreds* **scions**
and tongues and *nations* **goyim**
shall see their *dead bodies* **carcasses**
three days and an half,
and shall not *suffer* **allow** their *dead bodies* **carcasses**
to be put in *graves* **tombs**.
10 And they that *dwell* **settle** upon the earth
shall *rejoice* **cheer** over them, and *make merry* **rejoice**,
and shall send *gifts* **honorariums** one to another;
because these two prophets *tormented* **tortured** them
that *dwelt* **settled** on the earth.
11 And after three days and an half
the spirit of life from *God* **Elohim** entered into them,
and they stood upon their feet;
and *great fear* **mega awe**
fell upon them which *saw* **observed** them.
12 And they heard a *great* **mega** voice
from *heaven* **the heavens**
saying **wording** unto them, Come up **Ascend** hither.
And they ascended *up* to *heaven* **the heavens** in a cloud;
and their enemies *beheld* **observed** them.
13 And *the same* **in that** hour
was there **became** a great earthquake **mega quake**,
and the tenth *part* of the city fell,
and in the *earthquake* **quake**
were *slain of men* **slaughtered**
seven thousand **names of humanity**:
and the *remnant* **rest** *were affrighted*
became awestricken, and gave glory to the
God **Elohim** of *heaven* **the heavens**.
cp 11:5
and it is sweet as honey in my mouth:
and as soon as I eat it, my belly embitters.
11 And he words to me,
You must prophesy again in front of many peoples
and goyim and tongues and sovereigns.

THE NAVE MEASURED

11 And I am given a reed like a scion:
and the angel stands, wording,
Rise and measure the nave of Elohim
and the sacrifice altar and those worshipping therein:
2 and cast out the courtyard outside the nave
and measure it not;
because it is given to the goyim:

REVELATION/HAGILU NATAN ELOHIM 11

and they trample the holy city forty—two months.

THE TWO WITNESSES

3 And I give to my two witnesses to prophesy
a thousand two hundred and sixty days,
arrayed in saq.
4 These are the two olives and the two menorah
standing in sight of the Elohim of the
earth. Zechar Yah 4:2—6, 11—14
5 And if anyone wills to injure them,
fire proceeds from their mouth
and consumes their enemies:
and if anyone wills to injure them,
thus must they be slaughtered.
cp 11:13
6 These have authority to shut the heavens,
so that the rain rains not in the days of their prophecy:
and they have authority over waters
to turn them to blood
and to smite the earth with all plagues
as often as ever they will.
7 And when they complete/shalam their witness,
the beast ascends from the abyss
makes war with them
and triumphs over them and slaughters them:
8 and their carcasses
are on the broadway of the megalopolis,
which spiritually is called, Sedom and Misrayim
— where also our Adonay was staked.
9 And they of the people and scions
and tongues and goyim
see their carcasses three and a half days
and allow not to put their carcasses in tombs.
10 And they who settle on the earth
cheer over them and rejoice;
and send honorariums to one another;
because these two prophets tortured them
who settle on the earth.
11 And after three and a half days
the spirit of life of Elohim enters into them
and they stand on their feet;
and mega awe falls on them who observe them.
12 And they hear a mega voice from the heavens
wording to them, Ascend here!
— and they ascend to the heavens in the cloud;
and their enemies observe them.
13 And in that hour a mega quake becomes
and the tenth of the city falls;
and in the quake
seven thousand names of humanity are slaughtered:
and the rest become awestricken

and give glory to the Elohim of the heavens.
cp 11:5
14 The second woe is *past* **gone**;
and behold, the third woe cometh quickly.

THE SEVENTH TRUMP

15 And the seventh angel *sounded* **trumped**;
and there *were great* **became**
mega voices in *heaven* **the heavens**,
saying **wording**,
The *kingdoms* **sovereigndom** of this *world* **cosmos**
are become *the kingdoms* of our *Lord* **Yah Veh**,
and of his *Christ* **the Messiah**;
and he shall reign
for ever and ever **unto the eons of the eons**.
16 And the four and twenty elders,
which sat *before God* **in sight of Elohim**
on their *seats* **thrones**,
fell upon their faces, and worshipped *God* **Elohim**,
17 *Saying* **Wording**, We *give*
eucharistize thee *thanks*,
O *Lord God Almighty* **Yah Veh El Sabaoth**,
which art, and wast, and art to come
who is, and who was, and who is coming;
because thou hast taken to thee
thy *great power* **mega dynamis**, and hast reigned.
18 And the *nations* **goyim** were *angry* **wroth**,
and thy wrath is come,
and the *time* **season** of the dead,
that they should be judged,
and that thou shouldest give reward
unto thy servants the prophets,
and to the *saints* **holy**, and them that *fear* **awe** thy name,
small **minute** and *great* **mega**;
and shouldest destroy them which destroy the earth.
19 And the *temple* **nave** of *God* **Elohim**
was opened in *heaven* **the heavens**,
and there was seen in his *temple* **nave**
the ark of his *testament* **covenant**:
and there *were* **became** lightnings,
and voices, and thunderings,
and *an earthquake* **a quake**, and *great* **mega** hail.

THE PANORAMA OF SIGNS AND EVENTS THE WOMAN

12 And there appeared
a *great wonder* **mega sign** in *heaven* **the heavens**;
a woman *clothed* **arrayed** with the sun,
and the moon under her feet,
and upon her head a *crown* **wreath** of twelve stars:

2 And she *being with child* **having in womb** cried,
travailing *in birth*, and *pained*
tortured to *be delivered* **birth**.

THE DRAGON

3 And there appeared another *wonder* **sign**
in *heaven* **the heavens**;
and behold a *great red* **mega fiery** dragon,
having seven heads and ten horns,
and seven *crowns* **diadems** upon his heads.

4 And his tail
drew **dragged** the third *part* of the
stars of *heaven* **the heavens**,
and did cast them to the earth:
and the dragon stood *before* **in sight of** the woman
which was ready **about** to *be delivered* **birth**,
for to devour her child as soon as
it was born **she birthed**.

THE MALE SON

5 And she *brought forth* **birthed**
a *man child* **male son**,
who was *about* to *rule* **shepherd** all *nations*
goyim *with* **in** a *rod* **scion** of iron:
and her child was *caught* **seized** up unto *God* **Elohim**,
and *to* his throne.

6 And the woman fled into the wilderness,
where she hath a place prepared of *God* **Elohim**,
that they should *feed* **nourish** her there
a thousand two hundred *and threescore* **sixty** days.

WAR IN THE HEAVENS

7 And there *was* **became** war
in *heaven* **the heavens**:
Michael **Michah El** and his angels
fought **warred** against the dragon;
and the dragon *fought* **warred** and his angels,

8 And *prevailed* **was** not **mighty enough**;
neither was their place
still found *any more* in *heaven* **the heavens**.

14 The second woe is gone:
and behold, the third woe comes quickly.

THE SEVENTH TRUMP

15 And the seventh angel trumps;
and mega voices become in the heavens,
wording, The sovereigndoms of this cosmos
are become to Yah Veh and his the Messiah;
and he reigns to the eons of the eons.

16 And the twenty—four elders,
sitting on their thrones in sight of Elohim
fall on their faces and worship Elohim,

17 wording, We eucharistize you,
O Yah Veh El Sabaoth,
who is and who was and who is coming;
for you are taking your mega dynamis and reign:

18 and the goyim raved and your wrath is come:
also the season to judge the dead
and to give reward
to your servants the prophets and to the holy
and to them who awe your name
— minute and mega:
and to destroy them who destroy the earth.

19 And the nave of Elohim opens in the heavens
and the ark of his covenant is seen in his nave:
and there become lightnings
and voices and thunderings
and a quake and mega hail.

THE PANORAMA OF SIGNS
AND EVENTS THE WOMAN

12 And a mega sign appears in the heavens:
— a woman arrayed with the sun
and the moon under her feet
and a wreath of twelve stars on her head:

2 and having in womb, she cries,
travailing and torturing to birth.

THE DRAGON

3 And another sign appears in the heavens;
and behold, a mega fiery dragon
having seven heads and ten horns
and seven diadems on his heads;

4 and his tail drags the third
of the stars of the heavens
and casts them to the earth:
and the dragon
stands in sight of the woman about to birth
to devour her child as soon as she births.

THE MALE SON

5 And she births a male son,
who is about to shepherd all goyim in a scion of iron:
and her child is seized to Elohim and to his throne.

6 And the woman flees to the wilderness,
where she has a place prepared by Elohim,
to be nourished
a thousand two hundred and sixty days.

WAR IN THE HEAVENS

7 And war becomes in the heavens:
Michah El and his angels war against the dragon;

REVELATION/HAGILU NATAN ELOHIM 12, 13

and the dragon and his angels war;
8 and they are not mighty enough
and their place is not still found in the heavens.
9 And the *great* **mega** dragon was cast out,
that *old* **ancient** serpent,
called *the Devil* **Diabolos**, and Satan,
which *deceiveth* **seduceth** the whole world:
he was cast out *into* **unto** the earth,
and his angels were cast out with him.

VICTORY IN THE HEAVENS

10 And I heard a *loud* **mega** voice
saying **wording** in *heaven* **the heavens**,
Now *is come* **becometh** salvation, and *strength* **dynamis**,
and the *kingdom* **sovereigndom** of our *God* **Elohim**,
and the *power* **authority** of his *Christ* **the Messiah**:
for **because** the accuser of our brethren is cast down,
which accused them *before* **in sight of** our *God* **Elohim**
day and night.
11 And they *overcame* **triumphed over** him
by **through** the blood of the Lamb,
and *by* **through** the word of their *testimony* **witness**;
and they loved not their *lives* **souls** unto the death.
12 *Therefore* **For this** rejoice, ye heavens,
and ye that *dwell* **tabernacle** in them.
Woe to the *inhabiters* **settlers** of the earth and of the sea!
for the devil **because Diabolos**
is come down **descended** unto you,
having *great wrath* **mega fury**,
because he knoweth
that he hath but a *short time* **little season**.
Yahn 12:31, 32, Loukas 10:18

THE DRAGON PURSUES THE WOMAN

13 And when the dragon saw
that he was cast unto the earth,
he *persecuted* **pursued** the woman
which *brought forth* **birthed** the *man child* **male**.
14 And to the woman
were given two wings of a *great* **mega** eagle,
that she might fly into the wilderness, into her place,
where she is nourished
for a time, and times, and half a time,
from the face of the serpent.
15 And the serpent cast out of his mouth
water as a *flood* **stream** after the woman,
that he might cause her
to be *carried away of the flood* **streamborne**.
16 And the earth helped the woman,
and the earth opened her mouth,
and swallowed *up the flood* **stream**
which the dragon cast out of his mouth.

THE DRAGON WARS WITH THE SPERMA OF THE WOMAN

17 And the dragon was wroth with the woman,
and went to make war
with the *remnant* **rest** of her *seed* **sperma**,
which *keep* **guard**
the *commandments* **misvoth** of *God* **Elohim**,
and have
the *testimony* **witness** of *Jesus Christ* **Yah Shua Messiah**.

THE BEAST FROM THE SEA

13 And I stood upon the sand of the sea,
and saw a beast *rise up* **ascend** out of the sea,
having seven heads and ten horns,
and upon his horns ten *crowns* **diadems**,
and upon his heads the name of blasphemy.
2 And the beast which I saw
was like unto a *leopard* **panther**,
and his feet were as *the feet* of a bear,
and his mouth as the mouth of a lion:
and the dragon gave him his *power* **dynamis**,
and his *seat* **throne**, and *great* **mega** authority.
3 And I saw one of his heads
as *it were wounded* **slaughtered** to death;
and his *deadly wound* **death plague** was *healed* **cured**:
and all the *world* **earth**
wondered **marvelled** after the beast.
4 And they worshipped the dragon
which gave *power* **authority** unto the beast:
and they worshipped the beast, *saying* **wording**,
Who is like unto the beast?
who is able to *make* war with him?
9 And the mega dragon is cast out,
that ancient serpent called Diabolos and Satan,
who seduces the whole world:
he is cast to the earth
and his angels are cast out with him.

VICTORY IN THE HEAVENS

10 And I hear a mega voice in the heavens,
wording, Now becomes salvation and dynamis
and the sovereigndom of our Elohim
and the authority of his the Messiah:
because the accuser of our brothers is cast down
— who accused them in sight of our Elohim
day and night.
11 And they triumph over him

through the blood of the Lamb
and through the word of their witness;
and they love not their souls to the death.

12   For this rejoice, you the heavens
and you who tabernacle therein.
Woe to the settlers of the earth and of the sea!
— because Diabolos descends to you
having mega fury
because he knows he has but a little
season. Yahn 12:31, 32, Loukas 10:18

The Dragon Pursues The Woman

13   And when the dragon sees he is cast to the earth
he pursues the woman who birthed the male.

14   And the woman is given
two wings of a mega eagle
to fly to her place to the wilderness;
where she is nourished
for a time and times and half a time
from the face of the serpent.

15   And from his mouth,
the serpent casts water as a stream after the woman,
so that she is streamborne:

16   and the earth helps the woman
and the earth opens her mouth
and swallows the stream
the dragon cast from his mouth.

The Dragon Wars With The Sperma Of The Woman

17   And the dragon rages with the woman
and goes to make war with the rest of her sperma
who guard the misvoth of Elohim
and have the witness of Yah Shua Messiah.

The Beast From The Sea

13   And I stand on the sand of the sea;
and see a beast ascend from the sea
having seven heads and ten horns;
and on his horns ten diadems;
and on his heads the name of blasphemy.

2   And the beast I see is like a panther
and his feet as of a bear
and his mouth as the mouth of a lion:
and the dragon gives him his dynamis
and his throne and mega authority.

3   And I see one of his heads
as slaughtered to death;
and his death plague is cured:
and all the earth marvels after the beast.

4   And they worship the dragon
who gives authority to the beast:
and they worship the beast, wording,
Who is like to the beast?
Who is able to war with him?

The Beast Wars With The Holy

5   And there was given unto him a mouth
speaking *great things* **mega** and blasphemies;
and *power* **authority** was given unto him
to *continue* **deal** forty *and* two months.

6   And he opened his mouth in blasphemy
against *God* **Elohim**,
to blaspheme his name, and his tabernacle,
and them that *dwell* **tabernacle** in *heaven* **the heavens**.

7   And it was given unto him
to make war with the *saints* **holy**,
and to *overcome* **triumph over** them:
and *power* **authority** was given him
over all *kindreds* **scions**, and tongues,
and *nations* **goyim**.

8   And all that *dwell* **settle** upon the earth
shall worship him,
whose names are not *written* **scribed**
in the *book* **scroll** of life of the Lamb
slain **slaughtered**
from the foundation of the *world* **cosmos**.

9   If any *man* **one** have an ear, let him hear.

10   *He that leadeth*
If anyone gathereth together into captivity
shall go into captivity **goeth**:
he that killeth with
if anyone slaughtereth at the sword,
must be killed with **at** the sword **is slaughtered**.
Here is the *patience* **endurance**
and the *faith* **trust** of the *saints* **holy**.

The Beast From The Earth

11   And I *beheld* **perceived** another beast
coming up **ascending** out of the earth;
and he had two horns like a lamb,
and he spake as a dragon.

12   And he *exerciseth* **dealeth**
all the *power* **authority**
of the first beast *before* **in sight of** him,
and causeth the earth
and them which *dwell* **settle** therein
to worship the first beast,
whose *deadly wound* **death plague** was *healed* **cured**.

13   And he doeth *great wonders* **mega signs**,
so that he maketh fire

REVELATION/HAGILU NATAN ELOHIM 13

come down **descend** from *heaven* **the heavens**
on **to** the earth in sight of *men* **humanity**,
14   And *deceiveth* **seduceth** them
that *dwell* **settle** on the earth
by the means of **through** those *miracles* **signs**
which he *had power* **was given** to do in sight of the beast;
saying **wording** to them that *dwell* **settle** on the earth,
that they should make an *image* **icon** to the beast,
which had the *wound* **plague** by a sword,
and *did live* **lived**.
15   And he *had power* **was given**
to give life unto the *image* **icon** of the beast,
that the *image* **icon** of the beast should both speak,
and cause that as many as *ever*
would **should** not worship the *image* **icon** of the beast
should be *killed* **slaughtered**.

THE TATTOO OF THE BEAST

16   And he causeth all, both
small **minute** and *great* **mega**,
rich and poor, *free* **liberated** and *bond* **servant**,
to *receive* **give them** a *mark* **tattoo** in their right hand,
or in their foreheads:
17   And that no *man* **one**
might *buy* **be able to market** or sell,
save **except** he that had the *mark* **tattoo**,
or the name of the beast, or the number of his name.

THE NUMBER OF THE BEAST

18   Here is wisdom.
Let him that hath *understanding* **a mind**
count **compute** the number of the beast:
for it is the number of a *man* **human**;
and his number is Six hundred *threescore* **sixty** and six.

THE BEAST WARS WITH THE HOLY

5   And he is given a mouth
speaking mega and blasphemies;
and he is given authority
to deal forty—two months.
6   And he opens his mouth in blasphemy
against Elohim
— to blaspheme his name and his tabernacle
and them who tabernacle in the heavens.
7   And he is given to make war with the holy
and to triumph over them:
and he is given authority
over all scions and tongues and goyim.
8   And all who settle on the earth worship him
— whose names are not scribed
in the scroll of life of the Lamb
slaughtered from the foundation of the cosmos.

9   If anyone has an ear, hear.
10   If anyone gathers a captivity
into captivity he goes:
if anyone slaughters at the sword,
at the sword he is slaughtered.
Here is the endurance and the trust of the holy.

THE BEAST FROM THE EARTH

11   And I perceive another beast
ascending from the earth;
and he has two horns like a lamb
and he speaks as a dragon.
12   And he deals all the authority
of the first beast in his sight;
and causes the earth and them settled therein
to worship the first beast, whose death plague is cured.
13   And he does mega signs,
to make fire descend from the heavens to the earth
in sight of humanity;
14   and seduces those settled on the earth
through those signs
he is given to do in sight of the beast;
wording to them settled on the earth
who had the plague by a sword and lived
to make an icon to the beast.
15   And he is given
to give life to the icon of the beast,
so that the icon of the beast both speaks
and causes as many as ever
who worship not the icon of the beast
to be slaughtered.

THE TATTOO OF THE BEAST

16   And he has all
— both minute and mega,
rich and poor,
liberated and servant,
— to be given a tattoo
in their right hand or in their foreheads:
17   so that no one is able to market or sell,
except them having the tattoo
or the name of the beast
or the number of his name.

THE NUMBER OF THE BEAST

18   Here is the wisdom:
whoever has a mind,
compute the number of the beast:
for it is the number of a human;
and his number is six hundred and sixty—six.

The Seven Visions
The First Vision

14 And I *looked* **perceived**, and, *lo* **behold**,
a Lamb *stood* **standing** on the mount *Sion* **Siyon**,
and with him an hundred forty *and* four thousand,
having his Father's name
written **scribed** in their foreheads.

2 And I heard a voice from *heaven* **the heavens**,
as the voice of many waters,
and as the voice of a *great* **mega** thunder:
and I heard the voice of *harpers* **citherists**
harping with **cithering at** their *harps* **cithers**:

3 And they sung as *it were* a new *song* **ode**
before **in sight of** the throne,
and *before* **in sight of** the four *beasts* **live beings**,
and the elders:
and no *man* **one** could learn that *song* **ode**
but **except** the hundred *and* forty *and* four thousand,
which were *redeemed* **marketed** from the earth.

4 These are they
which were not *defiled* **stained** with women;
for they are virgins.
These are they
which follow the Lamb whithersoever he goeth.
These were *redeemed* **marketed**
from among *men* **humanity**,
being the *firstfruits* **firstlings**
unto *God* **Elohim** and to the Lamb.

5 And in their mouth was found no *guile* **deceit**:
for they are *without fault* **unblemished**
before **in front of** the throne of *God* **Elohim**.

The Second Vision

6 And I saw another angel
fly in the *midst of heaven* **midheavens**,
having the *everlasting gospel* **eternal evangelism**
to *preach* **evangelize** unto them
that *dwell* **settle** on the earth,
and to every *nation* **goyim**, and *kindred* **scion**,
and tongue, and people,

7 *Saying with* **Wording in** a *loud* **mega** voice,
Fear God **Awe Elohim**, and give glory to him;
for **because** the hour of his judgment is come:
and worship him
that made *heaven* **the heavens**, and earth, and the sea,
and the fountains of waters.

The Third Vision

8 And there followed another
angel, *saying* **wording**,
Babylon **Babel** is fallen, is fallen,
that *great city* **megalopolis**,
because she *made* **gave** all *nations* **goyim** drink
of the wine of the *wrath* **fury**
of her *fornication* **whoredom**.

The Fourth Vision

9 And the third angel followed them,
saying with **speaking in** a *loud* **mega** voice,
If any *man* **one** worship the beast and his *image* **icon**,
and *receive* **take** his *mark* **tattoo** in his forehead,
or in his hand,

10 The same shall drink
of the wine of the *wrath* **fury** of *God* **Elohim**,
which is *poured out without mixture* **mingled undiluted**
into the cup of his *indignation* **wrath**;
and he shall be *tormented* **tortured**
with **in** fire and *brimstone* **sulphur**
in *the presence* **sight** of the holy angels, and
in *the presence* **sight** of the Lamb:

11 And the smoke of their
torment **torture** ascendeth *up*
for ever and ever **unto the eons of the eons**:
and they have no rest day nor night,
who worship the beast and his *image* **icon**,
and *whosoever* **if any**
receiveth **taketh** the *mark* **tattoo** of his name.

12 Here is the *patience*
endurance of the *saints* **holy**:
here are they that *keep* **guard**
the *commandments* **misvoth** of *God* **Elohim**,
and the *faith* **trust** of *Jesus* **Yah Shua**.

The Seven Visions
The First Vision

14 And I perceive, and behold,
a Lamb standing on the Mount Siyon:
and with him an hundred and forty—four thousand
having the name of his Father
scribed in their foreheads.

2 And I hear a voice from the heavens,
as the voice of many waters
and as the voice of a mega thunder:
and I hear the voice of citherists
cithering at their cithers:

3 and they sing a new ode in sight of the throne
and in sight of the four live beings and the elders:
and no one can learn that ode
except the hundred and forty—four thousand,
who are marketed from the earth.

4 These are they who stained not with women
for they are virgins;
these are they who follow the Lamb
wherever he goes;
these are marketed from among humanity
— firstlings to Elohim and to the Lamb.
5 And no deceit is found in their mouth:
for they are unblemished
in front of the throne of Elohim.

THE SECOND VISION

6 And I see another angel fly in the midheavens;
having the eternal evangelism
to evangelize to them who settle on the earth
and to every goyim and scion and tongue and people:
7 wording in a mega voice,
Awe Elohim and give him glory;
because the hour of his judgment is come:
and worship him
who made the heavens and earth and the sea
and the fountains of waters.

THE THIRD VISION

8 And another angel follows, wording,
Babel is fallen, is fallen — that megalopolis;
because she gave all goyim drink
of the wine of the fury of her whoredom.

THE FOURTH VISION

9 And the third angel follows them,
speaking in a mega voice,
If anyone worships the beast and his icon
and takes his tattoo in his forehead or in his hand,
10 the same drinks of the
wine of the fury of Elohim,
mingled undiluted in the cup of his wrath;
and is tortured in fire and sulphur
in the sight of the holy angels
and in sight of the Lamb:
11 and the smoke of their torture ascends
to the eons of the eons:
and they who worship the beast and his icon
— also if any take the tattoo of his name
they have no rest day and night.
12 Here is the endurance of the holy:
here are they who guard the misvoth of Elohim
and the trust of Yah Shua.

THE FIFTH VISION
THE SECOND BEATITUDE

13 And I heard a voice from *heaven* **the heavens**
saying **wording** unto me, *Write* **Scribe**,
Blessed are the dead
which die in *the Lord* **Yah Veh** from henceforth:
Yea, *saith* **wordeth** the Spirit,
that they may rest from their labours;
and their works do follow **with** them.

THE SIXTH VISION THE HARVEST BY ONE LIKE UNTO THE SON OF HUMANITY

14 And I *looked* **perceived**,
and behold, a white cloud,
and upon the cloud
one sat like unto the Son of *man* **humanity**,
having on his head a golden *crown* **wreath**,
and in his hand a sharp sickle.
15 And another angel came out of the *temple* **nave**,
crying *with* **in** a *loud* **mega** voice
to him that sat on the cloud,
Thrust **Send** in thy sickle, and *reap* **harvest**:
for **because** the *time* **hour** is come
for thee to *reap* **harvest**;
for **because** the harvest of the earth is *ripe* **dried**.
16 And he that sat on the cloud
thrust **cast** in his sickle on the earth;
and the earth was *reaped* **harvested**.

THE SEVENTH VISION
THE HARVEST BY THE ANGEL

17 And another angel came out of the *temple* **nave**
which is in *heaven* **the heavens**,
he also having a sharp sickle.
18 And another angel came
out from the **sacrifice** altar,
which had *power* **authority** over fire;
and *cried* **voiced** with a *loud* **mega** cry
to him that had the sharp sickle, *saying* **speaking**,
Thrust **Send** in thy sharp sickle,
and *gather* **dry** the clusters *of the vine* of the earth;
for **because** her grapes are *fully ripe* **matured**.
19 And the angel *thrust* **cast**
in his sickle into the earth,
and *gathered* **dried** the vine of the earth,
and cast it into the *great winepress* **mega trough**
of the *wrath* **fury** of *God* **Elohim**.
20 And the *winepress* **trough**
was *trodden* **trampled**
without the city,
and blood came out of the *winepress* **trough**,
even unto the horse bridles,
by the space of **up to**
a thousand *and* six hundred *furlongs* **stadia**.

The Seven Final Plagues

15 And I saw another sign in *heaven* **the heavens**,
great **mega** and marvellous,
seven angels having the seven *last* **final** plagues;
for **because** in them
is *filled up* **completed/shalamed** the
wrath **fury** of *God* **Elohim**.

2 And I saw as *it were* a sea of
glass mingled with fire:
and them that had *gotten the victory* **triumphed**
over **from** the beast,
and *over* **from** his *image* **icon**,
and *over* **from** his *mark* **tattoo**,
and *over* **from** the number of his name,
stand on the sea of glass,
having the *harps* **cithers** of *God* **Elohim**.

3 And they sing the *song* **ode** of *Moses* **Mosheh**
the servant of *God* **Elohim**,
and the *song* **ode** of the Lamb,
saying **wording**,
Great **Mega** and marvellous are thy works,
Lord God Almighty **Yah Veh El Sabaoth**;
just and true are thy ways,
thou *King* **Sovereign** of *saints* **the holy**.

4 Who shall not *fear* **no way**
awe thee, O *Lord* **Yah Veh**,
and glorify thy name?
for **because** thou only art *holy* **merciful**:
for **because** all *nations* **goyim** shall come
and worship *before thee* **in thy sight**;
for **because** thy judgments are *made* manifest.

The Fifth Vision
The Second Beatitude

13 And I hear a voice from the heavens
wording to me,
Scribe,
Blessed — the dead who die in Yah Veh henceforth:
Yes, words the Spirit,
that they rest from their labors;
and their works follow with them.

The Sixth Vision
The Harvest By One Like
To The Son Of Humanity

14 And I perceive, and behold, a white cloud
— and on the cloud
one sitting like to the Son of humanity,
having a golden wreath on his head
and a sharp sickle in his hand.

15 And another angel comes from the nave,
crying in a mega voice to him sitting on the cloud,
Send in your sickle and harvest:
because the hour for you to harvest is come;
because the harvest of the earth is dried.

16 And he sitting on the cloud
casts in his sickle on the earth;
and the earth is harvested.

The Seventh Vision
The Harvest By The Angel

17 And another angel
comes from the nave in the heavens,
he also having a sharp sickle:

18 and another angel comes
from the sacrifice altar,
who has authority over fire;
and with a mega cry
voices to him having the sharp sickle,
speaking, Send in your sharp sickle
and dry the clusters of the earth;
because her grapes are matured.

19 And the angel casts in his sickle to the earth
and dries the vine of the earth
and casts it in the mega trough of the fury of Elohim.

20 And the trough is trampled outside the city
and blood comes from the trough
even to the horse bridles
— up to a thousand and six hundred stadia.

The Seven Final Plagues

15 And I see another sign in the heavens,
mega and marvellous:
seven angels having the seven final plagues;
because in them
the fury of Elohim is completed/shalamed.

2 And I see as a sea of glass mingled with fire:
and they who triumphed from the beast,
and from his icon,
and from his tattoo,
and from the number of his name,
stand on the sea of glass having the cithers of Elohim.

3 And they sing
the ode of Mosheh the servant of Elohim
and the ode of the Lamb;
wording, Mega and marvellous are your works,
Yah Veh El Sabaoth;
just and true are your ways,
Sovereign of the holy:

REVELATION/HAGILU NATAN ELOHIM 15, 16

4 Who never no way awes you, O Yah Veh,
and glorifies your name?
Because you only are merciful;
because all goyim come and worship in your sight;
because your judgments are manifested.

5 And after *that* **these** I *looked*
perceived, and, behold,
the *temple* **nave** of the tabernacle
of the *testimony* **witness** in *heaven*
the heavens was opened:

6 And the seven angels came
out of the *temple* **nave**,
having the seven plagues,
clothed **endued** in pure and *white* **radiant** linen,
and *having their breasts girded* **girt about the chest**
with golden girdles.

7 And one of the four *beasts* **live beings**
gave unto the seven angels seven golden *vials* **phials**
full of the *wrath* **fury** of *God* **Elohim**,
who liveth *for ever and ever* **unto the eons of the eons**.

8 And the *temple* **nave** was filled with smoke
from the glory of *God* **Elohim**,
and from his *power* **dynamis**;
and no *man* **one** was able to enter into the *temple* **nave**,
till the seven plagues of the seven angels
were fulfilled/**shalamed**.

16 And I heard a *great* **mega**
voice out of the *temple* **nave**
saying **wording** to the seven angels,
Go *your ways*,
and pour out the *vials* **phials**
of the *wrath* **fury** of *God* **Elohim**
upon **unto** the earth.

THE FIRST PLAGUE

2 And the first went,
and poured out his *vial* **phial** upon the earth;
and there *fell* **became**
a noisome and grievous sore **an evil ulcer**
upon the men **unto humanity**
which had the *mark* **tattoo** of the beast,
and *upon* them which worshipped his *image* **icon**.

THE SECOND PLAGUE

3 And the second angel
poured out his *vial* **phial** *upon* **into** the sea;
and it became as the blood of a dead *man*:
and every living soul died in the sea.

THE THIRD PLAGUE

4 And the third angel
poured out his *vial* **phial** *upon* **into** the *rivers* **streams**
and **into** fountains of waters;
and they became blood.

5 And I heard the angel of
the waters *say* **wording**,
Thou art *righteous* **just**, O *Lord* **Yah Veh**,
*which art, and wast, and shalt be**
who is, and who was*,
because thou hast judged *thus* **these**.
*most mss omit, and shalt be/who is coming

6 *For* **Because** they have *shed* **poured**
the blood of *saints* **the holy** and prophets,
and thou hast given them blood to drink;
for they are worthy.

7 And I heard another out of the *sacrifice* **altar**
say **wording**,
Even so **Yea**, *Lord God Almighty* **Yah Veh El Sabaoth**,
true and *righteous* **just** are thy judgments.

THE FOURTH PLAGUE

8 And the fourth angel
poured out his *vial* **phial** upon the sun;
and *power* **it** was given unto him
to scorch *men with* **humanity in** fire.

9 And *men* **humanity**
were scorched with *great heat* **mega scorch**,
and blasphemed the name of *God* **Elohim**,
which hath *power* **authority** over these plagues:
and they repented not to give him glory.

THE FIFTH PLAGUE

10 And the fifth angel
poured out his *vial* **phial** upon the
seat **throne** of the beast;
and his *kingdom* **sovereigndom**
was full of darkness **became darkened**;
and they gnawed their tongues *for* **from** pain,

11 And blasphemed the God
Elohim of *heaven* **the heavens**
because of **from** their pains and **from** their *sores* **ulcers**,
and repented not of their *deeds* **works**.

5 And after these I perceive, and behold,
the nave of the tabernacle
of the witness in the heavens opens:

6 and the seven angels having the seven plagues
come from the nave
endued in pure and radiant linen
and girt about the chests with golden girdles.

7 And one of the four live beings
gives the seven angels
who live to the eons of the eons
seven golden phials full of the fury of Elohim.

REVELATION/HAGILU NATAN ELOHIM 16

8 And the nave fills with smoke
from the glory of Elohim and from his dynamis;
and no one is able to enter the nave
until the seven plagues of the seven angels
are fulfilled/shalamed.

16 And I hear a mega voice from the nave
wording to the seven angels,
Go and pour out the phials of the fury of Elohim
to the earth.

THE FIRST PLAGUE

2 And the first goes
and pours his phial upon the earth;
and there becomes an evil ulcer to humanity
having the tattoo of the beast
— who worship his icon.

THE SECOND PLAGUE

3 And the second angel
pours his phial into the sea;
and it becomes as the blood of the dead:
and every living soul in the sea dies.

THE THIRD PLAGUE

4 And the third angel
pours his phial into the streams
and into fountains of waters;
and they become blood.

5 And I hear the angel of the waters wording,
You are just, O Yah Veh,
who is and who was*,
because you judge these.
*most mss omit, and who is coming

6 Because they poured
the blood of the holy and prophets;
and you give them blood to drink;
for they are worthy.

7 And I hear another from
the sacrifice altar wording,
Yes, Yah Veh El Sabaoth,
true and just are your judgments.

THE FOURTH PLAGUE

8 And the fourth angel
pours his phial on the sun;
and he is given to scorch humanity in fire:

9 and humanity is scorched with mega scorch:
and they blaspheme the name of Elohim
who has authority over these plagues: and
they repent not to give him glory.

THE FIFTH PLAGUE

10 And the fifth angel
pours his phial on the throne of the beast;
and his sovereigndom becomes dark;
and they gnaw their tongues from pain;

11 and blaspheme the Elohim of the heavens
from their pains and from their ulcers
— and repent not of their works.

THE SIXTH PLAGUE

12 And the sixth angel
poured out his *vial* **phial**
upon the *great river* **mega stream** Euphrates;
and the water thereof was dried up,
that the way of the *kings* **sovereigns**
of the *east* **rising of the sun** might be prepared.

13 And I saw three *unclean*
impure spirits like frogs
come out of the mouth of the dragon,
and out of the mouth of the beast,
and out of the mouth of the *false* **pseudo** prophet.

14 For they are the spirits of *devils* **demons**,
working miracles **doing signs**,
which *go forth* **proceed** unto the *kings* **sovereigns**
of the earth and of the whole world,
to gather them to the *battle* **war**
of that *great* **mega** day of *God Almighty* **El Sabaoth**.

THE THIRD BEATITUDE

15 Behold, I come as a thief.
Blessed is he that watcheth,
and *keepeth* **guardeth** his garments,
lest he walk naked,
and they see his *shame* **misbehaviour**.

16 And he gathered them together into a place
called in *the Hebrew tongue* **Hebraic**,
Armageddon **Har Megiddo**.

THE SEVENTH PLAGUE

17 And the seventh angel
poured out his *vial* **phial** into the air;
and there came a *great* **mega** voice
out of the *temple* **nave** of *heaven* **the heavens**,
from the throne,
saying **wording**, It *is done* **hath become**.

18 And there *were* **became** voices,
and thunders, and lightnings;
and there *was* **became** a *great earthquake* **mega quake**,
such as was not *since men* **from when humanity**
were **became** upon the earth,

REVELATION/HAGILU NATAN ELOHIM 17, 17

so *mighty an earthquake* **vast a quake**,
and *so great* **thus mega**.
19 And the *great city* **megalopolis**
was divided **became** into three parts,
and the cities of the *nations* **goyim** fell:
and *great Babylon* **mega Babel**
came in remembrance **was remembered**
before God **in sight of Elohim**,
to give unto her the cup of the wine
of the *fierceness* **fury** of his wrath.
20 And every island fled *away*,
and the mountains were not found.
21 And there *fell* **descended** upon *men* **humanity**
a *great* **mega** hail out of *heaven* **the heavens**,
every stone *about the weight of a talent* **as a talentweight**:
and *men* **humanity** blasphemed *God* **Elohim**
because of **from** the plague of the hail;
for **because** the plague thereof
was *exceeding great* **extremely mega**.

The Mega Whore

17 And there came one of the seven angels
which had the seven *vials* **phials**,
and *talked* **spake** with me, *saying* **wording** unto me,
Come hither; I *will* **shall** shew unto thee the judgment
of the *great* **mega** whore that sitteth upon many waters:
2 With whom the *kings* **sovereigns** of the earth
have *committed fornication* **whored**,
and *the inhabitants of* **they who settled on** the earth
have *been made drunk* **intoxicated**
with **from** the wine of her *fornication* **whoredom**.
3 So he *carried* **bore** me *away* in *the* spirit
into the wilderness:
and I saw a woman sit upon a scarlet *coloured* beast,
full of names of blasphemy,
having seven heads and ten horns.
4 And the woman was arrayed
in purple and scarlet *colour*,
and *decked* **gilded** with gold and
precious stones and pearls,
having a golden cup in her hand full of abominations
and *filthiness* **impurity** of her *fornication* **whoredom**:

The Sixth Plague

12 And the sixth angel
pours his phial on the mega stream Euphrates;
and the water thereof dries
to prepare the way
of the sovereigns of the rising of the sun.
13 And I see three impure spirits like frogs
from the mouth of the dragon
and from the mouth of the beast
and from the mouth of the pseudoprophet:
14 for they are spirits of demons doing signs
who proceed to the sovereigns of the earth
and of the whole world
— to gather them to the war
of that mega day of El Sabaoth.

The Third Beatitude

15 Behold, I come as a thief.
Blessed — he who watches and guards his garments;
lest he walk naked and they see his misbehavior.
16 And he gathers them together into a place
called in Hebraic, Har Megiddo.

The Seventh Plague

17 And the seventh angel
pours his phial into the air;
and a mega voice
comes from the nave of the heavens
— from the throne, wording, So be it!
18 And so be it,
voices and thunders and lightnings;
and a mega quake becomes
such as became not
since humanity became upon the earth
— so vast a quake and thus mega.
19 And so be it,
the megalopolis *is* in three parts
and the cities of the goyim fall:
and mega Babel is remembered in sight of Elohim,
to give her
the cup of the wine of the fury of his wrath:
20 and every island flees;
and the mountains are not found:
21 and a mega hail as a talentweight
descends from the heavens upon humanity:
and humanity blasphemes Elohim
from the plague of the hail;
because the plague thereof is extremely mega.

The Mega Whore

17 And one of the seven angels
having the seven phials
comes and speaks with me,
wording to me, Come here!
I show you the judgment of the mega whore
sitting on many waters:
2 with whom the sovereigns of the earth whored;

              and who settle on the earth
who intoxicate from the wine of her whoredom.
3   So he bears me in spirit to the wilderness:
and I see a woman sitting on a scarlet beast
full of names of blasphemy
having seven heads and ten horns.
4   And the woman is arrayed in purple and scarlet
and gilded with gold and precious stones and pearls;
having a golden cup in her hand
full of abominations and impurity of her whoredom:
5   And upon her forehead was
a name *written* **scribed**,
MYSTERY,
BABYLON **BABEL** THE *GREAT* **MEGA**, THE
MOTHER OF *HARLOTS* **WHORES** AND
ABOMINATIONS OF THE EARTH.
6   And I saw the woman
drunken with **intoxicated from** the blood
of the *saints* **holy**,
and *with* **from** the blood
of the *martyrs* **witnesses** of *Jesus* **Yah Shua**:
and when I saw her,
I *wondered with great admiration*
marvelled a mega marvel.

The Mystery Of The Woman And The Beast From The Sea

7   And the angel said unto me,
Wherefore didst **Why marvellest** thou *marvel*?
I *will tell* **shall say** thee the mystery of the woman,
and of the beast that *carrieth* **beareth** her,
which hath the seven heads and ten horns.
8   The beast that thou sawest
was, and is not;
and *shall* **is about to** ascend
out of the *bottomless pit* **abyss**,
and go into *perdition* **destruction**:
and they that *dwell* **settle** on the earth
shall *wonder* **marvel**,
whose names were not *written* **scribed**
in the *book* **scroll** of life
from the foundation of the *world* **cosmos**,
when they *behold* **see** the beast
that was, and is not, *and yet* **though** is.
9 And here is the mind which hath wisdom.
The seven heads are seven mountains, *on*
which **whereon** the woman sitteth.
10   And there are seven *kings* **sovereigns**:
five are fallen,
and one is,

and the other is not yet come;
and when he cometh,
he must *continue* **abide** a *short space* **little**.
11   And the beast that was, and is not,
even he is the eighth, and is of the seven,
and goeth into *perdition* **destruction**.
12   And the ten horns which thou sawest
are ten *kings* **sovereigns**,
which have *received* **taken** no *kingdom* **sovereigndom**
as yet;
but *receive power* **take authority** as *kings* **sovereigns**
one hour with the beast.
13   These have one *mind* **opinion**,
and shall *give* **distribute** their *power* **own dynamis**
and *strength* **authority** unto the beast.
14   These shall *make* war with the Lamb,
and the Lamb shall *overcome* **triumph over** them:
for **because** he is *Lord* **Adonay** of *lords* **adoniym**,
and *King* **Sovereign** of *kings* **sovereigns**:
and they that are with him are called,
and *chosen* **select**, and *faithful* **trustworthy**.
15   And he *saith* **wordeth** unto me,
The waters which thou sawest, where the whore sitteth,
are peoples, and multitudes,
and *nations* **goyim**, and tongues.
16   And the ten horns which
thou sawest upon the beast,
these shall hate the whore,
and shall make her desolate and naked,
and shall eat her flesh, and burn her *with* **in** fire.
17   For *God hath put* **Elohim gave** in their hearts
to *fulfil* **deal** his *will* **opinion**,
and to *agree* **deal one opinion**,
and give their *kingdom* **sovereigndom** unto the beast,
until the *words* **rhemas** of *God* **Elohim**
shall be fulfilled/**shalamed**.
18   And the woman which thou sawest
is that *great city* **megalopolis**,
which reigneth **having sovereigndom**
over the *kings* **sovereigns** of the earth.
5   and on her forehead, a name scribed,
MYSTERY!
BABEL THE MEGA
THE MOTHER OF WHORES
AND ABOMINATIONS OF THE EARTH.
6   And I see the woman
intoxicated from the blood of the holy
and from the blood of the witnesses of Yah Shua:
and when I see her I marvel a mega marvel.

The Mystery Of The Woman And The Beast From The Sea

7 And the angel says to me, Why marvel?
I say to you the mystery of the woman
and of the beast who bears her
— having the seven heads and ten horns.

8 The beast you see was, and is not:
and is about to ascend from the abyss
and go into destruction:
and they who settle on the earth marvel
— whose names are not scribed in the scroll of life
from the foundation of the cosmos
— when they see the beast
who was and is not and though is.

9 And here is the mind having wisdom:
the seven heads are seven mountains
whereon the woman sits.

10 And there are seven sovereigns:
five are fallen
and one is
and the other has not yet come;
and when he comes he must abide a little.

11 And the beast who was and is not
he is also the eighth
and is of the seven
and goes into destruction.

12 And the ten horns you see are ten sovereigns,
who take no sovereigndom as yet;
but take authority as sovereigns with the beast
one hour.

13 These have one opinion
and distribute their own dynamis and authority
to the beast.

14 These war with the Lamb
and the Lamb triumphs over them:
because he is Adonay of adoniym
and Sovereign of sovereigns:
and those with him
are called and select and trustworthy.

15 And he words to me,
The waters you see, where the whore sits,
are peoples and multitudes and goyim and tongues.

16 And the ten horns you see on the beast,
these hate the whore
and make her desolate and naked
and eat her flesh and burn her in fire.

17 For Elohim gives in their
hearts to deal his opinion;
and to deal one opinion
and give their sovereigndom to the beast,
until the rhemas of Elohim are fulfilled/shalamed.

18 And the woman you see is that megalopolis,
having sovereigndom over the sovereigns of the earth.

Babel Is Fallen, Is Fallen

18 And after these *things*
I saw another angel
come down **descend** from *heaven* **the heavens**,
having *great power* **mega authority**;
and the earth was lightened *with* **by** his glory.

2 And he cried *mightily* **in might**
with a *strong* **mega** voice, *saying* **wording**,
Babylon **Babel** the *great* **mega** is fallen, is fallen,
and is become the *habitation*
settlement of *devils* **demons**,
and the *hold* **guardhouse** of every *foul* **impure** spirit,
and a *cage* **guardhouse**
of every *unclean* **impure** and hateful *bird* **fowl**.

3 *For* **Because** all *nations*
goyim have drunk of the wine
of the *wrath* **fury** of her *fornication* **whoredom**,
and the *kings* **sovereigns** of the earth
have *committed fornication* **whored** with her,
and the merchants of the earth are *waxed rich* **enriched**
through **from** the *abundance* **dynamis**
of her *delicacies* **luxuries**.

4 And I heard another voice
from *heaven* **the heavens**,
saying **wording**, Come out of her, my people,
that ye be not *partakers* **co—partakers** of her sins,
and that ye *receive* **take** not of her plagues.

5 *For* **Because** her sins
have *reached* **followed** unto *heaven* **the heavens**,
and *God* **Elohim** hath remembered
her *iniquities* **injustices**.

6 *Reward* **Give** her
even as she *rewarded* **gave to** you,
and double unto her double according to her works:
in the cup which she hath *filled fill* **mingled**
mingle to her double.

7 *How* **As** much *as* she hath glorified herself,
and *lived deliciously* **luxuriated**,
so much *torment* **torture** and *sorrow* **mourning** give her:
for **because** she *saith* **wordeth** in her heart,
I sit a *queen* **sovereigness**, and am no widow,
and shall *no way* see no *sorrow* **mourning**.

8 *Therefore* **For this** shall her
plagues come in one day,
death, and *sorrow* **mourning**, and famine;
and she shall be *utterly burned with* **burnt in** fire:

for strong **because mighty**
is *the Lord God* **Yah Veh Elohim**
who judgeth her.

Sovereigns Weep Over The Fall Of Babel

9 And the *kings* **sovereigns** of the earth,
who have *committed fornication* **whored** and
lived deliciously **luxuriated** with her,
shall *bewail* **weep for** her, and *lament for* **chop over** her,
when they shall see the smoke of her *burning* **firing**,

10 Standing *from* afar *off*
for the *fear* **awe** of her *torment* **torture**, *saying* **wording**,
Alas **Woe**, *alas* **woe** that *great city*
Babylon **megalopolis Babel**,
that mighty city!
for **because** in one hour is thy judgment come.

Merchants Weep Over The Fall Of Babel

11 And the merchants of the earth
shall weep and mourn over her;
for **because** no *man* **one**
buyeth their merchandise **marketeth**
her wares *any* **no** more:

12 The *merchandise* **wares** of gold, and silver,
and precious stones, and of pearls,
and *fine* **white** linen, and purple, and silk, and scarlet,
and all *thyine wood* **incense timber**,
and all *manner* vessels of *ivory* **elephantine**,
and all *manner* vessels of most precious *wood* **timber**,
and of *brass* **copper**, and iron, and marble,

13 And cinnamon, and *odours* **incense**,
and *ointments* **myrrh**, and frankincense,
and wine, and *olive* oil,
and fine flour, and *wheat* **grain**,
and *beasts* **animals**, and sheep, and horses, and chariots,
and *slaves* **bodies**, and souls of *men* **humanity**.

14 And the *fruits* **evening hour**
that thy soul lusted after **of thy soul's panting**
are *departed* **gone** from thee,
and all *things which were dainty* **the greasy**
and *goodly* **radiant** are *departed* **gone** from thee,
and thou shalt find them no more *at all* **no way**.

Babel Is Fallen, Is Fallen

18 And after these
I see another angel descending from the heavens
having mega authority;
and the earth is lit by his glory.

2 And he cries in might with a mega voice,
wording, Babel the mega is fallen! Is fallen!
and becomes the settlement of demons
and the guardhouse of every impure spirit
and a guardhouse of every impure and hateful fowl.

3 Because all goyim drank
of the wine of the fury of her whoredom
and the sovereigns of the earth whored with her
and the merchants of the earth enriched
from the dynamis of her luxuries.

4 And I hear another voice from the heavens,
wording, Come from her, my people,
that you not co—partake of her sins
and that you not take of her plagues.

5 Because her sins follow to the heavens
and Elohim remembers her injustices.

6 Give to her even as she gave to you
and double to her double according to her works:
in the cup she mingles, mingle to her double:

7 as much as she glorifies herself and luxuriates
so much torture and mourning give her:
because she words in her heart,
I sit a sovereigness and am no widow
and never no way see mourning.

8 For this her plagues come in one day
— death and mourning and famine;
and she utterly burns in fire:
because mighty is Yah Veh Elohim who judges her.

Sovereigns Weep Over The Fall Of Babel

9 And the sovereigns of the earth
who whored and luxuriated with her,
weep for her and chop over her
when they see the smoke of her firing,

10 standing from afar for the awe of her torture,
wording, Woe!
Woe that megalopolis Babel! — that mighty city!
because in one hour is your judgment iis come.

Merchants Weep Over The Fall Of Babel

11 And the merchants of the earth
weep and mourn over her;
because no one markets her wares never more

12 — the wares of gold and silver
and precious stones and of pearls
and white linen and purple and silk and scarlet
and all incense timber and all vessels of elephantine
and all vessels of most precious timber
and of copper and iron and marble

13 and cinnamon and incense
and myrrh and frankincense and wine and olive oil
and fine flour and grain

REVELATION/HAGILU NATAN ELOHIM 19

and animals and sheep and horses and chariots
and bodies and souls of humanity.

14 And the evening hour of
the panting of your soul
is gone from you;
and all the greasy and radiant
are gone from you;
and you no way find them never more.

15 The merchants of these *things*,
which were *made rich* **enriched** by her,
shall stand *from* afar *off*
for the *fear* **awe** of her *torment* **torture**,
weeping and *wailing* **mourning**,

16 And *saying* **wording**, *Alas* **Woe**,
alas **woe** that *great city* **megalopolis**,
that was *clothed* **arrayed** in *fine* **white** linen,
and purple, and scarlet,
and *decked with* **gilded in** gold,
and precious stones, and pearls!

17 *For* **Because** in one hour
so *great* **vast** riches is *come to nought* **desolated**.

PILOTS, PASSENGERS, AND SAILERS CRY OVER THE FALL OF BABEL

And every *shipmaster* **pilot**,
and all the *company* **homogeneous crowd**
in *ships* **sailers**,
and *sailors* **ship crew**, and as many as *trade* **work** by sea,
stood *from* afar *off*,

18 And cried
when they saw the smoke of her *burning* **firing**,
saying **wording**,
What *city* is like unto this *great city* **megalopolis**!

19 And they cast dust on their heads, and cried,
weeping and *wailing* **mourning**,
saying **wording**, *Alas* **Woe**,
alas **woe** that *great city* **megalopolis**,
wherein were *made rich* **enriched**
all that had *ships* **sailers** in the sea
by reason of **from** her *costliness* **preciousness**!
for **because** in one hour is she *made desolate* **desolated**.

20 Rejoice over her, *thou heaven* **heavens**,
and ye holy apostles and prophets;
for God **because Elohim**
hath *avenged you on* **judged your judgment of** her.

21 And *a* **one** mighty angel took up a stone
like a great **as a mega** millstone, and cast it into the sea,
saying **wording**, Thus with violence
shall that *great city Babylon* **megalopolis Babel**
be *thrown down* **cast**,

and shall **never no way**
still be found *no more at all*.

22 And the voice of *harpers*
citherists, and musicians,
and of *pipers* **flutists**, and trumpeters,
shall **never no way still** be heard *no more at all* in thee;
and *no craftsman* **any technician**,
of whatsoever *craft he be* **technique**,
shall **never no way still** be found *any more* in thee;
and the *sound* **voice** of a millstone
shall **never no way still** be heard *no more at all* in thee;

23 And the light of a candle
shall **never no way still** *shine no*
more at all **manifest** in thee;
and the voice of the bridegroom and of the bride
shall **never no way still** be heard *no more at all* in thee:
for **because** thy merchants
were the *great men* **magistrates** of the earth;
for by **because in** thy *sorceries* **pharmacies**
were all *nations deceived* **goyim seduced**.

24 And in her was found the blood of prophets,
and of *saints* **the holy**,
and of all that were *slain* **slaughtered** upon the earth.

THE FOUR HALALU YAHS FROM THE HEAVENS

19 And after these *things* I heard a *great* **mega** voice
of *much people* **many multitudes** in *heaven* **the heavens**,
saying **wording**, *Alleluia* **Halalu Yah**;
Salvation, and glory, and honour, and *power* **dynamis**,
unto *the Lord* **Yah Veh** our *God* **Elohim**:

2 *For* **Because** true and *righteous*
just are his judgments:
for **because** he hath judged the *great* **mega** whore,
which *did corrupt* **corrupted** the earth
with **in** her *fornication* **whoredom**,
and hath avenged the blood of his servants *at*
from her hand.

3 And *again* **secondly** they
said, *Alleluia* **Halalu Yah**.
And her smoke *rose up* **ascended**
for ever and ever **unto the eons of the eons**.

15 Her merchants of these, whom she enriched,
stand from afar for the awe of her torture
— weeping and mourning

16 and wording, Woe!
Woe! — that megalopolis
arrayed in white linen and purple and scarlet
and gilded in gold and precious stones and pearls!

17 Because in one hour so vast riches are desolated.

Pilots, Passengers, And Sailers Cry Over The Fall Of Babel

And every pilot
and all the homogeneous crowd in sailers
and ship crew and as many as work
by sea stand from afar;
18   and seeing the smoke of her firing, they cry,
wording, What is like to this megalopolis!
19   And they cast dust on their heads and cry,
weeping and mourning, wording, Woe!
Woe that megalopolis,
wherein all who had sailers in the sea
enriched from her preciousnesses!
Because in one hour she desolated.
20   Rejoice over her,
O the heavens and you holy apostles and prophets;
because Elohim judges your judgment of her.
21   And one mighty angel takes a stone
as a mega millstone and casts it into the sea, wording,
Thus with violence is that megalopolis Babel cast;
and are never ever no way still found in you:
22   and the voice of citherists and musicians
and of flutists and trumpeters
are never ever no way still heard in you;
and any technician of whatever technique,
are never ever no way still found in you;
and the voice of a millstone
are never ever no way still heard in you;
23   and the light of a candle
are never ever no way still manifested in you;
and the voice of the bridegroom and of the bride
are never ever no way still heard in you:
because your merchants
are the magistrates of the earth;
because in your pharmacies
all goyim are seduced:
24   and in her
are found the blood of prophets and of the holy
and of all those slaughtered on the earth.

The Four Halalu Yahs From The Heavens

19   And after these
I hear a mega voice of many multitudes
in the heavens,
wording, Halalu Yah!
Salvation and glory and honor and dynamis,
to Yah Veh our Elohim:
2   because true and just are his judgments:
because he judged the mega whore
who corrupted the earth in her whoredom
and avenged the blood of his servants from her hand.
3   And secondly they say, Halalu Yah!
— and her smoke ascends to the eons of the eons.
4   And the four and twenty elders
and the four *beasts* **live beings** fell *down*
and worshipped *God* **Elohim** that sat on the throne,
saying **wording**, Amen; *Alleluia* **Halalu Yah**.
5   And a voice came out of
the throne, *saying* **wording**,
Praise **Halal** our *God* **Elohim**, all ye his
servants, and ye that *fear* **awe** him,
both *small* **minute** and *great* **mega**.
6   And I heard
as *it were* the voice of a *great* **vast** multitude,
and as the voice of many waters,
and as the voice of mighty thunderings,
saying **wording**, *Alleluia* **Halalu Yah**:
for **because**
the Lord God omnipotent **Yah Veh El Sabaoth** reigneth.

The Marriage Of The Lamb Is Come

7   Let us *be glad* **cheer** and *rejoice* **jump for joy**,
and give *honour* **glory** to him:
for **because** the marriage of the Lamb is come,
and his *wife* **woman** hath *made* **prepared** herself *ready*.
8   And to her was *granted* **given**
that she should be arrayed in *fine* **white** linen,
clean **pure** and *white* **radiant**:
for the *fine* **white** linen
is the *righteousness* **justification** of *saints* **the holy**.

The Fourth Beatitude

9   And he *saith* **wordeth** unto me, *Write* **Scribe**,
Blessed are they
which are called unto the marriage supper of the Lamb.
And he *saith* **wordeth** unto me,
These are the true *sayings* **words** of *God* **Elohim**.
10   And I fell *at* **in front of** his feet to worship him.
And he *said* **worded** unto me, See *thou do it* not:
I am thy *fellowservant* **co—servant**,
and of thy brethren
that have the *testimony* **witness** of *Jesus* **Yah Shua**:
worship *God* **Elohim**:
for the *testimony* **witness** of *Jesus* **Yah Shua**
is the spirit of prophecy.

REVELATION/HAGILU NATAN ELOHIM 19

THE SOVEREIGN OF SOVEREIGNS, ADONAY OF ADONIYM, AND WARRIORS IN THE HEAVENS SMITE THE GOYIM

11 And I saw *heaven* **the heavens** opened,
and behold, a white horse;
and he that sat upon him
was called *faithful* **Trustworthy** and True,
and in *righteousness* **justness**
he *doth judge* **judgeth** and *make war* **warreth**.

12 His eyes were as a flame of fire,
and on his head were many *crowns* **diadems**;
and he had a name *written* **scribed**,
that no man knew, *but* **except** he himself.

13 And he was *clothed* **arrayed**
with a *vesture* **garment**
dipped **baptized** in blood:
and his name is called The Word of *God* **Elohim**.

14 And the *armies which were*
warriors in *heaven* **the heavens**
followed him upon white horses,
clothed **endued** in *fine* white linen,
white and *clean* **pure**.

15 And out of his mouth
goeth **proceedeth** a sharp *sword* **sabre**,
that *with* **in** it he should smite the *nations* **goyim**:
and he shall *rule* **shepherd** them
with **in** a *rod* **scion** of iron:
and he *treadeth* **trampleth** the *winepress* **wine trough**
of the *fierceness* **fury** and wrath
of *Almighty God* **El Sabaoth**.

16 And he hath on his *vesture*
garment and on his thigh
a name *written* **scribed**,
KING **SOVEREIGN** OF *KINGS* **SOVEREIGNS**,
AND *LORD* **ADONAY** OF *LORDS* **ADONIYM**.

THE SUPPER OF THE MEGA ELOHIM

17 And I saw *an* **one** angel standing in the sun;
and he cried with a *loud* **mega** voice,
saying **wording**
to all the fowls that fly in the *midst*
of heaven **midheavens**,
Come and gather yourselves together
unto the supper of the *great God* **mega Elohim**;

4 And the twenty—four elders
and the four live beings
fall and worship Elohim sitting on the throne,
wording, Amen! Halalu Yah!

5 And a voice comes from the throne, wording,
Halal our Elohim,
all you his servants and you who awe him
— both minute and mega.

6 And I hear as the voice of a vast multitude
and as the voice of many waters
and as the voice of mighty thunderings,
wording, Halalu Yah!
because Yah Veh El Sabaoth reigns.

THE MARRIAGE OF THE LAMB IS COME

7 Cheer and jump for joy and give him glory!
because the marriage of the Lamb is come
and his woman prepares herself.

8 And she is given to be arrayed in white linen
— pure and radiant:
for the white linen is the justification of the holy.

THE FOURTH BEATITUDE

9 And he words to me, Scribe, Blessed
— those called to the marriage supper of the Lamb.
And he words to me,
These are the true words of Elohim.

10 — and I fall in front of his feet to worship him.
And he words to me, See — not:
I am co—servant of you and of your brothers
who have the witness of Yah Shua:
worship Elohim:
for the witness of Yah Shua is the spirit of prophecy.

THE SOVEREIGN OF SOVEREIGNS, ADONAY OF ADONIYM, AND WARRIORS IN THE HEAVENS SMITE THE GOYIM

11 And I see the heavens open;
and behold, a white horse;
and he sitting on him is called Trustworthy and True;
and in justness he judges and wars.

12 His eyes are as a flame of fire
and on his head are many diadems;
and he has a name scribed,
that no man knows — except he himself:

13 and he is arrayed with a
garment baptized in blood:
and his name is called The Word of Elohim.

14 And the warriors in the heavens
follow him on white horses,
endued in white linen — white and pure:

15 and a sharp sabre proceeds from his mouth
to smite the goyim
and to shepherd them in a scion of iron:
and he tramples the wine trough

of the fury and wrath of El Sabaoth.

16 And on his garment and on his thigh
he has a name scribed,
SOVEREIGN OF SOVEREIGNS,
AND ADONAY OF ADONIYM.

The Supper Of The Mega Elohim

17 And I see one angel standing in the sun;
and he cries with a mega voice
— wording to all the fowls that fly in the midheavens,
Come and gather yourselves together
to the supper of the mega Elohim

18 That ye may eat the flesh of *kings* **sovereigns**,
and the flesh of *captains* **chiliarchs**,
and the flesh of mighty *men*,
and the flesh of horses, and of them that sit on them,
and the flesh of all *men*,
both *free* **liberated** and *bond* **servant**,
both *small* **minute** and *great* **mega**.

19 And I saw the beast,
and the *kings* **sovereigns** of the earth,
and their *armies* **warriors**, gathered
together to make war
against **with** him that sat on the horse,
and *against* **with** his *army* **warriors**.

Beast And Pseudo Prophet Cast Into The Lake Of Fire

20 And the beast was *taken* **seized**,
and with him the *false* **pseudo** prophet
that *wrought miracles before him* **did signs in his sight**,
with **in** which he *deceived* **seduced** them
that had *received* **taken** the *mark* **tattoo** of the beast,
and them that worshipped his *image* **icon**.
These *both* **two** were cast alive
into a lake of fire burning *with brimstone* **in sulphur**.

The Slaughter Of The Rest

21 And the *remnant* **rest** were *slain* **slaughtered**
with **at** the *sword* **sabre** of him
that sat upon the horse,
which *sword* proceeded out of his mouth:
and all the fowls were filled *with* **from** their flesh.

Satan Bound

20 And I saw an angel
come down **descending** from *heaven* **the heavens**,
having the key of the *bottomless pit* **abyss**
and a *great chain* **mega fetter** in his hand.

2 And he *laid hold on* **overpowered** the dragon,
that *old* **ancient** serpent,
which is *the Devil* **Diabolos**, and Satan,
and bound him a thousand years,

3 And cast him into the *bottomless pit* **abyss**,
and shut him *up*, and *set a seal upon* **sealed**
him, that he should **never no way**
deceive **still seduce** the *nations* **goyim** no more,
till the thousand years
should be fulfilled/shalamed:
and after *that* **these**
he must be loosed a little *season* **time**.

The Axed Souls Reign With Messiah

4 And I saw thrones, and they sat upon them,
and judgment was given unto them:
and *I saw* the souls of them that were *beheaded* **axed**
for the witness of *Jesus* **Yah Shua**,
and for the word of *God* **Elohim**,
and which had not worshipped the beast,
neither his *image* **icon**,
neither had *received* **taken** his *mark* **tattoo**
upon their foreheads, or in their hands;
and they lived and reigned with *Christ* **Messiah**
a thousand years.

The First Resurrection

5 But the rest of the dead *lived* **relived** not *again*
until the thousand years
were finished **shall be fulfilled/shalamed**.
This is the first resurrection.

The Fifth Beatitude

6 Blessed and holy
is he that hath *part* in the first resurrection:
on such **over these**
the second death hath no *power* **authority**,
but they shall be priests
of *God* **Elohim** and of *Christ* **Messiah**,
and shall reign with him a thousand years.

Satan Loosed

7 And when the thousand years
are *expired* **fulfilled/shalamed**,
Satan shall be loosed out of his *prison* **guardhouse**,

8 And shall go *out* to *deceive*
seduce the *nations* **goyim**
which are in the four *quarters* **corners** of the earth,
Gog, and Magog, to gather them together to *battle* **war**:
the number of whom *is* as the sand of the sea.

18 to eat the flesh of sovereigns,
and the flesh of chiliarchs,
and the flesh of mighty,
and the flesh of horses,
and of those sitting on them,
and the flesh of all
— liberated and servant — minute and mega.

19 And I see the beast
and the sovereigns of the earth and their warriors
gather together to make war
with him sitting on the horse and with his warriors.

Beast And Pseudoprophet Cast Into The Lake Of Fire

20 And the beast is seized;
and with him
the pseudoprophet who did signs in his sight;
in which he seduced them
who took the tattoo of the beast
and them who worship his icon.
These two are cast alive
into a lake of fire burning in sulphur.

The Slaughter Of The Rest

21 And the rest are slaughtered
at the sabre of him sitting upon the horse,
proceeding from his mouth:
and all the fowls fill from their flesh.

Satan Bound

20 And I see an angel descending
from the heavens,
having the key of the abyss;
and a mega fetter in his hand:
2 and he overpowers the dragon
— that ancient serpent who is Diabolos and Satan
and binds him a thousand years:
3 and casts him into the abyss
and shuts him and seals him,
so that he never no way still seduces the goyim
till the thousand years are fulfilled/shalamed:
and after these he must be loosed a little time.

The Axed Souls Reign With Messiah

4 And I see thrones and those sitting thereon:
and they are given judgment:
and the souls of those axed for the witness
of Yah Shua and for the word of Elohim
who neither worshipped the beast nor his icon;
nor had taken his tattoo
on their foreheads or in their hands;
and they live and reign with Messiah
a thousand years.

The First Resurrection

5 And the rest of the dead relive not
until the thousand years are fulfilled/shalamed.
This is the first resurrection.

The Fifth Beatitude

6 Blessed and holy
whoever has part in the first resurrection;
over these the second death has no authority:
but they become priests of Elohim and of Messiah
and reign with him a thousand years.

Satan Loosed

7 And when the thousand years
are fulfilled/shalamed,
Satan is loosed from his guardhouse;
8 and goes to seduce the goyim
in the four corners of the earth
— Gog and Magog — to gather them together to war:
whose number is as the sand of the sea.
9 And they *went up* **ascended**
on the breadth of the earth,
and *compassed* **surrounded**
the *camp* **encampment** of the *saints about* **holy**,
and the beloved city:
and fire *came down* **descended** from *God* **Elohim**
out of *heaven* **the heavens**, and devoured them.

The Sentence Of Diabolos

10 And *the devil* **Diabolos**
that *deceived* **seduced** them
was cast into the lake of fire and *brimstone* **sulphur**,
where the beast and the *false* **pseudo** prophet are,
and shall be *tormented* **tortured** day and night
for ever and ever **unto the eons of the eons**.

The Judgment Of The Earth And The Heavens

11 And I saw a *great* **mega** white throne,
and him that sat on it,
from whose face the earth and the
heaven **heavens** fled *away*;
and there was found no place for them.

THE JUDGMENT OF THE HOLY

12 And I saw the dead, *small* **minute** and *great* **mega**,
stand *before God* **in sight of Elohim**;
and the *books* **scrolls** were opened:
and another *book* **scroll** was opened,
which is the book of life:
and the dead were judged out of those *things*
which *were written* **scribed** in the *books* **scrolls**,
according to their works.

THE JUDGMENT OF THE UNHOLY

13 And the sea gave up the dead which were in it;
and death and *hell* **Hades/Sheol**
delivered **gave** up the dead which were in them:
and they were judged
every man **each** according to their works.

THE SENTENCE OF DEATH AND HADES/SHEOL

14 And death and *hell* **Hades/Sheol**
were cast into the lake of fire.
This is the second death.

THE SENTENCE OF THE UNHOLY

15 And *whosoever* **if any** was not found
written **scribed** in the *book* **scroll** of life
was cast into the lake of fire.

THE NEW HEAVENS AND THE NEW EARTH

21 And I saw *a* **the** new *heaven*
heavens and *a* **the** new earth:
for the first *heaven* **heavens** and the first earth
were passed away;
and there was *no more* **not still** a sea.

THE NEW YERU SHALEM

2 And I *John* **Yahn** saw the holy city,
new *Jerusalem* **Yeru Shalem**,
coming down **descending** from *God* **Elohim**
out of *heaven* **the heavens**,
prepared as a bride adorned for her *husband* **man**.

THE NEW RELATIONSHIP OF ELOHIM WITH THE HOLY

3 And I heard a *great* **mega**
voice out of *heaven* **the heavens**
saying **wording**, Behold,
the tabernacle of *God* **Elohim** is with *men* **humanity**,

and he *will dwell* **shall tabernacle** with them,
and they shall be his *people* **peoples**,
and *God* **Elohim** himself shall be with them,
and be — their *God* **Elohim**.

4 And *God* **Elohim**
shall wipe *away* all tears from their eyes;
and there shall *be no more* **still becomes no** death,
neither sorrow, nor crying,
neither shall there **no way still** be *any more* pain:
for **because** the *former things* **first** are *passed away* **gone**.

5 And he that sat upon the throne said,
Behold, I make all *things* new.
And he *said* **worded** unto me, *Write* **Scribe**:
for **because** these words are true
and *faithful* **trustworthy**.

6 And he said unto me, It *is done* **hath become**.
I am Alpha and Omega **I AM the A and the Ù**,
the beginning and the *end* **completion/shalom**.
I *will* **shall** give unto him that is athirst
of the fountain of the water of life *freely* **gratuitously**.

7 He that *overcometh* **triumpheth**
shall inherit all *things*
and I *will* **shall** be *his* **to him**, *God* **Elohim**,
and he shall be *my* **to me,** son.

9 And they ascend on the breadth of the earth
and surround the encampment of the holy
and the beloved city:
and fire descends from Elohim from the heavens
and consumes them.

THE SENTENCE OF DIABOLOS

10 And Diabolos who seduced them
is cast into the lake of fire and sulphur
where the beast and the pseudoprophet are:
to be tortured day and night to the eons of the eons.

THE JUDGMENT OF THE EARTH AND THE HEAVENS

11 And I see a mega white throne
and him sitting thereon
from whose face the earth and the heavens flee;
and no place is found for them.

THE JUDGMENT OF THE HOLY

12 And I see the dead — minute and mega
standing in sight of Elohim; and the scrolls are opened:
and another scroll is opened — of life:
and the dead are judged
from that scribed in the scrolls
according to their works.

REVELATION/HAGILU NATAN ELOHIM 21

THE JUDGMENT OF THE UNHOLY

13 And the sea gives up the dead in it;
and death and Hades/Sheol give up the dead in them:
and they are each judged according to their works.

THE SENTENCE OF DEATH AND HADES/SHEOL

14 And death and Hades/Sheol
are cast into the lake of fire.
This is the second death.

THE SENTENCE OF THE UNHOLY

15 And if any are not found
scribed in the scroll of life
they are cast into the lake of fire.

THE NEW HEAVENS AND THE NEW EARTH

21 And I see the new heavens and a new earth:
for the first heavens and the first earth passed away;
and there is not still a sea.

THE NEW YERU SHALEM

2 And I Yahn see the holy
city — new Yeru Shalem
descending from Elohim from the heavens
prepared as a bride adorned for her man.

THE NEW RELATIONSHIP OF ELOHIM WITH THE HOLY

3 And I hear a mega voice
from the heavens, wording,
Behold, the tabernacle of Elohim is with humanity
and he tabernacles with them;
and they become his peoples
and Elohim himself becomes with them
— their Elohim.

4 And Elohim wipes all tears from their eyes;
and there still becomes
neither death nor sorrow nor crying;
and never no way still becomes pain:
because the first have gone.

5 And he sitting on the throne says,
Behold, I make all new.
And he words to me, Scribe:
because these words are true and trustworthy.

6 And he says to me, It is become!
I AM the A and the Ù,
the beginning and the completion/shalom.
To him who thirsts
I give of the fountain of the water of life gratuitously.

7 he who triumphs inherits all;
and I become to him, Elohim
and he becomes to me, son.

THE SEVERED RELATIONSHIP OF ELOHIM FROM THE UNHOLY

8 But the *fearful* **cowardly**,
and *unbelieving* **trustless**,
and the abominable, and murderers, and whoremongers,
and *sorcerers* **pharmaceutists**, and idolaters,
and all *liars* **pseudos**,
shall have their part in the lake
which burneth with fire and *brimstone* **sulphur**:
which is the second death.

THE BRIDE

9 And there came unto me one of the seven angels
which had the seven *vials* **phials**
full of the seven *last* **final** plagues,
and *talked* **spake** with me, *saying* **wording**, Come hither,
I *will* **shall** shew thee the bride, the Lamb's *wife* **woman**.

THE NEW YERU SHALEM

10 And he *carried* **bore** me away in *the* spirit
to a *great* **mega** and high mountain,
and shewed me that *great city* **megalopolis**,
the holy *Jerusalem* **Yeru Shalem**,
descending out of *heaven* **the heavens** from *God* **Elohim**,

11 Having the glory of *God* **Elohim**:
and her light *was* like unto a stone most precious,
even like **as** a jasper stone, *clear as crystal* **crystaline**;

12 And had a wall *great* **mega** and high,
and had twelve gates, and at the gates twelve angels,
and names *written thereon* **epigraphed**,
which are *the names* of the twelve *tribes* **scions**
of the *children* **sons** of *Israel* **Yisra El**:

13 *On* **By** the *east* **rising** three gates;
on **by** the north three gates;
on **by** the south three gates;
and *on* **by** the *west* **lowering** three gates.

14 And the wall of the city had twelve foundations,
and in them
the names of the twelve apostles of the Lamb.

THE MEASUREMENTS OF THE NEW YERU SHALEM

15 And he that *talked* **spake** with me
had a golden reed to measure the city,
and the gates thereof, and the wall thereof.

16   And the city lieth foursquare,
and the length is as *large* **long** as the breadth:
and he measured the city with the reed,
twelve thousand *furlongs* **stadia**.
The length and the breadth and the height of it are equal.
17   And he measured the wall thereof,
an hundred *and* forty *and* four cubits,
according to the measure of a *man* **human**,
that **which** is, of the angel.

The Materials Of The New Yeru Shalem

18   And the *building* **structure** of the wall of it
was *of* jasper:
and the city *was* pure gold, like unto *clear* **pure** glass.
19   And the foundations of the wall of the city
were garnished **adorned**
with all *manner of* precious stones.
The first foundation *was* jasper; the second, sapphire;
the third, *a* chalcedony; the fourth, *an* emerald;
20   The fifth, sardonyx; the sixth, sardius;
the seventh, chrysolyte; the eighth, beryl;
the ninth, *a* topaz; the tenth, *a* chrysoprasus;
the eleventh, *a* jacinth; the twelfth, *an* amethyst.
21   And the twelve gates were twelve pearls:
every several **each one** gate was of one pearl:
and the *street* **broadway** of the city was pure gold,
as *it were transparent* **diaphanous** glass.

The Severed Relationship Of Elohim From The Unholy

8   And the cowardly and trustless
and the abominable and murderers
and whoremongers and pharmaceutists
and idolaters and all pseudos
have their part in the lake
burning with fire and sulphur
— being the second death.

The Bride

9   And one of the seven angels comes to me
— who had the seven phials
full of the seven final plagues
and speaks with me, wording, Come hither!
I show you the bride, the woman of the Lamb.

The New Yeru Shalem

10   And in spirit,
he bears me to a mega and high mountain
and shows me that megalopolis
the holy Yeru Shalem
descending from the heavens from Elohim;
11   having the glory of Elohim:
and her light is like to a stone most precious
as a jasper stone, crystaline;
12   having a wall mega and high,
having twelve gates,
and at the gates twelve angels,
and names epigraphed,
being the twelve scions of the sons of Yisra El:
13   by the rising three gates;
by the north three gates;
by the south three gates;
and by the lowering three gates.
14   And the wall of the city has twelve foundations
and in them
the names of the twelve apostles of the Lamb.

THE MEASUREMENTS OF THE NEW YERU SHALEM

15   And he speaking with me has a golden reed
to measure the city and the gates and the wall:
16   and the city lies foursquare
and the length is as long as the breadth:
and he measures the city with the reed,
twelve thousand stadia.
The length and the breadth and the height are equal.
17   And he measures the wall
a hundred and forty—four cubits
— the measure of a human — being the angel.

The Materials Of The New Yeru Shalem

18   And the structure of the wall is jasper:
and the city is pure gold, like pure glass:
19   and the foundations of the wall of the city
are adorned with all precious stones:
the first foundation, jasper;
the second, sapphire;
the third, chalcedony;
the fourth, emerald;
20   the fifth, sardonyx;
the sixth, sardius;
the seventh, chrysolyte;
the eighth, beryl;
the ninth, topaz;
the tenth, chrysoprasus;
the eleventh, jacinth;
the twelfth, amethyst.
21   And the twelve gates are twelve pearls:
each one gate is one pearl:
and the broadway of the city is pure gold
— as diaphanous glass.

REVELATION/HAGILU NATAN ELOHIM 21, 22

THE OMISSIONS OF THE NEW YERU SHALEM

22 And I saw no *temple* **nave** therein:
for *the Lord God Almighty* **Yah Veh El Sabaoth**
and the Lamb are the *temple* **nave** of it.

23 And the city had no need of the sun,
neither of the moon, to *shine* **manifest** in it:
for the glory of *God did lighten* **Elohim lightened** it,
and the Lamb is the *light* **candle** thereof.

24 And the *nations* **goyim** of them which are saved
shall walk in the light of it:
and the *kings* **sovereigns** of the earth
do bring their glory and honour into it.

25 And the gates of it
shall not **no way** be shut *at all* by day:
for there shall be no night there.

26 And they shall bring the glory and honour
of the *nations* **goyim** into it.

27 And there shall *in* **not** no *wise* **way** enter into it
any thing **aught** that *defileth* **profaneth**,
neither *whatsoever worketh* **doeth** abomination,
or *maketh a lie* **lieth**:
but **except** they which are *written* **scribed**
in the Lamb's *book* **scroll** of life.

THE THRONE, STREAM, AND STAFF OF LIFE OF THE NEW YERU SHALEM

22 And he shewed me a pure *river* **stream**
of water of life,
clear **radiant** as *crystal* **crystaline**,
proceeding out of the throne of *God*
Elohim and of the Lamb.

2 In the midst of the *street* **broadway** of it,
and *on either side* **hence and hence** of the *river* **stream**,
was there the *tree* **staff** of life,
which *bare* **dealt** twelve *manner of* fruits,
and *yielded* **gave** her fruit *every* **each single** month:
and the leaves of the *tree* **staff**
were *for* **unto** the *healing* **therapy** of the *nations* **goyim**.

3 And there shall **not still**
be *no more curse* **any anathema**:
but the throne of *God* **Elohim** and of the Lamb
shall be in it;
and his servants shall *serve* **liturgize** him:

4 And they shall see his face;
and his name shall be in their foreheads.

5 And there shall be no night there;
and they need no candle, neither light of the sun;
for the Lord God **because Yah Veh Elohim**
giveth **lighteth** them *light*:

and they shall reign
for ever and ever **unto the eons of the eons**.

SUMMATION

6 And he said unto me,
These *sayings* **words** are *faithful* **trustworthy** and true:
and *the Lord God* **Yah Veh Elohim** of the holy prophets
sent **apostolized** his angel
to shew unto his servants *the things* **those**
which must *shortly be done* **quickly become**.

THE SIXTH BEATITUDE

7 Behold, I come quickly:
blessed is he that *keepeth* **guardeth** the *sayings* **words**
of the prophecy of this *book* **scroll**.

8 And I *John* **Yahn** saw these
things, and heard *them*.
And when I had heard and seen,
I fell *down* to worship
before **in front of** the feet of the angel
which shewed me these *things*.

9 Then *saith* **wordeth** he
unto me, See *thou do it* not:
for I am thy *fellowservant* **co—servant**,
and of thy brethren the prophets,
and of them
which *keep* **guard** the *sayings* **words** of this *book* **scroll**:
worship *God* **Elohim**.

10 And he *saith* **wordeth** unto me,
Seal not the *sayings* **words**
of the prophecy of this *book* **scroll**:
for **because** the *time* **season** is *at hand* **near**.

THE OMISSIONS OF THE NEW YERU SHALEM

22 And I see no nave therein;
for Yah Veh El Sabaoth and the Lamb
are the nave thereof:

23 and the city needs neither the sun nor the moon
to manifest therein:
for the glory of Elohim lights it
and the Lamb is the candle thereof.

24 And the goyim of the saved
walk in the light thereof:
and the sovereigns of the earth
bring their glory and honor therein:

25 and the gates thereof
are never no way shut by day;
for there is no night there:

26 and they bring the glory and honor
of the goyim therein:

27   and aught that profanes
or does an abomination or a lie
never no way enters therein
— except those scribed
in the scroll of life of the Lamb.

The Throne, Stream, And Staff Of Life Of The New Yeru Shalem

22 And he shows me a pure stream of water of life
radiant as crystaline
proceeding from the throne of Elohim and of the Lamb.
2   midst the broadway
and hence and hence of the stream
is the staff of life dealing twelve fruits;
giving her fruit each single month:
and the leaves of the staff
are to the therapy of the goyim.
3   And there is not still any anathema:
and the throne of Elohim and of the Lamb are therein;
and his servants liturgize him:
4   and they see his face;
and his name *is* on their foreheads.
5   And there is no night there;
and they need neither candle nor light of the sun;
because Yah Veh Elohim lights them:
and they reign to the eons of the eons.

Summation

6   And he says to me,
These words are trustworthy and true:
and Yah Veh Elohim of the holy prophets
apostolized his angel to show his servants
those which must quickly become.

The Sixth Beatitude

7   Behold, I come quickly:
blessed — whoever guards the words
of the prophecy of this scroll.
8   And I Yahn see and hear these:
and when I hear and see,
I fall to worship in front of the feet of the angel
who shows me these.
9   And he words to me, See — not:
for I am your co—servant,
and of your brothers the prophets,
and of them who guard the words of this scroll:
worship Elohim.
10   And he words to me,
Seal not the words of the prophecy of this scroll:
because the season is near.

11   He that *is* unjust **injureth**,
let him *be* unjust **injure** still:
and he which *is filthy* **fouleth**, let him *be filthy* **foul** still:
and he that is *righteous* **just**,
let him *be righteous* **justify** still:
and he that is holy, let him be *holy* **hallowed** still.
12   And, behold, I come quickly;
and my reward is with me,
to give *every man* **up to each**
according as his work shall be.
13   *I am Alpha and Omega* **I AM the A and the Û**,
the beginning and the *end* **completion/shalom**,
the first and the *last* **final**.

The Seventh Beatitude

14   Blessed are they that do his
commandments **misvoth**,
that they may have *right* **authority**
to the *tree* **staff** of life,
and may enter in through the gates into the city.
15   For without are dogs, and
sorcerers **pharmaceutists**,
and whoremongers, and murderers, and idolaters,
and whosoever *loveth* **befriendeth** and maketh a lie.

Epilogue

THE FINAL AFFIRMATION OF AUTHOR AND AUTHORSHIP

16   I *Jesus* **Yah Shua** have sent mine angel
to *testify* **witness** unto you
these in the *churches* **ecclesiae**.
I am **I AM** the root and the *offspring* **genos** of David,
and the *bright* **radiant** and *morning* **dawning** star.

The Final Invitation

17   And the Spirit and the bride *say* **word**, Come.
And let him that heareth**, let him** say, Come.
And let him that is athirst come.
And whosoever *will* **willeth**,
let him take the water of life *freely* **gratuitously**.

The Final Warning

18   For I *testify* **co—witness** unto every *man* **one**
that heareth the words of the prophecy
of this *book* **scroll**,
if **whenever** any *man* **one** shall *add*
place unto these *things*,
God **Elohim** shall *add* **place** unto him
the plagues that are *written* **scribed** in this *book* **scroll**:

19   And *if* **whenever** any *man*
one shall *take away* **remove**
from the words of the *book* **scroll** of this prophecy,
God **Elohim** shall *take away* **remove** his part
out of the *book* **scroll** of life, and out of the holy city,
and *from the things* **those**
which are *written* **scribed** in this *book* **scroll**.

The Final Promise And Prayer

20   He which *testifieth* **witnesseth** these *things*
saith **wordeth**,
Surely **Yea**, I come quickly.
Amen.
Even so **Yes**, come, *Lord Jesus* **Adonay Yah Shua**.

The Final Benediction

21   The *grace* **charism**
of our *Lord Jesus Christ* **Adonay Yah Shua Messiah**
be with you all.
Amen.

11   he who injures, still injures:
and he who fouls, still fouls:
and he who is just, is still justified:
and he who is holy, is still hallowed.

12   And behold, I come quickly;
and my reward is with me
to give to each as to his work.

13   I AM the A and the Ù,
the beginning and the completion/shalom,
the first and the final.

The Seventh Beatitude

14   Blessed — whoever does his misvoth;
that they have authority to the staff of life
and enter the city through the gates.

15   For outside are dogs,
and pharmaceutists,
and whoremongers,
and murderers,
and idolaters,
and whoever befriends and makes a lie.

Epilogue

THE FINAL AFFIRMATION OF AUTHOR AND AUTHORSHIP

16   I Yah Shua sent my angel to you
to witness these in the ecclesiae.
I AM the root and the genos of David,
the radiant and dawning star.

The Final Invitation

17   And the Spirit and the bride word, Come;
And whoever hears, say, Come.
And whoever thirsts, come.
And whoever wills, take the water of life gratuitously.

The Final Warning

18   For I co—witness to everyone
who hears the words of the prophecy of this scroll,
Whenever anyone places to these,
Elohim places to him
the plagues scribed in this scroll:

19   and whenever anyone removes
from the words of the scroll of this prophecy,
Elohim removes his part
from the scroll of life and from the holy city,
and those scribed in this scroll.

The Final Promise And Prayer

20   He who witnesses these,
words, Yes, I come quickly.
Amen.
Yes, come, Adonay Yah Shua.

The Final Benediction

21   The charism of our Adonay Yah Shua Messiah
be with you all.
Amen.

VOLUME SEVEN

LEXICON

FORWARD

This is a precious season in the annals of time – the hush preceding the parousia – when so many Messianists are eager to more fully understand the Scriptures. And never was it more easy to accomplish.

All Messianists ought to be ever grateful for the Authorized King James Version – for it brought to the English speaking world one of the most trustworthy versions of Scripture.

The greatest help to its fuller comprehension was the work of James Strong, when he prepared his Exhaustive Concordance – and his remarkable numbering system – all without the help of modern technological advances.

And now in this, our day, so many of the old standard research works are being republished keyed to Strong's Concordance.

Some of the most important and helpful are:

Theological Wordbook of the Old Testament,

The Englishman's Hebrew and Chaldee Concordance of the Old Testament by Wigram,

The Englishman's Greek Concordance of the New Testament by Wigram,

Vine's Expository Dictionary of Biblical Words,

and of course, the works on which these others are based,

Strong's Exhaustive Concordance, Complete and Unabridged Edition.

Note: Many of these volumes are still being offered without Strong's numbering system; and even Strong's Concordance is being offered in condensed versions. Insist on unabridged editions keyed to Strong. They will expand your ministry within the span of life Elohim has granted you, and save you countless hours.

These five volumes together with the *exeGeses parallel BIBLE* are all you will ever need to thoroughly research Scripture for yourself – even though English is your only language.

FORMAT:

All words are keyed to Strong's Concordance numbers, thus:

Old Covenant numbers and words are within braces, thus: {0000 Transliterated Hebrew, Arami Word};

New Covenant numbers and words are within brackets, thus: [0000 Transliterated Hellenic Word].

Any words not covered in the LEXICON may be researched by following the guidelines in Strong's Concordance.

PARTS OF SPEECH:

In most Versions, parts of speech have been altered to suit the translator. Where a manuscript would say, I rest you, the translators say, I shall give you rest – thus altering rest from a verb to a noun. Another similar example, I mercy you, the translators say, I shall shew you mercy.

The *exeGeses parallel BIBLE* adheres to the manuscripts.

TRANSLATION versus TRANSLITERATION:

Translating is transcribing a word from one **language** to another:

Transliterating is transcribing a word from one **alphabet** to another.

A number of words are treated as **transliterations**, even though they are imperfect; this may be due to alphabetic differences (c, ch, k, ts, z), or prefixes, and suffixes; yet they are offered to draw your attention to the association between languages.

Also included from time to time are words to enhance your understanding:

see draws your attention to a related word;

cp draws your attention to compare a contrasting word;
read draws your attention to a related Scripture;

note: draws your attention to a matter worth noting.

This LEXICON has two sections. **SUMMARIES:**
A grouping of words of similar and/or contrasting root or

subject matter. The HEADING presents the words of the grouping. Then each of the words under the HEADING is exposited.

For example, tabernacle, temple, and tent are used interchangeably in most versions; the definition and distinction of each is thoroughly exposited under the following SUMMARY:

TABERNACLE, TEMPLE, TENT:
tabernacle followed by the exegesis.
temple followed by the exegesis.
tent followed by the exegesis.

A thorough exegesis of each of the subjects under the HEADING will not only enlighten you on the various

subjects, but give you insight into the understanding of what Scripture doctrinates.

DEFINITIONS:

This section follows the SUMMARY, and contains the translated and transliterated words unique to the *exeGeses parallel BIBLE*.

May your spirit be as enriched as you read and research the unsearchable riches of the Holy Word of Elohim.

SUMMARIES:

ADONAY, ADONI, ADONIM:

Adonay, adoni, adonim *transliterated titles* {113 adoni, *plural* adonim} {*intensive plural* 136 adonay} [2960 kuriakos] [2961 kuriuo] [2962 kurios] Lord; one who has authority, whether deity, sovereign, landlord, slavelord, or a woman's man; in their original consonantal form, Adonay and adoni were one and the same, the vowels being added in the Masoretic Text between 600 and 800 A.D.; the Masoretic text also attempted to distinguish deity by using the intensive, plural Adonay; their fallibility is most evident in Psalm 110:1; and this error was also continued in the New Covenant; and we, in our fallibility, have attempted to correctly distinguish between Adonay, adoni, and adonim; **see** Gesenius, Theological Wordbook of the Old Testament; **cp** Yah Veh.

ANGEL:

angel *transliterated noun* {4397, 4398 malak} [32 angelos] messenger; an angel may be a messenger of Satan, of humanity, or of Elohim; angels are ministering spirits; this does not imply that they are either embodied or disembodied; the angel of Yah Veh in the Old Covenant is an embodied manifestation of Elohim, and may well have been Adonay Yah Shua; Yahn the Baptizer was the angel prophesied in the Old Covenant, and manifested in the New Covenant.

angels (equal to) *adjective* [2465 isangelos] like angels; angelic.

ANOINT, ANOINTED, ANOINTING, MESSIAH:

anoint, libate, pour *verb* {4886 mashach} {5258 nacak} {5260 necak} {5480 cuwk} {8210 shaphach} [218 alipho] [4689 spendomai] [5548 chrio] symbolic of setting apart by libating (pouring on) of oil; of pouring a molten image.

anointed *noun* **Messiah** *transliterated title* {4899 mashiach} [5547 christos] anointed; Messiah is a transliteration of the Hebrew mashiach, and a translation of the Hellene Christos; Yah Shua Messiah is the Anointed of Yah Veh; **see** Messias; **note:** the *exeGeses parallel BIBLE* indicates whenever Messiah is preceded by the article, as in "the Messiah".

anointed, libated *noun* {5257 necik} symbolic of one set apart by libating (pouring on) oil.

anointing *noun* {4888 moshchah} [5545 chrisma] a spiritual enduement; a chrism; **cp** charism.

anointing flask *noun* {610 acuwk} a container to hold anointing oil.

anointing oil *noun* {4887 meshach} oil used for anointing;.

BAPTISM, BAPTIZE, BAPTIZER:

baptism *transliterated noun* [908 baptisma] immersion in water; an outward expression of inward experience; of identification with the death, burial, and resurrection of the Yah Shua Messiah; of an inward experience in the Holy Spirit. **baptismal** *noun* {7366 rachats} an instrument used for baptizing.

baptize *transliterated verb* {7364 rachats} [907 baptizo] [909 baptismos] [911 bapto] [1686 embapto] to immerse in a body of water; to immerse in the Holy Spirit; **note:** in the Old Covenant, baptism was required for physical purification of humans and animals; in the New Covenant, the baptism of Yahn the Baptizer was unto repentance; those baptisms were **in** water; the new baptism is **in** the Holy Spirit; all who have taken Yah Shua as their Messiah have the Holy Spirit; all who have been metamorphosed by the renewing of the mind are baptized **in** the Holy Spirit; **see** metamorphose.

Baptizer *transliterated participle* [910 baptistees] one who baptizes; used only of Yahn the Baptizer.

CHARISM, CHARISMA, CHARISMATIC, CHEERS:

charism *transliterated noun* {2580 chen} [5485 charis] grace; an unmerited spiritual enduement bestowed on all who trust in Adonay Yah Shua Messiah as Savior.

charism (bestow) *verb* [5487 charitoo] verb of charism; to endue, or to be endued with charism.

charism (grant) *transliterated verb* {2589 channoth} {2603, 2604 chanan} [5483 charizomai] [5486 charisma] verb of charism; to grant charism.

charisma *transliterated singular noun* **charismata** *plural noun* {2594 chaninah} [5486 charisma] a spiritual enduement. **charismatic** *adjective* {2587 channun} having charisma.

cheers *noun* [5463 chairo] a salute of approval, of welcome; often used as a greeting; chairo is the prime root of words indicating charism.

COMPLETE, COMPLETELY, COMPLETER, COMPLETION:
complete *noun* [3651 holotelees] [5046 telios] perfect; finished; finalized; satisfaction, as in a state of being, or as payment of a debt.

complete *verb* [658 apoteleo] [4931 sunteleo] [5048 telioo] [5055 teleo] to perfect; to finish; to finalize; to satisfy.
complete (fully) *verb* [1615 ekteleo] [2005 epiteleo] to

fully finish, finalize, perfect, satisfy.

completely *adverb* [3651 holoteles] [3838 panteles] [5049 telios] fully; totally.

completer *noun* [5051 teliotees] one who completes, fully satisfies, pays in full.

completion *noun* [4930 suntelia] [5047 teliotees] [5050 teliosis] [5056 telos] full satisfaction; full payment.

completion (bring to) *verb* [5052 telesphoreo] to bring to full satisfaction. **see** SHALAM, SHALOM.

DOCTOR, DOCTRINE, DOCTRINATE, RABBI:
doctor *noun* [1320 didaskalos] one who doctrinates; the Hellene translation of rabbi, rabboni.

doctor of the torah *noun* [3547 nomodidaskalos] one who doctrinates the torah.

doctrinate *verb* [1318 didaktos] [1321 didasko] to teach.
doctrinate otherwise, other doctrine *verb* [2085

heterodidaskaleo] to doctrinate differently; to doctrinate different doctrines.

doctrinator of good *noun* [2567 kalodidaskalos] teacher of good.

doctrine *noun* {3948 leqach} [1319 didaskalia] [1322 didakee] teaching.

rabbi *noun* [1988 epistates] a doctor who doctrinates; the Hellene translation of the Hebrew and Arami word for rabbi; scribed only by Loukas who spoke no Hebrew.

rabbi *transliterated noun* {7227 rab} [4461 rhabbi] a great doctor who doctrinates; the Hebrew transliteration for doctor as scribed by Yahn, Matthaios, and Markos; **see** great.

rabboni *transliterated noun* {7229 rab} [4462 rhabboni] the Arami transliteration for doctor as spoken by others, and scribed by Yahn and Markos; **see** great.

EL, ELAH, ELI, ELOHAH, ELOHIM, ELOI:
Most versions translate the many Hebrew, Aramaic, and Hellene words of deity without any distinction.

The *exeGeses parallel BIBLE* transliterates all the Hebrew and Arami titles of deity of the Old Covenant, and translates all the Hellene titles of the New Covenant corresponding to the Hebrew and Arami.

El, Eli *transliterated title* {410 el} [2241 eli] El, as being almighty.

Elah, Elohah, Eloi *transliterated singular title* {426 elah} {433 elohah} [1682 eloi] a male god.

Elohim, elohim *transliterated plural title* {430 elohim} plural of {433 eloahh, elowahh}; this plural title has a dual interpretation; at times it refers to pagan gods, and at times to the triune Father, Son, and Holy Spirit.

Elohimic *adjective* [2304 thios] Elohim-like.

Elohimic *noun* [2305 thiotees] Elohim-likeness.

Elohimic *noun* [2320 theotees] the total essence of Elohim.
Elyon *transliterated title* **uppermost** *adjective* {5943 illay} {5945, 5946 elyon} [5310 hupsistos] an

uppermost place or position; a title of Elohim. **Elohim-doctrinated** *verb* [2312 theodidaktos] doctrinated by Elohim.

Elohim-hater *noun* [2319 theostugees] one who hates Elohim.

Elohim-opponent *noun* [2314 theomakos] one who opposes Elohim.

Elohim-resister *noun* [2313 theomakeo] one who resists Elohim.

Elohim-reverence *noun* [2317 theosebia] reverence to Elohim.

Elohim-revering *adverb* [2318 theosebees] reverent of Elohim. **Elohim-spirited** *verb* [2315 theopnustos] spirited by Elohim. **goddess** *title* [2299 thea] a female deity.

theos *title* [2316 theos] a male deity; **note:** when theos refers to Elohim, the *exeGeses parallel BIBLE* so translates.

EUCHARIST, EUCHARISTIC, EUCHARISTIZE:
eucharist *transliterated noun; also used verbally* [2169 eucharistia] an offering of charism: verb; to offer charism; usually related to the commemoration of memorial of our Lord's final communion service; **see** charism.

eucharistic *transliterated adjective* [2170 eucharistos] of good charism; **see** charism.

eucharistize *transliterated verb* [2168 eucharisteo] [2169 eucharistia] to express or offer charism; **see** charism.

EULOGIZE, EULOGY:
eulogize *transliterated verb* [1757 eneulogeomai] [2127 eulogeo] to word well.

eulogized *transliterated adjective* [2128 eulogeetos] well worded.

eulogy *transliterated noun* [2129 eulogia] a well word.

Evangelism, Evangelist, Evangelize:
evangelism *transliterated noun* {1309 besorah} {4400 malakuth} [31 angelia] [2098 euangelion] [3852 parangelia] the Helene is from the root, angel; the evangelism is Elohim's message to humanity.

evangelist *transliterated noun, participle* {1319 basar} [2099 euangelistees] one who evangelizes the evangelism.

evangelize *transliterated verb* {1319 basar} [312 anangello] [518 apangello] [1229 diangello] [1804 exangello] [2097 euangelizo] [2605 katangello] [3853 parangello] to disperse the evangelism.

evangelizer *transliterated noun* [2604 katangelus] one who evangelizes.

pre-evangelism *transliterated noun* [1860 epangelia] [1862 epangelma] an evangelism previously prepared, or previously evangelized; **see** evangelism; **cp** angel.

pre-evangelize *transliterated verb* [1861 epangello] [4279 proepangellomai] [4283 prouangelizomai] [4293 prokatangello] previously evangelized; an evangelism previously prepared for future evangelizing.

HOLY, HOLIES, HALLOW, NAVE:
holies *noun* {4720 miqdash} {6944 qodesh} [39 hagion] the outer court of the tabernacle; where the congregation congregated, where the doctrinating took place; the Old Covenant equivalent of the New Covenant priestal precinct; **cp** holy of holies; **see** congregation; **see** tabernacle.

holily *adverb* [55 hagnos] in a holy manner.

holiness *noun* [38 hagiasmos] [41 hagiotees] [42 hagiosunee] [47 hagnia] [54 hagnotees] the character of being holy.

holy (one) *adjective* {6918 qadosh} {6922 qaddish} spiritually whole; set apart unto Elohim.

holy (the) *noun* [40 hagios] that which has been hallowed; they who have been hallowed – set apart unto Elohim; whereas many versions interchange the words holy and saints, the *exeGeses parallel BIBLE* abides with holy.

holy of holies *noun* {6944 qodesh} [39 hagion] the inner court of the tabernacle; corresponds to the nave in the New Covenant; **see** SUMMARY: TABERNACLE, TEMPLE, TENT. **hallow, hallowing** *verb* {6942 qadash} [37 hagiazo] [48 hagnizo] [49 hagnismos] [53 hagnos] verb of holy; whereas many versions interchange the words sanctify and hallow, the *exeGeses parallel BIBLE* abides with hallow.

hallowed whore *noun* {6948 qedeshah} a female whore for religious service.

hallowed whoremonger *noun* {6945 qadesh} a male whore for religious service.

nave *transliterated noun* [3485 naos] one of two Hellenic words mistranslated temple; the nave corresponds to the holy of holies of the tabernacle where, prior to the staking of the Messiah, only the archpriest was allowed to enter; when the Messiah shalamed complete satisfaction for the sins of humanity, the veil of the nave was split from above to below so that all Messianists may now freely enter into his presence. Halalu Yah!

priestal precinct *noun* [2411 hieron] one of two Hellenic words mistranslated temple; the priestal precinct refers to the holies area of the tabernacle where the doctrinating took place; **see** SUMMARY: TABERNACLE, TEMPLE, TENT.

JUDGE, JUDGMENT, JUST,
JUSTNESS, JUSTIFICATION, JUSTICE:
judge, plead, examine *verb* {8199 shaphat} {8200 shephat} [350 anakrino] [2919 krino] to scrutinize; to investigate.

judge, judger *noun* {6414 palil} [1348 dikastees] [2923 kritees] [2924 kritikos] one that decides; one that sentences.
judgment (under) *verb* [5267 hupodikos] under sentence.
judgment *adjective, noun* {6416 pelili} {6417 peliliah} [2917 krima] [2920 krisis] [2922 kriterion] decision; crisis; criterion. **judgment, examination** *noun* [351 anakrisis] investigation. **judgment, justification** *noun* {1779 duwn} {4941 mishpat} {8196 shephut} {*plural* 8201 shephet} [1345 dikaioma] [1347 dikaiosis] [1349 dikee] a judicial verdict; a sentence; also, an unsentencing.

judicators *plural noun* {8614 tiphtay} ones who judge.
jurisdiction *noun* {4082, 4083 mediynah} a district under a judge.

just, justness *adjective* {6662 tsaddiq} {6664 tsedeq} {6665 tsidqah} {6666 tsedaqah} [1342 dikaios] [1343 dikaiosunee] [1738 endikos] having justness; innocent in the sense of not having unjustness: whereas most versions alternate between just, justness and righteous, righteousness, just and justness are more accurate; this is the root of the Hellene word, Sadducees, transliterated Sadoqiy; **see** Yah Veh Sidqenu.

just judgment *noun* [1341 dikaiokrisia] a just sentence.

justice *noun* {6415 pelilah} a right judgment that is just.

justification, judgment see judgment, justification.

justify, justified *verb* {6663 tsadaq} [1344 dikaioo] to cause to be just; **see** just.

justly *adverb* [1346 dikaios] **see** just.

KAPPORETH, KAPUR/ATONE, KIPPURIM/ATONEMENTS, KOPUR/ATONEMENT:

kapporeth *noun* {3727 kapporeth} [2435 hilasteerion] the atonement cover of the holy ark.

kapur/atone *verb* {3722 kapar} [2433 hilaskomai] [2436 hileos] to expiate the guilt of by sufferance of penalty or some equivalent; to make complete satisfaction for.

kippurim/atonements *plural transliterated noun* {3725 kippurim} expiations; **see** Yom Kippurim.

koper/atonement *noun* {3724 kopher} [2434 hilasmos] an expiation; **see** camphire, pitch.

OFFER, OFFERING:

note: most versions insert the words **offer** and **offering**, even though they are not indicated in the manuscripts; **cp** holocaust; sacrifice; libation; **read** Leviticus 23:37.

offer *verb* [4374 prosphero] to offer an offering.

offer up, bear up, bring up *verb* [399 anaphero] to offer up an offering; to take up.

offering *noun* {4503, 4504 minchah} [4376 prosphora] a tribute; **note:** most versions often imply offer and offering even when not in manuscripts; **see** qorban.

offering *noun* {5379 nisseth} an offering, as received.

PRIEST, PRIESTAL PRECINCT, PRIESTHOOD:

priest *noun* {3548 kohen} {3549 kahen} [2409 hierus] an officer of sacrifices and ministries of the holies and the holy of holies of the tabernacle; the emminent priests were classified as: **head** {7218 rosh}, **great** {1419 gadol}, and **arch** [749 archiereus] [758 archon].

priest, priested, priesting *verb* {3547 kahan} [2407 hieratuo] [2418 hierourgeo] to officiate as a priest.

priestal *adjective* [2413 hieros] hallowed.

priestal precinct *noun* [2411 hieron] one of two Hellenic words mistranslated temple; the priestal precinct refers to the holies area of the tabernacle where the doctrinating took place; **see** SUMMARY: TABERNACLE, TEMPLE, TENT.

priestal precinct stripper *noun* [2416 hierosuleo] [2417 hierosulos] one who strips priestal precincts, either by removing or desecrating.

priesthood *noun* {3550 kehunnah} [2405 hieratia] [2406 hieratuma] [2420 hierosune] the office of the priest.

priestlike, priestly *adjective* [2412 hieroprepes] hallowed.

SALVATION, SAVE, SAVIOUR:

salvation *noun* {3468 yesha} {8668 teshuah} [4991 soteria] [4992 soterion] the restoration to wholeness.

salvational *adjective* [4991 soteerios] rescue.

save, saviour *verb, noun* {3467 yasha} [1295 diasozo] [4982 sozo] to rescue; one who rescues; to restore wholeness. **Saviour** *title* [4990 soter] a title reserved for our Adonay Yah Shua Messiah; one who saves, rescues, restores to wholeness. **see** shalam, shalom.

SATIATE, SATISFY, SATURATE, SUFFICIENT:

satiate, satisfy *verb* {7646 sabea} to fill to satisfaction.

satiate, saturate *verb* {7301 ravah} to satisfy the appetite of hunger, or thirst.

satiated, satisfied *adjective* {7649 sabea} sufficiently satisfied; sufficiently satiated.

satiated, saturated *noun* {7310 revayah} satisfied.

satiation, saturated *noun, adjective* {7302 raveh} satisfaction. **satiaty, satisfaction** *noun* {7648 soba} {7654 sobah} sufficiently satisfied; sufficiently satiated.

satisfaction *noun* {7966 shillum} as a recompense for something owed; **see** shalom.

satisfied, sufficient *verb* [714 arkeo] to be satisfactory.

SHALAM, SHALOM, SHELAMIM:

also see SUMMARY: COMPLETE and fulfill.

shalam *verb* {transliterated 7999 shalam} {transliterated 8000 shelam} (to cause) to be at shalom; to complete; to fulfill; to satisfy a debt.

Note: The Hellene uses three different root forms which conform to the Hebrew **shalam** and **shalom**:

1. the first root form [1514 eireneuo *verb*] [1517 eirenopoieo *verb*] [1516 eirenikos *adjective*] [1518 eirenopoios *adjective*] relates primarily to the area of personal satisfaction and contentment: and it also conforms to the Hebrew noun, Shalom

2. the second root form [4137 pleero *verb*] in the Hellene, means to fill full, and to fulfull: and it also conforms to the Hebrew verb, Shalam:

3. the third root form [658 apoteleo *verb*] [4931 sunteleo *verb*] [5048 telioo *verb*] [5055 teleo *verb*] relates primarily to the area of satisfying a debt, spiritual, moral, material: and it also conforms to the Hebrew verb, Shalam.

shalom *noun* {7965 shalom} {7966 shillum} [5046 telios] complete satisfaction, as in a state of being, or as payment of a debt.

Mighty Important Consideration: The translators of the Septuagint, the Old Covenant from Hebraic and Aramaic into Hellene, have translated the words of **shalom** and **shalam** into the following Hellenic words: [467 autapodom] to recompense; [591 apadidom] to give back; [661 apotino] to repay; [1515 eireneuo] to be at peace; [1516 eirenikos] peace; [1517 eirenopoleo] to make peace; [3648 holokieuos] whole; [4982 sozo] heal, save; [4992 soteria] save; [5046 telios] perfect; [5055 teleo] finished: **see** Yahn 19:30. Since we know that Adonay Yah Shua Messiah spoke either Aramaic or Hebrew (and not Hellene) on the stake, is it possible that His word for **teleo** was literally, **shalam**?

shalom (of) *transliterated noun, adjective* {8001 shelam} {8003 shalem} [1515 eirene] [1516 eirenikos] of inward satisfaction.

shelamim *transliterated plural noun* {8002 shelamim} from {7999 shalam}; sacrifices of shalom.

SOUL, SOULICAL, SOULLESS:

soul *noun* {5315 nephesh} [5590 psuchee] the psyche; the soul is the center of the emotional attributes; the soul of the flesh is in the blood; **read** Leviticus 17:11; the inhalation of breath brings oxygen to the blood, which brings life to the flesh; the soul sustains life, but is not life itself; Yah Veh puffed (exsouled) into the nostrils of Adam; and Adam became a living soul; **see** puff; **read** Genesis 2:7; all live beings have souls; **note:** most versions render nephesh into more than forty differents words, and psuchee into seven; only soul is correct; **cp** spirit.

soulical *adjective* [5591 psuchikos] emotional; **cp** spiritual.

soulless *noun* [895 apsuchos] without soul; figuratively, without emotion.

SPIRIT, SPIRITS, SPIRITUAL, SPIRITUALS:

Spirit, spirit, spirits *name, noun* {7307, 7308 ruwach} [4151 pneuma] the Hebrew and Arami word ruwach has the twofold meaning of spirit and wind; the Hellene word pneuma has the single meaning of spirit; **cp** wind.

The Holy Spirit is that essence of triune Elohim who participated in the creation, and Who conceived the flesh body of Elohim, Yah Shua the Messiah; the Holy Spirit guides the spiritually unborn to the Messiah; **read** Yahn 3:1-8; the Holy Spirit guides the spiritually born into all truth; the Holy Spirit is the "another Paraclete" of the Messianist; **read** Yahn 15:26, 16:7-11; the Holy Spirit endues Messianists with the spirituals of energies, ministries, and charismata; **read** 1 Corinthians 12:1-11; the King James Version sometimes translates Holy Spirit as Holy Ghost; in Germanic languages, their word for spirit is rooted in our word for ghost; in Latin languages, their word for spirit is rooted in our word for spirit; in modern day English, ghost is a dead spirit; Yah Shua became flesh of the living Holy Spirit of Elohim, and thus we translate Holy Spirit throughout; we are well aware that many Spirit-filled Messianists prefer Holy Ghost – and this is by no means an effort to alter their personal convictions.

the human spirit is the center of the mental attributes; the will, memory, thought, including, but not limited to wisdom, knowledge, prophecy; all Messianists are born of, and have the Holy Spirit; but not all Messianists are filled with the Holy Spirit; Messianists may also have "in Spirit" experiences; **read** Apocalypse 4:2.

demon spirits are evil spirits which may possess and control the spiritually unborn, and attack the Messianist.

spiritual *adjective* [4152 pneumatikos] that mental attribute which is beyond that of the physical, or soulical.

spiritually *adverb* [4153 pneumatikos] in a spiritual manner. **spirituals** *noun* [4152 pneumatikos] the spirituals bestowed upon humanity are often referred to as spiritual gifts; they are, more accurately, spirituals which the Holy Spirit endues as He wills upon whom He wills; here are nine of the spirituals as presented in I Corinthians 12:1-11:

word of wisdom *nouns* [3056 logos] [4678 sophia] the spiritual of the promise of the ability to decide well.

word of knowledge *nouns* [3056 logos] [1108 gnosis] the spiritual of the promise of the awareness of facts not necessarily gained through experiences of self or others.

trust *noun* [4102 pistis] **note:** trust is a more accurate translation than the usual words, belief and faith; whereas belief and faith imply a directing of the mind, trust implies a total reliance of the being; the Hebrew word for trust is rooted in the word, amen; **see** amen.

charismata of healings *plural nouns* [5486 charisma] [2386 iama] the spiritual of having the abilities of healings of various ailments.

energizing *transliterated verb* **dynamis** *transliterated noun* [1755 energema] [1411 dunamis] the spiritual of energizing the ability; of having the energy and the ability.

word of prophecy *nouns* [3056 logos] [4394 prophetia] the spiritual of the promise of the ability to foretell; foretell is not to be confused with tell forth; **read** I Corinthians 12:10 with 2 Petros 1:19–21.

discernments of spirits *plural nouns* [1253 diakrisis] [4151 pneuma] the spiritual ability to distinguish species or qualities of spirits; to test the spirits, whether they be of Elohim.

genos of tongues *adjective/noun* [1085 genos] [1100 glossa] the spiritual of the ability to express in species of tongues other than those acquired through experience; including foreign and spiritual tongues.

translation of tongues *nouns* [2058 hermeneia] [1100 glossa] the ability to hear a tongue or language other than than learned by human experience, and rendering its meaning; **note:** dreams are interpreted; tongues are translated.

TABERNACLE, TEMPLE, TENT:

tabernacle *noun* {4907, 4908 mishkan} {7933 sheken} [4633 skene] [4636 skenos] [4638 skenoma] the structure surrounding the holies {6944 qodesh} [39 hagion] which is the priestal precinct [2411 hieron]; and the holy of holies {6944 qodesh} [39 hagion] which is the nave [3485 naos]; the holies/priestal precinct, the outer court of the tabernacle, is the place of doctrinating where Yah Shua doctrinated; although Yah Shua referred to the holy of holies/nave, He did not enter the holy of holies/nave until after he split the veil; tabernacle is also the housing of the human body; and the human body is also the nave of the Holy Spirit; **cp** manse; **see** holies, holy of holies, priestal precinct, nave; **note:** the *exeGeses parallel BIBLE* accurately distinguishes between tent, and tabernacle.

tabernacle (over) (upon) *verb* {7931 shakan} {7932 shekan} [1981 episkenoo] [4637 skenoo] to abide in a tabernacle; to abide over, upon.

tabernaclemaker *noun* [4635 skenopoios] a maker of tabernacles; **note:** it is quite possible that Paulos manufactured tabernacles in which to congregate; there is no evidence that Paulos was a tentmaker.

tabernacler (fellow) (nearby) *adjective* {7934 shaken} a fellow who tabernacles nearby; a neighbour.

tabernaclestaking *verb* [4634 skenopeegia] the setting up of the tabernacle; **see** Sukkoth/Brush arbor.

temple *noun*, in the Authorized King James and most other versions, are mistranslations; temple, as a place of worship, is unknown in Scripture: for {1964, 1965 heykal} **see** manse: for [2411 hieron] **see** priestal precinct: for [3485 naos] **see** nave. **tent** *noun* {168 ohel} a portable lodging; a portable covering of cloth and/or skins; tent is designated as the abode of the Yisra Eliy: and tent is also designated as the covering of the tabernacle; **note:** the *exeGeses parallel BIBLE* accurately distinguishes between tent and tabernacle.

tent *verb* {167 ahal} to abide in a tent.

TRUST, ENTRUST, TRUSTLESS, TRUSTWORTHY:

trust (little) *noun* [3640 oligopistos] literally, puny truster.

trust, amen, amenable *transliterated verb* {539 aman} to confirm; to confide it.

trust, entrust *verb* {539 aman} {540 aman} [4100 pistuo] [4104 pistoo] **see** amen; to confidently rely upon; **note:** whereas believing is a psyching up of the mental attributes, trust is the abandonment of self into the care of another.

trust, trustworthiness *noun* {529 emuwn} {2622 chacuth} [4102 pistis] **see** amen; the spiritual ability of total reliance in another; **note:** whereas faith is a psyching up of the mental attribute, trust is the abandonment of self into the care of another; **note:** the *exeGeses parallel BIBLE* indicates whenever trust is preceded by the article, as in "the trust".

trustless *adjective, noun* [571 apistos] without trust.
trustlessness *noun* [570 apistia] to not trust.

trustlessness, distrust *noun* [543 apeitheia] obstinate and rebellious.

trustworthily, trustworthiness, trustworthy, trusting *adjective, adverb* {530 emunah} [4101 pistikos] [4103 pistos].

YAH HUDAH, YAH HUDIY, YAH HUDIYM:

In Strong's Concordance, Old Covenant, between {3050 Yah} and {3068 Yah Veh} are most of the words that pertain to the people of Yah Veh who are called by His name (2 Chronicles 7:14). There is a difference of vowel points between the words referring to Yah, and the words referring to Yah Hudah. However, these vowel points were not added until the seventh century A.D. in the masoretic text – long after the Hebrews decided that it was not proper to refer to Yah Veh by His name – even though Yah Veh had so commanded; **read** Genesis 29:24, Exodus 3:15, 2 Chronicles 7:14, Psalms 68:4, 83:18, Yesha Yah 12:2, 42:8, 52:6, Yirme Yah 33:2, Ephesians 3:15, Apocalypse 14:1.

Yah Hudah, Yah Hudaim, Yah Hudiy; *transliterated names* {a place 3055 yehud} {the land, the people 3061 yehud} {the peoples 3062 yehudaim} {the scion 3063 yehudah} {a people, a person 3064, 3065 yehudi} [a land 2448, 2449 Ioudaia] [a people, a person 2453 ioudaios] [a people, a person, a scion 2455 ioudas] Celebrated of Yah.

Yah Hudaic, Yah Hudaically *transliterated name* {3066 yehudith} [2451, 2452 ioudaikos] the Yah Hudahiy tongue; as a Yah Hudiy.

Yah Hudaism *noun* [2454 ioudaismos] the Yah Hudahiy religion, and usages.

Yah Hudaize *participle* {3054 yahad} [2450 ioudaizo] to cause to be Yah Hudahiy.

YAH, YAH SHUA, YAH VEH, and compound names:

Yah *transliterated name* {3050 yah} name of Deity in basic form: Eternal Existent One; **see** following for compound forms.

Yah Shua *transliterated name* {3091 yehowshua} {3442, 3443 yeshuwa} [2424 ieesous] Yah Saves; the name of Mosheh's successor, the name of our Adonay Messiah, and the name of other persons.

Yah Veh *transliterated name* {3068, 3069 yehovah} Eternal Existent One.

Yah Veh Nissi *transliterated name* {3071 yehovahnissi} Yah Veh Ensign.

Yah Veh Raah *transliterated name* {3068 yehovah} {7462 raah} Yah Veh Tends; **see** Psalm 23:1.

Yah Veh Raphah *transliterated name* {3068 yehovah} {7495 raphah} Yah Veh Healer.

Yah Veh Sabaoth *transliterated name* {3068 yehovah} {6635 tsabaah *plural* sabaoth} [3841 pantokrator] Yah Veh of Hosts; **see** Sabaoth.

Yah Veh Sadakah *transliterated name* {3068 yehovah} {6666 sadakah} Yah Veh of Justness.

Yah Veh Shalom *transliterated name* {3073 yehovahshalom} Yah Veh Shalom; **see** complete.

Yah Veh Sham *transliterated name* {3068 yehovah} {8033 sham} Yah Veh's Presence; **see** Yechezq El 48:35.

Yah Veh Sidqenu *transliterated name* {3072 yehovahtsidqenuw} a combined form of {3068 yehovah} and {6664 tsedek} Yah Veh of Justness.

Yah Veh Yireh *transliterated name* {3070 yehovahyireh} Yah Veh Sees.

DEFINITIONS:

A

A and Ù *title* [1 alpha] [5598 omega] the first and final letters of the Hellene alphabet; a title that Adonay Yah Shua ascribes to Himself.

ab, abba, father *transliterated noun* {1 ab} {2 ab} [5 abba] [3962 pater] **ab** is Hebrew for father; **abba** is a Hellenic transliteration; **pater** is the Hellenic translation.

Abaddon *transliterated name, noun* {10 abaddoh} {11 abaddon} [3 abaddon] Destroyer; destruction; **cp** Apollyon. **abandon** *adjective* {2310 chadel} destitute.

abandon, allow, leave, let, set *verb* {3240 yanach} {5203 natash} to abandon; to allow to be; to allow to be set. **abandon, cease, decease, desist** *verb* {2308 chadai} to be lacking; to stop.

abandon, release *verb* {8281 sharah} to free.

abase, abate, belittle, slight, swift, trifle *verb* {6819 tsaar} {6985 qat} {7034 qalah} {7043 qalal} [2274 heetaomai] to belittle in contempt; to make light of; to lessen.

abase, lower *verb* {8213 shaphel} {8214 shephal} to humiliate.

abasement, abasing *noun* {7022 qiyqalown} {7036 qalown} {7045 qelalah} an intense disgrace.

LEXICON

abate, abase, belittle, slight, swift, trifle *verb* {6819 tsaar} {6985 qat} {7034 qalah} {7043 qalal} [2274 heetaomai] to belittle in contempt; to make light of; to lessen.

abate, lack *verb* {2637 chacer} to lack, to lessen; spoken of the prophecy of the Messiah having become flesh; **read** Psalm 8:5.

Abde El *transliterated name* {5655 abdeel} Serving El.

Abdi El *transliterated name* {5661 abdiel} Servant of El.

Abel *transliterated name* {59 abel} Meadow.

Abel *transliterated name* {1893 hebel} [6 abel] son of Adam.

Abel Beth Maachah *transliterated name* {62 abelbethmaachah} Meadow of the House of Piercing.

Abel Hash Shittim *transliterated name* {63 abelhashshittim} Meadow of the Shittim; **see** Shittim.

Abel Keramim *transliterated name* {64 abelkeramim} Meadow of the Vineyards.

Abel Maim *transliterated name* {66 abelmayim} Meadow of the Waters.

Abel Mecholah *transliterated name* {65 abelmecholah} Meadow of the Round Dance.

Abel Misrayim *transliterated name* {67 abelmitsrayim} Meadow of Misrayim; **see** Misrayim.

abhor *verb* {6973 quts} in the sense of cutting off from.

abhor, abhorrent *verb* {8581 taab} to shrink from with horror; to loathe.

abhorrence *noun* {8441 toebah} an extreme loathing, especially to idolatry.

Abi *transliterated name* {21 abi} Father.

Abi Albon *transliterated name* {45 abialbon} Father Valiant.

Abi Asaph *transliterated name* {23 abiasaph} {43 ebjasaph} Father Gatherer.

Abi Athar *transliterated name* {54 ebyathar} [8 abiathar] Father of the Remains.

Abi Dah *transliterated name* {28 abida} Father Knows.

Abi Dan *transliterated name* {27 abidan} Father Judge.

Abi El *transliterated name* {22 abiel} Father El.

Abi Ezer *transliterated name* {44 abiezer} Father of Help.

Abi Gail *transliterated name* {26 abigail} Father of Joy.

Abi Gibon *transliterated name* {25 abigibon} Father of Gibon (Hill).

Abi Ha Ezri *transliterated name* {33 abihaezri} Father of Help; **cp** Abi Ezer.

Abi Hail *transliterated name* {32 abihail} Father of Valour.

Abi Hu *transliterated name* {30 abihu} Father of Him.

Abi Hud *transliterated name* {31 abihud} [10 abioud] Father of Majesty.

Abi Mael *transliterated name* {39 abimael} Father Mael; meaning of Mael uncertain.

Abi Melech *transliterated name* {40 abimelech} Father Sovereign.

Abi Nadab *transliterated name* {41 abinadab} Father Volunteer.

Abi Ner *transliterated name* {74 abiner} Father Lamp.

Abi Noam *transliterated name* {42 abinoam} Father of Pleasantness.

Abi Ram *transliterated name* {48 abiram} Father Lofty.

Abi Shag *transliterated name* {49 abishag} Father of Error.

Abi Shai *transliterated name* {52 abishai} Father of Presents.

Abi Shalom *transliterated name* {53 abishalom} Father of Shalom; **see** shalom.

Abi Shua *transliterated name* {50 abishua} Father of Opulence.

Abi Shur *transliterated name* {51 abishur} Father of the Wall.

Abi Tal *transliterated name* {37 abital} Father of Dew.

Abi Tub *transliterated name* {36 abitub} Father of Goodness.

Abi Yah *transliterated name* {29 abiyah} [7 abia] Father Yah.

Abi Yam *transliterated name* {38 abiyam} Father of the Sea.

Abib *transliterated name*, **unripe** *adjective* {3, 4 eb} {24 abib} an unripened or tender produce; a month of the Hebrew calender; also a syllable in the name of the city, Tel Abib.

abide *verb* [1265 diameno] [1696 emmeno] [1961 epimeno] [2650 katameno] [3306 meno] [3887 parameno] [4357 prosmeno] [5278 hupomeno] the root, *meno*, with its various prefixes, carries various connotations; from remaining in a place, to having a oneship with Adonay Yah Shua; **read** Yahn 15:.

Abilene *transliterated name* [9 abilene] possibly, Of Abel.

able, can, enable, prevail *verb* {3201 yakol} {3202 yekel} {3546 kehal} [1410 dunamai] [2427 hikanoo] the dynamis to do; **see** dynamis.

abode *noun* [3438 mone] a staying, residence; the noun of abide; only in Yahn 14:2, 23.

abominable *adjective* [947 bdeluktos] stinky; loathsome; idolatrous.

abominate *verb* {8262 shaqats} [948 bdelussomai] to stink; to loathe.

abomination *noun* {8251 shiqquts} {8263 sheqets} [946 bdelugma] a stink; a loathing; especially in the nostrils of Elohim; usually refers to idols.

abort, bereave, bereft *verb* {7921 shakol} to miscarry or suffer abortion; to deprive of; to be deprived of.

abound by the myriads *verb* {7231 rabab} to increase innumerably; **see** myriad.

abound *verb* {6280 athar} to increase; to be abundant.

abound, greaten *verb* {7235 rabah} {7236 rebah} to increase; to be greatened, in any dimension.

above, up, upper *adverb* [507 ano] upward; the top.

above, upper, uppermost *adjective* [509 anothen] [510 anoterikos] [511 anoteron] from above; the source of the rebirth; **read** Yahn 3:1-8.

Abraham *transliterated name* {85 abraham} [11 abraam] Father of a Multitude; Abram's name after Yah Veh changed it.

Abram *transliterated name* {87 abram} Father Lofty; Abraham's name before Yah Veh changed it.

abroad (gone) *adverb* [590 apodemos] absent from one's own people.

abroad (went) *verb* [589 apodemeo] to go away from one's own people.

absent *adjective* [548 apeimi] away.

absinthe, wormwood *transliterated noun* {3939 laanah} [894 apsinthos] a bitter plant.

abstinence, private assembly *noun* {6116 atsereth} a sacrifice of self-restraint; **see** restraint.

abundance *noun* {6283 athereth} an ample supply.

abundance *noun* {8635 tarbuth} a greatening, in any dimension.

abundance, greatness, greatnesses *noun* {1420 gedullah} {1433 godel} {7230 rob} {7238 rebu} increase; magnitude; mighty acts.

abundance, throng *noun* {8229 shiphah} plenty; a crowd.

abundant, great, greater *adjective* {1419 gadol} {7227, 7229 rab} {7260 rabrab} {7690 saggiy} plentiful; large; older.

abuse, encourage *verb* {7292 rahab} in the sense of urging; of pressuring.

abusive *adjective* [486 antiloidoreo] to rail in reply.

abyss *noun* {6683 tsulah} {8415 tehom} [12 abussos] a deep, depthless chasm; sometimes refers to sheol and hades. **accusation, cause** *noun* [156 aita] [157 aitiama] [158 aition] as asked; as inquired into.

accustomed *verb* [1480 ethizo] [1486 etho] to accustom; customary; usage.

accustomed, use, used, useful *verb* {5532 cakan} to be familiar by use; to be serviceable to.

Ach Ab *transliterated name* {256 achab} Brother (Friend) of His Father.

Ach Archel *transliterated name* {316 acharchel} Behind the Intrenchment.

Ach Ban *transliterated name* {257 achban} Brother of Discerning.

Ach Rach *transliterated name* {315 achrach} After His Brother.

Ach Umay *transliterated name* {267 achuwmay} Brother of Water.

Ach Zay *transliterated name* {273 achzay} Possessor.

Achasbay *transliterated name* {308 achacbay} uncertain derivative.

achashtariy *transliterated noun* {326 achashtariy} courier; a designation, rather than a name.

Achashverosh *transliterated name* {325 achashverowsh} the title of a Persian sovereign.

Achaz *transliterated name* {271 achaz} [881 akaz] Possessor.

Achaz Yah *transliterated name* {274 achazyah} Possessed of Yah.

Acher *transliterated name* {313 acher} Next, Other.

Achi *transliterated name* {278 echiy} {277 achiy} Brotherly.

Achi Am *transliterated name* {279 achiyam} Brother of the Mother.

Achi Ezer *transliterated name* {295 achiezer} Brother of Help.

Achi 1-lud *transliterated name* {282 achihud} Brother of Majesty; **cp** Achi Hud {284}.

Achi 1-lud *transliterated name* {284 achichud} Brother of Propounding; **cp** Achi Hud {282}.

Achi Lud *transliterated name* {286 achilud} Brother of Birth.

Achi Maas *transliterated name* {290 achiymaats} Brother of Closure.

Achi Man *transliterated name* {289 achiman} Brother of a Portion.

Achi Melech *transliterated name* {288 achimelech} Brother of the Sovereign.

Achi Moth *transliterated name* {287 achimoth} Brother of Death.

Achi Nadab *transliterated name* {292 achinadab} Brother Volunteer.

Achi Noam *transliterated name* {293 achinoam} Brother of Pleasantness.

Achi Qam *transliterated name* {296 achiyqam} Brother of Rising.

Achi Ra *transliterated name* {299 achira} Brother of Evil.

Achi Ram *transliterated name* {297 achiram} Brother Lofty.

Achi Ramiy *transliterated name* {298 achiyramiy} Of Achi Ram.

Achi Samach *transliterated name* {294 achisamach} Brother Upholder.

Achi Shachar *transliterated name* {300 achiyshachar} Brother of the Dawn.

Achi Shar *transliterated name* {301 achishar} Brother Songster.

Achi Thophel *transliterated name* {302 achithophel} Brother of Slime.

Achi Tub *transliterated name* {285 achitub} Brother of Goodness.

Achi Yah *transliterated name* {281 achiyah} Brother of Yah.

Achlab *transliterated name* {303 achlab} Fatness.

Achlay *transliterated name* {304 achlay} O That.

Achoach *transliterated name* {265 achowach} Brotherly.

Achoachiy *transliterated name* {266 achowchiy} Of Achoach.

Achuz Zam *transliterated name* {275 achuzzam} Possession.

Achuz Zath *transliterated name* {276 achuzzath} Possession.

Achyan *transliterated name* {291 achyan} Brotherly.

Achyo *transliterated name* {283 achyow} Brotherly.

acknowledge, know *verb* [1921 epiginosko] to recognize; to become acquainted with.

acquaintance *noun* {4378 makkar} one who is recognized.

acquaintance, known *noun* [1110 gnostos] one who is known by another.

acquire *verb* {5239 nalah} to gain; **see** acquisition.

acquire *verb* {7408 rakash} to acquire; to lay up.

acquisition *noun* {4512 minleh} that which is acquired; that which is gained.

acquisition *noun* {7399 rekush} that which is acquired; that which is layed up.

acre, pair, team, yoke *noun* {6776 tsemed} two, as joined; an acre, as a day's task for one yoke.

acts *noun* {4566, 4567 mabad} in the sense of deeds. **acts, function** *noun* [4234 praxis] something done; a deed. ad **infinitum** *adjective* {6783 tsmithuth} without limit.

Adalya *transliterated name* {118 adalya} of Persian derivative; a son of Haman.

Adam *transliterated name* {121 adam} [76 adam] Human; the first human; **see** human, humanity.

adam *transliterated noun* {120 adam} ruddy, human, humanity.

Adbe El *transliterated name* {110 adbeel} Lanquished of El. **add, again, augment, increase** *verb* {3254 yacaph} to add to; to repeat.

Addar *transliterated name* {146 addar} Mighty.

Addi *transliterated name* {5716 adiy} [78 addi] Ornamental; **see** ornaments.

adhere *verb* {6821 tsaphad} to stick.

adhere, captivate, capture *verb* {3920 lachad} {3921 leked} [259 halosis] to catch; to cause to stick.

adhere, join, stick *verb* {1692 dabaq} {1693 debaq} [4347 proskollao] to join one's self to closely, stick to; to remain attached.

adhering *adjective* {1695 dabeq} joining closely; devoting.

Adi El *transliterated name* {5717 adiel} Ornament of El.

Adithayim *dual transliterated name* {5723 adiythayim} Double Prey.

adjudge *verb* [1948 epikrino] to decide or determine.

Adlay *transliterated name* {5724 adlay} the meaning uncertain.

Admatha *transliterated name* {133 admatha} a Persian nobleman.

administration *noun* [3622 oikonomia] management; oversight.

administrator *noun* [3621 oikonomeo] [3623 oikonomos] overseer; manager.

admonish, rebuke *verb* [2008 epitimao] to charge sharply.

Adoni; **see** SUMMARY: ADONAY, ADONI, ADONIM:

Adoni Bezeq *transliterated name* {137 adonibezeq} Adoni of Bezeq (in Pelesheth).

Adoni Qam *transliterated name* {140 adoniqam} Adoni of Rising.

Adoni Ram *transliterated name* {141 adoniyram} {151 adoram} Adoni Lofty.

Adoni Sedeq *transliterated name* {139 adonitsedeq} Adoni of Justness; **see** Sadoq.

Adoni Yah *transliterated name* {138 adoniyah} Adoni of Yah.

Adorayim *dual transliterated name* {115 adowrayim} Double Mound.

adorn *verb* {6286 paar} to embellish.

adornment *noun* {8597 tiphareth} ornament.

adornment, ornament, tiara *noun* {6287 peer} an embellishment; a tiara, as an adornment.

Adram Melech *transliterated name* {152 adrammelech} Mighty Sovereign.

Adri El *transliterated name* {5741 adriel} Drove of El.

Adullam *transliterated name* {5725 adullam} the meaning uncertain; a place in Pelesheth.

Adullamiy *transliterated name* {5726 adullamiy} Of Adullam.

adulterer *noun* [3432 moikos] male who commits sexual infidelity.

adulterer, adulteress *verbal noun* {5003 naaph} (adulterer) male and (adulteress) female who commit sexual infidelity.

adulteries *plural noun* {5004 niuph} {5005 naaphuph} sexual infidelities.

adulterize *verb* {5003 naaph} [3429 moikaomai] [3431 moikuo] to commit sexual infidelity.

adulterous *adjective* **adulteress** *noun* [3428 moikalis] given to sexual infidelity; a female who adulterizes.

adultery *noun* [3430 moikia] sexual infidelity.

advantage *noun* {3504 yithrown} {4195 mothar} gain.

adversary *noun* [476 antidikos] *plural noun* [480 antikimai] an opponent.

advocate *noun* {1781, 1782 dayan} one who pleads in behalf of another; **see** plead (for).

afar, far, distant past *adjective* {7350 rachoq} {7352 rachiq} {7369 racheq} remote; in time, or distance.

aftergrowth *noun* {3954 leqesh} a second growth or crop; metaphorically, development.

afterrain *noun* {4456 malqosh} the spring rain.

again, augment, increase, add *verb* {3254 yacaph} to repeat; to add to.

Age *transliterated name* {89 age} uncertain derivative. **age** *noun* {2207 zoqen} old age.

LEXICON

age *verb* {2204 zaqen} to become old; **see** beard; **see** elder.

age (old) *noun* {*plural* 2208 zaqun} {2209 ziqnah} old age.

aged, elder *noun* {2205 zaqen} {3453 yashish} {3486 yasheh} one who is aged; an elder of a family or congregation.

agitate *verb* {2000 hamam} {2111, 2112 zuwa} {6470 paam} to disturb; to cause commotion.

agitation *noun* {2113 zevaah} commotion; disturbance.

agonize against *verb* [464 antagonizomai] literally, to antagonize; to struggle against.

agonize *verb* [75 agonizomai] to struggle; to contend.

agony, contest *noun* [73 agon] [74 agonia] a struggle; a contest.

Agrippas *transliterated name* [67 agrippas] Wild Horse Tamer.

Aha *interjection* [1436 ea] let it be.

Aha *interjection* {1889 heach} [3758 oua] an exclamation.

Aha *transliterated interjection* {162 ahahh} an exclamation; in most places used with Adonay Yah Veh.

Aharon *transliterated name* {175 aharon} [2 aaron] the meaning uncertain; the brother of Mosheh.

Achan *transliterated name* {5912 achan} Troublesome.

Achar *transliterated name* {5917 achar} Troublesome.

Achbor *transliterated name* {5907 achbowr} possibly, Mouse.

Achish *transliterated name* {397 achiysh} of uncertain derivative.

Akkad *transliterated name* {390 akkad} Fortress.

Akko *transliterated name* {5910 akkow} Hemmed In.

Akor *transliterated name* {5911 akowr} Troubled.

Achsah *transliterated name* {5915 achsah} Tinkler.

Achshaph *transliterated name* {407 achshaph} Sorcery.

Achzib *transliterated name* {392 achziyb} Deceitful.

Al Tashcheth *transliterated name* {516 altashcheth} Destroy Not.

alabaster *transliterated noun* [211 alabastron] the name of a stone; a container made of alabaster.

Alemeth *transliterated name* {5964 alemeth} Covering.

algumim *transliterated plural noun* {418 algummim} sticks of algum wood.

alien *noun* [241 allogenees] of other genes; foreigner; stranger.

alienate *verb* [526 apallotrioo] to estrange.

alienate *verb* [1369 dichazo] to make apart; to set against another.

alienate *verb* {5361 naqa} to feel aversion.

alienation *noun* {8569 tenuwah} enmity.

alight, drive *verb* {6795 tsanach} to come down; to cause to descend; to drive down.

Allam Melech *transliterated name* {487 allammelech} Oak of the Sovereign.

allegorize *transliterated verb* [238 allegoreo] to present as an allegory, as a veiled presentation.

Allon Bachuth *transliterated name* {439 allownbachuwth} Oak of Weeping.

allot, smooth it over *verb* {2505 chalaq} literally, to smooth; as tossing smooth pebbles to allot lands, inheritances; smoothing over as through flattery.

allotment, portion, smooth *noun* {2506 cheleq} {2508 chalaq} {2511 challaq} {2513 chelqah} {2515 chaluqqah} {4255 machleqah} {4256 machaloqeth} {4521 menath} smoothness of tongue; usually an inheritance allotted by pebble.

allow *verb* [1832 exesti] to permit; often mistranslated lawful, but is unrelated to law.

allow, forgive, forsake, leave, release, *verb* [863 aphieemi] to send forth.

allow, give *verb* {5414 nathan} {5415 nethan} literally, to give; to give permission.

allow, leave, let, set, abandon *verb* {3240 yanach} {5203 natash} to allow to be; to allow to be set; to abandon.

Almighty *title* {46 abiyr} a title of Elohim; **cp** Shadday; **see** mighty.

Almodad *transliterated name* {486 almodad} [1678 elmodam] Wizard.

almond *noun* {8247 shaqed} the tree or nut, as the earliest in bloom.

almond shaped *adjective* {8246 shaqed} shaped like almonds.

almugim *transliterated plural noun* {484 almuggiym} sticks of almugim wood.

aloes *transliterated noun* [250 aloe] a gum.

altar (sacrifice) *noun* {4056 madbach} {4196 mizbeach} [2379 thusiasterion] a furniture on which sacrifices are sacrificed; the Hebrew is from the root of the verb, sacrifice {2076 zabach}; **see** sacrifice.

alter, change, double, duplicate, fold, reiterate, repeat *verb* {8132 shana} {8133 shena} {8138 shanah} to reinforce by folding, by doubling; may include disguise, camouflage.

altogether, together, unitedly *adverb* {3162 yachad} as one; **see** unite.

Alvah, Alyah *transliterated name* {5933 alvah, alyah} Wickedness.

Alvan, Alyan *transliterated name* {5935 alvan, alyan} Ascended.

always *adverb* [3842 pantote] at all times.

Am Ram *transliterated name* {6019 amram} High People.

Am Ramiy *transliterated name* {6020 amramiy} Of Am Ram.

Amaleq *transliterated name* {6002 amaleq} the meaning uncertain; Of Esav.

Amaleqiy *transliterated name* {6003 amaleqiy} Of Amaleq.

Amanah *transliterated name* {548, 549 amanah} Amenable; Trustworthy; from the root, amen.

Amar Yah *transliterated name* {568 amaryah} Saying of Yah.

amaranthine *transliterated noun* [262 amarantinos] [263 amarantos] an imaginary flower that is unfading in character.

Amas Yah *transliterated name* {558 amatsyah} Strength of Yah.

Amas Yah *transliterated name* {6007 amacyah} Burden of Yah.

Amasay *transliterated name* {6022 amasay} Burdensome.

Amashsay *transliterated name* {6023 amashcay} possibly, Burdensome.

ambassador *title* **pang** *noun* {6735 tsir} an ambassador, as a representative; a pang, as writhing.

ambassage *verb* {6737 tsayar} to send an ambassador.

amen *transliterated noun, interjection* {543 amen} {544 omen} [281 amen] trustworthy; worthy of trust; from the Hebrew and Arami root {539, 540 aman} meaning trust; one of two words which transliterates into every language.

amen, amenable, trust *transliterated verb* {539, 540 aman} to confirm; to confide in.

amethyst *transliterated noun* [271 amethustos] a stone as an anti-intoxicant.

amicable *adjective* [269 amachos] without strife.

Amittay *transliterated name* {573 amittay} Truly.

Ammi El *transliterated name* {5988 ammiel} People of El.

Ammi Hud *transliterated name* {5989 ammihud} {5991 ammichur} People of Majesty.

Ammi Nadab *transliterated name* {5992 amminadab} {5993 amminadib} [284 aminadab] People of Volunteers.

Ammi Shadday *transliterated name* {5996 ammishadday} People of Shadday (Elohim, as the Almighty).

Ammi Zabad *transliterated name* {5990 ammiyzabad} People of Endowment.

Ammon *transliterated name* {5983 ammown} People; Inbred.

Ammoniy *transliterated name* {5984 ammowniy} Of Ammon.

Ammoniyth *transliterated name* {5985 ammowniyth} a female Ammoniy.

Amnon *transliterated name* {550 amnon} Trustworthy; from the root of amen.

Amon *transliterated name* {526 amon} [300 amon] Trained.

among, inward, middle, midst, within *noun* {7130 qereb} {8432 tavek} the nearest part; the center.

Amoq *transliterated name* {5987 amowq} Deep.

Amorah *transliterated name* {6017 amorah} [1116 gomorrha] Bind; Heap.

Amos *transliterated name* {531 amots} [301 amos] Strong.

Amos *transliterated name* {5986 amos} Burdened.

Amsi *transliterated name* {557 amtsiy} Strong.

Ana Yah *transliterated name* {6043 anayah} Answer of Yah.

Anacharath *transliterated name* {588 anacharath} Snorting.

Anam Melech *transliterated name* {6048 anammelech} Answer of Melech.

Anan Yah *transliterated name* {6055 ananyah} Overclouding of Yah.

Anaq *transliterated name* {6061 anaq} Choker.

Anaqiym *transliterated name* {6062 anaqiym} Of Anaq.

anathema *transliterated noun* [331 anathema] [2652 katanathema] a curse.

anathematize *verb* [332 anathematizo] [2653 katanathematizo] to bind by a curse.

Anathoth *plural transliterated name* {6068 anathowth} Answers.

Anathothi Yah *transliterated name* {6070 anthothiyah} Answers of Yah.

Anathothiy *transliterated name* {6069 anthothiy} Of Anathoth.

Ancient *title* {6268 attiq} the enduring one.

ancient, antiquity, east, easterly, eastern, eastward, formerly, preceding *noun* {6921 qadim} {6924 qedem} {6925 qodam} {6926 qidmah} {6927 qadmah} literally, the forefront; from the front.

ancient(s), east, eastern *adjective* {6930 qadmon} {6931 qadmoniy} anterior.

ancients *plural noun* {6917 qadumim} of antiquity.

ancients, archaic (the) *transliterated noun, adjective* [744 arkaios] that has been from the beginning; original; primeval.

Andreas *transliterated noun* [406 andreas] Manly.

angel; see SUMMARY: ANGEL.

Ani Am *transliterated name* {593 aniyam} Mourning of People.

anile *adjective* [1126 graodees] old womanish.

animal *noun* {929 behemah} [2934 kteenos] a domesticated live possession; **see** behemoth; **cp** beast.

anise *noun* [432 aneethon] a seed used for flavoring.

ankles *dual noun* {7166 qarcol} the joints connecting the feet and legs.

anklet, march *noun* {685 etsadah} {6807 tseadah} a pacing; an ornament of that which paces; an ankle chain.

announce *verb* {3745 keraz} to proclaim.

announcer *noun* {3744 karoz} a proclaimer.

annul, disallow, discourage *verb* {5106 nuw} to refuse; dissuade.

anoint, anointed, anointing; see SUMMARY: ANOINT.

answer *noun* {4617 maaneh} response.

answer *verb* {6030, 6032 anah} to respond truthfully, as in witnessing.

ant *noun* {5244 nemalah} from its bisected appearance.

antelope *noun* {8377 tow} named after the white stripe on its cheek.

anticipate, confront, precede *verb* {6923 qadam} to front; **cp** east.

antimessiah *noun* [500 antikristos] one that opposes the Messiah; **cp** pseudo messiah.

Antipas *transliterated noun* [493 antipas] Stepfather.

antiquate, remove, transcribe *verb* {6275 athaq} that which has aged; to take away; to take down, as in transcribing.

antiquated, weaned *adjective* {6267 attiq} that which has endured; removed.

antique *adjective* {6266 athiq} {6276 atheq} that which has endured.

antiquity, east, easterly, eastern, eastward, formerly, preceding, ancient *noun* {6921 qadim} {6924 qedem} {6925 qodam} {6926 qidmah} {6927 qadmah} literally, the forefront; from the front.

antithesis *transliterated noun* [477 antithesis] an opposing thesis.

antitype *transliterated noun* [499 antitupon] the representation of a type.

Antothi Yah *transliterated name* {6070 antothiyah} Answers of Yah.

anus *noun* {6574 parshedon} the lower oriface of the alimentary canal.

anvil, step, support, time *noun* {6471 paamah} anvil, as a support; support, as a pedestal or column in a structure; a "stepper", as a supporter of the body; time, as an occasion or occurrence – but not as measured time.

anxiety *noun* [3308 merimna] excessive care or attention.

anxious *verb* [3309 merimnao] to be troubled with cares; to care for.

apart (from) *adverb* [5565 koris] separate; without making use.

apathetic *adjective* [524 apalgeo] to become apathetic; to cease to feel pain or grief.

apathetic (become) *verb* [120 athumeo] to become discouraged.

Apharesiym *plural transliterated name* {670 apharecay} Of a region in Ashshur.

Apharsechiy *transliterated name* {671 apharcechay} Of an Ashshur tribe.

Apheq, Aphiq *transliterated name* {663 apheq, aphiyq} Fortress.

Apheqah *transliterated name* {664 apheqah} Fortress.

Aphiach *transliterated name* {647 aphiyach} Puff.

aphis *noun* {2602 chanamal} a plant louse.

apocalypse *transliterated noun* [602 apokalupsis] a revelation, usually of the future; unveiling.

Apollos *transliterated name* [625 apollos] a sun deity.

Apollyon *transliterated name* [623 apolluon] Destroyer; the Hellene is a translation of the Hebrew Abaddon; **see** Abaddon.

apostasy *noun* {4878 meshubah} [647 apostasion] renunciation of a trust once held; renunciation of a marriage.

apostate *noun* {7726 shobab} {7628 shebiy} one who has turned from.

apostatize *verb* {5472 cuwg} [646 apostasia] renouncing a trust once held; renouncing a marriage.

apostle *noun* [652 apostolos] one who is commissioned; all apostles are disciples, but not all disciples are apostles; of his disciples, Yah Shua selected twelve to be his apostles; **cp** disciple.

apostleship *noun* [651 apostolee] the commission of the commissioned.

apostolize *verb* [649 apostello] [1821 exapostello] [4882 sunapostello] to commission as an apostle; **see** send.

Appayim *dual transliterated name* {649 appayim} Two Nostrils.

appear, look *verb* {8259 shaqaph} [398 anaphainoman] to become apparent; to gaze; **see** manifest.

appearance *noun* {7299 rave} aspect; from the root of {7200 raah} to see.

apple (tree) *noun* {8598 tappuach} the fruit or the tree.

appoint, bore, pierce *verb* {5344 naqab} to point out; to thrust or make a hole through.

appoint, number *verb* {4483 menah} {4484 mene} {4487 manah} to enumerate.

appointed *adjective* {2163 zahman} set; as in the setting of a time.

appointment *noun* {2165, 2166 zeman} a set period, usually of a specific time; **cp** time.

appraisal, arrangement *noun* {6187 erek} that which is lined up in a row for evaluation.

appraise, apprize, arrange, array, line up, rank *verb* {6186 arak} to line up in a row; to put in order.

approach *adjective* {7131 qareb} {7132 qerabah} used verbally; to bring near.

approach, bring near, oblate *verb* {7126 qarab} {7127 qereb} to draw near; to bring near; to offer for worship.

approve, prove, reprove *verb* {3198 yakach} [1381 dokimazo] to prove; to accept or reject the proving.

approved *adjective* [1384 dokimos] accepted; proved.

Aqan *transliterated name* {6130 aqan} Tortuous.

Aqqub *transliterated name* {6126 aqquwb} Restrained.

Aquila *transliterated name* [207 akulas] Eagle.

Arab *transliterated name* {694 arab} [690 araps] Lurker.

Arabahiy *transliterated name* {6164 arbathiy} Of (Beth Ha) Arabah.

Arabia *transliterated name* {6152 arab} [688 arabia] Sterile.

Arabiy *transliterated name* {6163 arabiy} Of Arabia.

Arach *transliterated name* {733 arach} Caravaning.

Aram *transliterated name* {758 aram} Highland.

Aram Naharaim *transliterated name* {763 aramnaharayim} Aram of the Two Rivers (Tigris, Euphrates).

Aramaic *transliterated adverb* {762 aramiyth} Of Aram: one of the languages of the Old Covenant and the New Covenant.

Aramiy, Aramiym *transliterated name* {761 arammiy} {*plural* 761 arammiym} Of Aram.

Ararat *transliterated name* {780 ararat} the meaning uncertain.

Aravnah *transliterated name* {728 aravnah} Strong.

arch *transliterated noun* [758 archon] chief, as being first in rank or power.

arch, back, bow, brow, rim *noun* {1354 gab} that which is bowed, curved; also the top or rim.

archaic (the), ancient(s) *transliterated noun, adjective* [744 arkaios] that which has been from the beginning; original; primeval.

archangel *transliterated noun* [743 archangelos] a hierarch angel; **see** hierarch; **see** angel.

Archippus *transliterated name* [751 archippos] an arch (ruler) of the horse.

architect *transliterated noun* [753 architekton] a chief constructor; **cp** Creator.

Archiy *transliterated name* {757 archiy} Of Erech.

archpriest *noun* [748 archieratikos] [749 archiereus] an arch priest.

archshepherd *noun* [750 archipoimeen] an arch shepherd.

Areli, Areliy *transliterated name* {692 areliy} Heroic; Of Areli.

Areopagus *transliterated name* [697 arios pagos] a compound name of Ares (a deity of war), and a stake (as a place to stake a tent).

Ari El *transliterated name* {739, 740, 741 ariel} Lion of El.

Ariday *transliterated name* {742 ariyday} the meaning uncertain; a son of Haman.

arise, arose, raise, rise, rose, rouse *verb* {6965, 6966 qum} [450 anisteemi] [1453 egiro] to stand forth; to rise; to be stirred up, awakened.

ark *noun* [2787 kibotos] a box; the Hellene refers to all arks; including Mosheh's coffin, Noach's ark, and the ark of the covenant.

ark *noun* {727 aron} a box of Yah Veh Elohim; a burial box; most often used of the ark of the covenant.

ark *noun* {8392 tebah} Noach's floating box.

arm, foreleg *noun* {2220 zeroah} [1023 brakion] arm (human), foreleg (animal); denoting force, strength.

armament, armor, armory, arms *noun* {5402 nesheq} military equipment; arsenal.

Arodiy *transliterated name* {722 arowdiy} Of Arod.

Aroer *transliterated name* {6177 aroer} Naked.

Aroeriy *transliterated name* {6200 aroeriy} Of Aroer.

aromas *plural noun* {5561 samim} those that have an aroma.

arose, raise, rise, rose, rouse, arise *verb* {6965, 6966 qum} [450 anisteemi] [1453 egiro] to stand forth; to rise; to be stirred up, awakened.

Arpachshad *transliterated name* {775 arpachshad} [742 arphaxad] the meaning uncertain; a son of Noach.

arrange *verb* [392 anatassomai] to ordain; to line up in order.

arrange, array, line up, rank, appraise, apprize *verb* {6186 arak} to line up in a row; to put in order.

arrange, fail, hoe, lack *verb* {5737 adar} to arrange a vineyard, as in hoeing; to miss having.

arrangement, appraisal *noun* {6187 erek} that which is lined up in a row for evaluation.

arrangement, formation, rank *noun* {4633 maarak} {4634 maarakah} {4635 maareketh} an arrangment (physical or mental).

array, line up, rank, appraise, apprize, arrange *verb* {6186 arak} to line up in a row; to put in order.

arrogance *noun* {2087 zadon} presumptuous; haughtiness.

arrogant *adjective* {2086 zed} presumptuous; haughty.

arrow, quarry *noun* {4551 macca} a missle, as projecting; a quarry, in which stones are ejected.

arrowsnake *noun* {7091 qippoz} as darting after its prey.

Arsa *transliterated name* {777 artsa} Earthiness.

arsenals *plural noun* {8530 talpiah} tall towers.

Artach Shashta *transliterated title* {783 artachshasta} a title of Persian sovereigns.

Artemis *transliterated name* [735 aretemis] a Hellene goddess; mistranslated Dianna.

Arubboth *plural transliterated name* {700 arubbowth} Windows.

Aryeh *transliterated name* {745 aryeh} Lion.

Aryoch *transliterated name* {746 aryowch} the meaning uncertain; the name of two Babeliy.

as to what *participle* {3964 ma} concerning.

Asa *transliterated name* {609 asa} [760 asa] name of a sovereign.

Asa Yah *transliterated name* {6222 asayah} Worked (Worker) of Yah.

Asah El *transliterated name* {6214 asahel} Worked (Worker) of El.

Asal Yah *transliterated name* {683 atsalyahuw} Set Aside of Yah.

Asar El *transliterated name* {840 asarel} Blithed of El.

Asar Elah *transliterated name* {841 asarelah} Blithed of El. **ascend** *verb* {5266 nacaq} {5559 celiq} [305 anabaino] [424 anerkomai] [4320 prosanabaino] to move upward; to go up; **cp** descend; **cp** descent.

ascend, holocaust, mount, regurgitate *verb* {5927, 5928 alah} to ascend, as a mountain; to mount an animal; to regurgitate food; to ascend a holocaust; **see** holocaust, *noun*.

ascent *noun* {4608 maaleh} a way, or steps of going up.
ascent, holocaust *noun* {5930 olah} an ascent to a higher area; an offering that has been holocausted; **see** holocaust, *verb*.

ascetics *plural noun* {3649 kamar} ones who withdraw to a solitary life.

Asel *transliterated name* {682 atsel} Set Aside.

Ash *transliterated name* {5906 ash} a constellation.

ashamed *adjective* [153 aiskunomai] [1870 epaiskunomai] humiliated; disgraced.

ashcake *noun* {5692 uggah} a round cake.

Ashchur *transliterated name* {806 ashchuwr} Dark.

Ashdod *transliterated name* {795 ashdod} [108 azotos] Ravager.

Ashdodiy *transliterated name* {796 ashdowdiy} Of Ashdod.

Ashdoth Pisgah *transliterated name* {798 ashdowthhappicgah} Springs of Pisgah.

Asher *transliterated name* {836 asher} [768 aseer] Blithesome.

Asherah *transliterated name* {842 asherah} a Phoenician goddess.

asherah, asherim *transliterated noun* {842 asherah, *plural* asherim} a wooden cultic altar or memorial.

Asheriy *transliterated name* {843 asheriy} Of Asher.

Ashkenaz *transliterated name* {813 ashkenaz} the meaning uncertain.

Ashqelon *transliterated name* {831 ashqelown} Weighing.

Ashqeloniy *transliterated name* {832 eshqelowniy} Of Ashqelon.

Ashshur *transliterated name* {804 ashshur} Blithesome.

Ashshuriy *transliterated name* {805 ashshuwriy} Of Ashshur.

Ashtaroth *plural transliterated name* {6252 ashtaroth} Phoenician gods of riches; also a place.

Ashtaroth Qarnaim *plural dual transliterated name* {6255 ashterothqarnayim} Ashtaroth of the Double Horns; **see** Ashtaroth.

Ashtarothiy *transliterated name* {6254 ashterathiy} Of Ashtaroth.

Ashtoreth *transliterated name* {6253 ashtoreth} Phoenician goddess of riches.

Asi El *transliterated name* {6221 asiel} Worked of El.

Asia *transliterated noun* [773 asia] thought to mean Asia Minor, the western shore of Asia.

Asians *transliterated noun* [774 asianos] of Asia.

Asiarch *transliterated noun* [775 asiarches] an arch of Asia.

ask, lend, loan *verb* {7592 shael} {7593 sheel} [154 aiteo] to inquire; to request or demand.

Asmon *transliterated name* {6111 atsmon} Bone-like.

asp *noun* {6620 pethen} [785 aspis] as a twister.

asphalt *noun* {2203 zepheth} as softened by the sun.

Asri El *transliterated name* {844 asriel} Blithed of El.

Asri Eliy *transliterated name* {845 asrieliy} Of Asri El.

assarion *transliterated noun* [787 assarion] a Roman coin.

assembly *noun* {3862 lahaqah} a gathering.

assessment *noun* {4371 mekec} a remuneration based on an enumeration (census); **see** evaluation.

assuage *verb* {7918 shakak} to appease; to allay fears.

astonish, desolate, stun *verb* {8074 shamem} {8075 shemam} to stun, as in to stupefy or devastate; to lay waste.

astonishment *noun* {8078 shimmamon} stun; **see** astonish.

Atha Yah *transliterated name* {6265 athayah} Reinforced of Yah.

Athach *transliterated name* {6269 athach} Lodging.

Athal Yah *transliterated name* {6271 athalyah} Constricted of Yah.

athanasia *transliterated noun* [110 athanasia] deathlessness.

Atharim *plural transliterated name* {871 atharim} Stepping Places.

athiest *noun* [112 atheos] without God.

Athlay *transliterated name* {6270 athlay} Constringent.

atom *transliterated noun* [823 atomos] minute; indivisible.

Atroth Beth Yah Ab *transliterated name* {5854 atrowthaddar} Crowns of the House of Yah Ab.

attach *verb* {2836 chashaq} to join; material to material; person to person.

attach, contrive, join *verb* {6775 tsamad} to link; to gird; mentally, to contrive.

attachments *plural noun* {2838 chashuq} rods connecting the posts or pillars.

attain, overtake, reach *verb* {5381 nasag} to attain by reaching for.

Attay *transliterated name* {6262 attay} Timely.

attend *verb* {7365 rechats} to tend at the bathing or baptizing.

attend, befriend, graze, tend *verb* {7462 raah} [5256 hupeereteo] to tend a flock or to pasture; to befriend, by attending to; to cause a flock to graze; **see** attendant; **see** Yah Veh Raah.

attendant *noun* [5257 hupeeretos] one who tends.

atonement *noun* **see kopur/atonement.**

audience, guard, hearing *noun* {4928 mishmaath} an audience; also obedience; a subject.

auditorium *noun* [201 akroateerion] a place of hearing.

aught, naught *noun* {3972 meumah} [3361 me] [3762 oudeis, oudemia, ouden] nil; several words, and combinations of words are used to indicate nil; these include the double negative, not aught, which the *exeGeses parallel BIBLE* renders as naught; most versions use the word, thing, which indicates an object; the *exeGeses parallel BIBLE* avoids thing; thing, as an object is not implied; **note:** ought is correctly aught, but the Authorized Version sometimes uses ought; when combined with the negative, naught, or nought.

augment, increase, add, again *verb* {3254 yacaph} to add to; to repeat.

Augustus *transliterated name* [828 Augoustos] August; Venerable.

aunt *noun* {1733 dodah} a father's or mother's sister.

authority *noun* [1849 exousia] to have the right.

authorize *verb* [1850 exousiazo] to grant the right.

authorize over *verb* [2715 katexousiazo] to be granted the right; to exercise authority.

automatically *adverb* [844 automatos] self-moved; acting without intervention or instigation of another.

avarice *noun* [147 aiskrokerdees] [150 aiskros] [4124 pleonexia] greedy gain.

avaricious *adjective* [146 aiskrokerdees] [4123 pleonektees] greedy of shameful gain.

avenge *verb* {5358 naqam} [1556 ekdikeo] to wreak vengeance; to exact satisfaction.

avengement, vengeance *noun* {5359 naqam} {5360 neqamah} revenge; **see** avenge.

avenger *noun* [1558 ekdikos] a punisher.

avow *verb* [1843 exomologeo] to vow; **see** vow *verb*. **Avva** *transliterated name* {5755 avva} Perverted.

EDC Hebrew / English Bible LEXICON

Avviy, Avviym *transliterated name* {5757 avviy} {*plural* 5761 avviym} Of Avva.

await *adjective* {3175 yachiyl} to wait expectantly.

await, expect, receive, wait *verb* {2442 chakah} {3176 yachal} {6960 qavah} [324 anadekomai] [362 anameno] [553 apekdekomai] [4327 prosdekomai] [4328 prosdokao] [4329 prosdokia] to anticipate; to wait expectantly, patiently; **cp** take.

awake, wake, waken *verb* {5782 uwr} {6974 quts} to wake up.

away from home *verb* [1553 ekdeemeo] to go abroad.

awe, awesome *adjective* {3373 yare} [127 aidos] [5398 phobeetron] [5401 phobos] reverential respect, fear.

awe, awesomeness *noun* {4172 morah} [5400 phobetron] [5401 phobos] reverential respect, fear.

awe, awestricken, awesome *verb* {3372 yare} [5399 phobeo] to respectfully reverence; to fear.

awe, dread, terrify *verb* {6206 arats} to reverence; to harass.

awl *noun* {4836 martsea} an instrument that bores; noun of bore.

Ay, Aya, Ayath *transliterated name* {5857 ay, aya, ayath} Heap.

Ayah *transliterated name* {345 ayah} Hawk.

Ayalon *transliterated name* {357 ayalown} Deer-field; **see** hart.

Ayin *transliterated name* {5871 ayin} [137 ainon] Fountain.

Az Buq *transliterated name* {5802 azbuwq} Strong Hollow.

Azan Yah *transliterated name* {245 azanyah} Hearkened of Yah.

Azar El *transliterated name* {5832 azarel} Helped of El.

Azar Yah *transliterated name* {5838, 5839 azaryah} Helped of Yah.

Azeqah *transliterated name* {5825 azeqah} Walled.

Azi El *transliterated name* {5815 aziel} Recouped of El.

Azzah *transliterated name* {5804 azzah} [1048 gaza] Strong.

Azzahiy *transliterated name* {5841 azzathiy} Of Azzah.

Azzur *transliterated name* {5809 azzuwr} [107 azor] Helper.

B

Baal, Baalim *transliterated title* {1168 baal} {*plural* 1168 baalim} [896 baal] a deity.

baal, married, mastered *transliterated noun* {1167 baal} {1169 beel} one who masters; one who is mastered.

baal, marry, master *verb* {*transliteration* 1166 baal} [1060 gameo] [1918 epigambruo] literally, baal means to be mastered; the ritual of one man and one woman becoming one flesh. **see** baalah.

Baal Berith *transliterated name* {1170 baalberith} Baal of the Covenant.

Baal Gad *transliterated name* {1171 baalgad} Baal of the Troop.

Baal 1-amon *transliterated name* {1174 baalhamon} Baal of a Multitude.

Baal 1-anan *transliterated name* {1177 baalhanan} Baal of Granting Charism.

Baal 1-asor *transliterated name* {1178 baalchatsor} Baal of the Courts.

Baal 1-ermon *transliterated name* {1179 baalhermon} Baal of Abruptness.

Baal Meon *transliterated name* {1186 baalmeon} Baal of Habitation.

Baal Peor *transliterated name* {1187 baalpeor} Baal of Peor (Gap); a deity.

Baal Perasim *transliterated name* {1188 baalperatsim} Baal of the Breaches.

Baal Sephon *transliterated name* {1189 baaltsephon} Baal of the North.

Baal Shalishah *transliterated name* {1190 baalshalishah} Baal of Tripling.

Baal Tamar *transliterated name* {1193 baaltamar} Baal of the Palm Tree.

Baal Yada *transliterated name* {1182 beelyada} Baal Knows.

Baal Yah *transliterated name* {1183 bealyah} Baal of Yah.

Baal Zebub *transliterated name* {1176 baalzebub} [954 beelzeboul] Baal of the Fly.

Baalah *transliterated name* {1173 baalah} places in Pelesheth; **see** baalah.

LEXICON

baalah *transliterated noun* {1172 baalah} feminine of baal.

Baalath *transliterated feminine name* {1191 baalath} rule of a baalah; **see** baalah *noun*.

Baalath Beer *transliterated feminine name* {1192 baalathbeer} Baalah of a Well.

Baali *transliterated name* {1180 baali} Master; a title of Yah Veh.

Baalim, Baal *transliterated title* {1168 baal} {*plural* 1168 baalim} [896 baal] a deity.

Baalim Bamoth *plural transliterated name* {1181 baalibamoth} Baalim of the Bamahs; **see** Bamah.

Baale Yah 1-ludah *plural transliterated name* {1184 baaliyehudah} Baalim of Yah.

Baase Yah *transliterated name* {1202 baaseyah} Work of Yah.

babble *verb* {981 bahtah} [5396 phluareo] to utter nonsense; to make empty charges.

babbler *noun* [5397 phluaros] of one indulging in empty and foolish talk.

Babel *transliterated name* {894, 895 babel} [897 babulon] Mingled; a place; an empire.

Babeliy *transliterated name* {896 babliy} Of Babel.

babes, babies *noun* [3515 neepiazo] [3516 neepios] literally, a very young person; figuratively, immature.

Bachurim *plural transliterated name* {980 bachuriym} Youths.

Bachurimiy *transliterated name* {978 bacharuwmiy} Of Bachurim.

back, bow, brow, rim, arch *noun* {1354 gab} that which is bowed, curved; also the top or rim.

backslide, backsliding *noun* [3900 paraptoma] a side-slip; a lapse or deviation from truth.

badger *noun* {8476 tachash} a clean furred animal; Strong suggests a species of antelope.

bag, bagpipe *noun* {5035 nebel} a skin bag to carry liquids; an instrument with an air supply bag.

bail *verb* {1802 dahlah} {7579 shaab} [501 antleo] to draw water; to let down a pail for drawing out water; verb of pail; **see** pail.

bakings, bakery *noun* {4580 maog} that which is baked, including bakery.

balance *verb* {8625 tekel} to balance, as in a balance scale.

balance, trample *verb* {5537 cala} {5541 calah} as suspended; as weighed; as trampled.

balance, weigh *verb* {8254 shakal} to suspend; to weigh by balancing a set weight against that being weighed; **see** shekel.

balances *dual noun* {3976, 3977 mozenim} a pair of scales to compare weights.

Balaq *transliterated name* {1111 balaq} [904 balak] Waster.

bald, baldy *noun* {7142 qereach} lacking hair on the back of the head.

balden *verb* {7139 qarach} to make bald.

balden, polish, rash *verb* {4178 mowrat} {4803 marat} {4804 merat} to rub (off); to pluck; to cause to be bald.

baldness *noun* {7146} a bald spot on the back of the head.

balm *noun* {6875 tseriy} balsam, as a balm.

Bamah, bamah *transliterated noun* {1116, 1117 bamah} [968 beema] [1041 bomos] Elevated; a tribunal; an elevated seat of judgment; **cp** ramah.

Bamoth Baal *plural transliterated name* {1120 bamothbaal} Baal of Heights; an elevated seat of judgment of Baal; **see** Bamah.

band, bond *noun* {4147 mocerah} {4562 masoreth} a restraint.

bandage *noun* {2848 chittul} loose material that is swathed; **see** swathe.

bandage, channel *noun* {8585 tealah} a bandage, as lifted on a wound; a channel into which water is raised.

bandage, sore *noun* {4205 mazor} in the sense of binding up, a bandage for a sore; an affliction.

bands *plural noun* {7196 qishshur} ornamental bands.

banish *verb* {5077 nada} to exclude.

banister *noun* {4552 micad} a railing of a stairway.

banner *noun* {1714 degel} a standard; a banner.

banner bearer *noun* {1713 dagal} one who carries a banner; to set up a standard; figuratively, to be noticeable.

banquet, drink *noun* {4960, 4961 mishteh} a banquet of eating and drinking; the act of drinking.

baptism, baptize, baptizer; **see** SUMMARY: BAPTISM.

Baqbaqqar *transliterated name* {1230 baqbaqqar} Searcher.

Baqbuk Yah *transliterated name* {1229 baqbukyah} Bottle (Emptying) of Yah.

Baqbuq *transliterated name* {1227 baqbuwq} Emptying, as a bottle emptying.

bar *verb* {5702 agan} disallow; prevent.

Bar, bar *transliterated noun* **son** *noun* {1247 bar, 1248 bar} heir apparent to the throne; also a prefix to a compound name indicating, son of; **cp** ben; **see** Psalm 2: where both bar and ben are used.

Bar Abbas *transliterated name* {1247 bar} {5 abagtha} [912 barabbas] Son of Abbas.

Bar Nabi *transliterated name* {1247 bar} {5029 nebiy} [921 barnabas] Son of a Prophet.

Bar Sabah *transliterated name* {1247 bar} {6638 tsabah} [923 barsabas] Son of a Host.

Bar Talmay *transliterated name* {1247 bar} {8526 talmay} [918 bartholomaios] Ridged Son.

Bar Tame *transliterated name* {1247 bar} {2931 tame} [924 bartimaios] Foul Son.

Bar Yah Shua *transliterated name* {1247 bar} {3091 yahshua} [919 barieesous] Son of Yah Shua.

Bar Yonah *transliterated name* {1247 bar} {3124 yonah} [920 barionas} Son of a Dove.

Barach El *transliterated name* {1292 barachel} Blessed of El.

Baraq *transliterated name* {1301 baraq} [913 barak] Lightning. **barb** *noun* {7899 sek} {7905 sukkah} a barb or briar, as pricking.

bare *adjective* {2835 chasiph} stripped off, as exposed.

bare, bear, beget, birth, born *verb* {3205 yalad} [1080 gennao] [5088 tikto] to produce from seed; of the male, to cause birth; of the female, to birth.

bare, strip *verb* {2834 chasaph} to strip off as to expose.

Bariach *transliterated name* {1282 bariyach} Fugitive.

barley *noun* {8184 seorah} a grain.

Barqos *transliterated name* {1302 barqos} of uncertain derivative.

barren *adjective* {6185 ariri} as stripped of children.

barren(s) *noun* {4629 maarch} {*plural* 4630 maarah} {*plural* 8205 shephee} bare areas; devoid of growth.

barren, expose *adjective* {8192 shaphah} bare.

Baruch *transliterated name* {1263 baruch} Blessed.

Barzillay *transliterated name* {1271 barzillay} Iron.

base, station *noun* {3653 ken} {4350 mekonah} {4369 mekunah} a base, as in furniture; a base, as in a station, or office.

Basha *transliterated name* {1201 basha} Offensiveness.

basket *noun* {5536 cal} *plural* {5552 calcillah} brush, as woven.

Baslith, Basluth *transliterated name* {1213 batsliyth, batsluwth} Peeling (onion).

bason, threshold *noun* {5592b saph} {5602 sephel} a container; as a vessel, or as a vestibule.

bastard *noun* [3541 nothos] an illegitimate person; **cp** mongrel.

bastinado *verb* [4463 rhabdizo] to beat with a rod or staff.

bath *transliterated noun* {1324, 1325 bath} [943 batos] a measure of liquids.

Bath, bath *transliterated noun* {1323 bath} daughter.

Bath Rabbim *transliterated name* {1337 bathrabbim} Daughter of Rabbim (Rabbis).

Bath Sheba *transliterated name* {1339 bathsheba} Daughter of an Oath.

Bath Shua *transliterated name* {1340 bathshua} Daughter of Opulence.

battering *noun* {6904 qabal} as in a battering ram.

battering ram *noun* {4239 mechiy} an instrument for striking.

Bavvay *transliterated name* {942 bavvay} the meaning uncertain; of Persian origin.

bay *adjective* {8320 saruq} fire colored.

Bayith *transliterated name* {1006 bayith} House; a place in Pelesheth.

bayith, beth, house, household, housing noun {1004, 1005 bayith, beth} [3613 oikeeteerion] [3614 oikia] [3624 oikos] usually translated house, as in family or dwelling, except when part of a name, as in Beth Abara; **cp** manse; nave; palace; priestal precinct.

bdellium noun {916 bedolach} a stone, separated or set apart. be, **became, become,** verb {1933, 1934 havah} {1961 hayah} [1096 ginomai] [2071 esomai] to come into existence; to exist; the (Logos) Word, who always existed, became flesh; hayah is the root of the *name* Yah {3050 yahh}.

beads noun {3558 kumaz} *plural* {2737 charuzim} jewels.

beam noun 4500 manohr} {6982 qorah} a frame; a structural support.

bear, beget, birth, born, bare verb {3205 yalad} [1080 gennao] [5088 tikto] to produce from seed; of the male, to cause birth; of the female, to birth.

bear, bore, borne verb {5445 sabal} [941 bastazo] to bear a burden or load; to lift.

bear, lade, lift, load, spare verb {5375 nacah} {5376 nesa} to lift, in a variety of applications.

bear, lift verb {5190 natal} {5191 netal} to raise; to lift as to impose.

bear fruit verb {6500 para} {6509 parah} [2592 karpophoreo] literally, or figuratively, to be fruitbearing.

bear up, bring up, offer up verb [399 anaphero] to take up; to offer up an offering.

beard noun {2206 zaqan} the beard as a sign of age; **see** aged, elder.

beast noun {1165 beiyr} literally, grazers; usually domesticated.

beautiful, handsome (very) adjective {3303 yapheh} {3304 yephehphiyah} {8209 shappir} [5611 horaios] timely; flourishing; beautiful.

beautify verb {3302 yaphah} to cause to be beautiful.

beauty noun {3308 yophiy}.

Bebay transliterated name {893 bebay} the meaning uncertain.

became, become, be verb {1933, 1934 havah} {1961 hayah} [1096 ginomai] [2071 esomai] to come into existence; to exist; the (Logos) Word, who always existed, became flesh; hayah is the root of the *name* Yah {3050 yahh}.

because conjunction [1360 dioti] on the account of; inasmuch as.

bed noun {4903, 4904 mishkab} from the verb, to lie (down); **see** lay, lie.

bed down, spread verb {3331 yatsa} to strew as a surface.

Bede Yah transliterated name {912 bedeyah} Servant of Yah.

bedstead noun {6210 eres} literally, an arch; a bedstead with a canopy.

Beer transliterated name {876 beer} Well (of water).

Beer Elim transliterated name {879 beerelim} Well of Elim.

Beer Lachay Roi transliterated name {883 beerlachayroiy} Well of Living Vision.

Beer Sheba transliterated name {884 beersheba} Well of an Oath.

Beera transliterated name {878 beera} Well (of water).

Beerah transliterated name {880 beerah} Well (of water).

Beeri transliterated name {882 beeri} Well (of water).

Beeroth plural transliterated name {881 beeroth} Wells (of water).

Beerothiy transliterated name {886 beerothiy} Of Beeroth.

Beeroth Bene Yaaqan plural transliterated name {885 beerothbeneyaaqan} Wells of the Sons of Yaaqan.

befall, fall, fell, happen verb {5307 naphal} {5308 nephal} {7136 qarah} to cause to bring about; fall, fall down, fall away; to fell, as in felling timber.

befit, befitting verb {4998 naah} [4241 prepi] to be at home; as to be suitable or proper.

befit, befitting adjective {5000 naveh} at home; as suitable or proper.

befriend, graze, tend, attend verb {7462 raah} [5256 hupeereteo] to befriend, by attending to; to cause a flock to graze; to tend a flock or to pasture; **see** attendant; **see** Yah Veh Raah.

befriend, kiss verb {5401 nashaq} [5368 phileo] [5370 phileema] the Hellene is the verb of friend; a soulical expression of fondness; to kiss as a form of attachment; **cp** love; **read** Yahn 21:15-17; **see** eros.

befriend brethren noun [5360 philadelphia] fraternal affection.

befriend brethren *verb* [5361 philadelphos] fraternal.

befriend children *verb* [5388 philoteknos] maternal.

befriend Elohim *verb* [5377 philotheos] pious.

befriend men *verb* [5362 philandros] affectionate of a woman to her man.

befriend pleasure *verb* [5369 philedonos] to be voluptuous.

befriend self *verb* [5367 philautos] to be selfish; conceited.

befriend silver *verb* [5365 philarguria] [5366 philarguros] to be fond of money; avaricious.

befriend strangers *verb* [5381 philoxeenia] [5382 philoxenos] to be hospitable.

befriendingly esteem *verb* [5389 philotimeomai] to be fond of honour; emulous.

beget, birth, born, bare, bear *verb* {3205 yalad} [1080 gennao] [5088 tikto] to produce from seed; of the male, to cause birth; of the female, to birth.

beginning, first(s), head, top *noun* {7218 rosh} {7221 rishah} {7225 reshith} {8462 rechillah} the head, in a variety of applications; the head of the body, of time, of the month, of archs.

beginning, hierarchy *noun* [746 arche] origin; chief; as being first, foremost.

behave, overturn, remain, return *verb* [390 anastrepho] [396 anatrepo] to turn; in the manner one turns (behaves); to turn over; to overthrow.

behavior *noun* [391 anastrophee] manner of turning about.

behemoth *transliterated noun* {930 behemoth} a large animal; **see** animal.

behold *interjection* {431 aluw} {718 aruw} {1887 he} {1888 ha} {2005 hen} {2009 hinneh} [2396 ide] [2400 idou] an exclamation of observing with surprise.

Becher *transliterated name* {1071 becher} Dromedary.

Becheriy *transliterated name* {1076 bachriy} Of Becher. **Bechorath** *transliterated name* {1064 bechowrath} Firstling. **Bel** *transliterated name* {1078 bel} the Baal of the Babeliy.

Bel Adoni *transliterated name* {1081 baladan} Bel (is his) Adoni.

Bel Shats Tsar *transliterated name* {1112, 1113 belshatstsar} a Babeliy sovereign.

belabour *adjective* {3023 yagea} weary of labour; **see** labour.

belabouring *noun* {3024 yegiah} weariness of labour; **see** labour.

Beli Yaal *transliterated name* {1100 beliyaal} [955 belial] Without Worth; a name ascribed to Satan.

belittle, slight, swift, trifle, abase, abate *verb* {6819 tsaar} {6985 qat} {7034 qalah} {7043 qalal} [2274 heetaomai] to belittle in contempt; to make light of; to lessen.

belly, matrix, womb *noun* {990 beten} {1512 gachon} {3770 keres} {4579 meah} {6896 qabab} {6897 qobah} {6898 qubbah} {7356 racham} (7358 rechem) [2836 koilia] the interior; a cavity as hollow; the abdominal cavity; sometimes refers to the womb.

beloved *noun* {3033 yediduwth} {3039 yedid} [27 agapeetos] a loved one.

beloved, lover, uncle *noun* {1730 dod} from the root, to boil; literally, an extremely warm caring for; a father's or mother's brother.

Belte Shats Tsar *transliterated name* {1095, 1096 belteshatstsar} the Babeliy name of Dani El.

Ben, ben, son *transliterated noun* {1121, 1122, 1123 ben} son, as builder of the family name; also a prefix to a name; **cp** bar; **note:** both ben and bar appear in Psalm 2:.

Ben Ammi *transliterated name* {1151 benammi} Son of the People.

Ben Deqer *transliterated name* {1128 bendeqer} Son of Stabbing.

Ben Geber *transliterated name* {1127 bengebar} Son of Man of Valour.

Ben 1-ladad *transliterated name* {1130 benhadad} Son of Hadad.

Ben 1-lail *transliterated name* {1134 benhail} Son of Valour.

Ben 1-lanan *transliterated name* {1135 benhanan} Son of Granting Charism.

Ben 1-lesed *transliterated name* {1136 bencheced} Son of Mercy.

Ben 1-lur *transliterated name* {1133 benhur} Son of Hur.

Ben Inu *transliterated name* {1148 beninu} Son of Ours.

Ben Oni *transliterated name* {1126 benoni} Son of Mischief.

Ben Regaz *transliterated name* {1123 son} {7266 regaz} [993 boanerges] Son of Rage.

Ben Yamin *transliterated name* {1144 binyamin} [958 beniamin] Son of the Right (as opposed to left).

Ben Yaminiy *transliterated name* {1145 binyaminiy} Of Ben Yamin.

Ben Zocheth *transliterated name* {1132 benzocheth} Son of Zocheth.

Bena Yah *transliterated name* {1141 benayah} Yah Builds.

bend, descend, penetrate, press, sink *verb* {5181 nachath} from the root, to sink; to go down; to press or lead down.

bend, pervert, twist *verb* {5753 avah} {5754 avvah} to crook; to overthrow.

Bene Beraq *plural transliterated name* {1139 beneberaq} Sons of Lightning.

Bene Yaaqan *plural transliterated name* {1142 beneyaaqan} Sons of Yaaqan.

beneficial *adjective* [5624 ophelimos] useful; advantageous.

beneficial *adjective* **benefit** *noun* [4851 sumphero] conducive; advantage.

benefit *noun* {8408 tagmuwl} [5622 ophelia] a bestowment; usefulness.

benefit *verb* {3276 yaal} [5623 opheleo] to be useful or valuable.

Beor *transliterated name* {1160 beor} [1007 bosor] Lamp.

Bera Yah *transliterated name* {1256 berayah} Created of Yah.

Berachah/blessing {1294 berachah} Blessing.

bereave, bereft, abort *verb* {7921 shakol} to deprive of; to be deprived of; to miscarry or suffer abortion.

bereaved, bereft *adjective* {7909 shakkul} deprived; left desolate.

bereavement(s) *noun* {7908 shekol} *plural* {7923 shikkulim} deprivation; childlessness.

Berech Yah *transliterated name* {1296 berechyah} [914 barakias] Kneel to Yah.

Bernice *transliterated name* [959 bernikee] Victorious.

Besal El *transliterated name* {1212 betsalel} In the Shadow of El.

Besay *transliterated name* {1153 becay} {1209 betsay} Trampled.

beseech *interjection* {577 anna} literally, Oh now!

beseech *participle* {4994 na} in the sense of pleading; **see** Hoshia Na.

beseech, console *verb* [3870 parakaleo] to invoke by consolation.

beseech, search, seek *verb* {1245 baqash} to search for, including a response to a petition; **cp** inquire, require.

Beser *transliterated name* {1221 betser} Digging (as an inaccessible spot).

besiege, bind, confine, form *verb* {6696 tsur} to confine; to form by shaping.

Besod Yah *transliterated name* {1152 becodyah} Counsel of Yah.

bestowing *verb* [632 aponemo] to confer as a gift.

Betach *transliterated name* {984 betach} Securely; Confidently.

Beth, beth, bayith, house, household, housing *noun* {1004, 1005 bayith, beth} [3613 oikeeteerion] [3614 oikia] [3624 oikos] usually translated house, as in family or dwelling, except when part of a name, as in Beth Abara; **cp** manse; nave; palace; priestal precinct.

Beth Abara *transliterated name* {1004 bayith} {5679 abarah} [962 beethabara] House of the Crossing.

Beth Anath *transliterated name* {1043 bethanath} House of Answers.

Beth Ania *transliterated name* [963 beethania] House of Dates.

Beth Anoth *plural transliterated name* {1042 bethanoth} House of Answers.

Beth Arbel *transliterated name* {1009 bethharbel} House of Lurking of El.

Beth Aven *transliterated name* {1007 bethaven} House of Mischief.

Beth Azmaveth *transliterated name* {1041 bethazmaveth} House of Azmaveth (Strong of Death).

Beth Baal Meon *transliterated name* {1010 bethbaalmeon} House of Habitation of Baal.

Beth Barah *transliterated name* {1012 bethbarah} House of the Plain (Raft).

Beth Biri *transliterated name* {1011 beythbiriy} House of the Creator.

Beth Dagon *transliterated name* {1016 bethdagon} House of Dagon (a fish deity).

Beth Diblathayim *dual transliterated name* {1015 beythdiblathayim} House of Two Lumps.

Beth Eden *transliterated name* {1040 betheden} House of Eden (Pleasure).

Beth El *transliterated name* {1008 bethel} House of El.

Beth Eliy *transliterated name* {1017 betheliy} Of Beth El.

Beth Eqed *transliterated name* {1044 beytheqed} House of Binding.

Beth Gader *transliterated name* {1013 bethgader} House of the Wall.

Beth Gamul *transliterated name* {1014 bethgamul} House of Dealing.

Beth I-la Arabah *transliterated name* {1026 beythhaarabah} House of the Plains.

Beth I-la Emeq *transliterated name* {1025 beythhaemeq} House of the Valley.

Beth I-la Esel *transliterated name* {1018 bethhaetsel} House Beside.

Beth I-la Ram *transliterated name* {1027 beythharam} House Lofted.

Beth I-la Ran *transliterated name* {1028 bethharan} House Lofted.

Beth I-la Yeshimoth *transliterated name* {1020 bethhayeshimoth} House of Desolations.

Beth I-lag Gilgal *transliterated name* {1019 bethhaggilgal} House of the Wheel.

Beth I-lak Kerem *transliterated name* {1021 bethhakkerem} House of the Vineyard.

Beth I-lam Merchaq *transliterated name* {1023 bethhammerchaq} House Afar.

Beth I-lash Shittah *transliterated name* {1029 beythhashshittah} House of Shittah (a species of tree).

Beth I-lesed *transliterated name* {1004 bayith} {2617 hesed} [964 bethesda] House of Mercy.

Beth I-loglah *transliterated name* {1031 bethchoglah} House of a Partridge.

Beth I-loron *transliterated name* {1032 bethchoron} House on the Boundary.

Beth Kar *transliterated name* {1033 beythkar} House of Meadow.

Beth Lebaoth *plural transliterated name* {1034 bethlebaoth} House of the Roaring Lionesses.

Beth Lechem *transliterated name* {1035 bethlechem} [965 bethleem] House of Bread.

Beth Lechemiy *transliterated name* {1022 bethhallechemi} Of Beth Lechem.

Beth Markaboth *plural transliterated name* {1024 bethmarkaboth} House of Chariots.

Beth Nimrah *transliterated name* {1039 bethnimrah} House of the Leopard.

Beth Pag *transliterated name* {1004 bayith} {6291 pag} [967 bethphagee] House of Unripened.

Beth Pases *transliterated name* {1048 bethpatsets} House of Scattering.

Beth Pelet *transliterated name* {1046 bethpelet} House of Escape.

Beth Peor *transliterated name* {1047 bethpeor} House of the Gap; a deity.

Beth Rapha *transliterated name* {1051 bethrapha} House of Healing.

Beth Rechob *transliterated name* {1050 bethrechob} House of the Broadway.

Beth Sayad *transliterated name* {1004 bayith} {6719 tsayad} [966 bethsaida] House of the Hunt.

Beth Shean, Beth Shan *transliterated name* {1052 beythshean, beythshan} House of Relaxation.

Beth Shemesh *transliterated name* {1053 bethshemesh} House of the Sun.

Beth Shemeshiy *transliterated name* {1030 bethhashshimshiy} Of Beth Shemesh.

Beth Sur *transliterated name* {1049 bethtsur} House of Rock.

Beth Tappuach *transliterated name* {1054 beythtappuwach} House of the Apple.

Bethu El *transliterated name* {1328 bethuwel} {1329 bethuwl} Desolated of El.

betray, deliver, surrender *verb* [3860 paradidomi] to deliver to an enemy; to release; to give to possession of another.

betroth, betrothe, congregate *verb* {781 aras} {3259 yaad} [718 harmozo] to join together as in marriage; to congregate.

betrothals *plural noun* {3623 kelulah} engagements for marriage.

better *adjective* [2909 kretton] more useful; more excellent.

beyond acme [5230 huperakmos] past the prime of youth.

Bezeq *transliterated name* {966 bezeq} Flash.

Bidqar *transliterated name* {920 bidqar} Stabber.

Bigvay *transliterated name* {902 bigvay} the meaning uncertain.

Bichri *transliterated name* {1075 bichriy} Firstling.

Bilam *transliterated name* {1109 bilam} [903 balaam] Not of the People.

Bilgay *transliterated name* {1084 bilgay} Relaxed.

Bina *transliterated name* {1150 bina} of unceratin derivative.

bind, bound *verb* {6123 aqad} {8244 saqad} to tie; to fasten.

bind, confine, form, besiege *verb* {6696 tsur} to confine; to form by shaping.

bind, conspire *verb* {7194 qashar} {7405 rakac} to tie; to tie together.

bind, harness *verb* {2280 chabash} to tie, or wrap.

bind, tyrranize *verb* {631 acar} {6014 amar} to bind with a bond; to bind a captive; to tyrranize.

Binnuy *transliterated name* {1131 binnuwy} Built Up.

bird *noun* {6833 tsippor} {6853 tsephar} a feathered vertabrate; **cp** flyer.

birth, born, bare, bear, beget *verb* {3205 yalad} [1080 gennao] [5088 tikto] to produce from seed; of the male, to cause birth; of the female, to birth.

Birzoth *plural transliterated name* {1269 birzowth} Holes (as pierced).

bit *noun* {4964 metheg} the bit of a harness.

bit, bit by bit, few, little, petty, shortly *adjective, adverb* {4592 meat} diminutive; a few; a little.

bit of land *noun* {3530 kibrah} a short distance.

bite, blink, nip *verb* {7169 garats} a pinch, of the lids, of the lips, of the hands as forming.

bite, usure *verb* {5391 nashak} literally, as in usury, to take a bite.

Bith Yah *transliterated name* {1332 bithyah} Daughter of Yah. **bitter** *adjective* {3992 maar} {4751 mar} {4815 meriri} {*plural* 8563 tamrurim} [4089 pikros] pungent; acrid; embittered; painful.

bitter, bitterness *noun* {4470 memer} {*plural* 4472 mamrorim} {4786 morah} {4787 morrah} {4814 meriruth} [4088 pikria] pungent; acridity; trouble; grief.

bitter, gall, venom *noun* {*plural* 4844 merarim} {4845 mererah} {4846 merorah} bile; venom; a bitter herb.

bitterly *adverb* [4090 pikros] with poignant grief.

bitumin *noun* {2564 chemar} as frothing to the surface.

Bizyoth Yah *transliterated name* {964 bizyotheyah} Despised of Yah.

black tile *noun* {5508 sochereth} tessara; a border tile.

blade, flame *noun* {3851 lahab} a flame of fire; a flashing blade of a sword.

blameless *adjective* **blamelessly** *adverb* [273, 274 amemptos] without blame.

blanket *noun* {8063 semikah} a large covering.

blaspheme *transliterated verb* {1442 gadaph} {4167 muq} {5006 naats} [987 blaspheemeo] to vilify; to slander.

blasphemous *transliterated adjective* [989 blaspheemos] vilifying.

blasphemy *transliterated noun* {5007 neatsah} [988 blaspheemia] a vilification.

blast *verb* {7710 shadaph} to scorch; to blight.

blast *verb* [4537 salpizo] to blast a trumpet.

blast, clang, clap, shout, stake *verb* {7321 ruwa} {8628 taqa} [4078 peegnumi] [4717 stauroo] to sound loudly; to celebrate by shouting, and/or blasting shophars and trumpets unto Yah Veh; to shout and/or blast a battle cry; to stake a tabernacle or tent; to stake for execution.

blast, blasting *noun* {7711 shedephah} a scorch; a blight.

blast(ing), clang(ing), clap(ping), shout(ing), stake(ing) *noun* {8619 taqowa} {8643 teruah} a loud sound; the celebration of shouting, and/or blasting shophars and trumpets unto Yah Veh; also of shouting, and/or blasting a battle cry; a stake of a tent, or tabernacle; a stake for execution.

bleeding, menstruous *adjective* {1742 davvay} sick, as in having a period.

blemish *noun* {3971 mum} [3470 momos] imperfection.

blemish *verb* [3469 momeomai] become imperfect.

bless, kneel *verb* {1288 barak} {1289 berak} [3107 makarios] to beatify; the Hebrew also means to kneel in adoration.

blessed *noun* [3106 makarizo] beatified.

blessedness *noun* [3108 makarismos] beatification.

blessing *noun* {1293, 1294 berakah} an adoration.

blind *verb* {5786 avar} to cause blindness.

blind, blindness *noun* {5787 ivver} {5788 ivvaron} literally, or figuratively, undiscerning; without sight; sightlessness.

blink *adverb* {6621 petha} to open momentarily.

blink *noun* {7281 rega} {8160 shaah} the blink of the eye; a quick look; a moment.

blink, calm, rest, split *verb* {7280 raga} this word is derived from two roots; blink and split, as momentary; calm and rest, as soothing.

blink, nip, bite *verb* {7169 qarats} to pinch the lids, the lips, or the hands as forming.

blister *noun* {3555 keviyah} a branding.

blister *verb* {3554 kavah} to prick; to penetrate, as to blister. **blithe** *noun* {835 esher} pleasant; **cp** blessed.

blithe *verb* {833 ashar} to please; **cp** bless.

blithesome *adjective* {837 ohsher} pleasing.

blood *noun* {1818 dam} [129 haima] the soul sustaining fluid in the arteries.

blood pouring *verb* [130 haimatekchusia] an effusion of blood.

bloody *adjective* {1741 devay} sickly; menstrous; loathing.

blossom *noun* {5322 nets} {5328 nitstsah} {5339 nitstsan} {5563 semadar} {6525 perach} {6733 tsitsah} {6734 tsitsith} [438 anthos] a bloom.

blossom, flourish *verb* {6524 parach} {6692 tsuts} to bloom.

blossom, wing *noun* {6731 tsits} a blossom, as blooming brightly; a wing, as gleaming.

blow *verb* {5380 nashab} to disperse; **cp** puff.

blow away *verb* {6284 paah} from the root of puff.

blush *verb* {2659 chapher} to express shame by blushing.

board *noun* {7175 qeresh} a slab or plank.

boast *verb* [2744 kaukaomai] to brag; to vaunt; in either a good or bad sense.

boast, boasting *noun* [2745 kaukeeme] [2746 kaukeesis] bragging; vaunting; in either a good or bad sense.

Boaz *transliterated name* {1162 boaz} [1003 booz] derivative uncertain.

bodily *adjective* [4984 somatikos] relating to the body; corporeal, or physical.

bodily *adverb* [4985 somatikos] relating to the body; corporeally, or physically.

body *noun* {1465 gevah} {1472 geviah} {1610 gaph} {1655 geshem} [4983 soma] the physical housing of the soul and spirit.

boil *verb* {7570 rathach} to boil.

boilings *noun* {7571 rethach} that which is boiled.

Bocheru *transliterated name* {1074 bocheruw} Firstborn.

Bochim *plural transliterated name* {1066 bochiym} Weepers.

boldly *adverb* **(having) boldness** *noun* [3954 parreesia] [3955 parreesiazomai] unreserved in speech; confident.

bond *noun* {632, 633 ecar} a binding declaration.

bond, band *noun* {4147 mocerak} {4562 masoreth} a restraint.

bonds *plural noun* {4575 maadannahoth} clusters.

bone, skeleton *noun* {1634, 1635 gerem} {6106 etsem} [3747 osteon] a framework; a substance; usually of the body.

boot *noun* {5430 seon} a military boot; a protection.

booted *participle* {5431 saan} shod with a military boot.

border, enclosure *noun* {1367 gebulah} {4526 micgereth} that outward bounds which encloses.

border, wing *noun* {3671 kanaph} {4020 migbalah} literally, extreme edge.

bore, pierce, appoint *verb* {5344 naqab} to point out; to thrust or make a hole through.

born *adjective* {3209 yillod} brought forth.

born *noun* {3211 yalid} that which is brought forth.

born, bare, bear, beget, birth *verb* {3205 yalad} [1080 gennao] [5088 tikto] to produce from seed; of the male, to cause birth; of the female, to birth.

borne, bear, bore *verb* {5445 sabal} [941 bastazo] to bear a burden or load; to lift.

borrow, join, lend *verb* {3867 lavah} literally, to entwine; to become wrapped up in; as a borrower, or as a lender.

Boses *transliterated name* {949 bowtsets} Bleached.

Bosmath *transliterated name* {1315 bosmath} Spices.

bosom *noun* {2436 cheq} {2683 chetsen} {2684 chotsen} [2859 kolpos] the breast; symbolic of one's inner self.

bosom, bowl *noun* {6747 tsallacheth} deep; as a bowl, as a bosom.

Bosqath *transliterated name* {1218 botsqath} Swell (of ground).

Bosrah *transliterated name* {1224 botsrah} Fold.

botany *transliterated noun* [1008 botanee] herbs and plants.

bound *noun* {615 acir} {616 accir} persons that are bound, as in imprisoned.

bound, bind *verb* {6123 agad} {8244 sagad} to tie; to fasten.

boundary *noun* [3725 horion] [3734 horothesia] as a boundary line; limit.

boundary, cord, line, pang *noun* {2256 chebel} literally, a rope; as a boundary line, or as binding one in a pang.

bounty *noun* {8228 shepha} {8636 tarbith} a premium; an abundance; an excess.

bow *noun* {7198 qesheth} {7199 qashshath} that which is bent; a bow in the heavens; the bow of an archer.

bow *verb* {6915 qadad} to bend in reverence or respect.

bow, brow, rim, arch, back *noun* {1354 gab} that which is bowed, curved; also the top or rim.

bowl, hollow, palm, paw, sole *noun* {3709 kaph} {6447 pas} {8168 shoal} a hollow of the hand, foot, paw, or body; also utensils with a hollow.

braggadocio *verb* [212 alazoneia] bragging.

braggard *noun* [213 alazon] one that brags.

braid *noun* {6616 pathil} that which is entwined.

braids *plural noun* {4253 machlaphoth} ringlets of hair.

branch *noun* {5342 netser} {6056, 6057 anaph} {*plural* 6073 opheim} {7754 sok} [902 baion] [2798 klados] [2814 kleema] a limb; a bough of a tree; a descendant; also of the Messiah; **cp** twig.

branch, ear, stream *noun* {7641 shibboleth} a branch or an ear of grain, as growing; a stream, as flowing.

branch, spear *noun* {7973 shelach} {7976 shilluchah} a spear, as a missile; a branch, as sprouting.

branching *adjective* {6058 aneph} as covering.

brand, etching, mark, tattoo *noun* {7085 qaaqa} {8420 tab} [5480 karagma] a scratched marking; a mark on animals; an x or a + as a signature of an illiterate; a mark of protection; **read** Yechezq El 9:4-6; **read** Apocalypse 13:16,17, 14:9-11, 15:2, 16:2, 19:20, 20:4; **cp** brand *verb*.

brand, mark, tattoo *verb* {8427, 8428 tavah} to mark an animal; to mark an x or + as a signature of an illiterate, or to mark for protection.

branded *verb* {5348 nagod} marked by piercing.

brander *noun* {5349 noqed} one who brands.

bray *verb* {5101 nahaq} a screaming from hunger; **cp** growl. **breach** *verb* {6561 paraq} {6562 peraq} {6555 parats} to breach; to separate from; to split.

breach, break *noun* {7667 sheber} {7670 shibron} a breach; a break; a ruin.

breach, break *verb* {7665 shabar} to breach; to break open.

breach, break (off) (loose), craunch, crunch, separate, split verb {6561 paraq} {6562 peraq} {6555 parats} to breach; to separate from; to split.

breach, plunder noun {6563 pereq} a breach; that which was broken away from.

breach, separate, split noun {6556 perets} a breach; a separation from; a split.

breaches dual noun {4370 miknac} in the sense of concealing.

bread noun {3899 lechem} literally, food; consider our Adonay Yah Shua Messiah as the food – that which sustains life.

break, breach noun {7667 sheber} {7670 shibron} a breach; a break; a ruin.

break, breach verb {7665 shabar} to breach; to break open.

break, broken verb {6565 parar} to break; to violate; especially a covenant.

break (down), dismay, terrify verb {2865, 2866 chathath} to cause to prostrate; to break down by violence, or fear.

break (forth) verb {6476 patsach} usually in singing; also break bones.

break (off) (loose), craunch, crunch, separate, split, break (open) verb {6626 pathath} to break open.

break neck verb {6202 araph} to break the neck, as to destroy.

breakers noun {4867 mishbar} a breaker of the sea.

breakwater noun {4664 miphrats} break is literal; water is implied; from the root, break.

breast noun {2373 chazeh} {7699 shad} [3149 mastos] the bosom; **see** bosom; **cp** chest.

breath noun {5396 nishma} {5397 neshamah} air inhaled and exhaled.

breathe verb [1709 empneo] to inhale and exhale; from the root of spirit.

breathe, puff verb {6315 puwach} to exhale the breath; to blow air; **cp** spirit {7307 ruwach}.

breathe cold verb [674 apopsucho] [5594 psucho] to inhale and exhale; from the root of soul.

breather noun {6314 pugah} breathing space.

bribe verb {7809 shachad} to donate.

bribe, ransom noun {7810 shachad} a donation.

bribes plural noun {8021 shalmon} extortions.

brick (make), whiten verb {3835 laban} to make a brick; to cause to be white; this is a derivative of two words; **see** brick noun; **see** white.

brick noun {3843 lebenah} a block of white clay.

bride noun [3565 numphee] a man's woman.

bridechamber noun [3567 numphon] bridal suite.

bridegroom noun [3566 numphios] a woman's man.

brier noun {5636 carpad} {8068 shamir} [942 batos] [5146 tribolos] a thorny or prickly stem.

brigandine noun {5630 siryon} a coat of mail.

bright vine noun {8321 soreqah} [288 ampelos] the Hebrew indicates a burning bright.

brilliance, brilliancy noun {5051 nogahh} {plural 5053 nogahoth} brightness; splendor.

brilliant copper noun {2830 chashmai} a polished metal.

bring, embark verb [321 anago] to bring out; to embark in sailing.

bring near, oblate, approach verb {7126 qarab} {7127 qereb} to draw near; to bring near; to offer for worship.

bring up, offer up, bear up verb [399 anaphero] to take up; to offer up an offering.

broad, large noun {7341 rochab} {7342 rachab} wide, width; roomy.

broaden, enlarge verb {7337 rachab} to widen; to make larger.

broadness noun {7338 rachab} width.

broadway noun {7339 rechob} [4113 plateia] a broad way; a wide street.

brocades plural noun {4865 mishbetsahim} fabrics into which gold, silk, or silver are woven.

brood verb {1716 dagar} to brood over eggs or chicks.

broom noun {4292 matate} an instrument for sweeping.

brother noun {251 ach} [80 adelphos] a male child born of one's parents; also used figuratively.

brotherhood noun {264 achavah} [81 adelphotees] brotherliness; a fraternity.

brow, rim, arch, back, bow *noun* {1354 gab} that which is bowed, curved; also the top or rim.

brush arbors, sukkoth, Sukkoth/Brush Arbors *transliterated noun* {5520 sok} {5521 sukkah} {5522 sikkuwth} {5523 sukkowth} {7900 sok} [4634 skeenopeegia] name of places in Pelesheth and Misrayim; a brush arbor to harbor animals; a celebration of harvest, of spreading of branches, of Hoshia Na; Leviticus 23:33-44, Yahn 7:37, Psalm 118:25,26, Matthaios 21:9-15, Markos 11:9,10, Yahn 12:13, Apocalypse 7:9,10; **see** Hoshia Na.

bubble *verb* {7370 rachash} to gush.

buck (goat) *noun* {6841 tsephir}{6842 tsaphir} a male goat.

buck, hairy *adjective* {8163 sair} shaggy; also a he goat.

buckler *noun* {4043 magen} {5507 socherah} a protector, as surrounding.

buckler *verb* {4042 magan} to protect to another's care.

bud, flee *verb* {5132 nuts} to flash, as in color; to flee in a flash.

build, edify *verb* {1124 benah} {1129 banah} [2026 epoikodomeo] [3618 oikodomeo] to build; to build up; to confirm; to construct; to erect.

building *noun* {1146, 1147 binyan} [3619 oikodomee] that which is erected or constructed.

bull *noun* {8450 tor} a male animal.

bullock *noun* {6499 par} a young bull, as breaking forth with strength.

bundle, kernel *noun* {6872 tseror} a package: as a parcel; as a particle.

Buqqi *transliterated name* {1231 buqqiy} Vacated; Evacuated.

Buqqi Yah *transliterated name* {1232 buqqiyah} Evacuating of Yah.

burden *noun* {2960 torach} {4614 maamacah} {4853 massa} {4858 massaah} [922 baros] a weight; **see** load; **see** overload.

burden *noun* {5447 sebel} {5448 sobel} {5450 sebalah} the load; the responsibility.

burden, lade, laden, load *verb* {6006 amas} to load a load; to impose a burden.

burden, uplift, uprise *noun* {4864 maseth} a raising; a reproach, as a burden.

burdenbearer *noun* {5449 sabbal} one that bears burdens; a porter.

burdened *adjective* [916 bareo] [925 baruno] weighed down.

burdenless *noun* [4 abares] not burdensome.

burn *verb* {6272 atham} to glow.

burn *verb* {8313 saraph} to fire; **see** seraph.

burn, kindle *verb* {3341 yatsah} {5400 nasaq} {6919 qadach} to set on fire; to desolate.

burn (down) *verb* {3344 yaqad} [2618 katakaio] to wholly consume.

burner, burnings *noun* {3350 yeqod} {4168 moqed} {4169 moqadah} a fire; a fuel.

burning *noun* {8316 serephah} a firing; a cremation; **see** seraph.

burning *participle* {3345 yeqad} {3346 yeqeda} a conflagration.

burning (coal) (flash) *noun* {7565 resheph} a burning coal; a burning flash as of a flaming arrow.

burnished *adjective* {7044 qalal} brightened.

burst (open), liberated *adjective* {6359 patir} {6362 patar} burst open, as a flower; liberate, as a person.

burster *noun* {6363 pitrah} a firstborn; the first to burst the matrix.

bury, hide *verb* {2934 taman} to hide by covering.

bush *noun* {5572 ceneh} a shrub with branches.

butler, drink (give), drown, moisten, wet *verb* {8248 shaqah} {8257 shaga} to butler, as a bartender; to drink to quench thirst; to drink unto drowning; to cause to be wet.

butlership, drinking, moistened, moisture *noun* {4945 mashqeh} to cause to be moistened, or drunken.

butt, push *adjective* {5056 naggach} butting, as vicious.

butt, push *verb* {5055 nagach} to butt with the horns; to war against.

buttocks *noun* {8357 shethah} the rump.

by, from, of *preposition* In most versions, these three words are used interchangeably as the translators desired; in the Hebrew, they are most often inferred; in the Hellene, two words [575 apo] [1537 ek, ex] (among others) are translated

into more than thirty words; most often the context must decide their proper use; for example, it is not feasible to build a doctrine on the phrase, the trust **of** Yah Shua Messiah.

byssus *noun* {3768 karpac} a yellow flax.

C

cage *noun* {5474 sugar} an inclosure.

cake *noun* {809 ashishah} a bakery, usually of grapes.

cakes *plural noun* {8601 tuphinim} those which have been caked by baking; **see** bake.

calamity *noun* {6365 pid} to ruin by piercing.

calcinations, cremations *plural noun* {4955 misraphahoth} calcinations as of lime; cremations of bones.

calf *noun* {5695 egel} male calf; as frisking round; **cp** heifer.

call back *verb* [479 antikaleo] to return an invitation.

call, proclaim, recall *verb* {7121 qara} {7123 qera} [1941 epikaleomai] [2564 kaleo] [4341 proskaleomai] [4377 prosphoneo] to call forth; to call out; to call upon; to address; **cp** name.

called *noun* {7148 qari} the called ones.

calling *noun* {7150 qeriah} having been called.

callous, heavy *adjective* {3515 kabed} [3975 pakunomai] as in grievous; as in thickskinned.

callous, heavy, honour *verb* {3513 kabad} to weigh down; to callous; to esteem.

callous, prevail, strengthen, uphold *verb* {553 amats} {555 omets} {2388 chazaq} {2393 chezqah} {5810 azaz} to become thickskinned; to enable physically.

calm, rest, split, blink *verb* {7280 raga} this word is derived from two roots; blink and split, as momentary; calm and rest, as soothing.

camel *transliterated noun* {1581 gamel} [2574 kameelos] burdenbearer.

camp *noun* {4264 machaneh} a tenting area; an army.

camp, encamp *verb* {2583 chanah} {8497 takah} [63 agrauleo] [835 aulizomai] to pass the night in the open air; to tent; **see** pull stakes; **see** court, courtyard.

camphire, koper/atonement, pitch *noun* {3724 koper} camphor, a medication; a sealant for the ark of the flood; also an atonement: **see** koper/atonement.

can, enable, prevail, able *verb* {3201 yakol} {3202 yekel} {3546 kehal} [1410 dunamai] [2427 hikanoo] the dynamis to do; **see** dynamis.

cankerworm *noun* {3218 yeleq} a devourer.

canon *transliterated noun* [2583 kanon] a measured rule or regulation.

canopy *noun* {2646 chuppah} a cover.

cap *noun* {3805 kothereth} {6858 tsepheth} the top cap of a column.

capable, possible *adjective* [1415 dunatos] having sufficient dynamis; **see** dynamis.

captivate, capture, adhere *verb* {3920 lachad} {3921 leked} [259 halosis] to catch; to cause to stick.

captive, captivity *noun, adjective* {7622 shebiyth} {7628 shebiy} {7633 shibyah} [161 aichmalosia] [162 aichmaloteuo] [164 aichmalotos] one that is captured; the state of being captured.

captive, captor *noun* **capture** *verb* {7617 shabah} [163 aikmalotizo] captive, as one captured; captor, as one who captures; capture, to transport into captivity; **see** survive.

capture, adhere, captivate *verb* {3920 lakad} {3921 leked} [258 halosis] to catch; to cause to stick.

capture, manipulate *verb* {8610 taphas} to manipulate; to seize with the hands; to use without warrant.

caravan *noun* {736 orechah} {1979 helikah} a group of travelers.

caravan *verb* {732 arach} to travel in groups.

carcase *noun* {1480 guphah} {5038 nebelah} {6297 peger} [2966 kolon] [4430 ptoma] corpse.

carcase heap *noun* {7419 ramuth} a heap of carcases.

carousal, potion *noun* {5435 cobe} a drinking revelry; a potion of carousing.

carouse *verb* **carouser** *participle* {5433 caba} to revel by drinking; one who carouses.

carousing *noun* [2970 komos] a drinking revelry.

carve *verb* {6605 pathach} {7049 qala} to hew in wood or stone; to plow the ground.

carve, chop *verb* {2404 chatab} to hew or cut.

carving noun {plural 2405 chatubah} {4734 miqlaath} {6603 pittuach} {6816 tsatsua} that which is carved or hewn.

cast, hurl, throw verb {7993 shalak} to throw out, down, or away.

cast, lie, put verb [906 ballo] to throw.

cast (away) (down) (forth) (out) verb {2904 tuwl} to pitch away, down, forth, or out.

castle noun {2038 harmon} a tall building.

castrated adjective {4790 meroach} literally, bruised testis.

castrated noun {1795 dakkah} literally, crushed testis.

cataract noun {8400 teballul} as flowing; a cataract in the eye.

catastrophe transliterated noun [2692 katastrophe] a calamity; a demolition.

catechize transliterated verb [2727 kateekeo] to doctrinate by question and answer.

cathedra transliterated noun [2515 kathedra] a seat of one in authority.

cathedra (preeminent) transliterated noun [4410 protokathedria] first seat of one in authority.

cauldron noun {4802 marchesheth} a stewing instrument.

cause, accusation noun [156 aitia] [157 aitiama] [158 aition] as asked; as inquired into.

causer noun [159 aitios] one that causes to be; **cp** Creator.
cauterize transliterated verb [2743 kauteriazo] to sear or burn with a caustic.

cavalry noun {6571 parash} combat troops on horseback.

cave, cavern noun {4631 mearah} {plural 4492 minharoth} [3692 opee] an opening in the earth.

cease verb {988 batel} {989 betel} to desist; to stop.

cease, consummate verb, participle {1584 gamar} {1585 gemar} to bring to conclusion.

cease, decease, desist, abandon verb {2308 chadai} to be lacking; to stop.

cedar noun {8391 teashshur} a species of tree.

ceil, ciel verb {5603 saphan} to cover with a ceiling.

ceiling, cieling noun {5604 sippun} a ceiling as a cover.

celebrate verb {2287 chagag} {8567 tanah} [1858 heortazo] to commemorate by ceremony.

celebration noun {2282 chag} [1859 heortee] a ceremonial commemoration; a festive occasion; Elohim's intent was for the earthly life of humanity to be one celebration after another.

cement noun {4423 melet} literally, smooth.

censer noun {4730 miqtereth} [2369 thumiasterion] an incense holder; **see** incense; **see** frankincenser.

census, mandate noun **specified** adjective {4662 miphqad} an enumeration; a designated spot; an order, or command.

centurion transliterated noun [1543 hekatontarchees] [2760 kenturion] an arch over a hundred.

ceremonial, ceremony noun [2356 threeskia] the form of commemorating an event.

ceremonious adjective [2357 threeskos] formal; ritual.

certain, secure adjective **certainly, securely** adverb {3330 yatstsib} [804 asphalees] [806 asphalos] assuredly; safely.

certainty, security noun {3321 yetseb} [803 asphalia] safety; an undoubtable truth.

cesspool noun {5122 nevaluw} from the root, to foul; a pool that collects filthy waste.

chaff noun {4671 mots} {5784 ur} [892 akuron] that which is winnowed from the grain.

chaff, flakes noun {4651 mappal} that which falls off; that which is pendulous.

chain noun {6060 anaq} {7242 rabid} a collar; a chain of adornment.

chain noun {7569 rattoq} {7572 rattiqah} {plural 7577 rethuqahoth} {8331 sharshah} {8333 sharsherah} a chain as woven; a chain as linked.

chain verb {6059 anaq} to adorn with a chain.

chain verb {7576 rathaq} to chain with a woven chain.
chalice noun {6907 qubbaath} a goblet.

chamber noun {3326 yatsuah} {3957 lishkah} {5393 nishkah} {8372 taah} a bedchamber; a cell; a room.

chameleon, swan noun {8580 tanshemeth} hard breather.
change, double, duplicate, fold, reiterate, repeat, alter verb {8132 shana} {8133 shena} {8138 shanah} to reinforce by folding, by doubling; may include disguise, camouflage.

change, exchange *verb* {3235 yamar} {4171 mur} [236 allasso] to alter; to change places.

changes *noun* {2487} chaliphah} alterations of ways of life; of clothing.

channel, bandage *noun* {8585 tealah} a channel into which water is raised; a bandage, as lifted on a wound.

charge *verb* [1291 diastellomai] to enjoin.

chariot, upper millstone *noun* {4817 merkab} {4818 merkabah} {7393 rekeb} {7396 rikbah} {7398 rekub} a vehicle; a rider; **cp** millstones.

charioteer *noun* {7395 rakkab} one that drives a chariot.

charism, charisma, charismatic; see SUMMARY: CHARISM.

charmer *noun* {2267 cheber} one who casts spells.

chart, inscribe *verb* {3789 kathab} {3790 kethab} {3799 katham} [1449 engrapho] to scribe; **see** scribe.

chase, flap, flee, wander *verb* {5074 nadad} {5323 natsa} to flap up and down; to shoo away.

chasm *noun* {6178 aruts} {7745 shuehah} [5490 chasma] a breach in a rock; an abyss.

chattel *noun* {4735 miqneh} {4736 miqnah} {7075 qinan} any human, animal, or material possession, except real estate.

chattel, chattelize *verb* {7069 qanah} to aquire chattel; to cause to be a chattel.

chatter *verb* {6527 parat} to scatter words.

cheat, deprive *verb* [650 apostereo] to deprive of some right.

checkered *adjective* {8665 tashbets} as reticulated.

cheek, jaw *noun* {3895 lechi} the side, or the bottom of the face.

cheer *noun* [5479 chara] cheerfulness; delight; **see** SUMMARY: CHARISM, CHEERS.

cheer *verb* {4010 mabliygiyth} {8055 samach} to cheer.

cheerful *adjective* {8056 sameach} blithe.

cheerfulness *noun* {8057 simehah} blithsomeness.

charm, join *verb* {2266 chabar} literally, to join objects; to cast spells.

cherish befriending *verb* [5387 philostorgos] to have affection for being a friend.

cherub, cherubim *transliterated noun* {*singular* 3742 cherub} [*plural* 5502 cheroubim] figures which guarded the Garden of Eden and the Ark; **cp** seraph.

chesnut *noun* {6196 armon} a nut bearing tree.

chest *noun* [4738 steethos] the thorax of the body; **cp** breast.

chew, cut *verb* {1262 barah} chew food; to cut as in choosing.

chew out *verb* {399 akal} to eat at; to gnaw at.

chew out *verb* {7170 qerats} to chastize verbally.

chicks *plural noun* {667 ephroachim} as in bursters of a shell.

child, children (young) *noun* {2056 valad} {3206 yeled} {3207 yeled} [3808 paidarion] [3813 paidion] [5043 teknon] young person or persons.

childbearer *noun* [5041 teknogoneo] a person who bears children.

childhood *noun* {3208 yalduth} [3812 paidiothen] the life period of a young person.

childless *adjective* [815 ateknos] without children.

children (fostered) *verb* [5044 teknotrophee] to bring up another person's children.

children (little) *noun* [5040 teknion] children of small stature.

chiliarch *transliterated noun* {441 alluph} [5506 chiliarchos] a ruler of a thousand.

chip away *verb* {7111 qetsaphah} to fragment.

chirp *verb* {6850 tsaphaph} to chirp or coo as a bird.

choice *adjective* {4004 mibchor} {4005 mibchar} select; best.

choir *plural noun* {1960 huyedah} a group of singers.

chomer, heap, mortar *transliterated noun* {2563 chomer} a dry measure as mixed, or heaped.

choose, chose *verb* {977 bacher} to select.

chop, carve *verb* {2404 chatab} to hew; to cut.

chop, chopping *noun* {4553 misped} [2870 kopetos] [2871 kopee] a beating of the breast as an expression of lamenting, mourning, or wailing.

chop, chopping *verb* {5594 saphad} [2875 kopto] to beat the breast as in expression of lamenting, mourning, or wailing.

chop, curtail, harvest, shorten *verb* {7114 qatsar} literally, or figuratively, to cut off.

chop off *verb* {7112 qatsats} {7113 qetsats} literally, or figuratively, to chop off.

chops, cuttings *noun* {1279 biryah} a cut or chop of meat.

chorus *transliterated noun* [5525 choros] a band of singers.

chosen *adjective* {972 bachirr} a select people whom Yah Veh chose.

ciel, ceil *verb* {5603 saphan} to cover with a ceiling.

cieling, ceiling *noun* {5604 sippun} a ceiling as a cover.

circle *noun* {2329 chug} a round.

circle *verb* {2328 chug} to go around.

circuit, crutch, spindle *noun* {6418 pelek} to be round; a spindle as whirled; hence a crutch.

circuit, revolution *noun* {8622 tequphah} a revolution of days; a revolving around.

circumcise *verb* {4135 mul} [4059 peritemno] to cut the foreskin; **cp** incise.

circumcision *noun* {4139 mulah} {*plural* 4139 muloth} [4061 peritomee] the cutting of the foreskin; **cp** decircumcision; **cp** incision; **cp** uncircumcision.

cistern *noun* [999 bothunos] a hole for storing water.

citadel *noun* {759 armown} a fortified dwelling.

citizen *noun* [4177 politees] a member of a nation.

citizenize *verb* [4176 polituomai] to cause to be, or become a citizen; citizenlike.

citizenship *noun* [4174 politia] [4175 polituma] membership in a nation.

city *noun* {5892 ayar} {6144 ar} {7149, 7151 qiryah} {7176 qereth} [4172 polis] (as in metropolis) a large town.

clamors *plural noun* {8663 teshuah} crashings; loud clamors.

clang, clap, shout, stake, blast *verb* {7321 ruwa} {8628 taqa} [4078 peegnumi] [4717 stauroo] to sound loudly; to celebrate by shouting, and/or blasting shophars and trumpets unto Yah Veh; to shout and/or blast a battle cry; to stake a tabernacle or tent; to stake for execution.

clang(ing), clap(ping), shout(ing), stake(ing), blast(ing) *noun* {8619 taqowa} {8643 teruah} a loud sound; the celebration of shouting, and/or blasting shophars and trumpets unto Yah Veh; also of shouting, and/or blasting a battle cry; a stake of a tent, or tabernacle; a stake for execution.

clap *verb* {4222 macha} to strike, especially hands.

clap, slap, slurp *verb* {5606 saphaq} as in clapping hands, slapping the thigh, slurping vomit; **see** gluttony.

clasp *noun* {6781 tsamid} a bracelet, as an arm clasp.

Claudius *transliterated name* [2804 klaudios] the name of a kaisar.

clay *noun* {2635 chacaph} [3749 ostrakinos] [4081 peelos] a substance of the earth; implies frailty.

clean *adjective* {5343 neqe} pure.

cleanse for sin, sin (against) *verb* {2398 chata} [264 hamartano] to misaim.

cleanse, polish, purge *verb* {1305 barar} [1571 ekkathairo] clarify, catharize; **cp** purify.

clear *adjective* [573 haplous] able to see distinctly, pure.

clear *adjective* **clearly** *adverb* {6703 tsach} bright; evident.

clear, gold *noun* {2091 zahab} literally, yellow shimmer.

clearing *adjective* {6708 tsechichi} as on the top of a rock.

clearing *noun* {6706 tsechiyach} as on the top of a rock.

cleave, pierce *verb* {6398 palach} to split in half; to pierce through.

cleaver *noun* {6393 peladah} a divider.

cleavered, cleft, clove, cloven *verb* {8156 shaca} {8158 shacaph} to split.

cleft *noun* {8157 sheca} a split.

cleft, clove, cloven, cleavered *verb* {8156 shaca} {8158 shacaph} to split.

cleft, twig *noun* {5585 caiph} a fissure of rocks; a small branch.

cliff *noun* [2911 kreemnos] the steep side of an elevation.

clip *verb* {5243 namal} to clip; to be clipped; as pruning; as circumcising.

clip *verb* {7094 qatsab} to clip or chop off.

clip, cut off *verb* {1219 batsar} to clip a crop; a city cut off by fortifying.

cloak *noun* {3737 karbela} {*feminine* 4304 mitpachath} a full outer garment.

cloak *verb* {3736 karbel} to put on a cloak; **see** cloak *noun*.

clot *noun* [2361 thronos] a large thick drop, especially of clotted blood.

cloth, clothes, covering *noun* {899 beged} {8008 salmah} {8071 simlah} that which is used to cover.

clothe *verb* {3271 yaat} [294 amphiennumi] to enrobe.

cloud *noun* {6050, 6051 anen} [3507 nephelee] [3509 nephos] a mist in the atmosphere.

cloud over, overcloud *verb* {6049 anan} to cover over with a cloud.

cloudiness *noun* {6053 ananah} the condition of mist in the atmosphere.

clove, cloven, cleavered, cleft *verb* {8156 shaca} {8158 shacaph} to split.

club *noun* {8455 tothach} a smiting instrument.

cluster *noun* [1009 botrus] a bunch or group.

coal *noun* [440 anthrax] anthracite.

coalfire *noun* [439 anthrakia] a fire of anthracite.

coat *noun* {3801 kethoneth} a covering; the first human covering in the Garden of Eden.

cocktail *noun* {4197 mezeg} {4469 mimcak} a mixed intoxicant.

cohabitation *noun* {5772 onah} the state of living together.

coil *verb* [1507 hellisso] [1667 helisso] to roll tightly; **cp** furl.

coincidence, incident *noun* {6294 pega} casual impact.

cold *noun* {7120 qor} {7135 qarah} chilly.

cold, hook, shield *noun* {6793 tsinnah} coldness, as piercing; a hook, as pointed; a shield, as a prickler.

colleague *noun* {3674, 3675 kenath} literally, one with the same title.

colts *plural noun* {5895 ayir} sons of a burro.

columns *plural noun* {8490 timarah} a round, vertical substance; a support; also of smoke.

comingle, mingle, pledge *verb* {6148, 6151 arab} to become colateral; **see** mingle.

comingling *noun* {8397 tebel} a mixing together; bestiality.

commander *noun* {5057 nagid} one who takes charge.

commander *noun* {7101 qatsin} one that determines.

commentary *noun* {4097 midrash} a treatise of notes or remarks.

common, profane *adjective* {2455 chol} [2839 koinos] that which is common; that which is held in common; that which is not hallowed.

commotion *noun* {7267 rogez} a quivering; **see** quiver.

commune *verb* [2843 koinonikos] to participate; to partake in common.

communicant, partaker *noun* [2844 koinonos] one who communes or partakes in common, or in communion.

communion *noun* [2842 koinonia] an act of sharing; the ceremony known as the Lord's Supper.

compacted *adjective* {4568 maabeh} compressed.

companion *noun* {2269 chabar} {2271 chabbar} {2270 chaber} {2273 chabrah} {2278 chabereth} {4828 merea} a personal associate.

companionship *noun* {2274 chebrah} personal association.

company *noun* {7277 rigmah} a throng.

compare, liken *verb* {1819 dahmah} [3666 homoioo] to liken unto; to compare; to resemble; to consider; homoioo is the verb of likeness.

compassion *noun* [3627 oikteiro] [3628 oiktirmos] empathy.

compassion, compassionate *participle* {2551 chemlah} commiseration.

compassion, spare *verb* {2550 chamal} [3629 oiktirmon] to exercise compassion; to spare.

compel *verb* [315 anagkazo] to necessitate; to oblige.

complete, completely, completer, completion; see SUMMARY: COMPLETE.

LEXICON

comprehend *verb* **comprehending, comprehension** *participle* {7919 sakal} {7920 sekal} [3539 noieo] [4920 sunieme] a mental grasp; to understand.

comprehending *adjective* [4908 sunetos] a mental grasping; understanding.

comprehension *noun* {7922 sekel} {7924 soklethanu} [3540 noeema] [4907 sunesis] a mental grasp; understanding.

compulsion *noun* [317 anagkastos] the act of compelling.

comrade *noun* [2083 hetairos] a close companion.

conceal, cover (over) *verb* {3680 kacah} to fill up hollows.

conceal, cut off *verb* {3582 kachad} to secrete by act or word; to destroy.

conceal, veil *verb* {5956 alam} to conceal; to veil from sight.

concealed, concealment *noun* {8587 taalummah} that which is veiled; covered over.

conceive *verb* {2029 harah} {3179 yacham} to become pregnant.

conceive, hath conceived *adjective* {2030 hareh} pregnant.

concentrate, shut *verb* {5462 sagar} {5463 segar} shut; shut tight; cold as shut tight, or concentrated.

conception *noun* {2031 harhor} {2032 heron} that which is conceived mentally, or physically.

concern *noun* {1674 dagah} to have care; anxiety.

concern *verb* {1672 deagah} to care about; to be anxious.

conclude, finish (off), fully finish *verb* {3615 kalah} {3635 kelal} to cease; to cause to decease; to bring to an end; **cp** complete.

conclusion *noun* {8502 tiklah} {8503 taklith} the finality.

conclusion, consummation, end *noun* {5490 soph} {5491 soph} {7093 qets} {7097 qetseh} {7098 qatsah} the end, of an eon, of a scroll.

concubine *noun* {3904 lechenah} {6370 pilegesh} one who cohabits without a marital relationship.

condemn *verb* [2607 kataginosko] to have knowledge against; to find fault with.

condemn *verb* [2613 katadikazo] [2632 katakrino] to judge against.

condemnation *noun* [2631 katakrima] [2633 katakrisis] a judgment against.

confide *verb* {982 batach} to place confidence in; **see** trust.

confidence *noun* {985 bitchah} [986 bittahchohn] with assurance.

confidence *noun* {4009 mibtach} a refuge; assurance; **cp** hope; **cp** trust.

confident *plural noun* {987 battuchoth} assured.

confidently *adverb* {983 batach} with confidence.

configuration *noun* {4976 scheema} a schematic; an arrangement of a form.

configure *verb* [4964 suscheematizomai] to form according to a schematic.

confine, form, besiege, bind *verb* {6696 tsur} to confine; to form by shaping.

confines, distress, narrows, straits *noun* {4689 matsoq} {4691 metsuqah} {4712 metsar} from the root, belly; a narrow place; a confinement.

confiscate *verb* {6065 anash} to penalize by confiscation; a confinement for a fine.

conform *verb* [4832 summorphos] [4833 summorpho] to bring to the same form of another; **see** metamorphose.

confront, meet *verb* {7122 qara} {7125 qirah} to encounter.

confront, precede, anticipate *verb* {6923 qadam} to front; **cp** east.

confusion *noun* {4103 mehumah} to question reluctantly; uproar.

congregate *verb* {6950 qahal} {7035 qahall} to congregate a congregation.

congregate, betroth, betrothe *verb* {781 aras} {3259 yaad} [718 harmozo] to join together as in marriage; to congregate.

congregating, expectation *noun* {4723 miqveh} a collecting of troops, of water, of expectation.

congregation *noun* {4721 maqhel} {6951 qahal} {6952 qehillah} the assemblage of Yah Veh's selected people; the Hebrew and Aramaic corresponds to the Hellene, ecclesia.

congregation, season *noun* {4150, 4151 moed} [2540 kairos] an assemblage; an occasion of celebration; a season of the year, of existence.

Congregationer *noun* {6953 qoheleth} the one that ministers to the congregation; the Preacher of Ecclesiastes.

consider, perceive *verb* [2657 katanoeo] to observe attentively.

consider (well) *verb* [2648 katamanthano] to examine thoroughly.

considering *verb* [872 aphorao] to consider attentively.

consolation *noun* {*plural* 8575 tanchumuhoth} [3874 parakleesis] [3889 paramuthia] [3890 paramuthion] [3931 pareegoria] compassion; solace.

console, beseech *verb* [3870 parakaleo] to invoke by consolation.

conspiracy *noun* {7195 qesher} a tying together.

conspiracy *noun* {7285 regesh} renunciation; resistance.

conspire *verb* {7283 ragash} {7284 regash} to renounce, resist.

conspire, bind *verb* {7194 qashar} to tie; to tie together.

constellations *plural noun* {4208 mazzalah} {4216 mazzaroth} the stellar heavens.

constricted *adjective* **tribulation, tribulator** *noun* {6862 tsar} {6869 tsarah} a constriction; a time of constriction; a constricted place; one that constricts.

consume, consummate *verb* **integrious** *adjective* {8552 tamam} to finish off; to cause to be in consummate wholeness.

consummate, cease *verb* {1584 gamer} {1585 gemar} to bring to conclusion.

consummate, consume *verb* {5486, 5487 suph} [355 analisko] to end; to finish off; to be used up.

consummation, end, conclusion *noun* {5490 soph} {5491 soph} {7093 qets} {7097 qetseh} {7098 qatsah} the end, of an eon, of a scroll.

consumption *noun* {8399 tablith} the consuming.

contain, maintain, measure, sustain *verb* {3557 kuwl} to keep in.

contemplate *verb* {6448 pacag} to disect; to analyze thoroughly.

contend *verb* {6229 asaq} to press upon.

contend, defend, plead, strive *verb* {7378 rub} to hold a controversy.

Contention *name* {6230 eseq} Strife.

contention *noun* {*plural* 4079 midyanim} {*plural* 4090 medanim} {4695 matstsuth} [119 athleesis] [2054 eris] argument.

contention, defence, plea, strife *noun* {7379 rib} a personal, or legal contest.

contest, agony *noun* [73 agon] [74 agonia] a struggle; a contest.

continual, continually, continuance *noun* {8548 tamid} to stretch out indefinitely.

contort, form, idolize *verb* {6087 atsab} to form; to contort; as in idolizing, to writhe in pain.

contorting *participle* {6088 atsab} writhing as in pain.

contorting, contortion, idol *noun* {6089 etseb} {6090 otseb} {6092 atseb} {6093 itstsabon} an earthen vessel; a writhing as in pain; **see** contort *verb*.

contortion, scar *noun* {6094 atstsebeth} contortion, as in pain; scars as causing contortion; **see** contort *verb*.

contradict *verb* [470 antapokrinomai] [483 antilego] to word against; to answer against.

contrive, join, attach *verb* {6775 tsamad} to link; to gird; mentally, to contrive.

control *noun* {4623 matsar} restraint.

controversy *noun* [485 antilogio] words against.

convocation *noun* {4744 miqra} a called meeting.

cool *adjective* {7119 qar} chilly.

cooling *noun* {4747 meqerah} a cooling off.

copper *noun* {5154 nechushah} {5174 nechash} {5178 nechosheth} a species of metal; that made of the metal.

copper, coppery *adjective* {5153 nachush} {5180 nechushtan} reddish; copper colored.

copulate *verb* {7250 raba} {7903 shekobeth} to squat; to lie out flat in copulation.

copulation, lying *noun* {7902 shekabah} the lying of the dew; the copulation of persons.

cord, hope *noun* {8615 tiqvah} hope, as to hang on to; a cord, to hang on to.

cord, line, pang, boundary *noun* {2256 chebel} literally, a rope; as a boundary line; as binding one in a pang.

LEXICON

cords *noun* {*plural* 4189 moshechoth} {4340 meythar} that which draws tight.

corner *noun* {4740 maqtsowa} {*plural* 4742 mequtsoth} an angle or recess.

corner *noun* {6434 pen} an angle; **cp** edge.

corner, chief *noun* {6438 pinnah} an angle; a pinnacle; a high person; **cp** edge.

corner, scrape *verb* {7106 qatsa} to corner off; to strip off.

corona *noun* {6843 tsephirah} as circling the head.

corrupt, corruptible *adjective* {7844 shechath} [5349 phthartos] decayable.

corrupt, destroy, destruct, lose, ruin, vanish *verb* {6 abad} {7 abad} {8 obed} {7843 shachath} [622 apollumi] [1311 diapthiro] [2704 kataphthiro] [5351 phthiro] to corrupt through decay.

corruption *noun* {7845 shachath} [1312 diaphthora] [5356 phthora] decay.

corruption, disfigured {*participle* 2763 charam} {*noun* 4893 mishchath} **see** devote; **see** destroy.

cosmic *transliterated adjective* [2886 cosmikos] [2887 cosmios] cosmetic; mundane; orderly.

cosmic power *noun* [2888 cosmokrator] power over the cosmos; **see** cosmos.

cosmos *transliterated noun* [2889 cosmos] the globe on which we now exist; **see** world; **cp** earth.

counsel (private), councilmen *noun* {*plural* 4176 moetsoth} {5475 cowd} {5483 eta} {6098 etsah} [1012 boulee] [1013 boouleema] purpose; advice; advisors.

counsel, consult *verb* {3272 yeat} {3289 yaats} {5779 uts} [1011 bouleuo] [4824 sumboulion] [4323 prosanatitheemi] to advise.

counsel, support *noun* {8454 tushiah} {*plural* 8458 tachbuloth} advice; support.

counsellor *noun* {*plural* 1907 haddabar} [1010 boulutees] [4825 sumboulos] adviser.

courage *noun* [2293 tharseo] [2294 tharsos] boldness; bravery.

courageous, encouraged *adjective* [2292 tharreo] to exercise courage.

courier *noun* {6432 pelethi} an official messenger (not angel); **cp** angel.

court, courtyard *noun* {2681 chatsir} {2691 chatser} [833 aulee] a residential court; a court of the tabernacle; a court for owls; a court as a village; often in conjuction with the name of the court.

court, ledge *noun* {*plural* 4052 migraah} {5835 azarah} {*plural* 7948 shalab} that which is surrounded; that which surrounds.

cousin *noun* [431 anepsios] the offspring of one's uncle or aunt.

covenant *noun* {1285 berith} [1242 diatheekee] literally, a cutting; in Scripture, a contract that was cut between Elohim and humanity; the shedding of blood is strongly implied.

covenant, covenantor *verb* [1303 diatithemai] [4934 suntitheemi] the act of covenanting; one who covenants.

covenant, cut *verb* {3772 karath} [4934 suntitheemi] literally, to cut; to covenant; to cut off; to cut down; to cut a cutting; to covenant a covenant.

cover *noun* {7184 qasah} a cover of an instrument.

cover *verb* {2643 chaph} {2645 chaphah} {2653 chophaph} in the sense of protection; of sins being covered.

cover *verb* {2926 talal} to strew over; to cover in.

cover *verb* {3728 kahphash} to cover, in the sense of atoning.

cover *verb* {7159 qaram} to cover.

cover, covering *noun* {3681 kacuy} {3682 kecuth} {4372 mikceh} {4374 mekeacceh} a protective covering; a veiling.

cover, covering *noun* {4539 masak} {4540 mesukkah} {4541 massekah} a cover as a veil, as a curtain.

cover, covert, covertly *noun, adjective* {5643 sether} a covering over; a concealment; also a hiding place of protection.

cover, demolish, hide *verb* {5641 sathar} {5642 sethar} to conceal by covering; to demolish and cover over.

cover, hedge *verb* {5526 sakak} to cover over; to hedge with a brush; **see** brush arbor.

cover, languish, veil *verb* {5848 ataph} {5968 alaph} to shroud; to cover over; to languish.

cover, vail, veil *verb* {3874 luwt} {5844 atah} {6809 tsaiph} [2619 katakaluptomai] to cover; to enrobe; to wrap; to withhold from view.

cover (over), conceal *verb* {3680 kacah} to fill up hollows.

coveralls *plural noun* {6446 pasim} a tunic many widths wide.

covering, cloth, clothes *noun* {899 beged} {8008 salmah} {8071 simlah} that which is used to cover.

covert *noun* {4563 mictowr} {4565 mictar} a protective cover; a refuge.

covertly *adverb* {2644 chapha} under cover.

covertly, enchantingly *adjective* {3909 lat} whispering a spell; under cover.

cowardice *noun* [1167 dilia] timidity.

cowardly *adjective* [1168 diliao] [1169 dilos] timid.

co-bound *verb* [4887 sundeomai] bound together.

co-citizens *noun* [4847 sumpolitees] citizens together.

co-destruct *verb* [4881 sunapollumi] to destroy or be destroyed in company with.

co-die *verb* [4880 sunapothneesko] die together.

co-elders *noun* [4850 sumpresbuteros] elders together.

co-enliven *verb* [4806 suzoopolio] enliven together.

co-heirs *noun* [4789 sunkleeronomos] heirs together.

co-judge *verb* [4793 sunkrino] judge together.

co-partake *verb* [4791 sunkoinonos] [4830 summetokos] to partake together.

co-partaker *noun* [4790 sunkoinoneo] [4829 summerizomai] [4830 summetokos] one who partakes with another.

co-scion *noun* [4853 sumphuletees] scions together.

co-seated *verb* [4775 sunkatheemai] [4776 sunkathizo] seated together.

co-servant *noun* [4889 sundoulos] servant together.

co-settle *verb* [4924 sunoikeo] [4925 sunoikodomeomai] to settle together.

co-souled *verb* [4861 sumpsukos] souled together.

co-staked *verb* [4957 sustauroo] staked together.

co-witness *verb* [4828 summartureo] [4901 sunepimartureo] to witness together.

crack, crush *verb* {2827 chashal} {7533 ratsats} {7779 shuph} to crack or crush to pieces; to weaken.

crafty *adjective* {3596 kiylay} withholding.

crag, ivory, tooth, tusk *noun* {8127, 8128 shen} {*plural* 8143 shenhabbim} [3599 adous] as being sharp.

cranium *transliterated noun* {1538 gulgoleth} [2898 kranion] the skull.

craunch, crunch, separate, split, breach, break (off) (loose) *verb* {6561 paraq} {6562 peraq} {6555 parats} to breach; to separate from; to split.

craunch bone, mighted, mightier, mightily, mighty *verb* {6105 atsam} to become mighty; to overpower a bone; to be powerful; to be numerous.

craw *noun* {4760 murah} an enlargement of the gullet of some birds to store food prior to gestation.

create, creator *verb* {1254 bara} [2936 ktizo] to cause to be; **cp** make; **cp** work.

creation *noun* {1278 beiryah} [2937 ktisis] that which is caused to be; **cp** work.

Creator *noun* [2939 ktistees] He who caused to be.

creature *noun* [2938 ktisma] that which the Creator caused to be.

creature, full breast *noun* {2123 ziyz} full breast in the sense of conspicuous, or "out in the open"; a moving creature.

creep *verb* {7430 ramas} to move on or near the ground.

creeper *noun* {2119 zachal} {7431 remes} [2062 herpeton] that which creeps.

cremate *verb* {5635 saraph} cremation of bones.

cremations, calcinations *plural noun* {4955 misraphahoth} cremations of bones; calcinations as of lime.

crimson *noun* {3758 karmil} carmine; a deep red.

crooked *noun* {4625 maaqash} [4646 skolios] bent; warped; wicked.

crooked, trap, trip *adjective* {6121 aqob} {6128 aqalqal} {6129 aqallathon} a trap; one that trips; crooked, as full of traps.

crop noun {1210 batssiyr} a harvest that has been cropped (clipped); **see** clip verb.

crop noun {1715 dagan} as an increase of growth.

crossway noun [296 amphodon] the place where two ways cross.

crotch noun {4667 miphsaah} the place of branching.

crouch verb {7251 raba} to sprawl on all fours.

crowd noun {5519 cak} a thicket of persons.

crown noun {5850 atarah} a circular headpiece; **cp** diadem; **cp** wreath.

crown noun {6936 qodqod} the circle of the head.

crown verb {5849 atar} to encircle with a crown.

crucible noun {4715 mitsreph} that in which metals are melted, and refined.

crumble, subjugate verb {7287 radah} to bring under; to conquer.

crumbs plural noun {5350 niqqud} as fragmented.

crunch, craunch, separate, split, breach, break (off) (loose) verb {6561 paraq} {6562 peraq} {6555 parats} to breach; to separate from; to split.

crush verb {1792 daka} {1794 dakah} {4277 machaq} to crush physically, or in spirit.

crush, crack verb {2827 chashal} {7533 ratsats} {7779 shuph} to crack or crush to pieces; to weaken.

crushed adjective {1793 dakkah} physically, or in spirit.

crutch, spindle, circuit noun {6418 pelek} to be round; a spindle as whirled; hence a crutch.

crutch, support noun {4938 mishenah} that on which one leans.

cry noun {2201 zaaq} {6818 tsaaqah} [2906 kraugee] an exclamation; a scream.

cry verb {2199 zaaq} {2200 zeiq} {4798 marzeach} {6817 tsaaq} {7768 shava} {7769 shua} {7773 sheva} {7775 shavah} [310 anaboao] [994 boao] [1916 epiboao] [2896 krazo] [2905 kraugazo] to exclaim; to scream; **note:** {7768 shava} is the verb of salvation.

crystal, frost, ice noun {7140 qerach} as being smooth.

cubit noun {520 ammah} a linear measure, thought to be a forearm in length.

cucumber field noun {4750 miqshah} a cucumbered field.

cucumbers plural noun {6498 paqquahoth} as splitting open to shed its seeds.

cultivation noun [1091 georgion] that which is cultivated.

cultivator noun {406 ikkar} [1092 georgos] a digger of the soil.

culvert noun {6794 tsinnur} a hollow.

cunning noun [3834 panourgia] [3835 panourgos] trickery.

cup, little owl noun {3563 kowe} a container; an owl, from the cup-like cavity of its eye.

curdle verb {7087 qapha} to thicken.

cure noun {1456 gahah} that which heals.

cure verb {1455 gahah} [2323 therapeuo] the Hellene is the verb of therapy; **see** therapy.

curl, trough noun {7298 rahat} {plural 4857 mashabim} {8268 shoqeth} a ringlet of hair; a drinking trough for animals.

curled adjective {4748 miqsheh} turned; rounded.

curse noun {8381 taalah} [2671 katara] an imprecation; a pronouncement of doom.

curse, cursing verb {779 arar} {3994 meerah} {6895 qabab} [685 ara] [1944 epikataratos] [2672 kataraomai] to pronounce doom.

curtail verb {2179 zanab} literally, to cut the tail; **see** tail.

curtail, harvest, shorten, chop verb {7114 qatsar} literally, or figuratively, to cut off.

custom noun [1485 ethos] a usage prescribed by habit or law.

custom noun {1983 halak} a toll on goods.

cut verb {1504 gazar} to cut down, cut off, cut out.

cut, chew verb {1262 barah} chew food; to cut as in choosing.

cut, covenant verb {3772 karath} {4934 suntitheemi} literally, to cut; to cut off; to cut down; to cut a cutting (covenant a covenant); Elohim's covenants were cut; this cutting may imply shedding of blood; **see** circumcision; **see** covenant.

cut, decide, determine, point verb {2782 charats} {2852 chathak} to be cut; to cut a decision, or a determination; to point.

cut, scrape *verb* {7096 qatsah} to cut off; to scrape off, by cutting; to destroy.

cut (off) *verb* {5533 sakan} from the root, knife.

cut off *verb* {1219 batsar} to clip a crop; a city cut off by fortifying.

cut off, conceal *verb* {3582 kachad} to destroy; to secrete by act or word.

cut off, loathe, lothe *verb* {6962 qut} {6990 qatat} literally, or figuratively, to be cut off.

cutting, separation *noun* {1508 gizrah} a cutting as of a stone; a place set apart.

cuttings, chops *noun* {1279 biryah} a cut or chop of meat.

cymbal, harpoon, locust, whirring *noun* {6767 tselatsal} a clattering, as of a cymbal; a whirring, as of wings; a rattling, as of a harpoon.

cymbals *dual noun* {4700 metseleth} large double jinglers; **see** jinglers.

cypress *noun* {8645 tirzah} a kind of tree.

D

Dabbesheth *transliterated name* {1708 dabbesheth} Hump.

Daberath *transliterated name* {1705 daberath} Word.

Dagon *transliterated name* {1712 dagon} a fish deity.

Dahava *transliterated name* {1723 dahava} of uncertain derivative.

daily *adjecive* [2184 epheemeros] for a day.

daily, by day *adjective* {3119 yomam} [2522 kathemerinos] during the period between sunrise and sunset, or sunrise to sunrise.

damage *noun* {2257 chabal} {5143 nezeq} hurt or injury.

damage (cause) (experience) *verb* {5142 nezaq} to suffer or inflict hurt, or injury.

damask *transliterated noun* {1833 demeshek} a fabric of Dammeseq.

Dammeseq *transliterated name* [*plural* 1153 damaskeenos] of Dammeseq.

Dammeseq *transliterated name* {1834 dammeseq} [1154 damaskos] a city of Syria; **see** damask.

Dan Yaan *transliterated name* {1842 dan yaan} Judge of Purpose.

dance *verb* {7540 raqad} [3738 orkeomai] to stomp; to spring about.

Dani El *transliterated name* {1840 daniel} {1841 daniel} [1158 daniel] Adoni of El.

darics *plural transliterated noun* {150 adarkon} Persian coins.

dark *adjective* {2841 chashrah} {7838 shachor} {7840 shecharchoreth} as in cloudy, dusky, swarthy.

dark *noun* {7835 shachar} dim, or dark in color.

darken *verb* {2821 chashak} {2825 chashekah} {6937 qadar} removing of light.

darkness *noun* {2816 chashok} {2821 chashach} {2822 choshek} {2824 cheshkah} {2825 chashechah} {3990 maaphel} {4285 machshak} {4588 mauph} {5890 eyphah} {6940 qadruth} {7815 shechor} absence of light.

darnel *noun* [2215 zizanion] darnel or false grain; resembling wheat except that the grains are black.

Darqon *transliterated name* {1874 darqown} of uncertain derivative; one of Shelomoh's servants.

dart *noun* {3591 kiydon} an instrument for striking.

Daryavesh *transliterated title* {1867, 1868 daryavesh} a title of several Persian sovereigns.

daughter *noun* {1323 bath} [2364 thugateer] a female offspring.

daughter in law *noun* {3618 kallah} a son's woman.

daughterling *noun* [2365 thugatrion] little daughter.

David *transliterated name* {1732 david} [1138 dabid] Loving.

dawn (at), dawning *noun* {4891 mishchar} {5053 nogahh} {7837 shachar} {7839 shacharuth} {8238 shepharphar} [827 augee] [3719 orthrizo] [3721 orthrios] [3722 orthros] daybreak.

dawn, dawning *verb* [1306 diaugazo] [2020 epiphosko] [3720 orthrinos] the breaking of day.

day, yom *transliterated noun* {3117, 3118 yom} [2250 heemera] including, but not limited to dawn to down, or dawn to dawn; 24 hours, or a nonspecific period such as the Day of Yah Veh, Yom Kippurim.

daylight *noun* {5105 neharah}.

dazzling white *verb* {6705 tsachach} as glaring.

dead *noun* [3498 nekros] necro; **see** necrosis; lifeless.

dead, death *noun* {4192 muth} {4193 moth} {4194 maveth} {*plural* 4463 mamoth} {8546 temuthah} [2288 thanatos] [5054 telutee] the cessation of life.

dead (half) *noun* [2253 heemithanees] as in entirely exhausted.

deaden *verb* [3499 nekroo] to cause to be lifeless.

deadly *adjective* [2286 thanasimos] fatal.

deal, ripen, wean *verb* {1580 gamal} transact.

dealing *noun* {1576 gemuwl} {1578 gemuwlah} transaction.

death (doomed to) *verb* [1935 epithanatios] destined to die.

deathbearing *adjective* [2287 thanateephoros] fatal.

deathify, die, necro- *verb* {4191 muth} [2289 thanatoo] to die; to put to death.

debate, discern, discriminate, doubt *verb* {995 biyn} [1252 diakrino] [1253 diakrisis] to distinguish; to thoroughly judge.

debtor *noun* [3781 ophiletees] used metaphorically of one who is under an obligation.

Decapolis *transliterated name* [1179 dekapolis] Ten City; a city which is tenth in size or influence; or a city over ten.

decease, desist, abandon, cease *verb* {2308 chadai} to be lacking; to stop.

deceased *noun* {2309 chedel} the state of the dead.

deceit *noun* **deceitful** *adjective* {4820 mirmah} {4860 mashshaon} {5231 nekel} {7423 remiah} fraud; treachery.

deceitfully/to Tormah *adverb, transliterated name* {8649 tormah} fraud.

deceive *verb* **deceiver** *participle* {5230 nakal} {8591 taa} to cheat.

deceive, deny, disown, emaciate *verb* {3584 kachash} [550 apeipomen] to be untrue in word, or deed.

deceive, hurl *verb* {7411 ramah} {7412 ramah} to throw; to betray.

deceive, mislead *verb* {5377 nasha} {7952 shalah} to lead astray; to wrong.

deception *noun* {7944 shal} a fault.

deception, denial, emaciation *noun* {3585 kachash} a failure of flesh.

deceptive *adjective* {3586 kechash} untrue in word, or deed.

decide, determine, point, cut *verb* {2782 charat} {2852 chathak} to be cut; to cut a decision, or a determination; to point.

decircumcision *noun* [1986 epispaomai] a circumcision which has been undone; **cp** circumcision.

decision *noun* {6600 pithgam} a judicial sentence.

decision, decisive, incision, incisor, ore, sickle, trench *adjective, noun* {2742 charuts} physically, soulically, or mentally, an incising.

decision, opinion *noun* [1106 gnomee] a personal judgment.

declaration *noun* [1335 diegesis] a setting forth in detail.

declare *verb* [1334 diegeomai] [1555 ekdiegeomari] [1834 exegeomai] the verb of exegesis; to set forth in detail.

decorous *adjective* [2158 uskeemon] respectable.

decorously *adverb* [2156 uskeemonos] in a seemly manner; decently.

decorum *noun* [2157 uskeemosunee] that which is befitting.

decree *noun* {1510 gezerah} {1881, 1882 dath} {2942 teem} [3724 horizo] a regulatory order.

decree, taste *noun* {2941, 2942 teem} judgment; flavor.

decreer *noun* {1884 dethabar} one who decrees.

dedicated *adjective* {2593 chaniyk} from hanukkah; initiated; practised.

deed *noun* {4659 miphalah} that which is done; noun of the verb do.

deed *noun* {6467 poal} {6468 peullah} an act or work; **see** do, make.

deep *noun* {4688 metsulah} far down; **cp** depths.

deep, deeper, depth *adjective* {6011 omeq} {6012 ameq} further below; far lower.

deep fried *verb* {7246 rabak} bake by soaking in oil.

deepen *verb* {6009 amaq} to be deep; to make deep.

defamation noun [1426 duspheemia] a bringing into disrepute; dishonour; disgrace.

defat, fatten verb {1878 dashen} depending on the case, to make fat, or to remove fat; to enrich.

defence, plea, strife, contention noun {7379 rib} a personal, or legal contest.

defend, plead, strive, contend verb {7378 rub} to hold a controversy.

defile verb [3392 miaino] contaminate.

defraud verb {6906 qaba} to cover over.

degrees, steps noun {4609 maalah} steps; stations; a progression; 1/360th of a circle.

Dela Yah transliterated name {1806 delayah} Bailed of Yah.

delay, slack verb [1019 braduno] to be slow.

delicacies noun {plural 4303 matammoth} {plural 4516 manamim} {6598 pathbag} dainties; delicious foods.

delicate adjective {6028 anog} dainty; luxurious.

delicate participle **delight, luxuriate** verb {6026 anag} to be, or to become soft; to delight in; to deride.

delicately adverb {4574 maadan} cheerfully.

delight, desire adjective {2655 chaphets} pleased with.

delight, desire noun {2531 chemed} {2532 chemdah} {2656 chephets} {2837 chesheq} {plural 3970 maavayim} {4261 machmad} {plural 4262 machmadim} {8588 taanug} a delight; a pleasure; an object of desire, or pleasure, or of value.

delight, desire verb {2654 chaphets} literally, to bend toward; to be inclined toward.

delight, luxuriate verb **delicate** participle {6026 anag} to be, or to become soft; to delight in; to deride.

delights plural noun {8191 shaashua} pleasant strokes.

deliver, surrender, betray verb [3860 paradidomi] to release; to give to possession of another; to deliver to an enemy.

delude verb [538 apatao] to cheat; to deceive.

delusion noun {plural 4123 mahathallahoth} [539 apatee] a misleading of the mind.

demand verb [523 apaiteo] to demand back.

demand verb [1809 exaiteomai] to demand (for trial).

demolish verb {2040 harac} utterly destroy; break; break through.

demolish, hide, cover verb {5641 sathar} {5642 sethar} to conceal by covering; to demolish and cover over.

demolition noun {2034 haricah} {2035 haricuwth} {2041 herec} utter destruction.

demon noun {7700 shed} [1140 daimonion] [1142 daimon] an evil spirit; **see** spirit; **cp** Diabolos.

demondreader noun [1174 disidaimonesteros] a kind of worshipper.

demondreading verb [1175 disidaimonia] the dreading of demons.

demonic adjective [1141 daimoniodees] demon in character.

demonized verb [1139 daimonizomai] to be infused or overtaken by a demon.

denarion transliterated noun [1220 denarion] a Latin coin; a silver tenthpiece (dime).

denial, emaciation, deception noun {3585 kachash} a failure of flesh.

deny verb [533 aparneomai] [720 arneomai] to disown; to recant; to renounce.

deny, disown, emaciate, deceive verb {3584 kachash} [550 apeipomen] to be untrue in word, or deed.

depart, remove verb {5253 nacag} to retreat.

dependant, necessary adjective [316 anagkaios] needed; depend upon.

depose, deposit, descend verb {5182 nechath} to go down; to bring away.

deprive, cheat verb [650 apostereo] to deprive of some right.

depth, deep, deeper adjective {6011 omeq} {6012 ameq} further below; far lower.

depths plural noun {4615 maamaqim} **cp** deep; lower region.

Deqer transliterated name {1857 deqer} Stab.

deride verb {3931 laab} {3932 laag} to ridicule.

derision noun {3933 laag} a ridicule.

descend verb [2597 katabaino] to go down.

LEXICON

descend, depose, deposit *verb* {5182 nechath} to go down; to bring away.

descend, lower, topple *verb* {3381 yarad} to go lower; to tip over.

descend, penetrate, press, sink, bend *verb* {5181 nachath} from the root, to sink; to go down; to press or lead down.

descendant *noun* [1549 ekgonon] one in the line of ancestors.

descending *adjective* {5185 nacheth} going down.

descent, festoon *noun* {4174 mowrad} a place of going down; an ornamental hanging; a garland or wreath.

desert dwellers *noun* {6728 tsiyiy} they who dwell in the desert.

desert *noun* {6707 tsechichah} {6723 tsiah} {6724 tsion} a barren place.

designate, indicate *verb* {5567 saman} [322 anadiknumi] to show; to appoint.

desirables *plural noun* {2532 chemdah} valuables.

desire *noun* {8375 taabah} {8378 taavah} {8669 teshuqah} a longing for; **cp** will.

desire *verb* {183 avah} {8373 taab} to long for; **cp** will.
desire *verb* {2530 chamad} to delight in.

desire, delight *adjective* {2655 chaphets} pleased with.

desire, delight *noun* {2531 chemed} {2532 chemdah} {2656 chephets} {2837 chesheq} {*plural* 3970 maavayim} {4261 machmad} {*plural* 4262 machmadim} {8588 taanug} a delight; a pleasure; an object of desire, or pleasure, or of value.

desire, delight *verb* {2654 chaphets} literally, to bend toward; to be inclined toward.

desist, abandon, cease, decease *verb* {2308 chadai} to be lacking; to stop.

desolate, dry, parch *adjective* {2720 chareb} {8076 shamen} parched; ruined.

desolate, dry, parch *verb* {2717, 2718 charab} {3456 yashem} {8045 shamad} {8046 shemad} [2049 ereemoo] to lay waste; to destroy.

desolate, strive *verb* {5327 natsah} to struggle; to lay waste.

desolate, stun, astonish *verb* {8074 shamem} {8075 shemam} to lay waste; to stun, as in to stupefy or devastate.

desolation *noun* **desolate** *adjective* {2723 chorbah} {*plural* 3451 yeshiymah} {3452 yeshimon} {4923 meshammah} {8047 shammah} {8077 shemamah} [2048b ereemos] [2050 ereemosis] an area which has been abandoned and left to ruin; **cp** wilderness.

despise *verb* {7750 suwt} to contemn.

despoil, pledge, spoil *verb* {2254, 2255 chabal} literally, to bind tightly; as in spoiling or as in binding a pledge.

despotes *transliterated title* [1203 despotes] a title ascribed to a lord of servants, to Yah Veh, and to Yah Shua; an absolute ruler; the present day connotation of tyrant did not appear until centuries later.

destroy, destruct, lose, lost *verb* {6 abad} {7 abad} [622 apollumi] to destroy fully.

destroy, destruct, lose, ruin, vanish, corrupt *verb* {6 abad} {7 abad} {8 obed} {7843 shachath} [622 apollumi] [1311 diapthiro] [2704 kataphthiro] [5351 phthiro] to corrupt through decay.

Destroyer *title* [3644 olothrutees] a ruiner; the Hellenic translation of the Hebrew, Abbaddon; **see** Abbaddon.
destroying *participle* {4892 mashcheth} ruining.

destruct, lose, lost, destroy *verb* {6 abad} {7 abad} [622 apollumi] to destroy fully.

destruction *noun* {8 obed} {12 abdan} {13 obdan} {3589 kiyd} {4889 mashchith} [684 apolia] [3639 olethros] ruin.

determine, point, cut, decide *verb* {2782 charat} {2852 chathak} to be cut; to cut a decision, or a determination; to point.

Deu El *transliterated name* {1845 deuel} Known of El.

devastation *noun* {7722 shoah} ruin.

deviate *noun* {7846 set} one who turns aside.

deviate *verb* {7847 satah} to turn aside.

devote, doom *verb* {2763 charam} to set apart for dedication; to set apart for destruction; **see** disfigure.

devoted, doomed *noun* {2764 cherem} that which is set apart in dedication; that which is set apart for destruction.

dewdrops *plural noun* {7447 raciyc} drippings; droppings.

Di Zahab *transliterated name* {1774 diyzahab} Of Gold.

Diabolos *transliterated name* **diabolic** *adjective* [1228 diabolos] the Hellenic name of Satan; also used adjectively; **see** Satan; **cp** demon.

diadem *transliterated noun* {3804 kether} [1238 diadeema] a royal headpiece; **cp** crown; **cp** wreath.

diadem *verb* {3803 kathar} to place a diadem.

dialect *transliterated noun* [1258 dialektos] a provincial form of a language; **read** Acts 2:8-11.

dialogue *transliterated noun* [1261 dialogismos] a reasoning of words.

dialogue *transliterated verb* [1256 dialegomai] [1260 dialogizomai] to reason words, in argument or exhortation.

diaphanous *transliterated adjective* [1307 diaphanees] transparent; translucent.

diaspora *transliterated noun* [1290 diaspora] dispersion.

diatribe *transliterated noun* [3859 paradiatribe] a harangue.

Diblayim *dual transliterated name* {1691 diblayim} Two Lumps.

dichotomize *transliterated verb* [1371 dikotomeo] to cut into two parts.

didactic *transliterated adjective* [1317 didaktikos] able to doctrinate.

didrachma *transliterated noun* [1323 didrachmon] double drachma.

die *verb* [599 apothneesko] [2348 thneesko] to become lifeless in the sense of dying off.

die *verb* [5053 telutao] to become lifeless in the sense of having come to completion.

die, necro-, deathify *verb* {4191 muth} [2289 thanatoo] to die; to put to death.

difficult *adjective* [1422 duskolos] impractible.

difficultly *adverb* [1423 duskolos] impractibly.

dig, explore *verb* {2658 chaphar} to pry into.

dig, pierce *verb* {3738, 3739 kahrah} to bore; to dig.

dig, undermine *verb* {6979 qur} to trench; to estop.

digging *noun* {4290 machtereth} a burglary committed by digging into a building.

Dilan *transliterated name* {1810 dilan} of uncertain derivative.

dilute *verb* {4107 mahal} to cut down; to reduce.

dim, fade *adjective* {3544 kehah} obscure; dull.

dim, fade *verb* {3543 kahah} to become obscure, dull.

diminish, lessen *verb* {4591 maat} to reduce; to pare off.

dimness *noun* [887 aklus] dimness of sight.

Dioscuri *transliterated noun* [1359 dioskouroi] Twins of Zeus.

Diotrephes *transliterated noun* [1361 diotrephes] Nourished of Zeus.

Diqlah *transliterated name* {1853 diqlah} of foreign origin; a region of Arabia.

disadvantageous *adjective* [255 alusiteless] without advantage; without gain.

disallow, discourage, annul *verb* {5106 nuw} to refuse; dissuade.

disappear *verb* {6461 pacac} to disperse.

disapproved *verb* [593 apodokimazo] to refuse to accept as true.

discern, discriminate, doubt, debate *verb* {995 biyn} [1252 diakrino] [1253 diakrisis] to distinguish; to thoroughly judge.

discern, distinguish, estrange, notice, recognize *verb* {5234 nakar} to acknowledge; to scrutinize; to distinguish between; to ignore, hence to be estranged.

discernment *noun* {998, 999 binah} distinguishment; understanding.

discernment *noun* {8394 tabun} [144 aistheesis] detection; distinguishment.

disciple *noun* [3101 matheetees] [*feminine* 3102 matheetria] a learner.

disciple *verb* {3925 lamad} [3100 matheetuo] to learn; to teach; **note:** not to be confused with discipline.

discipled *adjective* {3928 limmud} one who has learned, who has been taught; **see** learn, teach.

discipline *noun* {*plural* 4000 mabim} {4148 mucar} {4561 mocar} tutorial; may or may not include punishment; the Hellene is the verb of pedagogue; to tutor; **note:** not to be confused with disciple.

discipline *verb* {3256 yacar} {4148 mucar} [3809 paidia] [3811 paiduo] to tutor; may or may not include punishment; the Hellene is the verb of pedagogue; to tutor; **note:** not to be confused with disciple; **cp** disciple.

discourage, annul, disallow verb {5106 nuw} to refuse; dissuade.

discriminate, doubt, debate, discern verb {995 biyn} [1252 diakrino] [1253 diakrisis] to distinguish; to thoroughly judge.

disease noun {4064 madveh} {4245 machalah} {plural 4251 machluyim} sickness.

disesteem verb {2107 zuwl} [2706 kataphphroneo] to belittle.

disfigured, corruption {participle 2763 charam} {noun 4893 mishchath} see devote; see destroy.

disgrace, folly, wither verb {5034 nabel} from the root, to wilt; to fall away; to fail.

disguise, search verb {2664 chaphas} to discover; to uncover; to mask.

dish noun {7086 qearah} as hollowed.

dishonour noun [819 atima] [820 atimos] disesteem.

dishonour verb [818 atimazo] to disesteem.

dishonourably adverb [821 atimoo] disesteemingly.

disintegrate, harass verb {7492 raats} to break in pieces.

disintegrator noun {4660 mappats} {4661 mappets} that which disintegrates.

dislocated adjective {4154 muwedeth} as slipped out of place.

dismay, terrify, break (down) verb {2865, 2866 chathath} to cause to prostrate; to break down by violence, or fear.

dismember verb {5408 nathach} to separate members of a body, human or animal; see members.

disown, emaciate, deceive, deny verb {3584 kachash} [550 apeipomen] to be untrue in word, or deed.

disperse verb {5086 nadaph} [1287 diaskorpizo] [1289 diaspiro] to scatter.

disperse, express, wound verb {6567 parash} to separate; to specify; to wound.

disregard verb [272 ameleo] as being unconcerned.

disrespect noun {937 buwz} {939 buwzah} abasement.

disrespect verb {936 buwz} to abase.

dissipate noun {3988 maac} to flow away.

dissolve noun {8557 temec} liquifaction; disappearance.

dissolve, flow, melt verb {4529 masah} to dissolve.

dissolve, melt verb {4127 muwg} to soften; to dissipate.

dissolve, vanish verb {4743 maqaq} [1262 dialuo] to dissolve; to dwindle; to vanish.

distant past, far, afar adjective {7350 rachoq} {7352 rachiq} {7369 racheq} remote; in time, or distance.

distant, receive in full verb [568 apeko] to have out; to keep away.

distend, extend verb {8311 sara} to extend oneself, as in stretching out; to distend, as an appendage.

distinction noun [1293 diastoles] [1243 diairesis] the difference between; a variation.

distinctly participle {6568 perash} to separate, as in words.

distinguish verb {6395 palah} [1243 diairesis] to differentiate.

distinguish, estrange, notice, recognize, discern verb {5234 nakar} to acknowledge; to scrutinize; to distinguish between; to ignore, hence to be estranged.

distortion noun {4297 mutteh} a stretching out of shape.

distress noun **distressful** adjective {6695 tsuqah} a strait.

distress, narrows, straits, confines noun {4689 matsoq} {4691 metsuqah} {4712 metsar} from the root, belly; a narrow place; a confinement.

distress, oppress verb {6693 tsuq} to compress.

distrust verb [544 apitheo] [569 apisteo] to lack trust.

distrust, trustlessness noun [543 apeitheia] [570 apistia] without trust; obstinate and rebellious.

distrusting adjective [545 apithees] lacking trust.

divide verb {6385 palag} {6386 pelag} to split.

dividing noun {6387 pelag} the division of a half.

divination noun {4738 miqcam} {7081 qecem} foreknowledge by magic.

divine verb {7080 qacam} to foreknow by magic.

diviner noun {1505 gezar} one who foreknows by magic.

division, rivulet noun {6390 pelaggah} {6391, 6392 peluggah} division of families; a split in the ground where a rivulet flows.

divorce *noun* {3748 keriythuth} a cutting of the marriage bond.

divulge *verb* [1583 eklaleo] to speak out.

do, keep, make, serve *verb* {5648 abad} in the sense of serving.

do, make *verb* {6466 paal} [4160 poieo] to assemble; to practice; to perform; **cp** create.

doctor, doctrine, doctrinate; see SUMMARY: DOCTOR.

Doda Yah *transliterated name* {1735 dowdavahuw} Beloved of Yah.

Doday *transliterated name* {1737 dowday} Amatory.

doe *noun* {8166 seirah} a she animal.

doe goat *noun* {5795, 5796 ez} a she goat, as strong.

dogma *transliterated noun* [1378 dogma] a definite and authoritative doctrine.

dogmatic *transliterated adjective* [1379 dogmatizomai] true to the doctrine; **see** dogma.

dominant *noun* {7984 shilton} {7989 shalliyt} one that prevails.

dominate *verb* [2634 katakuriuo] [2961 kuriuo] to lord over.

dominate *adjective* {7990 shalliyt} mighty over; **cp** reign.

dominate *verb* {7786 sur} {7980 shalat} {7981 shelet} [831 authenteo] to be mighty over; **cp** reign.

domineering *adverb* {7986 shalleteth} ability to prevail.

doom, devote *verb* {2763 charam} to set apart for liturgy; to set apart for destruction; **see** disfigured.

doomed, devoted *noun* {2764 cherem} that which is set apart in liturgy; that which is set apart for destruction.

Dophqah *transliterated name* {1850 dophqah} Knock.

Dorcas, gazelle, Tabitha *noun* {6643 tsebiy} {6646 tsebiyah} [5000 tabitha] a gazelle, as beautiful; Tabitha is the Hellene transliteration of tsebiyah; Dorcas is the Hellene translation of tsebiyah.

double *adjective* [1362 diplous] two-fold.

double *verb* [1363 diploo] to repay or render two-fold.

double, duplicate, fold, reiterate, repeat, alter, change *verb* {8132 shana} {8133 shena} {8138 shanah} to reinforce by folding, by doubling; may include disguise, camouflage.

double, duplicate, second *noun* {4932 mishneh} a copy of; a double amount; a repetition.

doublemouthed *adjective* [1366 distomos] two-edged.

doublesouled *adjective* [1374 dipsukos] in the sense of being twofaced; **cp** doubleworded.

doubleworded *adjective* [1351 dilogos] as in wording differently on different occasions; in the sense of being twofaced; **cp** doublesouled.

doubt, debate, discern, discriminate *verb* {995 biyn} [1252 diakrino] [1253 diakrisis] to distinguish; to thoroughly judge.

doughboard *noun* {4863 mishereth} a board on which the dough rises.

downcast *adjective* {7807 shach} sunken.

downing *noun* {4606 meal} the downing, usually of the sun; **cp** dawn, dawning.

downing *verb* [1416 dumi] to go down, usually of the sun; **cp** dawn, dawning.

downpour *noun* {1653 geshem} [5494 kimon] a heavy rain.

downpour *verb* {1652 gasham} {1656 goshem} to rain heavily.

downward *adverb* {4295 mattah} in the direction of down.

dowry *noun* {4119 mohar} {*plural* 7964 shilluach} the price paid to marry a woman.

drachma *transliterated noun* [1406 drachme] a silver coin; literally, a handful of silver; **cp** didrachma.

drachmim *plural noun* {1871 darkmohneem} Persian coins.

drag *verb* {5498 sachab} to trail along.

drag net *noun* {4365 mikmereth} a net that is dragged; **see** net.

dragon *transliterated noun* [1404 drakon] a kind of serpent.

drape *noun* {7757 shul} that which hangs down; **cp** train.

draughts *plural noun* {8514 talubah} desications.

draw *verb* {8025 shalaph} as a drawn sword.

draw, pour *verb* {7324 ruq} to pour in; to pour out.

drawn *adjective* {8305 seriyqah} flax, as drawn.

dread, terrify, awe *verb* {6206 arats} to harass; to reverence.

dream *noun* {2472 chalom} {2493 chelem} [1798 enupnion] [3677 onar] thoughts, images, or emotions occurring during sleep.

dream *verb* {2492 chalam} [1797 enupniazomai] to experience a thought, image, or emotion during sleep.

dregs *plural noun* {8105 shemer} the settlings of the wine.

drift, shake, stagger, totter, wag, wander, waver *verb* {5128 nuwa} to waver.

drink (give), drown, moisten, wet, butler *verb* {8248 shaqah} {8257 shaga} to butler, as a bartender; to drink to quench thirst; to drink unto drowning; to cause to be wet.

drink *noun* {8354 shathah} a liquid.

drink, banquet *noun* {4960, 4961 mishteh} the act of drinking; a banquet of eating and drinking.

drink, moisture *noun* {8249 shiqquv} {8250 shiqquw} a beverage.

drinking *noun* {8358 shethy} intoxicating.

drinking, moistened, moisture, butlership *noun* {4945 mashqeh} to cause to be moistened, or drunken.

drip, drop *noun* {1812 deleph} a dripping.

drip, drop *verb* {1811 dahlaph} {5197, 5198 nataph} {6201 araph} {7491 raaph} to drip; to descend in drops; as in weeping.

dripping, fresh *adjective* {2961 tariy} to be moist.

dripping darkness *noun* {6205 araphel} gloom; as of a lowering sky.

drive, alight *verb* {6795 tsanach} to cause to descend; to come down; to drive down.

drive, ride *verb* {7392 rakab} to place upon; to dispatch.

drive (out), expel *verb* {1644 garash} {2957 terad} {5080 nadach} {5090 nahag} to expatriate; to push off; to carry away.

drop, spoil *verb* {7997 shalal} to let drop; to strip, or plunder.

dross *noun* {5509 sug} scoria.

drought, parch *noun* {2721 choreb} {2725 charabon} very dry.

drove *noun* {5739 eder} [34 agelee] an arrangement of; a herd, as being driven.

drown, moisten, wet, butler, drink (give) *verb* {8248 shaqah} {8257 shaga} to butler, as a bartender; to drink to quench thirst; to drink unto drowning; to cause to be wet.

drowsiness *noun* {5124 numah} {8572 tenuwm} sleepiness.

drudgery *noun* {6045 inyan} difficult task.

dry, parch, desolate *adjective* {2720 chareb} {8076 shamen} parched; ruined.

dry, parch, desolate *verb* {2717, 2718 charab} {3456 yashem} {8045 shamad} {8046 shemad} [2049 ereemoo] to lay waste; to destroy.

dry, wither *noun* {3002 yabesh} {3004 yabbashah} {3006, 3007 yabbesheth} lands and waters dry; plants, persons wither.

dry, wither *verb* {3001 yabesh} {5405 nashath} {7060 qamal} lands and waters dry; plants, persons wither.

dugout *noun* {1358 gob} {1360 gebe} a digging.

dull *verb* {6949 qahah} to unsharpen.

dumbfounded *verb* {1724 dahham} to cause to be speechless.

dung *noun* {*plural* 2755 charey yonim} {6569 peresh} {6675 tsoah} {6832 tsephua} excrement.

dungball *noun* {1557 gahlal} {1561 gehlel} a ball of excrement.

dunghill *noun* {830 ashpoth} {4087 madmenah} a heap of excrement.

dungy *adjective* {6674 tso} dunglike.

dupe, entice *verb* {6601 pathah} to delude; to tempt; **cp** test.

duplicate, fold, reiterate, repeat, alter, change, double *verb* {8132 shana} {8133 shena} {8138 shanah} to reinforce by folding, by doubling; may include disguise, camouflage.

duplicate, second, double *noun* {4932 mishneh} a copy of; a double amount; a repetition.

dusk, duskward *noun* {4628 maarabah} {5939 alatah} in the sense of shade.

dust *noun* {6083 aphar} [2868 koniortos] [5522 choos] fine particles of matter.

dust *verb* {6080 aphar} to dust with dust.

dusty *adjective* [5517 choikos] dirty; soil-like.

dwell, settle *verb* [1460 egkatoikeo] [2730 katoikeo] [3611 oikeo] to reside.

dye *noun* {6648 tseba} a dye.

dye *verb* {6647 tseba} to dip into a dye.

dyed scarlet *participle, verb* {8529 tala} to dye a scarlet color.

dynamic *adjective* [1414 dunateo] able; capable.

dynamis *transliterated noun* [1411 dunamis] dynamic ability.

dynamize *verb* [1412 dunamoo] [1743 endunamoo] to endue with dynamis.

dynast, dynasty *noun* [1413 dunastees] one endued with dynamis; the seat of dynamis; **see** dynamis.

E

eagle *noun* {5403 neshar} {5405 nesher} from the root, to lacerate; as a bird of prey.

ear *noun* {241 ozen} [5621 otion] the organ for hearing.

ear, stream, branch *noun* {7641 shibboleth} a branch or an ear of grain, as growing; a stream, as flowing.

early (rise) (seek) *verb* {7836 shachar} to be early.

early start, start early *verb* {7925 shakam} to start early.

earrings *noun* {5694 agil} as being round; **cp** nosering.

earth, land *noun* {772 ara} {776 erets} {778 araq} [1093 gee] **cp** soil; **cp** cosmos.

earthly *adjective* [1919 epigios] as of the earth.

east, easterly, eastern, eastward, formerly, preceding, ancient, antiquity *noun* {6921 qadim} {6924 qedem} {6925 qodam} {6926 qidmah} {6927 qadmah} literally, the forefront; from the front.

east, eastern, ancient(s) *adjective* {6930 qadmon} {6931 qadmoniy} anterior.

eat, fight *verb* {3898 lacham} literally, to feed on food, to feed on an enemy.

eating *verb* **food** *noun* [1034 brosimos] literally, feeding; the act of eating.

Ebed Melech *transliterated name* {5663 ebedmelech} Servant of the Sovereign.

Eben Ezer *transliterated name* {72 ebenhaezer} Stone of Help.

Eber *transliterated name* {5677 eber} [1443 eber] Beyond; Crossover.

Ebes *transliterated name* {77 ebets} Conspicuous.

Ebron {5683 ebron} Over Against.

ecclesia *singular* **ecclesiae** *plural transliterated noun* [1577 ekklesia] refers to the congregation of the Messianists, and corresponds to the Hebrew word, congregation (except in Acts 2:38); **see** congregation.

echo *transliterated noun* [2279 echos] a reverberation; figuratively a rumor.

echo *transliterated verb* [2278 echeo] to reverberate.

Echud *transliterated name* {261 echuwd} United.

eclipses *plural noun* {3650 kimriyrim} obscurages, as of lights.

ecstasis *transliterated noun* [1611 ekstasis] enraptured in a state of mental absorption.

Eden *transliterated name* {5729 eden} {5731 eden} Pleasure: **see** pleasure.

Eder *transliterated name* {5738 eder} Arrangement.

edge *noun* {6285 peah} {6366 peyah} from mouth, as the edge of the head.

edge, end *noun* {7093 qets} {7097 qetseh} {7098 qatsah} {7099 qetsev} an extremity.

edge, lip *noun* {8193 saphah} [5491 kilos] an edge; a shoreline; the physical lip; a language; **cp** tongue.

edict *noun* {3982 maamar} {3983 memar} {7010 qeyam} a spoken decree.

edify, build *verb* {1124 benah} {1129 banah} [2026 epoikodomeo] [3618 oikodomeo] to build; to build up; to confirm; to construct; to erect.

Edom, Edomiy *transliterated name* {123 edom} {130 edomi} [2401 idoumaia] Red; Ruddy; a region; people of the region; **cp** Adam.

effulgence *noun* [541 apaugasma] radiance.

effusion *verb* [401 anakusis] a pouring out.

Eglayim *dual transliterated name* {97 eglayim} Double Drops.

El, Eli *transliterated name, transliterated title* {410 el} [2241 eli] El, as being mighty. **see** SUMMARY: El, Eli.

El Ad *transliterated name* {496 elad} Witnessed of El.

El Adah *transliterated name* {497 eladah} El Adorns.

El Aleh *transliterated name* {500 elaleh} El Ascends.

El Asah *transliterated name* {501 elasah} El Works.

El Azar *transliterated name* {499 elazar} [1648 eleazar] [2976 lazaros] El Helps.

El Beth El *transliterated name* {416 elbeythel} El of the House of El.

El Daah *transliterated name* {420 eldaah} El Knows.

El Dad *transliterated name* {419 eldad} El Beloved.

El Elohe Yisra El *transliterated name* {415 eleloheyyisrael} Mighty El of Yisra El.

El Hanan *transliterated name* {445 elchanan} El Grants Charism.

El Naam *transliterated name* {493 elnaam} El Pleases.

El Nathan *transliterated name* {494 elnathan} El Gives.

El Paal *transliterated name* {508 elpaal} El Makes.

El Paran *transliterated name* {364 eylparan} El of Paran.

El Qanah *transliterated name* {511 elqanah} El Chattelizes.

El Sabaoth *transliterated title* {410 el} {6635 tsebaah} **see** Sabaoth.

El Saphan *transliterated name* {469 elitsaphan} El of Treasure.

El Teqeh *transliterated name* {514 elteqeh} of unceratin derivative.

El Teqon *transliterated name* {515 elteqon} El Straightens.

El Tolad *transliterated name* {513 eltolad} El of Generations.

El Uzay *transliterated name* {498 eluwzay} El Recoups.

El Yachba *transliterated name* {455 elyachaba} El Hides.

El Yah Enay *transliterated name* {454 elyehoweynay} Towards El are my Eyes.

El Yaqim *transliterated name* {471 elyaqiym} [1662 eliakeim] El Raises.

El Yasaph *transliterated name* {460 elyacaph} El Increases.

El Yashib *transliterated name* {475 elyashiyb} El Returns.

El Zabad *transliterated name* {443 elzabad} El Endows.

Elamiy *transliterated name* {5867 elam} [1639 elamiy] Of Elam.

Elamiy *transliterated name* {5962 almiy} Of Elam.

elbow *noun* {679 atstsiyl} literally, joint.

elder *noun* {2205 zaqen} {7868 sib} [4244 presbuterion] [4245 presbuteros] an elder, as grayed; a presbyter.

elephantine *transliterated adjective* [1661 elephantinos] of an elephant; ivory.

elevation *noun* {5131 noph} a raised area.

Eli *transliterated name* {5941 eli} [2242 heeli] Holocauster.

Eli, El *transliterated name, transliterated title* {410 el} [2241 eli] El, as being mighty. **see** SUMMARY: El, Eli.

Eli Ab *transliterated name* {446 eliab} El the Father.

Eli Ada *transliterated name* {450 eliada} El Knows.

Eli Am *transliterated name* {463 eliam} El of the People.

Eli Athah *transliterated name* {448 eliyathah} El of Consent.

Eli Dad *transliterated name* {449 elidad} El Beloved.

Eli El *transliterated name* {447 eliel} El of El.

Eli Enay *transliterated name* {462 eliyeynay} El the Eye; **see** El Yah Enay.

Eli Ezer *transliterated name* {461 eliezer} [1663 eliezer] El Helps.

Eli 1-loreph *transliterated name* {456 eliychoreph} El of Winter.

Eli 1-lu *transliterated name* {453 elihu} El of Him.

Eli Melech *transliterated name* {458 elimelech} El Sovereign.

Eli Phal *transliterated name* {465 eliphal} El of Prayer.

Eli Phaz *transliterated name* {464 eliphaz} El of Pure Gold.

Eli Phelehu *transliterated name* {466 eliyphelehuw} El Distinguishes.

Eli Phelet *transliterated name* {467 eliphelet} El of Escape.
Eli Qa *transliterated name* {470 eliyqa} El Vomits.

Eli Shah *transliterated name* {473 elishah} meaning uncertain.

Eli Shama *transliterated name* {476 elishama} El Hearkens.

Eli Shaphat *transliterated name* {478 elishaphat} El Judges.

Eli Sheba *transliterated name* {472 elisheba} [1665 elisabeth] El of Oath.

Eli Shua *transliterated name* {474 eliyshuwa} {477 eliysha} [1666 elissaios] El is Salvation.

Eli Sur *transliterated name* {468 elitsur} El of the Rock.

Eli Ud *transliterated name* {410 el} {1935 howd} [1664 eliud] El of Majesty.

Eli Yah *transliterated name* {452 eliyah} [2243 eelias] El of Yah.

Ellasar *transliterated name* {495 ellacar} an early country of Asia.

Elohah, Elohim, Eloi; see SUMMARY: EL, ELAH, ELI.

Elon *transliterated name* {356 elown} Oak Grove.

Elon Beth 1-lanan *transliterated name* {358 eylownbeythchanan} Oak Grove of the House of Charism.

Eloniy *transliterated name* {440 elowniy} Of Elon.

Elqoshiy *transliterated name* {512 elqoshiy} Of Elqosh.

Elyon *transliterated title* **uppermost** *adjective* {5943 illay} {5945, 5946 elyon} [5310 hupsistos] an uppermost place or position; a title of Elohim.

emaciate *verb* {7329 razah} to thin.

emaciate, deceive, deny, disown *verb* {3584 kachash} [550 apeipomen] to be untrue in word, or deed.

emaciated *adjective* {7330 razeh} {7534 raq} as flattened out; thin; skinny.

emaciation *noun* {7332 razon} {7334 raziy} thin; skinny.

emaciation *noun* {7829 shachepheth} as peeled thin.

emaciation, deception, denial *noun* {3585 kachash} a failure of flesh.

embalm, ripen, spice *verb* {2590 chanat} from the root, to spice.

embitter *verb* {4843 marar} [4087 pikraino] to cause to be bitter.

embroider *verb* **emroiderer** *participle* {7551 raqam} {7660 shabats} to variegate color; usually threads of gold.

embroidered mail *noun* {7661 shabats} a woven, or mesh armour.

embroidery *noun* {7553 riqmah} of variegated color.

embryo *noun* {1564 golem} a wrapped unformed mass.

Emim *plural transliterated name* {368 eymiym} Terrors.

eminence, eminent *noun* {5057 nagid} one that stands out.

eminent, oversee, perpetual, perpetuity (in) *adjective, participle* {5329 natsach} {5331 netsach} [1336 dieenekes] continual, on and on; to oversee work; to be eminent.

Emmaus *transliterated name* {3222 yem} [1695 emmaous] Warm Spring.

Emoriy *transliterated name* {567 emoriy} Mountaineer.

empower, overpower, prevail *verb* {8280 sarah} {8630 taqaph} [2616 katadunastuo] [2729 katiskuo] [2901 krataioo] [2902 krateo] to have ability over; to cause to have power.

empowerment *noun* {8632 teqoph} power.

empty, pour out, strip naked *verb* {6168 arah} {6379 pakah} to empty; to empty by pouring; to strip bare; **see** naked.

empty, req, vain, vanity, void *adjective* {1892 hebel} {*transliteration* 7385 riq} {*transliteration* 7386 req} {7723 shav} [*transliteration* 4469 rhaka] emptiness, voidness; figuratively, stupid.

empty, vainly, void *adverb* {7387 reqam} emptily; without effect; **cp** req.

En Eglayim *dual transliterated name* {5882 eyneglayim} Fountain of Two Calves.

En 1-laq Qore *transliterated name* {5875 eynhaqqowre} Fountain of Calling.

En 1-larod *transliterated name* {5878 eyncharod} Fountain of Trembling.

En 1-lasor *transliterated name* {5877 eynchatsowr} Fountain of a Court.

En Tappuach *transliterated name* {5887 eyntappuwach} Fountain of an Apple (Tree).

enable, prevail, able, can *verb* {3201 yakol} {3202 yekel} {3546 kehal} [1410 dunamai] [2427 hikanoo] the dynamis to do; **see** dynamis.

encamp, camp *verb* {2583 chanah} {8497 takah} [63 agrauleo] [835 aulizomai] to pass the night in the open air; to tent; **see** pull stakes; **see** court, courtyard.

encampment *noun* {8466 tachanah} [3925 parembolee] a place to camp, to pitch tents.

enchant *verb* **enchanters** *participle* {3907 lachash} to whisper a spell; whisperers of spells.

enchanter *noun* {825 ashshaph} {826 ashshaph} [1114 gooes] a conjurer; a whisperer of spells.

enchantingly, covertly *adjective* {3909 laht} whispering a spell; under cover.

enchantment *noun* {3908 lachash} a whispered spell.

enclose, inclose, lock, shod *verb* {5274 naal} {7000 qatar} to fasten; **see** shoe.

encounter, intercede, reach *verb* {6293 paga} to impinge. **encourage, abuse** *verb* {7292 rahab} in the sense of urging; of pressuring.

end, conclusion, consummation *noun* {5490 soph} {5491 soph} {7093 qets} {7097 qetseh} {7098 qatsah} the end, of an eon, of a scroll.

end, edge *noun* {7093 qets} {7097 qetseh} {7098 qatsah} {7099 qetsev} an extremity.

end, part *noun* {7117, 7118 qetsath} a portion; a termination.

endow *verb* {2064 zabad} {4117 mahar} a bestowment of a dowry or a valuable; **cp** endue.

endowment *noun* {2065 zehved} a bestowment, a dowry.
endurance *noun* [5281 hupomonee] constancy.

endure *verb* [4722 stego] to keep by covering, to bear.

endure, abide *verb* [5278 hupomeno] [5297 hupophero] to bear, persevere.

endure, tolerate *verb* [430 anekomai] to hold oneself up against.

endure evil *verb* [420 anexikakos] to forbear.

enemy *noun* {340 ayab} {341 oyeb} {6145, 6146 ar} [2190 ekthros] one who hates.

energize, energizing *transliterated verb* [1753 energeia] [1754 energeo] [1755 energeema] [1756 energees] to impart energy.

enfold, gather *verb* {3664 kanac} to collect; to wrap.

engrave, (set) statute *verb* **statute setter** *participle* {2710 chaqaq} [1795 entupoo] to engrave; to prescribe; **see** statue.
engrave *verb* **engraving** *participle, noun* {2707 chaqah} {2799 charosheth} {2801 charath} to carve; a carved work; **see** statute.

engrave, open, pethach *verb* {6605 pathach} {6606 pethach} [*transliterated* 2188 ephphatha] to open; to loosen; to engrave.

engraver *noun* {2791 cheresh} {2794 choresh} {2796 charash} {*plural* 2798 chaarashim} {2800 charosheth} a skilled engraver of any material.

engraving *noun* {2799 charosheth} {6603 pittuach} a sculpting.

enlarge, broaden *verb* {7337 rachab} to widen; to make larger. **enlighten** *verb* {2094 zahar} *participle* {2095 zehar} to cause to gleam; to cause to understand.

enliven *verb* [2227 zoopoieo] to bestow life.

enmity *noun* {342 eybah} {4895 mastemah} [2189 ekthra] hatred.

Enosh *transliterated name* {583 enosh} [1800 enos] Man, Mortal.

enquire, examine, inquire, require, seek *verb* {1875 dahrash} to ask; to seek; **cp** beseech.

enrage *verb* {2194 zaam} {2196 zaaph} {7107 qatsaph} {7108 qetsaph} [3949 parorgizo] [3951 parotruno] to cause one to rage; to rage.

enraged *adjective* {2198 zaeph} angered.

enrich *verb* {6238 ashar} to cause to be rich; **see** rich.

enrobe *verb* {3847 labesh} {3848 lebash} to wrap around; **cp** robe.

ensign, pole, sail *noun* **Nissi** *transliterated title* {5251 nec} an ensign; the pole of an ensign; part of the title, Yah Veh Nissi, which means, Yah Veh Ensign.

ensign, sign *noun* {226 owth} [3902 parasemos] [4592 seemion] as emblematic, or as a signal; the sun, moon, and stars are for signs and seasons; Yonah was a sign to the Ninevehiy and the Yah Hudiy; turning water into wine was Yah Shua's first sign; some signs are miraculous, some are not.

ensign (raise an) *verb* {5264 nacac} to lift up; as fluttering in the wind.

ensign bearer *noun* {5263 nacac} one who bears an ensign.

enslave *verb* [2615 katadouloo] to bring into bondage (to one's self).

ensnare, snare *verb* {3369 yaqosh} {5367 naqash} {6351 pachah} {6983 qosh} to lay, or spring a snare.

entangle *verb* {8308 sarqak} to interlace.

entangle, pawn, pledge *verb* {5670 abat} to entangle a people; to entangle a pledge by pawning.

enter *verb* {5954 alal} to enter, in the sense of thrusting.

entertain, laugh, ridicule *verb* {6711 tsachaq} {6712 tsechoq} {7832 sechag} to laugh; to laugh at; to laugh at in defiance.

entice, dupe *verb* {6601 pathah} to delude, to tempt; **cp** test.

entomb *verb* {6912 qabar} [2290 thapto] to deposit in a tomb; to bury, **see** tomb.

entombment *noun* {5027 taphee} burial.

entorahed *verb* [1772 ennomos] under the torah; **cp** untorahed.

entrap *verb* [64 agreuo] [1185 deleazo] to trap; to trip up.

entrust, trust *verb* {539 aman} {540 aman} [4100 pistuo] [4104 pistoo] **see** amen; to confidently rely upon; **note:** whereas believing is a psyching up of the mental attributes, trust is the abandonment of self into the care of another.

entwine *verb* {5440 sabak} {8276 sarag} [4553 sargane *a transliteration of the Hebrew 5440*] entangle; as woven.

enumeration *noun* {4510 minyan} a counting up of numbers.

environ, round, surround *noun* {3603 kikkar} literally, circle; the environs of an area; a round of material, usually of precious metals.

envy, jealousy, suspicion *noun* {7068 qinah} zeal, as jealousy, or envy.

envy, suspect *verb* **jealous, zealous** *adjective* {7065 qana} {7067 qanna} {7072 qannow} to be zealous, as jealous, or envious.

enwisen, wisen *verb* {2449 chakam} [4679 sophizo] to cause to be wise.

eon, eon of the eons *transliterated noun* [165 aion] unlimited; limitless periods of time.

Epaphroditus *transliterated name* [1891 epaphrodites] Devotee of Aphrodite (a deity).

ephah *transliterated noun* {374 ephah} a measure.

ephod *transliterated noun* {642 ephuddah} { 646 ephod} a shoulderpiece of clothing.

Ephrath *transliterated name* {672 ephrath} another name of Beth Lechem.

Ephrathiy *transliterated name* {673 ephrathiy} Of Ephrath.

Ephrayim *transliterated name* {669 ephrayim} {6085 ephron} [2187 ephraim] Double Fruit, or Fawn-like.

Epicurean *transliterated name* [1946 ephikourios] a follower of the philosopher Epikouroos.

epigraph *transliterated noun* [1923 epigraphee] a superscription; **cp** inscription.

epigraph *transliterated verb* [1924 epigrapho] to scribe an epigraph.

epiphanous *adjective* [2016 epiphanees] bright.

epiphany *noun* [2015 epiphania] a manifestation; usually, a manifestation of Christ as divine.

episcopate, visitation *transliterated noun* [1984 episcope] [1985 episcopos] one who scopes; an inspector; inspection.

epistle *transliterated noun* {104 iggera} {107 iggereth} {5406, 5407 nishtevan} [1992 epistolee] a letter.

epistolize *transliterated verb* [1989 epistello] to communicate by epistle.

Eqer *transliterated name* {6134 eqer} Uprooted.

Eqron *transliterated name* {6138 eqrown} Eradication.

Eqroniy *transliterated name* {6139 eqroniy} Of Eqron.

equal, reign *noun* {4915 moshel} equal, in the sense of being able to liken unto, or compare with; reign, of being more than equal, of being over.

equal to angels *adjective* [2465 isangelos] like angels; angelic. **see** SUMMARY: ANGEL.

equate, equalize *verb* {7737 shavah} {7739 shevah} to level; to resemble.

equidistant *participle* {7947 shalab} of equal distance.

equip, rescue, strip *verb* {2502 chalats} literally, to strip for hostility; to strip out of danger.

Er *transliterated name* {6147 er} [2262 er] Awake.

Eraniy *transliterated name* {6198 eraniy} Of Eran.

erase, wipe, wipe out *verb* {4229 machah} [1813 exalipho] to rub; to rub out; to erase sins, tears, names.

Erastos *transliterated name* [2037 erastos] of eros; **see** Eros.

erect *noun* {6968 qomemiuth} high, as straightened out.

erect *verb* {5446 sebal} to raise up.

Erech *transliterated name* {751 erech} Length.

Erechiy *transliterated name* {756 archevay} Of Erech; **see** Archiy.

Eri *transliterated name* {6179 eriy} Waken.

Eriy *transliterated name* {6180 eriy} Of Eri.

Eros *transliterated title* **eros** *transliterated noun* Although eros does not appear in Scripture, it is worthy of definition; a deity; the expression of the physical emotion, often sexual; **cp** love, the spiritual expression; **cp** befriend, the soulical expression; **see** Erastos.

err inadvertently, inadvertently err *verb* {7683 shagag} {7686 shagah} to err unintentionally.

error *noun* {4870 mishgeh} {4879 meshugah} {7691 shegiah} {8442 toah} a moral or spiritual mistake.

error (inadvertent) *noun* {7684 shegagah} {*plural* 7691 shegiyahoth} unintentional error.

erupt *verb* {8368 sathar} to break out.

Esav *transliterated name* {6215 esav} [2269 esau] Worker.

Esbon *transliterated name* {675 etsbon} of uncertain derivative.

escape, rescue *verb* {4422 malat} literally, to smooth; to slip away; to be slipped away.

escape, rescue, strip *verb* {5337, 5338 natsal} to snatch away; favorably, or unfavorably.

escape, slip (away) (out) *verb* {6403 palat} {6405 peletah}.

escapee, escaped, escaping *noun* {6412 palit} {6413 peleytah} that which has escaped.

Esem *transliterated name* {6107 etsem} Bone.

Eseq *transliterated name* {6230 eseq} Contend.

Eser *transliterated name* {687 etser} Treasure.

Esh Baal *transliterated name* {792 eshbaal} Man of Baal.

Eshan *transliterated name* {824 eshan} Lean.

Esheq *transliterated name* {6232 esheq} Oppression.

Eshkol *transliterated name* {812 eshkol} Cluster.

Eshtaol *transliterated name* {847 eshtaol} Ask.

Eshtaoliy *transliterated name* {848 eshtauliy} Of Eshtaol.

Esli *transliterated name* [2069 esli] meaning uncertain; possibly, Of El.

establish *verb* [950 bebaioo] to make sure.

establish, prepare *verb* {3559 kuwn} to set up.

establishment *noun* [951 bebaiosis] stability.

establishment *noun* {4349 makown} a base, as set up; **see** establish.

esteem *noun* {3367 yeqar} the regard; the value.

esteem *verb* {1921, 1922 hadar} to hold in honour; **cp** honour.

esteem *verb* {3365 yaqar} to value highly; to regard highly.

esteem, estimation *noun* {3366 yeqar} the value.

esteemed *adjective* {3357, 3358 yaqqiyr} highly valued; highly regarded.

Ester *transliterated name* {635 ecter} the meaning uncertain; of Persian derivative.

estimate *verb* {3699 kacac} to appraise.

estrange, notice, recognize, discern, distinguish *verb* {5234 nakar} to acknowledge; to scrutinize; to distinguish between; to ignore, hence to be estranged.

estrange, strange *verb* {2114 zuwr} to cause to be strange; although a verb, often carries the force of a noun; **see** strange.

Esyon Geber *transliterated name* {6100 etsyongeber} Spine- like of a Man.

et cetera *particiCourse* {3706 keeneth} and so on.

etching, mark, tattoo, brand *noun* {7085 qaaqa} {8420 tab} [5480 karagma] a scratched marking; a mark on animals; an x or a + as a signature of an illiterate; a mark of protection; **read** Yechezq El 9:4–6; **read** Apocalypse 13:16,17, 14:9–11, 15:2, 16:2, 19:20, 20:4; **cp** brand.

eternal, eternally, eternity, original *noun, adjective, adverbally* {5703 ad} {5769 olam} {5865 elom} {5957 alam} [126 aidios] [166 aionios] a limitless period – either past, present, or future.

Eth Qasin *transliterated name* {6278 ethqatsiyn} Time of a Commander.

ethnarch *transliterated title* [1481 ethnarchees] an arch over the ethnics.

eucharist, eucharistic, eucharistize; see SUMMARY: EUCHARIST.

eulogize, eulogy; see SUMMARY: EULOGIZE, EULOGY:

eunuch *transliterated noun* {5631 saric} {*plural* 5632 sarek} [2135 eunouchos] one who has gone beyond circumcision by castration.

eunuchize *transliterated verb* [2134 eunouchizo] to castrate; to become a eunuch.

euphonious *transliterated adjective* [2163 eupheemos] well sounding; praiseworthy.

euphony *transliterated noun* [2162 eupheemia] agreeableness of sound; a praise.

Euphrates *transliterated name* {6578 perath} [2166 euphratees] name of a river; Bursting; Rushing.

evaluation *noun* {4373 mikcah} an evaluation based on an enumeration (census); see assessment.

evangelism, evangelist, evangelize; see SUMMARY: EVANGELISM.

eve, even, evening *noun* {6153 ereb} [2073 hespera] [3796 opse] the end of day; dusk.

evening *adjective* [3797 opsimos] duskward.

evening, obscure *verb* {6150 arab} in the sense of dusking; of becoming obscure.

evening breeze *noun* {5399 nesheph} a breeze at dusk. **ever** *adverb* [104 ai] at any; at all; **cp** eon.

evil *adjective* {7451 ra} [2556 kakos] injurious.

evil *noun* {7455 ra} [4189 poneeria] [4190, 4191 poneeros] an opposition of all that is good, right, and whole.

evil (do) *verb* [2554 kakopoyeo] to injure; to sin; **see** vilify.

Evil Merodach *transliterated name* {192 eviylmerodach} possibly, Soldier of Merodach.

evildoer *noun* [2555 kakopoyos] one who does evil.

evilworker *noun* [2557 kakourgos] one who works evil.

ewe *noun* {7353 rachel} a young female.

ewe lamb *noun* {3535 kabsah} {3776 kisbah} a young female sheep.

exact *verb* **exactor** *participle* {5065 nagas} {5378 nasha} {5383 nashah} to extract; one that extracts by tax or tyrany.

exact, forget *verb* {5382 nashah} to neglect; to remove from.

exact, transact *verb* [4238 prasso] to extract dues; to execute; to perform repeatedly.

exactly as, even as *participle* [2509 kathaper] [2531 kathos] [5618 hosper] just as.

exalt, extol, raise (up) *verb* {5549 salal} from the root, to mound up; **see** selah; **cp** halal.

exalt, lift, loft, raise *verb* {7311, 7313 rum} {7318 romam} {7426 ramam} to lift hand, heart, offering, voice; to oath; **see** exalt.

exalt, loft *verb* {7682 sagab} to lift high.

exaltation *noun* {7319 romemah} {7427 romemuth} {7863 siy} elevation; praise.

exalting, lifting, swelling *noun* {7613 seeth} an elevation; from the verb, lift {5375}.

exaltment *noun* {8641 terumah} {8642 terumiah} the celebration of lifting a sacrificial exaltment unto Yah Veh.

examination, judgment *noun* [351 anakrisis] investigation.

examine, expect *verb* {7663 sabar} to scrutinize with expectation.

examine, inquire, require, seek, enquire *verb* {1875 darash} to ask; to seek; **cp** beseech.

examine, judge, plead *verb* {8199 shaphat} {8200 shephat} [350 anakrino] [2919 krino] to scrutinize; to investigate.

exceeding, greatly, increasing, many, mighty, much, very *adjective* {7689, 7690 saggiy} superlatively mighty, or large.

exceeding, remainder, remnant, rest *noun* {3499 yether} the remainder, those left over.

excellent, exceeding *adjective* **exceedingly** *adverb* {3493 yattiyr} preeminent; very.

exchange (in) *noun* {8545 temurah} [465 antallagma] to barter; to trade.

LEXICON

exchange, change *verb* {3235 yamar} {4171 mur} [236 allasso] to alter; to change places.

excise *noun* {1093 beloh} a tax on articles consumed.

excite *verb* [383 anasio] [2042 erethizo] to quake; to stir up.

exclaim *verb* [400 anaphoneo] to cry out.

exclusion *noun* {5079 niddah} one chased away; excluded, as a menstruous woman.

excrement *noun* {2716 chere} {*plural* 2755 charim} {*plural* 4280 macharaah} {6627 tsaah} human or animal dung.

executioners *plural noun* {3746 kariy} {3774 kerethi} guards in charge of executing.

exhale *adjective* {3307 yapheach} puffing.

exhaust, exhale *verb* {6313 pug} to exhale; to let out the breath.

exhausted *adjective* {4198 mazeh} sucked out.

exhausted *noun* {6296 pagar} to be exhaled; out of breath.

exile *noun* {1473 golah} {1546, 1547 gauwth} one who is expelled; an expulsion.

exile, expose *verb* {1540 galah} {1541 gelah} to expel; to expose.

exodus, exit *transliterated noun* {*plural* 8444 totsaahoth} [1841 exodos] an exit; of death as an exodus from life.

exonerate *verb* {5352 naqah} verb of innocent; to declare innocent; **see** innocent.

exonerated, innocent *adjective* {5355 naqi} [172 akakos] not guilty.

exoneration basins *plural noun* {4518 menaqqithoth} sacrifice basins which held blood; from the verb, exonerate.

expand *verb* {7554 raqa} to expand by pounding thin; verb of expanse.

expanded *adjective* {7555 riqqua} thinned.

expanse *noun* {4800 merchab} an enlargement.

expanse *noun* {7549 raqia} noun of expand; of the heavens; **read** Genesis 1:8.

expect, examine *verb* {7663 sabar} to scrutinize with expectation.

expect, receive, wait, await *verb* {2442 chakah} {3176 yachal} {6960 qavah} [324 anadekomai] [362 anameno] [553 apekdekomai] [4327 prosdekomai] [4328 prosdokao] [4329 prosdokia] to anticipate; to wait expectantly, patiently; **cp** take.

expectation *noun* {4007 mabbat} {7664 seber} anticipation.

expectation, congregating *noun* {4723 miqveh} this Hebrew word has two roots; a congregating of troops, of water; of expectation.

expel, drive (out) *verb* {1644 garash} {2957 terad} {5080 nadach} {5090 nahag} to carry away; to expatriate; to push off.

expiration *noun* {4646 mappach} an exhausting of breath.

expire *verb* {1478 gava} to breathe one's last breath.

expire soul, pressure, puff *verb* {5301 naphach} [1634 ekpsucho] to breathe away one's soul; to pressure, as in a pressure cooker; and to puff; **cp** expire spirit.

expire spirit *verb* [1606 ekpneo] to breathe away one's spirit; **cp** expire soul.

explain *verb* {874 bahar} [1956 epiluo] to make plain; **cp** interpret; **cp** translate.

explanation *noun* [1955 epilusis] a making plain; **cp** interpretation; **cp** translation.

exploit, exploitation *noun* {4611 maalal} {5949 alilah} {5950 aliliah} an act or accomplishment.

exploit, glean *verb* {5953 alal} to pick up after; in a good sense, to glean; in a bad sence, to exploit.

exploits, freaks *plural noun* {8586 taalul} deeds as exploitations.

explore, dig *verb* {2658 chaphar} {8446 tur} to pry into.

expose *verb* {5783 uwr} {6544 para} to loosen; to cause to be bare.

expose, exile *verb* {1540 galah} {1541 gelah} to expel; to expose.

expound *verb* [5419 phrazo] to define; to explain in detail.

express, wound, disperse *verb* {6567 parash} to separate; to specify; to wound.

exscind *verb* [1575 ekklao] [1581 ekkopto] to cut off or out.

exsynagogue *transliterated verb* [656 aposunagogos] to excommunicate from a synagogue.

extend *verb* {3447 yahshat} to reach out.

extend, distend verb {8311 sara} to extend oneself, as in stretching out; to distend, as an appendage.

extend, happen verb {4291 meta} to extend unto the heavens; to happen upon.

extend, send verb {7971 shalach} {7972 shelach} to send; to send forth.

extend, spread (thin), stretch verb {5186 natah} {5628 sarach} to bend away; to spread out; to stretch.

extend hands, wring hands participle {3029 yeda} {3034 yadah} {8426 todah} to extend hands in praise; to wring hands in sorrow.

extending, sending participle {4916 mishloach} a sending out; from the verb, send.

extention noun {5629 serach} an augmentation.

exterminate verb {6789 tsamath} to eradicate; to wipe out.

extermination noun {7171 qerets} extirpation.

extol, raise (up), exalt verb {5549 salal} from the root, to mound up; **see** selah; **cp** halal.

extort, oppress verb {6231 ashaq} to press out of; to oppress.

extortion, oppression noun {6233 osheq} a pressing out of; an oppressing.

extortioner of gold noun {4062 madhebah}.

eye, fountain noun {5869, 5870 ayin} [3788 ophthalmos] as the eye of the landscape; the organ for seeing; **see** fountain. **eye against** verb [503 antophthalmeo] to stare against.

eyelids plural noun {6079 aphaph} as fluttering.

eyeservice noun [3787 ophthalmodoulia] a deceitful ascent to agree; **cp** lipservice.

eyewitness noun [845 autoptees] one who physically witnessed.

Ezra transliterated name {5830, 5831 ezrah} Helper.

Ezrah transliterated name {5834 ezrah} Helper.

Ezri transliterated name {5836 ezri} Help.

Ezri El transliterated name {5837 ezriel} Help of El.

Ezri Qam transliterated name {5840 azriyqam} Help of an Enemy.

F

fabricate, machinate verb, participle {2803, 2804 chashab} to interpenetrate; to weave; to contrive; physically, to fabricate; mentally, to machinate.

fabricated adjective {6247 esheth} fabricated; machinated.

fabricated girdle noun {2805 chesheb} a girdle, as interlaced.

fabrication, machination noun {2808 cheshbohn} {plural 2810 chishshabonth} {4284 machashebeth} a contrivance of machine, or mind.

face noun {6440 paneh} [4383 prospon] the front of the head; also used verbally.

face verb {6437 panah} to turn face toward; facing.

face bread, prothesis bread compound noun {6440 paneh} {3899 lechem} [transliteration 4286 prothesis] [740 artos] the bread of the holy of holies as displayed; the face bread of the Old Covenant is identical to the prothesis bread of the New Covenant.

fade, dim adjective {3544 kehah} obscure; dull.

fade, dim verb {3543 kahah} to become obscure, dull.

fade, shade verb {6004 amam} in the sense of concealing; of fading.

fail, fall (away),(off) (out) verb [1601 ekpipto] to be without effect; to be driven out of one's course.

fail, hoe, lack, arrange verb {5737 adar} to miss having; to arrange a vineyard, as in hoeing.

failing noun {3631 killayon} as in finished off.

fall (away) (off) (out), fail verb [1601 ekpipto] to be without effect; to be driven out of one's course.

fall, fell, happen, befall verb {5307 naphal} {5308 nephal} {7136 qarah} fall, fall down, fall away; to fell, as in felling timber; to cause to bring about.

false adjective {3538 cedab} deceitful.

false, falsehood noun {8267 sheqer} an untruth.

falsify verb {8266 shaqar} to cheat; to be untrue.

falter, stumble, trip verb {3782 kashal} to totter; to waver.

fame, hearing, notoriety, report noun {8052 shemuah} {8088 shema} {8089 shoma} [189 akoee] that which is heard; an announcement; a rumor.

family *noun* {4940 mishpachah} parents and their offspring, ancestors and their descendants.

famine *noun* {7458 raab} {7459 reabon} a dearth of food.

famish *adjective* {7457 raeb} experiencing famine.

famish *verb* {7456 raeb} to experience famine.

far, afar, distant past *adjective* {7350 rachoq} {7352 rachiq} {7369 racheq} remote; in time, or distance.

far be it *interjection* {2486 chaliylah} in the sense of that which is profane.

far removed, removed far *verb* {7368 rachaq} from the root, to widen.

fascinate *verb* [940 baskaino] to lead away into error by wicked arts.

fast *verb* {6684 tsum} to abstain from eating.

fast, fasting *noun* {6685 tsom} {8589 taanith} [776 asitia] abstinence from eating.

fasting *adjective* [777 asitos] without food.

fat *adjective* {1879 dashen} {8082 shamen} fat symbolizes health and prosperity.

fat *noun* {6309 peder} the fat of the holocaust sacrifices.

fat, fatness *noun* {1880 deshen} {1881 dath} {2459 cheleb} {4924 mashman} the grease of the body; the richness, fertility; fat symbolizes health and prosperity.

Fate *name* {4507 meniy} Destiny; perhaps the name of an idol.

father, ab, **abba** *transliterated noun* {1 ab} {2 ab} [5 abba] [3962 pater] **ab** is Hebrew for father; **abba** is a Hellenic transliteration; **pater** is the Hellenic translation.

father in law *noun* {2524 cham} [3995 pentheros] the father of a man's woman or a woman's man.

fatherland *noun* [3968 patris] one's native home.

fatherless *adjective* [540 apator] without father.

fatling *noun* {4806 meriy} that which is stall fed.

fatten, defat *verb* {1878 dashen} {2954 taphash} {8080 shaman} depending on the case, to make fat, or to remove fat; to enrich.

fatten, plump *verb* {2492 chalam} {3780 kasah} to cause to be fat, to plump; to cover with flesh.

fattlings *plural noun* {4220 meachim} that which is fattened; prosperous.

faultless *adjective* [176 akatagnostos] literally, unfaulted.

fawn *noun* {6082 opher} from its dusty color.

fear *noun* {6343 pachad} {6345 pachdah} alarm; **cp** awe.

fear *verb* {3025 yagor} {6342 pachad} {7297 rahah} to be alarmed; to be afraid; **cp** awe.

feast *noun* [1403 doche] a reception.

feast *noun* {3900 lechem} literally, a feeding.

feast of mourning *noun* {4798 marzeach} a cry of grief.

feast of revelling *noun* {4797 mirzasch} a cry of joy.

feel, grope *verb* {4959 mashash} from the root, to feel of.

fell, happen, befall, fall *verb* {5307 naphal} {5308 nephal} {7136 qarah} to fell, as in felling timber; to cause to bring about; fall, fall down, fall away.

fellow settler *noun* [4040 perioikos] associates or mates who settle together.

female *noun* {5347 neqebah} [2338 theelia] the species that births, whether human, animal, or plant.

fennel flower *noun* {7100 qetsach} from its pungency.

ferment, foam *verb* {2556 chamets} {2560 chamar} [2220 zumoo] to cause to ferment; action of enzymes induced by yeast or bacteria.

fermentation *noun* {2557 chamets} {2561 chemer} {2562 chamar} [2219 zumee] the action of enzymes induced by yeast or bacteria; **see** yeast.

fermented *adjective* {2558 chomets} that which is fermented.

festive mantle *noun* {6614 pethigil} a mantle for festive occasions.

festoon, descent *noun* {4174 mowrad} a place of going down; an ornamental hanging; a garland or wreath.

fetter *noun* [254 halusis] a restraint.

fetus *noun* {7698 sheger} {7988 shilyah} that which is finally ejected.

fever *noun* {2746 charchur} {6920 qaddachath} as hot; inflamed.

few, few men, men *plural noun* {4962 mathim} **see** Theological Wordbook of the Old Testament, 1263.

few, little, petty, shortly, bit, bit by bit *adjective, adverb* {4592 meat} diminutive; a few; a little.

fewer, lesser, little, pinky, younger *adjective* {6810 tsaor} {6995 qoten} {6996 qatan} less in age, number, size; little finger.

field *noun* {7704 sadeh} {7709 shedemah} {*plural* 8309 sheremahoth} [68 agros] land set aside for tillage, pasture, or sport.

fiery *adjective* [4447 purinos] inflamed.

fiery *noun* [4449 purrazo] [4450 purros] reddened; flame colored.

fiery, fired *verb* [4448 puroomai] to be inflamed; to burn; of the heat of passions; of anger.

fig *noun* {8384 tenah} [4810 sukon] a species of fruit.

fight, eat *verb* {3898 lacham} literally, to feed on food; to feed on an enemy.

fighting *noun* {3901 lachem} literally, a feeding on the enemy.

figtree *noun* [4808 sukee] a species of fruit tree.

figurine *noun* {5566 semel} a likeness; a carved figure; a statuette; an idol.

fill *verb* [1072 gemizo] [1705 empiplao, empleetho] to occupy wholly, including liquid in a bottle, a position of leadership; **cp** fill full, fulfill.

fill full, fulfill, fully fill *verb* {4390 mala} {4391 mela} {4395 meleah} [378 anapleeroo] [4130 pleetho] [4137 pleeroo] [4845 sumpleero] to bring to a conclusion; **see** [4137 pleero] under SUMMARY: SHALAM **cp** complete; **cp** shalom; **see** worship.

filling, fulfillment *noun* {*plural* 4394 milluim} {4396 milluah} {4402 milleth} that which has filled; that which is fulfilled; of sacrifices; of stones which fill mountings.

filth *noun* {7516 rephesh} as mud; **cp** foul.

final, finality [2078 eskatos] extreme; last in time or in place.

find *verb* {7912 shekach} [429 anurisko] to discover.

finger *verb* [2345 thigo] to point out; to touch with the finger.

finger, toe *noun* {676 etsba} {677 etsba} [1147 daktulos] literally, a digit as a grasper; **cp** great toe, thumb.

finial *noun* {3730 kaphtor} a chaplet; the top of a stem, or column.

finish (full) (final) *noun* {3617 kalah} the end; full and final cessation; **cp** completion.

finish (off), fully finish, conclude *verb* {3615 kalah} {3635 kelal} to cease; to cause to decease; to bring to an end; **cp** complete.

finished off *adjective* {3616 kaleh} to cease.

finishing *noun* [535 apartismos] completion.

fire, fiery *noun* {5135 nur} also used adjectively; from the root, to shine.

firing *noun* [4451 purosis] trials as a test; burning by which metals are refined.

firing *noun* {801 ashshah} a celebration of a firing as a sacrifice unto Elohim.

firm, form, pour *verb* {3332 yatsaq} to pour out; to shape by pouring into a mold; to make firm.

first(s), head, top, beginning *noun* {7218 rosh} {7221 rishah} {7225 reshith} {8462 rechillah} the head, in a variety of applications; the head of the body, of time, of the month, of archs.

first, head *adjective* {7223 rishon} {7224 rishoniy} head, as at the top; first, as at the beginning.

firstborn *noun* {*feminine* 1067 bekirah} {*masculine* 1069 bakar} the first to burst the womb.

firstborn, firstling *noun* {1060 bekor} {*plural* 1061 bikkuwr} [536 *plural* aparkee] [4416 prototokos] the first offspring of a family or of a harvest.

firstrights, firstling *noun* {1062 bekorah} [4415 prototokia] the rights afforded a firstborn.

firstripe *noun* {1073 bakkurah} that which ripens first.

fists *dual noun* {2651 chophen} clenched hands.

fistsful *plural noun* {6653 tsebeth} as much as the clenched hand can hold.

flake *noun* [3016 lepton] a flake, or shaving.

flakes, chaff *noun* {4651 mappal} that which falls off; that which is pendulous.

flambeau *noun* {3940 lappid} a flaming torch.

flame *noun* {3827 labbah} {3852 lehabah} {7631 sebib} {7632 shabib} {7957 shalhebeth} a flame, or a flare of fire as split into tongues; **read** Acts 2:3.

flame, blade *noun* {3851 lahab} a flame of fire; a flashing blade of a sword.

flame, inflame *verb* **flaming** *adjective* {3857 lahat} {3859 laham} to blaze; that which is inflamed by fire.

flamed, inflamed *adjective* {6867 tsarebeth} [4092 pimpramai] as burning.

flamings *plural noun* {3858 lahatim} flames, as enwraping.

flank *noun* **flanks** *dual noun* {3409 yarek} {3410 yarka} {3411 yerechah} figuratively, the rear; the thigh, or thighs, as being soft.

flank, folly *noun* {3689 kecel} {3690 kiclah} silliness; the flank of the body; the flanks as symbolic of hope.

flap, flee, wander, chase *verb* {5074 nadad} {5323 natsa} to flap up and down; to shoo away.

flap, rebel *verb* {4754 mahrah} to flap one's self; to flap one's wings; to rebel.

flash, shine *verb* {3313 yapha} from the root, to shine.

flask *noun* {6378 pak} a container from which a liquid may flow.

flax *noun* {6593 pishteh} {6594 pishtah} flax as woven; flax as a wick

flee *verb* {5075 nedad} {5111 nud} {5127 nuwc} to depart; to flit.

flee, bud *verb* {5132 nuts} to flash, as in color; to flee in a flash.

flee, wander, chase, flap *verb* {5074 nadad} {5323 natsa} to flap up and down; to shoo away.

flesh *noun* {1320 basar} {1321 besar} [4561 sarx] literally, the substance of the living body; symbolically, the entire nature of man, sense and reason.

flesh, kinflesh *noun* {7607 sheer} {7608 shaarah} flesh, as food; flesh, as near of kin.

fleshly *adjective* [4559 sarkikos] under the control of animal appetites.

fleshy *adjective* [4560 sarkinos] consisting of flesh; soft.

flight, retreat *noun* {4498 manohs} {4499 menusah} a place to flee to; a fleeing.

flint *noun* {6862 tsar} {6864 tsor} a hard pebble; a tight place.

flip, flit, paddle *verb* {7751 shuwt} to flit forth and back; to flip oars.

flit, flitter, fly *verb* {5774 uph} {1675 daah} [4072 petomai] to move through the air.

flit, paddle, flip *verb* {7751 shuwt} to flit forth and back; to flip oars.

float, overflow *verb* {6687 tsuph} to float; to flow over.

flock *noun* {6629 tson} {6792 tsone} a group, usually of animals or birds.

flog *verb* [1194 dero] to scourge.

flood *noun* {2230 zerem} {3999 mabbuwl} an overflowing.

flood *verb* {2229 zaram} to overflow.

floor *noun* {7172 qarqa} a slab or board laid down.

flour *noun* {5560 soleth} flour, as stripped.

flour *noun* {7058 qemach} that which is ground.

flourish, blossom *verb* {6524 parach} {6692 tsuts} to bloom.

flourish, germinate *verb* {5107 nub} from the root, to germinate; to flourish.

flow, flux *verb* {2100 zoov} of land as flowing with milk and honey; of woman as fluxing with blood.

flow, melt, dissolve *verb* {4529 masah} to dissolve.

flow, pour *verb* {5047 negad} {5064 nagar} {5140 nazal} to flow out, as to clear the way; to pour out.

flow, sparkle *verb* {5102 nahar} to flow, as to assemble; to be cheerful; to sparkle.

flush {*adjective* 2447 chakliyl} {*noun* 2448 chakliluth} flush in color.

flushness *noun* {6289 parur} a glowing flushness.

flute *noun* {2485 chaliyl} as being perforated.

flute *noun* {4953 mashroqiy} {5155 nechiylah} [836 aulos] as a musical pipe, blown, or whistled.

flute *verb* [832 auleo] to blow or whistle the flute.

flutist *noun* [834 auleetees] one who flutes.

flux, flow *noun* {2101 zohv} {2231 zirmah} the flow as of blood or pus.

flux, flow *verb* {2100 zuwb} of land as flowing with milk and honey; of woman as fluxing with blood.

fly, flit, flitter *verb* {5774 uph} {1675 daah} [4072 petomai] to move through the air.

flyer *noun* {5775, 5776 oph} [4071 petinon] [4421 pteenon] that which flies.

foam, ferment *verb* {2556 chamets} {2560 chamar} [2220 zumoo] to cause to ferment; action of enzymes induced by yeast or bacteria.

fodder, mingle, mix up *verb* {1101 balal} to mix together; to mix up; **see** Beli Yaal; **see** comingle.

fold, reiterate, repeat, alter, change, double, duplicate *verb* {8132 shana} {8133 shena} {8138 shanah} to reinforce by folding, by doubling; may include disguise, camouflage.

foliage *noun* {6074 ophi} {6288 purah} {6788 tsammereth} whatever sprouts from a tree, vine, or plant.

foliage, rope, wreath, wreathen *noun* {5688 abothah} as entwined; a wreath of victory; **cp** crown; **cp** diadem.

folly *noun* {200 ivveleth} {5039 nebalah} {5529 sekel} {5531 sikluth} silliness; foolishness.

folly *verb* {5528 sakal} to do foolishly; to act silly.

folly, flank *noun* {3689 kecel} {3690 kiclah} silliness; the flank of the body; the flank, as symbolic of hope.

folly, wither, disgrace *verb* {5034 nabel} from the root, to wilt; to fall away; to fail.

food *noun* **eating** *verb* [1034 brosimos] that which is eaten.

food *noun* {3894 lachuwm} [1033 broma] that which is eaten.

food *noun* {3978 maakal} {4202, 4203 mazown} an edible.

fool, foolish *adjective* {5036 nabal} stupid.

fool *noun* **Kesil** *transliterated name* {3684 kecil} {5530 sakal} a constellation; stupid, or silly.

foolish *adjective* {191 eviyl} {196 eviliy} {3687 keciyluth} silly.

foolish *adjective* {3688 kecal} to be silly.

foot (on) *noun* {7273 ragli} persons on foot; infantry.

foot (step) *noun* {4772 margelah} {7271 regal} {7272 regel} [4228 pous] the foot; a footstep.

foot (to the) *noun* [4158 podeerees] full length.

foothold *noun* {4613 moomad} a place to secure the foot.

footstool *noun* {3534 kebesh} [5286 hupopodion] as trodden upon; as under foot.

forage *noun* [5527 chortasma] animal feed.

force, lizard, substance *noun* {3581 koach} {3981 maamats} pressure, physical or intellectual; also a lizard.

forehead *noun* {4696 metsach} [3359 metopon] the upper front of the head.

foreknow *verb* [4267 proginosko] to know prior to occurrence.

foreleg, arm *noun* {2220 zeroah} [1023 brakion] arm (human), foreleg (animal); denoting force, strength.

foresay *verb* [4280 proereo] to say prior to occurrence.

foresee *verb* [4308 proorao] to see prior to occurrence.

foreshabbath *transliterated noun* [4315 prosabbaton] shabbath eve.

foreskin, uncircumcised *noun* {6190 orlah} [203 akrobustia] the foreskin of the penis; the foreskin not removed; **cp** circumcision; **cp** decircumcision.

forespeak *verb* [4302 prolego] to speak prior to occurrence.

forest *noun* {2793 choresh} {3264 yaor} {3293 yaar} {3295 yaarah} [5208 hulee] a growth of trees.

foretell *verb* [4277 proepo] to tell prior to occurrence.

forget *adjective* {7913 shekach} oblivious.

forget *verb* {7911 shakach} to be oblivious of.

forget, exact *verb* {5382 nashah} to neglect; to remove from.

forging *noun* {4300 metil} a metal as hammered out.

forgive *verb* {5545 salach} to grant charism.

forgive, forsake, leave, release, allow *verb* [863 aphieemi] to send forth.

forgiveness *noun* {5547 celichah} [859 aphesis] charism granted.

forgiving *noun* {5546 callach} a granting of charism.

fork *noun* {4207 mazleg} {*plural* 4207 mezlagoth} an instrument to draw up.

form *noun* {3333 yetsukah} {*plural* 3338 yatsurim} {8389 toar} [3444 morphee] [3446 morphosis] that which is formed; **see** metamorphose.

form *noun* {3336 yetser} to form of the thought.

form *noun* {6699 tsurah} a form, as shaped.

form *verb* {3335 yatsar} [3445 morphoomai] to shape; **see** metamorphose.

form, besiege, bind, confine *verb* {6696 tsur} to confine; to form by shaping.

form, idolize, contort *verb* {6087 atsab} to form; to contort; as in idolizing, as in pain.

form, pour, firm *verb* {3332 yatsaq} to pour out; to shape by pouring into a mold; to make firm.

formation, rank, arrangement *noun* {4633 maarak} {4634 maarakah} {4635 maareketh} an arrangment (physical or mental).

formerly, preceding, ancient, antiquity, east, easterly, eastern, eastward *noun* {6921 qadim} {6924 qedem} {6925 qodam} {6926 qidmah} {6927 qadmah} literally, the forefront; from the front.

formula, quantity *noun* {4971 mathkuneth} a measured proportion of portions.

forsake, leave (behind), release, abandon *verb* {5800 azab} [1459 enkatalipo] to leave behind; in a good sense, to let remain over; in a bad sense, to abandon.

forsake, leave, release, allow, forgive, abandon *verb* [863 aphieemi] to send forth.

forsaking, leaving, releasing, abandoning *noun* {5805 azubah} a desertion.

fortifications *plural noun* {8284 sharoth} reinforcements.

fortified, fortress, fortressed *noun, adjective* {4013 mibtsar} [3794 okuroma] a reinforced building, or city.

forum *noun* [60 agoraios] a market; including a forum for open discussion, of the judiciary; **see** market.

foul *verb* {2930 tame} {2933 tamah} {2936 tanaph} {7515 raphas} [4510 rupoo] to become offensive to the senses; **cp** filth.

foul, foulness *noun* {2932 tumah} [4507 ruparia] [4508 ruparos] [4509 rupos] loathsome; offensive to the senses.

fouled *adjective* {2931 tame} loathed.

found, foundation *verb* {3245 yacad} [2311 themelioo] to lay a base or basis for.

foundation *noun* {3246 yecud} {3247 yecod} {3248 yecudah} {4143 muwcad} {4144 mowcad} {4145 muwcadah} {*plural* 4146 mowcadah} {4328 meuccadah} {4527 maccad} {8356 shathah} [2310 themelios] [2602 katabolee] the base or basis, whether of a fact, or ediface.

fountain *noun* {1543 gulah} {4002 mabbua} {4599 mayan} {5033 nebek} a source, usually of water.

fountain *noun* {4726 maqor} a gusher; including tears, and menstruation of a woman.

fountain, eye *noun* {5869, 5870 ayin} [3788 ophthalmos] as the eye of the landscape; the organ for seeing.

foursquare, square *verb* {7251 raba} to cause to be quadrate.

fowl *noun* {1257 barbur} {6853 tsephar} [3732 orneon] a species of flyer.

fracture *noun* {4386 mekittah} a crushing break.

fragment *noun* {7518 rats} {*plural* 7616 shabahim} [2801 klasma] of remnants of food, a broken piece.

frail *adjective* [770 astheneo] [772 asthenees] feeble.

frailty *noun* [769 asthenia] feebleness of body or mind.

frailty *noun* [771 astheneema] error arising from weakness of mind; a scruple of conscience.

framing *noun* {4746 meqareh} the frame of a building, as the meeting of timbers.

frankincense *noun* {3828 lebonah} [3030 libanos] a species of incense; **see** incense.

frankincenser *noun* [3031 libanoton] a censer for a species of incense; **see** censer.

fraud *noun* {8496 tok} {*plural* 8501 takakim} {*plural* 8595 tatuaim} in the sense of cutting up; also errors.

freaks, exploits *plural noun* {8586 taalul} deeds as exploitations.

fresh *adjective* {3892 lach} new, as unused; as undried.

fresh, dripping *adjective* {2961 tahiy} new, as moist.

freshness *noun* {3893 leach} vigor.

friend *noun* {5997 amith} {7453 rea} {7463 reeh} {7464 reah} {7468 reuth} {7474 raah} [5384 philos] a fond one; a soulical attraction.

friendly minded *noun* [5390 philophronos] [5391 philophron] agreeable.

friendship *noun* [5373 philia] relationship with a fond one.

fright *noun* {1205 beathah} extreme fear.

frighten *verb* {1204 baath} {7738 shavah} to cause extreme fear.

frivolity *noun* {8604 tiphlah} silliness.

frost, ice, crystal *noun* {7140 qerach} as being smooth.

froth *verb* [875 aphrizo] to foam at the mouth.

frothiness *noun* {6350 pachazuth} frothy; foamy; unimportant.

frothy *adjective* {6348, 6349 pachaz} frothy; foamy; as boiling over; as unimportant.

fruit (stray) *noun* {6528 peret} fruit left for strangers to glean.

fruit *noun* {5108 nob} {6529 peri} [2590 karpos] species of produce of the ground, usually self-seeded.

fuel *noun* {3980 maakoleth} a feed for fire.

fuel pile *noun* {4071 medurah} an accumulation of fuel.

fugitive *noun* {1280 beriach} {1281 bariach} {4015 mibrach} {5211 niye} one who flees.

fulfill, fully fill, fill full *verb* {4390 mala} {4391 mela} {4395 meleah} [378 anapleeroo] [4130 pleetho] [4137 pleeroo] [4845 sumpleero] to bring to a conclusion; **cp** complete; **see** shalom; **see** worship.

fulfillment, filling *noun* {*plural* 4394 milluim} {4396 milluah} {4402 milleth} that which has filled; that which is fulfilled; of sacrifices; of stones which fill mountings.

full, fulness *adjective* {4392 male} [1073 gemo] [4134 pleerees] filling; filled full.

fully finish, conclude, finish (off) *verb* {3615 kalah} {3635 kelal} [535 apartismos] to cease; to cause to decease; to bring to an end; **cp** complete.

fulness *noun* [4138 pleeroma] the whole filling; the totality.

fulness, fulfillment *noun* {4395 meleah} that which is brought to a conclusion; an abundance.

fuming *adjective* {2740 charon} {2750 choriy} burning anger; **see** kindle, inflame.

function *noun* {4612 maamad} job; assigned activity.

function, acts *noun* [4234 praxis] something done; a deed.

furl *verb* [4428 ptusso] to roll up; **cp** coil; **cp** unfurl.

furnace, oven *noun* {8574 tannur} a fire pot.

furrow *noun* {6170 arugah} {8525 telem} a furrow, as dug and piled.

fury *noun* {2528 chema} {5678 ebrah} [2372 thumos] an outburst of passion.

fury, poison *noun* {2534 chemah} heat; an outburst of passion as poison.

G

Gabbatha *transliterated name* {1355 gab} [1042 gabbatha] Arch, Bow.

Gabbay *transliterated name* {1373 gabbay} Collective.

Gabri El *transliterated name* {1403 gabriel} [1043 gabrieel] Man of El.

Gacham *transliterated name* {1514 gacham} Flame.

Gacher *transliterated name* {1515 gacher} Lurker.

Gad *transliterated name* {1408, 1410 gad} [1045 gad] Treasure.

Gaddi *transliterated name* {1426 gaddiy} Treasured.

Gadi *transliterated name* {1424 gadiy} Treasured.

Gadi El *transliterated name* {1427 gaddiyel} Treasure of El.

Gadiy *transliterated name* {1425 gadiy} Of Gad; a Yisra Eliy.

gain, greed *noun* {1215 betsa} that which is greedily gained; **see** the verb; **read** Yechezq El 22:27, where the noun and the verb are used together.

gain, greed *verb* {1214 batsa} gaining through greed; **see** the noun.

Gal Ed *transliterated name* {1567 galed} Heap of Witness; a memorial cairn east of the Yarden.

galbanum *transliterated noun* {2464 chelbenah} a gum.

Galiyl *transliterated name* {1551 galiyl} [1056 galilaia] Circle; Corona.

Galiyliy *transliterated name* [1057 galilaios] Of Galiyl.

gall, venom, bitter *noun* {*plural* 4844 merarim} {4845 mererah} {4846 merorah} bile; venom; a bitter herb.

Gamli El *transliterated name* {1583 gamliel} [1059 gamalieel] Reward of El.

Gammadim/warriors *plural transliterated name* {1575 gammadim} Warriors, as grasping instruments.

gangrene *transliterated noun* [1044 gangraina] an ulcer, as gnawing.

gape, gasp *verb* {6473 paar} {6475 patsah} to open the mouth in gasping, or in gaping.

garden *noun* {1588 gan} {1593 gannah} {1594 ginnah} [2779 keepos] a ground for growing edibles and flowers; **cp** paradise.

gardener *noun* [2780 keepouros] one who tends a garden.

garment *noun* {4063 medev} a garment, as measured.

garment (masculine) *noun* {7897 shith} a masculine garment, as being put on.

garrison *verb* {1598 ganan} to hedge round about.

Gath Rimmon *transliterated name* {1667 gathrimmown} Winepress of the Pomegranate.

Gath Shemen *transliterated name* {1660 gath} {8081 shemen} [1068 gethseemanee] Treader of (anointing) Oil.

gather *verb* {622 aseaph} {6908 qabats} {7197 qashash} to bring together; **cp** congregate.

gather, enfold *verb* {3664 kanac} {3673 kenash} to wrap; to collect.

gathering, ingathering *noun* {*plural* 624 acuppim} {625 oceph} {626 acephah} {*plural* 627 acuppah} {628 acpecuph} {6910 qebutsah} a collection of offerings, fruits, people, or learned persons.

gauge *noun* {8506 token} {8508 toknith} a measure of all dimensions; including, but not limited to size, volume, weight.

gauge *verb* {8505 takan} to measure all dimensions; including, but not limited to size, volume, weight.

Gay, valley *transliterated noun* {1516 gay} valley; sometimes transliterated when used in compound names.

Gay Chazi/Valley of the Seer *transliterated name* {1522 gechaziy} Valley of the Seer.

Gay I-laregah/Valley of Slaughter *transliterated name* {1516 gay} {2028 haregah} Valley of Slaughter.

Gay I-linnom/Valley of Burning *name* {1516 gay} {2011 hinnom} [1067 geenna] used figuratively, as a name for the place (or state) of everlasting punishment; may be transliterated, Gay Hinnom.

Gay I-lizzayon/Valley of Vision *transliterated name* {1516 gay} {2384 chizzayown} Valley of Vision.

Gay Melach/Valley of Salt *transliterated name* {1516 gay} {4417 melach} Valley of Salt.

gazelle, Tabitha, Dorcas *noun* {6643 tsebiy} {6646 tsebiyah} [5000 tabitha] a gazelle, as beautiful; Tabitha is the Hellene transliteration of tsebiyah; Dorcas is the Hellene translation of tsebiyah.

Geba *transliterated name* {1387 geba} Hillock.

Gedal Yah *transliterated name* {1436 gedalyah} Greatness of Yah.

Gederothayim *dual transliterated name* {1453 gederothayim} Double Wall.

Gemar Yah *transliterated name* {1587 gemaryah} Consummated of Yah.

genealogize *transliterated verb* {3187 yachas} [1075 genealogeo] literally, to sprout; to sequence by birth.

genealogy *transliterated noun* {3188 yachas} [1076 genealogia] the sequence by birth.

generation *noun* {1755 dor} {1859 dar} a revolution of time.

generation *noun* {*plural* 8435 toledahoth} [1074 genea] descendants; history.

genesis, genetics *transliterated noun* [1078 genesis] beginning; birth.

genos *transliterated noun* [1085 genos] species; kinds.

gerah *transliterated noun* {1626 gerah} a small measure of weight, a coin.

germinate, flourish *verb* {5107 nub} from the root, to germinate; to flourish.

Geshur *transliterated name* {1650 geshuwr} Bridge.

Geshuriy *transliterated name* {1651 geshuwriy} Of Geshur.

Geu El *transliterated name* {1345 geuel} Triumph of El.

ghosts *plural noun* {7496 raphaim} the spirits of departed beings; **cp** spirit.

Giach *transliterated name* {1520 giyach} Fountain.

Giba *transliterated name* {1388 giba} Hill.

Gibah *transliterated name* {1390 gibah} Hillock.

Gibath *transliterated name* {1394 gibath} Hilliness.

Gibathiy *transliterated name* {1395 gibathiy} Of Gibath.

gibe *noun* {8148 sheninah} a snide; a scoff.

Gibon *transliterated name* {1391 gibown} Hilly.

Giboniy *transliterated name* {1393 giboniy} Of Gibon.

Gichon *transliterated name* {1521 gichown} Stream; a river of Paradise.

Gidon *transliterated name* {1439 gidown} [1066 gedeon] Feller; Toppler.

Gidoni *transliterated name* {1441 gidoniy} Felled; Cut Off.

gift *noun* {4976 mattan} {4978 mattena} {4979 mattanah} {4991 mattath} {5379 nisseth} {7862 shay} {8670 teshurah} [1390 doma] that which is voluntarily presented without compensation in return; **note:** in some versions, the word is often inserted without reason, and at other times mistranslated.

Gilad *transliterated name* {1568 gilad} a region east of Yarden.

Giladiy *transliterated name* {1569 giladiy} Of Gilad.

Gilalay *transliterated name* {1562 gilalay} Dungy.

gird *verb* {2296 chagar} {8151 shanas} to bind.

girdle *noun* {2289 chagohr} {2290 chagorah} {4206 maziyach} {4228 machagoreth} a binding, or belt for the waist.

Girgashiy *transliterated name* {1622 girgashiy} [1086 gergesenos] of uncertain derivative; Of Kenaan.

girt *verb* [4024 perizonnumi] to fasten by a girdle, to equip.

Gishpa *transliterated name* {1658 gishpa} of uncertain derivative.

Gittayim *dual transliterated name* {1664 gittayim} Double Winepress.

give *verb* {3051 yahab} {3052, 3053 yehab} [1325 didomi] [1394 dosis].

give, allow *verb* {5414 nathan} {5415 nethan} literally, to give; to give permission.

give over *verb* [325 anadidomi].

give (over) *verb* [1929 epididomi] to surrender.

give (up) (back) *verb* [591 apodidomi] to give away.

giver *noun* [1395 dotees] one who gives.

glean (after) *verb* {3950 laqat} {3953 laqash} to pick up after the harvest.

glean, exploit *verb* {5953 alal} to pick up after; in a good sense, to glean; in a bad sence, to exploit.

gleaning *noun* {3951 leqet} that which is left after the harvest.

glitter, resound *verb* {6670 tsahal} to stand out; in color, or in sound.

glittering *participle* {6668 tsahab} from the root, to glitter.

glorify, glorifying *verb* {8231 shaphar} {8232 shephar} {8235 shiphrah} [1392 doxazo] [1740 endoxazomai] to brighten; to splendor.

glorious, glories *adjective* {8233 shepher} [1741 endoxos] splendorous; praiseworthy.

glory *noun* [1391 doxa] splendor; praise.

glory pavilion *noun* {8237 shaphrur} a canopy of splendor.

glutton, quake, shake *participle* {2151 zalal} to quake; to shake; to eat in excess; **cp** drunkard.

gluttony *noun* {5607 sepheq} overeating; **cp** drunkard.

gnash *verb* [1031 bruko] to grate the teeth in pain or rage.

gnashing *noun* [1030 brugmos] a grating of the teeth.

gnaw *verb* {6207 araq} to eat at; to pain.

gnawing *noun* {7469 reuth} {7475 rayah} a feeding upon, in the sense of desiring.

go, walk, went *verb* {3212 yahlach} literally, to walk.

go (about) (around), surround, turn (about) (around) *verb* {5437 cabab} to border; to revolve; to surround.

goad *verb* {5496 cuth} to prick; to stimulate.

goats (he) *plural noun* {6260 attud} as prepared; as full grown.

GOD see SUMMARY: EL, ELAH, ELI, ELOHAH, ELOHIM, ELOI:

Gog *transliterated name* {1463 gog} [1136 gog] derivative uncertain; an Yisra Eliy; a northern area.

gold, clear *noun* {2091 zahab} literally, yellow shimmer.

LEXICON

Golyath *transliterated name* {1555 golyath} Uncoverer (as in exposing).

Gomer *transliterated name* {1586 gomer} Ceased; Consumated.

good *adjective* [2570 kalos] valuable; praiseworthy.

govern *verb* {8323 sarar} to domineer.

governess *noun* {8282 sarah} the dominant female.

governing *noun* [2231 heegemonia] the time period of governing.

governor *noun* {6346, 6347 pechah} {8269 sar} {8660 tirshatha} [2230 hegemoneuo] [2232 hegemon] [2233 hegeomai] the dominant male; one who governs.

goy, goyim *transliterated noun* {*singular* 1471 goy} {*plural* 1471 goyim} [1484 ethnos] other nations; sometimes includes Yisra Eliy and Yah Hudiy; a transliteration of the Hebrew; a translation of the Hellene.

goyim (as the) *adverb* [1482 ethnikos] [1483 ethnikos] **see** goy, goyim.

grain *noun* {1250 bar} grain of any species.

granary *noun* {4200 mezev} {*plural* 4460 mammegoroth} a building for storing grain.

granary, terror *noun* {4035 megurah} a fright; a place to store grain.

grant *verb* [1433 doreomai] to permit.

grant charism; **see** charism (grant).

grapevines *plural noun* {8291 saruq} vines of grapes.

grass *noun* {2682 chatsir} the lawn of a courtyard.

gratis, gratuitous *adjective,* **gratuitously** *adverb* {2600 chinnam} [77 adapanos] [1432 dorean] free; freely; bestowed freely.

gratuity *noun* [1431 dorea] [1434 doreema] an honorarium.

gray *verb* {7867 siyb} to grow gray; to age.

grayed, grayness *noun* {7869 seyb} {7872 seybah} aged.

graze, tend, attend, befriend *verb* {7462 raah} [5256 hupeereteo] to cause a flock to graze; to tend a flock or to pasture; to befriend, by attending to; **see** attendant; **see** Yah Veh Raah.

great toe, thumb *noun* {931 bohen} literally, large digit.

great, greater, abundant *adjective* {1419 gadol} {7227, 7229 rab}{7260 rabrab} {7690 saggiy} large; older; plentiful.

greaten *adjective* {1432 gadel} large.

greaten, abound *verb* {7235 rabah} {7236 rebah} to be greatened, in any dimension; to increase.

greaten, grow *verb* {1431 gadal} to enlarge.

greatly, increasing, many, mighty, much, very, exceeding *adjective* {7689, 7690 saggiy} superlatively mighty, or large.

greatness, greatnesses, abundance *noun* {1420 gedullah} {1433 godel} {7230 rob} {7238 rebu} increase; magnitude; mighty acts.

greed, gain *noun* {1215 betsa} that which is greedily gained; **see** the verb; **read** Yechezq El 22:27, where the noun and the verb are used together.

greed, gain *verb* {1214 batsa} gaining through greed; **see** the noun.

green *adjective* {7387, 7488 raanan} as flourishing; as prosperous.

green, greens *noun* {3418 yereq} {3419 yareq} as edibles.

green (pale) *adjective* {3420 yeraqon} [5515 chloros] a paleness; of plants from drought, or of people from fright.

griddle *noun* {4227 machabath} a baking pan.

grief *noun* {3015 yagah} {8424 tugah} affliction; oppression.

grieve *verb* {3013 yagah} {5701 agam} to be sad.

grinderteeth *plural noun* {4459 maltaaoth} the teeth that grind; the molars.

grits *plural noun* {7383 riphah} grits, as pounded.

groan, groaning *noun* {5009 neaqah} an audible, nonverbal expressing of grief; **cp** growl; **cp** sigh.

groan, groaning *verb* {5008 naaq} to express an audible, nonverbal utterance expressing grief; **cp** growl; **cp** sigh.

grope, feel *verb* {4959 mashash} from the root, to feel of.

grow, greaten *verb* {1431 gadal} to enlarge.

grow, scatter, spread *verb* {6335 push} [837 auxano] to grow, to enlarge; as in spreading out.

growl *verb* {5098, 5099 naham} {5286 naar} to snarl; **cp** groan.

growling *noun* {5100 nahamah} snarling; **cp** groan.

growth *noun* [838 auxeesis] increase.

growth (spontaneous) *noun* {5599 caphiach} that which grows of itself, sometimes without nurturing.

guard *noun* {4929 mishmar} {4931 mishmereth} {*plural* 8109 shemurah} [5441 phulax] one that protects; the guard of the night.

guard *verb* [1314 diaphulasso] [5442 phulasso] to protect; to obey.

guard, guardhouse *noun* [5438 phulakee] a person or place that guards.

guard, hearing, audience *noun* {4928 mishmaath} an audience; also obedience; a subject.

guard, on guard, regard *verb* {5201 natar} {5202 nater} {5341 natsar} {8104 shamar} {*plural* 8107 shimmurim} {8108 shomrah} {8176 shaar} [5083 tereo] in the sense of protecting from harm, observing observances, obeying misvahs.

guide, sustain *verb* {5095 nahal} literally, to lead with light.

guilt (for the) *noun* {819 ashmah} an offering to Elohim for having guilted; **see** guilt.

guilt, guiltiness *noun* {817 asham} a breach of code; **cp** subject to.

guiltless *adjective* [121 athoos] without guilt.

guilty *adjective* {818 ashem} {2054 vazar} to bear guilt; to have breached.

guilty *verb* {816 asham} to have breached a code.

Gulgoleth *transliterated name* {1538 gulgoleth} [1115 golgotha] Cranium; **cp** cranium.

gullible *adjective* {6612 pethai} seducible.

gullible *noun* {6615 pethayuth} seducible.

gulp *verb* {3886 luwa} to swallow; to be rash.

gulp *verb* {7602 shaaph} to inhale; to gulp.

Gur Baal *transliterated name* {1485 gurbaal} Sojourn of Baal.

gush *verb* {5042 naba} to gush the Spirit, water, words.

H

Haba Yah *transliterated name* {2256 habayah} Hidden of Yah.

Habaqqaq *transliterated name* {2265 chabaqquwq} Embrace.

habergeon *noun* {8302 shiryonah} {8473 tachara} a mesh garment of metal as armour; of linen as woven.

habitation *noun* {4583 maon} {4585 meonah} a habitat; an area in which to abide.

habitation (rest in) *verb* {5115 navah} to abide in rest.

habitation of rest *noun* {5116 navah} a restful abode.

Hachal Yah *transliterated name* {2446 chachalyah} Flushness of Yah.

Hachilah *transliterated name* {2444 chachiylah} Flushness.

Hachmoni *transliterated name* {2453 chachmowniy} Enwisen.

Hadad *transliterated name* {111 adad} {2301 chadad} Sharp.

hades, sheol *noun* {7585 sheol} [86 hades] literally, the unseen; sheol is a transliteration of the Hebrew; hades is a transliteration of the Hellene, which is a translation of the Hebrew; both refer to a temporary abode of the body and soul; there is a progressive distinction of purpose of sheol/hades from its inception to its final state; **read** Yechezq El 31:15–17, 32:18–29, Loukas 16:19–31, Apocalypse 20:13,14; **cp** Psalm 16:10, Acts 2:27.

Hadrach *transliterated name* {2317 chadrach} of uncertain derivative; a Syriaiy deity.

Hagab *transliterated name* {2285 hagab} [13 agabos] Locust.

Hagaba *transliterated name* {2286 chagaba} Locust.

Hagar *transliterated name* {1904 hagar} [28 agar] mother of Yishma El.

Hagariy *transliterated name* {1905 hagriy} Of Hagar.

Haggay *transliterated name* {2292 chaggay} Celebrative.

Hah! *interjection* {1929 hahh} {1930 how} an expression of grief.

hair, hairy *noun* {8177 sear} {8181 saar} {8185 saarah} [2359 thrix, trikos] [5155 trikinos] a filament protruding from the skin; **cp** tresses.

hairy, buck *adjective* {8163 sair} shaggy; also a he goat.

Halach *transliterated name* {2477 chalach} of foreign origin; a region in Ashshur.

halal *noun* [133 ainesis] [136 ainos] [1868 epainos] laud.

halal *transliterated noun* {*plural* 1974 hillul} {4110 mahalal} {8416 tehillah} a hail; a reverent salutation; **cp** selah.

halal *transliterated verb* {1984 halal} to hail; to salute reverently; as in Halalu Yah.

halal *verb* [134 aineo] [1867 epaineo] to laud.

halaled one *transliterated title* {1966 heylel} hailed one; a title of Satan.

Halalu Yah *transliterated verb* {1984 halal} {3050 yah} [239 allelouya] Hail Yah.

Halchul *transliterated name* {2478 chalchuwl} Writhed.

half, mid-, midst *preposition* {2676 chatsoth} {2677 chetsiy} {4275 mechetsah} {4276 machatsith} among; a half of a whole; the middle of.

halloo *verb* [214 alalazo] to sound out loudly.

hallow; see SUMMARY: HOLY, HOLIES, HALLOW:

haloed, haloing *verb* [4034 perilampo] to encircle as with a halo; to shine around.

halve *verb* {2673 chatsah} to separate one whole into two halves.

Hamath *transliterated name* {2574 chamath} Walled.

Hamath Rabbah *transliterated name* {2579 chamathrabbah} Wall of Rabbah (Great).

Hamath Sobah *transliterated name* {2578 chamathtsowbah} Wall of Sobah (Station).

Hamathiy *transliterated name* {2577 chamathiy} Of Hamath.

hammer *verb* {1986 halam} to pound; to strike down.

hammer, quarry *noun* {4717 maqqabah} {4718 maqqebeth} that which is used to pound; a quarry, from which is pounded.

hammerings *plural noun* {4112 mahalummah} poundings of a hammer.

hammock *noun* {4412 maluwnah} a restingplace; **see** lodge.

Hammu El *transliterated name* {2536 chammuwel} Heat of El.

Hamor *transliterated name* {2544 chamor} [1697 emmor] Burro.

hamstring, uproot *verb* {6131, 6132 aqar} to pluck up the root; to cut the tendons.

Hanan El *transliterated name* {2606 chananel} Granted Charism of El.

Hanan Yah *transliterated name* {2608 chananyah} [367 ananias] [452 annas] Granted Charism of Yah.

hand *noun* {3027, 3028 yad} [5495 cheir] the body part below the wrist.

hand toss *verb* {3034 yadah} to toss by hand.

handle *noun* {5325 nitstab} a fixed handle.

handle *verb* {3032 yadad} {7061 qasmats} {7062 qomets} [5496 cheiragogeo] to manipulate with the hands.

handlead *verb* [5497 cheiragogos] to lead by the hand.

handmade *adjective* [5499 cheiropoietos] made by hand.

hands (extend) (wring) *participle* {3029 yeda} {3034 yadah} {8426 todah} to extend hands in praise; to wring hands in sorrow.

handscribing *noun* [5498 cheirographon] that which is scribed by hand.

handsome, beautiful (very) *adjective* {3303 yapheh} {3304 yephehphiyah} {8209 shappir} [5611 horaios] beautiful; timely; flourishing.

hang, suspend *verb* **prone** *participle* {8511 tala} {8518 talah} to suspend.

Hannah *transliterated name* {2584 channah} [451 anna] Endued with Charism.

Hanni El *transliterated name* {2592 channiel} Granted Charism of El.

Hanoch *transliterated name* {2585 chanoch} [1802 enok] Hanukkahed.

hanukkah *transliterated noun* {2597 chanukkah} {2598 chanukkah} [1456 enkainia] a celebration of hallowing.

hanukkah *transliterated verb* {2596 chanuk} [1457 enkainizo] to celebrate a hanukkah.

Haparayim *dual transliterated name* {2663 chapharayim} Double Pit.

happen, befall, fall, fell *verb* {5307 naphal} {5308 nephal} {7136 qarah} to cause to bring about; fall, fall down, fall away; to fell, as in felling timber.

happen, extend *verb* {4291 metah} to extend unto the heavens; to happen upon.

happening, occurrence *noun* {4745 miqreh} that which happens to occur.

Haqupha *transliterated name* {2709 chaquwpha} Crooked.

Har Megiddo *transliterated name* {2022 har} {4023 megiddo} [717 armageddon] Rendezvous Mountain.

Haran *transliterated name* {2771 charan} [5488 charrhan] Parched.

Harashim/engravers *plural transliterated name* {2798 charashiym} Engravers.

harass, disintegrate *verb* {7492 raats} to break in pieces.

harbor *noun* [3040 limeen] a shelter or haven, usually for boats.

Harchas *transliterated name* {2745 charchac} possibly, Shining.

Harchur *transliterated name* {2744 charchuwr} Inflammation.

hard, stern *adjective* {7186 qasheh} [4642 skleeros] harsh; severe.

hard, stern *verb* {7188 qashach} severe.

harden *verb* {7185 qashah} [4645 skleeruno] literally, or figuratively, to become obstinate.

hardheartedness *noun* [4641 skleerokardia] hardness of heart.

hardnaped *adjective* [4644 skleerotrakeelos] obstinate.

Harha Yah *transliterated name* {2736 charayah} Fearing Yah.

harness, bind *verb* {2280 chabash} to tie, or wrap.

harp *noun* {3658 kinnor} an instrument on which to twang.

harpoon, locust, whirring, cymbal *noun* {6767 tselatsal} a clattering, as of a cymbal; a whirring, as of wings; a rattling, as of a harpoon.

harrow *verb* {7702 sadad} to harrow a field.

hart *noun* {354 ayal} a stag; a male of the red deer.

Harum Aph *transliterated name* {2739 charuwmaph} Devoted Nostrils.

Harus *transliterated name* {2743 charuwts} Earnest.

harvest *noun* {7105 qatsir} [2326 therismos] the harvest as clipped.

harvest *verb* {103 agar} [2325 therizo] to ingather.

harvest, shorten, chop, curtail *verb* {7114 qatsar} literally, or figuratively, to cut off.

harvester *noun* [2327 theristees] one that harvests.

Hasad Yah *transliterated name* {2619 chacadyah} Mercy of Yah.

Hasar Addar *transliterated name* {2692 chatsaraddar} Court of Addar.

Hasar Enan *transliterated name* {2704 chatsareynan} Court of Springs.

Hasar Enon *transliterated name* {2703 chatsareynown} Court of Fountains.

Hasar Gaddah *transliterated name* {2693 chatsargaddah} Court of Treasure.

Hasar Hat Tichon *transliterated name* {2694 chatsarhattiychowa} Court of the Middle.

Hasar Maveth *transliterated name* {2700 chatsarmaveth} Court of Death.

Hasar Shual *transliterated name* {2705 chatsarshuwal} Court of the Fox.

Hasar Susah *transliterated name* {2701 chatsarcuwcah} Court of Cavalry.

Hasar Susim *plural transliterated name* {2702 chatsarcuwciym} Court of Horses.

Haserim *plural transliterated name* {2699 chatseriym} (masculine) Courts.

Haseroth *plural transliterated name* {2698 chatserowth} (feminine) Courts.

Haseson Tamar *transliterated name* {2688 chatsetsowntamar} Row of the Palm Tree.

Hashab Yah *transliterated name* {2811 chachabyah} Fabricated of Yah.

Hashabne Yah *transliterated name* {2813 chashabneyah} Machinated of Yah.

Hashbad Danah *transliterated name* {2806 chashbaddanah} Fabricated Rule.

Hashshub *transliterated name* {2815 chashshuwb} Fabricated.

LEXICON

Hasi Ham Menuchiy *transliterated name* {2680 chatsiyhammenachtiy} Of Hasi Ham Menuchoth.

Hasi Ham Menuchoth *plural transliterated name* {2679 chatsiyhammenuchowth} Midst of the Resting Places.

Hasor *transliterated name* {2674 chatsowr} Court.

Hasor Hadattah *transliterated name* {2675 chatsowrchadattah} New Hasor (Court).

haste *noun* {2649 chippazown} hurriedness.

haste, hasten *verb* {2363 chush} {2439 chiysh} {2648 chaphaz} {4116 mahar} to hurry up; to be eager.

hastily chew *verb* {3216 yala} to utter inconsiderately.

hasting, skillful *adjective* {4106 mahir} to hurry along; to be skillful; quick, as skillful.

hasty *adjective* **hastily** *adverb* {4118 maher} hurry; hurriedly.

hate *verb* {8130 sane} {8131 sene} [3404 misseo] to have an intense aversion.

hated *adjective* {8146 sani} disliked intensely.

hateful *adjective* [4767 stugeetos] full of hate.

Hathach *transliterated name* {2047 hathach} of foreign origin; a Persian eunuch.

hatred *noun* {8135 sinah} an intense aversion.

haughtily, high *adverb* {7315 rom} {7317 romah} aloft; proudly.

haughtiness, haughty, height *noun* {7312, 7314 rum} haughty, as in highminded; height, as altitude.

haven *noun* {2348 choph} a place of covering, protection; *see* spare.

Havran *transliterated name* {2362 chavran} Cavernous.

Havvah *transliterated name* {2332 havvah} [2096 Eva] Lifegiver; name of the first female; Adam's woman.

Haza El *transliterated name* {2371 chazael} Seer of El; Seer, as seeing into the future; **cp** prophet.

Haza Yah *transliterated name* {2382 chazayah} Seer of Yah; Seer, as seeing into the future; **cp** prophet.

Hazi El *transliterated name* {2381 haziel} Seer of El; Seer, as seeing into the future; **cp** prophet.

he burro *noun* {2543 chamor} a male burro.

he goat *noun* {8495 tayish} that which butts.

he goats *plural noun* {6260 attud} as prepared; as full grown.

head *noun* [2776 kephalee] the top of the body.

head, first *adjective* {7223 rishon} {7224 rishoniy} head, as at the top; first, as at the beginning.

head, sum *noun* {7217 resh} the top of the body; the sum total.

head, top, beginning, first(s) *noun* {7218 rosh} {7221 rishah} {7225 reshith} {8462 rechillah} the head, in a variety of applications; the head of the body, of time, of the month, of archs.

headpieces *plural noun* {4763 meraashoth} as a headrest.

headships *plural noun* {4761 marashoth} one that heads others.

headstone *noun* {68 eben} {7222 roshah}.

headstruck *verb* [2775 kephalaioo] a strike or wound on the head.

heal *verb* {7495 raphah} [2390 iaomai] to cause to be whole; *see* Yah Veh Raphah.

heal, healed, healthy [*verb* 5198 hugiaino] [*adjective* 5199 hugiees] to cause to be hygenized; to be hygenic; healthy, or healed in body, or in doctrine.

healer *noun* {*plural* 7499 rephuah} [2395 iatros] one who causes another to be whole, healthy; a medicine.

healing *noun* {724 arukah} {4832 marpe} {8644 teruphah} [2386 iama] [2392 iasis] wholeness.

health *noun* {7500 riphuth} the state of wholeness.

heap *noun* {5067 ned} {8510 tel} a mound; as piling up.

heap *noun* {6194 arem} {6652 tsibbur} a pile.

heap *verb* {6192 aram} {6651 tsabar} to pile up; to aggregate.

heap, mortar, chomer *transliterated noun* {2563 chomer} a dry measure as mixed, or heaped.

heaps *noun* {5856 iy} piles of rubble.

hear *verb* {8085 shama} {8086 shema} [191 akouo] to ear.

hearer *noun* [202 akroatees] one that hears.

hearing *noun* {4926 mishmag} that which the ear hears.

hearing, audience, guard *noun* {4928 mishmaath} an audience; also obedience; a subject.

hearing, notoriety, report, fame *noun* {8052 shemuah} {8088 shema} {8089 shoma} [189 akoee] that which is heard; an announcement; a rumor.

hearken *adjective* {7183 qashshab} attending to the ear.

hearken *verb* {238, 239 azan} emphatic of hear.

hearken *verb* {7181 qashab} {7182 qesheb} to attend to the ear.

heart *noun* {3820, 3821 leb} {3824, 3825 lebab} [2588 kardia] the blood pump of the body; symbolically of the center of the will.

hearth *noun* {4018 mebashshelah} a hearth for boiling, or cooking.

heartknowing *adjective* [2589 kardiognostees] knowing the heart.

heat *verb* {2552 chamam} to be, or cause to be hot.

heat, hot *noun* {2527 chom} literally, or figuratively.

heaven, heavens *noun* {*dual* 8064, 8065 shamayim} [3772 ouranos] the lofties; the name of the expanse surrounding the earth; **read** Genesis 1:6-8; in the Old Covenant, the heavens is always dual; in the New Covenant, sometimes singular, sometimes plural.

heavenlies *noun* [2032 epouranios] in the sphere of the heavens.

heavenly *adjective* [3770 ouranios] belonging to, or of the heavens.

heavens (from the) *adverb* [3771 ouranothen].

heaviness, heavy *noun* {3514 kobed} {3517 kebeduth} as in grievous.

heavy, callous *adjective* {3515 kabed} as in grievous; as in thickskinned.

heavy, heaviness *noun* {3514 kobed} {3517 kebeduth} as in grievous.

heavy, honour, callous *verb* {3513 kabed} to esteem; to weigh down; to callous.

Hebraic *transliterated adjective* [1444 hebraikos] [1446 hebrais] [1447 hebraisti] the Hebrew tongue.

Hebrew *transliterated name* {5680, 5681 ibriy} [1445 Hebraios] Of Eber.

hedge *noun* [5418 phragmos] a row of bushes; figuratively, a partition; a separation.

hedge *verb* {5473 cuwq} {7735 sug} {7753 suk} [5418 phragmos] to hedge in; to hem in; to inclose; to plant a row of bushes; to partition; to separate.

heel (restrain the) (trip the) *verb* {6117 aqab} to seize by holding the heel.

heel, heelprint, heel trippers, trip the heel *noun* {6119 aqeb} [4418 pterna] the back of the foot; a print made by the heel; ones that trip the heel by trapping.

Hege *transliterated name* {1896 hege} of Persian origin; a eunuch of Xerxes.

heifer *noun* {5697 eglah} {6510 parah} [1151 damalis] female calf; as being round; as being tame; **cp** calf.

height, haughtiness, haughty *noun* {7312, 7314 rum} haughty, as in highminded; height, as altitude.

height, high *noun* {6967 qomah} the highness.

heir *noun* [2818 kleeronomos] a possessor; one who received by allotment.

Helday *transliterated name* {2469 chelday} Transcient.

Heleph *transliterated name* {2501 cheleph} [256 alphaios] Change; Exchange.

Heleq *transliterated name* {2507 cheleq} Allotment.

Heleq Dam *transliterated name* {2506 cheleq} {1818 dam} [184 akeldama] Allotment of Blood.

Heleqiy *transliterated name* {2516 chelqiy} Of Heleq.

Heles *transliterated name* {2503 chelets} Equipped.

Helqath *transliterated name* {2520 chelqath} Smoothness.

Helgath Has Surim *plural transliterated name* {2521 chelqathhatstsuriym} Smoothness of the Rocks.

Hellas *transliterated name* [1671 hellas] the nation now known as Greece.

Hellene *transliterated name* [1672 hellen] Of Hellas.

Hellenic *transliterated name, adjective* [1673 hellenikos] [1676 hellenisti] the tongue of Hellas.

Hellenist *transliterated name* [1674 hellenis] [1675 hellenistees} Of Hellas.

helmet *noun* {3553 kowbah} as being arched.

help *noun* {5828 ezer} aid.

help *verb* **helper** *participle* {5826 azar} to protect; to aid.

LEXICON

Helqai *transliterated name* {2517 helqay} Allotted.

hemorrhage *noun* [131 haimorroeo] a heavy bleeding.

hemorrhoid, mound *noun* {2914 techor} a rising of earth; a rising by inflamation.

Hephsi Bah *transliterated name* {2657 chephtsiybahh} My Delight is in Her.

herb, herbage, herbs *noun* {6211 asab} {6212 eseb} [3001 lakanon] [5528 chortos] annual seed plants used primarily for healing and seasoning.

herbs *plural noun* {2235 zehrohgim} that which is sown.

heresy *transliterated noun* [139 hairesis] an opposing opinion.

Hereth *transliterated name* {2802 chereth} Forest.

heretical *transliterated adjective* [141 hairetikos] that of heresy.

Hermas *transliterated name* [2057 hermas] Of Hermes.

Hermes *transliterated name* [2060 hermees] An angel of Hellene deities.

Hermogenes *transliterated name* [2061 hermogenees] Of the genes of Hermes; **see** Hermes.

Herod *transliterated name* [2264 heerodees] Hero; Heroic.

Herodias *transliterated name* [2266 heerodias] Of Herod.

Herodion *transliterated name* [2267 heerodion] Of Herod.

Hesro *transliterated name* {2695 chetsrow} Court (inclosure).

Hesron *transliterated name* {2696 chetsrown} [2074 esrom] Courtyard.

Hesroniy *transliterated name* {2697 chetsrowniy} Of Hesron.

heterogenetic inductions *dual noun* {3610 kilayim} crossbreed; mix together.

Heth *transliterated name* {2845 cheth} Terrified.

Hethiy *transliterated name* {2850 chittiy} Of Heth.

hew *verb* {2672 chatsab} to cut or carve; as in lumbering, mining, or quarrying.

hewed, hewn *adjective* {4274 machtseh}.

hexsect *verb* {8338 shawshaw} {8341 shashah} to divide into sixths.

Hezyon *transliterated name* {2383 chezyown} Seer; One Who Foresees.

Hi El *transliterated name* {2419 chiel} Life of El.

Hidday *transliterated name* {1914 hidday} of uncertain derivative.

hidden treasure *noun* {4301 matmon} {*plural* 4362 mikman} {*plural* 4710 mitspunim} {6840 tsaphin} {8226 saphan} a secreted valuable.

Hiddeqel *transliterated name* {2313 chiddeqel} of foreign origin; the Tigris river.

hide *verb* {2244 chaba} {2247 chabah} to withhold from view.

hide, bury *verb* {2934 taman} to hide by covering.

hide, cover, demolish *verb* {5641 sathar} {5642 sethar} to conceal by covering; to demolish and cover over.

hide, treasure *verb* {6845 tsaphan} to hide by covering over; to reserve, or protect.

hiding *noun* {2253 chebon} a withholding from view.

Hierapolis *transliterated name* [2404 hieropolis] Holy City.

hierarch, vapour *noun* {5387 nasi} [747 archeegos] a chief leader; as being first, foremost; also a vapour, as a rising mist.

hierarchy, beginning *noun* [746 arche] chief; origin; as being first, foremost.

high, haughtily *adverb* {7315 rom} {7317 romah} aloft; proudly.

high, height *noun* {4791 marom} {5299 naphah} elevation; elation.

high, height *noun* {6967 qomah} the highness.

high forehead *adjective* {1371 gibbeagh} as a frontal balding.

high forehead *noun* {1372 gabbachath} frontal baldness.

highway *noun* {4546 mecillah} {4547 masluwl} [1327 diexodes] an exitway.

hilarious *noun* [2431 hilaros] merriness; promptness or willingness.

hilarity *adjective* [2432 hilarotees] merry; prompt or willing.

hill *noun* {5316 nephet} a height.

Hillel *transliterated name* {1985 hillel} Halal; **see** halal.

Hilqi Yah *transliterated name* {2518 hilqiyah} Alloted of Yah.

hin *transliterated noun* {1969 hiyn} a unit of liquid measure.

hind leg, leg *noun* {7785 shoq} the leg of a biped; the hind leg of a quadruped.

hindrance *noun* {4622 matsor} an obstacle.

hire *noun* {4909 maskoreth} {7938 seker} {7939 sakar} reward, or return of that earned as a hireling.

hire *verb* {7936 sakar} {8566 tanah} to employ.

hireling *noun* {7916 sakir} {7917 sekirah} [3407 misthios] [3411 misthotos] one that is hired; an employee.

hiss *verb* {659 epha} {8319 sharaq} the sound of a prolonged s; used to show disapproval.

hisser *noun* {660 epheh} {6848 tsepha} that which hisses.

hisses, hissing *noun* {*plural* 8292 sheruqah} {8322 shereqah}.

Hizqi *transliterated name* {2395 chiziqi} Strong.

ho *transliterated particle, interjection* {1945 howy} an interjection of surprise, delight, exultation.

hoarfrost, tankard *noun* {3713 kephor} a covering; hoarfrost, as covering the ground; a tankard, as a covered vessel.

Hodav Yah *transliterated name* {1938, 1939 hodavyah} Majesty of Yah.

Hodev Yah *transliterated name* {1937 howdevah} Majesty of Yah.

Hodi Yah *transliterated name* {1940, 1941 hodiyah} Majesty of Yah.

hoe *noun* {4282 macharesheth} {4576 mader} an instrument for picking; **cp** pick.

hoe, lack, arrange, fail *verb* {5737 adar} to miss having; to arrange a vineyard, as in hoeing.

Hoglah *transliterated name* {2295 choglah} possibly, a Partridge.

holding, holdings *noun* {4943 mesheq} {5232 nekac} {5233 nekec} [*plural* 5224 huparkonta] from the verb, hold: one's possessions including investments.

hole *noun* {3975 meurah} a crevice.

hole *noun* {5357 naqiyq} a boring in the rock.

hollow *noun* {5014 nabab} that which is empty inside.

hollow, palm, paw, sole, bowl *noun* {3709 kaph} {6447 pas} {8168 shoal} a hollow of the hand, foot, paw, or body; also utensils with a hollow.

hollow depressions *plural noun* {8258 sheqararah}.

holocaust *noun* {*plural* 1890 habhabim} {5928 alah} {5930 olah} [*transliteration* 3646 holokautoma] a sacrificial burning.

holocaust, ascent *noun* {5930 olah} an ascent to a higher area; an offering that has been holocausted; **see** holocaust, *verb*.

holocaust, mount, regurgitate, ascend *verb* {5927, 5928 alah} to ascend, as a mountain; to mount an animal; to regurgitate food; to ascend a holocaust; **see** holocaust, *noun*.

holy, holies; see SUMMARY: HOLY, HOLIES, HALLOW:

home (at) *verb* [1736 endeemeo] figuratively, as in the body.

home (away from) *verb* [1553 ekdeemeo] figuratively, as out of the body.

homolies *transliterated noun* [3657 homilia] wording together.

homologize *transliterated verb* [3656 homileo] [3662 homoiazo] to word together.

homosexual *noun* [733 arsenokoitees] sexual desires for one of the same sex.

honour *noun* {3519 kabod} esteem.

honour, heavy, callous *verb* {3513 kabad} to esteem; to weigh down; to callous.

honour, honourable *adjective* {3520 kebuddah} [1784 entimos] one of esteem.

honour, price *noun* [5092 timee] of esteem; of value; money paid.

honour, price *verb* [5091 timao] to esteem; to value.

hoof *noun* {6541 parcah} the horn-like foot of some animals.

hook *noun* {2397 chach} {2443 chakkah} {*dual* 8240 shaphath} as an ornament, or as a grappler.

LEXICON

hook, shield, cold *noun* {6793 tsinnah} coldness, as piercing; a hook, as pointed; a shield, as a prickler.

hook, thorn *noun* {5518 sirah} {*plural* 7165 qeresim} literally, a boiler; a hook; a thorn.

hope *noun* {3689 kecel} {8431 towcheleth} {8615 tiqvah} [1680 elpis] a high expectation.

hope *verb* [1679 elpizo] to fully expect.

hope, cord *noun* {8615 tiqvah} hope, as to hang on to; a cord, to hang on to.

1-lor 1-lag Gidgad *transliterated name* {2735 chorhaggidgad} Hole of the Cleft.

horn *noun* {7161, 7162 qeren} [2768 keras] a bonelike growth on the head of some animals; a music instrument.

1-loronayim *dual transliterated name* {2773 choronayim} Double Hole.

horoscopist *noun* {1895 habar} {2748 chartom} {2749 chartom} one who foretells events by the zodiac.

horrible *adjective* **horribly** *adverb* {8186 shaarurith} of horror.

horror, whirling *noun* {8178 saar} a whirling of a storm; a shuddering of horror.

horse, swallow *noun* {5483 cuc} {5484 cucah} a horse as leaping; a swallow as flitting.

1-losay *transliterated name* {2335 chowzay} Seer, as seeing into the future; **cp** prophet.

1-losha Yah *transliterated name* {1955 hoshayah} Salvation of Yah; **cp** Hoshia Na.

1-loshea *transliterated name* {1954 hoshea} [5617 hosee] Deliverer.

1-loshia Na *transliterated saying* {3467 yasha} {4994 na} [5614 hosanna] Save, we beseech; **see** beseech.

host, hosting *verb* {6633 tsaba} to assemble a host.

host, hosts *noun* **Sabaoth** *transliterated title* {6635 tsebaah *plural* tsabaoth} [3841 pantokrator] [*plural* 4519 sabaoth] of hosts; a vast array of warriors; often compounded with El and with Yah Veh; [4519 sabaoth] is the Hellenic transliteration of sabaoth, only in Romans 9:29, and Yaaqovos 5:4; [3841 pantokrator] is the Hellenic translation of sabaoth, only in 2 Corinthians 6:18, and throughout the Apocalypse; **see** host.

host, swell *verb* {6638 tsabah} to assemble a host; to swell up.

hot [2200 zestos] boiling hot; metaphorically of fervor of mind and zeal.

hot, heat *noun* {2527 chom} literally, or figuratively.

hot springs *plural noun* {3222 yamim}.

hour (half) *noun* [2256 heemiorion] one half of one literal hour.

hour *noun* [5610 hora] a specific period of time; an indefinite period of time, as the hour of Yah Shua's parousia.

house *noun* [3612 oikeema] a house to guard persons.

house, household, housing, bayith, beth *noun* {1004, 1005 bayith, beth} [3613 oikeeteerion] [3614 oikia] [3624 oikos] usually translated house, as in family or dwelling, except when part of a name, as in Beth Abara; **cp** manse; nave; palace; priestal precinct.

house (whole) *noun* [3832 panoiki] with the whole family.

houseguard *noun* [3626 oikouros] one who guards a house.

household *noun* [3609 oikios] [3615 oikiakos] members of a house; domestics, and all who are under the authority of the same householder.

housekeeper *noun* [3610 oiketees] one who keeps house.

housedespotes *masculine noun* [3617 oikodespotes] despotes (head) of the house; **see** despotes.

housedespotes *feminine verb* [3616 oikodespoteo] to be despotes (head) of the house.

hover *verb* {7363 rachaph} to hover over; to brood as a bird over her chicks.

howl (caused us to) *verb* {8437 tolal} to cause to emit a wailing cry.

howl *verb* {3213 yalal} a wailing cry.

howling *adjective* {3214 yelel} a wailing cry.

howling *noun* {3215 yelalah} a wailing cry.

hubris *transliterated noun* [5196 hubris] insolence; arrogance; violence.

hubs *plural noun* {2840 chishshur} as attached; **see** spokes.

human, humanity *noun* {119 adam} {120 adam} {121 adam} [444 anthropos] Adam {121 adam} is the name of the first adami (human) {120 adam}; who is the first anthropo (human) [444 anthropos]; Yah Shua Messiah,

the son of Yah Veh, was born by the Holy Spirit through a woman; He is the son of humanity, not the son of man; a human being consists of at least three attributes: body, soul, spirit.

human, humanly *adjective* [442 anthropinos] as human.

humanity pleaser *noun* [441 anthropareskos] one who tries to please humanity.

humble *adjective* {6035 anav} {6041 aniy} [5011 tapinos] lowered in esteem or status.

humble, humbling, subdue *verb* {3665 kana} {6031 anab} {6033 anah} {6039 enuth} {6800 tsana} [5013 tapino] to cause to bend the knee; to knuckle under; to lower in esteem or status.

humblemindedness *noun* [5012 tapinophrosunee] of humble mind.

humbleness *noun* {6037 anvah} lowered in esteem or status.

humbling, subdue, humble *verb* {3665 kana} {6031 anab} {6033 anah} {6039 enuth} {6800 tsana} [5013 tapino] to cause to bend the knee; to knuckle under; to lower in esteem or status.

humiliation *noun* {6040 oniy} a disesteeming humbling.

humility *noun* {6038 anavah} humbleness.

hunt *verb* {6679 tsud} [2614 katadioko] to lurk for, and hunt down.

hunt, hunter *noun* {6718 tsaid} {6719 tsaad} {6720 tsedah} that which is hunted; one that hunts.

hunthold, lair, lure *noun* {4679 metsadah} {4685 metsodah} {4686 matsudah} a hunter's hideout; a lair; a lure.

1-luqqoq *transliterated name* {2712 chuqqoq} Statute Setter.

1-lur *transliterated name* {2354 chur} White.

hurl, deceive *verb* {7411 ramah} {7412 ramah} to throw; to betray.

hurl, throw, cast *verb* {7993 shalak} to throw out, down, or away.

hurricane *noun* {5492 cuphah} {5591 caar} a violent cyclone.

hurricaned *verb* {5590 caar} to toss.

hurry *verb* {5789 uwsh} to hasten.

hush *verb* {*imperative* 2013 hacah} {2814 chashah} to quiet.

hush, plow *verb* {2790 charash} literally, to scratch; to silence.

hush, subside *verb* {8367 shathaq} from the root, to subside.

1-lushay *transliterated name* {2365 chuwshay} Hasty.

1-lymenaeus *transliterated name* [5211 humenaios] God of Marriage.

hymn *transliterated noun* [5215 humnos] a song of praise.

hymn *transliterated verb* [5214 humneo] to sing in praise.

hyssop *transliterated noun* {231 ezob} [5301 hussopos] an aromatic plant used as a remedy for bruises.

I

I AM *title* {1961 hayah} [1473 ego] [1510 eimi] the eternal existant one; **cp** Yah; **note:** Whenever the scripture presents Yah Veh or Yah Shua as the eternal existant one, the *exeGeses parallel BIBLE* indicates with all capital letters, thus: **I AM**.

Ibsan *transliterated name* {78 ibtsan} Splendid.

ice, crystal, frost *noun* {7140 qerach} as being smooth.

icon (sun) *noun* {2553 chamman} an image of the sun.

icon *transliterated noun* [1504 ikon] a likeness; an image.

idol *transliterated noun* {434, 457 eliyl} {*plural* 1544 gillul} {6091 azab} [1497 idolon] an image or other object of worship.

idol, contorting, contortion *noun* {6089 etseb} {6090 otseb} {6092 atseb} {6093 itstsabon} an earthen vessel; a writhing as in pain; **see** contort *verb*.

idol, worthless *noun* {434 elul} {457 elil} of no worth.

idol of awe *noun* {4656 miphletseth} an idol of reverence.

idol sacrifice *noun* [1494 idolothuton] a sacrifice to an idol. **idolater** *transliterated noun* [1496 idololatrees] an idol worshipper.

idolatrous (downright) *transliterated adjective* [2712 katidolos] utterly idolatrous.

idolatry *transliterated noun* [1495 idolatria] a worship of an idol.

LEXICON — EDC Hebrew / English Bible

idoleon *transliterated noun* [1493 idolion] a place of idol worship.

idolize, contort, form *verb* {6087 atsab} to form; to contort; as in idolizing, to writhe in pain.

if *conjunction, noun* [1487 ei] a condition. **cp** if ever [1437].

if not, unless *participle* {3884 looleh}.

if only, if though, O that *interjection* {3863 luw} as a petition.

if ever, whenever *adverb* [1437 ean] is a compound of [1487 ei] and [302 an] and may express the condition, if; or the opportunity, when. **cp if** [1487].

ignoble *adjective* [36 agenes] without genos.

Ilay *transliterated name* {5866 iylay} Ascended.

image *noun* {6754, 6755 tselem} semblance.

imagery, imagination *noun* {4906 maskiyth} images of stone; images of the imagination.

Immanu El *transliterated name* {6005 immanuel} [1694 emmanoueel] El With Us.

immeasurably *adverb* [280 ametros] without measure; unable to measure.

immoveable *adjective* [277 ametakineetos] not moveable.

immutable *adjective* **immutability** *noun* [276 ametathetos] unchangeable; unchangeability.

impartial *adjective* [87 adiakritos] not critical.

imparting, partaking *verb* [2841 koinoneo] communing and partaking by imparting.

impending, ready, treasured *adjective* {6259, 6264 athud} {6263 athid} prepared; treasured.

impossible *adjective* [418 anendekton] unable to be. **impossible, impotent** *adjective* [101 adunateo] [102 adunatos] not able; without ability.

impoverish *verb* [4433 ptokuo] to be poor.

impoverish *verb* {4134 mowk} to become lean.

impoverish *verb* {7567 rashash} to cause to be poor by demolishing.

impoverish, lack *verb* {7326 rush} verb of poverty; to be destitute; **see** poverty.

impudence *noun* [335 anaidia] insolence.

impudent *adjective* {6277 athaq} in the sense of being carried away.

impure *adjective* [169 akathartos] not pure; **cp** pure.

impurity *noun* [167 akatharsia] [168 akathartees] without purity; **cp** purity.

in law *noun* {2860 chathan} a relative through marriage.

in order to, on account of, so (as) (that) *participle* {4616 maan} {5668 abur} for the purpose of.

inactivate *verb* [2673 katargeo] to render inactive; to abolish.

inadvertent error *noun* {7684 shegagah} unintentional error.

inadvertently err, err inadvertently *verb* {7683 shagag} {7686 shagah} to err unintentionally.

incense *adjective* [2367 thuinos] fragrant.

incense *noun* {6988 qetorah} {7002 qitter} {7004 qetoreth} [2368 thumiama] aromatic fumes; **cp** frankincense.

incense *verb* {4729 miqtar} {6999 qatar} {7002 qitter} {7004 qetoreth} [2370 thumiao] to fume aromatics.

incident, coincidence *noun* {6294 pega} casual impact.

incise *verb* {8295 sarat} to cut the flesh; forbidden by Yah Veh; **cp** circumcise; **cp** eunuchize.

incision *noun* {8296 sareteth} a cutting in the flesh; forbidden by Yah Veh; **cp** circumcision; **cp** eunuchize.

incision, incisor, minings, sickle, trench, decision, incisors *noun* [2699 katatome] mutilators; **cp** circumcise; **cp** eunuchize.

incision, incisor, ore, sickle, trench, decision, decisive *adjective, noun* {2742 charuts} literally, mentally, or soulically, an incising.

inclose, lock, shod, enclose *verb* {5274 naal} {7000 qatar} to fasten; **see** shoe.

inconvenient *adjective* [428 anuthetos] not wellsuited.

incorruptibility *noun* [861 aphtharsia] not decayable.

incorruptible *adjective* [862 aphthartos] not subject to decay.

incorruptible *noun* [90 adiaphthoria] not corrupt.

increase *noun* {6451 piccah} an expansion.

increase *noun* {7679 saga} an increase through growth.

increase *noun, adjective* **increasingly** *adverb* {4766 marbeh} {4767 mirbah} {4768 marbith} an oversupply; an oversupplying.

increase *verb* {7680 sega} {7685 sagah} to increase through growth.

increase, add, again, augment *verb* {3254 yacaph} to add to; to repeat.

increasing, many, mighty, much, very, exceeding, greatly *adjective* {7689, 7690 saggiy} superlatively mighty, or large.

indebted *verb* [3784 ophilo] to be under obligation; to owe.

indeed *adverb* [3689 ontos] in reality; in truth.

indeed, therefore, then *adverb* [686 ara] truly; in point of fact; the idea of drawing a conclusion.

indescribable *adjective* [411 ankdieegeetos] unable to describe; **cp** inexpressible.

indicate, designate *verb* {5567 caman} [322 anadiknumi] to show; to appoint.

indignation *noun* [24 aganakteesis] resentment.

indignify *verb* [23 aganakteo] to resent.

indwell *verb* [1774 enoikeo] to dwell within.

inexcusable *adjective* [379 anapologeetos] without pleadability.

inexhaustible *adjective* [413 anekliptos] unable to explore competely.

inexpressible *adjective* [412 aneklaleetos] [731 arreetos] unable to express; **cp** indescribable.

infant *noun* {5768 olal} [1025 brephos] a young baby; **see** suckling.

inflame, flame *verb* **flaming** *adjective* {3857 lahat} {3859 laham} to blaze; that which is inflamed by fire.

inflame, kindle, scorch *verb* {2734 charah} {2787 charar} {6866 zarab} literally, or soulically, to glow; to blaze up.

inflamed, flamed *adjective* {6867 tsarebeth} [4092 pimpramai] as burning.

ingathering, gathering *noun* {*plural* 624 acuppim} {625 oceph} {626 acephah} {*plural* 627 acuppah} {628 acpecuph} {6910 qebutsah} a collection of offerings, fruits, people, or learned persons.

ingot *noun* {7192 qesitah} an ingot, as weighed and stamped for a coin.

ingraft *verb* [1461 enkentrizo] to cut into for the sake of inserting a scion; to graft in.

inherit *verb* {5157 nachal} [2816 kleeronomeo] [2820 kleero- omai] to come into possession by allotment.

inheritance *noun* {5159 nachalah} [2817 kleeronomia] the acquisition of a possession by allotment.

injure *verb* [91 adikeo] verb of injustice; to be unjust; **see** injustice.

injustice *noun* [92 adikeema] [93 adikia] an injury; **see** unjust. **inkling** *noun* {8102 shemets} a slight emission

inkwell *noun* {7083 qeceth} a container for ink.

inner, inward *adjective* {6442 peniymiy} the inside of; **cp** out, outward.

innermost depths *noun* {4278 mechqar} that which is scrutinized.

innocency *noun* {5356 niqqaon} guiltlessness.

innocent, exonerated *adjective* {5355 naqi} [172 akakos] not guilty.

inopportune *adjective* [170 akaieomai] without opportunity.

inopportunely *adverb* [171 akairos] without opportunity.

inquire precisely *verb* [198 akriboo] to interrogate exactly.

inquire, require, seek, enquire, examine *verb* {1875 darash} to ask; to seek; **cp** beseech.

insane *noun* {7696 shaga} one that raves.

insanity *noun* {7697 shiggaon} a raving.

inscribe, chart *verb* {3789 kathab} {3790 kethab} {3799 katham} [1449 engrapho] to scribe; **see** scribe.

inscribing *noun* {3791, 3792 kethab} {4385 miktab} [1121 gramma] a writing; **cp** scribe.

inscription *noun* {3793 kethobeth} a tattoo on the skin; a caption; **see** superscription.

insignificant *adjective* **lessen** *verb* {6994 qaton} [1642 elattoo] a diminishing in rank or influence.

inspection *noun* {4935 mishiy} to examine thoroughly.

instability *adjective* [181 akatastasia] disorder; **see** unstable.

instead, in stead *participle* {8478 tachath} in lieu of.

instrument *noun* {3627 keliy} including, but not limited to music, ornament, weapon.

insubordinate, unsubjected *adjective* [506 anupotaktos] not subject to; refusing subordination.

integrious *adjective* **integriously** *adverb* {8535 tam} {8549 tamim} in consummate wholeness.

integrious *noun* **consummate, consume** *verb* {8552 tamam} to finish off; to cause to be in consummate wholeness.

integrity *noun* {4974 methom} {8537 tom} {8538 tummah} consummate wholeness.

intent, intention *noun* {6656 tseda} {7454 rea} {7470 reuth} {7476 raon} that which one attends to do; **see** tend.

intently *adverb* [1616 ektenia] [1617 ektenesteron] earnestly.

intercede *verb* [1793 entunkano] to intervene in behalf of.

intercede, reach, encounter *verb* {6293 paga} to impinge.

interest *noun* {4855 mashsha} a loan, interest on a loan; **cp** usuary.

intermarry, in law *verb* {2859 chathan} to contract affinity by marriage.

interpret *verb* {6590 peshar} to give the meaning of; **cp** translate; **note:** dreams are interpreted; tongues are translated.

interpretation *noun* {6591 peshar} {6592 pesher} {6623 pithron} an explanation of the meaning of; **cp** translation; **note:** dreams are interpreted; tongues are translated.

interval *noun* [1292 diasteema] a space between.

intimidate *verb* [1286 diasio] to make timid or fearful.

intoxicant *noun* {7941 shekar} [4608 sikera] that which intoxicates; an intoxicating agent.

intoxicate *verb* {7937 shakar} [3182 methuskomai] [3184 methuo] to drink unto intoxication; to cause intoxication.

intoxicated *adj* {7910 shikkor} one who is intoxicated.

intoxicated, intoxication *noun* {7943 shekar} [3178 methee] the state of being intoxicated.

intoxicator *noun* [3183 methusos] one who intoxicates.

intreat *verb* {6279 athar} to petition with urgency.

intrigue *noun* {2154 zimmah} {2162 zamam} {4209 mezimmah} conspiracy; strategy.

intrigue *verb* {2161 zamam} to conspire, to strategize.

invalidate *verb* [208 akuroo] to unconfirm.

invigoration *noun* {4241 michyah} from the root of enliven; the sustenance of life.

inviolable *adjective* [531 aparabatos] not violated.

invisible *adjective* [517 aoratos] incapable of being seen.

inward, inner *adjective* {6442 peniymiy} the inside of; **cp** out, outward.

inward, middle, midst, within, among *noun* {7130 qereb} {8432 tavek} the nearest part; the center.

inwards *plural noun* {4577, 4578 meah} the innards; the intestines; figuratively, of sympathy, or empathy.

iota *transliterated noun* [2503 iota] the tenth letter of the Hebrew alphabet, and the eighth letter of the Hellenic alphabet; the minutest part.

Iqqesh *transliterated name* {6142 iqqesh} Perverted.

Ir Ham Melach/City of Salt *transliterated name* {5898 iyrhammelach} City of Salt.

Ir Nachash/City of the Serpent *transliterated name* {5904 iyrnachash} City of the Serpent.

iron *noun* {1270 barzel} {6523 parzel} as an ore; as an instrument of cutting.

irreverence *plural noun* [763 asebia] without reverence.

irreverent *adjective* [765 asebees] without reverence.

irreverently *adverb* [764 asebeo] to act without reverence for.

irritate, thunder *verb* {7481 raam} to agitate; to be agitated.

Ish Bosheth *transliterated name* {378 ishbosheth} Man of Shame.

Ish Hod *transliterated name* {379 iyshhowd} Man of Majesty.

Ish Tob *transliterated name* {382 ishtob} Man of Goodness.

island *noun* {336, 339 iy} [3520 nesos] a habitable spot of land.

island howlers *plural noun* {338 eieyim} a howler of an island.

isle *noun* [3519 neesion] a small island.

Ithi El *transliterated name* {384 ithiel} Blithed of El.

Ittay *transliterated name* {863 ittay} Near.

ivory, tooth, tusk, crag *noun* {8127, 8128 shen} {*plural* 8143 shenhabbim} [3599 adous] as being sharp.

Iy Ezer *transliterated name* {372 iyezer} No Help.

Iy Ezeriy *transliterated name* {373 iyezriy} Of Iy Ezer.

Iy Chabod *transliterated name* {350 iychabowd} No Honour.

Iy Thamar *transliterated name* {385 iythamar} Coast of the Palm.

Iy Zebel *transliterated name* {348 iyzebel} [2403 iezabeel] No Residing.

Iye Ha Abarim *plural transliterated name* {5863 iyeyhaabariym} Heaps of the Passers.

Iyim *plural transliterated name* {5864 iyiym} Heaps.

Iyob *transliterated name* {347 iyowb} [2492 iob] Persecuted.

Iyon *transliterated name* {5859 iyown} Heap.

J

Jambres *transliterated name* [2387 iambrees] the meaning uncertain.

jasper *noun* [2393 iaspis] a precious stone of divers colors; thought to be dark green or opalescent.

javelin *noun* {7420 romach} from being hurled.

jaw, cheek *noun* {3895 lechi} the side, or the bottom of the face.

jealous, zealous *adjective* **envy, suspect** *verb* {7065 qana} {7067 qanna} {7072 qannow} to be zealous, as jealous, or envious.

jealousy, suspicion, envy *noun* {7068 qinah} zeal, as jealousy, or envy.

jeering *adjective* {3934 laeg} **see** deride.

jinglers *plural noun* {4698 metsillah} little bells that jingle; **see** cymbals.

join *verb* {2338 chut} literally, to thread together; **see** thread.

join, attach, contrive *verb* {6775 tsamad} to link; to gird; mentally, to contrive.

join, charm *verb* {2266 chabar} literally, to join objects; to cast spells.

join, lend, borrow *verb* {3867 lavah} literally, to entwine; to become wrapped up in, as a borrower, or as a lender.

join, stick, adhere *verb* {1692 dabaq} {1693 debaq} [4347 proskollao] to join one's self to closely; stick to; to remain attached.

joint *noun* {2279 chobereth} {4225 machbereth} {*plural* 4226 mechabberoth} a place of joining.

journey *verb* [3593 hodeuo] [3596 hodoiporeo] [4922 sunodeuo] to travel; **see** sojourn.

journey, way *noun* {1870 derek} a road, as trodden; a walkway; figuratively, the journey of life.

journey, way *noun* {4550 macca} [3597 hodiporia] [3598 hodos] a trip; **see** sojourn.

joy *noun* {4885 masows} from the verb, rejoice.

jubilee *transliterated noun* {3104 yobel} the celebration of the year of jubile; **read** Leviticus 25:10–54, 27:17–24, Yah Shua 6:4—13.

judge, judgment; see SUMMARY: JUDGE, JUDGMENT:

juice *noun* {3955 leshad} {8492 tirosh} as freshly squeezed.

jump *verb* {5539 salad} to leap.

jump for joy *adjective* {5938 alez} {5947 alliyz} a physical expression of praise.

jump for joy *verb* {5937 alaz} {5970 alats} [20 agalliasis] [21 agalliao] to physically express praise.

jumping for joy *noun* {5951 alitsuth} a physical expression of praise.

juniper *noun* {7574 rethem} a species of evergreen shrub.

just, justness, justice, justification; see SUMMARY: JUDGE, JUDGEMENT, JUST:

K

Kaisar *transliterated title* [2541 kaisar] title of the Roman sovereign; the Hellene form for Tsar.

Kaisaria *transliterated name* [2542 kaisaria] Kaisar City.

Kaleb *transliterated name* {3612 kaleb} Dog.

Kaleb Ephrathah *transliterated name* {3613 kalebephrathah} Dog of Fruitbearing.

Kalebiy *transliterated name* {3614 kalebiy} Of Kaleb.

Kalkol *transliterated name* {3633 kalkol} Sustenance.

Kalubay *transliterated name* {3621 keluwbay} Dog.

Kaluhay *transliterated name* {3622 keluwhay} Finished.

kammon *transliterated noun* {3646 kammon} [2951 kuminon] a dill or fennel.

Kaphar Nachum *transliterated name* {3723 kaphar} {5151 nachum} [2584 kapernaoum] Comfort Village.

kapporeth, kapur/atone; see SUMMARY: KAPPORETH: **Karmel/orchard** *transliterated name, noun* {3759 karmel} a planting of fruit trees; an orchard.

Karmeliy *transliterated name* {3761 karmeliy} Of Karmel.

keep, make, serve, do *verb* {5648 abad} in the sense of serving.

Kelach *transliterated name* {3625 kelach} Maturity.

Kenaan *transliterated name* **merchant** *noun* {3667 kenaan} [5477 chanaan] merchant; made to bend the knee; humiliated; name of a person; name of a land.

Kenaanah *transliterated name* {3668 kenaanah} Humiliated.

Kenaaniy *transliterated name* {3669 kenaaniy} [2581 kananitees] [5478 chananaios] Of Kenaan; see Kenaan.

Kenan Yah *transliterated name* {3663 kenanyah} Planted of Yah.

Kepha *transliterated name* {3710 keph} [2786 keephas] Rock; Kepha is the Hellene transliteration of the Hebrew Keph; Petros is the Hellenic translation of Keph; **cp** Petros.

Keran *transliterated name* {3763 keran} of uncertain derivative.

kernal, bundle *noun* {6872 tseror} a package, as a parcel, as a particle.

kernel *noun* {*plural* 6507 perudah} {7666 shabar} {7668 sheber} [2848 kokkos] a seed within a hard shell; grain, as broken into kernels.

kernels (market for) *verb* {7666 shabar} to purchase kernels.

Kesediy, Kesediym *transliterated name* {3679 kacday} {*plural* 3778 kasdiym} {3779 kasday} {5466 chaldaios} Of Kesed.

Kesil *transliterated name* **fool** *noun* {3684 kecil} {5530 sakal} a constellation; stupid, or silly.

key *noun* [2807 klis] an instrument for shutting a lock; figuratively, used to denote power and authority.

Kil Ab *transliterated name* {3609 kilab} Restraint of His Father.

Kilyon *transliterated name* {3630 kilyown} Failing.

kin, kindred *noun* {4129 moda} {4130 modaath} {4138 moledeth} [4772 sungenia] [4773 sungenees] blood relatives.

kind, kinder, kindness {5543 kreestos} as useful; benevolent.

kindle, burn *verb* {3341 yatsah} {5400 nasaq} {6919 qadach} to set on fire; to desolate.

kindle, inflame, scorch *verb* {2734 charah} {2787 charar} {6866 zarab} literally, or soulically, to glow; to blaze up.

kinflesh, flesh *noun* {7607 sheer} {7608 shaarah} flesh, as food; flesh, as near of kin.

Kinneroth *transliterated name* {3672 kinnerowth} [1082 genneesaret] Harpist.

kippurim/atonements; see SUMMARY: KIPPURIM

kiss *noun* {5390 neshiqah} to touch with the lips.

kiss *verb* {5401 nashaq} as attaching; as fastening.

kiss, befriend *verb* {5401 nashaq} [5368 phileo] [5370 phileema] the Hellene is the verb of friend; a soulical expression of fondness; to kiss as a form of attachment; **cp** love; **read** Yahn 21:15-17.

kiss (ardently) *verb* [2705 kataphileo] to kiss earnestly.

Kithlish *transliterated name* {3798 kithliysh} Wall of a Man.

Kittiy *transliterated name* {3794 kittiy} Of Cyprus; an islander.

Kiymah *transliterated noun* {3598 kiymah} the name of a cluster of stars.

Kiyun *transliterated name* {3594 kiyun} [4481 remphan] an idolic statue; the Hellene is an incorrect transliteration of the Hebrew.

knee *noun* {1290, 1291 bereck} [1119 gonu] the joint between the upper and lower leg.

kneel, bless *verb* {1288 barak} {1289 berak} [3107 makarios] to beatify; the Hebrew also means to kneel in adoration.

kneel, knuckle under *verb* {3766 kara} [1120 gonupeteo] to bend the knee; to fall to the knee.

knife, razor, sheath *noun* {8593 taar} a knife, or a razor, as making bare; a sheath, as being bare.

knobs *plural noun* {6497 peqaim} literally, openers.

knock *verb* {5368 neqash} {6375 piq} as in knees knocking.

know *verb* [1097 ginosko] to be aware of facts.

know, acknowledge *verb* [1921 epiginosko] to recognize; to become acquainted with.

know, perceive *verb* {3045 yada} {3046 yeda} [143 aisthanomai] [1492 eido] [5274 hupolambano] to be aware through the senses.

know exactly *verb* [1231 diaginosko] to diagnose.

knower *noun* {3049 yiddoni} one who has the spirit (not necessarily holy) of knowledge; **cp** seer.

knowledge *noun* **knowingly** *adverb* {4093 madda} intelligence; conssciousness.

knowledge, perception *noun* {1843 dehag} {1844 dehgah} {1847 dahgath} [1108 gnosis] an awareness of facts.

known (become) (cause to be) *verb* [319 anagnorizomai] [1107 gnorizo] to cause to become known.

known, acquaintance *noun* [1110 gnostos] one who is known by another.

Kol Hozeh *transliterated name* {3626 kolchozeh} Every Seer.

Kon Yah *transliterated name* {3659 konyah} Established of Yah.

Konan Yah *transliterated name* {3562 konanyah} Established of Yah.

kopur/atonement; see SUMMARY: KOPUR.

kor *transliterated noun* {3734 kor} [2884 koros] a large dry measure.

Kor Ashan *transliterated name* {3565 kowrashan} Furnace of Smoke.

Koresh *transliterated name* {3566, 3567 koresh} a Persian sovereign.

Kush *transliterated name* {3568 kush} the son of Ham; that which is now Ethiopia.

Kushan Rishathaim *dual transliterated name* {3573 kuwshanrishathayim} Kushan of Double Wickedness.

Kushiy *transliterated name* {3569, 3570 kuwshiy} Of Kush.

Kushiyth *transliterated name* {3571 kuwshiyth} a female Kushiy.

Kuth *transliterated name* {3575 kuwth} the meaning uncertain; a province in Ashshur.

L

La El *transliterated name* {3815 lael} Of El.

labor, labour *noun* {3018 yegiya} {3022 yaga} the labor, including the result thereof.

labor, labour *verb* {3021 yaga} to labor; to toil; **see** belabour.

Lachmam *transliterated name* {3903 lachmam} Bread-like.

Lachmi *transliterated name* {3902 lachmiy} Bread.

lack *adjective* {2638 chacer} {2639 checer} {2640 chocer} {4270 machor} without; destitute of.

lack, abate *verb* {2637 chacer} to lack, to lessen; spoken of the prophecy of the Messiah having become flesh; **read** Psalm 8:5.

lack, arrange, fail, hoe *verb* {5737 adar} to miss having; to arrange a vineyard, as in hoeing.

lack, impoverish *verb* {7326 rush} verb of poverty; to be destitute; **see** poverty.

lacking *adverb* {2642 checrohn} deficiency.

lad *noun* {5288, 5289 naar} {5290 noar} {5958 elem} [3816 pais] male child; **cp** lass.

Ladah *transliterated name* {3935 ladah} the meaning uncertain.

Ladan *transliterated name* {3936 ladan} the meaning uncertain.

lade, laden, load, burden *verb* {6006 amas} to load a load; to impose a burden.

lade, lift, load, spare, bear *verb* {5375 nacah} {5376 nesa} to lift, in a variety of applications.

ladhood *noun* {5290 noar} the eon of being a lad.

lady *noun* {1377 gebiyrah} {1404 gebereth} [2959 kuria] feminine of lord.

lair, lure, hunthold *noun* {4679 metsudah} {4685 metsodah} {4686 matsudah} a hunter's hideout; a lair; a lure.

lake *noun* [3041 limnee] an inland body of water, as nearness of a shore.

Lamb (the), lamb *noun* [721 arnion] is used of Christ, as a sacrifice to expiate the sins of men; a small sheep.

lamb (ewe) *noun* {3535 kabsah} {3776 kisbah} a young female sheep.

lamb, lambs *noun* {563 immar} {2922 tela} {2924 taleh} {3532 kebes} {3775 keseb} {7716 seh} [286 amnos] [704 areen] small sheep.

lame *noun* [5560 kolos] limping; as deprived of a foot.

lament *verb* {5091 nahah} {6969 qun} [2354 threeneo] [2360 throeomai] to mourn; to express deep sorrow for.

lamentation *noun* {4553 micped} {5089 noahh} {5092 nehiy} {5093 niyah} {5204 niy} {7015 qinah} [2355 threenos] a mourning.

lamp *noun* {5216 nerah} that which glistens; a light.

land, earth *noun* {772 ara} {776 erets} {778 araq} [1093 gee] the soil; terra frima; **cp** cosmos.

languid *noun* {5889 ayeph} weak; wasted away.

languish *verb* {5888 ayeph} {5969 ulpeh} to weaken.

languish, veil, cover *verb* {5848 ataph} {5968 alaph} to shroud; to cover over; to languish.

Laodicea *transliterated name* [2993 laodikia] Laity of Judgment.

Laodicean *transliterated name* [2994 laodikus] Of Laodicea.

lap *verb* {3952 laqaq} to lick up with the tongue; **cp** lick.

Lappidoth *plural transliterated name* {3941 lappiydowth} Flambeaus.

Laqqum *transliterated name* {3946 laqquwm} possibly, Fortification.

large, broad *noun* {7341 rochab} {7342 rachab} wide; width; roomy.

largess *noun* {5023 nebizbah} liberality; a bounty as owed.

larynx *transliterated noun* [2995 larunx] the body structure housing the vocal cords.

lash *noun* {2250 chabburah} the wound of a lashing or whipping.

lass *noun* {5291 naarah} [3814 paidiskee] female child; **cp** lad.

latter rain *noun* {4456 malqosh} the spring rain.

lattice, net, netting *noun* {7638 sabak} that which is entwined.

laud, soothe *verb* {7623 shabach} {7624 shecach} to extol with words; to smooth it over.

laugh, ridicule, entertain *verb* {6711 tsachaq} {6712 tsechoq} {7832 sechag} to laugh; to laugh at; to laugh at in defiance.

laughingstock *noun* {4890 mischaq} an object of ridicule.

laughter, ridicule *noun* {7814 sechoq} a laugh; a laughing at; a laughing at in defiance.

launder *verb* {3526 kabac} to wash by treading; used only of ceremonial cleansing of clothing after their contamination, except in 2 Shemu El 19:24.

lay, lie (down) *verb* {7901 shakab} to lie down; **see** bed.

lay, repose *verb* [2621 katakimai] to lie down; recline at a meal.

lay waste *verb* {3765 kircem} to despoil.

layer *noun* {5073 nidbak} that which is laid vertically; a stratum.

laying aside *verb* [595 apothesis] to put away; to abandon for a time or permanently.

lead, led *verb* {5148 nachah} to guide; to transport.

leaders, leaderships *plural noun* {6546 parah} persons at the beginning; persons at the front.

leaf, leaves *noun* {5929 aleh} a foliage of a tree.

lean *verb* {8172 shaan} to rely on for support.

leap for joy *verb* {5965 alaz} to exult physically; **cp** jump for joy.

leap, lighten, loose *verb* {5425 nathar} [242 hallomai] to leap; to loosen; to untie.

leap, solidify *verb* {6339 pazaz} to become solid; to spring.

leaper *noun* {1788 dishon} that which leaps.

learn, teach *verb* {3925 lamad} literally, to goad; to disciple; to be discipled; **see** disciple *verb*.

lease *verb* [1554 ekdidomi] to give out; to let out for hire.

leave, let, set, abandon, allow *verb* {3240 yanach} {5203 natash} to allow to be; to allow to be set; to abandon.

leave, release, allow, abandon, forgive, forsake *verb* [863 aphieemi] to send forth.

leave (behind), release, abandon, forsake *verb* {5800 azab} [1459 enkatalipo] to leave behind; in a good sense, to let remain over; in a bad sense, to abandon.

leave off, loose *verb* [447 anieemi] to loosen; to let go of.

leaves *noun* [5444 phullon] as sprouts.

leaving, releasing, abandoning, forsaking *noun* {5805 azubah} a desertion.

lechery *noun* [766 aselgia] unrestrained lust; selfish pleasure.

Lechi *transliterated name* {3896 lechiy} Cheek.

ledge, court *noun* {*plural* 4052 migraah} {5835 azarah} {*plural* 7948 shalab} that which is surrounded; that which surrounds.

left *adjective* {8042 semaliy} leftward.

left *noun* {8040 semol} that which is opposite the right; **cp** right; example: when facing north, the west; most versions erroneously insert the words *hand*, or *side*; we sit not on Yah Shua's right hand, or on his left hand; but at his left, and at his right.

left over, leftovers *noun* {5736 adaph} a surplus.

left *verb* {8041 samal} to pass leftward.

leftover *noun* {5669 abur} that which has been passed over, or kept over.

leg *noun* {3767 kara} {8243 shaq} [4628 skelos] a limb of a human or animal.

leg, hind leg *noun* {7785 shoq} the leg of a biped; the hind leg of a quadruped.

Lekah *transliterated name* {3922 lekah} Walk.

Lemech *transliterated name* {3929 lemech} [2984 lamech] the meaning uncertain.

Lemu El *transliterated name* {3927 lemuel} Of El.

lend, borrow, join *verb* {3867 lavah} literally, to entwine; to become wrapped up in, as a borrower, or as a lender.

lend, loan, ask {7592 shael} {7593 sheel} [154 aiteo] to inquire; to request or demand.

lender *noun* {4874 mashsheh} {5386 neshiy} one to whom another is indebted.

lentiles *plural noun* {5742 adashim} an edible pealike vegetable, usually cooked whole, or ground.

leopard *noun* {5245 nemar} {5246 namer} as being spotted.

leper, leprous *verb* {6879 tsara} to be stricken with leprousy.

leprosy *noun* {6883 tsaraath} a disease of the skin.

Lesha *transliterated name* {3962 lesha} Break Through.

lessen *verb* **insignificant** *adjective* {6994 qaton} [1642 elattoo] a diminishing in rank or influence.

lessen, diminish *verb* {4591 maat} to pare off; to reduce.

lesser, little, pinky, younger, fewer *adjective* {6810 tsaor} {6995 qoten} {6996 qatan} less in age, number, size; little finger.

let (down) (fall) (go) (loose), loose, loosen up, slacken *verb* {7503 raphah} to slacken.

let, set, abandon, allow, leave *verb* {3240 yanach} {5203 natash} to allow to be; to allow to be set; to abandon.

lethek *transliterated noun* {3963 lethek} a dry measure.

level, plain, straight, straightness *noun* {4334 miyshor, *plural* miyshorim} {4339 meyshar} {6160 arabah} plain, as unadorned; as a level land area; as of straight character; as just.

Levi, Leviy, Leviym *transliterated name* {3878 levi} {*plural* 3879, 3881 leviym} [3018 lui] [*plural* 3019 luitees] Attached; Joined; name of a person; of a scion of Yisra El.

leviathan *transliterated noun* {3882 livathan} a wreathed monster.

levir *noun* {2993 yabam} the one who is to levirate.

levirate *verb* {2992 yabam} to impregnate a deceased brother's widow to preserve his seed.

Levitical *transliterated adjective* {3878 levi} [3020 luitikos] of Levi.

libate, pour, anoint *verb* {4886 mashach} {5258 nacak} {5260 necak} {5480 cuwk} {8210 shaphach} [218 alipho] [4689 spendomai] [5548 chrio] symbolic of setting apart by libating (pouring on) of oil; of pouring a molten image.

libated, anointed *noun* {5257 necik} symbolic of one set apart by libating (pouring on) oil.

libation, pouring *noun* {5261 necak} {5262 necek} a pouring of worship; a pouring of images.

liberal, liberty *noun* {1865 derowr} from the root, to move rapidly; freedom.

liberality *noun* [572 haplotees] not restricted in giving, granting, or yielding.

liberate *verb* {2666 chaphash} {7804 shezab} [1659 elutheroo] to release; to free.

liberated *adjective* {2670 chopshiy} [1658 elutheros] released.

liberated *noun* [558 apelutheros] one released.

liberated, burst (open) *adjective* {6359 patir} {6362 patar} burst open, as a flower; liberate, as a person.

liberation *noun* {2667 chophesh} {2668 chuphshah} a releasing.

liberty *adjective* {2669 chophshuth} spoken of a house; possibly in contrast to a guarded house.

lick *verb* {3897 lachak} to lap with the tongue; **cp** lap. **lie (down), lay** *verb* {7901 shakab} to lie down.

lie *verb* {3576 kazab} to deceive.

lie, put, cast *verb* [906 ballo] to throw.

life (physical) *noun* {2424 chayuth} [2222 zoee] the portion of existence following birth and preceding death wherein a being grows, decides, and decays; life is sustained by the soul; **read** Leviticus 17:11; physical life is superceded by eternal life with Yah Veh, or eternal death in the lake of fire.

life, live, lively, living *adjective* {2416, 2417 chay} {2422 chayeh} the Hebrew and Arami adjective is used as a noun in English; **see** live.

lifestyle *noun* [72 agogee] a mode of living.

lift *verb* {7213 raam} to raise.

lift, bear *verb* {5190 natal} {5191 netal} to lift, as to impose; to raise.

lift, load, spare, bear, lade *verb* {5375 nacah} {5376 nesa} to lift, in a variety of applications.

lift, loft, raise, exalt *verb* {7311, 7313 rum} {7318 romam} {7426 ramam} to lift hand, heart, offering, voice; to oath; **see** exalt.

lift, take *verb* [142 airo] to take up; to take away.

lifting, swelling, exalting *noun* {7613 seeth} an elevation; from the verb, lift {5375}.

light *noun* {3974 maor} a luminary.

light, lit *verb* [381 anapto] to light a fire.

lighten, loose, leap *verb* {5425 nathar} [242 hallomai] to leap; to loosen; to untie.

lightning *noun* {1300 baraq} {2385 chaziz} [796 astrapee] a flashing light produced by an atmospheric discharge.

like *adjective* [3664 homoios] similar to.

like, likewise *adverb* [3668 homoios] same as; samewise.

like manner (in) *adverb* [5615 hosautos] in the same way.

likeminded *noun* [3675 homophron] of similar thoughts.

liken, compare *verb* {1819 dahmah} [3666 homoioo] to liken unto; to compare; to resemble; to consider; homoioo is the verb of likeness.

liken, proverbialize *verb* {4911 mashal} to present as a proverb; liken, as being equal; **see** equal.

likeness *noun* {1823 demuwth} {1825 dimyohn} [3665 homoiotees] [3667 homoioma] [3669 homoiosis] resemblance; noun of liken.

likesouled *noun* [2473 isopsuchos] with similar emotions.

lilies *plural noun* [2918 krinon] plants possessing a bell-like blossom.

lily, trumpet *noun* **Shoshanna** *transliterated name* {7799 shoshanna} [4677 sousanna] lily, as a flower, or as an ornament; trumpet, from its lily shaped bell.

limp *verb* {6760 tsala} to limp; as one-sided.

limp, limping *noun* {6761 tsela}.

line *noun* {6957 qav} {6961 qaveh} a line for measuring.

line up, rank, appraise, apprize, arrange, array *verb* {6186 arak} to line up in a row; to put in order.

line, pang, boundary, cord *noun* {2256 chebel} literally, a rope; as a boundary line; as binding one in a pang.

linen *transliterated noun* [3043 linon] a thread or cloth made of flax.

linen (bleached) *noun* [4616 sindon] a cloth or clothing of linen that has been lightened by bleaching.

linen (white) *noun* {948 buwts} [1039 bussinos] [1040 bussos] made of flax.

linen (white), marble (white) *noun* {8336 shesh} white, as bleached.

linger *verb* {4102 mahahh} to question; to hesitate.

lintel *noun* {4947 mashqoph} an overhang.

lion *noun* {3918 layish} a lion, as a crusher, from his destructive blows.

lion (roaring) *noun* {3833 lebia, *plural* lebaim} {7826 shachal} a lion, as a roarer.

lioness (roaring) *noun* {3833 *singular* lebeoth, *plural* lebaoth} a female lion, as the fiercer.

lip (upper) *noun* {8222 sapham} as the place for hair.

lip, edge *noun* {8193 saphah} [5491 kilos] an edge; a shoreline; the physical lip; a language; **cp** tongue.

Liqchi *transliterated name* {3949 liqchiy} Learned.

litra *transliterated noun* [3046 litra] a measured weight.

little *noun* {4705 mitsar} little in size, or significance.

little owl, cup *noun* {3563 kowe} a cup; a little owl, from the cup-like cavity of its eye.

little, petty, shortly, bit, bit by bit, few *adjective, adverb* {4592 meat} diminutive; a few; a little.

little, pinky, younger, fewer, lesser *adjective* {6810 tsaor} {6995 qoten} {6996 qatan} less in age, number, size; little finger.

liturgist *transliterated noun* [3011 litourgos] one who ministers a religious service.

liturgize *transliterated verb* [3000 latruo] [3008 litourgeo] to minister a religious service.

liturgizing *transliterated adjective* [3010 litourgikos] of religious service.

liturgy *transliterated noun* [2999 latria] [3009 litourgia] religious service.

live beings *noun* {2423 cheva} [2226 zoon] as in animal sacrifices in Hebrews 13:11; of irrational blasphemers in 2 Petros 2:12 and Yah Hudah 10; of live beings who worship throughout the Apocalypse; **see** life; **see** live.

live *verb* {2418, 2421 chayah} {2425 chayay} [2198 zao] to live; to enliven; **see** life.

liver *noun* {3516 kabed} the largest glandular organ of the body.

living areas, Havoth *noun* {2333 chavvah} a residential area; **see** life; **see** live.

lizard *noun* {8079 semamith} as being poisonous.

lizard, substance, force *noun* {3581 koach} {3981 maamats} pressure; physical, or intellectual; also a lizard.

Lo Ammi *transliterated name* {3818 loammi} Not My People.

Lo Debar *transliterated name* {3810 lodebar} Not Pastured.

Lo Ruchamah *transliterated name* {3819 loruchamah} Not Mercied.

load *noun* {5385 nesuah} a load, as bearing, or lifting.

load, burden, lade, laden *verb* {6006 amas} to load a load; to impose a burden.

load, spare, bear, lade, lift *verb* {5375 nacah} {5376 nesa} to lift, in a variety of applications.

loan *noun* {4859 mashshaah} a loan; **cp** interest.

loan, lend, ask {7592 shael} {7593 sheel} [154 aiteo] to inquire; to request or demand.

loathe, lothe *verb* {1602 gaal} {2092 zaham} {5354 naqat} {8374 taab} to dislike intensely.

loathe, lothe, cut off *verb* {6962 qut} {6990 qatat} literally, or figuratively, to be cut off.

Lochesh *transliterated name* {3873 lowchesh} Enchanter.

lock *noun* {4514 manul} {4515 manal} a bolt.

lock, shod, enclose, inclose *verb* {5274 naal} {7000 qatar} to fasten; **see** shoe.

locksmith, lockup *noun* {4525 mager} one that makes or services locks; a place of lockup.

locust *noun* [200 akris] as pointed; or as lightning on the top of vegetation.

locust, whirring, cymbal, harpoon *noun* {6767 tselatsal} a clattering, as of a cymbal; a whirring, as of wings; a rattling, as of a harpoon.

Lod *transliterated name* {3850 lod} [3069 ludda] meaning uncertain.

lodge *noun* {4411 malown} a restingplace; **see** hammock.

loft, exalt *verb* {7682 saqab} to lift high.

loft, raise, exalt, lift *verb* {7311, 7313 rum} {7318 romam} {7426 ramam} to lift hand, heart, offering, voice; to oath; **see** exalt.

lofty *participle* {8524 talal} to elevate.

logic *transliterated noun* [3053 logismos] reasoning.

logical *transliterated adjective* [3050 logikos] rational.

logomachize *transliterated verb* [3054 logomakeo] to dispute words.

logomachy *transliterated noun* [3055 logomakia] disputation of words.

loins *noun* {*plural* 2504 chalats} {*dual* 4975 mothen} [*plural* 3751 osphus] the lower parts of the back; symbolically the seat of reproductive vigor.

long, longing *verb* {16 ebeh} to breathe after.

look (around) (at) (away) *verb* {5027 nabat} {8159 shaah} to look at; to regard favorably.

look, appear *verb* {8259 shaqaph} [398 anaphainoman] to become apparent; to gaze; **see** manifest.

lookout *noun* {8260 sheqeph} {*plural* 8261 shaquph} peep hole to look through.

lookout tower *adjective, noun* {969 bachown} a high structure for guarding by looking.

loose, leap, lighten *verb* {5425 nathar} [242 hallomai] to leap; to loosen; to untie.

loose, leave off *verb* [447 anieemi] to loosen; to release.

loose, loosen up, slacken, let (down) (fall) (go) (loose) *verb* {7503 raphah} to slacken.

loose, release *verb* [3089 luo] to set free, unbind.

lop (off) *verb* {7082 qacac} {8456 tazaz} to whack off. **lop** *verb* {5586 caaph} to detwig.

lord *noun* {1376 gebiyr} a dignitary; one who prevails mightily; **cp** lady.

lord, Lord *title*, **LORD** *name*: see SUMMARY ADONAY, ADONI, ADONIM: see SUMMARY YAH, YAH SHUA, YAH VEH.

lordship *noun* [2963 kuriotees] lord over; see lord.

lose *verb* [2210 zeemioo] to sustain damage; to suffer loss.

lose, lost, destroy, destruct *verb* {6 abad} {7 abad} [622 apollumi] to destroy fully.

lose, ruin, vanish, corrupt, destroy, destruct *verb* {6 abad} {7 abad} {8 obed} {7843 shachath} [622 apollumi] [1311 diapthiro] [2704 kataphthiro] [5351 phthiro] to corrupt through decay.

loss, lost *noun* {9 abedah} [2209 zeemia] loss; destruction.

Lot *transliterated name* {3876 lot} [3091 lot] Veiled.

lot *noun* [2819 kleeros] an object used for casting lots; that which is obtained by lot; an allotted portion.

lothing *noun* {1604 goal} intense dislike.

lotuses *plural noun* {6628 tseelim} of the lotus tree, as being slender.

Loukas *transliterated name* [3065 loukas] perhaps Enlightener.

Loukia *transliterated name* [3073 loukia] perhaps Enlightenment.

Loukios *transliterated name* [3066 loukios] perhaps Enlightening.

love *noun* {160 ahabah} [26 agapee] a spiritual caring for, above and beyond that which is soulical, or physical; **cp** friend; **cp** eros.

love *verb* {157 ahab} {*plural* 158 ahab} {*plural* 159 ohab} [25 agapao] to care for spiritually, above and beyond that which is soulical, or physical; **cp** befriend; **cp** eros.

loves, uncle, beloved *noun* {1730 dod} literally, from the root, to boil; an extremely warm caring for; an uncle.

low, lower, lowly *adjective* {8215 shephal} {8217 shaphal} humiliating; depressed.

lower, abase *verb* {8213 shaphel} {8214 shaphel} to humiliate.

lower, topple, descend *verb* {3381 yarad} to go lower; to tip over.

lowland *noun* {8218 shiplah} {8219 shephelah} a depression of land.

lowliness *noun* {8216 shephel} as in humility.

Lubiym *plural transliterated name* {3864 luwbiym} Of the interior of Africa.

Luchith *transliterated name* {3872 luwchiyth} Slab.

Lud *transliterated name* {3865 luwd} the meaning uncertain; the name of two nations.

Ludiy *transliterated name* {3866 luwdiy} Of Lud.

lump *noun* {1690 debelah} that which is pressed together; usually of figs.

lure, hunthold, lair *noun* {4679 metsudah} {4685 metsodah} {4686 matsudah} a hunter's hideout; a lair; a lure.

lurk *noun* {695 ereb} {3993 maarab} {6660 tsediah} a place from which to lie in wait; an ambush.

lurk *verb* {693 arab} {696 oreb} {6658 tsadah} [1747 enedra] [1748 enedreno] [1749 enedron] to lie in wait; to ambush.

lurking *noun* {698 orobah} that which is gained by lying in wait.

Lush *transliterated name* {3889 luwsh} Kneading.

luxuriate, delight *verb* **delicate** *participle* {6026 anag} to be, or to become soft; to delight in; to deride.

luxurious *adjective* **luxury** *noun* {6027 oneg} in luxury.

lyric poem *noun* {7692 shiggayon} a rambling poem.

M

Ma Halal El *transliterated name* {4111 mahalalel} [3121 malaeeel] Halal of El.

Maad Yah *transliterated name* {4573 maadyah} Adorned of Yah.

Maaday *transliterated name* {4572 maaday} Adornment.

Maachah *transliterated name* {4601 maachah} Pinched.

Maachahiy *transliterated name* {4602 maachathiy} Of Maachah.

Maas *transliterated name* {4619 maats} Closure.

Maase Yah *transliterated name* {4641 maaseyah} Work of Yah.

Maaz Yah *transliterated name* {4590 maazyah} Recouped of Yah.

Mach Nadbay *transliterated name* {4367 machnadbay} What is Like a Volunteer?

Machalath *transliterated name* {4258 machalath} Sickness.

Machanayim *dual transliterated name* {4266 machanayim} Double Camp.

Machaneh Dan *transliterated name* {4265 machanehdan} Camp of Dan.

Machath *transliterated name* {4287 machath} Erasure.

Machaviym *plural transliterated name* {4233 machaviym} Of Machaveh.

Machazioth *plural transliterated name* {4238 machaziyowth} Visions.

Machbena *transliterated name* {4343 machbena} Hilly.

Machbeniy *transliterated name* {4344 machbannay} Of Machbena.

Machi *transliterated name* {4352 machiy} Impoverished.

machinate, fabricate *verb, participle* {2803, 2804 chashab} to interpenetate; to contrive; physically, to fabricate; mentally, to machinate.

machination, fabrication *noun* {2808 cheshbohn} {*plural* 2810 chishshabonth} {4284 machashebeth} a contrivance of machine, or mind.

Machir *transliterated name* {4353 machiyr} Sell.

Machiriy *transliterated name* {4354 makchiyriy} Of Machir.

Machlah *transliterated name* {4244 machlah} Sickness.

Machli *transliterated name* {4249 machliy} Sick.

Machliy *transliterated name* {4250 machliy} Of Machli.

Machlon *transliterated name* {4248 machlown} Sick.

Machol *transliterated name* {4235 machowl} Round Dancing.

Machpelah *transliterated name* {4375 machpelah} Double.

Machse Yah *transliterated name* {4271 machceyah} Refuge of Yah.

Maday *transliterated name* {4074, 4075, 4076, 4077 maday} [3370 meedos] a country of central Asia.

madness *participle* {1947 holelah} {1948 holelooth} in the sense of folly.

Magdala *transliterated name* {4026 migdalah} [3093 magdala] Tower.

Magdalene *transliterated name* {4026 migdalah} [3094 magdalene] of Magdala.

Magdi El *transliterated name* {4025 magdiel} Precious of El.

maggot eaten *verb* [4662 skoleekobrotos] eaten by maggots.

maggot *noun* {7415 rimmah} [4663 skoleex] a wormlike larva.

maggot, scarlet *noun* {8438 tolaath} a wormlike larva; scarlet, the color of the maggot.

magi *plural*, **magus** *singular noun* {*plural* 2445 chakkim} {7248 rabmag} [3097 magos] a title of wise ones; and in Acts 13: 6, 8 of sorcerers.

magnificent *adjective* **magnificently** *adverb* [3171 megalos] [3176 megistos] very great.

magnify *verb* [3170 megaluno] to extol; to greaten.

Magog *transliterated name* {4031 magog} [3098 magog] a northern region of prophecy; **read** Yechezq El 38:2, 39:6; **cp** Gog.

Magor Mis Sabib *transliterated name* {4036 magowrmiccabiyb} Terror Round About.

Magpi Ash *transliterated name* {4047 magpiyash} Smiter of Herbage.

Maharay *transliterated name* {4121 maharay} Hasty.

maid *noun* {519 amah} {8198 shiphchah} [1399 doulee] female servant.

maiden *noun* {7361 rachamah} [2877 korasion] an unmarried woman.

maimed *participle* {7038 qalat} [376 anapeeros] castrated; crippled.

maintain, measure, sustain, contain *verb* {3557 kuwl} to keep in.

majesty *noun* **majestic** *adjective* {1925 heder} {1926 hadar} {1927 hadarah} [3168 megaliotees] [3169 megaloprepees] [3172 megalosunee] greatness; splendor.

make, do *verb* {6466 paal} [4160 poieo] to assemble; to practice; to perform; **cp** create.

make, serve, do, keep *verb* {5648 abad} in the sense of serving.

Malachi *transliterated name* {4401 malachiy} Angel.

male *noun* {2138 zakur} {2145 zakar} [730 arreen] the species that fertilizes the female, whether human, animal, or plant.

malice *noun* [2549 kakia] ill will.

Malkam, Milkom *transliterated name* {4445 malkam, milkown} the meaning uncertain; the national idol of the Ammoniy.

Malki El *transliterated name* {4439 malkiyel} Sovereign of El.

Malki Eliy *transliterated name* {4440 malkiyeliy} Of Malki El.

Malki Ram *transliterated name* {4443 malkiyram} Sovereign of Exaltation.

Malki Sedeq *transliterated name* {4442 malkiytsedeq} [3198 melkisedek] Sovereign of Justness; sovereign of the Sadoq priesthood.

Malki Shua *transliterated name* {4444 malkiyshuwa} Sovereign of Salvation.

Malki Yah *transliterated name* {4441 malkiyah} Sovereign of Yah.

mallet *noun* {4650 mephiyts} an instrument that breaks.

Malluch *transliterated name* {4409 malluwch} Reigned.

mammon *transliterated noun* [3126 mammonas] avarice.

mammy *transliterated noun* [3125 mammee] granny.

man *noun* {376 iysh} {582 enosh} {606 enosh} [435 aneer] the human male adult; **cp** woman; **cp** human.

Manachath *transliterated name* {4506 manachath} Rest.

manager *noun* [2012 epitropos] one in charge of.

mandate *noun* {7595 sheela} the decision of an asking.

mandate, census *noun* **specified** *adjective* {4662 miphqad} an enumeration; a designated spot; an order, or command.

mandrake *noun* {1736 duwday} an herb, considered to be aphrodesiac.

maneh *transliterated noun* {4488 maneh} a measure.

manger *noun* {18 ebuwc} a foddering place.

manifest *adjective* [5318 phaneros] apparent.

manifestation *noun* [5321 phanerosis] [5324 phantazomai] an exhibition; a spectacle.

manifestation *noun* {8544 temunah} from species {4327 miyn} a specification.

manifested *verb* [5319 phaneroo] to render apparent.

manifestly *adverb* [5320 phaneros] clearly; openly.

manipulate, capture *verb* {8610 taphas} to manipulate; to seize with the hands; to use without warrant.

manly *adjective* {377 iysh} [407 andrizomai] to behave in manner of a man.

manna *transliterated noun* {4478 man} literally, a whatever.

Manoach *transliterated name* {4495 manowach} Rest.

manse *noun* {1964, 1965 heykal} usually mistranslated temple or palace; a large house for rulers, and also for Yah Veh; **see** tabernacle; **cp** nave; **cp** priestal precinct.

manslayer *noun* [409 androphonos] one who slays man.

mantle (mighty) *noun* {145 eder} {155 adaereth} a covering as symbolic of authority, power.

mantle *noun* {*plural* 4254 mechalatsah} {4594 maateh} {*plural* 4595 maataphah} {4598 meiyl} {*plural* 5622 carbal} [4018 peribolaion] a covering, as easily stripped off.

manure *noun* {1828 domen} **cp** dung.

many, mighty, more, much *adjective* {3524 kabbiyr} vast.

many, mighty, much, very, exceeding, greatly, increasing *adjective* {7689, 7690 saggiy} superlatively mighty, or large.

Maoch *transliterated name* {4582 maowch} Pierced.

Maon *transliterated name* {4584 maown} Habitation.

Maoniym *plural transliterated name* {4586 meuwniy} Of Maon.

Maqas *transliterated name* {4739 maqats} End.

Maqheloth *plural transliterated name* {4722 maqheloth} Congregations.

Maqqedah *transliterated name* {4719 maqqedah} Branded.

maranatha [3134 maran atha] our Adonay comes.

marble (white), linen (white) *noun* {8336 shesh} white, as bleached.

march, anklet *noun* {685 etsadah} {6807 tseadah} a pacing; an ornament of that which paces; an ankle chain.

mare *noun* {7424 rammak} a brood mare.

Mareshah *transliterated name* {4762 mareshah} Summit.

mark, tattoo, brand *verb* {8427, 8428 tavah} to mark an animal; to mark an x or + as a signature of an illiterate, or to mark for protection.

mark, tattoo, brand, etching *noun* {7085 qaaqa} {8420 tab} [5480 karagma] a scratched marking; a mark on animals; an x or a + as a signature of an illiterate; a mark of protection; **read** Yechezq El 9:4–6; **read** Apocalypse 13:16,17, 14:9–11, 15:2, 16:2, 19:20, 20:4; **cp** brand.

market (for) kernels *verb* {7666 shabar} to aquire kernels at the market; **see** kernels.

market *noun* {5801 izzabon} [58 agora] a place to market, to purchase; **see** forum.

market *verb* [59 agorazo] [1805 exagorazo] to market in the sense of purchasing; Yah Shua marketed us to Elohim with His blood; Apocalypse 5:9.

Markos *transliterated name* [3138 markos] the meaning uncertain.

marriage *noun* [1062 gamos] the holy ritual wherein one man and one woman become one flesh.

married, mastered, baal *transliterated noun* {1167 baal} {1169 beel} one who masters; one who is mastered.

marrow *noun* {4221 moach} [3452 muelos] the tissue within the bone; fat.

marrowed *verb* {4229 machah} to fatten.

marry off *verb* [1547 ekgamizo] [1548 ekgamiskomai] to give in marriage.

marry, master, baal *verb* {transliteration 1166 baal} [1060 gameo] [1918 epigambruo] literally, baal means to be mastered; the ritual of one man and one woman becoming one flesh.

marsh, rush *noun* {98 agam} {99 agem} {100 agmone} a stagnant water, or that which grows therefrom.

Martha *transliterated name* [3136 martha] possibly Minister, in the sense of serving.

marvel *noun* {4652 miphlaah} {8540 temahh} a consternation; a miracle; a wonder.

marvel *verb* **marvels** *noun* **marvelous** *adjective* {6381 pala} {6382 pele} {6383 pali} [2295 thauma] [2297 thaumasios] [2298 thaumastos] an amazing miraculous sight.

marvel *verb* {8429 tevahh} {8539 tamahh} [2296 thaumazo] to be in consternation at the miraculous sight of.

Masay *transliterated name* {4640 masay} Workable.

masculine garment *noun* {7897 shith} a masculine garment, as being put on.

Masreqah *transliterated name* {4957 masreqah} Vineyard.

massage *verb* {4799 marach} to soften by rubbing.

Massah *transliterated name* **testing** *noun* {4531 maccah} Testing.

mast *noun* {8650 toren} a pole as a mast.

master *noun* {1397 geber} {1399 gebar} {1400 gebar} {1401 gibbar} one who prevails in power; **cp** mistress.

master *noun* {4756 marah} one that dominates.

master, baal, marry *verb* {transliteration 1166 baal} [1060 gameo] [1918 epigambruo] literally, baal means to be mastered; the ritual of one man and one woman becoming one flesh.

mastered, baal, married *transliterated noun* {1167 baal} {1169 beel} one who masters; one who is mastered.

mataeologist *transliterated noun* [3151 mataiologos] a babbler of words.

mataeology *transliterated noun* [3150 mataiologia] vain, unprofitable discourse or inquiry.

matricide *noun* [3389 meetraloees] mother murder.

matrix *noun* {4866 mishber} [3388 meetra] the mothering organ.

matrix, womb, belly *noun* {990 beten} {1512 gachon} {3770 keres} {4579 meah} {6896 qabab} {6897 qobah} {6898 qubbah} {7356 racham} (7358 rechem) [2836 koilia] the interior; a cavity as hollow; the abdominal cavity; sometimes refers to the womb.

matsah *transliterated noun* {4682 matstsah} [106 azumos] unfermented bakery.

Mattan *transliterated name* {4977 mattan} [3157 matthan] Gift.

Mattatha *transliterated name* [3160 mattatha] form of Gift of Yah.

Mattattah *transliterated name* {4992 mattattah} form of Gift of Yah.

Mattenay *transliterated name* {4982 mattenay} Gift.

Matthaios *transliterated name* [3156 matthaios] form of Gift of Yah.

Matthat *transliterated name* [3158 matthat] form of Gift of Yah.

Matthias *transliterated name* [3159 matthias] form of Gift of Yah.

Mattith Yah *transliterated name* {4993 mattithyah} [3161 mattathias] Gift of Yah.

maturity *noun* {3624 kelach} to be fully finished.

may, might *auxiliary verbs* these auxiliary verbs are not in the manuscripts. So they are either italicised or omitted in the *exeGeses parallel BIBLE*. **cp** shall, should; will, would.

Mayim Meribah/Waters of Strife *plural transliterated name* {4325 mayim, 4809 meriybah} Waters of Strife.

Mayim Nephtoach/Waters of Nephtoach *plural transliterated name* {4325 mayim, 5318 nephtowach} Waters of a Spring; **see** Nephtoach.

Me Hay Yarqon *transliterated name* {4313 meyhayyarqown} Waters of the Pale Green.

Me Zahab *transliterated name* {4314 meyzahab} Waters of Gold.

meadow *noun* {3741 karah} a grassland.

meadow, ram, saddle *noun* {3733 kar} literally, plumpness, as in a full grown lamb; padding, as in a saddle; a meadow for sheep.

measure *noun* {4884 mesurah} a liquid measure.

measure *verb* {4058 madad} to fit; to size up.

measure, measurement, tailoring *noun* {4060 middah} {4067 madown} {*plural* 4461 memadim} size.

measure, sustain, contain, maintain *verb* {3557 kuwl} to keep in.

Mebunnay *transliterated name* {4012 mebunnay} Built Up.

Mechida *transliterated name* {4240 mechiyda} Propound.

Mechir *transliterated name* {4243 mechiyr} Price.

Mecholathiy *transliterated name* {4259 mecholathiy} Of Abel Mecholah.

Mechuya El *transliterated name* {4232 mechuyael} Erased of El.

Medatha *transliterated name* {4099 medatha} the meaning uncertain; the father of Haman.

mediate *verb* [3315 mesituo] to be in the middle of persons, usually to resolve differences.

mediator *noun* [3316 mesitees] one who is in the middle of persons, usually to resolve differences.

meditate *verb* {7742 suwach} {7878 siyach} to muse pensively; to ponder.

meditate, mutter *verb* {1897 hagah} to contemplate upon; to utter in a low voice.

meditation *noun* {1899 hegeh} {1900 haguth} {1901 hagig} {1902 higgayon} {7808 seach} {7879 siyach} {7881 siachah} a pensive musing; a pondering.

meet *verb* {6298 pagash} to contact; **cp** reach.

meet, confront *verb* {7122 qara} {7125 qirah} to encounter.

mega *adjective* [3173 megas] great.

Megiddo *transliterated name* {4023 megiddo, megiddon} Troop; in the New Covenant, it is transliterated with the prefix, Har, as in Armageddon; the Valley of Troops; **read** Apocalypse 16:16.

Mehetab El *transliterated name* {4105 mehetabel} Well—pleased of El.

Mecherahiy *transliterated name* {4382 mecherathiy} Of Mecherah.

Mechonah *transliterated name* {4368 mechonah} Base.

Melech *transliterated name* {4428, 4429 melech} [3124 malchos] [3197 melchi] Sovereign.

melech *transliterated title* {4428 melech} {4430 melech} sovereign.

melt *verb* {4549 macac} to liquify.

melt, dissolve *verb* {4127 muwg} to soften; to dissipate.

melt, dissolve, flow *verb* {4529 masah} to dissolve.

melt, pour *verb* {5413 nathak} to flow; to liquify.

melt away *adjective* {4523 mac} as in pining away.

member *noun* [3196 melos] a body part.

members *noun* {5409 nethach} parts of a body, human or animal.

memorial *noun* {234 azkarah} {2143 zeker} {2146 zikron} [3422 mneemosunon] a remembrance.

memorialize, remember *verb* {2142 zakar} {7876 shayah} [3403 mimeeskomai] [3415 mnaomai] [3421 mneemonuo] [5279 hupomimneesko] an acting of the memory; to hold in remembrance.

Memuchan *transliterated name* {4462 memuwchan} the meaning uncertain; a Persian satrap.

men, few, few men *plural noun* {4962 mathim} **see** Theological Wordbook of the Old Testament, 1263.

men subduers *noun* [405 andrapodistees] they that bring men to their feet.

Menachem *transliterated name* {4505 menachem} Sigh.

Menash Sheh *transliterated name* {4519 menashsheh} [3128 manassees] Forgetful.

Menash Shiy {4520 menashshiy} Of Menash Sheh.

menorah *transliterated noun* {4501 menorah} {5043 nebresha} [3087 luchnia] the holy candelabrum with seven candles.

menstrual *plural adjective* {5708 ed} as of a woman's period.

menstruate *verb* {1738 dahvah} to be sick, as in menstruation; **cp** bleed.

menstruation *adjective* {1739 dahveh} **cp** bleed.

Meonothay *plural transliterated name* {4587 meownothay} Habitations.

Mephi Bosheth *transliterated name* {4648 mephiybosheth} Dispeller of Shame.

Merayah *transliterated name* {4811 merayah} Rebellion.

Merayoth *transliterated name* {4812 merayowth} Rebellions.

merchandise *noun* {4627 maarab} {*plural* 4728 maqqechoth} {4819 markoleth} articles of exchange.

merchandise *noun* {7404 rekullah} that which a merchant peddles.

merchandise *verb*, **palpitate** *verb* **merchant** *participle* {5503 cachar} to peddle; a peddler (pedlar); to merchandise by travelling; to pound.

merchandise, merchant *noun* {5504, 5505 cachar} {5506 cechorah} that which is peddled; a peddler (pedlar).

merchandising *noun* {4536 micchar} buying and selling.

merchant *noun* **Kenaan** *transliterated name* {3667 kenaan} [5477 chanaan] merchant; made to bend the knee; humiliated; name of a person; name of a land.

merchant *noun* {7402 rachal} an itinerant trader; a peddler (pedlar).

mercies *noun* {7356 racham} {*plural* 7356 rachamim} {7359 rechem} [1654 eleeemosunee] compassions; retributions withheld.

merciful, mercied *adjective* {2623 chacid} {7349 rachum} {7362 rachmani} [1655 eleeemon] [3741 hosios] compassionate.

mercifully *adverb* [3743 hosios] compassionately.

mercy *noun* [1656 eleos] [3742 hosiotees] compassion; a retribution withheld.

mercy *noun* {2617 checed} literally, a bowing of the neck in kindness.

mercy *verb* {7355 racham} [1653 eleeo] to give mercy; to be mercied; to give compassion; to withhold retribution. **mercy, shame** *verb* {2616 chaced} literally, to bow the neck in kindness; to reprove.

Meri Baal *transliterated name* {4810 meriybaal} Rebellion of Baal.

Merib Baal *transliterated name* {4807 meribbaal} Strife of Baal. **Meribah** *transliterated name* {4809 meribah} Strife.

Merodach Bel Adoni *transliterated name* {4757 merodachbaladan} a sovereign.

Merodach *transliterated name* {4781 merodach} an idol.

Meshach *transliterated name* {4335, 4336 meyshach} the meaning uncertain; the Babel name of Misha El.

Meshech *transliterated name* {4902 meshech} Sowing.

Meshelem Yah *transliterated name* {4920 meshelemyah} Shalom of Yah.

Meshezab El *transliterated name* {4898 meshezabel} Liberated of El.

Mesoba Yah *transliterated name* {4677 metsobayah} Found of Yah.

Messiah *transliterated title* **anointed** *noun* {4899 mashiach} [5547 christos] anointed; Messiah is a transliteration of the Hebrew mashiach, and a translation of the Hellene christos; Yah Shua Messiah is the Anointed of Yah Veh; **see** Messias; **note:** the *exeGeses parallel BIBLE* indicates whenever Messiah is preceded by the article, as in "the Messiah".

Messianists *title* {4899 mashiach} [5546 kristianos] of the Messiah; all who trust in the Messiah.

Messias *transliterated title* [3323 messias] the Hellene transliteration of the Hebrew, Messiah; **see** Messiah.

metamorphose *transliterated verb* [3339 metamorphoomai] to change from one form to another; only in Matthaios 17:2, Markos 9:2, Romans 12:2, 2 Corinthians 3:18; **see** form; **cp** transfigure.

meteorite *noun* [1356 diopetees] a body which has fallen from the heavens.

Methu Shelach *transliterated name* {4968 methushelach} [3103 mathousala] Man of Security; Man of Spear.

Methusha El *transliterated name* {4967 methushael} Man of El.

Mi Yamin *transliterated name* {4326 miyamin} From the Right.

Mibchar *transliterated name* {4006 mibchar} Choice.

Mibsar *transliterated name* {4014 mibtsar} Fortified.

Michah El *transliterated name* {4317 michahel} [3413 mikaeel] Who is Like unto El; or, O That El.

Michah *transliterated name* {4316, 4318 michah} Who is Like; or, O That.

Michah Yah *transliterated name* {4319 michahuw} {4320 miychayah} {4321 michayehuw} {4322 michayahuw} Who is Like unto Yah; or, O That Yah.

Michal *transliterated name* {4324 michal} Streamlet.

Michmash *transliterated name* {4363 michmash} Stored.

Michmethath *transliterated name* {4366 michmethath} Concealment.

Michri *transliterated name* {4381 michriy} Sell.

mid, middle, pupil *noun* {380 iyshown} literally, the middle man of the eye; the middle of the night.

middle *adjective* {8484 tikon} central.

middle, midst, within, among, inward *noun* {7130 qereb} {8432 tavek} the nearest part; the center.

midheaven *noun* [3321 mesouraneema] in the middle of the heavens.

midnight *noun* [3317 mesonuktion] the moment between two consecutive days.

midst, within, among, inward, middle *noun* {7130 qereb} {8432 tavek} the nearest part; the center.

Midyan *transliterated name* {4080 midyan} [3099 madian] Contentious; a son of Abraham.

Midyaniy, Midyaniym *transliterated name* {4084 midyaniy} {*plural* 4092 medyaniym} Of Midyan.

mid-, midst, half *preposition* {2676 chatsoth} {2677 chetsiy} {4275 mechetsah} {4276 machatsith} among; a half of a whole; the middle of.

Migdal Eder *transliterated name* {4029 migdaleder} Tower of Droves.

Migdal El *transliterated name* {4027 migdalel} Tower of El.

Migdal Gad *transliterated name* {4028 migdalgad} Tower of Troops.

Migdol *transliterated name* **tower** *noun* {4024 migdol} {4026 migdal} tower; a place in Misrayim.

might *noun* {353 eyal} {360 eyaluth} {1369, 1370 geburah} {6108 otsem} {6109 otsmah} {*plural* 6110 atstsumah} [2479 iskus] authority; power.

mighty *noun* {193 uwl} {352 ayil} strong; powerful.

mighty *verb* {142 adar} to be great.

mighty, mighted, mightier, mightily, craunch bone *verb* {6105 atsam} to become mighty; to be powerful; to be numerous; to overpower a bone.

mighty, mightier *adjective* {47 abbiyr} {117 addiyr} {1368 gibbor} {6099 atsum} {8623, 8624 taqqiph} [2478 iskuros] mighty; powerful; **see** Almighty.

mighty, mightily *adverb* {3966 meod} sometimes duple.

mighty, more, much, many *adjective* {3524 kabbiyr} vast.

mighty, much, very, exceeding, greatly, increasing, many *adjective* {7689, 7690 saggiy} superlatively mighty, or large.

mighty diviner *noun* {148 adargazer} mighty prognosticator.

mighty enough *adjective* [2480 iskuo] to have, or exercise force.

mighty mantle *noun* {145 eder} {155 adaereth} a covering as symbolic of authority, power.

mighty oaks *noun* {436 elown} a forest of strong oaks.

migrate *verb* {6813 tsaan} to load up.

Milalay *transliterated name* {4450 milaly} Utter.

Milchah *transliterated name* {4435 milchah} Sovereigness.

millstone (upper), chariot *noun* {4817 merkab} {4818 merkabah} {7393 rekeb} {7396 rikbah} {7398 rekub} a vehicle; a rider; **cp** millstones.

millstones *dual noun* {7347 recheh} an upper and a lower millstone, as used to mill grain.

Min Yamin *transliterated name* {4509 minyamiyn} From the Right.

mina *transliterated noun* [3414 mna] a Latin coin of a hundred weight.

mind *noun* [1271 dianoyia] [1771 ennoia] [1963 epinoia] [3563 nous] that mental facility of the spirit which remembers, and wills.

mingle, mix up, fodder *verb* {1101 balal} to mix together; to mix up; **see** Beli Yaal; **see** comingle.

mingle, pledge, comingle *verb* {6148 arab} to become colateral.

minister *noun* [1249 diakonos] one who serves.

minister *verb* {8120 shemash} {8334 sharath} [1247 kiakoneo] to serve.

ministry *noun* {8335 shareth} [1248 diakonia] the serving; the service.

Miqloth *transliterated name* {4732 miqlowth} Staffs.

Miqne Yah *transliterated name* {4737 miqneyah} Chattel of Yah.

mirage *noun* {8273 sharab} a mirage, as glaring.

Mirmah *transliterated name* {4821 mirmah} Defraud.

mirror *noun* {7209 reiy} that which reflects that which is seen.

Miryam *transliterated name* {4813 miryam} [3137 mariam] Rebellious; the true transliteration of Mary.

miscarriage *noun* {5309 nephel} as having fallen.

mischief *noun* {205 aven} {611 acown} {*plural* 8383 teunim} harm; hurt.

Misha El *transliterated name* {4332, 4333 mishael} Who is Like unto El; or: O That El.

mislead, deceive *verb* {5377 nasha} {7952 shalah} to lead astray; to wrong.

misleading *noun* {7955 shalah} {7960 shaluw} wrongful.

Mispeh *transliterated name* {4708 mitspeh} {4709 mitspah} Watchtower.

Misrayim *transliterated name* {4713 mitsriy} {*dual* 4714 mitsrayim} [124 aiguptios] [125 aiguptos] **note:** Misrayim of the Old Covenant is translated to Egypt in the New Covenant.

Misrephoth Mayim *plural transliterated name* {4956 misrephowthmayim} Calcinations/Cremations of Water.

missile *noun* [956 belos] [1002 bolis] as a spear, or arrow.

mistress *noun* {1404 gebereth} feminine of {1376 gebiyr} {1400 gebar}.

mistress *noun* {7694, 7695 shegal} one that copulates with.

mistress *transliterated title* {1172 baalah} feminine of {1167 baal}.

mistress of mistresses *noun* {7705 shiddah} a woman of the house.

misvah *verb* {6680 tsavah} [1781 entellomai] the Hebrew is from the noun misvah; **see** misvah *noun*.

misvah, *plural* **misvoth** *transliterated noun* {4687 mitsvah} {6673 tsav} [1785 entolee] [1778 entalma] a command; commandments; **see** command *verb*.

Mithqah *transliterated name* {4989 mithqah} Sweetness.

mix verb {4537 macak} as a cocktail.

mix up, fodder, mingle verb {1101 balal} to mix together; to mix up; **see** Beli Yaal; **see** comingle.

mixture noun {4538 mecek} a cocktail.

Moad Yah transliterated name {4153 moadyah} Congregation of Yah.

mock verb {2048 hathal} to deride.

mockers plural noun {2049 hathollim} deriders.

moist adjective {7373 ratob} moist with sap.

moist verb {7372 ratab} to wetten.

moisten, rain verb [1026 breko] to moisten by a shower.

moisten, wet, butler, drink (give), drown verb {8248 shaqah} {8257 shaga} to butler, as a bartender; to drink to quench thirst; to drink unto drowning; to cause to be wet.

moistened, moisture, butlership, drinking noun {4945 mashqeh} to cause to be moistened, or drunken.

moisture, drink noun {8249 shiqquv} {8250 shiqquw} a beverage.

molars plural noun {4973 methalleah} literally, biters.

mold verb [4111 plasso] to form by molding.

molded noun [4110 plasma] the product that was formed by molding.

Molech transliterated name {4432 molech} Sovereign; an Ammoniy deity.

Molecheth transliterated name {4447 molecheth} Reigned.

molten noun {4541 maccekah} that which has been cast by a molten metal.

momentary noun [3910 parautika] at that very instant.

mongrel noun {4464 mamzer} one born of parents of different races; **cp** bastard.

mongrel, woof noun {6154 ereb} a crossed race of persons; the transverse threads.

monolith, stump noun {4676 matstsebah} {4678 matstsebeth} a singular block of stone.

monster noun {8565 tan} {plural 8568 tannoth} {8577 tannim} [2785 keetos] a malformed and/or huge animal.

month noun {3393 yerach} [3376 men] the period between two new moons; **see** month, moon (new).

month, moon (new) noun {2320 chodesh} [3561 noumeenia] a period of time from which events were scheduled; **see** month.

monument noun {6725 tsiun} any substance to memorialize.

moon (full) noun {3677 keceh} its festival.

moon, month noun {3391 yerach} {3393 yerach} {3394 yareach} {3842 lebanah} [4582 seleenee] the sign in the heavens by which seasons are measured; the body in the heavens which reflects the sun; known as the lesser light; **cp** new moon.

Mordechay transliterated name {4782 mordechay} meaning uncertain.

more, much, many, mighty adjective {3524 kabbiyr} vast.

Moreshethiy transliterated name {4183 morashiy} Of Moresheth Gath.

Mori Yah transliterated name {4179 moriyah} Seen of Yah.

morning (early) noun {1242 boqer} [4404 proi] [4407 proinos] the first part of daylight.

morology transliterated noun [3473 morologia] silly words.

morphosis transliterated noun [3446 morphosis] form; figure; **cp** metamorphose.

morrow (the), tomorrow noun {4279 machar} {4283 mochorath} [839 aurion] [1887 epaurion] the following day.

morsel noun {6595 path} a bit.

mortal adjective [2349 thneetos] subject to death.

mortar, chomer, heap transliterated noun {2563 chomer} a dry measure as mixed, or heaped.

Mosa transliterated name {4162 mowsta} Proceeding.

Mosah transliterated name {4681 motsah} Wrung.

Moserah, plural **Moseroth** transliterated name {4149 mowcerah, mocerowth} Band(s).

Mosheh transliterated name {4872, 4873 mosheh} [3475 moseus, moses, mouses] Drawn (as from the water).

moth noun {5580 cac} {6211 ash} an insect known for eating cloth.

motheaten verb {6244 ashesh} eaten by moths.

mother *noun* {517 em} [3384 meeteer] a female parent.

mother in law *noun* {2545 chamoth} [3994 penthera] the mother of a man's woman, or a woman's man.

motherless *noun* [282 ameetor] without mother; possibly, unmothered.

moulding *noun* {2213 zer} a border.

mound, hemorrhoid *noun* {2914 techor} a rising of earth; a rising by inflamation.

mound, mount *noun* {5550 solelah} as raised.

mount, mountain *noun* {2022 har} {2042 harar} [3714 orinos] [3735 oros] a high landmass.

mount, regurgitate, ascend, holocaust *verb* {5927, 5928 alah} to ascend, as a mountain; to mount an animal; to regurgitate food; to ascend a holocaust; **see** holocaust, *noun*.

Mount El *noun, name* {2025 harel} Mount of El.

mourn *verb* {578 anah} to lament through groaning.

mourning *noun* {8386 taaniyah} a lamenting.

mouth *noun* {6310 peh} {6433 pum} [4750 stoma] in the sense of edge.

much, many, mighty, more *adjective* {3524 kabbiyr} vast.

much, very, exceeding, greatly, increasing, many, mighty *adjective* {7689, 7690 saggiy} superlatively mighty, or large.

muffle *verb* {3813 lahat}.

Multitude of Gog *noun, name* {1996 hamongog} Multitude of Gog.

murder *noun* {7524 retsach} the killing of a person with malice aforethought; **cp** slaughter.

murder *verb* {7523 ratsach} to kill of a person with malice aforethought; **cp** slaughter.

murderer *noun* [443 anthropoktonos] one that kills a person with malice aforethought; **cp** slaughter.

murmurings *plural noun* {8519 telunnoth} grumblings.

mustard *noun* [4615 sinapi] a plant which grows from a very small seed to a remarkable size; refers to a small quantity which becomes great.

muster, oversee, visit *verb* {6485 paqad} to visit with friendly intent, to oversee; or to visit with hostile intent, to take care of; to muster for display.

muster, overseer, oversight, visitation *noun* {6486 pequddah} a visit with friendly intent, to oversee; or a visit with hostile intent, to take care of; a muster for display.

mute *noun* {482 elem} a silenced one.

mute, tie *verb* {481 alam} as in silencing by tying the tongue, or lips; tying bundles.

Muth, Muth Labben *transliterated name* {4192 muwth, muwthlabben} To Die for the Son.

mutilator *verb* [2699 katatomee] cutter; one who would go beyond circumcision.

mutter, meditate *verb* {1897 hagah} to contemplate upon; to utter in a low voice.

muzzle *noun* {4269 machcown} a muzzle.

myriads *noun* {7233 rebabah} {*plural* 7239 ribboth} {7240 ribbo} [3461 murias] [3463 murioi] an innumerable abundance; the number of ten thousand.

myriads (abound by the) *verb* {7231 rabab} to multiply by the myriads.

myrrh (tincture of) *transliterated noun* [4669 smurnizomai] a myrrh concentrate.

myrrh *transliterated noun* {3910 lot} {4753 mowr} [3464 muron] [4666 smurna] an anointing ointment.

myrrh *transliterated verb* [3462 murizo] to anoint with myrrh. **mystery** *noun* {7328 raz} that which is hidden.

myth *transliterated noun* [3454 muthos] a religious legend.

N

Naaman *transliterated name* {5283 naaman} [3497 neeman] Pleasant.

Naamaniy *transliterated name* {5280 naamiy} Of Naaman.

Naarah *transliterated name* {5292 naarah} Lass.

Naaray *transliterated name* {5293 naaray} Youthful.

Nachali El *transliterated name* {5160 nachaliyel} Wadi of El; **see** wadi.

Nacham *transliterated name* {5163 nacham} Consolation.

Nachamani *transliterated name* {5167 nachamaniy} Consolatory.

Nachash *transliterated name* {5176 nachash} Serpent.

Nachath *transliterated name* {5184 nachath} Rest.

LEXICON

Nachbi *transliterated name* {5147 nachbiy} Hide.

Nachor *transliterated name* {5152 nachowr} [3493 nachor] Snorer.

Nachray *transliterated name* {5171 nachray} Snorter.

Nachshon *transliterated name* {5177 nachshon} [3476 naasson] Prognosticator.

Nachum *transliterated name* {5151 nachuwm} [3486 naoum] Comfortable.

nail *noun* {6856 tsipporen} the nail of a finger; a nail, as being pointy, for scratching.

Nain *transliterated name* [3484 nain] Home.

naked *adjective* [1131 gumnos] unclothed; scantily or poorly clothed.

naked, nakedness *adjective* {5903 eyrom} {6174 arom} nudity; partial, or total.

naked, nakedness *noun* {4626 maar} {*plural* 4636 maaromim} {6172 ervah} {6173 arvah} that which is stripped bare.

naked, nude *noun* {6181 eryah} stripped.

naked (be) *verb* [1130 gumneetuomai] to be stripped; to be scantily clothed.

naked tree *noun* {6176 arar} a tree, as stripped.

nakedness *noun* [1132 gumnotees] want of clothing, nakedness of the body.

nakednesses *noun* {*plural* 6169 arahoth} plots of land that are stripped bare.

Nachon *transliterated name* {5225 nachown} Prepared.

name *noun* {8034 shem} [3686 onoma] [5122 tounoma] a title by which a person is distinguished.

name *verb* [3687 onomazo] to bestow a title.

Naphtali *transliterated name* {5321 naphtali} [3508 nephthalim] Wrestler.

Naphtuchim *transliterated name* {5320 naphtuchiym} the meaning uncertain.

Narcissus *transliterated name* [3488 narkissos] Erotic.

nard *transliterated noun* {5373 nerd} [3487 nardos] an aromatic anointing oinment.

narrowness *noun* {4164 muwtsaq} a pressing in.

narrows, straits, confines, distress *noun* {4689 matsoq} {4691 metsuqah} {4712 metsar} from the root, belly; a narrow place; a confinement.

Nathan *transliterated name* {5416 nathan} [3481 nathan] Given.

Nathan Melech *transliterated name* {5419 nathanmelech} Given of the Sovereign.

nation *noun* {523, 524 ummah} {3816 leom} a people united by a government; **cp** goyim; **cp** people.

nature *noun* [5449 phusis] the natural according to physics.

naught, aught *noun* {3972 meumah} [3361 me] [3762 oudeis, oudemia, ouden] nil; several words, and combinations of words are used to indicate nil; these include the double negative, not aught, which the *exeGeses parallel BIBLE* renders as naught.

nave; see SUMMARY: HOLY, HOLIES, HALLOW:

navel *noun* {8270 shor} {8306 sharir} {8326 shorer} the umbilicus of the body.

navesweeper *noun* [3511 neokoros] one who sweeps the nave.

Navith *transliterated name* {5121 naviyth} Habitation.

Nazarene *transliterated name* [3479 nazareenos] [3480 nazoraios] of Nazareth; **cp** Separatist.

Nazareth *transliterated name* [3478 nazareth] derivation uncertain; not to be confused with Old Covenant separatist vow of separation.

Neapolis *transliterated name* [3496 neapolis] New City.

near, nearby, neighbor, nigh *adjective* {7138 qarob} near in place, kindred, or time.

Near Yah *transliterated name* {5294 nearyah} Lad of Yah.

Nebayoth *plural transliterated name* {5032 nebayowth} Fruitfulnesses.

Nebukadnets Tsar *transliterated name* {5019, 5020 nebukadnetstsar} a Tsar of Babel.

Nebushazban *transliterated name* {5021 nebuwshazban} the meaning uncertain; Nebukadnets Tsar's chief eunuch.

necessary, dependant *adjective* [316 anankaios] needed; depend upon.

necessity, need *noun* [318 anankee] distress.

Nechem Yah *transliterated name* {5166 nechemyah} Consolation of Yah.

Nechlamiy *transliterated name* {5161 nechelamiy} Dreamed; Of Nechlam.

Nechum *transliterated name* {5149 nechuwm} Sighed Over.

Nechushta *transliterated name* {5179 nechushta} Copper.

Nechushtan *transliterated name* {5180 nechushtan} Copper.

neck *noun* {1621 gargeroth} {4665 miphreketh} {6203 oreph} {6676, 6677 tsavvar} [5137 trakeelos] the part connecting the head to the body.

necklace *noun* {2002 hamniyk} necklace or neck chain.

necromancer *noun* {178 ob} {*plural* 328 atim} one who communicates with the dead.

necrosis *transliterated noun* [3500 nekrosis] decease.

necro-, deathify, die *verb* {4191 muth} [2289 thanatoo] to die; to put to death.

Nedab Yah *transliterated name* {5072 nedabyah} Volunteer of Yah.

need, necessity *noun* [318 anankee] distress.

needy *noun* {34 ebyon} one who lacks necessities; **cp** poor.

Nei El *transliterated name* {5272 neiel} Wanderer of El.

neighbor, nigh, near, nearby *adjective* {7138 qarob} near in place, kindred, or time.

neighbour *noun* [1069 geton] [4139 plesion] one who dwells nearby; a fellow.

neighing *noun* {*plural* 4684 mitshalah} a whinnying; a whining.

Necho *transliterated name* {5224 nechow} the meaning uncertain; a Misrayim sovereign.

Nemu El *transliterated name* {5241 nemuel} (at the) Right of El.

Nemu Eliy *transliterated name* {5242 nemuweliy} Of Nemu El.

neophyte *transliterated noun* [3504 neophutos] a new convert; a proselyte.

Nephilim *transliterated plural name* {5303 nephilim} literally, Fellers; they who cause others to be felled; that is, to be toppled; **see** fall.

Nephisim *plural transliterated name* {5300 nephuwsheciym} {5304 nephiyciym} Expansions.

Nephtoach *transliterated name* {5318 nephtowach} Opened, as a spring.

Neqeb *transliterated name* {5346 neqeb} Mounting.

Nergal Shareser *transliterated name* {5371 nergalsharetser} the meaning uncertain.

Neri Yah *transliterated name* {5374 neriyah} [3518 neeri] Light of Yah; Overseen of Yah.

Nesiach *transliterated name* {5335 netsiyach} Conspicuous.

Nesib *transliterated name* {5334 netsiyb} Station.

nest *noun* {7064 qen} a nest, as fixed; figuratively, a dwelling.

nest *verb* {7077 qanan} to build, or occupy a nest.

net (drag) *noun* {4365 mikmereth} [293 amphibleestron] a net that is dragged.

net *noun* {4346 makbar} {4364 makmar} {4365 mikmereth} {7568 resheth} {*plural* 7636 shabie} that which is woven; a hair net; **cp** screen.

net, netting, lattice *noun* {7638 sabak} that which is intwined.

Nethan El *transliterated name* {5417 nethanel} [3482 nathanaeel] Given of El.

Nethan Yah *transliterated name* {5418 nethanyah} Given of Yah.

nether, nethermost *adjective* {8481 tachton} {8482 tachti} the lower, or lowest.

Nethinim *transliterated plural noun* {5411 nathinim} {5412 nethinim} those devoted exclusively to holy worship.

new, fresh, anew *adjectice* [2537 kainos] new, especially in freshness, of a new kind.

new, newness *adjective* {2319 chadash} **see** renew, renovate. **new moon, month** *noun* {2320 chodesh} [3561 noumeenia] a period of time from which events were scheduled; **see** month.

newness *noun* [2538 kainotees] in a new state.

Nibchaz *transliterated name* {5026 nibchaz} the meaning uncertain; a deity of the Avviy.

Nicodemus *transliterated name* [3530 nikodemos] Public Triumphant.

Nicolaitees *transliterated name* [3531 nikolaitees] Laity Triumphant.

Nicolas *transliterated name* [3532 nikolainos] Triumphant.

Nicopolis *transliterated name* [3533 nikopolis] Triumphant City.

Niger *transliterated name* [3526 niger] Black.

nigh, near, nearby, neighbor *adjective* {7138 qarob} near in place, kindred, or time.

night *noun* {3915 layil} {3916 leyleyla} [3571 nux] literally, a twisting away (of the light); the part of day from sunset to sunrise.

nightday *noun* [3574 nuktheemeron] a full day; **cp** day.

Nineveh *transliterated name* {5210 nineveh} [3535 nineui] meaning uncertain.

Nineviy *transliterated name* [3536 ninuitees] of Nineveh.

nip, bite, blink *verb* {7169 qarats} a pinch; of the lids, of the lips, of the hands as forming.

nipple *noun* {1717 dad} the small protuberance of a breast or udder.

Nisroch *transliterated name* {5268 nisroch} the meaning uncertain; a Babel idol.

Nissi *transliterated title* **pole, sail, ensign** *noun* {5251 nec} an ensign; the pole of an ensign; part of the title, Yah Veh Nissi, which means, Yah Veh Ensign.

nitre *nun* {5427 nether} named from its effervescing acid.

Noach *transliterated name* {5146 noach} [3575 noe] Rest; the patriarch of the flood.

Noad Yah *transliterated name* {5129 noadyah} Congregated (Betrothed) of Yah.

Noah *transliterated name* {5270 noah} Movement; a Yisra Eliyth.

Nobach *transliterated name* {5025 nobach} Bark.

Nobay *transliterated name* {5109 nowbay} Fruitful.

noble *noun* {7261 rabreban} a magnate.

nobles *plural noun* {2715 chor} persons of eminent character.

nobles *plural noun* {6579 partam} grandees.

Nochah *transliterated name* {5119 nowchah} Rest.

nocturnal spectre *noun* {3917 lilith} a night spectre.

nod, nodding, nodded *verb* [1769 enneos] [1770 enneuo] [2656 kataneuo] [3506 neuo] to signal with the head.

Nogah *transliterated name* {5052 nogahh} [3477 naggai] Brilliant.

noncircumcised *verb* [564 aperitmeetos] not circumcised; **cp** circumcised; **cp** decircumcised.

nonpseudo *adjective* [893 apseudees] not phony; **cp** pseudo.

Noomi *transliterated name* {5281 noomiy} Pleasantness.

noon, window *dual noun* {6672 tsohar} double light, as a window; double light, as noon.

noose *noun* [1029 brokos] figuratively, a snare.

noose *noun* {5364 niqpah} a rope, as encircling.

Nophach {5302 nophach} Gust.

north, northerly, northern, northward, north quarter *noun* {6828 tsaphon} literally, of the dark; used only of the north.

northern *adjective* {6830 tsephoniy} of the north.

nosering *noun* {5141 nezem} meaning uncertain; a circular ornament.

nostril, snout, wrath *noun* {639 aph} {*plural* 5156 nechirim} [3709 orgee] the snorter, as in expressing wrath; **see** snorting.

nothing; **see** naught, nought, aught, ought.

notice, recognize, discern, distinguish, estrange *verb* {5234 nakar} to acknowledge; to scrutinize; to distinguish between; to ignore, hence to be estranged.

notoriety, report, fame, hearing *noun* {8052 shemuah} {8088 shema} {8089 shoma} [189 akoee] that which is heard; an announcement; a rumor.

nourish *verb* {2109, 2110 zuwn} to plumpen.

nourishment *noun* {4361 makkoleth} eats.

number, appoint *verb* {4483 menah} {4484 mene} {4487 manah} to enumerate.

Nun *transliterated name* {5126 nun} Perpetual.

nurture *verb* [397 anatrepho] soulically, and mentally, to nourish.

Nymphas *transliterated name* [3564 numphas] Veiled Oblation; a mythical Hellene goddess.

O

O, Oh *interjection* {994 biy} in the sense of pleading.

O that, if only, if though *interjection* {3863 luw} as a petition.

O that, whoever *participle pronoun* {4310 miy}.

oak *noun* {8410 tidhar} a species of tree.

oar, scourge *noun* {7885 shait} a whip; a paddle.

oath *noun* {7621 shebuah} [3727 horkos] literally, a seven; figuratively, the number of completion; a solemn affirmation.

oath *verb* {422 alah} {7650 shaba} [1964 epiokeo] [3660 omnumi, omnuo] [3726 horkizo] [3728 horkomosia] literally, to seven; figuratively, to complete; to solemnly affirm.

Obad Yah *transliterated name* {5662 obadyah} Server of Yah.

Obed *transliterated name* {5744 obed} [5601 obed] Server.

Obed Edom *transliterated name* {5654 obededom} Server of Edom.

oblate, approach, bring near *verb* {7126 qarab} {7127 qereb} to offer for worship; to draw near; to bring near.

oblation *noun* [1435 doron] an oblation; a transliteration of the Hebrew qorban, and of the Hellenic qorban; **see** qorban; **read** Markos 7:11.

oblivion *noun* {5388 neshiyah} forgotten.

obscure, evening *verb* {6150 arab} in the sense of dusking; of becoming obscure.

obscure, uncertain *adjective* [82 adelos] [83 adelotes] unclear.

obscurity *noun* {4155 muwaph} shielded from view.

observant *noun* {7907 sekviy} one that observes.

observation *noun* {7914 sekiyah} that which is observed.

observe, prowl *verb* {7789 shur} to spy out; to survey; **see** stroll.

observer, prowler *noun* {7790 shur} a foe, as lying in wait; **see** stroll.

obstinate *participle* {3267 yaaz} to be bold.

occasion *noun* {8385 taanah} opportunity; opportune time.

occurrence, happening *noun* {4745 miqreh} that which happens to occur.

ode *transliterated noun* [5603 ode] a poem set to music.

offer, offering; see SUMMARY: OFFER, OFFERING:

officer *noun* {2951 tiphcar} {7860 shoter} [4233 praktor] an official invested with an office.

offscouring *verb* {5501 cechiy} a scouring off; **see** scrape off.

offscraping *noun* [4067 peripsoma] what is scraped off; scum.

offspring *adjective* {3329 yetsiy} an issue.

offspring *noun* {5209 nin} {6526 pirchach} {*plural* 6631 tseetsim} that which issued of; progeny; produce; **see** posterity.

ogling *participle* {8265 saqar} to blink coquettishly, playfully.

Oholah *transliterated name* {170 oholah} Her Tent.

Oholi Ab *transliterated name* {171 oholiyab} Tent of Father.

Oholi Bah *transliterated name* {172 oholiybah} My Tent is in Her.

Oholi Bamah *transliterated name* {173 oholiybamah} Tent of the Bamah (Height).

oil *noun* {3323 yitshar} {8081 shemen} oil for anointing.

Ochran *transliterated name* {5918 ochran} Troubler.

old *adjective* [3820 palaios] not recent; worn out.

olive *noun* {2132 zayith} [*plural* 1636 elaia] an oily fruit.

olive (good) *noun* [2565 kallielaios] as cultivated; as improved.

olive (wild) *noun* [65 agrielaios] as uncultivated; as natural.

olive oil *noun* [1637 elaion] the oil of anointing.

olive orchard *noun* [1638 elaion].

Olympas *transliterated name* [3652 olumpas] Heavenly.

omega *transliterated noun* [5598 omega] the last letter of the Greek alphabet; figuratively, finality.

omen *noun* {852 ath} {*plural* 852 atheen} {4159 mopeth} [5059 teras] a phenomenon.

omer *transliterated noun* {5995 amir} {6016 omer} a dry measure of grain.

on account of, so (as) (that), in order to *participle* {4616 maan} {5668 abur} for the purpose of.

on guard, regard, guard *verb* {5201 natar} {5202 nater} {5341 natsar} {8104 shamar} {*plural* 8107 shimmurim} {8108 shomrah} {8176 shaar} [5083 tereo] in the sense of protecting from harm, observing observances, obeying misvahs.

onager *noun* {6167 arad} {6171 arod} a wild burro.

Onesimus *transliterated name* [3682 oneesimos] Profitable.

Onesiphorus *transliterated name* [3683 oneesiphoros] Tribute Bearer.

open, pethach, engrave *verb* {[*transliterated* 6605 pathach} {[*transliterated* 6606 pethach] [*transliterated* 2188 ephphatha] to open; to loosen; to engrave.

open, opening *verb* {6491 paqach} [455 anoigo] [457 anoixis] to open up.

opener *noun* {4668 maphteach} that which opens.

openeyed *adjective* {6493 piqqeach} clear sighted.

opening *noun* {4669 miphtach} as an arperture.

opening *noun* {6495 peqachqoach} as a way of escape.

opening, portal *noun* {6607 pethach} {6608 pethach} {6610 pithchon} {8179 shaar} {8651 tera} [2374 thura] an entrance or an exit.

Ophay *transliterated name* {5778 owphay} Flyer-like.

Ophel *transliterated name* {6077 ophel} Mound.

Opheniy *transliterated name* {6078 ophniy} Of Ophen.

opinion, decision *noun* [1106 gnomee] a personal judgment.

opinions *plural noun* {5587 saiphim} {8312 saraphim} literally, of divided mind; **see** skeptics.

opponent *noun* {7009 giym} one that rises against.

opponent *noun* {8324 sharar} one that opposes.

opportunity *noun* [874 aphorme] a starting point.

oppose *verb* [496 antipipto] [498 antitassomai] to set against.

oppose *verb* {7852 satam} to lurk for; for noun, **see** satan.

opposite, toward, -ward *adjective* {4136 mowl} [481 antikru] [492 antiparerkomai] [495 antiperan] across from.

opposition *noun* {7855 sitnah} **see** oppose.

oppress *verb* {3238 yanah} to maltreat.

oppress, distress *verb* {6693 tsuwq} to compress.

oppress, extort *verb* {6231 ashaq} to press out of; to oppress.

oppress, press *verb* {3905 lachats} literally, to press; to distress.

oppression *noun* {3906 lachats} {4157 muwaqah} {*plural* 4642 maashaqqah} {4835 merutsah} {6125 aqah} {*plural* 6217 ashuq} [2347 thlipsis] constraint; oppression; pressure.

oppression, extortion *noun* {6233 osheq} a pressing out; an oppressing.

oppression, race *noun* {4793 merots} {4794, 4835 merutsah} a test of running; the pressures of life.

oppressor *noun* {4160 muwts} {6216 ashoq} one who oppresses.

opulent, outcry *noun* {7771 showa} one that is opulent; an outcry; **see** cry.

oracle *noun* {5001 naam} {5002 neum} [3051 logion] [5538 chrematismos] a verbal revelation or affirmation.

oracle *verb* [5537 chrematizo] to utter an oracle.

orator *noun* [3052 logios] one who words.

orator *noun* [4489 reetor] one who rhetorizes.

orchard *noun*, **Karmel** *transliterated name* {3759 karmel} a planting of fruit trees; an orchard.

ordain *verb* [1299 diatasso] [5021 tasso] to set apart for ministry; to establish by appointment.

order *noun* [2003 epitage] [5001 tagma] [5010 taxis] an arrangement; a command.

order *verb* [2004 epitasso] [4367 protasso] [4929 suntasso] [5002 taktos] to arrange; to command.

ordinance *noun* [1296 diatage] [1297 diatagma] an order.

ore *noun* {3800 kethem} as carved out; as mined.

ore, sickle, trench, decision, decisive, incision, incisor *adjective, noun* {2742 charuts} literally, a mental, soulical, or material incising.

origin *noun* {4351 mekorah} as being dug; as if a mine.

original, eternal, eternally, eternity *noun, adjective, adverbally* {5703 ad} {5769 olam} {5865 elom} {5957 alam} [126 adidios] [166 aionios] a limitless period – either past, present, or future.

ornament *noun* {2481 chaliy} {2484 chelyah} a trinket as polished.

ornament *noun* {5716 adiy} an ornament that adorns.

ornament, adornment, tiara *noun* {6287 peer} an embellishment; a tiara, as an adornment.

orphan *transliterated noun* {3490 yathom} [3737 orphanos] without parents; bereft.

orphanize *transliterated verb* [642 aporphanizomai] to cause to become orphan.

Osem *transliterated name* {684 otsem} Strong.

Osnapper *transliterated name* {620 ocnapper} the meaning uncertain; an Ashshuriy sovereign.

ostriches *plural noun* {7443 renen} named from its cry.

other doctrine, doctrinate otherwise *verb* [2085 heterodidaskaleo] to teach differently; to teach different doctrines.

Othni *transliterated name* {6273 othni} Force.

Othni El *transliterated name* {6274 othniel} Force of El.

out, outside, outskirt, outward, outway, without *noun, adverb* {2351 chuts} a separated area.

outburst *noun* {8241 shetseph} an emotional outburst.

outcasts *plural noun* {6849 tsephiah} that which is cast out.

outcry *noun* {6682 tsevachah} a crying out.

outcry, opulent *noun* {7771 showa} one that is opulent; an outcry; **see** cry.

outresurrection *noun* [1815 exanastasis] a resurrection out of.

outrun, run *verb* **runner** *participle* {7323 ruts} {7325 rur} to run; to run faster than.

oven, furnace *noun* {8574 tannur} a fire pot.

overburden *verb* [1912 epibareo] to put a heavy load upon; to be burdensome.

overcast *verb* {5743 ub} to be dense.

overcloud, cloud over *verb* {6049 anan} to cover over with a cloud.

overflow *noun* {3502 yithrah} the surplus.

overflow *verb* {7857 shataph} to inundate.

overflow, float *verb* {6687 tsuph} {7783 shuq} to float; to flow over.

overflowing *noun* {7858 sheteph} an inundation.

overlay *noun* {6826 tsippuy} an encasement.

overlay, watch *verb* **watcher** *participle* {6822, 6823 tsaphah} to observe; to await; to sheet over.

overlay, subdue *verb* {7286 radad} to conquer; to sheet over.

overload *verb* {2959 tarach} to overburden; **cp** burden.

overlook *verb* [3865 paratheoreo] [5237 huperido] to disregard.

overlord *verb* [2634 katakuriuo] [2961 kuriuo] to lord over; **see** lord.

overpass, pass (over) (through), surpass, trespass *verb* {5674 abar} to cross over; this verb is unrelated to the mistranslation of passover.

overpower, prevail, empower *verb* {8280 sarah} {8630 taqaph} [2616 katadunastuo] [2729 katiskuo] [2901 krataioo] [2902 krateo] to have ability over; to cause to have power.

oversee, perpetual, perpetuity (in), eminent *adjective, participle* {5329 natsach} {5331 netsach} [1336 dieenekes] continual, on and on; to oversee work; to be eminent.

oversee, scope over *verb* [1983 episkopeo] to episcopate; to inspect over.

oversee, visit, muster *verb* {6485 paqad} to oversee; to visit with friendly intent, to visit with hostile intent, to take care of; to muster for display.

overseeing *noun* {6487 piqqadon} that which is being overseen, or watched over.

overseeing others *verb* [244 allotriepiskopos] in the sense of not minding one's own matters.

overseer *noun* {6488 peqiduth} {6496 paqid} one that oversees, or watches over.

overseer, oversight, visitation, muster *noun* {6486 pequddah} a visit with friendly intent, to oversee; or a visit with hostile intent, to take care of; a muster for display.

overshadow, overshadowing verb {6751 tsalal} to shade, as hovering over.

oversight, visitation, muster, overseer noun {6486 pequddah} a visit with friendly intent, to oversee; or a visit with hostile intent, to take care of; a muster for display.

overspread, spread over verb {5259 nacak} to interweave.

overspreading adjective {4473 mimshach} expanding over.

overtake, reach, attain verb {5381 nasag} to attain by reaching for.

overtake, take over verb [2638 katalambano] to lay hold of; to seize.

overthrow noun {2925 taltelah} {4072 midcheh} {plural 4073 medachphah} {4114 mahpechah} an overthrow; a rejection.

overthrow verb {1760 dahghah} to overthrow by pushing down.

overturn, remain, return, behave verb [390 anastrepho] [396 anatrepo] to turn over; to overthrow; to turn; in the manner one turns (behaves).

overworking [4020 periergazomai] [4021 periergos] to bustle about uselessly.

owl (little), cup noun {3563 kowe} a container; an owl, from the cup-like cavity of its eye.

ox, oxen noun {7794 shor} an ox, or oxen as strolling; **see** stroll.

P

Paaray transliterated name {6474 paaray} Yawning.

pace noun {4703 mitsad} {6806 tsaah} a marching pace; the measured movement from one step to another; **cp** step.

pace verb {6805 tsaad} to pace; to march; **see** march.

Pachath Moab transliterated name {6355 pachathmowab} Pit of Moab.

pacify verb [1514 iereneuo] [1517 eirenopoieo] the verb of peace; to make peace; to be peaceful.

Paddan transliterated name {6307 paddan} Plateau.

Paddan Aram transliterated name {6307 paddanaram} Plateau of Aram.

paddle, flip, flit verb {7751 shuwt} to flit forth and back; to flip oars.

Pagi El transliterated name {6295 pagiel} Coincidence of El.

pail noun {1805 deli} [502 antlema] a container for drawing water; noun of bail.

pail noun {5845 atiyn} container.

pain noun {3511 keeb} physically, soulically, or mentally, suffering.

pain verb {3510 kaab} to hurt; to feel pain.

palace noun {1001 bira} {1002 birah} {1055 bithan} {plural 1003 birahanith} a large house; **cp** house; manse; nave; priestal precinct.

Palal transliterated name {6420 palal} Prayer.

Palal Yah transliterated name {6421 palalyah} Prayer of Yah.

palanquin noun {668 appiryown} a passenger conveyance borne on shoulders by poles.

palanquin, tortoise noun {6632 tsab} a wagon, as covered; a tortoise, as covered.

palate noun {2441 chek} the roof of the mouth.

pale verb {2357 chavar} to turn pale; to blanch.

Pallu transliterated name {6396 palluw} Distinquished.

Palluiy transliterated name {6384 palluiy} Of Pallu.

palm, paw, sole, bowl, hollow noun {3709 kaph} {6447 pas} {8168 shoal} a hollow of the hand, foot, paw, or body; also utensils with a hollow.

palm (tree) noun {8558 tamar} {8560 tomer} {8561 timmor} a species of tree; symbolic of triumph; of being erect.

palm leaf noun {3712 kippah} as having a hollow as a palm.

palmspan verb {2946 taphach} to span with the palm.

palmspan, support noun {2947 tephach} {2948 tophach} the span of a palm; a support; **see** span.

Paloniy transliterated name {6397 pelowniy} Separate; Of Palon.

Palti transliterated name {6406 paltiy} Escaped.

Palti El transliterated name {6409 paltiel} Escape of El.

Paltiy transliterated name {6407 paltiy} Of Palti.

pamper verb {6445 panaq} to treat daintily.

pang noun **ambassador** title {6735 tsir} an ambassador, as a representative; a pang, as writhing.

pang noun {2427 chiyl} a throe, especially of childbirth.

pang, boundary, cord, line noun {2256 chebel} literally, a rope; as a boundary line, or as binding one in a pang.

pannag transliterated noun {6436 pannag} an article of trade or barter.

panoply transliterated noun [3833 panoplia] a full suit of armour.

pant (after) verb {5689 agab} [1937 epithumeo] to breathe hard after; **cp** sigh.

panter noun [1938 epithumeetees] one who pants.

panting noun {5691 agabah} {plural 5690 egeb} [1939 epithumia] a breathing hard after; **cp** the Hebrew agabah with the Hellenic agape.

parable transliterated noun [3850 parabole] similitude; a short narrative of a possible event in life, from which a moral or spiritual truth is drawn.

Paraclete transliterated noun [3875 parakleetos] one who consoles, guides, intercedes; Yah Shua is the Paraclete; 1 Yahn 2:1; the Holy Spirit is the "another Paraclete" whom Yah Shua sent after His rapture; **read** Yahn 14:16,26, 15:26, 16:7.

paradise, park noun {6508 pardec} [3857 paradisos] a park; refers to the original garden, the new garden in Apocalypse, as well as the third heaven in 2 Corinthians 12; **cp** garden.

paradox transliterated noun [3861 paradoxos] a contradiction.

Paran transliterated name {6290 paran} Ornamental.

parapet noun {4624 maaqeh} a rampart to protect warriors.

parcel noun [5564 chorion] a plot of land.

parch noun **parched** adjective {6704 tsicheh} {plural 6710 tsachtsachah} {6723 tsiyah} {6724 tsiywon} {7039 qaliy} parched land, throat, kernels.

parch, desolate, dry adjective {2720 chareb} {8076 shamen} parched; ruined.

parch, desolate, dry verb {2717, 2718 charab} {3456 yashem} {8045 shamad} {8046 shemad} [2049 ereemoo] to lay waste; to destroy.

parch, drought noun {2721 choreb} {2725 charabon} very dry.

parched (area) noun {2723 chorbah} {2724 charabah}.

parched adjective {6704 tsicheh} from the root, to glow; parched.

parchment noun [3200 membrana] membrane.

parents noun [1118 gonus] father and mother.

Parnach transliterated name {6535 parnach} of uncertain derivative.

Paroh transliterated title {6547 paroh} [5328 pharao] title of Misrayim sovereigns.

Paroh Hophra transliterated title and name {6548 parohchophra} a Misrayim sovereign.

Paroh Nechoh transliterated title and name {6549 parohnechoh} a Misrayim sovereign.

parousia, appearance transliterated noun [3952 parousia] the presence to be; of the coming of ministers; especially of the return of our Adonay Yah Shua Messiah.

Parpar transliterated name {6554 parpar} Rapid.

part, end noun {7117, 7118 qetsath} a portion; a termination.

partake, partaking verb [3335 metalambano] [3352 metochee] [3348 metecho] to take part together; to share in.

partake, support verb [482 antilambanomai] [484 antileepsis] to take part; to support.

partaker, communicant noun [2844 koinonos] one who communes or partakes in common, or in communion.

partaker, partner noun [3335 metalambano] [3336 metaleepsis] [3353 metokos] one who takes part.

partaking, imparting verb [2841 koinoneo] communing and partaking by imparting.

partiality noun [4380 prosopolepteo] [4382 prosopoleepsia] favoritism.

partiality noun {4856 massoh} as in lifting one above another.

Paruach transliterated name {6515 paruwach} Blossomed.

Parvayim transliterated name {6516 parvayim} an Oriental region.

Pas Dammim {6450 pacdammiym} Coverall of Blood.

pasach *transliterated noun* {6453 pecach} [3957 pascha] a celebration of Elohim's protection; a celebration sacrifice of a lamb; Adonay Yah Shua Messiah as our protection; often mistranslated passover; **cp** suffer [3958 pasko]; **read** Vine; **read** Theological Wordbook of the Old Testament.

pasach *transliterated verb* {6452 pacach} to protect.

Pasach *transliterated name* {6457 pasach} Protection.

Pashchur *transliterated name* {6583 pashchuwr} Liberation.

pass, passage *noun* {4569 maabarah} a place to cross over; **see** route.

pass (away) (over) (through) *verb* {2498, 2499 chalaph} from the root, to slide by; to pass on.

pass (over) (through), surpass, trespass, overpass *verb* {5674 abar} to cross over; this verb is unrelated to the mistranslation of passover.

pasture *noun* {4829 mireh} {4830 miriyth} {5097 nahalol} a place of feeding.

pasture *noun* {4999 naah} {7471 reiy} [3542 nome] grazing land.

patch *verb* {2950 taphal} literally, to patch clothes; to patch lies.

patch, spot *verb* {2921 tala} to color in spots; to repair in spots.

path, way *noun* {734, 735 orach} also includes the manner of a person.

pathos *transliterated noun* [3806 pathos] a suffering; a passion.

Pathrosiym *transliterated name* {6625 pathruciym} Of Pathros.

patriarch *transliterated noun* [3966 patriarches] [3967 patrikos] [3971 patroos] the arch fathers; the early fathers.

patriarchal tradition *noun* [3970 patroparadotos] the tradition of the arch fathers.

patriarchy *noun* [3965 patria] the reign of the arch fathers, past or present.

patricide *noun* [3964 patraloees] a parricide; a murderer of, or the murder of one's father.

patroness *noun* [4368 prostatis] a female who sponsors or supports.

pattern *noun* {8403 tabnith} a model to be reproduced or followed.

Paulos *transliterated name* [3972 paulos] Little.

pause *verb* [3973 pauo] to stop.

pavement, red hot stones *noun* {7528 ratsaph} {7529 retseph} as used for baking; as used for laying a pavement.

pavilion *noun* {643 appeden} {8237 shaphrur} a large tent.

paw, sole, bowl, hollow, palm *noun noun* {3709 kaph} {6447 pas} {8168 shoal} a hollow of the hand, foot, paw, or body; also utensils with a hollow.

pawn, pledge, entangle *verb* {5670 abat} to entangle a people; to entangle a pledge by pawning.

payoff *noun* {866 ethnah} {868 ethnan} {5078 nedeh} {5083 nadan} usually the price paid to a whore.

peacocks *plural noun* {8500 tukkim} a species of imported creature.

pearls *plural noun* {6443 paniyn} as being round.

pebble *noun* {1486 goral} casting pebbles was a common manner of determining who received what; **see** Apocalypse 2:17.

peculiar aquisition *noun* [4047 peripoiesis] private, personal property; Messianists are Elohim's private personal property.

peculiar people *adjective* [4041 periousios] private personal people; Messianists are Elohim's private personal people.

peculiar treasure *noun* {5459 cegullah} private treasure, as held close to the breast; private property.

pedagogue *transliterated noun* [3807 paidagogos] [3810 paidutees] one who disciplines children; a tutor.

Pedah El *transliterated name* {6300 pedahel} Redeemed of El.

Pedah Sur *transliterated name* {6301 pedatsur} Redeemed of the Rock.

Pedah Yah *transliterated name* {6305 pedayah} Redeemed of Yah.

peel *noun* {4286 machsoph} a peeling.

peel *verb* {6478 patsal} to strip, as tree bark.

peelings *plural noun* {6479 petsalah} that which is peeled.

peer *verb* {7688 shagach} to peep; to peer.

peeved *adjective* {5620 car} annoyed.

Pela Yah *transliterated name* {6411 pelayah} Marvel of Yah.

Pelat Yah *transliterated name* {6410 pelatyah} Escape of Yah.

Peleg *transliterated name* {6389 peleg} [5317 phalek] Split.

Pelesheth *transliterated name* {6429 pelesheth} Wallow; original name of Palestine.

Peleshethiy *transliterated name* {6430 pelishtiy} Of Pelesheth.

pelican *noun* {6893 qaath} from its vomiting.

penalize *verb* {6064 anash} to inflict a penalty; to fine.

penalty *noun* {6066 onesh} a fine; **see** confiscate.

pendant *noun* {7720 saharon} a round ornament for the neck.

pendants *plural noun* {5188 netiyphahoth} pendants for the ears.

pendulous *plural noun* {8534 taltalim} vibrations.

penetrate, press, sink, bend, descend *verb* {5181 nachath} from the root, to sink; to go down; to press or lead down.

Peni El *transliterated name* {6439 peniel} [5323 phanouel] Face of El.

pentecost *transliterated noun* [4005 pentekostee] fiftieth; the fiftieth day following the pasach; **read** Leviticus 23:15-17, Acts 2:1-4.

Penu El *transliterated name* {6439 punuel} Face of El.

people, peoples *noun* {5971, 5972 am} [2992 laos] the body of citizens of a place, group, or class; **cp** goyim; **cp** nations.

Peqach *transliterated name* {6492 peqach} Open.

Peqach Yah *transliterated name* {6494 peqachyah} Opened of Yah.

Peqod/visitation *transliterated name, noun* {6489 peqowd} refers to Babel as a place of Yah Veh's visitation.

perceive, consider *verb* [2657 katanoeo] to observe attentively.

perceive, know *verb* {3045 yada} {3046 yeda} [143 aisthanomai] [1492 eido] [5274 hupolambano] to be aware through the senses.

perception *noun* {4486 manda} [144 aitheesis] [145 aistheeteerin] an awareness through the senses.

perception, knowledge *noun* {1843 dehag} {1844 dehgah} {1847 dahgath} [1108 gnosis] an awareness of facts.

perennial, permanent *adjective* {386 ethan} {7011 qayam} continually abiding; lasting.

Peres *transliterated name* {6557 perets} [5329 phares] Separatist; **see** Peresiy.

Peres Uzza *transliterated name* {6560 peretsuzza} Separatist of Strength; **see** Peresiy.

Peresiy *transliterated name* {6558 partsi} [*plural* 5330 pharisaios] Separatist; one who separates from.

perfect *adjective*, **totality** *noun*, **totally** {3642 kaliyl} all inclusive; naught to be added.

perfect *verb* {3634 kalal} to finish to perfection.

perfection *noun* {*plural* 4357 miklah} {4359 miklal} splendid; with splendor.

perforated *adjective* {2751 choriy} full of holes.

perfume *noun* {7544 reqach} {7545 roqach} {*plural* 7547 raqquachim} an aromatic; a scented substance.

perfume *verb* {7543 raqach} to perfume.

perfumer *noun* {*masculine* 7546 raqqach} {*feminine* 7548 raqqachah} one that perfumes.

Perizziy *transliterated name* {6522 perizziy} Of the suburbs.

permanent, perennial *adjective* {386 ethan} {7011 qayam} continually abiding; lasting.

permit *noun* {7558 rishyon} a permission.

perpetual, perpetuity (in), eminent, oversee *adjective, participle* {5329 natsach} {5331 netsach} [1336 dieenekes] continual, on and on; to oversee work; to be eminent.

perpetually *adverb* {8411 tedira} continually on and on.

perpetuate *verb* {5125 nun} to continue on and on.

perplex *verb* {6323 pun} {7672 shebash} to confuse, to entangle.

persecuted, persecution *verb, noun* {4783 murdaph} {4788 marud} a maltreatment; to maltreat.

Persia, Persian *transliterated name* {6539, 6540 parac} {6542, 6543 parsciy} the land of Persia; including settlers.

perverse *adjective* {2019 haphakpak} [1294 diastrepho] devious; distorted.

perverseness *noun* {3891 lezuwth} {5758 ivya} {5558 seleph} a turning from; a mental twistedness.

perversion *noun* **perverted** *adjective* {6143 iqqeshuth} as in perversion of mouth.

perversion, perversity *noun* {5771 avon} deviation.

perversities *plural noun* {5773 aveh} deviations.

pervert *noun* {5760 avil} perverse.

pervert *verb* {3868 luwz} {6140 aqash} to distort; to turn away from.

pervert *verb* {5686 abath} to interlace.

pervert, subvert *verb* {5557 calaph} to turn from; to undermine.

pervert, twist, bend *verb* {5753 avah} {5754 avvah} to crook; to overthrow.

perverted *adjective* {6141 iqqesh} distorted; turned away from.

pestle *verb* {3795 kathiyth} {3806 kathash} {3807 kathath} to pulverize with a pestle.

pestle, socket *noun* {4388 maktesh} {5940 eliy} the pestle of a mortar; a socket.

pethach, engrave, open *verb* {[transliterated 6605 pathach} {[transliterated 6606 pethach] [transliterated 2188 ephphatha] to open; to loosen; to engrave.

Pethach Yah *transliterated name* {6611 pethachyah} Opened of Yah.

Pethu El *transliterated name* {6602 pethuel} Duped of El.

petition *noun* {7596 shelah} [1162 deesis] an asking; a solemn request.

petition *verb* {8469 tachanun} [1189 deomai] to solemnly request.

petrifaction *noun* [4457 porosis] rocklikeness; **see** Petros.

petrified *verb* [4456 poroo] become rocklike; **see** Petros.

Petros *transliterated name* {3710 keph} [4074 petros] Rock; **see** Kepha; **note:** Petros is a Hellene translation of the Hebrew Keph, whereas Kepha is a transliteration of the Hebrew.

petty, shortly, bit, bit by bit, few, little *adjective, adverb* {4592 meat} diminutive; a few; a little.

Peullthay *transliterated name* {6469 peullthay} Laborious.

phantasm *transliterated noun* [5326 phantasm] a figment of the imagination.

pharmacist *transliterated noun* [5332 pharmakus] [5333 pharmakos] drug pushers; originally pharmacists were associated with drugs in the occult.

pharmacy *transliterated noun* [5331 pharmakia] the dispensary of drugs.

Pharsin *verb* {6537 peras} separated; split.

Philadelphia *transliterated noun* [5359 philadelphia] Friendship City.

philanthropically *transliterated adverb* [5364 philanthropos] friendly giving.

philanthropy *transliterated noun* [5363 philanthropia] friend of humanity; also friend of giving.

Philemon *transliterated name* [5371 philemon] Friendly.

Philetos *transliterated name* [5372 philetos] Friendly.

Philippos *transliterated name* [5376 philippos] Friend of Horses.

Philologos *transliterated name* [5378 philologos] Friend of Words; Philological.

phoenix *transliterated noun* [5404 phoinix] a type of palm.

phylactery *noun* {2903 towphaphah} [*transliteration* 5440 phulakterion] a guardcase worn on the forehead containing scripture passages.

physical *adjective* [5446 phusichos] of the physique; instinctive.

physically *adv* [5447 phusichos] instinctively.

Pi Ha Hiroth *plural transliterated name* {6367 pihachiyroth} Mouth of the Holes.

pick *noun* {4281 machareshah} an instrument for picking; **cp** hoe.

pierce *verb* {3735 kara} to be pierced in spirit.

pierce, appoint, bore *verb* {5344 naqab} to point out; to thrust or make a hole through.

pierce, dig *verb* {3738, 3739 kahrah} to bore; to dig through.

pierce, pinch *verb* {4600 maak} from the root, to press; to pierce.

pierce, pluck, profane *verb* {2490 chalal} {2610 chaneph} [2840 koinoo] to pierce a person; to pluck an instrument; to desecrate the hallowed.

pierced, profane *adjective* {2455 chol} {2491 chalal} [952 bebeelos] of pierced (slaughtered) and profaned persons.

Pichol *transliterated name* {6369 piychol} Mouth of All.

Pilcha *transliterated name* {6401 pilcha} Slicing.

pilgrim *noun* [3927 parepidemos] a wanderer in a foreign land.

pillar *noun* {4690 matsuq} {5982 ammud} {*plural* 8564 tamrurim} [4769 stulos] a column; a vertical structural support; of smoke; of fire; **cp** statue.

Piltay *transliterated name* {6408 piltay} Escaped.

pinch, pierce *verb* {4600 maak} from the root, to press; to pierce.

Pinechas *transliterated name* {6372 piynechac} Mouth of a Serpent.

pinion *noun* {83 eber} {84 ebrah} the bone of the wing.

pinky, younger, fewer, lesser, little *adjective* {6810 tsaor} {6995 qoten} {6996 qatan} less in age, number, size; little finger.

Pirathoniy *transliterated name* {6553 pirathoniy} Of Pirathon.

Pisgah *transliterated name* {6449 picgah} Contemplation.

Pishon *transliterated name* {6376 piyshown} Spread.

Pisses *transliterated name* {6483 pitstsets} Dispersive.

pit *noun* {4379 mikreh} {6354 pachath} as dug.

pit, pitfall *noun* {7825 shechith} {7882 shichah} as a depression.

pitch, camphire, koper/atonement *noun* {3724 koper} camphor, a medication; a sealant for the ark of the flood; also an atonement: **see** koper/atonement.

pitted *noun* {6356 pecheheth} pitted with holes or blemishes as in oxidation.

place *noun* {8499 tekunah} a fixed, or certain place.

place, put, set *verb* {7760, 7761 suwm} {7896 shith} {8239 shaphath} {8271 shathah} to put in place.

place (by), set (by), stand (by), station (by) *verb* {3320 yatsab} {3322 yatsag} {5324 natsab} from the root, to place, so as to stay.

placing *noun* {8667 tesumeth} a placing of the hand.

plague *noun* {4046 maggephah} a pestilence.

plague *transliterated noun* {5061 nega} {5063 negeph} [4127 plege] a heavy touch, or strike; an infliction of disease.

plague, reach, touch *verb* {5060 naga} to touch heavily; to strike.

plain, straight, straightness, level *noun* {4334 miyshor, *plural* miyshorim} {4339 meyshar} {6160 arabah} plain, as unadorned; as a level land area; as of straight character; as just.

plant *noun* {3657 kannah} {3661 kanan} [5451 phutia] organic produce which cannot move of itself.

plant *verb* {5193 nata, *plural* natiaim} [5452 phutuo] to place seed in the ground.

plant, plantation *noun* {5194 neta} a planting; a place of planting.

plant, planting, plantation *noun* {4218 mizra} {4302 matta} a field, as planted.

plea, pleading *noun* {1779, 1780 diyn} a defence; a petition.

plea, strife, contention, defence *noun* {7379 rib} a personal, or legal contest.

plead *verb* [626 apologeomai] to defend.

plead, examine, judge *verb* {8199 shaphat} {8200 shephat} [350 anakrino] [2919 krino] to scrutinize; to investigate.

plead, strive, contend, defend *verb* {7378 rub} to hold a controversy.

plead (for) *verb* {1777, 1778 diyn} to petition; to act in defence of.

pleader *noun* {1781, 1782 dayan} one who pleads.

pleading *noun* [627 apologia] words in defence.

pleading, plea *noun* {1779, 1780 diyn} a defence; a petition.

pleasant, pleasure *adjective* {5273 naiym} {6156 areb} delightful.

pleasantness *adjective* {5278 noam} delightful; agreeableness.

please, be pleased, pleasing, (have the) (take) pleasure *verb* {5276 naem} {5727 adan} {6149 areb} {7521 ratsah} [700 aresko] [701 arestos] to please; to please (satisfy) a debt; **cp** shalom.

pleasing, pleasure *noun* {7522 ratson} a delight.

pleasure *noun* {5730 eden} **see** Eden.

pledge (heavy) *noun* {5667 abot} that which has been pledged, or pawned.

pledge *noun* {2258 chabol} {6161 arubbah} {6162 arabon} [728 arrabon] an agreement as bound; that which is pledged for colateral.

pledge, comingle, mingle *verb* {6148, 6151 arab} to become colateral.

pledge, entangle, pawn *verb* {5670 abat} to entangle a people; to entangle a pledge by pawning.

pledge, spoil, despoil *verb* {2254, 2255 chabal} literally, to bind tightly; as in spoiling or as in binding a pledge.

pledges *plural noun* {8594 taarubahoth} sons, as security.

plough *verb* {2758 charish} literally, to slice.

plow, hush *verb* {2790 charash} literally, to scratch; to silence.

plowed fields *plural* {3010 yageb} literally, plowings, as in fields to plow.

plowers *participle* {3009 yagab} diggers; ploughers.

pluck *verb* {5394 nashal} to pluck off.

pluck, plucking, psalm, psalming *noun* {2158, 2159 zamir} {2170 zemar} {2172 zimrah} {2176 zimrath} {4210 mizmor} a string, fruit, or twig as plucked.

pluck, profane, pierce *verb* {2490 chalal} {2610 chaneph} [2840 koinoo] to pierce a person; to pluck an instrument; to desecrate the hallowed.

pluck, pull, pull stakes *verb* {5265 naca} to pluck; to pull up; to pull the tent stakes when moving; **read** Numbers 33:3–48.

pluck, strip *verb* {6998 qataph} {7059 qamat} to pluck out; to strip off.

plucker, psalmist *noun* {2171 zammar} plucker.

plumage *noun* {5133 notsah} the entire covering of feathers on a bird.

plumbline *noun* {4949 mishqeleth} a weight with a line attached for surveying.

plump *noun* {2109 yahsan} {6371 pimah} fat.

plump, fatten *verb* {2492 chalam} {3780 kasah} to cause to be fat, to plump; to cover with flesh.

plunder *noun* {957 baz} {961 bizzah} {4933 mechiccah} [724 harpage] a pillage.

plunder *verb* {962 bazaz} {8154 shasah} {8155 shacac} [1283 diarpazo] to seize apart; to pillage.

pockets *plural noun* {2754 charitim} literally, cutouts.

poem *noun* {4387 miktam} a metrical composition.

poet *transliterated noun* [4163 poietes] one who composes metrical compositions.

point, cut, decide, determine *verb* {2782 charat} {2852 chathak} to be cut; to cut a decision, or a determination; to point.

point, pointen *verb* {8150 shanan} to point; to cause to be pointy; to pierce.

poison, fury *noun* {2534 chemah} heat; as anger, as poison.

Pochereth Sebayim *transliterated name* {6380 pocherethtsebayiym} Trap of Gazelles.

pole, sail, ensign *noun* **Nissi** *transliterated title* {5251 nec} an ensign; the pole of an ensign; part of the title, Yah Veh Nissi, which means, Yah Veh Ensign.

pole, yoke pole *noun* {4132 mowt} the slip pole of a yoke.

polish, purge, cleanse *verb* {1305 barar} [1571 ekkathairo] clarify, catharize; **cp** purify.

polish, rash, balden *verb* {4178 mowrat} {4803 marat} {4804 merat} to rub (off); to pluck; to cause to be bald.

polish, scour *verb* {4838 maraq} to polish, so as to sharpen.

politarche *transliterated noun* [4173 politarches] arch politicians of the city.

pollution *noun* [234 alisgeema] a contamination.

polylogy *transliterated noun* [4180 polulogia] multiwordedness.

pomp *noun* {1344 geah} {1346 gaavah} {1347 gaoun} {1348 qeuwth} ostentation; majesty.

pompous *adjective* {1341 ge} {1343 geeh} {1349 gaayon} ostentatious.

pond *noun* {4950 mishqa} a settling (of water).

poor *adjective* {1800 dal} weak; thin: **cp** needy; **note:** one can be poor without being needy.

poor *noun* [4434 ptokos] begging; lacking in anything.

Porkios *transliterated name* [4201 porkios] Porky.

portal, opening *noun* {6607, 6608 pethach} {6610 pithchon} {8179 shaar} {8651 tera} [2374 thura] an opening for entering and exiting.

portalguard *noun* {8652 tara} [2377 thuroros] one who guards a portal.

porter *noun* {7778 shoer} a janitor.

portico *noun* {4329 meycak} {4528 micderown} [4745 stoa] a porch, as being covered.

portion *noun* {4490 manah} a portion as measured out; **see** maneh.

portion, smooth, allotment *noun* {2506 cheleq} {2508 chalaq} {2511 challaq} {2513 chelqah} {2515 chaluqqah} {4255 machleqah} {4256 machaloqeth} {4521 menath} smoothness of tongue; usually an inheritance allotted by pebble.

possess *verb* {270 achaz} to have by seizing; verb of possession.

possess *verb* {3423 yaresh} [2932 ktaomai] to take hold; in some Hebrew stems, to dispossess.

possession *noun* {272 achuzzah} something seized.

possession *noun* {3424 yereshah} {3425 yerushshah} {4180 morash} {4181 morashah} {4476 mimshaq} that which is held on to.

possible, capable *adjective* [1415 dunatos] having sufficient dynamis; **see** dynamis.

posterity *noun* {5220 neked} from the root, to propagate; **see** offspring.

potentate *noun* {7333 razon} {7336 razan} one who possesses power.

Poti Phera *transliterated name* {6319 powtiyphera} the meaning uncertain; of Misrayim derivative.

potion, carousal *noun* {5435 cobe} a drinking revelry; a potion of carousing.

potsherd, pottery *noun* {2789 cheres} a piece of pottery.

pottage *noun* {5138 nazid} that which is boiled.

pouch *noun* {3219 yalqut} for gleanings, or for scrip.

pouch *noun* {3599 kiyc} [905 balantion] a money bag.

pounce *verb* {2907 tuws} to pounce upon, as a bird of prey.

pour, anoint, libate *verb* {4886 mashach} {5258 nacak} {5260 necak} {5480 cuwk} {8210 shaphach} [218 alipho] [4689 spendomai] [5548 chrio] symbolic of setting apart by libating (pouring on) of oil; of pouring a molten image.

pour, draw *verb* {7324 ruq} to pour in; to pour out.

pour, firm, form *verb* {3332 yatsaq} to pour out; to shape by pouring into a mold; to make firm.

pour, flow *verb* {5047 negad} {5064 nagar} {5140 nazel} to pour out; to flow out, as to clear the way.

pour, melt *verb* {5413 nathak} to flow; to liquify.

pour blood *verb* [130 haimatekchusia] as an effusion of blood.

pour (out) *verb* {6694 tsuwq}.

pour out, strip naked, empty *verb* {6168 arah} {6379 pakah} to empty; to empty by pouring; to strip bare; **see** naked.

poured (forth), (out) *verb* [1632a echeo] [1632b echuno] to pour forth; to bestow.

pouring *noun* {8211 shephek} a place where ashes are poured.

pouring, libation *noun* {5261 necak} {5262 necek} a pouring of worship; a pouring of images.

poverty *noun* {4544 mickenuth} {7389 rish} destitution.

power *noun* {2632 checen} {8632 teqoph} {8633 toqeph} [2904 kratos] ability.

powerful *adjective* {2626 chacin} {2634 chacon} [2900 krataios] [2903 kratistos] able.

praetorium *transliterated noun* [4232 praitorion] courtroom.

prancer *noun* {3753 karkarah} an animal that prances; probably a dromedary.

pray *verb* {6419 palai} {6739 tsela} [4336 proseuchomai] to entreat.

prayer *noun* {8605 tephillah} [4335 proseuche] an entreaty.

pre-evangelism *transliterated noun* [1860 epangelia] [1862 epangelma] an evangelism previously prepared, or previously evangelized; **see** evangelism; **cp** angel.

pre-evangelize *transliterated verb* [1861 epangello] [4279 proepangellomai] [4283 prouangelizomai] [4293 prokatangello] previously evangelized; an evangelism previously prepared for future evangelizing.

preach, preaching *verb* [2784 kerusso] to proclaim.

preacher *noun* [2783 keerux] proclaimer.

preaching *noun* [2782 keerugma] proclaiming.

prearrange *verb* [4384 protasso] previously arranged.

precede, anticipate, confront *verb* {6923 qadam} to front; **cp** east.

preceding, ancient, antiquity, east, easterly, eastern, eastward, formerly *noun* {6921 qadim} {6924 qedem} {6925 qodam} {6926 qidmah} {6927 qadmah} literally, the forefront; from the front.

precepts *plural noun* {6490 piqqudim} mandates.

precious (vastly) *adjective* [4185 polutelees] [4186 polutimos] extremely valuable.

precious *noun* {4022 meged} highly regarded.

preciousnesses *plural noun* {4030 migdanahoth} that which is highly regarded.

precipitate *verb* {4048 magar} to yield up; to hurl from a precipice; to hurry.

precise (most) *adjective* [196 akribestatos] most exact.

precisely (inquire) *verb* [198 akriboo] to be exact.

precisely (more) *adverb* [197 akribesteron] [199 akribos] more exactly.

preciseness *noun* [195 akribia] exactness.

predetermine *verb* [4309 proorizo] [4388 protitheemi] to determine prior to occurrence.

preeminent *noun* {5330 netsach} most prominent.

preeminent cathedras *noun* [4410 protokathedria] the foremost seat; preeminence in council.

preeminent leader *noun* [4414 protostates] the most prominent leader at celebrations.

preeminent recliner *noun* [4411 protoklisia] the most prominent reclining place.

preevident *adjective* [4271 prodelos] known before all.

prefect, statue, station *noun* {5333 netsib} {*plural* 5460 seganin} {*plural* 5461 saganim} {6346, 6347 pechah} a stationed officer; that which is stationary; a station; also a statue.

preinscribe *verb* [4270 prographo] to write previously.

premeditate *verb* [4304 promeletao] to meditate prior to occurrence.

preparation *noun* [2091 hetoimasia] a making ready.

prepare *verb* [2090 hetoimazo] [2680 kataskuazo] [3903 paraskuazo] to prepare; make ready; equip.

prepare, establish *verb* {3559 kuwn} to set up.

prepared *adjective* [2092 hetoimos] prepared; ready.

preparedly *adverb* [2093 hetoimos] readily.

presbyter *transliterated noun* [4243 presbuo] [4245 presbuteros] an elder representative; the Hellene word for the congregational and ecclesiastical representatives.

presbytry *transliterated noun* [4242 presbia] the office of elder representative; corresponds to Old Covenant elder.

present *noun* {7862 shay} a gift.

press *noun* {6333 purah} a grape crusher.

press oil *verb* {6671 tsahar} to press out oil.

press, oppress *verb* {3905 lachats} literally, to press; to oppress.

press, sink, bend, descend, penetrate *verb* {5181 nachath} from the root, to sink; to go down; to press or lead down.

pressure, puff, expire soul *verb* {5301 naphach} [1634 ekpsucho] to breathe away one's soul; to pressure, as in a pressure cooker; and to puff; **cp** expire spirit.

presume, swell *verb* {6075 aphal} to assume aforehand; an ascending, as swollen.

pretext *noun* {5931 illah} [4392 prophasis] a pretense.

prevail, able, can, enable *verb* {3201 yakol} {3202 yekel} {3546 kehal} [1410 dunamai] [2427 hikanoo] the dynamis to do; **see** dynamis.

prevail, empower, overpower *verb* {8280 sarah} {8630 taqaph} [2616 katadunastuo] [2729 katiskuo] [2901 krataioo] [2902 krateo] to have ability over; to cause to have power.

prevail, strengthen, uphold, callous *verb* {553 amats} {555 omets} {2388 chazaq} {2393 chezqah} {5810 azaz} to enable physically; to become thickskinned.

prevail mightily *verb* {1396 gabar} might in verbal form, for which there is no English equivalent.

previously preached *verb* [4296 prokerusso] that which was proclaimed in advance; **cp** pre-evangelize.

prewitness *verb* [4303 promarturomai] to witness prior to occurrence.

prey, tear *noun* {2964 tereph} {2966 terephah} {5706 ad} a prey, as an object of attack; as being torn.

price *noun* {4242 mechiyr} the payment.

price *noun* {4377 meker} the evaluation; the value to be paid; **cp** sell.

price, honour *noun* [5092 timee] of esteem; of value; money paid.

price, honour *verb* [5091 timao] to esteem; to value.

prickle *noun* {5544 cillon} a type of brier.

pride *noun* {7293 rahab} {7296 rohab} a vociferous boasting.

pride *noun* {7830 shachats} as in strutting.

priest, priestal precinct, priesthood; see SUMMARY: PRIEST.

prince *noun* {*plural* 4502 minnezarim} set apart.

prison guard *noun* [1200 desmophulax] one that guards a prison.

prison *noun* {3608 kele} {3628 kelu} [1201 desmoteerion] a place of binding.

prisoner *noun* [1202 desmotees] one that is bound.

private assembly *noun* {6116 atsereth} an assembly; a festival.

private counsel, councilmen *noun* {*plural* 4176 moetsoth} {5475 cowd} {5483 eta} {6098 etsah} [1012 boulee] [1013 boouleema] purpose; advice; advisors.

probe *verb* {2713 chaqar} to penetrate.

probe, probing *noun* {2714 chaqar} penetration.

proceeding, procedure, rising, springing *noun* {4161 motsa} {*plural* 4163 motsaoth} literally, the source of going forth, whether of persons, of water, of the sun.

procession *noun* {8418 tahalukah} an orderly walk; from the verb, to walk.

proclaim, recall, call *verb* {7121 qara} {7123 qera} [1941 epikaleomai] [2564 kaleo] [4341 proskaleomai] [4377 prosphoneo] to call out; to call upon; to address; **cp** name.

proconsul *noun* [445 anthupatuo] [446 anthupatos] the highest officer.

produce *noun* {2981 yebuwl} {8393 tebuah} {8570 tenubah} the product of the soil.

produce, progeny *noun* [1081 gennema] offspring.

produce, promote *verb* {6329 puq} to bring forth.

profane, common *adjective* {2455 chol} [2839 koinos] that which is common; that which is held in common; that which is not hallowed.

profane *noun* {1352 goel} desecration.

profane *verb* {1351 gaal} [953 bebeloo] to cross the threshold in the sense of desecrating the holy.

profane, pierce, pluck *verb* {2490 chalal} {2610 chaneph} [2840 koinoo] to pierce a person; to pluck an instrument; to desecrate the hallowed.

profane, pierced *adjective* {2455 chol} {2491 chalal} [952 bebeelos] of pierced (slaughtered) and profaned persons.
profaner *noun* {2611 chaneph} a desecrater.

profanity *noun* {2612 choneph} {2613 chanuphah} desecration.

profess *verb* [437 anthomologeomai] [3670 homologeo] to homologize; to agree with words.

professedly *adverb* [3672 homologoumenos] confessedly.

profession *noun* [3671 homologia] homology.

profound *adjective* {5994 amiq} as unsearcheable.

progenitors *noun* [4269 progonos] ancestors; forefathers.

progeny, produce *noun* [1081 gennema] offspring.

prognosis *transliterated noun* [4268 prognosis] foreknowledge.

prognosticate *verb* {5172 nachash} to predict.

prognostication *noun* {5173 nachash} a prediction.

prone *participle* **suspend, hang** *verb* {8511 tala} {8518 talah} to suspend.

proof *noun* [1382 dokime] a test; that which is tested.

proof *verb* {974 bachan} to test, as in a crucible.

proofing *verb* [1383 dokimion] that by which something is tested or proved.

prop, sustain, uphold *verb* {5564 camak} {8551 tamak} to prop up; with the hands, or with props.

proper *adjective* [433 aneko] to be proper; to attain unto.

prophecy *transliterated noun* {5016 nebuah} {5017 nebuah} [4394 prophetia] a foretelling prior to occurrence; does not mean a telling forth.

prophesy *transliterated verb* {5012 naba} {5013 neba} [4395 propheetuo] to foretell prior to occurrence; does not mean to tell forth.

prophet *transliterated noun* {5029 nebiy} {5030 nabiy} [4396 prophetes] one who foretells prior to occurrence; does not mean one who tells forth.

prophetess *transliterated feminine noun* {5031 nebiah} [4398 prophetis] a female who foretells prior to occurrence; does not mean one who tells forth.

prophetic *transliterated adjective* [4397 prophetikos] a foretelling; does not mean a telling forth.

propound *verb* {2330 chud} [394 anatithemi] to propose for consideration; **see** shew, show.

proselyte *transliterated noun* [4339 proselutos] one who has changed religions.

prosper, succeed *verb* {3787 kasher} {6743 tsaleach} {6744 tselach} to succeed; to press on.

prosperity *noun* {3574 kowsharah} {3788 kishron} success.

prostrate *verb* {5456 cagad} {5457 cegid} {7511 raphas} {7812, 7817 shachah} to lie with face to the soil as in doing obeisance.

protected *noun* {5336 natsiyr} delivered.

prothesis *transliterated noun* [4286 prothesis] a setting forth of a thesis; the bread of the holies as displayed.

prothesis bread, face bread *transliterated noun* {6440 paneh} {3899 lechem} [4286 prothesis] [740 artos] the bread of the holy of holies as displayed; the face bread of the Old Covenant is identical to the prothesis bread of the New Covenant.

prototype *noun* [5296 hupotuposis] a type to be patterned after.

proud *adjective* {7295 rahab} as insolent; **note:** Yah Veh was never proud of His Son; but well-pleased.

prove, reprove, approve *verb* {3198 yakach} [1381 dokimazo] to prove; to accept or reject the proving.

proverb *noun* {4912 mashal} {4914 meshol} [3942 paroimia] an adage; a general truth of conduct expressed in a sententious form.

proverbialize, liken *verb* {4911 mashal} to present as a proverb; liken, as being equal; **see** equal.

prowl, observe *verb* {7789 shur} to survey; to spy out; **see** stroll.

prowl, yearn *verb* {8264 shaqaq} to prowl as an animal; to greedily yearn for.

prowler, observer *noun* {7790 shur} a foe, as lying in wait; **see** stroll.

psalm *noun* [5568 psalmos] a sacred ode.

psalm, pluck *verb* {2167, 2168 zamar} [5567 psallo] as in plucking strings; **cp** strum.

psalm, psalming, pluck, plucking *noun* {2158, 2159 zamir} {2170 zemar} {2172 zimrah} {2176 zimrath} {4210 mizmor} a string, fruit, or twig as plucked.

psalmist, plucker *noun* {2171 zammar} plucker.

psalmpicks *plural noun* {4211 mazmerah} **note:** when the shalom of Yah Veh reigns, spears are turned into psalmpicks.

psalterion *transliterated noun* {6460 pecanterin} a transliteration of the Hellene psalterion; a lyre. *transliterated noun* [5571 pseudes] phony.

pseudo apostles *transliterated noun* [5570 pseudapostolos] phony apostles.

pseudo brothers *noun* [5569 pseudadelphos] phony brothers.

pseudo doctors *noun* [5572 pseudodidaskalos] phony doctors.

pseudo messiah *noun* [5580 pseudochristos] phony messiah.

pseudo prophets *transliterated noun* [5578 pseudoprophetes] phony prophets.

pseudo witnesses *noun* [5575 pseudomartur] phony witnesses.

pseudo witnessing *verb* [5576 pseudomarturia] phony witnessing.

pseudologists *transliterated noun* [5572 pseudologos] phony wordists.

pseudonym *transliterated noun* [5581 pseudonumos] phony name.

Puah, Puvvah *transliterated name* {6312 puwah, puvvah} Blow Away.

pudenda *noun* {*plural* 4016 mabushim} {4589 maor} exposed part.

pudenda, socket *noun* {6596 poth} literally, a hole.

puff *verb* [4154 pneo] [4157 pnoee] to blow hard; from pneuma (spirit).

puff *verb* {5301 naphach} [1720 emphusao] to blow hard; from nephesh; the Septuagint translates naphach to emphuzao; this word is used of Yah Veh puffing into Adam; of the Holy Spirit puffing into the dry bones; and of Yah Shua puffing into the disciples.

puff *verb* {5395 nasham} {5398 nashaph} to blow away; from nephesh.

puff, breathe *verb* {6315 puwach} **cp** spirit {7307 ruwach}.

puff, expire soul, pressure *verb* {5301 naphach} [1634 ekpsucho] to breathe away one's soul; to pressure, as in a pressure cooker; and to puff; **cp** expire spirit.

puffed up *adjective* [5448 phusioo] as in proud.

puffings up *noun* [5450 phusiosis] as in proud.

pull (down) (out) *verb* {5421 natha} {5422 nathats} to tear out; to tear down.

pull, pull stakes, pluck *verb* {5265 naca} to pluck; to pull up; to pull the tent stakes when moving; **read** Numbers 33:3–48.

pull, take, put (down) [2507 kathaireo] to take down, demolish.

pulling down *noun* [2506 kathairesis] a taking down, demolition.

pulpit *noun* {1687 debir} the furniture from whence the word is worded.

pulverize *verb* {1854 dahkak} {1855 dekak} {7833 shachaq} to crush to powder; to vapourize.

pulverized, thin *adjective* {1851 dak} thin; beaten small; emaciated.

punch *verb* [2852 kolaphizo] to strike with the fist; treat with violence.

Puniy *transliterated name* {6324 puwniy} Of Pun.

pupil *noun* {892 babah} the hollow of the eye.

pupil, mid, middle *noun* {380 iyshown} literally, the middle man of the eye; the middle of the night.

Pur, Purim *transliterated name, noun* {6332 puwr, *plural* puriym} a celebration of deliverance; **read** Ester 9:24–32.

Purah *transliterated name* {6513 purah} Foliage.

pure *adjective* {1249 bar} {2889 tahor} physically, soulically, or mentally, completely pure.

pure *adjective* {2134 zak} {2135 zakah} [2513 katharos] clean; clear; catharized.

pure *noun* {2890, 2891 tehor} completely pure.

pure *noun, participle* {6337 paz} {6338 pazaz} refined; made pure.

purge, cleanse, polish *verb* {1305 barar} [1571 ekkathairo] clarify; catharize; **cp** purify.

purification *noun* {*plural* 4795 maruqim} {8562 tamruq} clarification; catharization.

purify *verb* {2135 zakah} {2141 zakak} {2891 taher} [2511 katharizo] physically, soulically, or mentally, to cause to be completely pure.

purifying *noun* [2512 katharismos] [2514 katharotees] a washing off; an expiation.

purity *noun* {1252 bor} {2136 zakuw} clarity; catharized.

purity, purification *noun* {2890 tehor} {2891 taher} {2892 tohar} {2893 tohorah} physically, soulically, or mentally, completely pure.

pursue *verb* {7291 radaph} to run after.

pus *verb* {2990 yabbel} the excretion of a running sore.

push, butt *adjective* {5056 naggach} butting, as vicious.

push, butt *verb* {5055 nagach} to butt with the horns; to war against.

pustules *plural noun* {76 ababuah} eruptions of pus.

Put *transliterated name* {6316 put} a son of Ham; his descendants.

put, cast, lie *verb* [906 ballo] to throw.

put, set, place *verb* {7760, 7761 suwm} {7896 shith} {8239 shaphath} {8271 shathah} to put in place.

Puthiy *transliterated name* {6336 puwthiy} Hinge; Of Puth.

Puti El *transliterated name* {6317 putiel} Contempt of El.

putrefied *adjective* [4550 sapros] [4595 seepo] rotten; worthless.

putrid *adjective* {8182 shoar} offensive; **cp** horrible.

putridity *noun* {4716 maq} a moldy mess.

Python *transliterated name* [4436 puthon] a species of snake used in pagan worship.

Q

qab *transliterated noun* {6894 qab} a scoop of dry measure.

Qabse El *transliterated name* {6909 qabtseel} Gathered of El.

Qadesh *transliterated name* {6946 qadesh} Hallowed.

Qadesh Barnea *transliterated name* {6947 qadeshbarnea} Hallowed Field of Wandering.

Qadmi El *transliterated name* {6934 qadmiel} Ancient of El.

Qadmoniy *transliterated name* {6935 qadmoniy} Ancient.

Qallay *transliterated name* {7040 qallay} Trifle.

Qamon *transliterated name* {7056 qamown} Raised.

Qanah *transliterated name* {7071 qanah} [2580 kana] Reedy; **cp** Reed Sea.

Qareach *transliterated name* {7143 qareach} Balden.

Qarqa *transliterated name* {7173 qarqa} Floor.

Qarqor *transliterated name* {7174 qarqor} Undermine.

Qartah *transliterated name* {7177 qartah} City.

Qartan *transliterated name* {7178 qartan} City.

Qatan *transliterated name* {6997 qatan} Small.

Qattath *transliterated name* {7005 qattath} Littleness.

Qayin *transliterated name* {7014 qayin} [2535 kain] Chattelizer.

Qayiniy *transliterated name* {7014 qayin} {7017 qeyniy} Of Qayin.

Qedar *transliterated name* {6938 qedar} Drakened.

Qedemah *transliterated name* {6929 qedemah} Precedence.

Qedemoth *transliterated name* {6932 qedemowth} Precedings.

Qedesh *transliterated name* {6943 qedesh} Hallowed.

Qehath *transliterated name* {6955 qehath} Allied.

Qehathiy *transliterated name* {6956 qohathiy} Of Qehath.

Qehelathah *transliterated name* {6954 qehelathah} Congregated.

Qeilah *transliterated name* {7084 qeiylah} Citadel.

Qelayah *transliterated name* {7041 qelayah} Abased.

Qelita *transliterated name* {7042 qeliyta} Maiming.

Qemu El *transliterated name* {7055 qemuel} Raised of El.

Qenath *transliterated name* {7079 qenath} Chattel.

Qenaz *transliterated name* {7073 qenaz} Hunter.

Qenaziy *transliterated name* {7074 qenizziy} Of Qenaz.

Qeren I-lap Puch *transliterated name* {7163 qerenhappuwch} Horn of Stibium.

Qerioth *plural transliterated name* {7152 qeriyowth} Cities. **Qeros** *transliterated name* {7026 qeroc} Ankled.

Qesem *transliterated name* {7081 qecem} [2973 kosam] Divination.

Qesiah *transliterated name* {7103 qetsiyah} Cassia.

Qesis *transliterated name* {7104 qetsiyts} Chopped Off.

Qeturah *transliterated name* {6989 qetuwrah} Incensed.

Qeynan *transliterated name* {7018 qeynan} [2536 kainan] Nest.

Qibroth I-lat Taavah *plural transliterated name* {6914 qibrowthbattaavah} Tombs of Desire.

Qibsayim *dual transliterated name* {6911 qibtsayim} Double Heap.

Qidron *transliterated name* {6939 qidron} [2748 kedron] Dusky.

Qinah *transliterated name* {7016 qiynah} Lamentation.

Qir *transliterated name* {7024 qiyr} Wall.

Qir I-lareseth *transliterated name* {7025 qiyrchareseth} Wall of Pottery.

Qiryath Arba *transliterated name* {7153 qiryatharba} City of the Four Giants.

Qiryath Arim *transliterated name* {7157 qiryathariym} City of Forests.

Qiryath I-lusoth *plural transliterated name* {7155 qiryathchutsowth} City of Outways.

Qiryath Sannah *transliterated name* {7158 qiryathcannah} City of Twigs.

Qiryath Sepher *transliterated name* {7158 qiryathcepher} City of a Scroll.

Qiryathaim *dual transliterated name* {7156 qiryathayim} Double City.

Qish *transliterated name* {7027 qish} [2797 kis] Bow.

Qishi *transliterated name* {7029 qiyshiy} Bowed.

Qishon *transliterated name* {7028 qiyshown} Ensnared.

Qishyon *transliterated name* {7191 qishyown} Stubborn.

Qitron *transliterated name* {7003 qitrown} Incensed.

Qola Yah *transliterated name* {6964 qolayah} Voice of Yah.

Qorach *transliterated name* {7141 qorach} [2879 kore] Baldened.

Qorachiy *transliterated name* {7145 qorchiy} Of Qorach.

qorban *transliterated noun* {7133 qorban} [2878 korban] a hallowed oblation; **see** oblation.

Qore *transliterated name* {6981 qore} Called.

Qos *transliterated name* {6976 qowts} Thorn.

quadruped *noun* [5074 tetrapous] four footed.

quake *noun* {7494 raash} a vibrating; a quivering.

quake *verb* {1949 huwm} {7322 ruph} {7493 raash} to vibrate; to quiver.

quake *verb* {5120 noot} to quake.

quake, glutton *participle* {2151 zalal} to shake; to eat in excess.

quake, quiver *verb* {7264 ragaz} {7265 regaz} to quiver; in anger, or fear.

quake, shake, glutton *participle* {2151 zalal} to quake; to shake; to eat in excess; **cp** drunkard.

quantity, formula *noun* {4971 mathkuneth} a measured proportion of portions.

quarried rock *noun* [2991 laxutos] a rock, as fashioned, as distinct from a natural rock.

quarry, arrow *noun* {4551 macca} a quarry, in which stones are ejected; a missle, as projecting.

quarry, hammer *noun* {4717 maqqabah} {4718 maqqebeth} that which is used to pound; a quarry, from which is pounded.

quarter *noun* [2835 kodrantes] a quarter coin.

quickly *adverb* {4120 meherah} promptly.

quicksand *noun* [4950 surtis] sand that yields to pressure.

quietly *adverb* {3814 lat} silently; **cp** hush.

quit *verb* {2976 yaash} to desist.

quiver, quake *verb* {7264 ragaz} {7265 regaz} to quiver; in anger, or fear.

quiver, tingle *verb* {6750 tsalal} to vibrate. **quivering** *adjective* {7268 raggaz} timid.

quivering *noun* {7269 rogsah} trepidation.

Qusha Yah *transliterated name* {6984 qushayah} Snared of Yah.

R

Raam Yah *transliterated name* {7485 raamyah} Thunder of Yah.

Rab Shaqeh *transliterated name* {7262 rabshaqeh} Great Butler.

Rabbah *transliterated feminine name* {7237 rabbah} Feminine of {7227 rab} rabbi.

rabbi; see SUMMARY: DOCTOR, DOCTRINE, RABBI:

race *noun* [1408 dromos] figuratively, the course of life, or occupation.

race, oppression *noun* {4793 merots} {4794, 4835 merutsah} a test of running; the pressures of life.

Rachab *transliterated name* {7343 rachab} [4460 rhaab] [4477 rhachab] Large; Broad.

Racham *transliterated name* {7357 racham} Mercy.

Rachel *transliterated name* {7354 rachel} [4478 rhachel] Ewe (lamb).

Radday *transliterated name* {7288 radday} Domineering.

rafts *plural noun* {7513 raphcodah} as a flat on the water.

rage *noun* {2195 zaam} {7108 qetsaph} {7109 qetsaph} {7110 qetseph} [3950 parorgismos] raving anger.

rags *plural noun* {5499 cechabahoth} as ripped or torn.

Rahab *transliterated name* {7294 rahab} Proud.

railing *noun* {7507 rephidah} as spread along.

rain *noun* {4306 matar} [1028 brokee] [5205 huetos] showers; **cp** downpour.

rain *verb* {4305 matar} to rain; **cp** downpour.

rain, moisten *verb* [1026 breko] to moisten, as by a shower.

rain (early) *noun* {3138 yoreh} {4175 moreh} autumnal showers.

raise, exalt, lift, loft *verb* {7311, 7313 rum} {7318 romam} {7426 ramam} to lift hand, heart, offering, voice; to oath; **see** exalt.

raise, rise, rose, rouse, arise, arose *verb* {6965, 6966 qum} [450 anisteemi] [1453 egiro] to stand forth; to rise; to be stirred up, awakened.

raise (up), exalt, extol *verb* {5549 salal} from the root, to mound up; **see** selah; **cp** halal.

raisin cakes *plural noun* {6778 tsammuq} bakings of dried grapes.

Rachal *transliterated name* {7403 rachal} Merchant.

Ram *transliterated name* {7410 ram} [689 aram] Lofted.

ram, saddle, meadow *noun* {3733 kar} literally, plumpness, as in a full grown lamb; padding, as in a saddle; a meadow for sheep.

Ram Yah *transliterated name* {7422 ramyah} Lofted of Yah.

Ramah *transliterated name* {7414 ramah} [707 arimathaia] [4471 rhama] Lofty Altar; **cp** bamah.

Ramah *transliterated name* {7484 ramah} Thunder.

ramah *transliterated noun* {7413 ramah} a lofted altar; **cp** bamah.

Ramah I-lam Mispeh *transliterated name* {7434 ramathhammitspeh} Ramah of the Watch Tower.

Ramah Lechi *transliterated name* {7437 ramathlechiy} Ramah of a Jaw.

Ramahayim Sophim *transliterated name* {7436 ramathayimtsowphiym} Double Ramah of Watchers.

Ramahiy *transliterated name* {7435 ramathiy} Of Ramah.

ramble on *verb* {7300 rud} mentally, soulically, or physically, to wander about.

rampart, siege *noun* {4692 matsur} {4694 matsor} a mound for protection; a seizing.

rank, appraise, apprize, arrange, array, line up *verb* {6186 arak} to line up in a row; to put in order.

rank, arrangement, formation *noun* {4633 maarak} {4634 maarakah} {4635 maareketh} an arrangment (physical or mental).

rank, row, shingle *noun* {7713 sederah} {7795 sorah} that which is regulated in rows.

ranks of five *noun* {2571 chamush} regulated rows of five.

ransom, bribe *noun* {7810 shachad}.

rape *verb* {7693 shagal} to ravish in copulation; **see** ravage.

Rapha, Raphaim *transliterated name* {singular 7497, 7498 rapha} {plural 7497 rephaim} Healer.

Rapha El *transliterated name* {7501 raphael} Healer of El.

Rapha Yah *transliterated name* {7509 rephayah} [4488 rhesa] Healer of Yah.

Raphu *transliterated name* {7505 raphu} Healed.

Raqqath *transliterated name* {7557 raqqath} Expanded.

Raqqon *transliterated name* {7542 raqqown} Emaciated.

rash, balden, polish *verb* {4178 mowrat} {4803 marat} {4804 merat} to rub (off); to pluck; to cause to be bald.

rasp *noun* {4883 massor} an instrument for rasping.

ravage *noun* {7701 shod} a devastation.

ravage *verb* {7703 shadad} {7736 shud} to devastate.

razor, sheath, knife *noun* {8593 taar} a knife, or a razor, as making bare; a sheath, as being bare.

Rea Yah *transliterated name* {7211 reayah} Seen of Yah.

reach, attain, overtake *verb* {5381 nasag} to attain by reaching for.

reach, encounter, intercede *verb* {6293 paga} to impinge.

reach, touch, plague *verb* {5060 naga} to touch heavily; to strike.

read *verb* [314 anaginosko] to decipher.

reading *noun* 320 anagnosis] that which is read.

ready *verb* {6257 athad} to prepare.

ready, treasured, impending *adjective* {6259, 6264 athud} {6263 athid} prepared; treasured.

rebel *verb* {4775 marad} {4784 marah} {6586 pasha} {7279 ragan} to renounce; to resist.

rebel, flap *verb* {4754 mahrah} to flap one's self; to flap one's wings; to rebel.

rebellion *noun* {4776 merad} {4777 mered} {4805 meriy} {6588 pesha} renunciation; resistance.

rebellious *adjective* {4779 marad} {4780 maruth}.

rebirth *verb* [313 anagennao] to be reborn.

rebuild *verb* [456 anoikodomeo] to build again.

rebuke *noun* {1606 geahrah} a chiding.

rebuke *verb* {1605 gahgar} to chide.

rebuke, admonish *verb* [2008 epitimao] to charge sharply.

recall, call, proclaim *verb* {7121 qara} {7123 qera} [1941 epikaleomai] [2564 kaleo] [4341 proskaleomai] [4377 prosphoneo] to call out; to call upon; to address; **cp** name.

receive in full, distant *verb* [568 apeko] to have out; to keep away.

receive, wait, await, expect *verb* {2442 chakah} {3176 yachal} {6960 qavah} [324 anadekomai] [362 anameno] [553 apekdekomai] [4327 prosdekomai] [4328 prosdokao] [4329 prosdokia] to anticipate; to wait expectantly, patiently; **cp** take.

Rechab Am *transliterated name* {7346 rechabam} [4497 rhoboam] Enlarged the People.

Rechab Yah *transliterated name* {7345 rechabyah} Enlarged of Yah.

Rechob *transliterated name* {7340 rechob} Broadway.

Rechoboth *plural transliterated name* {7344 rechoboth} Broadways.

Rechum *transliterated name* {7348 rechuwm} Merciful.

recline *verb* [347 anaklino] the posture when eating; **cp** repose.

recognize, discern, distinguish, estrange, notice *verb* {5234 nakar} to acknowledge; to scrutinize; to distinguish between; to ignore, hence to be estranged.

recompense *noun* [468 antapodoma] [469 antapodosis] that which is given back.

recompense *verb* [467 antapodidomi] to give back.

reconcile (fully) *verb* [604 apokatallasso] completely restore.

reconcile *verb* [2644 katallasso] to restore.

reconciliation *noun* [2643 katallagee] restoration.

record *noun* {1799 dikrown} a register.

recoup *verb* {5756 uz} to restore strength.

red hot stones, pavement *noun* {7528 ratsaph} {7529 retseph} as used for baking; as used for laying a pavement.

redeem *verb*, **redeemer** *participle* {1350 gaal} {6299 padah} [3084 lutroo] [3086 lutrotes] to ransom; a ransomer; **cp** market.

redeemed *noun* {*plural* 6302 paduim} the ransomed.

redemption *noun* {1353 geullah} {6304 peduth} {6306 pidon} [487 antilutron] [629 apolutrosis] [3083 lutron] [3085 lutrosis] the ransom; the setting free.

Reed (Sea) *name* {5488 cuph} {5492 cuphah} [2063 eruthra] [2281 thalassa] of reeds; Reed Sea; **note:** Reed is mistranslated Red.

Reela Yah *transliterated name* {7480 reelayah} Shaken of Yah.

reem *noun* {7214 reem} a wild ox.

refine *verb* {2212 zaqaq} {6884 tsaraph} to purify; **cp** test; **cp** proof.

refiner *noun* {6885 tsorephi} one that refines.

refire *verb* [329 anazopureo] to fire up again.

reflourish *verb* [330 anathallo] to flourish again.

refrain, restrain, retain *verb* {3607 kala} {6113 atsar} to restrict; to hold back.

refresh *verb* [404 anapsuko] recovery of breath.

refreshing *noun* [403 anapsuxis] recovery of breath.

refuge *noun* {4152 muwadah} {4224 machabe} {*plural* 4224 machabeim} {4268 machaceh} {4733 miqlat} a place of protection.

refuge (seek) *verb* {2620 chacah} {2622 chacuth} to flee to for protection.

refuse *adjective* {3986 maen} {*plural* 3987 maenim} unwilling.

refuse *verb* {3985 maen} {3988 maac} to reject; to spurn; also to disappear.

refute *verb* [471 antepo] an answer instead of; as opposed to.

regard, guard, on guard *verb* {5201 natar} {5202 nater} {5341 natsar} {8104 shamar} {*plural* 8107 shimmurim} {8108 shomrah} {8176 shaar} [5083 tereo] in the sense of protecting from harm, observing observances, obeying misvoth.

regenesis *noun* [3824 palingenesia] rebirth; renovation; restoration.

region *noun* [5561 chora] an area.

regirt *verb* [328 anazonnumi] to girt again.

regret *verb* [3338 metamellomai] to be sorry; **cp** repent.

regurgitate, ascend, holocaust, mount *verb* {5927, 5928 alah} to ascend, as a mountain; to mount an animal; to regurgitate food; to ascend a holocaust; **see** holocaust, *noun*.

reign *noun* {4474 mimshal} {4475 memshalah} the office of a sovereign.

reign *verb* **sovereign** *participle* {4427 malak} {4910 mashal} [936 basiluo] to rule; the officiating of a sovereign; **see** sovereign.

reign, equal *noun* {4915 moshel} equal, in the sense of being able to liken unto, or compare with; reign; of being more than equal; of being over.

reinforce *verb* {5790 uth} to hasten; to encourage.

reinforcement *noun* {8136 shinan} to reinforce by doubling, or by duplicating.

reinforcing *participle* {4834 marats} pressuring; irritating.

reins *plural noun* {2910 tuwchah} {3629 keliy} [3510 nephros] literally, kidneys; symbolic of the innermost thoughts.

reiterate, repeat, alter, change, double, duplicate, fold *verb* {8132 shana} {8133 shena} {8138 shanah} to reinforce by folding, by doubling; may include disguise, camouflage.

reject *verb* {5010 naar} to not accept.

rejoice *verb* {2302 chadah} {2868 teeb} {7797 sus} to cheer.

rejoicing *noun* {8342 sason} a cheerfulness.

rejoicing *verb* {2304, 2305 chedvah} cheering.

rejuvenate *verb* {7375 rutaphash} made juvenile.

Rekah *transliterated name* {7397 rekah} Tenderized.

relax *verb* {7599 shaan} to loll.

relaxation, relaxed *noun* {7600 shaanan} [425 anesis] relaxation, as being secure; relief.

release *noun* {8059 shemittah} the negation of a debt.

release *verb* {8058 shamat} [525 apallasso] to loose; to let fall, or drop.

release, abandon *verb* {8281 sharah} to free.

release, abandon, forsake, leave (behind) *verb* {5800 azab} [1459 enkatalipo] to leave behind; in a good sense, to let remain over; in a bad sense, to abandon.

release, allow, forgive, forsake, leave *verb* [863 aphieemi] to send forth.

release, loose *verb* [3089 luo] to set free; to unbind.

release, unravel *verb* {8271 shere} to let loose.

released *noun* {8293 sheruth} set free; separate; freedom of persons.

releasing, forsaking, leaving *noun* {5805 azubah} the letting loose of, or from.

relive *verb* [326 anazao] to live again.

remain, remaining *verb* {3498 yathar} to be left over.

remain, return, behave, overturn *verb* [390 anastrepho] [396 anatrepo] to turn; in the manner one turns (behaves); to turn over; to overthrow.

remainder, remnant, rest, exceeding *noun* {3499 yether} the remainder, those left over.

Remal Yah *transliterated name* {7425 remalyah} Bedecked of Yah.

remeasure *verb* [488 antimetreo] to remeter.

remember, memorialize *verb* {2142 zakar} {7876 shayah} [3403 mimeeskomai] [3415 mnaomai] [3421 mneemonuo] [5279 hupomimneesko] an acting of the memory; to hold in remembrance.

remember, remind *verb* [363 anamimnesko] to recollect; to remind.

remembrance *noun* [364 anamneesis] [3417 mnia] [3420 mneemee] [5280 hupomneesis] a recollection; a memory.

remind *verb* [3560 noutheteo] to caution; to recall to mind; **see** mind.

remnant, rest, exceeding, remainder *noun* {3499 yether} the remainder, those left over.

remove *verb* [522 apairo] to lift off.

remove *verb* [851 aphaireo] to take away.

remove, depart *verb* {5253 nacag} to retreat.

remove, transcribe, antiquate *verb* {6275 athaq} that which has aged; to take away; to take down, as in transcribing.

removed far, far removed *verb* {7368 rachaq} from the root, to widen.

renew, renewing, renovate *verb* {2318 chadash} [340 anakainizo] [341 anakainoo] [342 anakainosis] [365 ananeoo] to make new again; to rebuild; to retore; **see** new.

repartee *verb* [2160 eutrapelia] to say in ready and witty reply.

repeat, alter, change, double, duplicate, fold, reiterate *verb* {8132 shana} {8133 shena} {8138 shanah} to reinforce by folding, by doubling; may include disguise, camouflage.

repent *verb* [3340 metanoeo] to be sorry afterwards; **cp** regret.

repentance *noun* [3341 metanoya] being sorry afterwards.

Rephach *transliterated name* {7506 rephach} Support.

report *verb* [1310 diapheemizo] to divulge; to tell thoroughly.

report, fame, hearing, notoriety *noun* {8052 shemuah} {8088 shema} {8089 shoma} [189 akoee] that which is heard; an announcement; a rumor.

repose *noun* {7258 rebets} a place of rest.

repose *verb* {7252 reba} [345 anakimai] [376 anapipto] [1879 epanapauomai] to prostrate; to rest; the posture when eating; **cp** recline.

repose, lay *verb* [2621 katakimai] to lie down; recline at a meal.

reproach *noun* {2781 cherpah} [3680 onidismos] [3681 onidos] a discredit; disgrace.

reproach *verb* {2778 charaph} [3679 onidizo] to discredit; to disgrace.

reproof *noun* {8433 tokachath} correction; refutation; noun of reprove; **see** reprove.

reprove, approve, prove *verb* {3198 yakach} [1381 dokimazo] to prove; to accept or reject the proving.

reputation *noun* {5082 nedibah} as of nobility.

req, vain, vanity, void, empty *adjective* {1892 hebel} {*transliteration* 7385 riq} {*transliteration* 7386 req} {7723 shav} [*transliteration* 4469 rhaka] emptiness; voidness; figuratively, stupid.

Reqem *transliterated name* {7552 reqem} Embroidered.

request *noun* {4862 mishalah} an asking.

require, seek, enquire, examine, inquire *verb* {1875 darash} to ask; to seek; **cp** beseech.

rescue *verb* {6308 pada} [4506 rhuomai] to retrieve; to pull from the current.

rescue, escape *verb* {4422 malat} literally, to smooth; to slip away; to be slipped away.

rescue, strip, equip *verb* {2502 chalats} literally, to strip for hostility; to strip out of danger.

rescue, strip, escape *verb* {5337, 5338 natsal} to snatch away; favorably, or unfavorably.

resend *verb* [375 anapempo] to send again.

Reseph *transliterated name* {7530 retseph} Red Hot Stones.

reservoir *noun* {650 aphiyq} a gathering of water; **see** gather.

reservoir *noun* {4724 miqvah} a congregating of waters; **see** congregate.

reside, residence *verb* {2082 zabal} {7871 shibah} to dwell.

residence *noun* {2073 zebul} a dwelling.

resident *noun* [1927 epidemeo] a dweller.

Resin *transliterated name* {7526 retsiyn} Pleasing.

resistance *noun* {8617 tequmah} ability to rise up against.

resound, glitter *verb* {6670 tsahal} to stand out; in color, or in sound.

respiration, respite *noun* {7305 revach} {7309 revachah} the inspiration and expiration; a spiritual respite; a spirit of rest; **see** spirit; **see** wind.

respire, scent *verb* {7304 ravach} {7306 ruwach} ruwach is the verb of spirit, wind; literally, to breathe freely; to refresh; to sense through the movement of air; **cp** breathe.

resplend *verb* [1584 eklampo] to be resplendent; to shine brilliantly.

respond, restore, return, turn (away) (back) (from) (to) *verb* {7725 shub} {8421 tub} from the root, to turn back; as to reply, to come back.

response, return, turn *noun* {8666 teshubah} a reccurence; a reply, as returned.

rest *adjective* {7282 ragea} restful.

rest *noun* {1679 dobe} {4494 manoach} {4496 menuchah} {4774 margeah} {5118 nuwach} {5183 nachath} {8253 sheqet} [372 anapausis] repose; tranquility.

rest *verb* {5117 nuwach} {8252 shaqat} [373 anapauo] to repose.

rest, exceeding, remainder, remnant *noun* {3499 yether} the remainder, those left over.

rest, split, blink, calm *verb* {7280 raga} this word is derived from two roots; blink and split, as momentary; calm and rest, as soothing.

rest in habitation *verb* {5115 navah} to rest, as at home; **see** habitation of rest.

restake *verb* [388 anastauroo] to stake again; **see** stake; **read** Hebrews 6:6.

resting place *noun* {4769 marbets} {4771 margoa} a place to rest.

restless *adjective* [180 akatapaustos] without rest; pauseless.

restore *verb* [600 apokathistemi] to reconstitute.

restore *verb* {8627 teqan} to set straight.

restore, return, turn (away) (back) (from) (to) respond *verb* {7725 shub} {8421 tub} from the root, to turn back; as to reply, to come back.

restrain the heel, trip the heel *verb* {6117 aqab} to seize by holding the heel.

restrain, retain, refrain *verb* {3607 kala} {6113 atsar} to restrict; to hold back.

restrainer *noun* {6115 etser} one that holds back; **see** abstinence.

restraint *noun* {6115 otser} a holding back; **see** abstinence.
resurrection *noun* [386 anastasis] a rising again.

retain, refrain, restrain *verb* {3607 kala} {6113 atsar} to restrict; to hold back.

retreat *verb* {7734 sug} to back off.

retreat, flight *noun* {4498 manohs} {4499 menusah} a place to flee to; a fleeing.

retribution *noun* {8005 shillem} {8011 shillumah} [489 antimisthia] retribution; reward in a negative sense.

return, behave, overturn, remain *verb* [390 anastrepho] [396 anatrepo] to turn; in the manner one turns (behaves); to turn over; to overthrow.

return, turn (away) (back) (from) (to) respond, restore *verb* {7725 shub} {8421 tub} from the root, to turn back; as to reply, to come back.

return, turn, response *noun* {8666 teshubah} a reccurence; a reply, as returned.

returning *noun* {7870 shibah} a turning back.

Reu *transliterated name* {7466 reu} [4466 rhagan] Friend.

Reu Ben *transliterated name* {7205 reuben} [4502 rouben] See a Son.

Reu Beniy *transliterated name* {7206 reuwbeniy} Of Reu Ben.

Reu El *transliterated name* {7467 reuel} Friend of El.

revere (well), reverence (well) *verb* [2124 eulabia] [2125 eulabeomai] [2150 eusebia] [2151 eusebeo] to well venerate.

reverently *adverb* [2153 eusebos] veneratively.

revolt *noun* {5627 carah} turned away.

revolt, revolting *verb* {5637 sarar} turning away.

revolution, circuit *noun* {8622 tequphah} a revolution of days; a revolving around.

rhema *transliterated noun* [4487 rhema] a verbalization; the noun of rhetorize; **cp** word.

rhetorically *transliterated adverb* [4490 rhetos] verbally.

rhetorize *transliterated verb* [4483 reo] to express verbally.

rib, side *noun* {5967 ala} {6763 tsela} literally, a curve or an arch; a rib of a body; a rib of a structure.

Ribay *transliterated name* {7380 riybay} Contentious.

Riblah {1689 diblah} {7247 riblah} Fertile.

Ribqah *transliterated name* {7259 ribqah} [4479 rhebekka] Fetterer.

rich, riches *noun* {6223 ashir} {6239 osher} {*plural* 6251 ashteroth} enriched with riches; **see** enrich.

riddle *noun* {2420 chidah} a question, proposition, or rhyme worded so as to rouse conjecture.

riddle, vertebrae *noun* {7001 qetar} a knot; as that which is to be unravelled.

ride, drive *verb* {7392 rakab} to place upon; to despatch.

ridges *plural noun* {7406 rekec} a mountain ridge.

ridicule *noun* {7047 qelec} {7048 qallacah} a disparagement.

ridicule *verb* [2606 katagelao] to laugh at; to deride.

ridicule *verb* {7046 qalac} to disparage.

ridicule, entertain, laugh *verb* {6711 tsachaq} {6712 tsechoq} {7832 sechag} to laugh; to laugh at; to laugh at in defiance.

ridicule, laugh, laughter *noun* {6712 tsechoq} {7814 sechoq} laughter; a laughing at; a laughing at in defiance.

right *adjective* {3227 yeminiy} {3233 yeminay} **see** right *noun*; **cp** left.

right *noun* {3225 yamiyn} that which is opposite the left; **cp** left; example: when facing north, the east; most versions erroneously insert the words *hand*, or *side*; we sit not on Yah Shua's right hand, or on his left hand; but at his left, and at his right.

right *verb* {3231 yaman} to cause to go to the right.

rim *noun* {3749 karkob} a rim as encircling.

rim, arch, back, bow, brow *noun* {1354 gab} that which is bowed, curved; also the top or rim.

Rimmon Peres *transliterated name* {7428 rimmonperets} Pomegranate Split (of Separation).

ringleaders, rims *plural noun* {5633 ceren} instigators; rims of wheels.

ringstraked *adjective* {6124 aqod} round, circular stripes.

rip, shred *verb* {7167 qara} from the root, to rend.

ripen, spice, embalm *verb* {2590 chanat} from the root, to spice.

ripen, wean, deal *verb* {1580 gamal} transact.

ripped *verb* [1284 diarrhesso] to tear apart with force.

rise early, seek early *verb* {7836 shachar} to be early.

rise, rose, rouse, arise, arose, raise *verb* {6965, 6966 qum} [393 anatello] [450 anisteemi] [1453 egiro] to stand forth; to rise; to be stirred up, awakened.

risen being *noun* {3351 yequm} a being who has risen.

rising *noun* {4217 mizrach} [395 anatole] the rising (of the sun); the east; **cp** lowering.

rising *noun* {7012 qimah} an arising.

rising, springing, proceeding, procedure *noun* {4161 motsa} {*plural* 4163 motsaoth} literally, the source of going forth, whether of persons, of water, of the sun.

Rispah *transliterated name* {7532 ritspah} Hot Stone.

Risya *transliterated name* {7525 ritsya} Pleased.

rivalry *noun* [2052 erithia] a desire to put one's self forward; factiousness.

river, rivulet *noun* {2975 yeor} {5103 nehar} {5104 nahar} {6388 peleg} a stream of water.

roaming *verb* {7904 shakah} to roam.

roar *verb* {1993 hamah} to hum, as in commotion.

roar *verb* {7580 shaag} to rumble.

roar, uproar, waste *noun* {7588 shaon} a rumble; a destruction.

roaring *noun* {7581 shagah} a rumbling.

roaring lion *noun* {3833 lebia *plural* labaim} {7826 shachal} a lion, as a roarer.

roaring lioness *noun* {3833 lebeoth *plural* lebaoth} a lioness, as the fiercer.

roaring waste *noun* {7584 shaavah} a wasting away.

robe, robing *noun* {1545 gelowm} {3830, 3831 lebush} {4403 malbwsh} {8509 takrik} {8516 talbosheth} a wraparound; **see** enrobe.

rock *noun* {2906 tur} {5553 cela} {6697 tsur} [4073 petra] [4074 petros] a rock; a piece of rock; **cp** Petros.

rock *noun* {*plural* 3710 kephim} a hollow rock; **cp** Kepha.

rocky *adjective* [4075 petrodees] rock-like; **cp** Petros. **rod** *noun* {2415 choter} [4464 rhabdos] rod, or twig; also a rod of royalty.

rod *noun* {4294 mattah} an offshoot, branch, sprout of a tree; of a people; **note:** both rod and scion are translated *tribe* in both covenants of most versions; **cp** scion; **cp** sceptre.

Rohagah *transliterated name* {7303 rowhagah} Outcry.

LEXICON

roll *noun* {1549 gillayon} {4039 megillah} something rolled up; a roll of a scroll; a little scroll.

roll *noun* {megillah} a roll of a scroll.

roll *verb* {1556 gahlal} to roll; to roll up; to roll away.

roll *verb* {6428 palash} to roll, as in dust or ashes; an expression of humbling.

Roman *transliterated name* [4513 rhomaikos] [4514 rhomaios] [4515 rhomaisti] of Rome.

Rome *transliterated name* [4516 rhome] Strength.

roof *noun* {1406 gag} usually the top of a house or altar.

rooster *noun* [220 alektor] a male fowl.

roostervoice *noun* [219 alektorophonia] the sound of a rooster.

root *noun* {8328 sheresh} {8330 shoresh} the underground part of a plant.

root, uproot *verb* {8327 sharash} {8332 sheroshu} to plant a root; to pull out by the root.

rope, wreath, wreathen, foliage *noun* {5688 abothah} as entwined; a wreath in victory; **cp** crown; **cp** diadem.

rose, rouse, arise, arose, raise, rise *verb* {6965, 6966 qum} [450 anisteemi] [1453 egiro] to stand forth; to rise; to be stirred up, awakened.

Rosh *transliterated name* {7220 rosh} Head; Top.

rosh *transliterated noun* {7219 rosh} a poisonous plant.

rot *verb* {5685 abash} to dry up.

rot *verb* {7537 raqab} to decay.

rotten, rotteness *noun* {7538 raqab} {7539 riqqabon} decay.

round *adjective* {5696 agol} circular.

round, strike (round about), surround *verb* {5362 naqaph} to strike; to strike all around; to surround; to round off the beard.

round, surround, environ *noun* {3603 kikkar} literally, circle; the environs of an area; a round of material, usually of precious metals.

round about *advery* {5439 cabiyb} all around; surrounding.

round dance *noun* {4246 mechol} a dance in which participants form a ring.

round dancing *verb* {4234 machol} to dance with participants forming a ring.

rouse, arise, arose, raise, rise, rose *verb* {6965, 6966 qum} [450 anisteemi] [1453 egiro] to be stirred up, awakened; to stand forth; to rise.

rouse up *verb* [387 anastatoo] soulically, to be roused.

route *noun* {4570 magalah} a rampart; a track; **see** pass, passage.

row, shingle, rank *noun* {7713 sederah} {7795 sorah} that which is regulated in rows.

row, turn *noun* {8447 tor} a succession of occasion; a row of.

rub, shake, wave *verb* {5130 nuph} to rub a bed with aromatics; to shake a hand; to wave an offering.

rub, sicken, stroke, worn (out) *verb* {2470 chalah} to wear out; to stroke the face as in appeasement.

rubbing rags *noun* {4418 malachim} literally, rubbers; that which is used to rub.

ruin *noun* {4288 mechittah} {4596 meiy} {4654 mappalah} {4658 mippeleth} {4875 meshoah} {4876 *plural* mashshooth} {6986 qeteb} {6987 qoteb} [3639 olethros] utter destruction; death.

ruin, vanish, corrupt, destroy, destruct, lose *verb* {6 abad} {7 abad} {8 obed} {7843 shachath} [622 apollumi] [1311 diapthiro] [2704 kataphthiro] [5351 phthiro] to corrupt through decay.

ruling *adverb* {4431 melak} adverb of reign.

rump *noun* {451 alyah} the hind of the body.

run, outrun *verb* **runner** *participle* {7323 ruts} {7325 rur} to run; one who runs; to run faster than.

rush *noun* {1999 hamullah} the sound of rushing.

rush, marsh *noun* {98 agam} {99 agem} {100 agmone} a stagnant water, or that which grows therefrom.

rushing *participle* {5584 caah} as a wind.

Ruth *transliterated name* {7327 ruth} [4503 routh] Friend.

S

Saanan *transliterated name* {6630 tsaanan} Flock.

Saanannim, Saanayim *plural transliterated name* {6815 tsaananniym, tsaanayim} Migrates.

Sabaoth *transliterated title* **host, hosts** *noun* {6635 tsebaah *plural* tsabaoth} [3841 pantokrator] [*plural* 4519 sabaoth] of hosts; a vast array of warriors; often compounded with El and with Yah Veh; [4519 sabaoth] is the Hellenic transliteration of sabaoth, only in Romans 9:29, and Yaaqovos 5:4; [3841 pantokrator] is the Hellenic translation of sabaoth, only in 2 Corinthians 6:18, and throughout the Apocalypse; **see** host.

Sabtecha *transliterated name* {5455 cabtecha} the meaning uncertain; a son of Kush, and the region settled by him.

sack *noun* {6861 tsiqion} a sack, as tied at the mouth; **cp** saq.

sackbut *noun* {5443 sabbeka} a lyre, as being stringed.

sacrifice *noun* {1685 debach} {2077 zebach} [2378 thusia] an offering – usually an animal; Yah Shua Messiah became our sacrifice as a lamb unblemished.

sacrifice *verb* {1684 debach} {2076 zabach} [2380 thuo] to offer up – usually an animal.

sacrifice (idol) *noun* [1494 eidolothuton] a sacrifice to an idol.

sacrifice altar *noun* {4056 madbach} {4196 mizbeach} [2379 thusiasterion] a furniture on which sacrifices are sacrificed; the Hebrew is from the root of the verb, sacrifice {2076 zabach}; **see** sacrifice.

saddle, meadow, ram *noun* {3733 kar} literally, plumpness, as in a full grown lamb; padding, as in a saddle; a meadow for sheep.

Sadoq *transliterated name* {6659 tsadowq} [4524 sadok] Just; a scion of the priesthood; **see** justness.

Sadoqiy *transliterated name* {6659 tsadowq} [4523 saddoukaios] of Sadoq; the name of a religious sect who claimed the virtue of justness; **see** Sadoq; **see** justness.

saffron *noun* {3750 karkom} the crocus.

sail, ensign, pole *noun* **Nissi** *transliterated title* {5251 nec} an ensign; the pole of an ensign; part of the title, Yah Veh Nissi, which means, Yah Veh Ensign.

sailer *noun* {2259 chobel} one that handles riggings of rope on a sailor.

Sair *transliterated name* {6811 tsaiyr} Little.

Sachar *transliterated name* {7940 sachar} Hire.

Sal Monah *transliterated name* {6758 tsalmonah} Shade of Death.

Sal Munna *transliterated name* {6759 tsalmunna} Shade is Withheld.

Salaph *transliterated name* {6764 tsalaph} the meaning uncertain.

Salchah *transliterated name* {5548 calchah} Walking. **sale** *noun* {4466 mimkereth} **see** sell.

Sallu, Sallay *transliterated name* {5543 calluw, callay} Balanced.

Salmah *transliterated name* {8009 salmah} Clothing.

Salmay *transliterated name* {8014 salmay} Clothed.

Salmon *transliterated name* {6756 tsalmown} Shady.

Salmon *transliterated name* {8012 salmon} [4533 salmon] [4534 salmone] Clothed.

salt *noun* **salty** *adjective* {4420 melechah} [358 analos] salted; an unfertile land caused by a high salt content.

salt *noun* {4415, 4416 melach} {4417 malach} [217 halas] [251 hals] [252 halukos] salt, as pulverized.

salt *verb* {4414 malach} [233 halizo] to rub on salt.

salutation *noun* [783 aspasmos] a greeting of welcome.

salute *verb* [782 aspazomai] to welcome.

salvation; see SUMMARY: SALVATION, SAVE:

Sancherib *transliterated name* {5576 cancheriyb} the meaning uncertain; an Ashshur sovereign.

sand *noun* {2344 chowl} [285 ammos] pulverized rock.

sanhedrim *transliterated noun* [4892 sunedriom] a Yah Hudiy tribunal.

Saphon *transliterated name* {6829 tsaphown} Northern.

saplings *plural noun* {3242 yeniqah} young trees.

sapphire *transliterated noun* {5601 sapir} a gem.

saq *transliterated noun* {8242 saq} [4526 sakkos] a mesh cloth; **cp** sack.

Sarah *transliterated name* {8283 sarah} [4564 sarrha] Marshaless (female marshal); **cp** Saray.

Saray *transliterated name* {8297 saray} Governess; **cp** Sarah.

Sardis *transliterated name* [4554 sardis] Asked.

Sarephath *transliterated name* {6886 tsarephath} [4558 sarepta] Refinement.

Sarethan *transliterated name* {6891 tsarethan} Pierced.

Sarsechim *transliterated name* {8310 sarcechiym} a Babeliy general.

satan *transliterated verb* {7853 satan} to oppose.

Satan *transliterated name* {7854 satan} [4566 satan] [4567 satanas] the Hebrew name of Diabolos; an opposer; the Hellene is a transliteration of the Hebrew; **see** satan; **see** Diabolos.

satiate, satisfy, saturate; see SUMMARY: SATIATE.

satrap *noun* {323, 324 achashdarpan} a governor.

savage *adjective* [434 aneemeros] uncivilized.

save, saviour; see SUMMARY: SAVE, SAVIOUR:

savour of rest *noun* {5207, 5208 nichoach} a species of offering.

saw *verb* {7787 sur} to saw with a saw.

say, said, saith, saying *verb* {559, 560 amar} [2031 epos] [2036 epo] [2046 ereo] [5345 pheemi] to express in words.

saying, sayings *noun* {561 emer} {562 omer} {565 imrah} a statement, usually quoted, often as a proverb.

scab *noun* {5597 cappachath} a mange, as falling off.

scale *noun* {7193 qasqeseth} a scale of a fish; a scale of an armor.

scall *noun* {5424 netheq} a scurf.

scalp *noun* {6936 qodqod} the scalp of the head.

scan, tan *verb* {7805 shazaph} to scan; to be scanned by the sun; hence, to tan.

scandal *transliterated noun* [4625 skandalon] a trap; a stumblingblock; **see** stumblingblock.

scandal, scandalize *transliterated verb* [4624 scandalizo] to entice to sin; to be a stumblingblock.

scapegoat *noun* {5799 azazel} a goat which bears the sins of another; **read** Leviticus 16:8–26.

scar, contortion *noun* {6094 atstsebeth} contortion, as in pain; scars as causing contortion; **see** contort *verb*.

scarlet *noun* {8144 shaniy} the color; **see** crimson.

scarlet, maggot *noun* {8438 tolaath} a wormlike larva; scarlet, as the color of the maggot.

scarring *noun* {3587 kiy} a scar or brand caused by searing.

scatter, shatter, splatter *verb* {5310 naphats} {5311 nephets} {6327 puts} {6340 pazar} {7376 ratash} to disperse; to disperse by shattering.

scatter, spread, grow *verb* {6335 push} [837 auxano] to grow, to enlarge; as in spreading out.

scattering *noun* {8600 tephowtsah} a dispersal.

scatterings *plural noun* {4215 mezarehim} of winds.

scent *noun* {7381, 7382 reyach} an inspiration and expiration of a being; an aroma that is emitted.

sceptre, scion *noun* {7625 shebat} {7626 shebet} {8275 sharbit} [5443 phule] an offshoot, branch, sprout of a tree; a family of people; a symbol of rule; **cp** rod.

scholar *noun* {8527 talmid} a teacher or learner.

scion, sceptre *noun* {7625 shebat} {7626 shebet} {8275 sharbit} [5443 phule] an offshoot, branch, sprout of a tree; a family of people; a symbol of rule; **cp** rod.

scion (another) [246 allophulos] **see** scion.

scions (twelve) *noun* [1429 diodekaphulon] the twelve scions of Yisra El.

scope over, oversee *verb* [1983 episkopeo] to episcopate; to inspect over.

scorch *adjective* [2739 kaumatizo] burn; scorch; sear.

scorch, kindle, inflame *verb* {2734 charah} {2787 charar} {6866 zarab} literally, or soulically, to glow; to blaze up.

scorch, scorching *noun* [2738 kauma] [2740 kausis] [2742 kauson] painful and burning heat.

scorches *plural noun* {2788 charim} parched areas.

scorn *verb* {3887 luwts} {5006 naats} to mouth off; to deride.

scorn, scorner *verb, participle* {3945 latsats} to despise; a despiser.

scorn, scorning *noun* {3944 latsohn} {5007 neatsah *plural* neatsahoth} a derision.

scorpion *transliterated noun* [4651 skorpios] a species of lizard with a sting in its tail.

scour, polish *verb* {4838 maraq} to polish, so as to sharpen.

scourge *noun* {7850 shotet} a whip.

scourge, oar *noun* {7885 shait} a whip; a paddle.

scrape (off) (away) (together) *verb* {5500 cachah} {5595 caphah} {5596 caphach} to scrape; **see** offscouring.

scrape, cut *verb* {7096 qatsah} to cut off; to scrape off, by cutting; to destroy.

scream *verb* {6463 paah} [349 anakrazo] to utter a shrill screech.

screen *noun* {4345 makber} as woven; **cp** net.

scribe *noun* {5613 capher} [1122 grammatus] a writer; one that scribes; **see** scripture; **see** scroll.

scribe *verb* {5608 saphar} [1123 graptos] [1125 grapho] to write; to scribe; **see** inscribe, chart.

scribing *noun* {5610 sephar} {5615 sephorah} [1121 gramma] that which is scribed; **see** scroll.

scripture *noun* [1124 graphee] the writing, especially of Elohim; scripture *singular* usually encompasses the whole scroll of Elohim; scriptures *plural* usually encompasses segments of scripture *singular*.

scroll *noun* {5609 cephar} {5612 ciphrah} [975 biblion] [976 biblos] a roll or series of rolls which contain scribings.

scrollette *noun* [974 biblaridion] diminutive of scroll; **cp** roll.

sculpt *verb* {6458 pacal} to sculpt a sculptile.

sculptiles *noun* {*plural* 6456 pecil} {6459 pecel} that which is sculpted.

sea, seaward *noun* {3220, 3221 yam} [2281 thalassa] a great expanse of salt water; toward the sea.

seah *transliterated noun* {5429 ceah} {5432 caceah} [4568 saton] a measure of grain.

seal *noun* {2368 chotham} [4973 sphragis] a signature ring used to seal scrolls to indicate that they have not been tampered with; **see** signet.

seal *verb* {2856, 2857 chatham} [4972 sphragizo] [5420 phrasso] to affix a seal; to close up.

search *noun* {2665 chephes} an uncovering; a discovery; a masking.

search *verb* [2045 erunao] to seek; to examine into.

search, disguise *verb* {2664 chaphas} to uncover; discover; to mask.

search, seek, beseech *verb* {1245 baqash} to search for, including a response to a petition; **cp** inquire, require.

season *noun* [2540 kairos] an occasion; a measure of time; a fixed or proper time.

season, congregation *noun* {4150, 4151 moed} [2540 kairos] an assemblage; an occasion of celebration, of the year, of existence.

seat *verb* [2525 kathistemi] to place down.

Sebaiym *plural transliterated name* {5436 cebaiym} Of Seba.

Sebam, Sibmah *transliterated name* {7643 sebam, sibmah} Spice.

Seboim *plural transliterated name* {6636 tseboiym} Gazelles.

Seboim *plural transliterated name* {6650 tseboiym} Stripes.

second, double, duplicate *noun* {4932 mishneh} a copy of; a double amount; a repetition.

secondly *adverb* {8579 tinyanuth} a second time.

section *noun* {1335 bether} that which has been cut.

section *verb* {1333 bathaq} {1334 bathar} to cut into sections.

secure *verb* [805 asphalizo] to make firm, secure.

secure, certain *adjective* **securely, certainly** *adverb* {3330 yatstsib} [804 asphalees] [806 asphalos] assuredly; safely.

secure loft *noun* {4869 misgab} a lofty place; figuratively, an elevated refuge.

security, certainty *noun* {3321 yetseb} [803 asphalia] safety; an undoubtable truth.

Sedad *transliterated name* {6657 tsedad} Side.

Sedom *transliterated name* {5467 cedom} [4670 sodoma] Scorch.

seduce, wander *verb* [4105 planao] to go; be led astray.

seducing *adjective* **seducer** *noun* [4108 planos] raving; a misleader.

seduction, wandering *noun* [4106 planee] a straying from.

seductions *plural noun* {4065 madduach} allurements.

see *adjective* {7202 raeh} as experiencing.

see *verb* {2370, 2372 chazah} to gaze; to envision; **see** seer.

see *verb* {7200 raah} [308 anablepo] the prime verb of to see; to see again.

see, spectacle noun {7210 roiy} from the root, sight.

seed noun {2221 zeruwa} {2233 zera} {2234 zerah} a seed, as planted; posterity.

seed verb {2232 zahrah} to plant seed.

seeing participle {7212 reith} sight.

seek verb [327 anazeeteo] to search for.

seek, beseech, search verb {1245 baqash} to search for, including a response to a petition; **cp** inquire, require.

seek, enquire, examine, inquire, require verb {1875 darash} to ask; to seek; **cp** beseech.

seek early, rise early verb {7836 shachar} to be early.

seek refuge verb {2620 chacah} {2622 chacuth} to flee to for protection.

seer noun {2374 chozeh} the former name of a prophet; one that sees into the future; **cp** knower.

seethe verb {2102, 2103 zuwd} literally, or soulically, to boil.

Seirah transliterated name {8167 seiyrah} Roughness.

Sechachah transliterated name {5527 sechachah} Covered; Hedged.

Sechu transliterated name {7906 sechuw} Observatory.

Sela transliterated name {6762 tsela} Limping.

Sela Ham Machleqoth plural transliterated name {5555 celahammachleqowth} Rock of the Allotments.

selah transliterated noun {5542 celah} a suspension in music; from the same root as halal; **see** exalt, extol; **cp** halal.

select verb [1586 eklegomai] to pick out; to choose.

selected [1588 eklektos] [1589 eklogee] picked out; chosen.

Selel Poni transliterated name {6753 tselelpowniy} Shadow-Facing.

Seleq transliterated name {6768 tseleq} Fissure.

self-control noun **control self** verb **self-controlled** adjective [1466 enkratia] [1467 enkratuomai] [1468 enkrates] restraint of one's own desires and passions, especially his sensual appetites.

sell (out) verb {4376 makar} {4465 mimkar} to sell merchandise; to sell persons; **see** price.

Seloph Had transliterated name {6765 tselophchad} the meaning uncertain.

Selsach transliterated name {6766 tseltsach} Clear Shade.

Semach Yah transliterated name {5565 semachyahuw} Upheld of Yah.

Semarayim dual transliterated name {6787 tsemarayim} Double Wool.

Semariy transliterated name {6786 tsemariy} Of the Kenaaniy.

semblance noun [1491 eidos] a likeness; resemblance.

Senan transliterated name {6799 tsenan} Flock.

send, extend verb {7971 shalach} {7972 shelach} to send; to send forth.

sending, extending participle {4916 mishlach} from the verb, to send; a sending out.

sending, shooting participle {4917 mishlachath} from the verb, send; a release; an army.

senesce verb [1095 gerasko] to grow old.

senescence noun [1094 geeras] a growing old; aging.

sentence noun {6599 pithgam} [610 apokrima] the verdict of a judgment.

sentiments plural noun {5587 saiph} mentally divided; mixed feelings.

Senuah transliterated name {5574 cenuwah} Pointed.

separate verb [673 apokorizomai] to rend apart.

separate verb {914 badal} to divide; to segregate; to distinguish.

separate verb {5144 nazar} to set apart; **see** separatist, separatism.

separate, split verb {6536 parac} {6537 perac} to separate from; to split.

separate, split, breach noun {6556 perets} a breach; a separation from; a split.

separate, split, breach, break (off) (loose), craunch, crunch verb {6561 paraq} {6562 peraq} {6555 parats} to breach; to separate from; to split.

separate, spread verb {6504 parad} to break through; to separate from; to spread out.

separation, cutting *noun* {1508 gizrah} a cutting as of a stone; a place set apart.

Separatist *title* **separatism** *noun* {5139 nazir} {5145 nezir} a person or object set apart for service; an emblem of the Separatist; sometimes mistranslated, Nazarite; **cp** Nazarene.

Sephan Yah *transliterated name* {6846 tsephanyah} Hidden (Treasured) of Yah.

Sepharvayim *dual transliterated name* {5617 cepharvayim} the meaning uncertain; a place in Ashshur.

Sepharviy *transliterated name* {5616 cepharviy} Of Sepharvayim.

Sephath *transliterated name* {6857 tsephath} Watcher.

Sephathah *transliterated name* {6859 tseph} Watcher.

Sephi *transliterated name* {6825 tsephiy} Watcher.

Sepho *transliterated name* {6825 tsephow} Watcher.

Sephon *transliterated name* {6827 tsephown} Watcher.

Sephoniy *transliterated name* {6830 tsephowniy} Of Sephon.

sequins *plural noun* {5351 nequddoth} those which are little and punctured.

Ser *transliterated name* {6863 tser} Narrow.

Sera Yah *transliterated name* {8304 serayah} Prevailed of Yah.

Seraph *transliterated name* {8315 saraph} Burning; **see** seraph, seraphim.

seraph, seraphim *transliterated noun* {8314 *singular* saraph *plural* saraphim} literally, on fire; a kind of serpent.

Seredah *transliterated name* {6868 tseredah} {6888 tserarah} Pierced.

Serediy *transliterated name* {5625 cardiy} Of Sered.

serenity *noun* {7959 shelev} {7962 shalvah} {7963 shelevah} complete satisfaction; **see** shalom *adjective*.

serene, serenity *adjective* {7961 shelevah}

serenely *adverb* {7987 sheliy}

serene, serenify serenize *verb* {7951 shalah, shalav} {7954 shelah} to make or become serene.

Sereth *transliterated name* {6889 tsereth} Splendor.

Sereth Hash Shachar *transliterated name* {6890 tserethhashshachar} Splendor of the Dawn.

Seri *transliterated name* {6874 tseriy} Balm.

Seror *transliterated name* {6872 tseror} Bundle.

serpent *noun* {5175 nachash} [3789 ophis] a reptile; figuratively of Satan, or one who is cunning.

Seruah *transliterated name* {6871 tseruwah} Leprous.

Serug *transliterated name* {8286 serug} [4562 sarouch] Tendril.

Seruyah *transliterated name* {6870 tseruyah} Balm.

servant *noun* {5649 abad} {5650 ebed} [1401 doulos] male servant; **see** serve; **cp** maid.

servantry *noun* {5657 abuddah} that which serves.

serve *verb* **server** *participle* {6399 pelach} to serve; that which serves.

serve, servient *verb* {5647 abad} [1398 douluo] to serve in servitude; to serve the soil, as in agriculture.

serve, do, keep, make *verb* {5648 abad} in the sense of serving.

service *noun* {5652 abad} {5656 abodah} {5673 abidah} a deed.

service *noun* {6402 polchan} as worship.

servient (be), (in) servitude, subservient *verb, adjective* [1396 doulagogeo] [1402 douloo] to enslave.

servitude *noun* {5659 abduth} [1397 douliei] [1400 doulon] slavery.

set (apart) *verb* [873 aphorizo] to set off by boundary. **set (apart)** *verb* {4560 macar} to separate from.

set (by), stand (by), station (by), place (by) *verb* {3320 yatsab} {3322 yatsag} {5324 natsab} from the root, to place, so as to stay.

set, abandon, allow, leave, let *verb* {3240 yanach} {5203 natash} to allow to be; to allow to be set; to abandon.

set, place, put *verb* {7760, 7761 suwm} {7896 shith} {8239 shaphath} {8271 shathah} to put in place.

set the torah *verb* [3548 nomothesia] to establish the torah.

settings *plural noun* {6183 ariph} the droopings of the sky.

settle *verb* {3427 yashab} {3488 yethib} [1460 enkatoikeo] [2730 katoikeo] [3611 oikeo] [3939 paroikeo] to settle down, as in a community, or as on a throne.

settle around *verb* [4039 perioikeo] to be a neighbor.

settlement *noun* {4186 moshab} [2731 katoikeesis] [2732 katoiketerion] [2733 katoikia] a place of settling; the act of settling; the state of being settled; **see** settle.

settler *noun* {8453 toshab} [3941 paroikos] one who has settled.

settling *verbal noun* [3940 paroikia] settlement.

seven *noun* {7651 shibah} a prime number; a week of days; symbolic of completion; the root of the verb, oath.

seven, seventh *adjective* {7637 shebiyiy} {7655 shibah} {7658 shibanah} [2033 hepta] **see** seven *noun*.

sevenfold *dual noun* {7659 shibathayim} literally, sevens; double seven.

sever *verb* {2685 chatsaph} {6991 qatal} {6992 qetal} {6993 qetel} {7088 qaphad} to cut off; to deathify.

severance *noun* {7089 qephadah} a cutting off.

Shaalbim *plural transliterated name* {8169 shaalbiym} Fox Holes.

Shaalbimiy *transliterated name* {8170 shaalboniy} Of Shaalbim.

Shaalim *transliterated name* {8171 shaaliym} Foxes.

Shaarayim *dual transliterated name* {8189 shaarayim} Double Portals.

shabbath *transliterated noun* {7676 shabbath} [2663 katapausis] [4521 sabbaton] a celebration of rest which Elohim commands humanity to guard.

shabbathism *transliterated noun* {4868 mishbath} {7674 shebeth} {7677 shabbathon} [4520 sabbatismos] a celebration of rest.

shabbathize *transliterated verb* {7673 shabath} [2664 katapauo] to celebrate a shabbathism.

Shabbethay *transliterated name* {7678 shabbethay} Restful.
Shacharayim *transliterated name* {7842 shacharayim} Double Dawn.

Shachasom *transliterated name* {7831 shachatsowm} Proudly. **shackle** *verb* {3729 kephath} to bind, or confine the limbs to prevent free motion.

shackles *noun* {3976 pede} a ring or band that confines the feet to prevent their free motion.

Shadday *transliterated title* {7706 shadday} Nourisher; Nurturer; sometimes compounded with El; **cp** Almighty; **see** Theological Wordbook.

shade *noun* {4699 metsullah} a hovering over.

shade *verb* {2927 telal} to cover over.

shade, fade *verb* {6004 amam} in the sense of concealing; of fading.

shade, shadow *noun* {6738 tsel} {6752 tselel} literally, or figuratively, shade; shadow.

shadow of death *noun* {6757 tsalmaveth} the shade, or shadow of death.

Shadrach *transliterated name* {7714, 7715 shadrach} the Babeliy name of one of Dani El's companions.

shaggy *adjective* {5569 camar} bristling.

shake *verb* {1607 gaash} {5287 naar} {5363 noqeph} {5426 nethat} {7477 raal} to thresh; **cp** quake.

shake, glutton, quake *participle* {2151 zalal} to quake; to shake; to eat in excess; **cp** drunkard.

shake, stagger, totter, wag, wander, waver, drift *verb* {5128 nuwa} to waver.

shake, wave, rub *verb* {5130 nuph} to rub a bed with aromatics; to shake a hand; to wave an offering.

shalam, shalom; see SUMMARY: SHALAM, SHALOM.

Shalem *transliterated name* {8004 shalem} [4530 salim] [4532 shaleem] Complete; **see** complete.

Shalishah *transliterated name* {8031 shalishah} Triple.

shall, should *auxiliary verbs* these auxiliary verbs are not in the manuscripts. They are italicised in the , and omitted in the . **cp** may, might; will, would.

Shallecheth *transliterated name* {7996 shallecheth} Cast.

Shalmaneser *transliterated name* {8022 shalmanecer} an Ashshuriy sovereign.

Shalmay *transliterated name* {8073 shamlay} Clothed; one of the Dedicates.

Shalome *transliterated name* {7965 shalom} [4539 salomee] Completely Satisfied; **see** shalom.

shame *noun* {955 buwshah} humiliation; disgrace.

shame *verb* {954 bush} {3001 yabesh} {3637 kalam} [1788 entrepo] [2617 kataiskuno] to humiliate; to disgrace.

shame, mercy *verb* {2616 chaced} literally, to bow the neck in kindness, or in reproof.

shame, shamefulness *noun* {1322 bosheth} {3639 kelimmah} {3640 kelimmuth} [149 aiskron] [151 aiskrotes] [152 aiskune] [1791 entropee] the feeling, and condition of shame; of disgrace.

shameful words *noun* [148 aiskrologia] disgraceful words.

Shammay *transliterated name* {8060 shammay} Destructive.

Shamsheray *transliterated name* {8125 shamsheray} Sunlike.

Shamur *transliterated name* {8053 shamuwr} Observed.

Shaphat *transliterated name* {8202 shaphat} Judge.

Shaphat Yah *transliterated name* {8203 shephatyah} Judge of Yah.

Shaphir *transliterated name* {8208 shapiyr} Glorified.

Sharay *transliterated name* {8298 sharay} Hostile.

Shareser *transliterated name* {8272 sharetser} the meaning uncertain.

Sharon *transliterated name* {8289 sharon} [4565 saron] Straight.

Sharoniy *transliterated name* {8290 sharowniy} Of Sharon.

sharp *adjective* {2299 chad} {*plural* 2303 chaddud} [3691 oxus] as pointed keen.

sharpen *verb* {2300 chadad} to cause to be sharp.

sharpen *verb* {3913 latash} to hammer out an edge.

sharpened *adjective* {4593 maot} an edge, as thinned.

Sharuchen *transliterated name* {8287 sharuwchen} Abode of Charism.

Shashaq *transliterated name* {8349 shashaq} Pedestrian.

Shashay *transliterated name* {8343 shashay} Whitish.

shatter, splatter, scatter *verb* {5310 naphats} {5311 nephets} {6327 puts} {6340 pazar} {7376 ratash} to disperse; to disperse by shattering.

shatter, vilify, vilifying *verb* {7489 raa} {7490 rea} [2551 kakologeo] [2558 kakoucheo] [2559 kakoo] verb of evil; to make or declare evil; to vilify by shattering; **see** evil.

Shaul *transliterated name* {7586 shaul} [4549 saoul] [4569 saulos] Asked; Loaned.

Shaveh *transliterated noun* {7740 shaveh} Plain; Plains; also a prefix to names of plains.

Shaveh Qiryathayim *dual transliterated name* {7741 shavehqiryathayim} Plain of a Double City.

she burro *noun* {860 athown} a female burro.

Shealti El *transliterated name* {7597, 7598 shealtiyel} [4528 salathieel] Asked (Loaned) of El.

shear *verb* {1494 gazaz} {3697 kacam} to cut, usually hair or fleece.

Shear Yah *transliterated name* {8187 shearyah} Guard of Yah.

Shear Yashub *transliterated name* {7610 shearyashuwb} A Remainder Returns.

shearing *noun* {1488 gez} {1492 gazzah} that which is sheared.

sheath *noun* {5084 nadan} {5085 nidneh} a receptacle of a sword; figuratively, the body, as a receptacle of the soul.

sheath, knife, razor *noun* {8593 taar} a knife, or a razor, as making bare; a sheath, as being bare.

Sheba *transliterated noun* {7652 sheba} Seven.

Sheba, Shebaiym *transliterated noun* {7614 sheba} {*plural* 7615 shebaiym} the meaning uncertain; three progeniters of scions; a district in Ethiopia.

Shebaiym *transliterated name* {7615 shebaiym} Of Sheba.

Sheban Yah *transliterated noun* {7645 shebanyah} Grown of Yah.

Shebat *transliterated noun* {7627 shebat} the name of a month.

Shebu El, Shuba El *transliterated noun* {7619 shebuel, shubael} Captured of El.

Shechar Yah *transliterated noun* {7841 shecharyah} Early Seeker of Yah.

Shedey Ur *transliterated name* {7707 shedeyuwr} Spreader of Light.

sheep *noun* [4263 probaton] a wooly domestic animal.

sheep gate *noun* [4262 probatikos] a gate through which sheep are led.

Sheerah *transliterated name* {7609 sheerah} Kinflesh.

sheets, snare *noun* {6341 pach} a sheet, as pounded thin; a snare of lumina, as made to spring shut.

Shekan Yah *transliterated name* {7935 shekanyah} Tabernacle of Yah.

shekel *transliterated noun* {8255 sheqel} a set weight of a balance scale.

Shechem *transliterated name* {7927, 7928 shechem} [4966 suchem] Shoulder.

Shechemiy *transliterated name* {7930 shichmiy} Of Shechem.

Shelach *transliterated name* {7974 shelach} [4527 sala] Spear; Branch.

Shelah *transliterated name* {7956 shelah} Ask; Loan.

Shelahiy *transliterated name* {8024 shelaniy} Of Shelah.

shelamim; see SUMMARY: SHALAM, SHELAMIM:

Shelem Yah *transliterated name* {8018 shelemyah} Completed of Yah; from {7965 shalom}; **see** complete.

Shelomi *transliterated name* {8015 shelomi} Complete; from {7965 Shalom}; **see** complete.

Shelomith *transliterated name* {8019 shelomith} Complete; from {7965 shalom}; **see** complete.

Shelomoh *transliterated name* {8010 shelomoh} [4672 solomon] Complete; from {7965 shalom}; **see** complete.

Shelomoth *transliterated name* {*feminine plural* 8013 shelomoth} Complete; from {7965 shalom}; **see** complete.

Shelumi El *transliterated name* {8017 shelumiel} Completed of El; from {7965 shalom}; **see** complete.

Shem *transliterated name* {8035 shem} [4590 seen] means Name.

Shem Eber *transliterated name* {8038 shemeber} Name of Pinion.

Shema *transliterated name* {8087 shema} {8090 shema} Annunciation.

Shema Yah *transliterated name* {8098 shemayah} Heard of Yah.

Shemar Yah *transliterated name* {8114 shemaryah} Guarded of Yah.

Shemer *transliterated name* {8106 shemer} Dregs.

Shemi Da *transliterated name* {8061 shemiyda} Name of Knowing.

Shemi Daiy *transliterated name* {8062 shemiydaiy} Of Shemi Da.

Shemi Ramoth *plural transliterated name* {8070 shemiyramowth} Name of Ramoth.

Shemu El *transliterated name* {8050 shemuel} [4545 samouel] Heard by El.

Shenassar *transliterated name* {8137 shenatstsar} Of Babel.

sheol, hades *noun* {7585 sheol} [86 hades] literally, the unseen; sheol is a transliteration of the Hebrew; hades is a transliteration of the Hellene, which is a translation of the Hebrew; both refer to a temporary abode of the body and soul; there is a progressive distinction of purpose of sheol/hades from its inception to its final state; **read** Yechezq El 31:15–17, 32:18–29, Loukas 16:19–31, Apocalypse 20:13,14; **cp** Psalm 16:10, Acts 2:27.

Shepham *transliterated name* {8221 shepham} Bare.

Shephamiy *transliterated name* {8225 shiphmiy} Of Shepham.

Shepher *transliterated name* {8234 shepher} Glorious.

shepherd *noun* [4166 poimen] one who tends.

shepherd *verb* [4165 poimaino] to tend.

shepherddom *noun* [4167 poimnee] [4168 poimnion] the sovereigndom of a shepherd.

Shephuphan, Shephupham *transliterated name* {8197 shephuwphan, shephuwpham} Adderlike.

Shereb Yah *transliterated name* {8274 sherebyah} Mirage of Yah.

Sheshach *transliterated name* {8347 sheshach} a symbolic name of Babel.

Sheshay *transliterated name* {8344 sheshay} Whitish.

Sheth *transliterated name* {8352 sheth} [4589 seeth] Set, as in authority; a son of Adam.

Shethar Bozenay *transliterated name* {8370 shetharbowzenay} the meaning uncertain; a Persian officer.

shew, show *verb* {2324 chava} {2331 chavah} to propose for consideration; **see** propound.

shewing, showing *noun* [323 anadixis] display.

Sheya *transliterated name* {7864 sheya} False.

Shibah *transliterated noun* {7656 shibah} Seven.

shibboleth *transliterated noun* {7641 shibboleth} a stream, as flowing; **cp** sibboleth; **see** Judges 12:6.

Shichor *transliterated name* {7883 shichor} Dark.

Shichor Libnath *transliterated name* {7884 shiychowrlibnath} Darkish Whiteness.

shield *noun* {{7982 shelet} a protector.

shield, cold, hook *noun* {6793 tsinnah} coldness, as piercing; a hook, as pointed; a shield, as a prickler.

Shikkeron *transliterated name* {7942 shikkerown} Intoxication.

Shilchi *transliterated name* {7977 shilchiy} Spear; Branch.

Shilchim *plural transliterated name* {7978 shilchiym} Spears; Branches.

Shillem *transliterated name* {8006 shillem} Retribution.

Shillemiy *transliterated name* {8016 shillemiy} Of Shillem.

Shiloach *transliterated name* {7975 shiloach} [4611 siloam] Spear; Branch.

Shiloh *transliterated title, name* {7886, 7887 shiloh} Tranquility; a title of the Messiah; a place in Pelesheth.

Shilohiy *transliterated name* {7888 shiloniy} Of Shiloh.

Shima *transliterated name* {8092 shima} Annunciation.

Shimah *transliterated name* {8039 shimah} {8093 shimah} Annunciation.

Shimahiym *plural transliterated name* {8101 shimathiym} Of Shimah.

Shimam *transliterated name* {8043 shimam} Annunciation.

Shimi *transliterated name* {8096 shimiy} [4584 semei] Famous.

Shimiy *transliterated name* {8097 shimiy} Of Shimi.

Shimon *transliterated name* {7889 shimon} Desolation.

Shimon *transliterated name* {8095 shimon} [4613 simon] [4826 sumeon] Hearer.

Shimoniy *transliterated name* {8099 shimoniy} Of Shimon {8095}.

Shimron *transliterated name* {8110 shimrown} Guardianship.

Shimroniy *transliterated name* {8117 shimroniy} Of Shimron.

Shimshay *transliterated name* {8124 shimshay} Sunny.

Shimshon *transliterated name* {8123 shimshon} [4546 sampson] Sunlight.

shine, flash *verb* {3313 yapha} from the root, to shine.

shine, think *verb* {6245 ashath} {6246 ashith} as polishing.

shingle *noun* {7824 shachiph} a board, as a chip.

shingle, rank, row *noun* {7713 sederah} {7795 sorah} that which is regulated in rows.

shinquards *plural noun* {4697 mitschah} a piece of armor protecting the shin.

ship *noun* {590 oniy} {591 oniyah} {6716 tsiy} a large boat.

ship *noun* {5600 sephinah} a vessel as ceiled; a ship with a deck; **see** ceiled; **cp** sailer.

Shitray *transliterated name* {7861 shitray} Official.

shittah, shittim *transliterated noun* {7848 *singular* shittah, *plural* shittim} a species of tree, or the timber thereof.

Shiyon *transliterated name* {7866 shiyown} Devastation.

Shobach *transliterated name* {7731 showbach} Thicket.

Shobay *transliterated name* {7630 shobay} Captor.

Shobeq *transliterated name* {7733 showbeq} Forsaking.

Shobyah *transliterated name* {7634 shobyah} Captive.

shod, enclose, inclose, lock *verb* {5274 naal} {7000 qatr} to fasten; **see** shoe.

shoe *noun* {5275 naalah} **see** shod.

Shomeron *transliterated name* {8111 shomeron} {8115 shomrain} [4540 samaria] Guard Station.

Shomeroness *transliterated name* [4542 samaritis] a female of Shomeron.

Shomeroniy *transliterated name* {8118 shomeroniy} [4541 samarites] Of Shomeron.

shoot *verb* {7232 rabab} to shoot an arrow.

shooting, sending *participle* {4917 mishlachath} from the verb, send; a release; an army.

Shophach *transliterated name* {7780 showphach} Poured.

shophar *noun* {7782 shophar} a Hebrew horn that sounds warning.

short *adjective* {7116 qatser} short, in a variety of applications.

shorten, chop, curtail, harvest *verb* {7114 qatsar} literally, or figuratively, to cut off.

shortly, bit, bit by bit, few, little, petty *adjective, adverb* {4592 meat} diminutive; a few; a little.

shortness *noun* {7115 qotser} impatience.

Shoshanna *transliterated name* **trumpet, lily** *noun* {7799 shoshanna} [4677 sousanna] Lily, as a flower, or as an ornament; trumpet, from its lily shaped bell.

shoulder *noun* {3802 katheph} {7926 shechem} [5606 omos] literally, a side piece; figuratively, the place of bearing a burden; the shoulder.

shoulder blade *noun* {7929 shikma} the bone of the shoulder.

shout *noun* {7440 rinnah} {7445 renanah} a shriek; a shout for joy.

shout *verb* {7438 ron} to shriek for deliverance; to shout for joy.

shout, blast *verb* {6681 tsavach} {7442 ranan} {7244 renen} {7321 ruwa} [2019 epiphoneo] to sound forth loudly, instrumentally or vocally.

shout, shouting *verb* {7442 ranan} {7444 rannen} to shriek; to shout for joy.

shout, stake, blast, clang, clap *verb* {7321 ruwa} {8628 taqa} [4078 peegnumi] [4717 stauroo] to sound loudly; to celebrate by shouting, and/or blasting shophars and trumpets unto Yah Veh; to shout and/or blast a battle cry; to stake a tabernacle or tent; to stake for execution.

shout, thunder *noun* {7452 rea} a crashing sound.

shout(ing), stake(ing), blast(ing), clang(ing), clap(ping) *noun* {8619 taqowa} {8643 teruah} a loud sound; the celebration of shouting, and/or blasting shophars and trumpets unto Yah Veh; also of shouting, and/or blasting a battle cry; a stake of a tent, or tabernacle; a stake for execution.

shove away *verb* [683 apotheomai] to push off; to reject.

shower *noun* {7377 riy} {*plural* 8164 saiyr} moisture.

shred *noun* {2636 chacpac} from the root, to peel; a shred; a scale.

shred, rip *verb* {7167 qara} from the root, to rend.

shreds *plural noun* {7168 qeraim} rags.

shriek *verb* {603 anaqah} to screech.

shrieker *noun* {604 anaqah} a shrieking animal.

shriveled *adjective* {5384 nasheh} shrunken and wrinkled.

shrub *noun* {7880 siach} bush.

Shu Telach *transliterated name* {7803 shuwthelach} Waste of Breakage.

Shu Telachiy *transliterated name* {8364 shuthalchiy} Of Shu Telach.

Shuach *transliterated name* {7744 shuwach} Dell.

Shuachiy *transliterated name* {7747 shuchiy} Of Shuach.

Shual *transliterated name* {7586 shauwl} [4549 saoni] [4569 saulos] Asked.

Shualiy *transliterated name* {7587 shauwliy} Of Shaul.

Shuchah *transliterated name* {7746 shuwchah} Chasm.

Shucham *transliterated name* {7748 shuwcham} Humbly.

Shuchamiy *transliterated name* {7749 shuwchamiy} Of Shucham.

shudder, whirl away *verb* {8175 saar} to storm; to shudder, as in fright; to be stormed away.

Shulammith *transliterated name* {7759 shuwlammiyth} Completely Satisfied.

Shumahiy *transliterated name* {8126 shumathiy} Garlic; Of Shumah.

Shunem *transliterated name* {7766 shuwnem} Quietly.

Shunemiyth *transliterated name* {7767 shuwnammiyth} a female of Shunem.

Shuni *transliterated name* {7764 shuwniy} Quiet.

Shuniy *transliterated name* {7765 shuwniy} Of Shuni.

Shuphamiy *transliterated name* {7781 shuwphamiy} Of Shephupham.

Shushanchiy *transliterated name* {7801 shuwshanchiy} the meaning uncertain.

shut, concentrate *verb* {5462 cagar} {5463 cegar} to shut; to shut tight; cold as shut tight, or concentrated.

shut (up) (in) *verb* {5534 sakar} {5535 sakath} to shut up, as a mouth; to shut in, as a people.

shut (up), stop (up) *verb* {5640 satham} to stop up; figuratively, to keep secret.

Siba *transliterated name* {6717 tsiyba} Station.

Sibbechay *transliterated name* {5444 cibbechay} Entwined.

sibboleth *transliterated noun* {5451 cibboleth} an ear of grain; **cp** shibboleth; **see** Judges 12:6.

Sibon *transliterated name* {6649 tsibown} Dyes.

Sibrayim *dual transliterated name* {5453 cibrayim} Double Will.

Sibya *transliterated name* {6644 tsibya} Gazelle.

Sibyah *transliterated name* {6645 tsibyah} Gazelle.

Sicha *transliterated name* {6727 tsicha} Parched.

Sichon *transliterated name* {5511 ciychown} Tempestuous.

sicken, stroke, worn (out), rub *verb* {2470 chalah} to wear out; to stroke the face as in appeasement.

sickle *noun* {2770 chermesh} an incisor.

sickle, trench, decision, decisive, incision, incisor, ore *adjective, noun* {2742 charuts} physically, soulically, or mentally, an incising.

sickness *noun* {2483 choliy} {*plural* 8463 tachalim} a malady.

Siddim *plural transliterated name* {6661 tsiddim} Sides.

side, rib *noun* {5967 ala} {6763 tsela} literally, a curve or an arch; a rib of a body; a rib of a structure.

Sidon *transliterated name* {6721 tsiydon} [4605 sidon] Hunt (as provision).

Sidoniy *transliterated name* {6722 tsiydoniy} [4606 sidonios] Of Sidon.

Sidqenuw (Yah Veh) *transliterated title* {3072 yehovah tsidqenuw} a combined form of {3068 yehovah} and {6664 tsedeq} Yah Veh of Justness.

Sidqi Yah *transliterated name* {6667 tsidqiyah} Justness of Yah; of the priesthood of Yah.

siege, rampart *noun* {4692 matsur} {4694 matsor} a mound for protection; a seizing.

sigh *verb* {584 anach} {3306 yaphach} {5162 nacham} [1690 embrimaomai] an expressing of emotion; to sigh over, as in empathy; does not mean regret.

sigh, sighing *noun* {585 anachah} {592 aniyah} {5164 nocham} an expression of emotion.

sigh deeply *verb* [389 anastenazo] to express deep emotion.

sight *noun* {7203 roeh} {7207 roeh} [309 anablepsis] a vision; a seeing again.

sign *verb* {7560 resham} to signature.

sign, ensign *noun* {226 owth} {3902 parasemos} [4592 seemion] as emblematic, or as a signal; the sun, moon, and stars are for signs and seasons; Yonah was a sign to the Ninevehiym and the Yah Hudahiym; turning water into wine was Yah Shua's first sign; some signs are miraculous, some are not.

signal *verb* [2678 katasio] to make a sign; to signal.

signet *noun* {2858 chothemeth} {2885 tabbaath} {5824 izqa} a signet ring used for sealing; **see** seal.

signify *verb* {7559 rasham} [4591 seemaino] [4593 seemioomai] to distinguish; to indicate; to signal.

silence *noun* {1745 duwmah} from the root, to be mute.

silent *adjective, adverb* {1747 duwmiyah} {1748 duwmahm} mute; still.

Sillah *transliterated name* {6741 tsillah} Shade.

Sillethay *transliterated name* {6769 tsillethay} Shady.

silver *noun* [693 argurous] made of silver.

silver *noun* {3701 keceph} [696 arguros] the metal, especially as a medium of exchange.

simplicity *noun* [858 aphelotes] smoothness.

simultaneously *adverb* [260 hama] at the same time.

Sin *transliterated name* {6790 tsin} Crag.

sin (against), cleanse for sin *verb* {2398 chata} [264 hamartano] to misaim.

sin (offering) (for the) *noun* {2399 chet} {2401 chataah} {2402 chattaah} {2403 chattath} {2408 chatiy} {2409 chattaya} [265 hamartema] [266 hamartia] a misaiming; in some instances implies an offering for sin.

Sinay *transliterated name* {5514 ciynay} [4614 sina] a mountain of Arabia.

sinew noun {1517 giyd} a tendon.

sing verb **songster, songstress** participle {7891 shiyr, shuwr} [103 ado] to sing; a male singer; a female singer.

singe verb {2760, 2761 charak} to scorch.

Siniy transliterated name {5513 ciyniy} Of one of the sons of Kenaan.

sink verb {7743 shuwach} literally, or figuratively, to sink.

sink, bend, descend, penetrate, press verb {5181 nachath} from the root, to sink; to go down; to press or lead down.

sinless adjective [361 anamartetos] one who is not misaiming.

sinner noun {2400 chatta} [268 hamartolos] one who misaims.

Sior transliterated name {6730 tsiyor} Belittle.

Siphyon transliterated name {6837 tsiphyown} Watcher.

Sippay transliterated name {5598 cippay} Bason-like.

Sippor transliterated name {6834 tsippowr} Bird.

Sipporah transliterated name {6855 tsipporah} Bird.

Siqlag transliterated name {6860 tsiqlag} uncertain derivative.

Sis transliterated name {6732 tsiyts} Blossom.

Sismay transliterated name {5581 cicmay} of uncertain derivative.

sister noun {269 achowth} [79 adelphe] a female child of the same parents.

sister in law noun {2994 yebemeth} the sister of a man's woman, or of a woman's man.

sistrum noun {plural 4517 menanaim} an instrument consisting of metal frame and metal rods, which jingle; **cp** tambourine.

Sithri transliterated name {5644 cithriy} Protective.

Siyon transliterated name {6726 tsiyown} [4622 sion] Monument.

skeleton, bone noun {1634, 1635 gerem} {6106 etsem} [3747 osteon] a framework; a substance, usually of the body.

skeptics plural noun {5588 ceeph} literally, of divided mind; **see** opinions.

skillet noun {6517 parur} {6745 tselachah} a utensil; as flattened, as being spread out.

skillful, hasting adjective {4106 mahir} to hurry along; to be skillful; quick, as skillful.

skin noun {1539 geled} {5785 owr} {5559 chros} the covering of the body.

skin noun {2573 chemeth} {4997 nod} as tied to hold contents, usually liquid.

skip about verb {6852 tsaphar}.

sky, powder noun {7834 shachaq} the upper atmosphere; a substance of pulverized particles.

slab noun [4109 plax] a slab for engraving.

slab noun {3871 luach} a slab, as polished; usually of stone; figuratively, of the heart.

slack adjective {7504 rapheh} lacking energy.

slack, delay verb [1019 braduno] to be slow.

slacken, let (down) (fall) (go) (loose), loose, loosen up verb {7503 raphah} to slacken.

slackness noun {7510 riphion} a lack of energy.

slander noun {1681 dibbah} [2636 katalalia] defamation.

slander verb [2635 katalaleo] to be a cause of sin to; to defame.

slanderer noun [2637 katalalos] one who slanders.

slap, slurp, clap verb {5606 saphaq} as in clapping hands, slapping the thigh, slurping vomit; **see** gluttony.

slaughter noun {2027 hereg} {2028 haregah} {2874 tebach} {2878 tibehah} {4293 matbeach} {7821 shechitah} [4967 sphagee] [4968 sphagion] to slaughter for sacrifice; a massacre.

slaughter verb {2026 harag} {2873 tabach} {7819, 7820 shachat} [615 apoktino] [2695 katasphatto] [4969 sphatto] [4372 prosphatos] to sacrifice; to massacre.

slaughterer noun {2876, 2877 tabbach} {2879 tabbachah} a butcher; an executioner.

slave noun {4522 mac, mic} one in forced servitude; **cp** servant; **cp** maid.

sledge noun {4173 morag} a sledge for threshing.

sledgehammers plural noun {3597 keylaph} from the root, to strike with noise.

sleep noun {8139, 8142 shenah} {8153 shenath} to slumber.

sleep *verb* {5123 nuwm} to slumber from drowsiness; **see** drowsiness.

sleep (sound) *noun* {8639 tardemah} also lethargy.

sleep soundly *verb* {7290 radam} to stun; to stupify with sleep, or with death.

slice *noun* {6400 pelach} a split; a division off a whole.

slice, slicer *noun* {2757 charits} slice of milk; may be cheese.

slight, swift, trifle, abase, abate, belittle *verb* {6819 tsaar} {6985 qat} {7034 qalah} {7043 qalal} [2274 heetaomai] to belittle in contempt; to make light of; to lessen.

slime *noun* {8602 taphel} soft, moist earth reduced to the consistency of slime; that which is slimy in consistency.

slime, saliva *noun* {7388 rir} from its broth texture.

sling *noun* {7050 qela} that which slings stones.

slinger *noun* {7051 qaila} one that slings stones.

slip (away) (out), escape *verb* {6403 palat} {6405 peletah}.

slothful *verb* {6101 atsal} *adjective* {6102 atsel} *noun* {6103 atslah} {6104 atsluth} slow; sluggish.

slurp, clap, slap *verb* {5606 saphaq} as in clapping hands, slapping the thigh, slurping vomit; **see** gluttony.

smite *verb* {5062 nagaph} to touch heavily.

smite, smitten *verb* {5221 nakah} to strike lightly, or heavily; **cp** strike.

smiter *adjective* {5222 nekeh} a traducer; **cp** striker.

smitten *adjective* {5223 nakeh} maimed; dejected; **cp** stricken.

smoke *noun* {6227 ashan} literal, figurative smoke.

smoke *noun* {7008 qitor} as the fume of a fire.

smoke *verb* {6225 ashan} literally, or figuratively, to smoke.

smoking, smoky *adjective* {6226 ashen} literally, or figuratively, smoky.

smooth *adjective* {2509 chalaq} {2512 challuq} smooth of tongue; smooth stones.

smooth it over, allot *verb* {2505 chalaq} literally, to smooth; as tossing smooth pebbles to allot lands, inheritances; as smoothing over through flattery.

smooth *verb* {4452 malats} as in soothing.

smooth, allotment, portion *noun* {2506 cheleq} {2508 chalaq} {2511 challaq} {2513 chelqah} {2515 chaluqqah} {4255 machleqah} {4256 machaloqeth} {4521 menath} smoothness of tongue; usually an inheritance allotted by pebble.

snare *noun* {4170 moqesh} {4204 mazor} {7407 rokes} that which entangles; as in turning aside from truth.

snare, ensnare *verb* {3369 yaqosh} {5367 naqash} {6351 pachah} {6983 qosh} to lay, or to spring a snare.

snare, sheets *noun* {6341 pach} a sheet, as pounded thin; a snare of lumina, as made to spring shut.

snarer *noun* {3352 yaqosh} {3353 yaqosh} one who snares.

snatch *verb* {6642 tsabat} to reach for.

snatch away *verb* {3261 yaah} from the root, to brush aside.

sneezing *noun* {5846 atiyshah} from the root, to sneeze.

snorting *participle* {5170 nacharah} as expressing wrath; **see** nostrils.

snout, wrath, nostril *noun* {639 aph} {*plural* 5156 nechirim} [3709 orgee] the snorter, as in expressing wrath; **see** snorting.

snow *noun* {7950 sheleg} {8517 telag} [5510 chion] frozen atmospheric vapor.

snow-white *verb* {7949 shalag} to be white as snow.

so *adverb* [686 ara] the idea of drawing a conclusion; in point of fact. **cp** thus.

so (as) (that), in order to, on account of *participle* {4616 maan} {5668 abur} for the purpose of.

Soan *transliterated name* {6814 tsoan} meaning uncertain.

Soar *transliterated name* {6820 tsoar} Belittle.

Sobah *transliterated name* {6678 tsowbah} Station.

Sobebah *transliterated name* {6637 tsobebah} Palanquin.

sober up *verb* [366 ananepho] [1594 eknepho] to become sober; metaphorically, to return to soberness of mind.

Sochar *transliterated name* {6714 tsochar} White.

socket, pestle *noun* {4388 maktesh} {5940 eliy} the pestle of a mortar; a socket.

socket, pudenda *noun* {6596 poth} literally, a hole.

soil *noun* {127 adamah} ruddy; the soil of the earth: **cp** Adam; **cp** cosmos.

sojourn *verb* {1481 gur} to travel; **see** journey.

sojourner, sojourning *noun* {1616 ger} {4033 magur} a traveler; a travelling; **see** journey.

Sochoh *transliterated name* {7755 sochoh} Hedge.

solaces *plural noun* {5150 nichum} consolings.

sole, bowl, hollow, palm, paw *noun noun* {3709 kaph} {6447 pas} {8168 shoal} a hollow of the hand, foot, paw, or body; also utensils with a hollow.

solidify, leap *verb* {6339 pazaz} to become solid; to spring.

son *noun* [5207 huios] a male offsrping; figuratively, kinship.

son, bar *noun* {1247, 1248 bar} a son; as heir apparent to the throne; also a prefix to a name; **cp** ben; **note:** both ben and bar appear in Psalm 2:.

son, ben, Ben *transliterated noun* {1121, 1122, 1123 ben} a son, as builder of the family name; also a prefix to a name; **cp** bar; **note:** both ben and bar appear in Psalm 2:.

song *noun* {7892 shir, shirah} words set to music.

songster, songstress *participle* **sing** *verb* {7891 shiyr, shuwr} [103 ado] to sing; a male singer; a female singer.

sonship *noun* [5206 huiothesia] the placing as a son; much closer than adoption.

soothe, laud *verb* {7623 shabach} {7624 shecach} to extol with words; to smooth it over.

soothings *plural noun* {2514 chalaqqah} {2519 chalaqlaqqah} smoothings over; **see** smooth.

soothsaying *verb* [3132 mantuomai] predicting.

Sophach *transliterated name* {6690 tsowphach} Breadth.

Sophar *transliterated name* {6691 tsowphar} Skip About.

Sophim *plural transliterated name* {6839 tsophiym} Watchers.

Sophnath Paneach *transliterated name* {6847 tsophnathpaneach} Yoseph's Misrayim name.

Sor *transliterated name* {6865 tsor} [5184 turos] Flint; often rendered as Tyre, Tyrus.

Sorah *transliterated name* {6881 tsorah} Hornet.

Sorahiy *transliterated name* {6882 tsorathiy} Of Sorah.

sorcerer {*participle* 3784 kashaph} {*noun* 3786 kashshaph} one who does sorceries through evil spirits.

sorceries *plural noun* {3785 keshephim} the use of powers of evil spirits.

sore, bandage *noun* {4205 mazor} an affliction; in the sense of binding up; a bandage for a sore.

Soreq *transliterated name* {7796 sowreq} Choice.

Soriy *transliterated name* {6865 tsor} {6876 tsoriy} [5183 turios] Of Sor.

sorrow *noun* {4341 makob} [3077 lupe] sadness; **note:** not to be confused with sorry.

sorrow *verb* [3076 lupeo] to be sad; **note:** not to be confused with sorry.

sort, straighten *verb* {8626 taqan} to unbend; to become upright; to sort out.

Sotay *transliterated name* {5479 cowtay} Swerving.

soul, soulical, soulless; see SUMMARY: SOUL.

sound sleep *noun* {8639 tardemah} also lethargy.

soundmind *verb* [4994 sophronizo] to make soundminded.

soundminded *noun, adjective* [4993 sophroneo] [4995 sophronismos] [4998 sophron] of a sound mind; figuratively, self-controlled.

soundmindedly *adverb* [4996 sophronos] to make mindfully; of sound mind.

soundmindedness *noun* [4997 sophrosunee] soundness of mind.

sounds (empty) *noun* [2757 kenophonia] vain voices; figuratively, a useless discussion.

sounds *noun* [5353 phthoggos] an audible sensation perceived by the ear.

soup *noun* {6564 paraq} soup, as full of crumbled meat.

sour grape *noun* {1154 becer} {1155 bocer} an unripe grape.

southerly, southward *adjective* {8486 teman} on the right when facing dawnward.

sovereign *adjective* [934 basilios] [937 basilikos] the character of the priesthood of the Messianists, of a person, place, or thing.

sovereign *noun* {4428, 4430 melech} [935 basilus] the office of a male who reigns over a sovereigndom; **see** reign; **cp** title.

sovereign *participle* **reign** *verb* {4427 malak} {4910 mashal} [936 basiluo] to rule; the officiating of a sovereign; **see** sovereign.

sovereign palace *noun* [933 basilion] the area in which a sovereign resides.

sovereigndom *noun* {4410 melukah} {4437 malku} {4438 malkuth, malkuyah} {4467 mamlakah} {4468 mamlakuth} [932 basilia] the area or peoples over which a sovereign reigns.

sovereigness *noun* {4436 malkah} {4433 malka} {4446 melecheth} [938 basilissa] a sovereign's woman; the title of a female who reigns over a sovereigndom.

sowing *participle* {4901 meshek} a sowing.

span *noun* {1574 gomed} {2239 zereth} the breadth of a hand.

Spania *transliterated name* [4681 spania] a region of Europe.

spanned in the palms *plural verb* {2949 tippuch} held in the span of a palm.

spare *verb* {2347 chue} to cover as in protection; **see** haven.

spare *verb* {2820 chasak} to preserve.

spare, bear, lade, lift, load *verb* {5375 nacah} {5376 nesa} to lift, in a variety of applications.

spare, compassion *verb* {2550 chamal} [3629 oiktirmon] to compassion; to spare.

sparkle, flow *verb* {5102 nahar} to flow, as to assemble; to sparkle, as to be cheerful.

speak *verb* [2980 laleo] [4354 proslaleo] to express thoughts or articulate sounds.

spear *noun* {2595 chaniyth} {7013 qayin} a lance for thrusting.

species (in), (to) species *noun* {2177, 2178 zan} {4327 min} by specific kinds.

specified *adjective* **census, mandate** *noun* {4662 miphqad} an enumeration; a designated spot; an order, or command.

spectacle, see *noun* {7210 roiy} from the root, sight; a vision.

speech *noun* [2981 lalia] that which is spoken.

speechless *noun* [216 alalos] without speech.

spelt *noun* {3698 kuccemeth} a variety of grain.

sperma *transliterated noun* [4690 sperma] the seed from which anything develops.

spermalogist *transliterated noun* [4691 spermologos] a seedy worder; an empty talker.

spice, embalm, ripen *verb* {2590 chanat} from the root, to spice.

spice, spicery *noun* {5219 nekoth} {5238 nekoth} an aromatic gum, as pounded out; **see** smitten.

spicy *plural adjective* {4840 merqachim} spicy seasonings.

spicy broth *noun* {4841 merqachah} an effusion of spiced seasonings.

spin, twirl, twist *noun* {1524 giyl} {1525 giylah} a physical expression of joy.

spin, twirl, twist *verb, noun* {1523 giyl, guwl} {3769 karar} [4761 strebloo] to spin around, as in rejoicing; **cp** whirl.

spindle, circuit, crutch *noun* {6418 pelek} to be round; a spindle as whirled; hence a crutch.

spine *noun* {6096 atseh} the backbone.

spinning *noun* {4299 matveh} that made by spinning.

spinnings, spun *noun* {4749 miqshah} turned, as in a lathe.

spiral stairs *plural noun* {3883 lowlim} circular steps.

spiral upward *verb* {55 abak} to coil upward.

spiraling *participle* {4141 muwcab} a coiling.

spirit(s), spiritual(s); see SUMMARY: SPIRIT, SPIRITUAL: **spit** *verb* {7556 raqaq} to expectorate.

spit, spittle *noun* {7536 roq} **cp** saliva.

splatter, scatter, shatter *verb* {5310 naphats} {5311 nephets} {6327 puts} {6340 pazar} {7376 ratash} to disperse; to disperse by shattering.

spleen *noun* [4698 splankna] a large lymphatic organ which modifies the blood structure, symbolic of compassion.

spleen (large) *noun* [4184 polusplanknos] the spleen as figurative of much compassion.

spleen (sympathetic) *noun* [4697 splanknizomai] the spleen as symbolic of sympathetic compassion.

spleen (tender) *noun* [2155 eusplanknos] the spleen as symbolic of tender compassion.

splendidly *adverb* {4358 miklowl} with splendor.

splendour *noun* {3314 yiphah} {*plural* 4360 miklulim} beauty.

split *verb* {1234 baqa} [4977 skizo] to separate into more than one.

split, blink, calm, rest *verb* {7280 raga} this word is derived from two roots; blink and split, as momentary; calm and rest, as soothing.

split, breach, break (off) (loose), craunch, crunch, separate *verb* {6561 paraq} {6562 peraq} {6555 parats} to breach; to separate from; to split.

split, breach, separate *noun* {6556 perets} a breach; a separation from; a split.

split, schism *transliterated noun* [4978 schisma] a gap; a split. **split, separate** *verb* {6536 parac} {6537 perac} to separate from; to split.

spoil *noun* {7998 shalal} that which is plundered.

spoil, despoil, pledge *verb* {2254, 2255 chabal} literally, to bind tightly; as in spoiling or as in binding a pledge.

spoil, drop *verb* {7997 shalal} to let drop; to strip, or plunder.

spokes *plural noun* {2839 chishshuq} as attached; **see** hubs.

spontaneous growth *noun* {5599 caphiyach} a self-growing growth.

spontaneous sprout *noun* {7823 shachic} a self-sprouting sprout.

spore *verb* [4687 spiro] the implanting or planting of sperma.

spot, patch *verb* {2921 tala} to color in spots; to repair in spots.

spread *verb* {3331 yatsa} {6566 paras} {6576 parshez} {6581 pasah} to disperse; to spread thin.

spread *verb* {4969 mathach} as in stretching nets, or tents.

spread *verb* {7502 raphad} {7849 shatach} to expend.

spread, bed down *verb* {3331 yatsa} to strew as a surface.

spread, grow, scatter *verb* {6335 push} [837 auxano] to grow, to enlarge; as in spreading out.

spread, separate *verb* {6504 parad} to break through; to separate from; to spread out.

spread, strip *verb* {6584 pashat} to spread out; to deploy; to strip clothing; to flay the skin.

spread (thin), stretch, extend *verb* {5186 natah} {5628 sarach} to bend away; to spread out; to stretch.

spread over, overspread *verb* {5259 nacak} to interweave.

spreads *plural noun* {4765 marbadim} oversized spreads.

sprigs *plural noun* {2150 zalzal} small twigs.

springing, proceeding, procedure, rising *noun* {4161 motsa} {*plural* 4163 motsaoth} literally, the source of going forth, whether of persons, of water, of the sun.

sprinkle *verb* {2236 zaraq} [4472 rhantizo] to sprinkle solids or liquids.

sprinkle *verb* {5137 nazah} {7450 racac} a ceremonious libating of blood, oil, or water.

sprinkler *noun* {4219 mizraq} a bowl or bason used to sprinkle.

sprout *noun* {1877 deshe} {1883 dethe} {3126 yoneq} {3127 yoneqeth} {4731 maqqelah} a sprout; a grass.

sprout *noun* {6780 tsemach} a sprout; also a prophetic title of the Messiah; **cp** rod; **cp** scion.

sprout *verb* {6779 tsamach} [985 blastano] to germinate; to sprout.

sprout (forth) *verb* {1876 dasha} [1631 ekphuo] [5453 phuo] to newly grow.

sprout (spontaneous) *noun* {7823 shachic} a self-sprouting sprout.

spurn *verb* {3973 maowc} to refuse with disdain.

spy, step, tread *verb* {7270 ragal} verb of foot; to measure out with the foot; **see** foot.

squad *noun* [4686 spira] a small group in a quad.

square, foursquare *verb* {7251 raba} to cause to be quadrate.

squeezed juice *nount* {6071 acic} juice, as freshly trodden.

squeezings *noun* {5332 netsach} as bright red juice of grapes.

stab *verb* {1856 daqar} {2944 taan} {*plural* 4094 madqarah} to stab through.

staff bearer *noun* [4465 rabdoukos] one that bears a staff.

staff, staves, timber *noun* {905 bad} {3586 xulon} [4464 rhabdos] timber, or staves made therefrom.

stagger *verb* {7478 raal} to reel; to stagger.

stagger, stray, wander *verb* {8582 taah} to reel; to stray.
stagger, totter, wag, wander, waver, drift, shake *verb* {5128 nuwa} to waver.

staggering *noun* {6330 puqah} stumbling; **see** waver, wiggle.

staggering *noun* {8653 tarelah} reeling.

stain *noun* [3436 molusmos] blackish.

stain *noun* [4696 spilos] soil.

stain *verb* [3435 moluno] to blacken.

stain *verb* [4695 spiloo] to soil.

stake *noun* {3489 yathed} [4716 stauros] a tabernacle or tent stake; an upright stake on which our Adonay was staked.

stake, blast, clang, clap, shout *verb* {7321 ruwa} {8628 taqa} [4078 peegnumi] [4717 stauroo] to sound loudly; to celebrate by shouting, and/or blasting shophars and trumpets unto Yah Veh; to shout and/or blast a battle cry; to stake a tabernacle or tent; to stake for execution.

stake(ing), blast(ing), clang(ing), clap(ping), shout(ing) *noun* {8619 taqowa} {8643 teruah} a loud sound; the celebration of shouting, and/or blasting shophars and trumpets unto Yah Veh; also of shouting, and/or blasting a battle cry; a stake of a tent, or tabernacle; a stake for execution.

stalk *noun* {7054 qamah} {7070 qaneh} the stem of a plant.
stallion *noun* {7409 rekesh} as set aside.

stalls *dual noun* {4942 mishpathim} stalls for animals.

stammerer, stammering *adjective* {5926 illeg} stuttering.

stand, standing, station *noun* {4673 matsab} {4674 mutstsab} {4675 mitstsabah} {5979 emdah} a stand; a military station.

stand, stay, withstand *verb* {5975 amad} {5977 omed} [436 anthistemi] [478 antikathistemi] to stand steady; to stand against.

stand (by), station (by), place (by), set (by) *verb* {3320 yatsab} {3322 yatsag} {5324 natsab} from the root, to place, so as to stay.

stand guard *verb* {7520 ratsad} to look with suspicion.

star *noun* {3556 kowkab} [792 aster] [798 astron] a luminous body in the heavens.

start early, early start *verb* {7925 shakam} to start early.

stater *transliterated noun* [4715 stater] a coin with a standard of value.

station, base *noun* {3653 ken} a base, as in furniture; a base as in a station, or office.

station, stand, standing *noun* {4673 matsab} {4674 mutstsab} {4675 mitstsabah} {5979 emdah} a stand; a military station.

station (by), place (by), set (by), stand (by) *verb* {3320 yatsab} {3322 yatsag} {5324 natsab} from the root, to place, so as to stay.

statute *noun* {2706 choq} {2708 chuqqah} a law engraved in stone; **cp** statue.

statute *noun* {2711 cheqeq} an enactment.

statue, station, prefect *noun* {5333 netsib} {*plural* 5460 seganin} {*plural* 5461 saganim} {6346, 6347 pechah} a stationed officer; that which is stationary; a station; also a statue.

statute (set) *verb* **statute setter** *participle* **engrave** *verb* {2710 chaqaq} [1795 entupoo] to engrave; to prescribe; **cp** statue.

staves, timber, staff *noun* {905 bad} [3586 xulon] [4464 rhabdos] timber, or staves made therefrom.

stay, withstand, stand *verb* {5975 amad} {5977 omed} [436 anthistemi] [478 antikathistemi] to stand steady; to stand against.

stay around, surround *verb* {3803 kathar} to enclose.

stay overnight *verb* {3885 lun, lin}.

steal *verb* {1589 ganab} to thieve; to deceive; **see** thief.

stedfast *adjective* [949 bebaios] stable.

steep steps *noun* {4095 madregah} a steep, or inaccessible place.

steepings *noun* {4952 mishrah} maceration; a steeped juice.

stench *noun* {6292 piggul} {6709 tsachanah} a stink; a putrefaction.

step *noun* {4096 midrak} a treading.

step, support, time, anvil *noun* {6471 paamah} anvil, as a support; support, as a pedestal or column in a structure; a "stepper", as a supporter of the body; time, as an occasion or occurrence – but not as measured time.

step, tread, spy *verb* {7270 ragal} verb of foot; to measure out with the foot; **see** foot.

Stephanas *transliterated name* [4734 stephanas] Wreathed.

Stephanos *transliterated name* [4736 stephanos] Wreathed.

steps, degrees *noun* {4609 maalah} steps; stations; a progression; 1/360th of a circle.

sterile *adjective* {1565 galmuwd} {6135 aqar} barren; desolate.

stern *adjective* **harden** *verb* {7188 qashach} severe; without feeling.

stern, hard *adjective* {7186 qasheh} [4642 skleeros] harsh; severe.

steward *noun* {4453 meltsar} the tsar over the household.

stibium *noun* {6320 puk} a stibium dye for the face.

stick, adhere, join *verb* {1692 dabaq} {1693 debaq} [4347 proskollao] to join one's self to closely; stick to; to remain attached.

stinger *noun* {3654 ken} a stinging insect.

stink *noun* {889 beosh} a bad smell.

stink *verb* {887 baash} {888 beesh} to smell bad; to be offensive.

stinkweed *noun* {890 boshah} {*plural* 891 beushiym} bad smelling weeds.

stitching *noun* {8278 serad} as pierced with a needle.

Stoic *transliterated name* [4770 stoikos] one of pantheistic philosophy.

stokade *noun* {4115 mahpecheth} a stokade, as being wrenched in.

stone *noun* {5619 caqal} [3035 lithinos] [3036 lithoboleo] [3037 lithos] a detached piece of rock.

stone *verb* {7275 ragam} [3034 lithazo] to hurl stones.

stoneheap *noun* {4773 margemah} a heap of stones.

stones (red hot), pavement *noun* {7528 ratsaph} {7529 retseph} as used for baking; as used for laying a pavement.

stood on end *verb* {5568 camar} to be erect; to bristle.

stool *noun* {1916 hadom} as a place to tromp or set the foot; **see** trample.

stop (up), shut (up) *verb* {5640 satham} to stop up; figuratively, to keep secret.

storage *plural adjective* {4543 mickenoth} an area to store valuables.

storm *noun* **stormy** *adjective* {5591 saar} {5592 caph} a weather storm.

storm *verb* {5590 caar} to agitate; to rush.

stoutness *noun* [100 hadrotes] plumpness in the sense of growth.

straight *adjective* {3474 yashar} {3477 yashar} [3717 orthos] as in upright; not crooked.

straight, straightness, level, plain *noun* {4334 miyshor, *plural* miyshorim} {4339 meyshar} {6160 arabah} plain, as unadorned; as a level land area; as of straight character; as just.

straight-footed [3716 orthopodeo] to go directly forward.

straighten *verb* [461 anorthoo] to straighten.

straighten, sort *verb* {8626 taqan} to unbend; to become upright; to sort out.

straightforward, straightforwardness *adjective* {5228 nakoach} {5229 nekochah} as integrious.

straightness *noun* {3476 yosher} {3483 yishrah} as in uprightness; as in integrious.

straightway *adverb* [2112 utheos] [2117 uthus] at once; immediately.

straits, confines, distress, narrows *noun* {4689 matsoq} {4691 metsuqah} {4712 metsar} from the root, belly; a narrow place; a confinement.

strange, estrange *verb* {2114 zuwr} to cause to be strange; although a verb, often carries the force of a noun.

strange, stranger *adjective* {5237 nokriy} [3579 xenizo] alien.

strange, stranger *noun* {2114 zur} {5235 noker} {5236 nekar} [3581 xenos] an alien; a cality.

strangers (lodge) *verb* [3580 zenodokeo] to be hospitable.

strangle *verb* {2614 chanaq} [519 apankomai] [4155 pnigo] [4846 sumpnigo] to choke.

strangled *noun* [4156 pniktos] that which is choked.

strangling *noun* {4267 machanaq} by choking.

strategize *verb* {6191 aram} to plot subtly.

strategoi *transliterated plural noun* [4755 strategos] strategists.

strategy *noun* {6193 orem} {6195 ormah} a subtle plot.

straw *noun* {8401 teben} stalk on which grain grows.

stray fruit *noun* {6528 peret} a stray fruit; a single fruit.

stray, wander, stagger *verb* {8582 taah} to reel; to stray.

stream *noun* {2988 yabal} {3105 yubal} a current of water.

stream, branch, ear *noun* {7641 shibboleth} a branch or an ear of grain, as growing; a stream, as flowing; **see** shibboleth.

streamlet *noun* {4323 miykal} a little stream.

street *noun* {7784 shuq} [4505 rhume] a road midst houses.

strength *noun* {202 own} {556 amtsah} {2391 chezeq} {2392 chozeq} {5797 oz} {5807 ezuz} physical ability.

strength *noun* {5326 nitsbah} {*plural* 8443 toaphah} firmness; speed.

strengthen, uphold, callous, prevail *verb* {553 amats} {555 omets} {2388 chazaq} {2393 chezqah} {5810 azaz} to enable physically; to become thickskinned.

stretch, extend, spread (thin) *verb* {5186 natah} {5628 sarach} to bend away; to spread out; to stretch.

stricken *adjective* {5218 naka} smitten.

stride *noun* {6587 pesa} a spread of the legs.

stride, spread *verb* {6585 pasa} {6589 pasaq} a spreading of the legs, or the lips.

strife *noun* {4066 maddown} {4683 matstsah} {4808 meribah} a struggle of words; a quarrel; a contest.

strife, contention, defence, plea *noun* {7379 rib} a personal, or legal contest.

strike (round about), surround, round *verb* {5362 naqaph} to strike; to strike all around; to surround; to round off the beard.

strike *verb* {4223 mecha} {4272 machats} to strike in pieces; to impale.

strip *verb* {1497 gazal} to flay, or cut.

strip, bare *verb* {2834 chasaph} to strip off as to expose.

strip, equip, rescue *verb* {2502 chalats} literally, to strip for hostility; to strip out of danger.

strip, escape, rescue *verb* {5337, 5338 natsal} to snatch away; favorably, or unfavorably.

strip, pluck *verb* {6998 qataph} {7059 qamat} to pluck out; to strip off.

strip, spread *verb* {6584 pashat} to spread out; to deploy; to strip clothing; to flay the skin.

strip bare *verb* {6209 arar} to bare; figuratively, to demolish.

strip naked, empty, pour out *verb* {6168 arah} {6379 pakah} to empty; to empty by pouring; to strip bare; **see** naked.

stripped *noun* {7758 sholal} bare.

stripped *verb* [554 apekduomai] [555 apekdusis] to despoil.

stripped, stripping *noun* {1498 gazel} {1499 gezel} {1500 gezelah} that which has been flayed, or cut.

strive, contend, defend, plead *verb* {7378 rub} to hold a controversy.

strive, desolate *verb* {5327 natsah} to struggle; to lay waste.

stroke *noun* {4273 machats} {4347 makkah} a strike.

stroke, worn (out), rub, sicken *verb* {2470 chalah} to wear out; to stroke the face as in appeasement.

stroll *verb* {6808 tsaah} to pace at leisure; **see** pace.

stroll *verb* {7788 shur} to wander about; as a whore, as a merchant.

strong, tough *adjective* {533 ammits} {554 amots} {2389 chazaq} {5794 az} {5808 izzuz} forceful; harsh; physically able.

stronger *adjective* {2390 chazeq} more powerful.

stronghold *noun* {4581 mauz} a place of protection.

strongly *adverb* {2394 chozqah} vehemently.

structure *noun* {8498 tekunah} the architecture.

strum *verb* **strummers** *participle* {5059 nagan} to strum, as on a musical instrument; one who strums; **cp** pluck.

strummer, strumming *noun* {5058 neginah} a musical instrument.

strums, strummings *plural noun* {4482 minim} a musical chord as parted into strings.

stubble *noun* {7179 qash} the stubs left in the soil after harvesting.

stumble *noun* {3783 kishshalon} ruin.

stumble *verb* [4417 ptaio] to trip up; to err; to sin.

stumble, trip, falter *verb* {3782 kashal} to totter; to waver.

stumbling *noun* [4348 proskomma] [4349 proskopee] an obstacle; to provide an occasion for sinning.

stumblingblock *noun* {4383 mikshol} {4384 makshelah} an obstacle; an enticement.

stump *noun* {6136 iqqar} the underground part of a tree.

stump, monolith *noun* {4676 matstsebah} {4678 matstsebeth} a singular block of stone.

stun, astonish, desolate *verb* {8074 shamem} {8075 shemam} to stun, as in to stupefy or devastate; to lay waste.

stupid *adjective* {1198 baar} gullible; one who swallows.

stupidity *noun* {6580 pash} degeneracy.

stylus *noun* {2747 cheret} {5842 et} {8279 sered} an instrument for engraving or inscribing.

Suach *transliterated name* {5477 cuwach} Sweeping.

Suar *transliterated name* {6686 tsuwar} Belittle.

subdue *verb* {3533 kabash} literally, to tread down.

subdue *verb* {4355 makak} literally, to tumble.

subdue, humble, humbling *verb* {3665 kana} {6031 anab} {6033 anah} {6039 enuth} {6800 tsana} [5013 tapino] to cause to bend the knee; to knuckle under; to lower in esteem or status.

subdue, overlay *verb* {7286 radad} to conquer; to sheet over.

subject to *noun* [1777 enochos] as in, liable to a penalty.

subject *verb* [5293 hupotasso] to obey; to subordinate.

subjugate, crumble *verb* {7287 radah} to bring under; to conquer.

submit *verb* [5226 hupiko] to yield; to surrender.

subside, hush *verb* {8367 shathaq} from the root, to subside.

substance, force, lizard *noun* {3581 koach} {3981 maamats} pressure, physical or intellectual; also a lizard.

substrata *noun* [2737 katoteros] underlayer; figurative of sheol/hades.

subterranean *noun* [2709 katakthonios] underground; of the world of departed souls.

subtil, subtle *adjective* {6175 arum} cunning.

suburb *noun* {4054 migrash} {6503 parbar} {6518 paraz} {*plural* 6519 perazah} a surrounding area.

suburban *adjective* {6521 peraziy; *plural* perozim} of a surrounding area.

suburbanite *noun* {6520 perazon} one that settles in a suburb; **cp** urbanite.

subvert, pervert *verb* {5557 calaph} to turn from; to undermine.

succeed, prosper *verb* {3787 kasher} {6743 tsaleach} {6744 tselach} to succeed; to press on.

successor *noun* {4497 manown} one who perpetuates.

such *noun* {6423 peloniy} a specific one.

such a one *noun* {6422 palmoniy} so and so.

suck (up) (out) *verb* {4041 megammah} {4711 matsats} {5966 ala} to suck up; to suck out.

suck, suckle, suckling *verb* {3243 yanaq} {5134 nuq} {5763 ul} to feed at the breast.

suck, sweeten *verb* {4985, 4988 mathaq} to be sweet; to relish.

suck, wring *verb* {4680 matsah} to wring, or squeeze out; to suck out.

suckling *noun* {5764 ul} {5768 olal} one who feeds at the breast; **see** infant.

sudarium *transliterated noun* [4676 soudarion] a cloth used to wipe perspiration from the face or to wrap the head of a corspe.

suddenly *adverb* {6597 pithom} instantly.

sufficiency *noun* {7647 saba} an overflow; plenty.

satire *noun* {4426 melitsah} {4485 manginah} a literary work holding up follies or shortcomings for ridicule.

sufficient *adjective* [566 apeki] adequate.

sufficient *adjective* [713 arketos] satisfactory.

sufficient, satisfied *verb* [714 arkeo] to be satisfactory. **see** SUMMARY: SATIATE, SATISFY, SUFFICIENT:

Suchahiy *transliterated name* {7756 suwchathiy} Of Sukah.

Sukkoth Benoth *transliterated noun* {5524 cukkowthbenowth} Brush Arbor of the Daughters.

Sukkoth/Brush Arbors, sukkoth, brush arbor *transliterated noun* {5520 cok} {5521 cukkah} {5522 cikkuwth} {5523 cukkowth} {7900 sok} [4634 skeenopeegia] Brush Arbor; name of places in Pelesheth and Misrayim; a brush arbor to harbor animals; a celebration of harvest, of spreading of branches, of Hoshia Na; Leviticus 23:33-44, Yahn 7:37, Psalm 118:25, 26, Matthaios 21:9-15, Markos 11:9,10, Yahn 12:13, Apocalypse 7:9,10; **see** Hoshia Na.

sulphur *noun* {1614 gophriyth} [2303 thion] as ignited.

sulphurous *adjective* [2306 thiodes] sulphur-like.

sum *noun* {6575 parashah} the full exposition; the total.

sum, head *noun* {7217 resh} the top of the body; the sum total.

sum up *verb* [346 anakephalaiomai] to total.

summer (fruit) (house) *noun* {7019 qaits} the summer season; summer fruit; a summer house.

summit *noun* {2872 tabbuwr} top of the pile.

summon *verb* {6817 tsaaq} [2753 keluo] [3343 metapempo] to call to convene.

summons *noun* [2752 keleuma] a call to convene.

sun *noun* {8121, 8122 shemesh} [2246 helios] the brightest body in the heavens.

sun icons *plural noun* {2553 chamman} sun pillars.

sup, supping *verb* [1172 dipneo] to dine.

superabound *verb* [4052 perissuo] [4121 pleonazo] to exceed adundantly.

superabundance *noun* [4051 perissuma] a surplus. **superabundant** *adjective, adverb* [4053 perissos] [5250 huperpleonazo] in the sense of beyond; excessive, supreme.

superabundantly (more) *adverb* [4054 perissoteron] [4055, 4056 perissoteros] [4057 perissos] [5249 huperperissos] more exceedingly.

superior *adjective* [5242 hupereko] to stand out; to excel; to be above.

Suph *transliterated name* {6689 tsuwph} Honeycomb.

supper *noun* [1173 dipnon] a formal meal usually in the evening

supplement *verb* [466 antanapleeroo] to fullfil; to fill up. **supplication** *noun* {8467 techinnah} {*plural* 8469 tachanunim} entreaty; petition.

support, counsel *noun* {8454 tushiah} {*plural* 8458 tachbuloth} advice; support.

support, crutch *noun* {4938 mishenah} that on which one leans.

support, palmspan *noun* {2947 tephach} {2948 tophach} the span of a palm; a span; a support.

support, partake *verb* [482 antilambanomai] [484 antileepsis] to take part; to support.

support, supply *noun* {4937 mishen} that on which one leans.

support, time, anvil, step *noun* {6471 paamah} anvil, as a support; support, as a pedestal or column in a structure; a "stepper", as a supporter of the body; time, as an occasion or occurrence – but not as measured time.

support, uphold *verb* {5582 scaad} to support; usually, figuratively; **cp** prop.

Sur *transliterated name* {6698 tsur} Rock.

Suri El *transliterated name* {6700 tsuriel} Rock of El.

Suri Shadday *transliterated name* {6701 tsurishadday} Rock of Shadday; **see** Shadday.

surpass, trespass, overpass, pass (over) (through) *verb* {5674 abar} to cross over; this verb is unrelated to the mistranslation of passover.

surrender, betray, deliver *verb* [3860 paradidomi] to give to possession of another; to deliver to an enemy; to release.

surround, environ, round *noun* {3603 kikkar} literally, circle; the environs of an area; a round of material, usually of precious metals.

surround, round, strike (round about) *verb* {5362 naqaph} to strike; to strike all around; to surround; to round off the beard.

surround, stay around *verb* {3803 kathar} to enclose.

surround, turn (about) (around), go (about) (around) *verb* {5437 cabab} to border; to revolve; to surround.

survey *verb* {8376 taah} {8388 taar} to mark off; to designate.

survive *verb* {7604 shaar} {8277 sarad} as having escaped.

LEXICON

survive, survivors *noun* {7605, 7606 shear} {7611 sheeriyth} {8300 sariyd} as escaped.

survivor *noun* {2475 chaloph} as being orphaned.

suspect, envy *verb* **jealous, zealous** *adjective* {7065 qana} {7067 qanna} {7072 qannow} to be zealous, as jealous, or envious.

suspend, hang *verb* **prone** *participle* {8511 tala} {8518 talah} to suspend.

suspicion, envy, jealous *noun* {7068 qinah} zeal, as jealousy, or envy.

sustain, contain, maintain, measure *verb* {3557 kuwl} to keep in.

sustain, guide *verb* {5095 nahal} literally, to lead with light.

sustain, uphold, prop *verb* {5564 camak} {8551 tamak} to prop up; with the hands, or with props.

swallow *verb* [2666 katapino] to drink down; to destroy; to be overwhelmed with sorrow.

swallow, horse *noun* {5483 cuc} {5484 cucah} a horse as leaping; a swallow as flitting.

swan, chameleon *noun* {8580 tanshemeth} hard breather.

swarmers *noun* {6157 arob} insects as swarming; **cp** teemers.

swathe *verb* {2853 chathal} {2854 chathullah} to wrap as a baby, as a bandage.

sway, wag over, wander, waver *verb* {5110 nud} to waver.

sweater *noun* {3154 yeza} a garment that causes sweat.

sweep (away) *verb* {5502 cachaph} to scrape off.

sweepings *noun* {5478 suwchah} that which is swept away.

sweeten, suck *verb* {4985, 4988 mathaq} to be sweet; to relish.

sweeter, sweetness *adjective* {4966 mathoq} {4986 metheq} {4987 motheq} sweet; pleasantness.

swell *adjective* {6639 tsabeh} swollen.

swell, host *verb* {6638 tsabah} to assemble a host; to swell up.

swell, presume *verb* {6075 aphal} to assume aforehand; an ascending, as swollen.

swelling, exalting, lifting *noun* {7613 seeth} an elevation; from the verb, lift {5375}.

swelling within *adjective* [1471 enkuos] pregnant.

swerve *participle* **swerver** *noun* {7750 sut} {*plural* 7750 sutim} one that turns to avoid.

swift *adjective* {7031 qal} rapid.

swift, trifle, abase, abate, belittle, slight *verb* {6819 tsaar} {6985 qat} {7034 qalah} {7043 qalal} [2274 heetaomai] to belittle in contempt; to make light of; to lessen.

swim *noun* {7813 sachu} from the verb, to swim.

swim *verb* {7811 sachah} to inundate; to swim.

swoop *verb* {5860 it} literally, or figuratively, to swoop down.

swooper *noun* {5861 ait} a being that swoops.

sword *noun* {2719 chereb} {4380 mekerah} a cutting instrument; a stabber.

sycamine fig *noun* [4807 sukaminos] a species of fig.

sycamore *transliterated noun* {8256 shaqam} [4809 sukomoraia] a species of tree.

Sychar *transliterated name* {7941 shekar} [4965 suchar] Intoxicant.

sycophant *transliterated noun* [4811 sukophanteo] a fig informer; a tattletale.

sympathy *noun* {4263 machmal} compassion.

symphonia *transliterated dual noun* {5481 ciyphoneya} Hellenic; literally, a sounding as one; a soundbag with dual pipes.

symphonize *verb* [4856 sumphoneo] [4859 sumphonos] literally, to sound as one; to harmonize; to agree.

symphony *transliterated noun* [4857 sumpheesis] [4858 sumphonia] literally, a sounding as one; harmony; a group of instruments sounding together.

synagogue *transliterated noun* [4864 sunagogee] Hellenic translation of the Hebrew congregation.

synagogue arch *transliterated noun* [752 archchisunagogos] the arch over a synagogue.

synagogue together *transliterated verb* [1997 episunagoge] to co-congregate.

Syria *transliterated name* {6865 tsor} [4947 suria] Rock; **cp** Sor.

Syriaiy *transliterated name* {6865 tsor} [4948 suros] Of Syria.

T

Taanak *transliterated name* {8590 taanak} the meaning uncertain; a place in Pelesheth.

Taarea *transliterated name* {8390 taarea} possibly, Earthly.

Tab Rimmon *transliterated name* {2886 tabrimmown} Goodly to Rimmon.

Tabe El *transliterated name* {2870 tabeel} Goodly of El.

tabernacle; see SUMMARY: TABERNACLE.

Tabitha, Dorcas, gazelle *noun* {6643 tsebiy} {6646 tsebiyah} [5000 tabitha] a gazelle, as beautiful; Tabitha is the Hellene transliteration of tsebiyah; Dorcas is the Hellene translation of tsebiyah.

table *noun* {7979 shulchan} a table, as spread out.

tablet *noun* [4093 pinakidion] a small slab for scribing; **cp** slab.

Tachan *transliterated name* {8465 tachan} Encamped.

Tachaniy *transliterated name* {8470 tachaniy} Of Tachan.

Tachash *transliterated name* {8477 tachash} Badger.

Tachath *transliterated name* {8480 tachath} Beneath.

Tachkemoni *transliterated name* {8461 tachkemoniy} Enwisen.

Tachpanches *transliterated name* {8471 tachpanchec} the meaning uncertain; a place in Misrayim.

Tachpenes *transliterated name* {8472 tachpeneyc} the meaning uncertain; a Misrayim woman.

Tachrea *transliterated name* {8475 tachrea} possibly, Earthly.

tail *noun* {2180 zahnab} literally, a flapper; **see** curtail.

tailoring *noun* {4055 mad} measured, or fitted clothing.

tailoring, measure, measurement *noun* {4060 middah} {4067 madown} {*plural* 4461 memadim} size.

take *verb* [618 apolambano] [2983 lambano] to take hold of; to take aside.

take, lift *verb* [142 airo] to take up; to take away.

take, undertake *verb* {6901 qabal} {6902 qebal} [353 analambano] to acquire; to take up; **cp** receive.

take heed *verb* [4337 proseko] to hold the mind towards; to be cautious about.

take out *verb* [336 anairesis] [337 anaireo] in the sense of deathifying.

take over, overtake *verb* [2638 katalambano] to lay hold of; to seize.

taken up *verb* [354 analepsis] ascended.

taking *noun* [3028 lepsis] receipt.

talebearer *noun* {7400 rakil} a scandalmonger, as travelling about.

Talmay *transliterated name* {8526 talmay} Ridged.

Tamar *transliterated name* {8559 tamar} [2283 thamar] Erect.

tambourine *noun* {8596 toph} {8611 topheth} as being shaken; a shallow drum, played with the hands.

tambourining *verb* {8608 taphaph} to play the tambourine.

tame *verb* {3711 kaphah} to bend into submission.

Tanchumeth *transliterated name* {8576 tanchumeth} Consolations.

tankard, hoarfrost *noun* {3713 kephor} a covering; hoarfrost, as coversing the ground; a tankard, as a covered vessel.

Taom *transliterated name* {8380 taomim} [2381 thomas] Twin; **see** Twin.

Tappuach *transliterated name* {8599 tappuwach} Apple.

target, target area *noun* {4307 mattarah} {4645 miphga} that which is aimed at; an area for aiming.

tarry *verb* [1304 diatribo] to remain.

Tarshish *transliterated name* {8659 tarshish} a place in the Mediterranean.

Tartaq *transliterated name* {8662 tartaq} the meaning uncertain; a deity of the Avviym.

Tartaros (incarcerate in) *verb* [5020 tartaros] possibly the lowest abyss in sheol/hades; **see** sheol/hades.

tassel *noun* {6731 tsits} as a tassel of hair; as an ornament.

taste *noun* {2940 taam} taste includes the full gestation.

taste *verb* {2938 taam} [1089 guomai] to taste; taste includes the full gestation.

taste, decree *noun* {2941, 2942 teem} judgment; flavor.

Tattenay *transliterated name* {8674 tattenay} the meaning uncertain; a Persian.

tattoo, brand, etching, mark noun {7085 qaaqa} {8420 tab} [5480 karagma] a scratched marking; a mark on animals; an x or a + as a signature of an illiterate; a mark of protection; **read** Yechezq El 9:4-6; **read** Apocalypse 13:16,17, 14:9-11, 15:2, 16:2, 19:20, 20:4; **cp** brand.

tattoo, brand, mark verb {8427, 8428 tavah} to mark an animal; to mark an x or + as a signature of an illiterate, or to mark for protection.

teach plural verb {4000 mabowm} to cause to discern.

teach, learn verb {3925 lamad} literally, to goad; to disciple; to be discipled; **see** verb disciple.

tear verb [1145 dakruo] to shed tears.

tear verb {6533 param} {6582 pashach} to rip.

tear, prey noun {2964 tereph} {2966 terephah} {5706 ad} a prey, as an object of attack; as being torn.

tear (away) (up) verb {5420 nathac} {5423 nathaq} to tear off; to tear up.

Tebach transliterated name {2875 tebach} Slaughter.

Tebal Yah transliterated name {2882 tebalyah} Dipped of Yah.

Tebes transliterated name {8405 tebets} Whiteness.

Techinnah transliterated name {8468 techinnah} Supplication.

teem verb {8317 sharats} to become prolific.

teemer noun {8318 sherets} one who becomes prolific; **cp** swarmer.

teeth, tusks plural noun {6374 piphiah} {8143 shenhabbim} teeth of a person, animal, or instrument.

Tel Aviv transliterated name {8512 telaviv} Heap of Unripe.

Tel Harsha transliterated name {8521 telcharsha} Heap of an Engraver.

Tel Melach transliterated name {8528 telmelach} Heap of Salt.

Telach transliterated name {8520 telach} Breach.

tell verb {5046 nagad} to relate.

Temach transliterated name {8547 temach} the meaning uncertain; one of the Dedicates.

Teman transliterated name {8487 teman} Southerly.

Temaniy transliterated name {8489 teymaniy} Of Teman.

temple noun {7541 raqqah} the side of the head as being thin.

temple, tent; see SUMMARY: TABERNACLE, TEMPLE:

tend, attend, befriend, graze verb {7462 raah} [5256 hupeereteo] to tend a flock or to pasture; to befriend, by attending to; to cause a flock to graze; **see** attendant; **see** Yah Veh Raah.

tender adjective {7390 rak} [527 apalos] tender; as soft, as weak.

tender noun {7473 roiy} one that tends flocks.

tender verb {7401 rakak} to tenderize; to soften; to weaken.

tenderness noun {7391 rok} tenderness; as softness; as weakness.

tendril noun {5189 netishah} {8299 sarig} a spiral shoot of a plant which attaches itself for support.

Teqoa transliterated name {8620 teqowa} Blast.

Teqoaiy transliterated name {8621 teqoiy} Of Teqoa.

Terach transliterated name {8646 terach} [2291 thara] derivative uncertain.

teraphim transliterated plural noun {8655 teraphim} family idols.

terrify verb {926 bahal} {927 behal} {1763 dechal} to panic; to hasten anxiously.

terrify, awe, dread verb {6206 arats} to harass; to reverence.

terrify, break (down), dismay verb {2865, 2866 chathath} to cause to prostrate; to break down by violence, or fear.

terror noun {928 behalah} {4032 magor} {4034 megorah} {7374 retet} panic.

terror noun {2844 chath} {2847 chittah} {2851 chittiyth} {plural 2849 chatchathim} in the sense of crushing.

terror, granary noun {4035 megurah} a fright; a place to store grain.

tertiary, thrice, tierce, triangle noun {7991 shalosh} an officer of the third rank; three times; an interval of a third; a three sided music instrument.

test noun [3984 pira] attempt.

test verb {5254 nacah} [426 anetazo] [1598 ekpirazo] [3985 pirazo] to test; to attempt; to try as in a court.

testi noun {6344 pachad} a testicle.

testing *noun* [3986 pirasmos] a putting to proof.

testing *noun* **Massah** *transliterated name* {4531 maccah} name means Testing.

tetrarch *transliterated title* [5075 tetrarcheo] [5076 tetrarchees] a ruler over a fourth part.

thatch *noun* [4721 stege] thatched roof.

then *adverb* {227 az} at that time, at that place: most versions, to avoid monotony, use **then** instead of **and**.

then *adverb* [687 ara] denoting an interrogation to which a negative answer is presumed: **see so**.

thence (from) [2547 kakithen] (of place) thence; (of time) thereafter, afterward.

Theo Philos *transliterated name* [2321 theophilos] Friend of God/Elohim.

therapist *transliterated noun* [2324 therapon] one skilled in therapeutics.

therapy *transliterated noun* [2322 therapia] cure.

thick (cloud), thicket, thickness *adjective* {5645, 5646 ab} {5672 abiy} {5687 aboth} thick; enveloping as a cloud.

thicken *verb* {5666 abah} to cause to be dense.

thicket *noun* {5441 cobek} {5442 cebak} {7730 sobek} trees or shrubs closely set.

thief *noun* {1590 gannab} one who steals.

thigh *noun* [3382 meros] the upper leg.

thin, pulverized *adjective* {1851 dak} thin; beaten small; emaciated.

thing, things *noun* **note:** These two word are never used throughout manuscripts; most often, they have been added by the translaters to satisfy the English idiom. At times, they are a mistranslation of the word, **word**, and a very few other words. These instances are brought out in the thus: *thing* **word.**

think, shine *verb* {6245 ashath} {6246 ashith} as polishing.

think, think well, well thinking *verb* [1380 dokeo] [2106 eudokeo] [2107 eudokia] [5426 phroneo] the (well) exercise of the mind.

think amiss *verb* [5422 phrenapatao] to be misled in mind.

thirst *noun* {6772 tsama} {6773 tsimah} a dryness.

thirst *noun* {6774 tsimmaon} a place of thirst.

thirst *verb* {6770 tsame} [1372 dipsao] literally, or figuratively, to thirst for; to long for.

thirsty *adjective* {6771 tsame} literally, to thirst; figuratively, to be longing for.

thistle *noun* {*plural* 5621 carabim} {7057 qimosh} {7063 qimmashon} a prickly plant.

thong *noun* [2438 himas] a strap or strip of leather; a whip to lash or to bind criminals; also a fastener, as a of a sandal.

thorn, hook *noun* {5518 sirah} {*plural* 7165 qeresim} literally, a boiler; a hook; a thorn.

thorn, thorns *noun* {5518 cirah} {5544 cillon} {6791 tsen} {*plural* 6796 tsaninim} {6975 qots} {7898 shaith} [173 akantha] [174 akanthinos] [4647 skolops] a sharp projection on the stem of a plant.

thought *noun* {*plural* 6248 ashtoth} {*plural* 6250 eshtonahoth} [1270 dianoema] [5424 phren] [5427 phronema] [5428 phronesis] that which results from thinking.

thought deluder *noun* [5423 phrenapates] a mind misleader; a deceiver.

thoughtful *adjective* [5429 phronimos] [5431 phrontizo] exercising thought.

thoughtfully *adverb* [5430 phronimos] in a thoughtful manner.

thoughtless *adjective* [878 aphron] without thought; as ignorant; as rash.

thoughtlessness *noun* [877 aphrosunee] unthoughtful.

thread *noun* {2339 chut} from the root, to sew; a string.

three yesters ago *adverb* {8032 shilshom} {8543 temol} these two words are usually used in combination; day before yesterday.

three yesters ago *noun* {865 ethmowl} may refer to day before yesterday, or recently.

thresh *verb* [248 aloao] to tread out grain.

threshing floor *noun* {1637 goren} [257 halon] a smooth and/or hard place to thresh grain.

threshold waiter *noun* {5605 saphaph} one that waits upon the threshold; a doorperson.

threshold, bason *noun* {5592 caph} {5602 cephel} a container; as a vessel, or as a vestibule.

thrice, tierce, triangle, tertiary *noun* {7991 shaloah} an officer of the third rank; three times; an interval of a third; a three sided music instrument.

throat *noun* {1621 gargeroth} {1627 garon} {3930 loa} the forepart of the neck.

throne *noun* {3676 kec} {3678 kicceh} {3764 korce} [2362 thronos] a seat of authority.

throng *noun* {6899 qibbuts} a crowd.

throng, abundance *noun* {8229 shiphah} a crowd, plenty.

throttle *verb* {1624 gahrah} to throttle the throat, to stir.

throw, cast, hurl *verb* {7993 shalak} to throw out, down, or away.

thrush *noun* {5693 aguwr} literally, to twitter; a species of bird.

thumb, great toe *noun* {931 bohen} literally, the large digit.

thunder *noun* {7482 raam} {7483 ramah} [1027 bronte] the voice caused by lightning.

thunder *verb* {7481 raam} to sound the voice caused by lightning.

thunder, irritate *verb* {7481 raam} to agitate; to be agitated.

thunder, shout *noun* {7452 rea} a crashing sound.

thunderstorm *noun* [3655 ombros].

thus *adverb* [3779 houto] in such manner. **see** Yahn 3:16.

tiara *noun* {4701 mitsnepheth} headpiece of a sovereign or archpriest.

tiara, ornament, adornment *noun* {6287 peer} an embellishment; a tiara, as an adornment.

Tibchath *transliterated name* {2880 tibchath} Slaughter.

tie, mute *verb* {481 alam} as in silencing by tying tongue, or lips; tying bundles.

tier, thirds, three, triple *noun* {8027 shalash} layers, or lofts; a whole, severed into three; three; threefold.

tierce, triangle, tertiary, thrice *noun* {7991 shaloah} an officer of the third rank; three times; an interval of a third; a three sided music instrument.

Tilgath Pilneser, Tilgath Pileser *transliterated name* {8407 tilgathpilnecer, tilgathpilecer} an Ashshuriy sovereign.

till *verb* {5214 niyr} to furrow the soil.

Timaeus *transliterated name* [5090 timaios] Fouled.

timber, staff, staves *noun* {905 bad} [3586 xulon] [4464 rhabdos] timber, or staves made therefrom.

timber, tree *noun* {6086 ets} {6097 etsah} a tree; timber; sticks of timber.

time *noun* {5732 iddan} not a specific measured period of time; rather an era of indeterminable length; as in this time, next time; of Arami origin, and appears only in Dani El.

time *noun* {6256 eth} [5550 chronos] chrono; a measured period of existence; including, but not limited to seconds, minutes, hours, days, weeks, months, years; **see** Apocalypse 10:6 for the prophecy when measured time ends and eternity begins; **cp** season.

time, anvil, step, support *noun* {6471 paamah} anvil, as a support; support, as a pedestal or column in a structure; a "stepper", as a supporter of the body; time, as an occasion or occurrence – but not as measured time.

time (at this) (by this) (from this) *adverb* {6258 attah} now; this present moment.

time (take) *verb* [5549 chronizo] to take a measured portion of time; **see** time.

time (waste) *verb* [5551 chronotribeo] to waste a measured portion of time; **see** time.

timely *adjective* {6261 itti} opportunely.

timidity *noun* {4816 morek} literally, soft.

timidsouled *adjective* [3642 oligopsukos] shy; lacking courage.

Timna *transliterated name* {8555 timna} Withhold.

Timnah *transliterated name* {8553 timnah} Portion.

Timnahiy *transliterated name* {8554 timniy} Of Timnah.

Timnath Heres *transliterated name* {8556 timnathcherec} Portion of the Sun.

Timo Theos *transliterated name* [5095 timotheos] Honoured of God/Elohim.

tingle, quiver *verb* {6750 tsalal} to vibrate.

tinkle *verb* {5913 akac} to tinkle with tinklers.

tinkler *noun* {5913 ecec} an ornament that tinkles.

Tiphsach *transliterated name* {8607 tiphcach} Ford.

Tiqvah *transliterated name* {8616 tiqvah} Cord.

Tirahiy *transliterated name* {8654 tirathiy} Gate; Of Tirah.

Tirchanah *transliterated name* {8647 tirchanah} the meaning uncertain; a Yisra Eliy.

Tireya *transliterated name* {8493 tiyreya} Awe.

Tirhaqah *transliterated name* {8640 tirhaqah} the meaning uncertain; a sovereign of Kush.

Tirsah *transliterated name* {8656 tirtsah} Pleasure.

Tisbehiy *transliterated name* {8664 tishbiy} Recourse; Of Tishbeh (in Gilad).

Tisiy *transliterated name* {8491 tiytsiy} Of Tis.

tithe *noun* {4643 maasrah} [1181 dekate] one tenth.

tithe *verb* {6237 asar} [586 apodekatoo] [1183 dekatoo] to offer or receive one tenth.

title *transliterated noun* [5102 titlos] the rank of a person; a caption; **cp** inscription; **cp** superscription; **cp** epigraph.

tittle *noun* [2762 keraia] an infintismal part.

Titus *transliterated name* [5103 titos] meaning uncertain.

Tormah/deceitfully *transliterated name* {8649 tormah} Fraud.

Toach *transliterated name* {8430 towach} Humbled.

Tob Adoni Yah *transliterated name* {2899 tobadoniyah} Goodly of Adoni Yah.

Tobi Yah *transliterated name* {2900 tobiyah} Goodly of Yah.

Tochu *transliterated name* {8459 tochuw} Abasement.

toddler *noun* {2945 taph} little ones that toddle.

toe, finger *noun* {676 etsba} {677 etsba} [1147 daktulos] literally, a digit as a grasper; **cp** great toe, thumb.

together, unitedly, altogether *adverb* {3162 yachad} as one; **see** united.

toil *adjective* {6001 amel} hard working.

toil *noun* {5999 amal} to work hard.

toil *verb* {5998 amal} hard work.

Token *transliterated name* {8507 token} Gauge.

Tola *transliterated name* {8439 towla} Maggot.

Tolaiy *transliterated name* {8440 towlaiy} Of Tola.

tolerance *noun* [463 anokee] ability to restrain.

tolerate, endure *verb* [430 anekomai] to hold oneself up against.

tomb *noun* {6900 qeburah} {6913 qeber} [5028 taphos] burial; **see** entomb; **cp** grave.

tomorrow, morrow (the) *noun* {4279 machar} {4283 mochorath} [839 aurion] [1887 epaurion] the following day.

tongue *name* {3956 leshonah} {3961 lishshan} [1100 glossa] the physical body part in the mouth; a language; **cp** lip.

tonguelash *verb* {3960 lashan} to wag the tongue.

tongues (divided) *noun* [1266 diamerizo] also implies distributed.

tongues (foreign) *noun* {3937 laaz} foreign languages.

tongues (other) *noun* [2084 heteroglossos] another language; only in 1 Corinthians 14:21.

tongues of fire *noun* [1100 glossa] [4442 pur] licking flames; **note:** in Acts 2:1-4, divided (or, distributed) tongues of fire sat on each of the apostles; they spoke in other tongues, and were heard in many dialects; **see** dialect.

tooth, tusk, crag, ivory *noun* {8127, 8128 shen} {*plural* 8143 shenhabbim} [3599 adous] as being sharp.

top, beginning, first(s), head *noun* {7218 rosh} {7221 rishah} {7225 reshith} {8462 rechillah} the head, in a variety of applications; the head of the body, of time, of the month, of archs.

Topheth *transliterated name* {8612 topheth} {8613 tophteh} meaning uncertain; Theological Wordbook suggests a place of spitting; Strong suggests a place of cremation; Scofield suggests a place in Gay Hinnom/Valley of Burning where humans were sacrificed; **read** Yesha Yah 30:33, Yirme Yah 7:31, 32, 19:6-14.

topple, descend, lower *verb* {3381 yarad} to go lower; to tip over.

topple, totter, waver *verb* {4131 mowt} {4571 maad} to waver; to fall over.

Toqahath *transliterated name* {8445 towqahath} Obedience.

LEXICON

torah *transliterated noun* {8451, 8452 torah} [3551 nomos] Elohim's holy statute; the first five scrolls of the Scripture.

torah (doctors of the) [3547 nomodidaskalos] doctrinators of the torah, including rabbis and rabbonis.

torah (set the) *verb* [3549 nomotheteo] to legislate the torah.

torah (setting the) *verb* [3548 nomothesia] legislating the torah.

torah (violating the) *noun* [3891 paranomeo] to be opposed to the torah.

torah setter *noun* [3550 nomothetees] one who legislates the torah.

torah violation, violation of the torah *noun* [458 anomia] [3892 paranomia] a disregarding of the torah.

torahically *adverb* [3545 nomimos] according to the torah.

torahist *noun* [3544 nomikos] an expert of the torah.

torrential *adjective* {5464 cagrid} rushingly.

tortoise, palanquin *noun* {6632 tsab} a wagon, as covered; a tortoise, as covered.

tossings *plural noun* {5076 nadud} flailings.

totality *noun*, **totally, perfect** *adjective* {3642 kaliyl} all inclusive; naught to be added.

totter, wag, wander, waver, drift, shake, stagger *verb* {5128 nuwa} to waver.

totter, waver, topple *verb* {4131 mowt} {4571 maad} to waver; to fall over.

touch *verb* {3237 yamash} (4184 muwsh) to touch.

touch, plague, reach *verb* {5060 naga} to touch heavily; to strike.

tough, strong *adjective* {533 ammits} {554 amots} {2389 chazaq} {5794 az} {5808 izzuz} forceful; harsh; physically able.

toward, -ward, opposite *adjective* {4136 mowl} [481 antikru] [492 antiparerkomai] [495 antiperan] across from.

tower *noun* **Migdol** *transliterated name* {4024 migdol} {4026 migdal} tower; a place in Misrayim.

tower *noun* {5470 cohar} a dungeon surrounded by walls.
tower *noun* {6877 tseriach} a citadel.

tracks *noun* [2487 ichnos] a way or path beaten by the feet; metaphorically used of imitating the example of another.

trail *noun* {5410 nathiybah} as trodden.

train *noun* {7640 shebel} the train of a gown, as flowing after; **cp** drape.

trample *verb* {1915 hadak} to crush with the foot; **see** stool. **trample** *verb* {6072 acac} {7429 ramac} {7512 rephac} [3961 pateo] to tread; to squeeze underfoot.

trample, balance *verb* {5537 cala} {5541 calah} as suspended; as weighed; as trampled.

trampled *adjective* {4001 mebuwcah} {4823 mirmac} {4833 mirpas} trodden; treaded upon.

trampling *noun* {8395 tebucah} a treading down.

tranquil *adjective* {7946 shalanan} serene.

transact, exact *verb* [4238 prasso] to extract dues; to execute; to perform repeatedly.

transcience *adjective* **transient** *adverb* {2465 cheled} the fleeting of life.

transcribe, antiquate, remove *verb* {6275 athaq} that which has aged; to take away; to take down, as in transcribing.

transcript *noun* {6572, 6573 parshegen} a copy.

transfigure *verb* [3345 metaschematizo] to alter the figure; **cp** metamorphose.

transgress *verb* [3845 parabaino] to overstep.

transgression *noun* [3847 parabasis] an overstepping of the basis.

transgressor *noun* [3848 parabatees] one who oversteps.

translate *verb* {8638 tirgam} [2058 hermenia] [2059 hermeenuo] [3177 methermenuo] the rendering of words from one language to another; **note:** languages are translated; dreams are interpreted; **cp** interpret.

translate thoroughly *verb* [1329 diermenuo] to translate exactly, in detail.

translator *noun* {3887 luwts} [1328 diermenutees] one who translates from one tongue to another; **cp** interpreter.

transparent *adjective* {3840 libnah}.

transplace *verb* [3346 metatithemi] to put in another place; to transpose.

transplant noun {8363 shethil} that which has removed and planted elsewhere.

transplant verb {8362 shathal} to remove and plant elsewhere.

trap, trip, crooked adjective {6121 aqob} {6128 aqalqal} {6129 aqallathon} a trap; one that trips; crooked, as full of traps.

trauma transliterated noun [5134 trauma] a wound.

traumatize transliterated verb [5135 traumatizo] to wound or injure.

travail noun [5604 odin] pain; a pang of birthing.

travail noun {8513 telaah} a distress.

travail verb [5605 odino] to experience the pains of birth.

tray noun {4289 machtah} a tray to remove live coals, or ashes.

tread, spy, step verb {7270 ragal} verb of foot; to measure out with the foot; **see** foot.

treason noun {4604 maal} a covert act.

treason verb {4603 maal} to act covertly.

treasure noun [2344 thesauros] something precious; a treasury, that which is laid up in a treasury.

treasure noun {5458 cegor} as withheld at the heart.

treasure verb {686 atsar} [2343 thesaurizo] to reserve; to store up.

treasure, hide verb {6845 tsaphan} to hide by covering over; to protect; to reserve.

treasure, treasury noun {214 owtsar} {plural 1595 genezim} {1596 genaz} {1597 ginzak} a gathering place of valuables.

treasure (hidden) noun {4301 matmon} {plural 4362 mikman} {plural 4710 mitspunim} {6840 tsaphin} {8226 saphan} a secreted valuable.

treasure (peculiar) noun {5459 cegullah} private treasure, as held close to the breast; private property.

treasured, impending, ready adjective {6259, 6264 athud} {6263 athid} prepared; treasured.

treasurer noun {plural 1411 gedabar} {1489 gizbar} {1490 gizbar} one that oversees a treasury.

tree noun {363 iylan} [1186 dendron].

tree, timber noun {6086 ets} {6097 etsah} a tree; timber; sticks of timber.

tremble verb {2729 charad} {2730 chared} {6426 palats} {7460 raad} to shudder with terror.

trembling noun {2731 charadah} {6427 pallatsuwth} {7461 raad} {8606 tiphletseth} a shudder; fear.

trench noun {2430 cheylah} {2434 chayits} a trench for protection.

trench, decision, decisive, incision, incisor, ore, sickle adjective, noun {2742 charuts} mentally, soulically, or physically, an incising.

trench, valiant noun {2426 chel} character of a person who protects; a trench for protection.

trespass, overpass, pass (over) (through), surpass verb {5674 abar} to cross over; this verb is unrelated to the mistranslation of passover.

tresses noun [2863 komao] [2864 kome] a long lock of hair; hair as hanging; **cp** hair.

triangle, tertiary, thrice, tierce noun {7991 shaloah} an officer of the third rank; three times; an interval of a third; a three sided music instrument.

tribulate verb [2346 thlibo] to press hard upon.

tribulate verb {6887 tsarar} to constrict.

tribulation noun [2347 thlipsis] a pressing together.

tribulation noun **tribulator** noun **constricted** adjective {6862 tsar} {6869 tsarah} a constriction; a time of constriction; a constricted place; one that constricts.

tribute noun {4061 middah} a tribute of money.

trickery noun {6122 oqbah} to trip or trap by trickery.

trifle, abase, abate, belittle, slight, swift verb {6819 tsaar} {6985 qat} {7034 qalah} {7043 qalal} [2274 heetaomai] to belittle in contempt; to make light of; to lessen.

trip, crooked, trap adjective {6121 aqob} {6128 aqalqal} {6129 aqallathon} a trap; one that trips; crooked, as full of traps.

trip, falter, stumble verb {3782 kashal} to totter; to waver.

trip the heel, heel, heelprint, heel trippers noun {6119 aqeb} [4418 pterna] the back of the foot; a print made by the heel; ones that trip the heel by trapping.

LEXICON

trip the heel, restrain the heel *verb* {6117 aqab} to seize by holding the heel.

troop against *verb* {1464 guwd} to attack with a troop.

troop *noun* {1409 gad} {1416 geduwd} a crowd, usually military.

trouble *verb* {5916 akar} to disturb.

trough *noun* {3342 yeqeb} a trough for treading wine.

trough, curl *noun* {7298 rahat} {*plural* 4857 mashabim} {8268 shoqeth} a drinking trough for animals; a ringlet of hair.

true (being) *noun* [226 aleethuo] to be true.

true *adjective* [227 alethes] accurate; genuine; honest.

true, truly, truth *noun* {571 emeth} [225 alethia] literally, of a truth.

truly *adverb* {551 omnam} {552 umnam} [230 alethos] **note:** the Hebrew are from the root of amen; **see** amen.

truly, truth *noun* {7187 qeshot} {7189 qoshet} from the root, to balance; equity.

trumpet, lily *noun* **Shoshanna** *transliterated name* {7799 shoshanna} [4677 sousanna] lily, as a flower, or as an ornament; trumpet, from its lily shaped bell.

trumpet, trump *noun* {2689 chatsotsrah} [4536 salpinx] a music instrument.

trump, trumpet, trumpeting *verb* {2690 chatsar} [4537 salpizo] to blow on a trumpet.

trumpeter *participle* {2690 chatsar} [4538 salpistees] one who trumpets.

trust, trustless, trustworthy; see SUMMARY: TRUST.

truthful *noun* [228 alethinos] factual.

Tubal Qayin *transliterated name* {8423 tuwbalqayin} Offspring of Qayin.

tubes *plural noun* {6804 tsantarah} hollows.

tuft *noun* {5296 neoreth} that which is shaken out, as the tuft from the flax.

Tulon *transliterated name* {8436 tuwlon} Lofty.

tumult *noun* {8351 sheth} [2351 thorubos] uprising; riot.

tumulting *verb* [2350 thorubeo] to make a noise or uproar; to disturb.

turban *noun* {*plural* 4021 migbaahoth} {6797 tsaniph} a wraparound headdress.

turn *noun* {5438 cibbah} a providential turn of affairs.

turn, response, return *noun* {8666 teshubah} a reccurence; a reply, as returned.

turn, row *noun* {8447 tor} a succession of occasion; a row of. **turn (about) (around), go (about) (around), surround** *verb* {5437 cabab} to border; to revolve; to surround.

turn (aside) (in), twist (off) *verb* {5493 sur} from the root, to turn off.

turn (away) (back) (from) (to) respond, restore, return *verb* {7725 shub} {8421 tub} from the root, to turn back; as to reply, to come back.

turtledove *noun* {8449 tor} a ringdove; a term of endearment. **tusk, crag, ivory, tooth** *noun* {8127, 8128 shen} {*plural* 8143 shenhabbim} [3599 adous] as being sharp.

tusks, teeth *plural noun* {6374 piphiah} {8143 shenhabbim} teeth of a person, animal, or instrument.

tutor *noun* [2519 kathegetes] teacher; **cp** doctor.

tweezers *noun* {*plural* 4212 mezammeroth} {*dual* 4457 malqachim} literally, pluckers or tweezers used to trim the menorah.

twig *noun* {2156 zemor} [2595 karphos] a small branch; figuratively, a smaller fault.

twig *noun* {5577 cancin} {5589 ceappah} {5634 carappah} **cp** branch.

twig, cleft *noun* {5585 caiph} a fissure of rocks; a small branch.

Twin, twins *name, noun* {*plural* 8380 taomim} [1324 didumos] Twin; **see** Taom.

twin, twinned *verb* {8382 taam} to bear twins; to twin; to twine; to duplicate.

twinkle *verb* {7335 razam} to twinkle the eye, as in mockery; **cp** blink.

twirl, twist, spin *noun* {1524 giyl} {1525 giylah} a physical expression of joy.

twirl, twist, spin *verb, noun* {1523 giyl, guwl} {3769 karar} [4761 strebloo] to spin around, as in rejoicing; **cp** whirl.

twirl, whirl, writhe *verb* {1752, 1753 duwr} {2342 chiyl} {3769 karar} {6801 tsanaph} to gyrate; to move in a circle; to dance.

twist (off), turn (aside) (in) *verb* {5493 sur} from the root, to turn off.

twist *verb* {5791 avath} {6127 aqal} to wrest away from. **twist, bend, pervert** *verb* {5753 avah} {5754 avvah} to crook; to overthrow.

twisted *adjective* {5494 cuwr} of a plant as being twisted.

twisted *adjective* {6129 aqallathon} {6618 pethaltol} contorted, tortuous.

type *noun* [5179 tupos] an example for imitation or warning.

tyranny *noun* {6531 perek} violence.

tyranny, tyrant *noun* {6184 aryts} a despotic rule; a despotic ruler.

tyrant *noun* **tyrannical** *adjective* {6530 perits} violent; one that is violent.

tyrranize, bind *verb* {631 acar} {6014 amar} to bind with a bond; to bind a captive; to tyrranize.

U

U El *transliterated name* {177 uel} possibly, Whether of El.

Ukal *transliterated name* {401 ukal} Devoured.

ulcer *noun* {7822 shechin} an inflamation.

umbilical cord *noun* {8270 shor} the navel cord connecting unborn infant to the mother.

unaccusable *adjective* [410 anegkletos] without cause of accusation.

unaccused *adjective* [338 anaitios] not accused; without accusation.

unadulterated *adjective* [185 akeraios] without mixture; without dilution.

unanxious *adjective* [275 amerimnos] without anxiety.

unapprehendable *adjective* [423 anepileptos] unable to take.

unapproved *adjective* [96 adokimos] not approved.

unashamed *adjective* [422 anepaischuntos] not ashamed.

unavaricious *adjective* [866 aphilarguros] undesiring of greedy gain.

unbend *verb* [352 anakupto] to rise; figuratively, to be elated.

unbeneficial *noun, adjective* [512 anopheles] without benefit.

unblemished *adjective* [298 amometos] [299 amomos] without imperfection.

unceasing *adjective* [88 adialiptos] not ceasing.

unceasingly *adverb* [89 adialiptos] not ceasingly.

uncertain, obscure *adjective* [82 adelos] [83 adelotess] unclear.

uncertainly *adverb* [84 adelos] unclear.

uncircumcise *verb* {6188 arel} as having the foreskin of the penis; as not having been circumcised; **cp** circumcision; **cp** decircumcision.

uncircumcised *adjective* {6189 arel} as having the foreskin of the penis; as not having been circumcised; **cp** circumcision; **cp** decircumcision

uncircumcised, foreskin *noun* {6190 orlah} [203 akrobustia] the foreskin of the penis; the foreskin not removed; **cp** circumcision; **cp** decircumcision.

uncle, beloved, loves *noun* {1730 dod} from the root, to boil; literally, an extremely warm caring for; an uncle.

uncomprehending *adjective* [801 asunetos] not having a mental grasp; without understanding.

uncontrollable *adjective* [193 akrates] not controllable.

uncovenantal *adjective* [111 athemitos] against, outside, or without covenant; **see** covenant.

uncovenanted *adjective* [113 athesmos] [802 asunthetos] against, outside, or without covenant; **see** covenant.

undeceitful *adjective* [97 adolos] not deceitful.

undergarment *noun* {6361 pattish} a thin garment.

undermine, dig *verb* {6979 qur} to trench; to estop.

undertake, take *verb* {6901 qabal} {6902 qebal} [353 analambano] to acquire; to take up; **cp** receive.

undiluted *adjective* [194 akratos] lliterally, without pouring together.

undisciplined *adjective* [521 apaidutos] without discipline; stupidly conjectured.

uneucharistic *adjective* [884 acharistos] without charism; **see** charism; **cp** eucharist.

LEXICON

unexplorable *adjective* [419 anexerunetos] unable to explore completely.

unfathered *verb* [540 apator] the negative of fathered; that is, no record of having been fathered; **cp** ungenealogized.

unfortunate *adjective* {2489 cheleka} literally, wretched.

unfortunates *plural noun* {2489 chelekim}.

unfriendly *adjective* [865 aphilagathos] not friendly.

unfruitful *adjective* [175 akarpos] barren.

unfurl *verb* [380 anaptusso] to unroll; **cp** furl.

ungenealogized *adjective* [35 agenealogetos] unrecorded genealogy; without genealogy.

ungrieving *adjective* [253 alupoteros] without grief.

unhypocritical *adjective* [505 anupokritos] without hypocrisy; sincere.

unintelligent *adjective* [801 asunetos] without intelligence.

unite *verb* {3161 yachad} to become one.

unitedly, altogether, together *adverb* {3162 yachad} as one; **see** unite.

unjust *adjective* [94 adikos] not just; **see** injure; **see** injustice.

unjustly *adverb* [95 akidos] without justness.

unknowing *adjective* [50 agnoeo] not knowing.

unknowingness *noun* [51 agnoema] [52 agnoia] [56 agnosia] without knowledge.

unknown *adjective* [57 agnostos] not known.

unlearned *noun* [261 amathes] [2399 idiotes] idiot.

unless, if not *participle* {3884 luwley} if not.

unlettered *adjective* [62 agrammatos] not grammatic; unable to scribe; illiterate.

unmarried *noun* [22 agamos] not married.

unmercied *adjective* [448 anileos] [462 anosios] without being mercied.

unmerciful *adjective* [415 anele emon] without compassion.

unmindful *noun* [453 anoetos] without mind.

unmindfulness *noun* [454 anoia] stupidity.

unmothered *adjective* [540 apator] the negative of mother; that is, no record of having been mothered; **cp** ungenealogized.

unpolluted *adjective* [283 amiantos] not polluted; **see** polluted.

unquestionable *adjective* [368 anantirrhetos] no room for rhetoric.

unquestioning *adverb* [369 anantirrhetos] without room for rhetoric.

unravel, release *verb* {8271 shere} to separate; to free.

unregrettable *adjective* [278 ametameletos] without regret.

unrepentant *adjective* [279 ametanoetos] without repentance.

unrestrained *adjective* [180 akatapaustos] [183 akatasketos] [192 akrasna] without restraint.

unripe *adjective* **Abib** *transliterated name* {3, 4 eb} {24 abib} an unripened or tender produce; a month of the Hebrew calender; also a syllable in the name of the city, Tel Abib.

unripe figs *noun* {6291 pag}.

unsentenced *adjective* [178 akatakritos] not sentenced.

unshod *adjective* {3182 yacheph} without footwear.

unstable *adjective* [182 akatastatos] not constant; **see** instability.

unstumbling *verbal noun* [679 aptaistos] not stumbling; without sin.

unsubjected, insubordinate *adjective* [506 anupotaktos] not subject to; refusing subordination.

unteased *adjective* [46 agnaphos] of cloth that has not been carded or combed.

untestable *adjective* [551 apirastos] unable to test.

untested *adjective* [552 apiros] inexperienced; ignorant.

until when *participle adverb* {4970 mathay} extent of time.

untorahed *adjective* [459 anomos] [460 anomos] without torah; **cp** entorahed; **see** torah.

untraceable *adjective* [421 anexichniastos] unable to track out.

untranslatable *adjective* [1421 dusermenutos] not translatable.

unutterable *adjective* [215 alaletos] unable to utter.

unveil *verb* [343 anakalupto] [601 apokalupto] to uncover.

unveil *verb* {8365 shatham} to lift the lid.

unveiled *adjective* [177 akatakaluptos] uncovered.

unwashen *adjective* [449 aniptos] not washed.

unwavering *adjective* [186 aklines] without wavering.

unwise *adjective* [781 asophos] not wise.

unwitnessed *adjective* [267 amaturos] without witness.

unworthily *adverb* [371 anaxios] undeservingly; **see** worthy.

unworthy *adjective* [370 anaxios] undeserving; **see** worthy.

up, upper, above *adverb* [507 ano] upward; the top.

uphold *verb* [472 antechomai] to hold on to.

uphold, callous, prevail, strengthen *verb* {553 amats} {555 omets} {2388 chazaq} {2393 chezqah} {5810 azaz} to enable physically; to become thickskinned.

uphold, prop, sustain *verb* {5564 camak} {8551 tamak} to prop up; with the hands, or with props.

uphold, support *verb* {5582 scaad} to support; usually, figuratively; **cp** prop.

upholding *participle* {5583 cead} aiding.

uplift, uprise, burden *noun* {4864 maseth} a raising; a reproach, as a burden.

upper, uppermost, above *adjective* [509 anothen] [510 anoterikos] [511 anoteron] from above; the source of the rebirth; **read** Yahn 3:1–8.

upper millstone, chariot *noun* {4817 merkab} {4818 merkabah} {7393 rekeb} {7396 rikbah} {7398 rekub} a vehicle; a rider; **cp** millstones.

upper room *noun* {5944 aliyah} {5952 alliyth} [508 anogeon] a space above earth; an upper loft.

uppermost *adjective* **Elyon** *transliterated title* {5943 illay} {5945, 5946 elyon} [5310 hupsistos] an uppermost place or position; a title of Elohim.

upright *plural adjective* {3651 ken} literally, set upright.

uprise, burden, uplift *noun* {4864 maseth} a raising; a reproach, as a burden.

uproar, waste, roar *noun* {7588 shaon} a rumble; a destruction.

uproot *verb* {5255 nacach} {5256 necach} {5428 nathash} to pluck up; to tear away.

uproot, hamstring *verb* {6131, 6132 aqar} to pluck up the root; to cut the tendons.

uproot, root *verb* {8327 sharash} {8332 sheroshu} to plant a root; to pull out by the root.

uprooted *adjective* {4535 maccach} {6133 eqer} usually of persons who are forced to move.

upset *verb* [384 anaskuazo] to pack up; figuratively, to upset.

Urbane *transliterated name* [3773 ourbanos] Urbane; of the city.

urbanite (the) *noun* {377 ish} {7149 qirah} [2469 iskariotes] City Man.

urge *verb* {6484 patsar} to peck at.

urgent *verb* {5169 nachats} to press for immediate action.

Uri *transliterated name* {221 uri} Flame.

Uri El *transliterated name* {222 uriel} Flame of El.

Uri Yah *transliterated name* {223 uriyah} [3774 ourias] Flame of Yah.

urinate *verb* {8366 shathan} from the root, to make water.

urines *plural noun* {7890 shain} the fluids secreted from the body.

Us *transliterated name* {5780 uwts} Consultation.

use, used, useful, accustomed *verb* {5532 cakan} to be familiar by use; to be serviceable to.

useful *adjective* [2173 euchreestos] easy to make use of.

useless *adjective* [888 achrios] [890 achreestos] unprofitable.

useless *verb* [889 achreioo] to render unserviceable.

usure, bite *verb* {5391 nashak} literally, as in usury, to take a bite.

usurpation *noun* [725 harpagmos] the act of seizing and holding in possession by force, or without right.

usury *noun* {5392 neshek} interest on a debt, usually excessive.

Uthay *transliterated name* {5793 uwthay} Reinforcing.

utter *verb* {4448 malal} {4449 melal} [2044 erugomai] [5350 phtheggomai] to express vocally; **cp** speak; **cp** word.

utterance *noun* {4008 mibta} {4405, 4406 millah} [669 apophtheggomai] a vocal expression; **see** utter.

Uzzen Sheerah *transliterated name* {242 uzzensheerah} Hearkened of Sheerah.

Uzzi El *transliterated name* {5816 uzziel} Strength of El.

Uzzi Eliy *transliterated name* {5817 ozziyeliy} Of Uzzi El.

Uzzi Yah *transliterated name* {5814 uzziya} {5818 uzziyah} [3604 ozias] Strength of Yah.

V

Veheb *transliterated name* {2052 vaheb} of uncertain derivative; a place in Moab.

vail *noun* {6532 poreketh} the separatrix in the tabernacle.

vail, veil *noun* {3875 lowt} {4044 meginnah} {4533 masveh} {*plural* 4555 micpachahoth} {5497 cuth} {6777 tsammah} {6809 tsaiph} {7289 radid} {7479 raalah} [2571 kaluma] a covering; that which is fastened on.

vail, veil, cover *verb* {3874 luwt} {5844 atah} {6809 tsaiph} [2572 kalupto] [2619 katakaluptomai] to cover; to enrobe; to wrap; to withhold from view.

vain (become) *verb* {1891 habal} to empty; to void; the Hebrew verb is not translatable into one English verb.

vain, vanity, void, empty, req *adjective* {1892 hebel} {*transliteration* 7385 riq} {*transliteration* 7386 req} {7723 shav} [*transliteration* 4469 rhaka] emptiness, voidness; figuratively, stupid.

vainly *adverb* [1500 eikee] [2756 kenos] idly; without reason.

vainly, void, empty *adverb* {7387 reqam} emptily; without effect; **cp** req.

valiant, trench *noun* {2426 chel} character of a person who protects; a trench for protection.

valiant, valour, valuable, virtue *noun* {2428, 2429 chayil} usually of persons of character; of valuables.

valley *noun* {1237 biqah} {6010 emeq} a lowland or split area between two heights.

Valley, Gay *transliterated noun* {1516 gay} sometimes transliterated when used in compound names.

Valley of Burning/Gay I-linnom *name* {1516 gay} {2011 hinnom} [1067 geenna] used figuratively, as a name for the place (or state) of everlasting punishment; may be transliterated, Gay Hinnom.

Valley of Engravers *transliterated plural name* {1516 gay} {2798 charashim} Valley of Engravers.

Valley of Salt/Gay Melach *transliterated name* {1516 gay} {4417 melach} Valley of Salt.

Valley of Slaughter/Gay I-laregah *transliterated name* {1516 gay} {2028 haregah} Valley of Slaughter.

Valley of Vision/Gay I-lizzayon *transliterated name* {1516 gay} {2384 chizzayon} Valley of Vision.

valour, valuable, virtue valiant *noun* {2428, 2429 chayil} usually of persons of character; of valuables.

Van Yah *transliterated name* {2057 vanyah} Answer of Yah. **vanish** *verb* {4414 malach} to rub away; **see** salt *verb*.

vanish, corrupt, destroy, destruct, lose, ruin *verb* {6 abad} {7 abad} {8 obed} {7843 shachath} [1311 diapthiro] [2704 kataphthiro] [5351 phthiro] to corrupt through decay.

vanish, dissolve *verb* {4743 maqaq} [1262 dialuo] to dissolve; to dwindle; to vanish.

vanity, void, empty, req, vain *adjective* {1892 hebel} {*transliteration* 7385 riq} {*transliteration* 7386 req} {7723 shav} [*transliteration* 4469 rhaka] emptiness, voidness; figuratively, stupid.

vanquish *verb* {2522 chalash} to cause to prostrate.

vanquished *noun* {2523 challash} one caused to prostrate.

vapour, hierarch *noun* {5387 nasi} [747 archeegos] a vapour, as a rising mist; a chief leader; as being first, foremost.

vassal *noun* {4522 mac} one that is under homage.

Vayezatha *transliterated name* {2055 vayezatha} of foreign origin; a son of Haman.

Vedan *transliterated name* {2051 vedan} the meaning uncertain; a place in Arabia.

veil, conceal *verb* {5956 alam} to conceal; to veil from sight.

veil, cover, languish, shroud *verb* {5848 ataph} {5968 alaph} to cover over; to languish.

venerable *adjective* [4575 sebastos] adorable in the sense of able to adore.

venerant *noun* [4586 semnos] worthy of adoration.

venerate *verb* [4573 sebazomai] [4576 sebomai] to adore.

veneration *noun* [4574 sebasma] [4587 semnotes] adoration.

vengeance *noun* [1557 ekdikesis] punishment inflicted in return for an injury, or an offense.

vengeance, avengement *noun* {5359 naqam} {5360 neqamah} revenge; **see** avenge.

venom *noun* [2447 ios] as emitted.

venom, bitter, gall *noun* {*plural* 4844 merarim} {4845 mererah} {4846 merorah} bile; venom; a bitter herb.

vermillion *noun* {8350 shashar} as a piercing red.

vertebrae, riddle *noun* {7001 qetar} a knot; as that which is to be unravelled.

very, exceeding, greatly, increasing, many, mighty, much *adjective* {7689, 7690 saggiy} superlatively mighty, or large.

vex *verb* {3707 kaac} [3791 ochleo] to harass; to irritate; to agitate; to trouble.

vexation *noun* {3708 kaac} an agitation; a harassment; an irritation.

vile *adjective* {5240 nemibzeh} evil.

vilification *noun* [2561 kakosis] a declared evil.

vilify, vilifying, shatter *verb* {7489 raa} {7490 rea} [2551 kakologeo] [2558 kakoucheo] [2559 kakoo] verb of evil; to make or declare evil; to vilify by shattering; **see** evil.

village *noun* [2968 kome] [2969 komopolis] a small assemblage of houses.

village, whelp *noun* {3715 kephiyr} a young lion, as covered with a mane; a village, as covered by walls.

vine (bright) *noun* {8321 soreqah} [288 ampelos] literally, a burning bright; a vine, as producing grapes.

vinedresser *noun* {3755 korem} [289 ampelourgos] one who tends the vines.

vineyard *noun* {3754 kerem} [290 ampelon] a plantation of grapevines.

violate *verb* [3845 parabaino] to go contrary.

violate *verb* {2554 chamac} to ravish.

violating the torah *verb* [3891 paranomeo] to disregard the torah.

violation *noun* [3847 parabasis] nonobservance; transgression.

violation of the torah, torah violation *noun* [458 anomia] [3892 paranomia] a disregarding of the torah; **see** torah.

violator *noun* [3848 parabates] one who violates the torah.

violence *noun* {2555 chamac} {4637 maaratsah} ravishment.

virgin *noun* {1330 bethulah} {5959 almah} {5961 alamoth} [3933 parthenos] one who has had no sexual intercourse.

virginity *noun* {1331 bethulim} [3932 parthenia] the quality or state of a virgin.

virtue valiant, valour, valuable *noun* {2428, 2429 chayil} usually of persons of character; of valuables.

visable *adjective* [3707 horatos] able to be seen.

visage *noun* [3799 opsis] appearance.

visage, vision *noun* {4758 mareh} {4759 marah} a vision, or visage, especially one of beauty.

vision *noun* {2376 chezev} {2377 chazon} {2378, 2379 chazoth} {2380 chazuth} {2384 chizzayon} {4236 machazeh} [3701 optasia] [3705 horama] [3706 horasis] that which is seen beyond eyesight.

visit, muster, oversee *verb* {6485 paqad} to visit with friendly intent, to oversee; or to visit with hostile intent, to take care of; to muster for display.

visitation, episcopate *transliterated noun* [1984 episcope] [1985 episcopos] one who scopes; an inspector; inspection.

visitation, muster, overseer, oversight *noun* {6486 pequddah} a visit with friendly intent, to oversee; or a visit with hostile intent, to take care of; a muster for display.

visitation/Peqod *noun, transliterated name* {6489 peqowd} refers to Babel as a place of Yah Veh's visitation.

voice *noun* {6963 qol} {7032 qal} [5456 phonee] sound.

voice *verb* [5455 phoneo] to voice out; to emit a sound.

LEXICON

voiceless *noun* [880 aphonos] without voice.

void *noun* {4003 mebuwqah} empty.

void *verb* {6331 pur} to cause to be empty.

void, empty, req, vain, vanity *adjective* {1892 hebel} {*transliteration* 7385 riq} {*transliteration* 7386 req} {7723 shav} [*transliteration* 4469 rhaka] emptiness, voidness; figuratively, stupid.

void, empty, vainly *adverb* {7387 reqam} emptily; without effect; **cp** req.

voluminous *noun* {6282 athar} increased in volume.

voluntary *noun* {4530 miccah} an offering, as flowing.

voluntary, voluntarily *noun, adverb* {5071 nedabah} a willing offer.

volunteer, voluntarily *verb* {5068 nadab} {5069 nedab} to offer willingly.

volunteers, voluntary *noun, adjective* {5081 nadyb} a willing offer; one who willingly offers.

voluptuous *adjective* {5719 adiyn} sensual gratification.

vomit *noun* {6892 qiy} that which is spewed.

vomit *verb* {6958 qow} {7006 qayah} to spew.

votive *noun* [334 anatheema] an offering of a vow; **cp** anathema.

vow *noun* {5088 neder} [2171 euchee] a binding word.

vow *verb* {5087 nadar} [2172 euchomia] to bind by word.

vulture *noun* {7201 raah} from its sharp sight.

vulva *noun* {5040 nabluth} the female pudenda.

W

wadi *noun* {5158 nachal} a watercourse which is dry, except in the rainy season.

wafers *plural noun* {3561 kavvanim} as prepared; wafers used in sacrifice.

wag over, wander, waver, sway *verb* {5110 nud} to waver.

wag, wander, waver, drift, shake, stagger, totter *verb* {5128 nuwa} to waver.

wagon *noun* {5699 agalah} that which has revolving wheels.

wait, await, expect, receive *verb* {2442 chakah} {3176 yachal} {6960 qavah} [324 anadekomai] [362 anameno] [553 apekdekomai] [4327 prosdekomai] [4328 prosdokao] [4329 prosdokia] to anticipate; to wait expectantly, patiently; **cp** take.

wake, waken, awake *verb* {5782 uwr} {6974 quts} to wake up.

waker *noun* {5894 iyr} one that is awake; one that wakens.

walk *noun* {4109 mahalak} literally, a walk; a passage.

walk, went, go *verb* {3212 yahlach} literally, to walk.

walk gently *verb* {1718 dadah}.

wall *noun* {1444 geder} {1447 gader} {1448 gederah} {7023 qir} an encircling enclosure.

wall *noun* {2346 chomah} a divider, or separator.

wall *noun* {2918 tiyrah} a protective wall.

wall *noun* {3796 kothel} {3797 kethal} a barrier that holds in confinement.

wall *noun* {7791 shur} as surrounding.

wall *verb* {1443 gadar} {5823 azaq} to install a wall; to wall in.

wallet *noun* [4082 pera] a leather pouch for carrying provisions.

wander (around) *verb* [4022 perierkomai] to go about.

wander, chase, flap, flee *verb* {5074 nadad} {5323 natsa} to flap up and down; to shoo away.

wander, seduce *verb* [4105 planao] to go or be led astray.

wander, stagger, stray *verb* {8582 taah} to reel; to stray.

wander, waver, drift, shake, stagger, totter, wag *verb* {5128 nuwa} to waver.

wander, waver, sway, wag over *verb* {5110 nud} to waver.

wandering *noun* **Nod** *transliterated noun* {5112, 5113 nod} exile.

wandering, seduction *noun* [4106 planee] a straying from.

war *noun* {7128, 7129 qerab} an encounter.

war, warfare, warrior *noun* {4421 milchamah} a fight; a fighter; **see** fight.

wardrobe *noun* {4458 meltachah} room where clothing is spread.

warp *noun* {8307 sheriruth} bent out of shape.

warp *noun* {8359 shethiy} a fixture; the warp in weaving.

warriors/Gammadim *plural noun* {1575 gammadim} as grasping instruments.

waste *noun* {7591 sheiyah} {7612 sheth} a devastation; a ruin.

waste *verb* {1110 balaq} {7582 shaah} to devastate; to ruin.

waste, roar, uproar *noun* {7588 shaon} a rumble; a destruction.

watch *verb* **watcher** *participle* **overlay** *verb* {6822, 6823 tsaphah} to observe; to await; to sheet over.

watch *verb* {8245 shaqad} [69 agrupmeo] to be alert; unsleeping.

watching *noun* {6836 tsephiah} [70 agrupnia] unsleeping.

watchtower *noun* {6844 tsaphith} a sentry post.

water *noun* {*dual* 4325 mayim} [5204 hudor] a common liquid.

waterless *adjective* [504 anudros] without water; dry.

wave *noun* {8573 tenuphah} the celebration of undulating a loaf or a breast unto Yah Veh.

wave, rub, shake *verb* {5130 nuph} to rub a bed with aromatics; to shake a hand; to wave an offering.

waver *verb* [1365 distazo] to stand in two ways, implying uncertainty of which way to take.

waver, drift, shake, stagger, totter, wag, wander *verb* {5128 nuwa} to waver.

waver, sway, wag over, wander *verb* {5110 nud} to waver.

waver, topple, totter *verb* {4131 mowt} {4571 maad} to waver; to fall over.

waver, wiggle *verb* {6328 puq} emotionally, to waver; physically, to wiggle.

way, journey *noun* {1870 derek} a road, as trodden; a walkway; figuratively, the journey of life.

way, journey *noun* {4550 macca} [3597 hodiporia] [3598 hodos] a trip; **see** sojourn.

way, path *noun* {734, 735 orach} also includes the manner of a person.

wean, deal, ripen *verb* {1580 gamal} transact.

weaned, antiquated *adjective* {6267 attiq} removed; that which has endured.

weapon *noun* {2021 hotsen} from the root sharp, and/or strong.

weary *adjective* {3287 yaeph} fatigued.

weary *verb* {3286 yaaph} {3288 yeaph} {3811 laah} to fatigue.

web *noun* {4545 macceketh} as expanded.

week, weeks *noun* {7620 shabua} literally, a seven; symbolic of an oath; **see** oath.

weigh *verb* {6424 palac} a literal weighing; a weighing (considering) of thought.

weigh, balance *verb* {8254 shakal} to weigh by balancing a set weight against that being weighed; **see** shekel.

weight *noun* {4946 mishqol} {4948 mishqal} a measure of heaviness.

weight *noun* {6425 pelec} a balance of a scale.

weighty *adjective* {5192 netel} a burden.

well *noun* {875 ber} {*plural* 877 bor} {953 bor} that which is dug; **cp** pit.

well-approve *verb* [2106 eudokeo] to well-please; to think well of.

well-approved *noun* [2107 eudokia] to be well-thought of.

well-please *verb* {3190 yatab} {3191 yetab} [2100 euaresteo] to cause to well-please.

well-pleasing *adjective* [2101 euarestos] fully agreeable.

well-receiving *adjective* [2126 eulabes] taking hold well.

well-souled *adjective* [2174 eupsucheo] of beneficient soul.

well-working *adverb* [2109 euergeteo] beneficently; doing well.

well-working *noun* [2108 uergesia] beneficence.

went, go, walk *verb* {3212 yahlach} literally, to walk.

whenever, if ever *adverb* [1437 ean] is a compound of [1487 ei] and [302 an] and may express the condition, if; or the opportunity, when. **cp if** [1487].

wet, butler, drink (give), drown, moisten *verb* {8248 shaqah} {8257 shaga} to butler, as a bartender; to drink to quench thirst; to drink unto drowning; to cause to be wet.

What trouble! *interjection* {4972 mattelaah} An Hebraic idiom.

wheat *noun* [4621 sitos] a cereal grain.

wheel, whirler *noun* {1534, 1535 galgal} {1536 gilgal} something that whirls.

whelp, village *noun* {3715 kephiyr} a young lion, as covered with a mane; a village, as covered by walls.

whip *noun* {7752 shot} literally, or figuratively, a lash. **whir** *noun* [4500 rhoizedon] a sound of whirling.

whirl *noun* {6802 tsenephah} a rapid revolving.

whirl, writhe, twirl *verb* {1752, 1753 duwr} {2342 chiyl} {3769 karar} {6801 tsanaph} to gyrate; to move in a circle; to dance.

whirl away, shudder *verb* {8175 saar} to storm; to shudder, as in fright; to be stormed away.

whirler *noun* {1754 dur} one who whirls.

whirler, wheel *noun* {1534, 1535 galgal} {1536 gilgal} that which whirls.

whirling *noun* {4070 medar} a spinning around, as in wandering.

whirling, horror *noun* {8178 saar} a whirling of a storm; a shuddering of horror.

whirlwind *noun* [2978 lailaps] a whirling wind.

whirring, cymbal, harpoon, locust *noun* {6767 tselatsal} a clattering, as of a cymbal; a whirring, as of wings; a rattling, as of a harpoon.

whisperer *noun* {5372 nirgan} [*plural* 5588 psithuristes] one who speaks without their vocal cords; figuratively, a slanderer.

whisperings *noun* {8103 shimtsah} [*plural* 5587 psithurismos] speaking without vocal cords; figuratively, slanderings.

white *adjective* {3836 laban}.

white linen, white marble *noun* {8336 shesh} white, as in bleached.

whiten, brick (make) *verb* {3835 laban} to make a brick; to cause to be white; this is a derivative of two words; **see** brick; **see** white.

whoever, O that *participle pronoun* {4310 miy} An Hebraic idiom.

whoop *verb* {6873 tsarach} to express a shrill sound.

whore *noun* [4204 porne] one who commits sexual acts for hire; in Scripture, also includes deviation from Elohim's misvoth.

whore, whoring *verb* {2181 zanah} [1608 ekpornuo] [4203 pornuo] to commit idolatry; to commit forbidden sexual acts for hire.

whore (hallowed) *noun* {6948 qedeshah} a female whore for religious service.

whoredoms *noun plural* {2183 zanunim} {2184 zenuwth} {8457 taznuth} [4202 pornia] physical or spiritual infidelity.

whoremonger (hallowed) *noun* {6945 qadesh} a male whore for religious service.

whoremonger *noun* [4205 pornos] a male whore.

wicked (deal) (declare) (do) *verb* {5765 avel} {7561 rasha} to do or declare evil.

wicked *adjective* {5766 avel} {7563 rasha} evil.

wicked *noun* {4849 mirshaath} {5767 avval} evil; an evil doer.

wickedly *adverb* {5766 avel} evilly.

wickedness *noun* {2248 chabulah} {5766 aval} {5932 alvah} {7562 resha} {7564 rishah} evil.

widow *noun* {490 almanah} [5503 chera] an unmarried woman whose man deceased.

widowhood *noun* {489 almon} {491 almanuth} the position of being a widow.

width *noun* {6613 pethay} the wideness.

wiggle, waver *verb* {6328 puq} emotionally, to waver; physically, to wiggle.

wild *noun* [66 agrios] as pertaining to the undeveloped, the natural, as the field.

wild olive *noun* [65 agrielaios] the natural growing olive.

wild runner *noun* {6501 pere} untamed runner.

wilderness *noun* {4057 midbar} [2047 eremia] [2048 eremos] an uninhabited and undeveloped area; **cp** desolation.

will *noun* {17 abowy} {35 abiyonah} {6640 tsebuw} [2307 thelema] [2308 thelesis] the volition; the attribute of the spirit that decides.

will, willing verb {14 abah} {2974 yaal} {5452 cebar} {6634 tseba} [1014 boulomai] [2309 thelo] to volitionate; the exercise to volition in deciding or determining; **cp** will, would, *auxiliary verbs*.

will, would, *auxiliary verbs* Whenever will and/or would appear as auxiliary verbs in the , they are changed to shall or should. They are omitted in the . **cp** will, willing; may, might; shall, should.

willceremony verb [1479 ethelothreskeia] a mental, or intellectual type ceremony.

wind noun {7307 ruach} [417 anemos] air in motion; ruach is the Hebrew word for both spirit and wind; great discernment must be exercised in some instances; therefore there are instances where the renders ruach as Spirit/wind; anemos is the Hellene word for wind; this distinction is important doctrinally; for most versions have mistranslated Spirit as wind in Yahn 3:8; **see** spirit.

window noun {2474 challown} as perforated.

window noun {4237 mechezah} as a look through.

window, noon dual noun {6672 tsohar} double light, as a window; double light, as noon.

windtossed noun [416 anemizo] tossed by the wind.

wine noun {3196 yayin} effervescence, as in fermentation.

wing noun [4419 pterugion] extremity; the top of the corner.

wing, blossom noun {6731 tsits} a blossom, as blooming brightly; a wing, as gleaming.

wing, border noun {3671 kanaph} {4020 migbalah} literally, extreme edge.

winnow verb {2219 zarah} to toss, as seed.

winnowing basket noun {4214 mizreh} a basket used to scatter chaff.

winnowing fork noun {7371 rachath} a fork used to scatter chaff.

winter (in) verb [3914 parakimazo] to stay with, or at a place over the winter season.

wipe, wipe out, erase verb {4229 machah} [1813 exalipho] to rub; to rub out; to erase sins, tears, names.

wisdom noun {2451, 2452 chokmah} {2454 chokmoth} [4678 sophia] the ability to decide well.

wise adjective {2450 chakam} [4680 sophos] deciding well.

wisen, enwisen verb {2449 chakam} [4679 sophizo] to cause to be wise.

withdraw noun {7873 siyg} removal into privacy.

withdraw verb {5756 uz} [402 anakoreo] to retire; to save by flight.

wither, disgrace, folly verb {5034 nabel} from the root, to wilt; to fall away; to fail.

wither, dry noun {3002 yabesh} {3004 yabbashah} {3006, 3007 yabbesheth} {7060 qamal} lands and waters dry; plants, persons wither.

wither, dry verb {3001 yabesh} {5405 nashath} {6798 tsanam} {7060 qamal} lands and waters dry; plants, persons wither. **within** adverb {6441 penimah} literally, faceward; inside; **see** inward; **cp** without.

within, among, inward, middle, midst noun {7130 qereb} {8432 tavek} the nearest part; the center.

without, out, outside, outskirt, outward, outway noun, adverb {2351 chuts} a separated area.

withstand, stand, stay verb {5975 amad} {5977 omed} [436 anthistemi] [478 antikathistemi] to stand steady; to stand against.

witness noun {5707 ed} {7717 sahed} {8584 teuwdah} [3141 marturia] [3144 martus] [3142 marturion] evidence.

witness noun {5712 edah} {5713 edah} a people as a witness.

witness noun {5715 eduth} the witness; especially the ark of the witness.

witness, witnessing verb {5749 ud} [1263 diamarturomi] [1957 epimartureo] [3140 martureo] [3143 marturomai] to give evidence; the Hellene is from the root, martyr; one who through martyrdom became a witness of Yah Shua.

witness against verb [2649 katamartureo].

woe interjection [3759 ouai] exclamation of grief

wolf noun [3074 lukos] a wild dog.

woman, women noun {802 ishshah} {*plural* 802 nashim} {*plural* 5389 nashin} {7695 shegal} {7705 shiddah} [1134 gunaiikios] [1135 gunee] an adult female; when married, the female becomes a man's woman.

womb (to have in) verb [1064 gaster] to be bearing in womb; pregnant.

LEXICON

womb, belly, matrix *noun* {990 beten} {1512 gachon} {3770 keres} {4579 meah} {6896 qabab} {6897 qobah} {6898 qubbah} {7356 racham} (7358 rechem) [2836 koilia] the interior; a cavity as hollow; the abdominal cavity; sometimes refers to the womb.

women (little) *noun* [1133 gunaikarion] used in a belittling sense.

woodwinds *noun* {5748 uggab} a breath controlled music instrument.

woof, mongrel *noun* {6154 ereb} the transverse threads; a crossed race of persons.

word *noun* {1697 dabar} {1699 dibber} {1700 dibrah} {1701 dibrah} {*plural* 1703 dabroth} [3056 logos] an utterance or scribing of a thought; a promise, or guarantee (to give one's word); a manifestation; **note:** the noun, logos, is the outward expression of the verb, lego (Adonay Yah Shua Messiah is the physical manifestation of Elohim's word); **read** Yahn 1:1–14.

word *verb* {1696 dabar} [3004 lego] in Hebrew and Hellene, word implies much more than uttering, or scribing one's thought; word also includes that of promising, or guaranteeing, or having been given one's word; when Yah Veh states, I have worded, or when Yah Shua states, Amen! Amen! I word unto you, they are saying, I have given my word, and that's final.

words (kind) *plural noun* [5542 chrestologia].

work *noun* {4639 maasch} {4399 melakah} an employment; a product; a transaction; **cp** creation.

work *verb* [2038 ergazomai] to do; to labor.

work *verb* {6213 asah} to be engaged in, or with; to do or make; **cp** create; **note:** {6213 asah} is the verb of work *noun* {4639 maasch}.

work, working, effort *noun* [2039 ergasia] [2041 ergon] occupation; toil.

worker *noun* [2040 ergates] a toiler.

world *noun* {8398 tebel} [3625 oikoumene] the inhabited earth; the universe; **cp** cosmos.

wormwood, absinthe *transliterated noun* {3939 laanah} [894 apsinthos] a bitter plant.

worn (out), rub, sicken, stroke *verb* {2470 chalah} to wear out; to stroke the face as in appeasement.

worship *verb* [4352 proskuneo] to do obesience, as by bowing and/or kissing.

worshipper *noun* [4353 proskunetes] one who worships.

worthily *adverb* [516 axios] deserving.

worthless, idol *noun* {434 elul} {457 elil} of no worth.

worthy (deem) *verb* [515 axioo] deserving.

worthy *adjective* [514 axios] deserving.

wound *noun* {6482 petsa} an open split.

wound *verb* {6481 patsa} to split open.

wound, disperse, express *verb* {6567 parash} to separate; to specify; to wound.

wraps *noun* {*singular* 5466 cadiyn} {*plural* 5156 nechirim} wraparounds.

wrath, nostril, snout *noun* {639 aph} {*plural* 5156 nechirim} [3709 orgee] the snorter, as in expressing wrath; **see** snorting.

wrathful *adjective* [3711 orgilos] intense anger.

wreath *noun* {3880 livyah} {*plural* 3914 loyoth} [4725 stemma] [4735 stephanos] as entwined; a wreath of victory; **cp** crown; **cp** diadem.

wreath, wreathen, foliage, rope *noun* {5688 abothah} as entwined; a wreath of victory; **cp** crown; **cp** diadem.

wreathe *verb* [4737 stephanoo] to wreathe in victory; **cp** crown; **cp** diadem.

wrestle *verb* {6617 pathal} to struggle; to entwine.

wrestlings *plural noun* {5319 naphtuim} strugglings.

wring hands, extend hands *participle* {3029 yeda} {3034 yadah} {8426 todah} to extend hands in praise; to wring hands in sorrow.

wring, suck *verb* {4680 matsah} to wring, or squeeze out; to suck out.

writhe, twirl, whirl *verb* {1752, 1753 duwr} {2342 chiyl} {3769 karar} {6801 tsanaph} to gyrate; to move in a circle; to dance.

writhing *noun* {5792 avvathah} twisting, as in pain.

wroth *adjective* [3710 orgizo] full of wrath.

Y

Yaalah *transliterated name* {3279 yaalah} Roe.

Yaanay *transliterated name* {3285 yaanay} Responsive.
Yaaqan *transliterated name* {3292 yaaqan} Tortuous.

Yaaqov, Yaaqovos *transliterated name* {3290 yaaqob} [2384 iakob] [2385 iakobos] Heel Seizer.

Yaaqovah *transliterated name* {3291 yaaqobah} Heel Seizer.

Yaare Oregim *plural transliterated name* {3296 yaarey oregiym} Forests of Weavers.

Yaaresh Yah *transliterated name* {3298 yaareshyah} of uncertain derivative and Yah.

Yaasi El *transliterated name* {3300 yaasiel} Worked of El.

Yaasu *transliterated name* {3299 yaasuw} They Work.

Yaazan Yah *transliterated name* {2970 yaazanyah} Hearkened of Yah.

Yaazi El *transliterated name* {3268 yaziel} Obstinate of El.

Yaazi Yah *transliterated name* {3269 yaaziyah} Obstinate of Yah.

Yabal *transliterated name* {2989 yabal} Stream.

Yabboq *transliterated name* {2999 yabboq} Pouring Forth.

Yabes *transliterated name* {3258 yabets} Sorrowful.

Yabesh *transliterated name* {3003 yabesh} Dry.

Yabin *transliterated name* {2985 yabyn} Discerning.

Yabne El *transliterated name* {2995 yabneel} Built of El.

Yabneh *transliterated name* {2996 yabneh} Built.

Yachath *transliterated name* {3189 yachath} Unity.

Yachazi El *transliterated name* {3166 yachaziel} Seer of El.

Yachazi Yah *transliterated name* {3167 yachaziyah} Seer of Yah.

Yachdi El *transliterated name* {3164 yachdiel} United of El.

Yachdi Yah *transliterated name* {3165 yechdiyah} United of Yah.

Yachdo *transliterated name* {3163 yachdo} United.

Yachle El *transliterated name* {3177 yachleel} Awaiting El.

Yachle Eliy *transliterated name* {3178 yachleeliy} Of Yachle El.

Yachmay *transliterated name* {3181 yachmay} Hot.

Yachse El *transliterated name* {3183 yachtseel} Halved of El.

Yachse Eliy *transliterated name* {3184 yachtseeliy} Of Yachse El.

Yachsi El *transliterated name* {3185 yachtsiyel} Halved of El.

Yachzerah *transliterated name* {3170 yachzerah} Protection.

Yada *transliterated name* {3047 yada} Knowing.

Yaddua *transliterated name* {3037 yadduwa} Knowing.

Yadon *transliterated name* {3036 yadown} Thankful.

Yael *transliterated name* {3278 yael} Wild Goats.

Yah; see SUMMARY: YAH, YAH SHUA:

Yah Ab *transliterated name* {3097 yowab} Yah Fathered.

Yah Ach *transliterated name* {3098 yowach} Yah Brothered.

Yah Achaz *transliterated name* {3059 yehowachaz} {3099 yowachaz} Yah Possessed.

Yah Addah *transliterated name* {3085 yehowaddah} Yah Adorns.

Yah Addan *transliterated name* {3086 yehaddan} Yah Pleases.

Yah Arib *transliterated name* {3080 yehowyariyb} Yah Contends.

Yah Ash *transliterated name* {3060 yehowash} Yah Fired.

Yah Ash *transliterated name* {3101 yowash} Yah Fired.

Yah Ash *transliterated name* {3135 yowash} Yah Hurries.

Yah Dai *transliterated name* {3056 yehday} Yudaic.

Yah El *transliterated name* {3100 yowel} [2493 ioeel] Yah El.

Yah Ezer *transliterated name* {3134 yowezer} Yah Helps.

Yah Ha *transliterated name* {3109 yowcha} Revived of Yah.

Yah 1-lanan, Yahn *transliterated name* {3076 yehowchanan} {3110 yowchanan} [contraction 2491 ioannees] Yah Grants Charism.

Yah 1-lanna, Yah 1-lannas *transliterated name* [2489 ioanna] [2490 ioannas] Yah Grants Charism.

Yah 1-lu *transliterated name* {3058 yewhu} Yah is He.

Yah 1-ludah, Yah 1-ludiy, Yah 1-ludiym; see SUMMARY: YAH HUDAH.

Yahudiah *transliterated name* {3057 yehudiyah} a female Yah Hudiy.

Yahudith *transliterated name* {3067 yehudith} a female Yah Hudiy.

Yah Chebed *transliterated name* {3115 yowchebed} Honoured of Yah.

Yah Nadab *transliterated name* {3082 yehownadab} {3122 yownadab} Yah Volunteers.

Yah Nathan *transliterated name* {3083 yehownathan} {3129 yownathan} Yah Given.

Yah Qim *transliterated name* {3137 yowqiym} [885 acheim] Yah Rises.

Yah Ram *transliterated name* {3088 yehowram} {3141 yowram} [2496 ioram] Yah Raises.

Yah Sadaq *transliterated name* {3087 yehowtsadaq} {3136 yowtsadaq} Yah Justifies.

Yah Shabath *transliterated name* {3090 yehowshabath} Yah Oaths; may be a form of Yah Sheba.

Yah Shah *transliterated name* {3144 yowshah} Equated of Yah.

Yah Shama *transliterated name* {1953 howshama} Yah Hears.

Yah Shaphat *transliterated name* {3092 yehowshaphat} {3146 yowshaphat} [2498 iosaphat] Yah Judges.

Yah Shavah *transliterated name* {3145 yowshavyah} Equated of Yah.

Yah Sheba *transliterated name* {3089 yehowsheba} Yah Oaths.

Yah Shua *transliterated name* {3091 yahshua} {3442, 3443 yahshua} [2424 ieesous] Yah Saves; the name of Mosheh's successor, the name of our Messiah, and the name of other persons; *see* SUMMARY: YAH, YAH SHUA, YAH VEH.

Yah Tham *transliterated name* {3147 yowtham} [2488 ioatham] Yah Integrious.

Yah Veh Shammah *transliterated name* {3074 yehovahshammah} Yah Veh's presence; symbolic name of Yeru Shalem.

Yah Yada *transliterated name* {3077 yehowyada} {3111 yowyada} Known of Yah.

Yah Yachin *transliterated name* {3078 yehowyachiyn} {3112 yowyachiyn} Yah Establishes.

Yah Yaqim *transliterated name* {3079 yehowyaqiym} {3113 yowyaqiym} Yah Raises.

Yah Yarib *transliterated name* {3114 yowyariyb} Yah Contends.

Yah Zabad *transliterated name* {3075 yehowzabad} {3107 yowzabad} Yah Endowed.

Yah Zachar *transliterated name* {3108 yahzachar} Yah Remembers.

Yah Veh; *see* SUMMARY: YAH, YAH SHUA, YAH VEH:

Yahn, Yah 1-lanan *transliterated name* {3076 yehowchanan} {3110 yowchanan} [*contraction* 2491 ioannees] Yah Grants Charism.

Yahsah *transliterated name* {3096 yahtsah} possibly, Threshing (floor); a place east of the Yarden.

Yair *transliterated name* {2971 yaiyr} [2383 iairos] Enlightener. **Yairiy** *transliterated name* {2972 yairiy} Of Yair.

Yachan *transliterated name* {3275 yachan} Troublesome.

Yachin *transliterated name* {3199 yachiyn} Establishes.

Yachiniy *transliterated name* {3200 yachiyniy} Of Yachin.

Yalam *transliterated name* {3281 yalam} Concealed; Veiled.

Yalon *transliterated name* {3210 yalown} Stay Overnight.

Yamin *transliterated name* {3226 yamiyn} Right.

Yaminiy *transliterated name* {3228 yemiyniy} Of Yamin.

Yamlech *transliterated name* {3230 yamlech} Reign.

Yanah *transliterated name* {3238 yanah} [2388 ianna] Oppressor.

Yanim *transliterated name* {3241 yaniym} Slumber.

Yanochah *transliterated name* {3239 yanowchah} Allowed to Stay.

Yaphia *transliterated name* {3309 yaphiya} Shining.

Yaphlet *transliterated name* {3310 yaphlet} He Escapes; He Slips Away.

Yaphletiy *transliterated name* {3311 yaphletiy} Of Yaphlet.

Yapho *transliterated name* {3305 yapho} [2445 ioppee] Beautiful.

Yaqeh *transliterated name* {3348 yaqeh} Obedient.

Yaqim *transliterated name* {3356 yaqiym} He Raises.

Yarah *transliterated name* {3294 yarah} Forest; Honeycomb.

Yarcha *transliterated name* {3398 yarcha} the meaning uncertain.

Yarden *transliterated name* {3383 yarden} [2446 iordanees] Descender.

Yareb *transliterated name* {3377 yareb} He Contends.

Yarib *transliterated name* {3402 yariyb} He Contends.

Yarmuth *transliterated name* {3412 yarmuwth} Lofty.

Yaroach *transliterated name* {3386 yarowach} Born At the New Moon.

Yarob Am *transliterated name* {3379 yarobam} Contender of People.

Yashen *transliterated name* {3464 yashen} Asleep.

Yashob Am *transliterated name* {3434 yashobam} People Return.

Yashub *transliterated name* {3437 yashuwb} He Returns.

Yashubi Lechem *transliterated name* {3433 yashubiylechem} Returner of Bread.

Yashubiy *transliterated name* {3432 yashubiy} Of Yashub.

Yathni El *transliterated name* {3496 yathniel} Saved of El.

Yattir *transliterated name* {3492 yattiyr} Remaining.

Yaur *transliterated name* {3265 yauwr} Forest; Honeycomb.

Yavan *transliterated name* {3120 yavan} Effervescing.

Yavaniy *transliterated name* {3125 yevaniy} Of Yavan.

Yazer *transliterated name* {3270 yazer} Helpful.

Ye 1-lalal El *transliterated name* {3094 yehallalel} Halal to El.

yea [3483 nai] [3513 ne] a particle of affirmation.

year, yearling *noun* {8140 shenah} {8141 shaneh} [1763 eniautos] [2094 etos] [4070 perusi] the time span of the revolution of the earth around the sun; that which is a year in age.

Yearim *plural transliterated name* {3297 yeariym} Forests.

yearn *verb* {3642 kamahh} {3648 kamar} {3700 kacaph} to pine after.

yearn, prowl *verb* {8264 shaqaq} to seek for greedily; to prowl as an animal.

yearning *verb* [2442 himiromai] desiring; longing for.

yeast *noun* {7603 seor} that which ferments.

Yeatheray *transliterated name* {2979 yeatheray} Stepping.

Yeberech Yah *transliterated name* {3000 yeberechyah} Blest of Yah.

Yebus *transliterated name* {2982 yebuwe} Trampled.

Yebusiy *transliterated name* {2983 yebuwciy} Of Yebus.

Yechezq El *transliterated name* {3168 yechezqel} Strengthened of El.

Yechi El *transliterated name* {3171 yechiel} Enlivened of El.

Yechi Eliy *transliterated name* {3172 yechiyeliy} Of Yechi El.

Yechi Yah *transliterated name* {3174 yechiyah} Enlivened of Yah.

Yechizqi Yah *transliterated name* {2396, 3169 yechiziqiyah} [1478 ezekias] Strengthened of Yah.

Yechubbah *transliterated name* {3160 yechubbah} Hidden.

Yeda Yah *transliterated name* {3042 yedayah} Extended Hands of Yah.

Yeda Yah *transliterated name* {3048 yedayah} Known of Yah.

Yedi *transliterated name* {3260 yediy} Congregate; Betroth.

Yedia El *transliterated name* {3043 yediyael} Known of El.

Yedid Yah *transliterated name* {3041 yedideyah} Beloved of Yah.

Yedidah *transliterated name* {3040 yedidah} Beloved.

Yeduthun *transliterated name* {3038 yeduthuwn} Extended Hands.

Yegar Sahadutha *transliterated name* {3026 yegarsahaduwtha} Heap of the Witness.

Yehuchal *transliterated name* {3081 yehuwchal} Able.

Yei El *transliterated name* {3273 yeiyel} Snatched Away of El.

Yeish *transliterated name* {3274 yeiysh} Hurried.

Yechol Yah *transliterated name* {3203 yecholyah} Yah Enables.

LEXICON

Yechon Yah *transliterated name* {3204 yechonyah} [2423 iechonias] Established of Yah.

Yemimah *transliterated name* {3224 yemiymah} Warm.

Yemu El *transliterated name* {3223 yemuel} Day of El.

Yepheth *transliterated name* {3315 yepheth} Delude; Entice.

Yephunneh *transliterated name* {3312 yephunneh} He Faces.

Yeqabse El *transliterated name* {3343 yeqabtseel} Gathered of El.

Yeqam Am *transliterated name* {3360 yeqamam} The People Rise.

Yeqam Yah *transliterated name* {3359 yeqamyah} Raised of Yah.

Yequthi El *transliterated name* {3354 yequthiel} Obedient of El.

Yerach *transliterated name* {3392 yerach} Moon.

Yerachme El *transliterated name* {3396 yerachmeel} Mercy of El.

Yerachme Eliy *transliterated name* {3397 yerachmeeliy} Of Yerachme El.

Yered *transliterated name* {3382 yered} [2391 iared] Toppler.

Yeremay *transliterated name* {3413 yeremay} Lofted.

Yeremoth, Yerimoth *plural transliterated name* {3406 yeriymowth, yereymowth} Elevations.

Yeri El *transliterated name* {3400 yeriel} Formed of El.

Yeri Yah *transliterated name* {3404 yeriyah} Formed of Yah.

Yeribay *transliterated name* {3403 yeriybay} Contentious.

Yericho *transliterated name* {3405 yericho} [2410 hieriko] Fragrant.

Yerioth *plural transliterated name* {3408 yeriyowth} Curtains.

Yerocham *transliterated name* {3395 yerocham} Merciful.

Yeru El *transliterated name* {3385 yeruel} Formed of El.

Yeru Shalem *transliterated name* {3389 yerushalaim} {3390 yerushalem} [2414 hierosoluma] [2419 hierousaleem] Founded Shalem.

Yeru Shalemiy *transliterated name* [2415 hierosolumites] Of Yeru Shalem.

Yerub Baal *transliterated name* {3378 yerubbaal} Contender of Baal.

Yerub Besheth *transliterated name* {3380 yerubbesheth} Contender of Shame.

Yerushah *transliterated name* {3388 yerushah} Possessed.

Yesar Elah *transliterated name* {3480 yesarelah} Straight Towards El.

Yeser *transliterated name* {3337 yetser} Form; Conception.

Yeseriy *transliterated name* {3340 yitsriy} Of Yeser.

Yesha Yah *transliterated name* {3470 yeshayah} [2268 hesaias] Saved of Yah.

Yeshanah *transliterated name* {3466 yeshanah} Old.

Yesheb Ab *transliterated name* {3428 yeshebab} Seat of His Father.

Yesher *transliterated name* {3475 yesher} Straight, as in right.

Yeshishay *transliterated name* {3454 yeshiyshay} Aged.

Yeshocha Yah *transliterated name* {3439 yeshochayah} Hungered of Yah.

Yeshurun *transliterated name* {3484 yeshuruwn} Straight, as in upright.

Yesima El *transliterated name* {3450 yesimael} Placed of El.

yesterday *adjective* [5504 chthes] the previous day.

Yetheriy *transliterated name* {3505 yithriy} Of Yether.

Yetheth *transliterated name* {3509 yetheth} of uncertain derivative.

Yetur *transliterated name* {3195 yetur} [2484 ituraea] Encircled.

Yeu El *transliterated name* {3262 yeuel} Snatched Away of El.

Yeus *transliterated name* {3263 yeuwts} Consultant.

Yeush *transliterated name* {3266 yeuwsh} Hurried.

Yezan Yah *transliterated name* {3153 yezanyah} Hearkened of Yah.

Yezav El *transliterated name* {3149 yezavel} Sprinkled of El.

Yezav Yah *transliterated name* {3150 yezziyah} Sprinkled of Yah.

Yibchar *transliterated name* {2984 yibchar} Choice.

Yible Am *transliterated name* {2991 yibleam} Swallowing People.

Yibne Yah *transliterated name* {2997 yibneyah} Built of Yah.

Yibni Yah *transliterated name* {2998 yibniyah} Building of Yah.

Yibsam *transliterated name* {3005 yibsam} Spice.

Yidalah *transliterated name* {3030 yidalah} of uncertain derivative.

Yidbash *transliterated name* {3031 yidbash} Honeyed.

Yiddo *transliterated name* {3035 yiddow} Praised.

Yidlaph *transliterated name* {3044 yidlaph} Tearful.

Yigal *transliterated name* {3008 yigal} Redeemer.

Yigdal Yah *transliterated name* {3012 yigdalyah} Greatened of Yah.

Yimlah *transliterated name* {3229 yimlah} Full.

Yimna *transliterated name* {3234 yimna} Withhold; Hinder.

Yimnah *transliterated name* {3232 yimnah} Prosperity.

Yimrah *transliterated name* {3236 yimrah} Exchange.

Yiphde Yah *transliterated name* {3301 yiphdeyah} Redeemed of Yah.

Yiphtach *transliterated name* {3316 yiphtach} [2422 iephthae] Opener.

Yiphtach El *transliterated name* {3317 yiphtachel} Opened of El.

Yiri Yah *transliterated name* {3376 yiriyah} Awed of Yah.

Yirme Yah *transliterated name* {3414 yirmeyah} [2408 hieremias] Raised of Yah.

Yiron *transliterated name* {3375 yirown} Awesomeness.

Yirpe El *transliterated name* {3416 yerpeel} Healed of El.

Yischaq *transliterated name* {3327 yitschaq} {3446 yischaq} [2464 isaak] Laughter; Ridicule.

Yischar *transliterated name* {3328 yitschar} He Shines.

Yishar *transliterated name* {3324 yitshar} Oil (anointing).

Yishariy *transliterated name* {3325 yitshariy} Of Yishar.

Yishay *transliterated name* {3448 yishay} [2421 iessai] Existent.

Yishbach *transliterated name* {3431 yishbach} He Lauds.

Yishbaq *transliterated name* {3435 yishbaq} He Leaves.

Yishbo Be Nob *transliterated name* {3430 yishbowbenob} He Settles in Nob.

Yishi *transliterated name* {3469 yishiy} Saving.

Yishma *transliterated name* {3457 yishma} Desolate.

Yishma El *transliterated name* {3458 yishmael} Hearkened of El.

Yishma Eliy *transliterated name* {3459 yishmaeliy} Of Yishma El.

Yishma Yah *transliterated name* {3460 yishmayah} Hearkened of Yah.

Yishmeray *transliterated name* {3461 yishmeray} Guarded.

Yishpah *transliterated name* {3472 yishpah} He Exposes.

Yishpan *transliterated name* {3473 yishpan} He Hides.

Yishshi Yah *transliterated name* {3449 yishshiyah} Exacted of Yah.

Yishvah *transliterated name* {3438 yishvah} He Equalizes.

Yishvi *transliterated name* {3440 yishviy} Equalized.

Yishviy *transliterated name* {3441 yishviy} Of Yishvi.

Yiskah *transliterated name* {3252 yickah} Observant.

Yismach Yah *transliterated name* {3253 yicmachyah} Upheld of Yah.

Yisra El *transliterated name* {3478, 3479 yisrael} [2474 israel] Ruled of El.

Yisra Eliy *transliterated name* {3481 yisreeliy} [2475 israeelitees] Of Yisra El.

Yisra Eliyth *transliterated name* {3482 yisreeliyth} a female Yisra Eliy.

Yisri *transliterated name* {3339 yitsriy} Formative.

Yissachar *transliterated name* {3485 yissachar} [2466 isakar] Exalted Hireling.

LEXICON

Yithlah *transliterated name* {3494 yithlah} It Hangs.

Yithmah *transliterated name* {3495 yithmah} Orphaned.

Yithnan *transliterated name* {3497 yithnan} Monster.

Yithra *transliterated name* {3501 yithra} Remainder.

Yithran *transliterated name* {3506 yithran} Remaining.

Yithre Am *transliterated name* {3507 yithream} Remainder of People.

Yithro *transliterated name* {3503 yithrow} His Remainder.

Yizliah *transliterated name* {3152 yizliyah} Drawn.

Yizrach *transliterated name* {3155 yizrach} Risen.

Yizrach Yah *transliterated name* {3156 yizrachyah} Risen of Yah.

Yizre El *transliterated name* {3157 yizreel} Seeded of El.

Yizre Eliy *transliterated name* {3158 yizreeliy} Of Yizre El.

Yizre Eliyth *transliterated name* {3159 yizreeliyth} a female of Yizre El.

Yobab *transliterated name* {3103 yowbab} Howler.

Yoed *transliterated name* {3133 yowed} Congregate; Betroth.

Yoelah *transliterated name* {3132 yowelah} Furthermore.

Yogbehah *transliterated name* {3011 yogbehah} Height.

Yogli *transliterated name* {3020 yogliy} Exiled.

yoke *noun* {5923 ol} [2218 zugos] that which joins; that which connects; figuratively, of bondage.

yoke *verb* {7573 ratham} to yoke a yoke pole.

yokepole, pole *noun* {4132 mowt} the slip pole of a yoke.

Yom Kippurim *transliterated plural noun* {3117 yom} {3725 kippurim} day of atonements; **see** kippurim/atonements. yom, day *transliterated noun* {3117, 3118 yom} [2250 heemera] including, but not limited to dawn to down, or dawn to dawn; 24 hours, or a nonspeific period such as the Day of Yah Veh; **see** Yom Kippurim.

Yonah *transliterated name* {3124 yonah} [2495 ionas] Dove.

Yoqde Am *transliterated name* {3347 yoqdeam} Burning of the People.

Yoqme Am *transliterated name* {3361 yoqmeam} The People Raise.

Yoqne Am *transliterated name* {3362 yoqneam} The People Lament.

Yoqshan *transliterated name* {3370 yoqshan} Ensnare.

Yoqtan *transliterated name* {3355 yoqtan} He Makes Little.

Yoqthe El *transliterated name* {3371 yoqtheel} Obedient of El.

Yorah *transliterated name* {3139 yowrah} Pouring.

Yoray *transliterated name* {3140 yowray} Pouring (rain).

Yorqe Am *transliterated name* {3421 yorqeam} People Pour Out.

Yoseph *transliterated name* {3084 yehowceph} {3130 yowceph} [2501 ioseph] Add; the name of several persons, including the name of the man of Miryam, the mother of Yah Shua.

Yoses *transliterated name* [2499, 2500 iosees] Add.

Yoshbe Qashah *transliterated name* {3436 yoshbeqashah} Hard Seat.

Yosheb Bash Shabbath *transliterated name* {3429 yoshebbashshebeth} Sitting in the Seat.

Yoshi Yah *transliterated name* {2977 yoshiyah} [2502 iosias] Founded of Yah.

Yoshib Yah *transliterated name* {3143 yoshibyah} Settled of Yah.

Yosiph Yah *transliterated name* {3131 yowciphyah} Yah Adds.

Yotbah *transliterated name* {3192 yotbah} Well-pleasing.

Yotbathah *transliterated name* {3193 yotbathah} Well- pleasing.

young *adjective* [3555 nossia] not born long.

younger, fewer, lesser, little, pinky *adjective* {6810 tsaor} {6995 qoten} {6996 qatan} less in age, number, size; little finger.

youngling *noun* {1469 gozal} [3502 neossos] [3556 nossion] the young of any species.

youngness *adjective* {6812 tseirah} smallness of age.

youth *noun* {970 bachur} {979 bechuroth} {979 bechurim} {*plural* 5271 neurah} {*plural* 5934 alum} [3494 neanias] [3495 neaniskos] [3503 neotees] a young person.

youthful *adjective* [3512 neoterikos] acting, being, or feeling young.

Yubal *transliterated name* {3106 yuwbal} Stream.

Yuchal *transliterated name* {3116 yuwchal} Able.

Yushab Hesed *transliterated name* {3142 yuwshabcheced} Mercy Returns.

Yuttah *transliterated name* {3194 yuttah} Extended.

Z

Zabdi El *transliterated name* {2068 zabdiel} Endowment of El.

Zabdi *transliterated name* {2067 zabdi} [2199 zebedaios] Endowment.

Zakkay *transliterated name* {2079 zabbay} {2140 zakkay} [2195 zakchaios] Pure.

Zakkur *transliterated name* {2139 zakkuwr} Memorialize.

Zamzomiym *plural transliterated name* {2157 zamzomim} Intriguing; Of Pelesheth.

Zanoach *transliterated name* {2182 zanowach} Abandoned.

zeal *noun* [2205 zelos] used favorably, ardor; unfavorably, jealousy.

zealot *transliterated noun, transliterated title* [2207 zelotes] one burning with zeal; a title of Shimon.

zealous *adjective* [2206 zeloo] to have warmth of feeling for or against.

zealous, jealous *adjective* **envy, suspect** *verb* {7065 qana} {7067 qanna} {7072 qannow} to be zealous, as jealous, or envious.

Zebach *transliterated name* {2078 zebach} Sacrifice.

Zebidah *transliterated name* {2080 zebiydah} Endowed.

Zebulun *transliterated name* {2074 zebulun} [2194 zaboulon] Residence.

Zechar Yah *transliterated name* {2148 zecharyah} [2197 zakarias] Memorial of Yah.

Zecher *transliterated name* {2144 zecher} Memorial.

Zemirah *transliterated name* {2160 zemiyrah} Psalm.

Zerach *transliterated name* {2226 zerach} [2196 zara] Rising, Dawn.

Zerach Yah *transliterated name* {2228 zerachyah} Rising of Yah.

Zerachiy *transliterated name* {250 ezrachiy} {2227 zarchiy} Of Zerach.

Zerub Babel *transliterated name* {2216, 2217 zerubbabel} [2216 zorobabel] Of Babel.

Zeus *transliterated name* [2203 zeus] deity of the Hellenes.

Zichri *transliterated name* {2147 zichriy} Memorable.

Ziph *transliterated name* {2128 ziyph} Flowing.

Ziphah *transliterated name* {2129 ziyphah} Flowing.

Ziphiy *transliterated name* {2130 ziyphiy} Of Ziph.

Zocheleth *transliterated name* {2120 zocheleth} Creeper.

Zocheth *transliterated name* {2105 zowcheth} of uncertain derivative.

Zuziym *plural transliterated name* {2104 zuwziym} Prominent; Of Pelesheth.

NOTES:

NOTES: